ROUTLEDGE HANDBOOK OF PHYSICAL CULTURAL STUDIES

Physical cultural studies (PCS) is a dynamic and rapidly developing field of study. This handbook offers the first definitive account of the state of the art in PCS, showcasing the latest research and methodological approaches. It examines the boundaries, preoccupations, theories and politics of PCS, drawing on transdisciplinary expertise from areas as diverse as sport studies, sociology, history, cultural studies, performance studies and anthropology.

Featuring chapters written by world-leading scholars, this handbook examines the most important themes and issues within PCS, exploring the active body through the lens of class, age, gender, sexuality, race, ethnicity, (dis)ability, medicine, religion, space and culture. Each chapter provides an overview of the state of knowledge in a particular subject area, while also considering possibilities for developing future research.

Representing a landmark contribution to physical cultural studies and allied fields, the *Routledge Handbook of Physical Cultural Studies* is an essential text for any undergraduate or postgraduate course on physical culture, sports studies, leisure studies, the sociology of sport, the body, or sport and social theory.

Michael L. Silk is a Professor of Sport and Social Sciences and Founder and Director of the Sport and Physical Activity Research Centre (SPARC) at Bournemouth University, UK. His research is interdisciplinary and focuses on the relationships between sport, physical activity, the governance of bodies, mediated spectacles, identities and urban spaces. He has published over 100 research articles and has written numerous books including *The Cultural Politics of Post-9/11 American Sport, Qualitative Research in Physical Culture, Sports Coaching Research, Sport and Neoliberalism, Sport and Corporate Nationalisms* and *Qualitative Research for Sports Studies*.

David L. Andrews is a Professor of Physical Cultural Studies at the University of Maryland, USA. His research examines physical culture as a complex empirical assemblage (including, but not restricted to, sport, fitness, exercise, recreation, leisure, wellness, dance and health-related movement practices). His publications include *Sport–Commerce–Culture, The Blackwell Companion to Sport* and *Sport and Neoliberalism*. He serves as the associate editor of the *Journal of Sport and Social Issues*, and on the editorial boards of the *Sociology of Sport Journal*, the *International Review for the Sociology of Sport, Communication and Sport* and *Leisure Studies*.

Holly Thorpe is an Associate Professor in the School of Human Development and Movement Studies at the University of Waikato, New Zealand. Her research interests include action sports, youth culture, women's health and critical sport for development studies. Running throughout these topics is a focus on the moving body, social theory and feminist theory. She has published over 60 journal articles and is the author of *Transnational Mobilities in Action Sport Cultures* and *Snowboarding Bodies in Theory and Practice*. She has also co-edited the *Berkshire Encyclopedia of Extreme Sports*, the Greenwood Guides to Extreme Sports series and *Women in Action Sport Cultures*.

ROUTLEDGE HANDBOOK OF PHYSICAL CULTURAL STUDIES

Edited by
Michael L. Silk, David L. Andrews and Holly Thorpe

LONDON AND NEW YORK

First published 2017
by Routledge
2 Park Square, Milton Park, Abingdon, Oxon OX14 4RN

and by Routledge
711 Third Avenue, New York, NY 10017

Routledge is an imprint of the Taylor and Francis Group, an informa business

© 2017 Michael L. Silk, David L. Andrews and Holly Thorpe

The right of Michael L. Silk, David L. Andrews and Holly Thorpe to be identified as the authors of the editorial material, and of the authors for their individual chapters, has been asserted in accordance with sections 77 and 78 of the Copyright, Designs and Patents Act 1988.

All rights reserved. No part of this book may be reprinted or reproduced or utilized in any form or by any electronic, mechanical, or other means, now known or hereafter invented, including photocopying and recording, or in any information storage or retrieval system, without permission in writing from the publishers.

Trademark notice: Product or corporate names may be trademarks or registered trademarks, and are used only for identification and explanation without intent to infringe.

British Library Cataloguing-in-Publication Data
A catalogue record for this book is available from the British Library

Library of Congress Cataloging in Publication Data
Names: Silk, Michael L., editor. | Andrews, David L., 1962- editor. | Thorpe, Holly, editor.
Title: Routledge handbook of physical cultural studies / edited by Michael L. Silk, David L. Andrews and Holly Thorpe.
Other titles: Handbook of physical cultural studies
Description: Abingdon, Oxon ; New York, NY : Routledge, 2017. | Series: Routledge international handbooks | Includes bibliographical references and index.
Identifiers: LCCN 2016033419| ISBN 978-1-138-81721-0 (hardback) | ISBN 978-1-315-74566-4 (ebook)
Subjects: LCSH: Physical education and training—Social aspects. | Sports sciences—Social aspects. | Human body—Social aspects.
Classification: LCC GV342.27 .R68 2017 | DDC 613.7—dc23
LC record available at https://lccn.loc.gov/2016033419

ISBN: 978-1-138-81721-0 (hbk)
ISBN: 978-1-315-74566-4 (ebk)

Typeset in Bembo
by FiSH Books Ltd, Enfield

CONTENTS

List of figures xi
Notes on contributors xii

Introduction 1
Michael L. Silk, David L. Andrews and Holly Thorpe

PART I
Groundings 13

1 Historicizing physical cultural studies 15
 Patricia Vertinsky and Gavin Weedon

2 Power and power relations 24
 Michael Atkinson and Kass Gibson

3 Theory and reflexivity 32
 Richard Pringle and Holly Thorpe

4 Interdisciplinarity and transdisciplinarity in physical cultural studies 42
 Leslie Heywood

5 The political imperative of feminism 51
 Rebecca Olive

6 Praxis 61
 Michael L. Silk and Joanne Mayoh

PART II
Practices   71

7 Therapeutic movement/leisure practices   73
   Stephanie Merchant

8 Exercise and fitness practices   84
   Nick Crossley

9 Dance practices   93
   Pirkko Markula and Marianne Clark

10 Subcultural formations and lifestyle sporting practices   102
   Belinda Wheaton

11 (High-)performance sport   111
   Jim Denison and J. P. Mills

PART III
Subjectified bodies   119

12 Classed bodies   121
   Alan Bairner

13 Raced bodies and black cultural politics   130
   Ben Carrington

14 Gendered bodies   141
   Clifton Evers and Jennifer Germon

15 Sexualized/sexed bodies   150
   Megan Chawansky and Satoko Itani

16 (Dis)abled bodies   159
   P. David Howe

17 Young bodies   167
   Louise McCuaig, Eimear Enright and Doune Macdonald

18 Ageing bodies   179
   Cassandra Phoenix

PART IV
Institutionalized bodies   **189**

19 Medicalized and scientized bodies   191
Parissa Safai

20 Digital bodies   200
Deborah Lupton

21 Spiritualized and religious bodies   209
Andrew Parker and Nick J. Watson

22 Aestheticized bodies   218
Julia Coffey

23 Fat bodies   228
Michael Gard

24 Mediated and commodified bodies   237
David Rowe

25 Spectacular and eroticized bodies   246
Toby Miller

26 Punished corporal bodies   257
Aaron L. Miller

PART V
Experiential bodies   **265**

27 Injured, pained and disrupted bodies   267
Jacquelyn Allen-Collinson

28 Risky/risking bodies   277
Mike Brown

29 Invisible (women's) bodies   286
Kim Toffoletti and Catherine Palmer

30 Affective and pleasured bodies   295
Adele Pavlidis

31 Mobile bodies   304
Phil Jones

| 32 | Pregnant bodies
Shannon Jette | 313 |

PART VI
Spaces — 321

33	'Natural', intimate and sensory landscapes *Gordon Waitt*	323
34	Physical cultural studies, sport and the environment *Brian Wilson and Brad Millington*	333
35	Urban and securitized spaces *Michael L. Silk and Andrew Manley*	344
36	Healthified spaces *Caroline Fusco*	355
37	Affective cities *Alan Latham and Derek P. McCormack*	369
38	Exercise and fitness spaces *Roberta Sassatelli*	378
39	Sport, migration and space *Thomas F. Carter*	389

PART VII
Contexts and sites of embodied practice — 399

40	Mind–body relations *Simone Fullagar*	401
41	Community and physical culture *Jacob J. Bustad and Bryan C. Clift*	412
42	Physical education, policy and embodied pedagogies *Lisette Burrows and Laura De Pian*	423
43	International development and policy *Simon C. Darnell*	432

44	Global mega-events, policy and legacy *Barbara Schausteck de Almeida*	441
45	Digital mediation, connectivity, and networked teens *Jessica Ringrose and Laura Harvey*	451

PART VIII
Methodological contingencies — 465

46	Critical discourse analysis *Toni Bruce, Jenny Rankine and Raymond Nairn*	467
47	Texts/representation *Cheryl Cooky*	476
48	Ethnographic approaches *Ryan King-White*	484
49	People in contexts *Natalie Barker-Ruchti and Astrid Schubring*	495
50	Narrative inquiry and autoethnography *Brett Smith*	505
51	Poetry, poiesis and physical culture *Katie Fitzpatrick*	515
52	Sensory, digital and visual methodologies *Sarah Pink, Vaike Fors and Martin Berg*	528
53	Digital media methodologies *Steph MacKay*	537

PART IX
Politics and praxis — 547

54	Physical cultural studies and public pedagogies *Emma Rich and Jennifer A. Sandlin*	549
55	Critical corporeal curricula, praxis and change *Jessica Francombe-Webb, Michael L. Silk and Anthony Bush*	558

56	Sport, development and social change *Shawn Forde, Devra Waldman, Lyndsay M. C. Hayhurst and Wendy Frisby*	568
57	Corporate social responsibility *Roger Levermore*	580
58	Embodiment and reflexive body politics *Joshua I. Newman, Michael D. Giardina and Christopher M. McLeod*	587
	Afterword: (Digital) physical cultural studies? *Tara Brabazon*	597

Index 604

FIGURES

17.1	Student assembly	171
17.2	Poster: handwashing technique	172
17.3	Poster: voice levels	173
17.4	Poster: eating time	174
17.5	Poster: wear your uniform well	176
36.1	Hallway spaces	358
36.2	Running in hallways	360
36.3	Banners of pride	361
36.4	Staircase	363
36.5	Blind spots	364
36.6	Viewpoints	365
49.1	The research meeting that researchers and research participants (as people-in-contexts) create	498
51.1	'Intro 1' by Alys Longley	522
51.2	'Intro 2' by Alys Longley	522
52.1	Screenshots from body monitoring app that automatically register body movement through a wristband	534

NOTES ON CONTRIBUTORS

Jacquelyn Allen-Collinson is professor in the sociology of physical culture, and director of the Health Advancement Research Team (HART) at the University of Lincoln, UK. Her current research interests cohere around sociological-phenomenological approaches to sporting embodiment; feminist phenomenology and women's embodiment in sport/exercise; the sociology of the senses; the lived experience of asthma in sport/exercise. She has published over 100 articles in 'mainstream' sociology, and sport sociology journals, with her recent work examining thermoception in sports/exercise, for example, in *Body and Society* on 'lived heat' in women's distance running and boxing. She is currently leading an international, multidisciplinary project on the lived experience of asthma in sport, including published work in the journal *Chest*.

David L. Andrews is a professor in the Physical Cultural Studies Research Group in the Department of Kinesiology, University of Maryland. He is an affiliate faculty member in the Department of Sociology, and the Maryland Center for Health Equity, as well as being an honorary professor in the Department of Health, Faculty of Humanities and Social Sciences, University of Bath, and an associate member, Sport and Physical Activity Research Centre, Bournemouth University. Professor Andrews's research critically examines physical culture as a complex empirical assemblage (including, but not restricted to, sport, fitness, exercise, recreation, leisure, wellness, dance and health-related movement practices). Among other foci, he analyses the complex interconnections linking physical culture with the structures and strictures of late capitalism, related systems of neoliberal governance, and the nature of life within the contemporary metropolis. Professor Andrews's publications include: *Sport-Commerce-Culture: Essays on Sport in Late Capitalist America* (Peter Lang, 2006), *The Blackwell Companion to Sport* (edited with Ben Carrington, Blackwell, 2013); and *Sport and Neoliberalism: Politics, Consumption, and Culture* (edited with Michael Silk, Temple University Press, 2012). He serves as the associate editor of the *Journal of Sport and Social Issues*, and on the editorial boards/editorial advisory boards of the *Sociology of Sport Journal*, the *International Review for the Sociology of Sport*, *Communication and Sport*, *Celebrity Studies* and *Leisure Studies*. In addition, he serves as the co-editor (with Stephen Wagg) of the Global Culture and Sport book series (Palgrave Macmillan).

Michael Atkinson is professor in the Faculty of Kinesiology Physical Education at the University of Toronto, where he teaches physical cultural studies and research methods. His central areas of teaching and research pertain to the experiences of human suffering as physical culture, radical embodiment, issues in bioethics, and ethnographic research methods. He is author/editor of nine books, and Michael's ethnographies have included the study of ticket scalping, tattooing, fell running, animal blood sports, Ashtanga yoga, critically ill athletes, Parkour, ice hockey violence and child abuse, and endurance sport cultures. Michael is currently co-editor of *Qualitative Research in Sport, Exercise, and Health*, and past editor of the *Sociology of Sport Journal*.

Alan Bairner was educated at the universities of Edinburgh and Hull, where he was awarded a PhD in political theory for his thesis on Antonio Gramsci's theory of the state. He is currently professor of sport and social theory at Loughborough University. He has written extensively on the relationship between sport and national identity. He is co-author of *Sport, Sectarianism and Society in a Divided Ireland* (1993) and author of *Sport, Nationalism and Globalization: European and North American Perspectives* (2001). He also edited *Sport and the Irish: Histories, Identities, Issues* (2005) and co-edited *Sport in Divided Societies* (1999), *The Bountiful Game? Football Identities and Finances* (2005) and *The Politics of the Olympics: A Survey* (2010). He is the founding editor of the *Asia Pacific Journal of Sport and Social Science* and serves on the editorial boards of the *International Review for the Sociology of Sport*, the *International Journal of Sport Policy and Politics*, the *Journal of Sport for Development* and *Soccer and Society*.

Natalie Barker-Ruchti is associate professor in sports coaching at the Department of Food and Nutrition, and Sport Science at the University of Gothenburg, Sweden. Her research interests lie in understanding how sport coaches and coaching affect athlete learning, identity and wellbeing, in particular in high-performance settings. In these works, the development of sustainable sporting practices forms a key aim. She has recently guest-edited a special issue of *Reflective Practice* on Sustainability in High Performance Sport, which also appeared in book form. She has also published in the journals *Sports Coaching Review*, *Sport, Education and Society*, the *International Journal of the History of Sport* and *Physical Education and Sport Pedagogy*. As an educator, she coordinates her department's sport coaching education programme and teaches in its sociological and pedagogical courses.

Martin Berg is associate professor of sociology at Halmstad University, Sweden. His research focuses mainly on digital methodologies and the mediatization of the body and everyday life. Currently, Berg is involved in the international research project 'Sensing, Shaping, Sharing: Imagining the Body in a Mediatized World', which is funded by the Swedish Foundation for Humanities and Social Sciences. In this project, his research engages with how body monitoring and self-tracking technologies and software are given form by designers in relation to their experiences and imaginaries. Berg has published within the areas of critical media studies and netnography.

Tara Brabazon is dean of graduate research and professor of cultural studies at Flinders University (Australia), Fellow of the Royal Society for the encouragement of Arts, Manufactures and Commerce (RSA) and director of the Popular Culture Collective. She has worked in nine universities in four countries, holding research professorships in media, creative media, communication and education. She is the author of 17 books and over 150 refereed articles and book chapters, and is a columnist for the *Times Higher Education*. Her best known books include the Digital Hemlock trilogy (*Digital Hemlock: Internet Education and the Poisoning of Teaching*, *The University of Google* and *Digital Dieting*), *Enabling University: (Dis)ability, Impairment and Higher Education*, *Thinking Popular Culture: War, Writing and Terrorism*, *Unique Urbanity: Renewal, Regeneration and Decay* and *From Revolution to Revelation: Generation X, Popular Memory, Cultural Studies*. Her research interests include city imaging, creative industries, cultural studies, physical cultural studies, digitization and higher education studies. She is committed to ensuring that Flinders is an enabling university, aligning excellence with social justice in the higher degree programme.

Mike Brown PhD is a senior lecturer in the Faculty of Education at the University of Waikato. His research interests include learning in outdoor environments, place-responsive learning and human relationships with the sea. He is the co-author of *A Pedagogy of Place* (2011) and *Adventurous Learning* (2016). He is also the co-editor of *Seascapes: Shaped by the Sea* (2015). Outside academia he is a keen sailor and avid collector of sailing literature.

Toni Bruce is a sport sociologist and cultural studies media scholar who has spent more than 25 years researching media representations of sport. Her research interrogates dominant discourses of gender, race/ethnicity, nationalism and dis/ability as they are represented textually and visually in media texts. She has co-edited two books on women in sport: *Sportswomen at the Olympics: A Global Comparison of Newspaper Coverage* (2010), with Jorid Hovden and Pirkko Markula, and *Outstanding: Research about Women and Sport in New Zealand* (2008), with Shona Thompson and Camilla Obel. She recently synthesized the vast body of research on media representation of sportswomen into 15 rules of representation, in 'New Rules for New Times: Sportswomen and Media Representation in the Third Wave' (*Sex Roles*, vol. 74, pp. 361–376). Her first academic novel – *Terra Ludus: A Novel about Gender, Media and Sport* – has been accepted for publication by Sense Publishers.

Lisette Burrows is a professor in the School of Physical Education, Sport and Exercise Sciences at the University of Otago, New Zealand. She has been researching and teaching health and physical education pedagogy for over 20 years. Her research draws on poststructural theoretical tools and insights from the sociology of education, sociology of youth, curriculum studies and cultural studies' perspectives to explore the place and meaning of physical culture and health in young people's lives. She is also interested in the ways health imperatives expressed at policy and government level are taken up and responded to in community contexts.

Anthony Bush is a lecturer in sports studies, education, and coaching at the University of Bath in the Department for Health. Dr Bush is an interdisciplinary scholar specializing on issues concerning the physically active body in multiple spaces and sites including, but not limited to, the elite sporting context. His work pushes at the ontological, epistemological and methodological boundaries of that which counts as the critical, social science-oriented study of sport and physical activity. He has recently co-authored (with Silk, Andrews and Lauder) a research monograph titled *Sports Coaching Research: Context, Consequences and Consciousness* (Routledge), and has published articles in journals such as *Reflective Practice* and the *Review of Education, Pedagogy, and Cultural Studies*.

Jacob J. Bustad is an assistant professor in the Department of Kinesiology at Towson University. Jacob completed his PhD in kinesiology at the University of Maryland, and his primary research interests include physical activity opportunity and governance in urban environments, and the relationships between sport, physical culture and urban development.

Ben Carrington is a professor in the Department of Sociology at the University of Texas, Austin. He also holds an appointment with the African and African Diaspora Studies Department. Professor Carrington studies a broad range of topics and areas generally concerned with mapping the circulation and reproduction of power within contemporary societies. More specifically, he is interested in how ideologies of race shape – and are themselves shaped by – cultural forms, practices and identities, and how popular culture is often a key site of both cultural resistance and domination. His work examines the mass media, music and sport as a way to understand key sociological dimensions of everyday life such as personal and communal identity and nationalistic identification and dis-identification. Professor Carrington currently serves on the editorial boards of *Sociological Theory*, *Identities: Global Studies in Culture and Power*, the *Journal of Sport and Social Issues*, the *Sociology of Sport Journal* and the *International Review for the Sociology of Sport*. Professor Carrington is a Carnegie Research Fellow at Leeds Metropolitan University, England and is a research associate of the Centre for Urban and Community Research, based at Goldsmiths College, University of London.

Thomas F. Carter is an anthropologist at the University of Brighton where he directs the Centre of Sport, Tourism, and Leisure Studies in Eastbourne, East Sussex. He has conducted ethnographic fieldwork in the US, Ecuador and Wales, with long-term fieldwork being conducted in Northern Ireland and Cuba. He is the author of two books: *The Quality of Home Runs* (published by Duke University Press) and *In Foreign Fields: The Politics and Experiences of Transnational Sport Migration* (published by Pluto Press). *The Quality of Home Runs* won the North American Society for the Sociology of Sport's Outstanding Book Award for 2009.

Megan Chawansky is interested in studies of gender, sport, sexualities and international development. Her research and consultancy experiences in the area of sport for development and peace (SDP) include work with partners in India, Zambia, Kenya, Sri Lanka and the Caribbean. She also served as a programme coordinator for PeacePlayers International-Cyprus from 2008 to 2009. She is a co-editor (with Dr Lyndsay M. C. Hayhurst and Professor Tess Kay) of *Beyond Sport for Development and Peace: Transnational Perspectives on Theory, Policy and Practice* (London: Routledge). Her academic work has appeared in the following journals: *Sociology of Sport Journal*, *Qualitative Research in Sport, Exercise and Health*, *Sport in Society* and *International Review for the Sociology of Sport*.

Marianne Clark PhD is currently a postdoctoral research fellow working in the School of Human Development and Movement Studies, University of Waikato, New Zealand. Key research interests include girls' and women's experiences of dance, physical activity and exercise, and the increasing use of technology in physical activity contexts. She draws on feminist, poststructuralist theoretical frameworks and has expertise in case study, ethnographic and autoethnographic research methods.

Bryan C. Clift is a lecturer (assistant professor) in the Department for Health at the University of Bath in the UK. Bryan's research and teaching focus on the context, structure and experience of sport, physical activity and the body. He is specifically interested in popular cultural practices, issues of contemporary urbanism and qualitative inquiry.

Notes on contributors

Julia Coffey is a lecturer in sociology at the University of Newcastle. Her research focuses on gender, youth, health and the body. Julia has published on young people's body work practices and identity, health and the body, and pedagogy. She is the author of two books: *Body Work: Youth, Gender and Health* (Routledge, 2016) and *Learning Bodies: The Body in Youth and Childhood* Studies (Springer, 2016, edited with Shelley Budgeon and Helen Cahill).

Cheryl Cooky is an associate professor of American studies at Purdue University. She received her PhD in sociology and gender studies from the University of Southern California. Cooky's research has been published in *Communication and Sport, Sex Roles, Feminist Studies, Journal of Sex Research, American Journal of Bioethics, Sociology of Sport Journal, Sociological Perspectives, Journal of Sport and Social Issues*, and in many edited books and anthologies. She is the president of the North American Society for the Sociology of Sport and serves on the editorial boards of the *Sociology of Sport Journal, Journal of Sport and Social Issues, Communication and Sport, Qualitative Research on Sport, Exercise and Health* and the *International Review for the Sociology of Sport*.

Nick Crossley is professor of sociology and co-founder/co-director of the Mitchell Centre for Social Network Analysis at the University of Manchester. He has published widely on issues on embodiment and, more recently, has been exploring the role of social networks in relation to collective action. His most recent book, *Networks of Sound, Style and Subversion* (Manchester University Press, 2015), analyses the rise of punk and post-punk 'music worlds' in Manchester, London, Liverpool and Sheffield during the late 1970s.

Simon C. Darnell is an assistant professor in the Faculty of Kinesiology and Physical Education at the University of Toronto. His research focuses on the relationship between sport and international development, the development implications of sports mega-events, and the place of social activism in the culture of sport. He is the author of *Sport for Development and Peace: A Critical Sociology* and co-author of *Sport and Social Movements: From the Global to the Local* (both published by Bloomsbury Academic). His research has also been published in the *Sociology of Sport Journal*, the *International Journal of Sport Policy and Politics* and *Progress in Development Studies*.

Jim Denison is an associate professor in the Faculty of Physical Education and Recreation at the University of Alberta, Edmonton, Canada. A sport sociologist and coach educator, his research examines the formation of coaches' practices through a Foucauldian lens. Along with his numerous book chapters and refereed articles, he edited *Coaching Knowledges: Understanding the Dynamics of Performance Sport* (A. & C. Black, 2007) and co-edited *Moving Writing: Crafting Movement in Sport Research* (Peter Lang, 2003) and *The Routledge Handbook of Sports Coaching* (Routledge, 2013).

Laura De Pian is a lecturer in sport and social sciences in the Physical Cultural Studies Research Group at the University of Bath, UK. Her teaching and publications to date involve critical engagement with obesity and health discourse, teachers' enactment of health policy and pedagogy in schools and young people's embodied learning through health education. Her interests in these areas pertain to issues of diversity and social class in particular, as well as innovative methods to engage young people in research.

Eimear Enright is a lecturer and the Bachelor of Health, Sport and Physical Education program convenor in the School of Human Movement and Nutrition Sciences at the

University of Queensland, Australia. She teaches, researches and writes primarily about youth voice and young people's participation and learning in health and physical education (HPE). This work includes projects on negotiating the HPE curriculum with post-primary and university students, supporting student-driven digital HPE experiences, and understanding how and what young people learn on their own terms in and through various movement subcultures. Her research draws on insights from the sociology of education, sociology of youth, cultural studies and curriculum studies, and often engages visual methods to support students in articulating their perspectives on health and physical culture.

Clifton Evers is a lecturer in the Department of Media Culture Heritage at Newcastle University, United Kingdom. Clifton conducts research about gender (particularly masculinity), surfing, space-place, digital media, bodies, as well as emotion and affect. A current research focus of his is improving sexual ethics practice by young men. Clifton has authored print and online articles, government reports, book chapters, and peer-reviewed academic articles. Civic engagement is at the heart of Clifton's work.

Katie Fitzpatrick is an associate professor in the Faculty of Education at the University of Auckland, New Zealand. Her research and teaching are focused on issues of health education, physical education and sexuality, as well as critical ethnographic methods, narrative and poetry. She is particularly concerned with the experiences of diverse youth in schools at the intersection of health, physicality, ethnicity, place, social class and gender/sexuality. She has published numerous articles and book chapters in these areas, as well as an international award-winning sole-authored book (*Critical pedagogy, physical education and urban schooling*, Peter Lang, 2013). She has also co-edited an international collection on health education in schools (*Health Education: Critical Perspectives*, Routledge, 2014). Katie is currently a recipient of a five-year Rutherford Discovery Fellowship from the Royal Society of New Zealand.

Shawn Forde is a PhD student in the School of Kinesiology at the University of British Columbia. His research focuses on sport, development, and social change. He has published in a number of peer-reviewed journals, including the *Sociology of Sport Journal*, the *International Review for the Sociology of Sport*, *Sport in Society* and *Sport Management Review*.

Vaike Fors is an associate professor in pedagogy at Halmstad University, Sweden. In her pursuit to contribute to further understandings of contemporary conditions for learning, she has studied people's interaction with new technologies in various research projects. She leads the project 'Sensing, Shaping, Sharing: Imagining the Body in a Mediatized World', which is funded by the Swedish Foundation for Humanities and Social Sciences (2015–2018). Her area of expertise lies in the fields of visual and sensory ethnography, and recent publications include *Visuell etnografi* (2015).

Jessica Francombe-Webb is a lecturer in sport and physical culture at the University of Bath, and co-convenor of the Lifelong Health and Wellbeing research group within the Department for Health. Her research draws from the discipline of feminist physical cultural studies in order to explore the contested politics of the (in)active body in relation to health, physical activity, body size and appearance. Her interests in these areas pertain to issues of power, gender, social class, race, (dis)ability across the lifespan, as well as the impact of the media and technology in everyday life. Her work has been published in *Sociology* ('Young Girls' Embodied Experiences of Femininity and Social Class'), *Leisure Studies* ('Learning to Leisure: Femininity and Practices of the Body') and *Television and New Media* ('Critically Encountering Exer-games and Young Femininity'), and she is the associate editor of *Leisure Sciences* and on the editorial board for the *Sociology of Sport Journal*. She is the co-PI (with Rachel Arnold) of an Age UK evaluation of Inspire and Include focused on the experiences of older disabled adults in sport and physical activity. Jessica maintains an active presence on Twitter: @jessfrancombe.

Wendy Frisby is a professor emeritus with the School of Kinesiology at the University of British Columbia. She has engaged with numerous community groups and has written extensively on participatory and community-based approaches to research. She has collaboratively worked with women living on low income, recent immigrants, those encountering mental illness, and a number of community partners. A key goal underpinning her research is to consider how power relations, organizational structures and policies can be changed to promote social equality in various sport and leisure contexts.

Simone Fullagar moved from Australia in 2014 to take up the position of chair in physical cultural studies at the University of Bath, UK. Simone is an interdisciplinary sociologist who undertakes qualitative research into inequality and the embodiment of sport, leisure and health practices (with funding from the Australian Research Council and other agencies). She has published widely using feminist poststructuralist perspectives to critically explore active living policy, women's depression and recovery, and alternative physical cultures (from cycle tourism, parkrun to roller derby). In recognition of her gender research, Simone was presented with the Shaw-Mannell Award for Leisure Research by the University of Waterloo, Canada, in 2015. Simone is currently working on a new book, *A Feminist Biopolitics of Depression and Recovery* (with W. O'Brien and A. Pavlidis), to be published by Palgrave in 2018.

Caroline Fusco is an associate professor in the Faculty of Kinesiology and Physical Education at the University of Toronto. She favours poststructuralist, feminist and cultural geography theories, and her work is grounded in the pursuit of ethical relations, equity and social justice. With funding from the Social Sciences and Humanities Research Council and the Canadian Institutes of Health Research, her research projects centre on the social and political landscapes of play and nurses' and young people's experiences of HPV vaccination spaces. She has also published in the area of sexualities in sport, and her future avenues of research will continue to focus on the ecological determinants of health and marginalized youth's experiences of neighbourhood change and critical animal studies. She recently won a Human Resources and Equity 2016 University of Toronto's Excellence Through Innovation Award (ETIA) for The Change Room Project (http://harthouse.ca/the-changeroom-project).

Michael Gard is associate professor of sport, health and physical education in the School of Human Movement and Nutrition Sciences at the University of Queensland. He has been/is a computer programmer, tournament squash player, music collector, frustrated rock star, church spotter and lycra-lout. He teaches, researches and writes about how the human body is and has been used, experienced, educated and governed.

Jennifer Germon is a research associate in the School of Social and Political Sciences and honorary affiliate of the Department of Gender and Cultural Studies, at the University of Sydney, Australia. She is the author of *Gender: A Genealogy of an Idea* (Palgrave 2009), and of articles, book chapters and commissioned reports on a range of gender, sexuality and disability issues. Her research interests include the medicalization of human sex-gender diversity, gendered violence (institutional and interpersonal), and the racialized militarization of women's bodies in Australia in World War II.

Michael D. Giardina is associate professor of media, politics and cultural studies in the Department of Sport Management at Florida State University. He is the author or editor of 18 books, including most notably *Sport, Spectacle, and NASCAR Nation: Consumption and the Cultural Politics of Neoliberalism* (with Joshua Newman; Palgrave Macmillan, 2011), which received the 2012 Outstanding Book Award from the North American Society for the Sociology of Sport (NASSS) and was named to the *Choice*'s 'Outstanding Academic Titles' list for 2012, and *Sporting Pedagogies: Performing Culture and Identity in the Global Arena* (Peter Lang, 2005), which received the 2006 NASSS Outstanding Book Award. He is the editor of the *Sociology of Sport Journal*, Special Issues Editor of *Cultural Studies ↔ Critical Methodologies*, co-editor (with Brett Smith) of the Qualitative Research in Sport and Physical Activity series for Routledge, co-editor (with Norman K. Denzin) of the ICQI series for Routledge, and Associate Director of the International Congress of Qualitative Inquiry.

Kass Gibson is a lecturer in the Faculty of Sport and Health Sciences at the University of St Mark and St John where he teaches physical cultural studies, research methods, and physical education and sports coaching pedagogy. His research draws on a range of theories (especially from neglected or 'forgotten' theorists) and methods in order to study meanings and experiences of sport, physical activity and exercise with a particular emphasis on science, technology and ethics therein. Prior to joining the University of St Mark and St John, Kass taught in schools, colleges and universities in New Zealand, Japan, Canada and the United Kingdom.

Laura Harvey is a lecturer in sociology at the University of Surrey. Her work takes an interdisciplinary approach, drawing on sociology, gender studies, social psychology and cultural studies. Her interests include sexualities, everyday intimacies and inequalities, research with young people, the mediation of sexual knowledge, feminist methodologies and discourse analysis.

Lyndsay M. C. Hayhurst is an assistant professor in the School of Kinesiology and Health Science at York University in Toronto, Canada. Her research interests include sport for development and peace, social justice, health, cultural studies of girlhood, postcolonial feminist theory, global governance, international relations and corporate social responsibility. She is a co-editor (with Tess Kay and Megan Chawansky) of *Beyond Sport for Development and Peace: Transnational Perspectives on Theory, Policy and Practice*, and her publications have appeared in *Women's Studies International Forum; Gender, Place and Culture; Third World Quarterly* and *Sociology of Sport Journal*. She has previously worked for the United Nations Development Programme and Right to Play.

Leslie Heywood is professor of English and creative writing at Binghamton University. Her academic work focuses on third wave feminism, the body and sport, and she has also published several books of poetry and creative nonfiction. She is the author of *Dedication to Hunger: The Anorexic Aesthetic in Modern Culture* (University of California Press), *Third Wave Agenda: Being Feminist, Doing Feminism* (University of Minnesota Press), and *Bodymakers: A Cultural Anatomy of Women's Bodybuilding* (Rutgers University Press). Most recently her work has been focused on approaches that integrate the sciences and the humanities, particularly intersections of affective neuroscience with gender, embodiment and sport cultures.

Notes on contributors

P. David Howe is reader in the social anthropology of sport in the School of Sport, Exercise and Health Sciences at Loughborough University. David is a leading figure in socio-cultural analysis of Paralympic sport and holds a guest professorship at Katholieke Universiteit Leuven, Belgium and an adjunct professorship at Queen's University, Canada. Trained as a medical anthropologist, he is the author of *Sport, Professionalism and Pain: Ethnographies of Injury and Risk* (Routledge, 2004) and *The Cultural Politics of the Paralympic Movement: Through the Anthropological Lens* (Routledge, 2008).

Satoko Itani is assistant professor in the Department of American and British Cultural Studies at Kansai University in Japan. Their research focuses on the issues of gender, sexuality, race and nation in sport and physical education through the lenses of postcolonial, queer and feminist theories. Their current research projects include: the experiences of 'transgender' athletes in Japan; Japanese gender and sexual politics in the health and physical education curriculum; and the queer politics and sports mega-events. They publish both in Japanese and English in diverse fields of study, including *The Journal of Sports and Gender Studies* and *Sociology of Diagnosis*.

Shannon Jette is an assistant professor in the Department of Kinesiology (School of Public Health) at the University of Maryland. Her research focuses on social, cultural and historical aspects of knowledge production in the disciplines of kinesiology, medicine and public health. She is particularly interested in studying exercise and fitness practices as technologies of health that have the potential to shape how we understand and experience our bodies. Shannon is currently examining lifestyle advice being provided to various groups of females who are considered 'at risk' in the context of the obesity epidemic, and is exploring how these individuals experience health, physical activity and weight gain in their everyday lives. She has published in such journals as *Sociology of Health and Illness* and *Health, Risk and Society*.

Phil Jones is senior lecturer in cultural geography at the University of Birmingham where he has worked since 2003. He is interested in issues around urban cultures, embodiment, affect and mobilities. Much of his work experiments with creative methods, including walking interviews, qualitative GIS and participatory co-design. He is the co-author of *Urban Regeneration in the UK* (2nd edition 2013), and co-editor of the collection *Creative Economies, Creative Communities* (2015). Beyond conventional academic outputs he also publishes in different media, including a comic book and short films as well as collaborating with artists on different projects. He tweets from @philjonesgeog.

Ryan King-White PhD is an associate professor of sport management at Towson University. His research interests revolve around critical pedagogy, praxis and (physical) cultural studies. Ryan was awarded the 2010 NASSS Article of the Year award for his research on Danny Almonte published in the *Sociology of Sport Journal*. His 2012 article on critical pedagogy in the same journal was designated as a 'spotlight' publication.

Alan Latham is a cultural and urban geographer whose research focuses on sociality, mobility and public-ness. After gaining bachelor and master's degrees in his native New Zealand, he moved to the UK to take up a Commonwealth Research Fellowship at the University of Bristol where he obtained his PhD. He has spent time working at the TU Berlin, and the Universities of Auckland and Southampton. He has published extensively in edited collections and academic journals and is the co-author of *Key Concepts in Urban Geography* and co-editor of *Key Thinkers on Cities*. His work has explored a range of sites in cities as diverse as Auckland,

London, New York, Eugene (OR), Malmo, Berlin and Champaign-Urbana. He is currently writing a contemporary history of sedentarism and practices of aerobic fitness. He teaches at University College London.

Roger Levermore is associate professor of business management education and associate director of the Hong Kong University of Science and Technology MBA programmes. He is based in the Management Department of the School of Business Management. His research interests are related to international relations, international development and CSR mainly focused on sports and in sub-Saharan Africa. He has published widely in these areas, with key publications being *Sport and International Relations* (Routledge, 2004) and *Sport and International Development* (Palgrave, 2009).

Deborah Lupton is centenary research professor in the News and Media Research Centre, Faculty of Arts and Design, University of Canberra. Her latest books are *Medicine as Culture* (3rd edition, Sage, 2012), *Fat* (Routledge, 2013), *Risk* (2nd edition, Routledge, 2013), *The Social Worlds of the Unborn* (Palgrave Macmillan, 2013), *The Unborn Human* (editor, Open Humanities Press, 2013), *Digital Sociology* (Routledge, 2015) and *The Quantified Self: A Sociology of Self-Tracking* (Polity, 2016). Her current research interests all involve aspects of digital sociology: big data cultures, self-tracking practices, digitized pregnancy and parenting, the digital surveillance of children, 3D printing technologies, digitized academia and digital health technologies.

Doune Macdonald is a professor and pro-vice-chancellor (teaching and learning) at the University of Queensland, Australia. The past decade has brought a number of changes to the field of health and physical education in the school and tertiary sector. Professor Macdonald's research interests have attempted to understand these shifts through the lens of professional socialization, discourse analysis and identity construction using predominantly qualitative methods. In particular, much of her work has addressed the challenges of curriculum reform and its impact upon teachers and teaching. More recently Professor Macdonald's interests have moved outside the formal education sphere to broader questions of physical activity and young people with two funded projects looking at at-risk young people and Aboriginal and Torres Strait Islanders. Currently the Australian Research Council, the National Health and Medical Research Council, Queensland Health and the Department of Education, Training and Youth Affairs fund some of her research projects.

Steph MacKay is an independent scholar who recently completed a Social Sciences and Humanities Research Council of Canada (SSHRC) Postdoctoral Fellowship in the School of Journalism and Communication at Carleton University in Ottawa, Canada. She has published in a range of scholarly journals, including *International Review for the Sociology of Sport* and *Sociology of Sport Journal*, and scholarly books on the topics of gender in digital skateboarding media, social theory, obesity and campus media. Her current project explores the role digital community media plays in facilitating women's entry into Great Lake surfing and providing female surfers with a space for the construction of cultural identities.

Andrew Manley is a lecturer in the Faculty of Humanities and Social Sciences at the University of Bath, UK. Adopting an eclectic mix of social theory, his research focuses on sport, leisure and physical cultures relational to globalization, urban regeneration and organizational identities. He has published on issues surrounding surveillance and securitization, international development, identity construction and organizational culture.

Notes on contributors

Pirkko Markula is a professor of socio-cultural studies of physical activity at the University of Alberta, Canada. Her research interests include poststructuralist, Foucauldian and Deleuzian analyses of dance, exercise and sport. She is the co-author with Michael Silk of *Qualitative Research for Physical Culture* (Routledge, 2011), co-author with Richard Pringle of *Foucault, Sport and Exercise: Power, Knowledge and Transforming the Self* (Routledge, 2006), editor of *Feminist Sport Studies: Sharing Joy, Sharing Pain* (SUNY Press, 2005) and *Olympic Women and the Media: International Perspectives* (Palgrave, 2009), co-editor with William Bridel and Jim Denison of *Endurance running: A Socio-cultural Examination* (Routledge, 2016), co-editor with Eileen Kennedy of *Women and Exercise: Body, Health and Consumerism* (Routledge, 2011), co-editor with Sarah Riley, Maree Burns, Hannah Frith and Sally Wiggins of *Critical Bodies: Representations, Identities and Practices of Weight and Body Management* (Palgrave, 2007), and co-editor with Jim Denison of *Moving Writing: Crafting Movement in Sport Research* (Peter Lang, 2003).

Joanne Mayoh is a senior academic in sport, physical activity and health at Bournemouth University, UK. Her research interests include women and embodiment within a physical activity context, the relationship between physicality and wellbeing, and the design and implementation of physical activity interventions that target women. Her recent work focuses on adopting a life world approach to explore how physical activity can provide pathways to wellbeing for women. She is particularly interested in how phenomenology can be used alongside sociological approaches (such as feminism) to help explore how groups of individuals (for example women) experience physical activity and their bodies in shared, meaningful ways.

Derek P. McCormack is associate professor at the School of Geography and Environment, University of Oxford, where he is also a fellow of Mansfield College. Derek is a human geographer whose work is informed by a wide ranging engagement with philosophy and social theory and is characterized by a commitment to creative approaches to methodology and writing. His research has made significant contributions to the development of a number of important conceptual agendas within human geography and beyond, particularly around the relations between non-representational theory, affect and materiality. Derek has a BA (Hons) from the National University of Ireland, Maynooth, an MSc in geography from Virginia Tech, and a PhD in geography from the University of Bristol. He is the author of *Refrains for Moving Bodies: Experience and Experiment in Affective Spaces* (Duke University Press).

Louise McCuaig is a senior lecturer in the School of Human Movement and Nutrition Sciences at the University of Queensland, Australia. Her research and teaching focus on the provision of quality health education in school settings. A focus of these endeavours is the training, preparation and professional development of pre-service and practising school teachers to enhance their school-based health education knowledge and skills. Drawing on social theory, salutogenic philosophies of health and qualitative approaches to research in HPE, Louise's research projects have explored the role of caring teachers, teacher education and school health and physical education in the social and moral education of young people. This work has inspired her current interest in research pertaining to the health of school teachers, salutogenic approaches to school health education, health literacy, health education teacher education and student transition.

Christopher M. McLeod is a doctoral candidate at Florida State University. His research interests include sport markets, biopolitics and materialisms, old and new. He has published research appearing in *Journal of Sport and Social Issues*, *Body and Society* and *Cultural Studies ↔ Critical Methodologies*.

Stephanie Merchant is a lecturer in the Department for Health at the University of Bath. Her research interests concern theorizing and exploring the mediative and affective elements of human perception in health, sport and leisure contexts, with a particular focus on the role of technology in altering experience of space and innovating methodological practice. Notable/recent publications include: 'The Body and the Senses: Visual Methods, Videography and the Submarine Sensorium' (*Body and Society*, 2011), 'Negotiating Underwater Space: The Sensorium, the Body and the Practice of Scuba-Diving' (*Leisure Studies*, 2011) and '(Re)constructing the Tourist Experience? Editing Experience and Mediating Memories of Learning to Dive' (*Leisure Studies*, 2016).

Aaron L. Miller PhD is annual lecturer in the Department of Kinesiology at California State University, East Bay, specializing in the study of education, sports, culture, power and violence. Between 2010 and 2015, he was assistant professor and Hakubi scholar at Kyoto University, and visiting scholar at Stanford University's Center on Adolescence. His first book, *Discourses of Discipline: An Anthropology of Corporal Punishment in Japan's Schools and Sports*, was published by the Institute for East Asian Studies at the University of California, Berkeley in 2013. Miller can be reached via email at amiller333@yahoo.com, and his website is www.aaronlmiller.com.

Toby Miller is emeritus distinguished professor at University of California, Riverside; Sir Walter Murdoch professor of cultural policy studies, Murdoch University; profesor invitado, Escuela de Comunicación Social, Universidad del Norte; professor of journalism, media and cultural studies, Cardiff University/Prifysgol Caerdydd; and director of the Institute of Media and Creative Industries, Loughborough University London. The author and editor of over 40 books, his work has been translated into Spanish, Chinese, Portuguese, Japanese, Turkish, German, Italian, Farsi and Swedish. His most recent volumes are *The Sage Companion to Television Studies* (edited with Manuel Alvarado, Milly Buonanno and Herman Gray, 2015), *The Routledge Companion to Global Popular Culture* (edited, 2015), *Greening the Media* (with Richard Maxwell, 2012) and *Blow Up the Humanities* (2012). He can be contacted at tobym69@icloud.com and his adventures scrutinized at www.tobymiller.org.

Brad Millington is a lecturer in the Department for Health at the University of Bath. His research involves the critical study of physical culture, with a specific focus on health and fitness technologies and on the relationship between sport and the environment. Brad is the co-author of *The Greening of Golf: Sport, Globalization and the Environment* (with Brian Wilson, Manchester University Press). His work also appears in a range of scholarly journals, including *The Sociological Quarterly*, *Critical Public Health*, *Geoforum* and *New Media and Society*. Brad's research has been funded by Sport Canada and by the Social Sciences and Humanities Research Council of Canada.

J. P. Mills PhD is currently an adjunct professor in psychology/sociology and kinesiology at St Mary's University in Calgary, Canada. A former international endurance runner, his research examines the formation of high-performance coaches' practices and knowledge, the formation of the sporting and physically active body and sport psychology through a post-structural lens.

Notes on contributors

Raymond Nairn MSc, PhD (Auckland) FNZPsS is a social psychologist with many years' experience in community education and action around Te Tiriti o Waitangi (Treaty of Waitangi), currently working as a research assistant in Whariki Research Group. With Waikaremoana Waitoki, Roseanne Black and Phillipa Pehi, he edited *Ka Tū, Ka Oho: Visions of a Bicultural Partnership in Psychology* (New Zealand Psychological Society, 2012). Raymond is a Pākehā New Zealander of Scots and English descent who has been analysing Pākehā discourses about the Indigenous peoples of New Zealand (e.g. 'Maori News is Bad News: That's Certainly So on Television', co-authored, *MAI Journal*, 2012) and media representations of those living with mental disorders (e.g. Nairn and Coverdale, 'Breakfast and Then Death': Imputations of Madness in Print Media Depiction of a Mass Killing', co-authored, *Australian Journal of Communication*, 2009) since 1990, routinely performing critical discourse analyses.

Joshua I. Newman PhD (Maryland) is director of the Center for Sport, Health, and Equitable Development and associate professor of sport, media, and cultural studies at Florida State University. He is also associate chair and director of doctoral studies in the Department of Sport Management. He has published two books and over 60 articles and chapters on issues related to social inequalities, cultural politics, and political economies and ecologies of sport and physical activity. His most recent book, *Sport, Spectacle, and NASCAR Nation* (Palgrave, with M. Giardina) was awarded NASSS's Outstanding Book for 2012 and was named as a Choice Outstanding Academic Title in 2013. His work has been published in top international journals such as the *Sociology of Sport Journal*, *Body and Society*, *Qualitative Inquiry* and the *Journal of Sport and Social Issues*. He is on the editorial boards of the *Journal of Global Sport Management*, *Sociology of Sport Journal*, and the *Journal of Amateur Sport* and is international scholar of excellence with the Shanghai University of Sport. He was recently elected president of the North American Society for the Sociology of Sport (NASSS).

Rebecca Olive lectures in cultural studies at Southern Cross University in Australia. Her research takes a feminist approach to issues of power, ethics and pedagogy, and how these relate to processes of cultural change and social activism. Using ethnographic approaches, her work focuses on lifestyle and action sports, in particular surfing, and social media. Rebecca has published in a range of journals and books including *International Journal of Cultural Studies*, *Media International Australia*, *Sport, Education and Society*, *Continuum: Journal of Media and Cultural Studies*, and the *Routledge International Handbook of Outdoor Studies*, and is the co-editor (with Holly Thorpe) of the forthcoming book, *Women in Action Sport Cultures: Politics, Identity and Experience*. She also continues to write for mainstream media and to publish her blog, *Making Friends with the Neighbours*.

Catherine Palmer is head of the School of Social Sciences and professor of sociology at the University of Tasmania. She has held appointments at Deakin University, Durham University, Flinders University and the University of Adelaide. Catherine's research spans a range of topics including sport and alcohol, social inequalities and sport, sport for development and peace, risk and lifestyle sport, as well as major sporting events such as the Tour de France. Her latest project is exploring fitness philanthropy and sports-based charity challenges.

Andrew Parker is professor of sport and Christian outreach and co-director (with Nick Watson) of the Centre for Sport, Spirituality and Religion (CSSR) in the Faculty of Applied Sciences at the University of Gloucestershire, UK. Andrew's research interests include sport and spirituality, sport and social identity, and physical activity and schooling. Published outputs reflect these interests and have appeared in periodicals such as the *Sociology of Sport Journal* and the *International Review for the Sociology of Sport*. He has served on the editorial boards of the *Sociology of Sport Journal* (2005–2008) (Human Kinetics), *Qualitative Research* (2001–present) (Sage), and is a former co-editor of the *International Journal of Religion and Sport* (2010–2012).

Adele Pavlidis is a research fellow at Griffith University, Australia. Her 2013 PhD explored roller derby in Australia and the gendered power relations at play in this dynamic and growing sport. She has published numerous peer-reviewed articles and chapters in quality outlets, including the monograph on roller derby in the world, *Sport, Gender and Power: The Rise of Roller Derby* (co-authored with Simone Fullagar). She is currently working on a range of projects, including a contract with Palgrave to co-author (together with Simone Fullagar and Wendy O'Brien) a book on the biopolitics of depression and recovery. Her interests traverse the field of feminist leisure and sport, with a focus on youth and wellbeing.

Cassandra Phoenix is a reader in the Department for Health at the University of Bath. Over the last decade, her research has spanned three complementary themes: the embodiment of ageing and physical activity; everyday experiences of chronic illness and impairment; and the use of outdoor spaces to manage and promote wellbeing. Edited books include: *Sport and Physical Activity in Later Life: Critical Perspectives* and *The World of Physical Culture in Sport and Exercise: Visual Methods for Qualitative Research*.

Sarah Pink is RMIT distinguished professor, and director of the Digital Ethnography Research Centre at RMIT University. She is also guest professor at the Swedish Centre for Applied Cultural Analysis at Halmstad University, Sweden. Her research often involves bringing together academic scholarship with applied practice to achieve novel approaches, and focused across fields including digital technologies in everyday life, futures, safety and sustainability. Her research is funded by national research councils and through industry partnerships internationally. Her recent books (mostly co-authored/edited) include *Digital Materialities: Anthropology and Design* (2016), *Digital Ethnography: Principles and Practice* (2016), *Screen Ecologies* (2016), *Media Anthropology and Public Engagement* (2015), *Un/Certainty* iBook (2015) and *Doing Sensory Ethnography* (2nd edition, 2015). Forthcoming books include *Theoretical Scholarship and Applied Practice*.

Richard Pringle is currently the associate dean of postgraduate study within the Faculty of Education and Social Work, University of Auckland. He is a critical qualitative researcher who examines diverse socio-cultural and pedagogical issues associated with sport, exercise, health, physical education, bodies and gender relations. He has an interest in exploring theoretical, historiographical and methodological issues associated with critical research. He is the co-author of *Foucault, Sport, and Exercise* (with Pirkko Markula), the co-editor of *Examining Sport Histories* (with Murray Phillips) and the co-author of *Sport and the Social Significance of Pleasure* (with Bob Rinehart and Jayne Caudwell).

Jenny Rankine is a PhD candidate at the University of Auckland, studying how to intervene in online racism against Māori. Born in Adelaide, she moved to New Zealand in 1979 and identifies as Pākehā, a Māori term for New Zealanders of European descent. She worked as a print journalist and in public relations before co-founding the Kupu Taea: Media and te Tiriti o Waitangi research group in 2003. The group is based at Massey University in Auckland. Jenny contributed to the group's academic and lay publications about how mass and Māori media report Māori issues and te Tiriti o Waitangi, New Zealand's founding constitutional document. These are available at www.trc.org.nz/research-about-media-and-te-tiriti. Her focus on alternatives to dominant colonial discourses about indigenous people led to the group's widely distributed booklet and website, *Alternatives to Anti-Māori Themes in News Media*, available at www.trc.org.nz/alternatives-anti-maori-themes-news-media.

Emma Rich is a reader in the Department for Health, University of Bath. Over the last decade she has been undertaking critical health research examining the recent changes in policies and practices geared towards tackling the perceived risks associated with obesity and the impact this has on young people's experiences of their bodies, weight and health practices. Her recent work is focused on digital health and the relationships between learning, technologies and health (e.g. exergaming, mobile health, social media). Her major publications (books) are *The Medicalization of Cyberspace* (Routledge, 2008) *Education, Disordered Eating and Obesity Discourse: Fat Fabrications* (Routledge, 2008) and *Debating Obesity: Critical Perspectives* (Palgrave, 2011).

Jessica Ringrose is professor of sociology of gender and education, Institute of Education, UCL. Her current research is on digital feminist activism and feminism in schools. She is interested in how feminist posthuman and new materialism theories transform empirical research relations. How can these approaches help us to rethink subjectivity, assembled power relations and sociological notions of agency, resistance and activism? Recent books include: *Post-Feminist Education? Girls and the Sexual Politics of Schooling* (Routledge, 2013), *Deleuze and Research Methodologies* (EUP, 2013) and *Children, Sexuality and Sexualisation* (Palgrave, 2015).

David Rowe is professor of cultural research, Institute for Culture and Society, Western Sydney University and honorary professor, Physical Cultural Studies Research Group, University of Bath. His main academic interests are in the sociology of media and popular culture. His books include *Popular Cultures: Rock Music, Sport and the Politics of Pleasure* (1995), *Sport, Culture and the Media: The Unruly Trinity* (1999, 2004), *Global Media Sport: Flows, Forms and Futures* (2011), *Sport Beyond Television: The Internet, Digital Media and the Rise of Networked Media Sport* (with Brett Hutchins, 2012), *Digital Media Sport: Technology, Power and Culture in the Network Society* (with Brett Hutchins, 2013) and *Sport, Public Broadcasting, and Cultural Citizenship: Signal Lost?* (with Jay Scherer, 2014). A frequent contributor to public debate on socio-cultural matters in print, broadcast and online media, Professor Rowe's work has been translated into several languages, including Chinese, French, Turkish, Spanish, Italian and Arabic.

Parissa Safai is an associate professor in the School of Kinesiology and Health Science in the Faculty of Health at York University. Her research interests focus on the critical study of sport at the intersection of risk, health and healthcare. This includes research on sports' 'culture of risk', the development and social organization of sport and exercise medicine, as well as the social determinants of athletes' health. Her research and teaching interests also centre on sport and social inequality with focused attention paid to the impact of gender, socio-economic and ethnocultural inequities on accessible physical activity for all. Her work has been published in such journals as the *Sociology of Sport Journal*, the *International Review for the Sociology of Sport*, *Sport History Review* and the *Canadian Bulletin of Medical History/Bulletin Canadien d'histoire de la médecine*.

Notes on contributors

Jennifer A. Sandlin is an associate professor in the social and cultural pedagogy programme in the School of Social Transformation at Arizona State University. Her research focuses on the intersections of education, learning and consumption, as well as on understanding and theorizing public pedagogy. Her work has been published in the *Journal of Consumer Culture*, *Adult Education Quarterly*, *Qualitative Inquiry*, *International Journal of Qualitative Studies in Education*, *Curriculum Inquiry* and *Teachers College Record*. She recently co-edited *Disney, Culture, and Curriculum* (Routledge, 2016) and *Teaching with Disney* (Peter Lang, 2016); other recent co-edited books include *Critical Pedagogies of Consumption* (Routledge, 2010), *Handbook of Public Pedagogy* (Routledge, 2010) and *Problematizing Public Pedagogy* (Routledge, 2014). She is co-editor of *Journal of Curriculum and Pedagogy* and serves on the editorial boards of several international journals. Jennifer received a BA in English literature from Millsaps College, an MA in anthropology from the University of New Mexico and a PhD in adult education from the University of Georgia.

Roberta Sassatelli is associate professor of sociology at the University of Milan (Italy). She has previously taught at the University of East Anglia (Norwich, UK) and the University of Bologna (Italy). Her research focuses on the theory of consumer action, the sociology of consumer practices and the politics of contemporary consumer culture as well as sociology of leisure and sport, sexuality and gender; she is also working on the sociology of emotions, visual studies and ethnography. She has done empirical research on ethical consumption, consumer movements, health and active leisure, consumption and class boundaries, lifestyles and the economic crisis, fashion and gender, quality food circuits. Among her recent books in English are *Consumer Culture: History, Theory and Politics* (Sage, 2007) and *Fitness Culture: Gyms and the Commercialisation of Discipline and Fun* (Palgrave, 2010).

Barbara Schausteck de Almeida completed a PhD in physical education at Universidade Federal do Paraná (UFPR) in Brazil. She is currently a post-doctoral researcher at the same institution. She was the editor of the *Journal of Latin American Association for the Socio-cultural Studies in Sport* (*JLASSS/ALESDE*) for the period 2014–2016. In 2012 and 2013, she was a visiting scholar at the University of Chichester, UK. Her researches focus on funding, politics and management of sport and sport mega-events.

Astrid Schubring is a senior lecturer at the Department of Food and Nutrition, and Sport Science at the University of Gothenburg, Sweden. Her research is socio-cultural in nature and evolves around topics such as youth sport, health and illness in elite sport, career development and coaching, and qualitative methods. Astrid has worked with different Olympic sport federations (e.g. biathlon, handball, gymnastics, wrestling, track and field) and is currently leading a longitudinal case study on health-related risk taking in elite athletes. She has published in journals, including *Sociology of Sport; Sport and Social Issues; Sport in Society; German Journal of Sports Medicine; Sport und Gesellschaft; Reflective Practice*.

Michael L. Silk is a professor of sport and social sciences and founder and director of the Sport and Physical Activity Research Centre (SPARC) at Bournemouth University, UK. His research is interdisciplinary and focuses on the relationships between sport, physical activity, the governance of bodies, mediated spectacles, identities and urban spaces. He has published over 100 research articles and has written numerous books including *The Cultural Politics of Post-9/11 American Sport* (Routledge), *Qualitative Research in Physical Culture* (with Pirkko Markula; Palgrave Macmillan), *Sports Coaching Research* (with Hugh Lauder, Anthony Bush and David

Andrews; Routledge), *Sport and Neoliberalism* (with David Andrews; Temple), *Sport and Corporate Nationalisms* (with David Andrews and C. L. Cole; Berg) and *Qualitative Research for Sports Studies* (with D. Mason and David Andrews; Berg). Professor Silk is managing editor of the journal *Leisure Studies*.

Brett Smith PhD is a professor within the School of Sport, Exercise and Rehabilitation Sciences at the University of Birmingham, UK. His research focuses on disability, sport and physical activity. He is also a methodologist in qualitative inquiry. Brett's research has been published widely in leading journals. In addition to over 100 publications, he has given over 150 invited talks to audiences in numerous countries around the world, including to the Royal Society of Medicine and in the UK Houses of Parliament. Brett is associate editor of two psychology journals and serves on seven editorial boards, including the *Sociology of Sport Journal*. He is co-editor (with Michael Giardina) of the Routledge book series on Qualitative Research in Sport and Physical Activity and co-editor (with Andrew C. Sparkes) of *The Routledge Handbook of Qualitative Methods in Sport and Exercise*. Brett is founder and former editor-in-chief of *Qualitative Research in Sport, Exercise and Health*.

Holly Thorpe is an associate professor in Te Oranga, School of Human Development and Movement Studies, at the University of Waikato in New Zealand. Her research interests have included action sports, youth culture, women's health, mobilities and critical sport for development studies. Running throughout these topics is a focus on the moving body, social theory, feminist theory and methodological approaches, ethnographic methods, and the challenges and potential of inter- and trans-disciplinarity. She has published over 60 journal articles and book chapters on these topics, and is the author of *Transnational Mobilities in Action Sport Cultures* and *Snowboarding Bodies in Theory and Practice*, and has co-edited various journals (*Sociology of Sport Journal* and *Journal of Sport History*) and collections, including the *Berkshire Encyclopedia of Extreme Sports* (with Douglas Booth), the Greenwood Guides to Extreme Sports series (with Douglas Booth), and *Women in Action Sport Cultures: Identity, Experience, Politics and Pedagogies* (with Rebecca Olive). She has been a recipient of both Fulbright and Leverhulme Fellowships, and in 2015 received the inaugural SSJ Early Career Researcher Award.

Kim Toffoletti is a senior lecturer in sociology at Deakin University, Australia, who specializes in the study of gender identities and relations in sport and leisure contexts. Kim's research is interdisciplinary, drawing on feminist, sociological and media studies paradigms to interpret the relationship between gender and other vectors of social difference in shaping women's sporting practices, experiences and representations. She has published on the gender–sport nexus in journals such as the *International Review for the Sociology of Sport*, *Journal of Sport and Social Issues* and *Communication and Sport*. Her current research projects include an examination of female athletes' use of social media and a forthcoming book, *Women Sport Fans: Identification, Participation, Representation* (Routledge), which uses transnational and critical postfeminist approaches to explore the production of the female sport fan as a transnational phenomenon.

Patricia Vertinsky is a distinguished university scholar and professor of kinesiology at the University of British Columbia. She is a social and cultural historian working across the fields of women's and gender history with a special interest in physical culture, physical education and modern dance. Her work focuses on the study of normalizing disciplinary regimes in kinesiology, sport science and physical culture, and the social, political and scientific context in which they have been conceived and promoted. She is particularly interested in regimes of risk and the gendered body in relation to patterns of physical culture and globalization in the late nineteenth and twentieth centuries. Dr Vertinsky is an international fellow of the American Academy of Kinesiology, past president of the North American Society of Sport History, and past vice-president of the International Society for Physical Education and Sport History.

Gordon Waitt is professor and head of the School of Geography and Sustainable Communities at the University of Wollongong, New South Wales, Australia. His current research and teaching interest cohere around feminist geographical approaches to vulnerabilities. He has published over 100 articles in geography journals including *Transactions of the Institute of British Geographers*, *Social and Cultural Geography*, *Antipode*, *Gender, Place and Culture*.

Devra Waldman is a doctoral student in the School of Kinesiology at the University of British Columbia. Her research is focused on the intersections of (post)colonialism, urban studies, international development, transnational corporatism, and physical culture. The focus of her dissertation is on the politics and implications of building branded, sport-focused, gated communities in suburbs of major metropolitan areas around India. She is published in the *International Review for the Sociology of Sport*, and has collaborated on chapters appearing in *The Handbook of Sport and Politics* (edited by Alan Bairner, John Kelly, and Jung Woo Lee) and *The Handbook of Feminism and Sport, Leisure and Physical Education* (edited by Jayne Caudwell, Louise Mansfield, Belinda Wheaton, and Rebecca Watson), on topics ranging from international development through sport, politics of international cricket, and postcolonial international relations.

Nick J. Watson is senior lecturer in sport, culture and religion at York St John University (YSJU) and co-director (with Andrew Parker) of the Centre for Sport, Spirituality and Religion (CSSR) at the University of Gloucestershire, UK. He has published widely on sport, spirituality and religion, including most recently *Sport and the Christian Religion: A Systematic Review of Literature* (with Andrew Parker, Cambridge Scholars Publishing, 2014), *Sports, Religion and Disability* (with Andrew Parker, Routledge, 2015), and *Sports Chaplaincy: Trends, Issues and Debates* (with Andrew Parker and John B. White, Routledge, 2016).

Gavin Weedon's research spans a range of somatic and communicative practices, from mud running and podcasting to labour migration in soccer and breathing in yoga. His recent work draws from science and technology studies, political ecology, and cultural studies, to explore the popularity of 'back to nature' health and fitness practices. Weedon is a postdoctoral research fellow in the School of Kinesiology at the University of British Columbia, Canada.

Belinda Wheaton is associate professor in sport and leisure studies in the Department of Te Oranga (Faculty of Education) at the University of Waikato, Aotearoa/NZ where she is postgraduate leader and teaches sociology papers and qualitative methodology. She is best known internationally for her research on the politics of identity in lifestyle sport, which spans 15 years and includes sport cultures including parkour, surfing, skateboarding, windsurfing and kitesurfing cultures. Key publications include *The Cultural Politics of Lifestyle Sports* (2013), and several edited collections including *Understanding Lifestyle Sport* (2004).

Brian Wilson is a sociologist and professor in the School of Kinesiology at the University of British Columbia. He is co-author of *The Greening of Golf: Sport, Globalization and the Environment* (with Brad Millington, Manchester University Press, 2016) and author of *Sport and*

Peace: A Sociological Perspective (Oxford University Press, 2012) and *Fight, Flight or Chill: Subcultures, Youth and Rave into the Twenty-First Century* (McGill-Queen's University Press, 2006). His other writing focuses on sport, social inequality, environmental issues, media, social movements and youth culture. He currently leads a Social Sciences and Humanities Research Council of Canada-funded project entitled 'Fostering "Sport Journalism for Peace" and a Role for Sociologists of Sport'.

INTRODUCTION

Michael L. Silk, David L. Andrews and Holly Thorpe

Over the past two decades or so, there has been a noticeable shift towards the identification of, and engagement with, physical culture as an empirical field of study (cf. Adair, 1998; Atkinson, 2010; Brabazon et al., 2015; Hargreaves and Vertinsky, 2007; Hughson, 2008; Kirk, 1999; McDonald, 1999; Phoenix and Smith, 2011; Pronger, 1998). While some may have utilized the more inclusive term 'physical culture' as little more than a descriptive antidote to the empirically limiting term 'sport', others clearly have broader aspirations in seeking to advance an intellectual project centred on the transdisciplinary study of physical culture: what has, at various points (Andrews, 2008; Atkinson, 2011; Brabazon et al., 2015; Ingham, 1997; Pavlidis and Olive, 2014; Silk and Andrews, 2011; Thorpe, 2011a; Vertinsky, 2015), been termed physical cultural studies (PCS). The emergent intellectual formation that is PCS engages neither the physical culture of the Soviet *spartakiad*, nor that of the late-nineteenth-century/early-twentieth-century physical culture movement. Rather, it incorporates a relational and pluralistic approach to, and understanding of, physical culture, whose various expressions of active embodiment (including, but certainly not restricted to, exercise, fitness, health, movement, leisure, recreation, dance, and sport practices) are approached as constituent elements of the broader conjunctural formation out of which they were constituted. Furthermore, this understanding is based on the assumption that the very nature of physical culture renders it a complex empirical site incorporating numerous interrelated levels that can be experienced, and thereby examined, from a variety of levels, including the socio-structural, discursive, processal, institutional, collective, communal, corporeal, affective, and subjective.

'Genesis' and germination

The very fact that each of the editors of this handbook possess their own – and markedly distinct – origin narratives for PCS, indicates that there are multiple spaces and times of origin for the project. Differently put, disparate researchers located around the world (some in groups, others in relative isolation) have, for various reasons (some empirical, others theoretical and/or methodological) navigated a physical cultural (studies) turn within their own work, and have, whether knowingly or otherwise, contributed to the loose coalescence of the intellectual formation, or sensibility, that we recognize PCS to be. Somewhat reworking Stuart Hall's (1992) reflections on the emergence of cultural studies, PCS has multiple trajectories, different ways of materializing, different histories in different disciplines and geographical locations; it is a set of different conjunctures, formations and moments.

Far from a coherent institutionalized formation, PCS is an intellectual assemblage perpetually in a state of becoming. It possesses no fixed origins, histories, disciplinary boundaries or trajectories, and is rather a site of both internal and external struggle for precisely what it should and could be now and, perhaps more importantly, in the future. So, there is a necessary and generative intellectual tension at the core of PCS; a dynamism that disrupts as much as it delineates, as the project responds to the unfolding conjunctures, or problem-spaces it confronts (Grossberg, 2010). Predictably, and again with Hall (1992: 277), the emergence of PCS as the 'new' kid on the block among the international community of sociology of sport scholars has been heralded by a degree of 'bad feeling, argument, unstable anxieties, and angry silences' derived, in part, from the over-eagerness and enthusiasm of some early advocates whose failures to attribute PCS's complex genealogy understandably rankled some (Adams et al., 2016). Looking to learn from previous oversights, within this handbook we seek to acknowledge both the complex derivation and extant plurality of PCS, by bringing together scholars from a multitude of ontological, theoretical, and methodological backgrounds, whose work helps to simultaneously establish, excoriate, and extend the always already contingent boundaries of PCS. Evidently, we are not looking to offer a definitive meta-narrative of what PCS is or should be, but instead as an attempt to bring together differing tensions, positionalities, debates, politics, and so on, so as to think productively about what an emergent PCS approach to active embodiment might, not ought, to look like.

While this handbook provides a forum for marking out the – necessarily fluid and permeable – boundaries of PCS in its current and complex iterations, this brief introduction provides the opportunity for us to proffer our own vantage point. Once again, out of a recognition that there are as many motivating factors behind people's turn to physical culture, as there are discrete expressions of PCS in practice, we can only offer an unavoidably personal and, some may argue, parochial genealogy of PCS. Rather than speaking from any sort of authority, we disavow any ascribed or achieved intellectual status and/or influence we may (or may not) have accumulated, and instead position ourselves as offering but one contribution to the ongoing PCS dialogue. According to our understanding, PCS is a collective and democratic project, incorporating a productive tension of divergent foci, viewpoints, and opinions (very) loosely united by a common concern with understanding the existence, operation, and effects of power and power relations as they are manifest within, and through, the complex and contextual field of physical culture. With such critical dynamism at is generative core, PCS fights off the inertia created by the all-too-easy adoption of empirical, theoretical, and/or methodological certainties. Differently put, and in a Freirean sense (Freire, 2000), we contend that PCS is a dialogic learning community, in that its advocates are in critical and constructive conversation, or dialogue, with each other as a core part of the learning process (as opposed to having knowledge and understanding imposed on them). Dialogue is thus understood as 'never an end in itself but a means to develop a better comprehension about the object of knowledge' (Macedo, 2000: 18). In this sense PCS aims to nurture dialogic 'reflection and action upon the world in order to transform it' (Freire, 2000: 51; see also Donnelly and Atkinson's discussion on a public sociology of sport, 2015). The ongoing PCS conversation, the basis of this handbook, aims to co-produce consciousness related to the field's object of knowledge: namely, physical culture in general, and, more specifically, the manner in which specific sites, forms, and/or expressions of physical culture are organized, disciplined, embodied, represented, and experienced in relation to the operations of social power.

Introduction

Promptings

As alluded to previously, it is important to acknowledge that PCS – or at least its constituent or complementary sensibilities – have been germinating, discussed and even centred in a number of academic and non-academic spaces. For us, physical culture, and more specifically physical cultural studies, is a response to a number of perceived intellectual (and institutional) threats, ambiguities, and/or inadequacies. Indeed, the seemingly unrelenting (bio)scientization of kinesiology/sports studies (and the accompanying devaluing of the humanities and social sciences of kinesiological thought) has been identified as a major contributory factor to the genesis and development of PCS (Andrews et al., 2013; Andrews, 2008; Ingham, 1997; Silk et al., 2013). However, the scientization of our academic field of study is certainly not the most compelling factor that can explain the inception and growth of PCS. Indeed, informed by a variety of intellectual influences (most notably, in our case, cultural studies, body studies, feminism, sociology, media studies, history, cultural geography, critical psychology, and urban studies), the unfolding transdisciplinary, transtheoretical, and transmethodological nature of our work placed it at odds with distinct disciplinary boundaries (such as sociology, or sub-disciplines such as the sociology of sport) as understood in the traditional sense of these disciplines. Indeed, we found such nomenclatures at best, to be increasingly vague and an imprecise descriptor of our research practice and objects of study. Additionally, our initial empirical focus on, and understanding of, high-profile, prolympic, or corporate *sport* (Andrews, 2006; Donnelly, 1996) was complicated by the recognition of the universality, yet imprecision, of sport as a collective noun. Thus, as our research ventured more into the realms of leisure, fitness, recreation, lifestyle, leisure, movement, popular culture, education, and health, we came to question the conceptual pertinence (and over-determining nature) of sport as a means of capturing the empirical breadth of our work. For us, and unlike some of its noted proponents (Harris, 2006), the sociology of sport failed to reflect the disciplinary and empirical diversity operating under the moniker, rendering the term at best, a term of relevance to only a segment of this diverse intellectual community, and, at worst, an anachronistic flag of convenience.

To date, the most considered and concerted contributions to the physical culture debate are arguably the varied contributions that comprise Jennifer Hargreaves and Patricia Vertinsky's (2007) edited anthology *Physical Culture, Power, and the Body*, those within the *Sociology of Sport Journal* special issue on *Physical Cultural Studies* (Silk and Andrews, 2011), and a number of contributors in Russell Field's (2015) *Playing for Change* (perhaps especially Vertinsky, and Donnelly and Atkinson). Evidenced within these works, the turn to physical culture is closely linked to – indeed, it has arguably been propelled by – an increased focus on the body and issues of embodiment within sociology of sport research. Furthermore, and as illustrated by numerous journal articles, conference foci, and conference presentations, once the sociology of sport acknowledged its unavoidably embodied emphasis, the field has gradually broken away from its narrow preoccupation with the sporting, and broadened its empirical scope to include a wider range of physical cultural forms.

As evidenced in this handbook, not all (in fact, perhaps a small minority) of PCS exponents are located within kinesiology/sport departments and/or have backgrounds within the field. Largely precipitated by the influential works of numerous feminist scholars (cf. Berlant, 1991; Bordo, 1993; Butler, 1993; Grosz, 1994; Haraway, 1991), the turn to the body within the wider academic community (specifically manifest in cultural studies and allied fields such as gender studies, health, social and cultural geography, leisure studies, media studies, queer studies, racial and ethnic studies, urban studies, youth studies etc.), and the accompanying increased attention paid to the processes, practices, and politics of embodiment, have spurred a rethinking of physical culture (in its myriad guises) as a relevant and resonant empirical domain. From displaying a palpable academic disregard, numerous scholars located outside the extant sociology of sport community have come to acknowledge physical culture as a legitimate, and indeed significant, avenue for critical intellectual inquiry into the relationship between the body, power, and culture. Indeed, over the past decade or more, there has been a discernible *physical culture creep*, whereby the inalienable social, cultural, political, and economic significance of physical culture has infiltrated even some of the most intransigent academic minds. Coupled with the breakdown (indeed, one could consider it almost to be an inversion) of traditional academic distinctions between high and low culture forms as legitimate objects of analysis, physical culture (including organized sport, dance, exercise, health, leisure, movement, recreation, and rehabilitative-related practices) has occupied the critical gaze of scholars from fields as diverse as American studies, anthropology, architecture, gender studies, geography, Latin American studies, media and communication studies, race and ethnic studies, and urban studies (cf. Barratt, 2012; Cook et al., 2015; Hill, 2016; Powers and Greenwell, 2016; Qviström, 2013; Worthen and Baker, 2016). While many of these researchers may be blissfully unaware of the field as they gleefully *discover* physical culture – oftentimes with little or no recognition of the work that preceded theirs – they nonetheless are making contributions to the body of knowledge. Yet, the recognition of physical culture as the central object of research was but a first (albeit an important) step towards imagining, and legitimating, PCS as an approach to studying the politics of (in)active embodiment.

A definitional effort

As indicated in our prefatory remarks, there has been a palpable (and we would argue healthy) mix of defensiveness, hostility, and outright disdain towards PCS, balanced with a growing and expanding (both intellectually and geographically) engagement and development of the field (to which this handbook is testimony). Within this context, this handbook is committed to developing ever more acute explanations of the focus, structure, purpose, critical edge, and value of PCS (cf. Atkinson, 2011; Silk and Andrews, 2011; Thorpe et al., 2011; Vertinsky, 2015). Further, and to avoid falling foul of the indeterminacy that hampered the growth of cultural studies more generally, we see this collection as a step towards – albeit far from a grand narrative – defining the possibilities of PCS. The collective unwillingness to delineate the parameters of the (vexed) cultural studies project created a situation wherein 'the refusal to define it becomes the key to understanding what it is' (Grossberg, 1997: 253). For PCS, this is simply not a sensible, strategic, or in any way sustainable state of affairs.

To this point, however, PCS has failed to delineate any coherent or consistent sense of its own parameters. This can be partly attributed to the criticism that unavoidably attends any definitional effort. Generally speaking, this takes two forms. The first is the anticipated, and indeed greatly welcomed, criticisms occasioned by the 'initial' definition (see Andrews, 2008), and those who (at times precociously, at times vivaciously, often both) advanced multiplicitous offshoots ground – to differing degrees – in the sensibilities of this definitional effort. Any attempt to define an intellectual phenomenon is bound to elicit disagreement and counter-definition of a particular element or elements (empirical, theoretical, methodological, or axiological), or, indeed, of the definitional effort *in toto*. Definitional efforts are thus the starting points, and subsequent stimulants, for the dialogic engagements through which the PCS project takes shape and consequently matures. Hence, those in any sense committed to the development of PCS are challenged to contribute to the definitional dialogue: to offer definitions and counter-definitions through which PCS can move forward, and realize its perpetual dynamics as a project always in the process of becoming. They need to be sufficiently bold to articulate their own definitional thoughts, recognizing that critique is the inevitable corollary, but dialogic advancement is the ultimate result – and this handbook is peppered with such accounts and advances. The second form of critique attending any definitional effort is linked to the position of authority that appears to be assumed by the definer(s). This leads to the interrogation of precisely what gives an individual, or collection of individuals, the right to speak for, in this case, a burgeoning intellectual project? What misguided sense of intellectual entitlement encourages such definitional efforts? This type of criticism is valid, but only if the definitions offered are positioned as being absolute and incomparable. Should they – as in the case of PCS – be framed as, hopeful, suggestive catalysts for considered deliberation, they cannot be critiqued for any totalizing ambitions. Others may read such assumed authority into the definitional effort, but it is not necessary there. Of course intellectual life is structured in such a way as to afford primacy and privilege to the voices of figures, whose status and influence is derived from their accrued intellectual capital. Although understandable in more established fields, PCS's recent emergence means it is a less hierarchical intellectual space, and one *presently* more open to a multitude of generational influences.

Definitions tend to divide as much as they unite; PCS incorporates numerous points of contestation that could alienate as much as they interpolate potential proponents. Yet, for us, PCS should not be reduced to being a generalist approach to the study of physical culture, and has to incorporate specific empirical, theoretical, methodological, and axiological dimensions through which researchers either do, or do not, recognize themselves and their work within it. This is not to say that any definition of PCS is fixed or inalienable, rather, the self-reflexivity inherent within the project demands constant critical reflection and revision. Hence, those involved and invested in PCS are charged with the responsibility for – they are the custodians of – its very being. It is in this sense that PCS should be considered a dialogic learning community, (re)generated through critical and constructive conversation (or dialogue), as opposed to being characterized by the imposition of externally derived knowledge (Freire, 2000). Any definitional effort then should be considered generative as opposed to being definitive. It is intended to be a stimulus for dialogue, rather than an act of intellectual domination. It is not written from any misguided sense of PCS authority or omnipotence; rather, it is offered by people who self-identify as members of the PCS learning community, yet who continue to struggle to adequately conceptualize the PCS project.

Having made the case for the importance for PCS of ongoing definitional practice, we are thus compelled to offer the following, as a starting point for what follows in this handbook:

PCS is a dynamic and self-reflexive *transdisciplinary* intellectual project, rooted in qualitative and critical forms of inquiry. Its research object is the diverse realm of physical culture (including, but not restricted to sport, fitness, exercise, recreation, leisure, wellness, dance, and health-related movement practices).

PCS is concerned with a process of theorizing the empirical, in identifying, interpreting, and intervening into the ways physical culture-related structures and institutions, spaces and places, discourses and representations, subjectivities and identities, and/or practices and embodiments, are linked to broader social, economic, political, and technological contexts.

By contextualizing physical culture in this way, PCS looks to explicate how active bodies become organized, disciplined, represented, embodied, and experienced in mobilizing (or corroborating), or at times immobilizing (or resisting), the conjunctural inflections and operations of power within a society.

As a form of critical pedagogy, PCS aims to generate and circulate the type of knowledge that would enable individuals and groups to discern, challenge, and potentially transform existing power structures and relations as they are manifest within, and experienced through, the complex field of physical culture.

From this definitional effort, we briefly expound upon what we consider to be the key elements of the PCS assemblage. However, unlike in previous discussions (Andrews and Silk, 2016), herein we are not advancing a prescriptive model of PCS. Rather, we envision PCS to be a dynamic intellectual assemblage that would incorporate some, if not necessarily all, of the following dimensions as researchers organically contour their research practice (Marcus and Saka, 2006) to the precise empirical scale and object of study:

- **Empirical:** PCS focuses on physical culture, and more specifically the way specific forms of physical culture are organized, disciplined, represented, embodied, and experienced in relation to the operations of social power. While acknowledging the human body as the subject and object of physical culture, PCS cannot be reduced to phenomenological studies of bodily movement. Physical culture, and therefore PCS, encompasses a breadth of empirical sites, and a depth of empirical dimensions/scales. Within its empirical reach, PCS includes activities ranging from sport, through fitness, exercise, recreation, leisure, wellness, dance, and health-related movement practices. Furthermore, the empirical dimensions/scales at which these physical cultural forms can be engaged range from the macro through the micro: from structure and institution, to discourse and representation, subjectivity and identity, to experiential practice and embodiment.
- **Contextual:** PCS offers an approach to the study of physical culture that is necessarily contextual in both form and objective. It is anti-reductionist, in that any physical cultural expression cannot be reduced to singular or simple effect (i.e. the social, economic, political, or technological). Rather, physical cultural phenomena are the aggregates of multiple and intersecting determinant relations and effects. Mapping the context (the aggregate of determinant relations) in which physical cultural expressions are structured, made meaningful, and experienced represents the contextual imperative and outcome of PCS. Moreover, PCS's contextuality is based on a dialectic assumption that, however minutely, physical cultural practices act as constitutive elements of the larger context through which they are simultaneously constituted.
- **Transdisciplinary:** PCS cannot be considered, nor should aspire to being, an academic discipline. Rather, its breadth of empirical engagement – focused as it is on a wide range of physical cultural forms and dimensions/scales – necessitates a truly transdisciplinary approach. As such, PCS selectively borrows from various field/disciplinary-based research objects, methods, and theories (such as those drawn from body studies, cultural studies, economics, gender and sexuality studies, history, media studies, philosophy, political science, race and ethnic studies, sociology, and urban studies). PCS's transdisciplinary formations are thus fluid, and wholly contingent on the form and dimension/scale of physical culture under scrutiny.
- **Theoretical:** PCS is characterized by a commitment to social and cultural theory as important frameworks informing empirical engagement and interpretation. However, this does assume a slavish adherence to a singular theoretical position, since the empirical diversity of the PCS project precludes the adoption of such a totalizing approach. PCS research requires a critical engagement with theory: a grappling with specific theories to see what is useful and appropriate within a particular empirical site, and

discarding/reworking that which is not. Hence, PCS requires the development of a broad-ranging and flexible theoretical vocabulary able to meet the extensive interpretive demands of its diverse empirical remit.
- **Political:** PCS is a political project, in that it is committed to the advancement of the social formations in which it is located. As such, PCS researchers adhere to an unequivocal understanding of politics of intellectual practice as being concerned with discerning the distribution, operations, and effects of power and power relations. PCS is based on the assumption that societies are fundamentally divided along hierarchically ordered lines of differentiation (i.e. those based on class, ethnic, gender, ability, generational, national, racial, and/or sexual norms), as manifest within the existence of socio-cultural inequities or injustices; advantages or disadvantages; enablements or constraints; empowerments or disempowerments. For this reason, and as part of their broader commitment to progressive social change, PCS researchers critically engage physical culture as a site where such social divisions and hierarchies are enacted, experienced, and at times contested. The sites of political struggle – or problem-spaces – within physical culture, through which social power becomes manifest and operationalized, are changeable and necessitate an equal dynamism in PCS's strategic emphases.
- **Qualitative:** PCS is a predominantly (though not exclusively) qualitative project, which seeks to interpret and understand (as opposed to predict and attempt to control) the diverse realm of physical culture as a social, cultural, political, economic, and technological construct. Through adherence to an approach rooted in specific forms of qualitative inquiry, PCS provides a counterpoint to the positivist scientism that increasingly dominates academic life. Qualitative research encompasses a diverse array of interpretive (as opposed to predictive) methods designed to elicit representations of the social world, through which that world, and experiences of it, are interpreted. PCS's value-laden approach to qualitative inquiry is rooted in a humanist intellectualism – a pathway paved by many who have put their heads above the parapet in a variety of disciplines – motivated by the identification and elimination of disparities and inequities, the struggle for social justice, and the realization of universal human rights.
- **Self-reflexive:** PCS research and researchers are motivated by subjective moral and political commitments, made explicit within and through the choices and enactment of research. Hence, PCS eschews the purported value-free objectivism of the positivist sciences in favour of a value-laden subjectivism, rooted in a critical approach guided by explicitly humanist goals. The self is thus unavoidably situated within research practice, and needs to be reflected upon as such. The variously located iterations of the PCS project are also more broadly reflexive, in that they recognize the need to be attentive to, and sometimes transform themselves in response to, the specific institutional, societal, and/or historical conditions they confront.
- **Pedagogical:** PCS represents a form of public pedagogy designed to impact learning communities within the academy, in the classroom, and throughout broader publics. Whether teaching, writing, presenting, consulting, advocating, protesting, agitating, mass communicating, and/or mentoring, PCS scholars utilize the products of their research labours in circulating knowledge to – and oftentimes co-producing knowledge with – wider constituencies. This pedagogical commitment is motivated by the aim of enabling individuals and groups to discern, challenge, and potentially transform existing power structures and relations, as they are manifest within, and experienced through, the complex field of physical culture.

Michael L. Silk, David L. Andrews and Holly Thorpe

Evolutions

From our viewpoint, PCS is a critical intellectual endeavour committed to the realization of progressive social change through the generation and dissemination of physical culture-related knowledge enabling individuals and groups to discern, challenge, and potentially transform existing power structures and relations. Yet, and while disconcerting for some, PCS's commitment to an ontological and epistemological conjuncturalism is at the root of its perpetual dynamism; it has an unremitting commitment to the future through the dialogic generation of ever-more acute understandings of the present. At any given moment, the struggle over defining PCS – over deciding what is the most prescient definition and formation of the project – will be waged. Uncomfortable conversations and confrontations will continue to be had in order to ensure that PCS retains its intellectual dynamism and political relevance (for fear of falling into the scientific method's trap of moribund knowledge generation resulting from adherence to the twin positivist pillars of replication and incrementalization). As the 'problem-spaces' that confront PCS change over time, so the project is compelled to reshape and refocus itself – to evolve – in order to be able to meet the interpretive and political demands of the new conjuncture (Grossberg, 2010: 1). PCS will constantly be reinventing itself in response to what are ever-changing institutional, societal, and/or historical conditions. The last generation's PCS may not be this generation's; something that has provoked, and will surely continue to fan, *stimulating* debates.

This intellectual conjuncturalism renders PCS an anti-relativist project: relativism in this sense understood as the uncritical embracement of any study of physical culture under the PCS umbrella as being an equally valid and/or credible interpretation as any other. Adopting a relativist stance would open PCS up to charges of an absence of intellectual coherence and credibility. While it may be an open and fluid project continually *in process*, at any given time, and in regards to any specific project, PCS needs to be subject to sustained challenges as to whether it adopts the most appropriate object of study, method, theory, and politics. Such challenges are in many respects its life-blood. Challenge stimulates debate (hopefully not retrenchment!), reflection, advances, new movements, and new moments; challenge, contestation and critique are centrally embedded in the often-allomorphic DNA of a constantly evolving PCS. This anti-relativism is not rooted in a realist assumption of the existence of a singular and truthful reality, that PCS researchers are driven to discover. No, this approach acknowledges a multiplicity of truth claims, yet equally establishes that some truth claims are more methodologically sound, theoretically informed, and politically prescient – they are more interpretively insightful – than others, based on fluid criteria for assessing the rigour, relevance, and quality of scholarship/research (see Amis and Silk, 2008, for a discussion of the politics of 'quality'). While advancing a temporal *authority of knowledge* claims, it is important to acknowledge their incompleteness and deficiencies, while (hopefully) demonstrating how they realize understandings more interpretively and politically insightful than their antecedents. PCS is not a discipline, but it must be disciplined (it must self-reflexively police the rigour and relevance of its research, through the establishment of generally accepted, though dynamic, criteria of evaluation). Only then will it be in a position to produce the 'best knowledge and understanding' of physical culture within the context at hand; knowledge and understanding to be used within the public pedagogical process of what is the 'daunting task of transforming the world' (Grossberg, 2010: 1) in whatever way possible. This is the intent of this handbook, a self-conscious and self-reflexive effort to (re-)produce a partial, political, theoretical, and practical PCS assemblage relevant to, and prompted by, our contemporary conjunctural moment. It will evolve, in part through the pages of this book, by holding the text together as a whole, or certain chapters with each other – each reader will use the book differently, for their own purposes and likely draw out multiple and competing uses, value, and meanings. It is a text that is necessarily held together by difference, contestation, and debate, and which, perhaps rather obviously, is marked by a unity in difference. By necessity, there was a need to/for order; in part this 'order' reflects an ephemeral and definitional assemblage, is perhaps prompted by our genesis (our differing starting points), and is certainly dictated by the strictures of corporatized academic publishing.

The opening two sections of the handbook provide a broad-based overview of the conceptual and empirical complexities of PCS. While some of this has been addressed in earlier discussions (Atkinson, 2011; Giardina and Newman, 2011; Silk and Andrews, 2011), herein contributors problematize, complicate, and extend the understanding of PCS's foundations and boundaries. *Groundings* (Part I) comprises six chapters that variously outline the historic, transdisciplinary, theoretical, self-reflexive, political, and praxis-oriented dimensions of PCS. The five chapters that comprise *Practices* (Part II) illustrate the empirical diversity of physical culture, incorporating discussions of leisure, health, movement, exercise/fitness, dance, lifestyle, and high-performance sport-related practices.

As we have suggested above, at least since the late 1980s and early 1990s, the physically (in)active body has garnered considerable academic attention (cf. Gruneau, 1991; Hargreaves, 1987; Harvey and Sparkes, 1991; Loy, 1991; Loy, Andrews and Rinehart, 1993; Theberge, 1991), such that the body and embodiment have increasingly become the 'empirical core' of the sociology of sport field (Andrews, 2008: 52). It is important to acknowledge that this turn to the moving body was informed by various disciplines, but particularly the strong foundation of feminist scholarship that had been reflexively engaging in research as an embodied act, and writing the body into the text for decades (England, 1994; Fonow and Cook, 1991; Lather, 1986, 2001; McLaren, 2002; Pillow, 2003; Stanley, 1990). Despite a renewed interest in sporting and exercising bodies, a number of critical sport scholars have expressed concern that the overspecialization and fragmentation of the parent field of kinesiology is limiting understandings of the 'body in motion' (Duncan, 2007: 56; Andrews, 2008; Booth, 2009; Duncan, 2007; Hargreaves and Vertinsky, 2007; Ingham, 1997; Woodward, 2009). Partly a response to such concerns, the transdisciplinarity and theoretical and methodological fluidity of PCS offers opportunities for reinvigorating and reconceptualizing understandings of the physically (in)active body.

In this handbook, three sections are dedicated to imagining the potential of PCS approaches for understanding the manner in which bodies become organized, represented, and experienced in relation to the operations of social power. The first of the three, *Subjectified Bodies* (Part III), features seven chapters that offer complex examinations of moving bodies as classed, raced, gendered, sexual and sexualized, (dis)abled, and aged, as well as the various ways that bodies press back upon existing social structures. The following section, *Institutionalized Bodies* (Part IV), builds upon the former with eight chapters revealing bodies as medicalized and scientized, technologized, spiritualized, aestheticized, healthized, mediated and commodified, spectacularized and eroticized, and disciplined and punished, across an array of global, national and local contexts. *Experiential Bodies* (Part V), then consists of six chapters that critically examine various dimensions of the lived moving body, including bodies as injured and pained, risk-taking, invisible, mobile, affective and pleasured, and pregnant. Of course, there are many intersections across the three sections dedicated to the moving body, and also with other parts of the handbook, and we encourage readers to take up the challenge to reimagine new connections for understanding (and intervening in) the ways power operates on and through moving bodies within and across disciplines, spaces, contexts, and sites.

As intimated throughout the constituent chapters of the handbook, the field of physical culture is empirically diverse, incorporating as it does a range of embodied practices. However, as the six chapters within *Contexts and Sites of Embodied Practice* (Part VII) illustrate, physical cultural practices are also manifest across a broad expanse of empirical dimensions. As such, the foci of these chapters range from health discourses, through pedagogical practices, to community and digital cultures, and both national and international policy. Our bodies, our physical practices are of course inherently spatialized; they are inseparable from, and serve to constitute (and are constituted by) the multifarious spaces they inhabit. Focusing on the relationships between power, privilege, and socio-spatio relations, the chapters in the *Spaces* section (Part VI) address the mutual constitution of bodies and spaces across a range of different scalar units. As such, the chapters focus on rethinking key geographical concepts of nature/landscape through the body, the important and active role played by non-humans in the environment in understanding physical culture, the neoliberal 'logics' of gyms in putting bodies to work, mobilities of migrants between spaces, the affective, material, and public spaces generated through exercise, sport and physical activities, the ways in which enclosures and functional sites, architecture and spatial technologies organize, survey and monitor bodies in 'healthified' spaces, and the relationships between, and legacies of, material and discursive urban renewal, sporting spectacle, mobility and securitized space.

Given our understanding of PCS as an organic and diffuse intellectual assemblage formed in response to the specific empirical scale and object of study, the methods utilized by PCS researchers are correspondingly diverse. As a result, *Methodological Contingencies* (Part VIII) comprises eight chapters that explicate varied approaches to identifying and engaging the physical cultural empirical, including autoethnographic and narrative, fictional and performative, contextual, ethnographic, textual, discursive, visual and sensory, and digital approaches. Donnelly and Atkinson (2015) ask if the critical study of sport and physical activity has tended to rest on its intellectual laurels, while all too infrequently engaging in concerted and unapologetic rituals of transformative praxis – a critique that has perhaps quite rightly been directed at PCS in its emergent forms (see Silk and Mayoh's Chapter 6 of this handbook on 'Praxis' for a fuller discussion). Given our understanding of PCS as both a political project, committed to the advancement of the social formations in which it is located, and a pedagogical project that can impact learning communities (within the academy, in the classroom, and throughout broader publics), we were keen to further debate about where and how PCS might (and has) enabled individuals and groups to discern, challenge, and potentially transform existing power structures and relations. As such, and in part influenced by Vertinsky (2015) who offers a compelling warning about striking the 'balance' between political desire, complexity, concreteness and the intellectual basis of the field, the *Politics and Praxis* section (Part IX) comprises five chapters that address the relationship between, and possibilities of, PCS, social change and publicness, the important place of the classroom and curriculum, the multiple complex relationships between sport, development and social change, the transformative possibilities in holding together two unlikely bedfellows in PCS and corporate social responsibility, and the complexities inherent in advancing the empirical and metaphysical bases of PCS relational to methodological reflexivities, flesh politics and embodiment.

References

Adair, D. 1998. Conformity, Diversity and Difference in Antipodean Physical Culture: The Indelible Influence of Immigration, Ethnicity and Race during the Formative Years of Organized Sport in Australia, c. 1778–1918. *Journal of Immigrants and Minorities*, 17, 14–48.

Adams, M. L., Davidson, J., Helstein, M. T., Jamieson, K. M., Kim, K. Y., King, S., McDonald, M. G. and Rail, G. 2016. Feminist Cultural Studies: Uncertainties and Possibilities. *Sociology of Sport Journal*, 33, 75–91.

Amis, J. and Silk, M. 2008. The Philosophy and Politics of Quality in Qualitative Organizational Research. *Organizational Research Methods*, 11, 456–480.

Andrews, D. L. 2006. *Sport-Commerce-Culture: Essays on Sport in Late Capitalist America*. New York, Peter Lang.

Andrews, D. L. 2008. Kinesiology's *Inconvenient Truth*: The Physical Cultural Studies Imperative. *Quest*, 60, 46–63.

Andrews, D. L. and Silk, M. L. 2016. Physical Cultural Studies on Sport. In R. Giulianotti (ed.), *Routledge Handbook of the Sociology of Sport*. London: Routledge.

Andrews, D. L., Silk, M. L., Francombe, J. and Bush, A. 2013. McKinesiology. *Review of Education, Pedagogy, and Cultural Studies*, 35, 1–22.

Atkinson, M. 2010. Entering Scapeland: Yoga, Fell and Post-Sport Physical Cultures. *Sport in Society: Cultures, Commerce, Media, Politics*, 13, 1249–1267.

Atkinson, M. 2011. Physical Cultural Studies [Redux]. *Sociology of Sport Journal*, 28, 135–144.

Ball, S. J. 2012. Performativity, Commodification and Commitment: An I-Spy Guide to the Neoliberal University. *British Journal of Educational Studies*, 60, 17–28.

Barratt, P. 2012. 'My Magic Cam': A More-Than-Representational Account of the Climbing Assemblage. *Area*, 44, 46–53.

Berlant, L. 1991. *The Anatomy of National Fantasy: Hawthorne, Utopia, and Everyday Life*. Chicago, IL: University of Chicago Press.

Booth, D. 2009. Politics and Pleasure: The Philosophy of Physical Education Revisited. *Quest*, 61, 133–153.

Bordo, S. 1993. *Unbearable Weight: Feminism, Western Culture, and the Body*. Berkeley, CA: University of California Press.

Brabazon, T., McRae, L. and Redhead, S. 2015. The Pushbike Song: Rolling Physical Cultural Studies through the Landscape. *Human Geographies: Journal of Studies and Research in Human Geography*, 9, 184–206.

Butler, J. 1993. *Bodies that Matter: On the Discursive Limits of 'Sex'*. New York: Routledge.

Cook, S., Shaw, J. and Simpson, P. 2015. Jography: Exploring Meanings, Experiences and Spatialities of Recreational Road-Running. *Mobilities*, 1–26.

Donnelly, P. 1996. Prolympism: Sport Monoculture as Crisis and Opportunity. *Quest*, 48, 25–42.

Donnelly, P. and M. Atkinson 2015. Where History Meets Biography: Toward a Public Sociology of Sport. In, R. Field (ed.), *Playing for Change: The Continuing Struggle for Sport and Recreation*. Toronto: University of Toronto Press.

Duncan, M. C. 2007. Bodies in Motion: The Sociology of Physical Activity. *Quest*, 59 (1), 55–66.

England, K. V. L. 1994. Getting Personal: Reflexivity, Positionality, and Feminist Research. *The Professional Geographer*, 46 (1), 80–89.

Field, R. (ed.) 2015. *Playing for Change: The Continuing Struggle for Sport and Recreation*. Toronto: University of Toronto Press.

Fonow, M. M. and Cook, J. A. (eds). 1991. *Beyond Methodology: Feminist Scholarship as Lived Research*. Bloomington, Ind: Indiana University Press.

Freire, P. 2000. *Pedagogy of the Oppressed*. New York: Continuum.

Giardina, M. D. and Newman, J. I. 2011. What is this 'Physical' in Physical Cultural Studies? *Sociology of Sport Journal*, 28, 36–63.

Grossberg, L. 1997. Cultural Studies: What's in a Name? (One More Time). In L. Grossberg (ed.), *Bringing It All Back Home: Essays on Cultural Studies*. Durham, NC: Duke University Press, 245–271.

Grossberg, L. 2010. *Cultural Studies in the Future Tense*. Durham, NC: Duke University Press.

Grosz, E. 1994. *Volatile Bodies: Toward a Corporeal Feminism*. Bloomington, IN: Indiana University Press.

Gruneau, R. S. 1991. Sport and 'Esprit de Corps': Notes on Power, Culture and the Politics of the Body. In F. Landry, M. Landry and M. Yerles (eds), *Sport ... The Third Millennium*. Les Sainte-Foy: Presses de L'Universite Laval, 169–185.

Hall, S. 1992. The Question of Cultural Identity. In S. Hall, D. Held and T. McGrew (eds), *Modernity and Its Futures*. Cambridge, MA: Polity Press, 273–326.

Haraway, D. J. 1991. *Simians, Cyborgs, and Women: The Reinvention of Nature*. New York: Routledge.

Hargreaves, J. 1987. The Body, Sport and Power Relations. In J. Horne, D. Jary and A. Tom-Linson (eds),

Sport, Leisure and Social Relations. London: Routledge and Kegan Paul, 139–159.
Hargreaves, J. and Vertinsky, P. (eds) 2007. *Physical Culture, Power, and the Body*. London: Routledge.
Harris, J. C. 2006. Sociology of Sport: Expanding Horizons in the Subdiscipline. *Quest*, 58, 71–91.
Harvey, J. and Sparks, R. 1991. The Politics of the Body in the Context of Modernity. *Quest*, 43, 164–189.
Hill, A. 2016. SlutWalk as Perifeminist Response to Rape Logic: The Politics of Reclaiming a Name. *Communication and Critical/Cultural Studies*, 13, 23–39.
Hughson, J. 2008. Ethnography and 'Physical Culture'. *Ethnography*, 9, 421–428.
Ingham, A. G. 1997. Toward a Department of Physical Cultural Studies and an End to Tribal Warfare. In J. Fernandez-Balboa (ed.), *Critical Postmodernism in Human Movement, Physical Education, and Sport*. Albany, NY: State University of New York Press.
Kirk, D. 1999. Physical Culture, Physical Education and Relational Analysis. *Sport, Education and Society*, 4, 63–73.
Lather, P. 1986. Research as Praxis. *Harvard Educational Review*, 56 (3), 257–278.
Lather, P. 2001. Postbook: Working the Ruins of Feminist Ethnography. *Signs*, 27 (1), 199–227.
Loy, J. W. 1991. Introduction – Missing in Action: The Case of the Absent Body. *Quest*, 43, 119–122.
Loy, J. W., Andrews, D. and Rinehart, R. E. 1993. The Body in Culture and Sport. *Sport Science Review*, 2 (1), 69–91.
Macedo, D. 2000) Introduction to the Anniversary Edition. In P. Freire, *Pedagogy of the Oppressed*. New York: Continuum.
Marcus, G. E. and Saka, E. 2006. Assemblage. *Theory, Culture and Society*, 23, 101–106.
McClaren, P. 2002. George Bush, Apocalypse Sometime Soon, and the American Imperium. *Cultural Studies ↔ Critical Methodologies*, 3 (2), 327–333.
McDonald, I. 1999. 'Physiological Patriots'?: The Politics of Physical Culture and Hindu Nationalism in India. *International Review for the Sociology of Sport*, 34, 343–358.
Pavlidis, A. and Olive, R. 2014. On the Track/in the Bleachers: Authenticity and Feminist Ethnographic Research in Sport and Physical Cultural Studies. *Sport in Society*, 17, 218–232.
Phoenix, C. and Smith, B. 2011. *The World of Physical Culture in Sport and Exercise: Visual Methods for Qualitative Research*. London: Routledge.
Pillow, W. S. 2003. Confession, Catharsis, or Cure? Rethinking the Uses of Reflexivity as a Methodological Power in Qualitative Research. *International Journal of Qualitative Studies in Education*, 16 (2), 175–196.
Powers, D. and Greenwell, D. 2016. Branded Fitness: Exercise and Promotional Culture. *Journal of Consumer Culture*.
Pronger, B. 1998. Post-Sport: Transgressing Boundaries in Physical Culture. In G. Rail and J. Harvey (eds), *Sport and Postmodern Times: Culture, Gender, Sexuality, the Body and Sport*. Albany, NY: SUNY Press.
Qviström, M. 2013. Landscapes with a Heartbeat: Tracing a Portable Landscape for Jogging in Sweden (1958–1971). *Environment and Planning A*, 45, 312–328.
Silk, M. L. and Andrews, D. L. 2011. Toward a Physical Cultural Studies. *Sociology of Sport Journal*, 28, 4–35.
Silk, M. L., Francombe, J. and Andrews, D. L. 2013. Slowing the Social Sciences of Sport: On the Possibilities of Physical Culture. *Sport in Society*, 1–24.
Stanley, L. 1990. *Feminist Praxis: Research, Theory and Epistemology in Feminist Sociology*. London: Routledge.
Theberge, N. 1991. Reflections on the Body in the Sociology of Sport. *Quest*, 42 (2), 123–134.
Thorpe, H. 2011a. Body Politics, Social Change, and the Future of Physical Cultural Studies. *Snowboarding Bodies in Theory and Practice*. New York: Palgrave Macmillan.
Thorpe, H., Barbour, K. and Bruce, T. 2011. Wandering and Wondering: Theory and Representation in Feminist Physical Cultural Studies. *Sociology of Sport Journal*, 28 (1), 106–134.
Vertinsky, P. 2015. Shadow Disciplines, or a Place for Post-Disciplinary Liaisons in the North American Research University: What Are We to Do with Physical Cultural Studies? In R. Field (ed.), *Playing for Change: The Continuing Struggle for Sport and Recreation*. Toronto: University of Toronto Press.
Woodward, K. 2009. Body Matters. *Embodied Sporting Practices: Regulating and Regulatory Bodies*. New York: Palgrave Macmillan.
Worthen, M. G. F. and Baker, S. A. 2016. Pushing Up on the Glass Ceiling of Female Muscularity: Women's Bodybuilding as Edgework. *Deviant Behavior*, 37 (5), 471–495.

PART I
Groundings

1
HISTORICIZING PHYSICAL CULTURAL STUDIES

Patricia Vertinsky and Gavin Weedon

Physical cultural studies (PCS) was born largely out of disciplinary struggles in kinesiology departments over the last few decades, where the moving body has increasingly become the site and source of conflict and contestation. Inheriting from cultural studies, PCS is ensconced in this language and conceptual apparatus of struggle, of epistemic crises and epistemological conflict, and this has become its modus operandi for understanding both the active body and the critical, emancipatory mission of the field. While this embattled mentality is somewhat merited by the 'kinesiological order of things' among those who clamor for expertise on matters of physical activity, it is also important, and impels us to emphasize that the study of physical culture has multiple lines of descent that complement its cultural studies heritage. These include the history of physical education, the birth of interdisciplinarity and the fields of 'studies' in the academic community, not to mention the extensive global reach of physical culture itself and its uptake outside of the Academy. In keeping with the recent trajectories of the somatic turn, we suggest that the unifying project of PCS – the 'end to tribal warfare' in kinesiology that Alan Ingham envisioned in 1997 – might be best pursued through more productive, albeit provocative conversations around the study of active physicality.

'The somatic turn': sociology of sport embraces the body

The sociology of sport's turn to the body (and more specifically to its physical culture) over the past two to three decades is closely linked to the concerted turn to embodiment in sociology and cultural studies during the same period.[1] Bryan Turner was among the first concerned to develop a genuine sociology of the body when he wrote *The Body and Society: Explorations in Social Theory* in 1984. During the decade that followed, leading up to the publication of the second edition of the book in 1996, Turner acknowledged that there had been 'a flood of publications concerned with the relationship between the body and society, the issue of embodiment with relation to theories of social action, the body and feminist theory and the body and consumer culture' (Turner, 1996: 1). Over a decade and a half into the twenty-first century (including a third edition of *The Body and Society* in 2012) there is now 'a generalized and enthusiastic recognition of the cultural and social significance of embodiment in every aspect of life among scholars throughout the humanities and the social sciences, as well as in areas of science and technology', paralleled by an explosion of interest in the active body in popular culture (Featherstone and Turner, 1995: 2; Shilling, 2005). 'Interest in the body', it seems, 'is everywhere' (Hargreaves and Vertinsky, 1996: 1).

As part of this intellectual shift, *Body and Society* was launched in 1995 with a mandate 'to cater for the expanding interest in the body as a topic of teaching and research within the academy; something which in turn can be related to the perceived importance of the body in popular culture, consumer culture and everyday life' (Featherstone and Turner, 1995: 1). Since its inception it has incorporated various dimensions of physical culture into its intellectual purview, citing the pertinent foundational works of Jean-Marie Brohm (1975), Michel Bernard (1976), Georges Vigarello (1978), Pierre Bourdieu (1978, 1980, 1988), Maurice Merleau-Ponty ([1945] 1962), Gilles Deleuze and Felix Guattari (1987), and many others, and pointing to a widening range of substantive topics requiring debate, such as the history of the body in art, technology, medicine, religion, gender and sexuality, ethnicity, fashion, the body and emotions, consumerism and sport. We now have an array of sophisticated theoretical lenses through which to broach questions around the political, economic, social and ecological moorings of physical cultural practices. Marcel Mauss ([1935] 1973), for example, was an early leader who wrote of the social dimensions exhibited in particular styles of movement such as walking, swimming and dancing. He was among the first to explicate the cultural importance of what he called 'techniques of the body', that is the ways in which, from society to society, people learn through education and imitation to use their bodies in a variety of instrumental ways. In this sense, as he demonstrated, the inculcation of specific body techniques was understood to involve not only the transmission of knowledge and skills but could be linked to larger social processes and purposes and to the proselytizing of particular schemes of preference, valuation and meaning (see Dyck and Archetti, 2003: 9).

Intellectual recognition of the body as a site of contested significance in the social sciences and humanities is inextricable from any historicizing of PCS (Hancock et al., 2000: 1). Indeed the ever broadening scope of the 'somatic turn' affirms that much is at stake in the struggle for the body in twenty-first-century kinesiology, and PCS has declared its intention to '*displace, decenter,* and *disrupt*' (Silk and Andrews, 2011: 29, original emphasis) natural scientific and otherwise objectivist understandings of active embodiment by way of a response. Yet there is a danger that anchoring the field within intra-departmental battles in kinesiology and the 'fields' and sub-disciplines of which it is comprised can underplay the multifarious histories of physical culture that promise to inform PCS. Physical culture movements and the global reach of somatic practices have long and storied histories, and any historicizing of PCS should not be conflated with, or made reducible to, the struggles within kinesiology, the mission of cultural studies or indeed the somatic turn.

Historicizing physical culture

The prevailing histories of physical culture take place in Europe and North America in the nineteenth and twentieth centuries, and show how an extended community of American and European actors, dancers, physical educators, health and fitness reformers and physical culture teachers created a spectrum of 'body cultures' that responded and contributed to modernity and artistic modernism. These body cultures, though heterogeneous in their form and contexts, collectively crafted and visualized a 'modern' body, ready for work, play, war and self-expression. Yet the obsession with physical culture apparent throughout the tense and formative modernist movement extended well beyond sport, games and purposive exercise, through gymnastics, body building and posture exercises to a wide range of holistic health practices and expressive activities.[2] Furthermore, interest in and knowledge about physical culture practices were circulating globally by the turn of the twentieth century through colonial struggles against imperial administrators and nationalist discourses as well as through the rise and expansion of new technologies and commodity culture (Ballantyne and Burton, 2005; Altglas, 2007). The map of domination of the world's spaces changed out of all recognition between 1850 and 1914 such that yoga, for example, could begin to develop into 'India's first global brand' of physical culture while simultaneously adapting many features to shifting local conditions (Alter, 2004, 2007).

We can see how the projects of PCS and of kinesiology are allied to the 'anatamo-politics' enacted by modern nation-states since the late eighteenth century (for Foucault in *The Order of Things*, at least), insofar as these fields of study and their members clamor to know, represent, advocate for, and be recognized as experts in matters pertaining to physical activity. Yet clearly any history of physical culture cannot simply be tied to the governance of bodies in modern, Western states but must be viewed more broadly as extending globally across centuries of human history. In his extensive work on physical cultures, Henning Eichberg has consistently called for a much greater focus upon the interlacement between Western histories of sport and physical culture and non-Western histories over time with attention to the political dimensions of body culture. Through body cultures, he says, especially in the clash between body cultures – cultural diversity becomes visible (Eichberg, 1998). Just as Foucault's take on the discursive production of European bourgeoisie identity has been critiqued for its curious omission of colonial bodies as articulatory forces in understandings of sexuality (Stoler, 1995), it is often the case that accounts of Western physical cultural expressions do not recognize their non-Western heritage, and so risk complicity in colonial projects.

What we want to emphasize here is that the study of physical culture has multiple lines of descent, including the myriad genealogies of physical cultural practices across the globe and their uptake outside of the Academy. Moreover, those lines are best conceived as dynamic, fluid and active in contemporary physical cultures as opposed to being statically rendered in accounts of the past for intellectual posterity, as if not subject to the turbulence of worlds in which histories are (re)written. Rather than rehearse the established story of the European diffusions and non-occidental encounters with physical culture, and so risk reifying the given history as a stable template for further research, it seems more prudent to underscore here that disentangling and reassembling the transnational complexity of physical cultural histories is imperative to the project of PCS.

Kinesiology's inconvenient truth

Nonetheless, PCS as it has been formalized as a field of study in recent years (in dialogue with Alan Ingham's vision for eponymous departments), has been historicized largely as emerging from disciplinary struggles within kinesiology departments, including the marginalization and much-debated 'demise' of the sociology of sport. The physical body in movement, the demands of high-level sport, and the rapidly growing arena of sports medicine and technology are increasingly prime foci of departments of kinesiology, or movement and exercise sciences, where those attached to sub-disciplines and professional accreditations vie with one another to garner research money, medically oriented business, and laboratory space. In this regard, the focus of kinesiology still reflects that envisaged by Dr R. Tait McKenzie, widely heralded as one of the leading pioneers of physical education, who said a century ago that 'the policy of the department may be said to contain something of the hospital clinic, a great deal of the classroom and laboratory and a little of the arena' (Berryman, 1995: 4). At the same time, the rapidly increasing move to a science and technology-based kinesiology, sport performance analysis and a return to a medical base (and a disease model) in pursuit of 'exercise is medicine' (Berryman, 2010), has tended to rigidify segmented groups with distinct cultures and organizational values, contributing to a heady mix of scholarly alienation. Among sociologists of sport, for example, there is a growing worry that the central implications of the body in questions of self-identity, the construction and maintenance of social inequalities, and the constitution and development of societies mean that it is far too important a subject for them to leave to the natural sciences and the sports medicine docs (Shilling, 1993: 204).[3]

These concerns found expression in David Andrews's 2007 address at the Academy of Kinesiology and Physical Education, (now the Academy of Kinesiology) meeting, in which he spoke passionately about the seemingly limitless and dominating effects of the sciences in kinesiology, and made the case for the 'physical cultural studies imperative' (Andrews, 2008). His critique, grounded in his own experience of the neo-liberal, corporate university, was of the instantiation of an epistemological hierarchy that privileged positivist over post-positivist, quantitative over qualitative, and predictive over interpretive ways of knowing active bodies. He took particular aim at a faculty that professed a focus and expertise on matters of human movement while failing to acknowledge that 'the active body is as much a social, cultural, philosophical, and historical entity as it is a genetic physiological, and psychological vessel and needs to be engaged as such through rigorous ethnographic, auto-ethnographic, textual and discursive, socio-historic treatment' (ibid.: 50). Kinesiology, he warned, was facing a crisis, at the very least manifest in terms of empirical ambiguity and political impotency. And policing that crisis was a response, he held, not only demanded by its urgency and high stakes, but informed by the cultural studies mantra derived from the classic study of that same name.[4]

At the same time, Andrews acknowledged that the sociology of sport community had been partly culpable in contributing to its own marginal status within a 'science-as-king-based' kinesiology, suggesting that its narrow focus on sport had limited the reach of that sub-discipline. Worse, he and his colleagues increasingly worried that sociologists of sport were climbing into bed with the scientists themselves; that evidence-based research was seeping into the critical sociological study of sport and threatening to neuter the political and critical potentialities of their sub-discipline. Public commentators such as Dave Zirin (2008) accused the sociology of sport of at its best, critically examining relationships of power, helping to fend off increasingly odious attacks on human freedom and equality, but at its worst drowning in a morass of incoherent, esoteric theoretical jargon where research is judged by the quantity of citations. Then there was Washington and Karen's (2001) damning review that sports sociology was professionally marginalized, scorned by sociologists and despised by sportspersons. Michael Atkinson (2011: 136) even hinted that 'perhaps in some ways the sociology of sport died some time ago without receiving a public eulogy or penned obituary'. Retrenchments in many departments of kinesiology or human movement studies units hinted that the sociology of sport was losing ground against science-oriented sub-disciplines which were teaming up with engineers, geneticists, orthopedic physicians and the applied health sciences more generally to expand their reach into emerging research funding possibilities and technically oriented job opportunities for their students (see for example, Lock, 2015). A central and compelling message in the history of medicine is the need to combine science and the humanities in understanding health and disease and in providing complementary tools to engineer improvements in the health of human populations (Jackson, 2014). Yet what Sir Burton Clark could say in 1963, 'that men of the sociological tribe [Ah, they were really men in those days!] rarely visit the land of the scientists and have little idea of what they do over there' continues to have a faint ring of truth (Clark, 1963: 54). That Andrews (2008: 46–47) had seen 'the fate of both the sociology of sport and kinesiology as being inextricably linked' did not bode well for either.

Without being drawn on the vitality or otherwise of the sociology of sport, we might say that as much as the somatic turn across the social sciences infused that sub-discipline with a renewed vigor and significance, as Hargreaves (1986) signposted nearly thirty years ago, it also opened up the space for broader empirical and theoretical ventures that have exceeded its disciplinary (sociological) heritage and empirical (sporting) focus, and so paved the way for PCS.

Cultural studies: promises and pitfalls

A common thread running through the sociology of sport and PCS is the influence of cultural studies, not as a 'parent discipline' but as an eclectic field of critical, politically engaged inquiry. Whereas sociology has historically held scant regard for matters of sport and the body, cultural studies' pursuit of the ways in which the communicative (and somatic) practices of everyday life are invested with power served to inform and to endorse social scientific studies of sport. According to Clifford Geertz, this broadening of interest in issues around the body in culture and society paralleled the blurring of disciplinary genres in the academy into an almost continuous field of interpretation, and propelled the emergence of new 'fields' or 'studies' (Geertz, 1980: 166). Indeed cultural studies was one among what James Chandler (2009: 737) called the emergence of 'shadow disciplines' since the 1960s – also including for example, area studies, gender studies, media studies, performance studies, science studies and, of course, sport studies. Each of these 'studies', according to Chandler, offered new approaches to subjects that linked existing disciplines and borrowed favored methodologies, and each also generated new demands on the whole system for different teaching arrangements, new contexts for collegial collaboration and management questions, new agendas for research and so on. This disciplinary destabilizing led detractors such as Bill Readings in *The University in Ruins* (1996: 90–91) to complain that the emergence of cultural studies was 'a mixture of Marxism, psychoanalysis, and semiotics promoted by those who are excluded from within, and who can neither stay nor leave'.

In spite of Readings's criticisms, the eclecticism of cultural studies in terms of theoretical lineages and methodological tools has often been considered one of its strengths. Samantha King (2005) has made the case for the productive confluence of cultural studies and sport studies on the basis of the former's refusal to rigidly adopt or apply methodological or theoretical 'frameworks' in favor of a 'radically contextualized' and contingent approach (ibid.: 24). It logically follows that the influence of cultural studies in the formation of PCS will likewise benefit from not being tied to the conventions of a disciplinary canon. In borrowing heavily from cultural studies, PCS scholars thus claimed to dedicate themselves to pursuing a 'contextually based understanding of the corporeal practices, discourses, and subjectivities through which active bodies become organized, represented, and experienced in relation to the operations of social power' (Silk and Andrews, 2011: 7).

It is important to remember that the history of Cultural Studies, as it emerged in post-war Britain, demonstrates how this emphasis on context and contingency is itself born out of struggles with certain traditions, notably Marx and Marxisms. The heyday of cultural studies in the 1960s through to the 1980s was part of a negotiation with Marxism, about what was overly reductive or determining, and what could be retained and reworked. The adage of a 'Marxism without guarantees' – later taken up by Andrews and Giardina (2008) as 'sport without guarantees' – is part of (and a response to) the 'post-Marxist' tendency to 'use Marxist concepts while constantly demonstrating their inadequacy' (Hall, 1986: 28); hence the influence of Gramsci's notion of hegemony among cultural studies' practitioners, which helped establish sport and (physical) culture as realms of contested, rather than foreshadowed significance. Many other influential figures have indelibly marked cultural studies before and since, not least De Saussure's writing on linguistics, Lacanian psychoanalysis and Althusser's reworking of ideology (see Hall, 1992), but Marxism's 'curious life-after-death quality' (Hall, 1986: 28) endures in PCS.

PCS has thus inherited from cultural studies a language, a theoretical lineage and a conceptual apparatus concerned with struggle and resistance.[5] In doing so it has harnessed that same critical, political sensibility that animated cultural studies in the 1970s and 1980s in order to interrogate active bodies and realize, as Giardina and Newman (2011) claimed, their 'emancipatory potential'. In addressing what constitutes 'the physical' in PCS they sought recourse in a dialectical ontology – an oscillation between self and society, agency and structure, that takes root in Marx and through Marxisms – that is to articulate the body as 'always already entangled in the dialectics of cultural production' (ibid.: 39–40). Through this inheritance, matters of epistemic crises and epistemological conflicts have emerged as its *modus operandi* for understanding both the active body and the critical, emancipatory mission of the field. And while this embattled mentality is somewhat merited by the present 'kinesiological order of things' (Foucault, 1973; Andrews, 2008), it also appears to harbor implications for the ways in which disciplinary relations within and outside of kinesiology are conceived, approached and represented by PCS advocates. This prompts the question as to whether the 'tyranny of the natural sciences' (Bairner, 2012: 115), disciplinary struggles and quests for 'mainstream' recognition, along with the dream of emancipation, are indeed the most fruitful orientations towards studying 'active' embodiment within and beyond PCS and kinesiology departments.

New vistas and trajectories

Despite the pronounced, and in many ways productive influence of cultural studies in the formation of PCS as a field of study, it may be the case that the project of PCS – the 'end to tribal warfare'[6] in kinesiology that Alan Ingham envisioned in 1997 – is best pursued through a broader and more productive ontological orientation towards (studying) active physicality. However, this need not equate to a call for interdisciplinarity insofar as that entails the unification of pre-existing disciplines applied to a common empirical form such as the active body. Indeed Ingham himself warned against borrowing the epistemological leanings of 'parent' disciplines and began to propose a program of study with an ontological basis that was honest to the focus of kinesiology and its requirement to study the body in motion. A PCS that can 'sensitize our students to movement as an anatomical, neural-physiological, *and* political-cultural problematic' without exacerbating disciplinary struggles and conflicts may well demand looking to new vistas and trajectories in the somatic turn, as well as to the multiple lines of descent beyond cultural studies that are also enveloped in the study of physical culture (Ingham, 1997: 178).

Just as the body became the locus of attention across the social sciences and humanities in the 1980s and 1990s, so the twenty first century is witnessing further shifts, twists and turns in its understandings around corporeality. These developments are multiple, and their genealogies dispersed and complex, though Blackman (2008) has aptly described the general shift from asking 'what the body is' (Shilling, 1993: 6) to the Deleuzian question of 'what a body can do?' (Deleuze and Guatarri, 1987). The relaunch of *Body and Society* in 2010 was intended as a metric of, and motor for these changing dynamics. The journal's editors (Blackman and Featherstone, 2010: 4) welcomed the 'renewed interest in relation to life and affect across the social sciences and humanities', and 'a new post-humanism' that conceived the *bios* as a vital force shared across and beyond the *anthropos*.[7] Advocating for a broad sensibility to bodies as more-than-human, regulated and productive, and always already in motion, there is a need, they said, to rethink the questions we might ask about bodies, and related concepts such as subjectivity, agency, power, technology, the human, the social and matter (Blackman and Featherstone, 2010: 5). Research pursuing the biopolitics of human movement (Newman and Giardina, 2014), such as those instances where disease brings the malleable borders of bodies into question (Newman, Shields and McLeod, 2015), and calls to recognize non-human animals in 'less speciesist' understandings of athletic cultures (Young, 2014: 388) are among recent examples of these sensibilities informing and enriching studies of sport and physical culture.

These developments suggest, somewhat paradoxically, that if the active body is to be the object of study for PCS, and perhaps even an empirical touchstone that might quell the 'tribal warfare' articulated by Ingham, lamented by Andrews and Silk, and that continues to colour the missions of both PCS and kinesiology, then it should not be unduly foregrounded or fixed in time and space in ways that forlornly tame its becomings. Put another way, calling into question the boundaries of the active human body necessarily calls into question the disciplinary boundaries that, in Bruno Latour's (1993) terms, have sought to 'purify' knowledge of the world along the axes of nature and culture. These are also, of course, the boundaries that continue to divide our multi-disciplinary kinesiology departments into bio-physical, socio-cultural, or pedagogical 'tribes'. Working at the margins of kinesiology, PCS practitioners might need to be nimble enough to track moving targets both in their empirical labor and in an ever shifting constellation of trans-disciplinarity across and beyond the social sciences and (post)humanities to breach these borders. In such projects, the historical body surely cannot be mere background or context, less still reducible to *either* human history *or* natural history. Active bodies that are generative, vital, lived and living, felt and feeling, human and otherwise, are always already historical.

Notes

1 The term 'sociology of sport' is generally favored over 'sport sociology'. Where the latter has been viewed as 'too applied', as per sport psychology, the sociology of sport declares itself as first and foremost a sociological enterprise, characterizing much of the work the field has produced. The distancing from the 'lesser' enterprise of applied/pedagogical work is important to note, as it demonstrates the specialization of expertise in kinesiology and human movement departments, often to the detriment of pedagogical and educational concerns.
2 For its extensive effects see Segel in *Body Ascendant: Modernism and the Physical Imperative* (1998), who shows how the obsession with physical culture resonated widely through the modernist movement and establishes the disturbing compatibility between the era's artistic and athletic celebration of the body and the rise of totalitarian nationalism and racism.
3 Bairner (2012: 115) has in this vein also asserted that the sociology of sport must be 'defended against the tyranny of the natural sciences'.
4 Policing the crisis being one of the most overt references to the heritage of cultural studies in this iteration of PCS (see Hall *et al.*, 1978).
5 Although we do not want to enter here the complex debate around the raison d'être of cultural studies, it is useful to remember that James Carey's theory of culture and the 'invention' of cultural studies was in large measure a response to the dominance of science and his vision for a non-positivist understanding of science that, in a manner akin to the remit of PCS, 'elevated the ethical over the epistemological' (Grossberg, 2009: 178).
6 A trope fully developed in Becher and Trowler's *Academic Tribes and Territories* (2001) with its sustained metaphor of the disciplines as tribal cultures distinguished by their respective languages, initiation rituals, folklore and so on.
7 Post-humanism is itself a heterogeneous body of theory and inquiry, often historicized in line with Foucault's declaration of the 'Death of Man' ([1970] 2003) and de-centring of the subject as agent in social life, and to which strands of feminist, post-colonial, de-colonial, and queer theory each make varied claims.

References

Alter, J. S., 2004. *Yoga in modern India*. Princeton, NJ: Princeton University Press.
Alter, J. S., 2007. Yoga and physical education: Swami Kuvalayananda's nationalist project. *Asian Medicine* 3 (1), 20–36.
Altglas, V., 2007. The global diffusion and westernization of neo-Hindu movements. *Religions of South Asia* 1, 217–237.
Andrews, D. L., 2008. Kinesiology's inconvenient truth: the physical cultural studies imperative. *Quest*, 60 (1), 46–63.
Andrews, D. L. and Giardina, M., 2008. Sport without guarantees: toward a cultural studies that matters. *Cultural Studies ↔ Critical Methodologies* 8, 395–422.
Atkinson, M., 2011. Physical cultural studies (redux). *Sociology of Sport Journal*, 28 (1), 135–144.
Bairner, A., 2012. For a sociology of sport. *Sociology of Sport Journal*, 29 (2), 102–117.
Ballantyne, T. and Burton, A., eds., 2005. *Bodies in contact: rethinking colonial encounters in world history*. Durham, NC: Duke University Press.
Becher, T. and Trowler, P., 2001. *Academic tribes and territories: intellectual enquiry and the culture of disciplines*. Philadelphia, PA: SRHE and Open University Press.
Bernard, M., 1976. Sport et institution ou les métamorphoses du pouvoir. In M. Bernard, ed., *Quelles pratiques corporelles maintenant?* Paris: Delarge.
Berryman, J. W., 1995. *Out of many, one: a history of the American College of Sports Medicine*. Champaign, IL: Human Kinetics.
Berryman, J. W., 2010. Exercise is medicine: a historical perspective. *Current Sports Medicine Reports*, 9 (4), 195–201.
Blackman, L., 2008. *The body: key concepts*. Oxford: Berg Publishers.
Blackman, L. and Featherstone, M., 2010. Re-visioning body & society. *Body and Society* 16 (1), 1–5.
Bourdieu, P., 1978. Sport and social class. *Social Science Information* 17 (6), 819–840.
Bourdieu, P., 1980. *The logic of practice*. Stanford, CA: Stanford University Press.
Bourdieu, P., 1988. A program for the comparative sociology of sport. In S. Kang, J. MacAloon and R. DaMatta, eds, *The Olympics and cultural exchange: the papers of the first international conference on the Olympics and east/west and south/north cultural exchange in the world system*. Seoul: Hanyang University Press.
Brohm, J. M., [1975] 1989. *Sport: a prison of measured time* (I. Frans, trans.). Worcester, UK: Pluto Press.
Chandler, J., 2009. Introduction: doctrines, disciplines, discourses, departments. *Critical Inquiry* 35 (4), 729–746.
Clark, B. R., 1963. Faculty culture. In T. F Lunsford, ed. *The study of campus culture*. Boulder, CO: WICHE.
Deleuze, G. and Guattari, F., 1987. *A Thousand plateaus: capitalism and schizophrenia*. Minneapolis, MN: University of Minnesota Press.
Dyck, N. and Archetti, E., eds., 2003. *Sport, dance and embodied identities*. Oxford: Berg.
Eichberg, H., 1998. A revolution in body culture. In J. Bale and C. Phil, eds, *Body cultures: essays on sport, spaces and identity*. London: Routledge, 128–148.
Featherstone, M. and Turner, B. S., 1995. Body and society: an introduction. *Body & Society*, 1 (1), 1–12.
Foucault, M., [1970] 2003. *The order of things: an archaeology of the human sciences*. London: Routledge.
Foucault, M., 1973. *The birth of the clinic: an archeology of medical perception*. London: Tavistock.
Geertz, C., 1980. Blurred genres: the re-figuration of social thought. *American Scholar* 49 (2), 165–179.
Giardina, M. D. and Newman, J. I., 2011. What is this 'physical' in physical cultural studies? *Sociology of Sport Journal* 28 (1), 36–63.
Grossberg, L., 2009. The conversation of cultural studies. *Cultural Studies* 23 (2), 177–182.
Hall, S., 1986. The problem of ideology: Marxism without guarantees. *Journal of Communication Inquiry* 10, 28–44.
Hall, S., 1992. Cultural studies and its theoretical legacies. In L. Grossberg, C. Nelson and P. Treichler, eds, *Cultural studies*. New York: Routledge, 277–294.
Hall, S., Critcher, C., Jefferson, T., Clarke, J. and Roberts, B., 1978. *Policing the crisis: mugging, the state and law and order*. London: Macmillan.
Hancock, P., Hughes, B., Jagger E., Paterson K., Russell R., Tulle-Winton E. and Tyler, M., 2000. *The body, culture and society: an introduction*. Buckingham, UK: Open University Press.
Hargreaves, J., 1986. *Sport, power and culture: a social and historical analysis of popular sports in Britain*. New York: St Martin's Press.

Hargreaves, J. and Vertinsky, P., 1996. *Physical culture, power and the body*. London: Routledge.
Ingham, A. G., 1997. Toward a department of physical cultural studies and an end to tribal warfare. In J. Fernandez-Balboa, ed., *Critical postmodernism in human movement, physical education, and sport*. Albany, NY: State University of New York Press, 157–182.
Jackson, M., 2014. *The history of medicine: a beginner's guide*. London: Oneworld Publication.
King, S., 2005. Methodological contingencies in contextual sports studies. In D. L. Andrews, D. S. Mason, and M. L. Silk, eds, *Qualitative methods in sports studies*. Oxford: Berg, 21–38.
Latour, B., 1993. *We have never been modern*. Cambridge, MA: Harvard University Press.
Lock, M., 2015. Comprehending the body in the era of the epigenome. *Current Anthropology* 56 (2), 151–177.
Mauss, M., [1935] 1973. Techniques of the body. *Economy and Society*, 2 (1), 70–88.
Merleau-Ponty, M., [1945] 1962. *Phenomenology of perception*. (C. Smith, trans.). New York: Routledge.
Newman, J. I. and Giardina, M. D., 2014. Moving biopolitics. *Cultural Studies ↔ Critical Methodologies* 14 (5), 419–424.
Newman, J. I., Shields, R., and McLeod, C. M., 2015. The MRSA epidemic and/as fluid biopolitics. *Body & Society*, doi: 10.1177/1357034X14551844 [published online before print].
Readings, B., 1996. *The university in ruins*. Cambridge, MA: Harvard University Press.
Segel, H. B., 1998. *Body ascendant: modernism and the physical imperative*. Baltimore, MD: The Johns Hopkins University Press.
Shilling, C., 1993. *The body and social theory*. London: Sage.
Shilling, C., 2005. *The body in culture, technology and society*. London: Sage.
Silk, M. L. and Andrews, D. L., 2011. Towards a physical cultural studies. *Sociology of Sport Journal* 28 (1), 4–35.
Stoler, A. L., 1995. *Race and the education of desire: Foucault's history of sexuality and the colonial order of things*. Durham, NC: Duke University Press.
Turner, B., 1996. *The body and society: explorations in social theory*, 2nd edn. Thousand Oaks, CA: Sage.
Vigarello, G., 1978. *Le corps redressé: histoire d'un pouvoir pédagogique*. Paris: Delarge.
Washington, R. E. and Karen, D., 2001. Sport and society. *Annual Review of Sociology* 27, 187–212.
Young, K., 2014. Towards a less speciesist sociology of sport. *Sociology of Sport Journal* 31 (4), 387–401.
Zirin, D., 2008. Calling sports sociology off the bench. *Contexts* (Summer), 27–31.

2
POWER AND POWER RELATIONS

Michael Atkinson and Kass Gibson

Power, power, everywhere and anywhere

Power is undoubtedly a core, if not the central, concept for physical cultural studies (PCS). The ways in which we define conceptually, analyze theoretically, identify empirically, or otherwise work to understand power in its manifest and latent complexity has profound implications for not only what we study in PCS but also how we can, or indeed should, go about studying it as a matter of both epistemology and praxis. While power sits symbolically at the center of the field through a concern to understand various forms (i.e. material, ideological or identity-based) of oppression in/through/as physical culture – and then deployed towards mapping, programming, seriously advocating or realizing progressive social change (Atkinson, 2011) – there is little consensus as to what actually constitutes power and how best to demonstrate its multifold effects empirically. Stated differently, there is no recognized canon of 'power thinking' in PCS or directional mandate of the field as such; despite what critics argue regarding the hegemonically enforced theoretical inclusions and exclusions in the burgeoning field. The problem of understanding power is complicated further given there is no shared understanding of *physical culture* itself.

Proponents of PCS are understandably reticent to demarcate the precise intellectual boundaries of PCS in part because of their explicitly relational and pluralistic axiologies. Resultantly, current theoretical variety in power arises partly from a lack of conceptual rigor in locating physical culture, but more fundamentally from the range of questions and theoretical traditions evidenced in PCS. PCS is thus left with empirical foci on power in physical cultural practices every bit as territorially murky as the sociology of sport, which has been of fundamental, but by no means exclusive, importance to the emergence of PCS. The object of our endeavor, true to PCS form, is not to impose orthodoxy or make normative and evaluative claims as to what legitimately counts as power or PCS scholarship, but to encourage communication about issues already addressed and to suggest new ones.

While PCS researchers account for the body as a subject of research, its objective materiality receives short shrift. There is a tendency to lose or obscure the obdurate materiality of human bodies behind densely theorized readings framing its central importance in the subject area. This chapter, then, sets out to clarify meanings of physical culture (and physical cultural studies) through a dialogue regarding how power can be understood through contextual definitions of physical culture. In this sense, we see power as the key conceptual project of PCS rather than defining bodies as passively docile or romantically resistant and resilient sites, billboards, or avenues of power. Our aim is to address an array of the theoretical problems germane to PCS where power is placed at the center of analysis and praxis. Our purpose is, therefore, clarification not systematically reviewing power in extant PCS literature. We begin with a broad-strokes sketch of key considerations of power as developed between two distinct but interlaced theoretical traditions informing PCS. First, theories of power as *power-over* address how certain groups or individuals have the ability to ensure another individual or group will do something at their behest, explicitly or otherwise, broadly reflecting Weber's (1968: 53) classic definition: 'the probability that one actor within a social relationship will be in a position to carry out his own will despite resistance'. Second, theories of power as the *power-to* are attentive to power as productive, agential and oftentimes understood in, as and through discourse influenced heavily, especially in PCS, by Michel Foucault. After briefly reviewing the general debates regarding power we then work toward defining physical culture by highlighting how different power perspectives focus our investigations across three main areas of interest: broad scale and institutionalized; small group and subcultural; and, phenomenological/existential.

From power-over to power-to

Important from the outset is that we must appreciate how conceptualizations of power are seldom total(izing). By this we mean traditions that theorize power as power-over do not exclude or deny agential capacity in power relations nor view power exclusively as repressive, analogous to absolutism, or tantamount to tyranny. Similarly, power-to perspectives, develop as explicit critiques of power-over accounts (e.g. Foucault, 1978, 1980; Parsons, 1963) need not dismiss force, constraint, or compulsion through material or ideological channels. If power is to be at the heart of PCS what is at stake is not whether differing perspectives recognize power as capacity, possession, repression, or production, but understandings and possibilities they enable. Power is relevant only as it enables us to define and understand physical culture (and vice versa). Power is neither inherently oppressive nor liberating. Power relations seldom, if ever, result in total control or even infer physical force or coercion, but rather shifting interactions and interdependencies. Thus, we maintain that all theories of power are fundamentally *relational and radically contextual*.

Power-over is arguably the form around which power became an explicit concern for social and political theorists and the predominant catalyst for the emergence of the critical theories of Lukács, Horkheimer, Fromm, Marcuse, Adorno, Pollock, Benjamin and others. A concentration on power-over serves as the schematic foundation of Marx and Engels's studies of capital–labor relations, is characteristic of Simmel's (1950) consideration of social differentiation as stemming from interaction and quantitative aspects of the group, and is integral to Durkheim's ([1897] 1951) studies of solidarity, collective consciousness, laws and patterns. C. Wright Mills's study of the common social background underpinning the convergence of political, economic and military power among privileged groups in *The Power Elite* (1956) promoted another foundational analysis of power as power-over. These perspectives tend to share attentiveness to the structural conditions under which social stratification takes place, which in turn views power relations as manifest in, through and about diffuse social inequalities. Addressing power through Marxist, feminist, postcolonial, race and queer theories conceptually as power-over has been integral to generating understandings of asymmetries between individuals and/or groups manifest through social (material-political) stratification and relationships between social groups, individualization and the emergence of (identifiable) dominant groups. The dominant critique of the metaphorical foundation of such perspectives, namely 'holding' power, is not as stark a divide as some might theorize. Power-over is not exclusively coercive. It requires neither demonstration nor exercise. It can be performative as both Goffman (1959) and Butler (1990) articulate.

Critiques of power-over perspectives, some of which are alluded to above, tend to be couched in terms that assume asymmetry presupposes power as held and repressive. Although not always the case, it is important to realize that all power-over views are far more nuanced than ruthless or 'governmental' authorities generating compliance through physical force or ideological manipulation. Moreover, despite such critiques being leveled directly at Marxist theorizing, largely in the wake of Foucault's (1980) famous critiques of Marx and Freud, we must realize that Gramscian hegemony theory (Gramsci, 1971) – as a power-over theory – has fundamentally shaped *virtually all* understandings of power in PCS (see Pringle, 2005). Valid empirical, political and philosophical criticisms of power-over perspectives have highlighted power as generating possibilities for action, positively and negatively, and constitutive of subjectivities and the social world.

The thrust behind theories of *power-to* is perhaps most succinctly defined by Arendt (1970: 44); as she writes, power is 'the human ability not just to act but to act in concert'. Arendt, like Max Weber to some degree, takes pains to distinguish power from authority, strength, force and violence. Similarly, as indicated above, Foucault (1978), like others, promotes changing perspectives on *what* was studied by moving away from addressing so-called social repositories of power. However, this does not deny the importance of such repositories, merely the idea of easily locatable ruled and ruler binaries. Resultantly, power-to analyses, especially those informed by Foucault, address how power produces certain experiences, perspectives, beliefs, desires, capacities and, apparently most distinctively, truths.

The focus of power-to in literature germane to PCS scholarship is on the reproduction of cultural understandings of physical cultural normality articulated in the relationship between knowledge produced and concomitant understandings and practices. To this end, power has been predominantly approached in PCS literature as shaping individuals' understanding of themselves as raced, classed, gendered, sexed, ethnicized, nationed, or spiritualized people in predominantly constraining manners. However, the problem of the relationship between social control and the body, or how we learn in, through and about our bodies, is not synonymous with, or always already, a problem of Foucauldian bio-power. A simultaneous success and failure of power-to theorizations, courtesy of foregrounding discursive formations within social relations, is to move away from seeking to account for power's dimensions given, from such perspectives, power is diffuse, dispersed and ultimately everywhere (and therefore, paradoxically, nowhere) to seeking understanding of the sources of power in certain forms of knowledge.

The above arguments accentuate that while advocates of certain traditions oftentimes vociferously champion the purported originality, if not uniqueness, of their theoretical orientation it is clear that multiple analytic paths tread on very similar conceptual territory. What accounts for the highly contested nature of the concept of power? Empirical complexity and multiplicity certainly, as Elias (1978: 92) comments, 'the difficulties encountered in reflecting on problems of power stem from the polymorphous nature of sources of power'. That being said, following Lukes (2004) and Said (1986), we believe that PCS conceptualizations of power are shaped by the theoretical and political orientations (not to mention the disciplinary training and exposure) of researchers at least as much as the empirical context of the study. Simply put, analyses influenced by critical race theory, will differ from those guided by postcolonial theories, feminisms, Marxisms and/or any combination of those. Resultantly, the academic and political utility of any given conceptualization of power is defined largely by the contextual nature of the analysis. However, the context of physical culture lacks any clear, or at least attempted, definition. Our purpose in the remaining section of this chapter, then, is to outline how an appreciation of power can actually lead us to a more productive understanding.

Broad-scale and institutional physical culture

At its broadest level, power is central to understanding the socio-historic conditions and socio-political contexts of the production and distributions of practices, goods, products, and ways and systems of knowing. As early functionalist theorists attest, wide-scale trends heuristically shape and organize society as 'social facts' confronting the human agent. Physical culture might be viewed as such as social fact via sets of ostensibly obdurate, dominant, pervasive, trending or statistically common characteristics about bodies and how they are collective shaped in a society; and the ways in which members within those social boundaries use relatively (culturally) normative tools, techniques, rituals and representations of these bodies. This sensitivity obviously leads to engaging with how, when, and under what circumstances different manifestations of power are important, to what extent, and the ways different sources and forms of power (or groups) interact. Studying how particular body cultures such as sport come to dominate economically, geographically and culturally over other body practices, patterns of sedentary living, the adoption and reliance on mobile technologies, the built physical geography of cities, obesity, and youth participation rates in sports are all forms of broad-scale physical culture PCS researchers address.

Extending the above, the exercise of power (over and/or to) through the performance of different activities is central to institutions, both internally and externally. How particular institutions and individuals therein gain the ability, rights, obligations, authority and/or legitimacy to influence the actions of others is a central question facing institutional(ized) physical culture. Thus, institutional(ized) physical culture accentuates stability in social structures and patterns when conflicts are de-escalated, demobilized, or quiescent through the dominance of certain interests and interest groups over, and/or through Others. Broad-scale physical culture brings into relief how particular social institutions, such as schools or medical communities for example, formulate understandings of bodies and encourage or dissuade certain practices in culturally distinctive ways. The contextual factors of broad-scale physical culture, shaped as they are by sociological problems of globalization, capital exchange and so forth, gives PCS cause to examine what would be traditionally identified as macro-sociological concerns. The changing corporate landscape, commodification of bodies, and the image have tremendous influence on socially relevant differentiations and exclusions through which practices are formulated. Yet PCS researchers can remain equally attentive to the interpretive practices shaped in no small manner by physical culture as mediating modes of practice. The ways in which beliefs become more coherent, consistent and systematic, namely rationalized, is potentially a core consideration in broad-scale and institutional physical culture. Power helps define the ways in which socialization occurs and social forms emerge that are hallmarks of contemporary bodily practices and values. In short, broad-scale physical culture accentuates 'system level' conditions.

Small group physical culture

At the 'micro' or small group level of physical culture, we focus on power as agency in so-called 'everyday lived experience'. In this sense, micro-logical studies of physical culture focus on small group, shared physical practices and how people express agency both in and as physical culture. This tradition of PCS research draws extensively on the history of intepretivism in the social sciences, and its unwavering emphasis on the power of human agents to define their lives through face-to-face (and we would add embodied) interactions in radically situated contexts. Central to such perspectives is rejecting fixed relationships and distinctions between structure and agency alike. Power, then, is indistinguishable from the situations and is therefore addressed not in and of itself but through carefully, considerately and critically attending to how and under what conditions certain people are able to do certain things, including to other people, especially relevant to the PCS agenda through authoritative categorization of people, individually and collectively, as subordinate or morally unacceptable in some way. On this point, Becker succinctly highlights how material means of cultural values as affording greater agency reflect power as constitutive of particular institutions, practices and subjectivities:

> the differences in the ability to make rules and apply them to other people are essentially power differentials (either legal or extralegal). Those groups whose social position gives them weapons and power are best able to enforce their rules. Distinctions of age, sex, ethnicity, and class are all related to differences in power, which accounts for differences in the degree to which groups so distinguished can make rules for others.
>
> *(Becker, 1963: 17–18)*

Mead's, Blumer's, Becker's and Goffman's emphasis on the reflexive aspects of (embodied) social performance as a marker of the power-to in everyday life is also starkly evident in a wide range of modernist and postmodernist theories including Norbert Elias, Simone de Beauvoir, Pierre Bourdieu and Michel Foucault. In another example, Thomas's theorem, 'if men define situations as real, they are real in their consequences', became the basis of *labeling theory* and one of the most fundamental power-sensitive concepts in modern sociology, and the *social construction of reality* principle (Berger and Luckmann, 1966), to which all contemporary theories of power owe a tremendous conceptual debt. Thus, as Prus (1999) pointedly identifies, interactionist studies of power are neither explicitly labeled as such nor do they resemble conventional studies of power so are not considered as studies of power despite generating conclusions, eerily familiar to those of Foucault, of the ubiquity of power and simultaneous shaping of individuals and society.

Radical existential physical culture

PCS has an almost non-existent relationship with existentialist theory and philosophy, and we find this condition rather peculiar given the overtly political and emancipatory thrust of the PCS *oeuvre* (Atkinson, 2011). Emphasizing reflexive individual existence, freedom, and choice, existentialism is a philosophy of agency unchained rooted in the collectively radical view that humans have an almost immeasurable capacity to define their own meanings in life, and must try to make 'authentic' decisions despite existing in an irrational, or as Albert Camus (1955) described it, utterly absurd, human (cultural) world. In terms of this chapter, a rebelliously reflexive perspective highlighting the need to remember in all contexts individuals have 'power-to(o)'. Do not, we would caution, lazily confuse humanitarian existentialism with economic neo-liberalism.

PCS research on power might well benefit by attending to existentialism's broad focus on the fabricated and anesthetic nature of human culture as a provider of purpose in life. Existentialists argue there is no rational order to the world, knowable teleological purpose or reasonable explanation regarding the essence of our existence. Belief otherwise indicates submission to power-over social structures, cultural practices and ideologies dictating existence. Power is therefore nothing to be found externally through given meaning structures. One cannot simply become liberated from one institution or another by tactical acts of resistance.

Contrary to the other power-over or power-to theories outlined in this chapter, the existentialism of Sartre, Camus, Nietzsche and others believes that because individuals are entirely free, they must therefore take personal responsibility for themselves; they have radical 'power too'. Such responsibility inevitably leads to profound anguish and dread that one's relationships, efforts, practice, sense of self, and overall life is devoid of purposeful meaning. Conscious thought on the meaninglessness of life leading to the general condition of suffering is the heart of human experience resulting from succumbing to a life of 'bad faith'. Existentialism therefore emphasizes individual action, freedom and decision as fundamental (power too), and holds that the only way to transcend the condition of humanity (the reality of inescapable suffering and inevitable death) is by exercising personal freedom and choice.

The existentialism articulated above is crystallized by the work of Sartre, Camus, de Beauvoir, Kierkegaard, Nietzsche, Heidegger, Merleau-Ponty, Jaspers, Husserl, Schopenhauer, Dostoevsky and Kafka. Existentialists assert human beings are thrown into a concrete, inveterate universe that cannot be thought away. Therefore, existence (*being-in-the-world*) precedes consciousness and is the ultimate reality. Individuals must embrace true agency and frighteningly choose their own way (as a radical form of personal power-to) without the aid of universal, objective standards. Thus, most existentialists believe that personal experience and acting on one's own convictions are essential in arriving at an experiential truth, and that the understanding of a situation by someone involved in that situation is superior to that of a detached, objective observer.

What we are specifically drawn to in existential theory as PCS researchers is the concrete examination of the sources of (embodied) human suffering in the face of postmodern meaning breakdown and anxiety, and the tracing back of such suffering to the roots of power (over). Along the lines of existential theory, physical culture provides empirical case studies of the absurd *and* how living in bad faith (or not) is a radical exercise in agency. To this end, existentialists' studies of physical practices might examine how diffuse existential suffering is reproduced through sports, exercise and physical activity; or by contrast, how recognizing and embracing the absurdity of meaning in any physical culture practice might actually produce radical and authentic moments of human pleasure.

Theoretically establishing physical cultural studies as the systematic study of both contextual and generic forms of existential human suffering and the possibility of self-determined pleasure through movement is not a difficult task requiring the total re-imagining of the PCS field. The early works of Marx, Durkheim and Weber envisioned how the power-over structuring aspects of society (i.e. its social hierarchies, divisions of labor and relations of power) lead to the dehumanizing conditions of mass alienation, anomie and rationalization. Frankfurt school theorists including Horkheimer, Adorno, Marcuse, Fromm and Pollock added depth in their collective dissection of ideology's role in producing differential access to power and culture. The Chicago School of micro-sociology's (i.e. Park, Sutherland, Thomas and Blumer) focus on marginality, deviance and the labeling of outsiders, modernist accounts of the complicated relationship between human agency and social structuration (i.e. Parsons, Elias, Merton, Bourdieu and Giddens), work from the Birmingham Centre for Contemporary Cultural Studies group (i.e. Hall, Jefferson, Bennett and McRobbie) and its emphasis on youth troubles in post-war England, the rise of feminist (i.e. Gilman, Butler, Bordo and hooks) and queer (i.e. Fausto-Sterling, Halperin, Sedgwick and Rich) scholarship and its focus on social inequalities grounded in identity, and the postmodern (i.e. Foucault, Jameson, Lyotard and Baudrillard) emphasis on the decentering of truth and the splintering of reality into a million mediated images all underscore how social conditions, practices, ideologies, institutions and micro experiences are laced with embodied suffering.

If PCS is emerging as a sub-discipline in which the empirical and theoretical unearthing of the social bases of suffering/pleasure is its long-term project, it might surely take its conceptual lead from extant social scientific research on health and illness. While there is a burgeoning pain, trauma, illness and health stream within the social scientific study of physical culture (see Malcolm and Safai, 2012; Sparkes and Smith, 2008), PCS is not openly marked as the existential study of social patterns in, and personal experiences with, physicality and human movement as means of better theorizing the forms, contexts and contours of the power-based roots of human suffering (or pleasure). Following Thin's (2014) argument, and echoing with the critical reflections of Frank (1994) and Wilkinson (2004), the systematic analysis of how both pleasure and suffering are existentially experienced and shapes people (in any number of ways) in the here and now of everyday life is critical for understanding how people make choices and enact personal power-to in radically embodied contexts.

Everyday accounts of existential pleasure through physical culture and sport are equally critical at this stage of inquiry. These feelings are two sides of the same substantive and theoretical coin, but the latter requires a fundamental shift in thinking about the mandate of physical cultural studies. Why? Within the past five years, there has been a renewed, and certainly contested, argument that the research act in the sociology of sport/physical culture must become more socially engaged and culturally meaningful (vis-à-vis the attention to, and work toward the alleviation of, human suffering) to retain its utility. Such an argument, coming perhaps most openly from advocates of physical cultural studies as a contender to the sociology of sport throne (Atkinson, 2011; Silk and Andrews, 2011; Giardina and Newman, 2011), rests upon the related premises that not only does theoretically driven research on physical culture offer much insight into a spectrum of social problems pertaining to human suffering, it also illustrates how life can be existentially pleasurable through physical culture as a site of meaning-making and choice exploration. Strangely enough, accounting for and documenting the pleasurable aspects of the human condition appears to be a radical interventionist task.

A forward-thinking, and existentialist, physical cultural studies might be one that sees encountering human suffering and the possibility of human pleasure through movement as a (if not *the*) core focus, is essentially the study of social life manifesting into and engaging with, as Burawoy writes (2004), the possibility/existence of better worlds. In the end, conceptually seeing actual persons as producers of authentic, agentic power in physical cultural practice very well may be the most radical PCS idea of all.

References

Arendt, H. (1970). *On Violence*. New York: Harcourt Brace.
Atkinson, M. (2011). Physical cultural studies [redux]. *Sociology of Sport Journal* 28(1), 135–144.
Becker, H. (1963). *Outsiders: Studies in the Sociology of Deviance*. New York: Free Press.
Berger, P. and Luckmann, T. (1966). *The Social Construction of Reality: A Treatise in the Sociology of Knowledge*. New York: Anchor Books.
Burawoy, M. (2004). Public sociologies: Contradictions, dilemmas, and possibilities. *Social Forces* 82(4), 603–618.
Butler, J. (1990). *Gender Trouble: Feminism and the Subversion of Identity*. New York: Routledge.
Camus, A. (1995). *The Myth of Sisyphus and Other Essays*. New York: Knopf.
Durkheim, E. ([1897] 1951). *Suicide*. Glencoe, IL: Free Press.

Elias, N. (1978). *What is Sociology?* London: Hutchinson.
Foucault, M. (1978). *The History of Sexuality, Volume 1: An Introduction.* London: Penguin.
Foucault, M. (1980). Prison talk. In C. Gordon (ed.), *Power/Knowledge: Selected Interviews and Other Writings 1972–1977.* Harlow: Harvester.
Frank, A. (1994). *The Wounded Storyteller.* Chicago, IL: University of Chicago Press.
Giardina, M. and Newman, J. (2011). What is this 'physical' in physical cultural studies? *Sociology of Sport Journal* 28(1), 36–63.
Goffman, E. (1959). *The Presentation of Self in Everyday Life.* New York: Doubleday Anchor.
Gramsci, A. (1971). *Selections from the Prison Notebooks.* New York: International Publishers.
Lukes, S. (2004). *Power: A Radical View*, 2nd edn. London: Palgrave Macmillan.
Malcolm, D. and Safai, P. (2012). *The Social Organization of Sports Medicine: Critical Socio-Cultural Perspectives.* London: Routledge.
Mills, C. W. (1956). *The Power Elite.* Oxford: Oxford University Press.
Parsons, T. (1963). On the concept of political power. *Proceedings of the American Philosophical Society* 107(3), 232–262.
Pringle, R. (2005). Masculinities, sport and power: A critical comparison of Gramscian and Foucauldian inspired theoretical tools. *Journal of Sport and Social Issues* 29(3), 256–278.
Prus, R. (1999). *Beyond the Power Mystique: Power as Intersubjective Accomplishment.* Albany, NY: SUNY.
Said, E. (1986). *After the Last Sky: Palestinian Lives.* New York: Pantheon Books.
Silk, M. and Andrews, D. L. (2011). Toward a physical cultural studies. *Sociology of Sport Journal*, 28(1), 4–35.
Simmel, G. (1950). *The Sociology of Georg Simmel.* New York: Free Press.
Sparkes, A. and Smith, B. (2008). Men, spinal cord injury, memories, and the narrative performance of pain. *Disability and Society* 23, 679–690.
Thin, N. (2014). Positive sociology and appreciative empathy: History and prospects. *Sociological Research Online* 19, 5.
Weber, M. (1968). *Economy and Society: An Outline of Interpretive Sociology.* New York: Bedminster Press.
Wilkinson, I. (2004). *Suffering: A Sociological Introduction.* Cambridge: Polity.

3
THEORY AND REFLEXIVITY

Richard Pringle and Holly Thorpe

In this chapter we introduce and discuss the significance of social 'theory' and 'reflexivity' with respect to their importance in conducting and producing *meaningful* qualitative research that has a clear *purpose* (see Markula and Silk, 2011). Given the tenets of physical cultural studies (PCS) and its concerns with social injustices and inequitable sets of relations of power, we focus predominantly on theories associated with what Sparkes and Smith (2014) call critical or openly ideological research. Accordingly, we focus on theories and associated research practices that eschew the notion of an objective or disinterested social scientist and with an underpinning purpose 'orientated toward social and individual transformation' (ibid.: 49–50). In this manner, we concur with Bourdieu's call against the fetishism of theory, within which some researchers seem more inclined to dwell on theoretical concepts 'instead of making them work … [and] putting them into action' (cited in Brandao, 2010: 231). In paraphrasing Marx we accordingly desire to make social theory and reflexive processes work, not just to know and represent the world but as tools to potentially change it.

Social theory is typically defined as a logically interrelated set of propositions that provides explanations of human actions, interactions and meaning-making processes. To explain this definition of social theory to undergraduate students we often draw from Chris Collins and Steve Jackson's (2007) analogy of theory as a road map. We explain that physical reality is complex and it can be difficult to navigate in unknown territories. Hence a map or GPS system can aid exploration by directing attention to aspects deemed relevant, such as roads, geographical features and relative distances. We then explain that social reality is perhaps more complex than physical geography and that a good social theory, like a map, can direct attention to select aspects of social reality – such as the workings of power or gender construction processes – that allow researchers to navigate, explore, interpret and draw conclusions. Thus we introduce and understand social theory as a tool, heuristic device and as a framework for interpretation (Thorpe, 2011).

Although social theory can illuminate, it can also work to obscure focus. We, accordingly, emphasize that social theory should not be understood as a definitive explanation of social reality but as a conceptual framework that needs ongoing testing, refining and critical reflection. As such, we highlight the necessary dialogue between theory and research, and concur with Bourdieu and Wacquant (1992: 16), who exclaimed that 'research without theory is blind, and theory without research is empty'. The relationship between theory and research, in this manner, is 'dynamically intertwined, mutually influential, and constantly changing' (Scott and Garner, 2013: 87).

Given the importance of theory to the research process it is not surprising that it has been defined as the 'heart and soul of sociology' (Thorpe, 2011: 12). Social theory, for example, encourages analysis of select topics, shapes the types of research questions asked and how researchers 'do' research (e.g. strategies for analysis of discourse), focuses interpretation of findings, impacts the quality of the research findings and, in turn, contours and refines theoretical understandings. Theory can correspondingly be understood as located within a discourse of methodology, with recognition that methodology involves an ongoing negotiation between theory and method (Scott and Garner, 2013). The research process, therefore, is never atheoretical and it is always more than just selecting a 'method' (Schwandt, 2000).

Yet perhaps the greatest indication of the significance of theory to critical research is with respect to how theory shapes the identities of researchers themselves. As examples, we know scholars who identify themselves, or at least their research selves, as Marxists, figurationalists or Foucauldians. This subjective investment can subsequently underpin academic debates and perhaps even influence power relations between scholars in a particular field of study or be associated with the acceptance or rejection of papers in select journals (e.g. see Dunning and Rojek, 1992, regarding the critiques and counter-critiques of figurational theory). A cultural studies approach, in contrast, would question the value of a researcher solely identifying with a specific theorist; as theory within cultural studies is always negotiated and developed in relation to diverse cultural contexts and changing political landscapes (King, 2005).

Commentators on research issues, however, more typically discuss the influence of biography on the research process. Indeed, the types of theories that researchers use depend, in part, on their life experiences, subjectivities and how they have been socialized/disciplined into the art of doing research. Sparkes and Smith contend:

> we conduct inquiry via a particular (research) paradigm because it embodies assumptions about the world that we believe in and supports values that we hold dear. And, because we hold these assumptions and values we conduct inquiry according to the precepts of that paradigm.
>
> *(Sparkes and Smith, 2014: 9)*

Correspondingly, they suggest that 'it is not the research "problem" or question that drives a study, but, either implicitly or explicitly, our assumptions and theoretical orientations' (ibid.: 9). This recognition underpins the importance, dare we say necessity, for researchers to critically reflect on the intimate links between their biographies, theoretical assumptions and research approaches.

Foundational, grounded and critical-reflexive theories

To further examine the links between self and theory, we explore a framework of thinking proposed by Scott and Garner (2013) that consists of the three broad types of theories: foundational, grounded and critical-reflexive. *Foundational theories* are broad ways of 'explaining what we observe in daily life at the microlevel and macrolevel' (ibid.: 88). A foundational theory (such as Marxism, symbolic interactionism or conflict theories) helps establish the purpose of the research, guides the types of questions asked, and provides somewhat 'grand' explanatory frameworks that can be generally applied to different contexts. Although clearly useful, foundational theories have been critiqued for producing 'normative' or seemingly circular research processes. That is, the prime conclusions reflect and/or reproduce the theoretical underpinnings and rarely produce findings that challenge or change the theoretical assumptions.

Grounded theories, in contrast, claim to begin analysis without *a priori* concepts through observations and the collection of empirical data in a manner that works towards building a theoretical perspective from the 'ground up'. Such an approach allegedly reduces the 'bias' of a theoretically driven examination and, therefore, counters the critique directed at foundational theories. Yet postmodern critiques of grounded theory suggest that it is disingenuous to claim that data is collected without theoretical guidance.

The broad criticisms directed at foundational and grounded theories have led to increased calls for *reflexive sociology* or for *critically reflexive theorizing*, in which researchers attempt to examine and acknowledge how their subjectivities, life experiences, theorizing and research approaches are interlinked. The subsequent 'theory-research-self' dialogue acknowledges that research is always inductive and deductive, and that theory always involves both foundational and grounded processes.

The calls for reflexive sociology can be traced back to the 1960s and the numerous 'turns' (e.g. linguistic, rhetorical, narrative, poststructural, ethical, reflexive) that have shaped the manner in which social science research has been conducted and represented. These 'multiple turns, which some refer to broadly as the postmodern turn, have blurred in a manner to disrupt universal truth claims, the possibility of researching from a position of "nowhere", and transcendent assertions of validity' (Pringle and Phillips, 2013: 2). The theoretical tools that gained favour in this context shunned the tenets of positivism or modernist ways of researching and were deemed to be post-positivist or, more specifically, *anti-positivist*, critical and self-reflexive (Markula and Silk, 2011). Within the sociology of sport and PCS, the postmodern turn has accordingly encouraged scholars to draw increasingly on qualitative research approaches and to be more transparent with respect to how 'data' is collected, analysed and represented. A greater awareness of the politics and responsibilities associated with the research act has also occurred (Denzin, 1997). This broad epistemological shift has been associated with the acknowledgement that 'truth' is not discovered by researchers but is *constructed* within the research process. Concomitantly, concern has also been directed to the processes associated with theorizing or how researchers 'do' theory.

Doing theory

Cultural studies, although difficult to demarcate, has been characterized in part through its interdisciplinary proclivities and its use of multiple theoretical and methodological approaches. As such, cultural studies has never been dominated by a particular theoretical approach. The PCS project similarly embraces a multiplicity of theoretical and research approaches. Grossberg (1997), however, noted that the underpinning linkage between these (perpetual) diversities was the need for cultural studies researchers to adopt a 'radical contextualism' as he argued that 'context is everything and everything is context for cultural studies' (ibid.: 7–8). This foregrounding of context is based on the understanding that cultural practices and entities can only be interpreted in relation to the context that constituted them. Hence, the need for researchers to examine the complex array of diverse factors that shape particular contexts and their respective articulations.

King (2005: 24) explained that within cultural studies the process of theorizing is 'developed in relation to changing epistemological and political conditions and thus is itself radically contextualised'. King drew from Nelson (1994: 202) to clarify further that the process of theorizing is 'inescapably grounded in contemporary life and current politics' and given that contemporary contexts are always in processes of change, researchers should constantly reflect upon the theoretical tools that they adopt: do they work? Do they help produce new insights? Or do they reaffirm what is already known? In this respect, researchers need to challenge their theoretical lens, test it in new contexts and if it is found wanting, be prepared to modify or search for alternative theoretical tools.

Hall (1992: 280) personalized this process of critically engaging with a theory by using the metaphor of 'wrestling with the angels'. He explained this metaphor with reference to his struggle to read and accept Althusser's version of Marx:

> I remember looking at the idea of 'theoretical practice' in *Reading Capital* and thinking, 'I've gone as far in this book as it is proper to go.' I felt, I will not give an inch to this profound misreading, this super-structuralist mistranslation, of classical Marxism, unless he beats me down, unless he defeats me in the spirit. He'll have to march over me to convince me. I warred with him, to the death.
>
> *(Hall, 1992: 280)*

Hall's vivid account of wrestling with, or testing, Althusser's theorizing reinforces the notion that research should not be theory-driven and theories should not be mobilized unreflexively. Taking inspiration from Hall's (1992) notion of wrestling with the angels, Thorpe (2011) adopts an explicitly PCS approach to theory, suggesting that one needs to push, pull and stretch a theory in relation to the empirical evidence to test its veracity for 'explaining particular aspects of contemporary society and/or the physically active body' (ibid.: 269). Similarly, Andrews and Silk (2015) suggest that a PCS approach to theory does not involve a 'slavish adherence to a singular theoretical position' but rather a 'critical engagement with theory: grappling with specific theories to see what is useful and appropriate within a particular empirical site, and disregarding/re-working that which is not' (ibid.: 88). Continuing, they proclaim that PCS requires 'the development of a broad-ranging and flexible theoretical vocabulary able to meet the extensive interpretive demands of its diverse empirical remit' (ibid.). As Hall (1992) suggests, all of this wrestling, stretching and grappling with social theory is a personal journey for the researcher in relation to their project, their politics, and individual ontological, epistemological and axiological assumptions. Thus, PCS approaches to theory must also be highly reflexive of how and why we are using theory in a particular historical context, and the strengths and limitations of such approaches (Andrews and Silk, 2015; Thorpe, 2011; King, 2005). In the following section, we explore the potential and concerns of the turn to reflexivity and the implication for our approaches to theory.

Reflexivity

The 'reflexive turn' in the social sciences and humanities has been such that many contemporary ethnographers seem to agree in the virtue of reflexivity in the theoretical and research practice (Foley, 2002), and consider it to be important to defining and judging the quality of research. At its most basic level, in the context of social research, reflexivity refers to 'a turning back on oneself, a process of self-reference', and understanding that the 'products of research are affected by the personnel and process of doing research' (Davies, 1999: 4). In other words, reflexivity is a 'continuing mode of self-analysis and political awareness' (Callaway, 1992: 33), in which the researcher is expected to be 'critically conscious through personal accounting' of how their own 'self-location (across, for example, gender, race, class, sexuality, ethnicity, nationality), position, and interests influence all stages of the research process' (Pillow, 2003: 178).

Reflexivity is a 'prevalent trend' in contemporary qualitative inquiry (ibid.: 180), yet the 'problem of reflexivity' and the ways in which 'our subjectivity becomes entangled in the lives of others' (Denzin, 1997: 27), is certainly not new. In fact, sociologists and anthropologists have been concerned with such issues for at least 40 years, and philosophers for considerably longer (see Lynch, 2000; Pillow, 2003). Despite a long history, many contemporary forms of reflexivity continue to be 'indebted to the Enlightenment conception of self-reflection as a uniquely human cognitive capacity that enables progressive understanding of the human predicament' (Lynch, 2000: 34). In the current cultural moment, reflexivity is most commonly used to refer to a method that all qualitative researchers 'can and should use to legitimize, validate, and question research practices and representations' (Pillow, 2003: 175).

According to Lynch (2000: 26), reflexivity, or being reflexive, 'is often claimed as a methodological virtue and source of superior insight, perspicacity or awareness', but it can be still very 'difficult to establish just what is being claimed'. In response to concerns that reflexivity is increasingly becoming an over-used, under-defined, and hollow term (also see Kenway and McLeod, 2004; Maton, 2003), some scholars have offered typologies to illustrate its multiple uses. For example, Denzin (1997: 218–223) identifies five differing types of reflexivity in use in qualitative research, including methodological, intertextual, standpoint, queer and feminist reflexivity; Pillow (2003) identifies four strategies of reflexivity that also 'highlight the difficulties and tensions in shifts from modern to postmodern understandings of doing qualitative research' (ibid.: 180); and Lynch (2000: 27) offers an 'inventory of reflexivities' with the aim to 'demonstrate the diversity of meanings and uses of the concept'. In this chapter, however, we focus on the critical social sciences, post-structuralist and feminist theoretical approaches to reflexivity, as we argue they have played the most important roles in yielding questions about what a researcher can know, their relationships with their projects and participants, and their ability to represent the lives of others. In fact, reflexivity and critical reflection have been developed and explored in feminist literature for several decades (Ryan and Golden, 2006). Groundbreaking feminist researchers have contributed concepts of 'strong reflexivity' (Harding, 1996) and 'situated knowledges' (Haraway, 1991) as part of a feminist critique of mainstream scientific methods that privilege particular notions of objectivity, scientific detachment and value neutrality (Speer, 2002; Daley, 2010). In so doing, feminist theory and feminist scholars have greatly extended our thinking about, and use of, reflexivity by 'situating reflexivity as primary to feminist research and methodology' (Pillow, 2003: 178). As Pillow reminds us, reflexivity under feminism is 'not only about investigating the power embedded in one's research' but also about 'doing research differently', including more equitable relationships with participants, creating research that is empowering for women, and always linked to political action (ibid.: 178).

Many critical scholars of sport and physical culture are also leaning into the so-called 'reflexive turn'. During the late 1990s and early 2000s, a group of sport researchers embraced autoethnography and narrative approaches to offer new ways of representing their own and others sporting, moving, researching bodies (see, for example, Denison and Rinehart, 2000), and this trend has been picked up again by a number of contemporary PCS scholars. Others opt to (re)write themselves into their methods. For example, Belinda Wheaton (2002) wrote openly about her multiple positions in windsurfing culture and how these enabled and constrained her access to various groups of participants; Ben Carrington (2008) developed an 'epistemological framework for a reflexive cultural studies/critical sociology of sport' based on a '*re*reading' of the 'moments of silence' in his previous ethnographic work on race, culture and identity in British cricket (ibid.: 424); and Jason Laurendeau (2011) presented an affective autoethnography that reveals his own reflexive engagements with issues of masculinity, family and the ethics of risk-taking in extreme sports such as BASE jumping.

Many other physical cultural scholars are also offering thoughtful, compelling and carefully crafted reflexive works, yet their acts and representations of reflexivity tend to be conducted individually and retrospectively, with few details as to *how* they developed such critical self-analysis and political awareness. In other words, we rarely hear about their 'methods of reflexivity', or the processes they have worked through to determine which aspects of their (fluid and multiple) identities are of significance at various stages in their projects (i.e. developing research questions, adoption of particular theoretical frameworks, interviewing, data analysis, writing up). As Grosz (1995) points out, there are 'limits to reflexivity' and to the extent to which we can develop a critical awareness of all the various 'influences on our research both at the time of conducting it and in the years that follow' (ibid.: 13). Continuing, she suggests that it may be more useful to think in terms of 'degrees of reflexivity' (ibid.), with 'some influences being easier to identify and articulate' at the time of our work, while others 'may take time, distance and detachment from the research' (Mauthner and Doucet, 2003: 425).

To date, few physical cultural scholars have explained the methods or strategies they have developed to help them critically reflect upon the multiple and fluid dimensions of their identities, and the influence their current positionings and personal histories have on their projects. Taking inspiration from post-structural feminist theorizing, however, a few feminist scholars of sport and physical culture are acknowledging the difficulties of developing such reflexivity, and are exploring the potential of collaborative approaches for facilitating and supporting more reflexive research practices and politics, both individually and collectively, and both during the research process and retrospectively (see, for example, Olive and Thorpe, 2011; Pavlidis and Olive, 2014; Thorpe, Barbour and Bruce, 2011). In so doing, some are engaging with Couldry's (1996) assertion that '"self-reflexivity" is not a license for autobiographical writing', but rather 'a theoretically informed examination of the conditions for the emergence of "selves"' (ibid.: 315). Thorpe (2009, 2011), for example, engages with the theoretical concepts of Pierre Bourdieu, Michel Foucault and post-structural feminist theorists, to inform her own reflexive research practices, as well as understandings of her participants' abilities to reflect critically on aspects of their own subjectivities. She further explores these ideas in collaboration with colleagues, and particularly the potential of Bourdieu's notion of field-crossing for enhancing researcher reflexivity (Thorpe, Barbour and Bruce, 2011; Olive and Thorpe, 2011). By no means does Bourdieu offer all the answers to 'doing' reflexivity, but by reflecting on the process these scholars point to the value of theoretically informed collaborations for enhancing researcher reflexivity at different stages in the research journey, and particularly for helping scholars access those 'blind spots' in their own identities that may 'never be comprehensively executed by the individual knower' (Pels, 2000: 17).

Criticisms of reflexivity

A growing number of scholars have expressed concerns about the growth in reflexive research (Lynch, 2000; Patai, 1994; Pels, 2000; Pillow, 2003), some of which might also be levelled at those adopting reflexive approaches in physical cultural studies. Lynch (2000), for example, argues that 'studies of "our own" investigative practices may, in some cases, be interesting, insightful and clearly written, or they may come across as tedious, pretentious and unrevealing' (ibid.: 47), whereas Pels (2000: 2) is concerned about the 'romance of reflexivity', and the tendency for authors to narrate their stories in particular ways that ultimately work to glorify their personal journeys and reflections. Similarly, while some remain adamant that reflexivity is not aiding our attempts to produce better, or more socially significant, research, others are engaging with such critiques with the aim of offering valuable suggestions as to how we might build upon and extend current understandings of reflexivity.

The work of Wanda Pillow (2003) is particularly noteworthy in her efforts to identify and overcome the pitfalls of reflexivity and to make the personal meaningful in a politically attuned manner. Concerned by the tendency for reflexivity to be used towards 'confession, catharsis or cure', she poses a series of questions to all purportedly 'reflexive' texts – 'Did I need the author's confessional tale to read the data? Did the use of "witnessing" as a metaphor for the researcher aid in my understanding of the research or close off my reading (for who can critique what another has "witnessed")?' (ibid.: 183). Continuing, she expresses concern that too many researchers are 'utilizing reflexivity in ways that are dependent on a modernist subject – a subject that is singular, knowable, and fixable' (ibid.: 192). However, rather than 'shrugging off reflexivity', Pillow advocates a 'tracing of the problematics of reflexivity' that involves a repositioning of reflexivity 'not as clarity, honesty, or humility, but as practices of confounding disruptions – at times even a failure of our language and practices' (ibid.). She calls for the interruption of 'comfortable reflexivities', and a move toward 'reflexivities of discomfort' (ibid.: 187). Whereas the former approach works 'against the critical impetus of reflexivity' and thus 'masks continued reliance upon traditional notions of validity, truth, and essence in qualitative research' (ibid.: 180), the latter postmodern approach to reflexivity 'accounts for multiplicity without making it singular' and 'acknowledges the unknowable without making it familiar' (ibid.: 181). Others have also offered valuable suggestions for how to engage in more politically inspired reflexivity with broader social, as opposed to individual, concerns at the core. Good examples include Fine's (1994: 70) deeply reflexive approach to 'working the hyphens' at which 'Self-Other join in the politics of everyday life', Richardson's (1999) guidelines for 'creative analytic practice' (CAP) ethnographic approaches with both personal and social impact, and Probyn's (1993: 3) aim to 'think the social through myself', all of which have been taken up and applied across an array of disciplines in highly creative and politically inspired ways.

Many sport and physical cultural scholars continue to use reflexivity as a form of 'confession, catharsis or cure' and with the modernist assumptions that positioning oneself in the research will enhance the 'validity' of the results and overall quality of the project (Pillow, 2003: 175). Yet others are embracing the more postmodern understandings of reflexivity espoused by Pillow. For example, Fiona McLachlan (2012: 72) drew on the concept of 'becoming' to 'embrace the disruption of linear, coherent, permanent, grounded understandings of objects, subjects and knowledge', which allowed her 'to conceptualise and problematise her own 'subjective involvement in analysing the plight of public swimming pools' (ibid.: 16). Also leaning toward a more postmodern understanding of reflexivity, Joshua Newman (2011) examines the 'politics of reflexivity and articulation' in relation to his past experiences and ongoing research on sport in Southern sporting fields. Concluding, he advocates for 'messier, bottom-up qualitative engagement with the body – a contemplative method of articulation(s) that situates the body among bodies and framed through both the *soi* and the *pour poi*' (ibid.: 553). For Newman (2011: 554), 'studying the complex relations of the body, the self, and reflexivity', is important for becoming more aware of, and thus working to limit, 'the violence created by our "embodied selves" along the way'.

Arguably, for reflexivity to make a valuable contribution to PCS it must be more than a 'methodological tool' (Pillow, 2003: 175), or theoretical concept. Rather, it must be conceived as an invaluable part of doing embodied, ethical, theoretically informed, and political ethnographic research (Carrington, 2008; England, 1994). In so doing, physical cultural studies scholars might also embrace the challenge of 'tracing the problematics' of their own (and others') variants of reflexivity (Pillow, 2003: 180), and perhaps consider joining the 'move[ment] away from comfortable uses of reflexivity' (ibid.: 175) towards more postmodern understandings of ourselves, and our participants, as 'multiple, as unknowable, as shifting' (ibid.: 180).

Conclusion

At the heart of the PCS agenda is the aim of constructing and disseminating 'potentially empowering forms of knowledge and understanding', particularly in relation to challenging power inequities and social injustices (Andrews, 2008: 54). With similar political intent, Denzin and Lincoln (2005) suggested that the literary and representative themes popularly associated with the postmodern turn in the 1990s, have been eclipsed in more recent years by the 'struggle to connect qualitative research to the hopes, needs, goals, and promises of a free democratic society' (ibid.: 3). As such, they encouraged researchers to reflect on processes to ensure their writings were of social and political importance. In following Denzin and Lincoln, we suggest that a key issue in the research process is to consider how *theoretically* sophisticated and *reflexive* research can be mobilized to imagine more 'politically expedient physical cultural possibilities' (Andrews, 2008: 57)?

In order to offer some insight into this question of political import we conclude by drawing from Butler's (2004) reflections on her groundbreaking text *Gender Trouble* published 14 years earlier. She reflexively acknowledged that in writing about the politics of parody, she used drag as an analogy as it resonated with her biography. She stated, 'you might as well know … the only way to describe me in my younger years was as a bar dyke who spent her days reading Hegel and her evenings, well, at the gay bar, which occasionally became a drag bar' (ibid.: 213). And it was in this 'cultural moment' that she became committed 'to the ideal that no one should be forcibly compelled to occupy a gender norm that is undergone, experientially, as an unlivable violation' (ibid.: 213). Consequently her political aims developed in relation to her life experiences and her desire to *theorize* gender as a performance.

Butler subsequently also developed her argument that 'theory is itself transformative' (ibid.: 204). Yet she did not believe that 'theory is sufficient for social and political transformation' as 'something besides theory must take place, such as interventions at social and political levels that involve actions, sustained labor, and institutionalized practice, which are not quite the same as the exercise of theory' (ibid.: 204–205). Of importance, however, she clarified 'that in all of these practices, theory is presupposed' (ibid.: 205). In other words, she stressed that theory underpins these overt political actions as it 'presupposes a vision of the world, of what is right, of what is just, of what is abhorrent, of what human action is and can be' (ibid.: 205).

In concluding this chapter, we have drawn closely from Butler to highlight the intersections between biography, reflexivity, theory, politics and the potential for social transformation. Yet we also acknowledge that the use of a particular theory or a reflexive writing style does not come with any political guarantee.

For many, reflexive analysis has the potential to 'reveal forgotten choices, expose hidden alternatives, lay bare epistemological limits and empower voices' that may otherwise be silenced by objective discourse (Lynch, 2000: 36). Yet there is also growing concern that the current focus on self-indulgent, narcissistic forms of reflexivity may be 'undermining the conditions necessary for emancipatory research' (Pillow, 2003: 176; Patai, 1994). As revealed in this chapter, there are multiple interpretations and usages of reflexivity, some with more emancipatory potential than others. With Lynch (2000), we are conscious that 'what reflexivity does, what it threatens to expose, what it reveals and who it empowers, depends upon who does it and how they go about it' (ibid.: 36). Thus, we conclude by arguing that the reflexive turn in PCS is important, only so long as we keep power relations and political injustices at the fore of our work.

References

Andrews, D. (2008). Kinesiology's *Inconvenient Truth* and the physical cultural studies imperative. *Quest, 60*, 45–62.

Andrews, D. and Silk, M. (2015). Physical cultural studies on sport. In R. Guilianotti (ed.), *The Routledge Handbook of the Sociology of Sport* (pp. 83–93). London: Routledge.

Bourdieu, P. and Wacquant, L. J. (1992). *An invitation to reflexive sociology*. Chicago, IL: University of Chicago Press.

Brandao, Z. (2010). Operating with concepts: with and beyond Bourdieu. *Educação e Pesquisa, 36*(1), 227–241.

Butler, J. (2004). *Undoing gender*. New York: Routledge.

Callaway, H. (1992). Ethnography and experience: gender implications in fieldwork and texts. In J. Okley and H. Callaway (eds), *Anthropology and autobiography* (pp. 29–49). New York: Routledge.

Carrington, B. (2008). 'What's the footballer doing here?' Racialized performativity, reflexivity, and identity. *Cultural Studies ↔ Critical Methodologies, 8*(4), 423–452.

Collins, C. and Jackson, S. J. (eds). (2007). *Sport in Aotearoa/New Zealand society*. Palmerston North: Dunmore Press.

Couldry, N. (1996). Speaking about others and speaking personally: reflections after Elspeth Probyn's 'Sexing the Self'. *Cultural Studies, 10*(2), 315–333.

Daley, A. (2010). Reflections on reflexivity and critical reflection as critical research practices. *Affilia, 25*(1), 68–82.

Davies, C. (1999). *Reflexive ethnography: a guide to researching selves and others*. New York: Routledge.

Denison, J. and Rinehart, R. (2000). Introduction: imagining sociological narratives. *Sociology of Sport Journal, 17*(1), 1–4.

Denzin, N. K. (1997). *Interpretive ethnography: ethnographic practices for the 21st century*. Thousand Oaks: Sage.

Denzin, N. and Lincoln, Y. (2005). Introduction: the discipline and practice of qualitative research. In N. Denzin and Y. Lincoln (eds), *The Sage handbook of qualitative research* (pp. 1–32). Thousand Oaks, CA: Sage.

Dunning, E. and Rojek, C. (eds) (1992). *Sport and leisure in the civilizing process: critique and counter-critique*. London: Macmillan,

England, K. V. L. (1994). Getting personal: reflexivity, positionality, and feminist research. *The Professional Geographer, 46*(1), 80–89.

Fine, M. (1994). Working the hyphens: reinventing self and other in qualitative research. In N. Denzin and Y. Lincoln (eds), *Handbook of qualitative research* (pp. 70–82). Newbury Park, CA: Sage.

Foley, D. E. (2002). Critical ethnography: the reflexive turn. *International Journal of Qualitative Studies in Education, 15*(4), 469–490.

Grossberg, L. (1997). Cultural studies, modern logic and theories of globalisation. In A. McRobbie (ed.), *Back to reality? Social experience and cultural studies* (pp. 7–35). Manchester: Manchester University Press.

Grosz, E. (1995). *Space, time and perversion: the politics of bodies*. Sydney, Allen & Unwin.

Guba, E. and Lincoln, Y. (1994). Competing paradigms in qualitative research. In N. K. Denzin and Y. Lincoln (eds), *Handbook of qualitative research*, 3rd edn (pp. 191–216). London: Sage.

Hall, S. (1992). Cultural studies and its theoretical legacies. In L. Grossberg, C. Nelson and P. Treichler (eds), *Cultural studies* (pp. 277–294). London: Routledge.

Haraway, D. J. (1991). *Simians, cyborgs, and women: the reinvention of nature*. London: Free Association Books.

Harding, S. (1996). Standpoint epistemology (a feminist version): How social disadvantage creates epistemic advantage. In S. P. Turner (ed.), *Social theory and sociology: the classics and beyond* (pp. 146–160). Oxford: Blackwell.

Kenway, J. and McLeod, J. (2004). Bourdieu's reflexive sociology and 'spaces of points of view': whose reflexivity, which perspective? *British Journal of Sociology of Education, 25*(4), 525–544.

King, S. (2005). Methodological contingencies in sport studies. In D. Andrews, D. Mason and M. Silk (eds), *Qualitative methods in sport studies* (pp. 21–38). Oxford: Berg.

Laurendeau, J. (2011). 'If you're reading this, it's because I've died': masculinity and relational risk in BASE jumping. *Sociology of Sport Journal, 28*(4), 404–420.

Lynch, M. (2000). Against reflexivity as an academic virtue and source of privileged knowledge. *Theory, Culture and Society, 17*(3), 26–54.

Markula, P. and Silk, M. (2011). *Qualitative research for physical culture*. Basingstoke: Palgrave Macmillan.

Maton, K. (2003). Reflexivity, relationism and research: Pierre Bourdieu and the epistemic conditions and social scientific knowledge. *Space and Culture, 6*(1), 52–65.

Mauthner, N. and Doucet, A. (2003). Reflexive accounts and accounts of reflexivity in qualitative data analysis. *Sociology, 37*(3), 413–431.

McLachlan, F. (2012). Poolspace: a deconstruction and reconfiguration of public swimming pools. Unpublished PhD. University of Otago.

Nelson, C. (1994). Always already cultural studies. In A. McRobbie (ed.) *Back to reality? Social experience and cultural studies*. Manchester: Manchester University Press.

Newman, J. (2011). [Un]comfortable in my own skin: articulation, reflexivity, and the duality of self. *Cultural Studies ↔ Critical Methodologies, 11*(6), 545–557.

Olive, R. and Thorpe, H. (2011). Negotiating the 'F-word' in the field: doing feminist ethnography in action sport cultures. *Sociology of Sport Journal, 28*(4), 421–440.

Patai, D. (1994). Response: when method becomes power. In A. Gitlen (ed), *Power and method* (pp. 61–73). New York: Routledge.

Pavlidis, A. and Olive, R. (2014). 'On the track/in the bleachers': authenticity and ethnographic research in sport and physical cultural studies, *Sport in Society: Cultures, Commerce, Media, Politics, 17*(2), 218–232.

Pels, D. (2000). Reflexivity: one step up. *Theory, Culture and Society, 17*(3), 1–25.

Pillow, W. S. (2003). Confession, catharsis, or cure? Rethinking the uses of reflexivity as a methodological power in qualitative research. *Qualitative Studies in Education, 16*(2), 175–196.

Pringle, R. and Phillips, M. (2013). Sport history, historiography and postmodern social theory: an introduction. In R. Pringle and M. Phillips (eds), *Examining sport histories: power, paradigms, and reflexivity* (pp. 1–25). Morgantown, WV: FIT Publishers.

Probyn, E. (1993). *Sexing the self: gendered positions in cultural studies*. London and New York: Routledge.

Richardson, L. (1999). Feathers in our cap. *Journal of Contemporary Ethnography, 28*(6), 660–668.

Ryan, L. and Golden, A. (2006). 'Tick the box please': a reflexive approach to doing quantitative social research. *Sociology, 40*(6), 1191–1200.

Schwandt, T. A. (2000). Three epistemological stances for qualitative inquiry: interpretivism, hermeneutics, and social constructionism. In N. K. Denzin and Y. S. Lincoln (eds), *Handbook of qualitative research*, 2nd edn (pp. 189–213). Thousand Oaks, CA: Sage.

Scott, G. and Garner, R. (2013). *Doing qualitative research: design, methods and technologies*. Upper Saddle River, NJ: Pearson.

Sparkes, A. C. and Smith, B. (2014). *Qualitative research methods in sport, exercise and health: From process to product*. Abingdon: Routledge.

Speer, S. A. (2002). What can conversation analysis contribute to feminist methodologies? Putting reflexivity into practice. *Discourse and Society, 13*, 783–803.

Thorpe, H. (2009). Bourdieu, feminism and female physical culture: gender reflexivity and the habitus-field complex. *Sociology of Sport Journal, 26*, 491–516.

Thorpe, H. (2011). *Snowboarding Bodies in Theory and Practice*. Basingstoke: Palgrave Macmillan.

Thorpe, H., Barbour, K. and Bruce, T. (2011). 'Wandering and wondering': playing with theory and representation in physical cultural fields. *Sociology of Sport Journal, 28*, 106–134.

Wheaton, B. (2002). Babes on the beach, women in the surf: researching gender, power and difference in the windsurfing culture. In J. Sugden and A. Tomlinson (eds), *Power games: a critical sociology of sport*. London: Routledge.

4
INTERDISCIPLINARITY AND TRANSDISCIPLINARITY IN PHYSICAL CULTURAL STUDIES

Leslie Heywood

The work of Basarab Nicolescu (2015), a theoretical physicist and founder of the International Center for Transdisciplinary Research and Studies, has perhaps gone the furthest in developing a working definition of transdisciplinarity that has influenced much research and provided a way into thinking about reconciling the often oppositional frameworks proceeding from the sciences and the humanities. In this chapter I argue that such a framework is necessary to a physical cultural studies (PCS), as indeed was called for in the foundational PCS agenda articulated by sport studies scholar David Andrews: PCS advocates 'a multi-method approach … from a variety of disciplines (including cultural studies, economics, history, media studies, philosophy, sociology, and urban studies) in engaging and interpreting the particular aspect of physical culture under scrutiny' (Andrews, 2008: 55). Similarly, Nicolescu is a scientist whose work challenges the dualistic, split nature of the modern scientific paradigm – a paradigm that PCS challenges at its foundations. But science – done in a particular way – remains a crucial part of his integrationist perspective. This is a move that is important for PCS to follow, because in its privileging of cultural constructivism over perspectives from the sciences, PCS has inadvertently violated its foundational intentions to operate within an inclusive, and necessarily interdisciplinary perspective. In fact, the stated aims of PCS actually make the field more transdisciplinary than interdisciplinary. But in its neglect of hard sciences such as neurobiology that, along with many levels of culture, work together inextricably to inform human movement, PCS has remained more interdisciplinary than transdisciplinary. Recent work within the field, such as that of Holly Thorpe on transdisciplinarity and embodiment, Jette, Vertinsky, and Ng's work on biomedical models of pregnancy and movement, John Evans's work on transdiciplinary models of sport and health, and my own work on the importance of affective neuroscience has heralded and embraced this direction (Thorpe, 2014, 2016; Jette et al., 2014; Evans, 2014; Heywood 2011, 2015; Heywood, Garcia and Wilson, 2010). For the field of PCS to fully achieve its stated aims, transdisciplinarity is an even more effective frame than the more interdisciplinarity model that privileges the constructivism of the cultural studies paradigm to the exclusion of the hard sciences.

Interdisciplinarity/transdisciplinarity: definitions and debates

In distinction from interdisciplinary approaches, transdisciplinary approaches incorporate holistic principles. This is put very clearly by, for instance, the Harvard Transdisciplinary Research in Energetics and Cancer Center:

> Transdisciplinary Research is defined as research efforts conducted by investigators from different disciplines working jointly to create new conceptual, theoretical, methodological, and translational innovations that integrate and move beyond discipline-specific approaches to address a common problem. Interdisciplinary Research is any study or group of studies undertaken by scholars from two or more distinct disciplines.
>
> *(Harvard Transdisciplinary Research in Energetics and Cancer Center, undated)*

Unlike a transdisciplinary model, which has a multidimensional perspective at its very inception, in an interdisciplinary model, the research retains distinct disciplinary frameworks but seeks to integrate them. It uses design and methodology that requires the use of perspectives and skills of the involved disciplines throughout the research process. But while transdisciplinary research emphasizes a 'moving beyond discipline specific approaches to a common problem', with an emphasis on the 'beyond', interdisciplinary research tends to involve collaboration between related fields and tends to not cross the major disciplinary divide between the sciences and the humanities (ibid.).

Therefore transdisciplinary research is much more inclusive of a posthumanist perspective that emphasizes levels and elements of cultural constructivism. For instance, according to an article in *Clinical and Investigative Medicine*:

> Multidisciplinarity draws on knowledge from different disciplines but stays within their boundaries. Interdisciplinarity analyzes, synthesizes and harmonizes links between disciplines into a coordinated and coherent whole. Transdisciplinarity integrates the natural, social and health sciences in a humanities context, and transcends their traditional boundaries ... The common words for multidisciplinary, interdisciplinary and transdisciplinary are additive, interactive, and holistic, respectively.
>
> *(Choi and Pak, 2006: 351)*

While multi- and inter-disciplinary work retain a disciplinary frame, the transdisciplinary approach aims to transcend disciplinarity altogether, and necessarily includes a (post)humanistic perspective that is invested in the investigation of cultural mechanisms, which would then involve questions of power and social inequality considered as an intricate part of an investigation of biological mechanisms. As the Holistic Education Network emphasizes, in transdisciplinarity there is:

> a focus on an issue such as pollution or hunger both within and beyond discipline boundaries with the possibility of new perspectives. The transdisciplinary vision goes beyond the exact sciences and demands dialogue with the humanities and the social sciences, as well as with art, literature, poetry and spiritual experience. The recognition of the existence of different levels of reality governed by different types of logic is inherent in the transdisciplinary attitude.
>
> *(Holistic Education Network, undated)*

For Nicolescu, who introduced the meaning of 'beyond disciplines' to the definition of transdisciplinarity in 1985, transdisciplinary knowledge has 'far-reaching consequences not only for science but also for culture and social life' (Nicolescu, 2015: 21).

The rethinking of the foundations of modern science that transdisciplinarity proposes – foundations based on 'a total separation between the knowing subject and Reality, which was assumed to be completely independent from the subject who observed it' (ibid.) is necessary because of its negative consequences:

> On the spiritual level, the consequences of scientism have been considerable: the only knowledge worthy of its name must therefore be scientific, objective; the only reality worthy of this name must be, of course, objective reality, ruled by objective laws. All knowledge other than scientific knowledge is thus cast into the inferno of subjectivity, tolerated at most as a meaningless embellishment or rejected with contempt as a fantasy, an illusion, a regression, or a product of the imagination.
>
> *(Nicolescu, 2015: 21)*

For Nicolescu, the absolute privilege given to scientism is such that even the general concept of 'spirituality' is suspect. Within this model, Subject becomes Object, opening the way for the 'exploitation of man by man' that subjects beings to scientific ideology and reduces them to their materiality, 'an object of scientific studies to be dissected, formalized, and manipulated' (ibid.). This would of course apply to nonhuman animals all the more so.

Nicolescu's critique of scientism has to do with the consequences of this kind of work for the human (and animal) subject. Rather than recognizing the value of individual life, scientism locates value in the production of 'objective' knowledge, an 'objectivity' that discounts emotion and any specific, located forms of knowledge. Yet, as the work of poststructuralist philosophers such as Jacques Derrida has long established (Derrida, 1968), simply flipping the binary to value the devalued term over the previously devalued term just repeats the same error. Instead, work in a transdisciplinary mode goes beyond oppositional pairs such as subject/object, consciousness/matter, or mind/body, and as such questions the usual privilege in academic inquiry awarded to cognition over affect or objective knowledge over subjective, quantitative over qualitative research. For Nicolescu, inquiry that looks at the mind in distinction from emotions and 'the body', and that doesn't take into account the impact of research activity and the production of truth claims on its subjects, would not be in the transdisciplinary mode.

From interdisciplinarity to transdisciplinarity, and the need for the engagement of science

While Nicolescu laments the exclusion of disciplinary principles that would consider human subjectivity, the exclusions can operate in the other direction as well. It is striking that the foundational principles of PCS make a call for work that sounds almost the same as the description of transdisciplinarity articulated by Nicolescu, while still excluding the hard sciences. A consideration of the 'three characteristics of PCS scholarship' found in the foundational model of Bush, Silk, Andrews, and Lauder (2013: 80) reveals aims that, unlike an interdisciplinary model that would not necessarily integrate perspectives from both the sciences and the humanities, a transdisciplinary perspective is being called for. Yet PCS, as it has been delineated thus far, remains within an interdisciplinary frame. According to 'A Brief Genealogy of Cultural Studies and Sport, Physical Cultural Studies, and the McUniversity', PCS recognizes the ontological complexity and interrelatedness of physical culture ... [It looks at] numerous ways of being *physically active* ... Second, the PCS project is ... radically contextual ... concerned with how active bodies become organized, represented, and experienced in relation to operations of social power ... Physical culture ... thus incorporates numerous 'events': the moments of 'practice that crystallizes diverse temporal and social trajectories' through which individuals negotiate their subjective – and for our interests embodied – identities and experiences ... Third, a PCS sensibility assumes that societies are fundamentally divided along hierarchically ordered lines of differentiation (i.e. those based on class, ethnic, gender, ability, generational, national, racial, and/or sexual norms), as realized through operations of power and power relations within the social formation.

(Bush et al., 2013: 80–82)

These 'three characteristics' as outlined do not directly include perspectives from the sciences, relying instead on a cultural studies model that tends to be constructivist in orientation. Yet a consideration especially of the second proposition, 'how active bodies become organized ... and experienced' points toward good reasons to include science. If 'power operates at every level of human life' (ibid.), one of the levels that must necessarily be considered is the biological – the impact of power on the actual, physical body and how that body physiologically responds to that power. An athlete who is slighted, for instance, for reasons pertaining to their gender, race, or sexuality, will have a stress response that then affects their experience of the sport context on many levels. A consideration of this kind of question – which involves the interaction effects between biological systems in the body and the social powers that impact and shape them – is necessarily a transdisciplinary question rather than an interdisciplinary one.

However, while Silk and Andrew's definitional article 'Toward a Physical Cultural Studies' includes a wide range of disciplines, none of the sciences are among them: 'PCS utiliz[es] concepts and theories from ... cultural studies, economics, history, media studies, philosophy, sociology, and urban studies in engaging and interpreting the particular aspect of physical culture under scrutiny' (Andrews, 2008: 54–55; quoted in Silk and Andrews, 2011: 7). Similarly, the call for a 'sacred-moral epistemology as a guiding principle' (Silk and Andrews, 2011: 14) that 'mak(es) a difference in the world instead of simply reflecting it' (ibid.: 17), necessitates a move beyond the reductionism of the scientific method and its claim to merely describe 'what is', examining the dynamic constructivism of 'the physical' that engages in social critique and moral dialogue within specific physical cultural contexts' (ibid.: 19). Yet my argument is that part of this contextualization should involve the consideration of biophysiological mechanisms as these interact with those contexts, and the work of Thorpe, Evans, and others is making interventions in this direction (Thorpe, 2014, 2016; Evans, 2014).

As this transformational direction suggests, the interaction effects between biological mechanisms and the cultural mechanisms that help give them shape offers a transdisciplinary standpoint crucial to the PCS mission. Biology is part of 'the physical' and the 'social totality' that informs sociality: 'the physical is a complex multilayered site replete with numerous types of events can and do "happen" – the product and producer of numerous overlapping systems and discourses (economic, political, aesthetic, demographic, regulatory, spatial) that creates a bewilderingly complex, and dynamic, coherent, social totality' (Silk and Andrews, 2011: 9–10). While presently anything scientific is missing from this description, the relationship between the physiological, psychological, and social body seems essential for realizing such aims. For instance, the ways an experience of trauma dysregulates an individual's primary process emotional systems, points to an important consideration of who is traumatized and why (social context) in relationship to the embodied effects of that trauma (biological context), and how that traumatization and its effects might in turn inform an individual's relationship to the practice of physical movement (psychological context). The way our bodies neurologically respond to cultural manifestations of difference – differential attributions of value, and the behaviors (hate crimes, for instance) influenced by those attributions – provides a fuller picture of what lived embodiment means. Silk and Andrews argue that 'we need an approach that can empower individuals by confronting injustices and promoting social change' (ibid.: 11). Yet the most effective way to 'empower' individuals is to reach them not just cognitively but emotionally as well. If PCS is a 'therapeutic project', meant to 'intervene in the world' (ibid.), it especially needs to engage the affective dimension, the primary process emotional systems that inform behavior and response simultaneously with power and discourse, and affective neuroscience provides this framework.

I have found the work of affective neuroscientists Stephen Porges and Jaak Panksepp to be particularly useful in this regard. I have used their work to formulate a transdisciplinary perspective in a reading of gender, sport, and sport cultures in 'Hunger, Emotions, and Sport: A Biocultural Approach' (Heywood, 2011a); to develop a neuropsychological perspective on sport performance in 'Affective Infrastructures: Toward a Neuropsychology of Sport' (Heywood, 2011b); and to analyze a gendered model of embodiment in neoliberalism in '"Strange Borrowing": Affective Neuroscience, Neoliberalism and the "Cruelly Optimistic" Gendered Bodies of CrossFit' (Heywood, 2015a). In all of these, I found that the insights coming from affective neuroscience complicated the cultural analysis so it became clearer how mind, body, affect, culture, and cognition all mutually inform one another in the ways I outlined above.

However, researchers coming from a constructivist perspective are right to feel suspicious about the ability of those scientists who claim to be transdisciplinary to not privilege the mechanistic perspective. A recent interview between evolutionary biologist D. S. Wilson and geneticist Eva Jablonka is indicative. While both scientists embrace the new paradigm that is concerned with the interaction effects between 'nature' and 'culture', in the interview Wilson slips unwittingly into a perspective that claims 'nature first', and Jablonka has to correct him:

> Wilson: You said that epigenetics had its breakthrough when it became mechanistically well-understood ... Everything has a physical mechanism. When learning and symbolic thought, as the physical mechanism, is better understood ... then maybe there will be a breakthrough there, in terms of seeing it, more clearly, as an inheritance system.
> Jablonka: I think it will help, but I worry about trying to reduce cultural phenomena ... just to the neurobiological mechanisms. This is a danger because there is a cultural level of description. Culture is indeed a system of interactions at many, many different levels, that crucially involve neurobiology, but the system is more than sum of its parts and requires its own level of analysis.
>
> *(Wilson, 2015)*

Jablonka's response, 'I worry about trying to reduce cultural phenomena ... just to the neurobiological mechanisms', points to the tension between traditional assumptions in the sciences and the newer models that have called those assumptions into question. It is through those newer models that scientific disciplines can contribute a vital level of analysis to PCS formulations, providing for a more multidimensional understanding of the moving body.

The evolution of scientific paradigms: the extended synthesis

That Nicolescu developed his transdisciplinary paradigm in a way that integrates humanistic concerns even though he is a highly trained scientist, shows that science is undergoing paradigm shifts, and not just in the sense of quantum physics and the way it resists reductionism. Similarly, Nikolas Rose, a British sociologist and social theorist, originally trained as a biologist, but who is now Head of the Department of Social Science, Health, and Medicine at King's College, London, and an expert in the work of Foucault who was originally trained as a biologist, has made a persuasive case for the integration of humanistic and scientific perspectives as an intellectual (and perhaps personal) necessity. As he puts it,

> There are good historical reasons why many in the social and human sciences have been highly critical of attempts to build a positive relation with the life sciences. But their dread of determinism, reductionism ... is now misplaced. We must configure a new double relationship with biology.
>
> *(Rose, 2013: 17)*

On the one hand, Rose argues, there is a need to 'recognise the provisonality of the knowledge claims in the life sciences' and to critically evaluate media representations of science. On the other hand, Rose calls for a move beyond the 'description, commentary and critique' characteristic of much social sciences' that will develop new ways of understanding the 'dynamic relations between the vital and its milieu' (ibid.).

A transdisciplinary PCS model would retain its critique of scientific knowledge production, for as Rose emphasizes, 'we need detailed social research to map out the interconnections between pathways for the production of truth and hopes about the generation of profit that have shaped investment, research priorities, and the interpretation of evidence and its implications' (Rose and Abi-Rached, 2013: 232). Yet that critique can work hand in hand with new scientific models that use some of the same concepts that PCS in the cultural studies tradition has long relied upon: an emphasis on context (environment) and changeability (plasticity) at the most basic biological levels. Even in the field of evolutionary biology, concepts like the 'selfish gene' and population genetics as the sole drivers of evolution through natural selection are under question by a more transdisciplinary focus that articulates a 'new way of understanding between the vital and its milieu' (Rose, 2013). The work of biologist Anne Fausto-Sterling on the gendered body (2012), biological anthropologist Sarah Blaffer Hrdy on cooperative breeding (2009), and biologist Patricia Gowaty's feminist revisions of evolutionary biology (2013) are all instrumental in this regard.

Key to thinking through how the integration of cultural studies perspectives might work in relation to biology are developments in evolutionary theory known as 'the extended synthesis', that begin to bridge the nature/nurture divide (Pigliucci and Muller, 2010). These developments can more readily include cultural studies perspectives because they demonstrate how the materiality of human behavior incorporates cultural developments at the biological level. In the words of geneticist Eva Jablonka and evolutionary biologist Marion Lamb, 'various inheritance systems (genetic, epigenetic, behavioral, symbolic) are instrumental in construction of the niche in which selection takes place ... organisms can engineer the environment in ways that affect the development and selection of their descendants' (Jablonka and Lamb, 2006: 237). Jablonka and Lamb's 'four dimensions' of evolution include the genetic, epigenetic, behavioral, and symbolic. All these occur in direct relationship to environment and context. Similarly, as epigenetics has established, genes themselves are expressed or not in constant negotiation with an organism's intracellular and extracellular environments, so that heritable changes in gene expression can arise from non-genetic sources. As Jablonka and Lamb put it, the extended synthesis sees

> human behavior and culture as consequences of hominids' extraordinary behavioral plasticity coupled with and enhanced by their powerful system of symbolic communication ... an important aspect of cultural evolution is the extremely variable ecological and social environments humans construct for themselves ... It is therefore wrong to think of them as passive objects of environmental selection. What we transmit through our behavioral and symbolic systems obviously has profound effect on the selection of the information that we transmit through our genes.
> (Jablonka and Lamb, 2006: 213, 286)

The extended synthesis as it is articulated here gives PCS research a more expanded ground on which to enter the conversation than did earlier scientific models. It stresses the need for examining behavioral and symbolic systems as they interact with genetics, since humans' 'elaborate cultural constructions form such a large part of their environment' (ibid.: 286). These developments provide possibilities for rapprochement between biological sciences and the humanities (e.g. Heywood et al., 2010; Thorpe, 2014, 2016).

With these integrative scientific models, 'nature versus nurture' is no longer an either/or proposition. When interaction effects between nature and nurture are taken into account, it highlights that 'human nature' and behavior does not occur in a vacuum, and that while millions of years of evolution have shaped humans to be a social species, with complex social and cultural practices that vary by ecology, the biological manifestations of that evolution by definition are subject to plasticity and change. While our very capacity to learn and respond to social context is necessarily built into our physiology, that physiology is itself affected by everything around it. It is in their interaction the most profound transdisciplinary possibilities for the analysis of physical movement lies.

The case for transdisciplinarity in physical cultural studies

'Science' understood in its models before the extended synthesis has informed PCS's interdisciplinary practice up to this point. As Silk, Francombe and Andrews write:

> The McDonaldizing rational productivity ethos of liberal capitalist society has seemingly found its epistemic corroboration in the positivist objectivism that underpins the scientific method, as conventionally understood. Both are constituents and simultaneously constitutors of a particular understanding of modernity, centred around linear evolutionary assumptions pertaining to the (assumed) inexorable progress of human civilization through the advancement of empirically grounded – often a euphemism for quantitatively driven and objectively reasoned – science.
>
> The self-evident epistemological hierarchy – what we can term the epistemological violence, that privileges specific 'scientific' ways of knowing – has structurally and intellectually constrained the potential and relevance of the social science of sport in terms of realizing its aims of developing a truly integrative and interdisciplinary approach to the study of physical activity and thereby of society.
> (Silk, Francombe and Andrews, 2014: 1272)

This rationale for the exclusion of science from the PCS paradigm, and thereby the argument for its interdisciplinarity instead of transdisciplinarity, makes perfect sense in these terms. But as I hope to have shown, many scientists have shifted in a different direction in terms of their truth claims, and that direction is a much more productive one for PCS since it reinforces PCS's most basic assumptions and claims as to the need to develop more multidimensional understandings of the moving body.

When Andrews writes in a refreshingly impassioned sense that 'either we develop truly comprehensive and integrative approaches to the stuff of human movement (incorporating everything from the genomic to the societal levels) or we end up using *kinesiology* as a euphemism for a collection of tangentially related, scientific endeavors' (Andrews, 2008: 59), he points to the necessity of including the genomic. Yet at the same time, if the motivation behind the project of PCS [is] 'a theoretically and empirically based understanding of various institutions, practices, and subjectivities through which physically active bodies are organized, regulated, and consumed in the service of particular power relations (prefigured on particular ability, class, ethnic, gender, generational, national, racial, and/or sexual norms and differences)' (Silk and Andrews, 2011: 10), these points of emphasis do not appear to include the genomic level. A transdisciplinary, interventionist project would also include and account for an interpretation of the neurobiological mechanisms that inform 'physically active bodies' from the inside out.

The transdisciplinary underpinnings of PCS, with its proclaimed focus on human movement in a radically contextual frame, makes it a primary site for exploring the 'affective shaping of human interaction' as that interaction is manifested in movement. This is one more necessary thread to the already extraordinarily complex PCS paradigm of 'a multi-method approach toward engaging the empirical (including ethnography and autoethnography, participant observation, discourse and media analysis, and contextual analysis)' (Andrews, 2008: 55) that includes specific attention to 'a theoretically and empirically based understanding of various institutions, practices, and subjectivities through which physically active bodies are organized, regulated, and consumed in the service of particular power relations (prefigured on particular ability, class, ethnic, gender, generational, national, racial, and/or sexual norms and differences)' (Silk and Andrews, 2011: 10). How our biological mechanisms related to affective, primary process emotions are informed, shaped, and impacted by power relations – how we differentially respond to power relations and why – is a crucial component to analyzing how 'physical bodies are organized, regulated and consumed'. The affect and effect of this organization is informed by biological mechanisms at the primary, secondary, and tertiary levels of the brain, and the relation between these mechanisms and the social institutions with which they have such a dynamic interaction should be a primary focus for transdisciplinary research on physical movement and embodiment more generally. Simply put, there is much potential for PCS in more transdisciplinary approaches to understanding, working with, and intervening in, moving bodies.

References

Andrews, D. L. (2008). Kinesiology's *Inconvenient Truth*: The Physical Cultural Studies Imperative. *Quest*, 60(1), 46–63.

Bush, A., Silk, M., Andrews, D. L. and Lauder, H. (2013). A Brief Genealogy of Cultural Studies and Sport, Physical Cultural Studies, and the McUniversity. In *Sport Coaching Research: Context, Consequences, and Consciousness*. London: Routledge, 71–85.

Choi, B. C. and Pak, A. W. (2006). Multidisciplinarity, Interdisciplinarity and Transdisciplinarity in Health Research, Services, Education and Policy: Definitions, Objectives, and Evidence of Effectiveness. *Clinical and Investigative Medicine*, 29(6), 351–364.

Derrida, J. (1968). *Of Grammatology* (trans. G. C. Spivak). Baltimore, MD: Johns Hopkins University Press.
Evans, J. (2014). Ideational Border Crossings: Rethinking the Politics of Knowledge Within and Across Disciplines, *Discourse: Studies in the Cultural Politics of Education*, 35(1), 45–61.
Fausto-Sterling, A. (2012). *Sex/Gender: Biology in a Social World*. New York: Routledge.
Gowaty, P. A. (2013). A Sex-Neutral Theoretical Framework for Making Strong Inferences About the Origins of Sex Roles. In M. L Fisher, J. Garcia, and R. S. Chang (eds), *Evolution's Empress*. Oxford: Oxford University Press, 85–112.
Harvard Transdisciplinary Research in Energetics and Cancer Center. (Undated). Definitions. Accessed August 29, 2015 from www.hsph.harvard.edu/trec/about-us/definitions.
Heywood, L. (2011a). Hunger, Emotions, and Sport: A Biocultural Approach. *Symploke*, 19(1–2), 119–142.
Heywood, L. (2011b). Affective Infrastructures: Toward a Neuropsychology of Sport. *Frontiers in Evolutionary Neuroscience*, 3, 1–5.
Heywood, L. (2015a). 'Strange Borrowing': Affective Neuroscience, Neoliberalism and the 'Cruelly Optimistic' Gendered Bodies of CrossFit. In C. Nally and A. Smith (eds), *Twenty-First Century Feminism: Forming and Performing Femininity*. Basingstoke: Palgrave Macmillan, 17–40.
Heywood, L. (2015b). The CrossFit Sensorium: Visuality, Affect and Immersive Sport. *Paragraph*, 38(1), 20–36.
Heywood, L., Garcia, J. and Wilson, D. (2010). Mind the Gap: Appropriate Evolutionary Perspectives Toward the Integration of the Sciences and Humanities. *Science and Education*, 19, 505–522.
Holistic Education Network. (Undated). Transdisciplinary Inquiry. Accessed August 29, 2015 from www.hent.org/transdisciplinary.htm.
Hrdy, S. B. (2009). *Mothers and Others: The Evolutionary Origins of Mutual Understanding*. Cambridge, MA: Harvard University Press.
Jablonka, E. and Lamb, M. J. (2006). *Evolution in Four Dimensions: Genetic, Epigenetic, Behavioral, and Symbolic Variation in the History of Life*. Cambridge, MA: Harvard University Press.
Jette, S., Vertinsky, P. and Ng, C. (2014). Biomedicine and Balance: Chinese-Canadian Women Negotiate Pregnancy-Related Lifestyle Directives and Risk. *Health, Risk & Society*, 16(6), 494–511.
Nicolescu, B. (2015). Transdisciplinary Methodology of the Dialogue Between Peoples, Cultures, and Spiritualities. *Human and Social Studies*, 4(2), 15–28.
Pigliucci, M. and Muller, G. B., eds (2010). *Evolution: The Extended Synthesis*. Cambridge, MA: MIT Press.
Porges, S. W. (2001). The Polyvagal Theory: Phylogenetic Substrates of a Social Nervous System. *International Journal of Psychophysiology*, 42, 123–146.
Rose, N. (2013). The Human Sciences in a Biological Age. *Institute for Culture and Society Occasional Paper* 3.1, 17–53.
Rose, N. and Abi-Rached, J. M. (2013). *Neuro: The New Brain Sciences and the Management of the Mind*. Princeton, NJ: Princeton University Press.
Silk, M. L. and Andrews, D. L. (2011). Toward a Physical Cultural Studies. *Sociology of Sport Journal*, 28(1), 4–35.
Silk, M., Francombe, J. and Andrews, D. L. (2014). Slowing the Social Sciences of Sport: On the Possibilities of Physical Culture. *Sport and Society*, 17(10), 1266–1289.
Thorpe, H. (2014). Moving Bodies beyond the Social/Biological Divide: Toward Theoretical and Transdisciplinary Adventures. *Sport, Education and Society*, 19(5), 666–686.
Thorpe, H. (2016). Athletic Women's Experiences of Amenorrhea: Biomedical Technologies, Somatic Ethics and Embodied Subjectivities. *Sociology of Sport Journal*, 33(1), 1–13.
Wilson, D. S. (2015). Beyond Genetic Evolution: A Conversation with Eva Jablonka. Accessed August 30, 2015 from https://evolution-institute.org/article/beyond-genetic-evolution-a-conversation-with-eva-jablonka/?source=tvol.

5

THE POLITICAL IMPERATIVE OF FEMINISM

Rebecca Olive

Physical cultural studies (PCS) scholars have been engaging in critical discussions about the ethics and politics of research, including special issues on these topics in *Cultural Studies ↔ Critical Methodologies* (2008) and *Sociology of Sport Journal* (2011). According to David Andrews and Michael Giardina (2008: 408), the goal of PCS is 'the deployment and (re)-realization of *a Cultural Studies that matters*, one that aims to produce the types of knowledge through which it would be in a position to intervene in the (broader social) world and *make a difference*' (emphasis original). Building on this, Michael Silk and David Andrews (2011: 14) argue that cultural research should be 'about helping people to empower themselves, determining what research can do for them (not us), and placing knowledge at their disposal to use in whichever way they wish'. In this way, the work we produce has the capacity to contribute to cultural change and thus researchers need to consider how we do our work, what we publish, and what the potential effects and affects of this might be?

Issues of theoretical and political research practices are issues of *praxis*, or 'that space between theory and practice where ideas are translated into concrete activities' (Hall, 1997: 5). Praxis asks that as scholars we do more than create knowledge, but that we practise that theory and knowledge in some way – that we do something with it to the benefit of the broader community (Davis, 1997; Hall, 1997; Lather, 1986). Such an approach to research bridges gaps between theory, knowledge production and activism, a challenge of academic work and writing that is implicit in the accusation that scholars operate from an ivory tower. With their focus on everyday and emancipatory research agendas, a call for praxis is a key component of the PCS manifesto (see for example, Andrews, 2008; Andrews and Giardina, 2008; Andrews and Silk, 2015; Atkinson, 2011; Silk and Andrews, 2011).[1] Such calls suggest PCS scholars 'embody the emancipatory notion of praxis in which knowledge is not only about finding out about the world, but also about changing it' (Silk and Andrews, 2011: 24). For Michael Atkinson (2011: 137), '[t]he merit, hope and future of the PCS movement ... lies in its call for engagement with real utopias, democracy and social intervention: simply, its call to committed praxis'.

While such aspirations are to be encouraged, Wheaton (2013) argues that 'despite the rhetoric, it is still the case that much of the discourse about this "new politics of possibilities" ... remains rooted in the ivory towers of academia, not civic engagement' (quoting Giardina and Denzin). Wheaton echoes Atkinson's critique of PCS's tendency to theorising;

> At present, PCS runs the very real risk of routinely resting on its own intellectual laurels – emerging far too often as an exercise in the philosophical reading of physical culture, power within social formations, or hegemonic representations of moving bodies and identities, and too infrequently as a concerted and unapologetic ritual of transformative praxis.
>
> *(Atkinson, 2011: 140, quoted in Wheaton, 2013: 10)*

Of course, such issues and concerns relating to praxis are not new, nor are they unique to PCS. Along with commentary in areas including education (Freire, 1972; Lather, 1986), cultural studies (Garbutt and Offord, 2012; Grossberg, 1993; Morris and Hjort, 2012; Turner, 2012) and history (Booth, 2011; Munslow, 2010), praxis remains fundamental to feminist scholarship, from the questions we ask to the knowledge we produce (Davis, 1997; Grosz, 2002; Hall, 1997; McLaren, 2002).

The political imperative of feminism

Feminist research explores and makes visible women's understandings and experiences of the world, as well as the patriarchal frameworks that have historically shaped these understandings and experiences (Ahmed, 1998; Grosz, 1994). Researchers engaged in feminist work have made significant contributions to not only how we think about 'women', but also how we think about history, bodies, gender, sexuality, race, ethnicity, and political-economy. The breadth of this body of work has led to great theoretical diversity where it is more useful to talk about feminisms than a unified feminist approach (Birrell, 2000; Hall, 1997). While often typologised as 'waves', Caudwell (2011: 117) argues that differentiating developments in feminist research, politics and activism in this way 'overly simplifies feminist theoretical expansion'.

A unifying link across this 'dynamic, continually evolving complex of theories' (Birrell, 2000: 61) is a commitment 'to producing frameworks of understanding that can serve as the basis for thoughtful and profound social change' (ibid.: 70). Feminist perspectives share a political orientation towards overcoming the subordination of women, 'must be relevant to the actual, concrete lives of women', and should 'both inform and reflect experience' (McLaren, 2002: 13; see also Davis, 1997; Hall, 1985; Probyn, 1993). In these terms, feminist research is not only a way of thinking and theorising, but is something we do. As Patti Lather (1986) wrote,

> We who do empirical research in the name of emancipatory politics must discover ways to connect our research methodology to our theoretical concerns and commitments. At its simplest, this is a call for critical inquirers to practice in their empirical endeavors what they preach in their theoretical formulations.
>
> *(Lather, 1986: 258, footnote 3)*

Navigating the tensions of using theory to remind us to privilege lived experiences, while critically analysing these experiences using theory, is an issue of praxis. In feminist studies of sport and physical cultures, this has manifested in a range of ways over time, including re-writing of histories, incorporation of ethnographic approaches, theoretical focus on lived experience, as well as community engagement and media contributions.

Feminism and praxis in the shift from sport to culture

The often competitive nature of sport and physical activity is seen as being measureable and quantifiable, with clear, objective outcomes, establishing sport as a male domain by embedding and reproducing established ideas about sex, gender and physical capabilities. A commitment to praxis has been clear in the political imperative of feminism to make visible and promote women's participation and achievements in sport, and to explore women's contributions to and understandings, experiences and knowledges about sport (Birrell, 2000; Birrell and Cole, 1994; Hall, 1985; Hargreaves, 1986, 1994). The contributions of feminist scholars to ways of thinking about and knowing women's contributions to and experiences of sport histories and organisations provided an essential foundation on which subsequent research about sex/gender, sport and bodies have built. This work showed how such structures marginalised women, and argued for active and explicit resistance against normalising processes in place through rules, uniforms, histories, traditions and relationships, which are stabilised as part of the game (Birrell and Theberge, 1994; Hargreaves, 1986, 1994; Lenskyj, 1994; Theberge, 1997). In these studies, power and resistance are seen in explicit terms, requiring collective and conscious political action to create change within sporting structures, organisations and administration (Birrell and Theberge, 1994; Hargreaves, 1994).

Since the 1990s, researchers have built upon these expanded ways of knowing sport, sex and gender, by increasingly using ethnographic approaches. Rather than asking questions based on existing assumptions, the use of interviews, observation and participation have allowed us to learn more about what media representations and participation mean for various women (Beal and Wilson, 2004; Bruce, 1998; Lenskyj, 1994; Markula, 1995; Theberge, 1997; Wheaton, 2002). These research approaches are contextual, engaged and reflexive, and reveal embodied accounts of how identity shapes experiences of participation. For example, Pirkko Markula (1995) found that women who took part in aerobics to reshape their bodies towards conventional 'firm but shapely, fit but sexy, strong but thin' feminine ideals also questioned the processes in which they were complicit. Nancy Theberge (1997) analysed the multiple and conflicting ways that women negotiate their participation in an adaptive version of ice-hockey, with rules that cut out body-contact but increase technical play. Jayne Caudwell (2007) used feminist and queer approaches to research football, women, gender and heteronormativity, to provide important insights on assumptions about lesbian communities and relationships, while in Beal and Wilson's (2004), Wheaton and Tomlinson's (1998) and Thorpe's (2009) research, participants in skateboarding, windsurfing and snowboarding explain complex hierarchies, with women employing a range of cultural tactics and performances to locate themselves as female participants and as women. In these studies, 'sport' was located in terms of physical cultural spaces and experiences within which women perform and negotiate identities and subjectivities in ways that challenge their own and broader socio-cultural gender discourses and stereotypes (Bruce, 1998; Cole, 1993; Pfister, 2010).

Understanding power relations in sport as engaged with cultural, contextual, embodied and relational moving bodies, helps to explore how sex and gender differences are constructed, understood, experienced and negotiated through subjectivities, participation, relationships, representations and performances in particular socio-cultural contexts. As well as critiquing the continued dominance of men and masculinities in sport and physical cultures, this research also highlights the enabling capacity of power relations, whereby women are always disrupting and contesting established discourses and norms. Rather than resistance and agency, such work engages with notions of power, ethics and pedagogies to imagine how we learn and transfer ways of knowing (Evers, 2004; Olive, 2016a; Pavlidis and Fullager, 2013; Rich, 2011a; Roy and Caudwell, 2014; Thorpe, 2009). This position connects with the premise that sports are 'constitutive, creative processes' (Hargreaves, 1994: 36) that contain potential for women to get beyond symbolic and physical forms of oppression and marginalisation, thus complicating issues of how we might contribute to cultural change in the knowledge we produce.

Feminist cultural studies: theory, embodiment, subjectivities and praxis

While research praxis is all very well in theory, translating it all into practice is tricky. In my own attempts at this, I have drawn on feminist cultural studies theories of bodies, subjectivities and space to image how cultural processes of change occur among individuals. Feminist cultural studies links the focus on power relations in everyday, lived, contextual experience, with feminist politics and commitments to praxis and equity. Feminist cultural studies researchers have explored the ways various aspects of our subjectivity – for example, sex, gender, sexuality, race, ethnicity, dis/ability – intersect, assemble and perform, within and through bodies, culture, relationships and place (Gatens, 1996; Grosz and Probyn, 1995; Hughes and Witz, 1997). That is, bodies are always actively constituting culture at the same time as culture is constituting subjectivities. Cole (1993: 86) argues that we cannot consider bodies and sport in isolation from cultures, politics, histories, economies and media that surround them, but instead as 'an ensemble of knowledges and practices that disciplines, conditions, reshapes, and inscribes the body', which diversifies not only how women play sport now, but possibilities for the future. Cole sees bodies as technologies for change, participating against the power structures they perform within. Further to this, Elizabeth Grosz (2002) points out that the ways we 'become' women (and men) are not situated in the past. Instead, they are always actively in the present as well as in the future – we are always in fact, becoming.

The implication of becoming is that we are in a constant relationship with the world around us and that neither is ever complete (Ahmed, 1998). In this way, bodies, experiences and culture are active and dynamic, with our complex identities, gender, sex, sexualities and so on playing out between us and the world in an ongoing exchange: always in place and time; always in context (Probyn, 2003). For example, research about surfing, has imagined the 'spatial imperative of subjectivities' (ibid.) of surfing bodies, cultures, spaces, subjectivities and power relations in a constant process of exchange (Evers, 2004; Olive, 2016a; Roy and Caudwell, 2014; Waitt, 2008), which has moved focus to the potential of everyday, cultural, grassroots approaches to translating theory into practice.

Thinking about theory, culture and experience in embodied terms incites new possibilities for research politics and praxis. Combined, these developments establish a research position that is messy, complex, lived and conceptual, and which allows for a 'politics of creative subversion' (Davis, 1997: 13). And it is here that feminist cultural studies theory is productive in thinking about praxis. By thinking about the potential of interactions between bodies, subjectivities, time, space and culture, arguments for explicit resistance lose their inevitability; resistance becomes implicit in participation, even if at times participation is complex and contradictory (see, for example, Bicknell, in press; Olive, 2016b). The productive potential has emerged in a range of ways, but in the next section I will focus on how feminist researchers have negotiated two: ethnographic methods and knowledge production.

Knowledge production, social justice and cultural change

> I propose that the goal of emancipatory research is to encourage self-reflection and deeper understanding on the part of the persons being researched at least as much as it is to generate empirically grounded theoretical knowledge. To do this, research designs must have more than minimal reciprocity.
>
> *(Lather, 1986: 266)*

As Lather highlights, issues of politics and knowledge production are woven throughout research design, methodologies, analysis and knowledge production. In this, reciprocity is not only about negotiating the complex social situation involved in qualitative research (especially fieldwork and interviews), and the ways participants are actively involved in these processes along with researchers (Harrison, MacGibbon and Morton, 2001). With theories of power, ethics and subjectivity so key to contemporary feminist research about sport and physical cultures, a number of researchers are engaging with issues of reflexivity and researcher positionality in their work (Adams, 2012; Evers, 2006; Francombe, 2013; Olive and Thorpe, 2011; Pavlidis and Olive, 2014; Popovic, 2010; Rich, 2011b; Thorpe, Barbour and Bruce, 2011). From engaging with participant perceptions of researcher subjectivities, to attempting greater accessibility and collaboration in their outputs, these researchers highlight the tensions and challenges of achieving more than minimal reciprocity in their research approaches and outputs. Feminist approaches have driven important developments in this area, contributing ways to account for and make use of researchers' existing subjective, embodied knowledges and understandings of sporting and physical cultural spaces. In particular, it is the drive to ensure that the research is about the lived experiences of participants that helps researchers avoid the very real prospect of 'navel gazing' in reflexive work, and instead to use these insights to explore assumptions and blind-spots, including feminist assumptions and perspectives, which can be as blinding as cultural insider status (Adams, 2012; Pavlidis and Olive, 2014; Thorpe, Barbour and Bruce, 2011; Wheaton, 2002).

This point about blind-spots should not be under-emphasised, as it is an integral part of researcher praxis. While feminists 'take as their point of departure the analysis of gender as a category of experience in society' (Birrell, 2000: 61), accounting for diversity recognises that 'that not all women share a common viewpoint. For some women, class and race will be much more significant' (Hall, 1985, 31; see also King and McDonald, 2007). As an example, the blind-spots around whiteness, heteronormativity, class and trans issues in my own research focus are glaring. As a white, heterosexual, (newly) middle class, Australian women who researches recreational action/lifestyle sports, I undeniably occupy a position of privilege, but which I have not adequately accounted for. Continuing to challenge the limitations of our view contributes to stronger arguments against continuing institutionalised and cultural discrimination and marginalisation based largely on perceived performance.

In a similar way, in our research fields and relationships it is possible to make use of relational and intersecting subjectivities to engage with various issues by drawing on our own subjectivity as (among other things) a woman, participant, feminist and researcher. As I have written elsewhere with Holly Thorpe:

> we have found that it is possible to engage in productive ethical and cultural conversations in the field, but this requires careful consideration of the unique social dynamics and local politics, a reflexive consideration of our role within it, as well as an intimate understanding of the broader culture within which we are working ...
> *(Olive and Thorpe, 2011: 432)*

Holly and I are 'intimately aware that simply performing individual acts of symbolic resistance is not enough to overturn the male-dominated social structures within action sport cultures' (ibid.: 435). However, for many researchers, enacting a consistent, disruptive and even resistant politics in the field is an important aspect of praxis.

Key questions also arise around what happens with the knowledge we produce? With contemporary research locating the most valuable and significant cultural changes as those that emerge from cultural participants themselves, how can contemporary researchers contribute resources to cultural change for good? How can we contribute back to the community and culture in ways that are relevant and concrete, to do a research that matters? As previously discussed, early feminist researchers including Jennifer Hargreaves, Patricia Vertinsky, Susan Birrell, Cheryl Cole and Nancy Theberge used forms of history to locate and understand women 'through the images of herself already deposited in history and the conditions of production of the work of man, and not on the basis of his work, his genealogy' (Irigaray, [1984] 2004: 11). Hargreaves (1982) argued for integrating critical theory into research about sport in order to counter existing analyses, which,

> Generally speaking, historical and comparative analyses of sport underestimate both the complexities of the social structures and the complexities of sport itself. They are based upon generalisations in relative isolation from the social, political and economic conditions of the time.
>
> *(Hargreaves, 1982: 3)*

By engaging with theory, these re-examinations highlighted issues women have faced in participation in sport and contributed important new perspectives that shape how we now think about sport, physical culture and bodies more broadly. That is, praxis was implicit in taking a female standpoint. While such approaches might not pass for praxis today, more recently researchers have been inspiring in the ways they have enacted their politics in community and cultural engagement. From Heather Skyes' participation in Pride House events with the Vancouver Olympic and Toronto Pan/Para Pan American Games (see, for example, PHTO, 2015), to Pirkko Markula's (2006, 2014) consideration about how to incorporate her critical theoretical insights into her fitness instruction and choreography practice, through to Kath Bicknell's (see, for example, Bicknell, 2014) ongoing contributions to technical developments in mountain biking equipment, feminist scholars are bringing their research into the world in affective and political ways.

Responding to the shift in thinking about sport as physical culture, a growing number of emerging academics have approached a call for praxis by making contributions within sports and physical cultures. In my case I have found leadership for this approach from a number of researchers who publish their work in a range of ways, including on blogs and websites, in niche magazines, in art exhibitions, on social media. I have practised this approach by continuing my blog, commenting on other websites, writing for art exhibitions, participating on discussion panels, speaking on radio, appearing in films, and publishing in (carefully selected) magazines (Olive, 2013, 2015, 2016b). While public intellectualism is not new, these forms of participation in mainstream media, online and social media, as well as artworks, exhibitions, workshops are growing in popularity among academics. This is about more than being an expert voice in a book or on a radio programme, but is about being visible, participating in debates, taking risks, and making oneself vulnerable. It is about being part of the discussion as it happens, bringing theory, methods, politics and critical analysis into cultural contexts outside of the proverbial ivory tower.

For me, publishing online in participatory media spaces continues to be a valuable part of my practice in my research about surfing, allowing me to continue to contribute female experiences, perspectives and voices into what (while changing) remains a largely male-dominated culture. To date, my contributions remain relatively small and exploratory, and my engagement with public intellectualism has remained largely within the confines of surfing cultural contexts. However, despite the limited scope of these contributions, I believe these efforts are not without impact. Contributing back to surfing culture is my attempt to open opportunities for surfing subjectivities to intersect out of the water but still in cultural space, where men who might not usually get to surf with women may have the chance to encounter a female way of knowing surfing (Olive, 2016a). These kinds of critical interventions can be rewarding and productive, but they also pose difficulties in that they require high levels of personal and professional vulnerability in cultural worlds with rules of engagement different than those in universities. Like social historian Jennifer Ho (2010), contributing back to the cultural community we are researching connects 'to the feminist ideals I believe in speaking truth to power and equality for all people ... I must hold myself accountable to practice in my scholarship what I preach in my blog (ibid.: 190).

Cultural change in this way is not necessarily fast or far-reaching, but for those it impacts, it can be significant. Writing into surfing culture was productive in contributing female perspectives, understandings and experiences, back to a culture dominated by men, as well as by providing opportunities for other women to join in the conversation (Olive, 2013, 2015). This was illustrated by a comment left by 'Karen' under one post, where she reflected that,

> despite constant encouragement from [my partner], the first post on K'baa [a collective blog] that I felt the urge to engage with was Bec writing on women in the surf. It was an entry point for me and, once I had got my toes wet, I kept coming back [to read and comment on posts].
>
> *(Quoted in Olive, 2015: 170)*

As a woman, Karen continues to be a minority in Australian surfing culture both at the beach and in historical and media representations of surfing. Although things are changing, women's voices remain notoriously rare to see or hear in surfing histories, magazines, films, photographs and other media (Olive, 2014). In this way, my own contribution to and participation in these online spaces as a woman and a surfer has aimed to encourage the participation of more female voices in a historically male-dominated cultural space.

Conclusion

Feminist calls to praxis that require me to privilege lived experience, remain relevant to the cultures I am researching and to contribute to change are the most challenging aspects of research I have encountered. They require me to walk a line of consistency between my research politics, theory, methods and outputs, as well as thinking about how this impacts on my subjectivity and behaviour outside of academic contexts. I take the lead from scholars before me who help me make sense of what it means to be political as a researcher, and how I can come to embody this across the research process and beyond. Enacting research praxis by developing a greater awareness of how my subjectivity limits my research, engaging with intersections of complex subjectivities in my thinking about sex/gender, and keeping research grounded in lived experience remain important contributions to what we can contribute as researchers and scholars, as well as pushing us to explore new ways to connect research back into the field to contribute to change towards greater equity, through community, policy, fieldwork and teaching.

Andrews and Silk (2015) have suggested that to date it has been students who have 'clearly led the way in demanding that PCS research does more than describe the *objects of PCS knowledge*' yet there are 'but a few examples of a PCS praxis that has *acted upon the world* in the manner that some individuals have argued for so passionately' (emphasis original). As PCS scholars continue to develop and strengthen their efforts at making media, policy, community and cultural contributions – at forms of praxis – there is much for them to draw upon from the significant, passionate and ever-developing body of feminist research in cultural studies, sociology, history, education, leisure studies and other fields. Such work has an established dialogue about so many of the qualities that PCS strives for – rigour, contextualisation, politics, reflexivity, social justice and praxis. Doing so is consistent with the PCS mandate for interdisciplinary, critical, reflexive scholarship and will contribute to greater accounting for diversity in efforts towards social change. In this chapter, I have drawn on feminist research about sport and physical cultures to illustrate the various ways that praxis has and continues to operate in a range of ways that have impacted women's representation and participation in sport and physical cultures. Whether through adopting a female standpoint, drawing on theory to develop greater ethics in methodologies, participating in policy development, engaging in community, or contributing to media, feminist researchers have always been interested in how sport and physical cultures connect with women's empowerment. In more recent cases, it has been through media contributions that emerging scholars have attempted to impact their various research fields. Yet as Gordon Waitt argues, approaching change through embodied subjectivities 'does not reveal a gender revolution that breaks the ideology of separate gender spheres' (Waitt, 2008: 92). And I agree. There are more radical and wide-ranging approaches of community engagement that we need to adopt. Yet in the meantime, by adopting praxis into our own everyday lives, by adopting theoretical understandings of embodied experience and knowledge as a relational process of cultural change, by making small, consistent contributions, by embodying the behaviours and attitudes we wish to see in others, we contribute to long-term, sustainable change for good.

Note

1   While there is a lack of explicit acknowledgement of the impact of the political imperative of feminist scholarship on PCS definitions the influence is clear. For example, although they do not engage with the politics driving the research, Silk and Andrews (2011) draw on the work of a range of feminist researchers as they develop their own research position and agenda.

References

Adams, C. 2012. (Writing Myself into) Betty White's Stories: (De)constructing Narratives of/through Feminist Sport History Research, *Journal of Sport History*, 39(3), 395–413.

Ahmed, S. 1998. *Differences that Matter: Feminist Theory and Postmodernism*. Cambridge: Cambridge University Press.

Andrews, D. 2008. Kinesiology's Inconvenient Truth and the Physical Cultural Studies Imperative. *Quest*, 60(1), 45–62.

Andrews, D. L. and Giardina, M. D. 2008. Sport without Guarantees: Toward a Cultural Studies that Matters. *Cultural Studies ↔ Critical Methodologies*, 8(4), 395–422.

Andrews, D. L. and Silk, M. L. 2015. Physical Cultural Studies. In R. Guilianotti (ed.), *Routledge Handbook of Sport Studies*. London: Routledge, 83–93.

Atkinson, M. 2011. Physical Cultural Studies [Redux]. *Sociology of Sport Journal*, 28(1), 135–144.

Beal, B. and Wilson, C. 2004. 'Chicks Dig Scars': Commercialisation and the Transformations of Skateboarders' Identities. In B. Wheaton (ed.), *Understanding Lifestyle Sports: Consumption, Identity and Difference*. London: Routledge, 31–54.

Bicknell, K. 2014. Tested: Specialised Women's Myth Saddle. Posted on Flow: Mountain Bike, 11 December. Accessed at http://flowmountainbike.com/tests/tested-specialized-womens-myth-saddle.

Bicknell, K. In press. Equipment, Innovation and the Mountain Biker's Taskscape. In H. Thorpe and R. Olive (eds), *Women in Action Sport Cultures: Identity, Politics, Experience, and Pedagogy*. Basingstoke: Palgrave Macmillan.

Birrell, S. 2000. Feminist Theories for Sport. In J. Coakley and E. Dunning (eds), *Handbook of Sports Studies*. London: Sage, 61–76.

Birrell, S., and Cole, C. L. 1994. *Women, Sport, and Culture*. Champaign, IL.: Human Kinetics.

Birrell, S. and Theberge, N. 1994. Feminist Resistance and Transformation in Sport. In D. M. Costa and S. R. Guthrie (eds), *Women and Sport: Interdisciplinary Perspectives*. Champaign, IL: Human Kinetics, 361–376.

Booth, D. 2011. History, Race, Sport: From Objective Knowledge to Socially-Responsible Narratives. In D. Adair (ed.), *Sport, 'Race' and Ethnicity: Narratives of Diversity and Difference*. Morgantown, WV: Fitness Information Technology, 13–39.

Bruce, T. 1998. Audience Frustration and Pleasure: Women Viewers Confront Televised Women's Basketball. *Journal of Sport and Social Issues*, 2(4), 373–397.

Caudwell, J. 2007. Queering the Field? The Complexities of Sexuality within a Lesbian-Identified Football Team in England. *Gender, Place and Culture*, 14(2), 183–196.

Caudwell, J. 2011. Sport Feminism(s): Narratives of Linearity? *Journal of Sport and Social Issues*, 35(2), 111–125.

Cole, C. L. 1993. Resisting the Canon: Feminist Cultural Studies, Sport, and Technologies of the Body. *Journal of Sport and Social Issues*, 17(2), 77–97.

Davis, K. 1997. Embody-ing Theory: Beyond Modernist and Postmodernist Readings of the Body. In K. Davis, ed. *Embodied Practices: Feminist Perspectives on the Body*. London: Sage, 1–23.

Evers, C. 2004. Men Who Surf. *Cultural Studies Review*, 10(1), 27–41.

Evers, C. 2006. How to Surf. *Journal of Sport and Social Issues*, 30(3), 229–243.

Francombe, J. 2013. Methods that Move: A Physical Performative Pedagogy of Subjectivity. *Sociology of Sport Journal*, 30(3), 256–273.

Freire, P. 1972. *Pedagogy of the Oppressed*. Harmondsworth: Penguin.

Garbutt, R. and Offord, B. 2012. A Scholarly Affair: Activating Cultural Studies. *Review of Education, Pedagogy and Cultural Studies*, 34(1–2), 3–7.

Gatens, M. 1996. *Imaginary Bodies: Ethics, Power and Corporeality*. New York: Routledge.

Grossberg, L. 1993. The Formations of Cultural Studies. In V. Blundell, J. Shepherd and I. Taylor (eds), *Relocating Cultural Studies: Developments in Theory and Research*. London: Routledge, 1–21.

Grosz, E. A. 1994. Sexual Difference and the Problem of Essentialism. In N. Schor and E. Weed (eds), *The Essential Difference*. Bloomington, IN: Indiana University Press, 82–97.

Grosz, E. A. 2002. Feminist Futures?. *Tulsa Studies in Women's Literature*, 21(1), 13–20.

Grosz, E. A. and Probyn, E. 1995. *Sexy Bodies: The Strange Carnalities of Feminism*. London: Routledge.

Hall, M.A. 1985. Knowledge and Gender: Epistemological Questions in the Social Analysis of Sport. *Sociology of Sport Journal*, 2(1), 25–42.

Hall, M. A. 1997. Women's Sport and Feminist Praxis: Bridging the Theory/Practice Gap. *Women in Sport and Physical Activity Journal*, 6(2), 213–224.

Hargreaves, J. 1982. Theorising Sport: An Introduction. In J. Hargreaves (ed.), *Sport, Culture and Ideology*, London: Routledge and Kegan Paul, 1–29.

Hargreaves, J. 1986. Where's the Virtue? Where's the Grace? A Discussion of the Social Production of Gender Relations in and through Sport. *Theory, Culture and Society*, 3(1), 109–121.

Hargreaves, J. 1994. *Sporting Females: Critical Issues in the History and Sociology of Women's Sports*. New York: Routledge.

Harrison, J., MacGibbon, L. and Morton, M. 2001. Regimes of Trustworthiness in Qualitative Research: The Rigors of Reciprocity. *Qualitative Inquiry*, 7(3), 323–345.

Ho, J. 2010. Being Held Accountable: On the Necessity of Intersectionality. *Journal of Women's History*, 22(4), 190–196.

Hughes, A. and Witz, A. 1997. Feminism and the Matter of Bodies: From de Beauvoir to Butler. *Body and Society*, 3(1), 47–60.

Irigaray, L. [1984] 2004. *An Ethics of Sexual Difference*. London: Continuum.

King, S. J. and McDonald, M. G. 2007. (Post)Identity and Sporting Cultures: An Introduction and Overview. *Sociology of Sport Journal*, 24(1), 1–19.

Lather, P. 1986. Research as Praxis. *Harvard Educational Review*, 56(3), 257–277.

Lenskyj, H. 1994. Sexuality and Femininity in Sport Contexts: Issues and Alternatives. *Journal of Sport and Social Issues*, 18, 356–376.

Markula, P. 1995. Firm but Shapely, Fit but Sexy, Strong but Thin: The Postmodern Aerobicizing Female Bodies. *Sociology of Sport Journal*, 12(4), 424–453.

Markula, P. 2006. Body–Movement–Change: Dance as Performative Qualitative Research. *Journal of Sport and Social Issues*, 30(4), 353–363.

Markula, P. 2014. The Moving Body and Social Change. *Cultural Studies ↔ Critical Methodologies*, 14(5), 483–495.

McLaren, M. A. 2002. *Feminism, Foucault, and Embodied Subjectivity*. Albany, NY: State University of New York Press.

Morris, M. and Hjort, M. 2012. *Creativity and Academic Activism*. Hong Kong: Hong Kong University Press.

Munslow, A. 2010. *The Future of History*. Basingstoke: Palgrave Macmillan.

Olive, R. 2013. Making Friends with the Neighbours: Blogging as a Research Method. *International Journal of Cultural Studies*, 16(1), 71–84.

Olive, R. 2014, Imagining Surfer Girls: The Production of Australian Surfing Histories. Accessed at www.girlmuseum.org/wp-content/uploads/2014/12/History-Rebecca-Olive-Imaginging-Surfer-Girls.pdf.

Olive, R. 2015. Interactivity, Blogs, and the Ethics of Doing Sport History. In G. Osmond and M. G. Phillips (eds), *Sport History in the Digital Age*. Champaign, IL: University of Illinois Press, 157–179.

Olive, R. 2016a. Women Who Surf: Female Difference, Intersecting Subjectivities and Cultural Pedagogies. In A. Hickey (ed.), *The Pedagogies of Cultural Studies*. Abingdon: Routledge, 179–197.

Olive, R. 2016b. Going Surfing/Doing Research: Learning How to Negotiate Cultural Politics from Women Who Surf. *Continuum: Journal of Media and Cultural Studies*, 30(2), 171–182.

Olive, R. and Thorpe, H. 2011. Negotiating the 'F-word' in the Field: Doing Feminist Ethnography in Action Sport Cultures. *Sociology of Sport Journal*, 28(4), 421–440.

Pavlidis, A. and Fullager, S. 2013. Narrating the Multiplicity of 'Derby Grrl': Exploring Intersectionality and the Dynamics of Affect in Roller Derby. *Leisure Sciences: An Interdisciplinary Journal*, 35(5), 422–437.

Pavlidis, A. and Olive, R. 2014. On the Track/in the Bleachers: Authenticity and Ethnographic Research in Sport and Physical Cultural Studies. *Sport in Society: Cultures, Commerce, Media, Politics*, 17(2), 218–232.

Pfister, G. 2010. Women in Sport: Gender Relations and Future Perspectives. *Sport in Society*, 13(2), 234–248.

PHTO. 2015. A History of the Pridehouse Movement. Accessed at www.podcastchart.com/podcasts/pridehouseto/episodes/2-the-very-first-gathering-of-the-phto-cafe-series-a-history-of-the-pride-house-movement.

Popovic, M. L. 2010. A VoIce in the Rink: Playing with Our Histories and Evoking Autoethnography. *Journal of Sport History*, 37(2), 235–255.

Probyn, E. 1993. *Sexing the Self: Gendered Positions in Cultural Studies*. London: Routledge.

Probyn, E. 2003. The Spatial Imperative of Subjectivity. In K. Anderson, M. Domosh, S. Pile and N. Thrift (eds), *Handbook of Cultural Geography*. London: Sage, 290–299.

Rich, E. 2011a. 'I See Her Being Obesed!' Public Pedagogy, Reality Media and the Obesity Crisis. *Health*, 15(1), 3–21.

Rich, E. 2011b. Exploring the Relationship between Pedagogy and Physical Cultural Studies: The Case of New Health Imperatives in Schools. *Sociology of Sport Journal*, 28(1), 64–84.

Roy, G. and Caudwell, J. 2014. Women and Surfing Spaces in Newquay, UK. In J. Hargreaves and E. Anderson (eds), *Routledge Handbook of Sport, Gender and Sexuality*. Abingdon: Routledge, 235–244.

Silk, M. L. and Andrews, D. L. 2011. Toward a Physical Cultural Studies. *Sociology of Sport Journal*, 28(1), 4–35.

Theberge, N. 1997. 'It's Part of the Game': Physicality and the Production of Gender in Women's Hockey. *Gender and Society*, 11(1), 69–87.

Thorpe, H. 2009. Bourdieu, Feminism and Female Physical Culture: Gender Reflexivity and the Habitus-Field Complex. *Sociology of Sport Journal*, 26(4), 491–516.

Thorpe, H., Barbour, K. and Bruce, T. 2011. 'Wandering and Wondering': Theory and Representation in Feminist Physical Cultural Studies. *Sociology of Sport Journal*, 28(1), 106–134.

Turner, G. 2012. *What's Become of Cultural Studies*. London: Sage.

Waitt, G. 2008. 'Killing Waves': Surfing, Space and Gender. *Social and Cultural Geography*, 9(1), 75–94.

Wheaton, B. 2002. Babes on the Beach, Women in the Surf: Researching Gender, Power and Difference in the Windsurfing Culture. In J. Sugden and A. Tomlinson, eds. *Power Games: A Critical Sociology of Sport*. London: Routledge, 240–266.

Wheaton, B. 2013. *The Cultural Politics of Lifestyle Sports*. New York: Routledge.

Wheaton, B. and Tomlinson, A. 1998. The Changing Gender Order in Sport? The Case of Windsurfing Subcultures. *Journal of Sport and Social Issues*, 22(3), 252–274.

6
PRAXIS

Michael L. Silk and Joanne Mayoh

Rather than some evangelical posturing with respect to the *right* way to conduct research for supposed *right* reasons, within this chapter we delineate our own positioning related to praxis – a term we understand as rooted in a feminist insistence that knowledge is useful, that understands theory and research as practice, and that is committed to understanding the social world and then changing it (Stanley, 1990, 2013). That is, we understand physical cultural studies (PCS) as being influenced by an emancipatory aspiration; one which offers a 'powerful opportunity for praxis to the extent that the research process enables people to change by encouraging self-reflection and a deeper understanding of their particular situations' (Lather, 1986). This aspiration has certainly been present in work to date; Andrews (2008: 54) for example argued that PCS is committed to producing and disseminating 'potentially empowering forms of knowledge and understanding', whilst Andrews and Giardina (2008: 408) advocated the importance of PCS 'activist-minded projects'. Yet, these motivations, despite such clarion calls, have perhaps yet to be realized to date; as Atkinson (2011: 141) suggested, 'the tallest and broadest hurdle [for PCS] is ultimately one of our collective commitments to engaged intervention and willingness to openly take sides in the process of policy development and reformation'.

Moorings/trajectories

Our journeys towards understanding praxis as an implicit component of scholarship are likely all different – we all have varying disciplinary, epistemological and theoretical moorings that are more or less likely to foreground (or not), centralize (or not), or position praxis as the (embodied) *raison d'être* (or not) for scholars/scholarship (a loose term deployed here to include a multitude of activities that we could place under such a banner). Of import for us herein, is not to pose our (or others) moorings as in any way being the right ones (how could they be, lest we were to close off a multiplicity of approaches/disciplines/knowledges that have critically and self-reflexively debated praxis) but rather to address how our understandings/influences/scholarly groundings and trajectories have led us to reflect on praxis within PCS scholarship. Indeed, if anything, and as indicated below, there is an uneven, unbalanced set of academic moorings that traverse the commitment to praxis and which have come to the fore (or not) in differing intensities, in theoretical, empirical and methodological explorations of PCS – praxis in PCS can be seen as a complex assemblage of scholarly trajectories that meet, clash, co-habit and exist in often uneasy coalescence within various efforts to contextualize physical culture. This we see as a healthy tension; our hope, our intent, is that we can hold together scholarly trajectories/ways of arriving at (or embedding) praxis (some of which are throughout this handbook), and that the tensions this creates can productively lead to debate that will invariably strengthen and develop discussion and further delineate physical cultural *praxes* ground in understandings from a differing array of scholarly trajectories, genealogies and histories.

If PCS is a collective and democratic project – incorporating a productive tension of divergent foci, viewpoints, and opinions that are (very) loosely united by a common concern with contextualizing the complex field of physical culture – then its generative core needs to demonstrate a critical dynamism that fights off the inertia created by the all-too-easy adoption of empirical, theoretical, and/or methodological certainties. That is, and in a Freirean sense (Freire, 2000), if PCS is a dialogic learning community, one in which there is a commitment to critical and constructive conversation, or dialogue, with each other as a core part of the learning process (as opposed to having knowledge and understanding imposed), there is a need to nurture dialogic 'reflection and action upon the world in order to transform it' (ibid.: 51). In this sense, and as a political project, and unsurprisingly historically entrenched in the work of the Birmingham Centre for Contemporary Cultural Studies, PCS is committed to the advancement of the social formations in which it is located and in which researchers display an unequivocal understanding of the politics of intellectual practice concerned with discerning the distribution, operations, and effects of power and power relations: hierarchically ordered societal lines of differentiation (i.e., those based on class, ethnic, gender, ability, generational, national, racial, and/or sexual norms) manifest in socio-cultural inequities or injustices; advantages or disadvantages; enablements or constraints; empowerments or disempowerments. For this reason, and as part of a broader commitment to progressive social change, PCS engages physical culture as a site where such social divisions and hierarchies are enacted, experienced, and at times contested. Indeed, given an understanding of the sites of political struggle – or problem-spaces – within physical culture and through which social power becomes manifest and operationalized as *changeable,* we would suggest there is a necessity for an equally fluid dynamism in PCS's strategic emphases, research practices and politics. In this sense, and rooted in a humanist intellectualism – a pathway paved by many who have put their heads above the parapet in a variety of disciplines – we would aver that PCS scholarship is motivated by the identification and elimination of disparities and inequities, the struggle for social justice, and the realization of universal human rights. These are subjective moral and political commitments, made explicit within and through the choices and enactment of research, and that recognizes the need scholars, researchers, and/or activists to be attentive to, and sometimes transform themselves in response to, the specific institutional, societal, and/or historical conditions they confront.

Thus, as a sensibility, and somewhat revising Denzin (2012), we feel PCS can, and should, be contributing to a range of conversations about, for example: gender-based violence and sexual health for disadvantaged women in the global south; healthcare provision among 'excluded' or 'marginalized' populations; the neoliberal governance of the body; the pathologized or abject body; immigration; racisms; personal identity; citizenship; freedom; patriotism; justice; democracy; perpetual war; violence; global social relations; political struggle; sporting bodies; class relations, gender inequalities, bodies in (urban) spaces; sexualities; (trans)gender bodily politics; and so on (a necessarily abbreviated list). To be *meaningful*, through connecting private troubles and public concerns, PCS scholarship can enable change when extending its critical, performative and utopian impulses to address urgent social issues in the interests of promoting social change (Giroux, 2001a). In so doing, PCS seeks to 'construct a political history of the (physical cultural) present' (Grossberg, 2006: 2) (parenthesis added), through which it becomes possible to construct politically expedient physical cultural possibilities out of the historical circumstances it confronts. Yet, as political theorist Jodi Dean (2000: 5) remarked: 'Cultural studies risks non-intervention by *presuming* its political purchase in advance' (emphasis added); it is for this reason that PCS needs to be attuned to developing a socio-historic imagination, that enables a 'quality of mind that will help [individuals] to use information and to develop reason in order to achieve lucid summations of what is going on in the world and of what may be happening within themselves' (Mills, 1959: 11). The *promise* then of PCS, like the promise of the sociological imagination, and indeed of those who have, in various guises in academe, taken up the sociological imagination as a motivation for their academic work (some explicitly acknowledged in PCS research to date, others implicit yet perhaps lacking formal recognition), is as a source of empowerment that can enable individuals to discern the nature of the society around them, and their location within it. PCS then, as a project, is ground within the various trajectories of academe that have an unequivocal 'commitment to progressive social change' (Miller, 2001: 1) and aims to *expose* and *render visible* unequal (physical cultural) power relations and produce the type of knowledge that can enable intervention into the broader social world. As such, PCS scholarship, and distinct from the vestiges of logical positivism found even within the most 'liberated' disciplines, should be unembarrassed by the label political, and like others before, unafraid to consummate a relationship with an emancipatory consciousness; a pragmatics of hope in an age of cynical reason (Kincheloe and McLaren, 2005).

As alluded to above, the enduring commitment to emancipatory practice is not especially new and draws on multiple scholarly trajectories; it is, however, especially indebted to feminist advances in knowledge, ontology, epistemology and methodology (especially within those focused on sport/physical cultural practices, see e.g. Birrell and Cole, 1994; Brabazon, 2002; Cole, 2003; Hall, 1996; Hargreaves, 1994; King, 2006; Lenskyj, 1986; Markula and Pringle, 2006; Olive and Thorpe, 2011; Pavlidis and Fullagar, 2014; Sykes, 2011; Thorpe, 2009; Vertinsky and Hargreaves, 2006; Young, 1980). Perhaps not surprisingly for an approach which people are coming to terms with, negating, thinking through, embracing (and so on), there is perhaps something of a publication lag with respect to any emergent synergy/difference between an emancipatory feminist politics and its convergence with PCS sensibilities, with explorations and dialogues in convergence, method, epistemology and knowledge (and marked difference) only beginning to emerge in academic outputs (see e.g. Francombe, 2010; Francombe-Webb et al., 2014, 2015; Olive, 2016; Chapter 5, this volume; Olive and Thorpe, 2011; Pavlidis and Fullagar, 2014; Pavlidis and Olive, 2014; Rich, 2011; Thorpe et al., 2011; cf. Adams et al., 2016). As such, and despite these early debates, the political projects of PCS and feminist scholars in sport and exercise have yet to fully realize a productive dialogue, fully converge, or build off each other. In part, this is due to something of lack of acknowledgement of empowering praxis and feminist approaches to research, or indeed early PCS dialogues ground in feminist sensibilities (cf. Adams et al., 2016; Thorpe et al., 2011), and we would aver, due to the nascent and sometimes provocative nature of some PCS writing. Feminist scholars (and scholarship) have certainly influenced the motivations among PCS advocates towards emancipation, power relations, embodiment, social change and a commitment towards social justice; perspectives that strive to translate research into concrete activities that make a difference to the world (Stanley, 2013). Likewise, there exists some similarities with respect to an attuned focus on the body as a site of power relations and negotiations, and a common call to centralize the body within research practice in the quest to further knowledge and ongoing discussions about (in)active embodiment.

Holding these concerns together, we can certainly begin to see how these debates are being played out and how a feminist-influenced praxis orientation is influencing an emergent and aspirational PCS (see e.g. the chapters in this handbook from Lesley Heywood, Clifton Evers and Jennifer Germon, Megan Chawansky and Satako Itani, Julia Coffey, Shannon Jette, Simone Fullagar, Lisette Burrows and Laura De Pian, Jessica Ringrose, Katie Fitzpatrick, Cheryl Cooky, Rebecca Olive, Emma Rich and Jennifer Sandlin). Thus, we hope the text serves as a productive and genuine attempt to hold together a plurality of approaches, an assemblage of moorings, scholars, theorizing and methodologies so as to further develop an emancipatory physical cultural imperative/praxes.

Borders/boundaries

If, as suggested above, and influenced by a feminist communitarian sensibility, PCS scholarship internalizes and centralizes morality, ethics, and *the political*, some would argue that there might be a need to rethink the civic and political responsibilities of academics. With Said (1994), we might need to embrace an intellectual amateurism in which we are physically and metaphorically exiled from our offices to connect with the political realities of society and in which we are encouraged to maintain critical distance from official or institutional bodies so as to speak truth to power (also, Rizvi and Lingard, 2006). Giroux's (2001b, 2004) border crossing advocates a view of intellectual work that re-theorizes the role of cultural workers and engaged artists in keeping justice and ethical considerations alive in progressive discourses and in revitalizing a broader set of social, political, and pedagogical considerations within a radical cultural politics. Drawing on the tradition of political work indebted to Williams and Hall (and continued through, among others, Mouffe, Fraser and Grossberg), Giroux (2001b) called for critical educators and cultural scholars to break down the artificial barriers, the separate spaces, and the different audiences that are supported through the infrastructure of disciplinary and institutional borders that 'atomize, insulate and prevent diverse cultural workers from collaborating across such boundaries' (ibid.: 7). We are not suggesting we all abandon our offices and inhabit such spaces, but we are suggesting that such *border crossings* should be held alongside the classroom, the journal, the book chapter, and the conference presentation as key spaces in which intervention, emancipatory action/practice and understanding can take place. Indeed, this is a notable, if emergent, trend; scholars addressing a range of physical cultural practices are increasingly inhabiting more public spaces – for example, the work of Mark Doidge's anti-discrimination community-based praxis among fan groups/ultras; Jules Boykoff's public writing and Olympic activism; Jim Denison's Foucauldian coach intervention project (see Chapter 11, this volume); Amanda De Lisio's work alongside sex worker support groups in Rio during the 2014 FIFA World Cup; Ian McDonald's award winning film documentaries addressing subjects from gay footballers (*Brighton Bandits*) to the experience of blindness and the game of chess (*Algorithms*); Simone Fullagar and Jess Francombe-Webb's media work related to the objectification and sexualization of the female body; or Rebecca Olive's blog focusing on marginalization and exclusion of female surfers – in the hope of contributing to broader cultural discussions and engaging in border crossing outside of academic contexts.

In keeping with the notion of a praxical PCS assemblage, each of these instances of intervention/emancipatory practice, are informed by the differing political, axiological, ontological and epistemological positions of the researchers; and illicit differing (political), policy and communitarian responses. Such emancipatory practice does somewhat reconceptualize the role and place of the 'academic' as traditionally understood; it is likely to rub against many of the 'standards' of the tenure review or promotion committee – how will they 'count' the oppositional art work created with the local artist, the poesis produced, the play performed at the community hall, the film created or, for that matter, the public talk given at a residents meeting? There are of course risks, especially for early career academics embedded within increasingly metric-oriented neoliberal institutions. Yet, and despite the reservations/critique of various metrics designed to measure scholarship, such systems (such as the REF in the UK and research councils) are demanding an impact agenda – however defined – that at the least suggests a passion/enthusiasm for meaningful social change as part of the boundaries of our academic lives. Conversely, and without being overly pessimistic, the institutionalization of praxis might well bring it with a multitude of constraints.

There are also potential concerns when considering ethics, as traditionally understood. One wonders how the Institutional Review Board (or ethics panels) – institutions ground in a liberal Enlightenment philosophy built on value-free social science that shies away from political and moral and which proffer research with a disinterested position – cope with any form of non-utilitarian ethics (Christians, 2005)? Following Christians, such a constricted understanding of ethics in 'science' does not seem at all adequate for intervention, for understanding 'science' and 'education' as a regime of power that helps to maintain the social order by normalizing subjects into categories designed by political authorities, for oppositional politics, for, emancipatory scholarship/praxis. Rather, we might need to rethink the boundaries of that which traditionally constitutes ethics: an ethical approach that does not search for neutral principles to which all parties can appeal, does not see people as receptacles for data, as outsiders excluded from the research process, and that breaks down the role of researcher as expert, might well be warranted. Such a reciprocal or social ethical approach erases any distinction between epistemology, aesthetics, and ethics and is located within a feminist communitarian model that rests on a complex view of moral judgments as integrating into an organic whole various perspectives – everyday experience, beliefs about the good, and feelings of approval and shame – in terms of human relations and social structures (Christians, 2005; Denzin, 2005). In practical terms, this is an ethical approach that is based on interpretive sufficiency (in which ethics is *measured* with regard to a politics of resistance, hope, and freedom and in which the researcher's responsibility is towards those studied) – rather than experimentalism or instrumental sufficiency (technical, exterior, statistically precise) – participates in a community's ongoing process of moral articulation, a representational adequacy free from racial, class, gender stereotyping, an effort to enable people to come to terms with their everyday experiences themselves, and the generation of social criticism, leads to resistance and empowers to action those who are interacting (Christians, 2005).

In this formulation, drawing on Christians (2000), the boundaries of scholarship are not just about empowering people; it is about helping people to empower themselves and imagine how things could be different, determining what research can do for them (not us), and imagines new forms of human transformation and emancipation. Again, we can begin to see these sensibilities influencing our academic practice. The work of Jessica Francombe-Webb is notable here (Francombe, 2013; Francombe-Webb and Silk, 2015) in which she deployed a reciprocal 'collaborative analytic element' (Francombe, 2013: 265) so as to heighten the critical social class awareness of teenage girls. Realized through workshops that posed relevant contemplative questions to the girls, she encouraged imaginative variation, facilitated personal reflection, and aided participants to 'deeply understand' (Lather, 1986) their own social world and offer powerful counter-narrative. Of course, the extent to which it makes a significant impact on the community, and the extent to which it could be considered wide-reaching is debatable (an issue on which the author critically self-reflects), yet, this work points to the centrality of reciprocity (see e.g. Harrison et al., 2001; Lather, 1986; Olive, Chapter 5, this volume), the need to critically reflect on how theoretical approaches translate into practice, and an avenue to developing, following Lather (1986), context-embedded data that dialectically generates theoretical propositions.

An emancipatory and reciprocal research sensibility works towards the desire for research practice ground in a sacred-moral humanistic discourse on care, solidarity, dignity and universal human rights (Denzin, 2005; Denzin and Giardina, 2006) – as opposed to a concern with how to 'get better data'. It points to how critical research into, on, and with, varying physical forms, subjectivities and experiences can enable praxis: encouraging community life to prosper, equipping people to come to mutually held conclusions, about community transformation and participation at all stages of the research process (from design through analysis through interpretation through implementation). This is a sacred-moral approach to physical cultural forms, structures, experiences and institutions; it is a civic, participatory, collaborative praxis, a project that joins the researcher(s) with the researched in an ongoing moral dialogue (Kemmis and McTaggart 2005: 568). There are of course a multitude of ways in which such a sacred-moral ethic can be enacted; Part IX (Politics and Praxis) of this handbook provides examples and offers critical (often self-) reflective considerations of such approaches.

An embodied and implicit sacred-moral praxis also speaks to an 'expressive praxis' (Harrison et al., 2001) in which we position ourselves as self-conscious, critical, participatory analysts, and engaged (although sometimes distinct from participants) co-contributors. This problematizes the hierarchical boundaries between researcher/the researched, asks us to reflect on that relationship as we minimize status difference, show our human side, and rather than hiding behind a cloak of anonymity recognize that our research products are co-produced accomplishments (cf. Fontana and Frey, 2005; Harrison, MacGibbon and Morton, 2001; Lather, 1986; Stanley, 2013). This is a position in which we need to be attuned to the extraordinary persistent residual of our own exilic marginality: an exile from our rigid professional affiliations and a recognition of detachment from those with whom we engage in order to produce resistive academic work that can 'write back' to (imperial) power, can read contrapuntally, can speak to justice, and can challenge injustice (Rizvi and Lingard, 2006; Said, 1994). In this regard then, we 'come clean at the hyphen' that separates and merges personal identities with our inventions of others, thereby offering a series of self-reflective points of critical consciousness around questions of how to represent responsibly, transform public consciousness and common sense about social injustice (see Fine, 1992; Harrison et al., 2001). To do so, and somewhat adapting Fine et al. (2000), a set of (partial) self-reflexive points of critical consciousness might be useful in providing a roadmap of what such an expressive praxis might look like, feel like and embody. Fine et al. (ibid.: 126–127) ask the researcher to consider whether they have connected the voices and stories of individuals back to the set of historic, structural, and economic relations in which they are situated (is the physical empirical addressed in context). Further, they ask if research has deployed multiple methods so that very different kinds of analysis have been constructed. They ask whether we have described the mundane (as opposed to the unique or startling) and provided the opportunity for some informants/constituencies/participants to review the material and interpret, dissent, or challenge interpretations. They ask us to consider how such disagreements in perspective would be reported and how we have thought through the theorizing of informants' words. Further, and perhaps most importantly, they ask whether the research has considered *how* these data could be used for progressive, conservative, repressive social policies? Has there been consideration of falling into the passive voice and has the (embodied) researcher decoupled responsibility for interpretations. Has there been thought given to who the researcher would be afraid will see these analyses and who is rendered vulnerable/responsible or exposed by these analyses. Finally, they ask if consideration has been given to the extent to which analysis offers an alternative to the commonsense or dominant discourse and the challenges different audiences might pose. Thus, and no matter where we aim to make a difference – in the classroom, through public ethnography, in the academic journal, in the community, on the street, influencing policy, through poetry, through campaigning, blogging or other forms of social media, film, and so on – PCS scholars should be critically reflexive with respect to how we want to live the lives of an emancipatory social inquirer (Schwandt, 2000).

On the possibilities of praxis

In this short coda, we use the term *possibilities* quite deliberately. With Stanley (2013: 15), we see possibilities for an ontological and political position 'in which knowledge is not simply defined as 'knowledge *what*' but also as 'knowledge *for*'. Yet, while there may be some form of unity with respect to PCS scholarship making a difference (in a multitude of diverse spaces/sites), the rhetoric is perhaps a little overplayed. For sure, and no matter how one comes to a position in which we want to do more than describe the *objects of PCS knowledge* (and there are a multitude of pathways to get here, drawing on differing knowledges, influences and disciplines, none of which are any better than any other; the point is that as individuals we have collectively arrived here through our own, often individual, scholarship, trajectories, training and thinking), at present there are few examples (see e.g. King-White, 2012; Thorpe, 2011; Thorpe et al., 2011) of how PCS praxes have *acted upon the world* in the manner that some proclaim. The pages of this handbook are peppered with accounts of research that have made various forms of impact in a multitude of sites/spaces; some publically proclaiming the transformative and emancipatory potential of their research, others more modest in describing praxis. History will likely be the judge, time will give a better indication of the ability of PCS scholars/scholarship to make a meaningful difference and the parameters of achievable action and transformation (however incremental, modest, and/or miniscule). Indeed, while there are a multitude of ways in which praxis can potentially transform, to date, it is perhaps in our educative work where we can (and have) most clearly taken strides (on this point, see for example Adams et al., 2016; Andrews et al., 2013; Silk et al., 2014, 2015; Levermore, Chapter 57, this volume). This is perhaps not surprising, for, if we consider our institutions as the roughest of neoliberal beasts that has created a new, soulless, academic performativity that makes us *more calculable than memorable* (Ball, 2012), our pedagogic practices (in the classroom, with communities, with publics), as a form of praxis, are activated by ethical imperatives and concerns – forms of pedagogy that can consider relations of freedom, authority, democratic knowledge and responsibility (Garbutt and Offord, 2010; Stevenson, 2010).

The possibilities of the future are indeed promising, although it is often difficult to measure impact (or social change) through such means (at least in a traditional sense). In this sense, and to date, praxis as realized is likely more closely equated to Freire's notion of conscientization, as we engage in work that can aid in 'breaking through prevailing mythologies to reach new levels of awareness – in particular, awareness of oppression, being an 'object' of others' will rather than a self-determining 'subject'. Despite the reality that we can likely never do enough, and more often than not our projects, no matter how well meaning, probably do not make as much of a difference as we would like, we have attempted to point towards exciting possibilities and deeply rooted yet emergent trajectories toward self-reflection, understanding, and emancipation that will come to define physical cultural *praxes*.

References

Adams, M. L. et al. (2016). Feminist Cultural Studies: Uncertainties and Possibilities. *Sociology of Sport Journal*, 33(1), 75–91.

Andrews, D. L. (2008). Kinesiology's *Inconvenient Truth*: The Physical Cultural Studies Imperative. *Quest*, 60(1), 46–63.

Andrews, D. and Giardina, M. (2008). Sport Without Guarantees: Towards a Cultural Studies that Matters. *Cultural Studies ↔ Critical Methodologies*, 8(4), 395–422.

Andrews, D. L., Silk, M., Francombe, J. and Bush, A. (2013). McKinesiology. *Review of Education, Pedagogy, and Cultural Studies*, 35(5), 335–356.

Atkinson, M. (2011). Physical Cultural Studies [Redux]. *Sociology of Sport Journal*, 28(1), 135–144.

Ball, S. J. (2012). 'Performativity, Commodification and Commitment: An I-Spy Guide to the Neoliberal University'. *British Journal of Educational Studies*, 60, 17–28.

Birrell, S. and Cole, C. L. (1994). *Women, Sport, and Culture*. Champaign, IL: Human Kinetics.

Brabazon, T. (2002). Fitness is a Feminist Issue. *Australian Feminist Studies*, 21(49), 65–83.

Christians, C. (2000). Ethics and Politics in Qualitative Research. In N. K. Denzin and Y. S. Lincoln (eds) *Handbook of Qualitative Research*, 2nd edn (pp. 133–155). Thousand Oaks, CA: Sage.

Christians, C. (2005). Ethics and Politics in Qualitative Research. In N. Denzin and Y. Lincoln (eds), *The Sage Handbook of Qualitative Research*. Thousand Oaks, CA: Sage.

Cole, C. L. (2003). Resisting the Canon: Feminist Cultural Studies, Sport and the Technologies of the Body. *Journal of Sport and Social Issues*, 17(2), 77–97.

Dean, J. (2000). Introduction: The Interface of Political Theory and Cultural Studies. In J. Dean (ed.), *Cultural Studies and Political Theory* (pp. 1–22). Ithaca, NY: Cornell University Press.

Denzin, N. K. (2005). Emancipatory Discourses and the Ethics and Politics of Interpretation. In N. K. Denzin and Y. S. Lincoln (eds), *The Sage Handbook of Qualitative Research*, 3rd edn (pp. 933–958). Thousand Oaks, CA: Sage.

Denzin, N. (2012). Afterword. In M. Silk and D. Andrews (eds), *Sport and Neoliberalism: Politics, Consumption and Culture* (pp. 294–302). Philadelphia, PA: Temple.

Denzin, N. and Giardina, M. (eds) (2006). *Qualitative Inquiry and the Conservative Challenge*. Walnut Creek, CA: Left Coast Press.

Fine, M. (1992). Passions, Politics and Power: Feminist Research Possibilities. In M. Fine (ed.), *Disruptive Voices: The Possibilities of Feminist Research*. Ann Arbor: The University of Michigan Press.

Fine, M., Weis, L., Weseen, S. and Wong, L. (2000). For Whom? Qualitative Research, Representations and Social Responsibilities. In Denzin, N. and Lincoln, Y. (eds) (2000). *Handbook of Qualitative Research*, 2nd edn (pp. 107–132). Thousand Oaks, CA: Sage.

Fontana, A. and Frey, J. (2005). The Interview: From Neutral Stance to Political Involvement. In Denzin, N. and Lincoln, Y. (eds). (2005). *The Sage Handbook of Qualitative Research*, 2nd edn Thousand Oaks, CA: Sage.

Francombe, J. (2010). 'I Cheer, You Cheer, We Cheer': Physical Technologies and the Normalized Body. *Television and New Media*, 11(5), 350–366.

Francombe, J. (2013). Methods that Move. A Physical Performative Pedagogy of Subjectivity. *Sociology of Sport Journal*, 30(3), 256–273.

Francombe-Webb, J. and Silk, M. (2015). Young Girls' Embodied Experiences of Femininity and Social Class. *Sociology: The Journal of the British Sociological Association*.

Francombe-Webb, J., Rich, E. and De Pian, L. (2014). I Move Like You … But Different: Biopolitics and Embodied Methodologies. *Cultural Studies ↔ Critical Methodologies*, 14(5), 471–482.

Freire, P. (2000). *Pedagogy of the Oppressed*. New York: Continuum.

Garbutt, R. and Offord, B. (2010). A Scholarly Affair. *Review of Education, Pedagogy, and Cultural Studies*, 34, 3–7.

Giroux, H. (2001a). 'Something's Missing': Cultural Studies, Neoliberalism and the Politics of Hope. *Strategies: Journal of Theory, Culture and the Politics*, 14(2), 227–252.

Giroux, H. (2001b). Cultural Studies as Performative Politics. *Cultural Studies ↔ Critical Methodologies*, 1, 5–23.

Giroux, H. (2004). War Talk, the Death of the Social, and the Disappearing Children: Remembering the Other War. *Cultural Studies ↔ Critical Methodologies*, 4(2), 206–211.

Grossberg, L. (2006). Does Cultural Studies Have Futures? Should it? (Or What's the Matter with New York? Cultural Studies, Contexts and Conjunctures. *Cultural Studies*, 20(1), 1–32.

Hall, M. A. (1996). *Feminism and Sporting Bodies: Essays on Theory and Practice*. Champaign, IL: Human Kinetics.
Harrison, J., MacGibbon, L. and Morton, M. (2001). Regimes of Trustworthiness in Qualitative Research: The Rigors of Reciprocity. *Qualitative Inquiry*, 7, 323–345.
Hargreaves, J. (1994). *Sporting Females: Critical Issues in the History and Sociology of Women's Sport*. London: Routledge.
Kemmis, S. and McTaggart, R. (2005). Participatory Action Research: Communicative Action and the Public Sphere. In N. Denzin and Y. Lincoln (eds), *The Sage Handbook of Qualitative Research*, 3rd edn (pp. 559–604). Thousand Oaks CA: Sage.
Kincheloe, J. and McLaren, P. (2005). Rethinking Critical Theory and Qualitative Research. In Denzin, N. and Lincoln, Y. (eds), *The Sage Handbook of Qualitative Research*, 3rd edn. Thousand Oaks, CA: Sage.
King, S. (2006). *Pink Ribbons, Inc. Breast Cancer Culture and the Politics of Philanthropy*. Minneapolis, MN: University of Minnesota Press.
King-White, R. (2012). Oh Henry! Physical Cultural Studies Critical Pedagogy Imperative. *Sociology of Sport Journal*, 29(3), 385–408.
Lather, P. (1986). Research as Praxis. *Harvard Educational Review*, 56(3), 257–277.
Lenskyj, H. (1986). *Out of Bounds: Women, Sport and Sexuality*. Toronto: Women's Press.
Markula, P., and Pringle. R. (2006). *Foucault, Sport and Exercise: Power, Knowledge and Transforming the Self*. Abingdon: Routledge.
Miller, T. (2001). What It Is and What It Isn't: Introducing ... Cultural Studies. In T. Miller (ed.), *A Companion to Cultural Studies* (pp. 1–20). Malden, MA: Blackwell.
Mills, C. W. (1959). *The Sociological Imagination*. London: Oxford University Press.
Olive, R. (2016). Women who Surf: Female Difference, Intersecting Subjectivities and Cultural Pedagogies. In A. Hickey (ed.) *The Pedagogies of Cultural Studies* (pp. 179–197). Abingdon: Routledge.
Olive, R. and Thorpe, H. (2011). Negotiating the 'F-Word' in the Field: Doing Feminist Ethnography in Action Sport Cultures. *Sociology of Sport Journal*, 28, 421–440.
Pavlidis, A. and Fullagar, S. (2014). *Sport, Gender and Power: The Rise of Roller Derby*. Farnham: Ashgate Publishers.
Pavlidis, A. and Olive, R. (2014). On the Track/in the Bleachers: Authenticity and Feminist Ethnographic Research in Sport and Physical Cultural Studies. *Sport in Society*, 17(2), 218–232.
Rich, E. (2011). Exploring the Relationship between Pedagogy and Physical Cultural Studies: The Case of New Health Imperatives in Schools. *Sociology of Sport Journal*, 28(1), 64–84.
Rizvi, F. and Lingard, B. (2006). Edward Said and the Cultural Politics of Education. *Discourse: Studies in the Cultural Politics of Education*, 27(3), 293–308.
Said, E. (1994). *Representations of the Intellectual*. New York: Pantheon.
Schwandt, T. (2000). Three Epistemological Stances for Qualitative Inquiry: Interpretivism, Hermeneutics, and Social Constructionism. In N. K. Denzin and Y. S. Lincoln (eds), *Handbook of Qualitative Research*, 2nd edn (pp. 189–214). Thousand Oaks, CA: Sage.
Silk, M., Francombe, J. and Andrews, D. L. (2014). Slowing the Social Sciences of Sport: On the Possibilities of Physical Culture. *Sport in Society*, 17(10), 1266–1289.
Silk, M., Francombe-Webb, J., Rich, E. and Merchant, S. (2015). On the Transgressive Possibilities of Physical Pedagogic Practices. *Qualitative Inquiry*, 21(9), 798–811.
Stanley, L. (1990). *Feminist Praxis: Research, Theory and Epistemology in Feminist Sociology*. London: Routledge.
Stanley, L. (2013). *Feminist Praxis (RLE Feminist Theory): Research, Theory and Epistemology in Feminist Sociology*. London: Routledge.
Stevenson, N. (2010). Critical Pedagogy, Democracy and Capitalism: Education Without Enemies or Borders. *Review of Education, Pedagogy and Cultural Studies*, 32(1), 66–92.
Sykes, H. (2011). *Queer Bodies: Sexualities, Genders and Fatness in Physical Education*. New York: Peter Lang.
Thorpe, H. (2009). Bourdieu, Feminism and Female Physical Culture: Gender Reflexivity and the Habitus-Field Complex. *Sociology of Sport Journal*, 26(4), 491–516.
Thorpe, H. (2011). *Snowboarding Bodies in Theory and Practice*. Basingstoke: Palgrave Macmillan.
Thorpe, H., Barbour, K. and Bruce, T. (2011). Wandering and Wondering: Theory and Representation in Feminist Physical Cultural Studies. *Sociology of Sport Journal*, 28(1), 106–134.
Vertinsky, P. and Hargreaves, J. (2006). *Physical Culture, Power and the Body*. London: Routledge.
Young, I. M. (1980). Throwing like a Girl: A Phenomenology of Feminine Body Comportment Motility and Spatiality. *Human Studies*, 3(1), 137–156.

PART II

Practices

7
THERAPEUTIC MOVEMENT/ LEISURE PRACTICES

Stephanie Merchant

Introduction

The links between physical activity and health have long been the subject of discussion within the fields of sociology of sport, health studies and the wider social and hard sciences. The effects of regular and moderate sporting/leisure-based movement on the body through associated physiological gains are well documented. Alongside this established and intricate body of literature, sits an emergent field of study that considers the affective, holistic and mental/psychological benefits of movement practices, both sport/leisure specific and more broadly related to everyday or organized social cultural activities such as dance, drama or artistic practice. As part of this emerging body of literature, which has been defined as physical cultural studies (PCS), there is a dedication to exploring the concept of 'therapeutic movement practices', in part in response to a research climate that increasingly values unearthing the impact of physicality and movement on specific wellbeing factors such as mental health, disease, cancer and ageing. Therapeutic movement practices are considered to be any embodied movement practices which either instill a sense of wellbeing in the practitioner, diminish trauma or distress, or aid a person to better understand themselves mentally and physically, whether they be organized/created specifically for the purpose of therapy or whether the therapeutic effect of movement is incidental to the activity. Broad as this notion is, it is not surprising that the number of 'practices' studied through a social and cultural lens in relation to therapeutic movement practices is prolific. From movement-centered clinical interventions, elite (cathartic) running, through recreational yoga, to community gardening, repeated studies in extremely varied contexts have documented similar personal and collective improvements in perceptions of wellbeing, mental attitude and sense of self as a consequence of engaging in activities that put the body in motion, a central concern of PCS. In this chapter I will initially highlight key themes that have evolved in academic research on therapeutic movement practices. Before concluding, I call for researchers to consider novel and holistic approaches to understanding the movement-therapy nexus, specifically by utilizing the creative and subject-centered tools for data collection and analysis open to and formed by existing PCS scholarship.

Therapeutic movement practices: an overview

As noted, the topic of therapeutic movement practices has been approached from a number of disciplines, albeit from slightly different perspectives all of which pay varying degrees of attention to a nexus of three key experiential elements:

1. bodily movement;
2. the space and context in which the bodily movement is taking place; and
3. the affective relationship between the body in motion, the space/context and any positive effects on one's sense of wellbeing.

In providing an overview of therapeutic movement practices to which PCS scholarship might be attuned, I will highlight three distinct but overlapping bodies of literature, that have emerged since the 1940s, but which have gained more concerted momentum since the cultural turn, that focus on the three key experiential elements noted above. First, I unpack the concept of dance/movement therapy (henceforth DMT), its theoretical groundings and purported benefits. Second, I consider sport/physical activity specific studies that concentrate on the less formalized yet implicit therapeutic benefits of being active for the management of mental health. Finally, I consider spatio-centric studies, in particular those that focus on the therapeutic benefits of taking part in nature-based activities.

Dance/movement therapy

Based on a combination of neuroscientific and phenomenological groundings, DMT has been developing as an organized practice since the 1940s (Koch and Fischman, 2011). Although it has its roots in the arts, DMT has evolved into its own discipline (Berrol, 1992). Berrol (ibid.: 19–20) explains that dance 'is a medium that orchestrates and fine tunes its inherent elements – time, space, weight and flow. The body, the conduit, objectifies all physical and emotional expression through structured motoric action, uniting indivisibly, process and product'. Drawing on the importance placed on dance and movement in ritual by human beings throughout the history of evolution, dance/movement therapists have argued that the intrinsic role of movement (kinesthesia) and the body (embodiment) in learning and development of the self, can be put to use to uncover and communicate, both the verbal and non-verbal traces/stores of trauma located in the body.

The healing primacy given to movement (or kinesthesia) over the other senses is elaborated by Sheets-Johnstone, who argues that, 'movement is at the core of life ... synergies of meaningful movement are part and parcel of the repertoire of all animate forms ... they evolve from human infancy onward ... they are the basis for self agency' (2010: 2–5). In her article 'Why is Movement Therapeutic?', Sheets-Johnstone (2010) argues that, the mind-body dualism is an errant concept, and as such reason and emotions needn't be thought of as solely pertaining to the mind. As Fitt (1988: 278) has argued, 'human reception, processing and response inextricably link the mind and body into a functional whole'. Thus instead of perceiving movement as located in the body and emotions as pertaining to the mind, movement is at the core of enabling human agency in the world. Sheets-Johnstone contends that it is as a result of this kinesthetic agency that we come to know the potentialities of our own bodies, or our realities. In her response, Sheets-Johnstone echoes the earlier words of Levy (1988), that movement is therapeutic as there is an 'integral relationship between our affective and tactile-kinesthetic bodies' and as a consequence our bodily movements and mobility are inherently linked to our emotions. Additionally she contends that, there is a pleasure associated with re-connecting to something we have lost – for example, the ability to communicate through multiple modalities (such as dance and movement), at a contemporary juncture that is dominated by words and vision. Therapists and researchers working in the field argue that, through a variety of approaches, DMT promotes healing, furthers wellbeing and facilitates self-discovery (Koch and Fischman, 2011).

A considerable number of studies that cite DMT as beneficial to practitioners are qualitative and even experimental in nature, enriched predominantly by phenomenological groundings (ibid.). Yet, since the discipline's early developments there has been a growing body of scientific research (Homann, 2010; Niedenthal, 2007), that employs significantly different language and terminology to similarly highlight the potential for healing and therapy offered through movement practices, particularly from a neuroscientific (Damasio, 2000; Winters, 2008) perspective. In relation to such studies it is reported that rhythm and movement indeed possess an ability to trigger neurophysiologic responses that can 'promote healing; and, alter affect … Viewing the human body as the vessel or container, and rhythmic movement as the medium, the receptor systems – kinesthetic, proprioceptive, vestibular, auditory, visual – can be systematically manipulated for therapeutic ends' (Berrol, 1992: 28). Consequently, as Koch and Fischman (2011: 61) argue, 'the embodied enactive approach becomes a unified scientific, philosophical, aesthetic, and potentially spiritual perspective with internal coherence'.

To this end, research that evaluates the merits of DMT has done so both in the context of clinical interventions and through less medically formalized settings. Thus, DMT has been employed to improve both psychological and physical issues in patients and practitioners. Examples of interventions that have targeted cancer patients are well documented (Aktas and Ogce, 2005; Bradt et al., 2011), and seek to address whether the hypothesized healing powers of movement can indeed aid recovery from the trauma faced by patients following, 'the removal of body parts, nausea, loss of hair and fatigue from radiotherapy and chemotherapy … [which] internally assault the physical body causing suffering and pain' (Ho, 2005: 337). Specific benefits witnessed in cancer patients include: improved shoulder range of movement, improved perception of body image and an enhanced sense of quality of life in women recovering from breast cancer (Dibbell-Hope, 2000; Sandel et al., 2005), and improved psychosocial coping in adolescents dealing with the emotional stress associated with cancer (Cohen and Walco, 1999). In addition to these markers of DMT success, broader attributes such as improvements to mood, reduction in distress and reduction in fatigue have also been noted as evident in relation to the interventions that focus on cancer patients (Bradt et al., 2011).

Further research on DMT initiatives targeted at young people has noted its potential to facilitate the expressive and dynamic abilities of at-risk 'African American youth in their struggle for affirmation and success' (Farr, 1997: 190), as well as enhanced sense of self and ability to build interpersonal relationships following torture (Gray, 2001; Harris, 2007). From a neuroscientific perspective there is also data to suggest that young people with mild depression who take part in DMT initiatives can experience a modulation of concentrations of serotonin and dopamine, ameliorating psychological distress (Jeong et al., 2005).

Therapeutic sporting practices

The above studies concerning dance/movement therapy, have at their core, a notion that the kinesthetic practice of dance and/or embodied movements themselves instigate some kind of problem/issue resolution or a diminishing effect on trauma. For this reason, contemporary DMT is more evident in trial- or intervention-based literature, rather than in studies that seek to uncover the incidental benefits of taking part in movement-centric activities, both for those actively seeking therapeutic effects and those who see therapeutic effects as added benefits of taking part. Indeed there have been a considerable number of studies that elaborate the inverse relationship between the occurrence of depressive symptoms and participation in physical activity (Lawlor and Hopker, 2001; Mutrie et al., 2000; O'Neal et al., 2000; Saxena et al., 2005; Strawbridge et al., 2002; Teychenne et al., 2008). Beyond the DMT discipline, there has been a concerted effort to consider the role that sport and physical activity more broadly has on people's recovery from, and management of, mental health problems (Biddle et al., 2003; Faulkner and Taylor, 2005; Leith, 2010; Morgan, 1997).

Carless and Douglas (2010) note, however, that as with the bulk of DMT literature, these studies are predicated on extolling the value that physical activity holds in *reducing* symptoms of mental disorder, with limited attention being given to developing a research agenda that seeks to better understand the additive/enriching qualities that are associated with engagement in sporting or leisure practices. Such 'qualities' include for example, 'feelings of accomplishment and wellbeing, enhanced self-esteem, a more positive mentality, greater mental alertness, increased energy and improved mood' (Carless and Douglas, 2010: 16). As Crone (2007) and Crone and Guy (2008) have noted, one of the main aspects of physical activity that is valued by people suffering from mental health issues, is not necessarily associated with symptom alleviation, but more to do with the fact that it provides a setting in which people can interact and take part as 'people-who-play-sport' as opposed to 'patients'. Further ways in which participation in sport can *add* to a sense of wellbeing rather than *diminish* mental health symptoms have been identified by Carless and Douglas (2010: 15) who, based on a review of existing literature (Davidson et al., 2005; Davidson and Strauss, 1992; Perkins, 2003), synthesize that physical activity can facilitate:

- the rebuilding of social roles and relationships;
- the development of meaning and purpose in one's life;
- the recreation of a positive sense of self and identity;
- a change in one's attitudes, values and goals;
- the enactment, acquisition and demonstration of ability;
- the pursuit of personal interests, hopes and aspirations; and
- the development and maintenance of a sense of hopefulness about one's future.

A final grouping of studies that somewhat bridge this body of work and the therapeutic landscapes literature presented below, have approached the therapeutic nature of sport participation by studying engagement with *specific* sports/leisure activities rather than physical activity generally. Such studies include for example Caddick et al.'s (2015) analysis of the effects of surfing on servicemen suffering from post-traumatic stress disorder. Among a host of studies focusing on the therapeutic nature of running (Hays, 1994; Pretty et al., 2005) sits Hockey and Allen-Collinson's phenomenographic elucidations of the road to recovery following injury, through road running (2007). The effect of yoga on spiritual development/mindfulness and as a complementary therapy in psychiatric disorders has also been given significant attention by researchers (Behere et al., 2011; Cabral et al., 2011; Duraiswamy et al., 2007; Khalsa, 2007). By focusing on a specific activity, as these studies do, there arises an opportunity to better understand the contextual elements of experience that enhance or give meaning to the activity, opening up for discussion the therapeutic nature of land/seascapes/spaces of sport and leisure, a topic elaborated further in the next section.

Therapeutic landscapes

The topics of human health, physical activity and wellbeing (in its widest guise) are beginning to form a significant body of literature when considered alongside the presence, use and construction of urban/rural green spaces. Academic work within human geography over the last 10 years has begun to argue that different landscapes have the power to affect those moving through and interacting with them in powerful and subjectively interesting ways (Conradson, 2005; Gesler, 1996, 1992; Kearns and Gesler, 1998; Merchant, 2011; Williams, 2007). Contemporary interest in 'nature' has stemmed from wider debates concerning political theory (Bennet, 2002; Haraway, 2004; Latour, 1993; Lingis, 2000, 2003), anthropology of perception (Gibson, 1986; Heidegger, 1962; Ingold, 2000; Merleau-Ponty, 1962, 1969) and theories of 'affect' (B. Anderson, 2009; J. Anderson, 2009; Deleuze et al., 2004; Dewsbury et al., 2002; Harrison et al., 2004; Thrift, 1996). Growing evidence supports the notion that exercising in and working on 'natural' landscapes can positively affect human wellbeing (Burns, 1998; Townsend, 2006). Links have been made between longevity and access to green space (Takano et al., 2002; Tanaka et al., 1996) and research participants who were asked to rank their own perceived levels of health, considered themselves healthier when they had access to green space (De Vries et al., 2003). Hartig et al. (2003) have considered more specific health measures in relation to participants exercising in natural areas and have found that being in natural environments can lower blood pressure, increase attention functioning and contribute to a sense of positive emotional wellbeing (Hartig, 2008; Hartig et al., 1991).

The cathartic nature of gardening and caring for plants and trees has also been shown to provide a form of therapy for those living in difficult circumstances. By engaging directly in tree planting activities it has been argued that volunteers both young and old can gain a sense of achievement or accomplishment 'that may be lacking [in their] day-to-day life' (Westphal, 2003: 139). This can translate to those whose lifestyles have suddenly significantly changed (for example military personnel who retire). In such cases, being active in and/or creating green spaces can aid recovery and ease trauma for those affected by crisis (Hewson, 2001; Miavitz, 1998).

A burgeoning new body of literature has begun to look at the potential for community gardening projects to act as expressions of community resilience in the wake of environmental, social or personal loss (Anderson, 2004; Miller and Rivera, 2007). Tidball et al. (2010: 592), drawing on Nucifora et al. (2007), define resistance as 'the ability of an individual, group, organization, or entire population to withstand manifestations of clinical distress, impairment, or dysfunction', and resilience as 'the ability of an individual, group, organization, or entire population to rebound from psychological perturbations, both in the context of critical incidents, terrorism, and mass disasters'. In New Orleans, for example, after the widespread devastation left by Hurricane Katrina in 2005, volunteers and local agencies set about planting over 6000 trees. Three local NGOs were developed specifically with this aim in mind, including Hike for KaTREEna, Replant New Orleans and Parkway Partners. This act was said to have boosted citizen morale by mobilizing a physical activity initiative and bringing the community together in a time of mourning (Tidball and Krasny, 2007; Tidball et al., 2010).

Similarly, after the 9/11 terrorist attacks on the United States of America, the U.S. Forestry Service sought to research the ensuing changes to the use and stewardship of trees (Tidball et al., 2010). The Living Memorials Project (set up by the USFS) involved the creation of 687 landscape memorials across the USA between 2001 and 2006. These landscapes were created through community planting of individual trees, small forests or bonsai gardens. While they were not promoted as initiatives aiming to target physical wellbeing, they inherently involved putting the body to work in a physically active manner, while fostering the development of community interaction and socialization. Indeed Tibdall et al. (2010: 592) have argued that, 'perhaps it is not surprising that interacting with nature through gardening offers a means of resistance and resilience for individual soldiers and civilians during war, given the large literature on the therapeutic benefits of plant–people interactions'.

This body of work evidently overlaps somewhat with the topic of therapeutic movement practices although it highlights the role of spatial characteristics as key to instilling a form of wellbeing in participants rather than explicitly focusing on the benefits of *movement* in itself. As such, these studies might be located more readily under the geocentric banner 'therapeutic landscapes' (Bodin and Hartig, 2003; Hansmann et al., 2007; Ingen, 2004; Pretty et al., 2005; Williams, 2007). As the majority of such studies do indeed focus on active movement and engagement with urban, rural and wild landscapes, I argue that the two fields of research should be considered in tandem when studying the therapeutic effects of movement in distinct spaces. Considering both the spaces of movement and movement itself as therapeutic further enriches the phenomenological groundings that have supported the theorization of both subgenres, notably the dissolution of both the mind-body distinction and the human-world distinction.

Researching therapeutic movement practices: a PCS perspective

The discussion presented above has at its core a human subject or multiple human subjects, moving bodies in context-specific ways (e.g. displaying sporting skill, artistic skill, practical skill, ritualistic co-ordination/balance, manipulations to and/or the traversal of land/seascapes). Either consciously or unconsciously the activities engaged in are dependent on mobility. More specifically, the above studies argue in each case that the body, in its act of movement, for whatever reason is instilling some kind of positive sense of wellbeing (in a variety of 'wellbeing's' guises). But being mobile is complex, it relies on the body's ability to perceive through the senses – to perceive where each body part is positioned in relation to the other and the environment (proprioception), and to perceive one's body moving in relation to that environment – including the beings and things which furnish that environment – (kinesthesia). For the most part, aside from a few conceptual (phenomenological) pieces of writing related to DMT (e.g. Sheets-Johnstone, 2010), the balance of scholarship does not actually seek to uncover or exemplify what it is about movement that is therapeutic, simply claiming admirably, yet limitedly, that engagement in movement practices *are* therapeutic:

> What is needed, therefore, in order to complement existing knowledge in this area is an alternative tack that can combine social, cultural and psychological approaches in order to provide insights into processes which, while perhaps involving biomedical change, cannot be reduced to biology or chemistry.
>
> *(Carless and Douglas, 2010: 17)*

If we are to research the therapeutic nature of movement practices qualitatively, then we need to think carefully about how we can capture the affective potentialities of proprioception and kinesthetic movement, in addition to wider environmental cues. As Carless and Douglas (2010: 17) note, to date there is 'little theoretical insight into *how* mental health changes come about through involvement in physical activity'. Building on the history and understanding illustrated within the studies examined above, PCS then is uniquely situated to innovate the field further by drawing on its traditional and experimental qualitative methodological approaches and focusing on the intricacies of context specific understanding of the body in motion.

What is it about the monotonous and repetitive plod of walking that puts the mind at ease? What does it feel like to be 'in the zone' or in a state of embodied 'flow'? How does chipping nails, heaving soil and watering seedlings bring solace to the grieving? Understanding the affective excess of human sensory perception in motion implicitly calls for researchers working under the umbrella of 'Therapeutic Movement Practices' to consider at once the body *and* the environment in which the physical activity is taking place. This provides an opportunity for PCS scholars concerned with the therapeutic nature of physical activity to bridge the theoretical divide between the sub-disciplines of DMT, therapeutic landscapes and medical sociology.

Getting at this kind of affective, sensuous, sometimes 'pre-reflective' and 'pre-objective' detail (Csordas, 1990: 6), studying aspects of life that seem almost insignificant; the fleeting encounters, immanent sensations, practical skills and sensuous dispositions (Lorimer, 2005), is a task that non- (or what Lorimer prefers to call 'more-than') representational theorists and phenomenologists have been grappling with particularly since the early 2000s (Dewsbury et al., 2002), following Nigel Thrift's influential book, *Spatial Formations* (1996). By stepping beyond the 'established academic habit of striving to uncover meanings and values that apparently await our discovery' (Lorimer, 2005: 84), and instead being open to what will become, or witnessing the unforeseen, it is possible to render visible many of the invisible aspects of embodied encounters with space that are often left outside the remit of traditional academic interest. After all, these aspects of experience deserve attention (especially as PCS scholars seek to enhance their commitment to social change/societal impact), since they contribute to the shaping of lives and worlds, whether routine or 'other', therapeutic or healing.

Despite the proliferation of work that takes seriously such elements of place, practice and performance, within the broader social sciences, Lorimer (2005) highlights the lack of methodological experimentalism accompanying this turn towards studying doings and becomings, and Latham (2003) similarly calls for more ingenuity in the research process. Indeed, Gordon (2008: 21) states that, 'our methods have thus far been less than satisfactory for addressing the very nature of the things and problems it is our responsibility to address'. This, seems particularly true yet surprising within the Therapeutic Movement Practices literature, with work such as Blackman and Venn's (2010: 7) special issue on 'affect' in *Body and Society* which explicitly aims to 'spark interest and ongoing engagements in questions of method and experimentation in light of the common ontologies emerging across the humanities and the natural, social and human sciences', to an extent failing to impact upon the field. With a broad acceptance, indeed celebration, of novel and experimental approaches to data collection, those working from a PCS perspective are ideally situated in this regard, to provide more holistic understandings of the precise ways in which movement and the environmental settings of movement are enriching for practitioners. As such, the arsenal of PCS-tested tools based on visual (Merchant, 2011), creative, participatory (Francombe-Webb et al., 2014), cartographic (Merchant, forthcoming), mobile (Allen-Collinson and Hockey, 2011; Francombe, 2013), narrative (Caddick et al., 2015; Sparkes, 2015), performative etc. methods offer a pathway from which to further innovate approaches to, and enrich knowledge of, the therapeutic characteristics of sport/leisure practices and the environments in which they take place.

Conclusion

In this chapter I have argued that therapeutic movement practices are being approached from a variety of different perspectives, but it is three subdisciplines in particular that have dedicated themselves specifically to exploring the intricacies of the concept. DMT, 'sport as therapy' and therapeutic landscapes studies, all have at their core an overlapping interest in understanding the affective, sensory and psychological impact that movement practices can yield. Studies in these domains do well to outline the breadth of applicability of therapeutic movement practices to different user groups, and the array of effects on symptom alleviation and emotional enrichment. The challenge for future work (from a PCS perspective) will be to overcome the isolated treatment of people (research participants) from the spatial contexts in which they find themselves. In this regard, potentially drawing on co-constructive and interrelational philosophies, and also mobilizing creative/innovative methodologies and ontologies, will aid in the development of understanding relating to the qualitative and subjective questions of *what* therapy is and means to an individual and *how* it occurs, feels and is manifest in everyday life.

References

Aktas, G. and Ogce, F. 2005. Dance as a therapy for cancer prevention. *Asian Pacific Journal of Cancer Prevention*, 6(3), 408.

Allen-Collinson, J. and Hockey, J. 2011. Feeling the way: notes toward a haptic phenomenology of distance running and scuba diving. *International Review for the Sociology of Sport*, 46(3), 330–345.

Anderson, B. 2009. Affective atmospheres. *Emotion, Space and Society*, 2(2), 77–81.

Anderson, J. 2009. Transient convergence and relational sensibility: beyond the modern constitution of nature. *Emotion, Space and Society*, 2(2), 120–127.

Anderson, K. 2004. *Nature, culture, and big old trees: live oaks and ceibas in the landscapes of Louisiana and Guatemala*. Austin, TX: University of Texas Press.

Behere, R. V. et al. 2011. Effect of yoga therapy on facial emotion recognition deficits, symptoms and functioning in patients with schizophrenia. *Acta Psychiatrica Scandinavica*, 123(2), 147–153.

Bennet, J. 2002. *The enchantment of modern life*. Princeton, NJ: Princeton University Press.

Berrol, C. F. 1992. The neurophysiologic basis of the mind–body connection in dance/movement therapy. *American Journal of Dance Therapy*, 14(1), 19–29.

Biddle, S. J. H., Fox, K. and Boutcher, S. 2003. *Physical activity and psychological well-being*. New York: Routledge.

Blackman, L. and Venn, C. 2010. Affect. *Body & Society*, 16(1), 7–28.

Bodin, M. and Hartig, T. 2003. Does the outdoor environment matter for psychological restoration gained through running? *Psychology of Sport and Exercise*, 4(2), 141–153.

Bradt, J., Goodill, S. W. and Dileo, C. 2011. Dance/movement therapy for improving psychological and physical outcomes in cancer patients. *Cochrane Database of Systematic Reviews*, 10, article CD007103.

Burns, G. W. 1998. *Nature-guided therapy: brief integrative strategies for health and well-being*. New York: Brunner/Mazel.

Cabral, P., Meyer, H. B. and Ames, D. 2011. Effectiveness of yoga therapy as a complementary treatment for major psychiatric disorders: a meta-analysis. *The Primary Care Companion to CNS Disorders*, 13(4), article 10r01068.

Caddick, N., Smith, B. and Phoenix, C. 2015. The effects of surfing and the natural environment on the well-being of combat veterans. *Qualitative Health Research*, 25(1), 76–86.

Carless, D. and Douglas, K. 2010. *Sport and physical activity for mental health*. Oxford: Wiley-Blackwell.

Cohen, S. O. and Walco, G. A. 1999. Dance/movement therapy for children and adolescents with cancer. *Cancer Practice*, 7(1), 34–42.

Conradson, D. 2005. Landscape, care and the relational self: therapeutic encounters in rural England. *Health and Place*, 11(4), 337–348.

Crone, D. 2007. Walking back to health: a qualitative investigation into service users' experiences of a walking project. *Issues in Mental Health Nursing*, 28(2), 167–183.

Crone, D. and Guy, H. 2008. 'I know it is only exercise, but to me it is something that keeps me going': a qualitative approach to understanding mental health service users' experiences of sports therapy. *International Journal of Mental Health Nursing*, 17(3), 197–207.

Csordas, T. 1990. Embodiment as a paradigm for anthropology. *Ethos: Journal of the Society for Psychological Anthropology*, 18, 5–47.

Damasio, A. R. 2000. *The feeling of what happens: body, emotion and the making of consciousness*. New York: Vintage.

Davidson, L. et al. 2005. Recovery in serious mental illness: a new wine or just a new bottle? *Professional Psychology: Research and Practice*, 36(5), 480.

Davidson, L. and Strauss, J. S. 1992. Sense of self in recovery from severe mental illness. *British Journal of Medical Psychology*, 65(2), 131–145.

De Vries, S. et al. 2003. Natural environments – healthy environments? An exploratory analysis of the relationship between greenspace and health. *Environment and Planning A*, 35(10), 1717–1732.

Deleuze, G., Guattari, F. and Massumi, B. 2004. *A thousand plateaus: capitalism and schizophrenia*. London: Continuum.

Dewsbury, J. D. et al. 2002. Enacting geographies. *Geoforum*, 33(4), 437–440.

Dibbell-Hope, S. 2000. The use of dance/movement therapy in psychological adaptation to breast cancer. *The Arts in Psychotherapy*, 27(1), 51–68.

Duraiswamy, G. et al. 2007. Yoga therapy as an add on treatment in the management of patients with schizophrenia: a randomized controlled trial. *Acta Psychiatrica Scandinavica*, 116(3), 226–232.

Farr, M. 1997. The role of dance/movement therapy in treating at-risk African American adolescents. *The Arts in Psychotherapy*, 24(2), 183–191.

Faulkner, G. E. J. and Taylor, A. H. 2005. *Exercise, health and mental health: Emerging relationships*. London: Taylor & Francis.

Fitt, S. 1988. *Dance kinesiology*. New York: Schirmer Books.

Francombe, J. 2013. Methods that move: a physical performative pedagogy of subjectivity. *Sociology of Sport Journal*, 30(3), 256–273.

Francombe-Webb, J., Rich, E. and De Pian, L. 2014. I move like you … but different biopolitics and embodied methodologies. *Cultural Studies ↔ Critical Methodologies*, 14(5), 471–482.

Gesler, W. 1996. Lourdes: healing in a place of pilgrimage. *Health and Place*, 2(2), 95–105.

Gesler, W. M. 1992. Therapeutic landscapes: medical issues in light of the new cultural geography. *Social Science and Medicine*, 34(7), 735–746.

Gibson, J. J. 1986. *The ecological approach to visual perception*. Hillsdale, NJ: Lawrence Erlbaum Associates.

Gordon, A. 2008. *An atlas of radical cartography*. New York: Journal of Aesthetics and Protest Press.

Gray, A. E. L. 2001. The body remembers: dance/movement therapy with an adult survivor of torture. *American Journal of Dance Therapy*, 23(1), 29–43.

Hansmann, R., Hug, S. M. and Seeland, K. 2007. Restoration and stress relief through physical activities in forests and parks. *Urban Forestry and Urban Greening*, 6(4), 213–225.

Haraway, D. 2004. *The Haraway reader*. London: Routledge.

Harris, D. A. 2007. Dance/movement therapy approaches to fostering resilience and recovery among African adolescent torture survivors. *Torture*, 17(2), 134–155.

Harrison, S., Pile, S. and Thrift, N. 2004. *Patterned ground: entanglements of nature and culture*. London: Reaktion.

Hartig, T. 2008. Green space, psychological restoration, and health inequality. *The Lancet*, 372 (9650), 1614–1615.

Hartig, T. et al. 2003. Tracking restoration in natural and urban field settings. *Journal of Environmental Psychology*, 23(2), 109–123.

Hartig, T., Mang, M. and Evans, G. W. 1991. Restorative effects of natural environment experiences. *Environment and Behavior*, 23(1), 3–26.

Hays, K. F. 1994. Running therapy: special characteristics and therapeutic issues of concern. *Psychotherapy: Theory, Research, Practice, Training*, 31(4), 725.

Heidegger, M. 1962. *Being and time*. Oxford: Blackwell.

Hewson, M. 2001. Horticultural therapy and post traumatic stress recovery. *Journal of Therapeutic Horticulture*, 12, 44–47.

Ho, R. T. H. 2005. Effects of dance movement therapy on Chinese cancer patients: a pilot study in Hong Kong. *The Arts in Psychotherapy*, 32(5), 337–345.

Hockey, J. and Allen-Collinson, J. 2007. Grasping the phenomenology of sporting bodies. *International Review for the Sociology of Sport*, 42(2), 115–131.

Homann, K. B. 2010. Embodied concepts of neurobiology in dance/movement therapy practice. *American Journal of Dance Therapy*, 32(2), 80–99.

Ingen, C. 2004. Therapeutic landscapes and the regulated body in the Toronto Front Runners. *Sociology of Sport Journal*, 21(3), 253–269.

Ingold, T. 2000. *The perception of the environment: essays on livelihood, dwelling and skill*. London: Routledge.

Jeong, Y.-J. et al. 2005. Dance movement therapy improves emotional responses and modulates neurohormones in adolescents with mild depression. *International Journal of Neuroscience*, 115(12), 1711–1720.

Kearns, R. A. and Gesler, W. M. 1998. *Putting health into place: landscape, identity, and well-being.* Syracuse, NY: Syracuse University Press.
Khalsa, S. B. 2007. Yoga as a therapeutic intervention. *Principles and Practice of Stress Management*, 3, 449–462.
Koch, S. C. and Fischman, D. 2011. Embodied enactive dance/movement therapy. *American Journal of Dance Therapy*, 33(1), 57–72.
Latham, A. 2003. Research, performance and doing human geography: some reflections of the diary–photograph, diary–interview method. *Environment and Planning A*, 35, 1993–2017.
Latour, B. 1993. *We have never been modern.* Cambridge, MA: Harvard University Press.
Lawlor, D. A. and Hopker, S. W. 2001. The effectiveness of exercise as an intervention in the management of depression: systematic review and meta-regression analysis of randomised controlled trials. *BMJ*, 322(7289), 763.
Leith, L. M. 2010. *Foundations of exercise and mental health.* Fitness Information Technology.
Levy, F. J. 1988. *Dance/movement therapy: a healing art.* ERIC.
Lingis, A. 2000. *Dangerous emotions.* Berkeley, CA: University of California Press.
Lingis, A. 2003. Animal body, inhuman face. In C. Wolfe (ed.), *Zoontologies: the question of the animal.* Minneapolis, MN: University of Minnesota Press, 165–182.
Lorimer, H. 2005. Cultural geography: the business of being more-that-representational. *Progress in Human Geography*, 29, 89–94.
Merchant, S. 2011. The body and the senses: visual methods, videography and the submarine sensorium. *Body and Society*, 17(1), 53–72.
Merchant, S. Forthcoming. The promise of biomapping for sport and leisure research. *Journal of Leisure Studies.*
Merleau-Ponty, M. 1962. *Phenomenology of perception.* Oxford: Routledge.
Merleau-Ponty, M. 1969. *The visible and the invisible.* Evanston, IL: Northwestern University Press.
Miavitz, E. 1998. Grief gardening. *Journal of Therapeutic Horticulture*, 9, 17–21.
Miller, D. and Rivera, J. D. 2007. Landscapes of disaster and place orientation in the aftermath of Hurricane Katrina. In D. Brunsma et al., *The sociology of Katrina: perspectives on a modern catastrophe.* Lanham, MD: Rowman & Littlefield, 141–154.
Morgan, W. P. 1997. *Physical activity and mental health.* London: Taylor & Francis.
Mutrie, N., Biddle, S. J. H. and Fox, K. R. 2000. The relationship between physical activity and clinically defined depression. *Physical activity and psychological well-being*, 46–62.
Niedenthal, P. M. 2007. Embodying emotion. *Science*, 316(5827), 1002–1005.
Nucifora Jr, F. et al. 2007. Building resistance, resilience, and recovery in the wake of school and workplace violence. *Disaster Medicine and Public Health Preparedness*, 1(Supplement 1), S33.
O'Neal, H. A., Dunn, A. L. and Martinsen, E. W. 2000. Depression and exercise. *International Journal of Sport Psychology*, 31(2), 110–135.
Perkins, R. 2003. *Social inclusion and recovery: a model for mental health practice.* Oxford: Elsevier Health Sciences.
Pretty, J. et al. 2005. The mental and physical health outcomes of green exercise. *International Journal of Environmental Health Research*, 15(5), 319–337.
Sandel, S. L. et al. 2005. Dance and movement program improves quality of life measures in breast cancer survivors. *Cancer Nursing*, 28(4), 301–309.
Saxena, S. et al. 2005. Mental health benefits of physical activity. *Journal of Mental Health*, 14(5), 445–451.
Sheets-Johnstone, M. 2010. Why is movement therapeutic? *American Journal of Dance Therapy*, 32(1), 2–15.
Sparkes, A. C. 2015. Ethnography as a sensual way of being. *Ethnographies in Sport and Exercise Research*, 45.
Strawbridge, W. J. et al. 2002. Physical activity reduces the risk of subsequent depression for older adults. *American Journal of Epidemiology*, 156(4), 328–334.
Takano, T., Nakamura, K. and Watanabe, M. 2002. Urban residential environments and senior citizens' longevity in megacity areas: the importance of walkable green spaces. *Journal of Epidemiology and Community Health*, 56(12), 913–918.
Tanaka, A. et al. 1996. Health levels influenced by urban residential conditions in a megacity – Tokyo. *Urban Studies*, 33(6), 879–894.
Teychenne, M., Ball, K. and Salmon, J. 2008. Physical activity and likelihood of depression in adults: a review. *Preventive Medicine*, 46(5), 397–411.
Thrift, N. J. 1996. *Spatial formations.* London: Sage.
Tidball, K. G. and Krasny, M. E. 2007. From risk to resilience: what role for community greening and civic

ecology in cities. In A. E. J. Wals (ed.), *Social learning towards a more sustainable world*. Wageningen: Wageningen Academic Publishers Books, 149–164.
Tidball, K. G. et al. 2010. Stewardship, learning, and memory in disaster resilience. *Environmental Education Research*, 16(5–6), 591–609.
Townsend, M. 2006. Feel blue? Touch green! Participation in forest/woodland management as a treatment for depression. *Urban Forestry and Urban Greening*, 5(3), 111–120.
Westphal, L. M. 2003. Urban greening and social benefits: a study of empowerment outcomes. *Journal of Arboriculture*, 29(3), 137–147.
Williams, A. 2007. *Therapeutic landscapes*. Farnham: Ashgate.
Winters, A. F. 2008. Emotion, embodiment, and mirror neurons in dance/movement therapy: a connection across disciplines. *American Journal of Dance Therapy*, 30(2), 84–105.

8
EXERCISE AND FITNESS PRACTICES

Nick Crossley

'Physical culture' embraces a range of different domains of activity. Indeed, all culture is embodied, engaged with by embodied beings in embodied ways and thus 'physical' in certain respects. 'Physical' often refers more narrowly to the human body, however, lending 'physical culture' an association with cultivation of the body – and this has certainly been a preoccupation within physical cultural studies. Bodies are cultivated in many ways and for many purposes. They are adorned with clothing and cosmetics; tanned or perhaps kept out of the sun so as to remain pale; disciplined, so as to move and communicate in particular ways; and they are subject to exercise regimes which work upon both their external appearance and such less visible properties as health and fitness. In this chapter I focus upon these exercise and fitness practices. My perspective on exercise and fitness is that of relational sociology, a perspective that encourages us to look beyond the individual and her experience to the social context in which physical culture is practised and, more especially, the connection of the individual and her practices to other individuals and their practices. As 'relational sociology' may be unfamiliar to some I begin with a brief introduction.

Relational sociology

There are different 'versions' of relational sociology (Powell and Dépelteau, 2013). In my version it is an approach in which social interaction, the more enduring relations or ties which interaction gives rise to and the networks formed by combinations of such ties are the primary focus and enjoy both an ontological and methodological privilege (Crossley, 2011, 2013, 2015). Interactions give rise to ties, which give rise to networks in this conception but the chain of causation moves equally in the other direction. Interaction is affected by the history and definition of the relation between parties to it and both relations and interactions are affected by their location within a wider network.

This approach is posited in opposition to individualism, both ontological and methodological, within social science and philosophy. Individual social actors, who may be either human beings or corporate entities, such as firms, trade unions or governments, are important but do not exist or act in isolation and are deemed emergent properties of social interaction. The newly born infant is a far cry from the social actor generally assumed in social scientific work and philosophy, for example, and only becomes a social actor, in the full sense, as an effect of interactions which transform her. All of the defining features of (human) social agency, from language use, through moral sensibilities and self-control to the various embodied forms of competence necessary to get by on a daily basis are formed in interaction with others.

While it opposes individualism-atomism, this approach equally opposes those forms of holism in which individual (human or corporate) actors disappear or are reduced to the status of mere bearers of structures/processes deemed to obey a 'higher logic'. The networked character of social life, and the fact that we are born into pre-existing networks, means that we never 'make history in circumstances of our own choosing', nor indeed in ways that we can foresee or intend. Our position in multiplex webs of social relations imposes situations upon us, generating constraints, opportunities and incitements; and the activities of others mediate the effects of our own, rendering outcomes unpredictable. In these ways social life has dynamics and mechanisms of its own, irreducible to individual participants. However, actors, human and corporate, collectively drive the interactions which, in turn, drive history. Furthermore, the networks in which we are enmeshed are always in-process and subject to change, and we exercise agency in relation to those changes and in relation to our position in the network. There are constraints, many of them, but we exercise inter-agency within them.

Reflexive embodiment and body techniques

This relational framework bears upon all that follows in this chapter. As a first step to linking it to the topics of exercise and fitness I will briefly introduce two concepts which are essential to a proper understanding of the latter: *reflexive embodiment* and *reflexive body techniques*.

Reflexive embodiment

In his celebrated phenomenology of lived embodiment, Merleau-Ponty (1962) argues, against Descartes' mind/body dualism, that we are our bodies and that our bodies connect us to the world through the sensuous (perceptual) apprehension of and mastery over it which they afford. However, he observes that, in the first instance, we are not reflectively aware of our bodies, as such. Our embodiment is our point of view on the world but not something that we have a point of view on, not something which we perceive as such (see also Crossley, 2001, 2006a; Leder, 1990). We are not, in the first instance, objects of our own experience. We are not self-conscious. We do become self-conscious, however, and in Merleau-Ponty's view this is an effect of our interactions and relations with others. We first become aware of ourselves, he argues, by becoming aware of the consciousness of others and specifically of their consciousness of us. On this basis we learn to project ourselves, imaginatively, into their shoes and from there to perceive ourselves as they might perceive us. Finally, in this process we acquire the habit of comparing ourselves to others.

Nobody experiences themselves, from within, as fat, tall or disabled, for example. There is no internal feeling corresponding to such states, no internal perception which might bring them to light. To view a body in this way is to view it from the outside, as an object, and indeed to compare it with other bodies which are thinner, shorter etc. The individual can only think of themselves in these ways, therefore, or indeed question whether they are fat, thin, short, tall, etc., by both adopting an external viewpoint upon themselves (seeing themselves as others see them) and comparing their self with others.

This same idea is explored by George Herbert Mead (1967), who labels the sense of self that we achieve by adopting the perspective of the other 'me' and who explores the role of play and games in this process. Through play, particularly role play, he observes, infants experiment with, try out and internalize the perspectives of specific others, particularly those who exert some form of authority over them (e.g. parents and teachers). This continues in the context of games but in the latter they also learn to perceive and conceive of themselves from the point of view of what he calls 'the generalised other'; that is, the view of a community taken as a whole, as captured in rules and norms. The infant becomes a reflexive actor by internalizing the perspectives of others.

This does not subordinate self to other. Turning back upon herself is only a first step for the actor in a dialogical process whereby she debates with herself about her life and potential courses of action. Through internalizing the role of the other she becomes an interlocutor with herself, conversing with herself as she might with others, and the outcome of that process is no less open or unpredictable that any other dialogue.

However, 'internal conversations' are embedded within wider conversational networks, connecting individual actors to one another, and these wider conversations and interactions feed into the actor's internal conversations, further shaping each actor's 'me'. C. H. Cooley's (1902) concept of the 'looking glass self' is a useful point of reference here. Like Mead and Merleau-Ponty, Cooley believes that human self-consciousness is an effect of our becoming conscious of the consciousness which others have of us. Furthermore, he suggests that others act like mirrors, reflecting back images of ourselves to us which, in many cases, shape our sense of ourselves. There is no determinism here. We are not forced to accept the views of others and, of course, their views may conflict. This is a complex process. However, as Cooley notes, the mirroring process is important to the formation of our sense of self. We rely upon others for feedback, both affective and informational, regarding our various qualities and states.

Such claims suggest one central way in which human agency, in its mature form, is an emergent property of social relations and they have many applications. Here we are interested in their relevance to embodiment. Although Mead's 'me' encompasses more than the purely physical properties of the actor, those properties are important to an actor's sense of self and the actor's perception of them often informs a decision to, for example, take up exercise. What we look like, our fitness, physical abilities and health are all important aspects of our sense of self, and these concerns are among the factors which inform the practice of exercise. What Mead, Merleau-Ponty and Cooley allow us to appreciate is that, however individual they may feel, these concerns and the embodied sense of self which underlies them take shape within the networks in which we live our lives.

I have developed these ideas elsewhere by reference to bodily blind spots, evidenced in the way that people put on weight, lose fitness, or age without noticing it (Crossley, 2004b, 2006a). They do not notice these bodily changes because they do not feel any different and because their perception of themselves in the mirror is conditioned by expectations which tend to evolve in tandem with the gradual process of bodily change itself (ibid.). It is the shock experienced when such bubbles are burst, I have suggested, that often precipitates a decision to take up (or restart) exercise (Crossley, 2006b). These shocks reveal the basic lack of embodied self-consciousness that we enjoy much of the time and also the importance of external reference points for increasing bodily awareness. They do not always involve others: we may learn that we have put on weight when we try on old clothes and may learn of loss of fitness when we struggle to perform an activity that we once performed well and with ease. Others often are the mirror which informs us of bodily change, however, and any worries, diagnoses and resolutions stemming from such shocks will always by mediated through the generalized other. We step out of our immediate lived embodiment and view our body as an object of concern; applying medical and/or aesthetic perspectives to our bodies which we have borrowed, qua perspective of the generalized other, from our wider networks.

Bodily shocks are a frequent cause of actors (re)turning to exercise. They are far from the full story, however. Motives for exercise are numerous (Crossley, 2006b). More importantly, however, they tend to change across the 'moral career' (Becker, 1961) of the exercising actor (Crossley, 2006b). The impetus derived from a body shock quickly wanes and, as innumerable gym attrition anecdotes testify, new recruits very quickly give up unless other incentives and 'lock-in' mechanisms come into play. Habit and routine may be a factor here, and these concepts play an important role in theories of practice (Shove et al., 2012). Habit is often insufficient, however, because for many people the chunk of time demanded for exercise is constantly under threat from competing demands, opportunities and unforeseen impositions such that priorities are always in question, routines are constantly being juggled and plans re-arranged. Regular exercise requires reflective thought and commitment. In what follows I will suggest that relational dynamics in the gym generate mechanisms which incentivize some actors to stick with it in spite of such obstacles. Before I do, however, we must introduce a further concept.

Reflexive body techniques

The relational embedding of our bodily life does not stop at our internalization of the roles of others. Its influence is also found in the ways in which we exercise and pursue fitness. Marcel Mauss's (1979) concept of body techniques provides a useful way in here. Mauss observes how 'uses of the body' vary across societies, historical periods and groups within society. In some cases this is a matter of the way in which something is done. He identifies differences in ways of walking between the French and Americans, for example, and differences between the ways in which he was taught to swim and the younger generation are taught. Similarly, we might point to differences in linguistic accents, which hinge upon different uses of the mouth, tongue etc. In other cases it is a matter of techniques in one society which have no equivalent in another. Most Westerners, if dropped into the Amazon rainforest, wouldn't last more than a few days, for example, because we lack the body techniques necessary to survival and flourishing in that environment, techniques which are taken for granted by human groups who live in the rainforest.

Body techniques, Mauss continues, are collective inventions which embody the practical reason of the network in which the actor is embedded. Differences of accent may be 'accidents' caused by gaps and concentrations within social-linguistic networks (Milroy, 1987), for example, but the basic technique of speaking to which they belong is a means that human beings have invented, collectively, for communicating. Speaking enhances an actor's capacity to engage with a particular type of environment (namely one involving other people) and to achieve whatever goals they may have within that environment. Likewise swimming: the techniques learned afford the actor an understanding of and mastery over a particular environment (deep water) which they can deploy flexibly in pursuit of their own goals.

Body techniques diffuse through social networks. This is why they manifest the uneven social distribution that Mauss observes, or rather it is because contact in social networks is unevenly distributed that body techniques are. It is no accident that most people in Liverpool speak with a Liverpool accent while most people in Manchester do not. We speak as we do as a consequence of contact with others and, where contact clusters geographically, so too do ways of speaking. Likewise with other body techniques. How we use our bodies is often habitual and, insofar as we are aware of it at all, feels natural, but both the struggles of neophytes to acquire these techniques and systematic comparison of their variation across space and time suggests that it is not. Again then, fundamental aspects of our (embodied) agency are found to be emergent properties of interaction within social networks.

This is relevant here because much of what we do when we exercise involves body techniques. Indeed, it involves what I have referred to elsewhere as 'reflexive body techniques' (Crossley, 2005, 2006a); that is, body techniques through which the embodied actor maintains and transforms herself qua body. Reflexive body techniques are uses of the body (and the resistance it meets in its environment) whose object is that self-same body. Though swimming can have various purposes, for example, including both sport and transport, it is frequently used as a means of increasing fitness and burning calories, and this goal affects the way in which the swimmer swims. They aim for an elevated heart rate, muscular burn and tiredness, reading these feelings, which they have often learned (against the grain) to enjoy, as signs that they are succeeding.

The same could be said for jogging, weight training, aerobics and, to use an example I return to, circuit training. This is one very clear way in which it makes sense to speak of fitness and exercise *practices*. When we exercise we take up one or more techniques that we have acquired from a collective stock which is stored and maintained within social networks to which we belong. Note also that many forms of exercise require resources (e.g. a pool for swimming) and the collective action of a network of others (pool attendants, managers, receptionists, coaches etc.) who maintain the environment which facilitates that exercise.

In the gym

Many forms of exercise are more social still. In what follows I elaborate upon this by reference to an ethnographic study that I conducted in a private health club during the late 1990s and early 2000s (Crossley, 2004a, 2006b, 2008). I will generalize my observations here, for purposes of widening the relevance of what I have to say. The evidential base for my claims is this ethnography, however.

In many cases exercise brings participants into contact. Joggers generally jog in public places, where they come into contact with other people, including but not exclusively other joggers (who often jog in the same places, such as parks, because they are the best places in the wider area to jog). Swimmers visit swimming pools, where they swim alongside others, and much weight training is conducted alongside others, in gyms. At a more collective level still, many people take exercise classes of some sort (e.g. aerobics, circuit training, yoga, Pilates). And many actors join health clubs or gyms (private or connected to public facilities) in order to achieve these ends. During the final decade of the twentieth century and first decade of the twenty-first the number of such clubs in many Western societies increased hugely (Sassatelli, 2010).

In these contexts exercise merges with social interaction and must accommodate its demands. Exercise in a public place impinges upon what Goffman (1983) calls the 'interaction order' and this places demands upon those involved. They must coordinate their activities with those of others, manage the impressions of self that they give off, fulfil any relationship obligations, show respect to others and help those others to maintain a positive impression of self ('face'), all of which can be difficult when one is hot and sweaty, engaged in physically demanding activity and in a state of semi-undress. This may entail a jogger adapting to the pedestrian traffic flow of a busy street, coping with teasing or harassment from casual observers ('keep those knees up fatty') or seeking to avoid such situations in the first place by being inconspicuous or rerouting/retiming a run (Smith, 1997). Alternatively, it may involve participants in a busy aerobics class coordinating their movements so as to avoid clashes, or friends adapting their exercises so that they can chat (Crossley, 2004a).

In this latter example the execution of body techniques is modified in order to facilitate sociability. Actors who may ordinarily stare straight ahead in exercise turn their head to talk.

The relational context may also transform the execution of body techniques through mirroring, however. Bodily blind spots are such that actors can be poor judges of whether they are performing an exercise properly or indeed safely. Such dangers are offset, however, when others observe them and offer feedback. Reflexive body techniques are not acquired once and for all in this respect and are not self-contained. They are situated within feedback loops constituted through the social nature of exercise and regulated by means of this relational mechanism. Exercising actors modify their exercise practice in response to the feedback of others.

As this point suggests, sociability, exercise and the reflexive body techniques that it involves interlock in ways which transform them. 'Having' a technique, in many instances, means being able to execute it in a sociable situation and adapting its execution in an ongoing manner to the demands of sociability, as indeed sociability must be adapted to the demands and effects of working out (usual decorum isn't possible when you are half undressed, dripping with sweat, exhausted and have ten minutes of gruelling exercise to go). 'Use of the body' is social not only in the respect that its forms vary across social groups but also because its execution is embedded in sociable situations.

Some of the interactions involved in exercise are 'one-shot', to borrow the language of game theory. The parties to it are unlikely to ever meet again and knowing this may affect their interaction in the here and now. The jogger suffering taunts from others may be tempted to shout abuse back and make a run for it if she knows that she will never be running that way or at that time again. Like most social activity exercise is often routinized, however, and this has the consequence that many alters become 'regulars'. They are repeatedly encountered and the actor will anticipate meeting them. This anticipation affects interaction. Knowing that she will undoubtedly meet her persecutors again, for example, the jogger will try to deal with them in a civil and friendly manner.

The history that actors share with their regulars constitutes a tie between them and in many cases, in contrast to the jogger and her tormentors, such ties are positive. Actors develop a 'nodding acquaintance' and light conversation becomes a norm between them. Each now expects the other to acknowledge their mutual acquaintance and expects that the other expects them to do the same. Though relatively minor, their tie entails obligations, and it may also entail rewards. Participating in exercise among unknown others can be alienating; actors feel out of place, reducing their incentive to train. Acknowledgement by others, conversely, creates a sense of belonging, and casual conversation can be enjoyable, adding to the incentive to train and also reframing the situation such that its meaning is not entirely pre-empted by the instrumental aims of 'training'. The gym becomes a source of sociability and even friendship as well as exercise. Furthermore, encouragement, informal competition and rivalry, and talk relating to the benefits of exercise can all incentivize both hard work in the moment and future gym visits, helping to form the 'gym habit'.

I return to incentives, meaning and framing. First, however, it is important to reflect upon this process of tie and network formation in a little more detail. It is widely observed in studies of social networks that actors are often disproportionately connected to alters who are like them in some salient respect, a phenomenon referred to as 'homophily' and sometimes broken down into 'status homophily', where individuals are disproportionately connected to others with whom they share social standing (e.g. social class, ethnicity, gender) and 'value homophily', where they are disproportionately connected to others with similar values, tastes and/or attitudes (McPherson et al., 2001; Lazarsfeld and Merton, 1964).

Value homophily can be an effect of one or both of two distinct processes: selection and influence. Similarity may come first and steer tie formation (selection) or connection may come first, leading to interaction and mutual influence, which in turn causes similarity (influence). Furthermore, selection may be affected by psychological and/or structural factors. That is, actors may choose to link to others who are like them from a largely unbiased pool (psychology) or their circumstances may be such that their 'pool' is biased towards alters who are like them, such that they disproportionately connect to others who are like them without choosing to.

One such structural mechanism is what Scott Feld (1981, 1982) calls the 'focus'. A focus is a space (sometimes also demarcated in time) where like-minded actors are likely to converge, thus increasingly their likelihood of forming ties. A shared interest draws them to the same place, at the same time, bringing them into contact and thereby increasing the likelihood that they will form a tie. Gyms, health clubs, sports clubs, swimming pools and, at least at certain times of the day and year, parks are all foci of this sort. They are time-places where actors with an interest in a particular type of fitness or exercise, and often similar aims of body modification/maintenance, converge and thus places where ties between such like-minded alters are forged.

Furthermore, in these cases there are often foci within foci. The muscle-conscious will head to the heavy weights room of a health club, thereby coming into contact with fellow bodybuilders, for example, while others may head to the aerobics suite. The martially minded will check out 'boot camp' and combat-related sessions, hooking up with other gym-soldiers, while new agers will gravitate towards meditation and yoga. And to bring in time, wider responsibilities relating to work, childcare etc. will all affect when an actor is able to work out, and in many cases will bring them into contact with others whose time demands are similarly structured.

The ties generated may simply be those of nodding acquaintance, as described above. However, in my aforementioned ethnography I found evidence of much stronger ties. Specifically, I belonged to a network of relatively strongly tied friends formed around two late evening circuit training classes, followed by a decamp (on behalf of some) to the sauna, further followed in some cases by a visit to a local pub and backed up by what became fairly frequent 'curry nights'. In one respect these ties were quite specific. When a participant stopped attending the circuit training class they very quickly dropped out of the network. In another respect, however, the ties were strong and multiplex. A range of forms of support, material, emotional and informational, were exchanged. Trust and mutual affection were strong, and contact was frequent.

Indeed in many cases these contacts were among the strongest friendships of those involved, at the time, not least because commitment to the circuit training class and also to this particular network of friends weakened the actor's ties to other potential commitments and friendships. This locked the actor into their gym network and activities. Coming to the gym and making friends there caused participants to lose contact with certain other friends, which in turn elevated the importance of gym-buddies and the gym context to which they were tied.

Furthermore, through repeated interaction a reservoir of shared experiences and tacit assumptions, and a common repertoire of rituals and role-relations was built up, collectively constituting a 'social world' (Crossley, 2011). For those involved this was generally positive. The existence of this world afforded them a sense of belonging in the gym, increased their incentives to attend and constituted an important source of social capital, in the sense in which both Lin (2002) and Coleman (1990) use that expression; that is to say, contacts within this social world both provided indirect access to resources which the actor did not otherwise enjoy access to and also counted as intrinsic goods in their own right.

My ethnography also pointed to certain negative externalities for those not involved in this world, however. In particular the network of regulars, albeit perhaps unintentionally, made ownership claims upon certain classes and spaces (e.g. the sauna), bending the constitutive interaction of those classes and spaces towards their own preferences and annoying and intimidating others in the process.

These relational dynamics had an important impact upon the motivation of those involved. Outsiders to the network of regulars may have been discouraged from further attendance by its negative externalities (I was not able to investigate this systematically). For insiders, however, the numerous goods generated by the group and the anticipated pleasure of interacting with their friends generated additional incentives and, as I have explained, a degree of lock-in, tying them to the gym and circuit training class. Furthermore, and no less importantly, discussion between insiders generated a 'vocabulary of motives', in Mills's (1940) sense, which many evidently drew upon when deciding whether or not to attend on a night when habit and routine were not enough. Even if their decision to attend was taken alone that decision and the reasons informing it were often discussed, building up a stock of reasons that each could call upon when they were in need of self-persuasion and generating a 'generalized other' which, when internalized by the actor, would motivate them to attend when the forces of inertia were pulling them in the other direction. Actors mutually persuaded one another and generated a moral pressure to attend.

Conclusion

Exercise and the pursuit of fitness are sometimes portrayed as solitary and narcissistic pursuits, and the techniques involved can seem narrowly instrumental in purpose and focus. In this chapter, via a relational sociology – I have presented an alternative perspective that offers important insights into understanding the cultivation of the body through the physical practices of exercise/fitness. Exercise, I have suggested, is both social and also often sociable. The desire to exercise, whatever its motivation (health, beauty etc.) presupposes that actors enjoy a reflexive relation to their selves which is, necessarily, mediated through their relations to and interactions with others. And the motives and discourses which inform such desires are themselves borrowed from our social networks. They are the discourses of a generalized other. Likewise the exercises which we perform in order to achieve our goals; they are reflexive body techniques which diffuse through our networks.

No less importantly, however, exercise often brings us into contact with others who, when their routines overlap with ours, such that we each become 'regulars' for one another, transform our working-out sessions in innumerable important ways. Dominant groups within an exercise space can dis-incentivize working out among outsiders but equally friendships and contacts can incentivize it in many ways, not least by reframing it as a fun experience and adding 'connection' to its other benefits.

References

Becker, H. (1961) *Outsiders*, New York: Free Press.
Coleman, J. (1990) *Foundations of Social Theory*, Cambridge, MA: Belknap.
Cooley, C. H. (1902) *Human Nature and Social Order*, New York: Charles Scribner and Sons.
Crossley, N. (2001) *The Social Body: Habit, Identity and Desire*, London: Sage.
Crossley, N. (2004a) The Circuit Trainer's Habitus: Reflexive Body Techniques and the Sociality of the Workout, *Body and Society* 10(1), 37–69.
Crossley, N. (2004b) Fat is a Sociological Issue: Obesity Rates in Late Modern, 'Body Conscious' Societies, *Social Theory and Health* 2(3), 222–253.
Crossley, N. (2005) Mapping Reflexive Body Techniques, *Body and Society* 11(1), 1–35.
Crossley, N. (2006a) *Reflexive Embodiment in Contemporary Society*, Buckingham: Open University Press.

Crossley, N. (2006b) In the Gym: Motives, Meanings and Moral Careers, *Body and Society* 12(3), 23–50.
Crossley, N. (2008) (Net)working Out: Social Capital in a Private Health Club, *British Journal of Sociology* 59(3), 475–500.
Crossley, N. (2011) *Towards Relational Sociology*, London: Routledge.
Crossley, N. (2013) Interactions, Juxtapositions and Tastes, in C. Powell and F. Dépelteau (eds), *Conceptualising Relational Sociology*, Basingstoke: Palgrave, 123–144.
Crossley, N. (2015) Relational Sociology and Culture, *International Review of Sociology* 25(1), 65–85.
Feld, S. (1981) The Focused Organisation of Social Ties, *American Journal of Sociology* 86, 1015–1035.
Feld, S. (1982) Social Structural Determinants of Similarity Among Associates, *American Sociological Review* 47, 797–801.
Goffman, E. (1983) The Interaction Order, *American Sociological Review* 48(1), 1–17
Lazarsfeld, P. and Merton, R. (1964) Friendship as Social Process, in M. Berger, T. Abel and C. Page (eds), *Freedom and Control in Modern Society*, New York: Octagon Books, 18–66.
Leder, D. (1990) *The Absent Body*, Chicago, IL: Chicago University Press.
Lin, N. (2002) *Social Capital*, Cambridge: Cambridge University Press.
Mauss, M. (1979) Techniques of the Body, in *Sociology and Psychology*, London: RKP.
McPherson, M., Smith-Lovin, L. and Cook, J. (2001) Birds of Feather: Homophily in Social Networks, *Annual Review of Sociology* 27, 415–444.
Mead, G. H. (1967) *Mind, Self and Society*, Chicago, IL: Chicago University Press.
Merleau-Ponty, M. (1962) *The Phenomenology of Perception*, London: Routledge.
Mills, C. W. (1940) Situated Actions and Vocabularies of Motive, *American Sociological Review* 5(4), 904–913.
Milroy, L. (1987) *Language and Social Networks*, Oxford: Blackwell.
Powell, C. and Dépelteau, F. (2013) *Conceptualising Relational Sociology*, Basingstoke: Palgrave.
Sassatelli, R. (2010) *Fitness Culture*, Basingstoke: Palgrave.
Shove, E., Pantzar, M. and Watson, M. (2012) *The Dynamics of Social Practice*, London: Sage.
Smith, G. (1997) Incivil Attention and Everyday Tolerance, *Perspectives on Social Problems* 9, 59–79.

9
DANCE PRACTICES

Pirkko Markula and Marianne Clark

Dance has had an ongoing, but somewhat uneasy, relationship with cultural studies. Already in early 1990s, Angela McRobbie critiqued the work of the Birmingham Centre of Contemporary Cultural Studies (CCCS) for ignoring women and girls' experiences in subcultures. 'Dance', she continued, 'is where girls were always found in subcultures. It was their only entitlement' (McRobbie, 1993: 419). In a series of studies, McRobbie then constructed girls' dance as the 'motivating force' for the entire subculture of the 'rave'.

In the context of the United States,[1] Jane Desmond (1993: 34) similarly argued that dance research could contribute to cultural studies by providing further insights into 'how social identities are signalled, formed and negotiated through bodily movement'. A few years later, she continued to observe how rare it was to find dance research in the journals of the broader field of cultural studies (Desmond, 1997). Despite an increasing interest in the 'body' or art forms such as (popular) music or film, cultural studies, she claimed, remained largely text-based with a major emphasis on literary texts (see also Morris, 2009). Desmond (1997) now specified that analysing the social codification of dance styles can enhance our understanding of how the dancing body is 'related to, duplicates, contests, amplifies, or exceeds norms of nondance bodily expression within specific historical contexts' (ibid.: 29). Like McRobbie (1993), who emphasised the 'liberatory potential' of rave dancing (see also Thomas, 2003), she further observed that dance, as a 'bodily' activity, has often been associated with 'nondominant' gender, races/ethnicities, classes or nationalities and therefore, it reflects the existing social inequalities as well as represents possible 'liberatory' impulses for these groups. According to Desmond (1997), dance should be designated as a primary text for social analysis (see also Bryson, 1997) that allows cultural studies scholars to ask new questions (Koritz, 1996). However, recognising the social production of identity in the body in motion requires special tools and Desmond urged cultural studies scholars to become 'movement literate' (Desmond, 1997: 50). Helen Thomas (2003: 202) echoed that cultural studies scholars do not currently '"know" how to "look" or write about movement'. Based on these arguments, a focus on dance can provide cultural studies with new methods that link theory closer to practice (see also Bryson, 1997; Manning, 2006).

More recently, Gay Morris (2009) indicated that dance studies' 'intertwined concerns of representation and the moving body as a concrete, though culturally permeated and perceived, entity' could expand the narrow focus on textual representation in cultural studies. Dance studies could work constructively with cultural studies for further interpretation of 'the place of human beings within historical conjunctures by working in the areas of tension between representations of the body and, in the broadest sense, the live body in performance' (ibid.: 94). In her vision for such interdisciplinary work, Morris advocated a conceptual focus of dance as a high-art theatrical form and its contributions to the larger society (see also Gard, 2006).

Unlike dance studies, the sociology of sport community has had close connection with cultural studies for more than three decades.[2] Although their research, justifiably, has focused primarily on competitive sport, there have been recent calls to include more diverse bodily practices and representations, including dance, under the umbrella of physical cultural studies (PCS). For example, according to David Andrews and Michael Silk (Andrews and Silk, 2015; Silk and Andrews, 2011), PCS is committed to critical and theoretically informed engagement with various expressions of active embodiment, such as dance, and their relationships between physical culture and power.

Michael Giardina and Josh Newman (2011a) recognised that the recent PCS calls for cultural studies of the body are 'per se nothing new' (ibid.: 28); such scholarship is shared with diverse fields including anthropology, dance studies, sociology and women's studies. They, nevertheless, envisioned PCS as a unique site where 'the body's emancipatory potential through bodily praxis' can be re-emphasised (ibid.: 38), a sentiment that continues the legacy of McRobbie's (1993) early cultural analysis of rave dance subculture. Similar to Desmond (1997) and Morris (2009), Giardina and Newman pointed to the limits and confines of text-based analysis preferring an increased emphasis on 'the study of bodily movement' through which the material body can be 'understood as a site of passage—moving as it does across temporal, metabolic, spatial, and discursive planes' (Giardina and Newman, 2011b: 41). Giardina and Newman further encouraged researchers to include their own bodily experiences, sensations and knowledges into their projects. Citing Judith Hamera, they noted that

> performance links experience, theory, and the work of close critique in ways that make precise analytical claims about cultural production and consumption, and expose how both culture and our claims are themselves constructed things, products of hearts and souls, minds and hands.
>
> *(Hamera cited in Giardina and Newman, 2011b: 525)*

Such engagement, they added, needs to go beyond 'traditional' field methods such as ethnography. To illustrate their view, they referred to an ethnographic work within a professional ballet company by Anna Aalten (2004). Although Giardina and Newman, ethnographers themselves, acknowledged the value of Aalten's detailed reports on the aesthetics, feminine embodiments and practices specific to ballet, she remained, they noted, a detached observer of the culture. For Giardina and Newman, the absence of Aalten's own 'body politics' disclosed a further detachment from the larger contextual forces, politics defining high-performance culture of ballet and the politics of qualitative research.

Fluid moves: physical cultural studies dance research

With an emphasis on the bodily practice (of dance) and performance, PCS should appeal to many researchers of dance. Despite its inclusion within the definitional efforts for PCS (Andrews and Silk, 2015; Giardina and Newman, 2011a, 20011b; Silk and Andrews, 2011), dance, nevertheless, remains at the margins of the current field of PCS. Then why should we promote a closer alliance with PCS when dance studies offers a viable cognate field for those interested in cultural study of dance?

We, naturally, continue to endorse dance studies as a location for dance scholarship. However, we acknowledge that in the North American contexts, the focus of dance studies is on 'high-art' theatrical dance performance and choreography examined through the disciplinary traditions of history, (literary) criticism and anthropology (e.g. Morris, 2009). Departing from this path, and following McRobbie (1994), we envision PCS as a meeting place, borrowing Giardina and Newman's term, for researchers interested in critical analysis of contemporary dance culture that enters our everyday lives from myriad directions. Expanding the analysis beyond the context of performing arts, we believe, allows the PCS dance scholar to tap into an ever-increasing field of diverse dance phenomena in the current culture. These can include analyses of mass media contexts of popular televised reality shows of dance, dance video games, popular web-based dance sites or dance in movies; recreational dance settings in multiple contexts where dancers of wide age ranges meet; 'casual' dance environments; contemporary dance-fitness fusions such as currently popular 'Barre' fitness; dance incorporated within other popular cultural forms such as sport events; 'new' popular dance forms; or dance in the neoliberalised society where it is now used to raise funds for charity or as a health practice to improve balance or reduce stress.

We further expand the dance studies agenda by emphasising non-professional dance settings in favour of professional dance. While professional, full-time employment in dance, particularly beyond ballet companies, continues to be rare, dance is a significant participatory physical activity. In Canada, for example, over 1 million people participate in community-based dance activities (Canada Council for the Arts, 2004). The experiences and stories, joys and pains, passions and disappointments of these dancers provide a large cultural archive through which a PCS researcher can theoretically and critically engage with the dancing bodies and selves as parts of physical culture and the larger politics of power.

We acknowledge that many of the 'popular cultural' dance phenomena and the dancers' experiences can be read and interpreted through established qualitative methods such as textual analysis, ethnography, participant observation or narrative inquiry. Like Desmond (1997) and Morris (2009), we stress that capturing the specific force of dance movement requires reaching beyond the traditional social science method arsenal. Methodological innovation, thus, should be an important aspect of the PCS dance research agenda.

We are both practising dancers. Our dancing bodies are, thus, deeply embedded in our research acts. If Giardina and Newman (2011b) were correct, we, as qualitative, dancing researchers, gain dual understanding of the bodily experiences of dancing and its location within the cultural, social, political and commercialised world of dance (entertainment). We concur that 'knowing' about dance movement first hand provides expertise in dance culture that an outsider has to learn throughout the research process. Personal experience, however, does not guarantee deep, theoretically informed, cultural analysis of dance. Although by no means a necessary requirement for a PCS dance project, we find a researcher's personal involvement in dance an asset if informed by well-justified, explicitly acknowledged, and coherently argued theoretical and methodological grounding. Dance research within PCS, in our view, can be guided by multiple theoretical frameworks aligned with appropriate methodological approaches. Nevertheless, we find simultaneous engagement with the larger power relations that locate dance within the intersections of current (health) politics for physical activity promotion, entertainment industry, or governance of performing arts AND an analysis of individual moving bodies within the micro-context of dance a crucial element for PCS analysis.

A body of existing research can be comfortably located under the PCS umbrella. For example, several scholars have explored the ballet studio (Hamera, 2005), ballroom dance (Picard, 2006), 'belly dance' (e.g. Kraus, 2014), tango (Olszewski, 2008; Savigliano, 2005; Viladrich,

2005), salsa (Atencio, 2008; Urquia, 2005) and social dance (e.g. Boyd, 2014; Beggan and Pruitt, 2014; Stivale, 2000, 2003) in recreational, non-professional settings. Drawing from a wide variety of theoretical perspectives, these scholars interpret the micro-context of dance to highlight how identities are constructed or verified through dance practice. Although they employ a set of methods ranging from interviews and participant observation to ethnography, they, almost without exception, participate, at various degrees, in dance themselves. In addition, some textual readings of theatrical performance of dance appear within sport history (e.g. Adams, 2005; Vertinsky, 2010a, 2014). Jennifer Metz's (2011) reading of the construction of masculine, athletic identity in the American televised reality show, *Dancing with the Stars*, nevertheless, exemplifies more closely the type of PCS dance project we suggest in this chapter. There are, however, only few existing works that openly embrace the PCS approach. In what follows, therefore, we provide further examples of our own work that we have purposefully, from their initial conception, located within the PCS project.

Dancing the self

Marianne's research project titled 'Dancing the Self: Constructing a Self through the Dancing Body' (Clark, 2014) was inspired by her curiosity about how adolescent female ballet dancers construct a self through the dancing body in commercial (or recreational) dance studios. Such studios are distinct from elite settings as they do not groom dancers for professional dance careers, but offer regular, organised classes by certified dance teachers.

To extend the previous analyses of the appearance of the dancing body in (elite) dance settings, Marianne was particularly interested in how adolescent girls make sense of their dancing bodies in motion. Many girls enjoy dance, and Marianne, thus, sought to examine the experiences and effects of the moving, doing, dancing body among adolescent female girls. Given the focus on everyday life and everyday contexts in PCS studies, Marianne chose to conduct a case study (Stake, 1995; Markula and Silk, 2011) in one ballet class. Case study designs have been widely used in many disciplines but she aligned its principles with her qualitative perspective. Like most case studies, this project involved participant observations and interviews. Additionally, Marianne participated in the ballet class with the girls. She considered that this approach provided a unique methodological contribution to PCS because the case study was conducted through a poststructuralist lens, which allowed for an explicit examination of power relations and emphasis on the moving body.

To situate the individual dancers' experiences within a larger cultural context of the current neoliberal understandings of health, femininity and physical activity, Marianne's PCS project required a critical cultural analytical lens. Therefore, she chose Foucault's (1979, 1988) theoretical concepts of disciplinary power, knowledge and the self to guide this study. This framework allowed her to consider how dancers draw upon multiple discourses, or systems of knowledge, available to them in contemporary society, to describe and make sense of their dancing bodies. For example, participants described their dancing bodies as expressive, careful and skilful. Indeed, developing the physical capacity to perform a complex movement repertoire was one of girls' favourite aspects of being a dancer. Participants also noted that through movement they were able to express that which they could not put into words or easily express in other areas of their life. These findings highlight the capacity of the moving body to express what exceeds textual understanding or analysis and both reflect and underline the importance of the interests of a PCS project.

Marianne further considered how the self was actively constructed through these discourses in the intersections of both technologies of dominance and the technologies of the self

(Foucault, 1979, 1988). Dancing with participants while occupying the dual role of researcher and dancer prompted Marianne to reflect on the politics of her own dancing and researching self. Through these multiple selves she was able to attend to her participants' and her own movement experiences from several perspectives and was impelled to acknowledge, however messily, the kinaesthetic, inarticulable forces of the dancing body not easily captured through text, or by her theoretical lens.

To summarise, Marianne's PCS dance project examined the everyday experiences of non-elite adolescent dancers. It explicitly considered the complex power relations that circulate within the ballet studio while also acknowledging the complex social context in which these adolescent girls live and construct a self. The Foucauldian analysis revealed that disciplinary power was deployed in the dance studio through the enclosure and partitioning of bodies in space, as well as the precise arrangement and use of time. However, the studio also acted as a unique and important space of respite from the specific adolescent feminine identities privileged in other social contexts (i.e. 'the good daughter' at home, 'the good student' at school). The studio also provided girls with an exclusive space in which to explore their physicality in creative, forceful ways not available or appropriate in other social spaces or movement settings in their lives. This project, therefore, privileged the complexity of embodied movement experiences for adolescent girls and pointed to their productive capacity. PCS provided the scholarly landscape to further explore the importance of skilful, expressive physicality in the everyday lives of adolescent girls and innovative ways to foster it. Finally, the project required ongoing reflection of the relationship between the dancing bodies and researching selves and explicit acknowledgment of the inextricable (power) relationship between the researcher's body and knowledge production.

Dance as a physical cultural practice

Pirkko has an established connection to socio-cultural study of the physically active body (e.g. Kennedy and Markula, 2011; Markula, 1995, 2001, 2006, 2013, 2014; Markula and Pringle, 2006). She nevertheless purposefully located her Social Sciences and Humanities Research Council of Canada (SSHRC)-supported grant study titled '"So You Think You Can Dance": Dance as a Physical Cultural Practice'[3] within the PCS agenda to find a home for dance research that did not sit comfortably with either dance studies or dance education. As a sport sociologist and a contemporary dancer, she wanted to examine the role of dance as an embodied and cultural practice and to analyse how the potentially 'subjugated and transformative' (Giardina and Newman, 2011b: 45) dancing body was represented in the popular culture.

To do this, she engaged in an analysis of the triad relationship between physical culture, power and the (moving) body through the televised dance reality show *So You Think You Can Dance* (SYTYCD). To follow her PCS agenda, she pictured SYTYCD as a 'billboard': a cultural practice that performs, provides and enables a variety of spaces and a variety of directions in its conjuncture with other aspects of contemporary culture (Grossberg, 1992: 109). Using Grossberg's (ibid.) Deleuzian-inspired 'map of territorialisation' as a theoretical guide, she examined how two 'machines', a differentiating machine and a territorialising machine, produced dance as a contemporary cultural formation.

The analysis of the territorialising machine revealed a system of circulation comprising the mediated entertainment industry and the (absence of) dance industry. This system produced limited possibilities for dance and dancers in contemporary society. While the televised reality show afforded huge visibility for dance, the dancers sank back to obscurity after the show due to a lack of an appropriate support provided, for example, by the music industry of SYTYCD's sister show, the *American Idol* or state support sustaining performing arts of opera, theatre and classical music. The entertainment industry, although profit driven and often exploitative capitalist enterprise, does ensure work opportunities and income for pop stars or film stars unavailable for the majority of dancers.

The analysis of the differentiating machine revealed a dominant dance identity of an emotional contemporary dancer or a 'sexy' ballroom dancer in favour of ballet. Although a variety of 'hip-hop' genres were popular among the auditioning dancers and frequently appeared in the show, these dancers did not typically advance to the final levels of the show. The construction of the dance identities was layered with representations of gender and ethnicity. It was noticeable that although dance is predominantly a women's activity, the majority of the winners in the Canadian SYTYCD were men. Grossberg (1992) identified also a third dimension of analysis, affect, that links the planes of the two machines. Although the analysis of the emotionality of the show is still incomplete, it was apparent that the emotional narrative lines of contemporary choreography sustained the popularity of these dancers. In addition, the emotional charge of each episode created a general narrative that arched towards the end of each season. Finally, as a PCS scholar, Pirkko was particularly interested in cultural analysis of the moving, dancing body. This aspect required methodological innovation that went beyond the textual analysis techniques of the previous phases of the project.

To analyse the role of the moving body, Pirkko drew from Deleuze's focus on what the body does (instead of what the body is). Consequently, in addition to structures of the cultural machinery, she was interested in what the dancing body actually does in the show. By creating multiple relationships, the body has force to join the large compounds, the machines, through which its affects carry further beyond a dance performance to the larger fields of popular culture, dance and research. The analysis of the force of the moving body required new methodological tools. To develop these, Pirkko designed and co-taught a graduate course titled 'Qualitative Movement Analysis for Dance' where she, alongside several dance students, explored interdisciplinary ways to analyse dance movement. Marianne also contributed to this course.

To summarise, Pirkko's project advances a dance research agenda in an emergent PCS through its focus on how dancing bodies join the large field of (popular) culture and the entertainment industry to produce certain types of representations that then circulate within the mass media. As a dancing researcher, Pirkko chose to analyse SYTYCD (instead of, for example, *Dancing with the Stars*) because it depicted aspiring dance professionals. Although not mapping everyday practices of a dance community, this study provided an in-depth cultural analysis of a dance reality TV show and its social and cultural depictions of the dancing body. Pirkko's study, thus, can be used as a starting point for further analysis of how these popular representations have impacted dance practice in the communities. Considering the popularity of dance reality shows (e.g. the Canadian SYTYCD garnered over one million viewers and the latest season of the US SYTYCD was watched by an average of five million viewers) the impact could be considerable. The analysis of the dancing body in SYTYCD required an engagement in methodologically innovative interdisciplinary dance movement analysis which expanded far beyond Pirkko's research to inform all the course participants' everyday practices as dancers, teachers, choreographers and researchers. Consequently, Pirkko's study contributed to, and pushed the boundaries of, PCS scholarship by locating dance on the axes of physical culture, power relations and the active body through an analysis of how popular TV culture constructs dance and dancers.

The physical cultural studies sensibility: the performance of dance research

While there is an existing corpus of work on the cultural study of dance—it appears in a wide range of journals located within a variety of academic disciplines—PCS can provide a meeting place where cultural research on everyday dance practices, collectively, can obtain more visibility. In this context, we envision that the fluid sensibility of PCS allows dance scholars to create connections to larger cultural scholarship of the body/physical culture/physical activity. For increased prominence, PCS dance research should be open to a divergent range of approaches, theoretical positions and methodologies that locate the individual embodied experiences or bodily representations within the larger relations of power.

The PCS field can further foster fruitful future connections between dance and other physical cultural forms such as exercise and sport through shared connections to, for example, larger political initiatives of health and/or dictates of commercialism. Similar to previous dance scholars, we advocate that cultural analysis of dance could inform further how embodiment and performance are understood in a variety of scholarly disciplines. For example, at the University of Alberta, we realised that there was a collective of researchers who, relatively independently, explored the representations and experiences of the contemporary ballet body from various disciplinary perspectives. These projects ranged from readings of ballet in children's picture books, creating ballet-based computer games or exploring the media frenzy around 'Barre fitness' to teaching less disciplinary adult recreational ballet classes and ballet training within non-normative dance. With the (moving) ballet body as the explicit focus but with an opportunity for broad conceptual scope, PCS presented an opportunity for purposeful, but creative engagement with multiple theoretical and methodological approaches. This could yield to further innovative advancements in the ways we study and understand all types of dancing bodies as they intersect with culture and power relations.

While this group of ballet researchers came together somewhat accidentally, PCS can, we believe, gather more of these types of collectives into research performances that link experience, theory and critique to analysis of cultural production and consumption of dance within contemporary society. The potential exists then for PCS to embrace diverse topics within everyday dance cultures, allowing researchers using various theoretical and methodological approaches to share ideas. For us, PCS has offered space to explore innovative theoretical and methodological avenues to understand contemporary physical (dance) culture; a space that we believe can flourish via centring dance as an embodied practice within the future trajectory of PCS scholarship.

Notes

1   We approach dance from the perspective of North American dance research. As international scholars who have collective experience living in Finland, the US, the UK, New Zealand, Norway and Canada, we acknowledge that the position of dance scholarship differs depending on cultural context. However, the migration of dance from physical education to fine arts characterises several of our academic contexts. In North America, dance as scholarly subject is often traced to physical education at the University of Wisconsin-Madison, where Margaret H'Doubler established a specialised major in dancing for women in 1927 (Vertinsky, 2010b). Since then, dance and dance scholarship has gradually migrated to Fine Arts faculties. This relocation has resulted in an additional binary division of dance education (of dance teachers) versus dance performance within the dance scholarship (Risner, 2010). In this formation, dance education focuses on improving how dance is taught at schools as well as at the university level pre-professional training programmes. Dance studies, in turn, generally refers to research on 'high-art' dance performance and choreography drawing from the disciplinary traditions of history, (literary) criticism and anthropology (e.g. Morris, 2009). The calls for closer connection with cultural studies have come from the dance studies scholars.

2   There is a noticeable gender division between dance studies and PCS: dance studies scholars are predominantly women whereas the most visible calls for the PCS have come from male sport researchers. The cultural image of dance as a feminine activity can reflect who advocates dance research. The majority of dancers, indeed, are girls and women. For example, in Canada 85% of all dancers are women (Canada Council for the Arts, 2004). Similarly, while 13% of Australian children participate in dance, only 3% are boys (Australian Bureau of Statistics, 2010). In the US, about 35% of girls dance, but only about 8% of boys are dancers (O'Neill, Pate and Liese, 2011). Against this background, it seems logical that women, having more cultural connection to dance, are also drawn to its cultural analysis.
3   This research was funded by the Social Sciences and Humanities Research Council, Canada.

References

Aalten, A. (2004). 'The moment when it all comes together': embodied experience in ballet. *European Journal of Women's Studies*, 11(4), 263–276.

Adams, M. L. (2005). 'Death to the prancing prince': effeminacy, sport discourses, and the salvation of men's dancing. *Body and Society*, 11, 63–86.

Andrews, D. L. and Silk, M. L. (2015). Physical cultural studies on sport. In R. Giulianotti (ed.), *The Routledge Handbook of the Sociology of Sport* (pp. 83–93). London: Routledge.

Atencio, M. (2008). 'Freaky is just how I get down': investigating the fluidity of minority ethnic feminine subjectivities in dance. *Leisure Studies*, 27(3), 311–327.

Australian Bureau of Statistics (2010). Arts and culture in Australia: a statistical overview. Accessed at www.abs.gov.au/ausstats/abs@.nsf/featurearticlesbytitle.

Beggan, J. K. and Pruitt, A. S. (2014). Leading, following and sexism in social dance: change of meaning as contained secondary adjustments. *Leisure Studies*, 33(5), 508–532.

Boyd, J. (2014). 'I go to dance, right?': representation/sensation on the gendered dance floor. *Leisure Studies*, 33(5), 491–507.

Bryson, N. (1997). Cultural studies and dance history. In J. C. Desmond (ed.), *Meaning in motion: new cultural studies of dance*. Durham, NC: Duke University Press, 55–77.

Canada Council for the Arts (2004). Facts on dance: then and now – and now what. Accessed at http://canadcouncil.ca/council/research/find-research/2004/facts-on-dance.

Clark, M. (2014). Dancing the self: constructing a self through the dancing body. Unpublished doctoral dissertation, University of Alberta, Edmonton, Canada.

Desmond, J. C. (1993). Embodying difference: issues in dance and cultural studies. *Cultural Critique*, Winter (26), 33–63.

Desmond, J. C. (1997). Embodying difference: issues in dance and cultural studies. In J. C. Desmond (ed.), *Meaning in motion: new cultural studies of dance*. Durham, NC: Duke University Press, 29–54.

Foucault, M. (1979). *Discipline and punish: the birth of the prison*. New York: Vintage Books.

Foucault, M. (1988). Technologies of the self. In L. H. Martin, H. Gutman and P. Hutton (eds), *Technologies of the self: a seminar with Michel Foucault*. Amherst, MA: University of Massachusetts Press, 16–49.

Gard, M. (2006). *Men who dance: aesthetics, athletics and the art of masculinity*. New York: Peter Lang.

Giardina, M. D. and Newman, J. I. (2011a). Physical cultural studies and embodied research acts. *Cultural Studies ↔ Critical Methodologies*, 11(6), 523–534.

Giardina, M. D. and Newman, J. I. (2011b). What is this 'physical' in physical cultural studies? *Sociology of Sport Journal*, 28, 36–63.

Grossberg, L. (1992). *We gotta get out of this place: popular conservatism and postmodern culture*. New York: Routledge.

Hamera, J. (2005). All the (dis)comforts of home: place, gendered self-fashioning, and solidarity in a ballet studio. *Text and Performance Quarterly*, 25, 93–112.

Kennedy, E. and Markula, P. (2011). *Women and exercise: the body, health and consumerism*. London: Routledge.

Koritz, A. (1996). Re/moving boundaries: from dance history to cultural studies. In G. Morris (ed.), *Moving words, re-writing dance*. London: Routledge, 88–103.

Kraus, R. (2014). Becoming a belly dancer: gender, the life course and the beginnings of a serious leisure career. *Leisure Studies*, 33(6), 565–579.

Manning, S. (2006). Letter from the president. *Society of Dance History Scholars Newsletter*, 26(1), 1–2.

Markula, P. (1995). Firm but shapely, fit but sexy, strong but thin: the postmodern aerobicizing female bodies. *Sociology of Sport Journal*, 12, 424–453.
Markula, P. (2001). Beyond the perfect body: women's body image distortion in fitness magazine discourse. *Journal of Sport and Social Issues*, 25, 134–155.
Markula, P. (2006). The dancing body without organs: Deleuze, femininity and performing research. *Qualitative Inquiry*, 12, 3–27.
Markula P. (2013). (Im)mobile bodies: contemporary semi-professional dancers' experiences with injuries. *International Review for the Sociology of Sport*, 50(7), 840–864.
Markula, P. (2014). Reading yoga: changing discourses of postural yoga on the *Yoga Journal* covers. *Communication and Sport*, 2(2), 143–171.
Markula, P. and Pringle, R. (2006). *Foucault, sport and exercise: power, knowledge and transformation*. London: Routledge.
Markula, P. and Silk, M. L. (2011). *Qualitative research for physical culture*. Basingstoke: Palgrave.
McRobbie, A. (1993). Shut up and dance: youth culture and changing modes of femininity. *Cultural Studies*, 7(3), 406–426.
McRobbie, A. (1994). *Postmodernism and popular culture*. London: Routledge.
Metz, J. (2011). Dancing in the shadows of war: pedagogical reflections on the performance of gender normativity and racialized masculinity. *Cultural Studies ↔ Critical Methodologies*, 11(6), 565–573.
Morris, G. (2009). Dance studies/cultural studies. *Dance Research Journal*, 41(1), 82–100.
O'Neill, J. O., Pate, R. R. and Liese, A. D. (2011). Descriptive epidemiology of dance participation in adolescents. *Research Quarterly for Exercise and Sport*, 82(3), 373–380.
Olszewski, B. (2008). Ed cuerpo del baile: the kinetic and social fundamentals of tango. *Body and Society*, 14, 63–81.
Picard, C. J. S. (2006). *From ballroom to dance sport: aesthetics, athletics, and body culture*. Albany, NY: State University of New York Press.
Risner, D. (2010). Dance education matters: rebuilding postsecondary dance education for twenty-first century relevance and resonance. *Journal of Dance Education*, 10(4), 95–110.
Savigliano, M. E. (1995). *Tango and the political economy of passion*. Boulder, CO: Westview.
Silk, M. L. and Andrews, D. L. (2011). Toward a physical cultural studies. *Sociology of Sport Journal*, 28, 4–35.
Stake, R. (1995). *The art of case study research*. Thousand Oaks, CA: Sage.
Stivale, C. J. (2000). Becoming Cajun. *Cultural Studies*, 14(2), 147–176.
Stivale, C. J. (2003). Feeling the event: spaces of affects and the Cajun dance arena. In J. Daryl Slack (ed.), *Animations [of Deleuze and Guattari]*. New York: Peter Lang, 31–58.
Thomas, H. (2003). *The body, dance and cultural theory*. Basingstoke: Palgrave.
Urquía, N. (2005). The re-branding of salsa in London's dance clubs: how an ethnicised form of cultural capital was institutionalized. *Leisure Studies*, 24(4), 385–397.
Vertinsky, P. (2010a). Isadora goes to Europe as the 'muse of modernism': modern dance, gender and the active female body. *Journal of Sport History*, 27, 19–39.
Vertinsky, P. (2010b). From physical educators to mother of the dance: Margaret H'Doubler and Martha Hill. *International Journal of the History of Sport*, 27, 1113–1132.
Vertinsky, P. (2014). Ida Rubinstein: dancing decadence and the 'the art of the beautiful pose'. *Nashim: A Journal of Jewish Women's Studies and Gender Issues*, 26, 1220146.
Viladrich, A. (2005). Tango immigrants in New York City: the value of social reciprocities. *Journal of Contemporary Ethnography*, 34, 533–559.

10
SUBCULTURAL FORMATIONS AND LIFESTYLE SPORTING PRACTICES

Belinda Wheaton

Introduction

My starting point in this chapter is that 'sport', as has been adopted by some sport sociology scholars, can be a narrow and restrictive concept, particularly in the USA where the influence of, and focus on the college and professional athlete has been pervasive. My central research interest, action/lifestyle sports sit on the margins of what has been conceptualized as *sport*. They are activities that take place predominantly in unbounded, unregulated and shifting spaces outside of institutional control, traversing the boundaries of play, games, leisure, sport and art.

In this chapter I present a personal and contextual account that illustrates key disciplinary influences in developing my understanding and conceptualization of lifestyle sporting cultures. I describe how the study of youth subcultures emerging from the British Cultural Studies tradition has influenced my understanding and conceptualization of lifestyle sporting cultures, and their cultural politics.[1] Despite wide-ranging critiques, *subculture* in its various manifestations has remained an enduring theoretical concept for making sense of both youth and sports formations and identities, particularly, within the study of action and lifestyle sports (Atkinson and Young, 2008; Beal, 1995; Wheaton, 2007). However, I also adopted a range of theoretical tools and including those popularized through critical sport and leisure studies. My chapter highlights the value of this eclecticism, driven by the empirical context rather than a commitment to a theoretical orthodoxy, or epistemology. It also supports physical cultural studies (PCS) calls to broaden the narrow definition of sport adopted by some (North American) sport sociology scholars (Andrews and Silk, 2011: 1).

The chapter takes the following structure. First I examine the historical impact of cultural studies on sport studies as institutionalized in the UK. I do not discuss what cultural studies is, nor its diverse applications to sport in different contexts; these histories and debates are well versed. Rather I illustrate that my positionality and national location defined 'what cultural studies is for me' (Turner, 2012: 8). While at this juncture, the 'PCS enterprise' still retains a degree of self-definition (Andrews and Silk, 2011: 1), here I understand it as a synthesis of influences drawing from fields including sociology, 'history of sport and physical activity, and the sociology of the body' (Andrews, 2008: 55), but which most closely follows the trajectory of cultural studies as institutionalized in the North American academy. Nonetheless, North

American and British variants of cultural studies share many foundational principles, histories and contemporary concerns. I then outline what I mean by lifestyle sports and their cultural politics, illustrating that many of the conceptual tools and methodologies I've found productive derive from British cultural studies. My conclusions, however, are more cautionary, reminding us that from its foundation cultural studies had a political imperative, yet has largely failed to live up to its interventionist praxis-based legacy.

British cultural studies, sport and its legacy

British cultural studies has had a deep-rooted and lasting influence on the development of sociological work in the English-speaking world, and sport is no exception (Carrington, 2001; Hargreaves and McDonald, 2000; Silk and Andrews, 2011; Tomlinson, 2001). Emerging from the foundational publications of Hoggart (1957), Williams (1958) and E. P. Thompson (1963), 'a radically different conception of culture' was established, challenging the ideal of high culture as being synonymous with literary texts and artifacts, previously dominant (Hargreaves and McDonald, 2000: 48). These texts paved the way for the study of working-class and popular cultures, and pointed 'towards a form of intellectual engagement that was openly interventionist' looking to see how oppressive social relations could be challenged (ibid.: 49).

The cultural studies agenda as institutionalized at the Birmingham Centre for Contemporary Cultural Studies (CCCS) gave centrality to everyday dimensions of cultural life such as the media, teenage magazines, popular music and sport (Tomlinson, 2001). Understanding popular culture 'as a *site of struggle*, as a contested terrain wherein dominant ideologies are found but also resisted', and how people created 'alternative waves of being and meaning-making' became a pillar of this intellectual project (Carrington and Andrews, 2013: 5). Although their publications on sport were intermittent, and focused exclusively on (working-class) male subjectivity, they were 'original, varied and well theorised' (Hargreaves and McDonald, 2000: 51). During the 1970s, the seminal body of research theorizing the emergence of post-Second World War British working-class youth subcultures emerged, published initially under the *Resistance through Ritual* working papers.[2] Despite wide-ranging critique, it continued to be seen as the 'benchmark' against which developments were measured (Muggleton, 2000: 4). It has had a significant impact on the theorizing of sport cultures (Atkinson and Wilson, 2002; Wheaton, 2007; Thorpe and Wheaton, 2013), including much of the pioneering work on action sports cultures (Beal, 1995; Thorpe and Wheaton, 2013).

As Hargreaves and McDonald (2000) outline, the CCCS opened the doors for a cultural studies of sport, which in the UK then became institutionalized in university departments of physical education, sport studies and leisure studies. They cite the publication of Jennifer Hargreaves's edited collection *Sport, Culture and Ideology* (1982) as a 'watershed' in this development of sport sociology. Interrogation of sport-based cultural contestation was also being developed across the Atlantic, for example in Gruneau's work (1983), and Ingham and Loy (1993), challenging the 'conventional, statistical neo-positivistic paradigm that had been dominant within North American sport studies' (ibid.: vii).

As a sport sociology student in Brighton, England in the 1990s, the influence of cultural studies on the sporting literature was pervasive. Being housed in institutional contexts where leisure and popular culture were celebrated as much as *sport*, I found that the sociology of sport was broad based, encouraging and embracing inter/multi-disciplinary connections, including cultural studies (see also Hargreaves and McDonald, 2000; Tomlinson, 1989, 2001). The institutional coupling of sport *and* leisure, in associations like the Leisure Studies Association, for example, where many British sports sociologists found a home, also consolidated this breadth.

As Tomlinson argues, sport is most usefully conceptualized as a part of the 'popular cultural leisure landscape' (Andrews, 2006: 262).

Towards an understanding of the cultural politics of lifestyle sports

My research's central empirical focus has been the understanding of what I have termed lifestyle sport cultures. Lifestyle sports refer to a range of participatory, informal and 'stoke'-seeking urban and rural sporting activities, including long-established sports like climbing and surfing through to emergent activities like kitesurfing and parkour (Wheaton, 2004, 2013). Many of these activities either originated (or like surfing were re-popularized) in North America around the 1960s. With their origins in the counter-cultural social movements of the 1960s and 1970s many had characteristics that were different to traditional rule-bound, competitive and institutionalized sport. Commentaries outlining the key characteristics of different lifestyle sport illustrate they are still marked by their negation of, or challenge to the dominant Western 'achievement sport' culture and values (e.g. Wheaton, 2004, 2013).

Different conceptual tools have been adopted for conceptualizing and mapping these sporting-based collectivities and their identities, including subculture, leisure lifestyles, neo-tribes, sub-worlds, serious leisure cultures (Stebbins, 2007), and Bourdieu's concepts of habitus, capital and field (Laberge and Kay, 2002). However, (re)conceptualizations of *subculture* or *subcultural formations* (Muggleton and Weinzierl, 2003), emerging from what has been termed post-CCCS youth studies, has been the central influence in my research, and is my focus here.

The conceptual tools for understanding lifestyle sports cultures: from subcultures to subcultural formations

Early research in sport sociology often used subculture in quite descriptive, atheoretical and ahistorical ways (Donnelly, 1985). However, from the 1990s, (British) cultural studies was increasingly influential (Beal, 2002). Researchers began focusing on incorporation and resistance, exploring apparent contradictions in sport participants' behavior, and highlighting how sport subcultures simultaneously resist and reproduce existing power arrangements. As Carrington argues, centering questions of cultural identity helps reveal 'the complex articulations of dominant ideologies while simultaneously recognizing the joy, creativity, and moments of resistance and occasionally, transformation that popular culture and sport provides us with' (Carrington, 2007: 62).

From the late 1990s subcultural scholarship within the youth culture field underwent substantial critique and revision (Muggleton and Weinzierl, 2003). *Subculture* was increasingly viewed as having limited applicability particularly in style-based youth contexts, which were characterized by more temporary, fluid and 'floating memberships' (Bennett, 1999: 600). Nonetheless more stable, bounded and distinctive group identities, that could be conceptualized as a re-working of subculture (Hodkinson, 2004) were also documented. Here I outline how this research (re)conceptualizing 'subculture' and subcultural identity helps to understand the cultural politics of lifestyle sports.

First, their conceptualization of (sub)cultural identity is influenced by cultural studies theorizations of identity as a dynamic process undergoing constant transformation; about 'becoming' as well as 'being' (Hall, 1990). As Muggleton (2000: 154) outlines, subcultural identity is constructed, shifting and fluid, a performance that is always in a state of flux. Essential to these performances are the ways in which we perceive others as locating us, and what differentiates us. Within empirical research on youth, claims to authenticity are recognized as central to the internal and 'external' status hierarchies, something that is practiced, fought over and reinvented. In this context I have found Sarah Thornton's conceptualization of subculture as 'taste cultures' particularly useful (Thornton, 1995: 8). Thornton's research focused on British dance/club cultures in the 1990s. Drawing on the subcultural sociology of the Chicago school (notions of status), and Bourdieu's (1984) work in *Distinction* (particularly the idea of cultural capital), she coined the term *subcultural capital*. Subcultural capital involves a series of *distinctions*, or *authenticity claims* such as the hip versus the mainstream. Thornton illustrates that taste can be a marker of identity that functions to classify social groupings, (not just class-based ones), including the cultural distinctions or hierarchies *within* popular culture. Thus, a politics of authenticity underpins subcultural statuses. As I expand on below, Thornton's approach highlights the importance of mapping the internal power hierarchies, and differential statuses, *within* as well as *between* lifestyle sport subculture, and the complexities of 'mainstream incorporation' (Thorpe and Wheaton, 2013).

The politics of incorporation

Much of the early research on the institutionalization and commercialization of lifestyle sports saw incorporation as a negative process that undermined the 'authentic' or resistant character of 'alternative' sports. Typically commercialization was conceptualized as 'a top-down process of corporate exploitation and commodification' (Edwards and Corte, 2010: 1137). The role of media and commerce was not given systematic attention, nor an explanation provided for what occurs after the subculture becomes public or 'mainstream'. Post-CCCS approaches, however, recognize the complex and shifting power relations involved in the commercialization of youth cultures before, during and after the group becomes incorporated into the mainstream. To do so they adopt various post-structuralist conceptions of power and resistance, such as advocated by Foucault, along with theoretical insights from Bourdieu, Maffesoli and Lefevbre (see Muggleton and Weinzierl, 2003). These approaches help explain how lifestyle sport consumers and participants re-work the images and meanings circulated in, and by global consumer culture (Beal and Smith, 2010; Edwards and Corte, 2010; Rinehart, 2008; Stranger, 2011; Wheaton and Beal, 2003). Commercialization processes have also led to many lifestyle sport subcultures fragmenting into multiple scenes, each with their own styles of participation such as the street and ramp skateboarders discussed by Atencio et al. (2009), or contested ideas of parkour as sport or performance art (Wheaton, 2013). A cultural politics underlies these status differences, played out *within* and *between* lifestyle sport cultures. Furthermore, as I outline below, the ways in which these status hierarchies underpin and contribute to (particularly gendered and racialized) exclusion processes is a central question.

Power hierarchies within and between a subculture: understanding exclusion and belonging

While early research on subcultures in both youth and sport traditions tended to focus on male (white heteronormative) experiences, feminist research helped me develop a greater sensitivity to the multiple voices, subjectivities and experiences *within* the subcultural group – including more marginalized and silenced voices – and to expose the ways in which forms of subcultural capital (economic, physical, embodied, etc.) underpin these power relations and status hierarchies.

My initial research had targeted the experiences of *female* windsurfers, and also attempted to map a range of (sub)cultural experiences and identities – particularly those on the *periphery* such as 'windsurfing widows'. Subsequently I've focused explicitly on subordinated experiences, such as those of non-white participants, older participants, and those outside of the global North (Wheaton, 2013). As I've argued, (Wheaton, 2007: 297) analyses of the cultural politics of lifestyle sport cultures need to explore 'the experiences of *all* participants – young and old, marginal consumers as well as "core" participants of different experiences, genders, sexualities, dis/abilities and ethnicities' – revealing how cultural power is reproduced and contested, and contributes to experiences of belonging and exclusion.

Towards theoretical eclecticism

The past decades have seen an ever-expanding and productive range of theoretical influences to understand the cultural politics of lifestyle sports. Following Bourdieu (1984) we can also conceptualize specific lifestyle sports as social *fields* that are characterized by the 'movement of the different types of *capital*' (Beedie, 2007: 25). These forms of capital are central to identity construction, and struggles over 'legitimate uses and meaning of the body, and subcultural space (e.g. Atencio, Beal, and Wilson, 2009; Thorpe, 2011). The impact of the spatial turn in the social sciences has also been influential in revealing how power inequalities are played out and reproduced through space. Different lifestyle sport groups appropriate and contest rural, urban and mediated sporting space (Drissel, 2012; Kidder, 2012; Waitt and Clifton, 2012). Thorpe has productively situated her work in the motilities paradigm, revealing global spatial flows in and across lifestyle sports, media and industries (Thorpe, 2014).

Methodological considerations

PCS, like cultural studies, promotes methodological eclecticism, and within the work of PCS proponents different methodological strands are evident, from textual to auto-ethnographic (Giardina and Newman, 2011). In developing the projects discussed in this chapter, I've also adopted diverse methodologies. However, in my endeavor to reveal power hierarchies within and between subcultural spaces, and to expose the marginal voices, I've found ethnographic or interview-based methodologies most useful. For example, I explored how among Zulu street children in post-apartheid South Africa, skateboarding represents a sporting space that exists outside of postcolonial white institutional control. I have also excavated the discursive association between surfing and whiteness. To do so I have explored the ways whiteness impacts (historically, materially, spatially, discursively) on the experiences of African America surfers in California, revealing their experiences of identity, belonging and exclusion, and the ways in which they consider their embodied practices are challenging white privilege and power. Following a long-standing feature of much feminist research (and as advocated by PCS researchers), I have attempted to attend to the ways in which my own radicalized, gendered and heterosexualized sporting body has articulated with the formations of power that exist within the research space (Wheaton, 2002, 2013).

Certainly such a focus on micro political struggles in the cultural realm can, as Grossberg (1997: 10) warns, fail to 'address the actual context of relations, the articulations, between popular culture and systemic politics'. Explorations of lifestyle sporting cultures, practices and identities must contextualize and illuminate their relationship to global and local cultural, economic and political processes in which they are embedded. But to understand this complex, shifting picture, research is required that foregrounds, 'the lived experience of people' (Saukko, 2003: 3). Only when we uncover *how* discourses are made meaningful, can our research contribute to illuminating the '[physical] cultural operations and experiences of power and power relations' (Silk and Andrews, 2011: 8) inherent in the PCS agenda, and in so-doing expose the political possibility of 'sport', leisure and physical activity.

Discussion: reclaiming the political legacy of cultural studies

Central to PCS's agenda is an emphasis on political engagement and public intellectualism, that academics need to go beyond theoretical inspection, to 'intervene in the operation and experience of power and power relations' in the social world around us (Andrews, 2008: 58). These are long-standing and deep-rooted issues. Debate about who cultural studies is for, and suggestions that it has lost its original commitment to 'critique in the public interest' (McGuigan, 2006: 138 cited in Turner, 2012: 161) are certainly not new, but embedded deep into cultural studies history and practice. Recently, important shifts in the academic landscape, particularly the intensification of the neo-liberalization of universities has contributed to the demise of the humanities and liberal arts generally (Turner, 2012) and *critical* leisure and sport studies programs (Andrews, 2008). However, I am not convinced that either cultural studies, or PCS as currently articulated, is well placed to challenge the neo-liberal university; nor, as is required, to intervene outside of academia more widely. As I have previously suggested with colleagues (Sugden, Tomlinson and Wheaton, 2012), we are not convinced that the Illinoisian-inflected version of performative cultural studies (Giardina and Denzin, 2011) advocated has, or indeed can lead to the kind of activist-minded, public intellectualism advocated. Despite the rhetoric, it is still the case that much of the discourse about this 'new politics of possibilities' (ibid.) remains rooted in academics' ivory towers, not civic engagement. As Turner (2012) has suggested, versions of cultural studies have proliferated that 'certainly nominated themselves political that would be more accurately described as a genre of academic performance':

> The insistence that cultural studies is political has, from time to time and in some contexts worked more like a legitimating discourse than a description of what is actually the case. … And as its activities have been more and more contained within the world of university, the claim to be engaged in a wider cultural politics is just not as convincing as it might once have been.
>
> *(Turner, 2012: 168–169)*

In the sphere of action/lifestyle sport research none of the projects I have been involved with could be considered to be the invested, interventionist and engaged role that some critical commentators call for (see e.g. McDonald, 2002). However, as outlined in Wheaton (2013) and Thorpe and Wheaton (2013), *some* action sports scholars are re-considering what 'constitutes socially responsible sociology' and investing in transforming the inequity in power relations they identify (Turner, 2012).

Thorpe and Wheaton (2013) suggest that central to initiating political change is 'our ability to explain and present a critical analysis in an accessible away so that readers can use them … to inform their involvement in political practice' (ibid.: 352). Efforts to 'strategically' disseminate potentially empowering forms of knowledge to wider audiences have included using new and social media to share information and inspire individual and collective political action (Olive, 2013), and addressing the gender politics of lifestyle sports through engaging with and in the action sport media (Wheaton, 1997). Most recently I have been engaging with policy makers and practitioners, particularly in parkour and surfing, working to co-produce knowledge and challenge dominant discourses, striving to re-imagine action sports identities and spaces (Thorpe and Wheaton, 2015; Wheaton, 2015a, 2015b). These types of initiatives might provide productive ways to intervene in, and even disrupt, our sporting social worlds.

Closing thoughts

This chapter has illustrated that cultural studies, especially post-CCCS youth formations, framed my research on the cultural politics of lifestyle sporting cultures. It drove a commitment to expose the multiple voices, subjectivities and experiences within the subcultural group – including the marginalized – and to expose the ways in which forms of subcultural capital underpin power relations. However, I've subsequently adopted a range of theoretical influences emerging from different interdisciplinary contexts. Such conceptual and theoretical eclecticism can enable the researcher to provide a more vivid picture of the complex and shifting cultural phenomenon under study (Andrews and Silk, 2011). As Thorpe demonstrates in her inspection of the snowboarding body, which she characterizes as PCS, 'strategically juxtaposing a selection of conceptual perspectives from commensurate paradigms' helps construct a 'multidimensional representation of the social, cultural, political, gendered, practiced, lived and interacting body'(Thorpe, 2011: 13).

PCS is certainly playing an important part in the struggle to retain sports legitimacy in the cultural studies 'canon'. As outlined here, while I have not explicitly located my research within PCS, my approach is sympathetic to, and shares many theoretical and methodological aims. Others like Holly Thorpe, do situate their research on action sports within the PCS project (Thorpe, 2011). However, as I have suggested elsewhere, from my British-based and multi-disciplinary academic grounding, the PCS label has appeared to be somewhat North American in terms of how it is historicized and driven (Sugden et al., 2012). I've experienced British sport studies as a broad church, encompassing and encouraging inter- and multi-disciplinary work generally and cultural studies specifically. It has provided a context to develop research that is, as Sugden and Tomlinson (2002) have argued, methodologically reflexivity, theoretically eclectic, and contextually grounded. Such an approach conceptualizes sporting cultures, economies and representations within the broader 'popular cultural leisure landscape'; centralizes power relations, and fosters political engagement and public intellectualism.

However, the ways in which 'engagement with real utopias, democracy and social intervention' (Atkinson, 2011: 137) can best be achieved in the twenty-first century requires continued reflection and engagement. These important and timely questions reflect cultural studies' legacy, its foundational political commitment rooted in 'real world' problems and forms of intellectual engagement that are interventionist. They are also problems that are essential to the 'merit, hope and future' of PCS (ibid.), and the sociology of sport more widely.

Notes

1 This discussion is drawn from a number of previously published sources, but primarily Wheaton (2013) and Thorpe and Wheaton (2013). My discussion about what PCS is, or might be, emerges from some earlier debate and presentations with my colleagues John Sugden and Alan Tomlinson, for which I am grateful (Sugden, Tomlinson and Wheaton, 2012).
2 Along with subsequent research (e.g. Hebdige, 1979) and review (McRobbie, 1980).

References

Andrews, D. L. (2006). Leisure studies: progress, phases and possibilities – an interview with Alan Tomlinson. *Leisure Studies*, 25(3), 257–273.

Andrews, D. (2008). Kinesiology's inconvenient truth and the physical cultural studies imperative. *Quest*, *60*(1), 45–62.

Andrews, D., and Silk, M. (2011). Physical cultural studies: engendering a productive dialogue. *Sociology of Sport Journal*, *28*(1), 1–3.

Atencio, M., Beal, B., and Wilson, C. (2009). The distinction of risk: urban skateboarding, street habitus and the construction of hierarchical gender relations. *Qualitative Research in Sport and Exercise*, *1*(1), 3–20.

Atkinson, M. (2011). Physical cultural studies [redux]. *Sociology of Sport Journal*, *28*(1), 135–144.

Atkinson, M., and Wilson, B. (2002). Bodies, subcultures and sport. In J. Maguire and K. Young (eds), *Theory, Sport and Society* (pp. 375–395). Oxford: JAI.

Atkinson, M., and Young, K. (2008). *Deviance and social control in sport*. Champaign, IL: Human Kinetics.

Beal, B. (1995). Disqualifying the official: an exploration of social resistance through the subculture of skateboarding. *Sociology of Sport Journal*, *12*(3), 252–267.

Beal, B. (2002). Symbolic interactionism and cultural studies: doing critical ethnography. In J. Maguire and K. Young (eds), *Theory, Sport and Society* (pp. 353–374). Oxford: JAI.

Beal, B., and Smith, M. (2010). Maverick's: big-wave surfing and the dynamic of 'nothing' and 'something'. *Sport in Society: Cultures, Commerce, Media, Politics*, *13*(7), 1102–1116.

Beedie, P. (2007). Legislators and interpreters: an examination of changes in philosophical interpretations of 'being a mountaineer'. In M. McNamee (ed.), *Philosophy, Risk and Adventure Sports* (pp. 25–42). London: Routledge.

Bennett, A. (1999). Subculture or neo-tribes? Rethinking the relationship between youth, style and musical taste. *Sociology*, *33*(3), 599–617.

Bourdieu, P. (1984). *Distinction: a social critique of the judgement of taste*. London: Routledge and Kegan Paul.

Carrington, B. (2001). Decentring the centre: cultural studies in Britain and its legacy. In T. Miller (ed.), *Cultural Studies: A Companion* (pp. 275–294). Oxford: Blackwell.

Carrington, B. (2007). Merely identity: cultural identity and the politics of sport. *Sociology of Sport Journal*, *24*(1), 49–66.

Carrington, B., and Andrews, D. (2013). (eds) *A companion to sport*. Chichester: Wiley Blackwell.

Donnelly, P. (1985). Sport subcultures. *Exercise and Sport Sciences Review*, *13*, 539–578.

Drissel, D. (2012). Skateboarding spaces of youth in Belfast: negotiating boundaries, transforming identities. *Spaces and Flows: An International Journal of Urban and Extra Urban Studies*, *2*(4), 115–138.

Edwards, B., and Corte, U. (2010). Commercialization and lifestyle sport: lessons from 20 years of freestyle BMX in 'Pro-Town, USA'. *Sport in Society: Cultures, Commerce, Media, Politics*, *13*(7), 1135–1151.

Giardina, M. D., and Denzin, N. K. (2011). Acts of activism ↔ politics of possibility: towards a new performative cultural politics. *Cultural Studies ↔ Critical Methodologies*, *11*(4), 319–327.

Giardina, M., and Newman, J. (2011). What is this 'physical' in physical cultural studies. *Sociology of Sport Journal*, *28*(1), 36–63.

Grossberg, L. (1997). *Dancing in spite of myself: essays on popular culture*. Durham, NC: Duke University Press.

Gruneau, R. (1983). *Class, sport and social development*. Amhurst, MA: University of Massachusetts Press.

Hall, S. (1990). Cultural identity and diaspora. In J. Rutherford (ed.), *Identity: Community, Culture, Difference*. London: Lawrence & Wishart.

Hargreaves, J. (1982). *Sport, culture and ideology*. London: Routledge.

Hargreaves, J., and McDonald, I. (2000). Cultural studies and the sociology of sport. In E. Dunning and J. Coakley (eds), *The Handbook of Sport Studies* (pp. 48–60). London: Sage.

Hebdige, D. (1979). *Subculture, the meaning of style*. London: Routledge.

Hodkinson, P. (2004). The Goth scene and (sub) cultural substance. In A. Bennett and K. Kahn-Harris (eds), *After Subculture: Critical Studies in Contemporary Youth Culture* (pp. 135–147). Basingstoke: Palgrave.

Hoggart, R. (1957). *The uses of literacy*. Harmondsworth: Penguin.

Ingham, A., and Loy, J. (eds). (1993). *Sport in social development: traditions, transitions and transformations*. Champaign, IL: Human Kinetics Publishers.

Kidder, J. (2012). Parkour, the affective appropriation of urban space, and the real/virtual dialectic. *City and Community*, *11*(3), 229–253.

Laberge, S., and Kay, J. (2002). Pierre Bourdieu's sociocultural theory and sport practice. In J. Maguire and K. Young (eds), *Theory, Sport and Society* (pp. 239–266). Oxford: JAI.

McDonald, I. (2002). Critical social research and political intervention: moralistic versus radical approaches. In J. Sugden and A. Tomlinson (eds), *Power Games: Theory and Method for a Critical Sociology of Sport* (pp. 100–116). London: Routledge.

McGuigan, J. (2006). The politics of cultural studies and cool capitalism. *Cultural Politics, 2*(2), 137–158.
McRobbie, A. (1980). Settling accounts with subcultures: a feminist critique. *Screen Education, 39*.
Muggleton, D. (2000). *Inside subculture: The postmodern meaning of style*. Oxford: Berg.
Muggleton, D., and Weinzierl, R. (2003). What is 'post-subcultural studies' anyway? In D. Muggleton and R. Weinzierl (eds), *The Post-Subcultures Reader* (pp. 3–23). Oxford: Berg.
Olive, R. (2013). 'Making friends with the neighbours': blogging as a research method. *International Journal of Cultural Studies, 16*(1), 71–84.
Rinehart, R. (2008). ESPN's X games, contests of opposition, resistance, co-option, and negotiation. In M. Atkinson and K. Young (eds), *Tribal Play: Subcultural Journeys Through Sport*, vol. IV, 'Research in the Sociology of Sport' (pp. 175–196). Bingley: JAI.
Saukko, P. (2003). *Doing research in cultural studies: an introduction to classical and new methodological approaches*. London: Sage.
Silk, M., and Andrews, D. (2011). Toward a physical cultural studies. *Sociology of Sport Journal, 28*(1), 4–35.
Stebbins, R. (2007). *Serious leisure: a perspective for our time*. London: Transaction publishers.
Stranger, M. (2011). *Surfing life: surface, substructure and the commodification of the sublime*. Farnham: Ashgate.
Sugden, J., and Tomlinson, A. (2002). Theory and method for a critical sociology of sport. In J. Sugden and A. Tomlinson (eds), *Power Games: Theory and Method for a Critical Sociology of Sport* (pp. 3–21). London: Routledge.
Sugden, J., Tomlinson, A., and Wheaton, B. (2012). Answering back: challenging the PCS (physical cultural studies) positioning within the sociology of sport. Paper presented at the Cross Roads in Cultural Studies, Paris.
Thompson, E. P. (1963). *The making of the English working class*. Harmondsworth: Penguin.
Thornton, S. (1995). *Club cultures: music, media and subcultural capital*. Cambridge: Polity Press.
Thorpe, H. (2011). *Snowboarding bodies in theory and practice*. Basingstoke: Palgrave Macmillan.
Thorpe, H. (2014). *Transnational mobilities in action sport cultures*. New York: Palgrave Macmillan.
Thorpe, H., and Wheaton, B. (2013). Dissecting action sports studies: past, present, and beyond. In D. Andrews and B. Carrington (eds), *A Companion to Sport* (pp. 341–358). Chichester: Wiley Blackwell.
Thorpe, H., and Wheaton, B. (2015). Understanding and responding to the trends of young people: action sports in New Zealand communities. Paper presented at the Connections 2015: Sport New Zealand Annual conference, Auckland.
Tomlinson, A. (1989). Whose side are they on? Leisure studies and cultural studies in Britain. *Leisure Studies, 8*(2), 97–106.
Tomlinson, A. (2001). Sport, leisure and style. In D. Morley and K. Robins (eds), *British Cultural Studies: Geography, Nationality, and Identity* (pp. 399–415). Oxford: Oxford University Press.
Turner, G. (2012). *What's become of cultural studies?* London: Sage.
Waitt, G., and Clifton, D. (2012). 'Stand out, not up': bodyboarders, gendered hierarchies and negotiating the dynamics of pride/shame. *Leisure Studies, 32*(5), 487–506.
Wheaton, B. (1997). Covert ethnography and the ethics of research: studying sport subcultures. In A. Tomlinson and S. Fleming (eds), *Ethics, Sport and Leisure: Crises and Critiques* (pp. 163–172). Aachen: Meyer and Meyer Verlag.
Wheaton, B. (2002). Babes on the beach, women in the surf: researching gender, power and difference in the windsurfing culture. In J. Sugden and A. Tomlinson (eds), *Power Games: Theory and Method for a Critical Sociology of Sport* (pp. 240–266). London: Routledge.
Wheaton, B. (ed.) (2004). *Understanding lifestyle sports: consumption, identity and difference*. London: Routledge.
Wheaton, B. (2007). After sport culture: rethinking sport and post-subcultural theory. *Journal of Sport and Social Issues, 31*(3), 283–307.
Wheaton, B. (2013). *The cultural politics of lifestyle sport*. London: Routledge.
Wheaton, B. (2015a). Opening address: exploring the social benefits of informal and action sports: an untapped potential? Paper presented at the Exploring the social benefits of informal and action sports (ESRC funded seminar series), Brighton.
Wheaton, B. (2015b). Understanding female board sport cultures and their potential for social good: A research informed perspective. Paper presented at the Surf + Social Good Bali, May.
Wheaton, B., and Beal, B. (2003). 'Keeping it real': subcultural media and the discourses of authenticity in alternative sport. *International Review for the Sociology of Sport, 38*(2), 155–176.
Williams, R. (1958). *Culture and society 1790–1950*. London: Chatto & Windus.

11
(HIGH-)PERFORMANCE SPORT

Jim Denison and J. P. Mills

Introduction

For many sports studies scholars high-performance sport is a dirty word. Oppressive. Neo-liberal. Exploitative. Disciplinary. But that does not necessarily have to be the case. At least that is how we read physical cultural studies and its promise to reject absolutes, fixed meaning and binaries: good–bad, agency–structure, theory–practice. Such divisions do not make sense within what Bush, Silk, Andrews and Lauder (2013) termed the physical pedagogic bricoleur's (PPB) epistemological framework; such divisions are simply not in the bricoleur's tool-kit. What does make sense within a PPB framework is a scholarship that problematizes in the name of change – lasting and ethical social change. In other words, an expansive and flexible methodological scholarship that produces work that '*make[s] a difference*' (Bush et al., 2013: 134, italics original). And so it is that high-performance sport, if we want it to be, can be studied and understood differently.

Not only do we *want* high-performance sport to be understood differently – to change – we believe it *needs* to be different to address many long-standing and recurring problems: burnout, drop-out, doping, corruption, under-performance … bodies objectified and made docile. More specifically, as Foucauldian-informed coach developers, to scrutinize the 'doing of high-performance sport', or to paraphrase Foucault (1983), to begin to notice all that high-performance sport does, means recognizing the multiplicity of meanings, experiences and relations of power that flow in and around every high-performance sporting context. Otherwise, how can we begin to create coach development programs that have the flexibility to prepare coaches to think more ethically about their athletes' unique qualities and specific developmental needs? How can we create coach development programs that 'do coaching justice' (Bush et al., 2013: 134)? In this chapter, we discuss how we have begun to answer these questions in an effort to (1) broaden high-performance coaches' understanding of effective coaching and (2) move high-performance sport beyond its disciplinary legacy so that it is no longer necessarily viewed as a dirty word by sports studies scholars.

A Foucauldian approach to high-performance sport

According to Michel Foucault (1978, 1995), in the transition to modern society the body became both the object and target of power. Central to the functioning of this power was an integrated system of control intended 'to make useful individuals'. To explain the precise details that characterized this transformation of the individual, Foucault (1995: 137) outlined four specific techniques, or 'disciplines', and illustrated how they 'made possible the meticulous control of the operations of the body'. These four techniques were: the *art of distributions* that involved how bodies were managed and used in spaces; the *control of activity* that involved how bodies were shaped by time in these spaces; the *organization of genesis* that involved the way specific bodily practices were categorized and grouped; and the *composition of forces* that involved the way bodies were brought together to function as a machine. Importantly for Foucault, these techniques did not operate in a disjointed or fragmented manner; rather they worked through three specific instruments, *hierarchical observation, normalizing judgment* and *the examination,* to exert their influence over the body. Foucault referred to the collective power of these techniques and instruments to assure the body's subjection – its docility – as anatomo-politics.

Underpinning Foucault's (1995) analysis of anatomo-politics and the making of docile bodies was his understanding of *panopticism*, a concept he based on Jeremy Bentham's architectural figure of the panopticon. According to Foucault, 'the panoptic mechanism arranges spatial unities that make it possible to see constantly and to recognize immediately ... assuring the efficient and automatic functioning of power' (ibid.: 201). Thus, from the total force of his analysis of an 'anatomo-politics of the human body', Foucault was able to show how disciplinary regimes operated in large social institutions such as factories, the military, schools, hospitals so that people could easily be transformed into cogs in a system where interaction, learning and personal growth were subservient to the large-scale production of all: 'an infinitesimal power over the active body ... its movements, gestures, attitudes, rapidity' (ibid.: 137).

While it could be argued that making bodies docile is an efficient way to develop 'coachable' athletes capable of winning, it is important to note, as a number of prominent sport scientists have shown, that winning and performance are relative (e.g. Noakes, 2005). In other words, a winning performance (as well as a losing performance) may not necessarily be an athlete's or a team's optimal performance. And could there be a greater travesty for a high-performer than this? Along similar lines, despite the general acceptance of many disciplinary coaching practices, including the approval from athletes who have been subjected to these practices (e.g. Jones and Standage, 2006; Williams and Manley, 2014), a number of Foucauldian scholars have shown that the repeated exposure to strict systems of control can limit and constrain athletes' growth and development, and undermine their ability to manage the demands of competitive sport (e.g. Barker-Ruchti and Tinning, 2010; Denison, 2007; Gearity and Mills, 2012; Jones and Denison, 2016). In response to these findings, some performance-minded and applied Foucauldian scholars have begun to argue for the importance of developing coaches' awareness and understanding of the problematic effects that anatomo-political power can have on athletes' bodies (Denison and Mills, 2014; Denison, Mills, and Jones, 2013; Denison, Pringle, Cassidy, and Hessian, 2015; Markula and Martin, 2007). More specifically, according to Denison, Pringle, Cassidy and Hessian (2015), who drew on Foucault's (1994) claim that 'freedom was the ontological condition of ethics', to provide athletes with greater opportunities to express their concerns, opinions, knowledge and emotions coaches need to begin to coach in a less disciplinary way. Or at the very least, coaches need to begin to coach with an awareness of all that anatomo-political power does to the body.

In contrast to coaching models that promote athlete empowerment as a solution to excessive coach control (e.g. Kidman, 2001; Miller and Kerr, 2002), coaching in a less disciplinary way would mean a coach problematizing sports' disciplinary legacy and the details – the disciplinary techniques and instruments – of his or her everyday coaching practices in an effort to minimize the harmful effects of anatomo-political power. For example, a coach could develop a more informed position with respect to the benefits and costs associated with surveying an athlete's diet or routinely measuring his or her fitness with lactate tests. Or, as Denison, Pringle, Cassidy and Hessian (2015) suggested, a coach could begin to focus on 'keeping his or her desires in check (e.g. aim to win but do not be a slave to such a desire), caring for his or her athletes' total well-being, seeking advice from appropriate mentors and recognizing that ethical coaching involves on-going work' (ibid.: 74). In this way, to 'coach with Foucault' would mean coaching with an awareness and sensitivity of how one is using his or her power 'to conduct himself [sic] properly in relation to others and for others' (Foucault, 1994: 287).

To further highlight how to coach with Foucault would mean going beyond simplistic pronouncements related to athlete empowerment, consider the following questions emanating from Foucault's (1995) historical analysis of discipline to transform the body: Do coaches need to manage the same problems faced by military leaders and factory owners? Is dissent a problem coaches are trying to prevent? Or looting? Or desertion? Do coaches, who in the main work as volunteers in club, community or educational settings, need to be concerned with maximizing profit or making life and death decisions? How are practices that were designed to serve as a 'general formula of domination' (ibid.: 137), 'a policy of coercions' (ibid.: 138), 'a calculated manipulation of [the body's] gestures, its behavior' (ibid.: 138) in order to enforce strict control to prevent disturbances and 'to render individuals docile' (ibid.: 231) relevant to effective coaching? Examine any definition, prescription or model of high-performance sport and effective coaching and nowhere will you see reference made to an effective coach as someone who dominates, coerces, manipulates and makes athletes docile. So then why are coaches' practices, as Shogan (1999) and more recently, Mills and Denison (2013) have so clearly illustrated, basically a blueprint or handbook for the transformation of athletes into disciplined bodies?

To go a step further with the seemingly contradictory association between discipline and coaches' practices, do coaches need to manage the same problems faced by prison wardens? Is recidivism a concern for coaches? Or violence? Or anger? Or troublemaking? Or rage? Because in effect a coach is saying, 'these are problems that concern me', when he or she employs the various disciplining techniques and instruments that Foucault (1995: 228) outlined made the prison 'the modern instrument of penality' – 'an indefinite discipline: an interrogation without end, an investigation that would be extended without limit to a meticulous and ever more analytical observation, a judgment … that was never closed … interlaced with the ruthless curiosity of an examination' (ibid.: 227). We recognize this analogy might seem extreme, but allow us to explain further the connection we are trying to make and why it is important to consider if coaches indeed wish, as they repeatedly say they do, to coach in ways that can increase their athletes' engagement and ownership over their athletic development.

Certainly we acknowledge that most coaches believe they encourage their athletes to think for themselves and that they believe they coach every one of their athletes as an individual (Mills and Denison, 2013). But can true 'thinking for oneself' or individualized coaching really occur within a training framework designed around the repetitive constraints of constant coach control? As a distance runner, how can knowing that you have to run all eight of your 400m repetitions in under 60 seconds for a workout to be deemed successful by your coach encourage independent thinking? Or as a soccer player, how can knowing that you have to maintain your 'disciplined' position on the field and 'do your job' encourage the sorts of spontaneity that an inspired performance requires?

Therefore, as Denison, Mills and Konoval (2015) argued in their critique of athlete-centred coaching, despite a coach believing that he or she is empowering his or her athletes and coaching in an autonomously supportive or holistic way, he or she will never develop engaged or open-minded athletes without first problematizing the effects produced by anatomo-political power and how it frames almost everything he or she does. To believe otherwise is to ignore, or worse mock, the workings of anatomo-politics and its effects on athletes' bodies – a folly we would certainly not recommend. It is akin to 'doing' the same thing but expecting a different response. Foucault (1995) argued similarly in his discussion of the extremely high rates of recidivism in French prisons in the mid-nineteenth century. Despite prison programs designed to reform, he argued:

> The prison cannot fail to produce delinquents. It does so by the very type of existence that it imposes on its inmates … it is supposed to apply the law, and to teach respect for it; but all its functioning operates in the form of an abuse of power.
> (Foucault, 1995: 266)

In other words, the idea of reform within a strict disciplinary apparatus is oxymoronic. For while a strict disciplinary framework may be effective when trying to get large numbers of people to all do the same thing such as produce identical 'widgets' for costumers across the world, such a framework has been shown to be a largely ineffective when trying to get a small number of elite athletes to perform their best (e.g. Barker-Ruchti and Tinning, 2010; Denison, 2007).

Accordingly, if a coach truly values developing thinking athletes or coaching each of his or her athletes as an individual (and we believe many coaches do), then his or her specific practices and pedagogies – the workouts and practice plans he or she designs and implements – need to reflect this aim. Slogans, truisms and tricks, or various types of behavioural or motivational interventions intended to foster and develop thinking, responsible or resilient athletes, will largely be ineffective if they are not accompanied by specific training practices and coaching pedagogies that disrupt sports' disciplinary legacy and the many unseen effects that anatomo-political power has on athletes' bodies. More to the point, through Foucault (1995), we believe for coaches to truly coach in holistic ways and not just pay lip service to this idea, they will need to destabilize specific relations of power present in their everyday training practices that can make athletes docile. Foucault recognized a similar need if indeed prisons were to educate their inmates: 'whether they [prisoners] are isolated in cells or whether they are given useless work ... [prison] creates an unnatural, useless and dangerous existence' (ibid.: 266). So again, whether to right the ills of the prison or to address the abuses, problems or shortcomings of disciplinary coaching practices, reforms at the level of behaviour, without also addressing relations of power, will largely be ineffectual.

However, knowing that coaches are unlikely to coach in new ways without being given time and support to reflect on their practices (Cushion, 2016), we have begun to consult with a number of high-performance coaches in order to help them 'notice' how their athletes' regular exposure to a range of disciplinary techniques and instruments could be jeopardizing their performance potential. And in what follows we discuss the specifics of what we do, and why we believe what we do can broaden the doing of high-performance sport and help coaches better understand 'what what they do does' (Foucault, 1983: 187).

Coaching with Foucault

As coaching scholars with a physical cultural studies sensibility we subscribe to the view that knowledge is contextual and 'reality' and 'truth' are multiple and subjective. We further recognize that knowledge, reality and truth are produced through dynamic and fluid (albeit non-egalitarian) power relations. More specifically, as Foucauldian-informed coach development consultants our intention is not to establish a general understanding of effective coaching or effective coach development. Rather, it is to illustrate the highly contextual and power-laden nature of coaching and how this in turn produces the limits and possibilities surrounding the formation of coaches' everyday training practices while also affording coaches the opportunity to change their practices and begin to coach differently. It is in this way, and in line with physical cultural studies, that our work as coach development consultants is inherently and unapologetically political.

Central to our practice as Foucauldian-informed coach developers is the recognition that every coaching context and every coach's learning needs are unique. Accordingly, we begin any collaboration with a coach by situating ourselves in his or her coaching context for an extended period of time. This allows us to notice the multiple relations of power that have formed around his or her coaching context, including the dominant discourses being enacted, how they get translated into practice and the effects they appear to be having. During this time we also meet regularly with our coach to discuss with him or her how thinking with Foucault could be a catalyst to problematize the many effects of anatomo-political power. Through these meetings we introduce our coach to a number of key Foucauldian concepts such as discipline, power, discourse and docility. It is in this way that we are able to bring to a coach's attention any number of unforeseen or taken-for-granted consequences or problems that might be resulting from how he or she is exercising his or her power.

A further way we try to help our coach begin to imagine what it might actually look like for him or her to coach in a less disciplinary way is through various 'what if scenarios'. For example, we might ask him or her what would it mean to question the power of the sport sciences to construct so-called 'best coaching practices'? Or what would it mean to stop using various techniques designed to observe, monitor and survey athletes' bodies? Or what would it mean to reconfigure how he or she partitions and encloses athletes in their training spaces? Or what would it mean to use movement progressions that are not so linear and technocratic? In other words, through these scenarios, we are attempting to illustrate to our coach how to destabilize the power of various disciplinary techniques and instruments that have been shown to make athletes docile.

One challenge we typically face in our work with coaches is being careful not to apply Foucault's analysis of anatomo-politics in a truncated or superficial way. For example, when suggesting to a coach that he or she reduce some of the techniques he or she uses to categorize and group his or her athletes, it is important that we keep in mind how disciplinary techniques for Foucault (1995), such as the organization of genesis in this case, operate through the deployment of discipline's instruments. In other words, with any Foucauldian-inspired practice we develop we always try to situate it within Foucault's broader theoretical framework of power/knowledge. At the same time, we recognize that we cannot expect a coach we are working with to engage wholly with every aspect of Foucault's analysis of anatomo-politics given the depth and complexity of Foucault's thinking. That is why we often suggest to a coach that he or she first try to change something very small about his or her coaching based on a specific Foucauldian concept. For example, he or she could reduce the number of workouts that he or she uses to rank or examine his or her athletes. Or he or she could reduce some of his or her 'normal' surveillance practices. Or he or she could reduce his or her use of fixed timetables and schedules. In other words, and as we have previously shown (Denison and Mills, 2014), there are many ways for a coach to think with Foucault to develop less disciplinary coaching practices. However, exactly what those practices might be for a particular coach is impossible for us to know before we situate ourselves in his or her coaching context. Again, this points to the nature of a Foucauldian-inspired project, whereby problematization, reflection and change can only be considered within the context of particular power relations (Foucault, 1978).

Thus, rather than trying to impose a new best coaching or training practice on a coach, our aim as Foucauldian-informed coach developers is to help coaches become more aware of the impact of some of their practices: an awareness that is likely to provide them with a number of different positions from which to operate. And it is from these multiple positions, and with multiple knowledges, that we believe coaches might begin to practice more fluidly and as a result develop new understandings of what it means to coach. It is in this way, therefore, that power's many taken-for-granted effects can be continually and constantly challenged.

Importantly, at all times during our work with any coach we are always very careful not to ignore his or her responsibilities to prepare his or her athletes to be competitive. Similarly, we are careful to keep in mind how the demands and priorities a coach faces are likely to vary over the course of our time working together. It might be possible for a coach to implement certain Foucauldian-inspired practices at one point during our collaboration that might be inappropriate at a different point in time. For example, early in the season we have found that coaches are much more open and willing to experiment with some of our suggestions. Whereas, in the heat of the competitive season, we have noticed, many coaches become reticent to try something new. Therefore, in order to forge a successful collaboration with a coach, and in accordance with our Foucauldian ethics, it is critical that we do not act in a way that undermines or disregards all that a coach knows and understands about coaching. To use our power ethically as Foucauldian-informed coach developers it is important that we respect the multiple meanings and experiences, including most importantly the different relations of power, present in and around a coach's coaching context. And to help us develop an awareness and appreciation for these meanings we utilize two primary strategies: observations and conversations.

When observing a coach we are working with we pay close attention to how he or she incorporates our Foucauldian-inspired suggestions into the flow of his or her everyday practices, including how he or she talks to his or her athletes about what these new practices mean. This allows us to determine the practicality, relevance and effectiveness of these practices to help our coach learn how to coach in a less disciplinary way. Through these observations we can also begin to understand how our coach's athletes might be responding to these new practices. For example, are they perceiving any differently their limits or potential? Are they beginning to view their coach differently or understand their involvement in sport in new ways? Similarly, are these new practices changing in any way the role of our coach? Is his or her effectiveness beginning to be understood differently? Are his or her motives for coaching changing at all? For example, perhaps he or she is beginning to question his or her role as an agent of normalization. What we also look for during our observations is whether any of the new practices we have suggested are having any unintended consequences. And in the case that they are, we always use this opportunity to discuss with our coach the importance of problematization as an ongoing and continuous coaching skill.

Of course observations on their own are never enough to fully understand the complex flow of meanings in and around any context, which is why having regular conversations with our coach is so important. Specifically, these conversations allow us to explore as well as ascertain any challenges our coach might be experiencing as he or she attempts to coach in a less disciplinary way. For example, there could be some coaching practices that he or she feels compelled to follow despite recognizing how they could contribute to athlete docility. Or he or she might be finding it difficult to convince his or her athletes to adopt certain practices because they seem strange or unconventional. Or perhaps he or she is beginning to feel that our presence could be influencing various relations of power affecting his or her ability to coach differently. In other words, through these conversations we can begin to assess whether our coach has been subjected to any panoptic structures of surveillance built into the routines of his or her everyday coaching existence that might be making it difficult for him or her to coach differently. And knowing this is critical to our work because we are not simply trying to change the coach we are working with; we are also trying to expose and change the many unseen effects of anatomo-political power that could be influencing the possibilities that a coach has to coach differently.

Conclusion

As we have tried to emphasize in this chapter, coaches' experiences are never pure or true but are instead shaped and informed through a range of power/knowledge relations that often privilege certain practices, pedagogies or perspectives, even if they are ineffective, while at the same time obscuring or marginalizing other approaches to coaching that in fact might be more beneficial. In this way, coaching can easily be conceptualized as unproblematic and made up of a sequence of fixed and supposedly known steps as opposed to being what it truly is: a dynamic, fluid and social process. Accordingly, central to our work as Foucauldian-informed coach development consultants is to expose and reveal the many problematic assumptions behind coaches' 'normal' understandings of 'how to coach'.

Markula and Martin (2007) argued similarly when they discussed that problems in coaching are often to do with relationships, ethics and specific contextual circumstances that cannot be approached with a fixed set of problem-solving strategies; decision making for coaches rarely arises following a logical and rational diagnosis where the coach draws on his or her long-term memory and a set of universal cognitive rules, as experts in more discrete domains like chess, mathematics or music might. In this regard, effective coaching is less about the accumulation of experience and more about the quality of reflection that a coach can bring to his or her experiences (Cushion, 2016).

Importantly, we believe that truly exceptional sport performances are unlikely to become more frequent if coaches' practices remain routine and method-bound and athletes' needs are fitted into preconceived systems, solutions and models formed around a range of disciplinary techniques and instruments. Becoming an effective high-performance coach should not be seen as a stage of development or a point to reach after a set period of time, or following a number of specific experiences, even if those experiences include completing a formal coaching certificate or coaching degree or coaching an Olympic gold medallist or a world championship team. Rather, becoming an effective coach should be a never-ending process of learning, discovery and self-transformation (Denison and Avner, 2011). Thus, like Markula (2011), who turned to Foucault to problematize a number of dominant fitness knowledges in order to transform fitness instructors' practices and the making of 'docile fitness bodies', we do not believe that athletes are doomed forever to be made docile by their coaches' everyday disciplinary training practices. Instead, by thinking with Foucault we believe coaches can begin to develop high-performance athletes and teams whose winning performances are not only their optimal performances but whose experiences in sport are more positive, ethical and healthy, an outcome that has the possibility of reversing the many negative effects that a commitment to high-performance sport has been shown to have on athletes' bodies, lives and futures. However, such an outcome is unlikely to occur until scholars see the value of developing theoretically informed practices that have the power to foster impactful change. Through a physical cultural studies framework we have attempted to forge such a direction in our work as Foucauldian-informed coach development consultants. And we can only hope that this is just the beginning of a physical culture studies that can serve a strong theory- and practice-based change agenda for high-performance sport.

References

Barker-Ruchti, N. and Tinning, R. (2010). Foucault in leotards: corporeal discipline in women's artistic gymnastics. *Sociology of Sport Journal*, 27, 229–250.
Bush, A., Silk, M., Andrews, D. and Lauder, H. (2013). *Sports coaching research: context, consequences and consciousness*. New York, NY: Routledge.
Cushion, C. (2016). Reflection and reflective practice discourses in coaching: a critical analysis. *Sport, Education and Society*, doi: 10.1080/13573322.2016.1142961.
Denison, J. (2007). Social theory for coaches: a Foucauldian reading of one athlete's poor performance. *International Journal of Sports Science and Coaching*, 2, 369–383.
Denison, J. and Avner, Z. (2011). Positive coaching: ethical practices for athlete development. *Quest*, 63, 209–227.
Denison, J. and Mills, J. P. (2014). Planning for distance running: coaching with Foucault. *Sports Coaching Review*, 3, 1–16.
Denison, J., Mills, J. P. and Jones, L. (2013). Effective coaching as a modernist formation. In P. Potrac, W. Gilbert and J. Denison (eds), *Routledge Handbook of Sports Coaching* (pp. 133–145). Abingdon: Routledge.
Denison, J., Mills, J. P. and Konoval, T. (2015). Sports' disciplinary legacy and the challenge of 'coaching differently'. *Sport, Education and Society*, doi: 10.1080/13573322.2015.1061986.
Denison, J., Pringle, R., Cassidy, T. and Hessian, P. (2015). Informing coaches' practices: towards an application of Foucault's ethics. *International Sport Coaching Journal*, 2, 72–76.
Foucault, M. (1978). *The history of sexuality, volume 1: an introduction*. New York: Random House.
Foucault, M. (1983). Power and truth. In H. L. Dreyfus and P. Rabinow (eds), *Michel Foucault: Beyond Structuralism and Hermeneutics*, 2nd edn (pp. 184–204). New York: Pantheon Books.
Foucault, M. (1994). The ethics of the concern of the self as a practice of freedom. In P. Rabinow (ed.), *Michel Foucault Ethics: The Essential Works 1* (pp. 281–301). London: Penguin Press.
Foucault, M. (1995). *Discipline and punish: the birth of the prison*. New York: Vintage Books.
Gearity, B. and Mills, J. P. (2012). Discipline and punish in the weights room. *Sports Coaching Review*, 1, 124–134.
Jones, L. and Denison, J. (2016). Immediate experiences of retirement in British professional and semi-professional football: the docile body in retirement. *The International Review for the Sociology of Sport*, doi: 10.1177/1012690215625348.
Jones, R. L. and Standage, M. (2006). First among equals: shared leadership in the coaching context. In R. L. Jones (ed.), *The Sports Coach as Educator: Re-Conceptualizing Sports Coaching* (pp. 65–76). London: Routledge.
Kidman, L. (2001). *Developing decision makers: an empowerment approach to coaching*. Christchurch, New Zealand: Innovative Communications.
Markula, P. (2011). Folding: a feminist intervention in mindful fitness. In E. Kennedy and P. Markula (eds), *Women and Exercise: The Body, Health and Consumerism* (pp. 60–78). New York: Routledge.
Markula, P. and Martin, M. (2007). Ethical coaching: gaining respect in the field. In J. Denison (ed.), *Coaching Knowledges: Understanding The Dynamics of Sport Performance* (pp. 51–82). Oxford: A. & C. Black.
Miller, P. S. and Kerr, G. A. (2002). Conceptualizing excellence: past, present, and future. *Journal of Applied Sport Psychology*, 14, 140–153.
Mills, J. P. and Denison, J. (2013). Coach Foucault: problematizing endurance running coaches' practices. *Sports Coach Review*, 2, 136–150.
Noakes, T. (2005). *Lore of running*, 3rd edn. Champaign, IL: Human Kinetics.
Shogan, D. (1999). *The making of high-performance athletes: discipline, diversity and ethics*. Toronto: University of Toronto Press.
Williams, S. and Manley, A. (2014). Elite coaching and the technocratic engineer: thanking the boys at Microsoft! *Sport, Education and Society*, 21, 828–850.

PART III
Subjectified bodies

12
CLASSED BODIES

Alan Bairner

Introduction: Why class?

In 2014, at a conference in Wuhan in China's Hubei Province where I gave a keynote lecture in sport and class in the United Kingdom, I was asked by a member of the audience what sports the British peasants play. It was a salutary reminder that our understanding of the concept of social class varies dramatically from place to place and from one era to another. Yet, the ways in which we use our bodies, not least when we play, watch and administer sport, are closely interwoven with social class through both time and space. This has been particularly true in Britain, where Karl Marx produced much of his influential analysis of class relations in nineteenth-century capitalist societies and modern sport was born. As Selina Todd (2015: 1) observes, 'Class has united and divided Britain since the Industrial Revolution.'

This chapter examines the relationships between sport, physical activity and class in Britain, with a specific focus on the Olympic Games and cricket, and the sociological theories that arguably best help us to understand these relationships. Although the emphasis is on sport, some consideration is also given to the wider social context in which bodies fulfil a range of classed functions. It is hoped that the chapter, written by a critical friend, can contribute to the development of physical cultural studies as a fluid sensibility towards scholarship on physical culture which incorporates a divergent range of theoretical perspectives in which the concept of class has a place, albeit not as sole determining factor.

According to Marx and Engels (1967: 79), writing in 1848, 'The history of all hitherto existing society is the history of class struggles.' Bourgeois society had 'established new classes, new conditions of oppression, new forms of struggle in place of the old ones' (ibid.: 80). Society as a whole, they claimed, 'is more and more splitting up into two great hostile camps, into two great classes directly facing each other: Bourgeoisie and Proletariat' (ibid.: 80). In addition, 'Of all the classes that stand face to face with the bourgeoisie today, the proletariat alone is a really revolutionary class' (ibid.: 91). It is worth noting that Marx recognized the presence of other classes in nineteenth-century capitalist societies. He chose to focus his attention, however, on what he regarded as the two largest blocs.

As a consequence of the apparent determinism of Marx's analysis, many followers have spent years apologizing for, or seeking to qualify, what were once their cherished beliefs. However, to those critics who view Marxism as nothing more than a crude form of economic reductionism, one could simply go on the offensive, accept that Marxism does reduce everything to economics and argue that there is nothing at all wrong with such an approach. My own inclination, as stated elsewhere, is to take a rather more cautious approach accepting that we should not ignore the importance of factors other than those that are essentially economic but insisting nevertheless that the economic realm and, in particular, social class remain of foremost significance (Bairner, 2007).

According to Boyne (2002: 121), 'Class appears to be less unrecognizably determinant of social action now than was the case just a quarter of a century ago.' It is certainly undeniable that 'it has long been fashionable to claim that conventional class analysis, Marxian or otherwise, is somehow deficient and in need of revision' (Grusky and Sørensen, 1998: 1187), and I agree with Standing (2014: 963) that 'understanding twenty-first century developments is surely easier if we see a more nuanced structure than the old Marxist dualism of capitalist (bourgeoisie) and proletariat'. What has not disappeared, however, is the significance of class as a broader concept as Standing's own work (2011) on 'the precariat' demonstrates – hence, the need for a more nuanced approach that does not equate class solely with one's position in the productive process. For example, as Sørensen (2000: 1553) suggests, 'Class as life conditions is a very useful concept for analyses of how patterns of attitudes, behaviors, and socialization vary by location in social structure.' In relation to sport and physical activity more generally, it is worth noting that, for the pioneering exponents of cultural studies, 'culture is neither an autonomous nor an externally determined field, but a site of social differences and struggle' (Johnson, 1986: 39). As for physical cultural studies (PCS), according to Silk and Andrews (2011: 10), its practice 'assumes that societies are fundamentally divided along hierarchically ordered lines of differentiation (i.e. those based on class, ethnic, gender, ability, generational, national, racial, and/or sexual norms), as realized through the operations of power and power relations within the social formation'.

The industrial proletariat described by Marx is a threatened species, at least in Western societies, where heavy manual labour is increasingly a thing of the past. In addition, because most adults can be described as workers in terms of their precise relationship to the means of production, Marx's original understanding of the idea of a working class inevitably becomes less tenable. Nevertheless, classes remain in the UK, arguably to a greater extent than in most northern and western European countries. Furthermore, in line with the concept of 'class as life conditions', they continue to exert a considerable influence not only on working bodies but also on sporting bodies, even those of participants who are not paid to play. Arguably the most important theorist in terms of teasing out this relationship was the French sociologist, Pierre Bourdieu.

Bourdieu and the embodiment of class

How Marxist was Bourdieu (Potter, 2000)? It has been suggested that a Bourdieusian analysis, identifies class as 'a shorthand term for roughly similar positions within a distribution of capitals, as opposed to referring to a set of causal or generative processes or relations, as has been a key feature of European class theory' (Flemmen, 2013: 333). This discussion has become further entangled with another conflict of opinions concerned with the extent to which Bourdieu was or was not a genuine voice of resistance. According to Ohl (2000: 147), while he was inspired by both Weber and Marx in his conceptualization of social classes, 'Bourdieu's construction of social space constitutes a break with Marxist theory'. Wolfreys suggested that the death of Pierre Bourdieu was a setback for the left both in France and internationally ... Bourdieu dismissed Marx's emphasis on workers' ability to consciously take control of their lives through the lived experience of class conflict as both voluntaristic, placing too much reliance on subjective consciousness, and deterministic, anticipating the 'maturing' of objective conditions.

(Wolfreys, 2002: 1–2)

This perspective is in line with a variety of critiques or, perhaps one should call them, reworkings of Marx's ideas that emphasize the need to escape from false dichotomies.

In an important study, Bourdieu (2004) discussed the relationship between the peasant and his body. His definition of the ways in which people behave at a village dance are specifically focused on French peasants, but they have more general implications. According to Bourdieu (ibid.: 584), one's 'bearing' [*tenue*] is immediately perceived by others, and especially by the girls, as a symbol of one's economic and social standing. 'Bodily *hexis*', he goes on, 'is above all a social *signum*.' Elsewhere, with specific reference to leisure activities, Bourdieu (1978: 823) argues that 'the bodily exercises of the "elite" are disconnected from the ordinary social occasions with which folk games remained associated (agrarian feasts, for example) and divested of the social (and, *a fortiori*, religious) functions still attached to a number of traditional games (such as ritual games played in a number of pre-capitalist societies at certain turning-points in the farming year)'. In addition, 'among the working classes, the abandonment of sport, an activity whose play-like character seems to make it particularly appropriate to adolescence, often coincides with marriage and entry into the serious responsibilities of adulthood'. Although the two developments described here have very different outcomes, it is clear that for Bourdieu, social class is the key explanatory factor for both.

For Bourdieu (1978: 826), 'the field of sporting practices is the site of struggles in which what is at stake, inter alia, is the monopolistic capacity to impose the legitimate definition of sporting practice and of the legitimate function of sporting activity'. With this in mind, he considers particular *classes* of body users, the term class now assigned a different but closely related meaning. Thus, 'the practice of sports such as tennis, riding, sailing or golf owes part of its "interest" to its distinguishing function and, more precisely, to the *gains in distinction* which it brings' (ibid.: 828). What was true in 1978 largely remains true today. As Bourdieu argues:

> the logic whereby agents incline towards this or that sporting practice cannot be understood unless their dispositions towards sport, which are themselves one dimension of a *particular relation to the body*, are reinserted into the unity of the system of dispositions, the habitus, which is the basis from which life-styles are generated.
>
> *(Bourdieu, 1978: 833)*

In sum, 'class habitus defines the meaning conferred on sporting activity' (ibid.: 835).

According to Rahkonen (1999: 16), although Bourdieu discusses class in many of his studies, 'he is more interested in elaborating relationships of domination or power than developing any class theory proper'. Nevertheless, it is undeniable that Bourdieu placed considerable emphasis on class, or more specifically, on what he described as class habitus. What becomes apparent here is that he saw his understanding of class as superseding that of Marx and the orthodox Marxist tradition. Thus, he suggested that 'the individuals grouped in a class that is constructed in a particular respect (that is, in a particularly determinant respect) always bring with them, in addition to the pertinent properties by which they are classified, secondary properties which are thus smuggled into the explanatory model' (Bourdieu, 1984: 102). According to Bourdieu, this means that a class or class fraction is defined not only by its position in the relations of production, as identified through indices such as occupation, income or even educational level, but also by numerous other factors. It is this apparently more nuanced approach to class, identifying other forms of capital than the solely economic and regarding habitus as only partially determined by one's economic position, that helps to explain Bourdieu's appeal for researchers looking at the relationship between sport, the body and class. Whether or not Bourdieu does in fact take us beyond Marxism's understanding of class, however, is best discussed by reference to studies which have sought to employ Bourdieu.

Using Bourdieu

An interesting example of the ways in which Bourdieu's work has been used in relation to physical cultures is provided by Stephanie Foote (2003) in her study of the manner in which Tonya Harding has been mediated in relation to identity and class. Foote (ibid.: 5) demonstrates effectively how 'Tonya's perceived loyalties and disloyalties to specific class styles and scripts became identified as a specific kind of improper – and therefore irreducibly – working-class identity'. In so doing, however, building upon Bourdieu, Foote seeks to replace class as a matter of economics with class as lifestyle. Thus, she concludes that class is 'a disposition that references a complex relationship to the world, a relationship that assigns cultural and personal values as it assigns economic values' (ibid.: 15). Given her background, Harding was exceptional. Having achieved success in her chosen sport, how she behaved is certainly a matter of interest. More arresting, however, is the fact that so few Tonya Hardings ever grace the ice rinks, the equestrian arenas or ballet schools of the world. The reasons for this will be discussed later in the chapter.

White and Wilson (1999) employ Bourdieu's concept of habitus in their study of the relationship between socioeconomic status and sport spectatorship in Canada. They note that 'the sociology of sport literature has consistently shown that social status is a positive predictor of sport involvement' (ibid.: 246) and that, with regard to sports spectatorship, 'existing research points to marked inequalities in attendance by income' (ibid.: 249). They add that, with regard to professional sport spectatorship, 'for both sexes, income was a stronger predictor than education, region, age, and language, suggesting that financial status is a powerful determinant of the ability to attend professional sport events in Canada' (ibid.: 260).

Collins and Buller (2003) also invoke the name of Bourdieu to counter arguments that social class has lost its saliency in the postmodern world. However, their analysis of social exclusion from high performance sport leads them to conclude that 'young people brought up in areas of social need are not being provided with sufficient support to enable them equal opportunities to perform at the highest level; they are not developing sufficient of Bourdieu's personal social capital' (ibid.: 438). As with White and Wilson's (1999) study, it would appear that the other forms of capital which Bourdieu highlighted are in fact secondary to and determined in the final analysis by economic capital. However, the cultural capital that can accrue from this is an essential component of class analysis in relation to access to sport.

Indeed, much that has been written about sport in this respect can also be applied more generally to physical activity and exercise. As Engström (2008: 324) notes, 'There is no doubt that in the Western World exercise is a social marker since a lifestyle that includes exercise signals a certain *cultural capital* that is both recognized by social groups and assigned a value.' It is further claimed that 'An individual's sport habitus is formed on the basis of their experience of different sporting activities undertaken in their leisure time and at school' (ibid.: 337). It is important to recognize, however, that leisure time itself and also the type of schooling that people receive, while instrumental in producing cultural capital, are ultimately the result of economic capital and, therefore, closely linked to an individual's social class. As Fitz et al. (2006: 10), remind us, 'class conditions, demands and interests lie at the centre of educational policy'. This is not to deny the importance of other categories of social exclusion. Indeed, as Evans (2004: 102) points out, class-based inequalities are 'compounded by other social characteristics, such as race, ethnicity, dis/ability, age, geography and sexuality that define people's lives'. Evans's point, however, is that class not only determines choice and preference in relation to sport and other forms of physical activity, 'it also determines a person's physical capacity, "their ability" to realize those choices and preferences, let alone extend them' (ibid.: 102). Furthermore, 'In health, as in PE and sport, being "middle class" offers massive advantages if your goal is either to achieve healthy longevity or perform in top level sport' (Evans and Bairner, 2012: 144). It is worth adding the caveat that these assertions are rooted in an analysis of British society and that, even there, in relation to top level sport, exceptions such as association football and boxing do exist. In the case of most Olympic sports, however, the general point is well made.

Sport and social class in Britain: an Olympic overview

On the day that Team GB's first gold medals of the 2012 London Olympic Games were awarded to two privately educated female rowers, Lord Moynihan, the chairman of the British Olympic Committee, announced that one of the worst statistics in British sport was that over 50 per cent of the UK's medallists in Beijing (at the 2008 Olympic Games) had come from independent schools. This meant that half the medals won came from just 7 per cent of the children in the UK. However, according to a defender of the contribution of private schools to British sport, not only are the figures cited by Moynihan exaggerated, they actually point to the failings of state schools in relation to sporting achievement rather than providing a critique of private schools or of contemporary British society more generally (Tozer, 2013).

In many respects, the emergence of modern sport in the United Kingdom was the consequence of what might be described as a grass-roots, or bottom-up, movement. Primitive forms of football had been played for centuries and rudimentary forms of cricket existed long before the sport was given formal rules. However, Marxist-informed analysis of the development of sport in Britain led to recognition of the central importance of class in terms of the exercise of bourgeois hegemonic power (Hargreaves, 1986; Jones, 1986, 1988). As Hargreaves (1986: 205) suggested, 'The successful achievement of bourgeois hegemony within the power bloc, as such, in the mid-Victorian period was signalled, notably, by the ascendancy of the ideology of gentlemanly amateurism.'

Thus, it was the private (or independent schools) such as Rugby and Eton College which played the major role in the process whereby traditional games were transformed into sports as we now know them. Furthermore, schools continued to play a major role in the development of British sporting talent well into the late twentieth century. This necessitated considerable reliance on the goodwill of school teachers, not necessarily trained in physical education, to make the UK a sporting country, since schools were where most children were first introduced to sport.

This approach to nurturing young sporting talent began to run into difficulties when, in the early 1990s, many teachers in the public sector (i.e. the sector in which state schools are located) legitimately refused to work additional hours in the evenings and at weekends to look after sports teams, a role for which most of them remained unqualified. In addition, school playing fields began to be sold off for housing developments by local authorities which had initially paid for them but could no longer afford to maintain their upkeep, a practice that has continued to the present day (reportedly three every week since the election of the Coalition Government in 2010). In such circumstances, it is not surprising that it is the independent schools, with their own facilities, better paid and better resourced teachers, and qualified coaches, that produce a disproportionate number of elite performers in numerous sports, albeit with the glaring exception of association football, in which the overwhelming majority of British-born players can be identified as working class.

In response to these developments, School Sport Partnerships (abbreviated as SSPs) were introduced in 2002 as part of a wider strategy by the previous Labour Government. From 2006, all schools in England were part of an SSP which was a family of secondary, primary and special schools working together to increase the quality and quantity of PE and sports opportunities for young people. In October 2010, the Department of Education informed the Youth Sport Trust, the relevant non-governmental agency which guaranteed funding for SSPs, would not be continued after March 2011 as part of a broader cost-cutting exercise which has been the present government's response to economic recession.

Thus, in the UK, as one education policy researcher has noted, 'after 13 years of New Labour control and investment in the school sport and physical education (PE) landscape, the election of the new coalition government in 2010 brought with it the potential for considerable change in the sector' (Mackintosh, 2014: 432). Among the most prominent changes was the dismantling of the SSP scheme which had achieved much in terms of ensuring that state school pupils were given opportunities to play sport. Arguably they may have played a part in recent British sporting successes particularly at the 2014 Commonwealth Games where several young athletes shone, notably English sprinters, male and female. Without schemes of this type, it is almost certain that the UK will become even more reliant for Olympic medal success on the products of private schools.

The hopes and expectations surrounding the 2012 London Olympics are now best approached in relation to the slippery concept of legacy, which embraces such diverse objectives as future sporting success, urban regeneration, employment opportunities, environmental sustainability and the emergence of a more physically active population. One hope was that young people would be inspired by the Games to take up sport. But how could that happen if schools could no longer provide the opportunities that had been made possible by the SSPs? As one commentator pronounced on the legacy of London 2012, 'Far from turning us into a sporting nation, we are danger of turning into a two tier one' (Gibson, 2015). Even in sports such as cycling and athletics, which should be accessible by almost anyone, 'the main growth is coming from those who have the time, the money and the opportunity to buy the kit, enter mass participation events and buy the expensive GPS sports watch' (ibid.). Moreover, despite the best efforts of those who are paid to identify potential athletic talent, people are not simply born to row or to sail any more than they are to box. They are taught to do so and, in the process, their bodies acquire different degrees of cultural habitus. In British sport, this has long been particularly apparent in cricket.

Cricket and social class in Britain

With reference to cricket in England during the 1920s and 1930s, Williams (1999: 114) writes, 'Few other cultural institutions can have made so clear the inequalities of economic status and social background or demonstrated to individuals their place in the social hierarchy.' This was particularly evident in the formal distinction between amateurs who belonged to a variety of elements of the middle and upper classes and professionals who played cricket for living. This was given even greater resonance through the use of the terms Gentlemen and Players to describe the two factions. As Williams (ibid.: 117) records, 'At most county grounds amateurs had separate changing rooms from professionals, though sometimes the amateurs from both sides shared the same dressing rooms.' Furthermore, 'the defence of amateur authority within county cricket by those with privileged backgrounds was related to their assumptions about the nature of social relations' (ibid.: 123). Describing amateur captains, Birley (1999: 254–255) comments, 'as a species they had too much power for their own good: over their humble professionals, over the umpires and over their committees'.

In terms of the body habitus of professional cricketers, there was a widespread tendency to see fast bowlers as the sporting equivalents of manual labourers. As former Somerset and England batsman Peter Roebuck (cited by Chalke, 2007: 8) commented on England bowler Tom Cartwright, a man with impeccable working-class credentials and socialist principles, 'He was a workingman, a proud working man, and he wanted to do his work. He wasn't lazy; he wanted to bowl his overs.' Cartwright himself observed, 'Bowling is bloody hard work' (cited by Chalke, ibid.). Among the most celebrated working-class bowlers were Harold Larwood and Bill Voce, both of whom grew up in the Nottinghamshire coalfield. Indeed, Larwood began working in the mines at the age of 14. Much of their subsequent renown can be traced to the infamous 'Bodyline' tour of Australia by the English cricket team in 1932–1933 when the patrician captain, Douglas Jardine (educated privately at Winchester College), deployed the two bowlers to carry out his leg theory, which resulted in injuries to opposing players and prompted the Australian captain Bill Woodfull to claim, 'There are two teams out there. One is playing cricket and the other is not' (Birley, 1999: 236).

Even in the post-Second World War era, fast bowlers of working-class origin, among them Freddie Trueman of Yorkshire and Brian Statham of Lancashire continued to represent a potent muscular force. Meanwhile, privately educated batsmen/captains were often still the order of the day – Peter May (educated at Charterhouse and Cambridge University), Colin Cowdrey (Tonbridge School and Oxford University), Ted Dexter (born in Milan and educated at Radley College and Cambridge University), Mike Brearley (City of London School and Cambridge University), and David Gower (King's School Canterbury and University College London). With the ending of the amateur–player divide, however, things undeniably changed. Fast bowler John Snow received part of his education at Christ's Hospital and, more recently, Chris Broad attended Oakham School. In addition, several post-war England captains have not only been bowlers but also state-educated. It is worth noting, nevertheless, that two of the three most recent test captains, Andrew Strauss (Radley and Durham University) and Alastair Cook (Bedford School), received an English public school education, and the third, Kevin Pietersen, was educated privately at Maritzburg College in his native South Africa.

Williams (1999) is largely sanguine about the class divide in English cricket even as it manifested itself in the inter-war years. He writes that 'A sense of class as an expression of fierce class antagonisms does not seem to have been the dominant narrative of social relations in first-class cricket' (ibid.: 131). Yet Marqusee (1994: 134) confidently asserts that 'Cricket today is disproportionately upper-class'. To that extent it can be compared with the Great Britain Olympic team and, in both cases, body habitus coexists alongside economic and cultural capital as determining factors.

Conclusion

I am somewhat sceptical about the relatively inclusive character of English cricket that Williams proposes. Indeed, although most governing bodies in the UK claim that opportunities do exist for young people from all social backgrounds to try their sports, cultural as well as financial barriers regularly stand in the way. However, according to exponents of PCS, 'the cultures of the body are neither *necessarily correspondent* to the overdetermining structural realm … nor *necessarily noncorrespondent*' (Giardina and Newman, 2011: 40). Thus, cultural capital and body habitus in and of themselves are also factors that help to explain why some sports are associated with the lower classes (Wilson, 2002). By further aiding such explanation, PCS makes its contribution to the development of a more nuanced understanding of the interplay between social class and body movement.

It is not impossible for people from subordinate classes to be accepted, to a degree, by those involved in, what are usually regarded, as elitist sports. Writing about his own youthful goal to be a member of a private golf club, Bradley S. Klein (2013: 151) writes, that this was 'More like a yearning, actually, one that I can link back to the feeling I had as a teenage caddie at Woodmere Club, when I marveled at the apparent ease with which these wealthy, comfortable, and well-dressed people all fit in so well with one another.' Klein suggests that 'The whole point of such an indulgence fantasy is to meet some need or fill up some emotional void. It's a feeling that was all tied up with simply wanting to belong and to be part of a place' (ibid.: 151).

Perhaps my father also felt such a need when, on his return from service in the Second World War, he found himself living in an unfamiliar Scottish town. He was working class, having served an apprenticeship before the war as a golf club maker in his native St Andrews. Growing up in that town had given him the opportunity to learn to play golf in a relatively democratic environment compared with the sport's reputation in most other parts of the world. When he arrived in Kirkcaldy, he was a two-handicap player and found himself in demand as a playing partner by the members of the local business and professional elite. Did this experience fill an emotional void? I doubt it very much. He belonged when he was on the course, but he was never fully integrated into the wider social life of the lawyers, the bankers and the entrepreneurs with and against whom he played. His sporting ability was never quite enough. Experiences of this sort may well help to explain why most people do not even try to enter into the classed world of other people's sports and pastimes.

References

Bairner, A. 2007. Back to basics: class, social theory and sport. *Sociology of Sport Journal*, 24 (1), 20–36.
Birley, D. 1999. *A social history of English cricket*. London: Aurum Press.
Bourdieu, P. 1978. Sport and social class. *Social Science Information*, 17 (6), 819–840.
Bourdieu, P. 1984. *Distinction: a social critique of the judgement of taste*. London: Routledge and Kegan Paul.
Bourdieu, P. 2004. The peasant and his body. *Ethnography*, 5 (4), 579–599.
Boyne, R. 2002. Bourdieu: from class to culture. *In memoriam* Pierre Bourdieu 1930–2002. *Theory, Culture and Society*, 19 (3), 117–128.
Chalke, S. 2007. *Tom Cartwright: the flame still burns*. Bath: Fairfield Books.
Collins, M. F. and Buller, J. R. 2003. Social exclusion from high performance sport: are all talented young sports people given an equal opportunity of reaching the Olympic podium? *Journal of Sport and Social Issues*, 27 (4), 420–442.
Engström, L. M. 2008. Who is physically active? Cultural capital and sports participation from adolescence to middle-age – a 38-year follow-up study. *Physical Education and Sport Pedagogy*, 13 (4): 319–343.
Evans, J. 2004. Making a difference? Education and 'ability' in physical education. *European Physical Education Review*, 10 (1), 95–108.
Evans, J. and Bairner, A. 2012. Physical education and social class. In G. Stidder and S. Hayes (eds), *Equity and inclusion in physical education and sport*, 2nd edn. London: Routledge, 141–158.
Fitz, J., Davies, B. and Evans, J. 2006. *Educational policy and social reproduction: class inscription and symbolic control*. London: Routledge.

Flemmen, M. 2013. Putting Bourdieu to work for class analysis: reflections on some recent contributions. *British Journal of Sociology*, 64 (2), 325–343.

Foote, S. 2003. Making sport of Tonya. *Journal of Sport and Social Issues*, 27 (1): 3–17.

Giardina, M. D. and Newman, J. L. 2011. What is this 'physical' in physical cultural studies? *Sociology of Sport Journal*, 28 (1), 36–63.

Gibson, O. 2015. Golden promises of London 2012's legacy turn out to be idle boasts. *The Guardian*, 25 March. Available from www.theguardian.com/uk-news/blog/2015/mar/25/olympic-legacy-london-2012-idle-boasts (accessed 30 March 2015).

Grusky, D. B. and Sørensen, J. B. 1998. Can class analysis be salvaged? *American Journal of Sociology*, 103 (5), 1187–1234.

Hargreaves, J. 1986. *Sport, power and culture: a social and historical analysis of popular sports in Britain.* Cambridge: Polity Press.

Johnson, R. 1986. What is cultural studies anyway? *Social Text*, 16, Winter, 38–80.

Jones, S. G. 1986. *Workers at play: a social and economic history of leisure 1918–1939.* London: Routledge and Kegan Paul.

Jones, S. G. 1988. *Sport, politics and the working class: organised labour and sport in inter-war Britain.* Manchester: Manchester University Press.

Klein, B. S. 2013. *Wide open fairways: a journey across the landscapes of modern golf.* Lincoln, NE: University of Nebraska Press.

Mackintosh, C. 2014. Dismantling the school sport partnership infrastructure: findings from a survey of physical education and school sport practitioners. *Education 3–13: International Journal of Primary, Elementary and Early Years Education*, 42 (4), 432–447.

Marqusee, M. 1994. *Anyone but England: cricket and the national malaise.* London: Verso.

Marx, K and Engels, F. 1967. *The communist manifesto.* London: Penguin Books.

Ohl, F. 2000. Are social classes still relevant to analyse sports groupings in 'postmodern' society? An analysis referring to P. Bourdieu's theory. *Scandinavian Journal of Medicine and Science in Sports*, 10, 146–155.

Potter, G. 2000. For Bourdieu, against Alexander: reality and reduction. *Journal for the Theory of Social Behaviour*, 30 (2), 229–246.

Rahkonen, K. 1999. *Not class but struggle: critical ouvertures to Pierre Bourdieu's sociology.* Helsinki: Department of Social Policy, University of Helsinki.

Silk, M. L. and Andrews, D. L. 2011. Toward a physical cultural studies, *Sociology of Sport Journal*, 28 (1), 4–35.

Sørensen, A. B. 2000. Toward a Sounder Basis for Class Analysis. *American Journal of Sociology*, 105 (6): 1523–1558.

Standing, G. 2011. *The precariat: the dangerous new class.* London: Bloomsbury Academic.

Standing, G. 2014. Understanding the precariat through labour and work. *Development and Change*, 45 (5), 963–980.

Todd, S. 2015. *The people: the rise and fall of the working class.* London: John Murray.

Tozer, M. 2013. 'One of the worst statistics in British sport, and wholly unacceptable': the contribution of privately educated members of Team GB to the Summer Olympic Games, 2000–2012. *International Journal of the History of Sport*, 30 (12), 1436–1454.

White, P. and Wilson, B. 1999. Distinction in the stands: an investigation of Bourdieu's 'Habitus', socioeconomic status and sport spectatorship in Canada. *International Review for the Sociology of Sport*, 34 (3), 245–264.

Williams, J. 1999. *Cricket and England: a cultural and social history of the inter-war years.* London: Frank Cass.

Wilson, T. C. 2002. The paradox of social class and sports involvement. *International Review for the Sociology of Sport*, 37 (1), 5–16.

Wolfreys. J. 2002. Pierre Bourdieu: voice of resistance. *International Socialism Journal*, 94. Available from http://pubs.socialistreviewindex.org.uk/isj94/wolfreys.htm (accessed 16 August 2005).

13
RACED BODIES AND BLACK CULTURAL POLITICS

Ben Carrington

'I am America,' he once declared. 'I am the part you won't recognize. But get used to me – black, confident, cocky; my name, not yours; my religion, not yours; my goals, my own. Get used to me.' That's the Ali I came to know as I came of age – not just as skilled a poet on the mic as he was a fighter in the ring, but a man who fought for what was right. A man who fought for us. He stood with King and Mandela; stood up when it was hard; spoke out when others wouldn't. His fight outside the ring would cost him his title and his public standing. It would earn him enemies on the left and the right, make him reviled, and nearly send him to jail. But Ali stood his ground. And his victory helped us get used to the America we recognize today.
(*Statement from President Barack Obama on the death of Muhammad Ali, June 4, 2016*)

The muscles of the colonized are always tensed.
(*Frantz Fanon,* Les Damnés de la Terre, *1961*)

On June 3, 2016, the boxer Muhammad Ali died, aged 74. Ali's passing generated global news coverage, as many commentators declared the Louisville-born, former world heavyweight champion to have been not only the greatest boxer of all time, but perhaps the greatest athlete of all time. For once the hyperbole of the media seemed to be appropriate. A common theme in the ensuing media commentary suggested that part of Ali's historic significance was the fact that he had 'transcended' sport into the political realm. That sport had given Ali a platform and enabled him to take various political stands such as his pronouncements against racism and religious discrimination towards Muslims in the United States and elsewhere, and most famously his refusal to be drafted into the US army during what he called a 'Christian war' in Vietnam, a stand that eventually led to his three-year ban from boxing. While there is some truth to this narrative, in this chapter I want to challenge a common understanding of 'sport and politics' that underpins such accounts. Rather than arguing, as the mainstream media did, that Ali's legacy and contemporary importance was to show how athletes could transcend sports *into* politics, I want to argue instead that Ali's enduring achievement was in fact to reveal how sport was *already inherently political*. Sport, as an embodied form of culture that is delimited in various ways by time and space, is given its meaning and significance because it creates the conditions for expressive forms of physicality that dramatize very human struggles around movement, aesthetics and freedom. The structures of sports organizations and their rules and codes, the ethics and ethos of games including how they should be played, questions concerning participation and ownership, and so on, the factors in other words that turn a particular form of physical movement into 'sport', are always complexly reflective of and in tension with wider social forces and the social relations of production within society. Much ideological work has to occur, then, in order for this simple and clearly verifiable fact of sports' politics to be overlooked. Ali thus lifted the veil and debunked the notion that sport and politics were and ever could be separate spheres and why he became such a controversial figure in the 1960s and 1970s (Marqusee, 2005).

There is now an impressive body of work that focuses on the experiences, commodification, representations and racialized power relations of the physically active body (see, for example, Adair and Rowe, 2010; Andrews, 2001; Carrington, 2010; Douglas and Jamieson, 2006; Hylton, 2008; Ifekwunigwe, 2009; Joseph et al., 2012; Leonard and King, 2011; Schultz, 2016; Spencer, 2004; Van Sterkenburg et al., 2010). Collectively, these important studies have contributed to our understandings of the contingent and highly mediated systems of racialized power relations that are implicated in the affective orientations and material experiences of everyday (physical cultural) life. Drawing on this literature, this chapter examines the ways in which certain sporting bodies become racialized as a way to think about embodied forms of politics and black cultural politics in particular. The chapter shows that the performative aspects of black physicality are, in and of themselves, important sources and sites of scholarly enquiry. In this context, the assumed apolitical nature of sports may be a useful and instructive starting point for producing an account of black politics that goes beyond *texts* (too often narrowly defined as speeches, literatures, manifestos and laws) as the primary modality for understanding politics. Instead, I make an argument for centering performative and creative forms of embodiment as expressive *of* and a site *for* politics (Carrington, 2010). In other words, the chapter attempts to understand the inherently political nature of sports and to read the political back into the assumed apolitical. The chapter discusses how forms of movement and physicality, sometimes taking violent forms, and often channeled through sports like boxing, have historically constituted a modality of black cultural politics. I then examine arguments that suggest that the hyper-commercialization of sports, driven by global capitalistic logics, has led to the commodification and depoliticization of the sporting black body. The result, it is claimed, is that rather than black athleticism challenging white supremacist discourses and promoting a broader notion of freedom, contemporary post/colonial racisms reduce blackness to the biological and black life to the body, thus curtailing black emancipatory politics. The chapter then looks briefly at contemporary forms of sporting politics that have grounded questions of race and sport alongside social justice movements. It is suggested that we may be witnessing the revival of a more critically conscious era of black athletic protest, in which the sporting body – whether it be quietly and silently at rest or symbolically and literally in motion (Farred, 2014; Quashie, 2012) – may once again serve to disrupt the social order, and in so doing help to shape a broader politics of social critique and transformation.

Sport as embodied black politics

As the political theorist Michael Hanchard (2006) has argued, because black subjects have historically been denied access to the public sphere of Western liberal democracies – due to both formal and informal acts of exclusion – an alternative black public sphere was created by New World Blacks that has broadened orthodox understandings of what constitutes 'politics'. Black protest and resistance have therefore called into question the oftentimes narrow definitions of politics, revealing how the seemingly inarguable distinctions between the political and the non-political are themselves political constructs, shaped in such a way as to favor the activities and interests of white, propertied elite males over others. Due to this exclusion, black politics has always had to find expression within those domains of civic life and cultural practices that have typically been categorized frivolous and marginal, that is to say, as 'non-political'. As Richard Iton notes, discussing the era when the Civil Rights movement had won legislative change concerning political representation:

> at the same time that blacks markedly increased their access to the arenas of formal political decision-making, and despite expectations that legalistic triumphs would orient most political energies toward these arenas, informal politics has continued to play a major role in mobilizing and shaping (and containing and circumscribing) black politics. In particular, the negotiation, representation, and reimagination of black interests through cultural symbols has continued to be a major component in the making of black politics.
>
> *(Iton, 2008: 4–5)*

With these observations in mind, we might identify two broad types of politics that have both shaped and come to define what we mean when we talk of black sporting politics. The first is when black athletes (and indeed others similarly subjected to racialized forms of oppression) 'take a stand' and issue demands or raise awareness about political projects with which they are aligned or simply use their platform as public figures to bring attention to issues that are seen to be of importance. Caribbean cricket player Viv Richards speaking out against the apartheid regime in South Africa, or Olympic athlete Cathy Freeman highlighting the conditions and social plight of Aboriginal Australians and the question of indigenous rights, being two of many examples we could think of here.

A second and perhaps less obvious but still important way to think about this question is to approach sport as an *embodied form of politics*. To consider how the very act or performance of athleticism can be read as a form of 'claim-making' on the world, that within bodily movement there is always a deeply aesthetic and therefore political dimension at play which is given wider racial significance in societies whose social structures are deeply racialized. Consider this section from *Les Damnés de la Terre* when Frantz Fanon, trying to make sense of liberation and freedom in the context of colonialism and what resistance against the colonial world looks like, states:

> The first thing which the colonial subjects learns is to remain in his place and not overstep its limits. Hence the dreams of the colonial subject are muscular dreams, dreams of action, dreams of aggressive vitality. I dream I am jumping, swimming, running and climbing; I dream that I burst out laughing, I am leaping across a river and chased by a pack of cars that never catches up with me. During colonization the colonized subject frees himself night after night between nine in the evening and six in the morning.
>
> *(Fanon, 1963: 15)*

Fanon's provocative insight, that subaltern freedom and emancipation from the colonial world are embedded within physicality (or at least within the dream-like fantasies of physicality), is a useful starting point from which to better appreciate why sport has often been an important, and at times almost metaphysical, site of self-actualization for those black subjects whose post-slavery freedoms and claims to citizenship were curtailed by white supremacy, whether that was in the US under Jim Crow laws, under Western colonial governance in Africa, the Americas and the Caribbean or later in post/colonial Europe and the former so-called settler colonies. Historically, for black people throughout the diaspora, 'freedom' was not some esoteric abstraction that defined the nature of modernity under the domination of instrumental rationality. Rather, freedom represented something more fundamental for those whose ethical and political demands for liberty were premised upon the simple desire to occupy the category of 'the human'.

Sport, as the structured pursuit of useless play, simultaneously serves to dramatize and accentuate the very conditions of racial subordination and freedom from constraint that the colonial world and anti-black racism inscribes onto black bodies. Both *negation* and *emancipation* are found in the autotelic pleasures of creativity and movement that sport produces for the racialized subaltern. The colonial subject's ludic-like dreams of muscular prowess, as Fanon puts it, imbue the category of sport with a form of physical release and symbolic power that resonates far beyond the playing fields. In this context we might suggest that sport becomes co-articulated with discourses of freedom and hope in the refiguring of the category of 'the human' (as *homo ludens*), simultaneously announcing black athleticism as a claim to and critique of western Modernity itself.

This idea of a reclaimed humanity that is found in a physically active forms of politics, one that refuses fixity and containment, can be read into and from Frederick Douglass's ([1845] 2003) recounting of the metaphysical emancipation that results from the fight with his master, Edward Covey. In *Narrative of the Life of Frederick Douglass, an American Slave*, Douglass writes:

> This battle with Mr. Covey was the turning-point in my career as a slave. It rekindled the few expiring embers of freedom, and revived within me a sense of my own manhood. It recalled the departed self-confidence, and inspired me again with determination to be free. The gratification afforded by the triumph was a full compensation for whatever else might follow, even death itself. He only can understand the deep satisfaction which I experienced, who has himself repelled by force the bloody arm of slavery. I felt as I never felt before. It was a glorious resurrection, from the tomb of slavery, to the heaven of freedom. My long-crushed spirit rose, cowardice departed, bold defiance took its place; and I now resolved that, however long I might remain a slave in form, the day had passed forever when I could be a slave in fact. I did not hesitate to let it be known of me, that the white man who expected to succeed in whipping, must also succeed in killing me.
>
> (Douglass, [1845] 2003: 69)

Douglass's account establishes, as Saidiya Hartman (1997: 3) notes, the centrality of violence in the making of not just the institution of slavery but the slave subject itself and 'identifies it as an original generative act equivalent to the statement "I was born"'. The 'blood-stained' birth of the slave subject becomes a 'primal scene' in the formation of the enslaved and also of the possibility for overcoming and transcending enslavement. If this 'terrible spectacle' is used to dramatize the originatory moment of slave subjecthood and marks the brutal dialectical conditions of domination of the black subject/white master, then violence also marks *the transformative moment of release* from subjugation both for the individual and, as Fanon also argues in *Les Damnés de la Terre*, for the coming into national consciousness of the colonial subject. The moment and act of physical struggle creates the conditions from which a post-slave consciousness, that is more fully and complexly human can emerge.

In his book *Forty Million Dollar Slaves*, journalist William Rhoden notes that, for Douglass it was the act of fighting and not necessarily the winning that was liberating. Summing up the courage to fight Covey was itself an act of liberation. Rhoden argues that Douglass 'translated the symbolism of confrontation in real terms. He fought a system of slavery, challenging it in a fundamental way by engaging his overseer in a life-or-death struggle. For many blacks, sports were similarly symbolic ways of physically transcending the system of bondage, a space of freedom (Rhoden, 2006: 49). I have used these seemingly disparate historical examples because they help us to better conceptualize how the physicality of "fighting" in a general sense and the role of the boxer more specifically (and ultimately that of the trope of 'the black athlete') have come to be seen as a revolutionary acts and spaces of resistance to even the most total forms of racial domination and white supremacy, and an important part of how we might begin to understand contemporary black sporting politics in relation to the black sporting body.

Politics of the apolitical

That such acts of (masculinist) violent resistance are contradictory should be immediately obvious. The 'productive' use of violence raises a number of profound ethical questions that should not be ignored. Indeed sport, as a form of regulated play, contains within it the paradoxes of freedom and constraint in its very constitution. It should not be a surprise to find that the use of sport by the subaltern reproduces and in fact accentuates these paradoxical elements – a kind of doubling of the effects of freedom and domination. However, rather than dismissing sport's political praxis as inherently 'compromised', as many critical theorists have tended to do (the master's games cannot dismantle the master's house) and seeking to avoid the oftentimes utopian embrace of black athletes as proto-revolutionaries found in the writings of those too eager to defend the complicated actions and lives of black athletes (resistance does not equal transformation), I want to suggest that we need to more dispassionately map these constitutive contradictions as inherent to the politics of sporting embodiment and to more precisely locate when and where such interventions may produce progressive political outcomes that are genuinely disruptive to the dominant heteropatriarchal capitalist racial order and of course, when they are not.

Discussing the freedom claims contained within the pragmatic, strategic and performative acts of defiance that structured black cultural practices and leisure during and after slavery, Hartman suggests that:

> since acts of resistance exist within the context of relations of domination and are not external to them, they acquire their character from these relations, and vice versa. At a dance, holiday fete, or corn shucking, the line between dominant and insurgent orchestrations of blackness could be effaced or fortified in the course of an evening, either because the enslaved utilized instrumental amusements for contrary purposes or because surveillance necessitated cautious forms of interaction and modes of expression.
>
> *(Hartman, 1997: 8)*

In other words, the cultural, symbolic and linguistic 'weapons of the weak' (Scott, 1985) have provided a powerful alternative to the public scripts of domination that underwrote racial exploitation and genocide. This is an infrapolitics that often operates under the radar of official political structures and precepts but that is never fully free from the residues of dominant ideologies. Extending these arguments, Hartman suggests that under such conditions of domination, in which access to the formal institutions of bourgeois state politics are greatly curtailed, such everyday acts and cultural practices nonetheless help to:

> illuminate inchoate and utopian expressions of freedom that are not and perhaps cannot be actualized elsewhere. The desires and longings that exceed the frame of civil rights and political emancipation find expression in quotidian acts labeled 'fanciful', 'exorbitant', and 'excessive' primarily because they express an understating or imagination of freedom quite at odds with bourgeois expectations.
>
> *(Hartman, 1997: 13)*

Especially during the Jim Crow era, sport's putatively apolitical framing enabled black athletes a degree of bodily creative expression in public that was nearly impossible in any other social or cultural arena at the time. For athletes such as the boxer Jack Johnson, the financial rewards accrued through professional sports provided a degree of relative autonomy from the racial strictures of Jim Crow America and the wider colonial world. But Johnson's triumphs, as with all black Atlantic athletes in the early twentieth century, as well as his failings, could never simply be read as personal achievements. Given the historical moment into which he came, his impact transcended the biographical to reshape broader social structures. Discussing Johnson's vernacular significance beyond the ring, James Scott notes:

> Whenever a rare event legitimately allowed the black community to vicariously and publicly savor the physical victory of a black man over a white man, that event became an epoch-making one in folk memory. The fight between Jack Johnson and Jim Jeffries (the 'White Hope') in 1910 and Joe Louis's subsequent career, which was aided by instant radio transmission of the fights, were indelible moments of reversal and revenge for the black community. "When Johnson battered a white man (Jeffries) to his knees, he was the symbolic black man taking out his revenge on all whites for a lifetime of indignities". Lest such moments be seen purely as a safety valve reconciling blacks to their quotidian world of white domination, there were racial fights in every state in the South and in much of the North immediately after the 1910 fight. The proximate causes varied, but it is clear that in the flush of their jubilation, blacks became momentarily bolder in gesture, speech, and carriage, and this was seen by much of the white community as a provocation, a breach of the public transcript. Intoxication comes in many forms.
>
> *(Scott, 1990: 41)*

Modern sport is able to symbolically impact the racial order precisely because it can claim to be a space 'removed from politics'. While the rules of the game would have to be learned, and the tactics and strategies of success may have initially been copied from the public scripts provided by British Victorian elites, over time the informal codes of behavior, how the game was really to be played, could be and eventually was re-written. Before Johnson, most black athletes simply followed these permissible scripts that defined their social roles and engaged in cautious modes of expression. Johnson took the play book, subverted it and turned it upside down, and in so doing revealed the inherently political nature of sports as a gendered site of racial contestation and conflict (among other axes of domination). The 'bold gestures' of subsequent black athletes and their 'physical victories', the refusal to be disciplined by white norms and the resistant acts to refuse to play sports with a deferential bow and instead to stand boldly or kneel silently in protest, all need to be understood as bodily expressions of a black politics of liberation that are as significant as any formal textual declarations of freedom.

Ben Carrington

Black sporting bodies as biopolitics

In *Race Men*, Hazel Carby charts the relationship between masculinity and politics within black culture. She examines the so-called 'race men' who have come to represent, that is to say, stand in for, black America and who were deemed morally obliged to provide intellectual leadership and moral uplift for the beleaguered black masses. Carby begins her discussion by noting how black culture has become inseparable from an increasingly globalized popular culture. The creative practices and products of black artists are now intertwined with the global circulation of capital and its concomitant ideologies:

> In these days of what is referred to as 'global culture', the Nike corporation produces racialized images for the world by elevating the bodies of Michael Jordan and Tiger Woods to the status of international icons. Hollywood too now takes for granted that black bodies can be used to promote both products and style worldwide ... But despite the multimillion-dollar international trade in black male bodies, and encouragement to 'just do it', there is no equivalent international outrage, no marches or large-scale public protest, at the hundreds of thousands of black male bodies languishing out of sight of the media in the North American penal system.
>
> *(Carby, 1998: 1)*

Writing in the late 1990s, Carby suggests that despite the hyper-visibility of particular black bodies within the global media culture, there has been little comparative mobilization within the broader public sphere around questions related to anti-black violence, black poverty and incarceration. Indeed some commentators have argued that the spectacle of 'the black body' has not only obscured the harsh social conditions that many black people continue to face, but that the very celebration of a narrow construction of blackness has diminished the space for progressive politics. For critics like Carby, the possibilities for a politics of social transformation have shifted in a negative direction; the focus of black politics becoming reduced instead to the bodies of (largely male) individual actors, musicians and athletes, social progress equated to the levels of wealth accumulated by select black celebrities. In this context, the advance of the individual via self-commodification now takes precedent over using such public positions as a space for oppositional speech. The agency and transformative power encapsulated by Muhammad Ali's declarative political demands for recognition, 'What's my name?', and the agency encapsulated in the assertion, 'I don't have to be what you want me to be', make for a stark contrast when compared to the voiceless icon of the Michael Jordan figurine stuck in mid-air clutching a ball, imploring us to 'Be like Mike' by consuming Nike's latest products.

This claimed shift in the culture of black politics during the 1990s can be seen in what Paul Gilroy previously termed a new racialized bio-politics, 'in which the person is defined as the body and in which certain exemplary bodies, for example, those of Mike Tyson and Michael Jordan, Naomi Campbell and Veronica Webb, become instantiations of community' (Gilroy, 1994: 55). Gilroy suggests that previously bodily and spiritual freedoms were sharply differentiated and that the most valuable forms of freedom espoused by black organic intellectuals (he mentions Douglass as an example) revolved around the liberation of the mind. Gilroy warns that with this move away from the liberation of the mind as the basis for black politics, today's bio-politics is increasingly only expressed via modalities of the body. Racialized bio-politics establishes the boundaries of the authentic racial community through 'the visual representation of racial bodies – engaged in characteristic activities – usually sexual or sporting that ground and solicit identification if not solidarity' (ibid.: 55). For Gilroy this is problematic as it marks the racial community exclusively as a space of heterosexual activity and confirms the abandonment of any politics aside from the ongoing oppositional creativity of gendered self-cultivation … If it survives, politics becomes an exclusively aesthetic concern with all the perils that implies.

(Gilroy, 1994: 55)

Earlier generations of athletes such as the boxers Jack Johnson and Joe Louis, the cricket player Garfield Sobers, and tennis star Althea Gibson, used sport to imagine and embody a form of black freedom and creativity that transcended the limits imposed upon black life by racism. In so doing, such athletes broke free from racism's formal and informal constraints to lay claim to a transfigurative politics of freedom. This form of black sporting politics has increasingly been displaced by media sponsors' requirements that athletes become first and foremost good corporate athletes. Put reductively, the charge is that the celebration of sporting black bodies obscures other types of bodies, those not endowed with athletic prowess, those languishing in prisons and detention centers, those in the shadows because on the run from law enforcement, those evicted onto the streets from their homes, those struggling to make a living on the sidewalks of our metropolitan cities. The hyper-visibility and celebration of the black athletic body, and the promotion of meritocratic myths about social mobility through sports, act as distorting mirrors, obscuring the lived everyday realities of black and brown bodies that are neither revered nor seen but increasingly abject and invisible, mundane disposable bodies. 'If the spectacle of the lynched black body haunts the modern age', notes Carby (1998: 2), 'then the slow disintegration of black bodies and souls in jail, urban ghettos, and beleaguered schools haunts our postmodern times'.

In the decades since Gilroy's and Carby's observations, the economic, cultural and political conditions and structural inequalities described have arguably accelerated and intensified. Select celebrity black bodies have become ever more visible. Globalized and integrated, multi-platform marketing strategies continue to commodify black bodies and remain fixated on displaying the black (usually but not exclusively male) athletic body as a synonym for power and strength on the one hand and as an object of (white) sexual desire on the other (Thrasher 2016). Similarly, and during the same period, levels of incarceration of African American women and men have reached such staggeringly high proportions that some have labelled the current moment as a new Jim Crow era (Alexander, 2010). And yet despite these deepening forms of racial injustice and inequality, and maybe even because of it, this conjuncture has also seen a new wave of athletic activism that suggests the earlier pessimistic critiques may be in need of substantial revision.

The return of the revolt of the black athlete?

Writing just after John Carlos and Tommie Smith had taken to the podium in Mexico City, bowed their heads, and each raised a black-gloved clenched fist in defiance at American society's denial of full human rights to African Americans, the scholar-activist Harry Edwards wrote of the emerging consciousness of athletes. 'The revolt of the black athlete in America', as Edwards phrased it, was a phase in the broader black liberation movement, which was 'as legitimate as the sit-ins, the freedom rides, or any other manifestation of Afro-American efforts to gain freedom' (Edwards, 1969: 38). In contrast to the 1960s, critical scholars, as we have just seen, have pointed to the decline in political activism among athletes, a general lack of political consciousness within the sports world, and suggested that there has been a contraction of the black public sphere linked to black politics becoming reduced to the aesthetic concerns of the body. Not only that, but black athletes stand accused of a certain complicity with systems of domination and inadvertently, through their inaction and passivity, aiding the white sports media complex that conceals rather than exposes contemporary forms of injustice and discrimination.

However, recent events have called into question such a pessimistic conclusion about sports, black athlete's consciousness and the regressive politics of the sports spectacle. In March 2012, for example, members of the Miami Heat NBA team, led by star players Dwayne Wade and LeBron James, published a photo of themselves on various social media platforms wearing 'hoodies' alongside the hashtag #WeAreTrayvonMartin. This, the players said, was an act of solidarity for the family of Trayvon Martin, a black teenager who was shot dead the month before after he was mistaken for a burglar by George Zimmerman, a self-styled neighborhood watch vigilante. In November 2014, several members of the St Louis Rams NFL team entered the field before the start of the game and dramatically paused live on national television, raising their hands in the air. This was a 'hands up, don't shoot' gesture that had become a symbol for protesters following the fatal shooting of 18-year-old Michael Brown by a police officer in nearby Ferguson, Missouri, earlier in the summer. A month later, in December 2014, players throughout the NBA wore warm-up T-shirts proclaiming 'I Can't Breathe'. This was in response to the killing of Eric Garner in Staten Island, New York City, earlier in the summer after police officers arrested Garner, using a chokehold around his neck. As Garner was taken to the ground, a recording caught his last words, 'I can't breathe'. The officers continued to restrain him and he died shortly after. In 2016, a number of WNBA players from multiple teams in the league, wore 'Black Lives Matter' t-shirts both before their games and afterwards during their press conferences, using social media and the national press to highlight the need to address racial discrimination and injustice in U.S. society.

It is apparent, in the context of a range of insurgent social movements such as Black Lives Matter that have highlighted the damaging effects of white supremacist discourses and structures of violence on black communities, that athletes are taking a stand and using their platforms to bring attention to matters beyond the playing field. In so doing, many athletes have faced backlash from white fans, mainstream sports writers, former players and right-wing commentators, often telling them to 'shut up and play' and worse. This very contestation, however, has once again revealed the inherently and already political nature of sports as a contested arena, and signals the reemergence of a more explicit political period in the world of sports that many claimed had disappeared by the 1990s.

In this context Jules Boykoff suggests that this increase in athlete activism has meant that power brokers who previously may have tried to prohibit any sign of politics are now having to allow and even sometimes (depending on the type of political protest and subject matter) endorsing such acts. Boykoff points out that when *People* magazine asked President Barack Obama about the 'I Can't Breathe' T-shirts worn by LeBron James and others, Obama replied:

> I think LeBron did the right thing. We forget the role that Muhammad Ali, Arthur Ashe, and Bill Russell played in raising consciousness. I'd like to see more athletes do that – not just around this issue, but around a range of issues.
>
> *(Cited by Boykoff, 2016: 252)*

Even Michael Jordan, for so long the 1990s embodiment of the apolitical black athlete who put corporate profit and image management before political consciousness and black activism, claimed he could no longer stay silent in the context of the Black Lives Matter social movement, black deaths at the hands of the police, and a series of shootings of police officers. As

Douglas Hartmann (2016) noted, 'When even Michael Jordan – that erstwhile poster child of the transcendent, apolitical, super-star athlete – jumps into the fray, you know something is up'. The combination of a broader shift towards a more active politics of anti-racism and the social movements driving this, the pervasiveness of social media enabling public discussion, dissent and dissemination of political ideas beyond the restricted spaces of the traditional corporate controlled dominant media and that crucially can offer forms of solidarity and support for those athletes who do speak out, and of course the central place of sports within global popular culture and the elevated status and standing of leading athletes, help to explain the evolving conjuncture of a new poetics of sporting politics.

Conclusion

Given that physical cultural studies 'looks to explicate how active bodies become organized, disciplined, represented, embodied, and experienced in mobilizing (and corroborating), or at times immobilizing (or resisting), the conjunctural inflections and operations of power and society' (Andrews and Silk, 2015: 87), this chapter has attempted to provide a brief exemplar of this approach by situating the (raced) sporting body in the context of black cultural politics, both past and present. By taking the sporting body seriously as a site for politics and a form of politics in and of itself, we might be better able to understand, trace and potentially challenge dominant relations of power that continue to circulate through sports today.

We can further conclude that is it now impossible to talk seriously about black politics without that discussion at some stage addressing and thinking carefully about that most peculiar and powerfully ludic form of physical culture we call 'sport'. From the threat to the racial order posed by Jack Johnson at the start of the twentieth century, to Muhammed Ali's courageous (if contradictory) acts of defiance to American imperialism abroad and white racism at home in the 1960s and 1970s, to today's creative athletic protests on and off the field, 'the black athlete' should be understood as a racial project capable of drawing attention to and occasionally challenging wider structures of feeling and racial formations. The much-lauded but poorly understood legacy of Ali shows us not just that social change is possible through sport but, as importantly, it helps us to see the ways in which sports are already and inherently political.

Acknowledgements

Parts of this chapter draw directly upon and update arguments first published in Carrington (2010), *Race, Sport and Politics*, particularly sections in Chapters 2 and 3 of that book.

References

Adair, D. and Rowe, D. (2010). Beyond boundaries: 'race', ethnicity and identity in sport. *International Review for the Sociology of Sport*, 45(3), 251–257.
Alexander, M. (2010). *The new Jim Crow: mass incarceration in the age of colorblindness*. New York: The New Press.
Andrews, D. L. (ed.). (2001). *Michael Jordan Inc.: corporate sport, media culture, and late modern America*. Albany, NY: State University of New York Press.
Andrews, D. L. and Silk, M. (2015). Physical cultural studies on sport. In R. Guilianotti (ed.), *The Routledge handbook of the sociology of sport*. London: Routledge.
Boykoff, J. (2016). *Power games: a political history of the Olympics*. London: Verso.
Carby, H. (1998). *Race men*. Cambridge, MA: Harvard University Press.

Carrington, B. (2010). *Race, sport and politics: the sporting black diaspora*. London: Sage
Douglas, D. and Jamieson, K. (2006). A farewell to remember: interrogating the Nancy Lopez farewell tour. *Sociology of Sport Journal*, 23, 117–141.
Douglass, F. ([1845] 2003). *Narrative of the life of Frederick Douglass, an American slave*. New York: Barnes & Noble Classics.
Edwards, H. (1969). *The revolt of the black athlete*. New York: Free Press.
Fanon, F. ([1963] 2004). *The wretched of the earth*. New York: Grove Press.
Farred, G. (2014). *In motion, at rest: the event of the athletic body*. Minneapolis, MN: University of Minnesota Press.
Gilroy, P. (1994). 'After the love has gone': bio-politics and etho-poetics in the black public sphere. *Public Culture*, 7, 49–76.
Hanchard, M. (2006). *Party/politics: horizons in black political thought*. Oxford: Oxford University Press.
Hartman, S. (1997). *Scenes of subjection: terror, slavery and self-making in the nineteenth century*. New York: Oxford University Press.
Hartmann, D. (2016). A new era of athlete awareness and advocacy. Available at https://thesocietypages.org/editors/2016/07/27/a-new-era-of-athlete-awareness-and-advocacy (accessed 28 July 2016).
Hylton, K. (2008). *'Race' and sport: critical race theory*. London: Routledge.
Ifekwunigwe, J. (2009). Venus and Serena are 'doing it' for themselves: theorizing sporting celebrity, class and black feminism for the hip-hop generation. In B. Carrington and I. McDonald (eds), *Marxism, cultural studies and sport*. London: Routledge, 130–153.
Iton, R. (2008). *In search of the black fantastic: politics and popular culture in the post-civil rights era*. Oxford: Oxford University Press.
Joseph, J., Darnel, S. and Nakamura, Y. (eds). (2012). *Race and sport in Canada: intersecting inequalities*. Toronto: Canadian Scholars' Press.
Leonard, D. and King, C. R. (eds) (2011). *Commodified and criminalized: new racism and African Americans in contemporary sports*. Lanham, MD: Rowman & Littlefield.
Marqusee, M. (2005). *Redemption song: Muhammad Ali and the spirit of the sixties*, 2nd edn. London: Verso.
Quashie, K. (2012). *The sovereignty of quiet: beyond resistance in black culture*. London: Rutgers University Press.
Rhoden, W. C. (2006). *Forty million dollar slaves: the rise, fall, and redemption of the black athlete*. New York: Three Rivers Press.
Schultz, J. (2016). *Moments of impact: injury, racialized memory, and reconciliation in college football*. Lincoln, NE: University of Nebraska Press.
Scott, J. (1985). *Weapons of the weak: everyday forms of peasant resistance*. New Haven, CT: Yale University Press.
Scott, J. C. (1990). *Domination and the arts of resistance: hidden transcripts*. New Haven, CT: Yale University Press.
Spencer, N. (2004). Sister act VI: Venus and Serena Williams at Indian Wells: 'sincere fictions' and white racism. *Journal of Sport and Social Issues*, 28(2), 115–135.
Van Sterkenburg, J., Knoppers, A. and De Leeuw, S. (2010). Race, ethnicity and content analysis of sports media: a critical reflection. *Media, Culture and Society*, 32(5), 819–839.

14
GENDERED BODIES

Clifton Evers and Jennifer Germon

It is often assumed that the concept of gender – understood as masculinity and femininity – has always existed. It hasn't. The concept came about through the work of sexologist John Money (1952, 1978), who took the term from linguistics during the 1950s and used it initially to explain how intersexed persons learnt to embody the behaviours, tastes, values, attitudes, comportment, etc. of their assigned gender. In other words, those qualities attributed to one of two (legitimate) human sexes, male and female. By Money's reasoning, if intersex people could acquire an unequivocal identity as a girl/woman or a boy/man despite variant sexual anatomy and physiology then the relation between a gender and a sex had to be contingent rather than essential. Given physical cultural studies' aim is to make visible the specificity of cultural practices that ascribe meanings to bodies and give form to their representation, analyses of gendered bodies cannot ignore the conditions under which the concept of gender emerged.

Embodied gender by Money's account, is produced through interaction between cells, environment, and experience. At the heart of Money's model lies a neural template stimulated through familial and social relations. The template codes for masculine *and* feminine traits rather than for one *or* the other. That is, the template codes for human behaviour organized by sex-gender. The socialization of gendered subjectivity then, requires the synthesis of and reinforcement of what behaviours are appropriate and inappropriate for one's own gender. Money extended his theory to account for how everyone learnt their gender, heralding the concept's shift beyond clinical contexts into political, theoretical, and everyday social discourse.

Even as Money's research consolidated and extended the evidence base for human sex diversity (Germon, 2009, 2014), his scholarly and populist discourse[1] further cemented the common sense idea that human bodies come in two distinct types – 'male' or 'female'. This was achieved by framing gender relations as not simply oppositional but importantly, as complementary. This is another example of Money's skill for breathing new life into pre-existing concepts. Complementarity evoked nineteenth-century European ideas of sexual difference that situated woman as man's complement rather than his equal (Schiebinger, 1989). Gender complementarity works to naturalize tradition and in so doing functions to shore up existing hierarchies.

Under the terms of oppositional complementarity, men are assumed 'by nature' as tough, stoic, taciturn, analytical, rational, risk-taking, independent, competitive, strong, assertive people. Women by contrast are assumed to be 'naturally' talkative, emotional, intuitive, empathetic, irrational, cooperative, weak, self-sacrificing people. This is otherwise known as sexual essentialism. Gayle Rubin (2007: 156) highlights the axiomatic nature of sexual essentialism where bodily sex is understood as 'a natural force that exists prior to social life and shapes institutions'. This paradigm formulates a sex-gender arrangement that is 'eternally unchanging, asocial, and transhistorical' (ibid.). It institutionalizes gender-appropriate psychologies and bodies through differentiated (read unequal) affordances and constraints with regards to family, sport, labour, leisure, politics, business, education, religion, and all other realms of social activity (Connell, 2009).

Of course, many bodies do not fit within the prototypical biological determinations of sexual dimorphism; chromosomal, anatomical, and endocrinological configurations vary considerably across the lifespan and across populations so are neither clear-cut nor stable. Biology is interactive, functioning with and through a dynamic complex environment. The plasticity of biology reveals binary sexual difference and associated sexual essentialism as illusory, albeit with significant material consequences. Awareness of that plasticity is vital to how physical cultural studies engages with bodies as matter in space. It provides a means to circumvent the seductive pull of essentialist, reductionist, and determinist approaches to bodies that have been historically entangled in discriminatory, and exclusionary social relations and practices. For Julia Epstein (1990) the medical response to the intersexed offers a poignant example of such entanglement. Driven by an ongoing investment in a 'binary sex differentiation that is known not to exist in biomedicine', bodies that deviate furthest from the privileged two are routinely subject to 'corrective' surgical procedures and hormonal therapies intended to standardize diverse morphology and fix the intersexed 'condition'. Such efforts are surely analogous to the attempts of Cinderella's step-sisters to amputate their heels and toes to fit *that* shoe.

Drilling down further it is possible to discern the racialized dimension to gender as originally conceived. Zine Mugabane's (2014) provocative analysis of Money's model makes clear that gender was always already raced. That is because the ideal feminine or masculine intersexed subject was one who approximated to white middle-class ideals of femininity and masculinity. Mugabane's argument is made all the more compelling because black people in the USA remained subject to residential and occupational segregation at that time, and continued to live 'under conditions of racial terror' (ibid.: 778). Moreover black bodies have historically been marked by excess in the colonial imagination, whether in terms of excessively formed genitalia or excessive sexuality (Mugabane, 2014; Somerville, 1998).

The augmentation of sexuality as a key identifier of who we are in the modern era is key to the maintenance of sexual essentialism. That is because sexuality marked by a hierarchy of value situates heterosexual married reproductive couples 'at the top of the erotic pyramid' (Rubin, 2007: 158), monogamous domiciled couples below them, and so on in descending order. Thus to understand gendered bodies it is also necessary to consider sexuality. Sexual practices and identifications vary across time, place, and culture. The nineteenth century – according to that most influential historian of social and sexual organization, Michel Foucault (1981) – gave rise to a 'scientia sexualis' or science of sexuality, that sought to capture 'the truth' of sex.[2] The efforts of the first generation of sexologists manifested in a series of discursive regimes grounded in science and medicine – of which Money's scholarship later became part – that framed what was and what could be known about sexuality.

Foucault's (1977) elaboration of the interrelation between power and knowledge is relevant here. Foucault explains that 'power produces; it produces reality; it produces domains of objects and rituals of truth' (ibid.: 104). Power/knowledge co-constitutes the wider 'dispotif'.[3] Through the dispotif, gendered subjects are produced and regulated as living beings who come to know themselves, to think and act, and to orientate to the world. For Foucault (1980: 30), power 'reaches into the very grain of individuals, touches their bodies and inserts itself into their actions and attitudes, their discourses, learning processes and everyday lives'.

Judith Butler (1990) makes good use of the work of Foucault through a performative theory of gender that has held sway for over two decades now. It asserts that we repeat, recite, ritualize, and internalize gendered discourses. For Butler 'gender is the repeated stylization of the body, a set of repeated acts within a highly rigid regulatory frame that congeal over time to produce the appearance of a substance, a natural sort of being' (ibid.: 33).

The differential effects of discursive regimes producing and working through gendered bodies that produce discrimination, trauma, exclusion, and violence can be challenged with such a Foucauldian awareness and thus is of relevance to physical cultural studies. By interrogating discursive traces, historically produced axioms can be identified and undermined, allowing alternatives to push through and be realized. This is particularly effective when woven together with self-reflexive empirical work, as Elspeth Probyn has shown (1993, 1996). Holly Thorpe's (2014) work on action sports exemplifies such an approach within physical cultural studies. Working with one's own body as research method ensures that biology and its agential qualities do not recede from view when attending to the socialization of sex-gender. The latter represents a significant risk should the study of physical culture remain tethered to a social constructivist methodology. The body is more than the raw substrate upon which culture does its work since bodies are active in social situations (Connell, 1995). Given this, how can physical cultural studies account for the dynamic complexity of the inter- and intra-action of biology, environment, society with experience?

A phenomenological[4] approach provides another useful lens for physical cultural studies because it understands the body as thoroughly active (Merleau-Ponty, 1982). We inhabit and come to know the world through the agential orientations of a 'lived body' (Moi, 2001), whereby 'no nature-culture distinction is necessary' (Young, 2002: 410). That is because bodies are relational – politically, culturally, and sociologically as well as spatially, temporally, and materially.

Iris Marion Young (1980) beautifully demonstrates this by articulating how a third person view – inculcated by Western symbolic systems – enfolds with the motor performance of bodies in her classic phenomenological study of 'throwing like a girl'. Young notes a doubling of attention in feminine comportment where self-objectification can orientate timidity, uncertainty, self-consciousness, etc., leading to restrictive movement. To 'throw like a girl' is to concentrate motion in one body part rather than engaging the whole body in space with 'fluid and directed motion' (ibid.: 146).[5] By contrast to throw 'like a boy' is to extend one's body and take up space boldly and freely. This is not to say that girls cannot throw otherwise, or that all boys can throw fully. The lived body operates through a dynamic of the biological, spatial, and social resulting in nuanced, situated/contextual, and fleshly knowledge mediated through the senses.

Another fruitful approach for physical cultural studies scholarship is the application of a sociological sensibility to gendered bodies. Some feminists have mobilized the concept of 'habitus' to understand how gender is embodied (Adkins and Skeggs, 2005; McNay, 1999; Probyn, 2004; Thorpe, 2009, 2010). Habitus refers to an embodied practical knowledge of differentiations and dispositions across and within various and complex social structures and settings. These include logics, rules, laws, values, and institutions.

The anthropologist-sociologist Marcel Mauss ([1935] 1979) used the term 'habitus' to identify the embodied practical application (conscious and unconscious) of social knowledge. Mauss shunned a 'homo-duplex' understanding of groups and individuals structured through a binary of social versus biological. For Mauss, 'forms, postures, gestures, movements are, fundamentally, acts that are social … we are everywhere faced with physio-psycho-sociological assemblages or series of action' (ibid.: 123). Sociologist Pierre Bourdieu further developed the concept of habitus, analysing how class and culture are produced and reproduced by way of it. The same analysis has application to gender. Bourdieu's collaborator Loïc Wacquant (2004: 316) describes habitus as 'the way society becomes deposited in persons in the form of lasting dispositions, or trained capacities and structured propensities to think, feel and act in determinant ways, which then guide them'. Bourdieu (1990: 56) writes that 'The habitus – embodied history, internalized as second nature and so forgotten as history – is the active presence of the whole past of which it is the product'. Bodily comportment – gait, gesture, posture, etc. – represents the somatic realization of the habitus or 'bodily hexis' (ibid.). Added to this is a 'feel for the game'; a well-developed, sophisticated non-conscious form of embodied improvisation (Sterne, 2006). Wacquant (2014a: 10) instructs that through the habitus we are 'suffering creatures of the flesh, blood, nerves and sinews'.

While there are some differences between the phenomenological approach to lived bodies and the sociological approach to habitus, as Nick Crossley (2001) has shown in his theorizing of the 'phenomenological habitus' it is possible to bring them together. Crossley's aim is to get at the creativity that happens through lived bodies and their sensory orientations while accommodating social structuring processes. It's worth recalling that Bourdieu and Wacquant (1992: 133) have claimed that 'Habitus is an open system of dispositions that is constantly subjected to experiences, and therefore constantly affected by them in a way that either reinforces or modifies its structures.'

For Crossley (2014: 108) the 'embodied actor who, while always drawing upon their habits to some extent, is not reducible to them and is capable of innovation and creativity' whether by 'reflective or conscious activity' or otherwise. Wacquant (2014b: 118) contests Crossley's reading of Bourdieu, arguing habitus is actually a 'multiscalar notion with which to construct the epistemic individual and account for both reproduction and change, conformity and creativity, as well as self-revision'. While Crossley accepts Wacquant's understanding of habitus he notes that it represents an extension of the initial Boudieusian model. The broader point we wish to make here is that such debates and creative theoretical approaches offer models through which physical cultural studies can orientate itself as the catalyst for creative, critical, and generative exchange about gendered bodies.

Elspeth Probyn (2004, 2005) does just this by bringing emotion and affect into the heart of matters of habitus. Emotion and affect imbue social agents with a certain motility and sensuous quality and are a crucial part of understanding gendered bodies. Emotions are the vehicle through which we socially, culturally, and consciously interpret, dramatize, categorize, express, and manage the immediacy of bodily affect. The psychologist Silvan Tomkins (1962, 1963) pointed to how the skin, muscles, and face function as key sites for the manifestation of affect (e.g. goosebumps, shivering, cheek-flushing, muscle tensing, etc.). This is not to suggest that affect is pre-personal or extra-discursive but rather that emotion and affect are entangled and *work together* to produce 'embodied meaning-making' (Wetherell, 2012: 4) in what is simultaneously a conscious *and* unconscious process. Against the common assumption that men are less emotional, such an understanding reminds us that all gendered habitus are sensual (Evers, 2006, 2009).

Through emotion and affect we learn about our relations to others (Probyn, 2005: 35), whether coming into alignment or otherwise with them (Brennan, 2004). Appreciating such provides physical cultural studies with an approach to pedagogy and politics that sutures with affects and emotions. Sara Ahmed's (2004) work is instructive in this regard. Her examination of how bodies (individual and collective) are woven into a circulating 'cultural politics of emotion' that 'surface' embodied social relations in particular ways. For example gendered bodies that transgress norms may become 'sticky' with disgust, denigration, derision yet also be experienced as a joy (ibid.). If gendering is sensually learned, lived, and surfaced, then affects – with their capacity to leap from one body to another – work to 'evoke tenderness, incite shame, ignite rage, excite fear' (Gibbs, 2002). Once again we find social life inseparable from biochemical and neurological life (Brennan, 2004: 1).

This brings us back to the materiality of bodies and their concomitant psychic and historical weight (Fausto-Sterling, 2000; Gatens 1991, 1996; Grosz, 1994). Gendered life is experienced through the body; posturally, vascularly, neurally, chemically, to name but a few. Then there's differences in physical shape, size, and strength. The assortment of fluids that bodies produce – water, blood, pus, sweat, mucus, milk, and so on – are leaky, messy, and visceral. Homeostasis may function as a measure of good health but bodies are dynamic and notoriously unstable. Corporeality is bound up with an 'imaginary body' that 'is socially and historically specific in that it is constructed by: a shared language; the shared psychical significance and privileging of various zones of the body (for example, the mouth, anus, the genitals; and common institutional practices and discourses (for example, medical, juridical and educational) which act on and through the body' (Gatens, 1996: 151–152). This again points to the complex intra-activity that shapes how certain bodily capacities, capabilities, and experiences come to be differentially valued and organized through gendered hierarchies and segmented categories. It is tricky terrain to theorize so as to produce new possibilities, rather than simply explain. If physical cultural studies is to do so, a certain curiosity and willingness to take risks is needed.

An example of how to do so is offered by Elizabeth Grosz (1994) who uses the model of the Möbius strip (a single twisted ribbon) to represent the way biology entwists with culture and experience. For Grosz the Möbius strip offers a counterpoint to binaries such as subject/object, biology/social, matter/representation, mind/body precisely because the inside of the strip is co-constituted with the outside, each folding into the other. Grosz promotes an 'open materiality' (1994: 191), or what Moira Gatens calls an 'active nature' (1996: 148). Their 'corporeal feminism' offers yet another way to appreciate the distinctive capacities, capabilities, and experiences of situated bodies that pushes beyond dualistic intellectual traditions. Where else might we find grounded, dynamic models that enable physical cultural studies to engage with gendered bodies in ways that mobilize creativity, openness, activity?

Let us consider the notion of *becoming* (Deleuze and Guattari, 1987). Becoming refers to ongoing qualitative transformation of bodies through differentiation and activity. Rather than a difference from or a difference to, 'differing' refers to movement and a continual mode of differing (Currier, 2003: 330). There is what philosopher Henri Bergson calls the '*élan vital*' or vital impetus (in Deleuze, 1988b). For Grosz (1994: 165) this offers a 'way of understanding the body in its connections with other bodies, both human and non-human, animate and inanimate, linking organs and biological processes to material objects and social practices while refusing to subordinate the body to a unit of homogeneity'.

Clifton Evers's (2009) study of surfing and masculinity refers to gendered becoming and a stylistics of gender that stems from practice/activity. Evers frames 'style' as the enfolding of situated, fluid, embodied, sensual, social, cultural, ecological, and spatial intermingling and expression where everything shapes everything else (Evers, 2006, 2009, 2015). Waves like bodies are temporal and always travel differently. Their styles pitch fast or slow, curl awkwardly, 'edged with a multiplicity of smaller waves' (Serres, 1995: 82). In this sense it is the styles of bodies-in-relation that matter rather than bodies-as-objects since 'you do not know beforehand what a body or a mind can do, in a given encounter, a given arrangement, a given combination' (Deleuze, 1992:

628). From this perspective it is clear that gendered bodies are marked by an ongoing qualitative transformation – *affectus*[6] – and *elan vital*.

Such multiplicity is analogous to how bioscientists increasingly recognize human sex diversity to be more prevalent than previously imagined. While once estimates of intersex populations hovered around 1:2000 live births (a notoriously speculative figure), recent estimates (using a very inclusive definition) posit somewhere in the order of 1:100 (Ainsworth, 2015: 290). This gives pause for thought. Such quantification offers some useful data about prevalence. Moreover, as recent research demonstrates, human bodily sex is not fully determined at birth but can and does transform over the lifespan (ibid.). While there may be a tendency toward qualitative work in physical cultural studies we can see here how quantitative work can also be generative of new possibilities.

Still other approaches can help those working through physical cultural studies to creatively think about and through gendered bodies. For instance, we ask: What does human ethology have to offer physical cultural studies in this regard? Moira Gatens (1996) – following Deleuze (1988a) – encourages just such an ethological effort. Ethology is traditionally associated with the study of animals, their affects, capacities, and (ever changing) habitats, all grounded in a relational premise. There is always variability. Here bodies are understood as multiple, a 'multiplicity' where difference is continuous and continual rather than a problem to be remedied (Currier, 2003: 330). Yet caution is warranted since ethology has close historical links to fields that promote essentialized and prescriptive notions of sex-gender, evolutionary psychology and evolutionary biology being two examples.

Turning attention to ecology also seems promising for physical cultural studies. Within an ecological frame, variation is necessary to the ongoing health and wellbeing of populations, species, and habitats. Preservation becomes the aim rather than remediation. The work of Rosemarie Garland-Thomson (2012) is instructive. Garland-Thomson draws from the language and logics of ecology in response to eugenicist arguments that favour selecting against disability. Her counter-eugenic project is one of disability conservation in the interests of human biodiversity. The concept of human biodiversity also has purchase for thinking about the difference in sex-gender difference. If, as increasingly looks to be the case, all humans are to some degree sexual intermediaries (Hirschfeld, [1910] 1991), the pathological tendencies of dominant understandings of sex-gender can no longer 'stick'.

Consider how a century ago Magnus Hirschfeld (ibid.) proposed a radical model of sexual difference that he called the Doctrine of Sexual Intermediaries. For Hirschfeld the idea that there were pure types of men and pure types of women was an ideological fantasy, an impossibility. The homologous nature of sexual tissue led Hirschfeld to propose that all humans were in some sense sexual intermediaries. The Doctrine was not a theory per se but rather a typology consisting of four primary dimensions: sexual, psychosocial, genital, and corporeal. Each had a series of secondary dimensions that Hirschfeld calculated to be at least four to the power of sixteen (or 4^{16}). His was a hunch for which he had no evidence base upon which to draw. A hundred years later the evidence appears to bear out Hirschfeld's sense of the normalcy of sex-gender diversity.

There has emerged over the past decade – alongside feminist science studies – a feminist 'new materialism' (Barad, 2003; Braidotti, 2002; Currier, 2003; Probyn, 2014; Whatmore, 2006). This new materialism has not simply dismantled and left behind dualisms such as social/biological, science/humanities, human/nonhuman, and nature/culture but envisioned new possibilities. It's a difficult yet necessary political and intellectual task that we argue physical cultural studies can orientate itself through when considering gendered bodies to wilfully create 'new meaning, new loci of meaning, and new ways of being, together, in the world' (Penelope, 1992: 42).

The wide conceptual, theoretical, and methodological universe we have surveyed here anticipates difference and an endlessly diversifying (rather than complete) picture of gendered bodies. It's an unsettling and creative account of gendered bodies that we advocate physical cultural studies pursue. In this chapter we have shown how this can be achieved by moving across and working *between* numerous disciplines and academic traditions – biomedicine, history, sexology, psychology, sociology, philosophy, cultural studies, phenomenology, feminism, and ecology. Physical cultural studies can function as a gathering place. As such it represents more than trans-disciplinarity as commonly conceived since it requires working between a wide array of disciplines, theories, concepts, and methodologies, all the while applying due diligence and care to interpretations and contexts. This dynamic intra-activity replicates how gendered bodies play out and from which we take our cue.

Notes

1 During the 1960s and 1970s television provided sexologists in North America with an important platform for engaging the public. Money was among those with a high public profile who became for a time, a household name.
2 Before gender entered the English lexicon as an ontological category, the term sex carried the conceptual weight of anatomical and physiological differences, erotic practices/desires, as well as psychological and behavioural dispositions.
3 After Foucault (1980: 194), we understand dispotif as 'a thoroughly heterogeneous ensemble consisting of discourses, institutions, architectural forms, regulatory decisions, laws, administrative measures, scientific statements, philosophical, moral and philanthropic propositions – in short, the said as much as the unsaid'.
4 Phenomenology is an approach to considering 'what it is to be a participant in the world, and how things present themselves' (Sokolowski, 2000: 48).
5 While women's spatio-temporal situations have long been the subject of feminist phenomenology (De Beauvoir, 1972; Fisher and Embree, 2000; Heinämaa, 2003), phenomenological approaches to masculinity remain few and far between (cf. Seidler, 2006).
6 Earlier we made reference to a social psychological model of affect. However, affect theory is diverse spanning multiple schools of thought. A popular and oft-used understanding is via the work of Gilles Deleuze (1988a) – who draws on the work of philosopher Benedict Spinoza – who is more interested in how 'affectus' is ostensibly the capacity to affect and be affected and the epistemological and ontological implications of this.

References

Adkins, L. and Skeggs, B. 2005. *Feminism after Bourdieu*. Oxford: Wiley-Blackwell.
Ahmed, S. 2004. *The cultural politics of emotion*. London: Routledge.
Ainsworth, C. 2015. Sex redefined. *Nature*, 518 (7539), 288–291.
Barad, K. 2003. Posthumanist performativity: toward an understanding of how matter comes to matter. *Signs*, 28 (3), 801–831.
Bourdieu, P. 1990. *The logic of practice*. Cambridge: Polity Press.
Bourdieu, P. and Wacquant, L. 1992. *An invitation to reflexive sociology*. Cambridge: Polity Press.
Braidotti, R. 2002. *Metamorphoses: towards a feminist theory of becoming*. Cambridge: Polity Press.
Brennan, T. 2004. *The transmission of affect*. Ithaca: Cornell University Press.
Butler, J. 1990. *Gender trouble: feminism and the subversion of identity*. New York: Routledge.
Colebrook, C. 2000. From radical representations to corporeal becomings: The feminist philosophy of Lloyd, Grosz, and Gatens. *Hypatia*, 15 (2), 76–93.
Connell, R. 1995. *Masculinities*. Sydney: Allen & Unwin.
Connell, R. 2009. *Gender*. Cambridge: Polity Press.
Crossley, N. 2001. The phenomenological habitus and its construction. *Theory and Society*, 30 (1), 81–120.
Crossley, N. 2014. Embodied actors, sociability and the limits of reflexivity. *Body and Society* 20 (2), 106–112.

Currier, D. 2003. Feminist technological future: Deleuze and body/technology assemblages. *Feminist Theory*, 4 (3), 321–338.
De Beauvoir, S. 1972. *The second sex* (trans. H. Parshley). Harmondsworth: Penguin Books.
Deleuze, G. 1988a. *Spinoza: practical philosophy*. New York: City Lights Books.
Deleuze, G. 1988b. *Bergsonism*. New York: Zone Books.
Deleuze, G. 1992. Ethology: Spinoza and us. In S. Lotringer (ed.), *Incorporations*. New York: Zone.
Deleuze, G. and Guattari, F. 1987. *A thousand plateaus: capitalism and schizophrenia*. Minneapolis, MN: University of Minnesota Press.
Epstein, J. 1990. Either/or – neither/both: sexual ambiguity and the ideology of gender. *Genders* 7, 99–142.
Evers, C. 2006. Becoming-man/becoming-wave. PhD thesis, University of Sydney, Australia.
Evers, C. 2009. 'The point': surfing, geography and a sensual life of men and masculinity on the Gold Coast, Australia. *Social and Cultural Geography*, 10 (8), 893–908.
Evers, C. 2015. Researching action sport with a GoPro camera: an embodied and emotional mobile video tale of the sea, masculinity, and men-who-surf. In I. Wellard (ed.), *Researching embodied sport*. London: Routledge.
Fausto-Sterling, A. 2000. *Sexing the body*. New York: Basic Books.
Fisher, L., and Embree, L. E. 2000. *Feminist phenomenology*. Dordrecht: Kluwer Academic.
Foucault, M. 1977. *Discipline and punishment: the birth of the prison* (trans. A. Sheriden). New York: Vintage Books.
Foucault, M. 1980. *Power/knowledge: selected interviews and other writings, 1972–1977*. New York: Pantheon Books.
Foucault, M. 1981. *The history of sexuality, volume 1* (trans. R. Hurley). London: Penguin.
Garland-Thomson, R. 2012. The case for conserving disability. *Bioethical Inquiry*, 9, 339–355.
Gatens, M. 1991. A critique of the sex/gender distinction. In S. Gunew (ed.), *A reader in feminist knowledge*. London: Routledge.
Gatens, M. 1996. *Imaginary bodies: ethics, power and corporeality*. London & New York: Routledge.
Germon, J. 2009. *Gender: a genealogy of an idea*. New York: Palgrave Macmillan.
Germon, J. 2014. Researching masculinities: renarrating sexual difference. *Qualitative Research Journal*, 14 (1), 50–63.
Gibbs, A. 2002. Contagious feelings: Pauline Hanson and the epidemiology of affect. *Australian Humanities Review*. Available from www.lib.latrobe.edu.au/AHR.
Grosz, E. 1994. *Volatile bodies: toward a corporeal feminism*. Bloomington, IN: Indiana University Press.
Heinämaa, S. 2003. *Toward a phenomenology of sexual difference: Husserl, Merleau-Ponty, Beauvoir*. Lanham, MD: Rowman & Littlefield.
Hirchsfeld, M. [1910] 1991. *Transvestites: The erotic drive to cross-dress*, trans. M. Lombardi-Nash. Buffalo NY: Prometheus.
Mauss, M. [1935] 1979. *Sociology and psychology* (trans. B. Brewster). London: Routledge.
McNay, L. 1999. Gender, habitus and the field: Pierre Bourdieu and the limits of reflexivity theory. *Theory, Culture and Society*, 16 (1), 95–117.
Merleau-Ponty, M. 1982. *Phenomenology of perception*. New York: Routledge.
Moi, T. 2001. *What is a woman and other essays*. Oxford: Oxford University Press.
Money, J. 1952. *Hermaphroditism: an inquiry into the nature of a human paradox*. Cambridge, MA: Harvard University Press.
Money, J. 1978. Determinants of human gender identity/role. In J. Money and H. Musaph (eds), *Handbook of sexology: history and ideology*. Oxford: Elsevier.
Mugabane, Z. 2014. Spectacles and scholarship: Caster Semenya, intersex studies, and the problem of race in feminist theory. *Signs*, 39 (3), 761–785.
Penelope, J. 1992. *Call me lesbian: lesbian lives, lesbian theory*. Berkeley, CA: Crossing Press.
Probyn, E. 1993. *Sexing the self*. London: Routledge.
Probyn, E. 1996. *Outside belongings*. London: Routledge.
Probyn, E. 2004. Shame in the habitus. In L. Adkins and B. Skeggs (eds), *Feminism after Bourdieu*. Malden, MA: Blackwell Publishers, 224–248.
Probyn, E. 2005. *Blush: faces of shame*. Minneapolis, MN: University of Minnesota Press.
Probyn, E. 2014. Women following fish in a more-than-human world. *Gender, Place and Culture*, 21 (5), 589–603.
Rubin, G. 2007 [1984]. Thinking sex: notes for a radical theory of the politics of sexuality. In R. Parker

and P. Aggleton (eds), *Culture, Society and Sexuality: A reader* (2nd edition). New York & London: Routledge, 150–187.

Schiebinger, L. 1989. *The mind has no sex? Women in the origins of modern science*. Cambridge, MA: Harvard University Press.

Seidler, V. J. 2006. *Transforming masculinities: men, cultures, bodies, power, sex and love*. New York: Routledge.

Serres, M. 1995. *Angels: a modern myth*. Paris: Flammarion.

Sokolowski, R. 2000. *Introduction to phenomenology*. Cambridge: Cambridge University Press.

Somerville, S. 1998. Scientific racism and the invention of the homosexual body. In L. Bland and L. Doan (eds), *Sexology in culture: labelling bodies and desires*. Polity, Cambridge, pp. 60–76.

Sterne, J. 2006. Communication as techné. In G. J. Shepherd, J. St. John and T. Striphas (eds), *Communication as …: perspectives on theory*. Thousand Oaks, CA: Sage Publications, 91–98.

Thorpe, H. 2009. Bourdieu, feminism and female physical culture: gender reflexivity and the habitus-field complex. *Sociology of Sport Journal*, 26, 491–516.

Thorpe. H. 2010. Bourdieu, gender reflexivity and physical culture: a case of masculinities in the snowboarding field. *Journal of Sport and Social Issues*, 34 (2), 176–214.

Thorpe, H. 2014. Moving beyond the social/biological divide: Toward theoretical and transdisciplinary adventures. *Sport, Education and Society*, 19 (5), 666–686.

Tomkins, S. 1962. *Affect, imagery, consciousness. Vol. 1: The positive affects*. New York: Springer.

Tomkins, S. 1963. *Affect, imagery, consciousness. Vol. 2: The negative affects*. New York: Springer.

Wacquant, L. 2004. Habitus. In J. Beckert and M. Zafirovski (eds), *International encyclopedia of economic sociology*. London: Routledge, 315–319.

Wacquant, L. 2014a. Homines in extremis: what fighting scholars teach us about habitus. *Body and Society*, 20 (2), 3–17.

Wacquant, L. 2014b. Putting habitus in its place: rejoinder to the symposium, *Body and Society*, 20(2) 118–139.

Wetherell, M. 2012. *Affect and emotion: a new social science understanding*. London: Sage.

Whatmore, S. 2006. Materialist returns: practising cultural geography in and for a more-than-human world. *Cultural Geographies*, 13, 600–609.

Young, I. M. 1980. Throwing like a girl: a phenomenology of feminine body comportment, motility and spatiality. *Human Studies*, 3 (1), 137–156.

Young, I. M. 2002. Lived body vs gender: reflections on social structures and subjectivity. *Ratio*, 15 (4), 410–428.

15
SEXUALIZED/SEXED BODIES

Megan Chawansky and Satoko Itani

Physical cultural studies (PCS) offers many possibilities for scholars who wish to contextualize sexualized and sexed bodies, theorize the sexualization and sexing of bodies, highlight the (in-)visibility of certain sexualized bodies, question which bodies are sexualized, and examine the complexities of defining how, when, where, which and by whom might bodies be sexualized and sexed. In this chapter, we offer our suggestions on delineating what a PCS approach to the study of sexualized and sexed bodies might look like by identifying existing research on sexualized and sexed bodies which (we suggest) embraces a PCS approach. We then discuss our current research in terms of what a PCS sensibility offers to us as teachers/activists/researchers as a way of encouraging others to further contemplate the viability of PCS in this domain. As scholars who are particularly interested and involved in research that considers transnational perspectives on physical cultures, we hone in on sexualized/sexed bodies, but remain mindful of the impossibility of isolating one dimension of subjective or embodied experiences; it is the privilege of white bodies in a white supremacist society wherein one can imagine or see a body *only* as sexualized or sexed, since the white body can exist as universal, 'unmarked', and not racialized (Mohanram, 1999). The bodies we consider and research are simultaneously gendered, raced, classed and located within discourses of (dis-)ability, nation, ethnicity, beauty and (re-)productivity which privilege and marginalize them in complex ways. In this chapter, we choose to focus on sexualized and sexed bodies, which we suggest are highly interrelated and slightly different effects of the same thing: heteropatriarchy and racism. While we understand that all bodies are sexualized/sexed to certain degrees and in certain contexts, the bodies we consider in this chapter are oftentimes demarcated as homosexual, gay (G), lesbian (L), bisexual (B), trans- (T), intersex (I) and queer (Q) bodies. They may also be bodies ('diagnosed' or not) with hyperandrogenism. We include this brief list not to be exhaustive or to exclude but in order to provide some parameters for this chapter. While we readily acknowledge the multiple ways sexualized/sexed bodies (dis-)appear in physical culture, our work in this area primarily deals with bodies coded, read or asserted to be 'lesbian' (Chawansky) and 'queer' (Itani), and so we invariably drift towards work which includes these subjectivities.

In the next paragraphs, we outline the loose parameters of a PCS approach to the study of sexualized/sexed bodies through a select reading of illustrative examples. We should note that in most instances, it is *our* designation of these articles as of the PCS vein rather than the authors' demarcation of them as such, and we imagine some might resist our designation.

Indeed, our own responses to the promise of PCS and of writing and researching within this intellectual project are cautious. The area wherein PCS holds the most promise for us as emerging academics is in the practical challenges of helping us to find a 'room of our own' in a contemporary, corporatized university context, something that we would suggest that the writing on – or related to – PCS has addressed in multiple instances (see Andrews, 2008; Andrews, Silk, Francombe and Bush, 2013; Silk, Francombe and Andrews, 2014). A brief digression here helps to explain why this particular dimension is appealing. We met at the Ohio State University and subsequently completed postgraduate degrees in 'Sport and Exercise Humanities' (SEH) in 2008. The SEH programme aspired to train students to consider the historical, philosophical and sociocultural dimensions of sport and exercise and began with a healthy cohort of postgraduate students. However, it was eliminated shortly after we graduated and undergraduate students may now enrol in a 'Sport Industry' degree whereas graduate study is only offered within sport management. As early-career scholars, we routinely read through and have contemplated job adverts in the fields of physical education, kinesiology, gender studies, sexuality studies, movement sciences and sport management. The implications of this are not only of trying to 'fit' within particular vacancies, but also in locating suitable mentors, establishing supportive tracks for young scholars, and imagining viable career trajectories. Moreover, we are all too aware of how our teaching/activism/research on sexualized/sexed bodies gets catalogued as uncomfortable, unnecessary, triggering and un-fundable within an academic climate reliant on 'neoliberal educational rationalities' (Silk et al., 2014: 1266).

That said, we would be remiss if we did not acknowledge some of our tentativeness regarding the PCS mandate, specifically as it relates to sexualized and sexed bodies. For Chawansky, the hesitancy resides less with the merit of the approach or its premise and more with the 'politics of the citation' and what perspectives are underutilized in outlining the PCS vision. As one whose women's studies coursework forms the backdrop of her materialist feminist research and activism, Chawansky aligns with those feminists who study sport and who highlight the lack of full inclusion of feminist knowledge in the PCS domain thus far (Thorpe, Barbour and Bruce, 2011). For Chawansky, the frequently articulated feminist slogans of the 'personal as political' and the 'body as a battleground' reflect an academic field and intellectual project already engaged with many of the sensibilities of PCS, especially as they relate to dimensions of sex and sexualities. As such, this chapter and indeed this entire collection provides a space to reflect on previous knowledge and pull together varied approaches in the interests of furthering the academic study of (in)active sexualized/sexed bodies. For Itani, the hesitancy rests with the ongoing lack of the analysis of colonialism, whiteness, and knowledge imperialism within the scholarships that claim to uphold the PCS approach. From the perspective of a queer scholar of colour from Japan, the turn towards *physical culture* from the Eurocentric universalization of *sport* has not resulted in the vigorous interventions into the theoretical frameworks and research methodologies that challenge knowledge production about (in)active bodies that are white, Eurocentric, heteronormative, and colonizing. We use this chapter – in part – to reflect upon some of our own hesitancies in the hopes of furthering the discussion on the possibilities of PCS as an analytical tool to study sexualized/sexed bodies.

Physical cultural studies research involving sexualized/sexed bodies

While accepting that the PCS approach to research and scholarship is continuously being refined, we wish to highlight some of its key tenets in order to reflect on how sexualized/sexed bodies might be understood through this lens. We do this by primarily reviewing examples of existing scholarship and in identifying areas of specific social, economic, political and technological importance to sexualized bodies. These four broad themes are regularly cited as the realms of consideration when delivering on the radical contextualization that PCS seeks to offer. In terms of sexualized and sexed bodies, this includes analysis on changes in national and transnational polices regarding GLBTIQ rights; harassment, bullying and protection of GLBTIQ people; and (in-)visibility and representations of GLBTIQ athletes, coaches and fans. More expansively, and within sporting mega events, this can include the monitoring and regulation of sex workers at/around sporting mega events, the policing of intersex athletes who compete as women and those female athletes who are deemed 'too masculine' and subjected to 'gender testing' and public shaming. It may also include the use of sexualized bodies to represent and promote mega events and national sensibilities.

PCS also seeks 'to *move beyond writing and researching about bodies to writing and researching through bodies as a principle force of the research act*' (Giardina and Newman, 2011: 44, emphasis original). In this dimension, PCS encourages scholars to move beyond 'identity-based reflexivity' (Nagar, 2014: 94) to examine the messiness of sexualized/sexed researcher bodies that invariably shape and are being shaped by research experiences. It also, as done by Pavlidis and Fullagar (2014) in their study of subjectification of women who engage in roller derby, allows us to consider embodied experiences such as pain and pleasure through re-imagining the (sexed) sporting bodies of participants.

A PCS approach helps to understand the (im-)possibilities of sporting events which seek to create spaces for marginalized sexualized bodies such as the Gay Games or World OutGames (Davidson, 2012, 2013). Davidson's (2012, 2013) research combines with Puar's (2002) analysis on gay mobilities and travel to remind us of the import of critical contextualization of mega events targeting 'marginalized' sexualized bodies. That is, Puar (ibid.) implores us to remember that to participate in the Gay Games and World OutGames around the Atlantic and Pacific requires athletes to possess a specific combination of privilege based on race, class and nation. In addition to considering events, PCS research on sexualized bodies can interrogate specific sexualized bodies within sport. For instance, King (2009a) examines the connections between homonormativity, homonationalism and militarism through a case study of Mark Bingham and considers the racialization of homonormativity through an analysis of former US basketball star, Sheryl Swoopes (King, 2009b). Further studies of sexualized bodies interrogate sport leagues such as the US Women's National Basketball Association (WNBA) and its shifting perspectives on the bodies of lesbian fans and athletes (McDonald, 2002, 2008, 2012). As an example, McDonald's (2012: 219) commentary on the WNBA locates their more recent interest in acknowledging and including lesbian and gay fans 'alongside such increasingly commercialized entities such as gay and lesbian tourism, the globalization of Pride/Mardi Gras/Gay Games mega events' and the emphasis on the pink dollar (Jones and LeBlanc, 2005). The economic imperative to recognize and market certain lesbian sporting celebrities extends to individual 'success' stories, as is noted in research by Chawansky and Francombe (2011, 2013).

In terms of sexed bodies, Levy's (2009) highly contextualized study of South African athlete, Caster Semenya, combines well with Mitra's (2014) research and activist work with Indian athletes with intersex variations. Taken together, these two analyses offer nuanced accounts of athletes with intersex variations (ibid.) or those assumed to have intersex variations (Levy, 2009) and present keen insights on the ways in which conversations and assessment about sexed bodies bespeak legacies and realities of racism, colonialism, class and caste. Bavington (2014) does related work on this theme and employs feminist, queer and racial analysis to contextualize the International Olympic Committee's (IOC) regulations on hyperandrogenism in elite female athletes. Bavington (ibid.) demonstrates that, contrary to the IOC's claim, the policy is not only de facto 'sex' test, but also exemplifies Western policy intervention and biomedical control of young females from the Global South. These more recently published works build on Cavanagh and Sykes (2006) and Cole (2000) to provide updated and contextualized scholarship on the sexed body in sport.

The selected literature referenced above informs our own respective projects in the area of sexualized/sexed bodies. For instance, one of Chawansky's (2015) recent projects blends her interest in the 'sport for international development and peace' (SDP) sector with previous investigations into lesbian sporting celebrity (Chawansky and Francombe, 2011, 2013). While the use and recent inclusion of celebrities in the realm of international development efforts has been explored by scholars from various disciplines (e.g. Brockington, 2014) and is a common practice within the SDP sector, it has received limited attention within the SDP literature, with the notable exceptions of Darnell (2012) and Wilson, Van Luijk and Boit (2013). Moreover, to date there has been no exploration of how lesbian sporting celebrity might operate in the SDP context. In pursuing this project, this work aspires to illuminate the limited attention afforded to sexuality in international development contexts (Jolly, 2011) and to expand understandings of how heteronormativity operates in SDP spaces (Carney and Chawansky, 2014). This is done through a case study of celebrity footballer, Abby Wambach, who was named a 'Development Champion' by the United States Agency for International Development (USAID) in 2012 (USAID, 2015). In this capacity, Wambach assists the organization in its efforts to empower girls and women around the world through the use of sport. Wambach is also publicly known to be married to a former female footballer – Sarah Huffman – though in statements, she has downplayed the political implications of this event by noting that:

> I know that I'll end up being a role model for many, many people out there for all kinds of reasons … my first hope is for being a genuine, honest and good person, then a great soccer player and then down the line, the choice I've made to marry not only my best friend and teammate, but the love of my life.
>
> *(Associated Press, 2014)*

The choice of Wambach to de-politicize her marriage exists within a context of homonationalism (Puar, 2006) which is especially suited to Wambach's primary sporting subjectivity: that of the fearless forward for the US Women's National Soccer Team (USWNT) best known for scoring goals on diving, aggressive headers. That Wambach can now serve as a sporting celebrity diplomat in different parts of the world bespeaks Puar's (2006: 68) argument that 'contemporary forms of US nationalism and patriotism' rely on 'certain domesticated homosexual bodies [to] provide ammunition to reinforce nationalist projects'. One of these nationalist projects is the recent appointment of a Special Envoy for LGBT Rights, which (self-)appoints the US as a leader in global LGBT rights (NPR, 2015). In this project, then, a careful consideration of Wambach's lesbian celebrity necessarily includes unpacking the transnational social, political, economic contexts, with a particular consideration of the neo-colonial critiques of SDP initiatives.

Itani's work develops on and critically engages with Western literature that examines the gender and sexual politics in sports within North American society. Itani's (2015) research examined the ways in which Japanese gender, sexual, racial, ethnic, and national politics are articulated in the discursive construction of Japanese female and 'trans' athletes in 'masculine' sports (soccer and wrestling) in the Japanese mainstream media. They also explored the ways in which Japanese female and 'trans' athletes in these sports negotiate Japanese gender and sexuality norms in the formation of their gendered subjectivities. Although this research was conducted and situated in Japan, the analysis of 'micro' and 'macro' level genealogical discourse analyses revealed not only the interaction of different discursive fields, but also their colonial trajectories.

Itani's (2015) analysis illustrates that Japanese mainstream media used multiple normative and normalizing discursive tactics to construct Japanese female athletes within patriarchal, sexist, and heterosexist gender and sexual norms. These discourses were also mobilized in the reporting on international competitions, particularly after the year 2011, the year of the triple natural (and human-made) disasters which included an earthquake, tsunami and nuclear meltdown. In these discourses, the success of Japanese female athletes was used by the media to construct Japanese national identity in order to recuperate Japanese masculinity. This masculinity has been repeatedly threatened, first through the defeat of Japan in WWII, then during the economic recession in the 1990s and more recently via the triple disasters. In this process of normalization and appropriation, the subject of the modern Japanese female athlete – a *taiikukaikei* (athletic) woman – was constituted. *Taiikukaikei* women's masculinity was constructed as a sign of their devotion to sport, as true athletes dedicate all their energy and time for their sports, not in dating or in taking care of one's appearance. The media analysis also demonstrated that heteronormativity and normative femininity are constantly troubled and subverted; the meanings of 'Japanese women' are always shifting. Despite its normalizing function, the discourse of *taiikukaikei* women leaves a murky 'third gender space' in which a 'female *sporting* masculinity' may be accepted.

In Itani's research, the experiences of cisgendered (a person whose gender identify conforms with the identity assigned at birth) and non-cisgendered athletes illustrated the intricate negotiations with the domination of males in (their) sport, Japanese gender and sexual norms, the conflicting demands of athletic careers, and the medicalized discourse of 'gender identity disorder' (GID). Some cisgendered female athletes formed ambivalent subjectivities through the conflicting demands of their sport and society, while other athletes took pride in their masculinities and physical strength. The construction of the female athletes' masculinity as a sign of 'devotion' to the sport and their coach's demand 'not to be a woman' have strong resonances with the media constructions of *taiikukaikei* women. The discourse of 'female sporting masculinity' both provides and closes off different ways of being a woman. The 'third gender space' produced through this discourse tolerates a certain level of female masculinity and the absence of heterosexual relationships, while feminine expressions and interests may be policed. It also makes female masculinity as the expression of their gender *identity* unthinkable, thus erasing non-cisgendered athletes in women's sport.

This unthinkability of a *queer* identity provided non-cisgendered athletes with a small and precarious yet important space to express their masculinity more safely, compared to other social spheres. Through being made unrecognizable, non-cisgendered athletes entered into male-dominated sports without their gender identity or sexuality being questioned. They negotiated and utilized these otherwise hurtful discourses of sexism, heterosexism, and cisgenderism by identifying and dis-identifying with the discourses for their survival in sports and in Japanese society at large.

Taking physical cultural studies forward for sexualized/sexed bodies

As noted above, scholars analyse the ways in which certain bodies are sexed and sexualized in and through sports and physical culture in various ways. A good portion of the aforementioned scholarship analysed how sports reproduce and reinforce heteropatriarchy within the white European and settler societies in North America and Australia. In more recent years, scholars have critiqued the whiteness of queer analysis of sport, called for the intersectional analysis of racial, national, and colonial politics, and demonstrated the effectiveness of this type of analysis (e.g. Davidson, 2012, 2013; McDonald, 2002, 2006, 2014; King, 2008, 2009b; Sykes, 2006, 2014a, 2014b). We have tried to demonstrate the utility of this approach through discussions of our own respective research projects, and below we provide further justification for this emphasis through direct connections to PCS and its future.

In this section we overview the theoretical and analytical frameworks that enable the 'radical contextualization' (Grossberg, as cited by Andrews, 2002), of sexualized/sexed bodies in terms of the 'colonial matrix of power' (Mignolo, 2011) as a way of taking PCS forward. Scholars have warned that a queer analysis of sport that relies on a primary focus (such as homophobia and transphobia) without intersectional analyses of colonialism and the production of modern sexuality run the risk of reproducing racist and white supremacist thinking (Davidson, 2013; King, 2008; McDonald, 2006, 2014; Sykes, 2006). In order to contextualize the sexualized/sexed bodies at the intersection of racial, national, and colonial politics, attention to the 'sociocultural' *difference*, or a 'micro' analysis of sociocultural specificity alone is rarely sufficient. It must be accompanied by the analysis of the 'macro' context that investigates global, colonial power relations that underpin the 'micro' context. The recent theoretical convergence of postcolonial and queer theories and Indigenous theorization of settler colonialism (Morgensen, 2010; Smith, 2005, 2006, 2010) offers powerful guidance from which to investigate the 'macro' contexts of colonialism and settler colonialism. This 'macro' context is crucial in order to understand the geopolitically specific formation of 'homonormative' (Duggan, 2002) and 'homonational' (Puar, 2007) queer activisms within the North American and European societies in the twenty-first century.

The interrogation and analysis of modern sexuality in Europe and settler-societies and its contemporary articulation provides an important theoretical foundation and the conceptual tools to analyse the formation of the modern sexualized/sexed subject in and through sports. As early feminist and later queer sport sociologists and historians revealed, modern sports functioned to produce and demarcate healthy, strong, disciplined, properly masculine bodies (white and heterosexual) from *other* bodies (racialized, feminine and queer). When the hetero-patriarchal family is the condition of the modern subject, those who fall outside heteronormative and white masculinity – *queer* others – are sexualized, racialized and marginalized in sport and outside of it. However, the emergence and development of queer activisms and the permeation of neoliberal capitalist logics and values in North American and Western European societies in the late twentieth century began to shift the condition of the modern subject. As Duggan (2002) and Puar (2007) theorized, in the time of war on terrorism and neoliberalism, affluent and patriotic gays and lesbians began to be included as a modern subject. In part this is seen throughout the 2010s, as liberal queer sport activisms that seek visibility and inclusion into mainstream competitive sport receive significant popular support. Importantly then, Davidson's (2012, 2013) research on the Gay Games and OutGames reveals how shifting sexual, racial, national, and colonial politics have shaped the direction and political implication of sport mega events for gay and lesbian athletes. Davidson (2013: 59) argues that Gay Games and World OutGames came to be 'co-opted into the larger phenomena of sexual exceptionalism and homonationalism' due to their desire of and pursuit for (liberal) inclusion into neoliberal patriarchal citizenship via modern athletic and consumer subjectivities.

Future PCS research must remain mindful that race has always been sexualized and sexuality has consistently been racialized within discourses of colonialism, nationalism, human rights, citizenship and migration (Smith, 2005, 2006, 2010; Morgensen, 2010). Sykes' and her colleagues' recent works concerning sport mega events and anti-globalization, Indigenous, and queer activisms incorporate such Indigenous scholars' critique of the formation of modern sexuality in a settler society and the queer complicity in settler-colonialism (Sykes, 2014a, 2014b; Sykes and Itani, 2014; Sykes and Lloyd, 2012). For example, analysing the liberal queer politics in sport represented by the PrideHouse in the Vancouver Olympics, Sykes (2014a) demonstrates the ways in which the discourse of homonational inclusion of gay and lesbian athletes relies on the erasure of Canada's settler-colonial history and ongoing colonization of Indigenous peoples. The Vancouver Olympics were made possible through the forced eviction and displacement of marginalized people, and were built and took place on the unceded First Nations territory. Furthermore, celebrating gay and lesbian inclusion in sport within North American context as 'progress' and equating the degree of 'gay-friendliness' with a sign of civilization erases the history of genocide and gender and sexual violence against Indigenous peoples, whose family structures, gender and sexual norms fell outside heteropatriarchal norms of European settlers (Morgensen, 2010). The kind of queer analysis that focuses only on homophobia in sports in this context becomes complicit with the project of settler-colonialism and white supremacy by omitting/erasing the genealogical analysis of the settler-colonial violence that paved the way to such inclusion. Moving forward, we hope to see PCS scholarship on sexualized/sexed bodies follow the leads of the research noted in the above paragraphs, insofar as they offers new points of entry and analysis.

To conclude, the aim of this chapter has been to present a sample of the research on sexualized/sexed bodies that meets many of the criteria of what is being defined as PCS work, particularly scholarship that is deeply contextualized, theoretically rigorous, embodied, politically inspired, and intersectional. In so doing, we offer a blueprint for those who wish to build on previous scholarship by highlighting some of the key elements of this research. We also sought to highlight the ways in which PCS can shape research by identifying important considerations that must be integrated into the PCS vision in order to fully contextualize sexualized/sexed bodies. Finally, we see the encouragement of scholars to research *through* the body (and not just on or about it) as a more recent contribution to the understanding of PCS and one that offers an array of possibilities for increasing our understandings of sexualized/sexed bodies.

References

Andrews, D. L., 2002. Coming to terms with cultural studies. *Journal of Sport and Social Issues*, 26, 110–117.
Andrews, D. L., 2008. Kinesiology's inconvenient truth: the physical cultural studies imperative. *Quest*, 60, 46–63.
Andrews, D. L., Silk, M. L., Francombe, J. and Bush, A., 2013. McKinesiology. *Review of Education, Pedagogy, and Cultural Studies*, 35, 1–22.
Associated Press, 2014. Wambach: marriage not about politics. Available from www.foxsports.com/foxsoccer/usa/story/abby-wambach-marriage-to-teammate-sarah-huffman-was-not-about-politics-101813 (accessed 30 April 2015).
Bavington, L., 2014. 'Sex' testing in women's sport: an intersectional analysis. Paper presented at Intersectionality Research, Policy and Practice Conference, Simon Fraser University, Vancouver, British Columbia, 26 April.
Brockington, D., 2014. *Celebrity advocacy and international development*. Abingdon, Oxon: Routledge.
Carney, A. and Chawansky, M., 2014. Taking sex off the sidelines: challenging heteronormativity within 'sport in development' research. *International Review for the Sociology of Sport*. doi: 10.1177/1012690214521616
Cavanagh, S. L. and Sykes, H., 2006. Transsexual bodies at the Olympics: the International Committee's policy on transsexual athletes at the 2004 Athens Summer Games. *Body and Society*, 12 (8), 75–102.
Chawansky, M., 2015. The next Abby Wambach: lesbian sporting celebrity within Sport for Development and Peace (SDP) projects. Paper presented at Lesbian Lives conference, University of Brighton, Brighton, England.

Chawansky, M. and Francombe, J., 2011. Cruising for Olivia: lesbian celebrity and the cultural politics of coming out in sport. *Sociology of Sport Journal*, 28 (4), 461–477.

Chawansky, M. and Francombe, J., 2013. Wanting to be Anna: examining lesbian sporting celebrity on *The L Word*. *Journal of Lesbian Studies*, 17 (2), 134–149.

Cole, C. L., 2000. One chromosome too many? In K. Schaffer and S. Smith (eds), *The Olympics at the millennium: power, politics and the games*. New Brunswick, NJ: Rutgers University Press, 128–146.

Darnell, S. C., 2012. *Sport for development and peace: a critical sociology*. London: Bloomsbury.

Davidson, J., 2012. Racism against the abnormal? The twentieth century gay games, biopower and the emergence of homonational sport. *Leisure Studies*, 1–22.

Davidson, J., 2013. Sporting homonationalisms: sexual exceptionalism, queer privilege, and the 21st century international lesbian and gay sport movement. *Sociology of Sport Journal*, 30, 57–82.

Duggan, L., 2002. The new homonormativity: the sexual politics of neoliberalism. In R. Castronovo and D. D. Nelson (eds), *Materializing democracy: toward a revitalized cultural politics*. Durham, NC: Duke University Press, 175–194.

Giardina, M. D. and Newman, J. I., 2011. What is this 'physical' in physical cultural studies? *Sociology of Sport Journal*, 28(1), 36–63.

Itani, S., 2015. Japanese female and 'trans' athletes: negotiating subjectivity and media constructions of gender, sexuality, and nation. Unpublished doctoral thesis. University of Toronto.

Jolly, S., 2011. Why is development work so straight? Heteronormativity in the international development industry. *Development in practice*, 21 (1), 18–28.

Jones, R. and LeBlanc, R., 2005. Sport sexuality and representation in advertising: the political economy of the pink dollar. In S. Jackson and D. J. Andrews (eds), *Sport, culture and advertising*. London: Routledge, 119–135.

King, S. J., 2008. What's queer about queer sociology now? A review essay. *Sociology of Sport Journal*, 25, 419–442.

King, S., 2009a. Virtually normal: Mark Bingham, the war on terror, and the sexual politics of sport. *Journal of Sport and Social Issues*, 33, 5–24.

King, S., 2009b. Homonormativity and the politics of race: reading Sheryl Swoopes. *Journal of Lesbian Studies*, 13, 272–290.

Levy, A., 2009. Either/or: sports, sex and the case of Caster Semenya. *The New Yorker*, 30 November. Available from www.newyorker.com/magazine/2009/11/30/eitheror (accessed 27 April 2015).

McDonald, M., 2002. Queering whiteness: the particular case of the Women's National Basketball Association. *Sociological Perspectives*, 45 (4), 379–396.

McDonald, M., 2006. Beyond the pale: the whiteness of sport studies and queer scholarship. In J. Caudwell (ed.), *Sport, sexualities and queer/theory*. London: Routledge, 33–45.

McDonald, M., 2008. Rethinking resistance: the queer play of visibility politics, the Women's National Basketball Association and late capitalism. *Leisure Studies*, 27 (1), 77–93.

McDonald, M., 2012. Out-of-bounds plays: the Women's National Basketball Association and the neoliberal imaginings of sexuality. In D. L. Andrews and M. Silk (eds), *Sport and neoliberalism*. Philadelphia, PA: Temple University Press, 211–224.

McDonald, M. G., 2014. Mapping intersectionality and whiteness: troubling gender and sexuality in sport studies. In J. Hargreaves and E. Anderson (eds), *Routledge handbook of sport, gender and sexuality*. Abingdon: Routledge, 151–159.

Mignolo, W. D., 2011. *The darker side of western modernity: global futures, decolonial options*. Durham, NC: Duke University Press.

Mitra, P., 2014. Male/female or other: the untold stories of female athletes with intersex variations in India. In J. Hargreaves and E. Anderson (eds), *Routledge handbook of sport, gender and sexuality*. Abingdon: Routledge, 384–394.

Mohanram, R., 1999. *Black body: women, colonialism, and space*. Minneapolis, MN: University of Minnesota Press.

Morgensen, S. L., 2010. Settler homonationalism: theorizing settler colonialism within queer modernities. *GLQ: A Journal of Lesbian and Gay Studies*, 16 (1–2), 105–131.

Nagar, R., 2014. *Muddying the waters: coauthoring feminisms across scholarship and activism*. Urbana, IL: University of Illinois Press.

NPR, 2015. US Appoints first-ever special envoy for LGBT rights. Available from www.npr.org/blogs/thetwo-way/2015/02/23/388482554/u-s-appoints-first-ever-special-envoy-for-lgbt-rights (accessed 30 April 2015).

Pavlidis, A. and Fullagar, S., 2014. The pain and pleasure of roller derby: thinking through affect and subjectification. *International Journal of Cultural Studies*, 18 (5), 483–499.

Puar, J. K., 2002. Circuits of queer mobility: tourism, travel, and globalization. *GLQ: A Journal of Lesbian and Gay Studies*, 8 (1–2), 101–137.

Puar, J. K., 2006. Mapping US homonormativities. *Gender, Place and Culture*, 13 (1), 67–88.

Puar, J. K., 2007. *Terrorist assemblages: homonationalism in queer times*. Durham, NC: Duke University Press.

Silk, M. L., Francombe, J. M. and Andrews, D. L., 2014. Slowing the social sciences of sport: on the possibilities of physical culture. *Sport in Society*, 17(10), 1266–1289.

Smith, A., 2005. *Conquest: sexual violence and American Indian genocide*. Cambridge, MA: South End Press.

Smith, A., 2006. Heteropatriarchy and the three pillars of white supremacy: rethinking women of color organizing. In INCITE! (ed.), *Color of Violence: INCITE! Women of Color Against Violence*. Cambridge, MA: South End Press.

Smith, A., 2010. Queer theory and native studies: the heteronormativity of settler colonialism, *GLQ: A Journal of Lesbian and Gay Studies,* 16 (1–2): 42–68.

Sykes, H., 2006. Queering theories of sexuality in sport studies. In J. Caudwell (ed.), *Sport, sexualities and queer/theory*. New York: Routledge, 13–32.

Sykes, H., 2014a. Sport within/against the US empire: queer complicity, anti-colonial activism. Paper presented at 2014 Annual Conference Meeting for North American Society for Sociology of Sport, Portland, Oregon.

Sykes, H., 2014b. Un-settling sex: researcher self-reflexivity, queer theory and settler colonial studies. *Qualitative Research in Sport, Exercise and Health*, 6 (4), 583–595.

Sykes, H. and Itani, S., 2014. Homonational inclusion and anti-colonial resistance at the Vancouver, Sochi and Rio de Janeiro Olympics. Paper presented at Second International Conference on Mega-Events and the City. Rio de Janeiro, Brazil, April/May.

Sykes, H. and Lloyd, J., 2012. Gay pride on stolen land. Paper presented at American Educational Research Association, Curriculum Studies Division B, Vancouver, BC, April.

Thorpe, H., Barbour, K. and Bruce, T., 2011. Feminist journeys: playing with theory and representation in physical cultural fields. *Sociology of Sport Journal*, 28, 106–134.

USAID, 2015. Sport for development: Abby Wambach. Available from www.usaid.gov/news-information/videos/sport-development-abby-wambach (accessed 30 April 2015).

Wilson, B., Van Luijk, N. and Boit, M., 2013. When celebrity athletes are 'social movement entrepreneurs': a study of the role of elite runners in Run-for-Peace events in post-conflict Kenya in 2008. *International Review for the Sociology of Sport*, doi: 10.1177/1012690213506005.

16
(DIS)ABLED BODIES

P. David Howe

Over the past thirty years, my research has focused on Paralympic bodies (Howe, 2008a). In part, my entry into this field was via my own body. Using my body both as researcher and subject (Howe, 2008b, 2011b), this work celebrates the physical nature of physical cultural studies (PCS) (Giardina and Newman, 2011). It also strives to achieve the aim of praxis that is another key tenet of PCS. Because of my very personal involvement in this research, it has always had a political agenda. I embrace the understanding of McDonald (2002) who highlights two different approaches to a political agenda in research – radical and moralistic. The radical approach highlights how 'critical' social research separates intervention from activism whereas the moralistic merges research with social activism. As such my research attempts to be at one and the same time both radical and moralistic. The praxis focus I take towards my research, while advocated by those who practice PCS, is at one and the same time often criticized for its lack of theoretical depth.

Scholarly activity looking at the importance of the disabled body in a variety of social environments (see Turner, 2001) have championed this importance of being theoretically robust. Likewise, in the field of sport studies, critical researchers have taken inspiration from theorists of the body (Blake 1996), including social theorists such as Bourdieu (1977, 1984, 1990), Foucault (1977) and Merleau-Ponty (1962, 1965). My work on the Paralympic bodies has been hugely influenced by Brian Pronger (2002), and particularly how he perceives sport as a controlling embodied practice. One of the triumphs of PCS is the use of multiple theoretical lenses that is articulated so nicely in Pronger's work, and developed further by other sociologists of sport and those working in the emerging field of PCS. Another connection between my own works on Paralympic bodies and PCS approaches is the centrality of participant-observations and an acknowledgement of the researching body. Over the past 25 years, there has been an increase of the use of participant observation as a primary ethnographic tool for researching sporting communities. Important ethnographic studies have been produced by anthropologists, such as Armstrong (1998) on football hooligans, Foley (1990) on American football, Klein (1991, 1993) on baseball and bodybuilding. Work by sociologists of sport has also celebrated this method, by de Garis (1999) focusing on professional wrestling, by Wheaton (1997, 2000) on wind surfing and by Thorpe (2006, 2008) on snowboarding. All of these authors celebrate the physical nature of their cultural investigation, and I would suggest that ethnography of sport should be further articulated following de Garis (1999) as sensuous ethnography. It is the sensuous nature of participant observation that I feel should be more often celebrated within PCS.

This chapter's focus on Paralympic bodies is not to suggest that these are not the only bodies that engage in disability sport, but rather since these are the most high-profile they can serve as good examples of (dis)abled bodies. In referring to Paralympic bodies I wish to make a distinction between congenital and acquired impairment as the two avenues into International Paralympic Committee (IPC) events. This should give the reader an understanding of the cultural specificity of the body central to Paralympic sporting practice while also setting the stage for the more theoretically driven discussion to follow.

Paralympic bodies

The running, jumping, swimming or simply moving bodies of impaired athletes have continually been judged in relation to an able-bodied 'norm' and the standards of play and performance are compared with those of mainstream competitions. This can have an adverse effect on participation rates within sport for the disabled as most bodies do not match up to the able-bodied norm. I use the term 'able-bodied' here because it is the term used by athletes within the cultural context of the Paralympic Games. As a former Paralympic athlete and ethnographer, I think it is important to use this term rather than the commonly used non-disabled. Since the late 1980s there has been a considered effort on the part of the IPC to force the issue of sport for the disabled into mainstream consciousness (Steadward, 1996). The problem is that it is a particular type of impaired body that is celebrated over others. The hierarchy inside and outside Paralympic Sport places those bodies that use mobility technologies to facilitate the participation above those who do not (Sherrill and Williams, 1996; Howe, 2008a; 2008b). In other words some disabled bodies are further marginalized within the confines of sport for disabled and as such there is a need to re-evaluate what is an acceptable sporting body. In an environment where the body is essential such as sport, imperfection becomes evident. Arguably, this is particularly evident in the Paralympic spectacle, where the presence of less than able bodies are in stark contrast to mainstream televised high-performance sport (Howe, 2008a; Howe and Parker, 2012). Karen DePauw (1997) examines how sport marginalizes the impaired and argues that we need to re-examine the relationship between sport and the body as it relates to disability:

> It is through the study of the body in the context of, and in relation to, sport that we can understand sport as one of the sites for the reproduction of social inequality in its promotion of the traditional view of athletic performance, masculinity, and physicality, including gendered images of the ideal physique and body beautiful.
> *(DePauw, 1997: 420)*

Sport is an embodied practice and as such many people who possess less than normal bodies may shy away from the masculine physicality associated with sport. For sportsmen and women with impairment, the manner in which they are embodied often marks them out for 'special' treatment in society as their bodies highlight these individuals in a meaningful way as imperfect and therefore inadequate. This is because a lack of a physical impairment is seen as 'normal' – so the imperfect body highlights the opposite – a lack of normality.

In the context of Paralympic sport there are two broad types of bodies that exist – those with either congenitally or acquired impairments. Both types of bodies will have travelled different roads before they became involved in Paralympic sport. Individuals with congenital impairments may have until recently attended what in the West are commonly referred to as 'special' schools. Early congenitally impaired Paralympians would have perhaps got their first exposure to sport through adapted physical activity classes at their school. These early experiences will have been instrumental in shaping the sporting experiences of these individuals. Today in many cases congenitally impaired individuals are schooled in inclusive environments but depending on the nature of the impairment they may or may not engage in a segregated physical education environment. Regardless of the type of access they have to organized sport the socialization of these young people will be distinct from those who went to special schools.

Those who come to Paralympic sport as a result of a traumatic accident, such as a car crash, are often socialized differently from congenitally impaired individuals. If a traumatic injury occurs in their youth these individuals may also have attended a special school or had adapted physical activity classes as their introduction to sport. If the traumatic injury happens after the age when young people attend school there is bound to be a period of transition to the new bodily circumstances. These individuals, regardless of age, go through a process of rehabilitation where their bodies need to be retrained often in the most basic tasks such as the management of daily hygiene regimes. Following Seymour, these individuals can be seen to be re-embodied. That is 'embodiment is our life-long obsession. Eating, sleeping, washing, grooming, stimulating and entertaining our bodies dominate our lives' (Seymour, 1998: 4) regardless of whether we are abled-bodied or not. After these individuals have relearned basic tasks or perhaps alongside these activities they in essence become re-embodied, that is learning some of what their 'new' body can and cannot do in an adaptive physical activity setting where sport will feature.

A body that engages in disability sport, from the grassroots to the Paralympics, should potentially be treated differently than an able body because the goals of the sport that celebrate higher, faster and stronger are more often than not unattainable for people with impairments (Howe, 2011a). However, the Paralympic movement adopts the same sport paradigm as the Olympic movement where judgement is made in performance terms and therefore is ultimately about physical superiority of one body over another (Howe and Jones, 2006). In other words,

> ability is at the centre of sport and physical activity. Ability, as currently socially constructed, means 'able' and implies a finely tuned 'able' body. On the other hand, disability, also a social construction, is often viewed in relation to ability and is, then, most often defined as 'less than' ability, as not able. To be able to 'see' individuals with disabilities as athletes (regardless of the impairment) requires us to redefine athleticism and our view of the body, especially the sporting body.
>
> *(DePauw, 1997: 423)*

This is a laudable goal which to date has not been achieved. While cyborg bodies, a blend of the human and space age technology such as Oscar Pistorius (Howe, 2011a) have been celebrated throughout the sporting world for his ability to transcend his impairment and compete at the Olympic Games, such celebrations have led to further marginalization of the most impaired Paralympians (Howe and Parker, 2012).

As the Paralympic Games continues its professionalization, there has been increased emphasis placed upon marketing the event with some bodies garnering most of the attention and coverage. In particular, the bodies in focus tend to be the less impaired and more often than not those who benefit from movement technologies such as prosthetic limbs and high-performance wheelchairs (Purdue and Howe, 2013). This creates tension between those bodies who are more severely impaired and the ones that are getting all the attention – not simply for their achievements but for what they represent to society at large. At this stage it is important to be mindful that the disabled bodies I have been talking about are not simply objects to be analysed from afar but are sensuous and as such it requires multiple lens to understand and articulate them appropriately. As previously noted, a strength of the PCS approach is its adoption of participant observation as its cornerstone (see for example de Garis, 1999; Klein, 1993; Thorpe, 2008). As I have explained elsewhere, there is considerable potential in using various French social theorists for understanding the sensuousness of less-abled bodies:

> a sensuous body ... can be understood through a marriage of the concepts highlighted from the work of Foucault, surrounding the disciplining of body, Bourdieu and his interpretation of the habitual nature of social practice and last but by no means least Merleau-Ponty's reflection upon the sedimentary nature of action and the multiplicity of perspectives any-body can get from 'being in the world'.
>
> (Howe, 2011b: 287)

Using multiple theoretical lenses, I suggest scholars within physical cultural studies can truly put the 'physical' into their work and importantly this can be used to articulate the social phenomenon of the ever-present impaired body in sport. The major apparatus that is both at the heart of Paralympic culture and that is central to the control of (dis)abled bodies is the classification process that all Paralympians must go through in order to be eligible for competition. Here we see the ways power operates on and through (dis)abled sporting bodies in multiple and nuanced ways, which is a key focus for those working in the emerging field of PCS (see Howe, 2008b).

Classified (dis)abled bodies

Classification is simply a structure for competition similar to the systems used in the sports of judo and boxing where competitors perform in distinctive weight categories (Jones and Howe, 2005; Howe and Jones, 2006). Within sport for the disabled, competitors are classified by their body's degree of function within their chosen sport. Classification takes the form of a series of functional tests that determine the appropriate category in which to place the athlete in order to provide equitable sporting contests. This process is conducted by a group of qualified classifiers who have between them an expertise in physical and/or sensory impairments and the sporting practice in which they are classifying athletes. It is therefore important that the classification that is the result of the process of examination of the impaired bodies[1] of athletes is robust and achieves equity across the Paralympic sporting practice and enables athletes to compete on a 'level playing field' (Sherrill, 1999).

The IPC currently organizes and administers both the Paralympic Games and the quadrennial World Championships for individual Paralympic sports such as athletics, using athletes who have been through a process of classification. Using the resources of the International Organisations of Sport for the Disabled (IOSD) (including athletes, volunteer administrators and classification systems) the IPC made the Paralympic Games into the most recognizable and influential vehicle for the promotion of sport for the disabled. The federations are the Cerebral Palsy International Sport and Recreation Association (CP-ISRA), International Blind Sport Association (IBSA), International Sports Federation for Persons with Intellectual Disability (INAS) and the International Wheelchair and Amputee Sport Association (IWAS). This is a federation that was launched in September 2004 at the Athens Paralympic Games. It is the result of a merger of two federations, the International Stoke Mandeville Wheelchair Sports

Federation (ISMWSF) and the International Sport Organisation for the Disabled (ISOD), that have been part of the Paralympic movement since its inception.

The classification system within Paralympic sport has continued to be very complex simply because of the nature of various impairments that the IOSDs service. This complexity and the number of classes that were produced made it initially difficult for the IPC to attract the desired media attention simply because there were so many events that it was hard for them to know where to focus. For example there are two 100 metre races at the Olympics, one for men and one for women. At the Paralympics Games in London in 2012 on the other hand there were 15 for men and 14 for women. Since the establishment of the IPC, in 1989, there has been constant pressure to remove the IOSDs from decisions regarding classification systems in order to streamline Paralympic programmes. However, many of the first officials of the IPC had previously held posts within these founding federations. Consequently, there was initially carte blanche acceptance of the IOSD's classification systems in the early days of the Paralympic movement. According to Bob Steadward, the IPC's first president, 'the potential benefit of decreasing classes by using a functional integrated classification system is that it may simplify the integration into the rest of the sports world' (Steadward, 1996: 36). Such a functional integrated classification system was developed in some sports such as swimming and downhill skiing. In this system athletes are classified according to what they can and cannot achieve physically within the sport rather than by the severity of their disability, as is the case with the disability specific classification system. The use of the functional integrated classification system reduces the number of classes for a group of athletes by focusing upon functional ability rather than disability and ultimately leads to an increase in the number of viable events at major championships (Vanlandewijck and Chappel, 1996).

Classification of course can be seen as a fundamental component of Paralympic culture (Howe, 2008a), but it is the insistence that the system is somehow socially neutral that is problematic (Dupré, 2006). The original classification system was developed by the International Stoke Mandeville Wheelchair Sports Federation (ISMWSF) an organization that has subsequently become known as the International Wheelchair and Amputee Sport Association (IWAS). This system classified athletes with spinal cord injuries according to where the lesion was in their spine because back function is of great importance in sport. It was believed that athletes with a greater level of function in their spine should be in a different class from those athletes that have less. Athletes who were leg amputees could easily be fitted into this system in the most able class that had full use of the spine. As more and more athletes with different impairments wished to get involved in sport for the disabled, ISMWSF established a broad class known as *les autre*. *Les autres* is a French phrase used within disability sport circles meaning 'the others'. Originally the term refers to athletes with a disability who did not directly fit into the classification system established by ISMWSF. Today *les autres* is used to highlight any athlete who is not specifically referred to in the classification systems of the IOSDs and that is able to be slotted into an existing classification system. I use the term here specifically to refer to athletes with a disability who do not use either a wheelchair or prosthesis while competing in athletics. Some athletes who use wheelchairs that were *les autre* including people with spina bifida and polio were able to be slotted into the ISMWSF system, but it was and never has been an exact science. However many *les autre* were ineligible because they did not need to use a wheelchair which eventually led to the development of the remaining IOSDs and ultimately the development of the IPC. As a result the classification system that led to the development of sport for the disabled was not political or culturally neutral.

What is clear from this overview is that classification of (dis)abled bodies has shaped (and continues to shape) Paralympic sporting culture and the control of Paralympian bodies (Howe,

2008a, 2008b), and disability sport more broadly. However, while it can be argued that the body is also controlled in the case of mainstream high-performance sport, the fact marginalizes (dis)abled bodies which means that in an odd way when they are present and highly visible they are markers of difference.

The every-present impaired body

For many with mobility impairments, bodily appearance is a constant consideration because to a great or lesser extent the impaired have to continually evaluate the physical environment in an attempt to physically manage their bodies. Leder (1990) has argued that the human body is a vehicle for living in the world (following the tradition of Merleau-Ponty, 1962) but suggests the normal able body is often absent from our attention. As a result our attention is only drawn to our own body either through illness, soreness (such as that of muscles) or impairment. Only in its appearance can it become a focal point for the personal analysis of social interaction. The perception that people are staring at your body may impact the many ways in which you respond to questions and/or contribute to discussion and therefore experience sport and its distinct spaces.

In his classic ethnography of impairment Murphy (1987: 12) highlights how his body both becomes an object of attention for him as well as others: 'The body no longer can be taken for granted, implicit and axiomatic, for it has become a problem. It no longer is the subject of unconscious assumption, but the object of conscious thought.' This is the case for both the impaired individual as well as the society that needs to deal with the 'problem' created by the abnormal body. This strain that is placed upon various social systems can be seen as the catalyst for attitudes that negatively impact upon the sporting experiences of impaired individuals. These attitudes as a collective, if left unchecked, can lead to disablism.

Disablism is, according to Miller et al. (2004: 9), 'discriminatory, oppressive or abusive behaviour arising from the belief that disabled people are inferior to others'. Over the last two decades there have been both national and international legislation passed by governments that has greatly reduced overt disablism. The elimination of overt disablist attitudes makes the lives of impaired people better, opening up opportunities for work and leisure although some feel there is a long way to go before equity is achieved. As Deal suggests,

> Not all forms of prejudice and discriminatory behaviour, however, are blatant and therefore easily identifiable, as subtle forms of prejudice also exist. Therefore any attempt to tackle prejudice towards disabled people must not only focus on overtly discriminatory behaviour but also recognize subtle forms of prejudice, which can be equally damaging.
>
> *(Deal, 2007: 94)*

Disablism is hard to detect and the able majority may be unaware that they are being disablist. I would suggest that disablism is at least as pervasive as homophobia in sport. However, neither homophobia nor disablist attitudes should be tolerated in sport or society more broadly. The diversity of society should be celebrated and this should be reflected in the tableau of sport. This is one of the strengths of PCS. Theoretically the use of multiple theoretical lenses to add flesh to the bones of the bodies that should I feel be central to the endeavour of PCS. Only by embracing the physical or rather the sensuous nature of sport and physical activity can PCS engage in both a radical and moralistic dance. Methodologically, participant observation and more embodied methods should be central to the PCS agenda. My own embodiment has allowed me to engage in such research in the Paralympic realm but there is a need to encourage more students and scholars alike to get up from their armchairs and embrace sensuous methods and theoretical diversity. In my research I long to see a world where Paralympic or (dis)abled does not stand for less than able! In order to do this, I leave you with a 'call to arms' from Atkinson:

> A practical and radical PCS may involve the deconstruction and destabilization of identities, practices, logics, institutions, and images of power in sports and health worlds, suggesting concrete policy amendments, rule changes or progressive cultural adaptations to foster more equitable and pleasurable sport, health and physical activity environments for all. PCS ventures beyond philosophy and critique; it must engage with the process of resolution.
>
> *(Atkinson, 2011: 139)*

I echo Atkinson's sentiments. The goal of my work is to be relevant at the level of praxis. In terms of Paralympic embodied research this means engaging with the practice community face to face (Howe and Jones, 2006) which also means leaving the academic armchair behind. This insight into my research should act as a reminder to both those new to PCS as well as established scholars who preach praxis 'from the armchair' that to attempt positive impact it is always better to get your hands dirty.

Note

1. In the case of athletes with mental impairments the classification focuses on determining mental ability. Athletes from the International Sports Federation for Persons with Intellectual Disability (INAS-FID) were banned from competition in IPC events from autumn 2000 due to a perceived lack of robustness in their classification process. The process of classification has been changed and these athletes did compete once again at the 2012 Paralympic Games.

References

Armstrong, G. 1998. *Football hooligans: knowing the score*. Oxford: Berg.
Atkinson, M. 2011. Physical cultural studies [Redux]. *Sociology of Sport Journal*, 28 (1), 135–144.
Blake, A. 1996. *The body language: the meaning of modern sport*. London: Lawrence & Wishart.
Bourdieu, P. 1977. *Outline of a theory of practice*. Cambridge: Cambridge University Press.
Bourdieu, P. 1984. *Distinction: a social critique of the judgement of taste*. London: Routledge.
Bourdieu, P. 1990. *The logic of practice*. Cambridge: Polity Press.
Deal, M. 2007. Aversive disablism: subtle prejudice toward disabled people. *Disability and Society*, 22 (1), 93–107.
De Garis, L. 1999. Experiments in pro wrestling: toward a performative and sensuous sport ethnography, *Sociology of Sport Journal*, 16 (1), 65–74.
DePauw, K. 1997. The (in)visibility of disability: cultural contexts and 'sporting bodies.' *Quest*, 49 (4), 416–430.
Dupré, J. 2006. Scientific classification. *Theory, Culture and Society*, 23 (2–3), 30–2.
Foley, D. 1990. *Learning capitalist culture*. Philadelphia, PA: University of Pennsylvania Press.
Foucault, M. 1977. *Discipline and punish: the birth of the prison*. London: Hammonworth.
Giardina, M. D. and Newman, J. I. 2011. What is this 'physical' in physical cultural studies? *Sociology of Sport Journal*, 28 (1), 36–63.
Howe, P. D. 2008a. *The cultural politics of the Paralympic movement: through the anthropological lens*. London: Routledge.
Howe, P. D. 2008b. The tail is wagging the dog: classification and the Paralympic movement. *Ethnography*, 9 (4), 499–518.

Howe, P. D. 2011a. Cyborg and Supercrip: The Paralympics technology and the (dis)empowerment of disabled athletes. *Sociology*, 45 (5), 868–882.

Howe, P. D. 2011b. Sporting bodies: sensuous, lived, and impaired In F. E. Mascia-Lees (ed.), *Companion to the anthropology of bodies/embodiment*. Oxford: Wiley-Blackwell, 102–116.

Howe, P. D. and Jones, C. 2006. Classification of disabled athletes: (dis)empowering the Paralympic practice community. *Sociology of Sport Journal,* 23 (1), 29–46.

Howe, P. D. and Parker, A. 2012. Celebrating imperfection: sport, disability and celebrity culture. *Celebrity Studies*, 3 (3) 270–282.

Jones, C. and Howe, P. D. 2005. The conceptual boundaries of sport for the disabled: classification and athletic performance. *Journal of Philosophy of Sport*, 32 (2), 133–146.

Klein, A. 1991. *Sugarball: the American game, the Dominican dream*. London: Yale University Press.

Klein, A. 1993. *Little big men: bodybuilding subculture and gender construction*. Albany, NY: State University of New York.

Leder, D. 1990. *The absent body*. Chicago, IL: University of Chicago Press.

McDonald, I. 2002. Critical social research and political intervention: moralistic *versus* radical approaches. In J. Sugden and A. Tomlinson (eds), *Power games: a critical sociology of sport*. London: Routledge, 100–116.

Merleau-Ponty, M. 1962. *Phenomenology of perception*. London: Routledge & Kegan Paul.

Merleau-Ponty, M. 1965. *The structure of behaviour*. London: Methuen.

Miller, P., Parker, S. and Gillinson, S. 2004. *Disablism: how to tackle the last prejudice*. London: Demos.

Murphy, R. F. 1987. *The body silent*. London: Dent.

Pronger, B. 2002. *Body fascism: salvation in the technology of physical fitness*. Toronto: University of Toronto Press.

Purdue, D. E. J. and Howe, P. D. 2013. Who's in and who is out? Legitimate bodies within the Paralympic Games. *Sociology of Sport Journal*, 30 (1), 24–40.

Seymour, W. 1998. *Remaking the body: rehabilitation and change*. London: Routledge.

Sherrill, C. 1999. Disability sport and classification theory: a new era. *Adapted Physical Activity Quarterly*, 16 (2), 206–215.

Sherrill, C. and Williams, T. 1996. Disability and sport: psychosocial perspectives on inclusion, integration and participation. In *Sport Science Review*, 5 (1), 42–64.

Steadward, R. 1996. Integration and sport in the Paralympic movement. *Sport Science Review*, 5 (1), 26–41.

Thorpe, H. 2006. Beyond 'decorative sociology': contextualizing female surf, skate and snow boarding. *Sociology of Sport Journal*, 23 (3), 205–228.

Thorpe, H. 2008. Foucault, technologies of self, and the media: discourses of femininity in snowboarding culture. *Journal of Sport and Social Issues*, 32 (2), 199–229.

Turner, B. S. 2001. Disability and the sociology of the body. In G. L. Albrecht, K. D. Seelman and M. Bury (eds), *Handbook of disability studies*. London: Sage, 252–267.

Vanlandewijck, Y. C. and Chappel, R. J. 1996. Integration and classification issues in competitive sports for athletes with disabilities. *Sport Science Review*, 5, 65–88.

Wheaton, B. 1997. Covert ethnography and the ethics of research: studying sport subcultures. In A. Tomlinson and S. Fleming (eds), *Ethics, sport and leisure: crises and critiques*. Aachen, Germany: Meyer and Meyer, 163–171.

Wheaton, B. 2000. Just do it: consumption, commitment, and identity in windsurfing subculture. *Sociology of Sport Journal*, 17 (3), 254–274.

17
YOUNG BODIES

Louise McCuaig, Eimear Enright and Doune Macdonald

Introduction

The contemporary child is at risk of countless unseen dangers, while burdened with the responsibility for assuming the skills and knowledge necessary to achieve economic and social success (Nadesan, 2010: 19). It follows that schools are critical sites for the management and promotion of hygienic, safe, compliant, disciplined and healthy bodies. In keeping with a view of physical cultural studies (PCS) that embraces transdisciplinarity (Silk and Andrews, 2011), this chapter sits at the interface of philosophy, sociology and pedagogy to explore the normalizing of bodies in schools. It is also consistent with the intellectual project that is PCS, imbued with a desire to create the type of knowledge that might mobilize progressive social change (ibid.) with, by and for young people in schools. Our aim in this paper is to illuminate the school's potential as both a site of physical culture injustice and of empowering forms of corporeal knowledge and understanding (Andrews, 2008). We will do so through a discussion of how various scholars have arrived at particular understandings of the corporeal practices, discourses and subjectivities through which young bodies become civilized and represented in schools, and the presentation of data we have recently generated within a larger project looking at the 'health work' undertaken in schools (Macdonald et al., 2013–2015).

We draw primarily on Foucauldian concepts to explain the surveillance of young bodies in schools and how technologies of domination and technologies of the self define young bodies in schools. In so doing, we recognize that the subjectivities, practices and discourses of young bodies are always in a particular set of complex social, economic, political and technological relationships that comprise the social context (Silk and Andrews, 2011).

Civilizing young bodies

Schooling has historically been implicated in 'civilizing' young bodies (Kirk, 1998; Shilling, 2004). The child in Western liberal democratic societies is 'positioned as a special category of person who lacks for a time the complete range of capacities necessary to function fully as a citizen' (Tyler, 1993: 35). As an innocent and natural state, childhood must therefore be preserved, a state of affairs that has led to more rather than less adult surveillance, supervision and control (Bessant, 1991). The modern child has become the focus of innumerable projects that purport to safeguard it from physical, sexual or moral danger, to ensure its normal development, to actively promote certain capacities such as intelligence, educability and emotional stability (ibid.). Subsequently, Western societies have witnessed the development of a plethora of experts and apparatuses established in the interests of children's welfare.

Researchers who have interrogated the history of childhood governance drawing on Rose and Foucault's work (e.g. Meredyth and Tyler, 1993), have considered the diversity of practices employed to survey, discipline and shape the corporeality of childhood. As Tyler (1993: 44) demonstrates, it is largely through placement in the space of the kindergarten that 'better children would be produced, children who had to learn to use themselves [and their bodies] in particular ways'. Practices such as the construction of child-sized furniture and toilets with glass partitioning above four feet, provides a unique adaptation of Foucault's Panopticon of surveillance, with the teacher functioning 'as a mobile observation post, able to see everything, everyone, everywhere from her giant status in a Lilliputian world' (ibid.: 47). The much desired 'better child' of the 1930s was thus a product of both psychological knowledges and architectural arrangements that positioned and regulated children's bodies to promote self-regulation as opposed to a fickle obedience to authority.

Operating within the 'Sociology of the Body', Chris Shilling's work has also shown how schools are implicated in monitoring and shaping young bodies. Drawing on a host of social theorists including Durkheim, Bourdieu, Bernstein, Elias and Mauss, Shilling has explored the embodied nature of schooling (Shilling, 1993), and the relationship that exists between general forms of body pedagogy dominant within a society as a whole, and the specific types of body pedagogies evident in curricula and schools (Shilling, 2010). Furthermore, some of Shilling's more recent work has highlighted the importance of understanding how social norms and policy initiatives relating to the body and health are mediated and recontextualized within schools and society more generally (ibid.).

As with other subject disciplines, the physical education (PE) profession contributes to modern schooling's role as a primary governmental technology that provides solutions to problematics surrounding the citizen's body. Unlike its fellow disciplines, PE is charged explicitly with the task of ensuring the health, strength and wellbeing of the nation's population through the training of apprentice citizens in the arts of healthy living. Over the past three decades PE scholarship has sought to understand PE as a privileged site of bodily control and discipline within schooling (Tinning, 2001). Interrogation of this 'civilization' or regulation of the young body in and through schooling, and PE specifically, has been subject to sustained theoretical, empirical and historical analysis (Armour, 1999; Evans et al., 2004; Kirk, 1998; McCuaig and Tinning, 2010; Wright and Macdonald, 2010). These various analyses highlight how the young body has been constructed over time and in different cultures, and draw on a range of theoretical and methodological tools to better understand and explain varied dimensions of active physicality and pedagogical work on and for the body.

Earlier studies drew attention to the field's bodily focus and the privileging of a specific type of body, the mesomorph. Tinning (1990) identifies how the predominantly 'fat free' muscularity of the mesomorph body shape, came to signify a range of positive social attributes. Mesomorphic children '"naturally" represent success in sport, high peer-group status, embody healthiness, discipline and positive personality traits such as trustworthiness and loyalty' (Evans and Davies, cited in Tinning, 1990: 24). Such studies revealed the value-laden, moralistic judgements regarding body shape within PE practice, with muscularity and slimness defined as 'good', while fatness signifies 'lazy' and 'bad'. Later, Kirk's (1998) *Schooling Bodies* drew extensively on historical material to explore the social construction of children's bodies in Australian and British schools between 1880 and 1950. He argued that discursive practices within three interlocking sites of physical training, medical inspection and sport in schools, reflected strategies of bodily construction undertaken in modernity, which Foucault labelled the disciplinary society. The onset of the First World War, Kirk argues, resulted in a disruption and reconstruction of the meticulous practices of the 'disciplinary society' towards a more liberalized form of schooling bodies, exemplified in the widespread adoption of competitive team games.

Powerful contributions on the ways in which young bodies and emotions are controlled in the interest of specific agendas have also come from feminist scholars. For example, Wright (2000) demonstrates how schools and PE programmes are sites of body work that have been implicated in the process of objectification and alienation of young bodies, and argued that pedagogical practices contribute to the shaping of particular forms of subjectivity. As Paechter (2003) argues, different forms of school PE and sport contribute to the construction of different forms of heterosexual masculinities and femininities. Feminist poststructuralist scholars have explored young people's gendered, classed and racialized body meanings and how these affect participation within and beyond PE (e.g. Azzarito and Solmon, 2006), adding to the lineage of research that enriches the study of physical culture.

Schooling young bodies: the more things change the more they stay the same

Schools are constructed, as Foucault put it, to be 'pedagogical machines', sites where multiple pedagogies and multiple regimes of truth operate. As such, schools have become a pre-eminent institution wherein the strategies of biopower are employed. Biopolitics addresses the vital processes of human existence and, in so doing, has given birth to 'the techniques, technologies, experts and apparatuses for the care and administration of the life of each and all' (Rose, 2001: 26). In his theorizing of power, Foucault devised a biopower model that incorporates two axes of operation.

Along one axis there is the deployment of biopower techniques which address the *individual* human body as a machine, acknowledging its capacity for greater efficiency, productivity and economy of movement (Rabinow, 1999). Along a second axis, biopower demonstrates a focus on the body collective, 'the population', where techniques of government are deployed in order to maximize a state's wealth, longevity, health and productivity (ibid.). The population itself, thus becomes a site of governmental intervention, informed by problematizations of the population's attributes and the subsequent identification of failures that provide the *raison d'être* for intervention (Tait, 2000).

Importantly, the exercise of biopower relies upon the deployment and representation of knowledge in forms that can render a population governable (Foucault, 1994). For example, the gathering of health statistics serves not only to measure the population's capacities and dispositions, but facilitates the creation of discriminating health-related norms, and the determination of those who are failing to meet them and in need of intervention. Norms are equalizing. They allow each individual to be compared to all others through a standard of measurement, and from the moment the norm is established, no one can 'escape its purview' (Ewald, 1990: 154). As Lemke (2011) points out, however, the operation of norms differs across the two, disciplinary and regulatory, axes of biopower. Disciplinary technologies assume a prescriptive norm, where 'hierarchical differentiations are used to establish a clear demarcation between those considered normal and abnormal, suitable and capable, and the others' (ibid.: 47). On the other hand, technologies of security take the empirical norm as a starting point, a regulative norm that acknowledges and 'allows for further differentiations' (ibid.).

As Rose (2000b) summarizes, persons and activities are governed through acting upon them in relation to social norms, behavioural and moral expectations constructed by expertise, and communicated through institutions as truths that individuals are required to consider in the shaping of their conduct. Governmentality within contemporary societies thus comprises an assemblage of biopolitical technologies which allow authorities to 'govern at a distance' (Rose, 2000a: 324), acting through the 'autonomous choices of relatively independent entities' (ibid.). As we noted earlier, Kirk's research confirms this transformation of governmental strategies in PE, where selves were 'regulated less coercively and externally by others and more often internally, by the self' (Kirk, 1998: 25).

Engaging with a political history of the construction of young bodies in schools (as we have done thus far) arguably makes it easier for us to imagine and construct alternative physical cultural possibilities for the subjectivities, practices and discourses of the young body. Understanding what is now going on in schools is enabled not only by reflecting on the historical circumstances the young body confronts (Silk and Andrews, 2011) but also by confronting the 'concrete' material realities and complex relationships within which the young body is articulated. We now draw on data we have recently generated to enable further empirical theorization.

Disciplining young bodies in Australian schools

Photographic evidence and associated discussion of the corporeal control of young bodies was gathered within a larger project looking at the 'health work' of teachers (Macdonald et al., 2013–2015). Multimethod data was collected within 12 primary and secondary schools across the state of Queensland, Australia with its primary focus seeking to measure and understand the extent to which teachers' time is invested in health rather than educative outcomes (see Rossi et al., 2016). In the following analysis of our data, we provide insight into the ways in which contemporary schools provide a unique site through which a cluster of biopolitical technologies are mobilized as a means of shaping and achieving desired bodies and citizens.

We first return to Foucault's (1977) explanation of the essential techniques of disciplinary power to explore the range of policy and pedagogical practices that include routines, uniforms and surveillance. In so doing we draw attention to the remarkable endurance of a 'political anatomy' (ibid.: 138), the blueprint of which Foucault claims emerged within secondary education and then spread to primary schools. Following this, we question the extent to which young people respond to, or are engaged by, the Panopticon of health and behaviour messages and the biopolitical technologies circulating within their school communities.

Prescriptive disciplinary technologies in school health work

Disciplining young bodies within the institutional space can be clearly demonstrated in the school assembly photo (Figure 17.1). More than any other artefact, this picture represents the continued reliance on disciplinary technologies that employ the principle of 'elementary location or partitioning' (Foucault, 1977: 43). On numerous occasions, researchers witnessed this disciplinary technique which aims to 'establish presences and absences, to know where and how to locate individuals, to set up useful communications, to interrupt others, to be able at each moment to supervise the conduct of each individual' (ibid.: 143). As a succession of teachers provided the student body with information on the organization, wellbeing and performance of the school community, teachers were afforded a position of surveillance over young bodies that was 'both general and individual' (ibid.: 145), and from which they could evaluate each and every student's presence and engagement.

Figure 17.1 Student assembly

In his commentary concerning the control of activity, Foucault (1977: 150) argues that the disciplinary technique of the timetable seeks to 'assure the quality of the time used', employing a sustained supervision that eliminates 'anything that might disturb or distract' (ibid.). This emphasis on extracting the most out of available time can be identified in the commentary of Simon, who provides insight into the literal training of students' bodies in order to achieve the optimal learning environment:

> You've basically got to be vigilant all the time, have eyes in the back of your head, be watching their behaviour 24/7 and you have to train them, really. Like you've got to have all these little strategies in place so you can actually start a group on time and not spend 20 minutes waiting for someone to waltz in the door. So we talk about right time, right place, right action. We talk about PLP, perfect listening position, and now we'll say it's the perfect learning position.
>
> *(Simon)*

Foucault further argues that time literally penetrates the body. Each act, for example listening, is broken down into its elements, where the position of the body, direction of the head, duration and aptitude are clearly defined. Within the context of Simon's explanation we see the relationship between disciplinary technologies and the prescriptive norm. There is no equivocation here, students must know the exact time that they can talk, act and be. Discipline, as Lemke (2011: 47) further explains, 'functions by designing an optimal model and its operationalisation, that is, by employing techniques and procedures to adjust and adapt individuals to this standard'. Exemplary cases of this can be found in the visuals located on school walls and noticeboards which provide exacting demonstrations of health-oriented practices, such as handwashing, reflective of a prescriptive norm (see Figure 17.2).

Perhaps ironically for some, it is within the context of free play, that we find the most powerful evidence of an enduring disciplinary technology. Teacher explanations of their duties during school breaks are particularly evocative of a disciplinary power that seeks to re-channel bodily forces towards a docility-productivity relation. Once again, an emphasis on time partitions is at work, as demonstrated by Leah, who explains that in the 'first break, they will eat from 11:00 to 11:15 and then they will have the opportunity if they've finished eating to play for 10 minutes. So it's only that 10 minutes but it is free play'.

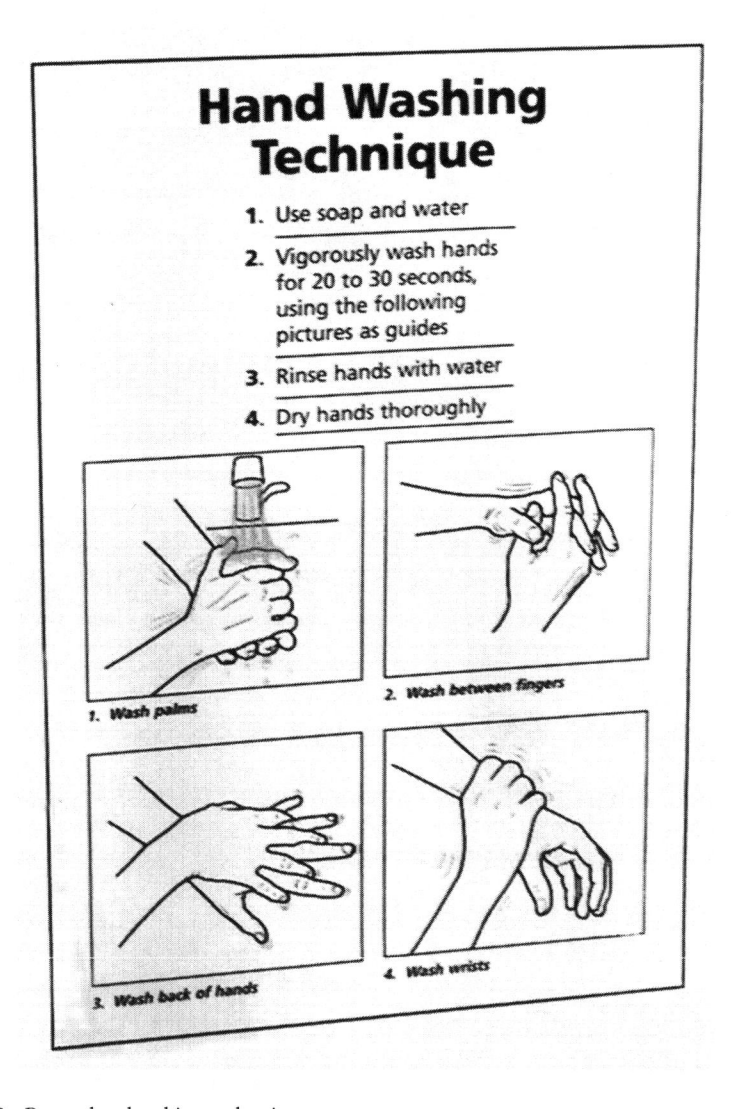

Figure 17.2 Poster: handwashing technqiue

Young bodies

Leah reveals here, the meticulous operations of time segments and constant surveillance conducted by the supervisory teacher, who ensures that students are exclusively engaged, first in the act of consuming a meal, and then in the exercise of their bodies through play. Not surprisingly, however, play is rarely 'free', but is positioned as a reward and offered to those who abide by a range of conditions that determine young people's engagement.

> We've brought in, *hard policies now for the school regarding play time*. I think you might have heard that in class the other day. Primary's had it for years, no hat, no play. PE's been pretty good the last couple of years, we now make it no hat, you can't go out and participate.
>
> *(Leah)*

Elsewhere, the meticulous fussiness of a politics of anatomy are depicted in the variations of voice levels that students can employ within the contexts of their school community (see Figure 17.3). Yet within this poster we also see evidence of a subtle shift towards a 'looser form' of biopower. While handwashing and attendance at assembly are characterized by a single

Voice Levels

0 — **Silence is Golden** – Absolute silence. No one is talking.

1 — **Spy Talk** – Whispering, only 1 person can hear you.

2 — **Low Flow** – Small group work, only the group can hear you.

3 — **Formal Normal** – Normal conversation voice.

4 — **Loud Crowd** – Presenting voice. Everyone can hear you.

5 — **Out of Control** – Playground voice, never used inside.

Figure 17.3 Poster: voice levels

benchmark of performance, the voice level poster encourages students to monitor their voices according to a spectrum of normative indicators, and choose a volume commensurate with the activity and location.

Likewise, the provision of a spectrum of normative health-related behaviours that incite students' decision-making processes, finds expression in the plethora of practices and messages surrounding the consumption of food (see Figure 17.4).

A broad continuum of behaviours, attitudes or actions that imply the possibility of options and personal choice is evident here. For example, training students in the art of healthy eating involves the provision of information in the form of colour-coded foods, which facilitates the shaping of students' choice and decision-making activities. Christian tries to explain the manner in which this regulatory power is operationalized:

> In terms of eating we have the green foods and amber. I think green is you're supposed to have that every day and you're allowed one amber day where the kids can eat, they have I think some special foods that aren't so healthy but in terms of the green foods, I think they have to be a certain size ... That's something that the kids I suppose are involved in now. They're starting to be a little bit more aware of what they can and can't eat.
>
> *(Christian)*

As this excerpt suggests, healthy citizens of the future need pedagogical environments that incite them to become critically aware of their bodies and an obligation to tame, train or enhance bodily capacities. For Foucault (1994: 137), the principle aim of disciplinary power is not simply a mastery of others, but seeks an 'increase in the mastery of each individual over his own body'. Achieving the much desired goal of a healthy active citizenry, demands strategies

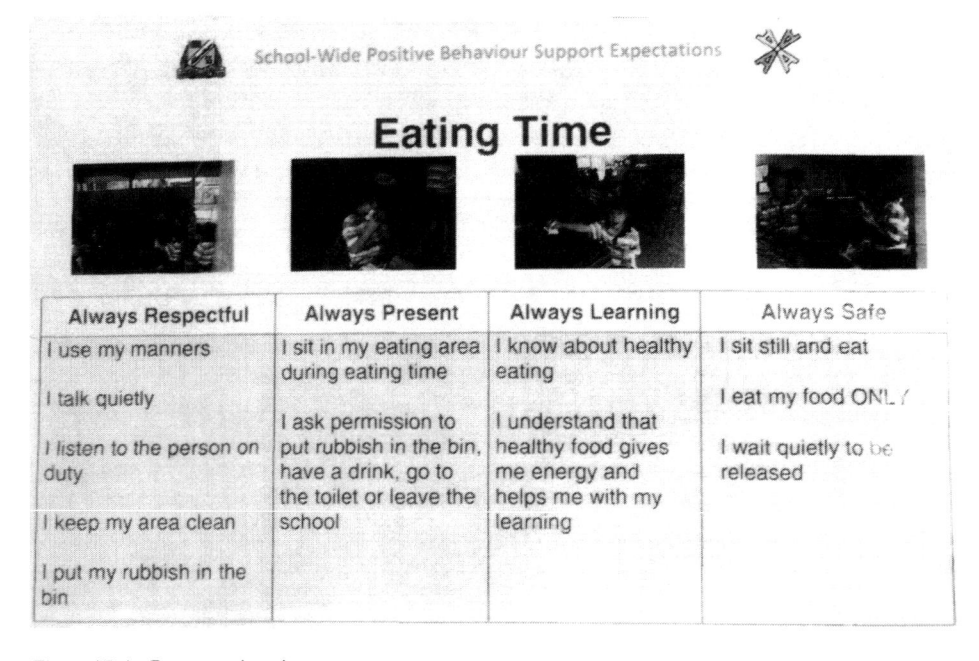

Figure 17.4 Poster: eating time

that incite corporeal confessions (McCuaig and Tinning, 2010), where apprentice citizens' bodies are provoked into revealing individual abilities, deviancy, deformity, character traits and health states. Teachers draw upon these performances to shape students according to sanctioned practices and behaviours, as demonstrated by Jane, who states that 'health work needs to happen in school, because otherwise when do they talk about it with their peers, *when can you control that conversation to make sure that it's correct and accurate*, and not going down the wrong track?'.

Nevertheless, in an era that has been characterized as offering new times, new technologies and 'new kids' (Gardner and Davis, 2013), many researchers have found the resiliency of disciplinary technologies to be, at best, dispiriting. Despite increasing commentary on youth as global citizens who are neither limited by time nor territoriality (Enright and Gard, 2016; Kenway and Bullen, 2008), it was difficult to find evidence of schools' engagement with the global or indeed the popular (Sholle and Denski, 1995). As Foucault (1977: 141) suggests, disciplinary institutions enclose their subjects in a 'protected place of disciplinary monotony', the techniques of which are 'acts of cunning' (ibid.: 139), profoundly suspicious mechanisms that involve an 'attentive "malevolence" that turns everything to account' (ibid.: 139). In one of his final interviews, Foucault (1994: 298) claimed that 'the freer people are with respect to each other, the more they want to control each other's conduct'. By contrast, given our understanding of the potential and strengths posed by the diversity of young people we saw in our research sites, the game of disciplining young bodies within schools was, for the most part, unappealing. To paraphrase Foucault (1990), perhaps humans are not particularly inventive when it comes to either disciplines or pleasures.

Indeed, there was little evidence that young bodies were afforded an opportunity to speak back or resist the ever watchful 'teacher's eye' and the Panopticon of behaviour and health instructions. In our efforts to explore the possibilities for resistance, it is critical that we understand the techniques by which subjects are hailed into thinking or acting according to their membership of a particular group or community (Lemke, 2011). Althusser's concept of 'hailing' captures a significant moment of subjectivation, wherein the individual is 'stitched' into discourse, recognizing and being 'rendered a subject and subjected to relations of power through discourse' (Youdell, 2006: 517). Evidence of this process and the hailing of the 'good student', can be found in a school poster on the wearing of uniform (see Figure 17.5), where the nebulous use of the word 'we' effortlessly recruits each and every student onto the school team that is 'working hard to create a good impression'. Instead of nominating school authorities as those who seek respectful bodily attire beyond the school gates, the term 'we' suggests that any student failing to meet this obligation is letting down the entire school community.

To what extent students complied with the call to 'wear their uniform well' was beyond the scope of this study. Still, we were surprised that an appreciation of youth voice and agency was largely absent in the visual data we generated. Increasingly, youth voice and participation is viewed as a vehicle for strengthening young people, their schools and communities, but our data revealed 'more of the same' in the construction of young people as passive recipients of health knowledge. One PE teacher's thoughts on the 'No hat, no play' policy, however, provides one of the few indicators of students' capacity to manipulate biopolitical strategies:

> Although there is that issue of what do you do about students who don't want to play and therefore don't bring a hat … we have noticed that it's almost killed off any activity on the ovals, which is good that they're wearing protection or not going out in the sun, but in an obesity epidemic that we're going through at the moment with teenagers, it's a concern that then no-one's out running around.
>
> *(Grant)*

> At school
> we work hard together
> to create a good
> impression
> When you leave
> we need you to continue
> that good impression
> Be respectful on
> public transport
> and
> wear your uniform well

Figure 17.5 Poster: wear your uniform well

While Grant's confusion regarding the greater good in terms of promoting healthy young bodies provides insight into students' options for resistance, there was little evidence, or indeed support for, young people's unique wisdom on how to keep their bodies safe, or promote the health of their bodies and school communities (Mayall, 1996). Neither was there recognition that many young people have significant experience negotiating complex health- and body-related issues at home. Instead, as our data analysis suggests, the schooling of young bodies continues to decontextualize young people from the social and economic environments within which they experience their lives. Pleasure, desire, class and gender are stripped away in the delivery of a one-size-fits-all, risk-reduction bag of biopower techniques. As Castel (1991) poignantly offers, the mere sharing of the trait 'youth', guarantees an endless parade of strategies that seek to tame and train the healthy citizen of the future.

Conclusion

At a time when, internationally, school curricula are aiming for the production of critical, creative and active citizens, ready to contribute to a globalized, entrepreneurial landscape, the discourses of hygienic, managed and disciplined bodies are an intriguing juxtaposition. And within these discourses, there are further tensions for teachers as, for example, the imperative for promoting physical activity that meets the imperative for sun safety, or the imperative for children eating at specified times that meet the contents of errant lunch boxes. At a time when neoliberal schools and schooling are competing in a market that promises to optimize individual children's potential, the schools' control of bodies/movement in space/time provides a particularly rich stream of inquiry.

Given this study has drawn on a multimethod approach and a multidisciplinary body of literature, it sits comfortably within physical cultural studies. Indeed, the rubric of physical cultural studies provides our collective work with the encouragement to be inclusive of paradigms and disciplines, structures and fluidities, geographies and time. It provides the spaces to recognize the complexity in both understanding and predicting the tensions, multifarious locations and trajectories of young bodies.

References

Andrews, D. L., 2008. Kinesiology's inconvenient truth: The physical cultural studies imperative. *Quest*, 60 (1), 46–63.

Armour, K. M., 1999. The case for a body focus in education and physical education. *Sport, Education and Society*, 4 (1), 5–15.

Azzarito, L. and Solmon, M. A., 2006. A feminist poststructuralist view on student bodies in physical education: Sites of compliance, resistance, and transformation. *Journal of Teaching in Physical Education*, 25 (2), 200–225.

Bessant, J., 1991. Described, measured and labelled: Eugenics, youth policy and moral panic in Victoria in the 1950s. *Journal of Australian Studies*, 31, 8–28.

Castel, R., 1991. From dangerousness to risk. In G. Burchell, C. Gordon and P. Miller, eds, *The Foucault Effect: Studies in Governmental Rationality*. Hemel Hempstead: Harvester Wheatsheaf, 281–298.

Enright, E. and Gard, M., 2016. Media, digital technology and learning in sport: A critical response to Hodkinson, Biesta and James. *Physical Education and Sport Pedagogy*, 21 (1), 40–54.

Evans, J., Davies, B. and Wright, J., ed., 2004. *Body Knowledge and Control: Studies in the Sociology of Physical Education and Health*. Hove: Psychology Press.

Ewald, F., 1990. Norms, discipline and the law. *Representations Special Issue: Law and the Order of Culture*, 30, 131–161.

Foucault, M., 1977. *Discipline and Punish: The Birth of the Prison* (A. Sheridan, trans.). New York: Vintage Books.

Foucault, M., 1990. *The Use of Pleasure: The History of Sexuality, Vol. 2* (R. Hurley, trans.). New York: Vintage Books.

Foucault, M., 1994. *Power: The Essential Works of Foucault 1954–1984*, Volume III (J. D. Faubion, ed.; R. Hurley and others, trans.). London: Penguin Books.

Gardner, H. and Davis, K., 2013. *The App Generation: How Today's Youth Navigate Identity, Intimacy, and Imagination in a Digital World*. New Haven, CT: Yale University Press.

Kenway, J. and Bullen, E., 2008. The global corporate curriculum and the young cyberflâneur as global citizen. In N. Dolby and F. Rizvi, eds, *Youth Moves: Identities and Education in Global Perspective*. London: Routledge, 17–32.

Kirk, D., 1998. *Schooling Bodies: School Practice and Public Discourse 1880–1950*. Leicester University Press.

Lemke, T., 2011. *Foucault, Governmentality, and Critique*. London: Paradigm Publishers.

Macdonald, D., Tinning, R., Rossi, A., Mangan, J. and McCuaig, L., 2013–2015. *Educating Healthy Citizens: The Health Work of Teachers in Australian Schools*. ARC Discovery Project.

Mayall, B., 1996. *Children, Health and the Social Order*. Open University Press.

McCuaig, L. and Tinning, R., 2010. HPE and the moral governance of p/leisurable bodies. *Sport, Education and Society*, 15 (1), 39–61.

Meredyth, D. and Tyler, D., ed., 1993. *Child and Citizen: Genealogies of Schooling and Subjectivity*. Brisbane: Institute for Cultural and Policy Studies, Griffith University.

Nadesan, M. H., 2010. *Governing Childhood into the 21st Century*. New York: Palgrave Macmillan.

Paechter, C., 2003. Power, bodies and identity: How different forms of physical education construct varying masculinities and femininities in secondary schools. *Sex Education: Sexuality, Society and Learning*, 3 (1), 47–59.

Rabinow, A., 1999. Artificiality and enlightenment: From sociobiology to biosociality. In C. Samson, ed., *Health Studies: A Critical and Cross-Cultural Reader*. Oxford: Blackwell, 50–60.

Rose, N., 2000a. Identity, genealogy, history. In P. Du Gay, J. Evans and P. Redman, eds, *Identity: A Reader*. London: Sage Publications in association with The Open University, 313–326.

Rose, N., 2000b. Government and control. *British Journal of Criminology*, 40 (2), 321–339.

Rose, N., 2001. Biopolitics in the twenty first century – notes for a research agenda. *Distinktion: Scandinavian Journal of Social Theory*, 2 (3), 25–44.

Rossi, A., Macdonald, D., McCuaig, L. and Johnson, R., 2016. Teachers as health workers: Patterns of Australian teachers' health work. *British Education Research Journal*, 42 (2), 258–276.

Shilling, C., 1993. Body, class and social inequalities. In J. Evans, ed., *Equality, Education and Physical Education*. Lewes: Falmer Press.

Shilling, C., 2004. *The Body in Culture, Technology and Society*. London: Sage.

Shilling, C., 2010. Exploring the society–body–school nexus: Theoretical and methodology issues in the study of body pedagogics. *Sport, Education and Society*, 15 (2), 151–167.

Sholle, D. and Denski, S., 1995. Critical media literacy: Reading, remapping, rewriting. *Rethinking Media Literacy: A Critical Pedagogy of Representation*, 4, 7–32.

Silk, M. L. and Andrews, D. L., 2011. Toward a physical cultural studies. *Sociology of Sport Journal*, 28 (1), 4–35.

Tait, G., 2000. From the Panopticon to the playground: Disciplinary practices. In D. Meadmore, B. Burnett and G. Tait, eds, *Practising Education: Social and Cultural Perspectives*. Frenchs Forest, NSW: Prentice Hall-Sprint Print, 7–18.

Tinning, R., 1990. *Ideology and Physical Education: Opening Pandora's Box*. Sydney: UNSW Press.

Tinning, R., 2001. *Physical Education and the Making of Citizens: Considering the Pedagogical Work of Physical Education in Contemporary Times*. AIESEP, Taipei: Taiwan.

Tyler, D., 1993. Making up children. In D. Meredyth and D. Tyler, eds., 1993. *Child and Citizen: Genealogies of Schooling and Subjectivity*. Brisbane: Institute for Cultural and Policy Studies, Griffith University.

Wright, J., 2000. Bodies, meanings and movement: A comparison of the language of a physical education lesson and a Feldenkrais movement class. *Sport, Education and Society*, 5 (1), 35–49.

Wright, J. and Macdonald, D., ed., 2010. *Young People, Physical Activity and the Everyday*. London: Routledge.

Youdell, D., 2006. Subjectivation and performative politics – Butler thinking Althusser and Foucault: Intelligibility, agency and the raced–nationed–religioned subjects of education. *British Journal of Sociology of Education*, 27 (4), 511–528.

18
AGEING BODIES

Cassandra Phoenix

Introduction

Over the past decade, research at the intersection of the ageing body and human movement has been slowly shifting from an almost exclusive focus on the health benefits of physical activity in older age (Chodzko-Zajko et al., 2009), to encompass the diverse and situated positions of older adults within a physical culture. Debates and discussions surrounding the intersection of ageing and physicality are taking place across a range of disciplines including social gerontology, sociology of sport, geography and health sciences to name but a few and subsequently incorporates a divergent range of approaches, theoretical positions and methodologies. This work illuminates how the ageing body is a key site for encountering, shaping and displaying the social and cultural context of physicality. It also highlights how individuals' experiences of physicality can be diverse, shaped by a variety of socio-economic factors and lifestyle choices that cannot be separated from the wider context and culture within which they take place (Gullette, 2004). In this chapter I provide an overview of how, from a sociocultural perspective, the ageing body is currently understood. I then draw attention to three specific strands of research within this domain, which I believe have much to offer physical cultural studies. Finally, I discuss how a focus on the ageing body can continue to contribute towards physical cultural studies as a fluid sensibility between critical scholarship on (in)active embodiment and power relations.

The ageing body in context

The ageing body has traditionally been framed by biomedical knowledge, which has encouraged an understanding of growing older primarily in terms of corporeality and bodily manifestations (Tulle-Winton, 2000). The implications of this have encompassed not only biological, but also cultural processes in that ageing has typically been perceived as a medical and social 'problem' with images of older people and the meaning of ageing itself being conflated with ill health, frailty, disability, disengagement, and dependency on the health care system (Blaikie, 1999). Such a scenario has allowed our relationship in Western society with the ageing process to be dominated by the narrative of decline (Gullette, 1997); a narrative that portrays 'a tragedy of accumulating deficits, diminishing reserves, and deteriorating attractiveness and strength: nothing more than denouement' (Randall and McKim, 2008: 4). The prevalence of this narrative has damaging implications for the ageing body because it presents ageing as a process of passively *getting* rather than actively *growing* old. This seemingly legitimizes the increased levels of risk, control and surveillance that the ageing body is subjected to via welfare and health professionals. It also further facilitates the management and movement of ageing bodies out of public spaces including the labour market and visual media (Tulle, 2008a). Indeed, as Tulle rightly reminds us, 'older bodies are subjected to forms of professional control and surveillance, whether at home or in institutions, justified and legitimated by their declining properties' (ibid.: 3). For her, these forms of domination are imposed on ageing bodies by broader structures and narratives that encompass socially contingent expectations of age appropriate behavior. These have consequences for individual agency and include, for example, dress (see Twigg, 2013), movement within certain public spaces (see Sparkes, 2015) and consumption (see Gilleard and Higgs, 2000).

According to Gilleard and Higgs (2000, 2013; see also Jones and Higgs, 2010), the practices of choice and consumption can provide opportunities for protecting identity and retaining a sense of agency alongside an ageing, changing body. Ageing, they assert, is not what it once was, to the extent that 'old age as a distinct social category has collapsed while ageing itself has lost much of its former coherence. Age as "old age" has been replaced by the feared social imaginary of a "fourth age" … while the ageing "process" has become caught up in the puzzling cultural complexity that is the "third age"' (Gilleard and Higgs, 2013: vii). Emerging from this blend of fear, hope and confusion, a number of scholars have noted a new kind of ageing appearing, characterized by 'the expansion of more promising possibilities of self-construction' in later life (Gergen and Gergen, 2000: 282). This 'new' model of ageing has entailed various descriptions including, but not limited to, 'successful ageing', 'positive ageing', 'productive ageing', 'healthy ageing' and 'ageing well'. While potentially empowering ageing social actors to move beyond the decline narrative, some of these conceptualizations have been critiqued for the role they play in reinforcing neoliberal ideologies of health, in which 'good' older adults are encouraged to take personal responsibility for their health and wellbeing via a physically active lifestyle (Holstein and Minkler, 2003). In this regard, physical cultures have played, and continue to play, a significant role in both shaping and constraining the *new ageing* and the experiences of active embodiment that it entails.

The ageing body in physical culture

Empirical research examining the experiences of adults who 'do' ageing through various forms of physicality has grown in recent years (see e.g. Paulson, 2005; Dionigi, 2006; Phoenix and Sparkes, 2009; Kluge et al., 2012; Hudson et al., 2014; Evans and Sleap, 2015). Amongst this are a number of examples where scholars have focused more specifically on the ways in which physical cultures are organized, embodied and experienced in relation to operations of social power (e.g. Tulle, 2008a; Griffin, 2010; Pike, 2012; Griffin and Phoenix, 2014; Nettleton, 2015; Jette and Vertinsky, 2015). Indeed, as this increase in empirical interest might suggest, participation in physical culture is now promoted as a legitimate, if not expected way to age. Yet this has not always been the case and, traditionally, strenuous activities were believed to be too demanding, even life threatening for the ageing body. This was particularly the case for women where conceptions of the female body were deeply rooted in reproductive biology and philosophy condoning separate, gendered spheres that constrained women's space and physicality (Vertinsky, 2002). Certainly, as we progress into the twenty-first century, Grossman and Stewart (2003) assert that many older women continue to report feeling physically and socially vulnerable when participating in exercise of mild to moderate intensity, worried about 'wearing out' their body or incurring sudden injury. That noted, it has also been argued that older women participating in sport profit from changing gender arrangements. For example, older sporting females can challenge the notion of the 'weaker sex' and are actively redefining traditional views on appropriate activities for women in later life (Pfister, 2012). These diverse and multiple meanings point to the relevance of physical cultural practices for understanding the ageing body and indeed the larger contexts through which it's constituted.

Resisting decline in older age

One significant strand of research within this domain offers insights into older adults' embodied responses to the competing (personal and social) narratives of ageing (see Dionigi, 2006; Tulle, 2007, 2008a; Dionigi et al., 2013; Ronkainen et al., 2013). This work has illuminated how physical cultural practices can be utilized as a key resource in older age for embodied resistance to the dominant narrative of decline. For example, as part of a larger ethnographic study of a women's running group, Griffin and Phoenix (2014) documented the complex picture of how 'Justine' (pseudonym) became aware of her own ageing as she learned how to run during midlife. They discussed the strategies she put in place to manage it and how she negotiated new forms of embodiment to challenge narrative foreclosure; an eminently social phenomenon that connects to the reification of cultural storylines and the tendency 'to internalize storylines in such a way as to severely constrict their own field of narrative expression' (Freeman, 2000: 83). Similarly, through her work with veteran elite runners, Tulle (2007, 2008a) suggested that sports participation in later life may reflect and can even instigate social change, by increasing embodied agency and widening the range of culturally available ageing identities beyond that of unitary, universal and inevitable decline. Both of these studies show how participation in sport and physical activity in later life has the potential to generate *counterstories* through which social actors might develop these 'resistant' identities as they age.

Counterstories are the stories which people tell and live that offer resistance to dominant cultural narratives such as the narrative of decline (Nelson, 2001). When told collectively, these 'new' stories present the possibility for both individual and social change. Phoenix and Smith (2011) used the notion of counterstories as a theoretical framework to problematize the common interpretation of resistance to ageing through physical cultural practices as being a uni-dimensional construct. Drawing upon the experiences of mature natural bodybuilders, they illustrated how *what* exactly was being resisted and precisely *how* it was being resisted, differed depending upon the message, intended audience and consistency of the counterstory being told. For example, the mature natural bodybuilders who told counterstories offering 'occasional and monadic resistance' displayed an awareness of the exclusionary and identity damaging nature of the narrative of decline, yet purposefully distinguished and distanced themselves from other ageing bodies. As such, their intent was not to question the unjustness of the narrative of decline, but to emphasize how their experiences of the ageing process (to which being a natural bodybuilder was central) did not fit this 'natural' ageing script. In contrast, other participants in their study displayed 'regular and dyadic resistance' to the narrative of decline by telling counterstories, which directly and openly contested it. What differed for this group was their acute awareness of the socially constructed nature of the ageing process. For them, it was people's assumptions about ageing, rather than ageing itself that directed older adults away from certain physical activities and toward others. Resistance to the narrative of decline, therefore, was patchy at best.

This research demonstrated how physical culture was not used as an arena to resist the binaries of either ageism or the ageing, changing body itself, but instead as a domain whereby the capacity for a *continuum of resistance* could be created. Awareness of such nuances, that are inherent to resisting the narrative of decline through physical cultural practices, can contribute to a more sophisticated understanding of *how* resistance is accomplished along with *the nature* of that resistance and the development of more comprehensive theorizing regarding how counter-stories can be facilitated and used more effectively to promote creative, meaningful embodied experiences of ageing through physicality.

Understanding how resistance to the notion of inevitable decline in older age might be enacted through sport and physical activity is important. Not least because exercise is commonly positioned as a key weapon in the fight against disease and, by extension the ageing process. This has been accentuated, argues Tulle (2008b) by the attentions of the discipline of human kinesiology / sport sciences, wherein researchers have become increasingly concerned with the impact of increasing age on performance, the potential impact of exercise on ageing processes, and the role played by exercise on illness prevention and life extension. In doing so, she argues, sport science (and by association sport and exercise) is a powerful constituent of the anti-ageing project (Vincent, 2006), and as such 'may perhaps be actively involved in the increased medicalization of ageing by reconstructing the ageing body as malleable, open to intervention' (Tulle, 2008b: 341–342). The danger in such a construction is that it becomes geared towards the elimination of ageing as process and burden. In doing so, it reinforces the social construction of ageing as associated with decline, a problem to map out and solve via science.

Pleasures of later life physicality

Being active in older age has been almost entirely overshadowed by health initiatives (with health outcome measures) and the slightly more elusive anti-ageing narratives alluded to above. To that end, a particularly noteworthy strand of inquiry, which has much to offer critical scholarship on the ageing body in physical culture, coheres around the embodied pleasures of physicality in later life. This area of analytical interest reflects and extends an increasing interest in affect, emotion and in some instances, the use of phenomenological approaches to understand physical cultural practices (see Pringle, 2009; Thorpe and Rinehart, 2010; Wellard, 2012; Throsby, 2013; Allen-Collinson and Leledaki, 2015; Allen-Collinson and Owton, 2015).

Although still in its infancy, the small amount of research that examines the pleasures of physicality in relation to the ageing body has illustrated how encountering pleasure with and through the moving, ageing body goes some way to challenging foreclosing assumptions about what the ageing body can and should, do, produce and represent. For example, informed by a 'carnal sociology', Nettleton (2013, 2015) argues that attention to the visceral basis of meaning gives insight into why older fell runners continue to participate in this intense, transformative activity in later life. Such an approach, she asserts, highlights the often profound, existential reasons for sustained participation that go beyond health pronouncements and the notion of a responsible citizen. Indeed, Nettleton explains how the imperative to run and experience a passion inherent (and to a certain extent exclusive) to the fell running community ensures that many older adults continue running, often against recommendations from health professionals that they should 'slow down' and engage in activity less risky to the older body.

Differing ideas around the benefits and risks of exertion is a theme also discussed by Jette and Vertinsky (2015). Conscious that health care policies and lifestyle prescriptions often lack sensitivity to social location, cultural nuance, and the power relations that they (re)produce, these authors turned their attention to traditional Chinese understandings of health geographies of the body (that differ vastly from those in Western society) to examine how varying body ontologies lead to a divergence in bodily practices that are conducted in the name of health. Drawing from in-depth interview data with Chinese origin women aged 65 and over and now living in Canada, Jette and Vertinsky argued that these women undertook their physical activity practices in pursuit of happiness and life balance. This was characterized by their practice of T'ai Chi as 'playing T'ai Chi' and a counter to neoliberal notions of personal responsibility for health based upon a Western conceived calculus of risk.

Pleasure, however, is not a singular, uni-dimensional concept, but can be experienced as different 'types' in, with and through the ageing body. Furthermore, it can be encountered across various temporalities and spaces, in some instances beyond where and when the activity was undertaken. These were the findings of research conducted by Phoenix and Orr (2014), which employed in-depth interviews and photo elicitation techniques to understand the impact of physical activity on older adult's perceptions and experiences of (self-)ageing (see Orr and Phoenix, 2015). Their analyses revealed four different types of pleasure, which were used to construct a typology of pleasure in later life. For example, they noted how pleasure could be *sensual* by coming into being through the senses (i.e. the smell of a freshly mown pitch, the touch of water against one's body as it moves in the swimming pool). It could also be encountered through the process of *documenting* one's activities (i.e. times, routes, descriptive accounts) or by *immersing* oneself in the moment of that activity (i.e. meditative state often accomplished in yoga). For some of the participants, pleasure was not induced through the act of physicality itself, but via the sense of routine and *habit* it brought to the rhythm of their daily life.

The studies outlined above mark some progress in a largely under-researched and under-theorized area of physical cultural studies. They go some way to broaden our understanding of how pleasures intersect within assemblages of bodies, objects and spaces. This provides an interesting starting point for discussions around how we might consider the accessibility of pleasures through physical culture particularly for those older adults who do not experience the sensations of movement itself as something pleasurable. This line of analysis has the potential to further develop recent theorizing around the 'taking place' of health and wellbeing, whereby 'wellbeing might not be taken *from* the environment but instead might emerge *as* the affective environment' (Andrews et al., 2014: 210).

The ageing body in (physical cultural) space and place

A third salient, but similarly rather neglected strand of research within this domain focuses on the significance of space and place for how the ageing body is enacted and encountered within physical cultural settings. This neglect mirrors a wider absence of 'geographical gerontology', a discipline which, according to Andrews et al. (2007: 158) has the potential to offer a 'nuanced, theoretically informed understanding of the role of place as a multi-layered, dynamic, historically and spatially contextualized process that both shapes and is shaped by the lives and experiences of older people'. In parallel, while 'geographies of movement and fitness' are gaining some traction within both the human / cultural geography and physical cultural studies literatures (e.g. see Andrews et al., 2005, 2012; Atkinson, 2010; Cosgriff et al., 2010), this has rarely extended to include a direct analytical concern with the ageing body.

One exception in this regard is Sparkes's (2010, 2015) autoethnographic reflections on performing age inside the gym. The visibility of the ageing body in everyday practice, he rightly reminds us, is contingent on the complex intersection of one's ageing corporeality and the social circumstances in which that corporeality is directly encountered. The landscape of the gym is neither fixed nor stable but an assemblage of physical objects, happenings, events, regimes, utterances and so forth. It is within this territory, Sparkes (2015) explains, that he becomes situated and aware of himself as an aged (and gendered) being both objectively and subjectively in relation to the bodies of others. Moreover, through his evocative stories Sparkes – himself a former high-level athlete – *shows* (rather than merely *tells*) what it's like to, for example, undress, bench press, stretch, observe and interact with other – often younger – bodies in this space and the consequences this has for the temporality of ageing embodiment. Not only are his felt and performed experiences of ageing shaped by the temporal movements (order and routine of sets, rest, repetition) and timescapes ('peak' and 'off-peak' within the gym) of the gym, but also by a life history in which his sporting body has been at the forefront of his body–self relationship.

The poignancy of certain spaces and places for body–self relationships can also have implications for where people seek out experiences of embodied activity. As part of a broader study adopting an interpretive 'geo-narrative' approach (see Bell et al., 2015), Bell and Wheeler (2015) explored the role of place characteristics in older adults' use of outdoor activity space. Noting the interdependent nature of wellbeing, they demonstrated how for some older adults, activity-based place interactions (e.g. favorite walking routes) were often tailored to promote opportunities for shared experiences with others and connections to their past. In response to Bell and Wheeler's call for a greater appreciation of the complex personal and structural factors that define and drive individual choices regarding the use of green (countryside) and blue (coastal) spaces for wellbeing over time, scholars sympathetic to the sensibilities of physical cultural studies might find themselves well placed to respond to this.

Future directions

In this chapter, I have presented a limited selection of key issues emerging within a growing interest in how the ageing body intersects with physical culture. Until relatively recently, biomedical perspectives and positivist methodologies have dominated our knowledge of the ageing body in relation to physicality. These have often reduced the experiences and meanings of physical cultural practices in older age almost exclusively to health pronouncements and contributed to a broader social 'war on old age' (see Vincent, 2007). Yet, using a divergent range of approaches, theoretical positions and methodologies, critical scholarship focusing upon active embodiment in later life has highlighted how 'doing' ageing, within the context of physical culture is also political. Here, I have alluded to the ways in which it provides a site for resistance that can be enacted and encountered, and bring to the fore new ways of relating to the ageing body (i.e. as a site of pleasure) that are currently excluded from narratives of ageing, health and active embodiment.

There remains, however, much work to be done. As examples, given the under-representation of older women in all spheres of sport and physical activity, along with the limited scope of current masculinity scripts for ageing men in Western society, a comprehensive theorizing of the intersections between gender, ageing and physical culture is required. There is also a need to critically interrogate current trends to demonize sedentary behavior, particularly in older age (see Tulle, 2015, for an excellent starting point). At the other end of the continuum, scholarship might focus on the seemingly confused boundary between health and fitness, and the implications this has for how individuals confront embodied active ageing (see Gilleard and Higgs, 2013). Finally, those with a dual commitment to physical cultural studies and the ageing body are well positioned to respond to recent calls to 'rethink our approach to physical activity' (see Das and Horton, 2012). This would involve diluting the traditional tendency toward 'prescription' and 'guidelines', and expanding critical scholarship beyond the level of the individual. By continuing to explore the 'emplaced' (Pink, 2011) experiences of sport, fitness, health-related movement practices and so forth in older age, along with the manner in which these are intrinsically linked to the wider social and cultural context in which we live, we shall, to borrow from Gullette (2004), be more sensitized to how people are *aged into* physical culture.

References

Allen-Collinson, J. and Leledaki, A., 2015. Sensing the outdoors: a visual and haptic phenomenology of outdoor exercise embodiment. *Leisure Studies*, 35 (4), 457–470.
Allen-Collinson, J. and Owton, H., 2015. Intense embodiment: senses of heat in women's running and boxing. *Body and Society*, 21 (2), 245–268.
Andrews G. J, Sudwell, M. and Sparkes, A. C., 2005. Towards a geography of fitness: an ethnographic case study of the gym in bodybuilding culture. *Social Science and Medicine*, 60, 877–891.
Andrews, G. J., Cutchin, M., McCracken, K., Phillips, D. R. and Wiles, J., 2007. Geographical gerontology: the constitution of a discipline. *Social Science and Medicine*, 65 (1), 151–168.
Andrews, G. J., Hall, E., Evans, B. and Colls, R., 2012. Moving beyond walkability: on the potential of health geography. *Social Science and Medicine*, 75 (11), 1925–1932.
Andrews, G. J., Chen, S. and Myers, S., 2014. The 'taking place' of health and wellbeing: towards non-representational theory. *Social Science and Medicine*, 108, 210–222.
Atkinson, M., 2010. Fell running in post-sport territories. *Qualitative Research in Sport and Exercise*, 2 (1), 109–132.
Bell, S. L. and Wheeler, B. W., 2015. Local environments and activity in later life: meaningful experiences in green and blue spaces. In E. Tulle and C. Phoenix (eds), *Physical activity and sport in later life: critical perspectives*. Basingstoke: Palgrave, 175–186.
Bell, S. L., Phoenix, C., Lovell, R. and Wheeler, B. W., 2015. Using GPS and geo-narratives: a methodological approach for understanding and situating everyday green space encounters. *Area*, 47 (1), 88–96.
Blaikie, A., 1999. *Ageing and popular culture*. Cambridge, UK: Cambridge University Press.
Chodzko-Zajko, W., Schwingel, A. and Park, C. H., 2009. Successful aging: the role of physical activity. *American Journal of Lifestyle Medicine*, 3 (1), 20–28.
Cosgriff, M., Little, D. E. and Wilson, E., 2010. The nature of nature: how New Zealand women in middle to later life experience nature-based leisure. *Leisure Sciences*, 32, 15–32.
Das, P. and Horton, R., 2012. Rethinking our approach to physical activity. *The Lancet*, 380 (9838), 189–190.
Dionigi, R., 2006. Competitive sport as leisure in later life: negotiations, discourse and aging. *Leisure Sciences*, 28 (2), 181–196.
Dionigi, R. A., Horton, S. and Baker, J., 2013. Negotiations of the ageing process: older adults' stories of sports participation. *Sport, Education and Society*, 18 (3), 370–387.
Evans, A. B. and Sleap, M., 2015. Older adults' lifelong embodied experiences of leisure time aquatic physical activity in the United Kingdom. *Leisure Studies*, 34 (3), 335–353.
Freeman, M., 2000. When the story's over, narrative foreclosure and the possibility of self-renewal. In: M. Andrews, S. Sclatter, C. Squire and A. Treader (eds), *Lines of narrative*. London: Routledge, 81–91.
Gergen, K. J. and Gergen, M. M., 2000. The new aging: self construction and social values. In R. W. Schaie and J. Hendricks (eds), *The evolution of the aging self: the societal impact of the aging process*. New York: Springer, 281–306.
Gilleard, C. and Higgs, P., 2000. *Cultures of ageing, self, citizen and the body*. Harlow: Prentice Hall.
Gilleard, C. and Higgs, P., 2013. *Ageing, corporeality and embodiment*. London: Anthem Press.
Griffin, M., 2010. Setting the scene: hailing women into a running identity. *Qualitative Research in Sport and Exercise*, 2 (2), 153–174.
Griffin, M. and Phoenix, C., 2014. Learning to run from narrative foreclosure: one woman's story of ageing and physical activity. *Journal of Aging and Physical Activity*, 22, 393–404.
Grossman, M. D. and Stewart, A. L., 2003. 'You aren't going to get better by just sitting around': physical activity perceptions, motivations, and barriers in adults 75 years of age or older. *The American Journal of Geriatric Cardiology*, 12 (1), 33–37.
Gullette, M. M., 1997. *Declining to decline: cultural combat and the politics of the midlife*. Charlottesville, VA: University of Virginia Press.
Gullette, M. M., 2004. *Aged by culture*. Chicago, IL: University of Chicago Press.

Holstein, M. B. and Minkler, M., 2003. Self, society and the 'new gerontology'. *The Gerontologist*, 43 (6), 787–796.
Hudson, J., Day, M. C. and Oliver, E. J., 2014. A 'new life' or 'delaying the inevitable'? Exploring older people's narratives during exercise uptake. *Psychology of Sport and Exercise*, 16 (3), 112–120.
Jette, S. and Vertinsky, P., 2015. The contingencies of exercise science in a globalizing world: ageing Chinese Canadians and their play and pleasure in exercise. In E. Tulle and C. Phoenix (eds), *Physical activity and sport in later life: critical perspectives*. Basingstoke: Palgrave, 113–123.
Jones, I. R. and Higgs, P. F., 2010. The natural, the normal and the normative: contested terrains in ageing and old age. *Social Science and Medicine*, 71, 1513–1519.
Kluge, M. A., Tang, A., Glick, L., LeCompte, M. and Willis, B., 2012. Let's keep moving: a dance movement class for older women recently relocated to a continuing care retirement community. *Arts and Health: An International Journal for Research, Policy and Practice*, 4 (1), 4–15
Nelson, H. L., 2001. *Damaged identities, narrative repair*. New York: Cornell University Press.
Nettleton, S., 2013. Cementing relations within a sporting field: fell running in the English Lake District and the acquisition of existential capital. *Cultural Sociology*, 7 (2), 196–210.
Nettleton, S., 2015. Fell running in later life: irresponsible intoxication or existential capital? In E. Tulle and C. Phoenix (eds), *Physical activity and sport in later life: critical perspectives*. Basingstoke, UK: Palgrave, 124–136.
Orr, N. and Phoenix, C., 2015. Photographing physical activity: using visual methods to 'grasp at' the sensual experiences of the ageing body. *Qualitative Research*, 15 (4), 454–472.
Paulson, S., 2005. How various 'cultures of fitness' shape subjective experiences of growing older. *Ageing and Society*, 25 (2), 229–244.
Pfister, G., 2012. It is never too late to win: sporting activities and performances of ageing women, *Sport in Society*, 15 (3), 369–384.
Phoenix, C. and Orr, N., 2014. Pleasure: a forgotten dimension of ageing and physical activity. *Social Science and Medicine*, 115, 94–102.
Phoenix, C. and Smith, B., 2011. Telling a (good?) counterstory of aging: natural bodybuilding meets the narrative of decline. *The Journals of Gerontology, Series B*, 66 (5), 628–639.
Phoenix, C. and Sparkes, A. C., 2009. Being Fred: big stories, small stories and the accomplishment of a positive ageing identity. *Qualitative Research*, 9 (2), 83–99.
Pike, E., 2012. Aquatic antiques: swimming off this mortal coil? *International Review for the Sociology of Sport*, 47, 492–510.
Pink, S., 2011. From embodiment to emplacement: re-thinking competing bodies, senses and spatialities. *Sport Education and Society*. 16 (3), 343–355.
Pringle, R., 2009. Defamiliarizing heavy-contact sports: a critical examination of rugby, discipline and pleasure. *Sociology of Sport Journal*, 26, 211–234.
Randall, W. L. and McKim, A. E., 2008. *Reading our lives: the poetics of growing old*. New York, NY: Oxford University Press.
Ronkainen, N., Ryba, T. and Nesti, M., 2013. 'The engine just started coughing!' – limits of physical performance, aging and career continuity in elite endurance sports. *Journal of Aging Studies*, 27 (4), 387–397.
Sparkes, A. C., 2010. Performing the ageing body and the importance of place: some brief autoethnographic moments. In B. Humberstone (ed.), *'When I am old …' Third age and leisure research: principles and practice*. LSA publication 108. Eastbourne: Leisure Studies Association, 21–32.
Sparkes, A. C., 2015. Ageing and embodied masculinities in physical activity settings: from flesh to theory and back again. In E. Tulle and C. Phoenix, eds. *Physical activity and sport in later life: critical perspectives*. Basingstoke: Palgrave, 137–148.
Thorpe, H. and Rinehart, R., 2010. Alternative sport and affect: non-representational theory examined. *Sport in Society*, 13 (7–8), 1268–1291.
Throsby, K., 2013. 'If I go in like a cranky sea lion, I come out like a smiling dolphin': marathon swimming and the unexpected pleasures of being a body in water. *Feminist Review*, 103, 5–22.
Tulle, E., 2007. Running to run: embodiment, structure and agency amongst veteran elite runners. *Sociology*, 41 (2), 329–346.
Tulle, E., 2008a. *Ageing, the body and social change: running in later life*. Basingstoke: Palgrave MacMillan.
Tulle, E., 2008b. Acting your age? Sports science and the ageing body. *Journal of Aging Studies*, 22 (4), 291–294.
Tulle, E., 2015. Physical activity and sedentary behaviour: a vital politics of old age? In E. Tulle and C. Phoenix (eds), *Physical activity and sport in later life: critical perspectives*. Basingstoke: Palgrave, 9–20.

Tulle-Winton, E., 2000. Old bodies. In P. Hancock, B. Hughes, E. Jagger, K. Paterson, R. Russell, E. Tulle-Winton and M. Tyler (eds), *The body, culture and society: an introduction*, Buckingham, UK: Open University Press, 64–84.

Twigg, J., 2013. *Fashion and age: dress, the body and later life*. London: Bloomsbury.

Vertinsky, P., 2002. Sporting women in the public gaze: shattering the master narratives of aging female bodies. *Canadian Woman Studies/ le cahiers de la femme*, 21 (3), 58–63.

Vincent, J., 2006. Ageing contested: anti-ageing science and the cultural construction of old age. *Sociology*, 40 (4), 681–698.

Vincent, J., 2007. Science and imagery in the 'war on old age'. *Ageing and Society*, 27 (6), 941–961.

Wellard, I., 2012. Body-reflexive pleasures: exploring bodily experiences within the context of sport and physical activity. *Sport, Education and Society*, 17 (1), 21–33.

PART IV

Institutionalized bodies

19
MEDICALIZED AND SCIENTIZED BODIES

Parissa Safai

Known for the diversity of its residents and neighborhoods, the City of Toronto (Ontario, Canada) is home to just under three million people (City of Toronto, 2012). A careful drive through one such neighborhood – called New Toronto, ironically – reveals a community in flux. Newly built multi-million dollar lakefront mansions sit next to dilapidated rent-by-the-month low-rise apartment buildings. Post-Second World War bungalows that have enjoyed the same owners for decades are prime properties for developers looking to scoop them up for a steal, sever their large lots into two, then rebuild and sell new, more modern and expensive homes to younger buyers looking to find a house of their own (and willing to take on outrageous levels of debt in order to do so) anywhere in the increasingly unaffordable city (Canadian Press, 2015; Toronto Foundation, 2014). After the First World War, New Toronto was a hotbed for industry and many people worked in the various manufacturing plants situated close to the railroad tracks that cut through the northern tip of the neighborhood. But, starting in the 1980s, the departure of various factories from New Toronto to other (cheaper) locations, including the exit of the area's largest employer (Goodyear), left behind a wake of unemployment and great swaths of unused industrial buildings and brownfields (ibid.). Given its proximity to the lake as well as to the downtown core of the city, New Toronto has been called the next 'it' place to live by Toronto trendsetters (e.g. blogTO, 2014) and yet, although one can see gentrification creeping in, the loss of those factories and lack of employment in the area continue to permeate its bones.

Along one of its major streets, just north of the local employment assistance center, there are a series of interconnected brown brick factory buildings, formerly home to some manufacturer or another. New business focused on fitness has settled into these buildings and four large banners advertise what one can find behind the doors. Feeding off of the original intent of the building, one banner boasts 'fitness at the factory' through Pilates, yoga, Zumba and dance. The next banner advertises a martial arts studio with the letters TNT (the chemical compound used in explosive materials) boldly highlighted and, following that, a third sign invites you to 'feed the warrior within' at CrossFit Colosseum (www.crossfitcolosseum.com). There are logos and images associated with each of these banners but the fourth one, right next to the CrossFit sign, simply has big, bold red letters declaring 'sports medicine clinic.' The taglines of the CrossFit gym (or 'box' in CrossFit parlance) and the sports medicine clinic make it clear that the clinic is part of the gym – the tagline for CrossFit Colloseum reads 'Forging Elite Fitness' and the tagline for the sports medicine clinic reads 'Reforging Elite Athletes.'

At first glance, these buildings and their signs seem unremarkable and perhaps even banal; yet what seems ordinary is, in fact, a rich tableau for the study of spaces, places, symbols and practices that construct, and are constructed by, the active body in the contemporary historical moment (Frow and Morris, 2000). As PCS scholars, we are compelled to 'excavate' these buildings and interrogate these businesses and banners in efforts to 'radically contextualize' the dis/connections between physical culture, health and medicine amidst the 'complex social, economic, political and technological relationships that comprise the social context' (Silk and Andrews, 2011: 9). For example, we must not minimize or overlook the fact that these former industrial buildings, once places of employment for many, are now spaces promoting fitness and exercise (the healthful benefits of which are implied) for those who can afford the registration and membership fees in a community with a high degree of unemployment (Urban HEART @ Toronto, 2014). A critical reading of this highlights the contradictions of health in contemporary neoliberal regimes where such key determinants of health as job in/security and un/employment are supplanted by the promotion of individualized lifestyle approaches, such as fitness and exercise, as a cure-all for illness and injury (Raphael, Bryant and Rioux, 2010). Ingham (1985) draws clear lines between the ideological construction of lifestyle as 'implausible panacea for the relational and distributive problems of advanced capitalism' (ibid.: 47) and its role in '[diverting] attention away from the *structural* impediments to well-being by framing health issues in terms of *personal*, moral responsibilities – a "pull yourself up by the bootstraps" alternative to state intervention in health care' (ibid.: 43, italics in original; see also Bercovitz, 2000). The buildings, the banners, the heightened (hyper-)promotion of fitness for the betterment of health rather than critical and sustained public interrogation of the negative health consequences of the exodus of industry, as contextualized by broader political and economic processes that favor market forces and the mobility of industry, is not unique to New Toronto (Coburn, 2004). Throughout Canada, there is a notable lack of public discussion and debate on the social, political and economic nature of health, and Raphael (2009) goes so far as to suggest that our collective 'health preoccupations with behavioral and "lifestyle" approaches rooted in individualized approaches to disease prevention' (ibid.: 193–194) block vitally needed discussions and responses to the social, political and economic inequities of health (Armstrong, Armstrong and Coburn, 2001; Raphael et al., 2010; Wilkinson and Pickett, 2009).

Crawford's (1980, 2006) influential work on healthism, the ideology of individual responsibility for health and health care, continues to figure prominently in critical health research exploring the ways in which the social production of illness and disease is neglected and collective responsibility for health care is hidden behind the individualization of health and illness and the promotion of lifestyle approaches within neoliberal regimes. Healthism positions poor health as the product of individual failure where 'people are blamed for both their acts and their omissions – what they do wrong and what they fail to do right' (Yoder, 2002: 26 as cited in Cheek, 2008). Even if and when the cause of illness is known to originate from outside of the individual, poor health is framed as the inability of the individual to 'resist culture, advertising, institutional and environmental constraints, disease agents, or, simply, lazy or poor personal habits' (Crawford, 1980: 368).

The concentrated focus on the individual is especially marked in neoliberal capitalism where the dogma of individual responsibility for health is both the result of and support to those pressures that orient success (for both the individual and the nation) as tied to the preservation and progress of the marketplace – including the health and healthcare marketplace – at all costs (Broom, 2008; Crawford, 1977; Struthers, 2013). The neoliberal turn in national and international politics in the late 1970s and 1980s, as influenced by and influencing the various fiscal crises of the time, offered fertile soil in which healthism took root and, in turn, the notion of *'individual responsibility for health, although not without challenge, proved to be particularly effective in establishing the "common sense" of neoliberalism's essential tenets'* (Crawford, 2006: 410, italics in original). Amidst this political right turn, there was a collective reorientation to the behavioral and lifestyle approaches that so characterize healthist ideology:

> In the convergence of new right ideology and right-thinking common sense, policing the crisis of the Welfare State requires the policing of the body ... It is an idea and/or policy which, in short, elevates the personal etiology of illness over the societal-structural etiology of illness. It is an idea and/or policy which is riddled, in both senses of the term, with voluntaristic assumptions that *a priori* define problems as personal and not as problems of milieu, structure, or egregious and invalidating ideologies such as racism, sexism, or ageism.
>
> *(Ingham, 1985: 50)*

Within neoliberal capitalism, individual responsibility is privileged above notions of public goods and community (Coburn, 2000; Evans, 1997; Salter and Salter, 1997) and, buoyed by the entrenchment of middle-class ideology (cf. Crawford, 2006), such language/concepts as willpower, self-discipline and lifestyle operate to define health as a personal trouble rather than public issue (cf. Mills, [1959] 2000; see also Howell and Ingham, 2001). In so doing, contemporary health promotion, as grounded in the ideology of individual responsibility, diverts our attention away from the politics of health, the structural forces and processes that shape health in our lives and, more significantly, undermines our abilities to – including our belief that we can – enact structural change (Bambra, Fox and Scott-Samuel, 2005).

Medicine is implicated within healthism as 'notions of health and illness, in whatever context used, in large measure retain a medicalized meaning' (Crawford, 1980: 370). Crawford writes:

> Health practices, therefore, cannot be understood without an accounting of the impact of the biomedical project – the state of medical knowledge, the forms of medical practice, political and economic uses and applications, and the transforming reach of medical constructions in social life. Neither can the concept and meaning of health be grasped without appreciating medicine's symbolic dimensions – meanings that traverse both the mundane and the sacred of an instrumental-rational culture, and meanings that, in being camouflaged as natural, become powerful vehicles for authorizing and validating social practices.
>
> *(Crawford, 2006: 404)*

As more and more social phenomena become identified as health-related through the process of medicalization, medicine – as tangible and symbolic practice *as well as* institution 'camouflaged as natural' – consolidates its institutionalized claim of power as the expert authority of all that is health (cf. Illich, 1977). Medicine reproduces healthist ideology and, as a way of managing populations, medicalization fosters 'a medical way of seeing' that transfers 'power over and responsibility for health from individuals, the public and therefore political life, to powerful elites, namely the medical and health professions and the multinational pharmaceutical companies' and 'this depoliticization of health, via the transfer of power and responsibility to these professional and/or commercial groups, means that we do not acknowledge our power over our own health or our autonomy over our own bodies (Bambra et al., 2005: 191). Set amidst this critical analytical backdrop, the seemingly banal tableau described earlier in this chapter is replete with significance – how can one 'feed the warrior within' if they are struggling with food insecurity as a consequence of unemployment?

How does sport and the myriad of other practices that are located under the wide label of physical culture weave through these themes? The seemingly ordinary series of banners is once again full of significance here as the two key taglines 'forging elite fitness' and 'reforging elite athletes' speak volumes about how we produce athletic bodies in the contemporary moment as well as the medicalization of those bodies. The key words of interest in those taglines are 'forging' and 'reforging'. According to Oxford Dictionaries (n.d.), the word 'forge' (/fôrj/) as a verb means:

1   Make or shape (a metal object) by heating it in a fire or furnace and beating or hammering it.
    1.1 Create (a relationship or new conditions)
2   Produce a copy or imitation of (a document, signature, banknote, or work or art) for the purpose of deception.

And, as a noun, means:

1   A blacksmith's workshop; a smithy.
    1.1 A furnace or hearth for melting or refining metal.
    1.2 A workshop or factory containing a furnace for refining metal.

The allusion to forging is fitting to this chapter's focus insofar as the ways in which we produce athletic bodies in this contemporary moment involves the beating or the hammering of the body into shape much like a piece of iron or steel hammered, welded, bent and chiseled as part of its transformation from raw metal to finished object. For the blacksmith, the hammering and manipulation of the raw metal results in stronger metal; in sport and fitness, whether at high performance levels or otherwise, the body is hammered and manipulated in order to produce stronger performance (Beamish and Ritchie, 2006). In one of a series of reports on Canadian sprinters and hurdlers preparing or the 2015 Pan Am Games in Toronto, a journalist describes the aftermath of one training session:

> Fawn Dorr is on her hands and knees calling out for God. Kimberly Hyacinthe is in the hallway, throwing up in a garbage can. Sam Effah is sitting down and someone is trying to pull him up, saying, 'I can't let you sit still.' Tremaine Harris is walking – well, swaying really – and moaning. Philip Osei looks fine but they call him the beast for a reason. He's barely human. It's an odd scene to come across in an old Downsview airplane hangar repurposed into a soccer facility and now, with the coach's shoe laces tying back the mesh netting, repurposed again to serve as a training space for many of Canada's fastest men and women. Those are the people rolling around on the ground, half hoping some act of magic will take away the pain coursing through every fiber of their being. That's their human side. Their athletic side is actually pretty happy about the pain. This is how they are supposed to feel; it's how they know they're working hard.
>
> Their effort on the track and in the weight room on this day in November, and the months on either side of it – long before the competition season even starts – is

what will decide if these athletes are good enough to stand on the podium at the Toronto Pan Am Games in July.

(Gillespie, 2015)

This deliberate forging of the body may be most obvious at the highest levels of organized, competitive sport, yet it is not exclusive to those looking to wear a gold medal around their necks or to those looking to hoist a trophy above their heads. One can easily be forgiven for mistaking a description of a CrossFit workout-of-the-day for a description of hard labor borne by prison inmates (McKeon, 2014). The all-encompassing imperative to perform and to excel acts as the furnace in which contemporary athletic bodies, as well as the 'boundaries of health and health care are being pushed, pulled, and reshaped' (Cheek, 2008: 975).

It is within this context that we see the forging of health not in the sense of its transformation from raw material to finished object but, rather, its imitation and deception. Athletes are often seen as symbols of strength and vitality, but this is a superficial façade in that they often sacrifice their health and well-being in the pursuit of success and idealized athleticism (Safai, 2013; Theberge, 2008). The pervasiveness of the 'culture of risk' depends in large part on the imperative to perform (Bridel, 2010) and, as performance becomes their 'default position' (Theberge, 2009: 181), 'health ... is linked overtly to performance' (Cheek, 2008: 975). As performance ascends to become the 'super-value' (cf. Crawford, 2006) against which all is measured, athletes are expected to pledge unconditional allegiance to the performance principle and are exalted as dedicated, disciplined, hard-working and perseverant when they do so (cf. Hughes and Coakley, 1991). Yet unquestioned allegiance to the performance principle requires constant training and competition at the edges of human capacity and the staggering rates of sport- and even fitness-related injury, disability and even death demonstrate that there are limits to our bodily quests for 'limitless performance' (Safai, 2013; see also McKeon, 2014). For example, Zirin (2011, 2015) routinely decries the forgery of health in the National Football League (NFL) – dissecting carefully crafted media releases from the league declaring the game 'safer than ever' with sobering statistics of the 100 per cent risk of injury for and the grossly shortened lifespans of players.

Within the privileging of performance at all costs, we see pain, injury and even death constructed as individual troubles or failings and not the consequence of the particular depoliticized, individualized and medicalized ways in which we produce athletic bodies. Crawford writes:

> In sum, medical practice is an individualized treatment mode, a mode which defines the client as deficient and which reconstructs the individual's understanding of the problem for which help is being sought. That reconstruction individualizes and compartmentalizes the problem, transforming it into its most immediate property: the biological and physical manifestations of the individual, diseased, human body. The answer to the problem is then logically held to be found in the same professionalized and individualized treatment, not in the reordering of the social, political, and environmental circumstances in which the individual exists.[1]
>
> *(Crawford, 1980: 373)*

In this sense, sports medicine plays a collusive role in the forged athletic body and the re/production of performance-related health at all costs. Rather than occupying space outside of contemporary sport and fitness regimes – and thereby being in a better position to contribute to the 'reordering of the social, political, and environmental circumstances' that frame and are framed by contemporary sport and fitness culture – sports medicine clinicians find their raison d'être within the performance principle (Hoberman, 1992; Safai, 2007). Theoretical and technical advances in sports medicine are made from and through the athletic body; as Young (1993: 376) has argued, 'sports workplaces are simultaneously sites of medical mastery and extraordinary medical neglect'. Furthermore, sports medicine clinicians come to occupy powerful roles within 'sport workplaces', not as safeguards of athletes' bodies and lives, but as managers of the negative consequences of sport and fitness practices (i.e. pain, injury and death) (Safai, 2013). As numerous athletes and some sport officials decried the alarming speed of the sliding track in Whistler, British Columbia prior to the death of Nodar Kumaritashvili in 2010 or the problematic and dangerous design of the ski cross course that claimed the life of Nik Zoricic in Grindewald, Switzerland in 2012, no sports medicine clinician involved in either of those events rang the alarm of the potential catastrophe awaiting participants (Safai, 2013). Danger lies in sports medicine that is integrated into contemporary sport and fitness (much like the sports medicine clinic that reforges the damaged bodies of those forged in the CrossFit box) as the performance imperative frames 'the interdependent relationships in which [clinicians] are enmeshed' and shapes 'not only clinicians' behavior, but also *their understanding of medical conditions*' (Malcolm, 2009: 206; italics in original).

It is important to acknowledge, in keeping with PCS's call for more transparent, democratic and 'openly incomplete' scholarship, that this chapter offers but a partial reading of the nature of health and medicine in contemporary social life broadly, and in contemporary physical culture more specifically (Silk and Andrews, 2011: 17). For example, we would be negligent to not acknowledge that there are some clinicians who do identify and agitate against the physical dangers imposed on people and/or the dangerous physical practices assumed by people as part of their participation in sport and fitness (e.g. Fainaru-Wada and Fainaru, 2013; McKeon, 2014). It would also be careless to neglect what happens in the micro-spaces between athlete-as-patient and healthcare provider since, 'like any other "key word", health is constructed in relation to social structures and experience and systematically articulated with other meanings and practices' (Crawford, 2006: 405). For example, despite the growth in scholarship on the complex synergies, tensions and contradictions between sport, health and medicine (see Baker, Safai and Fraser-Thomas, 2014; Malcolm, 2014), researchers have still not yet explored (fully or otherwise) athletes' resistance to the conceptualization and construction of the body as machine to be reforged or reassembled when hurt or damaged. What of those athletes who resist (sports) medicine's collusion in high-performance sport? What of those healthcare providers who refuse the imperative of the performance principle in their negotiations with patients? Furthermore, what of those athletes or clinicians who engage in acts of resistance within the confines of the performance principle in efforts to preserve a sense of agency or to temper the negative and isolating consequences of the pursuit of excellence at all costs (e.g. Hoberman, 2002)? Robust explorations of these questions (and others) will help to flush out our understandings of the multiple, dynamic, contradictory, constituting and constitutive meanings and practices associated with health, medicine and the active body. It is also important to acknowledge that, despite the growth in the critical study of health, medicine and the active body over the past few decades, we have not yet fully explored or advocated for more humane sport and fitness. In other words, there has been a relative absence of active, political engagement in the dismantling of health-compromising social practices and institutions by scholars who, in at least their writings, are '[committed] to progressive social change' (Miller, 2001: 1).

The articulation, construction and advancement of humane physical culture – in particular, sport and fitness – offers resistance to the instrumentalized and individualized ethos of the performance principle and resonates with PCS's political and moral imperative to make difference in our lives. Humane physical culture does not see the 'culture of risk' as accidental or a product of individual failings, but recognizes it as an embedded structural element of contemporary sport and fitness production systems built on human labor pushed to the edge. In so doing, humane physical culture respects the vulnerability of the body and actively resists the pressure, fear or moralizing narratives of worth associated with the tolerance (or lack of) of pain/injury. Humane physical culture privileges the ethics of care *and* a collective responsibility for well-being (itself a concept that has been poorly unpacked and addressed in physical cultural studies) at all costs (Duquin, 1994), demanding that those charged with health care similarly prioritize well-being above all. Humane physical culture does not disassociate health in sport and fitness from the larger social, political and economic determinants that frame health more broadly – in fact, humane physical culture recognizes health as a public political issue: 'The political question about danger is which ones will be identified as requiring public attention and which will be relegated to the private sphere ... this problem-defining, boundary-setting and solution-forming dimension is the locus of volatile politics and ideology of health' (Crawford, 2006: 403). This demands the encouragement of athletes' political engagement in sport and fitness around their rights to health – destabilizing commonplace assumptions that politics is only the purview of government, rejecting understandings of health as only medicalized care (cf. Bambra et al., 2005), and resisting the all-encompassing imperative to perform in contemporary sport and fitness. Such rejection of the dangerous ways in which we forge athletic bodies and the encouragement of humane physical culture, in turn, require active and sustained political engagement from the academic community. This resonates with the PCS project in its call to researchers to not make 'theoretical work ... an end in itself', but to forge insightful connections between private-public/academic-lay theories, methods and knowledges that 'is part of an effort to enable [us] to come to terms with [our] everyday experiences ... and, through the generation of social criticism, leads to resistance and empowers to action those who are interacting' (Silk and Andrews, 2011: 13).

Note

1   It is important to acknowledge that there are medical practitioners who are paying closer attention to the material conditions of life as integral parts of clinical practice. For example, in Toronto, Dr Gary Bloch has dedicated his career to addressing poverty as an underlying cause of illness. He and his staff actively work with patients and their families not just with medical diagnosis and treatment but also with social assistance, housing and legal aid (Porter, 2015). The Canadian Medical Association (CMA) has also recognized the negative health consequences of income inequality and poverty in various reports and position statements (e.g. CMA, 2013) but it is unclear, at this time, how such reports and statements influence government action or daily clinical practice.

References

Armstrong, P., Armstrong, H. and Coburn, D., eds, 2001. *Unhealthy times: Political economy perspectives on health and care in Canada*, Oxford University Press, Toronto.
Baker, J., Safai, P. and Fraser-Thomas, J., 2014. *Health and elite sport: Is high performance sport a healthy pursuit?* Routledge, London.
Bambra, C., Fox, D. and Scott-Samuel, A., 2005. Towards a politics of health. *Health Promotion International*, 20 (2), 187–192.
Beamish, R. and Ritchie, I., 2006. *Fastest, highest, strongest: A critique of high-performance sport.* Routledge, New York.
Bercovitz, K. L., 2000. A critical analysis of Canada's 'active living': Science or politics? *Critical Public Health*, 10 (1), 19–39.
blogTO, 2014. The top 5 neighbourhoods on the rise in 2015. Available from www.blogto.com/city/

2014/12/the_top_5_toronto_neighbourhoods_on_the_rise_in_2015 (accessed May 28, 2015).
Bridel, W. F., 2010. 'Finish … whatever it takes' exploring pain and pleasure in the ironman triathlon: A socio-cultural analysis. PhD thesis, Queen's University, Kingston, Ontario.
Broom, D., 2008. Hazardous good intentions? Unintended consequences of the project of prevention. *Health Sociology Review*, 17 (2), 129–140.
Canadian Press, 2015. Homes in Toronto, Vancouver became more unaffordable this year. *The Star*, 22 June. Available from www.thestar.com/business/2015/06/22/homes-in-toronto-vancouver-became-more-unaffordable-this-year.print.html (accessed June 23, 2015).
Cheek, J., 2008. Healthism: A new conservatism? *Qualitative Health Research*, 18 (7), 974–982.
City of Toronto, 2012. *2011 Census: Population and dwelling counts*. Available from www1.toronto.ca/city_of_toronto/social_development_finance__administration/files/pdf/2011-census-backgrounder.pdf (accessed June 21, 2015).
CMA, 2013. *Health care in Canada: What makes us sick?* Available from www.cma.ca/Assets/assets-library/document/fr/advocacy/What-makes-us-sick_en.pdf (accessed May 28, 2015).
Coburn, D., 2000. Income inequality, social cohesion and the health status of populations: The role of neo-liberalism. *Social Science and Medicine*, 51 (1), 135–146.
Coburn, D., 2004. Beyond the income inequality hypothesis: Class, neo-liberalism and health inequalities. *Social Science and Medicine*, 58 (1), 41–56.
Crawford, R., 1977. You are dangerous to your health: the ideology and politics of victim blaming. *International Journal of Health Services*, 7 (4), 663–680.
Crawford, R., 1980. Healthism and the medicalization of everyday life. *International Journal of Health Services*, 10 (3), 365–388.
Crawford, R., 2006. Health as meaningful social practice. *Health: An Interdisciplinary Journal for the Social Study of Health, Illness and Medicine*, 10 (4), 401–420.
Duquin, M. E., 1994. The body snatchers and Dr. Frankenstein revisited: Social construction and deconstruction of bodies and sport. *Journal of Sport and Social Issues*, 18 (3), 268–281.
Evans, R. G., 1997. Going for the gold: The redistributive agenda behind market-based health care reform. *Journal of Health Politics, Policy and Law*, 22 (2), 427–465.
Fainaru-Wada, M. and Fainaru, S., 2013. *League of denial: The NFL, concussions and the battle for truth*. Penguin Random House, New York.
Frow, J. and Morris, M., 2000. Cultural studies. In N. K. Denzin and Y. S. Lincoln, eds, *Handbook of qualitative research*, 2nd edn. Sage, Thousand Oaks, 695–727.
Gillespie, K., 2015. The race to the Pan Am Games – and the pain it takes to make it. *The Star*, 17 June. Available from www.thestar.com/news/gta/panamgames/2015/06/17/the-race-to-the-pan-am-games-and-the-pain-it-takes-to-make-it.html (accessed September 11, 2016).
Hoberman, J. M., 1992. *Mortal engines: The science of performance and the dehumanization of sport*. Free Press, New York.
Hoberman, J., 2002. Sports physicians and the doping crisis in elite sport. *Clinical Journal of Sport Medicine*, 12 (4), 203–208.
Howell, J. and Ingham, A., 2001. From social problem to personal issue: The language of lifestyle. *Cultural Studies*, 15 (4), 326–351.
Hughes, R. and Coakley, J., 1991. Positive deviance among athletes: The implications of overconformity to the sport ethic. *Sociology of Sport Journal*, 8 (4), 307–325.
Illich, I., 1977. *Limits to medicine*. Penguin, Harmondsworth.
Ingham, A., 1985. From public issue to personal trouble: Well-being and the fiscal crisis of the state. *Sociology of Sport Journal*, 2 (1), 43–55.
Malcolm, D., 2009. Medical uncertainty and clinician-athlete relations: The management of concussion injuries in Rugby Union. *Sociology of Sport Journal*, 26 (2), 191–210.
Malcolm, D., 2014, Sport, health and medicine: A sociological agenda, *Asia Pacific Journal of Sport and Social Science*, 3(1), 51–63.
McKeon, L., 2014. Save me from my workout. *Toronto Life Magazine*. Available from www.torontolife.com/informer/features/2014/06/23/save-me-from-my-workout/?page=all#tlb_multipage_anchor_1 (accessed June 21, 2015).
Miller, T., 2001. What it is and what it isn't: Introducing … cultural studies. In T. Miller, ed., *A companion to cultural studies*. Blackwell, Malden, 1–20.
Mills, C. W., [1959] 2000. *The sociological imagination*. Oxford University Press, Oxford.
Oxford Dictionaries, n.d. Forge. Available from www.oxforddictionaries.com/us/definition/

american_english/forge (accessed September 5, 2016).

Porter, C., 2015. St. Michael's health team offers prescription for poverty. *The Star*, May 23. Available from www.thestar.com/news/insight/2015/05/23/st-michaels-hospital-health-team-offers-prescription-for-poverty.html (accessed on May 23, 2015).

Raphael, D., 2009. Escaping from the Phantom Zone: Social determinants of health, public health units and public policy in Canada. *Health Promotion International*, 24 (2), 193–198.

Raphael, D., Bryant, T. and Rioux, M., eds, 2010. *Staying alive: Critical perspectives on health, illness, and health care*, 2nd edn. Canadian Scholars' Press, Toronto.

Safai, P., 2007. A critical analysis of the development of sport medicine in Canada, 1955–80. *International Review for the Sociology of Sport*, 42 (3), 321–341.

Safai, P., 2013. Sports medicine, the state and the politics of risk. In D. L. Andrews and B. Carrington, eds, *A companion to sport*. Wiley-Blackwell, Malden, 112–128.

Salter, L. and Salter, R., 1997. Displacing the welfare state. In W. Clement, ed., *Understanding Canada: Building on the new Canadian political economy*. McGill-Queen's University Press, Montreal, 311–337.

Silk, M. L. and Andrews, D. L., 2011. Toward a physical cultural studies. *Sociology of Sport Journal*, 28 (1), 4–35.

Struthers, J., 2013. Historical perspective on care and the welfare state: The rise, retreat, return, and reframing of a key concept. In P. Armstrong, B. Clow, K. Grant, M. Haworth-Brockman, B. Jackson, A. Pederson and M. Seeley, eds, *Thinking women and health care reform in Canada*. Women's Press, Toronto, 159–170.

Theberge, N., 2008. 'Just a normal bad part of what I do': Elite athletes' accounts of the relationship between health and sport. *Sociology of Sport Journal*, 25, 206–222.

Theberge, N., 2009. 'It's not about health, it's about performance': Sport medicine, health and the culture of risk in Canadian sport. In P. Vertinsky and J. Hargreaves, eds, *Physical Culture, Power and the Body*. Routledge, London, 176–194.

Toronto Foundation, 2014. *Toronto's vital signs 2014 report*. Available from http://torontosvitalsigns.ca/full-report.pdf (accessed June 21, 2015).

Urban HEART @ Toronto, 2014, *Centre for Research on Inner City Health – St Michael's Hospital*. Available from www.torontohealthprofiles.ca/urbanheartattoronto/UrbanHeart_ExecutiveReport.pdf (accessed June 21, 2015).

Wilkinson, R. and Pickett, K., 2009. *The spirit level: Why equality is better for everyone*, Penguin, London.

Yoder, S. D., 2002. Individual responsibility for health: Decision not discovery. *Hastings Centre Report*, 32 (2), 22–31.

Young, K., 1993. Violence, risk and liability in male sports culture. *Sociology of Sport Journal*, 10 (4), 373–396.

Zirin, D., 2011. NFL labor pains and the press release that redefined chutzpah. *Edge of Sports*. Available from www.edgeofsports.com/2011-03-14-607/index.html (accessed June 22, 2015).

Zirin, D., 2015. 'It gets really disgusting': Dave Zirin unloads on Roger Goodell, concussions and NFL's demented culture. *Salon*. Available from: www.salon.com/2015/03/20/it_gets_really_disgusting_dave_zirin_unloads_on_roger_goodell_concussions_nfls_demented_culture (accessed June 22, 2015).

20
DIGITAL BODIES

Deborah Lupton

Introduction

Human bodies have always interacted with technologies. However, the nature of the technology has changed over the millennia. In the contemporary digital era, bodies are digitized as never before, both by individuals on their behalf and by other actors and agencies seeking to portray and monitor their bodies. From Facebook status updates and images, Instagram selfies, YouTube videos and tweets to exergames, sophisticated digital medical imaging technologies and the ceaseless generation of data from sensor-based devices and environments, human bodies now emit vast quantities of digital data. A major change in digitized embodiment is the ways in which detailed data are now generated on the geolocation, movements, appearance, behaviours and functions of bodies and the uses to which these data are put as part of the digital data knowledge economy. The cyborg body has transformed into the digital body, whose data outputs possess commercial, managerial and research as well as personal value and status to a range of actors and agencies beyond the individual.

Researchers contributing to physical cultural studies have drawn attention to how recent digital technologies are employed to monitor and measure moving bodies in diverse ways. They have analysed the representations and practices of embodiment that are portrayed in apps and exergames such as Wii Fit, for example, that bring together exercise and fitness routines with gaming devices. In such games, certain bodily shapes and degrees of fitness are normalized, while others are stigmatized. Stereotypical gendered, lean, vigorous and youthful bodies are frequently reproduced and celebrated in these games. Participants are encouraged to engage in self-care practices directed at attempting to develop these attributes (Francombe, 2010; Millington, 2014a, 2014b). Via such technologies (among a plethora of many other practices and devices), the biopolitics of movement (Newman and Giardina, 2014) are configured. These technologies enact forms of biopedagogies that privilege the active, physically fit and therefore (assumed) productive and self-responsible body.

In this chapter, I extend this previous work by examining the ways in which human bodies interact with and are configured by digital technologies and how these technologies generate new knowledges and practices about bodies. I use infants and young children as a case study to explain these aspects. From before they are even born, children's bodies are now frequently represented and monitored by digital technologies, including medical imaging and monitoring devices as well as social media sites, surveillance and self-tracking technologies. In my discussion, I draw on literature from sociocultural theorizing of the body, childhood, digital technologies and big data, particularly that by scholars adopting the sociomaterial perspective. The chapter is divided into two main parts. The first presents a general overview of theoretical approaches to conceptualizing the interactions between bodies and technologies, while the second part is devoted to outlining the ways in which infants' and young children's (moving) bodies are digitized.

Theorizing digital bodies

Scholars in the sociology of the body and technocultures developed an interest in the entanglements of human bodies with computerized technologies following the advent of personal computing in the mid-1980s. The terms 'cyborg' and 'cyberspace' (among many other 'cyber' neologisms) were adopted to discuss the ways in which computer users interacted with their PCs and with each other online. Donna Haraway's work on the political implications of the cyborg as a heterogeneous, ambiguous and hybrid entity has been particularly important in drawing attention to the fluidities of embodiment and selfhood (Haraway, 1991, 1997). Many other social researchers into the 1990s and early 2000s seized on the concept of the cyborg to investigate the forms of embodiment that are generated or mediated by digital technologies across a range of contexts: including, for example, computer users, IVF embryos, menopausal women, athletes and older people (Lupton, 1995; Buse, 2010; Franklin, 2006; Rayvon, 2012; Leng, 1996).

Cyber terminology is not as often employed in discussions of the social, cultural and political dimensions of computer technology use now that academic terminology has moved more to a focus on the 'digital' (Lupton, 2015b). However, the important work of Haraway and others writing on cyborg bodies developed an argument that acknowledges the complexity of relationships between human and nonhuman actors and calls into question ideas about the fixed nature of identity and embodiment (Lupton, 2015c). Such a perspective is now often referred to as 'sociomaterialism'. It recognizes that subject and object co-configure each other as part of a relationship. Objects are viewed as participating in specific sets of relations, including those with other artefacts as well as with people (Latour, 2005; Law, 2008; Fenwick and Landri, 2012). The term 'assemblage' is often used to capture these entanglements. Assemblages of human flesh and nonhuman actors are constantly configured and reconfigured. They facilitate modes of knowing and living the body.

People domesticate technologies by bringing them into their everyday worlds, melding them to their bodies/selves and bestowing these objects with biographically specific meanings. They become 'territories of the self', marked by individual use, and therefore redolent of personal histories (Nippert-Eng, 1996). This concept of territories of the self acknowledges that bodies and selves are not contained to the fleshly envelope of the individual body, but extend beyond this into space and connect and interconnect with other bodies and objects. These processes are inevitably relational because they involve embodied interactions and affective responses (Lupton, 2015b, 2016; Labanyi, 2010). As Merleau-Ponty (1968) argues, our embodiment is always inevitably interrelational or intercorporeal. We experience the world as fleshly bodies, via the sensations and emotions configured through and by our bodies as they relate to other bodies and material objects and spaces. We touch these others, and they touch us. Our bodies are distributed throughout the spaces we inhabit, just as these spaces and the others within them inhabit. Embodiment, then, is primarily a relational assemblage. The concept of 'the person' (including the person's body) becomes distributed between the interactions of heterogeneous elements (Lee, 2008).

In the digital age, practices of embodiment are increasingly becoming enacted via digital technologies. We now no longer refer to the separate environment of 'cyberspace' as our everyday worlds have become so thoroughly digitized. Where once the figure of the cyborg was a science-fiction creation of superhuman powers (Lupton, 1995), our bodies now engage routinely with digital technologies to the extent that it is taken for granted. It is now frequently argued that online and offline selves cannot be distinguished from each other any longer, given the pervasiveness and ubiquity of online participation. Instead categories of flesh, identity and technology are porous and intermeshed (Elwell, 2014; Hayles, 2012). Our bodies are digital data assemblages (Lupton, 2015c).

Digital social theorists have drawn attention to the increasingly sensor-saturated physical environments in which people move, which add to the pre-existing technologies for visually observing and documenting human movements in public spaces, such as CCTV cameras (Kitchin and Dodge, 2011; Kitchin, 2014; Lyon and Bauman, 2013). Kitchin and Dodge (2011) use the term 'code/space' to describe the intersections of software coding with the spatial configurations of humans and nonhumans. They underline the power of code to shape, manage, monitor and discipline the movements of bodies in space and place, including both public and private domains. Digital representations of bodies and digital data on many aspects of embodiment are generated from the various sites, devices and spaces with which individuals interact daily. These include the transactional data produced via routine encounters with surveillance cameras in public spaces, sensors or online websites, platforms and search engines or from the content that people upload voluntarily to social media sites or collect on themselves using self-tracking devices. These technologies create and recreate certain types of digital data assemblages which can then be scrutinized, monitored and used for various purposes, including intervention.

The collection and analysis of digitized information about people's behaviours are now becoming increasingly advocated and implemented in many social contexts and institutions: the workplace, education, medicine and public health, insurance, government, marketing, advertising and commerce, the military, citizen science, and urban planning and management. The growing commodification and commercial value of digital data sets and their use in these domains are blurring the boundaries between small and big data, the private and the public. People are now encouraged, obliged or coerced into using digital devices for monitoring aspects of their lives to produce personal data that are employed not only for private and voluntary purposes but also for the purposes of others. These data have begun to be appropriated by a range of actors and agencies, including commercial, managerial, research and governmental (Lupton, 2016).

Critical data scholars have drawn attention to the valorization of quantifiable information in the digital data economy and the algorithmic processing of this information as part of new forms of soft power relations and the production of inequalities (Lupton, 2015b; Kitchin, 2014; Cheney-Lippold, 2011). Digital data can have tangible material effects on people's actions, including the ways in which their bodies are conceptualized, managed and disciplined by themselves and others. The calculations and predictions that are generated by software algorithms are beginning to shape people's life chances and opportunities: their access to insurance, health care, credit and employment, and their exclusion from spaces and places, as in the identification of potential criminals and terrorists (Crawford and Schultz, 2014).

It is difficult, if not impossible, to separate digital technologies from their users, as both are viewed as mutually constituted. Technologies discipline the body to assimilate better to their requirements, their ways of seeing, monitoring and treating human flesh. However, bodies also shape technologies. The new mobile and wearable devices are carried or worn on the body, becoming a body prosthetic, an extension of the body. When people handle or touch technologies, they may leave the marks of their bodies on the devices: body oils, sweat, skin flakes. Software is also transformed by use. Now that digital technologies are increasingly used as part of the practices of selfhood, digital archives have become important storage places for personalized bodily data. Images, descriptions and markers of users' bodies are entered into the memories of their digital devices: photographs and videos of themselves, records of their geolocation, the detailed biometric information that is generated by self-tracking apps. Digital devices and software have become repositories of selfhood and embodiment (Lupton, 2015b, 2016).

Young children's embodiment and digital technologies

All human bodies are understood to be in the process of constant transformation, requiring engaging in work on the self and reflexive self-monitoring as part of performing selfhood and embodiment. Foucault refers to these ethical practices of citizenship as 'technologies of the self' (Foucault, 1986, 1988). Beck uses the term 'reflexive biography' (Beck, 1992; Beck and Beck-Gernsheim, 1995) to denote the ways in which people are encouraged to seek knowledge and use it to improve their life chances, health and wellbeing. The idea of the unfinished body is particularly true of children's bodies, which are viewed as requiring constant monitoring, assessment and improvement from themselves and other actors and agencies to achieve the ideal of the civilized body (Jenks, 2005; Uprichard, 2008; Lupton, 2013a).

While developing *in utero* and following birth, children's bodies are measured and observed for signs of 'normal' growth and development, and they are continually subjected to practices that seek to socialize and normalize their bodies. Children's bodies – and especially those of the unborn, infants and the very young – are regarded as particularly precious and vulnerable, requiring the intense surveillance of their caregivers as part of efforts to protect them from risk and ensure their optimum health and development (Lupton, 2013a, 2014). These efforts are now often rendered into digital forms with the use of an array of devices and software.

The sociomaterialist perspective has been taken up by several scholars writing about children's bodies, particularly within cultural geography, but also by some sociologists and anthropologists (Horton and Kraftl, 2006a, 2006b; Lee, 2008; Woodyer, 2008; Prout, 1996). Researchers using a sociomaterialist approach have conducted studies on, for example, children's use of asthma medication (Prout, 1996), the surveillant technologies that have developed around controlling children's body weight in schools (Rich et al., 2011), children's sleep and the objects with which they interact (Lee, 2008), the interrelationship of objects with pedagogy and classroom management of students' bodies (Mulcahy, 2012) and sociomaterial practices in classrooms that lead to the inclusion or exclusion of children with disabilities (Söderström, 2014). Outside sociomaterialist studies, young children's interactions with digital technologies have attracted extensive attention from social researchers, particularly in relation to topics such as the potential for cyber-bullying, online paedophilia and for children to become unfit and overweight due to spending too much time in front of screens (Holloway et al., 2013). However, few researchers thus far have directed their attention to the types of digital technologies that visually represent children's bodies or render their body functions, activities and behaviours into digital data; or, in other words, how children's bodies become digital data assemblages.

From the embryonic stage of development onwards, children's bodies are now routinely monitored and portrayed using digital technologies. A plethora of websites provide images of every stage of embryonic and foetal development, from fertilization to birth, using a combination of digital images taken from embryo and foetus specimens and digital imaging software (Lupton, 2013b). 3/4D ultrasounds have become commodified, used for 'social' or 'bonding' purposes instead of the traditional medical diagnostic and screening scan. Many companies offering 3/D ultrasounds now come to people's homes, allowing expectant parents to invite family and friends and turn a viewing of the foetus into a party event. This sometimes involves a 'gender reveal' moment, in which the sonographer demonstrates to all participants, including the parents, the sex of the foetus. Some companies offer the service of using 3D ultrasound scan files to create life-sized printed foetus replica models for parents.

The posting to social media sites such as Facebook, Twitter, Instagram and YouTube of the foetus ultrasound image has become a rite of passage for many new parents and often a way of announcing the pregnancy. Using widgets such as 'Baby Gaga', expectant parents can upload regular status updates to their social media feeds automatically that provide news on the foetus's development. While a woman is pregnant, she can use a range of digital devices to monitor her foetus. Hundreds of pregnancy apps are currently on the market, including not only those that provide information but those that invite users to upload personal information about their bodies and the development of their foetus (Tripp et al., 2014). Some apps offer a personalized foetal development overview or provide the opportunity for the woman to record the size of her pregnant abdomen week by week, eventually creating a time-lapse video. Other apps involve women tracking foetal movements or heartbeat. Bella Beat is a smartphone attachment and app that allows the pregnant women to hear and record the foetal heartbeat whenever she likes and to upload the audio file to her social media accounts.

YouTube has become a predominant medium for the representation of the unborn entity in the form of ultrasound images and of the moment of birth. Almost 100,000 videos showing live childbirth, including both vaginal and Caesarean births, are available for viewing on that site, allowing the entry into the world of these infants to be viewed by thousands and, in the case of some popular videos, even millions of viewers. Some women even choose to live-stream the birth so that audiences can watch the delivery in real time. Following the birth, there are similar opportunities for proud parents to share images of their infant online on social media platforms. In addition to these are the growing number of devices on the market for parents to monitor the health, development and wellbeing of their infants and young children. Apps are available to monitor such aspects as infants' feeding and sleeping patterns, their weight and height and their development and achievements towards milestones. Sensor-embedded baby clothing, wrist or ankle bands and toys can be purchased that monitor infants' heart rate, body temperature and breathing, producing data that are transmitted to the parents' devices. Smartphones can be turned into baby monitors with the use of apps that record the sound levels of the infant.

As children grow, their geolocation, educational progress and physical fitness can be tracked by their parents using apps, other software and wearable devices. As children themselves begin to use digital technologies for their purposes, they start to configure their own digital assemblages that represent and track their bodies. With the advent of touchscreen mobile devices such as smartphones and tablet computers, even very young children are now able to use social media sites and the thousands of apps that have been designed especially for their use (Holloway et al., 2013). Some such technologies encourage young children to learn about the anatomy of human bodies or about nutrition, exercise and physical fitness, calculate their body mass index, collect information about their bodies or represent their bodies in certain ways (such as manipulating photographic images of themselves). These technologies typically employ gamification strategies to provide interest and motivation for use. Some involve combining competition or games with self-tracking using wearable devices. One example is the Leapfrog Leapband, a digital wristband

Digital bodies

connected to an app that encourages children to be physically active in return for providing them with the opportunity to care for virtual pets. Another is the Sqord interactive online platform with associated digital wristband and app. Children who sign up can make an avatar of themselves and use the wristband to track their physical activity. Users compete with other users by gaining points for moving their bodies as often and as fast as possible.

In the formal educational system, there are still more opportunities for children's bodies to be monitored, measured and evaluated, and rendered into digitized assemblages. Programmable 'smart schools' are becoming viewed as part of the 'smart city', an urban environment in which sensors that can watch and collect digital data on citizens are ubiquitous (Williamson, 2014). The monitoring of children's educational progress and outcomes using software is now routinely undertaken in many schools, as are their movements around the school. In countries such as the USA and the UK, the majority of schools have CCTV cameras that track students. Many use biometric tracking technologies such as RFID chips in badges or school uniforms and fingerprints to identify children and monitor their movements and their purchases at school canteens (Taylor, 2013; Selwyn, 2015). A growing number of schools are beginning to use wearable devices, apps and other software for health and physical education lessons, such as coaching apps that record children's sporting performances and digital heart rate monitors that track their physical exertions (Lupton, 2015a).

We can see in the use of digital technologies to monitor and represent the bodies of children a range of forms of embodiment. Digitized data assemblages of children's bodies are generated from before birth via a combination of devices that seek to achieve medical- or health-related or social and affective objectives. These assemblages may move between different domains: when, for example, a digitized ultrasound image that was generated for medical purposes becomes repurposed by expectant parents as a social media artefact, a way of announcing the pregnancy, establishing their foetus as new person and establishing its social relationships. Parents' digital devices, and later those of educational institutions and those of children themselves when they begin to use digital devices, potentially become personalized repositories for a vast amount of unique digital assemblages on the individual child: from images of them to descriptions of their growth, development, mental and physical health and wellbeing, movements in space, achievements and learning outcomes. These data assemblages, containing as they do granular details about children, offer unprecedented potential to configure knowledges about individual children and also large groups of children (as represented in aggregated big data sets).

Conclusion

As I have shown in this chapter, new forms of bodies are being configured via contemporary digital technologies. Devices that can monitor, portray, measure and compare bodies generate unceasing flows of data about individuals that then move into the digital data economy and are repurposed by a range of actors and agencies. I have employed the example of young children's bodies to demonstrate the manifold ways in which such digitized bodily assemblages are created and the uses to which they are put. Digital data are forms of 'lively capital' in four major ways. First they are generated from life itself, in terms of documenting humans' bodies and selves. Second, as digital data they are labile and fluid as they are generated and circulate in the digital data economy. Third, because with the advent of interconnected smart objects, aggregated data sets and predictive analytics, personal digital data have potential effects on the conduct of life and life opportunities. And finally, as valuable commercial and research entities, they contribute to people's livelihoods (Lupton, 2016).

In this age of unceasing collection of often very intimate and personal information about people via digital technologies, questions of data security and data privacy have become paramount. Once personal digital data enter the computing cloud, people lose control over how they are protected and controlled. Recent scandals and controversies, have revealed the precariousness of personal data security and privacy. These include such events as the former CIA and the US National Security Agency contractor Edward Snowden's release of documents that demonstrate how national security agencies in Western countries are conducting surveillance on citizens' online interactions and various events of hacking into personal data databases.

Thus far we know very little about how people are engaging with the digital data assemblages that are generated on them, how they contribute to, manage, manipulate and make sense of these assemblages and what impacts they have on people's sense of selfhood and embodiment. This is a particularly pressing issue for individuals such as the current generation of children whose lives and bodies have been so thoroughly digitally documented. As humans are entering into technological entanglements that can document their lives from pre-birth to death in ever-finer detail, many issues and implications remain to be explored. These include who has the right to collect data on people, who controls and has access to the repositories of personal data that are now configured on individuals, how these data are used by those who do have access and what happens to people's data assemblages after death.

Digital data assemblages are always mutable, dynamic and responsive to new inputs. A recursive feedback loop is established in which information is generated from digital technologies that then are used by the individual to assess her or his activities and behaviour, and modify them accordingly, which then configure a renewed data assemblage – and on the cycle goes. Indeed, one major novel aspect of people's encounters with digital technologies is the ways in which these technologies are now often designed to 'nudge' users into taking up certain practices. Instead of merely providing information, as in older forms of internet engagement, software is coded to algorithmically manipulate users' personal data and send them 'push' notifications to encourage them to purchase more goods and services or change their behaviour to optimize their health, wellbeing or productivity.

More and more, our digital machines are taking on the role of managers, task-masters or disciplinarians of our bodies. Commentators are now beginning to envisage a world in which interconnected smart devices, as part of the Internet of Things, interact with the personalized data that each generates to provide advice to users. Thus, for example, the wearable body tracker can interact with smart objects in the user's home (such as the smart fridge, smart thermostat, smart television and smart bed) to determine what kind of food users should consume, what types of television programmes they should watch, what temperature level their home should be set at and for how long and what time they should go to sleep and wake up, based on such features as their mood, body weight, calories burnt and physical activity data.

Such entanglements of human bodies with technological devices potentially represent further major changes to concepts and practices of embodiment. For the field of physical cultural studies, they constitute a new and important element of understanding how knowledges, practices, objects, emotion, discourse, data and humans intertwine.

References

Beck, U. 1992. *Risk Society: Towards a New Modernity*. London: Sage.
Beck, U. and Beck-Gernsheim, E. 1995. *The Normal Chaos of Love*. Cambridge: Polity.
Buse, C. E. 2010. E-scaping the ageing body? Computer technologies and embodiment in later life. *Ageing and Society*, 30(6), 987–1009.

Cheney-Lippold, J. 2011. A new algorithmic identity: soft biopolitics and the modulation of control. *Theory, Culture and Society*, 28(6), 164–181.

Crawford, K. and Schultz, J. 2014. Big data and due process: toward a framework to redress predictive privacy harms. *Boston College Law Review*, 55(1), 93–128.

Elwell, J. S. 2014. The transmediated self: life between the digital and the analog. *Convergence*, 20(2), 233–249.

Fenwick, T. and Landri, P. 2012. Materialities, textures and pedagogies: socio-material assemblages in education. *Pedagogy, Culture and Society*, 20(1), 1–7.

Foucault, M. 1986. *The History of Sexuality, Volume 3: The Care of the Self*. New York: Pantheon.

Foucault, M. 1988. Technologies of the self. In L. Martin, H. Gutman and P. Hutton (eds), *Technologies of the Self: A Seminar with Michel Foucault*. London: Tavistock, 16–49.

Francombe, J. 2010. 'I cheer, you cheer, we cheer': physical technologies and the normalized body. *Television and New Media*, 11(5), 350–366.

Franklin, S. 2006. The cyborg embryo. *Theory, Culture and Society*, 23(7–8), 167.

Haraway, D. 1991. *Simians, Cyborgs and Women: the Reinvention of Nature*. London: Free Association.

Haraway, D. 1997. *Modest_Witness@Second_Millennium: FemaleMan©Meets_OncoMouse™: Feminism and Technoscience*. New York: Routledge.

Hayles, N. K. 2012. *How We Think: Digital Media and Contemporary Technogenesis*. Chicago, IL: University of Chicago Press.

Holloway, D., Green, L. and Livingstone, S. 2013. *Zero to Eight: Young Children and Their Internet Use*. London: LSE London, EU Kids Online.

Horton, J. and Kraftl, P. 2006a. Not just growing up, but going on: materials, spacings, bodies, situations. *Children's Geographies*, 4(3), 259–276.

Horton, J. and Kraftl, P. 2006b. What else? Some more ways of thinking and doing 'Children's Geographies'. *Children's Geographies*, 4(1), 69–95.

Jenks, C. 2005. *Childhood: Critical Concepts in Sociology*. New York: Routledge.

Kitchin, R. 2014. *The Data Revolution: Big Data, Open Data, Data Infrastructures and Their Consequences*. London: Sage.

Kitchin, R. and Dodge, M. 2011. *Code/Space: Software and Everyday Life*. Cambridge, MA: MIT Press.

Labanyi, J. 2010. Doing things: emotion, affect, and materiality. *Journal of Spanish Cultural Studies*, 11(3–4), 223–233.

Latour, B. 2005. *Reassembling the Social: An Introduction to Actor-Network-Theory*. Oxford: Clarendon.

Law, J. 2008. On sociology and STS. *The Sociological Review*, 56(4), 623–649.

Lee, N. 2008. Awake, asleep, adult, child: an a-humanist account of persons. *Body and Society*, 14(4), 57–74.

Leng, K. W. 1996. On menopause and cyborgs: or, towards a feminist cyborg politics of menopause. *Body and Society*, 2(3), 33–52.

Lupton, D. 1995. The embodied computer/user. *Body and Society*, 1(3–4), 97–112.

Lupton, D. 2013a. Infant embodiment and interembodiment: a review of sociocultural perspectives. *Childhood*, 20(1), 37–50.

Lupton, D. 2013b. *The Social Worlds of the Unborn*. Basingstoke: Palgrave Macmillan.

Lupton, D. 2014. Precious, pure, uncivilised, vulnerable: infant embodiment in Australian popular media. *Children and Society*, 28(5), 341–351.

Lupton, D. 2015a. Data assemblages, sentient schools and digitised health and physical education (response to Gard). *Sport, Education and Society*, 20(1), 122–132.

Lupton, D. 2015b. *Digital Sociology*. London: Routledge.

Lupton, D. 2015c. Donna Haraway: the digital cyborg assemblage and the new digital health technologies. In F. Collyer (ed.), *The Palgrave Handbook of Social Theory in Health, Illness and Medicine*. Basingstoke: Palgrave Macmillan, 567–581.

Lupton, D. 2016. *The Quantified Self: A Sociology of Self-Tracking*. Cambridge: Polity Press.

Lyon, D. and Bauman, Z. 2013. *Liquid Surveillance: A Conversation*. Oxford: Wiley.

Merleau-Ponty, M. 1968. *The Visible and the Invisible*. Evanston, IL: Northwestern University Press.

Millington, B. 2014a. Amusing ourselves to life: fitness consumerism and the birth of bio-games. *Journal of Sport and Social Issues*, 38(6), 491–508.

Millington, B. 2014b. Smartphone apps and the mobile privatization of health and fitness. *Critical Studies in Media Communication*, 31(5), 479–493.

Mulcahy, D. 2012. Affective assemblages: body matters in the pedagogic practices of contemporary school classrooms. *Pedagogy, Culture and Society*, 20(1), 9–27.

Newman, J. I. and Giardina, M. D. 2014. Moving biopolitics. *Cultural Studies ↔ Critical Methodologies*, 14(5), 419–424.

Nippert-Eng, C. 1996. *Home and Work: Negotiating Boundaries through Everyday Life*. Chicago: University of Chicago Press.

Prout, A. 1996. Actor-network theory, technology and medical sociology: an illustrative analysis of the metered dose inhaler. *Sociology of Health and Illness*, 18(2), 198–219.

Rayvon, F. 2012. Aren't athletes cyborgs? Technology, bodies, and sporting competitions. *Women's Studies Quarterly*, 40(1), 281–293.

Rich, E., Evans, J. and De Pian, L. 2011. Children's bodies, surveillance and the obesity crisis. In E. Rich, L. F. Monaghan and L. Aphramor (eds), *Debating Obesity: Critical Perspectives*. Basingstoke: Palgrave Macmillan, 139–163.

Selwyn, N. 2015. Data entry: towards the critical study of digital data and education. *Learning, Media and Technology*, 40(1), 64–82.

Söderström, S. 2014. Socio-material practices in classrooms that lead to the social participation or social isolation of disabled pupils. *Scandinavian Journal of Disability Research*, online first.

Taylor, E. 2013. *Surveillance Schools: Security, Discipline and Control in Contemporary Education*. Basingstoke: Palgrave Macmillan.

Tripp, N. et al. 2014. An emerging model of maternity care: smartphone, midwife, doctor? *Women and Birth: Journal of the Australian College of Midwives*, 27(1), 64.

Uprichard, E. 2008. Children as 'being and becomings': children, childhood and temporality. *Children and Society*, 22(4), 303–313.

Williamson, B. 2014. Smart schools in sentient cities. *dmlcentral*. Available from http://dmlcentral.net/blog/ben-williamson/smart-schools-sentient-cities (accessed 14 May 2015).

Woodyer, T. 2008. The body as research tool: embodied practice and children's geographies. *Children's Geographies*, 6(4), 349–362.

21
SPIRITUALIZED AND RELIGIOUS BODIES

Andrew Parker and Nick J. Watson

Introduction

Those who have written about the relationship between sport and religion are in general agreement that academics outside of the traditional social science sports studies disciplines (i.e. sociology, history, anthropology, philosophy and psychology), such as theologians and philosophers of religion, have been slow to recognize the cultural significance of modern-day sports (see Watson, 2011a). In this chapter,[1] we argue that this trend is slowly changing. In addition to the emergence of research centres, academic journals and sport–faith initiatives, contributors to recent monographs and anthologies that analyse the different facets of the sport–religion relationship have emanated from a plethora of disciplinary fields and subject areas.

It is widely accepted that links between the sacred and sport have been evident across a number of historical periods. These include primitive times when ritual-cultic ball games were played to appease the gods (for fertility), the athletic spectacles of ancient Greece and the Olympic games that were held in honour of mythological deities, the gladiatorial contests of Rome, the festivals and folk-games of the Middle Ages in Britain and Europe, Puritanical suspicion and prohibitions against sports, and, of course, Victorian muscular Christianity (*c.*1820–1910), a socio-theological movement that significantly shaped the character of modern sports (see Guttman, [1978] 2004; Mangan, 1981; Shilling and Mellor, 2014). Additionally, there is a small corpus of work that has explored how sport interacts with other monotheistic and eastern (pantheistic) world religions, such as Islam, Judaism, Buddhism and Shintoism (see Magdalinski and Chandler, 2002; Prebish, 1993). These accounts provide useful comparative insight for those examining the sport–Christianity relationship which is our primary focus in this chapter.

Given Christianity's Hebraic roots and its inseparable ties to Jewish history, faith and tradition, contemporary debates surrounding Judaism and sporting pursuit undoubtedly assist scholars when examining the sport–Christianity nexus, especially in relation to historical, theological and sociological research on embodiment and identity. In the following discussion our central aim is to review a selection of existing academic work on sport and spiritualized/religious bodies. We begin with a brief overview of the more general literature on sport and religion, focusing thereafter on a topic around which our own recent research has been located, that is, sport and the disabled body. To this end, the chapter is structured around four main themes: (i) sport, spirituality and religion, (ii) sport, religion and the body, (iii) sport, religion and the disabled body, and (iv) sport, religion and re-embodiment. We have chosen these themes to demonstrate the contribution which a physical cultural studies approach might bring to the academic interrogation of sport and spiritualized/religious bodies (Silk and Andrews, 2011). We take as our starting point the notion that such investigations seek to explore and locate physically active bodies within the social, political and economic contexts which they inhabit and how they are represented, organized and regulated by the power structures in and against which they sit (Andrews, 2008). Drawing ideas from a range of key disciplinary areas (i.e. theology, sociology and disability studies), we highlight the way in which the study of spiritualized/religious bodies might, at the same time, shape the contours of physical cultural studies itself. Needless to say, it is to an exploration of the first of our four themes that we initially turn.

Sport, spirituality and religion

Over the past 30–40 years there has been a steady growth in the academic literature surrounding sport and religion, (see Watson and Parker, 2013, 2014). Within this literature a key historical theme has been that of muscular Christianity – a narrative that locates the development of modern-day sport in mid-nineteenth-century Britain amidst the alleged transformation of unruly pastimes into a series of structured and codified games, primarily via the English public schools (Parker and Weir, 2012). A key player in this transformational process was Thomas Arnold, head teacher at Rugby School between 1828 and 1841, whose desire it was to mould his (male) students into 'good Christian gentlemen' by way of competitive games, an education in the classics, and generous helpings of discipline, respect and morality (Mangan, 1981). Most notable among documentary representations of Arnold's legacy is Thomas Hughes's fictional account *Tom Brown's Schooldays* (published in 1857), the story of a young boy (Tom Brown) whose character is shaped during his days at Rugby School around what came to be known as 'muscular Christianity'; a term encapsulating the development of Christian manliness in line with notions of spiritual, moral and physical purity (Simon and Bradley, 1975). Of course, in reality, muscular Christianity had its roots in a whole range of wider ethical and moral concerns which were prevalent in Britain during the 1800s; the protection of the weak, the plight of the poor, and the promotion of moral virtue. The incorporation of these (and other) issues into a framework of physical and spiritual 'wholesomeness' resulted in the establishment of a series of core values which, in time, came to characterize the relationship between sport and religion: fair play, respect, strength, perseverance, subordination, obedience, loyalty, co-operation, self-control, endurance. Especially significant here was a fervent Christian faith and stoic masculinity which collectively engendered the formation of personal character and a respect for the disciplined, physical body. Revered too were virtues such as courage, temperance and *esprit de corps* – the 'holy trinity' of moral stature – subsequently expressed by the sporting ventures of Baron Pierre de Coubertin, the founder of the International Olympic Committee (IOC) and the modern Olympic Games.

Of course, as modern sporting forms evolved and professionalization and commercialization ensued, muscular Christian values became less prevalent amidst a backdrop of moral and ethical decline (see Watson and Parker, 2013). In turn, considerations of the spiritual and religious aspects of sport became somewhat marginalized within the broader orbits of sports studies, an issue which Shilling and Mellor (2014: 351) have highlighted as 'potentially antagonistic' to broader attempts to establish the societal importance of sport especially given the cultural and political significance of religion (and religious practice) in modern-day life. That said, vestiges of the underpinning values of the muscular Christian era persist in commercialized sport where physical/bodily 'perfection' continues to be celebrated, glorified and revered. Advertising, the media and the contemporary marketing techniques of consumer culture have largely been responsible for the promotion and ubiquitous perpetuation of the 'perfect body' amidst a spontaneous life course outlook where impulsivity and mass consumption reign and where ideals of youth, fitness and beauty have come to represent a central focus of social existence (see Featherstone, 1991, 2010; Shilling, 2012). Such values sit in stark contrast to the realities of life for those whose experiences of embodiment are less straightforward, especially in relation to disability sport (Howe and Parker, 2012; Watson and Parker, 2012). Before exploring in more detail how embodiment is negotiated and reconciled within this specific context and to what extent notions of spirituality and religion might feature as a part of this overall picture, we first turn our attentions to a broader analysis of the connections between embodiment and religion.

Sport, religion and the body

In his brief history of the relationship between mind and body within the context of religion and sport, Hopsicker (2014) has outlined the extent to which dualistic thinking dominated early religious conceptions of the human body with Ancient Greek philosophy (and in particular the work of Plato and Aristotle) positing intellectual thought as superior to physical activity. Platonism advocates that there are two distinct realms: the visible material world and the invisible spiritual world, which results in the material (including the body) being viewed as inferior. Reinforced by Gnostic and Manichean philosophies, such inferences were perhaps most (in)famously played out during the Enlightenment period by the Roman Catholic philosopher René Descartes whose work frequently featured the promotion of cerebral over corporeal pursuit (Cartesian mind–body dualism). Not surprisingly, these ideas influenced many within the Christian church where theological discussions concerning the body historically carried negative connotations concerning the potential evils of its undisciplined form (Scarpa and Carraro, 2011). In turn, physical and intellectual ventures were often framed as polar opposites in theological circles with the former being portrayed as spiritually unworthy.

As we have seen, in Britain at least, the nineteenth century brought with it a change of heart on the part of the church with regards to the value of the body and the role that physical activity might play in holistic wellbeing (see Collins, 2014). Such changes aligned with widespread social upheaval surrounding processes of industrialization and secularization. Denominational debates persisted about the irrelevance and distractive potential of sport to spiritual and moral development. Yet, church leaders addressed these tensions in various ways and over time there emerged a general acquaintance between the church and sport and a growing acknowledgement in religious circles of the value of physical activity and of the physical body.

Despite the fact that the church–sport relationship is now firmly established and that more recent theological analyses have identified sports participation as both embodied and corporeal (see Ellis, 2014; Harvey, 2014), dualistic tensions remain especially in some evangelical (Christian) quarters where a propensity to perpetuate the mind/body dichotomy continues. There are, of course, complex historical and cultural reasons for this, not least the church's general drift away from its Hebraic roots and *holistic* understandings of human beings and the sacredness of the body. As Wilson (1989) notes, for the Hebrews, there is no separation of the secular and the sacred. To them, life is a unified, theological whole:

> In Hebrew thought, a person is a soul-body ... viewed as a single entity, an indivisible whole ... 'soul' or 'spirit' refers to the whole person or individual as a living being ... One's body (i.e., entire being) is to be offered daily in joyful obedience as a 'living sacrifice' (Rom. 12: 1). On the one hand, pleasure and satisfaction are not ends to be pursued in themselves; on the other, enjoyment of the material and physical aspects of this life is far more than mere preparation for higher things. To enjoy is an opportunity to bring blessing to one's Creator, 'So whether you eat drink or whatever you do, do it all for the glory of God' (1 Cor. 10:31).[2]

As Watson (2011b) goes on to point out, these understandings are predicated on the biblical position that *all* humans are made in the image of God – *imago Dei* (Gen. 1:27) and comprise soul, body and spirit (1 Thessalonians 5:23). The Platonic–Cartesian dualism deeply entrenched in Western thought is further combatted in such traditions by referring to the soul, body and spirit holistically as the *heart*, a Hebrew and Pauline perspective. This view maintains that though comprising different elements, human beings are thoroughly integrated entities. Against this historical backdrop, it is clear that mind and body are integral to the sport–religion interface. So how then might we frame these historical debates when developing a theology of disability sport?

Sport, religion and the disabled body

Following the publication of Eiesland's seminal work, *The Disabled God* (1994), which focuses solely on physical disability, a growing literature has emerged on the theology of both physical and intellectual disability (see Brock and Swinton, 2012; Yong, 2007). Predating Eiesland's work, scholarship has specifically examined intellectual disability through a Christian lens (see for example Hauerwas, 1986). This body of empirical research has evolved across all of the major Christian denominations and within a number of related disciplines, (i.e. religious studies, sociology, ethics, education and psychology) (Swinton, 2011). Prior to the mid-1990s there was some theological reflection on disability – albeit more common within the orbits of the Catholic church – which was born out of the disability rights and other civil rights movements of the 1970s but one might argue that this was, and still is, viewed as an area of 'specialist interest'. Hauerwas and Vanier (2009), however, suggest that the biblical themes of weakness, vulnerability, mutuality, hospitality, humility and love are at the heart of the Christian faith and thus integral to sound theological debate.

The reasons for the relative lack of theological reflection on disability are many but as Reynolds (2008: 68) states, a major determinant in this respect is that theology has been 'taken captive by the cult of normalcy', that is, it has often adopted a starting point rooted in Enlightenment philosophies and ideas, especially utilitarianism, rationalism, free-market capitalism, ableism and intellectualism. In thinking about and interacting with those people in society who have disabilities, it may well be that we are also confronted with our own fragilities and weaknesses (physical and intellectual) and therefore, disability can 'disturb us' (Yong, 2007). As we have seen, the pervasive influence of Platonic–Cartesian dualism in theology (Wilson, 1989) and sport (Twietmeyer, 2008) has also been a factor in de-emphasizing and devaluing the role of the body, and able-bodied and disabled sport as a whole, in Western culture. Theological reflection on the 'full diversity of experiences of human embodiment' has, in turn, been lacking in theology (Creamer, 2009: 117), until that is, the emergence of the more recent 'body craze' in the discipline, as is the case in the field of sports studies since the 1990s. This focus on the body in academic studies of sport is, of course, embedded in the central importance of the 'perfect body' in both sporting and wider social contexts.

To varying degrees publications on the theology of disability critique the socio-cultural structures and institutions that marginalize, alienate, oppress and devalue the disabled. Disability sport scholars following the foundational work of the Marxist sociologist Michael Oliver (1990), mainly advocating the social constructionist model of disability, have analysed how access, provision of facilities in schools and communities, funding, media and cinematic representations, and the overall status and perceived importance of disability sports, is significantly different to able-bodied sport, for example, the Olympic Games (Thomas and Smith, 2009; Howe, 2008). A particularly thorough and nuanced analysis of negative socio-cultural structures is presented by Reynolds, who discusses the 'economies of exchange' that fuel the 'cult of normalcy' and ultimately configure the lens through which modern society views the disabled:

> Consciousness of worth is something that transpires according to what I call an *'economy of exchange'*, a system of reciprocity that regulates interactions in a community ... The attribution of worth never occurs in isolated form as an individual's thought process, but rather within a complex set of social arrangements and reciprocal relationships that distribute, and appraise values ... Economics of exchange, therefore, revolve around identification markers that display what I call *body capital* ... All kinds of cultural productions are involved, such as beauty, athleticism and intelligence ... The body is an icon representing the effects of power ... cast in the form of the dominant culture's sense of the good.
>
> *(Reynolds, 2008: 56–70)*

The dominant culture of our age born from the Enlightenment modernist principles of individuality, self-sufficiency, materialism, rationalism, free-market capitalism and power, encourage a 'cult of normalcy' that, Reynolds (ibid.: 62) goes on, 'tells people with disabilities who they are, forcing them by various societal rituals to bear a name that is 'depersonalizing', and this leads to 'alienation', both socially and personally'. This 'tyranny of normality', as Hauerwas (2004) has called it, so grips our culture that we are often in denial as to its existence, preferring to suppress our own fears and insecurities and thus maintain the status quo. Such practices of unconscious denial comprise what Kierkegaard ([1849] 1989: 74) labels a 'spiritless sense of security', a 'fictitious health' that underpins many of the institutions of our society (Brueggemann, 2010), including sport (Watson, 2014; Stringfellow, [1973] 2004). This empirical reality has been evidenced in a burgeoning sports ethics, and fast-developing theology of sport literature, an example of which we now consider.

Sport, religion and re-embodiment

In their qualitative study of the interconnections between historical conceptions of sport and contemporary arguments surrounding re-embodiment, Howe and Parker (2014) highlight the importance of religious engagement for a group of high performance (elite, Paralympic) athletes dealing with issues of impairment and how the act of re-embodiment (being metaphorically 're-born') in line with Christian beliefs and understandings was something to which they turned in order to make sense of their place in the world. The specific focus of the authors is the extent to which the life stories of the athletes concerned were layered with religious symbolism and inference, and how the spiritual 'journeys' or 'pilgrimages' that these individuals embarked upon gave new meaning to their lives.

In their analysis of the personal accounts provided by their respondents, Howe and Parker (2014) illustrate how the transition from life as an able-bodied individual to one with impairment was seen by a number of athletes as a pilgrimage through which they found spiritual significance in relation to the changes that had occurred to their bodies and to their lives more generally. Coming to terms with disability (and an accompanying sense of 'reduced' social status) was a key turning point for many and alongside this came a process of self-reflection which engendered a consideration of 'greater purpose' and 'religious calling' around advocacy and support for others with disability. Given that such support processes were located – for this particular group at least – within the context of elite sport, crucial to this calling was a sense of re-embodiment. Because of the relationship between the origins of modern-day sport and Christianity (i.e. the benefits of a healthy body and healthy mind), and of the moral and ethical connections between physical activity, embodiment and the Christian faith, there is a sense in which one might argue that the spiritual journey evident within these re-embodiment narratives is somewhat unsurprising. That said, and as Howe and Parker (2014) are quick to point out, not all high performance athletes who experience a sense of post-accident vulnerability seek to make sense of their 'new world' in this way. On the contrary, for some the journey to re-embodiment takes place on an entirely secular basis while others find solace via alternative belief systems. Nevertheless, for a number of the athletes concerned, a holistic 'healthy body, healthy mind' ethos was integral to their sense of purpose and calling and, perhaps more importantly, their understandings of their bodies post-impairment, this in line with the sporting activity which they sought to undertake. In this way, spiritual and religious reflection allowed these athletes to positively re-imagine their 'physical selves' which, in turn, facilitated a renewed sense of hope in relation to their futures and their potential contribution to individuals in similar circumstances and to wider society. Indeed, so powerful was this re-imagining process and the spiritual journeys and pilgrimages that these athletes experienced, that some came to reflect upon their re-embodiment as a process of 'transformation' and (metaphorical) 'resurrection'.

As Howe and Parker (2014) note, such acts of re-embodiment inevitably demand new understandings of personhood around a re-conceptualized integration of mind and body (Csordas, 1994; Seymour, 1998). In turn, one of the ways they suggest we might make sense of these spiritual journeys is to think of religion as a mechanism for facilitating a re-configuration of 'wholeness' in line with Csordas's (2002) three stages of ritual healing: (i) predisposition, (ii) empowerment and (iii) transformation. Utilizing this framework, Howe and Parker (2014) argue that it may well be that high performance athletes who have experienced impairment by way of traumatic accident journey through these stages as part of a rite of passage to re-embodiment. The first stage (predisposition) requires that the individual believes that a level of rehabilitation is possible – a belief that is devoid of any false sense of hope that they will somehow overcome their impairment and which follows instead an acceptance of and adjustment to their new social reality. The second stage (empowerment) is where the individual realizes that the healing of the body and the mind are linked by some form of spiritual power, where they begin to articulate a faith that is beyond the realities of the social world in which they live, and where a close allegiance to religious doctrine and spiritual experience form. The final stage, comprising the transformation from 'able-bodied non-believer' to 'impaired believer' follows, it seems, a process of resurrection. This necessarily requires a wholesale acceptance by the individual of their re-configured life and the expectations and behaviours which go with it, yet at the same time this acceptance is grounded in a sense of renewed purpose and calling around physical re-embodiment, spiritual positivity and social contribution.

On the basis of the empirical evidence which Howe and Parker (2014) present, it appears that spiritual and religious belief may provide disabled athletes with new understandings of embodiment and of their position in the social world. As a consequence, rather than allowing their lives to be hindered by impairment, such individuals 'take the symbolism associated with Christ's broken (and subsequently resurrected) body as a powerful and transformative means by which they … can come to view their journey to re-embodiment afresh: as one of fate and destiny; as a road to emancipation; as a blessing in disguise' (ibid.: 21). In this sense, these athletes not only determine to accept and adjust to their impaired bodies, but can be seen as being metaphorically 'born again' into a whole new social existence in and through which they use their new-found religious/spiritual experiences to positively impact their own lives and those of others.

Conclusions

It has been our intention throughout this chapter to consider the relationship between spirituality, religion and embodiment within the context of sporting participation and, in particular, we have explored disability sport as a site where this relationship might manifest itself most clearly. In so doing, we have examined the interconnections between historical conceptions of religion and embodiment, and how spiritual and religious attachments might shape everyday sporting realities. In turn, and by way of an interdisciplinary perspective, we have attempted to explore some of the social, political and theological complexities that impact spiritualized/religious bodies and how they might be represented, organized, regulated and ultimately emancipated. To this end, we have attempted to demonstrate the contribution which a physical cultural studies approach might bring to the academic interrogation of the sport–religion relationship.

Of course, we recognize that there are many additional ways in which such interconnections and attachments might be explored. For example, scholars and empirical researchers may wish to examine notions of embodiment in sporting locales from different faith perspectives (i.e. Judaic and Islamic). These kinds of investigations may necessarily stimulate discussion around the nuances of denominational affiliation, geographical circumstance, and political affiliation. Additionally, theological research on the disabled body (Watson and Parker, 2015) and the genetically modified body (Trothen, 2011, 2013) is at an embryonic stage and requires further theoretical and empirical development. Research from a religious perspective on the gendered sporting body is, to date, relatively sparse but this has been identified as a key area for future research (see Watson and Parker, 2014). Investigations into varying modes of religious and spiritual embodiment will inevitably help scholars to think more critically about the potential relationship between sporting participation and theological anthropology. In turn, such work has the potential to (re)locate spirituality and religion more firmly as topics of discussion within sport studies as a whole.

Notes

1   This chapter includes extracts and ideas from previously published work (see Howe and Parker, 2014; Watson, 2007, 2011a, 2011b; Watson and Parker 2013, 2014, 2015).
2   This quotation comprises extracts from the following sections of Wilson's (1989) text: 'Foundational not Optional' (ibid.: 131–132); 'Everything is Theological' (ibid.: 156–159); 'Dynamic Unity versus Dualism' (ibid.: 167–171); and 'Spirituality: Heavenly or Earthly' (ibid.: 174–178).

References

Andrews, D. L. 2008. Kinesiology's Inconvenient Truth: The Physical Cultural Studies Imperative. *Quest*, 60 (1), 46–63.
Brock, B. and Swinton, J. 2012. *Disability in the Christian Tradition: A Reader*. Grand Rapids, MI: Wm. B. Eerdmans Publishing.
Brueggemann, W. 2010. *Out of Babylon*. Nashville, TN: Abingdon Press.
Collins, M. 2014. Sport, Religion and Wellbeing, and Cameron's Big Society. *Implicit Religion*, 17 (2), 139–165.
Creamer, D. B. 2009. *Disability and Christian Theology: Embodied Limits and Constructive Possibilities*. Oxford: Oxford University Press.
Csordas, T. J. (ed.). 1994. *Embodiment and Experience: The Existential Ground of Culture and Self*. Cambridge: Cambridge University Press.
Csordas, T. J. 2002. *Body/Meaning/Healing*. New York: Palgrave Macmillan.
Eiesland, N. L. 1994. *The Disabled God: Towards a Liberation Theology of Disability*. Nashville, TN, USA: Abingdon Press.
Ellis, R. 2014. *The Games People Play: Theology, Religion and Sport*. London: Wipf & Stock.
Featherstone, M. 1991. *Consumer Culture and Postmodernism*. London: Sage.
Featherstone, M. 2010. Body Image and Affect in Consumer Culture. *Body and Society*, 16 (1), 193–221.
Guttman, A. [1978] 2004. *From Ritual to Record: The Nature of Modern Sports*. New York: Columbia University Press.
Harvey, L. 2014. *A Brief Theology of Sport*. London: SCM Press.
Hauerwas, S. 1986. *Suffering Presence*. Notre Dame, IN: University of Notre Dame Press.
Hauerwas, S. 2004. Community and Diversity: The Tyranny of Normality. In J. Swinton (ed.), *Critical Reflections on Stanley Hauerwas' Theology of Disability: Disabling Society, Enabling Theology*. New York: Haworth Press, 37–43.
Hauerwas, S. and Vanier, J. 2009. *Living Gently in a Violent World: The Prophetic Witness of Weakness*. Downers Grove, IL: Intervarsity Press.
Hopsicker, P. M. 2014. A Modern Conception of Flesh: Towards a Theology of Disability Sport. *Journal of Religion, Disability and Health*, 18 (1), 82–96.
Howe, P. D. 2008. *The Cultural Politics of the Paralympic Movement: Through an Anthropological Lens*. London: Routledge.
Howe, P. D. and Parker, A. 2012. Celebrating Imperfection: Sport, Disability and Celebrity Culture. *Celebrity Studies*, 3 (3), 270–282.
Howe, P. D. and Parker, A. 2014. Disability as a Path to Spiritual Enlightenment: An Ethnographic Account of the Significance of Religion in Paralympic Sport. *Journal of Disability and Religion*, 18 (1), 8–23.
Kierkegaard, S. [1849] 1989. *The Sickness Unto Death: A Christian Exposition of Edification and Awakening*. London: Penguin Books.
Magdalinski, T. and Chandler, T. J. L. (eds). 2002. *With God on Their Side: Sport in the Service of Religion*. London: Routledge.
Mangan, J. A. 1981. *Athleticism in the Victorian and Edwardian Public School: The Emergence and Consolidation of an Educational Ideology*. Cambridge: Cambridge University Press.
Oliver, M. 1990. *The Politics of Disablement*. Basingstoke: Macmillan/St Martin's Press.
Parker, A. and Weir, J. S. 2012. Sport, Spirituality and Protestantism: A Historical Overview. *Theology*, 114 (4), 253–265.
Prebish, C. S. 1993. *Religion and Sport: The Meeting of Sacred and Profane*. London: Greenwood Press.
Reynolds, T. E. 2008. *Vulnerable Communion: A Theology of Disability and Hospitality*. Grand Rapids, MI: Brazos Press.
Scarpa, S. and Carraro, A. N. 2011. Does Christianity Demean the Body and Deny the Value of Sport: A Provocative Thesis. *Sport, Ethics and Philosophy*, 5 (2), 110–123.
Seymour, W. 1998. *Remaking the Body: Rehabilitation and Change*. London: Routledge.
Shilling, C., 2012. *The Body and Social Theory*, 3rd edn. London: Sage.
Shilling, C. and Mellor, P. A. 2014. Re-conceptualizing Sport as a Sacred Phenomenon. *Sociology of Sport Journal*, 31, 349–376.
Silk, M. L. and Andrews, D. L. 2011. Toward a Physical Cultural Studies. *Sociology of Sport Journal*, 28, 4–35.
Simon, B. and Bradley, I. (eds). 1975. *The Victorian Public School: Studies in the Development of an Educational Institution*. Dublin: Gill & Macmillan.

Stringfellow, W. [1973] 2004. *An Ethic for Christians and Other Aliens in a Strange Land*. Eugene, OR: Wipf & Stock.

Swinton, J. 2011. Who is the God We Worship? Theologies of Disability: Challenges and New Possibilities. *International Journal of Practical Theology*, 14 (2), 273–307.

Thomas, N. and Smith, A. 2009. *Disability Sport and Society: An Introduction*. London: Routledge.

Trothen, T. J. 2011. Better than Normal? Constructing Modified Athletes and a Relational Theological Ethic. In J. Parry, M. S. Nesti and N. J. Watson (eds), *Theology, Ethics and Transcendence in Sports*. London: Routledge, 64–81.

Trothen, T. J. 2013. The Technoscience Enhancement Debate in Sports: What's Religion Got To Do with It? In N. J. Watson and A. Parker (eds), *Sports and Christianity: Historical and Contemporary Perspectives*. London: Routledge, 207–224.

Twietmeyer, G. 2008. A Theology of Inferiority: Is Christianity the Source of Kinesiology's Second-class Status in the Academy. *Quest*, 60, 452–466.

Watson, N. J. 2007. Muscular Christianity in the Modern Age: Winning for Christ or Playing for Glory? In J. Parry, S. Robinson, N. J. Watson and M. Nesti (eds), *Sport and Spirituality: An Introduction*. London: Routledge, 80–94.

Watson, N. J. 2011a. Introduction. In J. Parry, M. Nesti, and N. J. Watson (eds), *Theology, Ethics and Transcendence in Sports*. London: Routledge, 1–11.

Watson, N. J. 2011b. Identity in Sport. A Psychological and Theological Analysis. In J. Parry, M. Nesti and N. J. Watson (eds), *Theology, Ethics and Transcendence in Sport*. London: Routledge, 104–147.

Watson, N. J. 2014. Special Olympians as a 'Prophetic Sign' to the Modern Sporting Babel. *Journal of Religion, Disability and Health*, 18 (1), 24–48.

Watson, N. J. and Parker, A. 2012. Christianity, Sport and Disability: A Case Study of the Role of Long-Distance Running in the Life of a Father and his Son who is Congenitally Blind and has Profound Intellectual Disabilities. *Practical Theology*, 5(2), 189–207.

Watson, N. J. and Parker, A. (eds). 2013. *Sports and Christianity: Historical and Contemporary Perspectives*. London: Routledge.

Watson, N. J. and Parker, A. 2014. *Sport and the Christian Religion: A Systematic Review of Literature*. Newcastle upon Tyne: Cambridge Scholars Press.

Watson, N. J. and Parker, A. (eds). 2015. *Sports, Religion and Disability*. New York: Routledge.

Wilson, M. V. 1989. *Our Father Abraham: Jewish Roots of the Christian Faith*. Grand Rapids, MI: Wm. B. Eerdmans Publishing.

Yong, A. 2007. *Theology and Down Syndrome: Reimaging Disability in Late Modernity*. Waco, TX: Baylor University Press.

22
AESTHETICIZED BODIES

Julia Coffey

This chapter explores the gendered dimensions of aesthetic body work practices. Currently, the aesthetic body is a site of intense focus and concern. The aesthetic body is both the target of a range of growing commercial industries, as well as a key focus of academic and theoretical study. Drawing on data from a qualitative study of young people's body work practices, this chapter explores the aesthetic body work practices of muscle-building and cosmetic surgery. The chapter mobilizes concepts of affect, assemblage and becoming to understand the aesthetically motivated practices of muscle-building and cosmetic surgery. This approach contributes to developing the use of post-human concepts in empirical research. The chapter concludes with a discussion of possible implications for the use of such concepts for physical cultural studies.

Current context of the aesthetic body: health and gender

The current emphasis on the body's appearance, or the aesthetic body, can be linked to a range of social, cultural and economic factors including the expansion of health, leisure, cosmetic, beauty and fitness industries since the 1980s (Shilling, 2003; Lupton, 1995); all of which are key areas of focus in the broad field of physical cultural studies. Sociological work has traced these shifts to cultural changes in advanced capitalist societies which occurred during the second half of the twentieth century in which conspicuous consumption became central in the ethos accompanying hard work in the realm of production (Shilling, 2007; Featherstone, 1982). As a result of this shift, embodiment and the physical body came to be treated as both a 'project' and a 'form of physical capital' (Bourdieu, 1977; Shilling, 2003, 2007; Mears, 2014). The increasing focus on 'health' in all spheres of life is particularly important for understanding the significance of the aesthetic body (Atkinson and Monaghan, 2014). The media is a crucial dimension of the growing industry of health through health and fitness magazines (Dworkin and Wachs, 2009), the popularity of reality television shows promoting weight-loss and fitness (Moore, 2010) and new social media sites such as Instagram, Twitter, Tumblr and Facebook which are fast becoming the prime means of marketing and advertising (Holmes, 2014).

The connections between feminized practices of health and beauty for women (the 'fashion-beauty complex') and broader gendered inequality have been widely critiqued (Wolf, 1991; Bordo, 2003; Bartky, 1990; McRobbie, 2009), particularly in relation to cosmetic surgery

Aestheticized bodies

(Davis, 1995; Leve et al., 2012; Banet-Weiser and Portwood-Stacer, 2006). A particular feature of the current social and cultural context is that men too are 'increasingly drawn into the consumer culture body image game and are becoming more critical and vulnerable about their bodies' (Featherstone, 2010: 202). Although the (young) female body continues to be particularly visible in the context of consumer culture through what McRobbie (2009) terms 'spectacular femininity' and the emphasis on slenderness, the young athletic and muscular male body embodies 'spectacular masculinity' and is increasingly visible in popular culture and the media (see Gill et al., 2005). Consumer culture is a central factor in men's concern for the body's appearance as men are increasingly 'invited to enjoy the dubious equality of consumers in the market place'; a position which women have traditionally occupied (Featherstone, 1982: 22). Consumer culture is 'obsessed with the body', as the cosmetic, beauty, fitness and leisure industries are geared towards marketing the ever-expanding sale of commodities associated with the body's appearance and 'wellbeing' (Featherstone, 2010). The body in consumer culture is involved in a complex relationship with images, advertising and desire. These factors are central in understanding the current concern for, and focus on the body for young men as well as women (ibid.: 197).

Along with the invitation to care about the body's appearance and to consume products to aid in the body's aesthetic improvement, a growing emphasis on individual responsibility for health is also central in understanding the rise in a concern for the body's appearance in general (Featherstone, 2010). Bell and McNaughton, however, argue that men's current concern with their bodies is not particularly new, and that men have been susceptible to aesthetic pressures for some time, particularly surrounding 'fatness' (Bell and McNaughton, 2007: 112).

This chapter explores body work practices as a way of understanding the gendered dimensions of the focus on the aesthetic body. 'Body work' is defined as the practices or 'work' one performs on one's own body (Gimlin, 2007). 'Body work' can also refer to all forms of bodily labour such as in caring and welfare industries and domestic labour (Shilling, 2011: 336). Recent work by Mears has also developed the term 'aesthetic labour', distinct from body work, to describe 'the practice of screening, managing, and controlling workers on the basis of their physical appearance' (Mears, 2014: 1330). In this chapter, as described elsewhere (Coffey, 2013a, 2013b, 2014), I use the term body work to describe work performed on one's own body that connects to aesthetic modifications or maintenance of the body. The practices of muscle-building and cosmetic surgery are the particular focus of this chapter, which aims to sketch possibilities for how Deleuzian concepts can be mobilized in empirical research in the field of physical cultural studies.

Theorizing the body

Because of the centrality of the body in consumer culture and popular discourse on gender, the body is a key area of academic study in the fields of physical cultural studies, sociology and gender studies. Exploring how people live their bodies and explain their practices of body work is crucial for understanding the processes and connections between societal forces and bodies. There are particular theoretical, ontological and epistemological questions associated with making the body the prime focus of attention; namely, the problem of dualism (Grosz, 1994). Understandings of the body which position bodies as involved in etiological relations with social structures are underpinned by a dualistic ontology. Finding ways to theorize bodies beyond dualisms has been a central tenet of much post-structural feminist work (Witz, 2000), and has also contributed to recent empirical approaches to the body (Coleman, 2009; Jackson, 2010).

This concern has led to different approaches being sought to think through some of the most important sociological problems, including the relations between people and social structures and processes associated with how individuals negotiate 'structure' and 'agency' (Coffey and Farrugia, 2013). Here, Deleuzian understandings of bodies as processes (not entities) which are constantly shifting and being redefined based on their relations with other bodies and forces in the world, have been proposed as offering a way of conceptualizing bodies beyond the most problematic dualisms in both feminist and sociological theory (see Coleman, 2009; Grosz, 1994; Budgeon, 2003). Following recent feminist philosophical discussions and emerging empirical studies of the body drawn from the work of Deleuze and Guattari and Spinoza (Ringrose and Harvey, 2015; Renold and Ringrose, 2011; Budgeon, 2003; Coleman, 2009) the body can be understood not as an object but as an event of becoming. I extend this work to argue that body work practices and the configurations of consumer culture and spectacular forms of femininity and masculinity are important because they are implicated in the mediating forces which work to form the body as an event (Budgeon, 2003). Studying aesthetic body work practices is one way of studying the processes of becoming associated with gender and the body.

Key concepts: assemblage, becoming, affect

The main concepts drawn upon in this chapter to assist analysis of gendered, aesthetic body work practices are assemblage, becoming and affect. Assemblage is a key concept in Deleuzian work, and is described by Potts as comprised through 'a kind of chaotic network of habitual and non-habitual connections, always in flux, always reassembling in different ways' (Potts, 2004: 19). As 'things', assemblages can also be understood as 'temporary unities' which are composed of multiple heterogeneous objects. It can only be termed an assemblage, however, because of the ways these multiple aspects *function together*, and it is this function that creates an assemblage, the unity of which 'comes solely from the fact that these items function together, that they "work together" as a functional unity' (Patton, 1994: 158). At a more practical level, assemblages can be understood as the process of connections and engagements between bodies (including human, animal and inanimate) and the world. As Fox describes, 'unpacking an individual's assemblages can enable an understanding of how a person may respond to his/her environment' (Fox, 2011: 365). Assemblages may resemble what we understand to be relatively stable norms of ways of being (gendered practices such as cosmetic surgery, for example); however, the concept of assemblage highlights the ways things form in contestation, and in relation to myriad other aspects. Another way of describing an assemblage is as a range of relations including norms, discourses, ideals and practices which are dynamic and change over time. Human bodies (which too can be understood as assemblages rather than strictly whole, unified entities) engage with other assemblages, and in this process, the conditions for further engagement and possibility are generated. Deleuze's (1992) framework of becoming refers to the process of connections and relations that forms (and reforms) the assemblage.

Rather than asking 'what are bodies?', or questioning the *being* of bodies, Deleuze (1992) asks 'what can a body do?' To study becoming is to study the micro-processes of change that occur through affect and relations. Affects mediate action, or becomings (Deleuze, 1988: 256). Affects can 'motivate embodied responses', which can lead us to think about ourselves and the world differently, and to move and behave differently (Hickey-Moody and Malins, 2007: 9). From a practical perspective, affect can be used to relate to the psychological, emotional and physical connections a body has: with other people, ideas and activities (Fox and Ward, 2008). The utility of these concepts for understanding aesthetic gendered body work practices is discussed in relation to two case study examples focusing on practices of muscle-building and cosmetic surgery.

Body work practices and broader understandings of health and gender were explored through 22 in-depth semi-structured interviews with men and women aged 18–33 in Melbourne, Australia. I recruited through asking personal contacts to forward electronic advertisements to their friends (not known to me) through Facebook and email, which enabled participants to self-select to be involved in this research. Participants were mainly white, middle class and heterosexual; but they came from a range of professions and education levels. The aim was to explore how body work is done and how bodies are understood by those who self-selected to participate. Participants discussed a range of body work practices related to their identities such as exercising through jogging, attending classes at a gym or weights training, as well as diet, wearing make-up, tattooing and cosmetic surgery (Coffey, 2013a, 2013b, 2014). Many of these practices were undertaken by both men and women, with the exception of wearing make-up, tanning and cosmetic surgery, which were exclusive to women in this study. In this chapter I only discuss two body work practices (muscle-building and cosmetic surgery) through drawing on two case-study examples from participants Ben and Kate. Almost all of the eleven men interviewed described a desire to be more muscular, and Ben's example has been chosen to illustrate this widely shared concern. Of the eleven women interviewed, only two had undergone cosmetic surgery. As discussed elsewhere (Coffey, 2016), though Kate and Isabelle had the same procedure (breast implants), they had quite divergent aims and experiences related to the surgery. Kate's example has been chosen to illustrate the tensions and complexities associated with her experience of the practice as she discussed this in more detail than Isabelle. For a more fulsome discussion of this see Coffey (2016).

'Bigger, stronger': aesthetic muscle-building and masculinity

Ben, aged 32, had been a professional baseball player for around 12 years, from the age of 16 to around 28. During this time he lived mostly in America where he played, and travelled back and forth. He moved back to Australia about four years prior to the interview, and lived with his wife (whom he married earlier in the year) in an inner-North suburb of Melbourne, Australia. Since returning to Australia, Ben studied for a couple of years, and now works full-time as a sales representative for a health food company. Throughout the interview he described his time as a professional baseballer as formative in his perception of the 'ideal male' body type; one which he had continued to 'keep up' in the four years since he had played professionally:

> There's definitely an ideal body type [for men]. If you see how popular in the last 10–15 years gyms are now. And the advent of companies like GNC [health supplement and vitamin franchise[1]], those health nutrition type places. 20 years ago no one did that, it was only gym rat type guys. But now everyone does that, everyone goes to gym, everyone now wants to look like the wrestlers and stuff. Especially myself, being a professional athlete, there was a big emphasis on the way you looked, not just the way you played, but how you looked in the uniform. You know, being tall, strong. I was a sort of skinny kid and worked out pretty hard in the gym and put a lot of emphasis on it.

Ben discusses the recent normalization of a particular, masculine, muscular aesthetic of health which previously had been the reserve of 'gym rat types', which he connects to the increase in health and fitness industries such as 'health and nutrition' companies. He describes that while he was a professional baseballer there was a 'big influence' on *looking* tall and strong; an important component alongside his actual physical performance as an athlete. He describes when he was younger and had just become a professional he 'would have done anything to get the ideal body', and that the pressure to be 'bigger, stronger' was intense:

> Men want to be that alpha male type. And associated with that is being big and strong … [The pressure came] from the club, and from your own idea of what the ideal, you know, look is. You would see guys and, you would look at them and you'd think, oh they look like athletes, they look like baseball players, and then you'd try and emulate that. And always, you know, in the club, they were always like 'bigger, stronger'. 'Bigger, stronger', you've gotta strive for that. That's just what it always was. So yeah I mean, it was just something that was hammered into you, the ideal, what you're supposed to look like.

Understanding Ben's examples through the concept of assemblage (Fox, 2011; Duff, 2014) draws attention to the range of relations, affects, discourses, ideals and practices related to the muscular aesthetic. The muscular assemblage in this case is closely interwoven with masculine ideals of strength, capability and potency ('bigger, stronger'). The professional baseballing community is also implicated at personal, interpersonal and institutional levels; and includes the physical spaces of the club rooms and training gyms, as well as the baseball field of play. Ben's description of the required 'look' of the baseballer also clearly links to Atkinson and Monaghan's description of muscles as 'culturally idealised' as the epitome of masculinity (Atkinson and Monaghan, 2014). Looking muscular is broadly understood as a way of affirming or ensuring recognition of possessing a normative masculine identity (Waquant, 1995).

The process of looking and comparing with other 'ideal' bodies and the men who 'look like athletes' in these spaces are also clearly important. Practices of the muscular assemblage for Ben include the physical effort of lifting heavy weights, as well as eating protein-rich foods and a range of vitamins and supplements (both illegal and legal); and the increased commercialization of health products. Ben engages with all of these aspects (and a multitude of others). This process of engagement can be termed becoming. Deleuze's (1992) framework of becoming refers to the process of connections and relations that forms (and reforms) the assemblage. The process informs what a body can do; the range of possibilities that are available stemming from engagement with the many dimensions of the assemblage. What can Ben's body do in relation to this aesthetically muscular assemblage?

Ben describes finding it difficult to 'get out of the habit' of doing the training he did when he was a professional, and that he 'can't bring' himself to not go to the gym for more than two days:

> It's funny, I can't really get out of the habit of still doing a lot of training. I can't bring myself to go for more than two days without going to the gym. I've sort of built up a reputation for being, like a big strong guy, and even if I get on the scales and weigh myself and I'll still be the same weight, I feel like if I don't go for a few days I feel not as strong, not as confident. I have to keep going and doing it. [I feel] a lot of pressure on that. I'm 32 and I wonder how long I can keep that up for.

Ben's exercise of lifting weights is something he 'has to keep going and doing'; he 'has to keep it up', though he worries he may not be able to continue in this identity for much longer. Body work, for Ben, has significant repercussions that extend beyond discourses of health and masculinity, though both of these discourses are implicated in the meanings of his body work.

Body work practices to do with exercise and lifting weights go towards shaping both the physical body and (hegemonically masculine) sense of self. As a result, body work practices are powerful in how the body is experienced and felt. This also means that if the practices of body work are not 'kept up' for whatever reason – through circumstances associated with injury, age, or other life changes such as increased work or family commitments – the embodied consequences and impact on sense of self may be profound. In this sense, the 'pressure' to 'keep it up' places significant constraints on the possibilities for living available to Ben. In this sense, Ben's engagement with the muscular assemblage (including affects, discourses, norms, ideals and practices) informs the range of possibility available for him. This is a crucial dimension in understanding Ben's aesthetically motivated body work through building muscle.

As Fox has argued in reference to becoming-fat and becoming-slim bodies (Fox, 2014), circulations of matter and desire affect the production of and experience of 'muscles', constituting 'affective economies' (Ahmed, 2004) which surround Ben's body as he attempts to maintain the muscular physique of a professional baseballer; an image and identity from five years prior. Ben's examples shed some insight into the intensive dynamics of aesthetic body work practices related to muscularity and masculinity as he strives to 'keep it up'.

'There's so much pressure to have this perfect body, you know': aesthetic cosmetic surgery and femininity

Kate was 22 and lived in Melbourne's south. She had a University qualification and worked part time as a nanny and administrative assistant. Kate spoke extensively about the portrayal of women in the media and what she perceived to be 'unfair' broader expectations of a particular appearance for women:

> Women are supposed to be a size 8 and they're supposed to you know, be tall and slim and tanned and toned and all those sorts of things. Men don't have that pressure that's on women. That's what I think. Men are more superficial, they expect [a particular ideal appearance] more. They expect that women … you know, it's sort of unfair, like women are supposed to have kids and then bounce back and have this perfect body and it just doesn't really happen like that! Um, like, my boyfriend says, 'Are you still gonna love me when I get old and fat?' and I'm like 'Yes! Are you going to love me if I get older and fat?' and he goes 'No!' And that is so what it's like and it's not fair!

Three years ago, before she was with her current partner, Kate had breast implant surgery. She describes that the decision came at what was a very low point in her life. Her boyfriend of three years 'just packed up one day and moved to Perth'. After this, she 'hit rock bottom', and decided 'all I wanted was boobs':

> So I saved up for it and I did all this research on it and it wasn't, like, an uneducated decision. But for me, that was a mental thing I couldn't get over. Because I've never once looked back on that decision and thought 'oh that was a bad decision'. And I researched absolutely everything, in front of the muscles, behind the muscle, saline, silicone, breast cancer, can you still breastfeed, I did this research for a *year*, it wasn't like I woke up one day and went 'Hey, I want big boobs!' When I told my parents, who are really like, hippies, I'm getting a boob job, mum was like, 'Oh no darling we just love you the way you are', and I was like 'Mum, seriously, I haven't grown boobs, I'm 21 years of age, it's not going to happen for me!'

She said that although it was difficult to 'go against' the advice of her family and friends who told her not to have surgery the decision was integral to her overall happiness and sense of comfort in her body:

> All my girlfriends were like, 'Don't do it'. So you're making a decision and you're going against everyone else. And it's a massive, it's a massive thing. But over time, you can't put a price on being happy with your body. I've never once looked back and regretted my decision. And over time, I've had so many moments where I just *feel* … like I don't have this feeling in my stomach where I'm worried about wearing bathers … Not stressing about summer, and enjoying your life, and just really living it.

Kate described breast implants as a solution to alleviating her suffering (cf. Davis, 1995), enabling her to live more fully. She described how she used to be teased and 'humiliated' at high school and would feel anxiety and stress related to any activities which involved a swimming pool or the beach. This may have particular significance in Australia where beach culture frames the experience of youth for those living on the coastline (Booth, 2012). She said before the surgery she could never wear the clothes she wanted to wear, and felt self-conscious even while showering. She contrasted the 'feeling' she had following the surgery with the feeling she had prior to it 'in her stomach' of anxiety, worry and 'stress' that 'eats away at you'. After her surgery Kate felt able to 'just really live [her] life'.

Understanding Kate's example through the concept of assemblage (Fox, 2011; Duff, 2014) draws attention to the range of relations, affects, discourses, ideals and practices related to the aesthetic, bodily aspects of femininity achieved through cosmetic surgery body work practices. Norms and discourses related to femininity, appearance, image and consumer culture logics of transformation and self-improvement are crucial aspects of Kate's cosmetic surgery assemblage. As in Leve et al.'s (2012) study, in Kate's example, ideologies of neoliberalism shape her decisions about cosmetic surgery as a lifestyle choice:

> I think if it makes you feel more confident … It's one of those things, I would never judge someone for a decision they make on their body. Um, I'm all for plastic surgery or make up or anything, if it makes you feel better, and you're on the earth for such a short time, you know?

This example also reflects the normalization of beauty practices such as cosmetic surgery as 'work on the self' that has the potential to lead to better self-esteem and a healthier 'body image' (Banet-Weiser and Portwood-Stacer, 2006; Featherstone, 2010). These are all important dimensions of the cosmetic surgery assemblage; as are interpersonal relationships with friends and family, and heterosexual norms of attractiveness in Kate's described self-consciousness with partners prior to the surgery. Spaces of the school, beach and the pool are also important, as are items of clothing, specifically dresses and swimming costumes, which she mentions on numerous occasions. These in particular can be understood as affective dimensions of the assemblage, as she describes the feeling of humiliation, stress and anxiety 'in [her] stomach' in these situations, where she was often teased. Interestingly, a critique of the 'unfair expectations' of women's bodies and 'pressures of femininity' could also be considered an important dimension of the assemblage. According to Deleuze (1988), what we are capable of is directly related to embodied sensation (affect), and it is the relations of affect that produce a body's capacities (Coleman, 2009). The process informs what a body can do; the range of possibilities that are available stemming from engagement with the many dimensions of the assemblage. Kate's engagement with the cosmetic surgery assemblage (including affects, discourses, norms, ideals and practices) informs the range of possibility available for her. In some sense, the critical aspect of Kate's engagement with femininity as part of the cosmetic surgery assemblage enables Kate to envisage a broader range of possibilities for her body beyond its appearance. She says: 'You've sorta gotta have that balance where, it is important to go out and feel great and look good … but it shouldn't be the most important thing in your life.'

She is adamant that 'it's ok not to be this perfect person', and reconceptualizes 'the ideal body' as 'just someone who's comfortable in their body' whatever shape or size. This has implications for her broader engagement with the practice of cosmetic surgery as she says she has no intention of having further cosmetic procedures. Kate's engagement with the cosmetic surgery assemblage can be understood as being more 'open' to possibilities beyond bodily aesthetic practices than Ben's. Unlike Ben, Kate does not feel locked in to 'keeping up' this body work practice. Rather than attributing Ben's example to individualized notions of poor body image based on the 'effects' of media images for example (following Coleman, 2009), the concepts of assemblage, affect and becoming enable an analysis of the unpredictable micro-forces that affect the body and mediate action.

Conclusion

This chapter has explored the gendered aesthetics associated with cultures of the physical through two case-study examples of two body work practices: muscle-building and cosmetic surgery. The chapter mobilizes concepts of affect, assemblage and becoming to understand these gendered, aesthetically motivated practices. I have argued that these concepts enable an analysis of the unpredictable micro-forces that affect the body and mediate action. This approach contributes to developing the use of post-human concepts in empirical research centring on the body and the politics of embodiment. This has implications for the use of such concepts for physical cultural studies. Through these brief examples, I have aimed to sketch possibilities for how Deleuzian concepts can be mobilized in empirical research in the field of physical cultural studies. Following Andrews and Silk (2015), drawing on empirical research on body work practices, I have hoped to contribute examples of how expressions of physical cultural studies are embodied through drawing on a burgeoning Deleuzian theoretical approach to the body as active potentiality. This perspective can enable analysis of the ambiguities and contradictions associated with the embodiment of physical cultures such as those related to muscle-building and cosmetic surgery, and I argue, one which has great potential to add to the rich theoretical territory currently informing analyses of the complex field of physical cultural studies.

Note

1 The company GNC LiveWell is described on its website as 'the world's largest retailer specializing in vitamins, herbs, weight management and sports nutrition. Established in Pittsburgh, USA by David Shakarian in 1935, GNC now has over 8000 stores in 49 countries.' See www.gnclivewell.com.au/about.asp?id=2&t=About+Us&cid=3&cat= (accessed 15 December 2014).

References

Ahmed, S. 2004. Affective Economies. *Social Text*, 22, 117–139.
Andrews, D.L., and Silk, M.L. (2015). Physical Cultural Studies on Sport. In R. Guillianotti (ed.)., *The Routledge Handbook of the Sociology of Sport* (pp. 83–93). London: Routledge.

Atkinson, M. and Monaghan, L. F. 2014. *Challenging Myths of Masculinity: Understanding Physical Cultures*. Farnham: Ashgate Publishing.

Banet-Weiser, S. and Portwood-Stacer, L. 2006. 'I Just Want to Be Me Again!': Beauty Pageants, Reality Television, and Post-Feminism. *Feminist Theory*, 7, 255–272.

Bartky, S. 1990. *Femininity and Domination: Studies in the Phenomenology of Oppression*. New York: Routledge.

Bell, K. and McNaughton, D. 2007. Feminism and the Invisible Fat Man. *Body and Society*, 13, 107–131.

Booth, D. 2012. *Australian Beach Cultures: The History of Sun, Sand and Surf*. Abingdon: Routledge.

Bordo, S. 2003. *Unbearable Weight: Feminism, Western Culture and the Body*. Berkeley, CA: University of California Press.

Bourdieu, P. 1977. *Outline of a Theory of Practice*. Cambridge: Cambridge University Press.

Budgeon, S. 2003. Identity as an Embodied Event. *Body and Society*, 9, 35–55.

Coffey, J. 2013a. Bodies, Body Work and Gender: Exploring a Deleuzian Approach. *Journal of Gender Studies*, 22, 3–16.

Coffey, J. 2013b. 'Body Pressure': Negotiating Gender through Body Work Practices. *Youth Studies Australia*, 32, 39–48.

Coffey, J. 2014. 'As Long as I'm Fit and a Healthy Weight, I Don't Feel Bad': Exploring Body Work and Health through the Concept of 'Affect'. *Journal of Sociology*, 51(3), 613–627.

Coffey, J. 2016. 'What Can I Do Next?' Cosmetic Surgery, Femininities and Affect. *Women: A Cultural Review*, 27(1), 79–95.

Coffey, J. and Farrugia, D. 2013. Unpacking the Black Box: The Problem of Agency in the Sociology of Youth. *Journal of Youth Studies*, 17, 464–471.

Coleman, R. 2009. *The Becoming of Bodies: Girls, Images, Experience*. Manchester: Manchester University Press.

Davis, K. 1995. *Reshaping the Female Body*. New York: Routledge.

Deleuze, G. 1988. *Spinoza: Practical Philosophy*. San Francisco, CA: City Lights Books.

Deleuze, G. 1992. Ethology: Spinoza and Us. In J. Crary and S. K. Winter (eds), *Incorporations*. New York: Zone.

Duff, C. 2014. *Assemblages of Health*. New York: Springer.

Dworkin, S. and Wachs, F. 2009. *Body Panic: Gender, Health and the Selling of Fitness*. New York: University of New York Press.

Evers, C. 2006. How to Surf. *Journal of Sport and Social Issues*, 30, 229–243.

Featherstone, M. 1982. The Body in Consumer Culture. *Theory, Culture and Society*, 1, 18–33.

Featherstone, M. 2010. Body, Image and Affect in Consumer Culture. *Body and Society*, 16, 193–221.

Fox, N. J. 2011. The Ill-Health Assemblage: Beyond the Body-with-Organs. *Health Sociology Review*, 20, 359–371.

Fox, N. J. 2014. The Micropolitics of Obesity: Materialism, Neoliberalism and Food Sovereignty. Paper presented at British Sociological Association Medical Sociology Annual Conference, Birmingham.

Fox, N. J. and Ward, K. J. 2008. What are Health Identities and How May We Study Them? *Sociology of Health and Illness*, 30, 1007–1021.

Gill, R., Henwood, K. and Mclean, C. 2005. Body Projects and the Regulation of Normative Masculinity. *Body and Society*, 11, 37–62.

Gimlin, D. 2007. What Is 'Body Work'? A Review of the Literature. *Sociology Compass*, 1, 353–370.

Grosz, E. 1994. *Volatile Bodies: Towards a Corporeal Feminism*. St Leonards: Allen & Unwin.

Hickey-Moody, A. and Malins, P. (eds). 2007. *Deleuzian Encounters: Studies in Contemporary Social Issues*. New York: Palgrave Macmillan.

Holmes, C. 2014. Health Messaging through Social Media. Paper presented at 142nd APHA Annual Meeting and Exposition, 15–19 November.

Jackson, A. Y. 2010. Deleuze and the Girl. *International Journal of Qualitative Studies in Education (QSE)*, 23, 579–587.

Leve, M., Rubin, L. and Pusic, A. 2012. Cosmetic Surgery and Neoliberalisms: Managing Risk and Responsibility. *Feminism and Psychology*, 22, 122–141.

Lupton, D. 1995. *The Imperative of Health: Public Health and the Regulated Body*. London: Sage.

McRobbie, A. 2009. *The Aftermath of Feminism: Gender, Culture and Social Change*. London: Sage.

Mears, A. 2014. Aesthetic Labor for the Sociologies of Work, Gender, and Beauty. *Sociology Compass*, 8, 1330–1343.

Moore, S. 2010. Is the Healthy Body Gendered? Toward a Feminist Critique of the New Paradigm of Health. *Body and Society*, 16, 95–118.

Patton, P. 1994. Metamorpho-logic: Bodies and Powers in a Thousand Plateaus. *Journal of the British Society for Phenomenology*, 25, 157–169.
Potts, A. 2004. Deleuze on Viagra (Or, What Can a 'Viagra-Body' Do?). *Body and Society*, 10, 17–36.
Renold, E. and Ringrose, J. 2011. Schizoid Subjectivities? Re-theorizing Teen Girls' Sexual Cultures in an Era of 'Sexualization'. *Journal of Sociology*, 47, 389–409.
Ringrose, J. and Harvey, L. 2015. Boobs, Back-Off, and Small Bits: Mediated Body Parts, Sexual Reward and Gendered Shame in Teens' Networked Images. *Continuum: Journal of Media and Cultural Studies*, 29, 205–217.
Shilling, C. 2003. *The Body and Social Theory*. London: Sage.
Shilling, C. 2007. Sociology and the Body: Classical Traditions and New Agendas. *Sociological Review Monograph*, 55, 1–18.
Shilling, C. 2011. Afterword: Body Work and the Sociological Tradition. *Sociology of Health and Illness*, 33, 336–340.
Waquant, L. 1995. Pugs at Work: Bodily Capital and Bodily Labour among Professional Boxers. *Body and Society*, 1, 65–93.
Witz, A. 2000. Whose Body Matters? Feminist Sociology and the Corporeal Turn in Sociology and Feminism. *Body and Society*, 6, 1–24.
Wolf, N. 1991. *The Beauty Myth: How Images of Beauty are Used Against Women*. New York: William Morrow.

23
FAT BODIES

Michael Gard

For people inclined to have faith in the day-to-day toil of scientists and the inexorable progress of scientific knowledge, these are unsettling times. This is not at all to say that a golden age of scientific progress is behind us or that scientists as a population are not quite what they used to be. But something has changed. The relatively recent explosion in the number of journal articles produced in most scientific fields of enquiry sits alongside a pervasive concern about the value of all this output. As I write, a spirited, bruising but ultimately vital international conversation about the quality of the work that researchers do is unfolding and, in turn, changing the way this work is done.

Perhaps the most well-known single contribution to this conversation is John Ioannidis's 2005 article 'Why Most Published Research Findings are False'. As close as modern academic life comes to an instant classic, the paper argued that far more published studies presented statistically significant findings than was statistically plausible. The reasons for this are numerous, but they include publication bias, poor study design and the tendency of scientists to interpret their data in ways that confirm their pre-existing beliefs. As a result, Ioannidis claims, most science is unreproducible, not just because of a lack of methodological clarity but also because most positive findings turn out to be wishful thinking on the part of the researchers. His startling and much-quoted conclusion, published in a more recent paper (Ioannidis, 2014: 1) is that 'many published research findings are false or exaggerated, and an estimated 85 per cent of research resources are wasted'.

Ioannidis's work is a rare example of detailed and careful science that has produced unequivocal findings which have then been reported with uncompromising forthrightness. There is no shilly-shallying or conditional language about the need to suspend judgement and conduct further research. In fact, it is a compelling mix of the empirical with the polemical; a 'cut through' moment in which scientific business as usual was suddenly – at least for those who were inclined to listen – no longer possible. Of course, Ioannidis has not been a lone voice and authors from a range of disciplines appear to share his views. For example, writing in *Nature*, Begley and Ellis (2012) have suggested that an important cause of the slow progress in cancer treatments has been the dismal consistency with which pre-clinical scientific 'discoveries' have turned out to be wrong. As a result, clinical trials of potential new treatments have low success rates because they tend to be based on flawed basic science; a case of garbage in, garbage out.

To a large extent, obesity research has escaped this kind of scrutiny, probably because of its relatively low scientific status. However, as I will show, there are rumblings of disquiet. They point to a malaise which shares some of the features that Ioannidis and others have described, but which also point to the peculiar baggage that seems to attach to the study of fatness. In other words, my interest here is in what we might call the *epistemological culture* of obesity research.

By focusing on epistemology, my invitation to the reader is to move beyond the identity politics that are now commonplace in social scientific analyses of science. That is, I offer a conception of physical cultural studies that approaches the study of body weight pragmatically and without allegiance to any particular kind of social science. At the same time, I contend that a critical engagement with the science of body weight cannot afford to lose sight of the 'science-ness' of this field of study. What I advocate, therefore, is for a simultaneously fluid and coherent traversing between science and social science in which neither ultimately gains the upper hand. Rather, the kind of physical cultural studies I attempt to offer in this chapter is one that should be able to speak to multiple intellectual and academic constituencies. In fact, there should be something both comforting and infuriating for all readers, precisely because this text sets out to both exploit and trouble some of the intellectual conventions that have been brought to bear on the study of body weight. If I have a contribution to make to physical cultural studies it is to aspire towards a form of social science that is eclectic, multiply literate and suspicious of any academic position that claims methodological or theoretical primacy.

A statistical disease

Most readers will be aware that a relatively recent globally mobile narrative has come to dominate the ways in which we are invited to think about human body weight. By this telling, the number of overweight and obese bodies has increased rapidly since the 1970s, continues to do so and now represents a serious threat, if not the greatest of all threats, to human health. The increase in human body weights is widely glossed as the 'obesity epidemic', thus conjuring images of rapid and uncontrolled spread of a serious medical condition.

The primary discursive element in this story has been the body mass index (BMI), a measure of a person's weight divided by their height. In fact, the BMI's rise to international notoriety is a remarkable story in itself. Invented in the middle of the nineteenth century and then first popularized in the twentieth century by Ancel Keys and colleagues in a 1972 article for *The Journal of Chronic Diseases*, the BMI is an instructive practical example of reductionism in action. In the face of the complexities of human body composition and the subtle aetiology of body weight fluctuation, it presents a radically simplified account of an individual's bodily health. On the one hand, its limitations are widely acknowledged by obesity researchers who point out that it was never intended as a diagnostic tool. At the same time, however, it is precisely on the strength of BMI statistics that virtually all of pronouncements about a body-fat led decline in human life expectancy are made. Moreover, following much debate, obesity has now been designated a 'disease' by organizations such as the American Medical Association (2013). Designating a certain condition a disease naturally implies the ability to form a judgement about when an individual moves from a non-diseased to a diseased state and at present this diagnostic choice is usually made via the putatively non-diagnostic BMI.

The pros and cons of the BMI have been voluminously debated and, in the main, a scientific consensus has been reached to the effect that its imperfections are outweighed by its usefulness. The BMI allows researchers to collect a large amount of data in relatively quick and inexpensive fashion and thereby present a snapshot of the prevalence of 'excessive' fatness in particular populations. This is not an indefensible position and it is clear, at least to me, that most researchers who take this position do so with good intentions. What I want to describe in the remainder of this chapter, however, are the consequences of this 'near enough is good enough' stance on the epistemology of body weight and human health.

For example, most undergraduate students of anatomy will know that a person can be relatively heavy for their height – and therefore be classified as overweight or obese – without having much body fat. Likewise, a low or 'normal' BMI score may obscure the existence of high levels of subcutaneous or visceral fat. In other words, if adipose tissue is the problem then the BMI – or any of its other suggested substitutes – may not be very useful. To put the point simply, a person with a 'normal' BMI between 20 and 25 may actually be very fat while a person with a BMI of 33 – which is well beyond the minimum obesity threshold of 30 – may have very little body fat at all. But, as I have said, these anomalies are well known and generally considered a price worth paying.

Slightly less well known are the problems that begin to accumulate once rigid classification systems such as the BMI are used to collect data on different human sub-populations. First, there are the problems associated with body proportions. The BMI assumes a mathematically standardized relationship between a person's height and weight. As a result, people who are shorter or taller than average are likely to record very different BMI scores even if their bodies are composed of the same percentages of body fat (Nevill, Stewart, Olds and Holder, 2006). This, in turn, has implications for the efficacy of the BMI with women, children and the anthropometric variation that comes with human ethnic diversity. For example, questions about the validity of using the BMI with Polynesians, Asians and people with African ancestry continue to occupy the minds of scholars (Deurenberg, 2001; Deurenberg and Deurenberg-Yap, 2003).

Putting the dimensions of different kinds of human bodies to one side, there is an equally complex set of issues concerning the *medical* significance of BMI measurements. Three particularly consequential examples stand out among many others. First, there is accumulating evidence that for any given elevated BMI – that is, a BMI above the 29.9 upper cut-off for 'normal' weight – the health risks may vary significantly across ethnic groups; a high BMI may be less risky for some groups compared to others (Dubbert et al., 2002; Chiu et al., 2011). Second, while adult BMI categories have at least some basis in human morbidity and mortality statistics, the same cannot be said for children. This is because very little compelling longitudinal data exist on which to base normative judgements about how fat children should or should not be. This means that classifying a child as 'normal' or 'overweight' or 'obese' is essentially guesswork and will probably remain so for the foreseeable future (Freedman et al., 2001; Freedman and Sherry, 2009). Third, it is becoming increasingly evident that the long-assumed 'U' shaped relationship between BMI and health outcomes may not hold for different age groups. In this model there is a healthy sweet spot of body weight normality (a BMI between 20 and 24.9) between the 'underweight' and 'overweight' zones wherein disease and premature death lie. That this might be a flawed assumption for people above 50 years of age was first reported three decades ago (Andres, Elahi, Tobin, Muller and Brant, 1985). Since then, a consistent flow of epidemiological data has questioned robustness of the 'U'-shaped relationship for all ages (Flegal, Graubard, Williamson and Gail, 2007).

I want to stress that these are not purely scientific matters. Rather, historically located social conditions, such as the pressure to continually produce publishable, generalizable and comparable body weight statistics, encourage obesity researchers to act as if some somatically and physiologically archetypal human existed and against which all others might be compared. Of course, notions of bodily normality and deviance have been present in all cultures across time and space. There is nothing especially singular or modern about the tendency of obesity researchers to want to classify people and draw artificially sharp distinctions between the good and the bad and the well and the unwell. What is specific to the present moment is the intersection between a set of epistemological practices (research methods, academic conventions, publishing practices, increased emphasis on the pursuit of research funds etc.) and a particular material field of study: human body weight and its consequences for bio-medical health. To put the point more succinctly, what are the *specific* consequences when we turn human body weight into raw material for the work of epidemiologists and public health researchers at this particular moment in academic history?

More is less?

In light of my opening comments about the work of Ioannidis and others, it will not surprise readers that one of the consequences I will highlight here is the apparent elusiveness of certainty about human body weight and health. A long list of examples could be offered but I will restrict myself to a conspicuous few.

Although as time goes by there are more researchers prepared to question it, the idea that human body weight is primarily the end product of the balance – or imbalance – between energy consumed and expended in the course of daily life remains fundamental to the purpose, practices and output of obesity research across the world. From a culturally anthropological point of view, we might characterize the 'energy in/energy out' account of human body weight as one of obesity research's founding stories or myths. This is why, for example, a huge amount of research work and resources have been devoted to trying to find out how many calories people consume, how many they expend and how to encourage or force people to alter these behaviours. In the case of energy consumption, thousands of research papers published in the last thirty years, based primarily on various kinds of indirect data such as interviews, diaries and questionnaires, have attempted to quantify the contribution of food and drink consumption to rising body weights. This has been a largely futile exercise. As Jan Wright and I pointed out a decade ago (Gard and Wright, 2005), it is not difficult to find researchers who confidently make diametrically opposed claims about whether average daily calorie intake has changed. More recently, the value of dietary research has been called into question and, in fact, some have been prepared to call it essentially worthless (Dhurandhar et al., 2015).

A virtually identical state of affairs exists in the field of energy expenditure research. As with energy intake, techniques for *directly* measuring energy expenditure suffer from three serious drawbacks; they are expensive, almost impossible to administer 'in situ' rather than the artificially controlled environment of the laboratory, and invasive. This last factor is perhaps the most intractable. If a research participant knows that their behaviour is being monitored, no matter how painlessly, there will always be doubt about whether the data collected is a valid measure of their behaviour when it is not being monitored (for more detailed discussions of energy expenditure research see Westerterp, 1999; Dishman, Washburn and Schoeller, 2001; Tremblay, 2004).

These issues are not mere irritants in the push for scientific certainty. The preoccupation with the minutiae of individual body weight management has been blamed for a widely acknowledged lack of progress towards viable and efficacious solutions to the 'obesity epidemic' (Karasu, 2016). In fact, a number of commentators have drawn specific critical attention to the small amount of useful knowledge that has been delivered despite remarkable increases in the number of published energy consumption and expenditure research papers (for an early example, see Garner and Wooley, 1991; for more recent commentary, see Herbert et al. 2013). And at the risk of labouring the point, the problem here is not simply one of slow progress. The argument being made here is that the effect of more and more poor quality research offering contradictory research findings is increasing confusion.

This epistemological state of affairs has had other consequences. In particular, the failures of 'energy in/energy out' research is cited by researchers who propose a range of other mechanisms to explain increasing body weights. These mechanisms vary widely in their plausibility but their proponents share a dissatisfaction with mainstream theories based purely on energy consumption and expenditure. They include theories about obesity viruses, the effect of antidepression medications, assortative human mating, the increasing age at which women have children, chemicals in the environment, increased use of air conditioners, and disrupted sleep patterns (see McAllister et al., 2009 for an extended assessment of these theories). We might think of these ideas as obesity research's equivalent of 'new age' spirituality or, perhaps slightly less pejoratively, 'alternative medicine'. That is, in cultural contexts thirsting for the answers science seems unable to deliver, people will look to and invent other answers no matter how speculative they might seem.

More prosaically, advocates for bariatric surgery and weight loss drugs tend also to base their arguments on the glaring failure of 'energy in/energy out' research to make a difference to the lives of people seeking treatments to help them lose weight (Mauro, Taylor, Wharton and Sharma, 2008; Atkinson, 2014). In the world of obesity research, these are the pragmatists, often infused with an entrepreneurial spirit to connect with corporate capitalism, most obviously in the shape of the pharmaceutical industry. The epistemological turn here is instrumentally away from what is 'true' towards 'what works'. The pursuit of trying to understand the behavioural pathways that lead people to put on weight has, they argue, got us nowhere. Indeed, pursuing the 'less is more' theme of this chapter, they argue that the overwhelming bias towards behavioural research and interventions has stymied progress towards more humane and effective obesity treatments.

I will return to the problem of the integrity of energy consumption and expenditure data shortly. For now I want to juxtapose what is widely held to be the failure of behavioural 'energy in/energy out' obesity research with the vast intervention literature I have just alluded to.

First, despite the existence of a lively scholarly dialogue about the limitations of behavioural research, anti-obesity interventions based on behavioural research continue to proliferate and find their way into the scholarly literature. At this point we find ourselves back with Ioannidis's basic insight that 'many published research findings are false or exaggerated'. In the fifteen years I have been reading obesity intervention research it is difficult to recall a single published study that concluded that the intervention that was studied failed to achieve worthwhile outcomes and that no further research into it should be carried out. Research into the phenomenon of publication bias tells us that this may have something to do with the reluctance of academic journals to publish null findings.

And yet there is surely more to it than this. For example, reviews of literature consistently point to the poor efficacy of school-based public health interventions and, in particular, those that target childhood overweight and obesity (see Gard and Pluim, 2014 for a summary). At the level of the individual paper, however, unpromising findings are routinely presented as hints of future success. For example, in the abstract for Datar and Sturm's (2004: 1501) paper 'Physical Education in Elementary School and Body Mass Index: Evidence from the Early Childhood Longitudinal Study' for the *American Journal of Public Health*, the authors claim that 'Expanding physical education programs in schools, in the form in which they currently exist, may be an effective intervention for combating obesity in the early years, especially among girls.' The data presented in this paper actually show that extra physical education classes were not associated with any BMI variation for any of the children in the study except a minority subset of the girls. Moreover, although they imply it in the paper's abstract, the study's design does not allow for any conclusion about causation. There is simply no way of knowing whether the small BMI 'effect' on a distinct minority of children had anything whatsoever to do with their physical education classes.

To reiterate, the reason why I think it is prudent to dispute Datar and Sturm's conclusion that physical education classes 'may be an effective intervention for combating obesity in the early years' is that reviews of the research literature uniformly conclude that physical education classes do not have this effect. There is a long list of school-related reasons why we might have doubted the efficacy of physical education classes to fight childhood obesity in the first place. But the more pertinent thing to say is that school-based interventions, such as physical education programmes, are based on the same behavioural assumptions that underpin intervention research in general and which have also proved misleading.

In fact, what is most remarkable about the proliferation of anti-obesity interventions is that their proponents appear to believe so vehemently in their importance and chances of success that they see targets of intervention wherever they look. To name just a few, advocates for these interventions have proposed:

- A complete ban on the sale to and possession of sweetened drinks of any kind (soft drinks, flavoured milk, etc.) by young people in public places (Hodge, Barrazza, Russo, Nelson and Measer, 2014). Under this ban, these drinks could only be consumed by young people indoors at the family home.
- Mandating that the recipes cooked on celebrity cooking shows, and the books that celebrity chefs produce, all be accompanied by nutrition labels (Howard, Adams and White, 2012). This recommendation has been made despite food labelling's widely reported lack of health impact.
- A range of strategies for monitoring and changing the energy consumption and expenditure of children beginning with newborn babies (Hesketh and Campbell, 2010).
- Frameworks for action that would require national governments to factor obesity prevention into all areas of policy deliberation, including taxation, public infrastructure and education (Sacks, Swinburn and Lawrence, 2009).

In short, within the epistemological culture of obesity research, obesity regularly trumps all other concerns such that there is no such thing as an 'off limits' field of intervention. Scholars now write openly about the need for a new paternalism with a view to limiting people's personal freedom to make their own food and physical activity behaviour choices (Dawson, 2014). Perhaps most telling of all, regardless of the sphere of activity, each actual or proposed line of intervention is justified with the same 'crisis' rhetoric. That is, the case in favour of particular interventions is rarely prosecuted with convincing reference to the intervention's past history of efficacy because, invariably, this history does not exist.

One might imagine that the lack of success in an area of intervention might discourage its advocates. In fact, the opposite is true. Because interventions so rarely have their intended effect, obesity researchers tend to conclude that body weight is exquisitely 'complex' and that this is why we need to target it on such a broad front. In other words, the war on obesity will only be won by achieving many small but cumulative victories. In an epistemological context of this kind where failure equals success, no measure is ever worthless.

Interestingly, with the rise of personal micro computing, social media and 'big data', obesity researchers are turning enthusiastically to digital technology in the war on obesity. Advocates for digital intervention into people's food and physical activity behaviours do so by pointing to the failure of past interventions and by celebrating the potential of these technologies to immerse people in new and intensified cultures of institutional and personal self-surveillance. In particular, they point to the potential for digital technology to solve the data integrity issues of the past because soon we will be able to wear sensors that will upload precise data about our behaviour in real time. In fact, the digital turn in obesity research has allowed many of its practitioners to draw a line under the field's less than glorious past and imagine that it will all be different this time.

Normal people working in extraordinary times

The conclusion that I want to offer will be familiar enough although my contention is that I have arrived here via a less conventional route. First the conclusion: there are instructive reasons to think of obesity research not as an evolving body of knowledge, but as a specific culture in itself. As such, it has its sub-cultures – the mainstream and its various offshoots and splinter groups – which exist within its own peculiar mixture of material and discursive conditions of possibility.

On the one hand, this conclusion is not a return to the various 'postmodernism versus science' debates in which discussion tended to turn on important though somewhat intractable questions of ontology and the limits of epistemology. In keeping with my opening remarks about physical cultural studies, nothing that I have talked about in this chapter is necessarily hostile to either extremes of postmodern constructionism or hardline scientific positivism. On the other hand, as I have argued elsewhere (Gard, 2011), I am disinclined to impugn the ideological, moral or intellectual fibre of the people who do obesity research. To put the point directly, while there have been no shortage of scholars prepared to accuse obesity science of sexism, racism, neo-liberal individualism and a long list of other sins, these arguments are either simply mistaken or at least vulnerable to the same charge of ideological excess that they level at others. In fact, it is this movement away from moral certainty and accusation towards a more intellectually generous and agile way of working that I see as one of physical cultural studies' most important potential contributions. In other words, in the midst of the intellectual promiscuity that I have advocated here, there is the hope that the people in our research will look less heroically admirable or morally deficient and simply more human.

My contention in this chapter has been that there are important questions about the nature and future of knowledge work that a cultural analysis of obesity research allows us to explore. Fanelli and Ioannidis (2013) have claimed that the overestimation of effect size be a particular problem in health and medical research which focuses on behavioural variables, a claim that is particularly relevant for obesity research. In fact, they found that effect size overestimation may be highest where academic competition is the most intense, most obviously in the United States. Their conclusion, like my own here, is that the pursuit of knowledge is being harmed by the interaction of new reward systems (particularly the pressure for more grants and more publications) and old ways of doing science. In essence, Fanelli and Ioannidis are telling us that where these rewards and the pressures they unleash are the highest, the higher the amount of ever more erroneous research is likely to be.

But rather than simply a matter for the science of obesity, these findings are relevant for all of us who study the body and physical culture, particularly those who study it most 'productively'. The cultural problems with obesity research are acute and, as I have argued, partly a product of its particular subject matter. That obesity has been hailed as a global crisis and has attracted the eye of research funding bodies the world over has also added fuel to that particular fire. But obesity research's problems are all our problems and any consideration of the quality of the work we do, whether physical or social science, cannot be divorced from the academic cultures in which it is produced.

References

American Medical Association. 2013. AMA adopts new policies on second day of voting at annual meeting. Available from www.ama-assn.org/ama/pub/news/news/2013/2013-06-18-new-ama-policies-annual-meeting.page (accessed 24 August 2015).

Andres, R., Elahi, D., Tobin, J. D., Muller, D. C. and Brant, L. 1985. Impact of age on weight goals. *Annals of Internal Medicine*, 103 (6, Part 2), 1030–1033.

Atkinson, R. L. 2014. Current status of the field of obesity. *Trends in Endocrinology and Metabolism*, 25 (6), 283–284.

Begley, C. G. and Ellis, L. M. 2012. Drug development: raise standards for preclinical cancer research. *Nature*, 483 (7391), 531–533.

Chiu, M., Austin, P. C., Manuel, D. G., Shah, B. R. and Tu, J. V. 2011. Deriving ethnic-specific BMI cutoff points for assessing diabetes risk. *Diabetes Care*, 34 (8), 1741–1748.

Datar, A. and Sturm, R. 2004. Physical education in elementary school and body mass index: evidence from the Early Childhood Longitudinal Study. *American Journal of Public Health*, 94 (9), 1501–1506.

Dawson, A. 2014. Information, choice and the ends of health promotion. *Monash Bioethics Review*, 32 (1–2), 106–120.

Deurenberg, P. 2001. Universal cut-off BMI points for obesity are not appropriate. *British Journal of Nutrition*, 85 (2), 135–136.

Deurenberg, P. and Deurenberg-Yap, M. 2003. Validity of body composition methods across ethnic population groups. *Acta Diabetologica*, 40 (1), S246–S249.

Dhurandhar, N. V., Schoeller, D., Brown, A. W., Heymsfield, S. B., Thomas, D., Sørensen, T. I. A., Speakman, J. R., Jeansonne, M., Allison, D. B. and the Energy Balance Measurement Working Group. 2015. Energy balance measurement: when something is not better than nothing. *International Journal of Obesity*, 39 (7), 1109–1113.

Dishman, R. K., Washburn, R. A. and Schoeller, D. A. 2001. Measurement of physical activity. *Quest*, 53 (3), 295–309.

Dubbert, P. M., Carithers, T., Sumner, A. E., Barbour, K. A., Clark, B. L., Hall, J. E. and Crook, E. D. 2002. Obesity, physical inactivity, and risk for cardiovascular disease. *The American Journal of the Medical Sciences*, 324 (3), 116–126.

Fanelli, D. and Ioannidis, J. P. 2013. US studies may overestimate effect sizes in softer research. *Proceedings of the National Academy of Sciences*, 110 (37), 15,031–15,036.

Flegal, K. M., Graubard, B. I., Williamson, D. F. and Gail, M. H. 2007. Cause-specific excess deaths associated with underweight, overweight, and obesity. *Journal of the American Medical Association*, 298 (17), 2028–2037.

Freedman, D. S. and Sherry, B. 2009. The validity of BMI as an indicator of body fatness and risk among children. *Pediatrics*, 124 (Supplement 1), S23–S34.

Freedman, D. S., Khan, L. K., Dietz, W. H., Srinivasan, S. R. and Berenson, G. S. 2001. Relationship of childhood obesity to coronary heart disease risk factors in adulthood: the Bogalusa Heart Study. *Pediatrics*, 108 (3), 712–718.

Gard, M. 2011. *The end of the obesity epidemic*. London: Routledge.

Gard, M. and Pluim, C. 2014. *Schools and public health: Past, present, future*. Lanham, MD: Lexington Books.

Gard, M. and J. Wright. 2005. *The obesity epidemic: Science, morality and ideology*. London: Routledge.

Garner, D. M. and Wooley, S. C. 1991. Confronting the failure of behavioral and dietary treatments for obesity. *Clinical Psychology Review*, 11 (6), 729–780.

Hebert, J. R., Allison, D. B., Archer, E., Lavie, C. J. and Blair, S. N. 2013. Scientific decision making, policy decisions, and the obesity pandemic. *Mayo Clinic Proceedings*, 88 (6), 593–604.

Hesketh, K. D. and Campbell, K. J. 2010. Interventions to prevent obesity in 0–5 year olds: an updated systematic review of the literature. *Obesity*, 18 (S1), S27–S35.

Hodge, J. G., Barrazza, L., Russo, S., Nelson, K. and Measer, G. 2014. A proposed ban on the sale to and possession of caloric sweetened beverages by minors in public. *Journal of Law, Medicine and Ethics*, 42 (1), 110–114.

Howard, S., Adams, J. and White, M. 2012. Nutritional content of supermarket ready meals and recipes by television chefs in the United Kingdom: cross sectional study. *British Medical Journal* 345, e7607, doi:10.1136/bmj.e7607.

Ioannidis, J. P. A. 2005. Why most published research findings are false. *PLoS Medicine*, 2 (8), e124.

Ioannidis, J. P. A. 2014. How to make more published research true. *PLoS Medicine*, 11 (10), e1001747.

Karasu, S. R. 2016. The obesities: an overview of convergent and divergent paradigms. *American Journal of Lifestyle Medicine*, 10 (2), 84–96.

Keys, A., Fidanza, F., Karvonen, M. J., Kimura, N. and Taylor, H. L. 1972. Indices of relative weight and obesity. *Journal of Chronic Diseases*, 25 (6), 329–343.

Mauro, M., Taylor, V., Wharton, S. and Sharma, A. M. 2008. Barriers to obesity treatment. *European Journal of Internal Medicine*, 19 (3), 173–180.

McAllister, E. J., Dhurandhar, N. V., Keith, S. W., Aronne, L. J., Barger, J., Baskin, M., Benca, R. M., Biggio, J., Boggiano, M. M., Eisenmann, J. C., Elobeid, M., Fontaine, K. R., Gluckman, P., Hanlon, E. C., Katzmarzyk, P., Pietrobelli, A., Redden, D. T., Ruden, D. M., Wang, C., Waterland, R. A., Wright, S. M. and Allison, D. B. 2009. Ten putative contributors to the obesity epidemic. *Critical Reviews in Food Science and Nutrition*, 49 (10), 868–913.

Nevill, A. M., Stewart, A. D., Olds, T. and Holder, R. 2006. Relationship between adiposity and body size reveals limitations of BMI. *American Journal of Physical Anthropology*, 129 (1), 151–156.

Sacks, G., Swinburn, B. and Lawrence, M. 2009. Obesity Policy Action framework and analysis grids for a comprehensive policy approach to reducing obesity. *Obesity Reviews*, 10 (1), 76–86.

Tremblay, M. 2004. The need for directly measured health data in Canada. *Canadian Journal of Public Health*, 95 (3), 165–166.

Westerterp, K. R. 1999. Assessment of physical activity level in relation to obesity: current evidence and research issues. *Medicine and Science in Sports and Exercise*, 31 (11 (suppl)), S522–S525.

24
MEDIATED AND COMMODIFIED BODIES

David Rowe

Introduction: the imaged body for sale

The body has always been central to sport, but it is also constantly being reconfigured and repurposed through a range of interconnected processes. This chapter is concerned with two of those processes – mediation and commodification – that relentlessly work on and, to a significant degree, problematize the sporting body. The term 'mediation' is used here to describe how the diverse elements of the social world become meaningful through various media and their symbolic representations. This is not a neutral process of translation, but one that is produced out of the power relations that enable some ways of interpreting the world to dominate others – that is, those that are 'hegemonic' (Rowe, 2004a). Furthermore, the body can be regarded not just as *mediated* (symbolically represented in certain ways as, for example, gendered, sexualized and racialized) but, in fact, *mediatized* (Frandsen, 2014). The latter is a process by which the constituents of society and culture – in this case, bodies and the processes that encircle them – are transformed 'into forms or formats suitable for media representation' (Couldry, 2008: 376). This chapter will focus on the wider process of mediation, although it is recognized that there is also considerable evidence of mediatization.

To describe the sporting body as 'commodified' is similarly transformative. It does not mean that the bodies of athletes are used in the practice of paid labour in precisely the same way as, for example, factory workers, farm labourers or nightclub bouncers. The commodification of the sporting body occurs when what was once used (in pre-industrial, pre-capitalist times) for the purposes of fun and ritual is now deployed not only in remunerated athletic labour, but can be bought and sold by clubs, corporations, entrepreneurs, and even by governments, while its image is used to sell itself and other goods and services. Thus, it is important to appreciate that the mediated and commodified sporting body is not merely captured and displayed in various ways for profit, but also changed in ways that blur the boundaries between the physical and the immaterial. The sporting body is also heavily institutionalized – being both disciplined by sports organizations and their rules and (re-)presented by formal media organizations – but it also necessarily strains against institutional control. So-called lifestyle and extreme sports have resisted in various ways institutional sport's rule governance and performativity (Wheaton, 2013), while both athletes and fans have sought to circumvent institutional media gatekeeping through direct communication via the internet and social media. Multiple struggles for control over the sporting body occur, including those relating to privacy, image rights, remuneration, exploitation and return on private and public investment. This contestation is over corporeal conduct, meaning and value, the analysis and historically informed understanding of which is central to the multiple perspectives and mixed methods of physical cultural studies.

Body control

Sport as a leisure practice was once located primarily in the realm of free, playful physical culture, where the body adopts the loosely agreed rules, postures and movements that frame various forms of 'folk' sport contest. In capitalist modernity, though, sport has been increasingly characterized as the taking of human (and in cases such as horse-racing, non-human) bodies and subjecting them to increasingly rationalized, regulated and competitively oriented physical play. This does not mean that contemporary sport is inherently unpleasurable – men and women throughout the world voluntarily engage in sport at levels that range from the casual to the determinedly serious. Compulsory sport for the unwilling is decidedly not a pleasure, as has been the experience of those subjected to it at school as part of a programme of physical and moral fitness (Miller, 2001). Sport within formal educational institutions and for pleasure has an economic dimension – sportswear and equipment must be purchased, and land reserved, shaped and prepared – but the spirit of *amateurism* (which is etymologically derived from the Latin *amare*, meaning 'to love') in some respects is inconsistent with the idea of being paid to play. The amateur sporting body does not have high exchange value, because unremunerated sport is ostensibly pursued for its own sake or for some higher purpose. The investment here is primarily ideological, such as through the state's use of the sport team as a model for the disciplined citizen–worker, or mythological, as with peak sports organizations' construction of a sporting world that transcends quotidian struggle for the means of life.

However, not all have been enamoured of amateur sport. As it became more institutionally established and bodies more athletically skilled, sport attracted co-present audiences, at which point it could be asked why, if attendees of other cultural spaces such as theatres and concert halls paid for admission, could not sport do the same? Similarly, its more adept and celebrated participants wondered why they could not be compensated for lost earnings and time (including through injury) for their bodily expertise, or even to make a partial or full living from its exploitation. There was also no shortage of entrepreneurs willing to use sports gatherings to supply goods and services to those present. This burgeoning industrialization of sport (Clarke and Critcher, 1985) inevitably eroded its amateur ethos, enabling the progressive enclosure of sports grounds, stadium building, charging for attendance, payment of sportspeople, extension of competition through leagues and tournaments, professionalization of a mobile sports labour force, and so on – in other words, all the constituents of readily recognizable modern capitalist sport.

This intensified valorization of the sporting body led inexorably to its commodification. Sport clubs could exchange athletes for profit as part of a transfer system where every player had their value, inevitably attenuating local ties and loyalties. While many sports (such as association football, tennis, rugby union and cricket) were governed by a neo-feudal order that made it very difficult for sportspeople to maximize their earnings, the most prominent athletes increasingly used their market value to wrest more of the growing revenue from sport from its owners and controllers. This did not mean a 'level playing field' for athlete workers – as sport's celebrity system developed, so did its inequality of rewards. But the possibilities of exploiting and commodifying the body were limited as long as sport's economy and culture remained space-based and required the bodies of the audiences to go to the same place as the sport bodies were performing.

Newspapers and magazines could carry photographic image and text about sport to their homes. Later, they could hear about it (including 'live' commentary) on radio or go to cinemas to see highlights of filmed sport contests in newsreels. But when sport on television entered most homes, the commodified sport body became highly mediated, thereby reinforcing its commodification in ways that prompted even more thoroughgoing mediation in an ascending spiral of sport labour value and cultural visibility (Rowe, 2004b). After the introduction of television, and especially with the inception of satellite broadcasting, the sporting body became available to many people in the world to view, most of whom would never share the same physical location as their sports idols. A physical cultural studies approach, therefore, must attend closely to the ways in which the sporting body can become substantially disembedded from its origins in spatially and demographically concentrated communities, and its valorization vastly enhanced by extending the spectatorial possibilities of performance through mediation, in some cases on a global scale.

Mediating the sporting body

The mediated sporting body is much more 'saleable' than the elemental form that performs before the 'naked eyes' of co-present spectators. Of course, this does not mean that its physical performance becomes irrelevant – indeed, it massively intensifies the surveillance and minute inspection of the body in motion. Mediation enabled a 'second wave' of commodification of the sporting body that made it the notional property of anyone with access to still and, especially, moving images of it. Initially, as noted above, the economy of sport revolved around enclosed stadiums, paying customers, local sponsors, hospitality, betting, and sport-associated print advertising. Remarkably in retrospect there was some reluctance to allow television to capture and relay performing sport bodies for fear of deterring co-present spectators. However, once it became clear that major sport contests could function as a means of attracting and holding vast, dispersed audiences for exposure to advertising (Whannel, 1992), the major paying customer became the purchaser of sport broadcast rights. The stadium was then transformed into the equivalent of a 'live' film set, with both sportspeople and crowds 'acting' in front of distant viewers.

Once sport on screen had been fully commodified – not least after free-to-air public service or advertising-dependent television had been supplemented (and often supplanted) by subscription television, which then produced paying viewers – the bodies of both sport players and crowds were enlisted in the production of commercial sport spectacle. Without the on-screen drama of the sport crowd generating the requisite atmosphere, sport events can appear lifeless and even bizarre. The bodies of the co-present crowd – colourfully dressed in the merchandise of rival nations and teams, displaying sponsors' logos, cheering, booing, chanting, gesturing, swaying, waving banners, expressing deep emotions, and even engaging in verbal abuse and violence – are in some sense commodified without being paid because the most expensively purchased television sport demands the spectacle of the 'sell-out' crowd. At the same time, performing sports bodies are paid to play and display, with large leisure and sportswear brands like Nike and Adidas intimately involved in their presentation in ways that maximize their sign value.

The commodified sporting body, therefore, while it must have (either currently, in the past or in prospect) a demonstrable capacity to do something physically notable in the domain of sport, cannot be 'de-commodified' off the field of play. The process of mediation has produced a celebritized sporting body that is at least notionally available at all times. These off-field duties usually mean wearing appropriately endorsed corporate brands, including those, such as watches or cars, which usually have little direct relationship with sport. At the very least, they mean *not* displaying or using unendorsed rival branded products. Thus, the disciplining of the contemporary commodified and mediated sporting body is as much semiotic and economic as it is physical, its training requiring much more than the refinement of athletic skill and the enhancement of fitness. Physical cultural studies, therefore, should appreciate the ways in which physical conditioning of the sporting body is analogous to its preparation for mediation and commodification. Long before it becomes quasi-public property, the sporting body is subjected to often-tortuous regimes of training, diet, and sometimes-traumatic collisions that make something of a mockery of compulsively repeated claims that the principal rationale for sport is bodily integrity, preservation and improvement. It is not uncommon for it to absorb performance-enhancing substances, many of them dangerous (Beamish, 2011), acquiring an exchange value that constantly redoubles as, paradoxically, it symbolically travels far beyond the actual human subject that it 'houses'. Mediation and commodification are processes with few clear constraints – their governing logics (as influentially addressed by Altheide and Snow, 1979 in relation to the media) appear to be an absence of any logic other than to expand. So, in the light of this necessarily abstract theoretical and historical foundation, how can actual mediated and commodified bodies be analysed in the context of the intellectual agenda of physical cultural studies?

Reading the sporting body

Sporting bodies generally achieve elite status when they are engaged in high performance sport under the gaze of large co-present and mediated audiences. Not all of them are commodified to a substantial extent – for example, Olympic athletes in less 'glamorous' sports such as archery, fencing and trampoline. Nor are they consistently mediated, often receiving extensive media coverage at intermittently staged large tournaments but virtually ignored by the media in between them, with many Olympians quickly forgotten by those who watched them perform with great interest at a Games via television. The sporting bodies with the highest commodity value are, in broad terms, the most visible. This conspicuity involves a range of sites, including the field of play, advertisements, merchandising, sponsor appearances, and media gossip pages. Such consistent and widespread exposure is indispensable to sporting stardom and celebrity. Although these concepts are often used interchangeably, they are not exactly synonymous. It is not necessary or desirable here to rehearse well-known arguments about how stars and celebrities are made, or to analyse value-based assessments of their contribution to culture and society (Rojek, 2012). But it is useful to suggest that, at least in the domain of sport, there are many more stars than celebrities (or, to put it another way, only a few people who play sport at an elite level qualify as both). The appellation 'sport star' is routinely attached to almost any moderately functioning professional sportsperson (especially sports*men*).

But the fame of a sport celebrity travels far beyond the world of sport and even to those who do not care for or know much about the person in question. This sporting celebrity is a product of the mediation of the sporting body, the image of which is projected across and between whole societies and may even be described as global. Superlative sporting performance is not essential to becoming a sports celebrity, although it can clearly help. The mediated sporting body becomes significantly detached from its physical origins, and transition to sports celebrity status means that a process of 'hypercommodification' takes place by which the body's exchange value increasingly lies in its omnipresent, multi-form image. Its shelf life can, therefore, be extended far beyond that of the usually short elite sport-playing career and its image sold in markets that have little or nothing to do with sport.

A pivotal example of this process is that of the now-retired English footballer David Beckham (Cashmore, 2004). As is well documented, Beckham's is initially the familiar tale of a boy of humble origins devoting his life to sport at an early age. Instead of becoming a tradesperson like his father, Beckham left the family home in suburban London in seeking to be signed by the leading club Manchester United. Unlike most aspiring professional footballers he went on to be a senior player and to have a remarkable career, captaining his country on 59 occasions and playing for the glamorous Real Madrid, AC Milan and Paris St Germain clubs. But while there is no doubt that Beckham was a footballer of uncommon ability – although he was seldom regarded as the best player of his generation – his corporeal performance on the pitch alone could not deliver him the status of global celebrity. Beckham's early attention to style – most notably in haircuts, tattoos, designer watches and clothes – meant that his image became familiar to those who were not close followers of football. When he met, 'courted' and then married a member of a famous pop group (Victoria 'Posh Spice' Adams who, as Victoria Beckham, went on to make a mark in another key area of the image economy – fashion), the mediation of Beckham (and so his commodification) reached extraordinary heights. The butt of jokes about his cognitive and speech abilities, Beckham's highly sexualized appearance in Emporium Armani underwear advertisements, and as a model for the company's sophisticated dress suits, foregrounded the exchange value of his body in a manner that tended to replicate class-based notions that cognitive and physical competence are incompatible for those of humble origins (Hargreaves, 1986).

In David Beckham's case, he could be reduced to his bodily disposition by activating structures of social class (his skilled manual working-class origin) and masculinity (the form of maleness associated with team-based, contact sport). Both, though, are complicated by the 'metrosexual' aspects of his presentation of self, which introduced the power dimensions surrounding sexuality and, specifically, homosexuality (Coad, 2008). Still other social variables of embodiment can be brought more repressively to bear in the domain of sport. The bodies of black sportsmen such as boxers Jack Johnson and Mike Tyson or basketballers Dennis Rodman and LeBron James invoke hegemonic discourses of 'race' which redouble the hierarchization of the mind-body dualism (Carrington, 2010; van Sterkenburg, 2011). When the racialized female sports body is, in turn, brought into the frame in instances such as tennis player Serena Williams and Olympian hurdler Lolo Jones (Adjepong and Carrington, 2014), the corporeal politics of sport is further exposed. Here the sexualization of sportswomen as, alternatively, masculinized (and so implicitly or explicitly lesbian) or hyper-heterosexual feminized, is overlaid with a racist reduction of black women to their sexual status.

Such sexualized mediation also problematizes precisely what constitutes a sporting body – does it have to be that of a well-credentialled athlete, and/or does it have to be active when captured? For example, the weekly US magazine *Sports Illustrated* has published a big-selling (with claimed sales of 18 million) swimsuit issue since 1964 featuring women who are predominantly models rather than athletes. Their bodies have become associated with sport as a consequence of being in a sport media site, and sometimes in the context of sporting accoutrements, such as equipment and venues. This so-called 'celebration of the female form' – in the absence of a corresponding presentation of the male form in decorative swimming attire and sexualized pose – involves a commodification of a *faux* sporting body through mediation alone. This point is made clearer in the light of the under-representation of women on the all-important cover of the magazine. As Weber and Carini have found on the basis of their content analysis research (which excluded the swimsuit issue):

> From 2000 through June 2011, there were 716 opportunities to depict a figure (or figures) from the sports world on the cover of *SI*. Women appeared on only 4.9 percent of covers, a representation similar to that found by Salwen and Wood (1994) from 1987 to 1989.
>
> (Weber and Carini, 2013: 199)

The female body in this influential media sport publication is less associated with that of a sportswoman than of a beauty/fashion model, despite criticisms from many academics and journalists (for example, Barkhorn, 2011; Ford, 2015; Kim, Sagas and Walker, 2013). An obvious way, then, of making the female sporting body more valuable beyond the sporting stadium is to present it as that of a glamour model. As Kim, Sagas and Walker (2013: 161) report of their content analysis of the *Sports Illustrated Swimsuit Issues* between 1997 and 2009, an increasing use after 1997 of female athlete models – women who had a claim to be in the magazine on their athletic merits but who were carefully made up to look like conventionally beautiful professional models – did not downplay women's sexual objectification, but instead '*Sports Illustrated* alternates athleticism with sexuality by continuously placing female athlete models [unlike the sportsmen who appeared in the same issue] in positions that are unrelated to sport'.

Thus, while men rarely appeared alone or in a directly sexualized position in relation to the camera, female athlete models frequently did so in fashion photo-spread style. But they were also increasingly supplemented by players' wives, dancers and cheerleaders (ibid.: 155). While these women all have relationships to sport and to athletes, their bodies are not instruments for the performance of sport. In strict labour market terms, therefore, they are competitors with sportswomen in the sphere of sign value. It is not surprising, therefore, that some sportswomen have taken the logic of sexually focused commodification and mediatization to the limit – as in the case of retired Russian tennis player Anna Kournikova and, in a group context, the nude calendars of sportswomen that proliferated in the last decade of the twentieth century (Mikosza and Phillips, 1999). These brief examples – many more could have been cited – reveal that commodification and mediatization are not blind or arbitrary processes, but are profoundly shaped by wider socio-cultural forces. In this instance, the stubborn masculine domination of sport, itself carried over from other institutional settings (not least the family and the workplace) and circulated across the media sports cultural complex (Rowe, 2004b), consistently reproduces forms of commodification and mediatization of sportswomen that privilege feminine sexuality over athletic excellence. Physical cultural studies can make sense of these processes in a range of ways, encompassing political economic approaches and the sociologies of class, 'race', gender and so on, and the repertoire of methods familiar to media studies, including quantitative content analysis enriched by critical discourse analysis and qualitative approaches including interview, focus and qualitative method that shift the focus from production and text to audiences (see, for example, Millington and Wilson, 2012).

Other 'intersectional' phenomena, such as ableism (Gilbert and Schantz, 2008) and ageism (Gibson and Singleton, 2012), are important factors in the commodified and mediated cultural economy of sport. Both are highlighted in the vast differences between the commercial value of broadcast rights for the Summer and Winter Olympics compared with the Paralympics or World Masters Games. Although sport is routinely advocated in terms of broadly pro-social values such as recreation and health, there has been a progressive separation between highly valued athletic bodies whose performance and image can be easily packaged for dedicated and incidental audiences, and those that are less instantly marketable because they do not conform to ready-made images of the beautiful and the youthful. There are exceptions to this rule, and it is useful to consider one instance of a Paralympian who crossed the 'ableist divide' only to become the source of one of sport's most notorious (and tragic) scandals. The champion Paralympian South African sprinter Oscar Pistorius, who acquired the nickname of the 'Blade Runner' on account of his prosthetic lower limbs (having been born without fibula), became world-renowned after qualifying to compete in elite able-bodied events (the 2011 World Championships in Athletics and 2012 London Olympics). There was widespread interest in Pistorius's athletic body and its use of advanced technology, including disputes over whether his prosthetics gave him an advantage over athletes who only had their congenital lower limbs at their disposal. Therefore, Pistorius became the world's best-known and most marketable Paralympian on the grounds of athletic excellence, pioneering movement into mega media able-bodied competition, conventional good looks, and a capacity to engender news coverage over his use of officially approved (although sometimes criticized) prosthetic technology (Carlin, 2014).

The move to the able-bodied global sport world created the opportunity for Pistorius, whose congenital absence of the fibula in both legs would usually have impeded his capacity to become affluent through sport performance, to become both more visible through the media and to generate greater corporeal commodity value. He acquired lucrative sponsorship and endorsement contracts with companies such as the Össur orthopaedics company, Oakley sunglasses and Nike leisurewear. But the case of Pistorius reveals how mediation can, in some instances, undermine commodification. When on St Valentine's Day 2013 he shot his girlfriend Reeva Steenkamp, claiming that he believed her to be an intruder, there followed a trial that received enormous media coverage and culminated in a five-year custodial sentence for culpable homicide the following year. A South African media monitoring service subsequently reported that, 'worldwide the Oscar trial is bigger in media than the FIFA 2014 World Cup' (*City Press*, 2014; although this was in the lead-up to the event in Brazil). This media coverage of the wrong kind led to the cancellation of sponsorships and advertisements involving Pistorius (including Nike's) as the corporations who once saw advantages in association with the sport celebrity's brand severed links in order to avoid damage to their own brands. Mediated scandals of varying seriousness, ranging from the death occasioned by Pistorius; spousal violence as in the case of American footballer Ray Rice; use of performance-enhancing drugs by Lance Armstrong, or serial philandering by Tiger Woods, all diminish the value of the sportsperson as commodity.

While their image may be partially rehabilitated and a narrative of rise, fall and rise can restore some of their branded sign value, the ease with which information about sport celebrities' crimes and misdemeanours can be globally recirculated via the media acts as a constant check on their return to esteemed pre-scandal status. In many cases it is off-field conduct that undermines present or past celebrated sporting performances. While mediation of the sporting body is indispensable to its advanced commodification, ironically it is that same process of mediation that can strip it of substantial commodity value.

Conclusion: the way of all sporting flesh

In November 2014, Australian cricketer Phillip Hughes was struck in the neck by a ball while batting and never recovered consciousness. Massive displays of public grief and media coverage in Australia and across the world followed, including tributes at English Premier League football and international rugby matches and, most poignantly, through the globally 'trending' hashtag #putoutyourbats. Even the Google landing page, which carefully rations content other than its brand, displayed the #putoutyourbats image of a lone cricket bat leaning against a wall (Rowe, 2014). Hughes's was not the only death in cricket that year nor in sport in general –

for example, there were many in horse racing. But genuine tragedy in sport (as opposed to those routinely described by excitable commentators when a failure of performance occurs) is its *memento mori* (reminder of mortality) – that is, for all the multiple imaging and the media's manipulation of time and space, there are ultimately actual human bodies involved that, despite their extraordinary attributes, are vulnerable and fragile. But, of course, even in death the linked processes of mediation and commodification do not simply stop – indeed, they may be enhanced. The death of a sportsperson, especially on the field of play, creates (if audio-visually recorded) the opportunity repeatedly to watch the fatal moment, and from many angles and speeds in the same manner as conventional sporting action. Furthermore, after a 'decent' lapse of time, commercial opportunities emerge for commemorative merchandising and sale of personal sporting paraphernalia, which becomes (as with gallery art) scarcer and more valuable because of premature death.

The sporting life cycle is produced out of this combination of the living, the imagined and the immaterial. If the corporeal element were to be lost in its entirety it could no longer be classified unproblematically as sport *per se*. For this reason, *pace* some arguments that the brain is a muscle involved in 'mind sports', card games such as bridge struggle for official recognition as *bona fide* sports (Cooper, 2015). Nonetheless, the 'bare, forked animal' (as the human being is described in Shakespeare's *King Lear*) is, as noted, often overshadowed and rendered almost non- or trans-human by the media apparatus of contemporary sport. Various forms of pharmacological and technological enhancement of the sporting body (Miah, 2010) problematize even more the nature of the human, its relationship to mediation, and the ethics of corporeal commodification. Like sport itself, physical cultural studies returns constantly to a focus on the body and subjects it to close scrutiny in a quest to divine its secrets. But equally, it must grasp how strange and remote the body becomes when re-fashioned by the forces of sporting mediation and commodification.

References

Adjepong, L. A. and Carrington, C. 2014. Black female athletes as space invaders. In J. Hargreaves and E. Anderson (eds), *Routledge handbook of sport, gender and sexuality*. New York: Routledge, 169–178.

Altheide, D. L. and Snow, R. P. 1979. *Media logics*. Thousand Oaks, CA: Sage.

Andrews, D. L. and Jackson, S. J. (eds). 2001. *Sport stars: the cultural politics of sporting celebrity*. New York: Routledge.

Barkhorn, E. 2011. 9 ways women get on the cover of *Sports Illustrated*. *The Atlantic*, 20 July, www.theatlantic.com/entertainment/archive/2011/07/9-ways-women-get-on-the-cover-of-sports-illustrated/242251 (accessed 7 March, 2015).

Beamish, R. 2011. *Steroids: a new look at performance-enhancing drugs*. Santa Barbara, CA: Praeger.

Carlin, J. 2014. *Chase your shadow: the trials of Oscar Pistorius*. London: Atlantic.

Carrington, B. 2010. *Race, sport and politics: the sporting black diaspora*. London: Sage.

Cashmore, E. 2004. *Beckham*, 2nd edn. Cambridge: Polity Press.

City Press. 2014. Oscar Pistorius trial bigger than World Cup, 11 March, www.citypress.co.za/news/oscar-pistorius-trial-bigger-world-cup (accessed 29 April, 2015).

Clarke, J. and Critcher, C. 1985. *The devil makes work: leisure in capitalist Britain*. London: Macmillan.

Coad, D. 2008. *The metrosexual: gender, sexuality, and sport*. Albany, NY: State University of New York Press.

Cooper, C. 2015. Bridge – a bid too far? The game's advocates want it classed as a sport. *The Independent*, 2 May, www.independent.co.uk/sport/general/others/bridge—a-bid-too-far-the-games-advocates-want-it-classed-as-a-sport-10221710.html (accessed 2 May 2015).

Couldry, N. 2008. Mediatization or mediation? Alternative understandings of the emergent space of digital storytelling. *New Media and Society*, 10(3), 373–391.

Ford, C. 2015. Stop turning Robyn Lawley into a symbol of diversity. *Daily Life*, 11 February, www.dailylife.com.au/news-and-views/dl-opinion/stop-turning-robyn-lawley-into-a-symbol-of-diversity-20150211-13b9ut.html (accessed 7 March 2015).

Frandsen, K. 2014. Mediatization of sports. In K. Lundby (ed.), *Mediatization of communication*. Berlin: Mouton de De Gruyter, 525–546.

Gibson, H. J. and Singleton, J. F. (eds). 2012. *Leisure and ageing: theory and practice*. Champaign, IL: Human Kinetics.

Gilbert, K. and Schantz, O. J. (eds). 2008. *The Paralympic Games: empowerment or side show?* Maidenhead: Meyer & Meyer.

Hargreaves, J. E. 1986. *Sport, power and culture: a social and historical analysis of popular sports in Britain*. Cambridge: Polity.

Kim, K., Sagas, M. and Walker, N. A. 2013. Replacing athleticism with sexuality: athlete models in *Sports Illustrated* swimsuit issues. *International Journal of Sport Communication*, 4(2), 148–162.

Miah, A. 2010. Towards the transhuman athlete: therapy, non-therapy and enhancement. *Sport in Society*, 13(2), 221–233.

Mikosza, J. M. and Phillips, M. G. 1999. Gender, sport and the body politic: framing femininity in the *Golden Girls of Sport* calendar and the *Atlanta Dream*. *International Review for the Sociology of Sport*, 34(1), 5–16.

Miller, T. 2001. *Sportsex*. Philadelphia, PA: Temple University Press.

Millington, B. and Wilson, B. 2012. Media analysis in physical cultural studies: from production to reception. In K. Young and M. Atkinson (eds), *Qualitative research on sport and physical culture*. Bingley: Emerald, 129–150.

Rojek, C. 2012. *Fame attack: the inflation of celebrity and its consequences*. London: Bloomsbury Academic.

Rowe, D. 2004a. Antonio Gramsci: sport, hegemony and the national-popular. In R. Giulianotti (ed.), *Sport and modern social theorists*. Basingstoke: Macmillan, 97–110.

Rowe, D. 2004b. *Sport, culture and the media: the unruly trinity*, 2nd edn. Maidenhead: Open University Press.

Rowe, D. 2014. After Phillip Hughes' death, it's time for a post-traumatic Test. *The Conversation*, 9 December, https://theconversation.com/after-phillip-hughes-death-its-time-for-a-post-traumatic-test-34971 (accessed 7 March, 2015).

Salwen, M. B. and Wood, N. 1994. Depictions of female athletes on *Sports Illustrated* covers, 1957–1989. *Journal of Sport Behavior*, 17, 98–107.

Van Sterkenburg, J. 2011. *Race, ethnicity and the sport media*. Amsterdam: Pallas.

Weber, J. D. and Carini, R. M. 2013. Where are the female athletes in *Sports Illustrated*? A content analysis of covers (2000–2011). *International Review for the Sociology of Sport*, 48(2), 196–203.

Whannel, G. 1992. *Fields in vision: television sport and cultural transformation*. London: Routledge.

Wheaton, B. 2013. *The cultural politics of lifestyle sports*. London: Routledge.

25
SPECTACULAR AND EROTICIZED BODIES

Toby Miller

Introduction

Across the past three decades, sport has transformed itself through the media into an internationalist capitalist project – and new pressures accompany the spoils. As part of the desire to address media spectators and capture their attention for advertisers, the sporting body has become an object of lyrical rhapsody and gendered money. It is up for grabs as a sexual icon. Sculpted features, chiseled waistelines, well-appointed curves, dreamy eyes, administered hair, and an air of casual threat are the currency of the day. And like beauty and fitness of all kinds, the years will attenuate them and the media will identify new names, new bodies, new Eros, new euros to take their places.

Sports and gender jumble together in a complex weave of commodification. They live cheek by capital, torso by Totti, boot by Beckham. The paradox of sport, its simultaneously transcendent and imprisoning qualities and capacity to allegorize, is most obvious, most dangerous, and perhaps most transformative when it comes to sex. With the advent of consumer capitalism and postmodern culture, the body has become an increasingly visible *locus* of desire. It's not just women who are objects of this gaze, not just women who are physically damaged in the interests of social expectations, and not just men who inspect the bodies of others for foibles and follicles.

The objectification of the male body is not universally welcome (Nelson, 2002; Weissman, 2010). But it compromises hitherto powerful assumptions about spectator sports. To explain such developments, physical cultural studies intersects with feminist and queer analyses in addition to Marxist political economy and media studies.

Any spectacle is potentially both pleasurable and dangerous, joyous and risky. The word implies something special, big, and uncertain. Just as a spectacular collision is harmful, a spectacular leap is exhilarating. Erotic experience is similar: the height of *jouissance* and the peril of exchange are mutually heightened in a spiral of bodily connection. All these contradictions and paradoxes are evident in the case of sporting bodies.

Such bodies are signs of free will, self-control, health, productivity, and transcendence – and their antonyms – in a very public way. As a consequence, there is an almost inevitable and chaotic oscillation between good and bad conduct among athletes, with dividing lines that are frequently unclear, or products of culture, time, and place rather than essence, eternity, and

Spectacular and eroticized bodies

ubiquity. So we see unstable binaries aplenty: high-performance dietary supplements versus illegal drugs; cultivated familial display in advertisements and clandestine exogamous affairs in private; professions of team or brand loyalty followed by identical and instant professions of cathexis onto other teams or products; days of devotion by contrast with nights of neglect. There are many other movements between and within the written and unwritten rules that distinguish good conduct from bad in the world of sporting spectacle. These topics are the stuff of physical cultural studies' concern with limit cases of subjectivity, those complex zones where the normal and the abnormal meet and mutually define one another through an uncomfortable *frottage*.

This chapter surveys some of the scholarly literature related to this tendency. For those readers who like to keep things relatively real as well as comfortably cloistered, to see things exemplified and applied, I also provide two short case studies. The first engages media coverage of a prominent Olympic swimmer coming out as gay. The second looks at the discourse surrounding women who are romantically involved with male sports stars.

Survey

Where did spectacular bodies start their association with sports? Norbert Elias investigated how European ruling classes and imperialist adventurers began globalizing sport in the sixteenth century, blending macrosociological and microsociological insights about class, nation, conduct, and fashion (Elias, 1978; Elias and Dunning, 1986).

Elias' disciples in sports studies focus, *inter alia*, on the spectacular body, focusing on discipline, mirroring, dominance, and communication (Maguire, 1993). The disciplined body is remodeled through diet and training; the mirroring body functions as a machine of desire, encouraging mimetic conduct via the purchase of commodities; the dominating body exercises power through physical force; and the communicative body is an expressive totality, balletic and beautiful, wracked and wrecked.

The media and fans frequently invest in these bodies as extensions of themselves – sites for playing out desire and anger. Hence the rage directed at the Australian rower Sally Robbins, who refused to perform towards the end of a 2004 Olympic race. The media criticized her, and public grief and anger erupted at this bizarre and unexplained negation of one's supposed duty as a citizen and patriot. Sporting trauma is not necessarily dealt with in the same way: when Canadian Ben Rutledge did the same thing in the next race, he was not berated, while content analysis shows that the British media respond to poor Olympic results with retribution, the Chinese with forgiveness, and the Russians with analysis (McKay and Roderick, 2010; Project for Excellence in Journalism, 2008).

They do share concerns with bodily passion and perfection. For its utility and unreliability alike mark it out for disappointment and excess as well as fulfillment and success. The athlete stands for the lifetime of sadness and happiness experienced by ordinary people, hysterically compressed into a star's career of dynamic highs and lows, followed by a descent into effective senility – at an age when others are still finding their way in life.

Umberto Eco explains the process like this:

> In an industrial society … where man becomes a number in the realm of the organization which has usurped his decision-making role, he has no means of production and is thus deprived of his power to decide. Individual strength, if not exerted in sports activities, is left abased when confronted with the strength of machines which determine man's very movements. In such a society the positive hero must embody

to an unthinkable degree the power demands that the average citizen nurtures but cannot satisfy.

(Eco, 1972: 14)

What was the old boy on about here? (Actually, he was only forty when he published this.) Eco was referring to the fantasy of secular transcendence, of surviving and thriving beyond the dross of the diurnal, the faff of the factory, the orality of the office. Sports stars embody and embrace spectacle as an exit from everyday *ennui*.

How does this happen, according to physical cultural studies? As key myths and symbols of gender, race, and happiness, sporting stars are reified by capitalistic, sexual, national, and governmental processes that fabricate personal qualities and social signs as resources for commerce, fantasy, art, and the state. In the process, they are transformed into models and celebrities, displacing the traditional role of royalty as symbols of status and exemplars of conduct. Sports stars form a labor aristocracy – people from working-class backgrounds who become fleetingly wealthy and famous at a young age, flickering as incendiary, mystificatory signs of a putative *bourgeois* mobility.

Thanks to the work of spectacle, we know almost too much about these stars, most notably what they look like *in extremis*: dirty, sweaty, teary, demoralized, undressed, furious, joyous, unguarded, unconscious, and otherwise diminished, injured, or exposed (like ourselves when vomiting or coming). Athletes' vulnerabilities and victories, tragedies and triumphs grow all too apparent as they are magnified with each replay and diagnosis, their gifts quickly undone, never to be wrapped again in the same pristine paper.

Athletes turn into celebrities of this kind when their social and private lives become as important as their professional qualities, providing stereotypes of success, power, and beauty through spectacle and sex. As figures of consumption and mimesis, they incarnate dramatic roles and fashions that index the limitations and promises of an age (Bueno, 2002). This tendency is subsidized and commodified – even governed – by tabloid media that draw in seemingly equal measure on celebration and condemnation, on press releases and *paparazzi*, as corporate photo shoots of big weddings are supplanted by unwanted candid shots of big waistlines. The lifestyle contractually favors beauty, reliability, and decency; but it finds those qualities hard to separate from ugliness, shock, and excess.

Corporate sponsors pay sizeable sums to associate their products with sports stars, attracted by the publicity afforded by celebrities. Such endorsements cost over a billion dollars a year in the US alone, based on a wager that audiences will seek to transfer fetishized qualities onto themselves by purchasing commodities associated with stars, through what marketing mavens call 'associative learning' (Till et al., 2008; Thrall et al., 2008).

The psy-function (psychology, psychoanalysis, and psychopharmacology) is by turns fascinated and horrified by the commercial potential and social impact of sports fans' contradictory relaxation, relief, arousal, aggression, entertainment, and identification. These venerable Aristotelian categories about drama are of course endowed today with the marvel of modern, scientific labels: the 'Sport Fan Motivation Scale' is in a battle to the death for scholarly hegemony with the 'Motivation Scale for Sport Consumption' to count them. Such research typically finds that men watch more media sport than women, are more animated by it, and are likelier to define themselves through it. The experience is deemed to be a means of experiencing closeness without profound intimacy (Sloan, 1989; Wann, 1995; Trail and James, 2001; Tang and Cooper, 2012; Arehart-Treichel, 2012).

There are culturalist as well as scientific versions of this mythology (Earnheardt et al., 2012; Markovits and Albertson, 2012; Weed, 2008; Benkwitz and Molnar, 2012). Critics deride cathectic responses onto celebrity athletes as evidence of pathological erotomania (McCutcheon et al., 2002), and studies of US TV sports fans indicate high correlations with support for imperialist warmongering, principally among white men (Stempel, 2006). These methods are some distance from physical cultural studies, though they touch on some core questions, especially as applied to gender.

Physical cultural studies is closer to a Marxist-feminist perspective, which suggests that athletes elicit desire by wooing consumers, glancing at them sexually and looking pretty in ways that are borrowed from romantic love but then reverse that relationship: people learn about romantic love from commodified humanity hyperextended beyond the norm. This is 'commodity aesthetics' (Haug, 1986), a complex mixture of marketing methods, social signs, and national emblems. Sports stars are understood within this perspective as products of capitalism and individualism and objects of personal and collective consumption – a necessarily unsteady relationship. Each tendency imbricates the public with the private and publicity with intimacy.

Such marketing has historically been targeted at men. For example, in the early 1990s, the Canadian beer company that owned The Sports Network (TSN) adopted 'We deliver the male' as its cable motto. In 1998, an advertisement for Disney's US equivalent, ESPN, promised 'More tackles, less tutus' (TSN quoted in Sparks, 1992: 330, 334; Broadcasting and Cable, 1998). During the same period, Australian women spectators felt excluded from TV's 'discourse of football' despite their pleasurable voyeurism at men playing the game (Poynton and Hartley, 1990: 144). And gay fans were present in increasing numbers but lacked media recognition (Klugman, 2015).

By the turn of the century, there was clearly a lack of fit between established marketers and emerging audiences. Commercial and cultural changes were exerting pressure on sport's gender normativity, weakening the seemingly rock-solid straight maleness at its core. Female US spectators had tuned to the Olympics in large numbers. The 1992 Winter Games drew 57 percent of its US TV audience from women. Women's figure skating out-rated that year's men's baseball World Series and National Collegiate Athletic Association basketball championship game. And the women's technical skating program at the 1994 Winter Games achieved the fourth-highest ratings in US history. In 1995, UK female spectators for Wimbledon on television outnumbered male, and the numbers were nearly equal for boxing. In the 1998 National Basketball Association (NBA) play-offs, more women were attracted to Game Seven than to *Veronica's Closet* (1997–2000) or *ER* (1994–2009) (Miller, 2001).

Meanwhile, male TV sports spectatorship in the US is in partial decline. The National Football League (NFL) saw 1998–1999 and 1999–2000 ratings for *Monday Night Football* at record lows – and a third of the audience was female. In 1999, more men aged 18–34 watched professional women's softball on ESPN2 than Arena football, the National Hockey League (NHL), or Major League Soccer. The NFL suffered a 13 percent decrease in TV ratings in the five seasons from 1997 and Disney exiled *Monday Night Football* from its broadcast network ABC to ESPN in 2006. The League increasingly relied for its survival on women, who made up perhaps 40 percent of the NFL audience by 2012; and women comprise half of ESPN's US viewers overall (Wenner and Gantz, 1998; Daddario, 1997; Miller, 2001, 2010; Oates, 2012; McBride, 2011).

The 2015 women's World Cup of football[1] attracted 1.35 million people to games and television coverage in 188 countries (Blatter, 2015). The Final drew more US TV viewers than any football match in history: 20.4 million spectators and a rating of 15.2. That was within touching distance or a margin for error of the Rose and Sugar Bowls and the NBA Championship game, and three times the number for the NHL finals. Fox benefited to the tune of US$26.8 million in advertising revenue over the tournament (Crupi, 2015; Campany, 2015).

Clearly, businesses with saturated 'natural' markets had settled on new objects of desire. Every major professional men's league in the US now has a women's media marketing plan. Hence ABC's coverage of Super Bowl 2000 featuring this from reporter Meredith Vieira: 'It is all about the butt' (Miller, 2001). TSN, which undertook to 'deliver the male' twenty-five years ago, now promises that 'Sponsorship programs on TSN.ca can be tailored to your target audience'.[2]

Of course, this is no utopic tale. The World Cup women of 2015 had to play on poor, even dangerous, pitches; opposing teams shared hotels; the President and Secretary-General of the Fédération Internationale de Football Association failed to attend; seeding was not based on success; and the prize money was 38.5 times less than for the men's competition (Campany, 2015). Meanwhile, in August 2015, Google offered 27,500 hits for 'Soccer is gay', a homophobic US remark about anything that escapes popular ken. Many of these sites attack the sexuality of football's players and followers (Mercado, 2008; though they also include *The Onion*'s parody of soccer coming out – see Onion, 2015).

Which is where we encounter our first case study.

Ian Thorpe

There is a historic identification of swimming with homoeroticism, as per young men frolicking naked in *The Swimming Hole*, a painting done by Thomas Eakins over 1884–1885, and Duncan Grant's 1911 work *Bathing* (LoveBrighton Blog, 2011). On the one hand, swimming is regarded as masculine because of its self-sufficiency and demand for fitness, strength, and skill. On the other, the sport's lack of violence marks it out from body-contact games (Miller, 2001; Stallings, 2012).

Elite male swimmers on television are outlined in form-hugging briefs or bodysuits, hair trimmed for minimal drag, lean, leggy, ducking, diving, turning, and speeding, seemingly oblivious to the gaze of others and even the actions of fellow-competitors. Bug-eyed in goggles, their muscles strain with each eruption from the water. Our vision of them is from a multitude of angles – warming up, swimming (seen from above and below the water), atop the podium in victory, and shivering in interviews.

The uncomfortable sense of the male body straining while almost naked can lead to some interesting practices of compensation in the media. The BBC advised its camera operators at the 1976 Olympic Games to capture swimmers' 'straight lines' in order to suggest 'strength, security, vitality and manliness,' rather than the 'grace and sweetness' of 'curved lines' (Peters, 1976).

And gay men in the pool? Bruce Hayes, a swimmer who won relay gold at the 1984 Olympics, became a key figure in a Levi Strauss campaign after coming out, but champion diver Greg Louganis lost sponsors when he did so, perhaps due to simultaneously announcing his HIV-positive status. And when Matthew Mitcham, one of ten out athletes from a total of ten thousand at the Beijing Games in 2008, won diving gold, NBC found itself unable to acknowledge his sexuality or the presence of his boyfriend in the stands (Miller, 2001; Louganis with Marcus, 2006; Billings et al., 2015: 146).

Enter Ian Thorpe, a hugely successful Australian swimmer and national hero, a winner of five Olympic gold medals who came out in 2014. The story drew major news coverage within and beyond the Anglosphere (McClymont and Bagshaw, 2014; Lallo, 2014; Dauphine, 2014; Herrera, 2014).

Thorpe is unpopular with some critics. The issues are money and courage. Finance's intrication with sex made his public declaration and its timing as much about mammon as men.

Thorpe was apparently warned prior to the 2000 Games about the financial impact on the Canadian swimmer Mark Tewksbury, who came out six years after winning the 1992 100-metre Olympic backstroke and lost a 'six-figure speaking contract' for being 'too openly gay' (McClymont and Bagshaw, 2014; Moore, 2006). The Australian stayed in the closet for over a decade.

That led to critique as well as embrace from many gay people when he came out (Holas, 2014). Thorpe also supposedly riled some colleagues. For when he resumed training post-retirement in the vain hope of selection for the 2012 Olympics, his fellow swimmers allegedly demanded that their governing body reveal the background to this comeback amid rumors of 'six-figure handshakes'. Swimming Australia was in a tight spot at the time, with ratings drooping and prime-time TV coverage at risk. If payments *were* made, they were presumably an investment in star power to regain media attention and boost revenues (Telegraph, 2012). A similar frenzy surrounded Thorpe's decision to come out on television (interviewed by lapsed British celebrity Michael Parkinson, with whom he shared an agent). The controversy was again to do with dollars, as the network that screened his revelation apparently agreed to hire Thorpe as a commentator for the 2014 Commonwealth Games as a *quid pro quo* (Lallo, 2014).

Wives and girlfriends

Let's now consider the most powerful yet derided form of female sports spectatorship: wives and girlfriends (WAGs). For while watching their national teams play in, most notably, the World Cup of men's football, spectators may have their attention drawn away from the 'beautiful game' *on* the pitch to beautiful people *off* the pitch – footballers' wives and girlfriends. Suddenly the spectacle is provided as much by other – albeit very special and privileged – audience members as their sporting *paramours*. That might provide certain viewers with welcome distractions from nil-nil draws, but critics ask: do they distract the footballers too?

The English media agonize over their men's national team. The two principal competitions it enters – the World Cup and the European Championships – are perennial disasters. The 2006 World Cup finals in Germany offered a new explanation. The press constructed WAGs as distractions from the players' mission: triumph on the pitch (Taipei Times, 2006). Shopping, sex, and celebrity supposedly sent the national team askew. Among hundreds of media stories that focused on WAG bodies and romantic histories, a favorite was the *Daily Star*'s guide for them on what to do during the Cup. It highlighted 'selfies, shopping and skinny mojitos' (Buchan, 2014). For the next World Cup finals, families were banned from training camp and could only join the team later if visits suited the side's schedule (Huffington Post, 2014).

England is not alone in such anxieties. Prior to the 2014 men's World Cup finals, several national teams issued policies limiting or proscribing heterosexual intercourse during the tournament (Graham, 2014):

- Mexico, Chile, and Bosnia and Herzegovina prohibited sexual activity by their national teams (Yahoo!, 2014; Magazine Monitor, 2014; Caamaño, 2014);
- Brazil and Mexico warned against overly frisky 'acrobatics' (Prensa, 2014);
- Spain demanded no funny business the night before matches – only on days off (Magazine Monitor, 2014); and
- Australia, France, and the US allowed varying degrees of action (Denholmes, 2014; Local, 2014; Bonesteel, 2014).

Why this focus on sex? The question leads to a much longer and more complex history than the one given by tabloid newspapers in their denunciations of WAGs or national associations' restrictions on them.

For example, Indian wrestling has long required men to forgo sex, the better to capitalize on the semen they produce (Alter, 1992). And with the emergence of sexology and internationally competitive sport in the twentieth century came scientific claims about sex and performance. Cyclists and swimmers ingested liquid extracts from bull testicles a hundred years ago, while the 1939 English Football Association Cup Final was allegedly decided on the strength of which team took monkey-gland tablets in training (the losers). And consider the mythology that still swirls around the 1974 men's World Cup final between the Netherlands and the then Federal Republic of Germany. The Dutch were supposedly instructed to have sex the night before. Having scored in the first minute (so to speak) they flagged. The Germans, ordered to abstain, triumphed, courtesy of two late goals (Miller, 2001).

Many great sporting achievements have supposedly followed nights of denial:

- Khalid Khannouchi's marathons;
- Muhammad Ali's fights;
- the 1996 Canadian Olympic swim team;
- Mike Ditka's Chicago Bears;
- John Elway's Super Bowl victories; and
- Carl Frosch's knockouts.

Readers may recall Robert De Niro pouring icy water into his underpants before a fight in *Raging Bull* (1980).

But such instances are contrasted with great performances that come hard on the heels of nocturnal indulgence:

- Wilt Chamberlain's hundred-point basketball game;
- Bob Beamon's Olympic long jump;
- Brazil's 1994 World Cup victory;
- Kerrin-Lee Gartner's Olympic skiing gold;
- Marty Liquori's mile record; and
- Joe Namath's Super Bowl success (Miller, 2001).

Pace these pleasurably fetishistic, gossipy anecdotes, the scientific evidence for a link between loving and losing versus chastity and success is sparse (McGlone and Shrier, 2000). The information we have is a blend of *macho* mysticism, media gossip, and minor scholarship.

Clearly, as long as women are routinely valued for their looks and the men they accompany, and conventionally devalued for other qualities, the WAG charade will come around every four years. One thing was always likely to occur in 2014, and duly came to pass: the World Cup ended in tears for England – perhaps private, orgasmic ones, perhaps endured/enjoyed alone or in company.

Conclusion

The capacity of sport to incarnate masculine hegemony has been destabilized. More and more women have become spectators and athletes, and over the past twenty years, sports and the media have belatedly sought them out as consumers. But the political economy of women's spectatorship is not matched by the political economy of women's sport. Emblematically, Fara Williams, one of England's most-capped and greatest footballers, acknowledged the month before the 2015 finals that she had lived homeless for much of her international career (Creighton, 2014). The ethical and political aspects of both private and public cultural policies that generate such inequalities necessitate inspection and publicity from physical cultural studies.

The hyper-masculinity that remains characteristic of newsrooms presents additional issues. In the US, there are 48 male sportscasters for every female, 94 percent of sports editors are men, and so are 90 percent of their assistants. The corollaries of inattention to female fans are clear (Schreiber, 2012; Adams and Tuggle, 2004). The Australian *bourgeois* media continue to discriminate as well: in 2008–2009, 9 percent of non-news TV was dedicated to women's sport. The figure was 86 percent for men (Australian Sports Commission, 2009: v). When women are directly addressed as fans of male bodies in motion, the result can be trivializing. The Colombian cable network Claro boasts a daytime discussion program aimed at female spectators called *Futbol y Tacón* (*Football and High Heels*). Its co-hosts, Jhoana Uribe and Sonia Cubides, are conventionally beautiful, light-skinned, and thin. They wear sexually arresting clothing and high heels on the program, other than when depicted in soft-core style having a shower together. The official version of this strategy calls it a search for diversity that can pull at the heartstrings of passionate fans (Espectador, 2014). Right.

Media attention and gossip continue to consign elite sportswomen to a different sphere from elite men. And as spectators, their expertise and commitment are rarely foregrounded or respected. The struggles of women and other marginalized spectators and stars continue. The erotic spectacle of sports remains structured in profound inequality. The task for physical cultural studies is to historicize and criticize such inequalities and theorize the pleasures they simultaneously incarnate and exclude.

The first lesson of this chapter: sporting spectacle and Eros are linked through money, in ways that suit the politicized interdisciplinary focus of physical cultural studies. A second lesson: the importance of looking at elderly, middle-aged, and new media, and in an international frame, in accordance with a multilingual cosmopolitanism that must characterize physical cultural studies' future.

Notes

1 It should go without saying that I use the term 'football' in this paragraph and below in the same way as 96% of the world's population, not the 4 percent whose 'footballers' have to wear body armor to play for the few seconds they are required to perform in a given season, and virtually none of them are capable of putting foot to ball in a meaningful way.
2 This promise was found at www.tsn.ca/contact/#advertsing_contact when this chapter was first written, but the link no longer works.

References

Adams, T. and Tuggle, C. A. 2004. ESPN's SportsCenter and coverage of women's athletics: 'It's a boys' club'. *Mass Communication & Society*, 7 (2), 237–248.

Alter, J. S. 1992. *The Wrestler's Body: Identity and Ideology in North India*. Berkeley, CA: University of California Press.

Arehart-Treichel, J. 2012. Why sports evoke passion, for better or worse. *Psychiatric News*, 47 (9), 13.

Australian Sports Commission. 2009. *Towards a Level Playing Field: Sport and Gender in Australian Media January 2008–July 2009*. Canberra: Australian Sports Commission.

Benkwitz, A. and Molnar, G. 2012. Interpreting and exploring football fan rivalries: An overview. *Soccer and Society*, 13 (4), 479–494.

Billings, A., Moscowitz, L., Rae, C. and Brown-Devlin, N. 2015. The art of coming out: Traditional and social media frames surrounding the NBA's Jason Collins. *Journalism and Mass Communication Quarterly*, 92 (1), 142–160.

Blatter, J. S. 2015. Message of the FIFA President. Available from www.fifa.com/mm/document/footballdevelopment/technicalsupport/02/67/08/90/fwwc2015_report_web_neutral.pdf, 4–7.

Bonesteel, M. 2014. US soccer coach Juergen Klinsmann says American players can have sex during World Cup. *Washington Post*, June 3. Available from www.washingtonpost.com/blogs/early-lead/wp/2014/06/03/u-s-soccer-coach-juergen-klinsmann-says-american-players-can-have-sex-during-world-cup/.

Broadcasting and Cable. 1998. There's life outside sports. There's also ballet. *Broadcasting and Cable*, May 11: 24–25.

Buchan, E. 2014. Selfies, shopping and skinny mojitos: WAGs' guide to Brazil 2014. *Daily Star*. Available from www.dailystar.co.uk/travel/party/381437/Holiday-like-a-WAG-in-Brazil.

Bueno, G. 2002. La canonización de Marilyn Monroe.' *El Catoblepas*, May 30, 9, 2.

Caamaño, C., 2014. Samapoli ya fijó las reglas de la 'Roja' en Brasil. *La Tercera*, May. Available from www.latercera.com/noticia/deportes/futbol/mundial/2014/05/2836-579980-9-sampaoli-ya-fijo-las-reglas-de-la-roja-en-brasil.shtml.

Campany, R. 2015. TV ratings for the Women's World Cup Final were 3 times bigger than the Stanley Cup Final, so why did FIFA give it short shrift? *Brookings Institution Press*, July 6. Available from www.brookings.edu/blogs/brookings-now/posts/2015/07/fifa-womens-world-cup-final-tv-ratings-three-times-stanley-cup.

Creighton, J. 2014. England midfielder Fara Williams: I was homeless for six years. *BBC News*, May 31. Available from www.bbc.co.uk/sport/0/football/27644997.

Crupi, A. 2015. US victory delivers record ratings for Fox. *AdAge*, July 6. Available from http://adage.com/article/media/u-s-victory-deliv/299341/.

Daddario, G. 1997. Gendered sports programming: 1992 Summer Olympic coverage and the feminine narrative form. *Sociology of Sport Journal*, 14 (2), 103–120.

Dauphine. 2014. Ian Thorpe, quintuple champion olympique, fait son coming-out. *Le Dauphine*, July 15. Available from www.ledauphine.com/sport/2014/07/14/ian-thorpe-quintuple-champion-olympique-fait-son-coming-out.

Denholmes, A. 2014. Australian football team won't ban sex during the World Cup. *Fanatix*, June 7. Available from www.fanatix.com/news/australian-football-team-wont-ban-sex-during-the-world-cup/258493/.

Earnheardt, A. C., Haridakis, P. and Hugenberg, B. (eds). 2012. *Sports Fans, Identity, and Socialization: Exploring the Fandemonium*. Lanham, MD: Lexington Books.

Eco, U. 1972. Towards a semiotic inquiry into the television message. Trans. Paolo Splendore. *Working Papers in Cultural Studies*, 3, 103–121.

Elias, N. 1978. On transformations of aggressiveness. *Theory and Society*, 5 (2), 229–242.

Elias, N. and Dunning, E. 1986. *Quest for Excitement: Sport and Leisure in the Civilizing Process*. Oxford: Basil Blackwell.

Espectador. 2014.'Claro Colombia' busca diversidad. *El Espectador*, March 18. Available from www.elespectador.com/entretenimiento/unchatcon/claro-colombia-busca-diversidad-articulo-481682.

Graham, B. 2014. Is your team allowed to have sex at the World Cup? *Sports.Mic*, June 5. Available from www.mic.com/articles/90517/is-your-team-allowed-to-have-sex-at-the-world-cup.

Haug, W. F. 1986. *Critique of Commodity Aesthetics: Appearance, Sexuality and Advertising in Capitalist Society* (trans. R. Bock). Cambridge: Polity Press.

Herrera, F. M. 2014. Ian Thorpe, leyenda mundial de la natación, se confiesa gay. *La Nación*, July 14. Available from www.nacion.com/ocio/farandula/Ian-Thorpe-mundial-natacion-confiesa_0_1426657487.html.

Holas, N. 2014. The backlash to Ian Thorpe's sexuality is coming from us. *Gay News Network*, July 13. Available from http://gaynewsnetwork.com.au/feature/the-backlash-to-ian-thorpe-s-sexuality-is-coming-from-us-14432.html.

Huffington Post. 2014. England WAGs banned from World Cup warm-up camp. *Huffington Post*, April 2. Available from www.huffingtonpost.co.uk/2014/04/02/england-wags-banned-world-cup-camp_n_5074593.html.

Klugman, M. 2015.'I love him in an absolutely gay way': Heterodox fragments of the erotic desires, pleasures, and masculinity of male sports fans. *Men and Masculinities*, 18 (2), 193–213.

Lallo, M. 2014. Did early start to Ian Thorpe interview cost Channel 10? *Sydney Morning Herald*, July 14. Available at: www.smh.com.au/entertainment/tv-and-radio/did-early-start-to-ian-thorpe-interview-cost-channel-10-20140714-zt6nr.html.

Local. 2014. French team to be spared World Cup sex ban. *The Local*, May 14. Available from www.thelocal.fr/20140514/french-players-allowed-world-cup-sex-within.

Louganis, G. with E. Marcus. 2006. *Breaking the Surface*. Naperville, IL: Source Books.

LoveBrighton Blog. 2011. Radical Bloomsbury. Available from http://visitbrighton.blogspot.co.uk/2011/04/radical-bloomsbury.html.

McBride, K. 2011. Can a sports network known for its male brand serve the female fan? *Poynter*, December 26. Available from www.poynter.org/latest-news/top-stories/157096/can-a-sports-network-known-for-its-male-brand-serve-the-female-fan.

McClymont, K. and Bagshaw, E. 2014. Deal or no deal: Why Thorpe kept quiet. *Sydney Morning Herald*, July 14. Available from www.smh.com.au/sport/swimming/deal-or-no-deal-why-thorpe-kept-quiet-20140713-3bv2m.html#ixzz37Y5aM0tT.

McCutcheon, L. E., Lange, R. and Houran, J. 2002. Conceptualization and measurement of celebrity worship. *British Journal of Psychology*, 93 (1), 67–87.

McGlone, S. and Shrier, I. 2000. Does sex the night before competition decrease performance? *Clinical Journal of Sport Medicine*, 10 (4), 233–234.

McKay, J. and Roderick, M. 2010. 'Lay down Sally': Media narratives of failure in Australian sport. *Journal of Australian Studies*, 34 (3), 295–315.

Magazine Monitor. 2014. The prevailing myth of sex before sport. *Magazine Monitor*, June 6. Available from www.bbc.co.uk/news/blogs-magazine-monitor-27734048.

Maguire, J. 1993. Bodies, sportscultures and societies: A critical review of some theories in the sociology of the body. *International Review for the Sociology of Sport*, 28 (1), 33–52.

Markovits, A. S. and Albertson, E. 2012. *Sportista: Female Fandom in the United States*. Philadelphia, PA: Temple University Press.

Mercado, M. 2008. Why America hates soccer. *Football*, March 25. Available from www.football.co.uk/football_features/story_306.shtml.

Miller, T. 2001. *SportSex*. Philadelphia, PA: Temple University Press.

Miller, T. 2010. *Television Studies: The Basics*. New York: Routledge.

Moore, D., 2006. Olympian Tewksbury reveals his struggles being gay. *Globe and Mail*, April 5. Available from www.theglobeandmail.com/news/national/olympian-tewksbury-reveals-his-struggles-being-gay/article18159890/.

Nelson, K. 2002. The erotic gaze and sports: An ethnographic consideration. *Journal of Sport History*, 29 (3), 407–412.

Oates, T. P. 2012. Representing the audience: The gendered politics of sport media. *Feminist Media, Studies* 12 (4), 603–607.

Onion. 2015. Soccer officially announces it is gay. Available from www.theonion.com/video/soccer-officially-announces-it-is-gay-17603.

Peters, R. 1976. *Television Coverage of Sport*. Birmingham: Centre for Contemporary Cultural Studies.

Poynton, B. and Hartley, J. 1990. Male-gazing: Australian Rules Football, gender and television. In M. E. Brown (ed.), *Television and Women's Culture: The Politics of the Popular*. Sydney: Currency Press, 144–157.

Prensa. 2014. Brasil 2014: Estas selecciones no tundra sexo durante el mundial. *La Prensa*, June 2. Available from http://laprensa.peru.com/deportes/noticia-brasil-2014-estas-selecciones-no-tendran-sexo-durante-mundial-26527.

Project for Excellence in Journalism. 2008. *The Media's Olympics*, August 22. Available from www.journalism.org/node/12484/feed.

Schreiber, K. 2012. Why don't we watch more women's sports? *Greatist*, August 2. Available from http://greatist.com/fitness/women-sports-viewership-080212/.

Sloan, L. R. 1989. The motives of sports fans. In J. H. Goldstein (ed.), *Sports, Games, and Play: Social and Psychological Motivations*. Hillsdale, NJ: Lawrence Erlbaum, 175–240.

Sparks, R. 1992. 'Delivering the male': Sports, Canadian television, and the making of TSN. *Canadian Journal of Communication*, 17 (1), 319–342.

Stallings, T. 2012. From beefcake to skatecake: Masculinity in the Swimming Pool. *KCET*, May 7. Available from www.kcet.org/arts/artbound/counties/riverside/from-beefcake-to-skatecake-masculinity-in-the-swimming-pool.html.

Stempel, C., 2006. Televised sports, masculinist moral capital, and support for the US invasion of Iraq. *Journal of Sport and Social Issues*, 30 (1), 79–106.
Taipei Times. 2006. World Cup: England WAGS keep the media distracted. *Taipei Times*, June 29, 19.
Tang, T. and Cooper, R. 2012. Gender, sports, and new media: Predictors of viewing during the 2008 Beijing Olympics. *Journal of Broadcasting and Electronic Media*, 56 (1), 75–91.
Telegraph. 2012. A pool full of sponsor gold for Thorpe. *Daily Telegraph*, March 14. Available from www.dailytelegraph.com.au/a-pool-full-of-sponsor-gold-for-ian-thorpe/story-e6freuy9-1226298572500.
Thrall, A., Jaime Lollio-Fahkreddine, T., Berent, J., Donnelly, L., Herrin, W., Paquette, Z., Wenglinski, R. and Wyatt, A. 2008. Star power: Celebrity advocacy and the evolution of the public sphere. *International Journal of Press/Politics*, 13 (4), 362–385.
Till, B. D., Stanley, S. M. and Priluck, R. 2008. Classical conditioning and celebrity endorsers: An examination of belongingness and resistance to extinction. *Psychology and Marketing*, 25 (2), 179–196.
Trail, G. T. and James, J. D. 2001. The motivation scale for sport consumption: Assessment of the scale's psychometric properties. *Journal of Sport Behavior*, 24 (1), 108–127.
Wann, D. L. 1995. Preliminary validation of the sport fan motivation scale. *Journal of Sport and Social Issues*, 19 (4), 377–396.
Weed, M. 2008. Exploring the sport spectator experience: Virtual football spectatorship in the pub. *Soccer and Society*, 9 (2), 189–197.
Weissman, N. 2010. A timely message about female sports fans. *Washington Post*, September 16. Available from http://voices.washingtonpost.com/box-seats/2010/09/a_timely_message_about_female.html.
Wenner, L. A. and Gantz, W. 1998. Watching sports on television: Audience experience, gender, fanship, and marriage. In L. Wenner (ed.), *MediaSport*. London: Routledge, 233–251.
Yahoo! 2014. No sex or alcohol for Mexico players during the World Cup. *Yahoo!*, May 21. Available from http://news.yahoo.com/no-sex-or-alcohol-for-mexico-players-during-the-world-cup-125007188-soccer.html.

26
PUNISHED CORPORAL BODIES

Aaron L. Miller

Introduction

Few issues may gain more from the perspective of physical cultural studies (PCS) than the issue of corporal punishment, the punishment of the body. Loosely defined as the beating, hitting, or kicking of the body to discipline or punish, by a person in a position of authority relative to a person in a subordinate position, corporal punishment is a social phenomenon common throughout the industrialized world. It is used in homes but also often in educational spaces by educators hoping to 'teach kids a lesson', and it raises important questions about power, violence, and cultural studies.

In Japan, where I have done much of my fieldwork, the linguistic roots of 'discipline' and 'punishment' are closely related to the body. One term for 'discipline' in Japanese, *shitsuke*, literally means 'beautifying' the 'body'. *Taibatsu*, the term for 'corporal punishment', and its Chinese character (*kanji*) ideographs maintain, literally mean the 'punishment' of the 'body'. Even the drawing of the *kanji* 'teach' is composed of three elements: 'parent', 'whip', and 'child'. In common parlance, *taibatsu* implies hitting any part of the body with the fist, palm, whip or bamboo stick, kicking, boxing of the ears, or making someone sit in *seiza* position (sitting on the knees with the legs curled up behind the buttocks). At times, it has also referred to forcing someone to stand holding buckets of water for long periods of time, starving someone of food or depriving them of the right to be in the classroom.

In this chapter, I will attempt to show why corporal punishment in Japan illustrates the pressing need for a sophisticated scholarly field such as physical cultural studies to guide us forward. In particular, physical cultural studies' call for 'committed praxis' offers a valuable extension upon Foucauldian theory, which can only help us understand this phenomenon but is limited in guiding us politically. When corporal punishment occurs, especially when it occurs in high-profile high school sports such as baseball and basketball, Foucauldian theory can help us explain why some who receive corporal punishment say they appreciate it and that it was 'good for them'. Foucauldian theory helps us make sense of the mechanism of power that allows corporal punishment to exist, even in a so-called 'civilized' society such as Japan, whose government has long ago banned the practice (Miller, 2013). However, Foucauldian theory is less sufficient in guiding us toward our proper role as scholar/activists. As scholars we need to take a stronger approach for the study of violence, power, and punishment in sport. We need our approach to be not merely explanatory or interpretive but also empirical, contextual, transdisciplinary, theoretical, qualitative, self-reflexive, pedagogical, and grounded in praxis, as the editors of this volume suggest. Physical cultural studies holds that promise.

According to Silk and Andrews (2015), PCS developed into a hybrid field drawing on sports sociology, cultural studies, and body studies, as well as 'dialogic learning community' aimed at providing scholars space to better understand their studies as well as impact progressive social change. Pioneers in this field see a 'seemingly unrelenting (bio)scienticization of kinesiology (and the accompanying devaluing of the humanities and social sciences)' and a need for more empirical, contextual, transdisciplinary, theoretical, political, qualitative, self-reflexive, and pedagogical studies. At the same time, there is a sense of radicalism in this scholarship. Giardina and Newman (2011) suggest that the goals of the PCS project are to use political and politicized bodies to engage and interact with human activity, foster an engaged social citizenship, and 'move beyond writing and researching about bodies to writing and researching through bodies as a principal force of the research act' (ibid.: 44). Atkinson similarly labels the movement a 'call to committed praxis' (Atkinson, 2001: 137).

I was trained as a socio-cultural anthropologist, so these aims all resonate deeply with me, and reassure me that like-minded scholars abound across departments different from my own. Socio-cultural anthropology has a long history of reflexivity and personal engagement in professional research, which echoes the passion of the leaders of this new field. Some anthropologists stop short of offering their two cents about their research, but I am not among them. To me, punished corporal bodies clearly generate and solidify power relations in Japan because bodies are not produced by society, they are also 'bodies about society'. That is to say, they tell us much about our political inequalities and call on us as privileged researchers to affect meaningful change (Giardina and Newman, 2011: 54). The very punishment of these bodies is a political act, and it serves to reproduce existing power relations.

We live in a present of plurality. There is no such thing as *the* Japanese physical culture. While some Japanese view their sporting bodies as unique and similar only to each other, not all Japanese sporting bodies are the same. While some Japanese athletes see their athletic bodies as inferior to those of Western (or Chinese) athletes, not all do (Miller, 2015). Similarly, the transition from 'sports for education' to 'sports for health' (Miller, 2011) and the transition from a reliance on samurai spirit to a reliance on sports science and sports medicine (Miller, 2009), are challenging 'traditional' views of the Japanese sporting body. Finally, the globalization of traditional Japanese 'sports' such as sumo and judo are challenging what used to be considered dominant and acceptable body postures, attitudes, and social graces in Japan. We cannot say there is only one Japanese physical culture; rather, there are many, and they vary across time, region, sport, gender, and class.

Japanese sports as physical culture

The moving body has increasingly become a key subject of academic inquiry in social science and humanities literature in recent years, including among scholars of sport, physical education, and the martial arts in the East (see e.g. Brownell, 1995; Sugimoto, 1995; Horne, 2000; Noguchi, 2004; Kelly, 2007; Otomo, 2007). Many scholars of Japanese sport have also taken a close look at the 'physical culture' or 'body culture' of Japan (e.g. Sugimoto, 1995; Ben-Ari, 1997; Horne, 2000; Spielvogel, 2003; McDonald and Hallinan, 2005: 198; Kelly and Sugimoto, 2007; Kelly, 2007; Light, 2008). But how might a PCS approach offer us a better understanding of Japanese physical culture? A major premise lurking behind much writing on 'Japanese physical cultural activities' – that is, martial arts, physical education, 'Western' sports, recreation, and dance – has been that there is something unique about the Japanese body and Japan's physical culture (see e.g. Nakamura, 1981, 2002; Ozawa, 2002; Otsuki, 1989, 2002; Murasaki, 2002; Kuraishi, 2005; Hayashi and Kuzuoka, 2004; Noguchi, 2004). These works assume that the ways in which Japanese people move their bodies in these physical cultural activities are 'uniquely Japanese'.

Part of the problem with this logic, however, as Kelly (2007: 13) notes, is that it is difficult to reconcile the sleek and well-trained physiques found in Tokyo fitness clubs (Spielvogel, 2003), with the corpulent bodies of Japan's sumo wrestlers (Whang, 2007). Can either of these bodies represent *the* Japanese sporting body? Given the rather different expectations of the bodies of high-performance athletes, dancers and fighters, and recreational exercisers involved in a wide array of physical cultural activities, how can anyone assert that there is such a thing as a single national physical culture of Japan? We must unpack the meanings of Japanese sports and the Japanese sporting body, and contextualize them in their political worlds.

Contextualizing Japanese physical cultural bodies

According to Sugimoto, Japanese began to see their sports as part of their 'physical culture' (*shintai bunka*) as early as the 1980s (Sugimoto, 1995: 156). But when sports, which are known as *supōtsu* in Japanese, were first introduced to Japan in the Meiji Period (1868–1912), they were considered modern and Western entities. At the time, the Japanese did not really understand the idea that 'competition' could be 'play'; indeed, the word for 'competition' (*kyōgi*) had yet to be invented (Collins, 2007: 7). In the decades that followed, Japan began to realize that sports were not simply diversionary pursuits or competitions, and that they were powerful ways to integrate with the international community, especially through the Olympic movement. Gradually, sports began to offer the Japanese a way to present their strengths to the world. At the same time, Western sports were gradually localized and ultimately became something 'Japanese', a process that was inherently tied to Japan's desire to at once be part of the world while also unique within it. The sporting body was a key political tool in this process.

Today, sports are an integral part of Japan's physical culture, and, as 'physical cultural activities', they deserve serious scholarly attention. The Japanese sporting body continues to have a role in furthering power or gender hierarchies, media representations help to form ideal body types, and the body is still perceived to be a unique 'ethnic entity' when considered in international comparative context. Yet current views of the Japanese sporting body are the result of particular historical circumstances, and the often traceable interplay between powerful and influential institutions acting throughout modern Japanese history (Kelly, 1998; Horne, 2000). These institutions include the state, the military, the education system, business groups, and advocates of science and medicine. To fully understand today's perceptions of Japanese sporting bodies, we must understand how these institutions have sought to establish their vision(s) of what the Japanese (body) should be.

Japan's modern 'encounter' with Western sports can be characterized by the acceptance of some Western physical, educational, and cultural ideas and techniques, and the adaptation of these ideas and techniques in particularly Japanese ways. This 'negotiation process' has been evident throughout Japanese sports history and has created a hybrid physio-educational sports culture (Miller, 2015). At first, Western sports were seen as subordinate to indigenously Japanese physical cultural activities such as the 'martial arts' (*budō*) or other traditional leisure activities. To Meiji Japanese, sports were perceived as 'Western' entities that must be made 'Japanese', and there were great attempts to localize them as such (Abe, 2006). During these periods of localization, there was often conflict between the so-called 'new Western sports culture' and 'old Japanese physical culture', the latter a notion that many associated with the martial arts. In the Meiji Period (1868–1912), for example, one writer opined, 'Japanese *bujutsu* ('martial arts') is our original exercise, which, down the ages, has ensured numerous feats, rendered good service to the state, and inspired the people' (quoted in Abe and Mangan, 2002: 107). In such articulations, martial arts were seen as powerful and indigenous activities that served the nation-state, so when sports were introduced, people initially denigrated them as 'Western' and 'foreign' and insisted that they required 'Japanization', which often meant 'sanitation'.

Before Japan opened itself to the West, restored the Meiji Emperor to the throne (1868), and embarked on an unprecedented modernization project, its long period of isolation (*sakoku jidai*; roughly mid-sixteenth to mid-eighteenth century) allowed socio-culturally specific ideas of the body to develop. These notions were not immediately compatible with those introduced by Westerners who visited Japan during the Meiji Period, and sports, among other cultural imports, challenged them. After a formal and nationalized education system was established in the late nineteenth century, however, Japanese schools – and school sports – have been a key conduit through which ideas of the Japanese sporting body have been disseminated, challenged, or changed. Educators have since debated how to best teach, guide, instruct, and discipline these bodies when they are young and learning how to 'play' sports. Chief among these educational debates has been the moral debate over corporal punishment.

Foucauldian theory and the punishment of Japanese sporting bodies

When I began researching corporal punishment in Japan, I applied the work of Michel Foucault, especially his ideas of 'power relations', and 'bio-power', because I thought they could help us better understand how sporting bodies have responded when punished physically. Foucault was skeptical of conventional definitions of 'power', insisting that he did not study 'power' per se; rather, he studied the history of 'how humans were made into subjects', or, in another articulation, how a new 'economy of power relations' was necessary (Foucault, 1982: 219). This 'economy', he believed, needed to start not from a study of those 'in power', but those in resistance to it. To Foucault, such 'power relations' were characterized by the 'governing' and 'structuring' of the 'possible field of action of others'; in other words, controlling the possible actions that one could or could not take (ibid.: 221). Such a conceptualization of power relations supposed that people being subjected to power were free and not slaves, and that each individual was 'thoroughly recognized and maintained to the very end as a person' (ibid.: 220). It also meant that subjects were free to decide for themselves whether or not they wanted to do what power demanded. Thus, in some cases, those 'in power' did not need to take any action to keep their subjects in line because subjects would willingly toe the line without coercion. Indeed, coercion was not a key component to Foucault's concept of power. Foucault calls this the 'productive nature of power'. He writes:

> If power ... never did anything but say no, do you really think one would be brought to obey it? What makes power good, what makes it accepted, is simply the fact that it doesn't weigh on us as a force that says no, but that it produces and traverses things, it induces pleasure, forms of knowledge, produces discourses. It needs to be considered as a productive network which runs through the whole social body, much more than a negative instance whose focus is repression.
>
> *(Foucault, 1980: 119)*

Such an approach prompts us to ask, what is the 'productive nature' of corporal punishment in Japanese sports? Various surveys suggest that many Japanese approve of physical discipline, even those who receive it themselves. Morita, for example, asserts that 75 percent of Japanese citizens believe that *taibatsu* is necessary for the disciplining of children (Morita, 2003: 21), and Goodman notes that there were surveys in the early 1980s, 'which suggested that the majority of parents (regularly about 70 percent) supported the use of discipline as being good for their children (*kodomo no tame*)' (Goodman, 2000: 167). Iwai's analysis of the 2008 Japan General Social Survey (JGSS) also showed that only a very few Japanese adults *categorically* condemned *taibatsu* by either parents or teachers (Iwai, 2008). Based on a study of approximately 5,600 participants, the JGSS revealed that only 6.3 percent of men and 8.6 percent of women were against *taibatsu* by parents, while 7.3 percent of men and 10.7 percent of women were against *taibatsu* by teachers (Iwai, 2008: 317). These surveys suggest that there has been rather widespread approval for *taibatsu*, and it is not only older Japanese who believe that *taibatsu* is necessary. A few studies that have analyzed the perceptions of young Japanese regarding *taibatsu* also suggest that young Japanese more often than not approve of its use (Ishikawa, 1998; Kobayashi et al., 1997; Imabashi, 1995; Sanuki, 2005).

In the case of corporal punishment in Japan, it seems Foucauldian power relations are useful for explaining why many Japanese have come to accept and even approve of physical discipline. Through its use of corporal punishment, Foucauldian 'power' routinizes behavior and shapes consciousness regarding what forms of behavior are acceptable or unacceptable, thereby 'producing' certain discourses and forms of knowledge, which in turn shape behavior.

Another Foucauldian concept – 'bio-power' – clarifies Foucault's argument. 'Bio-power' represents one of three ways that Foucault believed humans are made into 'subjects.' The first way was by 'dividing practices', in which people are separated into categories (e.g. separating the sane from the insane by putting the latter in mental hospitals). The second way is by objectifying people as subjects in a process called 'scientific classification', which is a process that often involves the physical appearance of the human body. Finally, for Foucault people are made into subjects by their own 'subjectification' of themselves (Rabinow, 1984: 7–11). This is 'bio-power': people apply 'technologies of power' upon themselves that 'power' would have applied had they not done so. This further explains how power produces, rather than only represses, behavior and discourse, and the body is a key part of this equation. 'Bio-power' creates a mechanism that routinizes physical behavior as people who are 'not in positions of power' begin to adapt their behavior and move their bodies in line with what those 'in power' would want. Foucault's theories of 'power relations' and 'bio-power' thus illustrate how Japanese bodies have been made into 'subjects' through the normalization of corporal punishment.

However, not all Japanese approve of corporal punishment, and more importantly Foucauldian theory does not guide us as scholar/activists toward any kind of meaningful action. Foucauldian theory may explain the societal mechanism by which people come to normalize, accept, and even approve of such 'violations' of individual bodies, but it does not explain who *should* have sovereignty over those bodies. Should it be the child him/herself, their parents, or the teacher or coach under whose charge he/she has been entrusted? Although Foucauldian theory does imply that those in power ought not abuse their power and inflict pain on an individual's body, is that implication enough?

Ultimately, the inability to answer this question indicates the limits of Foucauldian theory and the need for a more pro-active, progressive, and politically engaged approach, as encouraged (though not always easily realized) by many working within physical cultural studies. Rarely do post-modern social theorists who take a relativistic approach make the case for any 'ought' position – that is, recommending policy changes; describing the 'is' – that is, how things are – is apparently enough. Description is safe; prescription is dangerous, especially so in a hyper-competitive and increasingly impoverished academic landscape. Few wish to go out on a limb to make an 'ought' case, even as the public is crying out for research-based insights.

Yet burgeoning fields such as physical cultural studies promise a different approach and encourage scholars to engage the political, rather than shy away from it. PCS proclaims to value the role of academics as everyday activists or 'public intellectuals', with some impacting positive social change through teaching, policy, media production, and other social contributions. For my part, this means drawing on my research about corporal punishment to give voice to those who consider themselves victims of violence, and showing the errors of educators who continue to use corporal punishment. As Dr Martin Luther King, Jr once said,

> The ultimate weakness of violence is that it is a descending spiral, begetting the very thing it seeks to destroy. Instead of diminishing evil, it multiplies it. Through violence you may murder the liar, but you cannot murder the lie, nor establish the truth. Through violence you may murder the hater, but you do not murder hate. In fact, violence merely increases hate.
>
> *(King 1967)*

Despite Dr King's massive contributions to our understanding of human rights, many continue to beat our own (and others') children in the name of 'education' and 'discipline'. As scholars of physical cultures, we must strive to eliminate this violence to whatever degree possible.

As scholars, we occupy a privileged, yet precarious position. We are rarely directly involved in the violent acts we observe in sporting and movement contexts. Yet we see what happens, and as observers we have the obligation to report. We also have the obligation to tell both sides of the story, since that separates us from profit-minded journalism and gives our work meaning and, hopefully, impact. Telling both sides of the story, however, is not the same thing as resorting to morally relativistic conclusions. Our painstaking research has earned us the right to offer reasoned, empirically based recommendations. Certainly agenda-led research is a patent methodological mistake, and one that would surely doom any research project to failure before it even begins, but who can fault us for having a committed praxis and sharing our opinion after our research is complete?

Mine is certainly not a new position. In 1990, Myles Horton and Paolo Freire argued that scholarly activism could only be developed by those 'who make the road by walking it' (Horton and Freire, 1990), and critical scholars in the sociology and anthropology of physical culture have been walking their own roads for years. Still, it is worth asking ourselves a simple question again: if we as scholars do not help the public think critically about the ethics of our adult actions, especially as they relate to our children's lives, who will? My research on corporal punishment in Japan has led me to conclude that young students and athletes crave both attention and structure, and they want firm but fair, as well as strict but supportive, teachers and coaches. No matter where I speak about this issue, but especially in Japan, I am always asked to share my opinion, and I choose to share it in this way, regardless of whether the prevailing winds of today's academia might try to blow my opinion in another, apolitical and self-muted direction.

While I did not embark upon my research with this activist agenda, as my academic career progresses and I meet with like-minded scholars in fields such as physical cultural studies, I feel it increasingly growing. The 'dialogic learning community' of physical cultural studies has helped bring my professional experiences and political positions into clearer focus, and I can sense my role expanding from that of a myopic researcher to that of researcher and advocate, and in this new multi-dimensional role I charge myself with the task of limiting the amount of pain and suffering in the world in any way I can. As scholars who are committed to praxis, partiality, and the political, and given the fact that what we say and write may mean a great deal to the people we study, physical cultural studies scholars ought to be similarly committed to helping adults learn how to discipline without corporal punishment.

References

Abe, I. 2006. Muscular Christianity in Japan: The Growth of a Hybrid. *International Journal of the History of Sport* 5(23), 714–738.

Abe, I. and Mangan, J. A. 2002. Sportsmanship – English Inspiration and Japanese Response: F. W. Strange and Chiyosaburo Takeda. *International Journal of the History of Sport* 19(2), 99–128.

Andrews, D. L. and Silk, M. L. 2015. Physical cultural studies on sport. In R. Guilianotti (ed.), *Routledge Handbook of the Sociology of Sport*. New York: Routledge, 83–93.

Atkinson, M. 2001. Physical Cultural Studies [Redux]. *Sociology of Sport Journal* 28, 135–144.

Ben-Ari, E. 1997. *Body Projects in Japanese Childcare: Culture, Organization and Emotions in a Preschool.* Richmond: Curzon Press.

Brownell, S. 1995. *Training the Body for China: Sports in the Moral Order of the People's Republic.* Chicago, IL: University of Chicago Press.

Collins, S. 2007. *The 1940 Tokyo Games: The Missing Olympics.* Abingdon: Routledge.

Foucault, M. 1980. *Power/Knowledge.* New York: Pantheon Books.

Foucault, M. 1982. Afterword: The Subject and Power. In H. Dreyfus and P. Rabinow (eds), *Michel Foucault: Beyond Structuralism and Hermeneutics.* Chicago, IL: University of Chicago Press, 208–226.

Giardina, M. D. and Newman, J. I. 2011. What is the 'Physical' in Physical Cultural Studies? *Sociology of Sport Journal,* 28, 36–63.

Goodman, R. 2000. *Children of the Japanese State: The Changing Role of Child Protection.* Oxford: Oxford University Press.

Hayashi, S. and Kuzuoka, M. 2004. *Yakyugata vs. sakkagata: yutakasa e no kyōgibunkaron* [Soccer vs. Baseball: A Cultural Theory of Sport Seeking Wealth]. Tokyo: Heibonsha.

Horne, J. 2000. Understanding Sport and Body Culture in Japan. *Body and Society,* 6(2), 73–86.

Horton, M. and Freire, P. 1990. *We Make the Road by Walking: Conversations on Education and Social Change.* Philadelphia, PA: Temple University Press.

Imabashi, M. 1995. *NHK Ohayo Janaru: Taibatsu.* Tokyo: Nippon Hōsō Kyōkai.

Ishikawa, Y. (ed.) 1998. *Oya/Kyōshi ni yoru: Taibatsu no Jittai* [The State of Affairs of Corporal Punishment According to Parents and Teachers]. Matsue: Shimane University Law, Letters, and Society Research Institute.

Iwai, H. 2008. Gishiki toshite no taibatsu [Taibatsu as Ritual]. In I. Tanioka, M. Nitta and K. Iwai (eds), *Nihonjin no Ishiki to Kōdō: Nihonban Sōgōshakaichōsa: JGSS ni yoru Bunseki* [The Consciousness and Actions of the Japanese People: Analysis of the JGSS Comprehensive Social Survey]. Tokyo: Tokyo University Press, 313–328.

Kelly, W. W. 1998. Blood and Guts in Japanese Professional Baseball. In S. Linhart and S. Frühstuck (eds), *The Culture of Japan as Seen through its Leisure.* New York: SUNY Press.

Kelly, W. W. 2007. Introduction. In W. W. Kelly and A Sugimoto, eds. *This Sporting Life: Sports and Body Culture in Modern Japan.* New Haven, CT: Yale University Council on East Asian Studies, 1–24.

Kelly, W. W. and Sugimoto, A. (eds). 2007. *This Sporting Life: Sports and Body Culture in Modern Japan.* New Haven, CT: Yale University Council on East Asian Studies.

King, M. L. 1967. Speech Delivered at Ohio Northern University, Ada, Ohio. Available from www.onu.edu/library/onuhistory/king (accessed June 5, 2015).

Kobayashi, N., Tanimura, M. and Shimauchi, Y. 1997. Corporal Punishment in the Schools and Homes of Japan. Paper presented at the Ninth Asian Congress of Pediatrics, Hong Kong, March 22–23.

Kuraishi, O. 2005. *Basukettobōru no kochi o hajimeru tame ni* [An Introduction to Basketball Coaching]. Tokyo: Nihon Bunka Shuppan.

Light, R. 2008. Learning Masculinities in a Japanese High School Rugby Club. *Sport, Education and Society* 13(2), 163–179.

McDonald, B. and Hallinan, C. 2005. Seishin Habitus: Spiritual Capital and Japanese Rowing. *International Review for the Sociology of Sport* 40(2), 187–200.

Miller, A. L. 2009. Bushidō vs. Science: Beyond Conflicting Pedagogies of Japanese Basketball Coaching. DPhil thesis, University of Oxford.

Miller, A. L. 2011. From Bushido to Science: A New Pedagogy of Japanese Sports Coaching. *Japan Forum* 23(3), 385–406.

Miller, A. L. 2013. *Discourses of Discipline: An Anthropology of Corporal Punishment in Japan's Schools and Sports.* Berkeley, CA: Institute of East Asian Studies.

Miller, A. L. 2015. Foucauldian Theory and the Making of the Japanese Sporting Body. *Contemporary Japan* 27(1), 13–31.

Morita, Y. 2003. *Shitsuke to Taibatsu: Kodomo no Uchinaru Chikara wo Sodateru Michisuji* [Discipline and Corporal Punishment: The Path to Instilling Inner Power in Children]. Nagasaki: Dōwakan.

Murasaki, N. 2002. *Samurai: Sekai no jōshiki o kutsugaesu nihonjin asuriito no karada kankaku* [Samurai: The Body Sense of Japanese Athletes that is Overthrowing the Common Sense of the World]. Tokyo: Gentosha.

Nakamura, T. 1981. *Supōtsu no fūdo* [The Spiritual Features of Sports]. Tokyo: Taishūkan.

Nakamura, T. (ed.). 2002. *Nihonjin to supōtsu no aishō* [The Chemistry of Sports and the Japanese]. Tokyo: Sōbunkikaku, 222–225.

Noguchi, H. 2004. The Idea of the Body in Japanese Culture and its Dismantlement. *International Journal of Sport and Health Science* 2(1), 8–24.

Otomo, R. 2007. Narratives, the Body, and the 1964 Tokyo Olympics. *Asian Studies Review* 31(2), 117–132.

Otsuki, T. 1989. *Te no nihonjin, ashi no seiyōjin* [The Hands of Japanese, the Feet of Westerners]. Tokyo: Tokuma Shoten.

Otsuki, T. 2002. Nihonjin to seiyōjin no undōkan to supōtsu [Sports and Perspectives on Exercise by Westerners and Japanese]. In T. Nakamura (ed.), *Nihonjin to supōtsu no aishō* [The chemistry of sports and the Japanese]. Tokyo: Sobunkikaku, 15–46.

Ozawa, E. 2002. Nihonjin no haibokukan to supōtsu [Sports and the Japanese Sense of Victory and Defeat]. In T. Nakamura (ed.), *Nihonjin to supōtsu no aishō* [The Chemistry of Sports and the Japanese]. Tokyo: Sobunkikaku, 143–166.

Rabinow, P. (ed.). 1984. *The Foucault Reader.* New York: Pantheon Books.

Sanuki, H. 2005. *Gakkō to Ningen Keisei* [Character Formation and the School]. Tokyo: Hosei University Press.

Spielvogel, L. 2003. *Working Out in Japan: Shaping the Female Body in Tokyo Fitness Clubs.* Durham, NC: Duke University Press.

Sugimoto, A. 1995. *Supōtsu bunka no henyō* [Transformations in Sports Culture]. Kyoto: Sekaishisōsha.

Whang, S. H. 2007. The Body as Culture: The Case of the Sumo Wrestler. In W. W. Kelly and A. Sugimoto (eds), *This Sporting Life: Sports and Body Culture in Modern Japan.* New Haven, CT: Yale University Council on East Asian Studies, 193–210.

PART V

Experiential bodies

27
INJURED, PAINED AND DISRUPTED BODIES

Jacquelyn Allen-Collinson

Introduction

All too commonly, pain and injury constitute integral components of participation in many sports and physical cultures, even those not usually constructed as dangerous or 'high-risk'. This was highlighted in the news in 2014 by the untimely death of the young Australian cricketer Phillip Hughes, who was struck on the neck by a ball from a pace bowler while batting in a domestic game, and died two days afterward, never regaining consciousness. Gone. Killed playing the game he loved. While such a catastrophic injury is thankfully rare in cricket, nevertheless, pain, injury and bodily disruption are widespread and often normalized within sport and physical cultural domains, where a 'culture of risk' can be argued to prevail. Adopting a transdisciplinary approach commensurate with PCS, this chapter explores some of the extant sociological, anthropological and social-psychological research on active embodiment in relation to injured, pained and disrupted bodies. From the myriad different approaches available in researching this area, here I focus upon the impact of identity disruption and the role of 'identity work' in dealing with the injured body in the physical-cultural context of distance running, drawing on data from two automethodological projects. The concept of 'identity work' has been utilized within various disciplines, and here is theorized from a symbolic interactionist perspective specifically. This sociological theoretical framework investigates the relational, processual and subjective elements of identity and embodiment, and thus coheres with the PCS enterprise. It offers powerful analytic insights in examining the injured and pained body as experienced within physical cultures, including within the normative structures of those cultures.

In order to highlight the potential of this particular theoretical framework, I provide illustrative data derived from multiple sources: a collaborative autoethnographic project on long-term injury in distance runners (Allen-Collinson and Hockey, 2008), and an autophenomenographic study of female distance running. Here, I explore the role of 'identity work' in sustaining identity during the liminality of 'injury time', when the self–body relation is often experienced as severely disrupted. From a sport-psychological perspective, Petrie has highlighted the traumatic nature of injury experiences in physical cultures, and the deleterious consequences for identity:

> Serious injury is one of the most emotionally and psychologically traumatic things that can happen to an athlete ... Because athletes are so dependent upon their physical skills and because their identities are so wrapped up in their sport, injury can be tremendously threatening to them.
>
> (Petrie, 1993: 18–19)

In order to provide insight into the socio-cultural framing of pain and injury experiences in physical cultures, commensurate with a PCS perspective, I first consider some of the extant sociological (and anthropological) literature on sports pain and injury. Over the past 20 years, a corpus of such literature has developed, which examines pain and injury vis-à-vis key socio-cultural variables, and situates embodied experience within the specificities of particular physical cultures. In relation to gender, for example, Young and White (1995) examine the experiences of young, elite female athletes, and Pike (2005) explores the role of non-orthodox sports medicine in female rowers' efforts to maintain their identities during the disruptive processes of injury and illness. With regard to ageing processes, Wainwright and Turner (2006) consider embodiment issues in relation to older ex-dancers, highlighting that both injury and ageing generate epiphanies for these dancers, forcing them to reflect on their embodied selves and career. Tulle (2007, 2008) similarly addresses ageing and embodiment in her accounts of the experiences of veteran runners. At the other end of the age spectrum, Pike (2010) charts the worlds of elite child athletes and their exposure to injury risk.

The (sub)cultural context and ethos of specific physical cultures where endurance and training/performing through pain and injury are valorized and normalized has been analysed in physical cultures as diverse as rugby (Howe, 2004), distance running (Allen-Collinson and Hockey, 2008), boxing (Wacquant, 1995; Woodward, 2009; Paradis, 2012; Allen-Collinson and Owton, 2015), martial arts (Channon and Jennings, 2013) and mixed martial arts (Spencer, 2012). As Wiese-Bjornstal et al. (1998: 63) noted of the sport–pain–injury nexus, 'athletes learn to define sacrifice, risk, pain, and injury as the price one must pay to be a true athlete in competitive sports', and this applies not only at the elite level, but also to other highly committed participants. Sociological and anthropological research has focused on the enduring of pain as a subcultural practice in extreme and/or endurance sports (e.g. Reischer, 2001; Atkinson, 2008). Such practice often requires stoicism of body and mind; 'stoicism' being defined as the exercising of endurance in the face of adversity (Moore et al., 2012: 162). The normalization of sacrifice, risk, pain and injury is not, however, necessarily always positive or productive and the substantial corporeal (and psychological) dangers generated by acceptance of such a 'culture of risk' have also been highlighted (for example, Safai, 2003).

While running is not deemed a high-risk sport, within the distance runner's life-world, risk, sacrifice, endurance and stoicism in the face of pain and injury are normative (Hockey and Allen-Collinson, 2015). Indeed, distance running requires of its adherents the psychological and physical ability to tolerate on a regular and frequent basis the pervasive fatigue, discomfort and pain generated by everyday training routines that require 'putting in the miles', whatever the weather and state of bodily being. As distance running and racing require huge and sustained volumes of training at a certain intensity of pace, these practices develop physical and psychological endurance. Within the distance running subculture, the desire and ability to endure, to keep on running in the face of fatigue and pain – and also certain kinds of injury – is highly valorized. That being said, however endemic and normalized fatigue, exhaustion, discomfort, pain and routine injury are within the distance runner's life-world, serious injury is nevertheless often encountered as a threat to running identity, producing a 'disruption of self' (Turner and Wainwright, 2003: 272) that can require sustained remedial identity work.

To date, the literature on the identity work undertaken by participants in physical cultures who suffer disruption to their identity is relatively sparse. This lacuna is particularly noticeable in relation to those participating at non-elite or grassroots levels, but who are nevertheless *serious* and highly committed physical culture participants. For these individuals, enforced retirement or withdrawal from their chosen physical cultural activity can engender deep disruption to the body–self and to the physical–cultural life-world (*Lebenswelt*). Although authors have certainly challenged the inevitability of biographical disruption as a result of illness (e.g. Faircloth et al., 2004), the assault on identity generated by illness, pain and injury has been well documented in sociology generally (e.g. Becker, 1997) and in relation to sport specifically (e.g. Sparkes and Smith, 2003; Owton and Allen-Collinson, 2014). Given the centrality of the body in most sports and physical cultures, body-disruptive events and processes such as injury and illness often result in 'disrupted body projects' (Sparkes, 2002), and physical–cultural biographical disruption. Material, corporeal disruption can also have deleterious consequences for a person's felt and lived identity, for as Budgeon (2003) notes, subjectivity and the material body are aspects of the self which are irreducibly linked so that bodies are never just objects but part of a process of self-identity (re)negotiation and renegotiating. Such disruption can require of sports participants' sustained engagement with 'identity work' in order to provide some sense of identity continuity. Here, I draw specifically upon the conceptualization of identity derived from the micro-sociological theoretical perspective of symbolic interactionism, which theorizes identity as an interactional, ongoing achievement, and has some conceptual overlap with social-psychological theorizations. Below, I discuss the concept of identity work and its constituent components before portraying illustrative data from the two research projects on sports injury in distance running, in order to ground abstract theoretical insights in a specific physical-cultural context.

Symbolic interactionist perspectives on identity and identity work in sport

Sociological concepts of identity have been subject to intense scrutiny and critique during the last few decades (Callero, 2003), particularly from poststructuralist theorists, who problematize notions of any fixed, stable identity, and highlight the fluidity and mutability of subjectivities. Poststructuralist accounts highlight how subjectivity is formulated through discourses, given substance and pattern through storyline and deployed in social interaction (Davies and Banks, 1992). This perspective holds strong analogies with the older tradition of symbolic interactionism (SI), which also challenged notions of the existence of some 'true' inner self, as fixed and temporarily consistent. SI theorists argued for the construction, emergence and presentation of self and identity within interactional milieu (Blumer, 1969; Goffman, 1969). These theorizations of identity range along a continuum between structural and more 'processual' perspectives, with the latter focusing analytic attention on social agency and the processes of identity construction in interaction; elucidating the ways in which identities are actively negotiated in social contexts, but within overarching social-structural frames. Of further analytic relevance is the distinction made by some theorists (e.g. Snow and Anderson, 1995) between: *social* identities and *personal* identities. The former are conceptualized as those we attribute or impute to social others, whereas personal identities refer to meanings we ourselves attribute to self. Social and personal identities do not always necessarily coincide, and individuals may have to engage in sustained identity work to present a social identity congruent with their own felt personal identity, especially when challenged by those with greater social power, as Goffman (1973) acutely observed in relation to those with stigmatized social identities. This takes us to the symbolic interactionist concept of identity work, succinctly defined by Snow and Anderson as:

the range of activities individuals engage in to create, present and sustain personal identities that are congruent with and supportive of the self-concept. So defined, identity work may involve a number of complementary activities: a) arrangement of physical settings or props; b) cosmetic face-work or the arrangement of personal appearance; c) selective association with other individuals and groups; d) verbal constructions and assertion of personal identities.

(Snow and Anderson, 1995: 241)

A similar formulation has been adopted by Perinbanayagam (2000), who employs analogous categories of 'materialistic', 'associative' and 'vocabularic' identifications, which map on to Snow and Anderson's categories, but amalgamate physical settings, props and the arrangement of physical appearance under the category of 'materialistic' identification. Concepts of materialistic and vocabularic identification are utilized in the analysis below, which theorizes from data generated by two research projects on distance running, one collaborative autoethnographic project and one autophenomenographic; the former focusing on an extended injury (and rehabilitation) period of two years, and the latter incorporating several shorter injury periods.

The research projects

Although autoethnography is a research approach increasingly familiar in social-science communities (Allen-Collinson, 2013; Holman Jones et al., 2013), autophenomenography may be less familiar to readers. This approach is analogous to autoethnography but where the researcher analyses her/his own experiences of a *phenomenon* rather than specifically of a cultural/subcultural domain (Allen-Collinson, 2011), as would constitute the focus in autoethnography, although there is inevitable overlap. Running 1 (R1) was a collaborative autoethnography undertaken in conjunction with a fellow runner–researcher (see Allen-Collinson and Hockey, 2008), as two highly experienced 'veteran' distance runners. Systematic data collection was via highly detailed individual training/research logs, and a shared 'analytic log', over a two-year period of long-term injury and rehabilitation. In the analytic log, we shared emergent analytical themes and concepts, and wrote up longer, more evocative narratives based on field notes. Data recording was via notebooks and micro tape recorders, the latter accompanying us on training sessions, and sometimes to physiotherapy appointments. During the research process, we engaged in *epochē* or phenomenologically inspired bracketing, by, among other things, subjecting to analytic questioning the influence of our own personal embodiment on the meanings, beliefs and knowledge we utilized and generated. In Running 2 (R2), an autophenomenographic project on women's running, I similarly maintained detailed training/research logs for three years, initially commencing in 2008 and then recommencing in October 2012 having moved to a new city. These logs also incorporate various periods of injury, primarily relating to knees and also ongoing problems with an increasingly arthritic foot.

Autoethnographers and autophenomenographers analytically write themselves into fieldwork accounts, as an integral part of the research process, and some may choose to adopt a highly personal, emotional and evocative style (e.g. Douglas and Carless, 2006). Writing in such a personal, emotional style can involve risk in challenging notions – still prevalent within more traditional academic quarters – that researcher–authors should be 'neutral', more 'objective', distanced and 'silent' (Sparkes, 2002). Such a transgressive stance can make autoethnography/autophenomenography, and more novel forms of qualitative research in general, vulnerable to accusations of being 'irrational, particularistic, private, and subjective, rather than reasonable, universal, public, and objective' (Greenhalgh, 2001: 55). While this chapter does present autoethnographic and autophenomenographic findings, these are framed in a more traditional, ethnographic–realist manner, given my primary purpose here is to engage in theoretical analysis of identity work, rather than generate a more evocative account.

Commensurate with the automethodological approach, it is important to offer some accountable knowledge to situate myself – and my co-researcher[1] in R1 – within the research. Now into my mid-fifties, I have been running since my mid-twenties (being a 'late starter'), and a veteran runner (in the UK classificatory system) for 20 years. Together with my co-runner and co-researcher on the collaborative project, we regularly trained together, often six or seven times a week. The chronic knee injuries that we both suffered some years ago constituted the focus of the collaborative autoethnographic project, initiated in order to document engagement with the emotional oscillations of the injury and rehabilitation process. These injuries, painful, frustrating and running-career-threatening, were incurred in the same week of winter training when, on separate evenings, forced by work demands to train in the dark, I stumbled into a fallen branch, twisting my right knee viciously, and my partner slid on a muddy stretch, wrenching his left knee. Some few days subsequently, having adhered to the usual conventions of RICE – that is, *rest* (relative), *ice, compression, elevation* – to no avail, it became clear that the injuries were substantially more severe than the usual 'niggles' plaguing habitual runners. We decided to document systematically the injury–rehabilitation process via the methods described above. At this point, we engaged in what Frank (1995; see also Carless and Douglas, 2010) terms the 'restitution narrative', seeking a return to our former running 'gloried self' (see also Allen-Collinson, 2003). The return to full running fitness was not, however, a straightforward progression, but rather a fragmented and emotionally charged timeline of progression, regression, frustration. Only after two years of such oscillation, could we say with some degree of confidence that we had 'returned to running'.

Employing the conceptual framework of identity work, the data on the lived experience of running injury, pain and disruption, drawn from the above projects, are portrayed below. Commensurate with the PCS perspective, with its focus on embodiment as lived within social structure and (sub)culture, I situate these findings within the physical-cultural domain of running, and analyse them vis-à-vis the categories formulated by Perinbanayagam (2000) within identity work: 'materialistic' and 'vocabularic' identifications. First, materialistic identification is considered in relation to handling the corporeal and identity disruption engendered by running injuries.

Materialistic identification: running routes and the 'look'

The use of physical settings and presentation of a certain running-body appearance emerged as salient in the research findings. In relation to physical settings, in both R1 and R2, during periods of injury, the routes that had been utilized when in full running fitness were retained as walking routes during rehabilitation. This provided some continuity of geographical and temporal space during the disruption to normal athletic training, and to athletic identity. Not only was the same ground trodden (albeit at a much lower pace), but we also sought to retain the same time slot for exercise. This modified use of the same spatio-temporal training 'hour' represented a commitment to sustain some form of training and, importantly, to an eventual return to full running fitness. It did, however, engender considerable ambivalence, as highlighted in this extract from my field note in R1:

> Strange feeling tonight as we set off across Pittville Circus towards the park. Normally, it takes only a few minutes to arrive at the little café hut as we settle into our stride,

> but today of course we are only walking ... everything passes by much more slowly. We exchange mutual, somewhat forlorn looks, no need for words. As far as I recall, it's the first time we've both been injured and out of running at the same time, and, for what may be a little while ...

Under the rubric of this particular identification, in addition to the use of the same physical settings, the issue of personal appearance emerged strongly from our data. The commitment to undertake brisk walking as a (poor) substitute for usual running training, along with our stoic resistance to overdoing the 'comfort eating', resulted in a degree of retention of the distinctive runner's 'look', characterized by a low BMI, lean body and ('gaunt' as one friend described) features. Commensurate with Grosz's (1994) observation regarding the body in general, the runner's body constitutes not only a lived body, but also an inscriptive surface upon which running miles and demanding training practices are etched. While sharing somatic similarities with others (anorexics, heavy smokers and drug users, *inter alia*, as some have told me) my running-woman body was (and is, but less so nowadays) central to identity. So, despite enduring the identity disruption provoked by injury, the continuity of a certain materialistic identification, in the corporeal form of a running body, helped sustain both myself and my running partner through the pain and frustration of the injury process. As a symbolic commitment to running identity, a further element of material identification involved the practice of wearing running gear during our daily brisk walks around the local park:

> We've made a joint decision today: rather than undertaking the rehab in our usual street clothes, we are going to walk around the park in our training gear. At least we'll look like runners – to ourselves as much as to anyone else. Feel a bit ambivalent, however, as it's somewhat poignant pulling on the training gear when it's all too apparent we are not running!
>
> *(Field note, R1)*

Running kit thus constituted a visual prop signalling continuity with former running identity and our commitment to a future 'full' running identity. Our felt identity was that of runners subjected to enforced injury time and the training gear was utilized as a form of 'transitional object' (Silver, 1996) to carry us through the period of running disruption. By wearing running gear, such as trainers, tracksters and wet-weather Gore-Tex running tops, we engaged in materialistic identification as runners, to ourselves and also to others within the local running subculture. Materialistic identification thus intertwined closely with a second form of identity work: associative identification. We dressed for ourselves primarily, but also toward an 'audience' whose validating response was sought (Stone, 1977). So, for example, other runners encountered out on our running routes would identify us in our specific gear and either stop briefly or call out to enquire as to why we were not actually running, nodding in empathy and uttering encouraging remarks when informed of the bane of injury. These forms of utterance can also be theorized as a form of 'identity talk' or vocabularic identification (Perinbanayagam, 2000).

Vocabularic identification – runners' talk

Drawing on Snow and Anderson's (1995) category of verbal constructions and assertion of personal identities, Perinbanayagam's (2000) concept of vocabularic identification proved significant. In R1, for example, the data were replete with notes of conversations between my running partner and myself where we made reference to our running identities either directly or indirectly. As noted above, endurance is a key element and requirement of distance running, and exhortations and encouragement to endure the injury process, 'stay strong' and 'dig in' feature throughout our logs. 'Digging in' is UK running subcultural terminology often employed to describe persevering under difficult and challenging circumstances. So, when the injuries were particularly painful, frustrating or recalcitrant, we encouraged each other to persevere, to be determined and to 'dig in' when the going got tough, just as we would when encountering a 'bad patch' on a long run: 'C'mon, Rosa!' my running partner would growl, making reference to the Portuguese Olympic marathon runner, Rosa Mota, renowned for her capacity to endure. We also reminded each other of past times when we had encountered and overcome other difficulties requiring perseverance and endurance, for example when my running partner reminded me of struggles to reduce my asthma inhaler use:

> … we have been reminiscing about other struggles, like when I decided to try to reduce my asthma medication and eventually managed to come off it completely – even for running – much to my delight. 'God, there were times when I thought you were going to pass out with the effort', says J, 'but you always kept going, no matter how tough it got. I reckon you would pass 'P' Company [UK parachute forces selection test]!'
>
> *(Field note, R1)*

A field note from R2 similarly recounts my identity self-talk during a cold winter's run when suffering severe menstrual cramps, which the jarring motion of downhill running served only to exacerbate:

> … horrid run tonight. Even with the Ponstan Forte (prescription painkiller), had to stop, doubled up several times, or pretend I was refastening a shoe lace, just to bend down and catch my breath. Stumbled and staggered my way down to the river meadows through the college grounds, but the downhill strides sent sharp red stabs into my core. Under my breath, just kept repeating to myself: 'keep going, running-woman' …

Conclusion

The above sections portray some of the findings cohering around engagement in identity work in order to cope with the pain and disruption engendered by sports injury within the physical culture of distance running. The positive impact on identity of physical cultures has been highlighted in the literature (e.g. Carless and Douglas, 2010), as of course have the negatives (e.g. Brewer et al., 1993). For many of us, pain and injury, while disruptive to physical-cultural participation and identities, constitute an integral aspect of that very participation. We tread a fine line. The wider social-structural context is salient also, as a PCS perspective encourages us to address. In my case and that of my co-runner (and for many other full-time workers), the injuries were provoked primarily by being obliged to train post-work in the dark. For, however central to our identities, running had to be squeezed into the interstices of highly demanding, long, exhausting working days. We had no choice; if we wanted to run, it was either pre- or post-work. Our working biographies were/are written on and into our bodies. Both of us have/had to spend long hours in sedentary jobs; result: tight hamstrings, compressed lumbar spines, knee, back, neck, shoulder problems, etc. For other workers, the somatic consequences may be much more deleterious. The particular knee injuries we incurred that November week were not after all random, but had their genesis in our work (and social class) situations. Furthermore, with sports physiotherapy not available via the UK National Health Service (for which we pay substantial National Insurance contributions), we could afford very few private consultations, potentially extending the injury time considerably. As 'trained' sociologists, many of our runs together both pre- and post-injuries, were fuelled by anger (sometimes dark fury) against the social-structural forces that so fundamentally constrained us – and left their indelible, painful, somatic markers on our ageing (running) bodies.

Commensurate with a PCS approach, this chapter has adopted a transdisciplinary perspective in utilizing theoretical and conceptual frameworks drawn from sociology, anthropology and social psychology, and employed autoethnography/autophenomenography as a methodological synthesis. There are myriad different ways in which pained, injured and disrupted bodies can be studied and represented within PCS. Here, I have opted for what some more 'purist' colleagues might see as a great limitation, and a strange hybrid: autoethnography/autophenomenography represented in a 'quasi-realist' ethnographic mode. There is indeed a certain representational tension. But as an auto/ethnographer, feminist phenomenologist and sociologist (and much more), tensions and paradoxes are ontologically familiar; they come with the (uneven and often jarring) terrain.

Note

1 I am grateful to my co-runner and co-researcher, Dr John Hockey, for giving his permission to use his name and our co-produced data in this chapter.

References

Allen-Collinson, J. 2003. Running into injury time: Distance running and temporality. *Sociology of Sport Journal*, 20 (4), 331–350.
Allen-Collinson, J. 2011. Intention and epochē in tension: Autophenomenography, bracketing and a novel approach to researching sporting embodiment. *Qualitative Research in Sport, Exercise and Health*, 3 (1): 48–62.
Allen-Collinson, J. 2013. Autoethnography as the engagement of self/other, self/culture, self/politics, selves/futures. In S. Holman Jones, T. E. Adams and C. Ellis (eds), *Handbook of Autoethnography*. Walnut Creek, CA: Left Coast Press, 281–299.
Allen-Collinson, J. and Hockey, J. 2008. Autoethnography as 'valid' methodology? A study of disrupted identity narratives. *The International Journal of Interdisciplinary Social Sciences*, 3 (6): 209–217.
Allen-Collinson, J. and Owton, H. 2015. Intense embodiment: Senses of heat in women's running and boxing. *Body and Society*, 21 (2): 245–268.
Atkinson, M. 2008. Triathlon, suffering and exciting significance. *Leisure Studies*, 27 (2): 165–180.
Becker, G. 1997. *Disrupted Lives: How People Create Meaning in a Chaotic World*. Berkeley, CA: University of California Press.
Blumer, H. 1969. *Symbolic Interactionism: Perspective and Method*. Englewood Cliffs, NJ: Prentice Hall.
Brewer, B., Van Raalte, J. and Linder, D. 1993. Athletic identity: Hercules' muscle or Achilles heel? *International Journal of Sport Psychology*, 24: 237–254.
Budgeon, S. 2003. Identity as an embodied event. *Body and Society*, 9 (1): 35–55.
Callero, P. L. 2003. The sociology of the self. *Annual Review of Sociology*, 29: 115–133.
Carless, D. and Douglas, K. 2010. *Sport and Physical Activity for Mental Health*. Oxford: Blackwell.
Channon, A. and Jennings, G. 2013. The rules of engagement: Negotiating painful and 'intimate' touch in mixed-sex martial arts. *Sociology of Sport Journal*, 30 (4): 487–503.
Davies, B. and Banks, C. 1992. The gender trap: A feminist poststructuralist analysis of primary school children's talk about gender. *Journal of Curriculum Studies*, 24 (1): 1–25.
Douglas, K. and Carless, D. 2006. Performance, discovery, and relational narratives among women professional tournament golfers. *Women in Sport and Physical Activity Journal*, 15 (2): 14–27.

Faircloth, C. A., Boylstein, C., Rittman, M., Young, M. E. and Gubrium, J. 2004. Sudden illness and biographical flow in narratives of stroke recovery. *Sociology of Health and Illness*, 26 (2): 242–261.
Frank, A. W. 1995. *The Wounded Storyteller: Body, Illness and Ethics*. Chicago, IL: University of Chicago Press.
Goffman, E. 1969. *The Presentation of Self in Everyday Life*. Harmondsworth: Penguin.
Goffman, E. 1973. *Stigma: Notes on the Management of Spoiled Identity*. Harmondsworth: Pelican Books.
Greenhalgh, S. 2001. *Under the Medical Gaze: Facts and Fictions of Chronic Pain*. Berkeley, CA: University of California Press.
Grosz, E. A. 1994. *Volatile Bodies: Toward a Corporeal Feminism*. Sydney: Allen & Unwin.
Hockey, J. and Allen-Collinson, J. 2015. Digging in: The sociological phenomenology of 'doing endurance' in distance-running. In W. Bridel, P. Markula and J. Denison (eds), *Endurance Running: A Socio-Cultural Examination*. London: Routledge.
Holman Jones, S., Adams, T. E. and Ellis, C. (eds). 2013. *Handbook of Autoethnography*. Walnut Creek, CA: Left Coast Press.
Howe, P. D. 2004. *Sport, Professionalism and Pain: Ethnographies of Injury and Risk*. London: Routledge.
Mead, G. H. 1934. *Mind, Self and Society*. Chicago, IL: University of Chicago Press.
Moore, A., Grime, J., Campbell, P. and Richardson, J. 2012. Troubling stoicism: Sociocultural influences and applications to health and illness. *Health (London)*, 17 (2): 159–173.
Owton, H. and Allen-Collinson, J. 2014. Conformers, contesters, and creators: Vignettes of asthma identities and sporting embodiment. *International Review for the Sociology of Sport*, 51 (6): 699–714.
Paradis, E. 2012. 'Boxers, briefs or bras'? Bodies, gender and change in the boxing gym, *Body and Society*, 18 (2): 82–109.
Perinbanayagam, R. S. 2000. *The Presence of Self*. Lanham, MD: Rowman & Littlefield.
Petrie, G. 1993. Injury from the athlete's point of view. In J. Heil (ed.), *Psychology of Sport Injury*. Champaign, IL: Human Kinetics, pp. 17–23.
Pike, E. C. J. 2005. 'Doctors just say "rest and take Ibuprofen"': A critical examination of the role of 'non-orthodox' health care in women's sport. *International Review for the Sociology of Sport*, 40 (2): 201–219.
Pike, E. 2010. The elite child athlete and injury risk. In C. Brackenridge and D. Rhind (eds), *Elite Child Athlete Welfare: International Perspectives*. Brunel: Brunel University Press, pp. 51–59.
Reischer, E. L. 2001. Running to the moon: The articulation and construction of self in marathon runners. *Anthropology of Consciousness*, 12 (2): 19–34.
Safai, P. 2003. Healing the body in the 'culture of risk': Examining the negotiation of treatment between sports medicine clinicians and injured athletes in Canadian intercollegiate sport. *Sociology of Sport Journal*, 20 (2): 127–146.
Silver, I. 1996. Role transitions, objects, and identity. *Symbolic Interaction*, 19 (1): 1–20.
Snow, D. A. and Anderson, L. 1995. The problem of identity construction among the homeless. In N. J. Hermann and L. T. Reynolds (eds), *Symbolic Interaction: An Introduction to Social Psychology*. New York: General Hall.
Sparkes, A. C. 2002. *Telling Tales in Sport and Physical Activity: A Qualitative Journey*. Champaign, IL: Human Kinetics.
Sparkes, A. C. and Smith, B. 2003. Men, sport, spinal cord injury and narrative time. *Qualitative Research*, 3 (3): 295–320.
Spencer, D. C. 2012. *Ultimate Fighting and Embodiment: Violence, Gender and Mixed Martial Arts*. London: Routledge.
Stone, G. P. 1977. Appearance and the self. In A. M. Rose (ed.), *Human Behaviour and Social Processes: An Interactionist Approach*. London: Routledge & Kegan Paul.
Tulle, E. 2007. Running to run: Embodiment, structure and agency amongst veteran elite runners. *Sociology*, 41 (2): 329–346.
Tulle, E. 2008. *Ageing, the Body and Social Change: Running in Later Life*. London: Palgrave Macmillan.
Turner, B. S. and Wainwright, S. P. 2003. Corps de ballet: The case of the injured ballet dancer. *Sociology of Health and Illness*, 25 (4): 269–288.
Wacquant, L. J. D. 1995. Pugs at work: Bodily capital and bodily labour among professional boxers. *Body and Society*, 1 (1): 65–93.
Wainwright, S. P. and Turner, B. S. 2006. 'Just crumbling to bits'? An exploration of the body, ageing, injury and career in classical ballet dancers. *Sociology*, 40 (2): 237–255.
Wiese-Bjornstal, D. M., Smith, A. M., Shaffer, S. and Morrey, M. A. 1998. An integrated model of response to sport injury: Psychological and sociological dynamics. *Journal of Applied Sport Psychology*, 10: 46–69.

Woodward, K. 2009. Hanging out and hanging about: Insider/outsider research in the sport of boxing. *Ethnography*, Special edition, 10 (4–5): 536–560.

Young, K. and White, P. 1995. Sport, physical danger and injury: The experience of élite women athletes. *Journal of Sport and Social Issues*, 19: 45–61.

28
RISKY/RISKING BODIES

Mike Brown

Introduction to risk

It is widely suggested that contemporary Western society has become obsessed with reducing unnecessary risks (Caplan, 2000; Lupton 1999; Lupton and Tulloch, 2002a), yet the popularity of recreational activities involving voluntary risk-taking, gives credence to Donnelly's (2004: 30) assertion that society has a 'curiously ambivalent attitude' toward risk-taking. Given media coverage of risks over which people have little control, such as antibiotic resistant 'superbugs', global warming and terrorism, it has been argued that individuals now focus attention on alleviating danger and risks in events over which they have some control in their everyday lives (Hope, 2005). To this end Furedi (2002: 8) has claimed that in contemporary society safety has become a fundamental value governed by what he has termed the 'precautionary principle'. The premise of this principle is that one should not take a risk unless the outcome is known in advance. Furedi (ibid.) suggests that this new moral etiquette, based on a heightened level of risk consciousness, 'is a prescriptive and intrusive morality. It demands that individuals subject themselves to the core value of safety. It encourages behaviour to be cautious and self-limiting. At the same time, it condemns those who put others at risk' (ibid.: 148).

Debates about risks and risk-taking have become openly politicized and embedded in government, professional and public discourses (Booth and Thorpe, 2007; Douglas 1992; Furedi, 2002). The desire to eliminate or control risks has seen the rise of risk management consultants, official standards, and policies. Technical definitions of risk (e.g. the probability of an event multiplied by the magnitude of the consequences) have been critiqued for being too narrow in focus and for failing to acknowledge the social and political contexts from which understandings of risk are generated (Kasperson et al., 2000; Slovic, 2000). Factors such as social background, gender, level of choice, prior experience, motivation, and the potential outcome shape individual and collective responses to risk (Kasperson et al., 2000; Slovic, 2000; Thorpe, 2007). Larana (2001: 25) has suggested that the disenchantment with experts' explanations of risk has led to 'the emergence of a new *risk consciousness*'. With expert knowledge problematized, what is viewed as risky is now seen as culturally constructed, highly contextualized, individualized and differentiated across time, places and cultures (Booth and Thorpe, 2007; Hope and Oliver, 2005; Lupton and Tulloch, 2002b). As Brown and Penney (2014: 270) have pointed out, what is defined as risky is 'both a political and a moral statement. The positioning of risk as a negative or positive is itself a reflection of the shifting value statements of a society at any given time.'

In the context of physical cultural studies (PCS), Booth and Thorpe (2007) have pointed out that for participants in extreme sports there is no universal standard by which to objectively assess risks; participants are required to constantly define and re-evaluate shifting perceptions of what they view as acceptable risk. Others are adopting anthropological approaches to risk in sport (Palmer, 2002), philosophical justifications of the value of dangerous sport (Russell, 2005), and auto-ethnographic examinations of gender, risk and responsibility (Laurendeau, 2011). Arguably, it is here, at the intersection of socio-cultural, embodied, philosophical, historical and psychological ways of knowing, that PCS's inter- and trans-disciplinary approach has much potential to shed new insights into voluntary risk-taking as 'materially based and culturally mediated' practices (Atkinson, 2011: 139).

Voluntary risk-taking in physical culture(s)

Notions of a risk-averse society – where safety and the desire for predictability guide action – stand in contrast to the rise of voluntary risk-taking in both sport and recreational contexts. Lyng's (1990) identification of the contradiction between Western society's efforts to reduce communal risks and individuals' participation in activities courting danger (e.g. physical contact sports, mountaineering, BASE jumping etc.) raises interesting issues for those interested in physical cultural studies. For as Donnelly has pointed out,

> We frequently admire individuals who appear to put 'life and limb' on the line for what, in the greater scheme of things, may be only a symbolic reward (e.g. a record of some kind); but may criticize those same individuals when things go wrong.
>
> *(Donnelly, 2004: 30)*

Donnelly's comment illustrates the tension faced by sportspeople and adventurers in contemporary society (e.g. when injured rugby players stay on the field, or commentary on the movie *Touching the Void*). When risk is seen primarily in terms of negative outcomes (e.g. disease, injury, financial hardship, death) it is less likely that voluntary risk-taking will be viewed in a favourable light. Furedi (2002: 4) commented that 'when safety is worshipped and risks are seen as intrinsically bad, society is making a clear statement about the values that ought to guide life … to ignore safety advice is to transgress the new moral consensus'. In this environment voluntary risk-taking might be considered 'as foolhardy, careless, irresponsible, and even "deviant", evidence of an individual's ignorance or lack of ability to regulate the self' (Lupton 1999: 148).

However, as with definitions of risk, individuals' decisions concerning risk-taking are complex and multifaceted, depending on previous experience, motivation, cultural values and the consequences of one's actions (or inaction). Individuals' responses to, or desire for risk has been studied from a number of perspectives (e.g. physiology, anthropology, sociology and psychology). Mythen (2007) has pointed out that while it is tempting to see risks as bad, in some areas of life – such as medicine, finance and leisure – the taking of risks can be rewarding (and rewarded). He argues that a focus on the negative aspect of risk-taking 'encourages us towards the erroneous view that human beings are innately risk averse' (ibid.: 801). Lupton and Tulloch (2002b) discuss the potential positives of participation in activities involving risk as a means to reveal an alternative version of the social actor. Rather than being inhibited by risk, a person may see the opportunity for personal gain, self-actualization, or simply the value in living an exciting life. For some people, appropriate risk-taking appears to be worth pursuing as it may lead to positive outcomes. For example, Howe's (2008) exploration of risk sports in remote locations led her to assert that risk 'contributes to the clarification of who we are, what we value, and what we are willing to do about it. It is a valuable element in developing a knowledge of one's self' (ibid.: 13).

Lyng's (1990) study of skydivers also sheds light on the productive aspects of voluntary risk-taking. Lyng used the term edgework to describe the participants' experiences. Edgework involves negotiations at 'the edge' of cultural boundaries: such as those between life and death, consciousness and unconsciousness, sanity and insanity, and 'an ordered sense of self and environment versus a disordered sense of self and environment' (ibid.: 857). He considered edgework as a positive aspect of human behaviour, highlighting that those who engage in edgework are not typically interested in thrill seeking or gambling. Lyng reported that participants in edgework refrained from placing themselves in situations involving circumstances over which they had no control (e.g. an adventure tourist operation). What participants sought was 'the chance to exercise skill in negotiating a challenge rather than turn their fate over to the roll of a dice' (ibid.: 863). So while to the casual observer skydiving might be deemed risky, for the dedicated participant it provides the opportunity to experience a sense of self-actualization, self-realization, or self-determination. As Lyng concluded,

> It is certainly strange that people voluntarily place themselves at risk even as public organizations endeavor to reduce the risks of living in modern society. It is even more startling to realize that these people value risk taking because it is the only means they have for achieving self-determination and authenticity. The same society that offers so much in the way of material 'quality of life' also propels many of us to the limits of our mortal existence in search of ourselves and our humanity.
>
> *(Lyng, 1990: 883)*

While not denying that activities such as skydiving contain an element of risk (the effect of gravity is undeniable), the attraction of voluntary risk-taking does not reside in luck, nor is it viewed as a foolhardy endeavour by practitioners (Lyng, 1990). Rather risk-taking is associated with 'the reflexive project of the self in terms of achieving personal "growth"' (Lupton, 1999: 154). The attraction of voluntary risk-taking as a constituent component in the experiences of adherents to a range of sporting and recreational activities is of interest to scholars of PCS as these participants are both shaped by, and have the ability to reshape, broader understandings of risk in contemporary society. Thus from a PCS perspective we might ask questions such as:

- Who has the power to define a risk or risk-taking behaviour, and how does this influence participation?
- What pedagogical/political forces or strategies are at play and how do they shape experiences and perceptions?
- Who is able to participate in risk-taking practices, and how is participation enabled or constrained?
- Whose voices and experiences of risk are marginalized and how is power and authority negotiated?

A case study: politics, morality and power in voluntary risk-taking

As Lyng noted, individuals who voluntarily participate in what are loosely defined as risky recreational activities (e.g. BASE jumping, sky diving, mountaineering, ocean sailing, etc.) do so in order to exercise control and enhance their quality of life. Thus the notion that practitioners in such endeavours engage in 'risky practices' is contentious. The expert or experienced practitioner draws on judgement and experience to minimize risks and maximize self-awareness. This is in contrast to the perspective of regulatory bodies or the casual observer who question the desirability of exposing oneself to unnecessary risks. In a recent study Brown and Penney (2014) examined public responses to a proposed solo sailing circumnavigation by the 16-year-old Australian 'schoolgirl'[1] Jessica Watson. This study highlights some of the central issues relating to voluntary risk-taking and how a physical cultural studies perspective can shed light on the nuanced and complex ways in which discourses of risk are used to maintain or disrupt ideological positions and challenge existing power relations.

Jessica Watson departed Sydney Harbour in October 2009 and returned in May 2010, three days before her seventeenth birthday. During this period she completed a solo sailing circumnavigation by way of the three Great Capes (Hope, Africa; Leeuwin, Australia; Horn, South America). On completion of her voyage she laid claim to the unofficial record for the youngest circumnavigator.[2] Prior to beginning the voyage Watson and her family were the focus of intense media attention and many public figures entered the debate (e.g. the Premier of Queensland, Anna Bligh; Former MotoGP world champion, Mick Doohan; Australian Family Association, John Morrissey). Few of the commentaries focused on the 'actual risks' associated with such a voyage, nor was there substantial commentary on the seaworthiness of the vessel, recent advances in communication and safety technology, or the documented experience of the skipper. Media reporting and associated blog postings focused on Watson's age and sex as key touchstones to portray the riskiness of such an undertaking. From a PCS perspective, we are able to analyse how Jessica Watson is positioned as being at risk through being discursively positioned as a young girl.

Inhibiting narratives of risk

The following comments posted in response to Kellett's (2009) newspaper article 'Schoolgirl's Solo Sail "Irresponsible"',[3] illustrate the positioning of Watson as being at risk.

> What a load of garbage. The kid should be given a clip over the ear, told to get into her room and do her homework and the parents should be told to get a responsible attitude or they will be taken to task by authorities. This is a disgrace. The kid will never be seen or heard of again …
>
> *(Phil,* Brisbane Times *website, 14 May 2009, 8:19 a.m.)*

> This girl isn't even old enough to drive a car, let alone sail a boat 40,000 kilometres around the world. An admirable goal, but not a very bright idea on the part of the parents to get behind this.
>
> *(JackSparrow,* Brisbane Times *website, 14 May 2009, 9:43 a.m.)*

The use of terms such as 'a girl' or 'a kid' served to position Watson as incapable of making informed 'adult' decisions. Jackson and Scott (1999: 19) have argued that, 'Risks to children are represented as inherently more grave than risks to adults: it is almost beyond debate that we should "protect" children, that any potential risk to children should be taken very seriously'. Thus it goes without saying that reasonable caring adults should object to such a risky endeavour. Positioning Watson as under the legal driving age, as a means to indicate a lack of maturity, 'draws on the legislative model that tries to neatly define life stages and capabilities by age'

(Brown and Penney, 2014: 272). By positioning Watson as 'a girl' or 'a kid' opponents of the voyage make claims about the ability and right of young people to make independent decisions.

> A boy sailing around the world can do it, but a young lady is very vulnerable indeed. She had better tie herself to something or else she will be overboard in no time. She should have someone else with her.
> *(Lyn, Brisbane Times website, 14 May 2009, 7:46 p.m.)*

Lyn's post reflects a gendered discourse of vulnerability, portraying young women as 'passive victims of risk' (Batchelor, 2007: 205). Laurendeau (2008: 296) has noted that seeking out and accepting risk 'is an integral part of the versions of masculinity that occupy hegemonic positions in sport'. In contrast, for women risk-taking has historically been something to be avoided or managed so as not to challenge conceptions of femininity or jeopardize the potential for motherhood (ibid.). In an earlier paper Palmer argued that discourses of extremity have been highly gendered. She contended that, 'where women are involved in dangerous pursuits, all sorts of cultural definitions and limitations are placed on their behavior' (Palmer, 2002: 333). Donnelly (2004) has provided an excellent commentary on the differing reactions to the deaths of mountaineers Alison Hargreaves and Rob Hall that illustrates how the morality of risk-taking has been played out on gender lines. However, Thorpe's (2007) research suggests that contemporary young women are increasingly likely to engage in risky behaviours across a range of activities including sports. She describes how many female extreme sports participants have not only accepted but normalized male value systems, such that visible scars are worn as 'badges of honor' much like their male peers (ibid.: 105). It is clear that what represents a risk is a complex amalgam of factors and that gendered representations have both historically, and contemporaneously, featured in definitions of what constitutes a responsible individual.

Counter narratives: empowering narratives of risk

The following four posts indicate that risk-taking can also be seen to offer opportunities for growth and development.

> It's only been in recent decades that 15 year olds and younger haven't been expected to earn their keep, and it's already been done by someone else her age. What makes the kids of today any less capable of doing that which the kids of the past used to? … If you treat kids like precious little snowflakes, they will expect that for the rest of their lives.
> *(Arhu #23, Stuff website, 15 May 2009, 12:07 p.m.)*

Adopting a historical perspective, Arhu remembers the productive roles and responsibilities that young people have previously occupied in society. Arhu views young people as competent social actors and cites the achievement of 'someone else her age' as evidence of capability. This challenges the conception of young people as inherently incompetent or 'at risk'.

> Hooray for this girl … All you sad, negative doomsdayers would have been yelling at Christopher Columbus that the world was flat if you were alive in his day. The girl has a dream. Better to die trying to achieve it than to live a long and unfulfilled life.
> *(Patsy, Brisbane Times website, 14 May 2009, 9:05 a.m.)*

Patsy points out Watson's right to take risks rather than to 'live a long and unfulfilled life'. Patsy challenges restrictive conceptions of femininity that exclude women from embracing risk.

> Why didn't people kick up a fuss when Jesse Martin (a boy from Melbourne) did the same thing in the late 1990s? (I think it would have been about 1997 from memory.) Was it because he was a 16 year old guy rather than a 16 year old girl?
> *(Helen,* Brisbane Times *website, 14 May 2009, 11:34 a.m.)*

Helen, who clearly has knowledge of previous circumnavigations pointed out the obviously gendered natured of much of the criticism levelled at Watson. This posting shows that opportunities exist to challenge gendered discourses of risk.

The final posting reveals an understanding of the value of informed risk-taking as a means to achieving personal growth (Lupton, 1999). Embracing opportunity and living life to the full, through pushing the boundaries of culturally accepted norms, is viewed as a positive endeavour that indicates a pathway to maturity.

> Part of growing up is taking responsibility for taking the decisions that can get us killed. She's chosen to do this, her parents have agreed as they obviously think she's capable. Therefore she shouldn't be held back by people who want to blanket her and hold her back from showing other young people what they can do.
> *(PD,* Brisbane Times *website, 14 May 2009, 9:03 a.m.)*

The contested nature of risk-taking

Commentary on Watson's voyage highlights the importance of the politics of risk definition (Adam and van Loon, 2000) and reveals the contested nature of definitions of risk and the way in which risk-taking behaviour is portrayed. Douglas and Wildavsky (1982) contend that individuals and interest groups selectively attend to certain risks that reflect particular worldviews (e.g. condemnation by the Australian Family Association). As a young woman, Jessica Watson embodies intersecting discourses of vulnerability and being in need of protection. Her teenage 'at risk' body is, as Shilling (1993: 204) highlights, 'centrally implicated in questions of self identity, the construction and maintenance of social inequalities, and the construction and development of societies'. It is clear that discourses of risk-taking and risk aversion are inherently tied to representations of embodiment that in turn shape how individuals are positioned, and how they should act in society. Brown and Penney (2014: 280) noted that 'People downplay certain risks and emphasize others as a means of maintaining and exercising control and power.' They suggested that the debates around Watson's voyage might best be understood by considering how the promotion of risk-taking or warnings to avoid unnecessary risks served 'as moral acts that sustain or undermine social, cultural or political positions' (ibid.). The data presented above illustrates how discourses of risk can be used to *constrain* young people and maintain hierarchical power structures while the counter narrative positions risk as a means of *enablement* – young people are capable and inspirational.

It is clear that Jessica Watson attracted attention because she challenged normative frameworks that sit comfortably with some groups in Western societies (e.g. family groups, older male sailors). By voluntarily embracing risk she disrupted society's positioning of women as passive victims of risk (e.g. sexual assault) rather than as proactive risk-takers (Lupton, 1999). Her proposed voyage drew substantial commentary from politicians, prominent sportspeople, special interest groups and members of the public revealing the importance of physical culture as 'a place where social forces, discourses, institutions, and processes congregate, congeal, and are contested in a manner which contributes to the shaping of human relations, experiences, and subjectivities' (Andrews, 2008: 56).

The blog postings related to Watson's proposed voyage support Laurendeau's (2008) contention that the pressures that female edgeworkers experience within the sport and recreation context mirror the pressures that are also brought to bear on them in their daily lives. The postings demonstrate that there are multiple perspectives on risk, the role of young people within society, and a level of resistance to accepting established gender stereotypes. For example Olstead (2011: 91) has described how women edgeworkers actively resisted 'the gendered idea that harm is a fixed reality for women, and that women are "always already" at risk'. The participants in her study took risks as 'a creative way for these women to dispute the social limits of their gendered performances' (ibid.: 91). As a young woman who challenged established limitations, Watson represented a threat to those (typically older and in positions of authority) who sought to determine what was or was not possible for a teenage girl.

Through reference to the case study on Jessica Watson, I have briefly illustrated the diversity of opinions and perceptions of voluntary risk-taking in a recreational pursuit in contemporary society. Far from representing a homogeneous position of society as risk averse, these postings reveal the contested and contradictory perspectives that individuals and interest groups hold. These support Donnelly's (2004: 54) assertion that voluntary risk-taking in sport and recreation reflects society's ambivalence to risk – in that 'it continues to celebrate risk while also being troubled by it'.

Watson's voyage could be viewed from a number of theoretical perspectives and different traditions of scholarship may provide contrasting or complementary insights. Positioning Watson through the use of age and gender categories illustrates the 'embodied nature of power relations' (Friedman and Van Ingen, 2011: 86) that were played out on the public stage. The initial newspaper article (Kellett, 2009) and the ensuing blog postings revealed complex, contradictory and diverse views on risk-taking, young people, young women and the role of parents and state agencies in contemporary Western society. In keeping with the ethos of PCS, the findings revealed the complexity of social relations, the way in which social power is fluid, contested and thwarted (e.g. calls made for maritime authorities to intervene were discussed but rejected) and the mutability of existing conceptual frameworks (e.g. Beck's risk society thesis).

Discussion

Twenty-five years ago Frey (1991: 144) suggested that 'the concept of risk can be a sensitizing, organizing concept for sports sociologists to employ when building models and explanations of human behaviour and social arrangements in the context of sport'. Given that discourses of risk permeate our everyday lives (e.g. risks from certain foods, germs if we fail to use hand sanitizer, or cardiovascular disease if we don't exercise regularly), Frey's call remains relevant today and is worthy of further attention (Giulianotti, 2009). In the absence of established authority (e.g. church or state) and contestation of scientific expertise (e.g. politicization of the causes and effects of global warming) examination of discourses of risk provides a means to study the physical cultural practices of both individuals and groups as they negotiate risk as the new moral etiquette (Furedi, 2002). The politicization of risk, the connection of risk discourses with the process of globalization (Douglas, 1992), the intersection of risk and gender – Laurendeau's 'gendered risk regimes' (2008: 300) – and the rise of alternative/extreme/lifestyle sports celebrating the risky/risking body (combined with the rise of digital media enabling new forms of production and consumption), provides fertile ground for furthering the developing genre of PCS.

Critical examination of conceptualizations of risk, risk-taking, and the positioning of individuals and groups as 'recipients' of risk, as active agents in seeking risk, or as perpetrators of power and authority through the categorization of the 'other' as being at risk, requires critical examination of existing structures and discourses combined with the ability to recognize and engage with emerging and fluid shifts in how risk is being constantly renegotiated.

Various expressions of active embodiment (Andrews and Silk, 2015) situate participants (as embodied beings) in complex relationships with risk discourses that enable or constrain access, levels of participation and continuity of involvement (e.g. women-only gyms, aqua jogging for 'seniors'). Thinking of risk in terms of moral and political discourses opens up opportunities for political debate and social action (Furedi, 2002), a project that lies at the heart of PCS. As briefly indicated in the case study above, analysis of risk discourses can challenge, confront and indicate alternative 'realities'. As Beck (1992: 24) has noted, reframing risk can lead to 'a reorganisation of power and authority'. Both positive and negative blog postings 'indicate that there is no fixed status quo and that "dominant" social, cultural and political values and beliefs can be challenged and changed, otherwise there would be no need to try and uphold them' (Brown and Penney, 2014: 284). The analysis of how participants in the complex field of physical culture negotiate discourses of risk has the potential to liberate and empower those, who like Watson, are subject to constraints that potentially limit both their aspirations and actions (Furedi, 2002). As Atkinson (2011: 137) suggests, the merit and future value of PCS lies in its collective call to committed praxis. Watson's voluntary risk-taking provides PCS scholars not only with fruitful avenues to examine constructions of risk and gender but to also reflexively engage with the value of transgression as we seek to cross disciplinary boundaries and productively extend our own fields of practice.

Notes

1 Watson was referred to as a 'schoolgirl' in a newspaper headline that led to the posts that are discussed here. This article was published before her departure.
2 Official records for the oldest and youngest circumnavigator stopped being recorded in 1999.
3 This article was published in September 2009, prior to Watson embarking on her voyage. Kellet's (2009) article appeared in the *Brisbane Times* and on Fairfax media's website in New Zealand (http://stuff.co.nz/).

References

Adam, B. and van Loon, J. 2000. Introduction: Repositioning risk; the challenge for social theory. In B. Adam, U. Beck, and J. van Loon (eds), *The Risk Society and Beyond*. London: Sage, 1–31.
Andrews, D. 2008. Kinesiology's inconvenient truth and the physical cultural studies imperative. *Quest*, 60(1), 45–62.
Andrews, D. and Silk, M. 2015. Physical cultural studies on sport. In R. Giulianotti, ed. *The Routledge Handbook of Sociology of Sport*. Abingdon, UK: Routledge, 83–93.
Atkinson, M. 2011. Physical cultural studies [Redux]. *Sociology of Sport Journal*, 28, 135–144.
Batchelor, S. 2007. 'Getting mad wi' it': Risk-seeking by young women. In K. Hannah-Moffat and P. O'Malley (eds), *Gendered Risks*. Abingdon, UK: Routledge-Cavendish, 205–227.
Beck, U. 1992. *Risk Society: Towards a New Modernity*. London: Sage.
Booth, D. and Thorpe, H. 2007. Meaning of extreme, the. In D. Booth and H. Thorpe (eds), *Berkshire Encyclopedia of Extreme Sports*. Great Barrington, MA: Berkshire, 181–197.
Brown, M. and Penney, D. 2014. Solo sailing: An 'ordinary girl', voluntary risk-taking and (ir)responsibility. *Sociology of Sport Journal*, 31(3), 267–286. doi: 10.1123/ssj.2013-0121
Caplan, P. 2000. Introduction: Risk revisited. In P. Caplan, ed. *Risk Revisited*. London: Pluto Press, 1–28.
Donnelly, P. 2004. Sport and risk culture. In K. Young, ed. *Sporting Bodies, Damaged Selves: Sociological Studies of Sports-Related Injuries*. Oxford: Elsevier, 29–57.

Douglas, M. 1992. *Risk and Blame*. London: Routledge.
Douglas, M. and Wildavsky, A. 1982. *Risk and Culture*. Berkeley, CA: University of California Press.
Frey, J. 1991. Social risk and the meaning of sport. *Sociology of Sport Journal*, 8, 136–145.
Friedman, M. and Van Ingen, C. 2011. Bodies in space: Spatializing physical cultural studies. *Sociology of Sport Journal*, 28, 85–105.
Furedi, F. 2002. *Culture of Fear*. London: Continuum.
Giulianotti, R. 2009. Risk and sport: An analysis of sociological theories and research agendas. *Sociology of Sport Journal*, 26, 540–556.
Hope, A. 2005. Risk, education and culture; Interpreting danger as a dynamic, culturally situated process. In A. Hope and P. Oliver (eds), *Risk, Education and Culture*. Aldershot: Ashgate, 3–20.
Hope, A. and Oliver, P. 2005. Preface. In A. Hope and P. Oliver (eds), *Risk, Education and Culture*. Aldershot: Ashgate, ix–xii.
Howe, L. 2008. Remote sport: Risk and self-knowledge in wilder spaces. *Journal of the Philosophy of Sport*, 15, 1–16.
Jackson, S., and Scott, S. 1999. Risk anxiety and the social construction of childhood. In D. Lupton (ed.), *Risk and Sociocultural Theory: New Directions and Perspectives*. Cambridge: Cambridge University Press, 86–107.
Kasperson, R. et al. 2000. The social amplification of risk: A conceptual framework. In P. Slovic (ed.), *The Perception of Risk*. London: Earthscan, 232–245.
Kellett, C. 2009. Schoolgirl's solo sail 'irresponsible'. Available from www.stuff.co.nz/world/australia/2411813/Schoolgirls-solo-sail-irresponsible (accessed 9 December 2010).
Larana, E. 2001. Reflexivity, risk and collective action over waste management: A constructive proposal. *Current Sociology*, 49(1), 23–48. doi: 10.1177/0011392101049001003
Laurendeau, J. 2008. 'Gendered risk regimes': A theoretical consideration of edgework and gender. *Sociology of Sport Journal*, 25, 293–309.
Laurendeau, J. 2011. 'If you're reading this, it's because I've died': Masculinity and relational risk in BASE jumping. *Sociology of Sport Journal*, 28, 404–420.
Lupton, D. 1999. *Risk*. London: Routledge.
Lupton, D. and Tulloch, J. 2002a. 'Life would be pretty dull without risk': Voluntary risk-taking and its pleasures. *Health Risk and Society*, 4(2), 113–124. doi: 10.1080/13698570220137015
Lupton, D. and Tulloch, J. 2002b. 'Risk is part of your life': Risk epistemologies among a group of Australians. *Sociology*, 36(2), 317–334. doi: 10.1177/0038038502036002005
Lyng, S. 1990. Edgework: A social psychological analysis of voluntary risk taking. *American Journal of Sociology*, 95(4), 851–886. doi: 10.1086/229379
Mythen, G. 2007. Reappraising the risk society thesis: Telescopic sight or myopic vision? *Current Sociology*, 55(6), 793–813.
Olstead, R. 2011. Gender, space and fear: A study of women's edgework. *Emotion, Space and Society*, 4, 86–94. doi: 10.1016/j.emospa.2010.12.004
Palmer, C. 2002. 'Shit happens': The selling of risk in extreme sport. *The Australian Journal of Anthropology*, 13(3), 323–336.
Russell, J. 2005. The value of dangerous sport. *Journal of the Philosophy of Sport*, 32(1), 1–19. doi: 10.1080/00948705.2005.9714667
Shilling, C. 1993. *The Body and Social Theory*. London: Sage.
Slovic, P. 2000. Perception of risk. In P. Slovic (ed.), *The Perception of Risk*. London: Earthscan, 220–231.
Thorpe, H. 2007. Gender. In D. Booth and H. Thorpe (eds), *Berkshire Encyclopedia of Extreme Sports*. Great Barrington, MA: Berkshire, 103–111.

29
INVISIBLE (WOMEN'S) BODIES

Kim Toffoletti and Catherine Palmer

Introduction

This chapter approaches the issue of invisible bodies in physical cultural studies debates by considering Muslim women's experiences of sport. A number of feminist scholars have identified the invisibility of Muslim women in wider discussions about women's participation in sport and exercise and have sought to illuminate the plurality of Muslim women as a social category as well as the socio-cultural, political and geographic contexts that shape Muslim women's embodied experiences of physical activity (Benn, Pfister and Jawad, 2011; Hargreaves, 2007; Kay, 2006; Pfister, 2003; Walseth, 2006a, 2006b). Existing literature primarily perceives and responds to barriers and enablers to Muslim women's participation as players of sport, with less emphasis placed on leisure and recreational expressions of active embodiment (for instance, sports fandom). The current orientation of studies concerning Muslim women's active participation in organized sport and fitness largely conforms to social inclusion paradigms, where marginalized groups and individuals are incorporated into mainstream culture as players of, or active participants in, organized sport (Walseth and Fasting, 2004).

In this chapter we offer an alternative approach to Muslim women's experiences of physical activity and leisure beyond the commonplace deficit model of participation (Knez, Macdonald and Abbott, 2012: 109). Central to our discussion is an interrogation of the dynamics of power that frame Muslim women through a deficit lens, and advocates for more research that is attentive to the complex tensions, pleasures and contradictions that shape Muslim women's encounters with various domains of physical culture. We suggest that a PCS approach, by extending the parameters of how we conceive active embodiment, can bring Muslim women into view (beyond the dominant, yet limited, framing of them in terms of sport participation) to encompass the varied ways they experience their own bodies in motion and other active bodies they encounter across a range of sites. At the conclusion of this chapter we reflect on our own research on media representations, active experiences and fan practices to illustrate this point.

In tandem with highlighting the possibilities PCS offers to opening up how we 'make visible' Muslim women's encounters with and relationship to the wider domain of physical cultures, this chapter contributes to PCS's fluid sensibility by exploring how transnational feminist thinking can advance critical scholarship on Muslim women's engagements with physical cultural domains. As a theoretical frame, methodological tool and analytic device, transnational feminism draws attention to global operations of social power as they manifest along intersecting axes of gender, sexuality, race and nation to govern, organize and represent the experiences of Muslim female bodies. It offers a model for the production of feminist knowledge across cultural divides that is attentive to existing power structures between western and non-western women, in an attempt to transform inequitable social relations through practices of solidarity.

The chapter is divided into four sections. The first section details how Muslim women's bodies are rendered invisible in physical cultural domains such as sport, despite growing media attention being paid to Muslim women post-9/11. The second section introduces transnational feminist theory to consider how it can help transform the way Muslim women's relationships to the complex field of physical culture are conceptualized. In the third section, which evaluates existing feminist research into Muslim women's sporting activities, we explore where and how Muslim women's experiences of sport and physical activity have been made visible and the limits and possibilities of such approaches. The final section draws on our own research in areas that remain under-investigated in physical cultural studies of Muslim women – media, fandom and consumption – to illustrate our arguments. It is through our own research experience that we identify a need to examine Muslim women's encounters with, and embodied experiences of, the physical realm in new and more expansive ways.

By surveying the research literature in order to identify where and how Muslim women appear in studies of sport and physical culture, as well as highlighting their absence in sports fan and media scholarship, this chapter demonstrates the need to expand studies of Muslim women beyond sport, and to adopt theoretical perspectives like transnational feminism to disrupt the assumed position of the Muslim woman as socio-cultural 'Other'. In the tradition of PCS approaches, advocating for the production of new knowledges and understandings of Muslim women's embodied experiences and encounters with physical cultural domains is geared toward 'enabling individuals and groups to discern, challenge, and potentially transform existing power structures and relations', hence facilitate social change (Andrews and Silk, 2015).

The 'invisible' Muslim woman

Within western culture, Muslim women's bodies have been historically constructed and represented as 'Other'; rendered variously as unfamiliar, strange, exotic and different to western norms and standards (Mohanty, 2003). It has been suggested that growing attention on cultural diversity in the contemporary media has seen an increase in the number and types of representations of Muslim women; however, Muslim women continue to be portrayed in a manner that emphasizes difference and 'Otherness' (MacDonald, 2006).

The substantial media coverage devoted to African-American female Muslim fencer Ibtihaj Muhammad as she qualified for the Rio 2016 Olympic games is suggestive of the increased visibility being accorded to veiled Muslim women in sport. Notably, much of this media attention was framed in terms of the challenges of wearing a veil, including Muhammad's own tweets about being asked to remove her head covering for photo accreditation at a sport event and subsequently being given an incorrect ID belonging to another person with a Muslim sounding name (Bult, 2016). Writing about the journalistic commentary on elite female Muslim athletes at the 2012 London Olympics, Samie and Sehlikoglu (2015) suggest that this kind of visibility, while drawing attention to Muslim women's athletic participation, does so in ways that reinscribe entrenched ideas about Muslim women as marginalized and oppressed.

Their analysis of western media representations of Muslim female Olympians demonstrates that increased media visibility functions to reinscribe relations of power by characterizing veiled Muslim women in physical culture spaces as 'strange, incompetent and out of place' (Samie and Sehlikoglu, 2015: 363). The authors argue that although Muslim women athletes are garnering media attention, their athletic abilities and achievements are depicted in ways that position them as 'Other' to western norms. When veiled Muslim women (both in Islamic states and living in the west) participate in sport, particularly global mega-events such as the Olympic Games and Paralympics, their experiences tend to be characterized in western media portrayals as a struggle against oppressive forces – religious, political and patriarchal. As noted by Samie and Sehlikoglu, the veil becomes a marker of visibility which is strategically used by the west to claim superiority over Islam (ibid.: 368). Concomitantly, non-veiled Muslim athletes remain invisible in representational accounts. The authors argue that this is because the western gaze fails to 'see' or recognize Muslim women who do not fit within pre-established colonialist narratives of Muslim women as hidden, passive and silent (ibid.: 371).

Transnational feminism

Here we explore the productive possibilities of applying transnational feminism to studies of Muslim women, sport and physical culture, with a view to offering new directions for research concerned with communities who are socially marginalized, hence commonly rendered invisible. Nagar and Swarr define transnational feminism as:

> an intersectional set of understandings, tools, and practices that can: (a) attend to the racialized, classed, masculinized, and heteronormative logics and practices of globalization and capitalist patriarchies, and the multiple ways in which they (re)structure colonial and neo-colonial relations of domination and subordination; (b) grapple with the complex and contradictory ways in which these processes both inform and are shaped by a range of subjectivities and understandings of individual and collective agency; and (c) interweave critiques, actions, and self-reflexivity so as to resist a priori predictions of what might constitute feminist politics in a given place and time.
> *(Nagar and Swarr, 2010: 5)*

By foregrounding the asymmetries of globalization processes and imagining new ways to forge solidarities between women without recourse to existing power hierarchies, transnational feminism offers a conceptually innovative frame to approach questions about identity, difference and visibility within PCS.

As white, middle-class, heterosexual western feminist sport scholars working to re-orient the way Muslim women's relationship to sport is approached, we envision transnational feminist theory as a 'way to do feminist work across cultural divides' (Grewal and Kaplan, 1994: 2). Transnational feminism exposes the complicity of western feminisms in the agendas of modernity and colonialism, which rely on the economic exploitation and socio-cultural marginalization of the 'Other', differentiating it from related approaches, like intersectionality, which aims to theorize multiple vectors of difference. While western feminism has revealed the unequal power relations between the genders, it has been critiqued by transnational feminists for failing to recognize its own embeddedness in the hierarchies of power between different cultures (Grewal and Kaplan, 1994; Mohanty, 2003). Thus feminist practices built on a Eurocentric vision of global sisterhood risk 'creating essentialist and monolithic categories that suppress issues of diversity, conflict and multiplicity within categories' (Grewal and Kaplan, 1994: 3). A key dimension of transnational feminism, then, is a call for western feminism to identify and internally critique the sets of values and assumptions on which first world women's issues erroneously become the dominant frame of reference for understanding the situation of all women.

Within the existing literature, two key texts demonstrate an indebtedness to transnational feminism – Jennifer Hargreaves's *Heroines of Sport: The Politics of Difference and Identity* (2000) and Tansin Benn, Gertrud Pfister and Haifaa Jawad's (2011) edited collection *Muslim Women and Sport*. It is primarily through a critique of sport organizations, institutions and practices that both texts frame their consideration of 'invisible' women's embodied experiences. Building on this work, we suggest that transnational feminism can also be fruitfully used to encourage researchers and policy makers to reflect on *how* knowledge about Muslim women in sport is produced, *by whom* and *for what purposes* (Mohanty, 2003). For instance, in the next section we identify that studies of Muslim women in sport are almost exclusively focused on barriers and enablers to Muslim women's participation in physical activity. This approach, we argue, presupposes that Muslim women are marginalized within sporting practices and discourses, and our role is to seek explanations for their outsider status, reflect on how they negotiate their marginal identity, and develop strategies to facilitate greater inclusion. By failing to look beyond this particular orientation, we risk reproducing the idea that Muslim women are in perpetual struggle and conflict with physical cultural domains. In our call for a re-orientation of studies of Muslim women to look beyond sport we question the production of knowledge about Muslim women that starts from a position of deficit and the purposes it might serve in reinscribing hierarchies of power.

The transnational feminist emphasis on building connections and alliances between diverse groups of women offers another means through which to frame a more expansive consideration of Muslim women's experiences of sport and recreation. There is no prescriptive way to enact solidarity, as Chandra Mohanty notes, although she advocates for relationships between diverse groups that are underpinned by 'mutuality, accountability, and the recognition of common interests' (Mohanty, 2003: 7). By suggesting that we look more broadly at the ways Muslim women encounter active embodiment – by consuming traditional and social media, through fandom and spectator practices, and via a diverse range of physical activities – we contest the narrow focus on sport participation in relation to Muslim women, hence open up the field through which points of connection can be made between women from diverse backgrounds, both Muslim and non-Muslim, who participate in a broad range of physical cultural activities and sites variously as players, participants, fans, journalists, coaches, educators, health professionals, administrators, scholars and the like. In keeping with transnational feminist paradigms, this kind of generative project necessitates foregrounding the differing situations and histories shaping various Muslim women's expressions of active embodiment internationally. Alongside Hargreaves (2000) and Benn, Pfister and Jawad (2011), we suggest that accounting for the particular circumstances of diverse groups of Muslim women, as well as questioning the priority given to western feminist perspectives and agendas, fosters a more complex understanding of how Muslim women experience their own and others' moving bodies in the wider cultural imaginary and representational sphere. Exploring how women can share affinities and pleasures through leisure, sport, fitness, health and recreation begins from the position that Muslim women can occupy positions as agentic subjects with capacity to express and respond to wider social circumstances shaping their encounters with physical cultural realms.

Muslim women and physical activity

Muslim women have been the subjects of a growing body of literature concerned with female empowerment as a means of achieving global gender justice (Benn, Pfister and Jawad, 2011). To a large extent, these studies have relied on social capital (Walseth, 2008), social inclusion

(Maxwell et al., 2013) and feminist post-structural frameworks (McCue and Kourouche, 2010). The broader field of international scholarship on Muslim women and sport almost exclusively examines Muslim women who partake in physical activity (Knez, MacDonald and Abbott, 2012). In this context, participation is assumed to mean *active* participation – that is, the physical activity of playing sport or exercising. Other forms of participation as consumers of sport, fitness, leisure and media experiences have thus far been largely on the periphery of discussions about Muslim women's relationship to physical activity.

Studies of Muslim women and sport emphasize both the facilitation of and hindrances to involvement in physical activity by exploring the interrelated factors of family influence (Kay, 2006), socio-cultural expectations of Muslim femininities (Nakamura, 2002), patriarchy (Hargreaves, 2007), ethnic identity (Abdul Razak et al., 2010) and religion (Benn, Dagkas and Jawad, 2011; De Knop and Theeboom, 1996; Pfister, 2003; Walseth and Fasting, 2003). Kristen Walseth's qualitative study of Norwegian Muslim women's experiences of physical activity stands as a landmark study in this area (2006a, 2006b, 2008), although investigations of Muslim women's participation in physical activity spans a variety of countries and continents, as evidenced in the edited collection *Muslim Women and Sport* (Benn, Pfister and Jawad, 2011), which offers investigations of Muslim women's sporting experiences from countries in Europe, North Africa and what western commentators term the 'Middle-East'. A number of studies coming out of Australia have also investigated the potential of sport and organized physical activities (fitness) to foster Muslim women's social inclusion (Cortis, 2009; Maxwell et al., 2013), the relationship between sport and identity politics for Muslim women who play sport (McCue and Kourouche, 2010; Palmer, 2008, 2009), and the potential health benefits of physical activity for young Muslim-Australians (Knez et al., 2012).

The theoretical reliance on social inclusion paradigms in some studies of Muslim women's sport participation places its emphasis on Muslim women's lack of connection and agency in social life (Maxwell et al., 2013). Redressing some of the limitations of these frameworks are studies that adopt a feminist post-structuralist lens, which allows for a consideration of agency, resistance and the performance and negotiation of Muslim and feminine identities when partaking in physical activity (Ahmad, 2011; McCue and Kourouche, 2010; Walseth, 2006a). Such research plays an important role in recasting the Muslim woman as agentic, rather than oppressed, in her encounters with sport. It is important to recognize the significant contributions of sport feminists to addressing Muslim women's participation in physical activity. The leading work in the field mobilizes many of the principles of transnational feminist thinking, including practices of knowledge production, contesting relations of power and enacting solidarities between women. Considerable scope exists, we believe, for a more systematic application of transnational feminist theory and praxis in studies of sport and physical culture. We argue that, collectively, the writings of transnational feminists can provide an overarching theoretical framework and analytical tool to re-orient the way Muslim women's encounters with sport are conceptualized to account for the interrelated dimensions of power, knowledge and solidarity, relative to the global flows that shape Muslim women's identities and experiences. Transnational feminism's generative focus on alliance building between different groups of Muslim women, as well as between Muslim and non-Muslim women, also offers an alternative way of conceptualizing women's relationship to the physical cultural realm, beyond dichotomous narratives of inclusion/exclusion, inside/outside, barriers/enablers, invisibility/visibility. In this regard, transnational feminism as a form of political praxis appears to share synergies with aspects of PCS that seek out moments of potential liberation emergent from processes of collective recognition and critique of physical cultural processes across various domains (educative, geographical, communal) (Andrews and Silk, 2015).

What emerges from surveying the literature into Muslim women's sporting participation is the tendency of this research to identify obstacles to playing sport as a means of facilitating Muslim women's greater involvement in athletic pursuits and promoting gender equality. As a result, these findings do not offer a comprehensive picture of the ways in which different Muslim women encounter and respond to physical cultures and (im)mobile bodies. Such omissions suggest a need to extend previous studies by moving beyond a deficit view of Muslim women's participation, which is typically couched in terms of barriers to social inclusion through sport. Crucially, as advocated by a PCS embrace of methodological and conceptual fluidity, we argue that a more expansive consideration of Muslim women's experiences of sport and physical activity necessitates adopting theoretical approaches beyond social capital, social inclusion and post-structural paradigms. Here we also suggest that recognizing diversity among Muslim women requires broadening the definition of Muslim women's encounters with sport to encompass their wider engagements with physical cultural domains in various capacities, such as via sport media consumption. By exploring the varied means by which Muslim women participate in, consume and are represented by processes and discourses of physical culture at local, national and global levels, the possibility opens up for alternative articulations of both sporting and Muslim identity.

Research reflections

Through our own research we have identified notable gaps in how Muslim women's relationship to physical culture and sport is portrayed. The visibility accorded to Muslim women in physical culture settings is mainly limited to Muslim women as athletes (Amara, 2012; Hargreaves, 2000; Samie and Sehlikoglu, 2015). Outside the context of mainstream, organized sport, Muslim women's (in)active bodies (particularly unveiled bodies) remain largely invisible. As a result, what also remains invisible are the contextually specific experiences and perspectives of diverse Muslim women as they navigate their everyday expressions of and responses to active embodiment. In one of the authors' own (Toffoletti, 2014) investigation of a fictional film about Iranian women football fans, transnational feminist paradigms offered a conceptual framework through which to problematize populist ethnocentric characterizations of Muslim women as a singular, homogeneous group (Mohanty, 2003) and explores how the film in question contests such western imaginings of the Muslim woman. By analysing the cinematic depiction of female Muslim sport fans using a transnational feminist framework, it offers an example of the kind of critical interventions we are proposing in this chapter and which could be productively extended to the visual analysis of media portrayals of Muslim women across a multitude of physical culture sites that go beyond the sports field, for instance, fitness magazines, sportswear websites, social media platforms devoted to health, gym and exercise cultures.

Our own research in the field of sport fans studies has also illuminated the possibilities of PCS for advancing critical scholarship on Muslim women's embodied experiences of physical cultural domains that moves beyond a focus on the sporting body. Whereas research into Muslim women and sport is almost exclusively focused on active participation in sport and encouraging community engagement within a social inclusion agenda, there has been no corresponding examination of Muslim women's relationship to sport as non-playing participants. In using the term 'non-playing participants', we emphasize that the consumption of sport is a form of participation not typically recognized in the literature or in taken-for-granted assumptions about what involvement in sport might mean. Being a fan or doing fandom requires active engagement on behalf of the supporter, whether it be cheering at the stadium, tweeting on social media, or meeting up with friends to watch a televised game. In the context of this chapter, then, the term 'consumptive participation' is also used as a means to distinguish embodied encounters that do not require physical exertion from what is commonly understood as active participation; that is, the playing of sport. We highlight this distinction to emphasize the limited ways that Muslim women's experiences of physical culture are framed, hence bring into view alternative ways of conceptualizing the practices, process and politics of active embodiment for Muslim women. Palmer's (2008) work, for example explores the ways in which a group of young Muslim, refugee women use their shared experiences of playing in a soccer team as a way of establishing and embellishing a particular cultural identity that both affirms and challenges many of the traditions of Islam. Drawing on a series of qualitative interviews with and many hours of field observations of the players at training, competition and in other social settings, Palmer teases out some of the ways in which these young women negotiate what are, at times, quite complex cultural politics for young Muslim women growing up in Australia's fifth largest capital city.

With the commodification of sport has come a critical focus on those who consume sport – the supporters, followers, fans and flaneurs, who constitute the variety of spectator identities characteristic of the contemporary sport consumer (Giulianotti, 2002). Participation in this sense takes a variety of forms, which includes attending games (ibid.), following athletes and teams local and globally via sport media (Hutchins and Rowe, 2012), as well as contributing to wider sport discourse via mediated forums (Palmer and Thompson, 2007). There are documented benefits of sport fan engagement as a leisure activity for women that enhances well-being by fostering affirmative group identities and a sense of community, while providing pleasure and enjoyment to participants (Mewett and Toffoletti, 2011; Obel, 2012). Co-authored research by one of the authors (Toffoletti and Mewett, 2012: 6) has highlighted the absence of, and need for, further research into sports consumption by women to encompass more of the world's regions, as well as identifying the need for greater engagement with women from minority backgrounds. What remains absent from sport fan literature is an analysis of the practices, experiences and meaning of sporting spectatorship for women who do not fit the normative categories of 'woman' and 'sport fan' – particularly, but not exclusively, through religion or ethnicity. We assert that these kinds of insights can bring into view the pleasures and possibilities sport holds for Muslim women beyond the playing field to foster inclusion and affirm identities. The example of sport fandom raised here offers one instance of how PCS scholarship can extend our thinking beyond limited definitions of participation and the kind of social cohesion this entails to consider how Muslim women mediate and negotiate different physical cultural spaces across varying socio-cultural, political and national contexts.

Conclusion

This chapter has attempted to address the issue of the invisible female Muslim body in physical cultural studies to re-orient the way Muslim women's relationship to sport is conceptualized, moving away from discourses of inclusion towards a wider exploration of their leisure and recreational encounters with, and expressions of, active embodiment. We recognize that there are many domains of sport participation in which research on Muslim women is limited: Muslim women as media consumers, coaches, educators, managers, judges, officials and administrators remain largely invisible in the academic literature and wider cultural realm. This chapter begins to address this invisibility through an examination of fan practices and media representations, suggesting a transnational feminist framework as a way forward.

In this chapter we have challenged those approaches that privilege a singular emphasis to engaging with sport in favour of alternative theoretical and conceptual lines of inquiry that 'make visible' Muslim women's diverse experiences of physical culture. This multi-dimensional approach to Muslim women's engagement with sport, we argue, is urgently needed in a climate where difference on the basis of gender and ethnic identity is commonly understood in the wider cultural imaginary (including media portrayals and sporting life) as a problem to overcome. Rather than viewing difference per se as the cause of Muslim women's invisibility we suggest that transnational feminist theory can transform the way researchers and practitioners working in physical cultural spaces conceptualize Muslim women's experiences. By emphasizing the role of power relations in the production of knowledge, transnational feminist perspectives build on existing sport feminist research that has sought to pose a challenge to western tropes of Muslim women as 'Other', hence invisible. Our research highlights an important gap in sport studies, calling for further critical reflection and investigation to redress the limited understandings of Muslim women as they appear in representational accounts, in favour of a more holistic understanding of Muslim experiences through the study of physical cultures.

The emphasis on particular discourses, images and understandings through which Muslim women's engagement with sport and physical culture has been constructed also raises questions for research with other invisible subjects such as Indigenous women or women in the Global South. Indeed, transnational feminism enables us to reflect on the theoretical and empirical bias towards the Global North when writing about women's experiences of sport and underscores the need for dialogue that recognizes that 'social theory from the world periphery has power and relevance for understanding our changing world' (Connell, 2007: ix).

Acknowledgements

Sections of this chapter have been adapted from an article by the authors published in the *International Review for the Sociology of Sport* titled 'New Approaches for Studies of Muslim Women and Sport'.

References

Abdul Razak, M. T., Omar-Fauzee, M. and Abd-Latif, R. 2010. The perspective of Arabic Muslim women toward sport participation. *Journal of Asia Pacific Studies*, 1 (2), 364–377.
Ahmad, A. 2011. British football: Where are the Muslim female footballers? *Soccer and Society*, 12 (3), 443–456.
Amara, M. 2012. Veiled women athletes in the 2008 Beijing Olympics: Media accounts. *International Journal of the History of Sport*, 29 (4), 638–651.
Andrews, D. L. and Silk, M. L. 2015. Physical cultural studies on sport. In R. Guilianotti (ed.), *Routledge handbook of the sociology of sport*. New York: Routledge, 83–93.
Benn, T., Dagkas, S. and Jawad, H. 2011. Embodied faith: Islam, religious freedom and educational practices in physical education. *Sport, Education and Society*, 16 (1), 17–34.
Benn, T., Pfister, G. and Jawad, H. (eds). 2011. *Muslim women and sport*. London: Routledge.
Bult, L. 2016. Muslim American Olympic fencer Ibtihaj Muhammad was asked to remove her hijab while registering for SXSW. *New York Daily News*, 12 March. Available from: www.nydailynews.com/news/national/u-s-fencer-ibtihaj-muhammad-asked-remove-hijab-sxsw-article-1.2562503 (accessed 15 March 2016).
Connell, R. 2007. *Southern theory: The global dynamics of knowledge in social science*. Sydney: Allen & Unwin.
Cortis, N. 2009. Social inclusion and sport: Culturally diverse women's perspectives. *Australian Journal of Social Issues*, 44 (1), 91–106.
De Knop, P. and Theeboom, M. 1996. Implications of Islam on Muslim girls: Sport participation in Western Europe. *Sport, Education and Society*, 1 (2), 147–164.
Giulianotti, R. 2002. Supporters, followers, fans, and flaneurs. *Journal of Sport and Social Issues*, 26 (1), 25–46.
Grewal, I. and Kaplan, C. 1994. *Scattered hegemonies: Postmodernity and transnational feminist practices*. Minneapolis, MN: University of Minnesota Press.

Hargreaves, J. 2000. *Heroines of sport: The politics of difference and identity*. London: Routledge.
Hargreaves, J. 2007. Sport, exercise, and the female Muslim body. In J. Hargreaves and P. Vertinsky (eds), *Physical culture, power, and the body*. New York: Routledge, 74–100.
Hutchins, B. and Rowe, D. 2012. *Sport beyond television*. London: Routledge.
Kay, T. 2006. Daughters of Islam: Family influences on Muslim young women's participation in sport. *International Review for the Sociology of Sport*, 41, (3–4) 357–373.
Knez, K., Macdonald, D. and Abbott, R. 2012. Challenging stereotypes: Muslim girls talk about physical activity, physical education and sport. *Asia-Pacific Journal of Health, Sport and Physical Education*, 3 (2), 109–122.
MacDonald, M. 2006. Muslim women and the veil: Problems of image and voice in media representations. *Feminist Media Studies*, 6 (1), 7–23.
Maxwell, H., Foley, C., Taylor, T. and Burton, C. 2013. Social inclusion in community sport: A case study of Muslim women in Australia. *Journal of Sport Management*, 27 (6), 467–481.
McCue, H. and Kourouche, F. 2010. The identity of the 'Australian Muslim woman' in sport and recreation. In S. Akbarzadeh (ed.), *Challenging identities: Muslim women in Australia*. Victoria: MUP, 130–158.
Mewett, P. and Toffoletti, K. 2011. Finding footy: Female fan socialization and Australian rules football. *Sport in Society*, 14 (5), 670–684.
Mohanty C. T. 2003. *Feminism without borders: Decolonizing theory, practicing solidarity*. Durham, NC: Duke University Press.
Nagar, R. and Swarr, A. L. (eds). 2010. *Critical transnational feminist praxis*. Albany, NY: SUNY.
Nakamura, Y. 2002. Beyond the hijab: Female Muslims and physical activity. *Women in Sport and Physical Activity Journal*, 11 (1), 21–48.
Obel, C. 2012. Fantasy, fun and identity construction among female fans of rugby union. In K. Toffoletti and P. Mewett (eds), *Sport and its female fans*. New York: Routledge, 115–134.
Palmer, C. 2008. Policy from the pitch? Soccer and young refugee women in a shifting policy climate. *Social Policy Review*, 20, 173–190.
Palmer, C. 2009. Soccer and the politics of identity for young Muslim refugee women in South Australia. *Soccer and Society*, 10 (1), 27–38.
Palmer, C. and Thompson, K. 2007. The paradoxes of football spectatorship: On-field and online expressions of social capital among the 'Grog Squad'. *Sociology of Sport Journal*, 24 (2), 187–205.
Pfister, G. 2003. Women and sport in Iran: Keeping goal in the hijab? In I. Hartmann-Tews and G. Pfister (eds), *Sport and women: Social issues in international perspective*. London: Routledge, 207–223.
Samie, S. F. and Sehlikoglu, S. 2015. Strange, incompetent and out-of-place: Media, Muslim sportswomen and London 2012. *Feminist Media Studies*, 15 (3), 363–381.
Toffoletti, K. 2014 Iranian women's sports fandom: Gender, resistance, and identity in the football movie *Offside*. *Journal of Sport and Social Issues*, 38 (1), 75–92.
Toffoletti, K. and Mewett, P. 2012. *Sport and its female fans*. New York: Routledge.
Walseth, K. 2006a. Young Muslim women and sport: The impact of identity work. *Leisure Studies*, 25 (1), 75–94.
Walseth, K. 2006b. Sport and belonging. *International Review for the Sociology of Sport*, 41 (3–4), 447–464.
Walseth, K. 2008. Bridging and bonding social capital in sport. *Sport, Education and Society*, 13 (1), 1–17.
Walseth, K. and Fasting, K. 2003. Islam's view on physical activity and sport: Egyptian women interpreting Islam. *International Review for the Sociology of Sport*, 38 (1), 45–60.
Walseth, K. and Fasting, K. 2004. Sport as a means of integrating minority women. *Sport in Society*, 7 (1), 109–129.

30
AFFECTIVE AND PLEASURED BODIES

Adele Pavlidis

This chapter starts with an extended quote from a participant interviewed in 2011 about her involvement with roller derby in Australia. June (not her real name), in her early thirties, worked as a naturopath. She had recently gone through a breakup with her boyfriend and shared some of the ways roller derby affected her:

> It's just that it gave me that *strength*, I was feeling quite *broken* at the time that I started … I've always had the ability to pick myself up and dust myself off, but it's like a different kind of a *strength* cause you are part of a team, you feel *connected* to something, its outside of my friendship world and outside of everything else I do … it constantly *challenges* you, which I guess any sport must do but I've just never been part of a team sport … I feel like I am a strong person, but it just helped resurrect me at a time when I needed it most, you know, so I feel it has been *healing* in that respect … and even having that double identity, it's quite *fun*, you get to sort of disappear into something else, whatever you call yourself, you can sort of play this role of this kick-arse, *strong* person, whatever you create for yourself, and you can just disappear into that.

In Nancy Finley's widely cited 2010 article on roller derby she concludes by stating, 'Women can now kick ass, but it might not bring the society any closer to societal support of child care or equal pay, or sports that do not glorify bruises' (Finley, 2010: 384). But what if we take a different view?

Roller derby enabled June to be a 'kick-arse, strong person'. Physical cultural studies (PCS) provides a framework where June's (and many others', including my own) experiences of sport can be taken seriously, and considered, independent to whether they might make major impacts on structural inequalities. PCS is a framework that enables the taken-for-granted notions of sport and physical activity to be questioned and rewritten. This rewriting of sport creates, as Andrews states, 'potentially empowering forms of knowledge and understanding' that can 'illuminate, and intervene into, sites of physical cultural injustice and inequity' (Andrews, 2008: 54). The text above highlights just one example where taken-for-granted notions of sport can be questioned. For June, roller derby allowed her a relation to her body that privileged her strength, her resilience, her connections to other women, and *her pleasure*.

Feminist Emma Goldman has been misquoted as stating the now famous phrase, 'If I can't dance I don't want to be in your revolution'. In 1934 Goldman wrote

> that a cause which stood for a beautiful ideal … for release and freedom from conventions and prejudice, should demand denial of life and joy … If it meant that, I did not want it. I want freedom, the right to self-expression, everybody's right to beautiful, radiant things.
>
> *(Quoted in Sweeney, 2015: 27)*

This centering, of the affective and pleasurable body in feminist politics, is a vital one. And it speaks to the importance of sport and leisure, wellbeing and health, play and recreation, as keys to workable strategies for living (with sexual difference) in the twenty-first century. PCS provides a framework for understanding bodies as affective, and, perhaps more importantly, pleasurable.

Understanding bodies as pleasurable speaks towards a type of feminist joy – women's bodies, often sites of control and desire by men – can now be spoken of, seen, and indeed experienced, as pleasurable. Not *for* men, but for women themselves – *auto*eroticism. Through sport and physical cultures women can experience pleasure for their own purposes. Irigaray (1993) wrote of feminine *jouissance*, a formless, fluid, expansiveness. And so, in this short chapter I argue that physical cultural studies is a framework that can interrogate and support a type of feminist joy. This is not to say that all aspects of physical cultures are joyful. But this is more to the point. Physical cultures, such as sport, leisure, dance, for example, are often spaces of control and discipline, as well as joy and pleasure (see for example Pavlidis and Fullagar, 2014). In my own research, women in roller derby thought of themselves and experienced their bodies as tough, strong and even mean. Feeling, and even being the cause of pain, was all part of the experience (Pavlidis and Fullagar, 2015). Roller derby is not a space where happiness is conditional on a relationship of care and reciprocity (Ahmed, 2010b), although it sometimes is this too. Rather, in derby, and I would argue, in other physically demanding sport, women can be 'happy' regardless of (and sometimes because of) their effects on others. For example, she might experience her increased fitness as pleasurable, or her toned thighs and buttocks as pleasurable, or her speed on the track, or her position of leadership, or her strength and skill at knocking down the opposing team members. Or even pleasure at being part of a team exclusively of women (Donnelly, 2012), where men are not particularly welcome (see Pavlidis and Connor, 2015 for a discussion of men in the sport).

Roller derby and other physical cultures, I argue, embraces the killjoy, and the joyful; both positions pleasurable and affective – and, arguably, powerful. Roller derby is a space where feminist killjoys – those that point out moments of sexism, express anger about things, talk about 'unhappy topics', and 'disturb the fantasy that happiness can be found in certain places' (Ahmed, 2010a) – are welcome and embraced. Scowling is encouraged, swearing is acceptable, and women are always 'active' (unless injured) participants. But it is also a space of joy; a place where bodies can be affective and pleasurable. It is a space where women can revel in their toned bodies, where they can wear skimpy clothing, and present themselves to others in ways they want. They can *enjoy* themselves, their bodies in particular. They can enjoy the way their body looks, what it can do, and how it feels. In my own work I have explored *both* a critical and productive account of derby. Issues of exclusion, bullying, and power relations of discipline and control (Pavlidis and Fullagar, 2013, 2014); as well as focusing on feelings of love, belonging and empowerment experienced through the sport (Pavlidis and Fullagar, 2014). Yet these experiences did not always come about in rational or logical ways.

PCS is a framework where the politics of passion and affect can be negotiated as it enables a refusal of ontological–epistemological divides. This is imperative. For to privilege affective and pleasurable bodies is not to negate questions of marginalization, nor is it an embrace of 'the perfect' neoliberal feminine subject competing for the perfect balance between successful sexuality and domesticity (McRobbie, 2015). Yet at the same time this approach does not assume women's desire for competition, for fitness, for vitality and health is wrong, because it is not. As Longhurst notes in her personal reflections of losing weight and becoming 'slim', 'the process of transforming oneself opens up possibilities for new capacities and for reflecting on a newly emerging self' (Longhurst, 2011: 883). Physically active leisure, such as roller derby and other action sport present opportunities for women to experience pleasure in a myriad of ways. PCS allows for analysis and exploration of this pleasure, as well as a critical response.

In my research into the experiences of women who played roller derby I spent over a year skating, training, playing in games (bouts) and spending time with women all over Australia involved in the sport. What became clear throughout the research was the women's acknowledgement – and even privileging – of their affective and pleasured bodies. The ways roller derby made them *feel* was of prime importance. But what can this tell us about roller derby? About sport more generally? How can we, as scholars working in the area of sport and physical culture, understand the affective and pleasurable experiences of our participants (and ourselves)? In my own work, reflecting on the insights and theoretical innovations of others before me, I have found that the affective experiences of pleasure (and also of pain, see Pavlidis and Fullagar, 2015) are central to understanding individual and cultural change. This necessarily short chapter outlines the 'turn to affect' in sport and physical cultures, and then demonstrates how this 'turn' can make representable (via writing) individual and cultural transformation.

Alternative sport and the 'affective turn'

The role of emotion in sport is not a new concern for scholars. In a 1959 article in the journal *Social Forces* Donald and Havighurst report on interviews with 434 men and women from New Zealand and the United States about the meanings people gave to their participation in sport and leisure. The results highlighted meanings related to enjoyment, achievement, belonging, creativity, and self-respect (Donald and Havighurst, 1959). Since then, and more than likely before, scholars have been fascinated with the pleasure and allure of sports, particularly those that involve some form of risk or danger. Primarily, these studies have made assumptions about the inherent good of leisure and sport – these functional perspectives have been and are still part of our popular discourse in society. However, there have been some alternative perspectives of note.

Most famous is Elias and Dunning's work, together and individually, in their seminal text, *Quest for Excitement* (1986). In this edited collection, and elsewhere, Elias and Dunning (1986) articulate a theory of the individual as restrained, held back, and sometimes in tension; 'the public and even private level of emotional control has become high by comparison with that of less highly differentiated societies' (ibid.: 65). This tension, they argue, needs a counter-measure; and it is in sport where it is primarily found. They write, 'in advanced industrial societies, leisure activities form an enclave for the socially approved arousal of moderate excitement behavior in public' (ibid.). Boldly, Dunning argued that sport plays a reinforcing role, secondary to class, in regards to the production and reproduction of masculine identity (ibid.: 282).

Relatedly, Lyng (1990) developed the concept of 'edgework' to account for people's allure towards risky or dangerous physical activities. He writes, 'activities that can be subsumed under the edgework concept have one central feature in common: they all involve a clearly observable threat to one's physical or mental well-being or one's sense of an ordered self' (ibid.: 857).

Fear, giving way to exhilaration and omnipotence, are central emotions said to be produced through these experiences (ibid.: 860). This work, by both Elias and Dunning, and Lyng, represents key ideas in the sociology of sport in regard to emotions and affect. Their work has been taken up and used, critiqued, evaluated and deployed for a range of uses. But centrally to both is their focus on the cultural and social aspects of experience, rather than the psychological.

Emotions are usually understood as *subjective* affective states. For example, a beating heart (affect) might be interpreted as fear, or excitement depending on the context. Or the warmth of a blushing face (affect) might signify pride or shame, though neither exclusively (Probyn, 2005). Affect, on the other hand, as Woodward writes, 'refers to the two-way relationship whereby something … or someone, affects and is affected by someone … else' (Woodward, 2015: 143). Emotion and affect are often used interchangeably, and regardless of the varied definitions they are certainly interrelated. Woodward, in her work advancing the psychosocial approach to research discusses the ways this framework focuses on the relationality between people's affects and sense of their selves, and the social worlds they inhabit (and that inhabit them): 'the dilemma of the space between inside and outside' (Woodward, 2015: 17).

Post-structural researchers have refused this inside/outside distinction, instead finding new ways of thinking about emotion, affect and the social. Elspeth Probyn's work has been explicit in addressing this distinction and refocusing the debates. About shame Probyn wrote, 'by denying or denigrating it or trying to eradicate it (as in the countless self-help books against various strains of shame), we impoverish ourselves and our attempts to understand human life' (Probyn, 2005: 3).

In sport sociology there has been a tendency to focus on displeasure – on the 'problem' – rather than on the pleasures and joys embodied through the practice; however, there are exceptions that have moved the discipline forward. Douglas Booth is most notable for his 1995 paper on ambiguities in pleasure and discipline in the context of the development of professional surfing. As a sport often associated with 'freedom', the development of professional surfing raises a range of provocative and useful questions in thinking about emotions and affect in sport. Influenced by Booth's work are researchers such as Clifton Evers (2009) who have made significant advances in the ways gender, sport and affect can be thought about in relation to the embodied movement of sport. Booth and Evers, along with others (for example, Saville, 2008) advocate for the centrality of emotion and affect in sport research and the importance of interdisciplinary approaches to these ends. As Thorpe and Wheaton (2013: 347) recognize, 'affect and sensation, and power and politics, are not mutually exclusive'.

More recently, Pringle, Rinehart and Caudwell published *Sport and the Social Significance of Pleasure* (2015) where pleasure and the politics of sport are explored in length. In refocusing our attention through PCS on pleasurable bodies, a powerful shift is possible. Probyn wrote, 'desire is a profoundly upsetting force. It may totally rearrange what we think we want: desire skews plans, setting forth unthought-of possibilities' (1996: 43). The interdisciplinary of PCS supports an analysis of pleasure as productive, and, much like in leisure, as valuable in its own right.

Affective and pleasurable bodies in physical cultures are both textual and visceral – both the body image, and the body without image (Featherstone, 2010: 195) – both represented and 'felt'. Both the body image (how others see us) and the body without image (our affects) are implicated in the joy (or not) experienced. This could be read cynically – as the ultimate goal of consumer culture achieved:

> The ultimate power to change lives, not just to look and be looked at, but a body in movement, an affective body which is noticed and commands respect; a body which

has the power to affect others; which possesses social force in the urban milieu and the spaces of sociability. This is the self-improvement road which leads to not just bodily and self-transformation, but style and lifestyle transformation too.

(Featherstone, 2010: 196)

But, and this is a noteworthy but, the style and lifestyle transformations in many physical cultures are not commercial – although there are some commercial aspects. Nor are these physical cultures controlled by a few profit driven entities – indeed, sports such as skateboarding, roller derby, and snowboarding actively refuse formal incorporation to varying degrees (or among some pockets of participants). The affective body that is noticed and commands respect in physical cultures such as roller derby also values the capacity to affect – notably to push over/down/out of the way opposing players for the goal of winning.

I have found that the affective experiences of pleasure (and pain) are central to understanding individual and cultural change. Although theories of affect and emotion can appear dense at times, I argue, in line with Atkinson (2011: 138), that PCS can be a form of 'committed praxis'. PCS in this instance is being used to understand the practice and theory of pleasure in the lives of sporting bodies, and the political potential of such knowledge. This necessarily short chapter now turns to some examples from my research in roller derby to demonstrate the varied ways affective and pleasurable bodies are central to understanding not only the experiences of individual women, but also of cultural and social transformations that are possible as these women engage in their social worlds beyond derby.

Representation and affect: feminist joy in roller derby

June, who was first introduced at the beginning of this chapter, spoke about the ways roller derby has changed her, helped her, healed her and improved her body image. She articulates the ways her friendships and belonging among her derby peers enabled these transformations in how she feels (affect) and other people's perceptions of her. The remainder of this chapter will focus on June's interview responses (transcribed) and serves as a demonstration of the insights garnered from a PCS framework that privileges affective and pleasurable bodies. My analysis here follows the lead of Sara Ahmed (2004: 27) in that my commitment is to making visible, 'not just the textuality of emotions, but also the emotionality of texts'. What is presented is a form of narrative analysis (Andrews, Squire and Tamboukou, 2013), where June is a new 'conceptual personae' (Deleuze and Guattari, 1994; for more detail on methodology please see Pavlidis and Fullagar, 2014: 43–52).

My collaborative and solo work has demonstrated the ways women embody multiple relations in roller derby that enable them to *use* the sport as a pathway to alternative ways of living as gendered subjects. June's narrative tells the story of a young woman going through a 'romantic breakup' and taking up roller derby to help her get through. Her story helps demonstrate the relationship between representation and affect. This relation is central to PCS: where the focus of cultural studies has often been on film, television and other texts, PCS brings the body and its affects into a more prominent position.

In several instances June attempts to articulate the affects enabled through her participation in roller derby. As a naturopath, practicing acupuncture and massage, her work colleagues participate in yoga or chi gong to de-stress. But for June, this was not enough. After going through what she described as a 'horrendous' breakup (her ex-boyfriend broke into her house at one stage) she started participating in roller derby:

> I was going through a lot and trying to find the strength to get back on track again and that's what derby gave me, it really did, it's like I went to derby and it challenged me and threw me around, and getting pushed and shoved just made me completely forget about everything in my life and then starting to feel that sense of achievement as well.

Being 'pushed and shoved' helped June forget about everything, as well as feel a sense of achievement. This notion is somewhat contradictory. Yet it is this experience that gives June a challenge she can overcome and feel 'success'. She continues:

> It's just given me a bit of gumption, it's not like I wanted to become more aggressive, its more that I just wanted to put my energy into something positive rather than into something negative and I had a lot burning inside of me, like I was really angry at the time and I feel like it's helped level me out … be more calm.

In this interview excerpt June separates aggression from anger. She wants me to know that 'it's not like I wanted to become more aggressive' and that the 'pushing and shoving' that she does in derby is a positive, calming influence in her life. Georgina Roy (2014) discusses the 'hard to describe' affects experienced by herself and her participants in surfing and the ways that post-structural theories of affect enable an analysis that can account for these affects. In my research I too have had the challenge of analyzing and writing those 'hard to describe' affects experienced through physical cultures. Here, June uses language and metaphor to try and describe the transformative capacity of roller derby in her life. Yet she is clear in saying that there was nothing 'wrong' with her – instead, roller derby *added* something more. It was *expansive*.

> I'm not like this broken person that derby rescued, its more that it just gave me somewhere to put all my energy … after derby, you are just bouncing back again, you feel joy cause you are having a lot of fun, you're playing again, which that's the thing, it's like playing, I mean its hardcore … but we're all laughing and having a great time you know … it teaches you to take hits in life as well, and to just bounce back again.

Roller derby gave this woman, who was tough and strong and working through heartache and anger, a way to be joyful again. She was able to experience pleasure and joy not by negating injustices or ignoring the ongoing marginalization of women. But by enabling the embodiment of resilience – the opportunity to fall, hard, and get back up, over and over and over again. Bodies in roller derby are affective and pleasurable (and painful): they are 'hard to describe', while at the same time perfectly understandable.

In terms of body image, June describes the ways roller derby shapes her body: 'physically, it's great, cause obviously it tones those areas that women worry about the most, cause you are down in derby stance'. June's body image – what can be seen and 'captured' (Featherstone, 2010) – improved through roller derby. As she mentions, her thighs and buttocks were toned and shaped through the sport. June also spoke explicitly about the 'roll out' – where the derby team 'present' themselves to the audience, often in a choreographed manner, to music (Pavlidis, 2012). The roll out is a key moment in derby, where representation, rather than affect, is key. Like other sports where the players run onto the field, the roll out is a chance for the players to 'step into' their role and be admired and celebrated by fans. Whereas on the track June has the capacity to affect others – to push them, shove them, and win/lose – in the roll out she has a different capacity; one of representation. She stated: 'When we had our roll out I suddenly got really emotional, like "oh my god this is so beautiful, I love my team", I just love all the girls, like everyone, I just like, they're just all cool.'

For June roller derby most certainly was a social intervention. On a number of levels the sport worked to connect her with a community of women who supported her needs at the time. In turn, June supported other women. This social intervention provided the conditions for personal transformation. On a meta-level, roller derby is a social intervention that is facilitating cultural transformation – where a full contact sport played predominantly by women is becoming normalized. As Atkinson (2011: 137) noted, 'the merit, hope and future of the PCS movement, as a successor to the sociology of sport, then, lies in its collective call for engagement with real utopias, democracy and social intervention'. Highlighting June's story, as someone who used roller derby as a social intervention, is an example of what PCS can make possible. After Atkinson, I argue that, although power may oppress, structures may dominate, identities may be marginalized, and ideologies might conceal, roller derby can change a woman's (or man's) life and bring joy and affective pleasures.

Concluding remarks

As an emerging field of study, PCS is a framework that can understand multiple knowledge bases and methodological paradigms. The example above tells the story of June, a roller derby skater, who used the sport to, in her words, 'heal', from a relationship breakup. Drawing from transcriptions of in-depth interviews, I have created a new 'conceptual personae' (Deleuze and Guattari, 1994) to embody June's affective and pleasurable body in roller derby. Enjoying her toned and fit body, and the adoration of fans when she and her team rolled out, were central to her experiences of joy and pleasure in roller derby. Yet also central were her affective transformations – from anger to joy through the tough embodiment of roller derby.

Through a PCS framework scholars can study the physically active body in relation to the power relations, structures and social forces at play in critical and nuanced ways. In practice, this translates to an opening and expanding of our analysis – in this case an analysis of feminist joy through physical activity. For June, these included: wrestling with the power relations and entanglements of a relationship breakup, juggling financial commitments and leisure (she specifically mentioned the financial burden of roller derby, yet saw its value in her life and worth the loss of income), and negotiating perceptions of women and aggression to maintain a style of femininity coherent with herself.

In cultural studies, scholars such as Amy Dobson are engaged in critical and important work interrogating the ways girls and young women represent themselves and their femininity online (for example, Dobson, 2011, 2014). Others have taken a broader perspective, examining changing notions of femininity and risk in contemporary society. Anita Harris outlined the 'can-do girl' as the ideal contemporary female subject: self-assured, consumer citizens, experiencing success at work (or school) and delaying motherhood (2004: 16–25). This ties in with scholars such as Deborah Lupton and critical work in public health. 'Taking care of one's health' and maintaining good health are key priorities in contemporary society – failure to prioritize health is a type of failed citizenship in neoliberal times (e.g. Lupton, 1995, 2013). Juxtaposed to this are the young women 'at risk'. Harris notes, that the 'at-risk category operates in a particular way in relation to young women, for they are imagined as both passive victims of circumstances beyond their control; and also as willful risk takers who use girlpower to their own (self-)destructive ends' (Harris, 2004: 26).

PCS, with the physically active body at its center, expands these perspectives. Physically active women are 'can-do girls' and 'at risk' – they are taking responsibility for their health through participation in active leisure, but they are also risking injury and at times their femininity (see for example Thorpe, 2014). They are (becoming) self-assured, as demonstrated by June's story, and experiencing success in leisure (but not necessarily work). And, central to this chapter, their experience goes beyond these dualisms. They are affective and pleasurable bodies, capable of joy through affect, and representation.

I started this chapter with an extended quote from June. She was 'at risk' in some ways – a victim of domestic violence, and suffering through her breakup. Yet through roller derby, a nontraditional, contact sport, she was able to transform herself and experience joy and strength. This is a powerful story and one that PCS gives us the tools to analyze and present to a broader audience. Understanding bodies as pleasurable, for themselves (not only others, though this too) is key to an affirmative feminist politics where the power relations and social forces influencing men and women can be disentangled in the hope of a more inclusive future. In PCS the refrain might read: 'If I can't play, I don't want to be in your revolution.' And perhaps, more pertinently, it is in playing that revolution is enabled.

Acknowledgement

Gratitude and derby love always to the women who made this research possible. Thank you.

References

Ahmed, S. 2004. *The Cultural Politics of Emotion*. London: Routledge.
Ahmed, S. 2010a. Feminist killjoys (and other willful subjects). *The Scholar and Feminist Online*, 8(3), 1–8.
Ahmed, S. 2010b. Killing joy: Feminism and the history of happiness. *Signs*, 35(3), 571–694.
Andrews, D. L. 2008. Kinesiology's inconvenient truth and the physical cultural studies imperative. *Quest*, 60(1), 45–62.
Andrews, M., Squire, C. and Tamboukou, M. (eds). 2013. *Doing Narrative Research*. London: Sage.
Atkinson, M. 2011. Physical cultural studies [Redux]. *Sociology of Sport Journal*, 28(1), 135–144.
Booth, D. 1995. Ambiguities in pleasure and discipline: the development of competitive surfing. *Journal of Sport History*, 22, 189–206.
Deleuze, G. and Guattari, F. 1994. *What is Philosophy?* (trans. G. Burchell and H. Tomlinson). New York: Verso.
Dobson, A. S. 2011. Hetero-sexy representation by young women on MySpace: The politics of performing an 'objectified' self. *Outskirts*, 25.
Dobson, A. S. 2014. 'Sexy' and 'laddish' girls: Unpacking complicity between two cultural imag(inations)es of young femininity. *Feminist Media Studies*, 14(2), 253–269.
Donald, M. N. and Havighurst, R. J. 1959. The meanings of leisure. *Social Forces*, 355–360.
Donnelly, M. K. 2012. The production of women onlyness: Women's flat track roller derby and women-only home improvement workshops. Dissertation, McMaster University. Available from http://digitalcommons.mcmaster.ca/opendissertations/6717.
Elias, N. and Dunning, E. 1986. *The Quest for Excitement: Sport and Leisure in the Civilizing Process*. Oxford: Blackwell.
Evers, C. 2009. *Notes for a Young Surfer*. Carlton: Melbourne University Press.
Featherstone, M. 2010. Body, image and affect in consumer culture. *Body and Society*, 16(1), 193–221.
Finley, N. J. 2010. Skating femininity: Gender maneuvering in women's roller derby. *Journal of Contemporary Ethnography*, 39(4), 359–387.
Goldman, E. 2011. *Living my Life*. New York: Cosimo.
Harris, A. 2004. *Future Girl: Young Women in the Twenty-First Century*. London: Routledge.
Irigaray, L. 1993. *This Sex Which is Not One* (trans. C. Porter). New York: Cornell University Press.
Longhurst, R. 2011. Becoming smaller: Autobiographical spaces of weight loss. *Antipode*, 44(3), 871–888.
Lupton, D. 1995. *The Imperative of Health: Public Health and the Regulated Body*. London: Taylor & Francis.
Lupton, D. 2013. Quantifying the body: Monitoring and measuring health in the age of mHealth technologies. *Critical Public Health*, 23(4), 393–403.

Lyng, S. 1990. Edgework: A social psychological analysis of voluntary risk taking. *American Journal of Sociology*, 851–886.
McRobbie, A. 2015. Notes on the perfect: Competitive femininity in neoliberal times. *Australian Feminist Studies*, 30(83), 3–20.
Pavlidis, A. 2012. From Riot Grrrls to roller derby? Exploring the relations between gender, music and sport. *Leisure Studies*, 31(2), 165–176.
Pavlidis, A. and Connor, J. 2015. Men in a 'women only' sport? Contesting gender relations and sex integration in roller derby. *Sport in Society*, 19(8–9), 1349–1362.
Pavlidis, A. and Fullagar, S. 2013. Becoming roller derby grrrls: Exploring the gendered play of affect in mediated sport cultures. *International Review for the Sociology of Sport*, 48(6), 673–688.
Pavlidis, A. and Fullagar, S. 2014. *Sport, Gender and Power: The Rise of Roller Derby*. Farnham: Ashgate.
Pavlidis, A. and Fullagar, S. 2015. The pain and pleasure of roller derby: Thinking through affect and subjectification. *International Journal of Cultural Studies*, 18(5), 483–499.
Pringle, R., Rinehart, R. E. and Caudwell, J. 2015. *Sport and the Social Significance of Pleasure*. London: Routledge.
Probyn, E. 1996. *Outside Belongings*. London: Routledge.
Probyn, E. 2005. *Blush*. Sydney: University of New South Wales Press.
Roy, G. 2014. 'Taking emotions seriously': Feeling female and becoming-surfer through UK Surf Space. *Emotion, Space and Society*, 12, 41–48.
Saville, S. J. 2008. Playing with fear: Parkour and the mobility of emotion. *Social and Cultural Geography*, 9(8), 891–914.
Sweeney, F. 2015. 'Beautiful, radiant things': Aesthetics, experience and feminist practice: A response to Kathy Davis. *Feminist Theory*, 16(1), 27–30. doi: 10.1177/1464700114563244
Thorpe, H. 2014. Moving bodies beyond the social/biological divide: Toward theoretical and transdisciplinary adventures. *Sport, Education and Society*, 19(5), 666–686.
Thorpe, H. A. and Wheaton, B. 2013. Dissecting action sports studies: Past, present, and beyond. In D. L. Andrews and B. Carrington (eds), *A Companion to Sport*. Chichester: Blackwell Publishing.
Woodward, K. 2015. *Psychosocial Studies: An Introduction*. London: Routledge.

31
MOBILE BODIES

Phil Jones

Introduction

The neoliberal belief in frictionless flows is a seductive intellectual conceit – movement is progress, stillness is reactionary. A key element of the globalization discourse is in freeing the movement of people, things and ideas in order to foster ever faster economic growth. Of course, this fantasy has limits. Flows of migrant bodies into Europe from the Middle East and Africa prompt protest. Afghani heroin enters the United States covertly. Attempts are made to stop the spread of extremist ideologies. Thus the mobility being encouraged by globalization is of people, things and ideas that are *sympathetic to the neoliberal project*.

The challenge of globalization has led to new ways of theorizing movement within the social sciences, in particular the rise of a constellation of ideas around 'mobilities'. As a school of thought, mobilities operates at a number of radically different scales, all the way from the transmission of viruses through to the daily flows of global trade. Despite this diversity of scales within mobilities, the *body* is a key site of analysis. Thus the challenge posed by PCS to find ways of studying the politics of active embodiment has significant overlaps with the intellectual project of mobilities scholars. As with PCS, work within the mobilities school is notable for an emphasis on methodological innovation. There are significant commonalities in the ways that both mobilities and PCS scholars embrace mixed methods and a pragmatic, interdisciplinary approach to the theoretical frames deployed, seeking the most appropriate approach to the subject under investigation (Andrews, 2008). A number of PCS scholars have also reflected on the body of the researcher within the research (for instance, Giardina and Newman, 2011; Pavlidis and Olive, 2013; Thorpe, 2012), which speaks to a significant strand of autoethnographic work within mobilities research.

This chapter begins by reviewing the literature on mobilities, in particular the outpouring of scholarship that followed Sheller and Urry's (2006) provocative manifesto declaring the existence of a 'new mobilities paradigm'. I then move on to discuss the methodologies championed by mobilities scholars and reflect on the overlaps with PCS. In the final section of this chapter I discuss some of my own work, exploring the active body as a research tool, with a particular focus on the world of commuter cycling.

The new mobilities paradigm

Mimi Sheller and John Urry's much cited 2006 paper on the 'new mobilities paradigm' forms the introduction to a special issue of the journal *Environment and Planning A* (Sheller and Urry, 2006). In setting out an agenda for mobilities they make an explicit argument that social science research has for too long been underpinned by sedentary assumptions influenced by Heidegger, i.e. that people staying in one place is normal/authentic and that mobile populations are inherently abject. While one can raise doubts as to whether this is a fair critique of social science as it stood in the early 2000s, certainly sedentary perspectives are at odds with a globalizing world where movement has become more common within and between nations. Sheller and Urry went on to establish the journal *Mobilities* as the home for debates in this field and both have set up mobilities research centres respectively at Drexel and Lancaster. Mimi Sheller has subsequently acknowledged that describing mobilities as a new 'paradigm' was consciously provocative and that the 2006 paper was titled with 'a knowing wink' (Sheller, 2014: 790).

The ideas underpinning the new mobilities paradigm did not emerge from a vacuum, however, and partly reflected an earlier collaboration looking at how city spaces are shaped by the car (Sheller and Urry, 2000). Thus from the outset, the theoretical framing of mobilities has had a strong automotive component. This should be unsurprising given that mobilities is interested in movement across a wide range of scales (including the global) many of which require vehicular locomotion. The initial manifestations of mobilities research therefore had somewhat of a skew toward transport-based work, leading Newman and Falcous (2012: 39) to claim that there has been an undue focus on 'the transport of bodies ..., transported bodies, or transportable bodies, rather than bodily movements'.

Nonetheless, it would be unfair to characterize discussions around mobilities as solely focused on issues around transport and the body as moveable object rather than the body as moving subject. One can easily find mobilities-led and mobilities-sympathetic research on a range of non-vehicular, embodied mobilities, such as (to highlight a random selection) bull fighting (Pink, 2011), road running (Cidell, 2014), parkour (Kidder, 2012; Saville, 2008), pilgrimage walking (Slavin, 2003), action sports (Thorpe, 2012, 2014) and cycling (see below). From the outset, mobilities has focused on the ways in which movement is politicized and socially constructed. Cresswell (2006) suggests that movement is to mobility what location is to place – the visible element of a wider set of social processes. In short, mobilities is somewhat of a magpie theoretical frame, bringing together considerations of movement across different scales with a variety of pre-existing theoretical literatures; Sheller and Urry in particular identify Simmel's urban rhythms, science and technology studies, the spatial turn, non-representational theory, network analysis and complex systems analysis as key components of mobilities studies. A great deal of work has gone on to refine Sheller and Urry's original call to arms. Tim Cresswell (2010), for example, has identified a series of questions that need to be considered when analysing different forms of mobility: why move; how fast; with what frequency; how is that movement constrained; to what extent does it rely upon the body; and why stop? In each of these questions there are significant issues around power relations (for an extreme example see Moran et al., 2012 on forced mobility in the Russian penal system).

A key issue raised by thinking about the mobile body is that of individual identity. Bodily mobility and identity construction can be seen as co-constructed. Rickly's (2016) analysis of rock climbers in north America, for example, highlights the politics that informs the choice to engage in this kind of activity. In order to be a 'lifestyle' climber, a particular set of mobilities have to be enacted. On the one level this is the embodied capacity for climbing. More than this, however, climbers need sufficient resources of money and time to *move between* different iconic locations for climbing and, indeed, to discover new ones. Furthermore, climbers need to study different ascents, attempting multiple routes meaning that their bodies need to *stop* in particular locations for lengthy periods – camping or living out of vans parked close to key climbing sites. This raises questions around the kinds of bodies that are able to take on this (classed, gendered) climbing identity. In her review of lifestyle climbing's history, Rickly (ibid.) notes that it emerged as a parallel to the 1950s beat generation – middle-class men, usually with college degrees, using a dedication to climbing as a means of rejecting the bourgeois expectations of that era. While women adopting this lifestyle have become more common in recent decades, there are still significant barriers to female participation around accepted gender roles, homosocial bonding cultures and mundane issues of personal safety when camping in remote locations.

The rock-climbing example highlights the gendered politics of mobility and, more than this, raises issues of intersectionality (Valentine, 2007). Gender, social class, ethnicity and so on come together in different ways to enable or constrain the capacity of an individual to embody a particular set of mobility choices and their associated identity formation (a point highlighted by Thorpe, 2012, in relation to snowboarding cultures). Thus intersectionality fundamentally informs an individual's potential mobilities. Pavlidis and Fullagar's (2013) reading of roller derby is instructive in this light. On the one hand there is a standard discourse that participation drives empowerment through physical activity. At the same time there is a tension between the roller derby's 'sexualized hyperfemininity' and the way this is played out through masculinized aggression (ibid.: 675). More interestingly, while players *become* the 'derby grrrl' through participation, a defining element of the derby girl identity is precisely its lack of singular definition. Instead there is an emphasis on embracing individuals' complex, intersecting identities by valorizing a plurality of non-traditional femininities which participation in derby redefines as normal/acceptable. Thus the capacity of individuals to construct and valorize their own complex identities is marshalled and intensified by participation in this particular form of sporting mobility.

Mobile methods

Both PCS and mobilities emphasize the importance of working between conventional disciplines, which inevitably means embracing a variety of methods beyond the positivitist and quantitative. Andrews's (2008) call to escape the scientific trap of conventional kinesiology through the mixed method approach of PCS has similarities to the ways that mobilities studies originally sought to distance itself from conventional transport research – although some mobilities and transport researchers have since engaged in a productive dialogue about the benefits of bringing these different approaches together (for example Knowles et al., 2008). Unsurprisingly, perhaps, given the influence of cultural studies approaches within PCS (Silk and Andrews, 2011), the body of the researcher is often emphasized within the methodologies adopted (Giardina and Newman, 2011). Some PCS scholars have suggested that while the researcher-as-insider can be productive, there needs to be caution about potentially problematic claims around the 'authenticity' of the data thus produced (Pavlidis and Olive, 2013).

The body of the researcher is often brought to the fore in mobilities approaches as well. Indeed, Merriman (2013) fears that there has been a tendency (particularly within work influenced by non-representational theory) to privilege certain methods over others, with an emphasis on performative and ethnographic techniques. He thus raises similar concerns about claims to authenticity made for datasets emphasizing the embodied experience of the researcher, particularly whether such claims downplay the value of more traditional qualitative techniques such as interviewing and archival research. He is also worried about researchers who explore the possibilities offered by new technologies without reflecting on whether the techniques being developed offer genuinely useful insights.

It is important not to downplay the usefulness of more traditional qualitative techniques – both PCS and mobilities approaches rely on giving careful consideration to the research problem being addressed when considering choice of methods. Notwithstanding Merriman's caution, there has been considerable methodological innovation both within and beyond the mobilities debate that has been valuable in helping to analyse and conceptualize the mobile body. We can broadly divide these innovations into two categories: first, existing techniques deployed in novel ways; and second, exploring the potential offered by new technologies. In the first category, for example, we might look at the way that Spinney (2006) undertook qualitative interviews with club cyclists and recorded an audio field diary of his own reflections while in the act of riding a bicycle up Mont Ventoux. The techniques are standard but the spatial context gives an embodied, rhythmic *immediacy* to the materials collected. Of course, this does not necessarily mean that such data is 'better' than that collected in an interview room. Instead one should consider that one gets something *different* through such an approach, which may need to be triangulated with other methods. Indeed, embodied and mobile research might not always be advantageous to the researcher, for example in Spinney's case, the physical exhaustion while riding *might* preclude some of the more reflective commentary that a conventional sedentary interview could potentially elicit from a participant.

Nonetheless, the capacity to access more immediate reflections as events are unfolding means that there is significant appeal to these mobile, embodied approaches. The ethnographies and interviews undertaken as part of the *Travel time use in the information age* project, for example, reflect this pursuit of *immediacy*. Part of this project involved researchers making regular journeys on public transport, collecting detailed field notes and interviewing fellow passengers. Some of the observations are strikingly banal – the precise ways in which people unpack their bags and colonize space in train carriages for example – but they give important insights into the ways in which this form of mobility is *experienced* every day that would be impossible to uncover without being there *in the moment* (Watts and Urry, 2008).

The emergence of new technologies does not automatically have a disruptive effect on methods. Few qualitative scholars would mourn the replacement of tape and minidisc with digital recorders of higher quality and capacity. Other technological innovations, however, have made some scholars uncomfortable, with not entirely unjustified concerns that these technologies tempt a return to a positivist model of unreflexive *measurement*. Clearly new technology should not be deployed in an uncritical fashion. This caveat aside, however, there has been some very exciting work into the mobile body that has been enabled by new technologies. As geographical information systems (GIS) have become more sophisticated over the last thirty years they have developed greater capacity to map and analyse different forms of qualitative information (Cartwright, 1997; Kwan and Knigge, 2006) giving scholars new ways to reflect on how the experiential relates to the Cartesian spaces of formal maps. Similarly, GPS technologies have allowed movements within space to be tracked, allowing analysis of everyday mobilities at the scale of the individual (Parks, 2001). While GPS can be used for purely quantitative analysis, scholars and arts practitioners have also explored the possibilities for creating 'locative media' that play with ideas of movement, location and embodiment (Pinder, 2013).

As video camera technology has become cheaper and smaller, there have been new possibilities for exploring movement at the scale of the individual. Lightweight helmet cameras worn by cyclists, for example, can give a riders'-eye-view of the everyday experience of cycling, allowing the immediate embodied practices to be analysed post-hoc without interfering with the experience in the moment (Brown et al., 2008). More conventional filming – shooting the view *of* the subject, rather than *from* them – allows for the mobilities of individual bodies to be examined. Of course the use of video brings with it a number of major ethical considerations, not least the way that such material is published and the inherent threat to the anonymity of participants. Giving participants control over the cameras can partially offset the power imbalances that video generates but it remains a fundamentally panoptic technology, subjecting participants to the (masculinized) gaze and its ethical drawbacks need to be carefully weighed against its methodological gains.

The sheer volume of material produced when filming the everyday – facilitated not least by high capacity memory cards allowing for hours of uninterrupted recording – makes considerable demands in terms of how the analysis is undertaken (Pink, 2012). Indeed, the flood of materials that can be produced is both an attractive and problematic quality of much of the newer technologically driven methods being deployed in mobilities scholarship. This again reinforces the importance of selecting an appropriate method for the research questions being examined, lest the researcher drown in a sea of interesting but irrelevant data.

Liminal mobilities: the case of cyclists

In the remainder of this chapter I am going to talk a little about some of my own work on the embodied mobility of cycling. It has long been recognized that the bicycle occupies an in-between space – faster than walking, slower than the car, intimately engaged with the environment yet able to pass through quickly (Slater, 1969). All forms of transport have an embodied component; the private car, for example, is a highly managed sensory environment designed to maximize the bodily comfort of its users (Edensor, 2003). As I have argued elsewhere, however, the sensory experience of riding a bicycle is considerably less regulated, leading to an intense and not always pleasant form of embodied mobility (Jones, 2012). One can therefore think of the bicycle as propagating a liminal form of mobility, combining elements of human locomotion alongside vehicular qualities. The bicycle also creates a set of identities specifically framed around embodiment.

In order to explore the embodied experience of everyday cycling mobilities, I asked a group of commuter cyclists ($n = 28$) to record unstructured narratives ('whatever is going through your head') during their ride home. Gathered in tandem with GPS tracks, these audio recordings were then mapped and analysed alongside their geographic location (for a more detailed explanation of this method see Jones and Evans, 2012). Textual analysis within NVivo indicated that issues around the bodily came out very strongly within the commentaries, perhaps unsurprisingly given that the physical effort required for cycling keeps bodily response at the forefront of riders' thinking. Participants reflected on the joys of speed, the effort of hills and high winds, the challenges of near misses and accidents.

Sometimes the sheer physicality of the ride precluded commentary being recorded. Participants wore a heart rate monitor which forms a useful proxy for the effort required at different points during the ride home. Where walking rarely pushes people into the kind of cardio exercise that one might undertake in a gym, uphill sections of a bike ride often will. Participant 3, for example, who was otherwise quite talkative during her ride, largely stopped speaking during a long, steep ride along a dual carriageway heading out of the city, with her heart rate entering the 170s – quite high for someone in early middle age.

Of course, if we were to look at heart rate data in isolation we might be guilty of falling into the trap of new technology tempting us back toward positivist measurement. Listening to Participant 3's audio recording one hears deep panting, nose blowing and involuntary sighing, putting the listener into the messy embodied reality of this difficult section of her journey. She even wheezes an apology for being out of breath, embodying a cliché of Englishness. What we lose here in more reflective commentary, we gain in a sense of the bodily and the immediate – the experiential qualities of cycling mobility, which are only hinted at by the sterile flow of numbers from a heart rate monitor.

All the participants were commuter cyclists working professional jobs that required some degree of formality in workplace appearance. The physical effort of cycling brings to the fore the body's leaky, sweaty imperfections – the 'dirt' that can render the individual abject in a western culture obsessed with distancing from embodied reality (Kristeva, 1982; Douglas [1966] 2002). Riders adopt different tactics to manage that relationship between their identities and the bodily abject:

> My cycling style is definitely relaxed, i.e. slow. I wear normal clothes to work on the bike and I have a big comfortable upright continental bike and I just take it easy. You can go faster if you want to, but you just end up having to have a shower when you get to work …
>
> *(Participant 13)*

The individual rider has different bodily capacities to manage the challenges posed by this form of mobility. As Participant 17 put it 'Don't want to sweat, not nice sitting in chair, clammy shirt on your back.' Others had rituals of showering or changing clothes in order to manage the limits that the exercised body puts onto their capacity to perform the identity of office-based professional.

All participants discussed the weather to a greater or lesser extent. Environmental conditions have the potential to make the cycling body abject (exhausted, soaking, dirty), yet not all encounters with the environment were negative. The embodied feeling of mobility could engender intense pleasures, particularly speed: 'I like doing this at rush hour when there's a great queue of traffic all the way down here and I can just go whizzing by' (Participant 6).

Relating to Cresswell's (2010) discussion of the power issues in mobility, here we see the bicycle positioned as giving freedom to move juxtaposed with the denial of automobility imposed on the car driver by congestion. The rhythms of daily traffic mean, however, that the same space will be experienced differently by cyclists at different times of day. Thus one can see mobility as being co-constructed with space/time. For example, one participant chose to cycle along a traffic-free canal towpath listening to music. His mobility in the towpath space was very different to that where he transitioned into the city centre: 'big hill, you can just freewheel down by the [shopping mall] and then we start getting into taxis and buses. So I'm going to have to pay attention here, be a proper cyclist for a while' (Participant 24).

Adopting the identity and riding style of the 'proper cyclist' signals the greater embodied skill needed to manage the mobility challenges of riding in the spaces of heavy traffic. Again, this reminds us of the fluid and contingent identities constructed by embodied mobility.

The co-construction of mobility between bodies and spaces finds strong expression in discussions of cycling infrastructure. The UK, in contrast to countries such as the Netherlands and Denmark, pays limited attention to cycling within urban design. Where cycle lanes segregated from motorized vehicles do exist in the UK, they are rarely continuous, most frequently taking the form of lines painted on pedestrian sidewalks. These designs take little account of how such infrastructure is experienced from the perspective of the cycling body: 'There is a cycle lane along here, but I find it quite slow and there's often cars parked on it further up so I only use it when the traffic's really bad' (Participant 3).

In a similar vein, participants frequently discussed road surface. This again highlights the liminal qualities of the bicycle, existing between the needs of the pedestrian and the motorized vehicle. Lumps and bumps on a sidewalk that would pass unnoticed underfoot for a pedestrian can cause instability on a thin-wheeled bicycle – Participant 13 talking about 'natural speed bumps on this bit of path where the roots have grown under the tarmac, pushed it up' for example. Similarly the potholes on roads whose effects are damped by the suspension of cars can create serious dangers for cyclists:

> There's occasionally a very nasty pothole down here which could easily throw a cyclist off ... I'm always complaining to the council about it and they keep coming and filling it up and it keeps coming open again. ... It's the sort of one if you hit on two wheels you come flying off at a pretty nasty fashion.
>
> *(Participant 15)*

Again, this highlights how cycling as a form of liminal mobility is poorly managed within UK urban design, falling between the infrastructure needs of pedestrians and drivers. Thus mobility is not simply a product of the identity and bodily skills of individual riders, but is connected to a web of socio-cultural and policy networks that shape the capacity of individuals to enact different forms of mobility.

Conclusion

Emerging work in PCS finds common cause with the mobilities agenda. Despite its early skew toward transport, mobilities treats embodiment as a core, though not exclusive, concern. Mobilities and PCS can trace elements of their intellectual heritage to cultural studies and both place a strong emphasis on interdisciplinarity. A shared concern with moving beyond positivist measurement to mixed methods approaches is a consequence of this interdisciplinarity, as is a belief in drawing upon the most appropriate theoretical frame for the research question in hand, rather than doggedly sticking within a prescribed canon. This of course brings the risk for both research areas that they are concerned with everything and nothing, a concern that Andrews (2008: 52) sought to address by arguing that PCS was focused on 'bodily movement and activity' – a rather narrow definition that others might take issue with. Nonetheless, mobilities arguably takes in a wider empirical landscape than PCS as while both are concerned with the position of the mobile within broader socio-economic processes, mobilities goes far beyond the realm of the purely physical and embodied.

Mobilities helps us to think not just about how bodies (both human and non-human) move themselves as acting subjects, but also about how, as objects, they are moved or constrained by outside forces – and, indeed, the fuzzy boundaries between subject and object status. As Thorpe's (2014) work demonstrates, there is clearly a productive dialogue to be had between PCS and mobilities considering the multiple globalized scales through which bodily movement is constructed. But mobilities scholars could also learn from PCS. Silk and Andrews (2011), for example, argue strongly that PCS has a deep commitment to social engagement, with its underlying purpose being to address inequalities and drive social change rather than merely to collect and analyse data. This is clearly a commitment that the more abstract and detached elements of mobilities scholarship – particularly among those invested in non-representational approaches – would do well to engage with.

A rich seam of methodological innovation has been opening up to mobilities scholars in the last decade, partly driven by new technologies and partly by a willingness to deploy traditional techniques in new, mobile, contexts. There has, however, been a clear preference within mobilities research for qualitative techniques, particularly to find ways of exploring the experiential and the everyday. The intent is not to use these techniques to enable prediction or modelling, but instead to interpret and understand the object of study. This methodological work not only offers new techniques to PCS scholars but also offers intellectual justification for seeking to develop research in these directions. To end on a note of caution, however, in moving beyond mere 'measurement' it is important we resist the temptation to dismiss quantitative and more conventionally positivist techniques out of hand. The promise of PCS and mobilities is in their interdisciplinarity; in their intellectual heritage, both open the door to mixed methods approaches that critically engage with (and subvert) quantitative techniques – as with my cycling example above using GPS. There is thus great potential for productive dialogue across the quantitative/qualitative divide within both research areas. This dialogue also needs to be extended between PCS and mobilities, which have much in common and also much to learn from each other.

References

Andrews, D. L. 2008. Kinesiology's inconvenient truth and the physical cultural studies imperative. *Quest*, 60(1), 45–62.
Brown, K. M., Dilley, R. and Marshall, K. 2008. Using a head-mounted video camera to understand social worlds and experiences. *Sociological Research Online*, 13(6), article 1, http://socresonline.org.uk/13/6/1.html.
Cartwright, W. 1997. New media and their application to the production of map products. *Computers and Geosciences*, 23(4), 447–456.
Cidell, J. 2014. Running road races as transgressive event mobilities. *Social and Cultural Geography*, 15(5), 571–583.
Cresswell, T. 2006. *On the move: mobility in the modern western world*. London: Routledge.
Cresswell, T. 2010. Towards a politics of mobility. *Environment and Planning D: Society and Space*, 28(1), 17–31.
Douglas, M. [1966] 2002. *Purity and danger: an analysis of the concepts of pollution and taboo*. London: Routledge & Kegan Paul.
Edensor, T. 2003. Defamiliarising the mundane roadscape: M6 – junction 19–16. *Space and Culture*, 6(2), 151–168.
Giardina, M. D. and Newman, J. I. 2011. Physical cultural studies and embodied research acts. *Cultural Studies ↔ Critical Methodologies*, 11(6), 523–534.
Jones, P. 2012. Sensory indiscipline and affect: a study of commuter cycling. *Social and Cultural Geography*, 13(6), 645–658.
Jones, P. and Evans, J. 2012. The spatial transcript: analysing mobilities through qualitative GIS. *Area*, 44(1), 92–99.
Kidder, J. 2012. Parkour, the affective appropriation of urban space, and the real/virtual dialectic. *City and Community*, 11(3), 229–253.
Knowles, R., Shaw, J. and Docherty, I. (eds). 2008. *Transport geographies: mobilities, flows and spaces*. Oxford: Wiley-Blackwell.
Kristeva, J. 1982. *Powers of horror: an essay on abjection*. New York: Columbia University Press.
Kwan, M. P. and Knigge, L. 2006. Doing qualitative research using GIS: an oxymoronic endeavor? *Environment and planning A*, 38(11), 1999–2002.
Merriman, P. 2013. Rethinking mobile methods. *Mobilities*, 9(2), 167–187.
Moran, D., Piacentini, L. and Pallot, J. 2012. Disciplined mobility and carceral geography: prisoner transport in Russia. *Transactions of the Institute of British Geographers*, 37(3), 446–460.
Newman, J. and Falcous, M. 2012. Moorings and movements: the paradox of sporting mobilities. *Sites*, 9(1), 38–58.
Parks, L. 2001. Cultural geographies in practice: plotting the personal: Global Positioning Satellites and interactive media. *Cultural Geographies*, 8(2), 209–222.
Pavlidis, A. and Fullagar, S. 2013. Becoming roller derby grrrls: exploring the gendered play of affect in mediated sport cultures. *International Review for the Sociology of Sport*, 48(6), 673–688.

Pavlidis, A. and Olive, R. 2013. On the track/in the bleachers: authenticity and feminist ethnographic research in sport and physical cultural studies. *Sport in Society*, 17(2), 218–232.

Pinder, D. 2013. Dis-locative arts: mobile media and the politics of global positioning. *Continuum*, 27(4), 523–541.

Pink, S. 2011. From embodiment to emplacement: re-thinking competing bodies, senses and spatialities. *Sport, Education and Society*, 16(3), 343–355.

Pink, S. (ed.). 2012. *Advances in visual methodology*. London: Sage.

Rickly, J. M. 2016. Lifestyle mobilities: a politics of lifestyle rock climbing. *Mobilities*, 11(2), 243–263.

Saville, S. J. 2008. Playing with fear: parkour and the mobility of emotion. *Social and Cultural Geography*, 9(8), 891–914.

Sheller, M. 2014. The new mobilities paradigm for a live sociology. *Current Sociology*, 62(6), 789–811.

Sheller, M. and Urry, J. 2000. The city and the car. *International Journal of Urban and Regional Research*, 24(4), 737–757.

Sheller, M. and Urry, J. 2006. The new mobilities paradigm. *Environment and Planning A*, 38(2), 207–226.

Silk, M. L. and Andrews, D. L. 2011. Towards a physical cultural studies. *Sociology of Sport Journal*, 28(1), 4–35.

Slater, C. 1969. The bicycle as field aid. *Professional Geographer*, 21, 360–362.

Slavin, S. 2003. Walking as spiritual practice: the pilgrimage to Santiago de Compostela. *Body and Society*, 9(3), 1–18.

Spinney, J. 2006. A place of sense: a kinaesthetic ethnography of cyclists on Mont Ventoux. *Environment and Planning D*, 24(5), 709–732.

Thorpe, H. 2012. Transnational mobilities in snowboarding culture: travel, tourism and lifestyle migration. *Mobilities*, 7(2), 317–345.

Thorpe, H. 2014. *Transnational mobilities in action sports cultures*. Basingstoke: Palgrave Macmillan.

Valentine, G. 2007. Theorizing and researching intersectionality: a challenge for feminist geography. *The Professional Geographer*, 59(1), 10–21.

Watts, L. and Urry, J. 2008. Moving methods, travelling times. *Environment and Planning D*, 26(5), 860–874.

32
PREGNANT BODIES

Shannon Jette

Over the past few years, there has been a proliferation of health interventions that are testing the efficacy of using prenatal exercise as a strategy to limit gestational weight gain (Jette, 2014). These interventions (which include randomized trials with both animals and humans) are needed, the argument goes, because women who are overweight or obese prior to pregnancy – or who gain too much weight during pregnancy – are possibly 'programming' the foetus to be an overweight/obese adult. Physical activity in pregnancy, it is hypothesized, can help to mitigate this risk, enhancing the future life of the unborn child. As stated in one of the interventions (Seneviratne et al., 2014: 2) aptly titled Improving Maternal and Progeny Obesity Via Exercise (IMPROVE): 'it may be possible to alter programming of the offspring of obese women to a healthier phenotype by interventions in pregnancy.' When framed in this manner, prenatal exercise clearly serves a political function, taking on eugenic undertones even, as it is positioned as a technique to help a woman be a 'fit' mother who gives birth to a baby with a 'healthier phenotype' (see also Jette, 2006).

In what follows, and drawing upon my previous work on the production of medical knowledge about prenatal exercise (Jette, 2009, 2011; Jette and Rail, 2013), I contextualize this current focus on exercise as a technique to control pregnancy weight gain and to enhance birth outcomes, illustrating that it is but the latest example of a long history of using physical (in)activity in pregnancy as a way to regulate population health. With this background, I then share my experience organizing prenatal movement classes that encouraged women to experience their bodies in new ways, without a focus upon weight reduction or the improvement of their 'progeny.' In other words, I share my own intervention against mainstream public health interventions. The approach that I take and the story that unfolds is illustrative of a physical cultural studies perspective in that I draw upon social and cultural theory to help me both contextualize my work and to advance a political agenda that aims to '*expose and render visible* unequal (physical cultural) power relations and produce the type of knowledge that can enable intervention into the broader social world' (Andrews and Silk, 2015: 90, emphasis in original). I conclude with some thoughts concerning the potential of and challenges to implementing alternative body practices on a wider scale, and also reflect on how my research contributes to the PCS project.

Situating the (in)active pregnant body: governing risk, exercising caution

My examination of prenatal exercise has, in large part, been informed by an analytic of governmentality, a perspective originally put forth by Foucault (2003a, 2003b), subsequently developed into the field of governmentality studies (see Miller and Rose, 2008), and also utilized by critical public health scholars interested in how risk functions as a technology of governance (Lupton, 1995; Petersen and Lupton, 1997). Foucault's (2003a, 2003b) writings on governmentality are part of his attempt to develop an analytic that could account for the complex workings of power in modern society – and how humans are produced as subjects – without setting up a dichotomy of state/civil, public/private, or a view of power as emanating from one central source (O'Malley, 2008). According to Rose and Miller (1992), the problematics of government may be analysed in terms of their *political rationalities* (the broad discursive frame of reference through which political problems and solutions are identified and considered, and which determine the focus and objects of governance) and in terms of the *technologies of government* (which pertain to the level of operationalization and involves a consideration of the techniques, tools and means through which practical policies are devised and inserted). It is through an analysis of the intricate inter-dependencies *between* political rationalities and governmental technologies, note Rose and Miller (ibid.: 175–176), that we can begin to understand the multiple and delicate networks (or the various technologies – including public health interventions) that 'connect the lives of individuals, groups and organizations to the aspirations of authorities.'

While Foucault's most well-known governmental writings focused on the exercise of power in modern societies characterized by classical liberal values, his analytical approach has been taken up and further developed by scholars examining power relations in Western society from the nineteenth century to present (see for instance, Lupton, 1995; O'Malley, 2008; Rose and Miller, 1992). Of particular interest to many of these scholars is how 'risk' has functioned as a technique of governance, one of the 'heterogeneous governmental strategies of … power by which populations and individuals are monitored and managed so as to best meet the goals of democratic humanism' (Lupton, 1999: 4). Notably, the mobilization of 'risk' has shifted under varying political rationalities, from a model of risk sharing under welfarism (with its political rationality of the promotion of social responsibility and the mutuality of social risk) to one of individual responsibility for health in the neoliberal context (often cloaked in the language of 'freedom of choice'; O'Malley, 2008; Rose and Miller, 1992). Feminist scholars have illustrated how, throughout the twentieth century, 'risk' became a central construct around which pregnancy is described, organized and practised in both the popular and medical realm such that in contemporary developed societies, pregnant women are pressed to manage an ever-increasing number of risk factors in order to enhance the life of the unborn child and be considered a responsible mother (see Lupton, 2012; Weir, 2006).

It was using an analytic of governmentality – and insights from scholars exploring risk – that I explored medical and popular literature pertaining to exercise and pregnancy from the late nineteenth century to present, and demonstrated that the advice provided has never been neutral but contingent upon social context, and intricately bound up in relations of power (Jette, 2009, 2011; Jette and Rail, 2013). That is to say, what has been perceived as a 'problem' with regards to the reproductive female body has changed in line with the social, economic and political landscape, as have the exercise prescriptions that have been provided, but the focus has remained on exerting control over the reproductive, female body. In what follows, I provide a brief overview of these changing ideas to illustrate my point, focusing on what was perceived to be the 'problem' and how prenatal (in)activity was viewed as one possible solution.

In late-nineteenth-century Britain and North America, concern about the health and fitness of the population, and in particular, the reproduction of a strong white, imperial nation-state were fuelled by a decrease in the birth rate (especially among the middle and upper classes), and the emergence of the 'new woman' who was perceived to threaten the sanctity of nineteenth-century gender roles which constructed women as the 'moral guardians' of the race (Arnup, 1994; Lupton, 1995). It was in this context that women's reproductive health became a special object of medical interest, with advice from (predominantly male) physicians serving to reinforce dominant ideas about what constituted proper social roles and behaviour for women (Vertinsky, 1994). With regards to exercise in pregnancy, medical texts encouraged upper and middle class white women (the target audience) to engage in easy walking, simple calisthenics or light housework (although nothing too rigorous) such that they might have an easier and less painful labour – similar to that of poor women and women of colour who reportedly gave birth and were back working within hours (Jette, 2009). The assumption that the 'lower classes' had easier births likely reflected the widely held impression that they were multiplying at an excessive rate – and that these women were less delicate, 'civilized' and human than women of the higher classes. By living a less indolent and luxurious lifestyle, it was thought that birth could be made easier for middle- and upper-class women, suggesting that advice to train for childbirth was in large part meant to encourage these women to reproduce – preventing race suicide and preserving the health of the nation-state.

The first half of the twentieth century witnessed significant changes in the care of the pregnant body as high rates of infant and maternal mortality – trends captured by new data collection systems put into place – emerged as a problem (see Jette, 2009), providing the impetus for the widespread medicalization (and hospitalization) of childbirth and the advent of formalized and routine prenatal care for all women – working, middle and upper class (Arney, 1982; Arnup, 1994). With regard to exercise in pregnancy, medical advice changed slightly as it was now recognized that some of the recipients of prenatal care were women who worked rigorously in their daily lives (on farms, cleaning their houses and/or in factories), and that 'additional' exercise was unwise as well as often difficult to obtain (Jette, 2009). While leisurely walks remained the dominant medical prescription, pregnant women (especially working women) were also advised to rest in the hopes that this would help to stem the high rates of infant and maternal mortality. Significantly, the provision of prenatal care and education in Canada, the US and Britain was increasingly taken on by government agencies in the first half of the twentieth century (Browne, 1951), early indications of the growing welfare state concerned with instilling norms around health and hygiene in the population (Dodd, 1991; Rose, 2001). The prenatal movement was also inextricably tied to a positive eugenics platform intended to encourage the 'fit' segments of society to reproduce (Dodd, 1991; Kline, 2001). In the Canadian context, for instance, government documents and popular literature alike positioned engaging in prenatal care as a pregnant woman's patriotic duty, illustrating how prenatal care (including advice about appropriate exercise) was overtly linked to the nation building project (Jette, 2009).

The notion that pregnant women should rest and take it easy remained a cornerstone of medical advice – and gained purchase in the popular imagination – until the late 1960s and into the 1970s when, in line with the disruption of traditional gender roles that occurred with the second wave feminist movement, women continued to engage in more rigorous leisure pursuits while pregnant (Jette, 2009, 2011). Debates about what is safe ensued, spurring the growth of a new research area: pregnancy exercise science in which researchers tried to determine the upper limits of safe prenatal exercise through laboratory studies as well as observational (epidemiological) studies in which the birth outcomes of women who exercised in pregnancy were compared to those who did not exercise, in order to determine if prenatal exercise is a risk factor for negative birth outcomes (Jette, 2011).

This brings us to the current moment in which, after decades of debate about if exercise during pregnancy is safe and, if so, how much, there has been a shift in the focus of research towards ascertaining the risk of physical *inactivity* in the context of the obesity epidemic. That is to say, as concerns about an obesity epidemic emerged at the close of the twentieth century (Gard and Wright, 2005), we saw a corresponding rise in research focusing on how/if prenatal exercise can be used to help prevent overweight and obese women giving birth to overweight/obese babies that will become adults with a range of chronic diseases (Jette, 2009; Jette and Rail, 2013). However, there has been a shift in the scale (both visually and temporally) at which the impact of exercise on the future health of the foetus is being envisioned. While exercise scientists previously explored the way in which maternal exercise might have an immediate impact upon the foetus in terms of nutrient deprivation (as blood is redirected from the placenta to exercising muscles) or foetal overheating (associated with birth defects; Jette, 2009, 2011), they are now trying to understand changes at not only the cellular but also the metabolic and genetic level of the foetus. This shift appears to correspond with increased attention at the turn of the twenty-first century to the Developmental Origins of Health and Disease (DOHaD) or foetal programming: the study of how early exposures in the womb (often linked to the behaviours of the pregnant woman and/or environmental exposures) can influence developmental pathways and induce permanent metabolic changes and, in effect, 'program' the foetus for future chronic disease (Warin et al., 2011). While the biologic mechanisms underlying the DOHaD are not well understood, researchers are increasingly interested in the potential role of epigenetic mechanisms whereby certain exposures in utero (as well as early life) can, in effect, turn the 'volume' of a gene up or down, altering the way it is expressed (i.e. phenotype) as opposed to the actual DNA (genotype).

While much of the early DOHaD research focused on how exposure of pregnant women to inadequate nutrition and general conditions of poverty led to poor health outcomes in offspring (namely low birth weight associated with hypertension, heart disease and Type 2 diabetes), in the past decade (and in conjunction with the panic that we are in the midst of an obesity epidemic) attention has shifted to an examination of how excessive maternal weight gain can program adult obesity and other metabolic disease in the foetus (Jette and Rail, 2013; Warin et al., 2011). Thus, while the gene–environment interaction is crucial to foetal origins research, in much of the literature concerning pregnancy weight gain, there tends to be a very narrow (and decontextualized) view of the environment whereby it is reduced to a woman's behaviours, and prenatal exercise is one such behaviour that can be used to enhance the life of the future child. Just as in the late nineteenth century, prenatal exercise functions as a technique of governmentality – one solution to a problematic of governance – but the problem has shifted from a concern with the health and fitness of the nation-state amidst concerns of race suicide to the cost of unhealthy bodies in the context of the obesity epidemic.

Reimagining the pregnant body: 'release' through dance

It was with this contextualized understanding of the (in)active pregnant body that I began my engagement with a non-profit dietary centre located in downtown Montreal, Quebec (the 'Centre' from this point forward) that provides pregnant women on low income who are at least five months pregnant with free dietary advice and free food such as milk, eggs and bread, as well as group classes on a range of topics from healthy eating to breastfeeding. I initially approached the Director of the Centre to seek permission to recruit participants for in-depth interviews, part of a project to explore how pregnant women on low income understand maternal weight gain and exercise (see Jette and Rail, 2014). My request was granted and, in addition to interviews with 13 pregnant women from the Centre, I also interviewed five dieticians employed at the Centre about their understanding of obesity and how this influenced their prenatal care advice. In return, I offered to provide the dieticians with a summary of my findings upon completion of the interviews.

In my presentation I explained that, based on my interviews, it seemed that both groups (the clients and dieticians) took a very instrumental view of physical activity. Many of the pregnant clients viewed it as something to perform following pregnancy in order to regain their pre-pregnancy bodies (the majority did not view it as a priority during pregnancy, despite the fact that the majority listed physical activity as one element of how to have a healthy pregnancy). The dieticians, on the other hand, saw the value in having the women exercise in order to prevent gestational diabetes mellitus (GDM), and indicated that they would urge the women to exercise in pregnancy for this reason. My suggestion was to instead emphasize pleasure in movement, and more specifically, to focus on the participants' love of dance (in the interviews, it emerged that many enjoy dancing but do not view it as safe in pregnancy). The dieticians were very receptive, and asked if I knew of anyone who could teach such a class, and if I could perhaps even arrange it. I had, much to my own surprise, become engaged in an act of border crossing (Andrews and Silk, 2015) into the role of interventionist. While excited by the opportunity to potentially create change, I was presented with something of a dilemma. Given my view of exercise in pregnancy as a technique of governmentality, how might I try to provide an experience that did not attempt to discipline and regulate bodies (i.e. did not function as a traditional public health intervention)?

It was at this time that I came upon the work of Eryn Dace Trudell, a Juilliard-trained dancer and choreographer who created MamaDances, a family dance programme 'dedicated to promoting the holistic health of parents, children, families and communities through music and movement' (www.mamadances.com). While MamaDances is now a community (family) dance programme, it began as a performance-based entity in which mothers would perform improvised dances with their babies or young children on stage. In our initial discussion, Trudell explained that she has developed pedagogical tools for helping women redefine themselves in the cognitive and bodily sense (mind/body are connected in her view) and that her goal is to bring pleasure to movement, and doing so, encourage postnatal women to view/experience their bodies in a positive way. While she was currently working with new mothers and their babies, she indicated an interest in developing a programme for pregnant women and, in collaboration with my contact at the Centre, we arranged a series of four classes to take place in the Fall of 2011 at the Centre.

A key component of Trudell's practice and pedagogy is the combination of traditional dance practices with Skinner Releasing Technique (SRT). SRT is considered a 'somatic movement practice,' one of a range of approaches to mind–body integration that emerged over the course of the twentieth century (Eddy, 2009; Emslie, 2009). Developed by dancer and choreographer Joan Skinner in the 1960s, SRT works from the principle that the body needs to release 'blocks' in order to move more freely (Agis and Moran, 2002). Skinner's work was informed by her desire to repair a bodily injury that the traditional medical profession could not solve; at the same time, she was also questioning the traditional dance techniques in which she had been trained that forced one part of the body against another, inhibited one's ability to breathe properly and contributed to her injury. In response, she devised a releasing process that is guided by poetic imagery that represents kinaesthetic experiences (with which the students can try to align themselves) as opposed to direct anatomical imagery (Alexander, 2001). First person experience is thus central to the learning environment and students are encouraged to move creatively in ways to align with the imagery as opposed to being shown/taught how to move based on 'anatomical truths' (Alexander, 2003: 4). The aim of releasing is not to relax the body, but rather to let go of conscious control and preconceived ideas through acts of metaphoric play, freeing the imagination and making the body available to images in an ongoing and continual process (Agis and Moran, 2002; Skinner et al., 1979).

The use of creativity, play and poetic imagery in order to help women experience their bodies differently were apparent as I observed the first class at the Centre. For instance, before the class began, a dietician at the Centre asked Trudell for ideas on how to better 'sell' the class to clients, asking if she should talk about how it can relieve low back pain and help to prevent GDM. Trudell countered with the suggestion that the dieticians explain to the women that the class will allow them to learn about and experience their bodies differently; that it offers the potential to make new choices and to have agency in movement – something particularly useful for the birthing experience, especially when in a medicalized environment.

During the class, Trudell took us through several guided imagery practices. In one exercise, we were to move around like we had marionette strings attached to our heads. Thus, all our movement should be around the axis of the strings, supporting us, and we moved and danced around to this for a while. A magic ball of string that was described as being like gossamer- pliable and brilliant – was also used to encourage the women to engage in play, to move their arms and hands to this imagery.

As I observed (and participated in) the class, I noticed that some of the participants appeared uncomfortable being asked to engage in this creative, child-like play, myself included. One example relates to a warm-up exercise when we were down on all fours (i.e. like a baby crawling):

> At this point Eryn incorporated a playful aspect, and had us move forward with our hands, making growling sounds like an animal. Interestingly, only the young daughter of one of the clients engaged whole-heartedly, as the rest of us refrained from growling.
>
> *(Field notes, 6 September 2011)*

The hesitancy of the adults in the room to engage in this process of imagining – and the willingness of the young child to do just this – was striking and illustrative of how play is socialized out of our bodies as we move into adulthood. When I asked Trudell about the imagery, she explained that the purpose is to help the women be more 'internal' and connect with what is happening in their bodies, with less focus on the exterior. Because we often limit our bodily movements with the thoughts and habits that we have been taught, she uses the imagery to help the women let go of these habits and to connect with and listen to their bodies, allowing movement in new and uninhibited ways.

Conclusion

While only a preliminary engagement, SRT seems to offer interesting avenues of investigation for scholars looking to move beyond the mind–body dualism that continues to shape Western ontology whereby the mind and body are considered separate entities, with the mind subject to voluntary control and the body at the whim of unconscious and automatic regulatory processes (Blackman, 2008). Skinner's pedagogical approach (further developed by Trudell) is one that may enhance our understanding of the body as multiple and 'mediated by processes and practices that produce dynamic points of intersection and connection' (ibid.: 107), as opposed to being an autonomous, pre-formed entity or produced solely by discourse. Yet at the same time, we must not dismiss the utility of a (feminist) poststructuralist perspective that facilitates an examination of the power relations embedded in systems of knowledge that in turn shape our material social practices and produce particular gendered subjectivities – albeit multiple, fluid and open to change (Weedon, 1997). My contextual analysis of the changing ideas concerning exercise during pregnancy illustrates how the shifting political, economic and social landscape influenced medical knowledge concerning acceptable physical activity for pregnant women – while women's movement practices simultaneously shaped the questions being asked by medical practitioners, the knowledge produced and the prescriptions provided. This mapping of the context in which physical activity in pregnancy is structured and made meaningful is illustrative of, and contributes to, the contextual imperative that underpins the PCS approach (Andrews and Silk, 2015).

My analysis of pregnant bodies is also explicitly political and interventionist, an attempt at praxis that reflects my grounding in feminist theory and practice, and which further contributes to a PCS agenda, in part by making explicit the influence of feminist scholarship in my research, and in doing so furthering a feminist PCS that, with few exceptions (Thorpe et al., 2011) has been undeveloped (see also Adams et al., 2016). More specifically, I refer to my attempt to explore alternative ways of performing movement during pregnancy that are, if not freed, at least loosened from the disciplinary imperative so often seen in (kinesiological) public health interventions that come with a host of outcomes that can (and must) be quantitatively measured and analysed (Silk, Bush and Andrews, 2010). For this very reason, however, it is questionable as to how/if this practice is sustainable beyond select spaces such as the Centre which questions the dominant discourse concerning pregnancy weight gain and encourages women to advocate for a less medicalized birth procedure while also providing them with free prenatal services and a supportive environment (Jette and Rail, 2014). Given the current (neoliberal) imperative within the realm of health (Jette and Rail, 2013) and academia (Silk et al., 2010) to engage in evidence-based research that will allow for greater efficiency, accountability and economic profit, research grants to examine pregnant women's embodied experiences of dance are likely limited, and funding to create sustainable community-based programmes even more unlikely (especially given the absence of evidence-based outcomes). This is not to say that such projects should be abandoned, but rather that we must continue to use whatever capital (social, cultural and economic) that we have as scholars to engage in these politically informed and potentially transformative interdisciplinary projects.

References

Adams, M. et al. 2016. Feminist cultural studies: Uncertainties and possibilities. *Sociology of Sport Journal*, 33 (1), 75–91.

Agis, G. and Moran, J. 2002. In its purest form: A rare insight into the work of Joan Skinner. *Animated*, Winter, 20–22.

Alexander, K. 2001. You can't make a leaf to grow by stretching it: Some notes on the philosophical implications of Skinner Releasing Technique. *Performance Journal*, 18 (Winter/Spring), 8–9.

Alexander, K. 2003. Unraveling the dance: An exploration of dance's underdeveloped relationship with its kinaesthetic nature, with particular reference to Skinner Releasing Technique. Paper presented at the New Connectivity Conference, London.

Andrews, D. L. and Silk, M. L. 2015. Physical cultural studies on sport. In R. Guilianotti (ed.), *Routledge handbook of the sociology of sport*. New York: Routledge, 83–93.

Arney, W. R. 1982. *Power and the profession of obstetrics*. Chicago, IL: University of Chicago Press.

Arnup, K. 1994. *Education for motherhood: Advice for mothers in twentieth-century Canada*. Toronto: University of Toronto Press.

Blackman, L. 2008. *The body: The key concepts*. New York: Berg.

Browne, F. J. 1951. *Antenatal and postnatal care*. London: Churchill.
Dodd, D. 1991. Advice to parents: The Blue Books, Helen MacMurchy, MD, and the federal Department of Health, 1920–34. *Canadian Bulletin of Medical History*, 8 (2), 203–230.
Eddy, M. 2009. A brief history of somatic practices and dance historical development of the field of somatic education and its relationship to dance. *Journal of Dance and Somatic Practices*, 1 (1), 5–27.
Emslie, M. 2009. Skinner Releasing Technique: Dancing from within. *Journal of Dance and Somatic Practices*, 1 (2), 169–175.
Foucault, M. 2003a. *'Society must be defended': Lectures at the College de France, 1975–1976* (ed. M. Bertani and A. Fontana, trans. D. Macey). New York: Picador.
Foucault, M. 2003b. Governmentality. In P. Rabinow and N. Rose (eds), *The essential Foucault: Selections from essential works of Foucault, 1954–1984*. New York: The New Press, 229–245.
Gard, M. and Wright, J. 2005. *The obesity epidemic: Science, morality and ideology*. New York: Routledge.
Jette, S. 2006. 'Fit for Two?': A critical discourse analysis of *Oxygen* fitness magazine. *Sociology of Sport Journal*, 23 (4), 331–351.
Jette, S. 2009. Governing risk, exercising caution: Western medical knowledge, physical activity and pregnancy. PhD thesis, University of British Columbia, Canada.
Jette, S. 2011. Exercising caution: The production of medical knowledge about physical exertion during pregnancy. *Canadian Bulletin of Medical History/Bulletin canadien d'histoire de la medicine*, 28 (2), 383–401.
Jette, S. 2014. Epigenetics, exercise and ethopolitics? The production of scientific knowledge about prenatal exercise. Presented at the North American Society for the Sociology of Sport conference, Portland, OR, 5–9 November.
Jette, S. and Rail, G. 2013. Ills from the womb? A critical examination of evidence-based medicine and pregnancy weight gain advice. *Health: An Interdisciplinary Journal for the Social Study of Health, Illness and Medicine*, 17 (4), 407–421.
Jette, S. and Rail, G. 2014. Resisting, reproducing, resigned? Low income pregnant women's constructions and experiences of a healthy pregnancy and proper weight gain. *Nursing Inquiry*, 21 (3), 202–211.
Kline, W. 2001. *Building a better race: Gender, sexuality, and eugenics from the turn of the century to the baby boom*. Berkeley, CA: University of California Press.
Lupton, D. 1995. *The imperative of health: Public health and the regulated body*. Thousands Oaks, CA: Sage Publications.
Lupton, D. 1999. Risk and the ontology of pregnant embodiment. In D. Lupton (ed.), *Risk and sociocultural theory: New directions and perspectives*. Cambridge: Cambridge University Press, 59–85.
Lupton, D. 2012. 'Precious cargo': Foetal subjects, risk and reproductive citizenship. *Critical Public Health*, 22 (3), 329–340.
Miller, P. and Rose, N. 2008. *Governing the present: Administering economic, social and personal life*. Cambridge, UK: Polity Press.
O'Malley, P. 2008. Governmentality and risk. In J. Zinn, ed. *Social theories of risk and uncertainty: An introduction*. Malden, MA: Blackwell, 52–75.
Petersen, A. and Lupton, D. 1997. *The new public health: Health and self in the age of risk*. London: Sage.
Rose, N. 2001. The politics of life itself. *Theory, Culture and Society*, 18 (6), 1–30.
Rose, N. and Miller, P. 1992. Political power beyond the state: Problematics of government. *The British Journal of Sociology*, 43 (2), 173–205.
Seneviratne, S. et al. 2014. Antenatal exercise in overweight and obese women and its effects on offspring and maternal health: Design and rationale of the IMPROVE (Improving Maternal and Progeny Obesity Via Exercise) randomised controlled trial. *BMC Pregnancy and Childbirth*, 14, 148–155.
Silk, M., Bush, A. and Andrews, D. 2010. Contingent intellectual amateurism, or, the problem with Evidence-Based Research. *Journal of Sport and Social Issues*, 34 (1), 105–128.
Skinner, J. et al. 1979. Skinner releasing technique: Imagery and its application to movement training. *Contact Quarterly*, 1 (Fall), 1–6.
Thorpe, H., Barbour, K. and Bruce, T. 2011. 'Wandering and wondering': Theory and representation in feminist Physical Cultural Studies. *Sociology of Sport Journal*, 28, 106–134.
Vertinsky, P. 1994. *The eternally wounded woman: Women, exercise and doctors in the late nineteenth century*. Manchester: Manchester University Press.
Warin, M. et al. 2011. Telescoping the origins of obesity to women's bodies: How gender inequalities are being squeezed out of Barker's hypothesis. *Annals of Human Biology*, 38 (4), 453–460.
Weedon, C. 1997. *Feminist practice and poststructuralist theory*, 2nd edn. Oxford: Blackwell.
Weir, L. 2006. *Pregnancy, risk and biopolitics: On the threshold of the living subject*. New York: Routledge.

PART VI

Spaces

33
'NATURAL', INTIMATE AND SENSORY LANDSCAPES

Gordon Waitt

In recent years conversations in cultural geography about nature and landscape are enlivened by incorporating the body and issues of embodiment. The shift towards the body as an approach and the instigation of examining physical culture – including walking, swimming, running, diving, cycling – in cultural geography is part of a wider corpus of research that critiques dominant, apolitical ways of thinking about nature found within science as objective, external to people and inanimate. Rethinking key geographical concepts of nature and landscape through the body is a project that resonates with physical cultural studies as an interdisciplinary project focussed on critical forms of enquiry on how bodies are (im)mobilized. This chapter argues that a prerequisite for recognizing the bodily experience has to begin with a theorization of space as an integral part of bodily experience. In this regard it may be useful for physical cultural studies to embrace current re-workings of nature within the philosophy of geography figured as post-, or critical phenomenologies. When conceptualized in terms of cultures of natures, the bodily experience of nature is simultaneously one which is in part shaped not only be the ideas but also by the technologies, equipment, animals, plants, soil and climate. In turn, these various material things provide affordances by which we come to know the self and world in particular ways. Embodied actions (including touching, listening, looking and tasting) of physical cultural activities (including walking, running, surfing, sunbathing) are practices which draw on such affordances in the processes of sensing and making sense of self–world relationships. This chapter outlines the implications of bringing questions about what bodies do as the starting point of enquiry about nature, intimacy and landscape. The basic argument is that nature is never pre-existing nor singular but instead always embodied, emplaced, represented, disciplined, experienced and multiple. The chapter explores some of the implications of studying nature when conceived as a spatially situated embodied process under two themes:

1. *Doing 'natures'*: animating landscapes.
2. *Responsibility*: situating the experience of nature.

To conclude, the chapter outlines how a physical cultural approach demands writing knowledge of nature and natural landscape as always unfolding, and fosters our attention on the importance of the politics of affect and emotion.

Cultures of natures: multinatural ontologies

Nature sometimes seems to form an apparently passive background to human practices. Indeed, for many people living in Western cities, encounters with are nature are often deeply embedded in a social and material life born of the epistemology and ontology of the scientific method advanced in seventeenth-century Europe. Such ideas locate nature as 'out there' waiting to be discovered, observed and measured in a multiple of ways. At the same time, places for nature are often taken to be those where certain humans are absent and often rely on an imagined spatial frontier that separates the civilized from the wild, history from prehistory. This hierarchical separation of humans from nature is one example of the dualism that underpin much enlightenment thinking that favours the mind over the body, men over women, solids over fluids, European/British history over Indigenous people's storylines and humans over non-humans (Grosz, 1994; Plumwood, 2002). Nature is made to appear absent from our daily life by human presence; until a disaster or emergency brings us proximate with the processes on which our existence depends.

The turn towards the body and the study of (in)active embodiment in cultural geography is embedded in epistemological and ontological conversations that offer new theoretical approaches that troubles understanding of nature as pure, singular, stable and 'out there'. Within the context of poststructuralist approaches that advocate for thinking of culture and nature outside of binary thinking, cultural geographies now discuss embodied, 'more-than-human' and 'multinatural' worlds.

There are assorted research strands that bypass enlightenment thinking of nature by drawing on different philosophers. One strand draws on feminist scholarship including Haraway (1991), Grosz (1994), Plumwood (2002) and Probyn (2000) while another resonates with Thrift's (2007) non-representational theory (NRT) or affective geographies. There are similarities but also important differences between these conceptual positions of rethinking nature in more lively ways. Both approaches share an interest in:

1. conceptualizing modes of power as relational rather than oppositional;
2. bringing to the fore non-conscious bodily habits that underpin everyday practices, routine and rhythms;
3. emphasizing the emplaced sensuous body as active in feeling, shaping and reshaping our orientation in the world; and
4. highlighting the potential of affective intensities and emotion to shape and transform our self and the world we live in.

Equally, both approaches share conceptualization of the body not as a bounded solid whole, but rather as active, porous and permeable. Strongly influenced by Deleuzian concepts, each emphasizes thinking with the notion of assemblage and *agencement*. The starting point with the concept of assemblage is to investigate the ongoing, provisional process of bringing together diverse elements (ideas, technologies, institutions, materials and humans) into a working order that makes coherent sense, where agency does not lie solely within the body-subject. Attention can then turn to the Deleuzian idea of *agencement*, or the property or quality of an assemblage. Assemblages hold together, or fall apart, depending on how their diverse elements relate or connect. Finally, both approaches call for methods that put front and centre the living, breathing, sensual, emotional, affective bodies into geographical enquiry of nature.

Nonetheless, important differences can be identified within and between geographical research strands of cultures of nature; particularly around modes of relating to human agency, the body, affect and emotion (see H. Lorimer, 2008). First, following Haraway one strand of ecofeminist geography emphasizes the organism as the entry point for analysis. In contrast, drawing on the work of Thrift (2007), non-representational accounts focus on the capacity of bodies to affect and to be affected that precedes and exceeds any stratified formations of power-knowledge. Second, non-representational accounts make theoretical distinctions between bodily sensations, emotions and affect. Affective geographies working within the non-conscious realm often distance themselves from research which privilege subjectivity and nameable emotions. Whereas, Probyn (2000) works within the assumption that sensation, affect and emotion can be both pre- and post-cognitive. Hence, alongside the capacities of bodies to affect, and be affected, bodies are always located and entwined within discursively produced relations of power, including the most intense bodily sensations of affect communicated as emotions. Finally, feminist geographers argue that affective geographies often ignore bodily differences along aged, racialized, classed, sexed and gendered lines. Centre stage to this debate is how affective geographies restore dualist thinking of mind and body (see Thien, 2005). Bondi (2005: 438) concluded that 'feminist geographers find research informed by non-representational theory too abstract, too little touched by how people make sense of their lives, and therefore too "inhuman", ungrounded, distancing, detached and, ironically, disembodied'. The next two sections explore the implications arising from enlivening the notions of nature and landscape.

Doing natures: animating 'landscapes'

One strand of research drawing on non-representational theory rethinks landscapes as performative rather than some material entity located in the eye of the onlooker. Motivated by Thrift's (2007) ideas, Wylie (2007) extends the intellectual project of reading landscape as text that privileged sight. Instead, Wylie encourages scholars to engage with the material world, using all the senses including bodily movement (kinaesthetic). This strand highlights that landscapes that we may take for granted as places for nature are made and remade through what bodies 'do'. We sense, and make sense of landscapes as natural through the frictions and rhythms of our movement and how we orientate ourselves towards the world. Attention is drawn to how landscapes are formed in terms of the body's position and orientation in relation to the tensions between material, cultural, social and physiological processes that intertwine together the body and world. No longer are natural landscapes conceived as detached, objective space, located somewhere 'out there'. Instead, natural landscapes are understood as something in and through which lives are lived, subjectivities are stabilized, and imagined geographies or myths are made and remade. This conception of landscapes as performative requires thinking about people as dwellers not observers; as multi-sensuous participants not detached onlookers.

Following Wylie's view, people know landscapes and places for nature by doing. What we do is not solely a cognitive project. Integral to this process is what we have already learnt from how our embodied, habitual practical knowledge is co-constituted through encounters with the material world; how it affects us and we affect it. Hence, scholars must remain alert to how different bodies-in-motion become attuned to the various affordances of the material world. One challenge posed by Thrift's ideas is for scholars to remain alert to the connections between the cognitive and non-cognitive in fashioning the intelligibility of places for nature. Another is to remain alert to futures that are open, rather than prescribed. While bodily habits and sets of ideas may reconfigure dominant understandings of self in relationship to the world, both may be modified through the interplay of bodily sensations, affect and emotion.

For example, recent cultural geography research exploring ways of walking that draws on non-representational theory illustrates the implications of a performative approach to understand nature and places for nature. Following a performative approach, walking is envisaged as an active corporate engagement of human bodies with the sensed world. Landscapes surface as part of a kinaesthetic movement-space of walking, which includes paths, trees, weather, topography, animals, boots, back-packs, packed lunches and cameras, that become understood as meaningful places for residents, tourists, ramblers, trampers or bushwalkers. Rather than landscape being conceived as a backdrop on which everyday life plays out, as Wylie (2007: 1) argues, 'Landscape is tension' – a concept that encompasses both 'nature' and society, the material world 'out there' and the sensing, perceiving, thinking self/body/subject.

Attention to the performative first highlights 'the walking body' as an assemblage of material affordances, embodied dispositions and social practices. Some scholars draw attention to the bodily practices, sensations apprehended as bodies attune to long-distance walks and the affordances of different terrains to sustain or harbour the self (Wylie, 2006; Edensor, 2008; H. Lorimer and Lund, 2008). Discussing a long-distance leisure walk in Scotland, Edensor (2008) draws attention to the self–world tension. He argues that travelling by foot, after a few days offers 'a deeper, non-cognitive, sensual form of appreciation developed for the terrain traversed, experienced through the feet and legs, promoting an adaptation to the environment through a heightened sense of corporeal balance' (ibid.: 132). Such work draws attention to the agency of wood, stones, moss and water in creating pathways. Likewise, Hayden Lorimer and Katrin Lund (2008: 194) explore the creative self–world tensions through their investigation of how practices of hillwalking help to sustain the subject of the 'Munro bagger'; that is people who collect the 284 highest peaks in Scotland, known as 'the Munros'. Lorimer and Lund (ibid.) discuss how the 'sensations of closeness and familiarity' to the material world perceived through the reciprocal relations with the feet sustains as sense of self that may be articulated with pride.

This work has drawn attention to the importance of moments of detachment, or bodies belonging but not quite fitting in. Such moments may offer reflection or distancing from lived experience. They are important because they provide opportunities for opening on the world, possibilities to imagine different futures. Thus walking and being-in-the-flow may generate 'time out' or the feeling that time has 'stood still' from the usual comings and goings of life. For example, Waitt, Gill and Head's (2008) work on walking in an Australian suburban reserve illustrates the importance of routine scheduling of walking as a way of managing emotions. The daily route of walking through a reserve after work at the end of the day evoked responses such as peacefulness, enjoyment and relaxation. Walking at the end of the working day may be important for the change in emotional dispositions and therapeutic benefits through the practice of moving along particular routes in places thought of as designated for nature. Furthermore, participants spoke of walking as changing the flow of time, and creating possibilities to problem solve.

Moreover, Wylie (2006) argues that views of the horizon have the affective capacity for self-reflection, thereby providing possibilities to obtain 'openings' on the world. The reflective capabilities and capacities of views are provided by the medium of depth that recedes from the onlooker. As Lorimer and Lund (2008: 194) argue: 'There is a distant horizon-hovering openness … that enables people to raise to consciousness an aspirant version of their self.' Waitt and Macquarie's (2014) discussion of walking in and through the Illawarra Escarpment, New South Wales, Australia, confirms their argument. Walking on the Illawarra Escarpment is made pleasurable through possibilities to access certain views of the horizon. In turn these views are often described as 'inspiring'. Waitt and Macquarie conclude that the therapeutic benefits of walking increase the capacity of people to carry out everyday responsibilities, and increased orientation of favourite walks towards escarpment views.

Other scholars highlight the politics of self-formation through the practice of leisure walking. For example, Palmer (2005) draws attention to the embodied disposition of many Western tourists arriving at Kakadu National Park, Northern Territory, Australia, who expect to walk anywhere in the park, despite the traditional owners' request for respectful visitors not to visit certain sites. Walking routes may be understood as a place and boundary making process by helping to 'zone-off' particular locations as place for nature often entangled within particular classed, gendered and racialized geographies of belonging. The traditional owners and visitors speak very differently of their emotions toward tourists walking independently in Kakadu National Park, and this is reflected in the affordance of walking. For many visitors, walking in Kakadu National Park with global positioning technologies (GPS) offers a space of adventure, wilderness and discovery; an opportunity to find themselves. For the traditional owners, visitors walking independently are an unwanted intrusion to sites they spend in the company of ancestral beings.

Waitt, Figueroa and McGee (2007) draw on Probyn (2000) to explore the dynamics of pride and shame of people who visit Uluru Kata Juta National Park, Northern Territory. The traditional owners request respectful visitors not to climb Uluru, rather walk around the base. Yet, the historical weight of ideas circulated by the tourism industry has normalized climbing Uluru as Ayers Rock. Waitt et al. (2007) discuss how visitors must negotiate different understandings of this place in the decision to climb or walk, including as home of the Anangu, a wilderness, a national homeland, and a site of reconciliation between settler and Indigenous peoples. Drawing on interviews and participant observation they discuss how shame triggered by witnessing people climb, or learning of Aboriginal dispossession, may operate through visceral shame opening a moment of detachment through a heightened sense of self desperately seeking to belonging, but not quite fitting in. Shame does not work to prescribe the future. Some visitors who felt shame continued to climb, justified as performance of national pride. Others, chose not to climb, and instead walked around the base. Walking, rather than climbing, illustrates the possibilities of performing a different version of the Australian nation respectful of traditional owners.

Together this work points to landscape not as backdrop to life, but as part of ourselves and a crucial learning medium for the ongoing sustenance and maintenance of bodily sensibility, capacities and competences. While walking helps to articulate individual narratives, they are embedded with social norms and collective history. Walking is a sensuous process, the body-in-motion becoming attuned to the rhythms of other entities and presences that comprise the landscape. The material world provides a wealth of resources to sense, think and move with. The pleasures of the practice of leisure walking cannot be separated from how they create a change in emotional states, sense of time, connection to place and thinking space.

Responsibility: situating the experience of nature

Another strand of research provides insights to the moral and political accountability of the subject taking as an ontological starting point the intersections between embodied encounter, humanitarianism, affective and emotional relations. In the context of nature-based tourism experiences, attention is drawn to the importance of spatial proximity afforded by touch. Following theorists such as Merleau-Ponty's (1962) existential phenomenology, the sense and meaning of touch is extended beyond simply registering contact conveyed through sensory receptors and nerve endings on the skin as temperature, texture and pressure. Instead, touch is conceived as always multi-sensory, and one of the ways in which people make sense of themselves by finding and making meaning in the world. Inspired by commentators like Grosz (1994) and Sedgwick (2003) who rethink the body away from any universalism, this work resists the binaries of outside or inside the body-self, and the idea that experience flows through discrete senses. Touch (and indeed smell, sound, taste or sight) may provide important clues for investigating the dynamic nexus between self, space, practices, morals, ideas, emotion and affect that are always located within the context of uneven structures or power geometries.

Touch is often prioritized as a tourist practice, because when human and non-human bodies touch they are the physically closest they can be. Tourists are often willing to pay to become physically closer to 'nature'. For nature-based tourism, proximity is a means of commodification. And, touch is the most intimate encounter. Well documented in the literature are examples of paying for proximity to touch charismatic animals including elephants, seals, dolphins, wales and penguins (see J. Lorimer, 2012).

Scholars draw attention to the politics of touch because of the capacity of this practice and sensual experience to dissolve or confirm social boundaries, hierarchies and classifications as well as to make close that which is spatially or temporally far away. For example, Straughan (2012) draws attention to how the material affordances of the touch of water facilitates a therapeutic landscape, wherein a sense of well-being emerges. Waitt and Cook (2007) draw on empirical case studies of Thai sea-kayaking tour experiences targeting Western tourists. They illustrate how sea-kayaking activities are actively shaped by the proximity afforded by touch, and indeed facilitated by tour operators. In this case the touch of water is integral to confirming and unsettling visitors' ideas of Thailand as an earthly paradise.

Voluntourism provides an excellent example to illustrate the politics of touch. Voluntourism is one example of civic engagement pertaining to narratives that promote moral modes of consumption in a wide range of social arenas from fair trade to 'green' purchasing. What are the implications of affective and emotional relationships triggered by the practices and experiences of the haptic sense of touch, understood within the context of power geometries that shape ecotourism? To help explore this question, Waitt, Figueroa and Nagle (2014) draw on empirical materials to reveal how scientific voluntourism is performed, represented and negotiated via touch on Montague Island nature reserve, New South Wales, Australia. They research human–penguin relationships and their moral implications through paying to help a penguin survey of nesting boxes. They discuss how in a cultural matrix that anthropomorphizes penguins as cute and cuddly, the survey of little penguin nesting boxes gives paying visitors physical proximity. They explore the affective intensities of touching penguins, and the reciprocity of being touched by penguins. Conducting the survey, visitors must confront an affective intensity to reach out and touch penguins. Visitors often know this touch is unwanted. Indeed the visitor information sheet provided when booking, and again on arrival, reminds visitors of conservation science principles that position all bird species as 'untouchable'. Waitt et al. (ibid.) discuss how the intensity of the affective push in the context of voluntourism brought to the fore moral dilemmas around the simple preservationist principle of 'do not touch'. They report how paying to be involved in the survey activities sustains a sense of ownership over the penguins that opened voluntourists' bodies to touch. Touch became a consumer prerogative that bends conservation science principles. Penguins were no longer positioned with the relationships that sustain the spaces of voluntourism as untouchable. For Waitt et al. (ibid.), embodied relations of touch offer a starting point for a theoretical approach that explores a spatially inflected understanding of responsibility that shapes and is shaped by material, symbolic, embodied, emotional and affective relationships.

Another body of literature in cultural geography that draws on the concept of embodied encounters explores the fleeting happenstances with independently mobile birds that constitute the varied practices, places and subjectivities of bird-watching (J. Lorimer, 2008; Hui, 2013; Wilkinson et al., 2014). The growing academic interest in bird-watching mirrors the increasing enrolment of birds in leisure tourism capitalist production (Green and Jones, 2010; Kim et al., 2010) and people as volunteer labour for citizen science projects.

The starting point of this work that adopts a performative theoretical lens is that the subject of the bird-watcher is always unstable rather than given, produced and reproduced through the constellation of material, affective and emotional relationships that constituted the bird-watching space. This is a deliberate move away from the recreational specialization approach in leisure studies that draws on quantitative methods and works within assumed pre-existing categories of bird-watchers differentiated by commitment, knowledge, skill, motivation, setting preferences and expenditure (see Scott and Schafer, 2001; Moore et al., 2008). One outcome of this approach is that it helps reproduce a social hierarchy of bird-watchers often differentiated by skill and categorized as *advanced, intermediate, novice* and *casual* (see McFarlane, 1994: 361; Cole and Scott, 1999: 45). These categories are usually taken for granted with the leisure studies literature.

However, omitted from these accounts are the everyday lived experience, and how becoming a bird-watcher is always a spatially contingent practice that relies on a heightened, sensual form of appreciation of place. What might the sensuous body tell us about bird-watching? Fleeting encounters with charismatic birds usually rely on experiences through eyes and ears, rather than touch. Nevertheless, as illustrated by the work of Wilkinson et al. (2014), paying attention to the embodied dimensions of the sights and sounds triggered by bird-watching practices offers new insights to the spatial imperatives of making sense of place and subjectivities.

Wilkinson et al. (ibid.) draw on ethnographic fieldwork conducted on the East Coast of Australia with 21 people who watch birds as a leisure practice. Seventeen of these participants observed birds as members of bird organizations: the Illawarra Birders, Eurobodalla Natural History Society, and Far South Coast Bird Watchers Incorporated. To better understand the embodied, the fleeting and the ephemeral in practices of encountering and listing birds, the project design used semi-structured interviews alongside participant observation. Home and citizen science were two key emergent themes.

This ethnographic research revealed a great deal about how self and home as places of belonging are mutually constituted through affective and emotional relationship triggered by practices of bird-watching and listing. For some, making places home is grounded in a working scientific knowledge of birds. The process of learning to identify bird species becomes part of the emotional work of home-making. For others, this process of home-making was facilitated through the work of establishing and maintaining bird-watching organizations that facilitated building close social relationships with like-minded people. This shared sense of belonging from identifying and listing birds was articulated by some participants as fuelled by a passion for the scientific principles of ornithology to build an environmentally responsible community and the subject of the citizen scientist. For others beginning to learn how to attune to different bird calls, colouring and habitat, the opportunity to watch birds together was integral to help sustain a sense of belonging following a major life course event, including migration, retirement, separation or bereavement.

And yet for others who had a trip-list of birds, the shared sense of belonging from identifying birds was more closely aligned to mediating a sense of belonging while travelling regionally, nationally or internationally. Bird-lists were often a motivation to travel. Pre-departure activities may require acquiring scientific knowledge about particular destinations as bird habitats and sensitizing the body to the species, their calls and their colouring. This knowledge is crucial to gain close physical proximity to birds. Consequently, the ideas of 'home' and 'away' are blurred. Arriving at specific destinations with bird-lists, participants expressed a sense of belonging through their highly specialized embodied knowledge to identify a particular bird species. Pleasures are derived from an embodied closeness and familiarity with birds. In doing so, this work also makes trouble for arguments that suggest that the ideas and technologies of bird-watching (cameras, binoculars, close circuit television) that privilege the eye and shape how people look at birds serves to only further impose dualist understanding of nature as 'out there', distinct from humans (see Chambers, 2007).

The subject of the citizen scientist also emerged from the ethnographic fieldwork. The citizen scientist is a term usually employed to discuss the work of volunteers who collect data through survey techniques that is then used by biologists and climatologists. Wilkinson et al. (2014) point out the self–world tensions felt by people who watch birds when conducting a bird survey for a citizen science project. To see, hear and classify a bird according to specific techniques prescribed by the survey is an essential part of the labour of bird-based citizen science. Through the sensual appreciation of ears and eyes participants become aware performatively of becoming a citizen scientist. Eyes and ears are trained specifically for participating in prescribed survey techniques of a citizen scientist. While some participants spoke of the rewards and pleasures, all participants spoke of the pressure and intensity of such voluntary work. Some reported giving up in disgust. And, yet others spoke of how learning to identity and list birds for the work of citizen science reduced their sensual appreciation of simply witnessing rather than identifying birds. Such findings point to the politics of embodiment. Citizen science is a site where social divisions and hierarchies are experienced and enacted. Scientists enrolling the volunteer labour of people who watch birds as a leisure practice would do well to become mindful of how social power becomes manifest. The close emotional and affective embodied connections to place and birds for people who watch birds for pleasure may not neatly transfer into citizen science. Indeed a sense of self and home may by undermined by the embodied practice demands of becoming a citizen scientist.

Conclusion

In conclusion, poststructuralist epistemology and ontology opens up ways of thinking of nature and subjectivities as performative. Nature is always a relational achievement between human and non-human components in their material context, each with their own rhythm, operating across different geographical scales, and composed of a multiplicity of uneven forces (affective, cultural and social). Hence, to sense and to make sense of 'nature' and 'natural landscape spaces' can never exist in advance waiting to be discovered. Instead, nature and places for nature are conceived as always an immanent relational, political and spatial process of making sense of ourselves in and through space that involves material, cultural and social forces. Brought to the fore in this work are how nature, landscapes, senses and subjectivities are not separate realms but as co-constituted, multiple and immanent, and enlivened through bodily habits, skills/practices, sensations/feelings, emotions and affects. In this relational thinking, nature and landscape spaces are made and remade sense of through creative self–world relationships.

A physical cultural studies approach is a provocation to others to increase their sensibility to nature and natural landscapes as something indeterminate, formed and forming, rather than a pre-given starting point. Such an approach gives social scientists an important role in the politics of nature, facilitating possibilities to reconstitute nature, and advocate for other modes of living with the non-human world. A physical cultural studies approach brings our attention to the notion of not one fixed nature 'out there' which needs revealing through science, but is one that is multiple, performative, embodied, spatial, temporal and relational. A physical cultural studies approach brings to our attention that the political is not only about ideas of consent and dissent about nature, but affective and emotional matters that mobilize practices and may offer self-scrutiny. Physical cultural studies asks us to consider how political moments are enacted through the sensual body; that is always located somewhere and embedded in ideologies.

References

Bondi, L., 2005. Making connections and thinking through emotions: between geography and psychotherapy. *Transactions of the Institute of British Geographers* 30, 433–448.
Chambers, C. 2007. 'Well its remote, I suppose, innit?' The relational politics of bird-watching through the CCTV lens. *Scottish Geographical Journal* 123 (2), 122–134.
Cole, J. and Scott, D. 1999. Segmenting participation in wildlife watching: a comparison of casual wildlife watchers and serious birders. *Human Dimensions of Wildlife: An International Journal* 4 (4), 44–61.
Edensor 2008. Walking through ruins. In T. Ingold and J. L. Vergunst (eds), *Ways of Walking: Ethnography and Practice on Foot*. Aldershot: Ashgate, 123–142.
Green, R. and Jones, D. 2010. *Practices, Needs and Attitudes of Bird-Watching Tourists in Australia*. Gold Coast, QLD: CRC for Sustainable Tourism.
Grosz, E. 1994. *Volatile Bodies: Toward a Corporeal Feminism*. St Leonards, NSW: Allen & Unwin.
Haraway, D 1991. *Simians, Cyborgs and Women: The Reinvention of Nature*. London: Free Association.
Hui, A. 2013. Moving with practices: the discontinuous, rhythmic and material mobilities of leisure. *Social and Cultural Geography* 14 (8), 888–908.
Kim, A., Keyning, J., Robertson, J. and Kleindorfer, S. 2010. Understanding birdwatching tourism market in Queensland, Australia. *Anatolia: An International Journal of Tourism and Hospitality Research* 21 (2), 227–247.
Lorimer, H. 2008. Cultural geography: non-representational conditions and concerns. *Progress in Human Geography* 32: 551–559.
Lorimer, H. and Lund, K. 2008. A collectable topography: walking, remembering and recording mountains. In T. Ingold and J. Lee (eds), *Ways of Walking: Ethnography and Practice on Foot*. London: Ashgate, 185–200.
Lorimer, J. 2008. Counting corncrakes: the affective science of the UK Corncrake Census. *Social Studies of Science* 38 (3), 277–405.
Lorimer, J. 2012. Touching environmentalism: the place of touch in the fraught biographies of elephant captivity. In M. Paterson and M. Dodge (eds), *Touching Space, Placing Touch*. Farnham: Ashgate, 169–190.
McFarlane, B. 1994. Specialization and motivations of birdwatchers. *Wildlife Society Bulletin* 22 (3), 361–370.
Merleau-Ponty, M. 1962. *Phenomenology of Perception* (trans. C. Smith). New York: Routledge.
Moore, R., Scott, D. and Moore, A. 2008. Gender-based differences in birdwatchers' participation and commitment. *Human Dimensions of Wildlife: An International Journal* 13 (2), 89–101.
Palmer L. 2005. Bushwalking in Kakadu: a study of cultural borderlands. *Social and Cultural Geography* 5(1), 119–120.
Plumwood, V. 2002. *Feminism and the Master of Nature*. London: Routledge.
Probyn, E. 2000. *Carnal Appetites: Food Sex Identities*. New York: Routledge.
Scott, D. and Schafer, C. 2001. Recreational specialization: a critical look at the construct. *Journal of Leisure Research* 33 (3), 319–343.
Sedgwick, E. 2003. *Touching Feeling: Affect, Pedagogy, Performativity*. Durham, NC: Duke University Press.
Straughan, E. R. 2012. Touched by water: the body in scuba diving. *Emotion, Space and Society* 5, 19–26.
Thien, D. 2005. 'After or beyond feeling? A consideration of affect and emotion in geography.' *Area* 37: 450–456.
Thrift, N. 2007. *Non-Representational Theory: Space, Politics, Affect*. London: Sage.
Waitt, G. and Cook, L. 2007. Leaving nothing but ripples on the water. *Social and Cultural Geography* 8 (4), 535–550.
Waitt, G. and Macquarie, P. 2014. Travel-as-homemaking. In G. Lean, R. Staiff and E. Waterton (eds), *Travel and Imagination*. London: Ashgate, 97–122.
Waitt, G., Figueroa, R. and McGee, L. 2007. Cracks in the rock: rethinking pride and shame in the moral terrains of Uluru. *Transactions of the Institute of British Geographers* 32 (2), 248–263.

Waitt, G., Gill, N. and Head, L. 2008. Walking practice and suburban nature-talk. *Social and Cultural Geography* 10, 41–60.

Waitt, G., Figueroa, R. M. and Nagle, T. 2014. Paying for proximity: touching the moral economy of ecological voluntourism. In M. Mostafanezhad and K. Hannam (eds), *Moral Encounters in Tourism*. London: Ashgate, 167–184.

Wilkinson C., Waitt, G. and Gibbs, L. 2014. Understanding place as 'home' and 'away' through practices of bird-watching. *Australian Geographer* 45(2), 205–220.

Wylie J. 2006. Depths and folds: on landscape and the gazing subject. *Environment and Planning D: Society and Space* 24(4), 519–535.

Wylie J. 2007. *Landscape*. London: Routledge.

34
PHYSICAL CULTURAL STUDIES, SPORT AND THE ENVIRONMENT

Brian Wilson and Brad Millington

We begin with two anecdotes from our many years spent researching on sport and environmental issues. The first comes from a recent study we undertook on environmental issues and golf. We learned during this project that a trade association representing the pesticide industry – an association that had once legally contested proposed legislation that would restrict the use of pesticides – also featured prominently on a council responsible for accrediting golf courses in pesticide spraying (Millington and Wilson, 2016). In other words, and to our surprise, an organization once opposing pesticide legislation in court, and one with a financial interest in the sustained use of chemicals, was directly involved in the regulatory process.

In this same study, we found that the system used by the Canadian federal government for deciding whether chemicals should be approved for sale on the market was reviewed by a government-appointed standing committee in the year 2000. We learned that the committee concluded that the vetting system used by the government worked 'in favour of trade and economics' when it should be 'giving pre-eminence' to 'the protection of human health and the environment' (Parliament of Canada, 2000). In the committee's eyes, there was no compelling justification for industry representation on government bodies mandated to assess chemical safety. The committee ultimately recommended the abolishment of an industry-driven 'economic committee' that was integral to the government's pesticide evaluation process. *Yet the standing committee's recommendation was not adopted.* Once again, we were thoroughly surprised.

We begin this chapter on sport, the environment, and physical cultural studies (PCS) with these examples for a few reasons. First, these two examples speak to the types of concerns found in the emerging area of research on environmental politics and sport. In the first section below, we summarize some of the main topics that have been pursued in this area of research to date. Second, the above examples are drawn from work that we ourselves have carried out on golf-related environmental issues. Having first overviewed research on sport and the environment herein, we then turn to a more thorough assessment of our own work on golf's environmental past and present. Third and finally, these examples stem from research that was theoretically informed, transdisciplinary in its scope, and inclined towards delivering insight that could inform positive social change. On all three scores, we see our own work as aligned with the wider PCS project, though in this chapter we also consider how our research on golf might help 'push' PCS in new or relatively uncharted directions. We argue in relation to this latter point that PCS, with its focus to date on the (human) body within particular contexts, has thus far overlooked the important and active role that non-humans – grass, insects, fungus, and many more – play in contemporary physical cultures.

Sport, sociology and the environment: prominent themes

We begin by offering a necessarily selective overview of existing research on sport and the environment. Although the focus of this review lies mainly with critical sociological work – most of which is published in sociology of sport journals – scholars working in this area also commonly draw from fields such as cultural studies, geography, political science, and urban studies. Of course, these are all areas commonly considered to be under the 'PCS umbrella'.

Sport management and environmental issues

Perhaps the most prominent theme we identified in reviewing literature on sport and the environment concerns the 'management' of sport events, and especially mega-events. This is such a pronounced theme because the topics dealt with in this strand of literature extend well beyond what would conventionally be considered PCS-related. That is to say, this area of research includes studies and commentaries by those interrogating 'best practices' for using a 'sustainability' or 'sustainable development' approach to dealing with sport-related environmental problems – as well as work by those who are critical of the dominant and often taken-for-granted 'sustainability' approach.

The classic definition of sustainable development stems from the 1986 report *Our Common Future*: 'meet[ing] the needs of the present without compromising the ability of future generations to meet their own needs' (see WCED, 1987). Chernushenko et al. adapted this definition in their description of 'sustainable sport':

> Sport is sustainable when it meets the needs of today's sporting communities while contributing to the improvement of future sport opportunities for all and the improvement of the integrity of the natural and social environment on which it depends.
>
> *(Chernushenko et al., 2001: 10)*

Sustainable development is often seen as having economic, social, and environmental 'pillars'. These make up what is commonly known as the 'triple bottom line' (see Dryzek, 2005; Wilson, 2012).

Researchers and commentators in the 'pro-sustainability' group generally adopt a functionalist view of environmental issues. This means that the fundamental assumptions underlying the need for sport mega-events and particular environment-impacting sport management practices often go unquestioned, as attempts are made to tweak and improve sporting events to enhance the triple bottom line – ideally across the board (see Savery and Gilbert, 2011). We generally consider research in this tradition to be outside of the PCS umbrella because there is a tendency to *uncritically* adopt a 'sustainability' approach to dealing with environmental problems. Even so, there are scholars and practitioners doing sustainability-driven work that is more reflexive about the limits of and problems with sustainability. Along these lines, David Chernushenko's (1994) book *Greening Our Games: Running Sports Events and Facilities that Won't Cost the Earth* is important and unique in the sense that it is viewed by many as the original call to critical sport scholars and sport managers alike to take environmental issues seriously. The book includes a warning for readers about the problems with using the sustainability concept as a guide for action, noting that economic considerations commonly take priority over environmental concerns when attempts are made to balance these against one another.

Chernushenko's reflexivity in this regard is most welcome, though it is also important to point out that he has faced justifiable criticism – from Lenskyj (1998) especially – given that the sustainability concept ultimately lies at the heart of his work. The perceived problem is that by suggesting to sport managers that 'environmentally friendly sport can be good for business', as he does in his book, Chernushenko's approach is 'light green' in its orientation. What this means is that the environment is positioned by Chernushenko as a resource to be managed by humans, rather than as something with intrinsic worth. Without valuing nature intrinsically – that is, without a 'darker green' perspective – the risk is that environmental concerns will be addressed *to the extent* that they do not impede economic ones. Said otherwise, the sustainability concept is inherently flawed in that less environmentally friendly options can be the *most logical* options in that they also bolster the economic bottom line (also see Beder, 1994). Lenskyj's criticism of the 'light greening' of sport foreshadowed subsequent critical appraisals of the promotion and production of sustainable sport mega-events, especially the Olympics (e.g. Hayes and Horne, 2011; Karamichas, 2013; Wilson and Millington, 2015).

Sport, modernization and globalization

Other scholars concerned with sport-related environmental issues have linked their research with concepts like modernization and globalization, and in this sense have connected sport's environmental implications to wider social processes. Modernization is especially relevant here: it has been used to understand the activities of sport managers and others who are compelled to achieve 'progress' through the strategic use of science and technology – for example, in the design and upkeep of playing terrain. John Bale's (2001) foundational book *Sport, Space and the City* includes descriptions of various technologies and space management strategies that have been adopted to aid the creation of predictable and uniform (i.e. modernized) sporting environments. Of course, the creation of such environments is not only helpful for developing more rationalized sporting experiences, it is intended also to make sport events more relatable to consumers and tourists intent on viewing or participating in something more generically and predictably pleasurable.

It is here where research examining the modernization of sporting environments is most obviously linked to the concept of globalization – recognizing that global tourists are encouraged by 'space imagineers/engineers' to visit and consume generically spectacular sporting spaces and attend mass mediated sporting events (Hannigan, 2005; Silk, 2014). Brian Stoddart's (1990) and John Horne's (1998) early writing on golf, tourism, and the environment speak to this trend precisely. Stoddart offers an incisive analysis of how the evolution of the golf industry took place with the global tourist market in mind, and how its development was inextricably linked to environmental problems such as water (over-)consumption. Horne's (1998) research is a useful reminder that the pursuit of globalization and modernization in sport has also fomented resistance. Focusing especially on the late-century golf boom in the Asian-Pacific region, Horne documents the emergence of the global anti-golf movement in the late 1980s – a movement whose leader claimed responsibility for halting several hundred golf course proposals in Japan, in part due to golf's environmental implications. Indeed, activism is a prominent theme in the literature on sport and the environment. Included here is Lenskyj's (2008) research on environmentalist anti-Olympics movements, Stolle-McCallister's (2004) research on anti-golf protests, and Wheaton's (2007) research on the organization Surfers Against Sewage.

Sport, neoliberalism and environmental policy

Closely associated with modernization and globalization is neoliberalism – a concept that, ideologically, positions market-based mechanisms at the centre of attempts to address social and environmental (in addition to economic) problems and that, politically, privileges policies that indeed aim to optimize conditions for market-based exchange. The usual assumption among advocates of a neoliberal approach is that there is an economic 'trickle-down' (to the less wealthy) when private businesses are especially prosperous. From an environmental perspective, the logic works in the other direction too: if people want environmental responsibility from corporations, they will 'vote' with their dollars, choosing businesses that are green over others that are not. In this system, businesses are made environmental leaders, and the need for government regulation mandating 'green' business practices recedes (e.g. see Cao, 2015).

Although we do not have space in this chapter to outline the full range of criticisms of neoliberalism (for more detailed discussions, see Andrews and Silk, 2012) – we will point out that those studying environmental issues have offered pointed critiques of the problems with the neoliberal approach to environmental management (Heynen et al., 2007). The most obvious of these is that corporations attempting to appeal to environmentally concerned consumers are compelled to *appear* green, and not necessarily to adopt what we previously referred to as a 'dark green' environmental ethic. What this means is that claims about 'being green' can be misaligned with actual environmental practices (Lubbers, 2002). Giulianotti et al. (2015) point to an example of this in a wider discussion of public opposition to the London 2012 Olympics. With companies such as BP, Dow Chemical, and Rio Tinto sponsoring the London Games, a campaign called 'Greenwash Gold' emerged and took up protest activities such as spraying mock 'officials' from Olympic sponsors with green custard. There is also compelling evidence that many consumers who hold particular pro-environment values still actively make consumption choices that would seem to contradict these values. Stoddart's (2011) study of environmentally concerned skiers that knowingly participate in skiing-related activities that are environmentally unfriendly (e.g. driving long distances to ski hills) is but one example of a study demonstrating this.

The greening of golf: sport, the environment and social change

Our own research on golf's relationship with the environment owes a great debt to the above-described literature – particularly the work of Stoddart (1990) and Horne (1998), who also focus on golf (also see Wheeler and Nauright, 2006). At the same time, our work began from the premise that golf's environmental dimensions have not received the attention they merit. This point was made in a 2010 special issue of the *Journal of Sport and Social Issues* on the topic of 'critical golf studies'. In their introduction to the issue, editors Perkins, Mincyte and Cole (2010) recognize the range of important social and environmental issues related to golf – from ecosystem disruption resulting from course development to water over-usage in water-scarce areas to the use of pesticides that may threaten human and non-human health to the displacement of local residents or farmers as golf courses are made.

In striving to contribute to the (small) body of critical literature on golf, we undertook a programme of study focused on golf's environmental past and present, particularly (though not exclusively) in Canada and the United States. Golf only officially arrived in North America in the late 1800s; before 'migrating' from Europe it was a game played to a great extent on rugged Scottish terrain, as opposed to the well-manicured courses we are familiar with today (Bale, 1994). What we sought to provide through our research was insight into a range of related topics: whether and to what extent the environment was deemed an issue of concern at different points in time across the twentieth century; what practices existed at different moments for actually manipulating the environment; how golf industry representatives responded (and are responding now) to the environmental movement; how government officials have in turn responded to the golf industry's approach to environmentalism; and what alternatives exist to the status quo/dominant response to golf-related environmental concerns. Our methods were similarly diverse, and included: analysis of golf industry trade journals dating back to the early 1900s; interviews with golf industry members, environmental activists, and health officials; analysis of government policies affecting the golf industry (as suggested in the above introduction); and analysis of mainstream media coverage of golf's impacts on the environment.

Our main research findings from this work can be found across a range of articles (Millington and Wilson, 2013, 2014, 2016a). As described in greatest detail in Millington and Wilson (2016b), our main results are as follows:

- Members of the golf industry have embraced environmentalism (especially since the late 1970s) despite once taking an antagonistic stance towards environmentalists' cause (especially in the immediate postwar years).
- There are limits to the 'green' sensibilities of those representing the mainstream golf industry – specifically in that environmentalism seems to be embraced only to the extent that it does not impede economic growth, as per the 'light green' perspective described above.
- Governments have responded in kind to the golf industry's leadership on environmental matters – for example, by exempting golf courses from otherwise progressive legislation pertaining to the use of pesticides for cosmetic purposes.
- Local and global 'anti-golf' movements have emerged over time, with varying goals and levels of success.
- 'Organic golf' (i.e. golf that is free of synthetic pesticides) has gained some traction and publicity as an alternative to versions of golf that allow for chemical usage when applied 'responsibly' (i.e. in reduced amounts, in targeted areas, and only when non-chemical practices are ineffective) – though there are barriers that currently prevent organic golf from becoming a more mainstream option. Organic golf emerged from a critique of the idea that responsible chemical usage is, in fact, possible or necessary – and from questions about the need for pristine conditions in the first place.

When we said before that our own work on sport and the environment is indebted to previous research, it is because these findings to a great extent reflect themes found in existing academic literature. For example, the golf industry's approach to environmentalism is underpinned by the concept of sustainability, with pro-environment activities and social contributions balanced with the pursuit of economic growth. Indeed, the triple bottom line is embedded in the Vision Statement for the Environmental Institute for Golf, the research and education arm of the Golf Course Superintendents Association of America (GCSAA): 'With respect for the game and the environment, the EIFG inspires environmental, social and economic progress through golf for the benefit of communities' (GCSAA, n.d.). Moreover, this sustainable approach has been realized through the adoption of science and technology. That is to say, the greening of golf has involved the *modernizing* of golf course architecture and maintenance. For a moment in time, the adoption of science and technology put golf at odds with the environmental movement in a very obvious way. In the first decades of the postwar years, golf industry representatives both adopted and fervently defended their right to use the very potent chemical DDT – born out of wartime research – with the help of broad-based chemical application equipment such as hydraulic sprayers. More recently, however, science and technology have shown the way towards 'safer' chemicals (at least in the golf industry's eyes) as well as precise means for applying them. Thus, golf industry representatives can now proclaim their stewardship on matters pertaining to the environment, given how far they have come from a time when liberally applying DDT was seen as normal (Millington and Wilson, 2013).

In addition, our point above that governments have responded in kind to golf's green sensibilities is reflective of the contemporary neoliberal climate when it comes to policymaking in general. As one case in point, golf courses have been exempted from policies in Canada that ban the use of pesticides for cosmetic reasons – provided those applying pesticides on courses earn proper accreditation. In the province of Ontario, this has led to the situation described in the above introduction, whereby chemical industry representatives have been enlisted in the accreditation process – and by extension, the process of regulating pesticide usage on golf courses. The neoliberal approach to environmental management has been to entrust a combination of corporate social responsibility and consumer 'choice-power' in the achievement of positive environmental outcomes. In policy terms, this has meant favouring industry-led mechanisms for environmental regulation (Boyd, 2003; MacDonald, 2007; McKenzie, 2002) – precisely what we have seen in Ontario and elsewhere when it comes to golf.

Physical cultural studies and the environment

How does this 'critical golf study' align with the wider PCS project? Upon reflection, we feel our work is in many ways aligned with the proposed tenets of PCS, though at the same time it is suggestive of how research on the environment might push PCS in new directions going forward.

Alignment with physical cultural studies

Perhaps the clearest point of overlap between our research and PCS involves the *theoretically informed* nature of our work. Theory has been used across our research to illuminate and explain empirical findings; it has not simply been deployed for theory's sake. How can we explain (and not just describe) a situation whereby chemical industry representatives are included in the process of regulating pesticide usage on golf courses in the Canadian province of Ontario? From the industry side, the motivation for their involvement in the regulatory process is obvious. But what about for governments? Here, the theoretical concept of environmental managerialism is instructive. As John Hannigan (2006) explains, this concept refers to the process through which governments, in an attempt 'to legislate a limited degree of protection sufficient to deflect criticism [about environmental concerns] but not significant enough to derail the engine of economic growth', enact 'environmental policies that are complex, ambiguous and open to exploitation by the forces of production and accumulation' (ibid.: 21). In other words, in neoliberal times especially, the state is 'dually mandated' – charged with both protecting the environment and promoting economic growth. The Ontario Cosmetic Pesticides Ban Act – the policy barring cosmetic pesticide usage except on golf courses – indeed legislates environmental protection to some extent. Yet this provincial legislation, much like Canada's federal system of pesticide oversight, is also open to industry influence. The point, in part, appears to be to avoid 'derail[ing] the engine of economic growth'.

At the same time, our work on golf is *transdisciplinary*, with transdisciplinarity being another hallmark of a PCS sensibility (Andrews and Silk, 2015). Indeed, we have drawn from across the social sciences in carrying out this work – from organizational studies, social movement studies, science and technology studies, the sociology of sport, environmental sociology, and beyond. More to the point, even with the golf industry's adoption of 'safer' chemicals and more precise means of applying them, concerns over pesticides linger (e.g. that the synergistic effects of exposures to multiple pesticides not suitably accounted for in research – see Arya, 2005). Our own critique of pesticide usage on golf courses is to a great extent historical. Golf industry representatives have in the past vouched for chemicals that, in later years, were deemed too risky for use on golf courses (e.g. DDT). The concern is that golf will be 'wrong' again about the chemicals still used today. Yet this critique is also heavily informed and motivated by the research and writing of biologists, epidemiologists, medical doctors, health activists and environmentalists, and a range of other natural scientists concerned with the impacts of various human-driven and environment-impacting activities on the health of ecosystems, humans, and non-humans.

To be sure, we do not come at the topic of golf and the environment from the same ontological or epistemological perspectives as these other academics and critics. What we do share with those working in these other areas, however, is a commitment, in the spirit of PCS, to synthesizing findings, theories, and methods so as to enable a comprehensive and nuanced assessment of the complexities of environmental problems.

A third point of overlap involves what we see as the *critical pedagogical dimension* of our research – and here we return again to the examples with which we began this article. We see our research in this sense as aligned with Andrews and Silk's (2015) view of PCS as a critical pedagogical project that aims to 'generate and circulate the type of knowledge that would enable individuals and groups to discern, challenge, and potentially transform existing power structures and relations as they are manifest within, and experienced through, the complex field of physical culture' (ibid.: 87). We recognize here that raising awareness about societal problems is one thing, while offering suggestions that lead to the transformations Andrews and Silk refer to is a more challenging and ambiguous task. That said, our work on golf is also politically engaged in that we advocate, based on empirical insight, for an alternative and more precautionary approach to environmentalism than what has taken hold in the golf industry to date.

In particular, we conclude our book *The Greening of Golf* (Millington and Wilson, 2016b) by advocating for 'organic golf' – a form of golf course maintenance that, in its strictest form, involves the excising of synthetic chemicals completely. Beyond the PCS literature, our arguments in this regard are guided by the work of sociologist Eric Ohlin Wright and historian Jay Winter, who have written about what Wright terms 'real utopias' and Winter terms 'minor utopias'. According to Wright, it is crucial that those interested in making tangible changes to dominant systems 'identify harms that are generated by existing arrangements', 'formulate alternatives which mitigate those harms', and 'propose transformative strategies for realising those alternatives' (Wright, 2007: 26; see also Wright, 2010, 2013). For his part, Winter (2006: 208) recognizes the imperfection of any utopian vision, but sees minor utopias as 'partial transformations' and 'steps on the way to less violent and less unjust societies'.

Organic golf holds such transformative potential. In choosing not to purchase or use synthetic pesticides, the organic golf practitioners we interviewed in our research were, in effect, disrupting golf's usual supply chain. This is not insignificant considering the deep-seated affiliation that now exists between the chemical industry and the golf industry (e.g. sponsorships, research partners), as well as the fact that reducing, but not eliminating, synthetic pesticides has become golf's 'common sense' environmental solution. Organic golf is not to be romanticized: organic ingredients can still be environmentally damaging, and organic golf still must reckon with the issue of occupying massive tracts of land in the name of an exclusive leisure activity. Even so, it is a more precautionary alternative, and one that can inspire thinking about *the circumstances under which golf is viable at all*. Organic golf is in this sense 'dark green' in its inclination.

The physical in physical cultural studies

In an essay entitled 'What is this "Physical" in Physical Cultural Studies?', Michael Giardina and Joshua Newman (2011) are unambiguous in their commitment to a PCS project that foregrounds the human body and human experience. As they state:

> any discussion concerning the imperatives of, and for, Physical Cultural Studies starts (and perhaps ends) along the articulatory axes of politics and practice; and, more specifically, the body – of the researcher and researched alike – as locus of politics and praxis.
>
> *(Giardina and Newman, 2011: 37)*

This, we think, is an instructive passage. In our view, the (human) body has and should continue to hold a place of high prominence in PCS research. It is also a passage notable for its anthropocentrism.

The straightforward point to make in assessing how our research on golf and the environment might make a modest contribution to pushing PCS in new directions – or, at least, *relatively* uncharted directions – would be to say that the environment need be considered a topic of inquiry to a much greater extent than it has been to date. Physical cultures, among other things, are generally *physically demanding* on the environment. This goes not just for golf, as Perkins, Mincyte and Cole (2010) say in their call for 'critical golf studies', but for other physical cultural practices as well. Yet there is also a broader point to be made in this regard. With its centring of the physical and human body, even in relation to a highly inclusive range of topics and issues, PCS seems out of step with the wider trend towards critical inquiry that positions humans and non-humans to be non-hierarchically arranged – to be folded together, even if 'without guarantees'. In other words, and as suggested by many 'new materialist', posthumanist thinkers (see especially Latour, 2005; Coole and Frost, 2010), there is much to be gained from 'flattening' ontological approaches in ways that would seem to depart from how PCS has evolved to date.

We recognize in making this claim that context is indeed crucial to PCS, as it is to cultural studies in general. PCS is even a theory of contexts (Andrews and Giardina, 2008), with context understood in a non-reductionist sense. Indeed, the 'radically contextual' orientation of PCS has been highly influential in our work on golf. DDT spraying on golf courses was impossible before the Second World War (in that DDT had not yet been created) and in the final decades of the twentieth century (when it was banned for such uses). This was a practice made possible only in the early postwar years by the wider conditions of possibility of the time.

But thinking contextually is different from ascribing *agency* to that which surrounds the (human) body. As one example here, consider Paul Robbins's (2007) work on 'lawn people' – that is, people, or 'turfgrass subjects', pursuing the 'ideal' front lawn for their homes *even as they recognize that the idyllic lawn might not be good for their health* (e.g. to the extent that its maintenance requires heavy chemical inputs). By Robbins's account, our habits of explanation in making sense of lawn people 'overlook some of the most fundamental players in the process' (ibid.: 133). The lawn people phenomenon is not just down to consumer desire, nor to the machinations of the pesticide industry (e.g. in 'selling' the perfect lawn). For Robbins, *turfgrass too makes demands*; nature 'speaks' in that brown patches and dandelions compel lawn owners to engage in particular practices – even if these practices might be against their best interests. It was not a stretch for us in studying golf to see how the idyllic golf course could likewise make 'demands' on the golf course superintendent or on others charged with its care.

Mark Stoddart (2012) similarly takes a new materialist approach in his research on skiing and the environment. Stoddart draws on the works of Bruno Latour and Donna Haraway in describing how snow, weather, and animals – along with skiers and skiing technologies – form human/non-human assemblages on ski hills. More to the point, these various 'actants' can make an imprint in their own unique ways. High winds are described as an 'unruly actant' in Stoddart's account, capable of preventing ski lifts from operating (ibid.: 88). The weather conditions that failed to deliver enough snow on Whistler mountain ahead of the 2010 Olympics are characterized in much the same way. All told, Stoddart offers a less human-centric way of understanding physical culture (see also Weedon, 2015) – a perspective that would seem to be helpful as researchers attempt to illuminate how 'light green' physical cultural practices might still have undue effects on the environment.

Conclusion

Is the human body the locus of politics in Robbins's, Stoddart's, or our own analysis? Might our 'habits of explanation' lead us to overlook the agency of the non-human – weeds, fungus, insects, snow, animals, and so on – in understanding the politics of physical culture, whether in environment-focused research or not? In posing these questions, we are not suggesting a departure from research and writing about active and inactive bodies. Nor are we promoting a turn away from contextual thinking. We are suggesting, however, that the 'physical' in physical cultural studies should not confine us to a focus on the human body, even if the body is highly contextualized. A PCS sensibility might also include physical geographies and physical objects – non-humans as much as humans – as a way of acknowledging and even foregrounding the array of environmental factors and 'things' that are integral to environment-related research, and surely other research as well. Such an approach, we think, would yield important and perhaps surprising findings in our research going forward.

References

Andrews, D. L. and Giardina, M. D. 2008. Sport without guarantees: Toward a cultural studies that matters. *Cultural Studies/Critical Methodologies*, 8(4), 395–422.
Andrews, D. L. and Silk, M. L. 2012. *Sport and Neoliberalism: Politics, Consumption, and Culture*. Philadelphia, PA: Temple University Press.
Andrews, D. L. and Silk, M. L. 2015. Physical cultural studies on sport. In R. Giulianotti (ed.), *Routledge Handbook of the Sociology of Sport*. New York: Routledge, 83–93.
Arya, N. 2005. Pesticides and human health: Why public health officials should support a ban on non-essential residential use. *Canadian Journal of Public Health*, 96(2), 89–92.
Bale, J. 1994. *Landscapes of Modern Sport*. London: Leicester University Press.
Bale, J. 2001. *Sport, Space and the City*. London: Routledge.
Beder, S. 1994. Sydney's toxic Green Olympics. *Current Affairs Bulletin*, 70(6), 12–18.
Boyd, D. R. 2003. *Unnatural Law: Rethinking Canadian Environmental Law and Policy*. Vancouver: UBC Press.
Cao, B. 2015. *Environment and Citizenship*. New York: Routledge.
Chernushenko, D. 1994. *Greening Our Games: Running Sports Events and Facilities that Won't Cost the Earth*. Ottawa: Centurion.
Chernushenko, D., Van der Kamp, A. and Stubbs, D. 2001. *Sustainable Sport Management: Running an Environmentally, Socially, and Economically Responsible Organization*. United Nations Environment Programme.

Coole, D. and Frost, S. (eds). 2010. *New materialisms: Ontology, agency, and politics.* Durham, NC: Duke University Press.
Dryzek, J. 2005. *The Politics of the Earth: Environmental Discourses*, 2nd edn. Oxford: Oxford University Press.
GCSAA. n.d. Environmental institute for golf, mission and vision. Available from www.eifg.org/who-we-are/mission-and-vision.
Giardina, M. and Newman, J. 2011. What is this 'physical' in physical cultural studies? *Sociology of Sport Journal*, 28(1), 36–63.
Giulianotti, R., Armstrong, G., Hales, G. and Hobbs, D. 2015. Sport mega-events and public opposition: A sociological study of the London 2012 Olympics. *Journal of Sport and Social Issues*, 39(2), 99–119.
Hannigan, J. 2005. *Fantasy City: Pleasure and Profit in the Postmodern Metropolis.* New York: Routledge.
Hannigan J. 2006. *Environmental Sociology*, 2nd edn. New York: Routledge.
Hayes, G. and Horne, J. 2011. Sustainable development, shock and awe? London 2012 and civil society. *Sociology*, 45(5), 749–764.
Heynen, N., McCarthy, J., Prudham, S. and Robbins, P. (eds). 2007. *Neoliberal Environments: False Promises and Unnatural Consequences.* New York: Routledge.
Horne, J. 1998. The politics of sport and leisure in Japan: Global power and local resistance. *International Review for the Sociology of Sport*, 33(2), 171–182.
Karamichas, J. 2013. *The Olympic Games and the Environment.* New York: Palgrave Macmillan.
Latour, B. 2005. *Reassembling the Social: An Introduction to Actor-Network-Theory.* Oxford: Oxford Press.
Lenskyj, H. 1998. Sport and corporate environmentalism: The case of the Sydney 2000 Olympics. *International Review for the Sociology of Sport*, 33(4), 341–354.
Lenskyj, H. 2008. *Olympic Industry Resistance: Challenging Olympic Power and Propaganda.* Albany, NY: SUNY Press.
Lubbers, E. (ed.). 2002. *Battling Big Business: Countering Greenwash, Infiltration and Other Forms of Corporate Bullying.* Monroe, ME: Common Courage Books.
MacDonald, D. 2007. *Business and Environmental Politics in Canada.* Toronto: University of Toronto Press.
McKenzie J. I. 2002. *Environmental Politics in Canada: Managing the Commons into the 21st Century.* Toronto: Oxford University Press.
Millington, B. and Wilson, B. 2013. Super intentions: Golf course management and the evolution of environmental responsibility. *The Sociological Quarterly*, 54(3), 450–475.
Millington, B. and Wilson, B. 2014. The masters of nature: Golf, non-humans, and consumer culture. In J. Gillett and M. Gilbert (eds), *Sport, Animals and Society.* New York: Routledge, 52–66.
Millington, B. and Wilson, B. 2016a. An unexceptional exception: Pesticides, golf and environmental regulation in Canada. *International Review for the Sociology of Sport*, 51(4), 446–467.
Millington, B. and Wilson, B. 2016b. *The Greening of Golf: Sport, Globalization and the Environment.* Manchester: Manchester University Press.
Parliament of Canada. 2000. *Pesticides: Making the Right Choice for the Protection of Health and the Environment.* Report of the Standing Committee on Environment and Sustainable Development. Available from www.parl.gc.ca/HousePublications/Publication.aspx?DocId=1031697andLanguage=EandMode=1andParl=36andSes=2.
Perkins, C., Mincyte, D. and Cole, C. L. 2010. Special Issue: Making the critical links and the links critical in golf studies. *Journal of Sport and Social Issues*, 34(3), 267–375.
Robbins, P. 2007. *Lawn People: How Grasses, Weeds, and Chemicals Make Us Who We Are.* Philadelphia, PA: Temple University Press.
Savery, J. and Gilbert, K. (eds). 2011. *Sustainability and Sport.* Champaign, IL: Commonground Publications.
Silk, M. 2014. The London 2012 Olympics: The cultural politics of urban regeneration. *Journal of Urban Cultural Studies*, 1(2), 273–293.
Stoddart, B. 1990. Wide world of golf: A research note on the interdependence of sport, culture, and economy. *Sociology of Sport Journal*, 7(4), 378–388.
Stoddart, M. C. J. 2011. 'If we wanted to be environmentally sustainable, we'd take the bus': Skiing, mobility and the irony of climate change. *Human Ecology Review*, 18(1), 19–29.
Stoddart, M. C. J. 2012. *Making Meaning out of Mountains: The Political Ecology of Skiing.* Vancouver: UBC Press.
Stolle-McAllister, J. 2004. Contingent hybridity: The cultural politics of Tepoztlán's anti-golf movement. *Identities: Global Studies in Culture and Power*, 11, 195–213.
WCED. 1987. *Our Common Future.* Oxford: Oxford University Press.

Weedon, G. 2015. Camaraderie reincorporated: Tough Mudder and the extended distribution of the social. *Journal of Sport and Social Issues*, 39(6), 431–454.

Wheaton, B. 2007. Identity, politics, and the beach: Environmental activism in Surfers Against Sewage. *Leisure Studies*, 26(3), 279–302.

Wheeler, K. and Nauright, J. 2006. A global perspective on the environmental impact of golf. *Sport in Society*, 9(3), 427–443.

Wilson, B. 2012. Growth and nature: Reflections on sport, carbon neutrality, and ecological modernization. In D. Andrews and M. Silk (eds), *Sport and Neo-liberalism: Politics, Consumption, and Culture*. Philadelphia, PA: Temple University Press, 90–108.

Wilson, B. and Millington, B. 2015. Sport and environmentalism. In R. Giulianotti (ed.), *Routledge Handbook of the Sociology of Sport*. New York: Routledge, 366–376.

Winter, J. 2006. *Dreams of Peace and Freedom: Utopian Moments in the Twentieth Century*. New Haven, CT: Yale Press.

Wright, E. O. 2007. Guidelines for envisioning real utopias. *Soundings*, 36, 26–39.

Wright, E. O. 2010. *Envisioning Real Utopias*. London: Verso.

Wright, E. O. 2013. Transforming capitalism through real utopias. *American Sociological Review*, 78(1), 1–25.

35
URBAN AND SECURITIZED SPACES

Michael L. Silk and Andrew Manley

Under the influence of the market-oriented dictates derived from what are ascendant neoliberal policy regimes (deregulation, privatization, liberalization, enhanced fiscal austerity, symbolically oriented tourist economies), the organization and management of contemporary urban spaces has become preoccupied with the reconstitution of 'spectacular urban space' (Harvey, 2001: 92) – or more accurately, select parcels of urban space – into multifaceted environments designed for the purpose of encouraging consumption-oriented capital accumulation (Boland, 2010; Judd, 1999; MacLeod, 2002). Not denying the variations in experience in urban spaces – neoliberalism is an incoherent and discursively constituted governance paradigm, an open and active assemblage, that is intertwined with multiple, multidimensional and multiscalar co-evolving projects, practices, technologies and strategies (McGuirk and Dowling, 2009) – select pockets of contemporary cities have become, are in the process of becoming, or aspire to be what David Harvey (2001) called capital spaces: those spaces that (re)capitalize upon the economic landscapes of their cities through shopping malls, themed restaurants, bars, theme parks, mega-complexes for professional sport franchises, leisure environments, gentrified housing, conference complexes, and, waterfront pleasure domes (e.g. Brenner and Theodore, 2002; Macleod et al., 2003; Wilcox et al., 2003). Building upon scholars (see e.g. Brenner and Theodore, 2002; Harvey, 2001; Hodkinson, 2011; McGuirk and Dowling, 2009; Paton et al., 2012; Peck et al., 2013; Sheller and Urry, 2003; Sigler and Wachsmuth, 2015) who have addressed the careful orchestration of city space as an arena for market-oriented growth and elite consumption practices, within this chapter we are concerned with ongoing processes involved in the constitution of physical culture as they relate to the symbolic reconstitution of cityscapes.

Physical culture in the city

Having shed their industrial exo and endoskeleton and capitalized upon the cultural landscape of the city, the 'visually seductive' celebration of the commercial monumentalities of late capitalism – which elevates physical cultural forms, practices, structures and experiences to new heights – may well work to negate the unpredictability of preconceived urban experiences, yet, this is merely a sophisticated façade (Harvey, 2001) that belies deep structural inequalities in the contemporary cityscape. Scholars have thus often addressed city spaces as polarized or segregated; divided cities that contain multiple narratives within the context of transformation in the predominant mode of social regulation (Walks, 2001). Under the aegis then of a complex and active neoliberal assemblage, and fully in line with market-led approaches to regeneration that are predicted on assumptions that urban social ills are found primarily in working/lower class districts (Paton et al., 2012), new urban glamour zones conceal a brutalizing demarcation between winners and losers, included and excluded, lionized and demonized populations (MacLeod, 2002); crude binary distinctions between those included in social, political and cultural practices and those excluded, and in which the poor or degenerate are rigidly disciplined through a range of discursive, legal and architectural methods (MacLeod, Raco and Ward, 2003). There is thus an uneasy juxtaposition between those served by 'capital space' (Harvey, 2001) and those either servile to, or shunned by, its over-determining consumerist logics; which brings to the fore important questions for physical cultural studies scholars relational to the articulations between physical cultural forms and the bifurcation of urban spaces/citizens in 'scary cities' (England and Simon, 2010).

There has been a plethora of academic work on sport stadia as anchors of urban regeneration and differentiation (e.g. Friedman et al., 2004, 2012; Hannigan, 1998); the advancement of internally and externally identifiable places (e.g. Bale, 1994; Chalkley and Essex, 1999; Rowe and McGuirk, 1999; Whitson and Macintosh, 1996; Wilcox et al., 2003), sporting events and the militarization of urban civil society (Schimmel, 2012); the broader strategic spectacularization of urban space and the design of scrubbed and reinvented, entertainment districts concentrated in small areas, physically bounded 'tourist bubbles' (Judd, 1999: 53), that simultaneously cosset the desired visitor while warding off the threatening 'other' (e.g. Bélanger, 2000; Boyle and Haggerty, 2009; Harvey, 2001; Lash and Urry, 1994; Silk, 2004, 2007); and the interactions between urban spaces, gender, sexuality and race, ethnicity and migration (e.g. De Martini Ugolotti, 2015; Evers, 2009; Joseph, 2012; Schimmel, 2015; Stephens and Delamont, 2013; Silk, 2009; Waitt and Clifton, 2013; Waitt and Staynes, 2015). Others have focused on institutionalized patterns of health inequality – especially within the context of a diversity of traditionally public health issues and concerns that have become incorporated into the reach of the private sector (e.g. disease prevention, public health, juvenile curfews, medical services, day care, nutrition, substance abuse prevention, mental health and family counselling, teen pregnancy, services for the homeless). Within this context, some scholars have addressed various iterations of physical culture (ranging from walking practices, to cycling, to (free-)running, to a discursive positioning of fitness within city policy/promotions) within (and against) the concrete and symbolic strategizing of city spaces and spatial practices (cf. Atkinson, 2011; Bairner, 2011; Bramham and Wagg, 2009; Silk and Andrews, 2006, 2008).

The deployment of a broad range of specialized technologies and techniques (e.g. policy and educational initiatives, architectural arrangements, urban planning, measures of public order, health and safety regulations, self and other observations) that work together to produce 'healthified' spaces (and subjectivities) have also been of concern (see Fusco, this volume). Healthified spaces are, as Fusco (2007) argues, enclosures and functional sites, architectural and spatial technologies, for the inscription and prescription of the 'new public health' and which organize, survey and monitor bodies in space. In this sense, geographies of healthification are also geographies of exclusion; bio-pedagogies of healthification normalize and celebrate certain bodies – productive, neoliberal, responsible, self-governing healthified subjects/citizens – while pathologizing others. In addressing the intersections between health and the material conditions of space and place, and the discursive construction of spaces that have been designed and designated for health, scholars have focused on the body and mobility, especially related to 'active transport' (Steinbach et al., 2011). Some have focused on the barriers to active transportation (such as cycling schemes / cycle hire schemes that have appeared in many cities) that are especially pronounced for women (and even more so when articulated with class and ethnicity): these include fear of road danger and higher levels than men related to a self-assessment of cautiousness, the complexities of women's journey that may well incorporate childcare and shopping alongside work commuting, and the public visibility of women's bodies (see e.g. Horton, 2007; Steinbach et al., 2011). As Creswell and Uteng (2008: 2) suggested, 'how people move (where, how fast, how often, etc.) is demonstrably gendered and continues to reproduce gendered power hierarchies'. Thus, the focus has been on how active transportation merely *reorganizes* mobility in urban spaces through normalizing certain bodies – productive, male, consumptive citizens – sanctioning a new politics of conduct that seeks to reconstruct citizens as moral subjects of *responsible* communities (Rose, 2000) and which contributes towards processes of acute unequalization (Tonkiss, 2013). Slightly revising Urry (2007), scholars interested in the interaction of technologies, the physical world, corporeal movement and lumpy, fragile, aged, classed, gendered and racialized bodies, are cognizant of how some bodies are, simply put, more able to become citizens than others (Green et al., 2012).

Spectacle and urban space

There has been a relatively fertile interest in the articulations between urban space and sport mega-events. This is perhaps of little surprise given the development of stadia, attracting sporting franchises, bidding for/hosting sport mega-events has emerged as one of the most effective vehicles for the advancement of internally and externally identifiable places, the (re)imaging through the (re)organization of spectacular urban space, attracting (mobile) capital and people in a period of intense inter-urban competition and urban entrepreneurialism, resultant in viscerally affective and effective processes of subject formation, governance, regulation and social control (e.g. Paton et al., 2012; Waitt, 2000). Indeed, deeply embedded in the bidding process to host sporting mega-events (especially in IOC mandates; see e.g. Armstrong et al., 2011) and the resultant promises of 'legacy' are a host of assumptions predicated on the 'pathologization of problem populations' (Paton et al., 2012: 1471): geographical, strategic, political and cultural initiatives centred on discursive and material reconstitution of desired new urban populace and spaces, and social regulation that infuses desired subjects with the consumer 'freedoms' afforded to them as privileged groups in consumer capitalist society. Such strategies form part of the processes that aim to inculcate specific pockets of cities (e.g. London's East End, Rio's favelas, Delhi's Yumana Delta, Glasgow's East End, Sydney's Homebush Bay West, Vancouver's Downtown Eastside) that hitherto did not form part of a sparkling global neoliberal metropolis. This material refashioning of place is, however, one that utilizes gentrification *as governance:* these spaces of consumption providing the means for displacement and for civilizing, managing and securitizing unruly populations in 'problem' places through 'inviting' those positioned as problem populations into the gentrification process, often without providing the means for achievement (Paton et al., 2012). The 'normative universality' of the sporting spectacle then is fully bound with, and subject to, measures that aim to secure the extension, maintenance, reproduction and management of the consequences of market rule (Peck, 2003).

Alongside the tender contouring of sanitized space, re-imaging for the external tourist market unsurprisingly forms part of sporting spectacle strategizing given the opportunity to showcase a *specific* image of place: it provides an opportunity to construct and promote an image with real political value onto a global stage; the resultant return being the attraction of transnational capital and tourists to the city which act as legitimizing tools and accelerants for urban renewal projects that promote economic growth (Gibbons and Wolff, 2012). Indeed, tourist strategizing is often centred on the presentation of a particular 'capital' image and is relational to global understandings of what matters in, and for, a global city or aspirant city/MUR (see e.g. Silk, 2002 on Kuala Lumpur 98; Silk, 2011, 2014 on London 2012; Gaffney, 2013 on Rio 2014; or Waitt, 2000 on Sydney 2000). Scholars have tended to discuss *the (g)local* (see Robertson, 1995) that matters for such sporting spectacles (and its valorized consumer); those that present palatable or understandable – to dispersed consumers, tourists and investors – narratives of a (aspirant) world-city. The concern here is that only specific local assets and resources – those conducive to the market and the tourist gaze – become exploited and selected consumerized representations of place take centre stage to temporarily showcase one *preferred* spatial narrative to the world. Equally problematic, through marshalling political, media and private sector interests, the construction of these hegemonic and dramaturgical urban narratives remake and represent spectacular pockets of urban space around discourses of growth, reinforce 'global city' imagery and act to supress opposition and indeed oppositional places (Gibbons and Wolff, 2012). In this sense, *the* image of place presented often becomes abstracted from local culture and translated into marketable meanings of place that are sharply differentiated from the surrounding urban landscape (Judd, 1999).

There has also been attention to the, at times conflicting and competing, relationships between material transformations of place, contested signifiers of the (national) past, and the mutual constitution of bodies and place. In this sense, preferred images mobilized through sporting spectacle go beyond the function of representing *the* brand image of a city; as a source of image and memory, it can symbolize who *belongs* in specific places in the present (Zukin, 1995). In our own work for example on London 2012 (Manley and Silk, 2014; Silk, 2011, 2014, 2015) we attempted to hold together the preferred images of London and the regeneration of urban space to aid our understandings of the position of minority communities within *new hierarchies of belonging* (Back et al., 2012) in particular spatialized forms. In line with previous work on the demonization of internal and external 'others' in the sporting discourses in the post 9/11 moment (see Silk, 2012), we suggested, following Back et al. (2012), that in London 2012 the presence of 'the other' was tolerated as long as terms of the hierarchy itself are not challenged. Indeed, we suggested that sporting spectacle imposes order and control through the production of (demonized) subjects and provides the conditions and indeed rhetoric for the subsequent rationalization of ill-treatment, control and management predicated on the anticipation of risk and with reference to an invented criteria pertaining to characteristics closely associated with race and religion (Bigo, 2002: 80). With Whittaker (2011), we proposed that sporting spectacles are predicated on the creation of fantastical geographical utopias that are *sustained* by the exploitation of migrant bodies who nurture the creative class and the tourist image: 'dirty pretty cities' that *require* an (illegal) underclass to nurture the cossetted citizen/visitor. In this sense, we have pointed to ways in which sporting spectacles have simultaneously generated a double imaginary: a harmonious heterogeneous realm of opportunity and a hidden 'reality' of inequality that is integral to the growth of world-cities: narcissistic imaginings of localities/nation as generous, tolerant and hospitable; 'a utopian geography that is so powerful and all-encompassing that it ensures the very real processes of exploitation and social exclusion which sustain the vision remain out of sight' (ibid.: 126).

As such, through our own work (on major events in Kuala Lumpur, Salt Lake City, Beijing, Singapore, Delhi, London and Glasgow), we have suggested that while sporting spectacles operating within the context of an open and active neoliberal assemblage offer gleaming aesthetics, (sporting) cities collapsed into (simple) tourist images, and the presentation of a particular expression of self within the logics of the global market, there remain important questions about the relevance and morality of such spaces and their symbolism for the wider urban citizenry and for their civil liberties. As Bhan (2009) contended in the build-up to the Delhi 2010 Commonwealth Games, in the shadows of the presentation of self, the poor and those who are discursively constituted as 'different' or 'other' than purified national fantasies/citizens are denied the right to the city, to residency and to citizenship (either physically through forced displacement, by being 'priced out', or through discursive/surveillant technologies and an enhanced architecture of security, social control and militarization). Thus, the erosion of the claim of the poor/other to be *legitimate* urban/national citizens, and the simultaneous erasure of their presence is made possible through a changing urban political landscape; characterized by the sporting spectacle as either catalyst or legitimating force for a shift in the representation of the poor/other in a context of changing expectations of government, an increasing aestheticization of poverty and urban space, and the surveillance of a small number of people (often the ethnic other) who become trapped within the imperatives of mobility while the '*majority is normalized*' (Bigo, 2006: 35, our emphasis). Indeed, it has become difficult to understand the relationships between physical culture (especially major sporting events) and urban spaces without appreciation of the attendant discourses coalescing around the militarization of urban space (see e.g. Manley and Silk, 2014; Schimmel, 2012; Silk, 2014) urban securitization and cleansing (e.g. Bennett and Haggerty, 2011; Boykoff, 2011; Boyle and Haggerty, 2009; Guilianotti and Klauser, 2010; Kennelly, 2015) and the (perceived) threat of terror (or indeed, the terrorist other). One needs only to think, for example, of the enhanced militarization of urban space around a major event (see for example Stephen Graham, 2012 on 'Lockdown London'), the ways in which sporting discourses have been appropriated and mobilized by various power blocs in the 'war on terror' (Butterworth and Moskal, 2009; Silk, 2012) or the crabgrass entanglements between sport and 'terror' incidents ranging from 7/7 (see Falcous and Silk, 2010), the 2013 Boston Marathon, the 1972 Munich Olympic Games, the Atlanta 1996 Olympic bombing and 'state terror' (e.g. Andrews et al., 2010). While the study of surveillance itself, and its relationship with differing scales of space and place is not new, the intensification and spread of social control mechanisms have expanded to encompass a networked system of both public agencies and private organizations (Lippert and Walby, 2012; Murakami Wood, 2013) – and has become of central importance in exploring the relationships between physical culture and urban spaces.

Spectacle and securitization

Much has been written surrounding the concept of the 'surveillance society', with contemporary academic theorizing traversing an array of socio-cultural and geographic contexts through which to deconstruct and delineate the growing ability to observe, identify, extract, categorize and govern specific populations across differing sites and scales of inquiry (Aas, 2011; Haggerty and Samatas, 2010; Lyon, 2003; Monahan, 2011; Murakami Wood, 2009). The rise of a decentralized mode of observation, and the infiltration of a growing multiplicity of organizing bodies, has led to the evolution of surveillant practices that penetrate both formal and informal settings, encroaching beyond the confines of guarded space and administered through the proliferation of digital networks of data capture (Bogard, 2011; Murakami Wood, 2013); this has theoretically at least led us toward post-panoptic concepts that seek to challenge and extend our understanding of surveillance and social control (e.g. Andrejevic, 2005; Bigo, 2006; Boyne, 2000; Deleuze, 1992; Haggerty, 2011; Haggerty and Ericson, 2000; Latour, 2005; Poster, 1990). Progressing Foucauldian notions of disciplinary surveillance, and modalities of power that 'fixes, arrests or regulates movements' (Foucault, 1977: 218–219), the work of Gilles Deleuze (1992) has sought to extend our way of considering control mechanisms and former disciplinary sites of enclosure. The introduction of electronic technologies and digital data capture has enhanced the capabilities to control specific populations as surveillance becomes more mobile, dispersed and interconnected, transcending the borders and boundaries of fixed geographical locations or institutional spaces (Graham and Murakami Wood, 2007; Latour, 2005; Poster, 1990) – and interestingly, while not our focus in this chapter, sport/'health' apps that track our mobility (e.g. Strava, RunKeeper, Runtastic, Nike+ Running, Endomondo, Garmin Connect), can be conceived of in this way. Here the course of surveillance practices have altered to become representative of the 'fluid' nature of contemporary society, situating the evolution of such processes in a contextual manner that urges a consideration of the developmental, and progressive dimensions of surveillance and social control measures, questioning how they may be implemented, contested and viewed as 'an orientation' (Bauman and Lyon, 2013: 2).

Situated within the growth of surveillance studies, and heavily dictated by a post-9/11 environment infused by perceptions of (in)security and unease (Bigo, 2002, 2011), scholarly attention has recently turned toward notions of 'security' and 'securitization' upon considering the conceptualization and configuration of monitoring and control in contemporary urban spaces (Murakami Wood, 2009). Accelerated by the infiltration of computing and communications technology, and the dominance of the military-industrial complex, the importance of theorizing practices of urban surveillance in light of shifting and context-specific cultural trends has become increasingly apparent (Gad and Lauritsen, 2009; Monahan, 2011). In our work on London 2012 (see Manley and Silk, 2014), to decipher the spatial-territorial configurations attached to shifting patterns of social control, we drew upon Bigo's (2006, 2011) ban-opticon *dispositif*, a transversal apparatus that seeks to understand the contemporary age of surveillance under the aegis of suspicion and within the current climate of fear. Surveillance post-9/11 has been 'established in relation to a state of unease' (Bigo, 2011: 47) through the proliferation of a global (in)security based upon the perceived or actual threat of terror attacks. Translated to an understanding of urban and securitized spaces, this post-panoptic perspective exposes the normalization of surveillance practices in relation to managing the threat of 'terror', notions of risk and the shifting patterns of urban transformation that contribute towards socio-spatial practices of ordering and an increased fragmentation of the urban environment. In this sense, the evolving cityscape becomes part of a delocalized, decentralized and omnipresent approach towards urban surveillance, allowing for the normalized exclusion of specific individuals, groups and organizations perceived as a danger to (trans)national security (Manley and Silk, 2014).

The technologies and strategies involved in the re-imagining of 'place' and the material re-mapping of urban space – of which physical cultural forms are endemic – have increasingly been centred upon tactics of entrepreneurial urbanism that, 'monitor, censor, as well as promote behaviour in the city in ways that reflect and reinforce particular kinds of social space' (Coleman, 2005: 132). The imposition of enhanced surveillance measures and the (re)creation of safe and secure enclaves have led to the divisive splitting of urban terrain and a reproduction of unequal spatial relations, accelerating processes of 'social removal' (Coleman, 2004, 2005) or that of 'social sorting' (Lyon, 2003). The normalization of surveillance following 9/11 may well have driven the enhanced integration of surveillance technologies and an escalating attention towards the 'othering' of a minority population against a normalized majority. Therefore, with reference to Bigo's Ban-opticon *dispositif*, we may view this method of urban governance as insisting upon 'the success of the differentiation between a normalized population which is pleased to be monitored "against danger" and an "alienation" of some groups of people considered as dangerous "others"' (Bigo, 2011: 63). The exclusion of a particular 'other' thus becomes propagated and legitimized through the management of fear and unease arising from the perceived threat of attack and acts of global/local terrorism. This management of fear and unease has targeted those in the urban periphery, and has been utilized to instigate methods of surveillance and securitization through the 'safe' and sanitized enclaves of urban gentrification, while accelerating the collation of databases for government agencies to enhance administrative efficiency and promote the segregation of the normalized majority from the 'abnormal', or those identified as 'undesirable' (Bigo, 2006; Fiske, 1998).

The surveillant assemblage, sanitized spaces, and civil liberties in the control society

By way of conclusion, we hold together our discussion on capital space, sporting spectacle, mobility and securitized urban space. This leads us to conceptualize one of the buzz words that have come to define the relationships between sporting events and urban spaces: *legacy, or at least the ways in which legacy is the dominant leitmotif derived from hosting a sporting event that will serve as panacea to a range of urban ills.* We think of legacy rather differently. The 'legacies' and longer-term liberty-costs (Raco, 2012) for urban spaces once the sport, leisure or event infrastructure is in place (or has moved on to the next host) may well be a range of new punitive measures and potentially invasive laws which legitimize the use of force, new surveillance technologies, methods of dealing with protest, and precedents of joint army, municipal and private security action become 'normalized' (Gibbons and Wolff, 2012: 441). Borrowing from the Deleuzian conception of *control societies*, urban surveillance mechanisms operate as inclusionary and exclusionary tools, fixated less upon the reforming or reshaping of the individual, and, in part, more upon processes of social sorting that function through virtual codes of profiling and the production of information objects ('data doubles'), thus resulting in the distribution of status and access to civil liberties across populations (Bogard, 2011; Deleuze, 1992; Rose, 1999). Thus, the spatial divisions emerging through the gentrification of urban interiors – endemic to the 'logics' of sporting spectacle – serve to 'fence in' or confine an accepted or normalized population, while simultaneously excluding, or 'fencing out', that which does not belong (Bigo, 2006, 2011). This brings with it a quiet accretion of restriction that will likely have a harsher and longer-lasting legacy on minorities and the poor (closely associated with race and religion): a massive police presence for ethnic youth in the surrounding communities, new policing techniques such as stop and search, the further stigmatization of lower-/working-class communities in policy discourse, and the familiar security architecture of airports and international borders – scanners, checkpoints, ID cards, cordons, security zones – rolled out in the heart of the city (Gibbons and Wolff, 2012; Graham, 2012). These are new geographies of fear that serve to maintain the fluid boundaries between deviance and belonging, order and disorder, that are instrumental to the ways in which cities are planned, built, lived, experienced (England and Simon, 2010), and most crucially *controlled*. Such material and discursive actions serve to 'justify' authoritarian modes of control sustained through urban geographies of fear (ibid.), suspicion, Draconian forms of policing and scrutiny, the suspension of rights, and the promotion of an atmosphere of perpetual emergence and panic (Back et al., 2012). Furthermore, and following Kern (2010), such an institutionalized culture of fear is actually integral to the success and legitimation of urban gentrification: 'fear of the other *justifies* displacement and redevelopment' (ibid.: 210, our emphasis) that can be further mitigated through 'private security, rationalized through the potential for wealth accumulation, and even commodified as desirable qualities of urban regeneration' (ibid.: 225). Simply put then, while capital investment in sport, leisure, tourism and so on may well produce scrubbed (albeit ephemeral) spaces of consumption, gentrification and offer *unquestioned* be(long)ing, the embedded soft-surveillance, the culture of governance/fear ingrained in architectures of such physical cultural forms and structures, points to the attenuation of the poor/impoverished/'other', to the degree that they are denied the basic *human rights to exist* in public [spectacular] space (Rose, 2000). While such concerns might be felt/experienced differently, at different intensities we would aver that these are important concerns (to be negated, empiricized, fought against) for those looking to address the complex relationships between physical culture and urban spaces.

References

Aas, K. F. (2011). 'Crimmigrant' bodies and bonafide travellers: surveillance, citizenship and global governance. *Theoretical Criminology*, 15(3): 331–346.
Andrejevic, M. (2005). The work of watching one another: lateral surveillance, risk, and governance. *Surveillance and Society*, 2(4): 479–497.
Andrews, D. L., Schultz, J. and Silk, M. (2010). The Olympics and terrorism. In A. Bairner (ed.), *The Politics of the Olympics*. London: Routledge, 81–92.
Armstrong, G., Hobbs, D. and Lindsay, I. (2011). Calling the shots: the pre-2012 London Olympic contest. *Urban Studies*, 48(15): 3169–3184.
Atkinson, M. (2011). Fell running and voluptuous panic. *American Journal of Play*, 4(1): 111–132.
Back, L., Sinha, S. and Bryan, C. (2012). New hierarchies of belonging. *European Journal of Cultural Studies*, 15(2): 139–154.
Bairner, A. (2011). Urban walking and the pedagogies of the street. *Sport, Education and Society*, 16(3): 371–384.
Bale, J. (1994). *Landscapes of Modern Sport*. Leicester: Leicester University Press.
Bauman, Z. and Lyon, D. (2013). *Liquid Surveillance*. Cambridge: Polity Press.
Bélanger, A. (2000). Sport venues and the spectacularization of urban spaces in North America: the case of the Molson Centre in Montreal. *International Review for the Sociology of Sport*. 35(3): 378–397.
Bennett, C. J. and Haggerty, K. D. (2011). Introduction: security games: surveillance and control at mega-events. In C. Bennett and K. Haggerty (eds), *Security Games: Surveillance and Control at Mega-Events*. London: Routledge, 1–19.
Bhan, G. (2009). 'This is no longer the city I knew': evictions, the urban poor and the right to the city in millennial Delhi. *Environment and Urbanization*, 21(1): 127–142.
Bigo, D. (2002). Security and immigration: toward a critique of the governmentality of unease. *Alternatives: Global, Local, Political*, 27(1): 63–92.
Bigo, D. (2006). Globalized (in)security: the field and the Ban-Opticon. In B. Didier and A. Tsoukala (ed.), *Illiberal Practices of Liberal Regimes: The (In)Security Games*. Paris: l'Harmattan, 5–49.
Bigo, D. (2011). Security, exception, ban and surveillance. In D. Lyon (ed.), *Theorizing Surveillance: The Panopticon and Beyond*. London: Routledge, 46–68.
Bogard, W. (2011). Surveillance assemblages and lines of flight. In D. Lyon (ed.), *Theorizing Surveillance: The Panopticon and Beyond*. London: Routledge, 97–122.
Boland, P. (2010). 'Capital of culture – you must be having a laugh!' Challenging the official rhetoric of Liverpool as the 2008 European cultural capital. *Social and Cultural Geography*, 11(7): 627–645.
Boykoff, J. (2011). The anti-Olympics. *New Left Review*, 67: 41–59.
Boyle, P. J. and Haggerty, K. D. (2009). Spectacular security: mega-events and the security complex. *International Political Sociology*, 3: 257–274.
Boyne, R. (2000). Post-Panopticism. *Economy and Society*, 29(2): 285–307.
Bramham, P. and Wagg, S. (2009). *Sport, Leisure and Culture in the Postmodern City*. Farnham: Ashgate.
Brenner, N. and Theodore, N. (2002). Cities and the geographies of 'actually existing neoliberalism'. *Antipode*, 34(3): 349–379.
Butterworth, M. L. and Moskal, S. D. (2009). American football, flags, and 'fun': the bell helicopter armed forces bowl and the rhetorical production of militarism. *Communication, Culture and Critique*, 2(4): 411–433.
Chalkley, B. and Essex, S. (1999). Urban development through hosting international events: a history of the Olympic Games. *Planning Perspectives*, 14: 369–394.
Coleman, R. (2004). Reclaiming the streets: closed circuit television, neoliberalism and the mystification of social divisions in Liverpool, UK. *Surveillance and Society*, 2(2–3): 293–309.
Coleman, R. (2005). Surveillance in the city: primary definition and urban spatial order. *Crime, Media, Culture*, 1(2): 131–148.

Cresswell, T. and Uteng, T (2008). Gendered mobilities: towards an holistic understanding. In Creswell and Uteng (eds), *Gendered Mobilities*. Farnham: Ashgate Publishing, 1–14.

De Martini Ugolotti, N. (2015). Climbing walls, making bridges: children of immigrants' identity negotiations through capoeira and parkour in Turin. *Leisure Studies*, 34(1): 19–33.

Deleuze, G. (1992). Postscript on the societies of control. *October*, 59: 3–7.

England, M. and Simon, S. (2010) Scary cities: urban geographies of fear, difference and belonging. *Social and Cultural Geography*, 11(3): 201–207.

Evers, C. (2009). The point: surfing, geography and a sensual life of men and masculinity on the Gold Coast, Australia. *Social and Cultural Geography*, 10(8): 893–908.

Falcous, M. and Silk, M. L. (2010). Olympic bidding, multicultural nationalism, terror and the epistemological violence of 'making Britain proud'. *Studies in Ethnicity and Nationalism*, 10(2): 167–186.

Fiske, J. (1998). Surveilling the city: whiteness, the black man and democratic totalitarianism. *Theory, Culture and Society*, 15(2): 67–88.

Foucault, M. (1977). *Discipline and Punish: The Birth of the Prison*. London: Penguin.

Friedman, M., Andrews, D. and Silk, M. (2004). Sport and the façade of redevelopment in the post-industrial city. *Sociology of Sport Journal*, 21: 119–139.

Friedman, M., Bustad, J. and Andrews, D. (2012). Feeding the downtown monster: (re)developing Baltimore's 'tourist bubble'. *City, Culture and Society*, 3(3): 209–218.

Fusco, C. (2007). 'Healthification' and the promises of urban space: a textual analysis of place, activity, youth (PLAY-ing) in the city. *International Review for the Sociology of Sport*, 42(1): 43–63.

Gad, C. and Lauritsen, P. (2009). Situated surveillance: an ethnographic study of fisheries inspection in Denmark. *Surveillance and Society*, 7(1): 49–57.

Gaffney, C. (2013). Mega-events and urban regeneration in Rio de Janeiro: planning in a state of emergency. *International Journal of Urban Sustainable Development*, 5(2): 132–153.

Gibbons, A. and Wolff, N. (2012) Games monitor. *City: Analysis of Urban Trends, Culture, Theory, Policy, Action*, 16(4): 468–473.

Giulianotti, R. and Klauser, F. (2010). Security governance and sporting mega-events: toward an interdisciplinary research agenda. *Journal of Sport and Social Issues*, 34(1): 1–13.

Graham, S. (2012). Olympics 2012 security. *City: Analysis of Urban Trends, Theory, Policy, Action*, 16(4): 446–451.

Graham, S. and Murakami Wood, D. (2007). Digitizing surveillance: categorization, space, inequality. In S. P. Hier and J. Greenberg (eds), *The Surveillance Studies Reader*. Maidenhead: McGraw-Hill/Open University Press, 218–230.

Green, J., Steinbach, R. and Datta, J. (2012). The travelling citizen: emergent discourses of moral mobility in a study of cycling in London. *Sociology*, 46(2): 272–289.

Haggerty, K. D. (2011). Tear down the walls: on demolishing the panopticon. In D. Lyon (ed.), *Theorizing Surveillance: The Panopticon and Beyond*. London: Routledge, 23–45.

Haggerty, K. D. and Ericson, R. V. (2000). The surveillant assemblage. *British Journal of Sociology*, 51(4): 605–622.

Haggerty, K. D. and Samatas, M. (eds). (2010). *Surveillance and Democracy*. London: Routledge.

Hannigan, J. (1998). *Fantasy City: Pleasure and Profit in the Postmodern Metropolis*. London: Routledge.

Harvey, D. (2001) *Spaces of Capital: Towards a Critical Geography*. New York: Routledge.

Hodkinson, S. (2011). Housing regeneration and the private finance initiative in England: unstitching the neoliberal urban straitjacket. *Antipode*, 43(2): 358–383.

Horton, D. (2007). Fear of cycling. In D. Horton, P. Rosen, and P. Cox (eds), *Cycling in Society*. Aldershot: Ashgate.

Joseph, J. (2012). The practice of capoeira: diasporic black culture in Canada. *Ethnic and Racial Studies*, 35(6): 1078–1095.

Judd, D. (1999). Constructing the tourist bubble. In S. Fainstein and D. Judd (eds), *The Tourist City*. New Haven, CT: Yale University Press, 35–53.

Kennelly, J. (2015). 'You're making our city look bad': Olympic security, neoliberal urbanization and homeless youth. *Ethnography*, 16(1): 3–24.

Kern, L. (2010). Selling the 'scary city': gendering freedom, fear and condominium development in the neoliberal city, *Social and Cultural Geography*, 11(3): 209–230.

Lash, S. and Urry, J. (1994). Economies of signs and space. *Time and Society*, 5(1): 97–102.

Latour, B. (2005). *Reassembling the Social: An Introduction to Actor-Network-Theory*. Oxford: Oxford University Press.

Lippert, R. and Walby, K. (2012). Municipal corporate security and the intensification of urban surveillance. *Surveillance and Society*, 9(3): 310–320.
Lyon, D. (2003). *Surveillance after September 11*. Cambridge: Polity Press.
McGuirk, P. and Dowling, R. (2009). Master-planned residential developments: beyond iconic spaces of neoliberalism? *Asia Pacific Viewpoint*, 50(2): 120–134.
MacLeod, G. (2002). From urban entrepreneurialism to a 'revanchist city'? On the spatial injustices of Glasgow's renaissance. *Antipode*, 34(3): 602–624.
MacLeod, G., Raco, M. and Ward, K. (2003). Negotiating the contemporary city. *Urban Studies*, 40(9): 1655–1671.
Manley, A. and Silk, M. (2014). Liquid London: sporting spectacle, Britishness and ban-optic surveillance. *Surveillance and Society*, 11(4): 360–376.
Monahan, T. (2011). Surveillance as cultural practice. *The Sociological Quarterly*, 52: 495–508.
Murakami Wood, D. (2009). The 'surveillance society' questions of history, place and culture. *European Journal of Criminology*, 6(2): 179–194.
Murakami Wood, D. (2013). What is global surveillance? Towards a relational political economy of the global surveillant assemblage. *Geoforum*, 49: 317–326.
Paton, K., Mooney, G. and McKee, K. (2012). Class, citizenship and regeneration: Glasgow and the Commonwealth Games 2014. *Antipode*, 44(4): 1470–1489.
Peck, J. (2003). Geography and public policy: mapping the penal state. *Progress in Human Geography*, 27(2): 222–232.
Peck, J., Theodore, N. and Brenner, N. (2013). Neoliberal urbanism redux? *International Journal of Urban abd Regional Research*, 37(3): 1091–1099.
Poster, M. (1990). *The Mode of Information Poststructuralism and Social Context*. Cambridge: Polity Press.
Raco, M. (2012). The privatization of urban development and the London 2012 Olympics. *City: Analysis of Urban Trends, Theory, Policy, Action*, 16(4): 452–460.
Robertson, R. (1995). Glocalization: time-space and homogeneity-heterogeneity. In M. Featherstone, S. Lash, and R. Robertson (eds.), *Global Modernities*. London: Sage, 25–44.
Rose, N. (1999). *Powers of Freedom*. New York: Routledge.
Rose, N. (2000). Government and control, *British Journal of Criminology*, 40(2): 321–339.
Rowe, D. and McGuirk, P. (1999). Drunk for three weeks: sporting success and city image. *International Review for the Sociology of Sport*, 34(1): 125–142.
Schimmel, K. S. (2012). Protecting the NFL/militarizing the homeland: citizen soldiers and urban resilience in post–9/11 America. *International Review for the Sociology of Sport*, 47(3): 338–357.
Schimmel, K. S. (2015). Assessing the sociology of sport: on sport and the city. *International Review for the Sociology of Sport*, 50(4–5): 591–595.
Sheller, M. and Urry, J. (2003). Mobile transformations of public and private life. *Theory, Culture and Society*, 20(3): 107–125.
Sigler, T. and Wachsmuth, D. (2015). Transnational gentrification: globalisation and neighbourhood change in Panama's Casco Antiguo. *Urban Studies*.
Silk, M. (2002). Bangsa Malaysia: global sport, the city and the refurbishment of local identities. *Media, Culture and Society*, 24(6): 775–794
Silk, M. (2004). A tale of two cities: spaces of consumption and the façade of cultural development. *Journal of Sport and Social Issues*, 28(4): 349–378.
Silk, M. (2007). Come downtown and play. *Leisure Studies*, 26(3): 253–277.
Silk, M. (2009). Postcards from Pigtown. *Cultural Studies ↔ Critical Methodologies*, 10(2): 143–156.
Silk, M. (2011). Towards a sociological understanding of London 2012. *Sociology*, 45(5): 733–748.
Silk, M. (2012). *The Cultural Politics of Post 9/11 American Sport: Power, Pedagogy and the Popular*. New York: Routledge.
Silk, M. (2014). The London 2012 Olympics: the cultural politics of urban regeneration. *Journal of Urban Cultural Studies*, 1(2): 273–294.
Silk, M. (2015). 'Isles of wonder': performing the mythopoeia of utopic multi-ethnic Britain. *Media, Culture and Society*, 37(1): 68–84.
Silk, M. and Andrews, D. (2006). The fittest city in America. *Journal of Sport and Social Issues*, 30(3): 315–327.
Silk, M. and Andrews, D. (2008). Managing Memphis: governance and spaces of inequality. *Social Identities*, 14(3): 395–414.
Steinbach, R., Green, J., Datta, J. and Edwards, P. (2011). Cycling and the city: a case study of how

gendered, ethnic and class identities can shape healthy transport choices. *Social Science and Medicine*, 72(7): 1123–1130.
Stephens, N. and Delamont, S. (2013). I can see it in the nightclub: dance, capoeira and male bodies. *The Sociological Review*, 62: 149–166.
Tonkiss, F. (2013). *Cities by Design: The Social Life of Urban Form*. Cambridge: Polity Press.
Urry, J. (2007). *Mobilities*. Cambridge: Polity.
Waitt, G. (2000). Playing games with Sydney: marketing Sydney for the 2000 Olympics. *Urban Studies*, 36(7): 1062–1073.
Waitt, G. and Clifton, D. (2013). 'Stand out, not-up': body-boarders, gendered hierarchies and negotiating the dynamics of pride/shame. *Leisure Studies*, doi: 10.1080/02614367.2012.684397.
Waitt, G. and Staynes, E. (2015). Sweating bodies: men, masculinities, affect, emotion. *Geoforum*, 59: 30–38.
Walks, A. (2001). The social ecology of the post-Fordist/global city? Economic restructuring and socio-spatial polarisation in the Toronto urban regional. *Urban Studies*, 38(3): 407–447.
Whitson, D. and Macintosh, D. (1996). The global circus: international sport, tourism, and the marketing of cities. *Journal of Sport and Social Issues*, 20(3): 278–295.
Whittaker, T. (2011). Between the dirty and the pretty: bodies in utopia in *Dirty Pretty Things*. *International Journal of Cultural Studies*, 14(2): 121–132.
Wilcox, R., Andrews, D., Pitter, R. and Irwin, D. (2003). *Sporting Dystopias: The Making and Meaning of Urban Sport Cultures*. New York: SUNY Press.
Zukin, S. (1995). *The Culture of Cities*. Oxford: Blackwell.

36
HEALTHIFIED SPACES

Caroline Fusco

Space and place are, besides bodies, an integral part of physical cultural lives: we are, without a doubt, thoroughly emplaced (Pink, 2007). I began my interrogations into space in physical cultural studies (PCS) with an examination of an everyday mundane space – a locker room. Its everydayness, however, belied a profound connection to people's lives, their bodies and spatial practices. Locker rooms, I found had a regime of Archi-Texts and Body-Texts that worked intertextually to (re)produce proper and clean spaces and proper and clean citizens – violations were minimized, monitored, regulated, inspected, 'tracked'. I labelled the techniques to maintain propriety in locker rooms processes of 'healthification' (Fusco, 2006).

The concept of 'healthification' stemmed from a combination of Foucault's (1977) theories of power, discipline, panopticon and governance, and Lefebvre's (1991) concept of 'conceived space' (e.g. representations of space) and describes how a range of specialized strategies and technologies, expertise and techniques are imagined and continuously deployed in physical cultural spaces in order to govern and produce 'healthified' spaces and healthified subjectivities. Healthified spaces are akin to 'spatial practices' (ibid.) and are the realization of institutional and individuals' commitments to, and consumption of, regimes of healthification. The concept of healthified space also draws from Crawford's (1980) concept of healthism where individual citizens are encouraged to take responsibility for their own health and wellness in neoliberal times. While the effects of healthism have been taken up in PCS studies of biopedagogies and neoliberalism (see Rail, 2012; Wright and Harwood, 2009), few of those studies have explicitly accounted for how biopedagogies are emplaced despite the growing recognition that biopedagogies '… cannot be separated from the local spaces which mediate the ways knowledge is experienced, valued and acted upon' (Rich, 2011: 76). There have, of course, been important and notable empirical contributions to the PCS field on space studies this decade (see, for example, Friedman and Andrews, 2011; Silk and Andrews, 2006; van Ingen, 2003; Vertinsky and Bale, 2004), but according to Friedman and van Ingen's (2011) timely and important (re)invitation,[1] there is still more to be done to reassert a spatial theory lens to/with PCS. Within this chapter, I take up Friedman and van Ingen's challenge using an illustrative example of a PCS critical inquiry into one very specific healthified space in one particular school whose motto – 'Be Fit to Learn and Learn to Be Fit' – was insinuated into the very architecture of the school, thus engendering specific spatial imaginaries and practices.

Promising beginnings

There have been a handful of scholars whose work draws more explicitly on the intersections among physical cultural studies, health and cultural geography fields (Andrews, Sudwell and Sparkes, 2005; Evans, 2006; Evans and Colls, 2009). During an era in which 'the cult of efficiency' in health (Stein, 2001) dominates (re)productions of space, critical examinations of the intersections among health, space and place have emerged from the 'cultural turn' in medical and health geographies (Gesler and Kearns, 2002), in therapeutic landscape studies (Williams, 2007) and in studies of risk, poverty and circuits of privilege and dispossession (Fitzpatrick and LaGory, 2003; Hudson-Rodd, 1998), all of which have focused mostly on interrogations of how power, socio-cultural *and spatial* relations privilege, enable or disable health spaces (Duff, 2011).

This work from critical health and medical geographers, as well as cultural geographers who view space as always under construction (Crang and Thrift, 2000), 'a simultaneity of stories-so-far' (Massey, 2005: 9) and embedded in practices and processes of violence and domination (Gregory and Pred, 2007), continue to inspire me to bring a spatial lens to the study of healthified spaces and processes of healthification in PCS. Particularly, I have turned my attention to understanding how young people's spaces might be subjected to healthified and biopedagogical classifications (Fusco, 2007, 2012) and how young people themselves might think about their physical cultural geographies. There has been a proliferation of research in physical cultural studies about how youth are incited to be healthy citizens through discourses and practices of biopedagogies but again specifically, there is little explicit research about how youth experience physical cultural spaces per se (see Borden, 2003, and Vivoni, 2009 for notable exceptions). Dillabough and Kennelly (2010) in their book *Lost Youth in the Global City* state that forms of knowledge emerge from space and place, and these shape young people's understandings of themselves as members of that locale. Dillabough and Kennelly suggest that social practices that emerge in space – and any associated representations – serve both to organize and divide space in particular ways and provide a set of referential acts for the classification of oneself and others (ibid.: 79). Examining spatial practices in youth spaces, like schools, is particularly important because there is increasing vigilance, surveillance and regulation of youth in schools. Indeed, many youth are under severe scrutiny in school spaces, experiencing increasing insecurity at the same time as being subjects of increasing securitization (Means, 2013; Raby, 2012). Moreover, according to children's geographers, youth are subjected to ever-expanding moral geographies in which civilized and acceptable ways of using the body are increasingly linked to spatial interventions (Aitken, 2001; Philo and Smith, 2003). My research recognizes the fluid and dynamic nature of youth subjectivities but takes as its starting point the power geometries (Massey, 1994) that are articulated in the spaces/places where youth spend much of their daily lives.

Spatial methodologies for interrogating healthification

Methodologically, I have drawn on institutional and spatial ethnographies and youth-based participation methods, while trying to focus on the socially produced and interpreted nature of space and on space as relational, symbolic and material rather than absolute and abstract (Gregory, 1994). I have wanted to render explicit the complex interplay of factors that impact on how youth experience and discursively construct places, as well as how, within such places, they are interpolated by (and position themselves within) 'power geometries' (Massey, 1994). I draw on qualitative micro-genealogical approaches (e.g. interviewing, photo-voice, drawing/mapping, observations, thematically based discourse and content analysis) in order to pay attention to the specificity of local everyday lives, while not underplaying analyses of wider processes, discourses and institutions to which these connect. I attend to the spatial practices of everyday lives; how space is represented and imagined, how it is symbolically linked to aspirations and desires, as well as an interrogation of how space is deployed, and to what effects (Lefebvre, 1991). This (physical) 'cultural sociology of space' (Richardson and Jensen, 2003) focuses on how the spatialities and symbolic meanings that social agents attach to their environments are 'constructed' in and through discourses and material practices, which is important in neoliberal times (Ferguson and Gupta, 2002). If specific spatial strategies are based on micromanaging youth's physicality through the material and symbolic regulations of space, then the production of such spaces/places is problematic and must be interrogated. Considering space relationally, discursively, affectively and materially and engaging in a 'spatial ecologies' (Massey, 2005) approach attends to the spatial scales of youth's lives and has particular import for PCS because 'place matters' (Fitzpatrick and LaGory, 2003). Moreover, the spatial effects of the production of physical cultural lives and the reification of dominant social divisions of power and inequity in space and place are not always fully articulated in PCS approaches.

Healthified architectures: hallways of healthiness?

In City Secondary School, the social and cultural production of space was very much connected to the physicality of its students. Indeed, the architecture was intended to have specific social, cultural and physical effects given its mission – 'Be Fit to Learn and Learn to be Fit'.

> I had a vision of a sports school where kids would be involved in sports, but that was not well received by the Board and so I had to amend my vision to be a healthy active living school … the aesthetics are helpful. The layout and the size of the hallways in the forum areas have been very helpful. We've taken a couple of instructional spaces and converted them into physical activity spaces. And because physical activity has become such a part of the culture, we've forced the academic spaces to work around those. We've made those a priority … it's too important an aspect of our culture and we'd rather fit the academics in around other spaces … it is a trade-off but because we value that part, it's a trade-off we're willing to make.
>
> *(Principal, City Secondary School)*

In this principal's mandate to 'encourage physical activity' among the school population, teachers and, specifically, students, were imagined as investors in the school's new geography of health and physicality. The spatial design of the school was imagined to be emancipatory, offering salvation and transcendence, like Pronger's (2002) texts of physical fitness, from potentially unhealthy and physically inactive living: the space was conceived for projects of physical self-actualization and empowerment. The students' enthusiastic narratives about their school space confirm its place in their imagination. Students at City Secondary School described the physical space using words like 'big', 'clean' and 'open'. One student describes the space as the 'cleanest school I've ever known' while another student notes, 'About the building itself, it's awesome. Like I haven't seen a school this big ever.' Another student mentioned, 'It looks like a good school. It's pretty clean. It looks good. It looks strong.' The size of the school and its cleanliness are very much connected to the ways in which students envision what can be done in those clean, big and strong spaces.

Student: I think when they built the school they didn't mean for, like, physical activity spaces in school hallways. I don't think so but then when our principal, I think he kind of incorporated it, because our school's motto is 'Be Fit to Learn and Learn to be Fit'. So, I think the school is kind of like into physical activity, so they kind of like tried scouting places where they could have physical activity because it's a part of the program.
Interviewer: Mm-hmm. Well, it's not often that you see people doing physical activity in the hallways?
Student: In this school it's kind of become normal to see people doing that, but if you went to another school or if another school came here, they'd be like, 'What the hell is going on?'

(Male student, City Secondary School, 17 years old, Grade 11)

In this particular school, the hallways were the most photographed and talked about physical activity space, which was not surprising given the novelty of sanctioned running and playing in the hallways. Re-cognizing the hallway as a physical activity space required that students buy into and relish the unique aspect of their school. The hallway was taken up as a novel landscape for physical activity and health.

Yet architecture mediates power relations (Dovey, 1999), and school hallways produce specific asymmetric landscapes. Dillabough and Kennelly (2010: 117) suggest that the school corridor is a site for the performance of gendered and racialized forms of youth cultural style, authorized through language games and physical gestures of power, and as a highly visible and equally dangerous setting for territorial competition.

Figure 36.1 Hallway spaces

> Interviewer: Do you think all the students are as into physical activity in the hallways as you are?
>
> Student: Um, no. I'm not gonna be sexist but usually the girls just talk. They just stand there and talk while the guys are usually playing. Yeah, and the teachers are like, 'give the girls the ball'. But they won't actually participate in physical activity that much. They just stand there in groups and just chat.
>
> Interviewer: So you think that the girls are not as physically active as the boys in this school?
>
> Student: There's some girls that are more physically active than boys but percentage wise probably 90, 80 percent girls are not physically active.
>
> *(Male student, City Secondary School, 17 years old, Grade 11)*

That gendered hierarchies are exercised in youth school spaces is no surprise to physical cultural studies researchers. In this particular school, the hallway spaces are lauded for their openness and freedom but the over-sportification of the school space can engender the (hetero)normative, masculinist and exclusionary hierarchies that are characteristic of sports spaces. Indeed, school hallways can be terrifying spaces: they can be sites of surveillance, and for violence and bullying (Raby, 2012).

> In the beginning of this school year, I didn't really like running in the halls. Because like, whenever we do our long jog every day, we do it in the halls. And, it's kind of like weird whenever anyone is staring at you. If we have it in the early morning, people are coming in late or people have spares, all the older students have spares. And you see them watching the whole time. People are like, watching you and, like, it just seems kind of embarrassing or awkward, you can see them, and you just keep running past them in circles. So it just seems really weird. When people walk down the hallways, you're just like, jogging past them. You just think they're, like, staring at you.
>
> *(Female student, City Secondary School, 15 years old, Grade 10)*

In these open, clean, spacious healthified hallway spaces, where there seems to be little access to private space, students are hyper-visible, and engage in self-monitoring as their bodies, their movements, and their non-movements and non-participation, are constantly on display.

Healthified hallways: spaces of new prudentialism

> I've grown to like it, running in the hallway because people can see that like, 'those people are actually, like, energetic'. And, they can be aware that, like, 'you took gym again even though you don't have to'. And, you kind of grow to like it because it's so open.
>
> *(Female student, City Secondary School, 16 years old, Grade 11)*

The narrative here aligns with the participatory imperative (Lupton, 1995) and the 'new prudentialism' (Dean, 1999). Being seen to be physically active is valorized, and youth are encouraged to consume all the spaces that are conceived and built for them in productive ways. In our 'culture of choice' (Stein, 2001), choosing to participate and going above and beyond what is mandated 'facilitates' some youth's autonomy and *reimaginings* of themselves as active consumers of their physical spaces: students find salvation in the spatial choices that they make every day. Here, the self that is enabled is the prudent-self, one who is willing to take action

Figure 36.2 Running in hallways

and make choices to improve their health status. This specific student assumes that her fellow students are watching and are interested in how the runners are taking charge of their own health and physical destinies. Healthification here depends on the subject being dutiful and governable (Miller and Rose, 2008) and a 'human being who can act' (Dean, 1999: 13–14). Adults (teachers) in the school also participate in celebrating this new prudentialism.

> I think that all high schools or any school for that matter, should be designed with health in mind. And, I think that kind of space, well, it's better for everybody's mental health, physical health. Overall, it makes you feel good coming into work because my school is nice. It feels open, it feels welcoming. I'm not, you know, pushing through the hallways trying to get through kids … and when they're in the corridors, they, in fact, have space to roam. They do. They totally do. They are youth, they've gotta develop some sort of autonomy, and they need to figure out what they're capable of managing.
>
> *(Female physical education teacher, City Secondary School)*

Adults in the school expect that students be the agents and entrepreneurs of their own health and space. Seemingly benevolent discourses about freedom and space to roam can be connected to neoliberalist conceptions of health, wellness and responsibility. Youth are to be taken charge of and are to take charge of themselves.

Healthified spaces

Healthification, hallways and scales of normativity

This particular school has a large (older and recent) immigrant population. One student noted:

> It's multicultural, people speaking English in their own fashion, right? Someone speak in a different fashion, someone speak with a different accent. I like people that don't make fun of you at all, like you speak any way you want.
> *(Female student, City Secondary School, 14 years old, Grade 9)*

One physical education teacher noted that in such a 'multicultural' space, there are often challenges when it comes to physical activity:

> They're polite, they're great, they're not the most athletic, but they're working on it, I think physical activity wise, they're not the most athletic kids. Like, we do have issues with commitment, and culturally they're not used to like, rep programs.
> *(Male physical education teacher, City Secondary School)*

In such landscapes, spatial practices may be used and lauded as opportunities for salvation and projects of self-actualization, and opportunities to teach good citizenship.

> Once you walk into the main corridor, the first thing you see is the [school symbol]. Even as you're walking down the main stairway, you see it hanging there. And, every school year, [the principal] takes every grade there – grades 9, 10, 11 and 12, and he gives them this speech about how you have to have pride in the school and that school is what you make of it.
> *(Male physical education teacher, City Secondary School)*

Figure 36.3 Banners of pride

Thus far, I have focused mostly on the local geographic scale of the hallway where healthification is inexorably linked to the daily lives of students (and teachers) through aesthetic design and curricular mandates but these should also be regarded as part of a wider strategy to protect and defend hegemonic, normative and economic interests. Discursive tropes of choice, good citizenship, morality and self-responsibility often render invisible the larger spatial contexts of young people's lives in which poverty, sexism, heterosexism, racism, adult violence, exclusion and global exploitation are pervasive (Dillabough and Kennelly, 2010). Institutional spaces, like schools, are employed to mobilize what might be understood as national bio-civilizing projects (Halse, 2009), which seek to normalize bodies within the confines of normative subject positions.

> Interviewer: Are there any questions that you think I should've asked or were you expecting me to ask?
> Student: I think that, uh, I would have thought you would have asked me if I think that physical activity spaces should exist in the school, honestly.
> Interviewer: Ok. Do you?
> Student: Yeah. I think they should exist in every school but that is not the case because as I said earlier, obesity is slowly becoming a problem ... I think the spaces are important because, like, not even as a nation but as a continent, we're just slowly becoming obese, so I think everyone should try to stay fit.
> *(Male student, City Secondary School, 15 years old, Grade 10)*

Space and modernist architecture have been known to reinscribe gender and heteronormativity (Browne, Lim and Brown, 2007), imperial, colonial, racialized and classed discourses (Razack, 2002; Sibley, 1995), as well as ableist discourses (Parr and Butler, 1999). It is important then to continue to pay attention to how schools' architectures, their spatial organization and physical cultural practices may reproduce these kinds of discourses and material realities, despite claims to the contrary. For example, in this school the openness of the hallways, the freedom of movement experienced and 'earned' by students is often conflated with notions of safe space. One teacher notes: 'I think, for some reason, we've established a decent culture here, yeah, and it's new, the kids didn't come into a space with any vandalism, they came into a brand new beautiful space. And it makes a difference' (female physical education teacher, City Secondary School). This of course makes invisible some of the more violent geographies of exclusion that can also occur in big, bright, clean open hallway spaces.

> Two boys pass a girl in the corridor. She runs past them. She's white, one boy is white, the other boy is Asian. We are all passing in the centre stairwell, which is a gathering place for students and interestingly located outside the principal's office. The boys call out after the girl, 'Lose some weight, will ya?' She continues on up the stairs. As they follow her up the stairs they raise their voices and yell, 'lose some weight, bitch'. They turn around and see me staring at them. They move quickly up the stairs. I get a sense that there is more to this space that I have been led to believe. So much for HALE (Healthy Active Living Education) and the respectful and empathetic components of the school's 'Pride' motto.
> *(CF, field note, 24 February 2010)*

Here, students have situated themselves within healthified, sexist and gendered 'power geometries'. The excerpts above illustrate that space and place in physical culture can be

Healthified spaces

Figure 36.4 Staircase

(re)productive spaces and 'rather than a neutral backdrop to social relations, architecture, materiality and space can uphold dominant cultural discourses, social divisions and inequalities' (Gillespie, 2002: 211).

Disrupting healthified space: creating alternative geographies

Paying attention to how a school's physical cultural space is rife with discourses and practices of healthification is crucial, but being open to recognizing alternative youth geographies is also important.

> Teacher: In school spaces, kids are pretty much allowed to be wherever they want. And they can be doing almost whatever they want in those spaces. I think the school is set up to have almost like, a college feel to it? You can have like, 'This is your space, and you sit here, and you have your lunch there' and that's ok ... In the hallways, we set up the pods for them to hang out in ... They love that big staircase. They all hang out there.
>
> Interviewer: Right. So you are saying the space and its design help with the administration and management of students?
>
> Teacher: Mmm. I think, more we've set up our culture to adjust to them? We knew there was going to be all this space. We knew we were going to allow them out into the hallways. I think that the big space hinders that a bit, because the kids can hide away and do stuff [laughs]. It's harder to cover as much area. Like, if the kids weren't allowed out in the hallways, then they'd *all* be in the cafeteria. Right? And then you could watch them all. Whereas now kids can be wherever they want. And you know, one of the big things is guys and girls will go into whatever hallway ... and find a little niche and enjoy themselves [laughs].
>
> (Male physical education teacher, City Secondary School)

Figure 36.5 Blind spots

While some of these 'little niches' may appear to support normative practices, it is encouraging to note that some youth can at least 'hide away' and create alternative geographies that mingle and intersect with the dominant healthified ones, creating spaces of competing desires, values and discourses. These could perhaps signal a potential challenge to institutional ideologies and lead to moments of transformation and renegotiation in space. For example, school hallways could also be a potential thirdspace (see Dickar, 2008).

> Interviewer: Do you feel like everybody is watching you?
> Student: No, it's so big. I think it's so big and no one can watch you all the time.
> *(Male student, City Secondary School, 14 years old, Grade 9)*

Different youth may have different kinds of relationships with their environments. This points to them as possible agents of change with respect to physical cultural geographies – if their stories are proactively taken up in ways that allow them to be co-constructors of a socially, environmentally and politically just public sphere (Sutton and Kemp, 2006). While adults may assume that students like the new, big, open spaces, these are not necessarily for everyone.

> Interviewer: What would you like to see more of in your school?
> Student: I don't really know. 'Cause it's a new school, so it's not really ... it's just a building we have right now, 'cause it's only a few years old. So, like, I know in a lot of other schools they have like pictures of like athletes of the year and stuff like awards. But like in our school, we've only started. So, like, I'd rather have that but since it's new I guess, we can't. It's kind of hard to do that. But I'd rather have like, well, that's why I prefer older schools. 'Cause, I dunno, they're old and damaged, but I like the schools with more personality.
> *(Male student, City Secondary School, 16 years old, Grade 11)*

Figure 36.6 Viewpoints

While schools (and governments), principals, teachers and students continue to discursively and materially construct new spaces, spatial practices and biopedagogical regimes, these may often be at odds with the ways in which physical cultural spaces are imagined and engaged in by some youth. By creating enabling spaces of competing values, physical cultures of healthification may be resisted, creating 'spaces of hope' (Harvey, 2000) for transformation.

A place for final thoughts

Studying physical culture's healthified spaces means accounting for the range of spatial relations that come together to shape, and be reshaped by, (young) people's understandings of space, and how their aspirations, emotions and desires are produced and reproduced through (un)comfortable encounters with other bodies in emplaced contexts. These cartographies of the present take account of how youth manage, take up or disrupt, desire, take pride or experience anxiety through spatial relations. Space matters to physical culture (Friedman and van Ingen, 2011), and its (re)production enables and fails some people more than others. It is incumbent on researchers to engage in a sustained interrogation of how space/place, subjects and discourses are privileged, silenced, governed and produced, in the (re)production of the affective, substantive geographies of everyday life (Foucault, 1980). There is much more work to be done in PCS to interrogate the interactions between geography and social justice, the relationships between global and local spaces, the impacts of space and place on inequalities, as well as understanding policy encroachments on places and spaces of physical culture, and what new spaces and places of protest are produced as a result. Inspired by poststructuralist and physical cultural theories and methods and accounting for 'affect' and new materialism/actor–network theory, which accounts for the agentic capacity of material things (e.g. space and its elements in the environment are considered to be significant in their interactions and relations), PCS scholarship should aspire to be reflexive about how we are shaping the material environment/spaces/places in our productions of PCS in order to find those moments of smooth space (Deleuze and Guattari, 1987) because in such places there is more potential for spatial and social justice.

Note

1   Van Ingen (2003) had previously urged sociology of sport scholars to consider space in their deliberations of sport, physical activities and marginalization. Her call to do so followed 10 years of relatively little examinations of space/place in sociology of sport after a special issue of the *International Review for the Sociology of Sport* in 1993 was dedicated to sport spaces. Since then, to my knowledge, there has only been one more special issue in the field devoted to the space/environments in PCS (see *Journal of Sport and Social Issues*, volumes 2 and 3, 2009).

References

Aitken, S. (2001). *Geographies of Young People: The Morally Contested Spaces of Identity*. London: Routledge.
Andrews, G., Sudwell, M. and Sparkes, A. (2005). Towards a geography of fitness: An ethnographic case study of the gym in British bodybuilding culture. *Social Science and Medicine* 60(4), 877–891.
Borden, I. (2003). *Skateboarding, Space and the City: Architecture and the Body*. London: Berg.
Browne, K., Lim, J. and Brown, G. (eds). (2007). *Geographies of Sexualities: Theory, Practice and Politics*. Aldershot: Ashgate.
Crang, M. and Thrift, N. (eds). (2000). *Thinking Space*. London: Routledge.
Crawford, R. (1980). Healthism and the medicalisation of everyday life. *International Journal of Health Services*, 19, 365–388.

Dean, M. (1999). *Governmentality: Power and Rule in Modern Society*. London: Sage.
Deleuze, G. and Guattari, F. (1987). 1440: The smooth and the striated. In G. Deleuze and F. Guattari, *A Thousand Plateaus: Capitalism and Schizophrenia* (pp. 474–500). Minneapolis, MN: University of Minnesota Press.
Dickar, M. (2008). *Corridor Cultures: Mapping Student Resistance at an Urban High School*. New York: New York University Press.
Dillabough, J.-A. and Kennelly, J. (2010). *Lost Youth in the Global City: Class, Culture and the Urban Imaginary*. New York: Routledge.
Dovey, K. (1999). *Framing Places: Mediating Power in the Built Form*. London: Routledge.
Duff, C. (2011). Network, resources and agencies: On the character and production of enabling spaces. *Health and Place*, 17, 149–156.
Evans, B. (2006). 'I'd feel ashamed': Girls' bodies and sport participation. *Gender, Place and Culture: A Journal of Feminist Geography*, 13(5), 547–561.
Evans, B. and Colls, R. (2009). Measuring fatness, governing bodies: The spatialities of the body mass index (BMI) in anti-obesity politics. *Antipode*, 41(5), 1051–1083.
Ferguson, J. and Gupta, A. (2002). Spatializing states: Towards an ethnography of neoliberal governmentality. *American Ethnologist*, 29(4), 981–1002.
Fitzpatrick, K. and LaGory, M. (2003). 'Placing' health in urban sociology: Cities as mosaics of risk and protection. *City and Community*, 2(1), 33–46.
Foucault, M. (1977). *Discipline and Punish: The Birth of the Prison*. New York, Vintage Books.
Foucault, M. (1980). *Power/Knowledge: Selected Interviews and Other Writings, 1972–1977* (trans. C. Gordon). New York: Pantheon Books.
Friedman, M. J. and Andrews, D. L. (2011). The built sport spectacle and the opacity of democracy. *International Review for the Sociology of Sport*, 46(3), 181–204.
Friedman, M. and van Ingen, C. (2011). Bodies in space: Spatializing physical cultural studies. *Sociology of Sport Journal*, 28(1), 85–105.
Fusco, C. (2006). Inscribing healthification: Governance, risk, surveillance and the subjects and spaces of fitness and health. *Health and Place*, 12, 65–78.
Fusco, C. (2007). Healthification and the promises of urban space: A textual analysis of representations of Place, Activity, Youth (PLAY-ing) in the city. *International Review for the Sociology of Sport*, 423(1), 43–63.
Fusco, C. (2012). Governing PLAY: Moral geographies, healthification and neo-liberal urban imaginaries. In D. Andrews and M. Silk (eds), *Sport and Neo-liberalism* (pp. 143–159). Philadelphia, PA: Temple University Press.
Gesler, W. and Kearns, R. (2002). *Culture/Place/Health*. London: Routledge.
Gillespie, R. (2002). Architecture and power: A family planning clinic as a case study. *Health and Place*, 8, 211–220.
Gregory, D. (1994). *Geographical Imaginations*. Cambridge, MA: Blackwell.
Gregory, D. and Pred, A. (eds). (2007). *Violent Geographies: Fear, Terror, and Political Violence*. New York: Routledge.
Halse, C. (2009). Bio-citizenship: Virtue discourse and the birth of the bio-citizen. In J. Wright and V. Harwood (eds), *Biopolitics and the Obesity 'Epidemic': Governing Bodies* (pp. 45–59). New York: Routledge.
Harvey, D. (2000). *Spaces of Hope*. Berkley, CA: California University Press.
Hudson-Rodd, N. (1998). Nineteenth century Canada: Indigenous place of dis-ease. *Health and Place*, 4(1), 55–66.
Lefebvre, H. (1991). *The Production of Space*. Oxford: Blackwell.
Lupton, D. (1995). *The Imperative of Public Health: Public Health and the Regulated Body*. London: Sage.
Massey, D. (1994). *Space, Place and Gender*. Minneapolis, MN: University of Minnesota Press.
Massey, D. (2005). *For Space*. London: Sage.
Means, A. (2013). *Schooling in the Age of Austerity: Urban Education and the Struggle for Democratic Life*. New York: Palgrave Macmillan.
Miller, P. and Rose, N. (2008). *Governing the Present*. Cambridge: Polity Press.
Parr, H. and Butler, R. (eds). (1999). *Mind and Body Spaces: New Geographies of Illness, Impairment and Disability*. London: Routledge.
Philo, C. and Smith, F. (2003). Guest editorial: Political geographies of children and young people. *Space and Polity*, 7(2), 99–115.

Pink, S. (2007). *Doing Visual Ethnography*. London: Sage.
Pronger, B. (2002). *Body Fascism: Salvation in the Technology of Physical Fitness*. Toronto: University of Toronto Press.
Raby, R. (2012). *School Rules: Obedience, Discipline, and Elusive Democracy*. Toronto: University of Toronto Press.
Rail, G. (2012). The birth of the obesity clinic: Confessions of the flesh, biopedagogies and physical culture. *Sociology of Sport Journal*, 29(2), 227–253.
Razack, S. (ed.). (2002). *Race, Space and the Law: Unmapping a White Settler Society*. Toronto: Between the Lines Press.
Rich, E. (2011). Exploring the relationship between pedagogy and physical cultural studies: The case of the new health imperatives in schools. *Sociology of Sport Journal*, 28, 64–84.
Richardson, T. and Jensen, O. (2003). Linking discourse and space: Towards a cultural sociology of space in analyzing spatial policy discourses. *Urban Studies*, 40(1), 7–22.
Sibley, D. (1995). *Geographies of Exclusion*. London, Routledge.
Silk, M. and Andrews, D. (2006). The fittest city in America. *Journal of Sport and Social Issues*, 30(3), 315–327.
Stein, J. (2001). *The Cult of Efficiency*. Toronto: Anansi.
Sutton, S. and Kemp, S. (2006). Young people's participation in constructing a socially just public sphere In C. Spencer and M. Blades (eds), *Children and their Environments: Learning, Using and Designing Spaces* (pp. 256–276). London: Cambridge University Press.
Van Ingen, C. (2003). Geographies of gender, sexuality and race: Reframing the focus on space in sport sociology. *International Review for the Sociology of Sport*, 38(2), 201–216.
Vertinsky, P. and Bale, J. (2004). *Sites of Sport: Space, Place, Experience*. London: Routledge.
Vivoni, F. (2009). Spots of spatial desire: Skateparks, skateplazas, and urban politics. *Journal of Sport and Social Issues*, 33(2), 130–149.
Williams, A. (ed.). (2007). *Therapeutic Landscapes*. Aldershot: Ashgate Publishing.
Wright, J. and Harwood, V. (eds). (2009). *Biopolitics and the Obesity 'Epidemic': Governing Bodies*. New York: Routledge.

37
AFFECTIVE CITIES

Alan Latham and Derek P. McCormack

Introduction

Contemporary western cities are full of people engaging in exercise, sport, and fitness-related activities. The scope of these activities is broad, and includes such relatively solitary practices as walking, running, and jogging; collective field sports like cricket, football, and softball; and a range of somatic movement-practices such as dance, t'ai chi, and yoga. Yet despite their diversity, these activities all share a number of characteristics. Perhaps most obviously, they all work upon and modify the capacities of bodies in some way: to that extent they can each be understood to focus attention on the somatic dimensions of experience. They also all involve the mobilization and monitoring of effort and exertion: in other words, to engage in them demands some kind of corporeal work and the expenditure of energy, even if the level and intensity of this expenditure varies enormously. Furthermore, most (if not all) foreground *kinaesthetic* experience: that is, each involves and generates the sense of movement through space, even if the range and scope of this movement varies enormously – from the scale of miles to the micro-gestural.

Many of the activities listed above are not distinctively urban. And indeed a great deal of work in physical cultural studies has analysed these activities without stressing their urban-ness. So what does focusing on the urban environment add for those of us interested in physical culture? In the following chapter we aim to highlight four reasons why attending to the urban environment can contribute to physical cultural studies and equally how physical cultural studies might contribute to work within urban studies:

1. The link between urbanites' physical activity levels and urbanization is an area of long-standing concern among both serious and popular commentators. Writers such as Simmel (1903) and Mumford (1936) argued that urban environments generate a certain somatic passivity, anticipating more recent speculations on the link between the changing organization of cities and the increased incidence of obesity (see, for instance, Sui, 2003). At the same time, cities have also been understood as the key sites for the development and experiment of a range of techniques for encouraging bodies to become active through different techniques (Schwartz, 1992).
2. The relation between physical activity and cities provides a crucial way of understanding how a range of cultural, social, and political ideals are articulated, reproduced, and regulated

through what bodies do in particular sites and spaces (see Bale, 2001). The nature of the activities undertaken at these sites is constrained and facilitated by a range of social, cultural, economic, and political processes, including gender, income, and ethnicity (see, for example, Evans, 2006; Fusco, 2006; Hargreaves and Vertinsky, 2007; Leeds Craig and Liberti, 2007; McCormack, 1999; Panter, Jones and Hillsdon, 2008). At the same time, exercise, sport and fitness activities have the potential to rework and rearticulate some of these processes (Borden, 2001).

3   The materiality of cities is both relational and processual, in ways that complicate any neat juxtaposition of the 'material' and the 'immaterial' (Latham and McCormack, 2004; Latham, 2016). Exercise, sport, and fitness complicate questions of urban materiality because they are profoundly affective: the materiality of the spaces of which they are generative is not just a matter of concrete structures or, indeed, of flesh. It is also about the production and circulation of affective energies and atmospheres whose materiality is distributed, vague, *and* felt.

4   Thinking about exercise, sports, and fitness activities in relation to urban environments provides an opportunity to explore the ways in which physical cultures are entangled with how cities are imagined, engineered, and inhabited through techniques and technologies of experience and public involvement. This can involve critical investigation of how such activities are mobilized as part of collective spectacles – most obviously through mega sporting projects such as the Olympics – designed to revive or boost urban economies (Gratton, Shibli and Coleman, 2005; Howell, 2005; Gold and Gold, 2007), and as part of deliberate strategies of place promotion (Silk and Amis, 2005; L'Etang, 2006). But on a much more mundane level, exercise, sport, and fitness provide significant modes of experiencing urban space – through ways of moving and feeling. Put another way, these activities are important techniques for sensing urban space.

Practices of affective activity

To begin, we wish to consider exercise, sport, and fitness activities in relation to a growing recognition of the *affective* dimensions of urban life: those aspects of urban life characterized by the emergence, circulation, and experience of emotions, moods, feelings, passions, and affect (Thrift, 2008). While the affective dimensions of urban life have been remarked upon by a number of important historical figures, the analysis of these dimensions has recently been developed in important ways. There is a growing recognition of the need to articulate a differentiated understanding of and vocabulary for affectivity (Massumi, 2002; McCormack, 2013; Thrift, 2008). There is a greater focus on the specific processes and techniques through which affectivity circulates and is distributed within and across cities (Katz, 1999; Sheller, 2003). And, there is a greater recognition that affectivity is not a kind of experiential or representational veil that obscures the real structures underpinning urban life, but that it is a crucial part of the everyday infra-structural materialities of urban experience. This, in turn, means that the affective life of cities has many different valences: cities are full of fears, traumas, and anxieties, but they are also full of a range of 'affective possibilities' offering opportunities for inhabiting cities in manifold ways (Conradson and Latham, 2007).

That exercise, sport, and fitness are affective is all too obvious – their enactment is both motivated by and generative of a range of intensely affective experiences, from anxiety, to hope, to fear, and joy. Beyond this observation, however, we can make a number of important claims about the affective dimensions of exercise, sport, and fitness activities, these practices reveal, albeit in different ways, the differentiated quality of urban affectivity. To begin, participation in these activities provides a particularly useful way of foregrounding the pre-personal relations of intensity that form a sensate background to urban life, and from which affective economies of belonging emerge with varying degrees of extensity and duration. This is perhaps most obvious in field sports such as football, in which a set of simple attractors – goals, a ball, players – potentializes a more than personal space of affective intensity (Massumi, 2002). But such fields are never just a matter of affect: their intensities are also registered as feeling in the moving bodies of both participants and spectators – for many people, whether live or via TV, it is impossible to just watch a game. A game that is worthy of the name will be felt – and expressed – as so many shared movements, collective anticipations, and demonstrative frustrations. And both participants and spectators will also express these felt intensities as collectively recognizable emotions.

Then, and second, exercise, sport, and fitness have increasingly become understood and undertaken as deliberate techniques for affective self-monitoring and management within contemporary metropolitan life. An analysis of these activities as techniques of the reflexive self is nothing new (see Mauss, 1979): but whereas earlier work focused on their importance in relation to the expenditure/accumulation of symbolic capital, more recent writing has emphasized their role as techniques of affective embodiment through which emotions, moods, and feelings are routinely generated (Monaghan, 2001; Crossley, 2004). The affective 'effect' of many kinaesthetic practices has become an integral part of popular discourses about health and fitness, with activities such as walking and running regularly promoted as techniques for combating a range of urban ills including depression, anxiety, and panic attacks.

Such comments obviously need some qualification. There is a real risk of taking at face value the 'effects' of these affects (see Kolata, 2003). In many respects the question of how they work is below the onto-epistemological thresholds of the social sciences. Yet this should not mean that they should be dismissed, or written out of socio-culturally inflected accounts of physical activity: indeed, these affects serve as an important reminder of how pre-cognitive and physiological processes are integral to the experience of urban space (Hitchings and Latham, 2016).

Third, insofar as physical activities are important techniques for amplifying, modulating, and circulating affectivity in cities, these activities are also generative of distinctive spaces whose emergence and organization is determined, at least in part, by the possibilities of generating forms of collective affective experience at different scales. As Ehrenreich (2007) argues large stadiums are particularly obvious in this regard – they are designed as much to produce affective atmospheres as to conjure a symbolic statement about the meaning of a city on the make. Sport is a machine for generating collective affects. But the amplification, modulation, and circulation of affectivity also take place in spaces of more modest scale. We might think, for instance, of a range of playing fields, parks, and recreational spaces. And we might think here of the streets in which urban marathons and fun runs take place, an example to which we will return later in the paper. In each case, the affective ecology of these sites is not just a by-product of the activity that takes place there. It is part of the felt materiality of the site, part of what gives it its distinctive quality – an atmosphere or background that is not just a way of sugar-coating something that would otherwise seem irrational, or whose significance is reducible to economies of representational meaning (Latham and McCormack, 2004).

Techniques and technologies of kinaesthetic involvement

In addition to the affective qualities of their spaces, sport, exercise, and fitness activities also provide an important way of thinking through the materiality of distinctive kinds of kinaesthetic 'movement-spaces' (Thrift, 2008) within cities. We can think of kinaesthesia as a kind of background proprioception that 'translates the exertions and ease of the body's encounters with objects into a muscular memory of relationality' (Massumi, 2002: 59). While all forms of somatic experience involve this kinaesthetic sense, certain kinds of physical activity – such as running, jogging, and walking – place primacy on this element of somatic practice, albeit with different degrees of intensity, and with different degrees of mediation through apparel, technology, and technique.

As we noted in the introduction, working upon and foregrounding the kinaesthetic experience of cities through techniques and technologies is not necessarily new. For instance, Hillel Schwartz has identified the emergence at the end of the nineteenth and beginning of the twentieth century, of a set of cultural and corporeal tendencies organized around the relationship between movement and emotional expression: 'from nursery school play and grammar school penmanship on through organized sports to adult gymnastics and beyond, to the design of prosthetic devices. The training of large- and small-muscle movements was regularly if not always allied to the new kinaesthetic in both its expressive and operative aspects, with which technology was often concordant' (Schwartz, 1992: 106).

This urban kinaesthetic has developed in various ways, not least through various kinds of technical enhancement. One of the more obvious of these is the running shoe, which has evolved into one of the key interfaces through which urban space is imagined, engineered, and experienced (Tenner, 2003; Lash and Lury, 2007). At the same time, practices like running and walking have been reinvented in deliberate ways, often with the aid of specific technical devices (see Shove and Pantzer, 2005; Latham, 2015; also Ingold, 2004). Consider, for instance, the case of Nordic walking, around which has developed a distinctive material-kinaesthetic culture. Originating in Finland, Nordic walking has become increasingly popular throughout Europe and North America. The key characteristic of Nordic walking is the cultivation of a distinctive walking technique with the aid of two poles. Compared with unaided walking, the advantages of using these poles are, apparently, a more relaxed walking rhythm, a longer (and more regular) stride, with an increased level of calorie burn.

As Shove and Pantzer (2005: 43) have argued, the growth of Nordic walking can be understood as a series of 'successive, but necessarily localized (re)invention' in different sites. What is also remarkable about this process is the degree to which it involves re-imagining and re-inhabiting urban space – one no longer needs to go out into the country to walk seriously – and how it generates its own forms of associations and collective events.

What is more, the process of activating bodies in cities is being facilitated by new alignments between kinaesthetic techniques and a range of other technologies. The most obvious in this regard is the use of a range of bio-data and geo-data technologies such as pulse monitors and GPS devices in order to record physiological activity and physical location, in addition to providing motivation (see Buttussi et al., 2006). At the same time, there is an emerging synchrony between techniques for mapping and managing the routes and rates of exercise, and technologies of affective modulation, most notably music. A perhaps more surprising example is provided by video games. Where once it was seen as one of the key factors in encouraging a more sedentary lifestyle the video game has now emerged as a possible solution for generating modes of physical/virtual interactivity in cities (see van Borries, Waltz and Böttger, 2007).

Of these 'exergames', Konami's Dance Dance Revolution (DDR) is one of the most famous. Developed in the late 1990s DDR involves a dance pad on the floor, on which players need to move in time with the rhythm of an accompanying track. Tremendously popular, DDR has also generated its own online user groups, and there is some evidence that it and other exergames do allow players to increase the intensity of effort and exertion (Tan et al., 2002; see also Mokka et al., 2003; Warburton et al., 2007). A slightly more recent variation on this is

Nintendo's Wii Fit. According to Nintendo, the Wii Fit 'combines fun and fitness in one product' and 'can change how you exercise, how you balance, and even how you move', using an interactive 'balance board' (cf. Francombe-Webb, 2016).

As the examples above illustrate, techniques and technologies of popular kinaesthetic activity are highly commodified. In itself this claim is rather unremarkable: such activity has always been commodified (see Smith Maguire, 2008). But what has changed is the extent to which the experience of movement promised by kinaesthetic techniques and technologies has become part of complex processes of branding urban space. While some analyses focus on the representational dimensions of this branding (Duncan, 1994; Eskes, Duncan and Miller, 1998), there is a growing recognition that the brand has become more than a representational phenomenon. As Celia Lury (2004: 1) has argued, the brand 'is a platform for the patterning of activity, a mode of organizing activities in time and space … a site – or diagram of interactivity, not of interaction'. There is a close association between the brand and the kinaesthetic and affective aspects of sport and fitness practices, given that it 'is in and of movement' (ibid: 15).

Exercising publics

If exercise, sport, and fitness provide important techniques for working on the affective and kinaesthetic registers of urban space, they are also important insofar as they are generative of distinctive kinds of collective events and experiences. Think here of the myriad marathons, half-marathons, 10K runs, and fun runs of all kinds that take place in cities. Of these, the urban marathon is perhaps the most interesting. Why? For one reason, it is one of the most distinctively urban of mass participation events (Berking and Neckel, 1993), literally requiring the commandeering of city streets for an activity that inconveniences many other urban inhabitants. Furthermore, it is an event that genuinely transcends the categories of exercise, sport, and fitness, involving many participants who do not even describe themselves as 'runners'.

Take for, example, the annual Berlin city marathon. Every year 40,000 runners, in-line skaters, walkers, wheelchair and pedal-chair riders, assemble in Berlin to compete in this event. Witnessed by close to a million spectators, the Berlin marathon is broadcast live not only by the local television station Radio Brandenburg and Berlin (RBB), but also by the national television channel ZDF. In terms of its sheer operational logistics, the Berlin Marathon is a significant event in the life of this city, requiring the registration and regulation of tens of thousands of contestants, the marshalling the crowds of viewers, and the organization of the necessary road closures.

How then to make sense of this kind of event? One way is to understand participation in the urban marathon through the lens of post-modern critiques of sport. In this vein, Helmuth Berking and Sighard Neckel (1993: 67) argue that the marathon offers itself 'directly for the symptomatic reading of the relationship between urbanity and individualization'. In these terms, the marathon recasts 'the personal experience of the city as a test of character, a challenge and existential struggle in dramatic form' (ibid.: 76). And, as Berking and Neckel observe (drawing upon Bourdieu, 1978), the demands marathon participation places on the individual means that it tends to be the pursuit of the urban middle classes seeking self-transformation (see also Reischer, 2001). The marathon runner may well be the embodiment of the modern pursuit of an urban ethic of individuality through the discipline and training of the body: yet the urban marathon is also an event through which individual participation becomes articulated through collective economies of charity and generosity. Commenting on this, Nettleton and Hardey (2006) suggest that the urban marathon reproduces certain problematic relations between 'fit' and 'needy' bodies in urban space.

Clearly these comments do provide some purchase on the phenomenon of the urban marathon. Yet to read urban marathons solely in these terms is rather limited, not least because the kinaesthetic and affective elements of participation in these events become factors that need to be explained through an appeal to broader sociological structures. But the kinaesthetic and affective dimensions of these events are not a kind of veneer that needs to be stripped away in order to explain the phenomena of urban marathons: they are crucial to its experiential and organizational consistency. In the marathon there is a very real sense in which this affective atmosphere is co-produced by both spectators and participants. This is not just a matter of the runners and their audience/supporters transforming ordinary streets into a kind of mobile carnival. It is also about the establishment of relational affective economy in which there is a mutual and resonant feedback loop between the affects and emotions of the participants and those of the spectators. The spectators respond to the visible signs of affective intensity – sweat, grimace, smile – with their own gestures – waves, cheers, applause (Latham and McCormack, 2012).

To what extent can these kinds of collective involvements be considered as forms of publicness? Recent work across the social sciences suggests that our definitions of publicness, and of the kinds of practices of involvement of which they consist, need some revising (Amin, 2012). At the very least, publics are understood increasingly to be differentiated, distributed, and of varying duration, and certainly not coterminous with the classical model of public space as an area within which citizens gather to articulate their political involvement. Yet, on one level exercise, sport and fitness events remind us of the continued importance of providing particular sites of publicness in the city – streets, playgrounds, parks, and recreational spaces of different kinds, and of varying degrees of porosity (see Ryan, 2006; Roth, 2006; Iverson, 2007). At the same time they also push us to think about the materiality of spaces of publicness as more ephemeral and less obviously structural. Importantly, the kind of publicness of which these practices are generative is not only a matter of participating in a communicative democracy (Habermas, 1989). It works on a more affective register, in the sense that it engages, amplifies, and circulates the affects, felt qualities, and intensities of experience. This publicness is also enactive, depending on the capacity of a multiplicity of practices to produce particular forms of association. And the space of this kind of publicness is eventful: it is a form of public spacing rather than public space.

Conclusion

In this chapter we have considered the relation between exercise, sport, and fitness activities and urban life, with a particular emphasis on how these activities can be traced through the affective, kinaesthetic, and collective registers of urban space. Our argument is that there is much physical cultural studies can gain from attending to the urban environment, just as there is much urban studies might gain from thinking more critically about cities' various and varied physical cultures. In the process, our tone has been reasonably affirmative: without ignoring some of the problems associated with these activities, we have nevertheless sought to avoid the common academic tendency to incorporate them within a narrative of critical disenchantment, as evidence of how contemporary urban life and the bodies that inhabit them are becoming alternately too fast, too slow, too sedentary, too active, too individualized, too competitive, or too unthinking.

Rather than vehicles for this kind of diagnosis, we see the ongoing enactment and evolution of forms of physical activity in cities as providing reasons to be hopeful about the life of cities. Part of the reason for this hopefulness is the fact that they continued to affectively animate cities in all kinds of ways. Part of the reason is that they are continuing to evolve, particularly through the alignment of different techniques and technologies, in ways that are giving rise to new landscapes of encounter and experiment. And part of the reason for such hopefulness is the fact that, like Spinoza and Deleuze, *we still do not know what a body can do* (Spinoza, 1990). It is perhaps easier to make this claim in relation to more obviously creative practices such as skateboarding or the more spectacular Parkour, both of which can be understood to actively work and rework space in novel ways – as well as being incorporated into a range of commodified circuits of value generation (see Borden, 2001; Thomson, 2008). But this claim can also be made in relation to more prosaic activities such as running and walking, in which it is also possible to experience a kind of 'focused intensity', a state which 'encompasses not just the ability to exclude a multiplicity of potential distractions but also a concentrated openness for something unexpected to happen. Something whose coming is not under our control and will therefore always appear to be sudden' (Gumbrecht, 2006: 52). It is because of their potential to generate the unforeseen in this way that exercise, sport, and fitness need to be situated on an ethico-political cartography of affective relations, and not on the plane of critical judgement, especially when thinking about how they participate in urban life. Equally, this is an ethos that might be carried into physical cultural studies. The bodies are not simply surfaces upon which power writes, they also expressive, caught up in the making of worlds.

To end, we would like to reaffirm the importance of a variation on the Spinozist question. Not only do we not know what bodies can do: we also do not know of what kinds of spaces they are generative. Or put another way, we might say we *still don't know what a city can do*. This is more than a matter of the physical sites in and at which exercise, sport, and fitness activities take place: it refers also to the kinds of affective, material, and public spaces of which they are generative. Thinking through these spaces, and the forms of being and becoming urban, is one of the most important aspects of understanding contemporary urban life. And furthering that claim, it suggests that physical cultural studies too needs to be attuned to the making collective that is so often at the centre of physical cultures. Physical cultural studies needs to be as much about the environments and spaces it helps perform, as the somatic practices through which such spaces are called forth.

References

Amin, A. 2012. *Land of Strangers*. Cambridge: Polity.
Bale, J. 2001. *Sport, Space, and the City*. Caldwell, NJ: Blackburn Press.
Berking, H. and Neckel, S. 1993. Urban marathon: The staging of individuality as an urban event. *Theory, Culture and Society* 10, 63–78.
Borden, I. 2001. *Skateboarding, Space and the City: Architecture and the Body*. Oxford: Berg.
Bourdieu, P. 1978. Sport and Social Class. *Social Science Information* 17, 819–840.
Buttussi, F., Chittaro, L. and Nadalutti, D. 2006. Bringing mobile guides and fitness activities together: A solution based on an embodied virtual trainer. *ACM International Conference Proceeding Series* 159, 29–36.
Conradson, D. and Latham, A. 2007: The affective possibilities of London: Antipodean transnationals and the overseas experience. *Mobilities* 2, 231–254.
Crossley, N. 2004. The circuit trainer's habitus: Reflexive body techniques and the sociality of the workout. *Body and Society* 10, 37–69.
Deleuze, G. 1990. *Expressionism in Philosophy: Spinoza* (trans. M. Joughin). New York: Zone Books.
Duncan, M. 1994. The politics of women's body images and practices: Foucault, the panopticon, and *Shape* magazine. *Journal of Sport and Social Issues* 18, 48–65.
Eskes, T. B., Duncan, M. C. and Miller, E. M. 1998. The discourse of empowerment: Foucault, Marcuse, and women's fitness texts. *Journal of Sport and Social Issues* 22, 317–344.
Evans, B. 2006. 'I'd feel ashamed': Girls' bodies and sports participation. *Gender, Place and Culture* 13, 547–561.

Francombe Webb, J. 2016. Critically encountering exer-games and young femininity. *Television and New Media* 17(5), 449–464.

Fusco, F. 2006. Spatializing the (im)proper subject: The geographies of abjection in sport and physical activity space. *Journal of Sport and Social Issues* 30, 5–28.

Gold, J. and Gold, M. 2007. *Olympic Cities: City Agendas, Planning, and the Worlds Games, 1896–2012*. London: Routledge.

Gratton, C., Shibli, S. and Coleman, R. 2005. Sport and economic regeneration in cities. *Urban Studies* 42, 985–999.

Gumbrecht, H. 2006. *In Praise of Athletic Beauty*. Cambridge, MA: Harvard University Press.

Habermas, J. 1989. *The Structural Transformation of the Public Sphere*. Cambridge, MA: MIT Press.

Hargreaves, J. and Vertinsky, P. (eds). 2007. *Physical Culture, Power, and the Body*. London: Routledge.

Hitchings, R. and Latham, A. 2016. Indoor versus outdoor running: Understanding how recreational exercise comes to inhabit environments through practitioner talk. *Transactions of the Institute of British Geographers* 41(4), 503–514.

Howell, J. 2005. Manufacturing experiences: Urban development, sport and recreation. *International Journal of Sport Management and Marketing* 1, 56–68.

Ingold, T. 2004. Culture on the ground: The world perceived through the feet. *Journal of Material Culture* 9, 315–340.

Iverson, K. 2007. *Publics and the City*. Oxford, Blackwell.

Katz, J. 1999. *How Emotions Work*. Chicago, IL: University of Chicago Press.

Kolata, G. 2003. *Ultimate Fitness: The Quest for Truth about Exercise and Health*. New York: Farrar, Strauss & Giroux.

Lash, S. and Lury, C. 2007. *Global Culture Industry*. Oxford: Polity.

Latham, A. 2015. The history of a habit: Jogging as a palliative to sedentariness in 1960s America, *Cultural Geographies*, 22(1), 103–126.

Latham, A. 2016. Materiality. In M. Jayne and K. Ward (eds), *Urban Theory: New Critical Perspectives*. London: Routledge.

Latham, A. and McCormack, D. P. 2004. Moving cities: Rethinking the materialities of urban geographies. *Progress in Human Geography* 28, 701–724.

Latham, A. and McCormack, D. P. 2012. Globalizations big and small: Notes on urban studies, actor-network theory and geographical scale. In I. Farias and T. Bender (eds), *Urban Assemblages: How Actor-Network Theory Changes Urban Studies*. London: Routledge, 53–72.

Leeds Craig, M. and Liberti, R. 2007. 'Cause that's what girls do': The making of a feminized gym. *Gender and Society* 21, 676–699.

L'Etang, J. 2006. Public relations and sport in promotional culture. *Public Relations Review* 32, 386–394.

Lury, C. 2004. *Brands: The Logos of the Global Economy*. London: Routledge.

McCormack, D. 1999. Body-shopping: Reconfiguring the geographies of fitness. *Gender, Place and Culture* 6(2), 155–177.

McCormack, D. 2013: *Refrains for Moving Bodies*. Durham, NC: Duke University Press.

Massumi, B. 2002. *Parables for the Virtual: Movement, Affect, Sensation*. Durham, NC: Duke University Press.

Mauss, M. 1979. Body-techniques. *Sociology and Psychology*. London: Routledge, 95–123.

Mokka, S. Väätänen, A., Heinilä, J. and Välkkynen, P. 2003. Fitness computer game with a bodily user interface. *Proceedings of the Second International Conference on Entertainment Computing* 38, 1–3.

Monaghan, L. 2001. Looking good, feeling good: The embodied pleasures of vibrant physicality. *Sociology of Health and Illness* 23, 330–356.

Mumford, L. 1936. *The Culture of Cities*. New York: Harcourt Brace.

Nettleton, S. and Hardey, M. 2006. Running away with health: The urban marathon and the construction of 'charitable bodies'. *Health* 10, 441–460.

Panter, J., Jones, A. and Hillsdon, M. 2008. Equity of access to physical activity facilities in an English city. *Preventative Medicine* 46, 303–307.

Reischer, E. 2001. Running to the moon: The articulation and construction of self in marathon runners. *Anthropology of Consciousness* 12, 19–35.

Roth, J. 2006. A mean-spirited sport: Japanese Brazilian croquet in São Paulo's public spaces. *Anthropological Quarterly* 79, 609–632.

Ryan, Z. (ed.). 2006. *The Good Life: New Public Spaces for Recreation*. New York: Van Alen Institute.

Schwartz, H. 1992. Torque: The new kinaesthetic of the twentieth century. In J. Crary and S. Kwinter (eds), *Incorporations*. New York: Zone, 71–126.

Sheller, M. 2003. Automotive emotions. *Theory, Culture and Society* 21, 221–242.
Shove, E. and Pantzer, M. 2005. Consumers, producers and practices: Understanding the invention and reinvention of Nordic walking. *Journal of Consumer Culture* 5, 43–64.
Silk, M. and Amis, J. 2005. Sport tourism, cityscapes and cultural politics. *Sport and Society* 8, 280–301.
Simmel, G. [1903] 1997. The metropolis and mental life. In D. Frisby and M. Featherstone (eds), *Simmel on Culture*. London: Sage.
Smith Maguire, J. 2008. *Fit for Consumption: Sociology and the Business of Fitness*. London: Routledge.
Sui, D. 2003. Musings on the fat city: Are obesity and urban forms linked? *Urban Geography* 24, 75–84.
Tan, B., Aziz, A., Chua, K. and The, K. 2002. Aerobic demands of the dance simulation game. *International Journal of Sports Medicine* 23, 125–129.
Tenner, E. 2003. *Our Own Devices: The Past and Future of Body Technology*, New York: Knopf.
Thomson, D. 2008. Jump city: Parkour and the traces. *South Atlantic Quarterly* 107, 251–263.
Thrift, N. 2008. *Nonrepresentational Theory: Space, Politics, Affect*. London: Routledge.
Van Borries, F., Waltz, P. and Böttger, M. (eds). 2007. *Space Time Play: Computer Games, Architecture and Urbanism*. Berlin: Birkhäuser.
Warburton, D., Bredin, D., Horita, L., Zbogar, D., Scott, J., Esch, B. and Rhodes, R. 2007. The health benefits of interactive video game exercise. *Applied Physiology, Nutrition and Metabolism* 32, 655–663.

38
EXERCISE AND FITNESS SPACES

Roberta Sassatelli

The contemporary world of gyms is an extremely complex and varied reality that is attracting increasing critical interest from many quarters as it is linked with consumer capitalism and how neo-liberal logic puts bodies at work in urban spaces (Sassatelli, 2015). The creation of specialized, typically commercial, spaces defined by the possibility of 'taking care of the body' strengthens the impression that modern urban living otherwise is and must be unhealthy, unnatural and harmful to the body. As a highly specialized and separated institution, the fitness gym reinforces the functionalized structure of consumer capitalist urban living and its emphasis on individualized (self) control of conducts furthering individualization and de-politicization of active leisure. Its diffusion, for example, has probably rendered less urgent the provision of parks, outdoor exercise tracks, cycling paths and other public gymnastic solutions, which may incidentally be less prone to commercialization, more universally available and more incisive in changing urban living. It has certainly had the effect of globally reinforcing the neo-liberal, middle-class idea that health and well-being matters are matters of individual will and consumerism (Maguire Smith, 2007; Sassatelli, 2010; Spielvogel, 2003).

Still, fitness gyms and health centres receive a general token of approval by mainstream pop and consumer culture as a solution to urban sedentary and functionalized patterns of living. If we take just a little step back in history, we can say that it is since the late 1970s that there has been a considerable growth in commercial recreational centres which have presented themselves in a new way: gyms have been closely associated with the notion of 'fitness', and in professional texts old labels have been replaced by neologisms such as 'fitness centres' and 'fitness clubs', and more recently 'health centres' or 'wellness clubs'. These neologisms come with the extra bonus of luxury and sociability. They also divert attention from the competitive, harsh and often very masculine world which was originally associated with the term 'gymnasium' and activate a semantics gravitating towards the area of 'leisured healthism'. While female pop icons (from Jane Fonda's aerobics to Madonna's 'Candy Fitness', a franchised global brand) often play important roles, this is not just a female province. Commercial gyms match the current governmental public campaigns for healthy lifestyle and longevity for the entire population in what has recently been termed 'mindful fitness' (Markula, 2011). Fitness in such a guise, may be seen as a rather apparently all-inclusive territory where functionalized, rationalized and individualized enjoyment must be displayed while working towards a normalized healthy-looking, young and efficient embodied self. Within this context, and attuned to the politics of the body and exercise that has been central to PCS approaches to understanding power relations in institutionalized spaces, such as gyms, I draw on ethnographic data (Molnar and Purdy, 2016; Sassatelli, 2012a) in this chapter to address the spatiality of commercial fitness gyms and their productive effects on embodied selves.

Commercial recreational exercise, hybridization and affects

Fitness gyms are supposedly non-competitive environments aimed at providing recreational exercise to boost physical form and well-being. As typically late-modern, urban, commercial and global institutions, fitness gyms are culturally branded as offering individuals the possibility to relax from everyday duties and take care of their bodies. Typically located in urban contexts, fitness gyms are a special breed of leisure institution (Rojek, 2000). Large metropolitan areas are those where commercial fitness penetration among the population is generally stronger. Gyms are different from social clubs – both working-class and upper-class – in that a set of specific tasks are to be carried out, with sociability being important as either a by-product or a facilitator of those tasks. In some respects, going to a fitness gym is a form of 'serious leisure' (Stebbins, 2009) that allows the development of a project and to a degree a 'career' within one's own free time. In others, it is a form of 'therapeutic leisure' (Caldwell, 2005) which is believed to prevent negative life events, can help us cope with the demands of ordinary life, and generally has healing functions for our bodies (and souls). In this sense, fitness gyms are best understood under the banner of 'rational recreation'. A notion of Victorian origin, according to Foucault (1975), rational recreation stresses that recreational activities should be morally uplifting for the participant, good for his or her body, and have positive benefits for the wider society. As distinct from more informal, spontaneous forms of leisure, or sub-cultures of commodity appropriation (Willis, 1979), they appear, functional to social order and dominant classifications. Fitness gyms may thus be considered at the opposite pole of Wacquant's (2003) boxing gym, where class and community are central and anti-structural or subversive elements are quite evident.

Emphasis on individuality is paramount in fitness culture. Fitness participants are constituted through an overarching rhetoric central to global consumer capitalism especially in its neo-liberal variant (see Bourdieu and Waquant, 2001) and evident in the discourse on, for example fat (Silk, Francombe and Bachelor, 2009) or addiction (Eccles, 2002; Reith, 2004; Sassatelli, 2007). This rhetoric points at the duties and pleasure of 'taking care of oneself' within a model of 'individual choice' and 'personal responsibility'. The politics inherently in this are further misrecognized as the model speaks in the seemingly universalistic voice of a fight against the ills of (global) urban living and its deskbound bureaucratized and rationalized patterns. Keep-fit activities in the gym may be understood as part of a larger process of individualization and commercialization that matches the shift of the bourgeois spirit (Beck and Gernsheim, 2001) from the nation to the market. They have been sustained through a commercialized imperative of health and were related to the progressive incorporation of more and more social strata into commercial relations. Indeed, the strong symbolic and institutional tie which had been created between gymnastics and politics in the nineteenth and early twentieth centuries has withered, leaving room for the development of apparently de-politicized health-oriented and fun-seeking, recreational forms of gymnastic which were gradually integrated by the emerging commercial gyms addressing a (potentially segmented) mass of individual consumers. Whereas recreational gymnastic activities were initially attached to public goals such as, notably, loyalty to the Nation, participants' individual desires are now presented as legitimizing commitment to exercise. Bodies and places, training and building acted upon each other with the 'immuring of physical exercise' (Eichberg, 1998) as part of a longer, civilizing trend towards the enclosure of the body.

Fitness culture is commercial at its core. Targeted at clients or customers, fitness aims at being qualified as an expression of consumers' desires and stresses individual strategies. The fit body is thereby linked not to the citizen or the worker, but to the sovereign consumer, a new sacred persona characterized as autonomous and choosy as well as responsible for him or herself. While different countries across the global West may work through different forms of provision, fitness gyms in Italy correspond to what might be considered the dominant model as evident, to different degrees, in the UK and the US. They are thus heavily imbued with promotional culture and commercial relations. More broadly, the commercialization of keep-fit activities essentially responds to its cultural configuration: it reflects the official objective of fitness training, namely the maintenance or improvement of individual well-being and body qualities. Managers are keen to structure through temporality and spatiality the variety of activities on offer as well as to provide what, in their words, is a 'fulfilling', 'total', 'complete' *experience*. An impression of variety, and an emphasis on experience, are reinforced by gym staff, who insist that all clients can 'discover their own way' to train by using the alternatives available in the gym. In their manner of speech, preference for different techniques is presented as a 'personal choice' rendered through a selection from the pre-packaged range of techniques available in the particular centre. The incessant introduction of new techniques and the role of trainers, both employees and self-employed personal trainers, in pushing innovation and differentiation forward is clearly a feature of today's fitness industry matching its commercial character. And it is inbuilt in the small details of gym initiation and participation. When the gym staff approach a new client with the fitness application form or a trainer proceeds with the ritual of the fitness test on a new client, they highlight both *variety* and *equivalence* of activities: most typical is a litany suggesting that the vast assortment of techniques are all finely tuned to fitness, albeit differentiated, and cater for individual needs. The selection and/or combination of different techniques is symbolically supported by all of them being presented as close substitutes (i.e. sound, guaranteed alternatives and 'safe options to choose from').

For a generalist fitness gym, one that provides many techniques to a fairly generalized public, variety is indeed crucial, becoming an experiential participation resource for clients. While irregular clients – or, even more so, leavers – consider variety confusing, regular gym-goers typically come to master it. Dedicated clients are usually quite familiar with the different activities and areas in their gym. They are often the first to take advantage of innovations and they feel relatively in control of the gym environment; even when they are not interested in new techniques, they typically relish the gym because, in their words, it makes an effort to be 'varied', potentially 'rich in new and diverse activities' and, therefore, always 'stimulating'. The rigidity (of movements, schedules, etc.) of each specific body technique is matched, for these clients, by a horizon of *combinatory freedom*. Enthusiasts insist on the possibility of using relatively rigid elements of training in a multitude of different personal combinations, describing their own fitness basket as something of a 'personal achievement'.

By and large, fitness gyms are indeed built on the provision of what I have called *structured variety* (Sassatelli, 2010). Modern markets thrive on the generation of differences, and consumers as well as producers are quite willing to collaborate in the process. Growth and control by managed, marginal diversification (or structured variety) is a well-known dynamic within consumer capitalism as developed in the large cities of today. The organization of different techniques in spatially differentiated areas helps project the idea that the fitness gym is not so much a total institution as it provides a *total service*: it is an elective place that supplies all that is needed for transforming the embodied subject towards the goal of fitness, a goal which takes on totalizing accents by taking care of the self as much as the body. Structured variety therefore is at the core of the cultural politics of fitness: it has a legitimating function as well as pushing for a continuous negotiation of boundaries of the fitness field.

In actual fact, the boom of the fitness industry has been matched by an equal growth in the range of workout options available: aqua exercise, boxing training, cardiovascular machines, circuit training, combat-style workouts, core stability workouts such as pilates, exercise to music such as step and aerobics, free weight exercise, and indoor cycling including spinning. Leaving behind monolithic exercise salons devoted entirely to body building or aerobics, commercial fitness gyms increasingly draws on cognate areas – such as sports, martial arts, dance, meditation – to provide different blends of aerobic and anaerobic, free-body and equipment-based exercises. Fitness is an increasingly hybrid endeavour, mixing Eastern and Western techniques. It draws from a truly global reservoir of body techniques and emotional codes which are consequently fast-changing: Colombian-born zumba, a form of exercise-to-music mixing Caribbean dance and aerobic exercises and sustained by a sensuous emphasis on fun and (female) togetherness, has quickly become popular, as have fitness boot camps, mimicking US Marines military training, emphasizing (masculine) strength and resistance, harsh and muscular discipline. Originally, fitness boot camps expanded fitness outside the gym into parks and nature, realizing the gyms', and indeed instructors', attempts at extending control of activities well beyond the immured, managerially driven reality of the club. But these muscular techniques found their way back into the gym, bringing with them new dress codes drawing on military outfits and opening the way for a renewed emphasis on strength training as opposed to aerobic exercise. Incidentally, this results in formats such as body weight training, which, mixing acrobatic elements and an emphasis on bare body performance, somehow mimics the extraordinary stunts of super-heroes and super-heroines from the film industry. As we shall see, this is well adjusted to the enhancement of a sense of 'fun' which normatively is associated with commercial fitness spaces.

From a broad cultural perspective, much of the generated difference in fitness culture happens through the ever-shifting hybridization and reshuffling of precepts and precincts which once appeared as irreconcilable and distant, thus for example renegotiating the boundary of sport and gymnastics. And much of it has to do with managing contradictions, evident more generally in urban commercial culture. Fitness culture thus presents itself as a skilful reconciliation of opposites. Indeed, the ever new techniques and practices available in the fitness gym show the current *dual* direction of the fitness industry towards *excitement* on the one hand, and *relaxation* on the other: to incorporate simulated activities which draw on the domestication of combat, conquest or competition to provide excitement, on the one hand; to include soft, mind-body techniques and pampering spaces (jacuzzi, saunas, etc.) to provide relaxation, on the other. As we shall see, the organization of this duality is crucial for the space the gym occupies in urban contexts: urban life is deemed both too exciting (typically for the mind) and too dull (typically for the body). The attention to both ills of urban life, a feature of commercial culture at large, is thus not surprisingly a dynamic factor in the development of current fitness trends.

More broadly, fitness training is justified as the most rational and effective way to transform the body, yet pleasurable involvement is of the essence. Keep-fit practices harbour a daunting contradiction between *ascetic rationality* and *hedonistic passion*, a central conundrum of consumer capitalism and its affective shaping of consumers' subjectivities through various forms of therapeutic pedagogies (Sedgwick, 2003). As suggested, dominant in consumer capitalism are ever-shifting but resilient forms of 'tamed hedonism' which accentuate the 'authenticity' of the consumer as a self-controlling self (Sassatelli, 2001). The various forms of fitness training are presented by trainers and expert discourse as the most 'rational' instrument to keep fit, take care of the body, get slim, toned, healthy and so on. Fitness training is accounted for as a rationally instrumental activity, but it does not take place in a coercive, compulsive and hierarchically organized institution. Gym spatiality and temporality is coded also through elements of popular culture, especially through pop music and fashion sportswear, which stress leisure and recreation, something that is furthered by the cheerful, welcoming attitude of gym staff towards 'clients'. Rationalization can make workouts quite dull and dry, which fits badly with the fact that going to a gym is, after all, an activity to be practised in one's own leisure time. Thus, fitness gyms must also provide hedonistic incentives, stressing emotional involvement, pleasure and fun. Involvement and fun are also linked to the 'natural' quality attributed to keep-fit activities in the gym, a quality that contrasts markedly with the clearly artificial, precisely planned and continuously managed concentration of a structured variety of elaborated body techniques in one single, indoor space.

Fitness gyms clearly live through another contradiction which is central to their urban nature: they may be distinguished by reference to 'nature', yet they are clearly artificial environments; they are seen as balancing out the ills of urban living, yet they are integral to it. Indeed, instead of displacement – looking for a space or moment of re-immersion in nature, such as mushrooming (Fine, 1998), climbing (Lewis, 2000) or windsurfing (Dant, 1998) – fitness gyms provide *emplacement*: they supply an interstice, integral to urban living and environment, where the body may be awakened to its nature. Broadly speaking, a number of different dimensions may be considered in looking at the use of space for fitness and sporting reasons. On the one hand, even re-immersion in nature can happen via more rationalized – fitness-like – procedures, such as the current development of Nordic walking (Shove and Pantzar, 2005). Nordic walking combines displacement and emplacement in that paths come complete with expected times, lights and even calorie counters. On the other, phenomena such as parkour for sport, fun and fitness purposes, appear to rely on forms of non-commercial institutionalization akin to sub-cultural formations of an 'anarcho-environmental kind' (Atkinson, 2009). There seems to be a dialectic between the 'immuring of physical activity' and the aspiration to 'go back into the open' (Eichberg, 1998) which finds expression, among other things, in the provision of virtualized natural settings inside ever greener, rounder, more natural-looking gym environments.

Broadly speaking, exercise is said to have a *balancing effect* for the embodied self if taken regularly and if it is the basis of a holistic healthy lifestyle. For one thing, fitness discourse as expressed by fitness magazines and manuals, as well as medical discourse in Italy, the UK and the US, regularly associates keep-fit exercise with food management (Sassatelli, 2010; see also Maguire Smith, 2007; Markula, 2011). More generally and not surprisingly, fitness manuals stress the centrality of keep-fit training with respect to one's own body conduct and knowledge. Fitness fans collude with such public rendering of fitness training. In their words, the body knowledge acquired in the gym helps define body priorities, and bodywork becomes a 'benchmark' for managing other body practices (food, rest, sex, etc.). For fitness fans, the way the body 'looks' and 'responds' to the exercise, and, conversely, the need to be 'ready' for the exercise, become self-monitoring devices. To some extent, this may even have a subversive potential as it may allow for various forms of individual appropriation. Yet, it may also lead to exercise addiction, which is of course an unwanted side-effect of consumer capitalist emphasis on desire and control (Sassatelli, 2007). A therapeutic instrumentality and its display via external bodily signs, such as muscle tone and stamina, are at the core of today's fitness culture. Manuals stress that a fitness workout in the gym is a muscle tonic, it is the most effective medicine which, providing 'strength and energy', helps you relax and sleep better, and more broadly works as a *cure-all practice*. The therapeutic ethic, so central to consumer capitalism (see Furedi, 2004; Hochschild, 2003; Illouz, 2008), is typically accompanied by reference to nature, both in fitness expert discourse and among fitness fans. Reference to nature begs the question of the cultural politics of fitness culture, especially when one addresses its urban characterization and its individualistic rationalization.

Leisure and duty

Time spent in the gym is typically coded as 'leisure' by both expert discourse and actual participants. This is so, even though many gym-goers, especially regular and keen participants, submit themselves to relatively demanding bodywork. Many sociologists have indeed interpreted their role as the de-mystification of the leisure, free-time, cheerful quality attributed to fitness (Glassner, 1992; Le Breton, 1990; Maguire and Mansfield, 1998). In such views, fitness is the example of an allegedly body-loving era which is in fact obsessed with the body to the point that inactivity is not an option and work enters the sphere of leisure. The ultimate objective of many such diagnoses is to maintain that as commercial institutions, gyms are *consumption generation devices*: while mere 'resting' costs nothing, keep-fit exercise needs a paraphernalia of commodities to be carried out. While this is an interesting line to pursue if we are to consider the relative advantages of different systems of leisure provision (commercial or not), it does not allow us to focus seriously on the way the experience of leisure is organized in contemporary consumer societies. Fitness gyms are, to a degree, entertainment industries: they largely manage involvement as fun. In this section, experiences of fun as narrated by a variety of participants are taken seriously and placed in the context of the emotional structure of the fitness scene. The fitness industry runs after clients' pleasures – to the point that clients may be classified by the palette of pleasures provided by fitness and how they manage to respond to it. While regular clients embrace a mix of hedonism and asceticism, estranged and marginal clients, or even gym dropouts, are as much recalcitrant to discipline as they are to 'positive thinking' and institutionally governed 'cheerfulness'. Regulars' vocabulary is rich in pleasure. Pleasure is present in many ways in the gym, tales told by regular and enthusiastic clients. There is surely a vocabulary of duty in regular clients' justifications for training, but they invariably also view fitness as 'recreation', 'entertainment', 'fun', 'diversion', 'play', 'leisure', 'a hobby'.

While play offers the possibility of 'sanctioned exhibition', or the 'opportunity to exhibit attributes valued in the wider social world' (Goffman, 1961: 61; see also Perinbanayagam, 2006), fitness gyms are backstage institutions. In other terms, they allow preparatory activities through which bodies may acquire attributes that are positively valued in other, often decisive, social occasions. Keep-fit exercise is not, in the final analysis, an end in itself: clients' efforts are justified as they produce embodied qualities that appear as external incentives to the activity's progress. However, fitness activities do offer the possibility of temporarily playing down their own seriousness and consequentiality. If games are 'mimeses of the interaction life of human agents who live in organized societies' (Perinbanayagam 2006: 25), fitness is a body discipline that, in a way, mimics games. The *emotional structure* of keep-fit workout – the spirit participants are required to embrace while training, irrespective of their own emotions – is characterized by the same 'surrealistic clarity' (Bateson, 1972) as that of play, only inverting its poles. Fitness reflects and subverts play by trading on its conventional meanings and turning them upside down. Play is a domain of non-serious seriousness, a reality separate from the wider social world by means of a membrane which makes it relatively non-consequential, important in itself and highly absorbing. Exercise, by contrast, is a domain of *serious playfulness*, a field of serious social action that plays down its own seriousness in order to encourage involvement in the proceeding of action. Fitness activities thus rest on a precise paradox: physical exercise is presented as having serious effects on clients' bodies, but is to be carried out as something which, like play, is relevant in itself and allows participants a sanctioned self-centredness. Clients are encouraged to experience workout as a time which has the quality of a meaningful, enjoyable present – in the dual meaning of *heightened perception of the here-and-now* and of *gift*, something special for oneself. As a result, clients may become more seriously involved.

As emotional leaders, trainers have an important role in promoting this emotional structure. Their job is primarily to manage the playfulness of exercise as a local experience, balancing this against its consequential seriousness. This is a delicate task. They must promote a relaxed and informal atmosphere, but must not undermine the ultimate value of bodywork, reducing it to a game with no purpose. They encourage clients by inducing concentration on the movements to be carried out, coding such concentration as 'fun' while simultaneously claiming that exercise will have tangible body 'pay-offs' for those who work hard. In exercise-to-music classes, rhythmic incitements are used as a way to provide a playful twist to the routine. Reference to fatigue is typically matched by cheerful expressions and appreciative comments. What Nina Loland (2000) found in her study of aerobics in Norway – namely a strong emphasis on 'corporeal work ethic' emphasizing the instrumentality of aerobic workout – was matched by a variety of playful, cheerful accompanying expressions in most of the training scene I witnessed across both Italy and Britain. Merely ascetic expressions, such as 'I know this isn't fun ... it shouldn't be fun ... however, it will be good afterward' reported by Loland (ibid.: 120) as spoken from an aerobics instructor during training, were indeed rather infrequent. Common instead was the qualification of training as a pleasurable duty, and not only because it may respond to deferred gratification. To be sure, a 'duty plus treat' logic certainly impinges on the training scene – with exercise being coded as work which allows for relaxation or relaxed sociable consumption afterwards, of food and drink, for example (Spielvogel, 2003; Crossley, 2006), but even more so of the wellness variety (saunas, spas, massages) which is increasingly offered in large, upmarket premises. However, rather more frequently, bodywork is itself coded via reference to involvement, energy and fun. *Cheerfulness* strongly qualifies the emotional fashioning of training as strenuous self-challenging commitment.

Considering the Italian and British fitness scene, and a broader set of activities besides classic aerobics which are now a tiny minority of what is going on in gyms, it is evident that all fitness participants indeed work hard at supporting cheerfulness, coding the sweat produced by physical exertion as effort *and* enthusiasm, considering the repetitiveness of moments as providing energy and exaltation (Sassatelli, 2010). In this sense, fitness also inverts the emotional structure of many contemporary sports and leisure activities which have been understood under the rubric of 'a quest for excitement' (Elias and Dunning, 1986): rather than 'mimetic excitement', fitness training is shaped as excited mimesis and cheerful enactment of a quest. In particular, if we go back to boxing, we find an interesting inversion. As suggested by Loic Wacquant (2003: 94–95), the boxer's 'learning of indifference to physical suffering is inseparable from the acquisition of the form of sangfroid specific to pugilism': the boxer has to develop a gradual resistance to being violently punched at and has to offset his own 'initial reflex of self-preservation that would undo the coordination of movements and give the opponent a decisive advantage'. By and large, what fitness participants display with strenuousness is not so much an indifference to fatigue, pain or fear – such as in the case of boxers which have to become 'resistant to excitement'. And not only because in the fitness gym there is very little physical fear, much less and much different pain, and relatively less fatigue. Leaving new combat keep-fit techniques aside, the hazardous excitement of games organized through strategic conversational structures (Perinbanayagam, 2006), the 'euphoric interaction' of a practice of 'uncertain outcome' (Goffman, 1961: 68) are not there and somewhat need to be artificially recreated. So fitness clients have rather to become – to paraphrase Wacquant – *excited to resist*. They need to display their will to work dutifully and laboriously, to perform their tasks vigorously (in resistance training) or precisely (in postural gymnastic), as fast as required (in aerobics and spinning) or as slow as required (in Pilates). As compared to boxing narratives, fitness fans' comments appear sanitized and ceremonial (Sassatelli, 2012b). Exercising bodies in the fitness gym do sweat and get tired, but indifference has to be acquired more to the ceremonial exposure which workout commands than to actual physical effort or danger. Being looked at may be as tough as fatigue, and taking responsibility for one's own body while accepting its defects is indeed a major, if different, challenge to one's own reflex of self-preservation.

To steer emotions in this direction, quite often gym instructors include themselves in the scene as training partners, and they use phrases such as 'we are really warm now!', 'I'd like to stop, but it's not finished', 'you really made me work hard today!'. They may even draw attention to imperfections in their own body, and they do so to downplay both body ideals and fatigue, to then stress both by complimenting achievement. In doing so they balance the internal meaningfulness of the exercise with its external effectiveness, 'fun' with consequentiality, local experience with embodied performance. Their role in managing the emotional structure of keep-fit exercise accounts for trainers' centrality in the success of any club and has, in many ways, become objectified in fitness culture, in manuals, fitness videos and more broadly in marketing. Current fitness marketing indeed also posits fun as crucial to exercise adherence: managers and trainers are thus encouraged to put emphasis on the provision of entertainment and clients should learn to take charge of their exercise programmes, including the activities that they enjoy most. There is, thus, clearly a normative element in 'fun'. And the institutionally sustained re-framing of training as 'fun' circularly legitimates the fitness gym as a commercial institution.

'Fun' has important rhetorical uses and materializes the cultural politics of fitness. As such, it is an extremely serious element. On one hand, it is geared towards something more than simple entertainment (i.e. body modification, keeping fit). On the other, it produces effects on the perception of what exercise is, and what it offers. Involvement experiences are important for their *effects of reality* (see Goffman, 1961). When coded as 'fun', involvement experiences are also crucial for their *effects of subjectivity* (see Foucault, 1984). They become part of reflexive narrative about self and participation or consumption. So many regulars describe bodywork in the gym as 'not work, but a space which must remain entertaining', something which needs 'commitment' and yet 'you must feel that you are not forced to do it'. The sequence of exercises may thus be described not just an external given, but as something alive in the clients' experiences. Fun is both predicated on, and confirms, the intrinsic relevance of keep-fit exercise. By and large, regular clients are adamant that they have learned to enjoy themselves *and* to use enjoyment in order to continue training. This duality of feeling – which entails both real engrossment and reflexive, even instrumental agency – is not to be understood as evidence of the merely ideological nature of fitness. It is rather a feature of all engrossment or 'flux' experiences in games: as Robert Perinbanayagam (2006) has quite convincingly argued, it becomes the basis of the possibility of stabilizing and narrating the self through games. The successful gym-goers whom I have met both in Italy and Britain mention self-challenge, on the one hand, and informality, on the other, as sources of fun (Sassatelli, 2010). In their words doing fitness is 'entertaining' because it provides a 'moment of concentration: try to do better every day'; because it furnishes a clear arena for self-evaluation: 'to find out how far I can go, and I really like being able to measures my performance'. But, to be fun, self-challenge is coded via the relational and emotional structure of the fitness gym. Courtesy, little informal exchanges during the exercises, a cheerful ambiance which allows for a respectful joke from time to time, the staging of a supportive attitude, all these small interaction devices are managed to make strenuous exertion and self-challenge pleasant. Rather than friendship, carnal fraternity or shared membership in 'a small guild renowned for toughness and bravery' which are the small pleasures of boxing training (Wacquant, 2003: 68), fitness training provides a rather more detached, urban, polished sociability to brighten up the monotony of training with a chance for diversion. But, this is 'real fun' imbued with an entrenched neo-liberal cultural politics, one that is largely based on individualized self-control. This results in the nestling of rationalized instrumentalization into embodied subjectivities that are well adjusted to the neo-liberal variant of consumer capitalism.

Concluding remarks

While the contemporary fitness workout in the gym is clearly man-made, and may require the use of machines and take place indoors in quite artificial environments, it is typically presented as a natural solution to re-establish what is defined as a 'natural balance'. The historian Roberta Park (1994: 62) has shown that what once might have been a measuring instrument, exercise, is now co-extensive with the notion of fitness: 'fitness is often linked to muscularity, the shape of the body, and/or the ability to perform an exercise session of 30 minutes'. This normalizes 'the natural body' as that of physical education and medical science: a body rationalized through the articulation of time and space via precisely codified exercise. By and large, fitness producers and consumers articulate the notions of nature and balance as against the ills of modern, urban life. Fitness fans portray their gym routines as counteracting the increasing levels of emotional stress and physical inactivity accompanying urban living, 'with its cars and pollution', where 'you don't even have to walk up the stairs' and where 'everything is done at breakneck speed', with 'tight schedules', and 'full agendas'. Reference to urban life as inescapably nervy and physically draining may be nuanced slightly differently in local renderings of global fitness discourse, yet this is a culturally overarching and historically deep script in Western culture as documented by many historical studies (Sassatelli, 2010). As typical of consumer capitalist extensions of the commodity frontier to the domains of personal affectivity and embodied selves (Hochschild, 2012), its current variant places emphasis on individual enjoyment and is spoken in an upbeat tone. Gym instructors and trainers all deploy slight variations on the same script: movement is natural, but only organized, disciplined and engrossing movement done regularly and enthusiastically in the gym works well when our daily life in the city has become, as they often comment, 'unnatural'. Their claims on embodied subjectivity extend well beyond the gym: fitness training is naturalized as objective and universal knowledge, something which can help all of us to 'feel our own body' not only 'inside', but also 'outside the gym'.

Fitness gyms are as much opposed to, as they are symbiotic with, hectic urban living. Fitness culture as shaped by consumer capitalism shares, and in many ways intensifies, the latter's fast pace, instrumentality and emphasis on visuality as well as its finely guarded social mixing. It allows people to address their body, but does not allow much strategic self-investment in the highly prescriptive, non-dialogic moves characterizing keep-fit training. It does so in a fashion which resembles the bureaucratic slant of many urban lower-middle to middle-class jobs, peppered with the buzz of personal, creative investment defining what has been called the 'new spirit of capitalism' (Boltanski and Chiappello, 1999) and incidentally getting nourishment from the incorporation of counter-cultural critiques. It goes well with the home–work–home pattern that characterizes the urban, self-contained bourgeois family while providing individualistic refuge from it. It offers space to move, but in an indoor space, sanitized and courteous. It provides for sociability, but one made of casual chats, without the risks of hazardous encounters in the park or sidewalk, rather than one made of more deep emotional attachments.

With all their sense of variety and pluralistic enjoyment fitness gyms are perfect places to study how differences are both effaced and put at work. Much current research, in PCS and beyond, thus addresses the cultural politics of fitness relational to how external, social identities are negotiated. Indeed, a sense of artificiality and rationality in fitness training is fostered by the blurring of external identities; a number of different studies have documented the way ethnicity (Sherman, 2009) and gender (Dworkin, 2003) are deployed, engaged and kept under control in various gym environments. While different gyms may cater for different populations (in terms of ethnicity, class, sexuality and gender, see for example Leeds Craig and Liberti, 2007; Bakken Ulseth and Seippel, 2011), by and large, especially in global fitness chains, the clientele is mixed and gym etiquette is at work. More research is needed on the politics of exercise involvement and adherence in terms of the management of social mixing and division. We need to consider more closely how different external social identities are positioned to manage local ceremonial risks that may be in the way of involvement and self-control, and how differentiated are the visions of involvement and self-control that different people get to develop.

To conclude, fitness training may work for the individual balancing of body and mind-self, but this looks very much like therapeutic, solitary coping rather than some kind of empowerment vis-à-vis the ills of urbanization. On the contrary, fitness culture tends to thrive on a rather toxic image of the city and a limited possibility of appropriation by citizens. Thus, quite often sold as a handy balancing trick, the gym may much less frequently work as such. Furthermore, predicated on the notion of balance, it requires more than a quick therapeutic fix and yet often, at its most commercial edge, training is presented as a quick fix. To be sure, fitness expert discourse is currently growing in reflexivity, participating in a current trend towards *promotional reflexivity* (Sassatelli, 2009). Fitness discourse increasingly acknowledges the contradictions of contemporary urban living, and that the gym may just add to it. However, if we consider with a critical eye, this only suggests that a sense of balance may require quite fundamental choices, other than a simple gym pass or exercise adherence. These are choices that require a more radical, less individualistic take on urban life – from the possibility of reconsidering mobility and spatiality in urban spaces to the way food is provided from rural areas to the city. All in all, how fitness exercise gets naturalized, and sometimes resisted, tell us much of the way we learn as urban consumers to govern ourselves and our bodies, incorporating marginal novelties that drive the extension of the commodity frontier.

References

Atkinson, M. F. (2009) Parkour, Anarcho-Environmentalism and Poiesis. *Journal of Sport and Social Issues*, 33(2), 169–194.

Bakken Ulseth, A. L. and Seippel, Ø. (2011) Fitness, Class and Culture: Social Inequality in Fitness. Nordic Sport Science Forum, idrottsforum.org.

Bateson, G. (1972) *Steps to an Ecology of Mind*. New York: Chandler Publishing Company.

Beck, U. and Gernsheim, E. (2001) *Individualisation*. London: Sage.

Boltanski, L. and Chiappello, E. (1999) *Le nouvel esprit du capitalisme*. Paris: Gallimard.

Bourdieu, P. and Wacquant, L. (2001) Newliberalspeak: Notes on the New Planetary Vulgate. *Radical Philosophy*, 105, 2–5.

Caldwell, L. L. (2005) Leisure and Health: Why is Leisure Therapeutic? *British Journal of Counselling and Psychology*, 1, 7–26.

Crossley, N. (2006) In the Gym: Motives, Meanings and Moral Careers. *Body and Society*, 12(3), 23–50.

Dant, T. (1998) Playing with Things: Objects and Subjects in Windsurfing. *Journal of Material Culture*, 3(1), 77–95.

Dworkin, S. L. (2003) A Woman's Place is in the Cardiovascular Room? Gender Relations, the Body and the Gym. In A. Bolin and J. Granskog (eds), *Athletic Intruders: Ethnographic Research on Women, Culture and Exercise*. Albany, NY: SUNY Press.

Eccles, S. (2002) The Lived Experiences of Additive Consumers. *Journal of Research for Consumer Issues*, 4, 1–17.

Eichberg, H. (1998) *Body Cultures: Essays on Sport, Space and Identity* (eds J. Bale and C. Philo). London: Routledge.

Elias, N. and Dunning, E. (1986) *The Quest for Excitement: Sport and Leisure in the Civilizing Process*. Oxford: Basil Blackwell.

Fine, G. A. (1998) *Morel Tales: The Culture of Mushrooming*. Cambridge, MA: Harvard University Press.

Foucault, M. (1975) *Discipline and Punish*. London: Penguin.

Foucault, M. (1984) *L'usage des plaisirs*. Paris: Gallimard.
Furedi, F. (2004) *Therapy Culture: Cultivating Vulnerability in an Uncertain Age*. London, Routledge.
Glassner, B. (1992) *Bodies: Overcoming the Tyranny of Perfection*. Chicago, IL: Contemporary Books.
Goffman, E. (1961) *Encounters: Two Studies in the Sociology of Interaction*. London: Penguin.
Hochschild, A. R. (2003) *The Commercialization of Intimate Life: Notes from Home and Work*. Berkeley, CA: University of California Press.
Hochschild, A. R. (2012) *The Outsourced Self*. New York: Metropolitan Books.
Illouz, E. (2008) *Saving the Modern Soul: Therapy, Emotions and the Culture of Self-Help*. Berkeley, CA: University of California Press.
Le Breton, D. (1990) *Anthropologie du corps et Modernité*. Paris: PUF.
Leeds Craig, M. and R. Liberti (2007) 'Cause That's What Girls Do: The Making of a Feminized Gym. *Gender and Society* 21(5), 676–699.
Lewis, N. (2000) The Climbing Body: Nature and the Experience of Modernity. *Body and Society*, 6(3), 58–80.
Loland, N. W. (2000) The Art of Concealment in a Culture of Display: Aerobicizing Women's and Men's Experience and Use of Their Own Bodies. *Sociology of Sport Journal*, 17, 111–129.
Maguire, J. and Mansfield, L. (1998) 'No-body's Perfect': Women, Aerobics and the Body Beautiful. *Sociology of Sport Journal*, 15(2), 109–137.
Maguire Smith, J. (2007) *Fit for Consumption: Sociology and the Business of Fitness*. London: Routledge.
Markula, P. (2011) 'Folding': A feminist intervention in mindful fitness. In E. Kennedy and P. Markula (eds), *Women and Exercise: The Body, Health and Consumerism*. Abingdon: Routledge, 60–78.
Molnar, G. and Purdy, L. (2016) *Ethnographies in Sport and Exercise Research*. Abingdon: Routledge.
Park, R. J. (1994) A Decade of the Body: Researching and Writing about the History of Health, Fitness, Exercise and Sport, 1983–1993. *Journal of Sport History*, 21(1), 59–82.
Perinbanayagam, R. (2006) *Games and Sport in Everyday Life. Dialogues and Narratives of the Self*. Boulder, CO: Paradigm Publishers.
Reith, G. (2004) Consumption and its Discontents: Addiction, Identity and the Problems of Freedom. *British Journal of Sociology*, 55(2), 283–300.
Rojek, C. (2000) *Leisure and Culture*. Basingstoke: Palgrave Macmillan.
Sassatelli, R. (2001) Tamed Hedonism: Choice, Desires and Deviant Pleasures. In A. Warde and J. Gronow (eds), *Ordinary Consumption*. London: Routledge, 93–106.
Sassatelli, R. (2007) *Consumer Culture: History, Theory and Politics*. London: Sage.
Sassatelli, R. (2009) Promotional Reflexivity, Irony, Defetishization and Moralization in The Body Shop Promotional Rhetoric. In L. Avellini et al. (eds), *Cultural Studies*. Bologna: I Libri di Emil.
Sassatelli, R. (2010) *Fitness Culture: Gyms and the Commercialization of Discipline and Fun*. Basingstoke, Palgrave Macmillan.
Sassatelli, R. (2012a) Body Politics. In K. Nash and A. Scott (eds), *Blackwell Companion to Political Sociology*, 2nd edn. Oxford: Blackwell, 347–358.
Sassatelli, R. (2012b) Self and Body. In F. Trentmann (ed.), *Handbook of the History of Consumption*. Oxford, Oxford University Press, 633–652.
Sassatelli, R. (2015) Healthy Cities and Instrumental Leisure: The Paradox of Fitness Gyms as Urban Phenomena. *Modern Italy*, 20(3), 237–250.
Sedgwick, E. K. (2003) *Touching Feeling: Affect, Pedagogy, Performativity*. Durham, NC: Duke University Press.
Sherman, J. (2009) The Colour of Muscle: Multiculturalism at a Brooklyn Bodybuilding Gym. In A. Wise and S. Velayutham (eds), *Everyday Multiculturalism*. London: Palgrave Macmillan, 161–176.
Shove, E. and Pantzar, M. (2005) Consumers, Producers and Practices: Understanding the Invention and Reinvention of Nordic Walking. *Journal of Consumer Culture* 5(1), 43–64.
Silk, M. L., Francombe, J. and Bachelor, F. (2009) The Biggest Loser: The Discourse Constitution of Fatness. *Studies in Communication and Culture*, 1(3), 383–403.
Spielvogel, L. (2003) *Working Out in Japan: Shaping the Female Body in Tokyo Fitness Clubs*. Durham, NC: Duke University Press.
Stebbins, R. A. (2009) Serious Leisure and Work. *Sociology Compass*, July.
Wacquant, L. (2003) *Body and Soul: Ethnographic Notebooks of an Apprentice Boxer*. New York: Oxford University Press.
Willis, P. (1979) *Profane Culture*. London: Routledge.

39
SPORT, MIGRATION AND SPACE

Thomas F. Carter

That our bodies move through space is an undeniable reality. In sport, those movements are often disciplined and conform to a specific sport's rules both when in competition and between competitions. The vast majority of attention outside physical cultural studies (PCS), scholarly and other, is paid to how bodies move during sporting contests. Attention is now growing on the movement of people outside competition, most especially their migration from one part of the world to another. How and why people migrate is an age-old question but sport-related migration is a relatively new phenomenon in comparison.

To better understand the movement of sport around the world and how contemporary labor migration coincides with other global processes, international sport migration needs to be analyzed from a context in which it is understood as a social process with its own dynamics that can be summed up in three interrelated principles:

1 the importance of migrant agency embodied in the ways which mobility is produced;
2 the self-sustaining nature of migratory processes that link movement with places as migratory points in sportspeople's lives; and
3 the trend towards structural dependence in the form of regulatory governance designed to control the movements while continuing select, established migratory processes.

Most sport migration studies place the emphasis upon the third of these principles as being *sui generis* generative structures without acknowledging the control of individuals' movements on and off the pitch underpins sport governance. Further, some credence is given to the second, mostly as sustaining already existing networks, and the first principle is almost completely ignored. This first principle needs the greater attention for it is the bodies of the sportspeople, their movements, and the ways in which they engender that movement that feeds the processes, weaves the patterns, and sustains NEOsport infrastructures (Carter, 2011a).

Taking these principles into account, this chapter makes distinctions between movement and migration. Movement is not the equivalent of migration. Migration itself is a particular kind of movement usually understood to involve a multitude of people. Migration, then, is not based on individuals' movements but is usually understood in broader, more sweeping understanding of the movements of populations. Migration is a global phenomenon but who moves, how migrants move and why they move depends on their ability to produce mobility. This conceptual distinction leads to a consideration of the recent rise of the mobilities paradigm and how a concept of mobility speaks to the power relations informing migrants' ability to travel. Following on from that discussion, assumptions about space embedded in analyses of international sport migration are examined. Using the notion of sportscape to understand the shifting conceptual models of space and place, it becomes clear that space and place are not what they are presumed to be. The emphasis on place rather than space helps us to understand migrant knowledges, experiences, and movements of professional sportspeople.

The globality of migration

The heightened awareness of people moving around the globe gives the impression that everyone is rushing about. That no one is staying put. It is commonly presumed our contemporary global era comprises greater migratory movements of people around the world than any preceding moment in time. Of course, there are millions of migrants, but the quantity of people engaged in international migration has not increased; more people migrated in the thirty years surrounding the turn of the twentieth century than at the turn of the twenty-first (Chatterjee, 2004: 83–87). Rather, what has changed is that the control of space by regulatory regimes through which people move has increased enormously over the past century (Koslowski, 2011).

Consequently, there is a significant political dimension to these common understandings of migration. Most often seen as an undifferentiated mass, whether classified as refugees, asylum seekers, or job seekers, the underpinning presumption is that migrants are unskilled, uneducated, impoverished, and often deemed undesirable unless those migrants are coming to fulfill a role the existing populace does not seem to take on. However, sport-related migrants provide a particularly valued form of labor that often is regulated in such a way as to make travel easier (Beaverstock et al., 2010). High-skilled labor migration generates particular kinds of mobility and specific kinds of movements in space, and sport-related migration does so in industry-specific ways. Thus, international sport migrants are valued over other migrants.

Sport-related migration, like all migration, is shaped by a wide array of social, economic, political, and historical factors. One's citizenship, race, gender, family, religion, and sport all help to determine whether one ever becomes an international sport migrant. Growing attention has been on questions of regulatory schema, especially citizenship, and migrants' experiences with these regimes (Carter, 2011a, 2011b). Gender, of course, shapes migratory experiences of women and men in decidedly different ways (Hondagneu-Sotelo, 1994) and Sine Agergaard's attention to these concerns indicate this differential importance within international sport migration (Agergaard, 2008; Agergaard and Botelho, 2011; Agergaard and Tiesler, 2014; Botelho and Agergaard, 2011; Engh and Agergaard, 2015). Race is widely acknowledged within sport-related scholarship but how it shapes international sport migration has only attracted some indirect attention, most particularly in the contexts of African football players traveling to Europe (Cornelissen and Solberg, 2007; Darby, 2011; Poli, 2006) and how Latin American baseball players are labeled by North American professional institutions (Klein, 1995), although there is the rare other example (e.g. Grainger, 2006). Other factors have not really been explored fully, such as migrants' families (Carter, 2007, 2011a: 127–151; Roderick, 2012), and religion (Rial, 2013).

The regulatory developments and seeming ease of high-skilled labor's movement leads to a further misconception regarding migration: that migration is effectively a frictionless movement around a global world – that migration is not bodies moving around in space, or more accurately, from place to place, but bodies moving through a singularly global space. This particular misconception has led to the development of the mobilities paradigm.

Mobility: the movement inherent in the system

To facilitate our understanding of international sport migration, it is important to understand what is meant by mobility. The dominant paradigmatic understanding of mobility asserts that mobility comprises a set of systems that structure the movement of various sets of social objects (Adey, 2009; Creswell and Merriman, 2012; Elliot and Urry, 2010; Urry, 2007). In effect, this paradigm rests upon the same inherent presumptions found within globalization theory while problematizing the nature of movement within the abstract space of the global. Situated within geography and sociology, much of the work on mobility focuses on technologies of mobility, whether that is transport systems (Cwerner et al., 2010), infrastructure (Kingsley and Urry, 2009) or other mobile technologies like mobile phones.

Networked, location-aware technologies certainly facilitate intense forms of social engagement. Their ability to seemingly transcend space through the production of simultaneity transforms space into movement, evoking 'movement-spaces' (Thrift, 2004). These technologies are changing the ways we understand our world, leading Merriman (2012) to question whether such notions of mobility ultimately rely upon conventional epistemologies of space and time. The ideology of globalization underpins such speculations, transmuting space and time as discrete aspects of life into a new merged form of space-time in which space is rendered immaterial, both in terms of one's physical reality and in terms of consequence, and time becomes the everlasting present while past and future lack substance.

This abstract global space exists as some enveloping atmosphere-like space that permeates all, insinuating itself into the tiniest nook or cranny of social life. The array of mobilities invoked by 'spaces of flows' (Appadurai, 1996), and 'liquid modernities' (Bauman, 1998) are ensconced in an amorphous, featureless space. Leading mobilities paradigm thinkers' focus on technologies, especially transport and communication, emphasizes the ways in which mobilities become the systems by which social beings, whether that is people, capital, money, or other entities, all move in this globalized space (Adey et al., 2014). Creswell's definitive formula combining movement, meaning, and power (2006) to distinguish mobility from movement is an appropriate first step. But even his widely cited formula does not shift the fecund ground from which mobility actually is produced. All too often seen as friction-less, effort-less, and more a mental journey than a physical one, the sense emerges that mobility bestows certain forms of social life. Those versions of life, however, eliminate human contingency and the specific cultural contexts in which the conditions for mobility are enacted.

To suggest that one's existence depends on being mobile and that mobility somehow exists outside of one's own life as a systemic set of social structures conflates mobility with personhood and society, respectively. Living beings certainly can move, and movement may be an inherent condition of life, but mobility is not an inherent biological condition. Furthermore, mobility is an aspect of the social conditions in which some people find themselves. The ability to become mobile frequently necessitates that others become immobile. How those relations are contested, formulated, and challenged is part of the intricate power relations within a society but not society in and of itself. Therefore, mobility should not be understood as a system or set of systems within a globalized world but as a kind of social relation, a form of capital that individuals produce in their relationships with specific, sometimes global, sporting institutions.

If mobility is understood as a form of capital, then it becomes rooted in the power relations found within global capitalism. The proliferation of new forms of capital generates new kinds of social relations as Marx thoroughly demonstrated (1992). Yet Marx also demonstrated that capital itself is a peculiar form of social relation that produces the fetishism of commodities;

each fetish obscures the actual relations that lie behind the form of each commodity. Instead of mobility being the systemic, generative structure permitting new social relations, mobility is a form of social relation produced through obscured relationships of power. As a form of capital, mobility manifests via the interrelationships between a number of different social actors all working in concert to produce and control that capital, whether those actors are family members, friends, bureaucrats, state officials, coaches, and other professionals and is used to produce the commodity we know as 'the athlete' within NEOsport (Carter, 2011a).

At stake here is an apparent conflation of mobility with movement. It would be ludicrous to assert that sports people, whether or not athletes, cannot move. Movement is inherent to the practice of sport, although where, when, and how one can move is often dictated and regulated by the strictures of that given sport. But that is movement within the rules of a game. What is not so apparent is that there are rules governing how, when, and where sports people can move outside the field of competition. Movement is also the individual capacity to physically shift from one locality to another. When that movement involves crossing an international border then that is often deemed to be migration. Authorities often attempt to dictate, restrict, and regulate the when, where, and means of effecting any such movement. But not all movement is migration, not all movement is generated via mobility and, most important, not all mobility is migration.

Therefore, mobility is not merely a question of who moves and who does not. Rather, the question revolves around the power to effect specific kinds of movement. How mobility is produced – materially and conceptually – requires asking 'How and why do people move?' The answers manifest in diverse, locally deployed power-geometries, embodied in various forms of social distinction (such as class, race, and gender), help determine who can and cannot travel within a given polity, as well as who is allowed to enter or leave said polity. Mobility, then, is consciously produced out of social relations and is not a result of mechanistic systems (Carter, 2011a, 2014). Thus, mobility is inextricably produced in social relations that transcend boundaries and link seemingly disparate places. The conditions in those places and the relations between them affect migrants' abilities to produce their own mobility but those conditions do not affect migrants' movements. Whether mobility can be produced at all, and the extent to which it can be produced, often results in, but does not determine, conditions of immobility for some even as others generate their own mobility.

Escaping space and emplacing migration

Global space is a placeless, timeless, unchanging, simultaneous present that, by virtue of being everywhere, is nowhere. Migrants do not move through some featureless world; rather, they move through a convoluted array of places governed by various and often overlapping authorities. It is then necessary to understand how those migrants' engagement with these places, most often recognized as states, act to shape their own understandings of specific localities and the dynamic relationships between them. Their ability to move from one locality to another depends on their relationships with the global regimes that attempt to contour how mobility is created and deployed.

A widely cited, significant approach for envisioning how global space might be more comprehensible has been Arjun Appadurai's (1996) invocation of various global -scapes as a means to frame and understand the movements of technologies, finance, information, and peoples around the world. These '-scapes' are different streams or flows in which material move across national boundaries. Indicating deeply inflected historical, linguistic, and political positionings, such amorphous constructs cannot be considered objective since these building blocks constitute historically situated imaginations of the world. Appadurai argues that many of these -scapes are predicated upon Western ideas that emerged from the Enlightenment thereby implying a direct link with civilizational discourses and moralistic value-laden judgments embedded in globalization projects.

Appadurai's uniform, unified, featureless -scapes reduce social differences to banal markers that denote the same manner of difference worldwide thereby reducing all difference to the same kinds of 'global' difference. Such a perspective has been adopted in which 'global sport' has become 'universal' while also engendering the same kinds of 'global' sporting difference (Giulianotti and Robertson, 2007; Maguire, 1999, 2005; Miller et al., 2001; Sage, 2011). This perspective necessitates a view of the world as a singular whole so that a common activity called sport can be seen to be going on everywhere in which it is assumed that its practitioners share identical values, mores, and norms as they engage in global sport. All too often, sport-related migration slips into this global space in which movement is unfettered and frictionless because the global space is an empty, conceptual space in which the realities of everyday, lived experience are situated in national or local spaces and not in the global. Painting pictures of relative ease of movement, readily available wealth, and overall positive experiences, global models whitewash the power relations inherent in any international journey as well as the lived experience of migration.

Appadurai does not talk about 'sportscapes' but the logic of his ethno-, techno-, finance-, media-, and ideoscapes sets up a logical framework for the realization that there must be global sportscapes as well. In this context, the concept of the sportscape, whatever the sport, conjures up an abstract space. If sportscapes are to be understood as specific flows formed out of interwoven movements of mobile persons, technology, media, finance, and ideologies informed by economies of scale, degrees of political control, and localized market rationalities, then any sportscape is as devoid of substance as the overall global space in which such -scapes supposedly exist.

Another version of sportscape evades the all-encompassing void of abstract space. For Bale (2001), a sportscape is a physically demarcated field of competition and the immediate material surroundings that encompass that sports field. Bale openly identifies sportscapes as socially circumscribed spaces completely separate from the natural landscape in which specific activities are staged and performed (Bale, 1994). Nevertheless, an abstract notion of space still underpins Bale's concept as he draws upon theorists for whom space pre-exists human activity (Harvey, 2006; Lefebvre, 1991; Soja, 1989; Tuan, 2001). Space, here, is also abstract but this abstract space is made manifest and is physically experienced by spectators, athletes, and officials moving through that space. As part of the urban fabric, stadiums and other sporting spaces have been a focus of sport-oriented scholars (Bale and Moen, 1995; Friedman et al., 2004; Friedman and Andrews, 2011; Gaffney, 2008; Vertinsky and Bale, 2004) yet analyses of stadiums normally do not move beyond the activities that occur within those physically and socially defined spaces. Thus, bodies move through Bale's sportscapes where playing fields become named stadiums as opposed to the physical topography of global sport that never materializes.

The concept of sportscape does not help us understand migration. For migrants do not move from one space to another or through some abstract space, whether immaterially global or geographically circumscribed. Rather migrants travel from place to place. Typically seen as closed, local, and stable whereas the 'global' is commonly and popularly equated with openness, infinity, and instability, place and globalization have been wrongly treated as separate entities both spatially and analytically (Escobar, 2001). Places are relational, not isomorphic, and the connections between places are multiply specific, simultaneously historical and ephemeral, imagined and lived, and coherent yet constantly contested. Emerging out of the intersections and interactions of concrete social relations, places are enacted (Casey, 2013). The focus on place in relation to the production of mobility makes it necessary to conceive of an alternative to global modes of thinking. Instead of conceiving of places as discrete entities within a global sportscape *à la* Appadurai or as parts of discrete, topographic sportscapes *à la* Bale, it is necessary to distinguish between migratory places and migratory points throughout migrants' lives. As distinct categories, places and points intertwine to create specific patterns of migratory movements.

As outlined elsewhere (Carter, 2013), migratory places are localities, experienced or imagined, that form part of the life narrative of a migrant. The two crucial ones are 'places of origin' and 'places of destination'. A place of origin is the locality a migrant identifies as the place from which one originates. Although often articulated in terms of nationality, especially ethnic-based nationality, places of origin are not assumed to be the equivalent of birthplace or citizenship. A place of destination is the ultimate goal of a migrant's travels. That place may be an immediate goal in some cases, but for others it may be a destination to be reached sometime in the distant future. It is possible that the place of destination is no more than a vague, imagined place or even an assumed return to one's place of origin. Whether defined distinctly and deliberately or vaguely and fuzzily, a migrant may never arrive at one's place of destination.

In contrast to the relative stability of migratory places in the life trajectory of a migrant, migratory points are distinctly multiple and fluid. Points of departure are those localities from which an individual leaves to travel to a new locale. Points of arrival, logically, are those localities at which transnational migrants complete a journey. Tracking these migratory points demonstrates the malleability of migrants' movements evidenced in their multiple points of departure and points of arrival. Points of arrival are distinguishable from places of destination. Places of destination are the intentional, ultimate goal of a migrant, whereas points of arrival are the localities at which a migrant has just finished a journey. Pursuing these movements also allows for tracking the shifting place of destination as a migrant's life experiences accumulate.

While migratory places certainly inform the various routes migrants pursue, it is the *related* local material conditions of migratory points that shape the means by which (and the route undertaken) a particular person will move. These localities are concrete, lived environs, even if only via one's imagination, that directly impact the ways in which people live their lives. Places are the locations of a multiplicity of forms of cultural politics that shape people's varied movements around the world. The strategic forging of migratory points to build one's career in global sport, shaped by some extent by global institutions asserting authority over that particular sport, engenders the production of mobility and thus results in international sport migration.

Concluding remarks

The spectacles, the mega events, and other sporting events will go on. The places where these events occur must have the highly skilled workers on and off the field for such shows to happen. Although athletes move through circumscribed competitive spaces when engaged in sport, they do so in designated places around the world. Their lives are emplaced. To move from place to place requires one to become mobile. Mobility informs how migrants engender their movements and facilitate their move across national borders and through geopolitical space. Understanding how mobility is a product of social relations rather than a power-laden structure shaping movement illuminates migration processes and experiences that earlier globalized formulations cannot quite capture.

Theoretically informed research about international sport migration has evolved: from the initial, groundbreaking 'global sporting arena' (Bale and Maguire, 1994) to global sport (Maguire, 1999) to transnational sport, the ways of conceptualizing the movements of sports professionals around the world. A variety of useful theoretical approaches, from globalization theory, to global commodity chains (Darby, 2011), to network theory (Poli, 2010), to transnationalism (Carter, 2011a), have been used to better explain the seemingly worldwide explosion of sport. Sport's pervasive, everyday, ubiquitous presence gives the appearance of a homogeneous global culture since everyone, everywhere is playing the same game(s). That appearance provides a globalized sense of the world as a singular spatial whole. Yet, there remains, quite simply, no global sense of place.

Much of global sport migration studies still consider place in a spatially demarcated, nested fashion in which the local sits within the national which resides in the regional surrounded by the global. Of course, people continue to construct some sort of boundaries around their places. Nevertheless, these constructs remain grounded in local social practices as do the relations people forge between those places. People do not work their way up through the nested spaces of local, national, regional, and global, they move from one locality. The privileging of global flows and connections means other foundations of social life are in danger of being overlooked (Wilding, 2007). The notion of place as a form of lived and grounded space is political (Lefebvre, 1991) but politics, including global projects, are located in places.

Scholarly approaches to migration are incredibly diverse and the ability to reach across disciplinary boundaries is often difficult (Brettell and Hollifield, 2000). Although there is increased interdisciplinary approaches to such topics (Portes and DeWind, 2008), the disciplinary divides remain. The theoretical stance one takes regarding international sport migration informs the kinds of questions one will ask, the kinds of data one will obtain, and ultimately the kinds of knowledge that will be produced. While the emphasis has been on the global structures of international sport migration, a turn towards the transnational lives of the professionals engaged in this enormous global industry has more recently emerged providing alternative ways of theorizing about sport migration. However scholars choose to frame their work, there remains a great deal more to be done and the debates between the various approaches and the emphases these approaches place on the embodied nature of migration should only further enhance our knowledge of the worldwide movements of sport and the people involved.

References

Adey, Peter (2009) *Mobility*. London: Routledge.
Adey, Peter, Bissel, David, Hannam, Kevin, Merriman, Peter, and Mimi Sheller, eds (2014) *The Routledge Handbook of Mobilities*. London: Routledge.
Agergaard Sine (2008) Elite athletes as migrants in Danish women's handball. *International Review for the Sociology of Sport* 43(1): 5–19.
Agergaard, Sine and Vera Botelho (2011) Female football migration: motivational factors for early migratory processes. In J. Maguire and M. Falcous, eds, *Sport and Migration: Borders, Boundaries and Crossings*, 157–169.
Agergaard, Sine and Nina Clara Tiesler, eds (2014) *Women, Soccer and Transnational Migration*. London: Routledge.
Appadurai, Arjun (1996) *Modernity at Large: Cultural Dimensions of Globalization*. Minneapolis, MN: University of Minnesota Press.
Bale, John (1994) *Landscapes of Modern Sport*. Leicester: Leicester University Press.
Bale, John (2001) *Sport, Space and the City*. Caldwell, NJ: Blackburn Press.
Bale, John and Joseph Maguire, eds (1994) *The Global Sports Arena: Athletic Talent Migration in an Interdependent World*. London: Frank Cass.
Bale, John and Olof Moen, eds (1995). *The Stadium and the City*. Keele: Keele University Press.
Bauman, Zygmunt (1998) *Globalization*. Cambridge: Polity Press.
Beaverstock, Jonathan V., Derudder, Ben, Faulconbridge, James, and Frank Witlox, eds (2010) *International Business Travel in the Global Economy*. Aldershot: Ashgate.

Botelho, Vera L. and Sine Agergaard (2011) Moving for the Love of the Game? International Migration of Female Footballers into Scandinavian Countries. *Soccer and Society* 12(6): 806–819.
Brettell, Caroline B. and Hollifield, James F., eds (2000) *Migration Theory: Talking Across Disciplines*. New York: Routledge.
Carter, Thomas F. (2007) Family Networks, State Interventions and the Experience of Cuban Transnational Sport Migration. *International Review for the Sociology of Sport* 42(4): 371–390.
Carter, Thomas F. (2011a) *In Foreign Fields: The Politics and Experiences of Transnational Sport Migration*. London: Pluto Press.
Carter, Thomas F. (2011b) What Happens while the Official Looks the Other Way? Citizenship, Transnational Sport Migrants and the Circumvention of the State. *Sport in Society* 14(2): 223–240.
Carter, Thomas F. (2013) Re-placing Sport Migrants: Moving beyond the Institutional Structures Informing International Sport Migration. *International Review for the Sociology of Sport* 48(1): 66–82.
Carter, Thomas F. (2014) On Mobility and Visibility in Women's Soccer: Theorizing an Alternative Approach to Sport Migration. In Sine Agergaard and Nina Clara Tiesler, eds, *Women, Soccer and Transnational Migration*. London: Routledge, 161–174.
Casey, Edward S. (2013) *The Fate of Place: A Philosophical History*. Berkeley, CA: University of California Press.
Chatterjee, Partha (2004) *The Politics of the Governed: Reflections on Popular Politics in Most of the World*. New York: Columbia University Press.
Cornelissen, Scarlett and Erik Solberg (2007) Sport Mobility and Circuits of Power: The Dynamics of Football Migration in Africa and the 2010 World Cup. *Politikon: South African Journal of Political Studies* 34(3): 295–314.
Creswell, Tim (2006) *On the Move: Mobility in the Western World*. London: Routledge.
Creswell, Tim and Peter Merriman (2012) *Geographies of Mobilities: Practices, Spaces, Subjects*. Aldershot: Ashgate.
Cwerner, Saulo, Sven Kesselring, and John Urry (2010) *Aeromobilities*. London: Routledge.
Darby, Paul. 2011 Out of Africa: The Exodus of Elite African Football Talent to Europe. In J. Maguire and M. Falcous, eds, *Sport and Migration: Borders, Boundaries and Crossings*. London: Routledge, 245–258.
Elliot, Anthony and John Urry (2010) *Mobile Lives*. London: Routledge.
Engh, Mari Haugaa and Sine Agergaard (2015) Producing Mobility through Locality and Visibility: Developing a Transnational Perspective on Sports Labour Migration. *International Review for the Sociology of Sport* 50(8): 974–992.
Escobar, Arturo (2001) Culture Sits in Places: Reflections on Globalism and Subaltern Strategies of Localization. *Political Geography* 20(2): 139–174.
Friedman, Michael T. and David L. Andrews (2011) The Built Sport Spectacle and the Opacity of Democracy. *International Review for the Sociology of Sport* 46(2): 181–204.
Friedman, Michael T., Andrews, David L., and Michael Silk (2004). Sport and the Facade of Redevelopment in the Postindustrial City. *Sociology of Sport Journal* 21(2): 119–139.
Gaffney, Christopher T. (2008) *Temples of the Earthbound Gods: Stadiums in the Cultural Landscapes of Rio de Janeiro and Buenos Aires*. Austin, TX: University of Texas Press.
Giulianotti, Richard and Roland Robertson (2007) *Globalization and Sport*. Chichester: John Wiley & Sons.
Grainger, Andrew (2006) From Immigrant to Overstayer: Samoan Identity, Rugby, and Cultural Politics of Race and Nation in Aotearoa/New Zealand. *Journal of Sport & Social Issues* 30(1): 45–61.
Harvey, David (2006) *Spaces of Global Capitalism*. London: Verso.
Hondagneu-Sotelo, Pierrette (1994) *Gendered Transitions: Mexican Experiences of Immigration*. Berkeley: University of California Press.
Kingsley, Dennis and John Urry (2009) *After the Car*. Cambridge: Polity Press.
Klein, Alan M. (1995) Headcase, Headstrong, and Head-of-the-Class: Resocialization and Labelling in Dominican Baseball. In M. Malec, ed., *The Social Roles of Sport in the Caribbean*. Amsterdam: Gordon and Breach, 125–154.
Koslowski, Rey (2011) *Global Mobility Regimes*. New York: Palgrave Macmillan.
Lefebvre, Henri (1991) *The Production of Space*. Oxford: Blackwell.
Maguire, Joseph (1999) *Global Sport: Identities, Societies, Civilizations*. Oxford: Polity Press.
Maguire, Joseph (2005) *Power and Global Sport: Zones of Prestige, Emulation and Resistance*. London: Routledge.
Maguire, Joseph and Falcous, Mark, eds (2011) *Sport and Migration: Borders, Boundaries and Crossings*. London: Routledge.

Marx, Karl (1992) *Capital, Volume 1: A Critique of Political Economy*. New York: Penguin.
Merriman, Peter (2012) *Mobility, Space and Culture*. London: Routledge
Miller, Toby, Geoffrey Lawrence, Jim McKay, and David Rowe (2001) *Globalization and Sport*. London: Sage.
Poli, Raffaele (2006) Migrations and Trade of African Football Players: Historic, Geographical, and Cultural Aspects. *Afrika Spectrum* 41(3): 393–414.
Poli, Raffaele (2010) Understanding Globalization through Football: The New International Division of Labour, Migratory Channels and Transnational Trade Circuits. *International Review for the Sociology of Sport* 45(4): 491–506.
Portes, Alejandro and Josh DeWind, eds (2008) *Rethinking Migration: New Theoretical and Empirical Perspectives*. New York: Berghahn.
Rial, Carmen (2013) Banal Religiosity: Brazilian Athletes as New Missionaries of the Neo-Pentecostal Diaspora. *Vibrant* 9(2): 129–158.
Roderick, Martin (2012) An Unpaid Labor of Love: Professional Footballers, Family Life, and the Problem of Job Relocation. *Journal of Sport and Social Issues*, 36(3): 317–338.
Sage, George (2011) *Globalizing Sport: How Organizations, Corporations, Media, and Politics are Changing Sport*. Boulder, CO: Paradigm Publishers.
Soja, Edward W. (1989) *Postmodern Geographies: The Reassertion of Space in Critical Social Theory*. London: Verso.
Thrift, Nigel (2004) Movement-space: Changing Domain of Thinking Resulting from the Development of New Kinds of Spatial Awareness. *Economy and Society* 33(4): 582–684.
Tuan, Yi Fu (2001) *Space and Place*. Minneapolis, MN: University of Minnesota Press.
Urry, John (2007) *Mobilities*. Cambridge: Polity Press
Vertinsky, Patricia and John Bale, eds (2004) *Sites of Sport: Space, Place, Experience*. London: Routledge.
Wilding, Raelene (2007) Transnational Ethnographies and Anthropological Imaginings of Migrancy. *Journal of Ethnic and Migration Studies* 33(2): 331–348.

PART VII

Contexts and sites of embodied practice

40
MIND–BODY RELATIONS

Simone Fullagar

This chapter pursues a line of critical questioning concerning how we come to 'know' the embodied, discursive and biopolitical dimensions of mental health and illness in the context of physical cultures. In terms of a physical cultural studies (PCS) sensibility I situate my engagement with both epistemic and everyday issues of injustice within a feminist context that understands the personal as political. Over the past decade I have explored questions about the cultural formation of 'normal and abnormal' subjectivities in everyday contexts with respect to shifting public discourses about increasing mental health problems. This intellectual inquiry has also been shaped by my family biography that was severely disrupted by the iatrogenic effects of psychiatry in 1950s Australia (Ehrenberg, 2009). My grandmother and uncle (her son) were both diagnosed as 'paranoid schizophrenics' and endured therapeutic treatment that was informed by emerging theories of brain dysfunction, failure of maternal bonding and genealogical impurities. Mental illness was a shameful infliction that brought institutional confinement, over-medication, electric shock treatment and the violation of basic rights. By the 1980s Australian mental health policies embraced the shift to deinstitutionalization as the medical model was increasingly challenged by advocacy and human rights movements that were gathering momentum in the US, Canada and the UK. Thirty years after his 'breakdown' during the pressure of final school exams (he was dux at the time), my uncle moved into a house, learned to cook, manage his own money and began to enjoy the freedom of everyday movement.

Those wasted years of his institutionalized existence offer a stark example of how the minds and bodies of pathologized populations are governed through therapeutic imperatives that seek to restore normality in the pursuit of health. Connecting critical health and sport perspectives Genevieve Rail's keynote at the recent International Sociology of Sport conference in Paris 2015 examined the 'imperative of wellbeing' with respect to how 'other' bodies are positioned, erased through normalized thinking or pathologized as unhappy, dissenting or unapologetic. In his critical work Metzl et al. (2010: 2) have argued that '"health" is a term replete with value judgments, hierarchies, and blind assumptions that speak as much about power and privilege as they do about wellbeing. Health is a desired state, but it is also a prescribed state and an ideological position.' These points echo the radical contextualism informing my PCS approach to mental health that situates biomedical, psychotherapeutic and health promotion intervention practices within a genealogy where truth claims about healing, restoring or optimizing mental health are historicized. Such an approach also makes visible the effects of power–knowledge relations on embodied subjects in order to disrupt the normative and open up other ways of knowing and being.

In writing this chapter my aim is twofold, first to consider how the 'physical' within Physical Cultural Studies has been theorized with respect to questions of mental (ill) health in the context of an historical dualism of mind and body. Second, I explore how the broader cultural, economic and political context of the United Kingdom (UK) has positioned mind–body relations within mental health policy, research, advocacy and practice. It is now commonplace to read that 'exercise is medicine' and I argue that active embodiment has been subsumed within a new *corporeal therapeutics* (with a nod to Nikolas Rose) aimed at ameliorating mental (ill) health. The physically active self is being mobilized through converging mental health discourses to treat and prevent a growing population 'problem'. Depression, for example, has been identified by the World Health Organization (2013) as a growing public health issue that affects about 400 million people (and it is gendered in ways that classify more women as depressed than men). There is a growing body of behavioural research that has identified the benefits of exercise for treating and managing depression (Harvey et al., 2010); however, what is missing is a more nuanced understanding of corporeal experience as social.

What might be the discursive effects of particular manifestations of truth – 'healthy bodies, healthy minds' – on how mental health is embodied within advanced liberalism? The corporeal self is being reimagined and acted upon through a range of somatic discourses about mental (ill) health that emphasize the physical as biological (the neurochemical brain of pharmacology and the physiological self of exercise medicine). While the shift to exercise as medicine may appear to counter the normative treatment of depression through drug therapies, I argue that it is intertwined with the growth of neuroscience and the pharmaceutical imaginary (Jenkins, 2010) that significantly shapes representations of mental (ill) health in the global north. In the next section I turn to my first question about how the embodied mind figures in PCS and what other trajectories of thought about physicality are possible. These are both theoretical and practical concerns about the cultural resources that we have (and desire) to respond in critical and creative ways to the experience of emotional distress in this conjunctural moment.

Mind–body relations in Physical Cultural Studies

Extending a line of reflexive questioning that has recently opened up the knowledge practices of PCS (Atkinson, 2011; Giardina and Newman, 2011; Rich, 2011; Silk and Andrews, 2011; Newman and Giardina, 2014; Pavlidis and Fullagar, 2014; Pavlidis and Olive, 2014; Thorpe, 2014), I am interested in the *limitations and promise* of theorizing physicality in relation to notions of embodied subjectivity. My analysis is focused on these broader epistemological concerns given the lack of specific attention that mind–body relations (and mental health) have received to date within the emerging debates around PCS as an inter- or transdisciplinary project (see Thorpe, 2014). The absence of critical attention paid to the embodied mind and mental (ill) health raises the question of whether the PCS imaginary has simply reversed the mind–body dualism rather than troubling the hierarchical relation? Bodies are the object and subject of contextual analysis with respect to different physical cultures, yet the politics of our embodied entanglement with emotion, affect or mind are often left unsaid. As Andrews and Silk (2015) argue, PCS is a fluid set of knowledge practices that can enable a theoretical and political responsiveness to emerging social problems. As an emergent field of study there is a danger of being hampered by recent didactic exchange that seeks to define (ironically from a universalized, disembodied and rather masculine standpoint) the object and subject of physical culture, right or wrong 'sides' and paradigmatic boundaries as well as new 'mandates' for praxis-oriented critique. I am concerned with the limiting way that 'bodies' or 'the body' have often been conjured up as fleshy physical containers in which resides a unified, rational subject that is acted upon and/or resists various neoliberal power relations. Yet, I am also drawn to the promise of PCS in terms of the creatively critical, relational and visceral ethos that can open different ways of knowing and disrupt manifestations of truth concerning embodied subjectivity. As a counter-move, this handbook opens up different intellectual trajectories for thinking through physicality.

The diversity of intellectual biographies in the handbook highlights how PCS-identified scholars engage in a politics of embodied knowledge that far exceeds the critique of an historical sociological imagining of sport. Having been drawn to PCS from the multidisciplinary field of leisure studies and the cultural turn within Australian post-structuralist sociology (Probyn, 2005; Game, 1991), I feel ambivalent about identifying with an origin story that seeks to heroically replace the epistemic object of 'sport' with that of 'physicality' (Cauldwell, 2011). My feminist sensibilities and long engagement with embodiment through feminist philosophy lead me to consider whether privileged claims are another masculine appropriation of 'the body'? This is also a reflexive question about the intellectual genealogies of different fields that appear politically aligned with PCS but start with a different set of problematizations (gender studies and disability studies, for example). On the one hand, by privileging the 'physical' PCS has *aligned* with feminist theories that trouble the assumed value of rationality, objective logic and self-present knowing that historically underpins the mind–body, masculine–feminine, reason–emotion dualisms. We see this politics in Giardina and Newman's (2011: 37) engagement with the physicality of the PCS project that 'reemphasizes the body's emancipatory potential through bodily praxis'. They position PCS as an intellectual meeting point for a diverse body politics and echo the sentiment of feminist philosophers of the body who argued for a shift in knowledge produced 'about' women's bodies to knowledge created 'through' writing the embodiment of gender as a force for change (Grosz, 1994). Although, beyond the work of feminists themselves in PCS there has been little deeper engagement with the extensive and diverse theoretical debates across feminist philosophy, cultural theory, sociology and critical psychology (Braidotti, 2013; Blackman, 2012; Wetherell, 2012; Probyn, 2005; Grosz, 1994).

Productive tensions are important in shaping PCS as different intellectual histories and fields enable points of engagement across diverse embodied experiences, subject positions, technologies and institutional practices (Silk and Andrews, 2011). As Newman and Giardina (2014: 421) suggest, physical movement is a central concern as 'there is biopolitics in how the body moves, why it moves, and how we come to make sense of that movement'. However, unless we assume a voluntaristic subject or functional physicality we are faced with the task of understanding the complex forces of movement that produce subjectivity as a biopsychosocial assemblage – thoughts, emotions and affects – that we indeed try to make sense of through the discourses available to us (Ahmed, 2004; Rose, 2007; Cvetkovich, 2012; Braidotti, 2013).

A PCS ethos that identifies the shifting conditions of possibility for contestation and change offers a means of critically examining the embodied formation of the 'inner world' of the self that we have come to 'know' through the rise of the psy-disciplines. Without a more critical thinking through of mind–body relations we lack any comprehension of how the everyday emotional lives (injustices and suffering) of (bio)citizens are shaped by normalized imperatives and forces of global capital. Hence, mental health problems are all too often imagined, felt and represented as 'private troubles' (chemical imbalances and personal failings) (Ehrenberg, 2009), rather than understood as 'public feelings' (Cvetkovich, 2012) that are shaped within the nexus of culture, power and inequality. Hence, there is a need for critical exploration of how sport, exercise and other physical cultures are increasingly positioned as 'good' for mental health. As embodied practices they are also sites of subjectification through which the exterior world is enfolded into the self with particular effects and affects.

By neglecting the complex mind–body, reason–emotion and social–biological interrelationships, there is a danger that PCS scholars will overlook the power–knowledge relations that shape cultural notions of health and mental health that also map across subject positions of normal–abnormal, masculine–feminine, white–black, expert–patient. At the heart of a critical perspective on mental health is the issue of the cultural (il)legitimacy afforded to particular forms of knowledge about sport, physical activity and exercise (policy, self-help, biomedical) and whose voices are privileged (citizens, experts, advocate organizations) (Cvetkovich, 2012). Newman's (2013: 400) call to move PCS beyond the desire for an embodied form of post-Enlightenment reason and towards an 'ecology of a kinesis affect' does promise to open up new trajectories and methods. Yet, curiously Newman overlooks the extensive body of work on cultural theories of affect and feminist trajectories that have pursued an embodied politics of knowledge (and with a significant contribution to rethinking the corporeality of mental 'illness', see Cvetkovich, 2012; Blackman, 2012). Of particular relevance here is Rosi Braidotti's (2013: 100) rethinking of an 'ontological relationality' that explores the formation of subjectivity through multiple desires and affects that connect culture, biology and technology through 'intelligent flesh and an embodied mind'. While there is not space to do justice to the extensive literature on affect and post-humanism, I would like to highlight the rich potential for PCS to engage with new theorizations of the subject as somatic, contingent and relational in a far broader sense (non-human nature, technology). Without a further exploration of physicality there is a danger that 'the body' within PCS will remain a rather static object of analysis in ways that marginalize other relational and inseparable dimensions of subjectivity, such as mind and emotion or affect.

PCS research is also profoundly affective in terms of how we are moved by injustices, contradictions and possibilities for change. The contradictions of performing feminine subjectivity that were evident in my qualitative research into depression and recovery have powerfully shaped the way that I approach the question of physicality. The women in our Australian study articulated the depths of their little-heard social suffering through depression in terms of embodied metaphors (heaviness, numbness, trapped in a black hole, feeling the weight of the world) (Fullagar and O'Brien, 2012). Their stories also spoke back to the dominant therapeutics of pharmacology and psy-discourses through visceral responses that voiced subjugated knowing. When asked about the everyday experiences that significantly enabled their recovery (beyond biomedical and psy-expertise) they identified a host of practices from swimming, gardening, team sport, yoga, walking, running that were active, creative and connected. Active embodiment worked for many as a counter-depressant and was vital to their sense of 'feeling alive' again (Fullagar, 2008b). Yet, these mind–body-affect relations were not simple 'physical activities' nor were they stable nor easily pinned down as some kind of 'cure' for depression. Rather, women's diverse stories of understanding their own mental (ill) health in the context of gender relations opened up a discursive space to explore everyday practices that sustain and undo particular experiences of subjectivity in the context of normalized neurochemical selfhood.

While mind–body relations have been largely absent in PCS theorizing there is an emergent literature that is broadly aligned with a PCS sensibility and critically explores the cultural nuances of embodied experiences of mental health. In terms of cultural difference Jette and Vertinsky (2011) question the limits of a normalized whiteness in mental health discourses. They identified how Western notions of self-responsibility for physical health were less dominant among older Chinese immigrant women in Canada. While the neoliberal imperative to manage oneself was not strong, mental health was still steeped in the socio-political context of Chinese culture where exercise was a 'way to regain health/balance and to improve their emotional state' (ibid.: 283). In a different Canadian study on immigrant women's mental health and physical activity Lee et al. (2014) identified the limitation of policy discourses within immigration, sport and physical activity and the value of participatory methods opened up a space for alternative voices to contribute legitimate knowledge. These are several examples of an emergent literature that aligns well with PCS as scholars offer a more nuanced understanding of the complex material and discursive forces shaping embodied subjectivity through diverse physical cultures (Lafrance, 2011; Carless and Douglas, 2012; Smith, 2013; Caddick, et al., 2015; Cauldwell, 2014). Jane Cauldwell writes a powerful autoethnographic account of feeling blue and provides a counter-narrative to make visible the mundane pleasures of active embodiment that are intertwined with the silence and stigma surrounding sportwomen's experience,

> accent on timing and duration is no surprise given that the dominant cultural practices of sport and physical activity aim to promote achievement and success through measurement of time. I avoid this framing because, for me, highly structured plans of progression have forged a form of personal stoicism, which on reflection served to mask my desperate emotional landscapes. Instead, I consider the routine and sustained physical activity of rowing (on an indoor-gym machine) as a habitual companion to feelings of low affect. Despite echoing the repetitions characteristic of intense negative rumination, the sequential rowing motion opens the possibilities for bodily pleasures found within the mundane.
>
> *(Cauldwell, 2014: 313)*

The emergent literature in this area reveals how minds, bodies and emotions are experienced in critical and productive ways that emphasize the importance of locating physicality within a cultural context, rather than an individualized corporeal therapeutics where 'expert' knowledge prevails.

The rise of a new corporeal therapeutics: exercise as medicine

Extending insights from scholarship on the biopolitics of mental health I turn to consider how mental (ill) health is rendered thinkable in terms of a form of somatic selfhood that privileges active physicality. Contemporary mental health policy, practice and research positions physical activity as a lifestyle intervention that has become part of what I refer to as a *corporeal therapeutics* of wellbeing within public mental health. We are urged to constantly improve our wellness, active lifestyles and sense of happiness, while balancing mind and body, work and life through a desire to prevent illness, improve productivity (reducing the burden of disease and profitability) and thus be valued as self-managing citizens. Although there is nothing new about the moral imperative to work on the body and self in the name of health (Fullagar, 2002), there is a noticeable deployment of biomedical metaphors that link scientific expertise and a notion of individual agency that is expressed through active physicality (behaviours and choices free of social context). Recently the Academy of Medical Royal Colleges (2015: 5) in the UK framed the value of exercise as a practice that can be prescribed by medical experts to cure ill health, 'the message is simple. Exercise is a miracle cure too often overlooked by doctors and the people they care for.' The promotion of physical activity for good mental health has been incorporated into UK policy (Department for Health, 2011). There has also been a shift in the recent House of Commons Health Committee Report (2015: 7) where physical activity is repositioned from an instrumental means of reducing obesity and to an activity that promotes a range of mind–body benefits including 'good mental wellbeing'. In terms of the translation of research and policy into treatment practices, the National Institute for Health and Care Excellence (2009) guidelines recommend structured group exercise as part of their evidence base for lifestyle interventions for depression. The National Health Service working through local authorities (and third party providers as part of the shift to privatization) provides a range of individualized 'exercise on prescription' and 'social prescribing' programmes for patients diagnosed with depression or experiencing social isolation and those who are 'frequent attenders' at GP surgeries. While these examples suggest that there is some state provision of exercise-based interventions, the economic and moral imperative extends the individual responsibility for physical activity and health, to mental health and wellbeing. Curiously the discursive framing of 'exercise as medicine for the soul' simplifies and renders invisible the complex issue of agency and the 'social determinants' of mental health that are well recognized (also impacting upon participation in exercise via the expert constructions of 'adherence and compliance') (Friedli, 2012). Despite the rhetoric of person-centred care and consumer-focused health that pervades the logic of care within advanced liberalism in the UK, there is a clear shift from the rights of the person to access state support to the responsibility to manage one's condition and maintain an active lifestyle with 'expert guidance'. The rise of exercise as medicine is situated within the broader policy context of what Hunter et al. (2010: 234) have called lifestyle drift, 'whereby governments start with a commitment to dealing with the wider social determinants of health but end up instigating narrow lifestyle interventions on individual behaviours, even where action at a governmental level may offer the greater chance of success'. In the context of mental health, the phenomenon of lifestyle drift is also shaped by the contemporary intersection of two forms of expertise – exercise science and neuroscience.

In response to new public health concerns about 'lifestyle diseases' an epistemic optimism has fuelled the growth of the health and exercise science research (physical activity promotion, exercise physiology, behaviour change psychology). Through the identification of specific biological processes, dose-response rates, behavioural triggers and measurable benefits of physical activity, the new exercise sciences seek to establish a positivist evidence base that will be recognized alongside the authority of medical knowledge (Piggin and Bairner, 2016; Neville, 2013). While there is conflicting evidence about the specific kinds of health and wellbeing outcomes that structured exercise can afford people experiencing mental ill health, there is a general consensus in this growing literature and policy that physical activity is beneficial for prevention and recovery (Harvey et al., 2010). Nikolas Rose (2007: 26) makes a compelling point about new public health imaginaries around somatic and neurochemical notions of personhood where 'exercise, the corporeal vitality of the self has become the privileged site of experiments with the self'. The corporeal self is being reimagined and acted upon through a range of somatic discourses about mental (ill) health that emphasize the physical as biological (the neurochemical brain of pharmacology and the physiological self of exercise medicine). While the shift to exercise as medicine may appear to counter the normative treatment of depression through drug therapies, I argue that knowledge production is intertwined with the growth of neuroscience and thus has implications for extending rather than questioning the pharmaceutical imaginary (Jenkins, 2010).

There is a large body of critical work that identifies how psychiatric classifications of mental illness work to *produce* a range of disorders and individualized pathologies that position biocitizens as abnormal, dysfunctional and unproductive individuals (Foucault, 2003; Ehrenberg, 2009). Rose's (2007) careful analysis illustrates how psy-discourses intersect with the economic and political rationalities of advanced liberalism to produce new forms of 'somatic subjectivity', and with the rise of brain science we have entered an era of 'neurochemical' selfhood (Fullagar, 2008b, 2009; Rose and Abi-Rached, 2013). Neuroscience has significantly influenced how mental illnesses are conceived of as biological problems and treated with drugs, electroconvulsive treatment or other forms of deep brain stimulation (vagus nerve stimulation, repetitive transcranial magnetic stimulation, magnetic seizure therapy).

The molecular focus of neuroscience also permeates popular discourses and mental health promotion where the effects of exercise are identified as acting through and upon our physicality. In 2015 you can read on the UK Mental Health Foundation website (www.mentalhealth.org.uk) that, 'Research has shown that exercise releases chemicals in your brain that make you feel good – boosting your self-esteem, helping you concentrate as well as sleep, look and feel better'. To extend Rose's (2007) argument about the molecular gaze of neuroscience, I suggest that the shift towards understanding the self in terms of molecular or neurochemical changes in the brain, is converging with a figure of the mobile body as organism (a mobile biopsychosocial assemblage, Braidotti, 2013). Changing the embodiment of mental ill health through exercise is conceived at the cellular level and through behaviours that move the whole body through instrumental relationships (dose–response) that aim to facilitate the self-management of depression.

The positioning of sport, exercise and physical activity within this new corporeal therapeutics is promising in one sense as it is a move away from pharmacological interventions that have been shown to be problematic in so many ways (Fullagar and O'Brien, 2013; Jenkins, 2010). However, it is a move that remains firmly within the scientific grip of biomedicine and as such the experience of embodied (in)activity is reduced to an individualized, asocial context. Exercise becomes good medicine for all, providing a moral imperative for the expansion of expertise that fuels a particular policy and practice industry. Critical engagement with this discourse is vital to identify the knowledge 'gaps' and other forms of 'evidence' and ways of knowing that can incorporate the complexity of experience as shaped through material–discursive–affective processes. Unpacking key assumptions underpinning such truth claims can provide a deconstructive moment to open up debate about researcher reflexivity, the limits of knowledge, the politics of truth and the profoundly social context of active embodiment. If medical ethics require practitioners to 'do no harm', then how might the disciplines embracing exercise as medicine consider the negative implications of active embodiment?

One of the major assumptions within the 'exercise is medicine' agenda is the normalized view of sport and physical activity as 'good' for the mental health of everyday and elite participants. Yet, the issues of over-training, compulsive exercising, post-elite career identity loss, performance anxiety, eating disorders and body shame abound (Caddick, Smith and Phoenix, 2015; Burrows and Sinkinson, 2014; Smith, 2013; Hughes and Leavey, 2012). Sport is a site of exclusion of all kinds where normalized masculine norms of toughness, invincibility and competitiveness contribute to a culture that stigmatizes 'failure' and reinscribes hegemonic ideals (Spandler and McKeown, 2012). A number of sport organizations (Football Association, Time to Change campaign) are attempting to collectively act to address stigma particularly in relation to masculine norms that prevent men from seeking help (The Mental Health Charter for Sport and Recreation, UK, www.sportandrecreation.org.uk/policy/campaigns-initiatives/the-mental-health-charter-for-sport-and-recre). While issues of over-exercising and the desire for bodies that are thin or heterosexy are well documented in feminist critiques (Francombe, 2014; Rich and Evans, 2013), they appear less recognized as sites of change to address mental health within sport and recreation organizations or research (McMahon, Penney and Dinan-Thompson, 2012; Fullagar, 2008a; Fullagar and Brown, 2003). Policy and practice 'solutions' to mental health problems that involve sport and physical activity have largely ignored the complexity of social context, diagnostic classification and thus participate in the expansion of healthism that regulates active minds and bodies in particular ways (Lupton, 2012; Crawford, 2006).

Concluding remarks

Across the spectrum of 'disorders' from 'enduring mental illness' (schizophrenia or bipolar) to 'common mental health issues' (depression or anxiety), the proliferation of medical, psychological and lifestyle treatments point towards the need for cultural analyses of emotional distress and wellbeing. Mental (ill) health is profoundly embodied as a manifestation of social suffering and diverse cultural meaning about mind–emotion–body relations (Harrington, 2008; Cvetkovich, 2012; Trivelli, 2014). This cultural framing of subjectivity remains undervalued and difficult to articulate within the biomedical apparatus of care/cure and promotion/prevention frameworks that are steeped in an ethos of individualized responsibility for physical and emotional wellbeing (Crawford, 2006; Bendelow, 2010). Mental health and illness are contested terms and the authority of research and policy also needs to be understood in relation to a range of publics that include activist websites, charity campaigns and survivor networks across a range of sites, spaces and practices as they all converge through an assemblage of wellbeing (Atkinson, 2013). Artist Justine Cooper parodies drug consumption in her critical illustration of how pharmaceuticalization is changing our understanding of (ab)normality as we are urged to desire particular relations to self (attractive, productive, unproblematic). Her website advertises a fictitious drug that promises idealized wellbeing, 'HAVIDOL: when more is not enough. HAVIDOL is the first and only treatment for dysphoric social attention consumption deficit anxiety disorder DSAC-DAD' (Cooper, 2009). The meaning and mobilization of mental health and illness categories, identities and technologies is ongoing as evidenced in the rise of the anti-psychiatry and 'mad' social movements (for example, the hearing voices network; LeFrançois, Menzies and Reaume, 2013). They articulate an emancipatory politics that values difference, lived experience as a form of expertise and self-defined notions of life, identity and recovery in the context of individual and collective notions of wellbeing, human rights and health service provision.

In this chapter I have argued that physical activity, sport and exercise programmes can be understood as part of an emerging *corporeal therapeutics* that brings together scientized expertise and an individual lifestyle orientation in new public mental health discourse. This shift appears to offer a non-pharmacological alternative that may contribute to improve quality of life for individuals, but the traces of new modes of neurochemical selfhood persist through the discourse of exercise as medicine. Solutions are highly individualized, ignore questions of social injustice and legitimize professional knowledge over diverse lived experiences. With the growth of community-based treatment and recovery-oriented (exercise prescription) programmes (inclusive sport) that have been funded by the State or charities there are tensions emerging in the current political context of intensified 'austerity'. Within the UK, legislative changes in 2013 allocated greater responsibility for public health to local governments (Health and Wellbeing Board, Clinical Commissioning Groups; Marks, 2015). At the same time local authorities are working with the effects of Conservative Government budget cuts of 40 per cent over the past five years (with more cuts announced in 2015). The vision of a physically active, mentally healthy, economically productive and self-governing citizenry exists alongside the closure of leisure centres, long waiting lists for community mental health support, increasing user-pays orientation in physical activity provision and reduced staff in sport and recreation delivery (Parnell, Millward and Spracklen 2014). These everyday and theoretical tensions open up possibilities for deeper conversations and more sophisticated analyses of how physicality is deployed in the name of health and wellbeing. Within the context of an emerging Physical Cultural Studies field the words of Rosi Braidotti (2013: 100) can help us think of physicality as 'intelligent flesh and an embodied mind'.

References

Academy of Medical Royal Colleges, 2015. *Exercise: The miracle cure and the role of the doctor in promoting it.* London: Academy of Medical Royal Colleges. Available from www.aomrc.org.uk/general-news/exercise-the-miracle-cure.html.
Ahmed, S., 2004. *The cultural politics of emotion.* Edinburgh: Edinburgh University Press.
Andrews, D. and Silk, M. 2015. Physical cultural studies on sport. In R. Guilianotti (ed.). *The Routledge Handbook of the Sociology of Sport* (pp. 83–93). London: Routledge.
Atkinson, M., 2011. Physical cultural studies [Redux], *Sociology of Sport Journal*, 28(1), 135–144.
Atkinson, S., 2013. Beyond components of wellbeing: the effects of relational and situated assemblage. *Topoi*, 32(2), 137–144.
Bendelow, G., 2010. Emotional health: challenging biomedicine or increasing health surveillance? *Critical Public Health*, 20(4), 465–474.
Blackman, L., 2012. *Immaterial Bodies: Affect, Embodiment, Mediation.* London: Sage.
Braidotti, R., 2013. *The posthuman.* Cambridge: Polity Press.
Burrows, L. and Sinkinson, M., 2014. Mental health in corporeal times. In K. Fitzpatrick and R. Tinning, eds, *Health Education: Critical Perspectives.* London: Routledge, 157–168.
Caddick, N., Smith, B. and Phoenix, C., 2015. Male combat veterans' narratives of PTSD, masculinity, and health. *Sociology of Health and Illness*, 37(1), 97–111.
Carless, D. and Douglas, K., 2012. The ethos of physical activity delivery in mental health: a narrative study of service user experiences. *Issues in Mental Health Nursing*, 33(3), 165–171.
Cauldwell, J., 2011. Sport feminism(s): narratives of linearity? *Journal of Sport and Social Issues*, 35(2), 111–125.
Cauldwell, J., 2014. 'Feeling blue': the ordinary pleasures of mundane motion. *Qualitative Research in Sport, Exercise and Health*, 7(3), 309–320.
Cooper, J., 2009. HAVIDOL. Available from http://havidol.com (accessed 6 July 2015).
Crawford, R., 2006. Health as a meaningful social practice. *Health*, 10(4), 401–420.
Cvetkovich, A., 2012. *Depression: a public feeling.* Durham, NC: Duke University Press.
Department of Health, 2011. *No health without mental health: a cross-government mental health outcomes strategy for people of all ages.* London: UK Government.
Ehrenberg, A., 2009. *Weariness of the self: diagnosing the history of depression in the contemporary age.* Montreal: McGill-Queen's Press.
Foucault, M., 2003. *Abnormal: lectures at the College de France 1974–75* (trans. G. Burchell). London: Verso Books.
Francombe, J., 2014. Learning to leisure: femininity and practices of the body. *Leisure Studies*, 33(6), 580–597.
Friedli, L., 2012. Mental health, resilience and inequalities: a social determinants perspective. *European Psychiatry*, 27(Supplement 1), 1–7.
Fullagar, S., 2002. Governing the healthy body: discourses of leisure and lifestyle within Australian health policy. *Health*, 6(1), 69–84.
Fullagar, S., 2008a. Leisure practices as counter-depressants. *Leisure Sciences*, 30(1), 1–18.
Fullagar, S., 2008b. Sites of somatic subjectivity: e-scaped mental health promotion and the biopolitics of depression. *Social Theory and Health*, 6, 323–341.
Fullagar, S., 2009. Negotiating the neurochemical self: anti-depressant consumption in women's recovery from depression. *Health*, 13(4), 389–406.
Fullagar, S. and Brown, P., 2003. Everyday temporalities: leisure, ethics and young women's emotional wellbeing. *Annals of Leisure Research*, 6(3), 193–208.
Fullagar, S. and O'Brien, W., 2012. Immobility, battles, and the journey of feeling alive: women's metaphors of self-transformation through depression and recovery. *Qualitative Health Research*, 22(8), 1063–1072.
Fullagar, S. and O'Brien, W., 2013. Problematizing the neurochemical subject of anti-depressant treatment: the limits of biomedical responses to women's emotional distress. *Health*, 17(1), 57–74.
Game, A., 1991. *Undoing the social: towards a deconstructive sociology.* Milton Keynes: Open University Press.

Giardina, M. D. and Newman, J. I., 2011. What is this 'physical' in physical cultural studies. *Sociology of Sport Journal*, 28(1), 36–63.

Grosz, E., 1994. *Volatile bodies: towards a corporeal feminism*. Sydney: Allen & Unwin.

Harrington, A., 2008. *The cure within: a history of mind–body medicine*. New York: Norton.

Harvey, S. B., Hotopf, M., Øverland, S. and Mykletun, A., 2010. Physical activity and common mental disorders. *The British Journal of Psychiatry*, 197(5), 357–364.

House of Commons Health Committee Report. 2015. *Impact of physical activity and diet on health*. Sixth Report of Session 2014–15. HC845. London: The Stationery Office.

Hughes, L. and Leavey, G., 2012. Setting the bar: athletes and vulnerability to mental illness. *The British Journal of Psychiatry*, 200(2), 95–96.

Hunter, D., Popay, J., Tannahill, C. and Whitehead, M., 2010. Getting to grips with health inequalities at last? Marmot review calls for renewed action to create a fairer society. *British Medical Journal*, 340(c684), 323–324.

Jenkins, J., ed., 2010. *The pharmaceutical self: the global shaping of experience in an age of psychopharmacology*. Santa Fe, NM: School of Advanced Research Press.

Jette, S. and Vertinsky, P., 2011. 'Exercise is medicine': understanding the exercise beliefs and practices of older Chinese women immigrants in British Columbia, Canada. *Journal of Aging Studies*, 25(3), 272–284.

Lafrance, M. N., 2011. Reproducing, resisting and transcending discourses of femininity: a discourse analysis of women's accounts of leisure. *Qualitative Research in Sport, Exercise and Health*, 3(1), 80–98.

Lee, D. S., Frisby, W. and Ponic, P., 2014. Promoting the mental health of immigrant women by transforming community physical activity. In L. Greaves, A. Pederson and N. Poole, eds., *Making It Better: Gender Transformative Health Promotion*. Toronto: Canadian Scholars' Press, 111–122.

LeFrançois, B. A., Menzies, R. and Reaume, G., 2013. *Mad matters: a critical reader in Canadian mad studies*. Toronto: Canadian Scholars' Press.

Lupton, D., 2012. *Medicine as culture: illness, disease and the body*. London: Sage.

Marks, L., 2015. *Governance, commissioning and public health*. Bristol: Policy Press.

McMahon, J., Penney, D. and Dinan-Thompson, M., 2012. Body practices – exposure and effect of a sporting culture? Stories from three Australian swimmers. *Sport, Education and Society*, 17(2), 181–206.

Metzl, J., Kirkland, A. and Kirkland, A. R. (eds), 2010. *Against health: how health became the new morality*. New York: NYU Press.

National Institute for Health and Care Excellence, 2009. *Depression in adults: recognition and management*. London: The Stationery Office.

Neville, R. D., 2013. Exercise is medicine: some cautionary remarks in principle as well as in practice. *Medicine, Health Care and Philosophy*, 16(3), 615–622.

Newman, J. I., 2013. Arousing a [post-]Enlightenment active body praxis. *Sociology of Sport Journal*, 30(3), 380–407.

Newman, J. I. and Giardina, M. D., 2014. Moving biopolitics. *Cultural Studies ↔ Critical Methodologies*, 14(5), 419–424.

Parnell, D., Millward, P. and Spracklen, K., 2014. Sport and austerity in the UK: an insight into Liverpool 2014. *Journal of Policy Research in Tourism, Leisure and Events*, 7(2), 200–213.

Pavlidis, A. and Fullagar, S., 2014. *Sport, Gender and Power: The Rise of Roller Derby*. Farnham: Ashgate.

Pavlidis, A. and Olive, R., 2014. On the track/in the bleachers: authenticity and feminist ethnographic research in sport and physical cultural studies. *Sport in Society*, 17(2), 218–232.

Piggin, J. and Bairner, A., 2016. The global physical inactivity pandemic: an analysis of knowledge production. *Sport, Education and Society*, 21(2), 1–17.

Probyn, E. 2005. *Blush: Faces of Shame*. Minneapolis, MN: University of Minnesota Press.

Rail, G., 2015. Keynote address. The wellbeing imperative: On bio-others, rescue missions and social justice, *International Sociology of Sport World Congress*, Paris, 7–12 June, 2015.

Rich, E., 2011. Exploring the relationship between pedagogy and physical cultural studies: the case of new health imperatives in schools. *Sociology of Sport Journal*, 28(1), 64–84.

Rich, E. and Evans, J., 2013. Physical culture, pedagogies of health, and the gendered body. In: D. L. Andrews and B. Carrington, eds., *A Companion to Sport*. Oxford, UK: John Wiley and Sons, 179–195.

Rose, N., 2007. *The politics of life itself: biomedicine, power and subjectivity in the twenty-first century*. Princeton, NJ: Princeton University Press.

Rose, N. S. and Abi-Rached, J. M., 2013. *Neuro: the new brain sciences and the management of the mind*. Princeton, NJ: Princeton University Press.

Silk, M. L. and Andrews, D. L., 2011. Toward a physical cultural studies. *Sociology of Sport Journal*, 28(1), 4–35.

Smith, B., 2013. Disability, sport and men's narratives of health: a qualitative study. *Health Psychology*, 32(1), 110–121.
Spandler, H. and McKeown, M., 2012. A critical exploration of using football in health and welfare programs: gender, masculinities, and social relations. *Journal of Sport and Social Issues*, 36(4), 387–409.
Thorpe, H., 2014. Moving bodies beyond the social/biological divide: toward theoretical and transdisciplinary adventures. *Sport, Education and Society*, 19(5), 666–686.
Trivelli, E., 2014. Depression, performativity and the conflicted body: an auto-ethnography of self-medication. *Subjectivity*, 7(2), 151–170.
UK Mental Health Foundation, 2015. Exercise and mental health. Available from www.mentalhealth.org.uk/help-information/mental-health-a-z/E/exercise-mental-health (accessed 11 January 2015).
Wetherell, M., 2012. *Affect and emotion: a new social science understanding*. London: Sage Publications.
World Health Organization, 2013. *Mental Health Action Plan 2013–2020*. Geneva: World Health Organization.

41
COMMUNITY AND PHYSICAL CULTURE

Jacob J. Bustad and Bryan C. Clift

Introduction

As physical cultural studies is primarily focused on the practices and experiences of the (in)active body, we suggest that there exists within physical cultural studies (PCS) an inherent concern for 'community'. As both an academic keyword and a concept and term readily used within everyday experience, community often connotes a multiplicity of meanings that are at once commonly understood and yet remain relatively opaque. While daily life may be characterized by discourses of community, the term is increasingly used in reference to vastly different groups of people and places in regards to scale, size, levels of social cohesion, and political identification. Whether a specific collection of homes and the families that live in them (e.g. a residential 'community'), or a broad understanding of political unity based in part on ideas about gender and sexuality (e.g. the LGBTQ 'community'), the word itself has increasingly been invested with multiple definitions and intentions, including in regards to sport, recreation, leisure and other forms of bodily movements and practices.

In our view, this seemingly (physical) cultural ubiquity means that the importance of engaging with forms of community within the contextual specificities of the contemporary moment must not be underestimated or undervalued, as these concerns are critical to how PCS might respond to social inequalities and contribute to dialogues about the communities in which we work and live. In this chapter, we derive our understanding of community by tracing meanings of this concept across a variety of scholarly fields, first through conceptualizations of community as anchored to philosophy and sociology, and in particular in regards to spatial and social relations. Following this, we further contextualize community within the lineage of cultural studies, as well as literature relevant to human movement and the active body. Lastly, we offer some specific directions and possibilities that constitute a specific approach to thinking about and engaging with community within PCS. In seeking to develop this approach as a response to the different and diverse framings of community that often permeate our everyday lives, we understand this concept to be part and parcel of the social, economic and political conjunctures within which specific communal forms and experiences take shape.

Philosophies and theories of community

As a core concept in social and cultural theory, the idea of community often eludes clear and concise definition. At the same time, the concept is flexible to and for those seeking to use it, and that flexibility has meant the concept is often taken-for-granted, and adopted uncritically (Cohen, 1985; Collins, 2010). Conceptually, community can be taken to include a range of scales, such as those in a neighborhood, city, nation, or global 'community'; it can also be mobilized to reference and explain associations among groups of people, such as those of a particular ethnic grouping, religion, nation, gender, sexuality, and so forth. As a starting place, we assert that community be understood in regards to spatial and cultural dimensions – that is, community is an idea that references groups of people living within specific areas and time frames, and who share a sense of belonging and meaning derived from shared social experiences.

As a philosophical and sociological concept, community is often initially associated with the work of Ferdinand Tönnies. In *Community and Civil Society*, first published in 1887 as *Gemeinschaft und Gesellschaft*, Tönnies outlined two concepts representative of social life or human associations: Gemeinschaft (community) and Gesellschaft (civil society). Gemeinschaft refers to those kinds of associations among and between human beings that can be characterized as small-scale and based on kinship, or the more 'real and organic life' wherein individuals act toward or with one another on the basis of historical and collective interest (Tönnies, 2001: 33). In contrast, Gesellschaft refers to those kinds of associations that are based in larger-scale and competitive, market-driven societies, wherein individuals act toward one another on the basis of competitive personal interest.

Tönnies focused on examining constructions of selfhood within the ever-present struggle between these two types of sociality. Focusing on the struggle between communal and civil society, his concepts remain important commentaries on modernity today and the effects of modernization resulting in the erosion of Gemeinschaft by Gesellschaft. Putnam (2000) illustrated the tension between Tönnies's ideal types within modern American society, arguing that the United States populace experienced lower membership in civic organizations in the final two-thirds of the twentieth century (Putnam, 1995, 2000). Although he explores a range of civic-minded organizations, Putnam (2000) uses the physical cultural practice of bowling as a broader metaphor for civil decline – the title *Bowling Alone* references the concurrent increase in number of bowlers in the US and decrease in community-based bowling leagues.

In his dedicated examination of religion, Durkheim (1965) suggested that religion was constructed and constituted not only through belief but also several kinds of beliefs and practices in relation to those things sacred (i.e. a church or ritual). Together, beliefs and practices integrate into a more unified system than one would be without the other. Around these sets of beliefs and related practices communities take shape, and for Durkheim these were morally based. In this sense, 'collective representations' are ways in which individuals and groups commonly shared among one another through institutions or experiences express and derive a sense of we-ness. Community, then, is comprised of and derived from those representations and experiences.

Another important conceptualization of community introduces more substantively the language of imagination and the expressions of collective belonging and identity. Anderson ([1983] 2006: 6) framed the nation as an 'imagined political community': '*imagined* because members of even the smallest nation will never know most of their fellow-members, meet them, or even hear of them, yet in the minds of each lives the image of their communion'.

Thinking through the relationship between the nation state, nationalism, and national identity, Anderson considered the nation an 'imagined' community because 'regardless of the actual inequality and exploitation that may prevail in each, the nation is always conceived as a deep, horizontal comradeship' (ibid.: 7). However, Anderson emphasizes that all communities, of all relative scales and sizes, are imagined in so far as they bring together individuals based on perceptions and feelings of a greater sense of collectivity, explaining that 'all communities larger than primordial villages of face-to-face contact (and perhaps even then) are imagined' (ibid.: 6). This conceptualization therefore asserts the socially constructed and experienced bonds which often characterize forms of community, through those moments that bring about a sense of connection with other individuals.

Another extension on the idea of community is found in Victor Turner's (1969: 26) sense of 'communitas'. Ingham and McDonald (2003) explain communitas as 'a special experience during which individuals are able to rise above those structures that materially and normatively regulate their daily lives and that unite people across the boundaries of structure, rank, and socioeconomic status'.

Ingham and McDonald (ibid.) agreed with Turner's assertion that the conditions out of which communitas could emerge on a more permanent basis are difficult to locate or create, and that community and communitas are objects and sites of ideological work. Acknowledging Turner's contributions, they importantly break from Turner by linking together the structural and the ideological, rather than maintaining some level of exclusivity between the two.

Importantly, these conceptualizations of communitas bring temporal specificity to the fore in discussions of community. Communitas in this sense responds in part to the turmoil of modernity (Weber, 1978; Cooley, 1967), the modern and industrial city and world, and the post-modern and post-industrial city and world. Whereas community previously suggested a stronger relationship between people and places across time, communitas acknowledges the post-war context through emergent and more impermanent ideas of community. As such, 'community' was decreasingly conceived as located only in specific places with fixed physical or spatial and temporal boundaries. Instead, shifting demographic patterns, population migration within and across countries, civil rights and feminist movements, and urban reformations all worked to unhinge prior ideas about community in relation to time and space.

Community and cultural studies – definitions and interpretations

A focus on the practices, experiences, and representations of different forms of community has also been evident in the lineage of cultural studies, extending back to the development of the Centre for Contemporary Cultural Studies (CCCS) at the University of Birmingham in the 1960s. This research looked to focus on how and why individuals interacted with particular elements of culture, including the formation of social groups based in and on cultural signs, symbols, meanings and practices. As evidence of the importance of conceptualizing community within social and cultural research, the term was included as one of Raymond Williams's 'keywords' for cultural studies, defined as 'a warmly persuasive word [used] to describe an existing set of relationships' (1976: 76). The initial incorporation of community into cultural studies therefore centered on engaging with forms of 'togetherness' that were characterized by particular social dynamics, and expressed through particular actions and experiences that demonstrated the dialectic relations between culture and society.

Specifically, the work of two scholars from the lineage of cultural studies reflect how issues and ideas of community were integral, if not often implicit, to the development of the field – one involved in the formation of the CCCS and British cultural studies in the early 1960s, and the other in the expansion and popularization of cultural studies in the late 1970s and early 1980s. The former, Richard Hoggart, helped to establish cultural studies in Britain through his own research and social commentary regarding the dynamics of English working-class families in the post-war era. In this mode, Hoggart (1957) focused on analyzing and describing how traditional working-class forms of culture and community were changing in the face of popular cultural imports from abroad.

As cultural studies continued to develop over the next several decades, ongoing discussions regarding the dynamics and representations of social groupings resulted in different theories linking culture and community. However, as Gelder (2007) notes, these theorizations were framed by previous work in cultural studies – including that of Hoggart and Williams, as well as E. P. Thompson – which shaped any understanding of community within the field:

> First, their focus was on the English working class, understood as a community bound to a neighbourhood and tied together by family. Second, these prehistories ... established a 'them' and 'us' binary with varying degrees of dissent, as well as a programme for writing 'history from below'. Third, the emphasis was cultural: on rituals, traditions and practices, and the meanings they conveyed. Fourth, contemporary life, defined through mass communication, mass cultural forms, entertainment and consumerism was seen as a threat to all this and therefore viewed negatively.
>
> *(Gelder, 2007: 87)*

These ideas therefore often characterized an understanding of community within cultural studies as both an integral aspect of lived experience, as well as a particular form of working-class identity that should be preserved and celebrated, especially against the rising tide of commercialism and consumerism.

In the late 1970s, this view of community was articulated through the work of Dick Hebdige, which specifically focused on the notion of 'subculture' as a particular formation or interpretation of intra-personal interaction and identification. According to Hebdige (1979), by this period more traditional forms of community were giving way to emergent forms of social togetherness, based on different aspects of daily life. In lieu of ties founded on family and neighborhood, an increasing number of youth expressed forms of communal relationships formed through culturally specific spaces and symbols. As his primary case in point, Hebdige identifies the 'moment of punk' as an example of subcultural practices and expressions, including the symbolism and aesthetics of punk as both musical form and as a source of shared identity (ibid.: 19). Following this work, the concept of 'subculture' within cultural studies was recognized as a form of social togetherness that was both related to and yet essentially different from the notion of community. On the one hand, both subcultures and communities were understood to be made up of shared cultural practices and experiences, but within this framework subcultures were also in part the result of an erosion, displacement and nullification of 'traditional' working-class forms of community.

Within the context of the 1980s and 1990s, the changing dynamics of the field of cultural studies were made evident via increased concerns for aspects of social identity beyond social class, including race, ethnicity, gender and sexuality (see Grossberg, Nelson and Treichler, 1992). This also meant that the previous understandings of 'community' as a disappearing form of working-class relations were problematized, as notions of social togetherness were recognized as not necessarily rooted within class position and status. Following McRobbie (1978, 1991), cultural studies increasingly acknowledged the potential limits of prioritizing class analysis over other axes of social difference, and in particular worked to incorporate forms of critical feminism within cultural research.

Similarly, Hall (1993) sought to discuss ideas of community in regards to national identity, race and ethnicity, and re-define the term in comparison to the conceptualization of community put forth by earlier cultural studies scholars. Taking on Williams's notion of community as based primarily in particular forms of race, ethnicity, national identity and social class, as evinced by the primary focus on English white working-class cultures, Hall (1993) asserts that this understanding is inherently limited in its ability to apprehend and analyze multiple types and kinds of 'community' that are a part of lived experience:

> the emphasis on 'actual and sustained social relationships' as the principal basis of identification and cultural 'belongingness' presents many difficulties which take us back to that original stress, in Williams's work, on culture and community as a 'whole way of life'. Whose *way*? Which *life*? One way or several? Isn't it the case that, in the modern world, the more we examine 'whole ways of life' the more internally diversified, the more cut through by complex patterns of similarity and difference, they appear to be?
>
> *(Hall, 1993: 359, original emphasis)*

These definitions and debates regarding community have continued in both cultural studies and related fields, including within research focused on the practices and experiences of the active body. While different authors have engaged with the idea of community in regards to diverse topics and issues, there have been two primary uses or understandings of the term within the study of human movement – the first of these incorporates 'community' to denote a form of social togetherness, evoking the Tönniesian and sociological definition to describe how physical movement can be involved in the development of social ties and cultural linkages between individuals. In her work focusing on female ice hockey players, Theberge (1995) utilizes this conception of community as social togetherness in exploring how gender and sport are interconnected within these athlete's experiences. Noting that 'women athletes face the challenge of constructing a community within a broader social context marked by ambivalence toward their endeavors', Theberge explains how both a commitment and identity related to the sport, as well as specific dynamics of gender and sexuality, are evident in the 'construction of community' (ibid.: 390).

American football has been one physical culture at the focus of discussions of community. As demonstrated by Foley's research in a small town in Texas, for the nearly 8,000 residents of North Town the rituals of high school football 'enlivened the community's social life … Community sports was the patriotic, neighborly thing to do' (Foley, 1990: 113). Yet at the same time, football often 'socializes people into community structures of inequality' (ibid.: 112). While these various rituals affirmed a collective solidarity, they also became the source of division through existing social hierarchies.

These discussions of community in relation to physical cultures have therefore both reflected an understanding of shared practices and identities, while also placing the concept within theoretical dialogue. In particular, Helstein (2005) argues that community, 'as normatively representative of solidarity and unification, is understood to be productive', in that most often our ideas of community are centered on the ways in which individuals come together to form a group identity that provides the opportunity to 'share in mutual identification and to pursue mutual rights' (ibid.: 2). However, while community represents a 'powerful construct' for both feminists and for female athletes, Helstein cites the Derridean concern for recognizing both the threat and promise of community as a form of social and political 'consensus' – instead, her analysis focuses on how community might work as a post-structural concept that will 'open up' to different theories and uses (ibid.).

More recently, developments in technology and forms of social media have once again suggested the re-defining of community within contemporary forms of sport and physical activity (Olive, 2015; Thorpe, 2014; Wilson and Hayhurst, 2009). While the approach to studying physical cultural communities offered here is primarily focused on non-digital contexts, the overlying understanding of community as open to different interpretations and definitions signals a clear re-constitution of the term away from its uses within sociology and earlier British cultural studies, and no longer attached to a particular historical moment or population. Instead, studies of physical culture have increasingly sought to explore how specifically different forms of contextually bound communal experience are characterized by particular cultural practices and expressions. To reiterate, we suggest that community within these works is discussed as an idea that references groups of people living within specific spatial and temporal contexts, and who share a sense of identity, belonging and meaning derived from common interests and practices.

Community and physical cultural studies

As evidenced by the preceding sections, future research concerning ideas of community in relation to the active body will have a number of philosophical, sociological and theoretical understandings to draw from and engage with, including previous work focused specifically on sport and physical activity. However, in the remaining space we branch off from these valuable contributions in order to offer a flexible and yet principled approach to thinking about and studying the myriad forms, practices and experiences of community that are related to physical culture and PCS.

In particular, this approach follows the theoretical formation of PCS as put forth by Ingham (1997) and Silk and Andrews (2011), as the position that we outline below is necessarily predicated on several guiding ideas about the nature of physical cultural research. In particular, while our approach is characterized by specific theories and methods, we would argue for an intellectual openness that means when thinking about physical cultures and community, 'no epistemology should be privileged' – and we would add ontology and methodology as well (Ingham, 1997: 171). This indicates that there is no singular, established and defined way of understanding and engaging with forms of community, but rather an open dialogue about how and why different theories and methods are, or might be, valuable to both the specific research agenda at hand, as well as to the larger development of PCS. Further, while multiple theories and methods are seen as possibilities, our approach follows Silk and Andrews's (2011) framework for a 'radically contextual' PCS, in which 'physical cultural forms ... can only be understood by the way in which they are *articulated* into a set of complex social, economic, political and technological relationships that comprise a social context' (ibid.: 9, original emphasis). In our view, this insistence on the inter-dependent nature of ideas of 'community' on the particular set of actors, spaces and forces involved means that any interpretation of communal experience and social togetherness must be developed in and through the acts of the researcher(s).

Given this context-specific understanding of social relations, rather than attempting to develop a singular and comprehensive theory of community within PCS, we would offer several guiding principles that can provide a basis for thinking about social cohesion and communal relationships in regards to physical culture and the active body. First, this includes Collins's (2010) assertion of community as a political construct, in that it functions as a culturally ubiquitous concept and term, as well as a contested form of social and political interaction within contemporary global societies. In this view, 'as the construct of community constitutes both a principle of actual social organization and an idea that people use to make sense of and shape their everyday lived realities, it may be central to the workings of intersecting power relations in heretofore unrecognized ways' (ibid.: 8). This 'elastic' conceptualization of community allows for 'a variety of contradictory meanings around which diverse social practices and understandings occur' (ibid.: 10). The emphasis is therefore on the ways in which forms of community are always and only enacted through particular cultural practices and experiences, and lived through specific social relations.

Moreover, by implicating any focus on community within existing relations of power, this framework aims to deconstruct and decenter many of the academic and popular meanings that have been ascribed to this term, including those within sociology and cultural studies. That is, instead of applying ideas about community that come pre-loaded with a specific definition or reference to a particular social group, researchers within PCS would recognize that forms of community are always experienced in and through practices that are to be described and defined in relation to their own context. This approach can also help to avoid what Joseph (2002) refers to as the 'romanticism' that has characterized several cultural understandings of community, including those in previous formations of cultural studies, wherein the researcher posits the given culture and population being focused on as simultaneously threatened and inherently valuable. Instead, PCS can and should seek to examine how particular 'communities' are both constituted by and constitutive of different subjectivities and social identities that are always embedded within specific configurations of power. Our approach thereby follows Helstein (2005) and others within the social study of human movement in recognizing the ways in which power always operates not only between a particular form of community and other forces and institutions, but also in and through the practices and experiences that make up any specific form of organized social relations.

These theoretical concerns often overlap with discussions about how researchers within PCS can methodologically engage with and study different community formations. At the core of a physical cultural method is *articulation*, or the active reconstructing of a context within and through which practices and *events*, or effects of power, and indeed communities, take shape (Grossberg, 1989; Hall, 1992; Andrews, 2002; Silk and Andrews, 2011). Working from an articulatory base, embracing a fluid yet critical adoption of the idea of community – from the organic communal to extended networks of communitas – as well as maintaining a sensitivity to Saukko's (2003; Silk and Andrews, 2011) three methodological currents/validities – contextual, dialogic, and self-reflexive – engaging with communities requires making use of the research bricolage (Kincheloe, 2001); that is, drawing upon a 'diverse methodological arsenal' (Silk and Andrews, 2011: 17) that allows researchers to work across disciplines, with multiple methods of inquiry, and within the complexity of the research task. As such, PCS may be regarded as resistant to methodologies and more embracing of methods.

No singular method represents the best way in which to do research on communities. The only method worth having, to paraphrase Stuart Hall (1992) on theory, is that which you have to fight off, not that which you speak with profound fluency (ibid.: 280). From interviewing, textual analysis, narrative analysis, and field methods (Markula and Silk, 2011), the practice and politics of the doing of research offers much in the way for qualitative, physical cultural researchers interested in studying communities. Decisions about which method(s) to make use of should be orchestrated not around rigid templates but rather oriented toward better understanding and negotiating the I-thou dialogue (Johnson, Chambers, Raghuram, and Tincknell, 2004). Community-based practice research (CBPR) and participatory action research (PAR) represent more common and useful approaches for working with communities. As approaches, and not methods or methodologies, CBPR and PAR seek to maintain commitments that, like politically inspired PCS projects, address forms of collective, self-reflexive, and political-inspired research (Kemmis and McTaggart, 1988, 2005; Levine-Rasky, 2015).

Instructively, Baker, Homan, Schonhoff, and Kreuter (1999) offer a useful distinction between three kinds of research on/with communities in terms of who drives and controls a project. The first understands the researcher as driving the inquiry. Control over the process of research – of shaping questions, approaches, and responses – rests in the hands of the researcher. In the second, community members might assist in some ways to shaping questions but are uninvolved in the rest of the process. Control largely lies in the hands of the research, and participants remain marginal contributors and sources of data. The third, and more recent form, involves the researcher and participants collaboratively and jointly conceiving and carrying out the research. Approached in this sense, community-based work does not rely on a singular approach but rather highlights a way of *practicing* the research process. For a useful discussion and series of examples of these types within sport and physical activity, see Schinke, McGannon and Smith's (2013) special issue in *Qualitative Research in Sport, Exercise and Health*.

In the last 15 to 20 years a few scholars have begun to take up the third type of community-based research on sport and physical activity put forward by Baker et al. (1999), most notably in the work of Wendy Frisby and Audrey Giles. While these are not the only people to engage with community-based scholarship, they do advance scholarship consistent with a collectively inspired and politically based impetus. Frisby and colleagues, for example have worked with low-income women and issues of sport and recreation involvement (Frisby and Millar, 2002) as well as Chinese immigrant women and inclusion in physical activity across a range of peoples, organizations, and institutions (Frisby, 2011). Audrey Giles and colleagues focus primarily on health-based research with aboriginal communities (e.g. Nicholls and Giles, 2007; Giles and Forsyth, 2007). What is compelling about the work of Wendy Frisby and Audrey Giles, and colleagues, is not just that they are mobilizing community-based work, but they work also to better understand the process of research *with* communities. They acknowledge and examine the difficulties in conducting research that integrates participants in every step of the research process (Frisby, Reid, Millar and Hoeber, 2005), works to understand issues of power through participatory and community research (Golob and Giles, 2013), and considers the dangerous potential for colonizing indigenous methodologies (Darroch and Giles, 2014). Doing so, they have laid the groundwork for community-based scholarship that, in paralleling Schinke, McGannon and Smith (2013), seek not definitive notions of what constitutes community-based research or practice but rather seek a diversity of perspectives. Such an orientation searches for a productive dialogue among several aspects of the research process. These aspects include, among others: a diversity of the ways in which community is conceptualized and carried out; a range of theoretical and methodological approaches; and a critical approach, meaning identifying and working with relations of power.

To conclude, we would like to further support the approach to thinking about community that has been outlined here by re-asserting the importance and relative usefulness for the term and concept within PCS. In particular, this utility is based in two different ways in which we hope to characterize dialogues regarding community within the ongoing and future development of PCS.

In the first sense, this refers to the ways in which critical analyses of specific physical cultural forms, practices and experiences of community and *communitas* can be aligned with research goals of apprehending and addressing existing relations of social, economic and political power. Following Collins (2010), there are several aspects of studying community that therefore make the concept a 'promising candidate' for engaging with myriad forms of social inequality. First, communities are manifest through actions by individuals in all social positions, and thus are experienced by both the 'elite' and 'everyday' – and the formation and experience of community is often characterized by 'strong, deep feelings' that can resonate powerfully along and across lines of social difference and identity (ibid.: 10). Further, the cultural pervasiveness of community as political construct means that it functions as an integral aspect of how people 'make sense of' social inequalities, and how social structures and institutions are organized and experienced (ibid.: 12).

These characteristics demonstrate how a critical theoretical and reflexive methodological approach can accentuate the ways in which forms of community involving active bodies – moving and/or consuming together – are always experienced in and through relations of power. At the same time, the value and potential for this approach to community within PCS incorporates not only the study of existing social relations and shared practices and identities, but also the fostering and development of a PCS community of researchers that aims to engage various publics through scholarly work. This means that along with interrogating what is meant by community when the term is used by and applied to particular social groupings, we would argue for a continual dialogue regarding the ongoing development of critical perspectives on human movement as the 'becoming of a community' in itself, by recognizing the various interests, aims and purposes that constitute PCS (Grossberg, 1996: 88). In this sense, studying community and communities would therefore also involve establishing an 'open-ended' form of community that is enacted through the personal and professional lives of 'practitioners' of PCS, and within the interactions between researchers and a variety of places, people and institutions. Following from the approach to community that has been explicated within this chapter, this would allow for and encourage different interpretations, identifications and experiences as an integral aspect of PCS – therefore we might utilize the conceptual 'elasticity' of community towards developing and realizing forms of praxis that allow those involved in PCS to both critically examine and engage with the worlds in which we live.

References

Anderson, B. ([1983] 2006). *Imagined communities: Reflections on the origin and spread of nationalism*, revised edn. London: Verso.
Andrews, D. L. (2002). Coming to terms with cultural studies. *Journal of Sport and Social Issues*, 26(1), 110–117.
Baker, E. A., Homan, S., Schonhoff, S. R. and Kreuter, M. (1999). Principles of practice for academic/practice/community research partnerships. *American Journal of Preventive Medicine*, 16(3), 86–93.
Cohen, A. P. (1985). *The symbolic construction of community*. London, UK: Tavistock Publications.
Collins, P. H. (2010). The new politics of community. *American Sociological Review*, 75(1), 7–30.
Cooley, C. (1967). *Social organization*. New York, NY: Schocken.
Darroch, F. and Giles, A. R. (2014). Decolonizing health research: Community-based participatory research and postcolonial feminist theory. *Canadian Journal of Action Research*, 15(3), 22–36.
Durkheim, E. (1965). *The elementary forms of the religious life*. New York, NY: Free Press.
Foley, D. E. (1990). The great American football ritual: Reproducing race, class, and gender inequality. *Sociology of Sport Journal*, 7, 111–135.
Frisby, W. (2011). Promising physical activity inclusion practices for Chinese immigrant women in Vancouver, Canada. *Quest*, 63(1), 135–147.
Frisby, W. and Millar, S. (2002). The actualities of doing community development to promote the inclusion of low income populations in local sport and recreation. *European Sport Management Quarterly*, 2(3), 209–233.
Frisby, W., Reid, C. J., Millar, S. and Hoeber, L. (2005). Putting 'participatory' into participatory forms of action research. *Journal of Sport Management*, 19(4), 367–386.
Gelder, K. (2007). *Subcultures: Cultural histories and social practice*. London: Routledge.
Giles, A. R. and Forsyth, J. (2007). On common ground: Power, knowledge, and practice in the study of Aboriginal sport and recreation. *Journal of Sport and Leisure*, 1(1), 1–20.

Golob, M. I. and Giles, A. R. (2013). Challenging and transforming power relations within community-based participatory research: the promise of a Foucauldian analysis. *Qualitative Research in Sport, Exercise and Health*, 5(3), 356–372.

Grossberg, L. (1989). The circulation of cultural studies. *Critical Studies in Mass Communication*, 6(4), 413–420.

Grossberg, L. (1996). Identity and cultural studies: Is that all there is? In S. Hall and P. Du Gay (eds), *Questions of cultural identity*. London: Sage, 87–107.

Grossberg, L., Nelson, C. and Treichler, P. (eds) (1992) *Cultural Studies*. London: Routledge.

Hall, S. (1992). Cultural studies and its theoretical legacies. In L. Grossberg, C. Nelson and P. Treichler (eds), *Cultural studies*. New York: Routledge, 277–294.

Hall, S. (1993). Culture, community, nation. *Cultural Studies*, 7(3), 349–363.

Hebdige, D. (1979). *Subculture: The meaning of style*. London: Routledge.

Helstein, M. (2005). Rethinking community: Introducing the 'whatever' female athlete. *Sociology of Sport Journal*, 21(1), 1–18.

Hoggart, R. (1957). *The uses of literacy: Aspects of working-class life with special references to publications and entertainments*. London: Chatto & Windus.

Ingham, A. G. (1997). Toward a department of physical cultural studies and an end to tribal warfare. In J. Fernandez-Balboa (ed.), *Critical postmodernism in human movement, physical education, and sport*. Albany, NY: SUNY Press.

Ingham, A. G. and McDonald, M. G. (2003). Sport and community/communitas. In R. C. Wilcox, D. L. Andrews, R. Pitter and R. L. Irwin (eds), *Sporting dystopias: The making and meanings of urban sport cultures*. Albany, NY: University of New York Press, 17–33.

Johnson, R., Chambers, D., Raghuram, P. and Tincknell, E. (2004). *The practice of cultural studies*. London, UK: Sage.

Joseph, M. (2002) *Against the romance of community*. Minneapolis, MN: University of Minnesota Press.

Kemmis, S. and McTaggart, R. (eds) (1988). *The action research planner*, 3rd edn. Geelong, Australia: Deakin University Press.

Kemmis, S. and McTaggart, R. (2005). Participatory action research: Communicative action and the public sphere. In N. Denzin and Y. Lincoln (eds), *The Sage handbook of qualitative research*, 3rd edn. Thousand Oaks, CA: Sage, 559–603.

Kincheloe, J. (2001). Describing the bricolage: Conceptualizing a new rigor in qualitative research. *Qualitative Inquiry*, 7(6), 679–692.

Levine-Rasky, C. (2015). Research for/about/with the community: A montage. *Cultural Studies ↔ Critical Methodologies*, 15(6), 455–467.

McRobbie, A. (1978) *'Jackie': An ideology of adolescent femininity*. Birmingham: Birmingham Centre for Contemporary Cultural Studies (CCCS Stencilled Papers), University of Birmingham.

McRobbie, A. (1991). *Feminism and youth culture: From 'Jackie' to 'Just seventeen'*. London: Macmillan.

Markula, P. and Silk, M. (2011). *Research physical culture: A qualitative handbook*. Basingstoke: Palgrave Macmillan.

Nicholls, S. and Giles, A. R. (2007). Sport as a tool for HIV/AIDS education: A potential catalyst for change. *Pimatisiwin: A Journal of Aboriginal and Indigenous Community Health*, 5(1), 51–85.

Olive, R. (2015). Reframing surfing: Physical culture in online spaces. *Media International Australia, Incorporating Culture and Policy*, 155(June), 99–107.

Putnam, R. D. (1995). Bowling alone: America's declining social capital. *Journal of Democracy*, 6(1), 65–78.

Putnam, R. D. (2000). *Bowling alone: The collapse and revival of American community*. New York: Simon & Schuster.

Saukko, P. (2003). *Doing research in cultural studies: An introduction to classical and new methodological approaches*. London: Sage.

Schinke, R. J., McGannon, K. R. and Smith, B. (2013). Expanding the sport and physical activity research landscape through community scholarship: Introduction. *Qualitative Research in Sport, Exercise and Health*, 5(3), 287–290.

Silk, M. and Andrews, D. L. (2011). Toward a physical cultural studies. *Sociology of Sport Journal*, 28(1), 4–35.

Theberge, N. (1995). Gender, sport, and the construction of community: A case study from women's ice hockey. *Sociology of Sport Journal*, 12(2), 389–402.

Thorpe, H. (2014). *Transnational Mobilities in Action Sport Cultures*. Basingstoke: Palgrave Macmillan.

Tönnies, F. (2001). *Community and civil society* (trans. J. Harris and M. Hollis, ed. J. Harris). Cambridge, UK: Cambridge University Press.

Turner, V. (1969). *The ritual process: Structure and anti-structure.* Chicago, IL: Aldine.
Weber, M. (1978). *Economy and society* (ed. G. Roth and C. Wittich). Berkeley, CA: University of California Press.
Williams, R. (1976). *Keywords: A vocabulary of culture and society.* London: Fontana/Croom Helm.
Wilson, B. and Hayhurst, L. (2009). Digital activism: Neoliberalism, the internet, and sport for youth development. *Sociology of Sport Journal*, 26(1), 155–181.

42
PHYSICAL EDUCATION, POLICY AND EMBODIED PEDAGOGIES

Lisette Burrows and Laura De Pian

Overview

Physical education (PE), its policy and its pedagogy are in what some may regard as an enviable position currently. Amid claims that everyone, everywhere is enmeshed in an obesity epidemic, schools and subjects like PE and/or health education (HE) have been positioned as saviours, places where work can be done to stem the obesity tide (Evans, Rich, Davies and Allwood, 2008; Gard, 2004, 2008). In both the United Kingdom (UK) and New Zealand (NZ), the notion that there are too many fat children who become fat adults has inspired a proliferation of programmes focused predominantly on improving nutrition and addressing the presumed sedentary lifestyles of young people (Burrows, Petrie and Cosgriff, 2013; Evans, De Pian, Rich and Davies, 2011; Evans et al., 2008; Petrie, Penney and Fellows, 2014). PE has seemingly found its place in the sun. But has it?

Several compelling critiques have been levelled against both the idea that obesity is a growing problem (see Gard, 2010; Gard and Wright, 2005) and the notion that, even if obesity is a problem, schools are locales where anti-obesity work should take place (Gard and Pluim, 2014). Suffice to say at this point, that in the context of broader concerns about obesity prevention, PE has sometimes given way to physical inoculation (Burrows, Wright and McCormack, 2009). That is, PE and/or HE as a subject concerned with learning 'about' PE or health has been subsumed by an orientation toward the subject that positions PE as a health-enhancing tool – that is learning *for* health (Fitzpatrick, 2011). The latter orientation is certainly one embraced by many US initiatives, such as health-optimizing physical education (HOPE). In the UK, PE has traditionally focused on competition and sport (Penney and Chandler, 2000), with HE being a part of personal, social and health education (PSHE). However, over the last decade, the UK government's National Healthy Schools programme has encouraged schools to adopt a 'whole school approach' to the design and delivery of their HE programmes. This has prompted a number of PE and school sport initiatives to 'combat obesity' by improving the quality of PE provision and encouraging increased participation in sport and physical activity. For example, in July 2011, the UK's Department of Health published revised recommendations of 'vigorous intensity activity for school-age children of at least 60 minutes a day' (National Audit Office, 2012: 24). In NZ, despite a mandated curriculum that suggests PE and HE are about 'learning' and producing creative, critical thinkers (Burrows, 2005, 2011; Burrows and

Wright, 2004a, 2004b; Gillespie and Culpan, 2000; Tasker, 1996–1997), evidence suggests that many continue to regard the health and physical education (HPE) subject area as one that has a pivotal role to play in stemming the tide of childhood obesity *and* inoculating young people against the 'risks' of all manner of other health concerns (e.g. drug taking, teen pregnancy, sexually transmitted diseases, depression) arising (Burrows and Sinkinson, 2014; De Pian, 2013; Fitzpatrick and Tinning, 2014).

As De Pian (2013) and others (e.g. Cale and Harris, 2013; Evans et al., 2008; Kirk, 2006) have suggested, a complex interweaving of policy, public health priorities together with the emergence of panics and crises about children's health, is responsible for the ease with which PE is positioned as both the problem and the solution to global health problems, and obesity, in particular. What is interesting to us, is the fact that much of the rhetoric and policy generated with a view to improving young people's health pays scarce attention to how children and young people themselves understand health, nor their embodied responses to the volume of health imperatives currently infusing their school and home environments (Burrows and Wright, 2004b). In this chapter we are interested in reading this situation alongside research that endeavours to understand the ways young people embody the pedagogies deployed. We draw on Ball, Maguire and Braun's (2012) notion of policy as process and Foucault's theorization of the 'subject' to understand something of what Blackman (2012) refers to as 'body subjects'. That is, the notion that embodiments are assembled, performed and enacted in situ.

First, we briefly map some of the ways schools are currently *doing* health policy and how they think about it. Next, we draw on empirical research in the UK (a doctoral study completed by the second author, which explored the emplacement, enactment and embodiment of health policies in UK schools) and NZ (a study by the first author seeking to understand the place and meaning of health and physical activity in young people's lives) to paint a picture, albeit a 'located' one, of how young people seem to be thinking, feeling and embodying policy aspirations in their schools and homes. We conclude by discussing to what extent examining the intersections of PE, policy and embodied pedagogies can contribute to the physical cultural studies (PCS) brief and how this brief might be informed and developed by PE and other school-based interests in the future. We consider what PCS and critical HPE researchers seem to already share in terms of their orientations toward the study of physical culture and what PCS tenets potentially inspire in relation to ongoing work in the HPE sphere.

Doing and thinking policy in physical education

UK government health policies tend to assume a behaviour change approach to health, underpinned by an oversimplified relationship between knowledge and behaviour (De Pian, 2013; Rich, De Pian and Francombe-Webb, 2015). School health policies have therefore been designed to educate and inform all young people about the risks associated with a poor diet, lack of exercise and excess weight, with the intention of urging them to take responsibility for their own health by altering their behaviour accordingly (e.g. by eating the 'right' foods, doing the correct amount of physical activity etc.). Findings from the UK study conducted by the second author highlighted that physical educators tend to draw uncritically on this dominant discourse, firstly in understanding and justifying their role in this endeavour ('a duty to educate and teach', 'raise awareness', 'reinforce messages', 'help pupils to recognize and realize the value and importance of health', and 'inform, guide and encourage pupils to make the right choices' were just a few of the phrases used by physical educators in interview) and secondly, in reading the 'health' of their pupil intake (through their lifestyle choices and the options available to them in their locale). However, the 'situated', 'professional' and 'material' contexts (Ball et al.,

2012) of the schools were found to enable or constrain the extent to which the educators could enact government health policy, and these contextual dimensions shaped the pedagogies that were employed in each school setting. Thus, ubiquitous health imperatives, even when driven and shaped by dominant political ideology, were emplaced and 'recontextualized' (Bernstein, 1990) and evidently generated very different curricula in each school. Generally speaking, the 'wealthy, well-educated and healthy' pupils attended schools located in affluent rural/suburban areas, which afforded ample time and funding to health-related resources and facilities. Conversely, the 'deprived, uneducated and unhealthy' pupils attended inner-city schools, where time and funding for health-related resources and facilities were restricted due to weight, and health more generally, being positioned as one of several pathologies in the pupils' lives.

In NZ, the formal curriculum is undergirded by a vision of developing 'young people who will be confident, connected, actively involved learners' (Ministry of Education, 2007: 9). Unlike the UK government school health policies described above, NZ's HPE curriculum explicitly embraces the notion that young people should develop capacities to think critically, understand health in a holistic sense (e.g. mental, spiritual, social and physical dimensions), pursue social justice agendas and understand the interrelationships that exist between the individual, others and society (ibid.). As is the case elsewhere, however, the official curriculum is not the only policy that informs what goes on in the name of health and/or physical education in schools. As others have catalogued (e.g. Petrie, Penney and Fellows, 2014; Powell, 2011), health promotion agencies, regional sports bodies, and an ever-expanding array of commercial enterprises (see Powell, 2014) are working in schools, transmitting messages about what matters most in health and PE in ways that do not necessarily align with the spirit of the HPE curriculum. Further, the healthism triplex (knowledge changes attitude and therefore behaviour) referred to in the UK context, remains an undergirding assumption in much teachers' work, despite efforts to complicate the simplistic notion that information will change what young people think and do for their health. Health policy in NZ, then, is a contested arena. Teachers, students and their families are perpetually negotiating and making sense (or not) of multiple messages and directives, some of which are ideologically disparate.

Embodying health policy in UK and NZ schools

UK children's voices

Given the UK physical educators' uncritical acceptance of dominant health and obesity discourse, it was perhaps to be expected that the majority of pupils in the UK study would define health by drawing on the same dominant notions of individual responsibility for the 'achievement' of health through enactment of an appropriate diet, exercise regime and body weight:

- 'I would like to be a bit thinner (I won't eat too much fat)' (Florence, aged 13);
- 'I do exercise all the time' (Nicholas, aged 10);
- 'I am not overweight' (Emily, aged 9).

Hence, all pupils were aware of what they *ought* to be doing in the name of achieving health, as endorsed by government guidelines and their school health pedagogies. Again, however, the extent to which this was possible was largely shaped by the economic resources of their schools and families. Nevertheless, the affective force of the biopedagogies enacted in the schools urged the pupils to repeatedly assess their own bodies and diet and exercise 'choices' in relation to the 'expert knowledge' endorsed by their health educators, to understand *who they are* in relation to *who they should be* and to take responsibility for making appropriate modifications where necessary. These pedagogies left 'little obvious space for resistance among the young people who [were] subjected to them' (Rich and Evans, 2009: 158). As such, the pupils and their teachers were largely unaware of the processes of subjectification that were occurring through their passive and uncritical engagement with the health imperatives of their school and wider society.

When asked how they feel about their own bodies, the data painted a far more complex and multifaceted picture, however. Sixteen per cent ($n = 183$) of the young people in this study reported that they were 'never' happy about their weight/size. Elsewhere, these young people have been referred to as 'troubled' bodies (De Pian, 2013; Evans, Davies, Rich and De Pian, 2013). However, just under half of the young people (44%, $n = 507$) reported that they were happy about their weight/size 'all the time'. These have previously been defined as 'emboldened' bodies (ibid.). The 40 per cent of participants ($n = 466$) who indicated that they were 'sometimes' happy about their weight/size are considered to have a more ambivalent, indifferent and/or transitory relationship with their body's weight/size. These have been described elsewhere as 'insouciant' bodies (ibid.). Of all three groups, it is this latter group of pupils, we would argue, which most clearly exemplifies the fluid nature of young people's relationships with their own bodies within and across time, place and space.

Closer analysis of this data, however, revealed that relatively low percentages of 'troubled' bodies and high percentages of 'emboldened' bodies reside in schools populated by predominantly white, middle-class children, and high proportions of 'troubled' bodies and low proportions of 'emboldened' bodies were generally found in the culturally diverse, lower-middle and working-class schools. Thus, the physical educators' uncritical acceptance of dominant obesity discourse inadvertently positioned their school – their staff and pupils – in relation to dominant health and obesity discourse, privileging those already 'privileged', and marginalizing the more deprived. These findings, at least on the surface, appear to offer some serious check on the perspective of previous research (e.g. Allwood, 2010; Evans et al., 2008; Halse, Honey and Boughtwood, 2007), which has emphasized only the potentially determining, all-consuming and destructive effects of obesity discourse for young people's embodiment.

The imperative to perform/achieve 'health' when emplaced within these school PE contexts where 'intense power relations' were at play (Tamboukou, 2003: 209) constructed a series of dichotomous distinctions (e.g. healthy/unhealthy, normal/pathological), which replicated wider societal values, whereby 'we make uniformity the criteria for belonging [and] we exclude people *because* of their diversity' (Kunc, 1992: 32). Thus, conformity was 'privileged' and indeed celebrated (e.g. through healthy snack awards and certificates) and difference became its 'negative counterpart', marginalized or 'othered' in terms of diet and exercise behaviour and body weight/size (e.g. being 'picked on' for being 'fat' or eating the 'wrong' foods). This created an intense desire among most pupils to not only 'be healthy' but to be recognized as such by their teachers and peers and indeed wider society for being a responsible biocitizen (Halse, 2009). As such, pupils were required to (l)earn their right to belong, through displaying the 'correct' body weight/size and health behaviours, which would equip them with a valuable passport to 'fit in' with their school's accepted 'healthy' normalized body ideal. However, through this process, pupils learnt that 'their worth as individuals [was] contingent upon being able to jump through the prescribed hoops' (Kunc, 1992: 32) and, hence, just as important as cultivating a slender physique was the imperative to command respect and a sense of belonging from teachers and peers.

NZ children's voices

In NZ, a growing cadre of research studies have sought to understand how children and young people think about their own and others' health, what they do with the messages they are exposed to and how they feel about these (e.g. Burrows and Wright, 2004a, 2004b; Burrows, 2010; Burrows, Wright and McCormack, 2009; Cosgriff, Burrows and Petrie, 2013; Powell, 2011; Powell and Fitzpatrick, 2013). In most of these studies, students repeatedly annex health to weight, body size and shape, and express a belief that achieving health is mainly a matter of eating well and exercising a lot (Burrows, 2009). Fruit and vegetables are foods ascribed an especially coveted status in children's views (Burrows and McCormack, 2014).

Similarly definitive convictions about the health-fulfilling properties of deliberate exercise are expressed across a range of NZ studies (e.g. Burrows and McCormack, 2014; Powell, 2011). Running, in particular, has particular purchase with NZ cohorts. Some expressed a view that any potentially debilitative effects of overconsumption of 'bad' food could be counteracted by doses of deliberate exercise. Others spoke of how exercise could stop one from becoming a 'couch potato' – a peculiarly NZ metaphor, used widely to refer to lazy, chip munching, TV-watching young people who become 'fat' through inactivity.

On one level, the seemingly widespread acceptance of this message, one promulgated regularly in health promotion campaigns, in pedagogical work in schools and on television advertisements, could be conceived as evidence of policy working. Yet as ethnographic work with young people suggests, what children do, think and feel about the 5+-a-day message and the imperative to exercise, is far from straightforward. As is the case with UK cohorts, some children express a ready familiarity with the message yet don't necessarily enact it in their daily lives. Others take the message to heart, declaring that they feel guilty if their dietary regimen departs too far from the 'prescription' or if they have not exercised enough. Some, whose familial or cultural proclivities preclude eating recommended foods, express fear that their own and their families' health, and indeed, their futures, will be jeopardized because of their failure to comply with healthy food recommendations. As one of the young boys, Jono, in Burrows's (2011) study put it:

> I'm very nervous about my weight too … Cause my um mum and dad their weight's kind of getting bigger. My dad yeah … Sometimes he doesn't eat it (the healthy stuff) and he gets much bigger and that's what I'm worried about, my parents' weight and my weight. Sometimes … my sister Helen she's in Room 8 at our school; her weight's kind of getting bigger too.
>
> *(Burrows, 2011: 6)*

Food, weight and subjectivity are intimately entwined in Jono's statement. In this case, healthy food policy yields evaluations of his own and his family's prospects that are far from liberatory. For Jono, and other young people in NZ cohorts, healthy food prescriptions can serve as reminders of all they are not, and may not be. In other instances, young NZ children called upon their health knowledge to cast aspersions on others, suggesting that ignorant and/or uncaring parents were producing fat and therefore unhealthy children (see Burrows, 2010). Still others spoke of the guilt, worry and confusion health imperatives produced for them, especially when their efforts to abide by health food and exercise regimens failed to produce the body shapes they were promised in health rhetoric. Others puzzled about why their friends could eat what they liked yet retain their slim shape, while they felt themselves growing fatter through consuming similar foods.

Further, what is clear from ethnographic work with young people in NZ are the ways class and culture contour not only how young people may receive health messages but also what they can and desire to do with them. Distinctly different orientations toward health promotion policies in two schools, a mere kilometre away from each other were noted in Burrows's (2011) work. When the NZ government introduced healthy food guidelines for schools, including recommendations regarding what can be sold in school canteens, the decile 10 school was aware of these but not overly bothered about following them. As teachers in this school declared, obesity (and by association, 'health') is not an issue in their school and the predominantly well-off parents provided quality lunches for their offspring. In the lower decile school largely populated by Māori and/or Pasifika students, teachers and parents tended to respond more concertedly, acutely aware that they were responsibilized (McCormack, 2012) and in some ways culpable, for improving the health of children in their school. In so saying, parents, students and some teachers (see Burrows and McCormack, 2012) actively resisted the imperative to think and behave in mainstream health-promoting ways, expressing discomfort at feeling like 'the food police or the water police … and enforcing rules about healthy lunches' (ibid.: 10).

This discomfort is not something so easily expressed by young people, yet on the odd occasion students in the study did express it. For example, one young man in Burrows (2011) study poked fun at his teacher's lecture on the perils of coke. Another declared that he didn't have any desire to eat like a palangi (non-Pasifika New Zealander). One young Samoan woman wondered why in her culture stick thin body shape was reviled, yet health education policy celebrated the thin ideal (Burrows, 2011). While rarely expressed, the occasional instance of strongly or delicately expressed sentiments about the disjuncture of health imperatives with the realities of daily lives lived is enough to shake up the universalism undergirding much health promotion rhetoric.

Concluding thoughts

Our research in two markedly different locales has produced remarkably similar conundrums. Across both UK and NZ cohorts, the visceral and lived impact of health policies is evident. Whether it be the insouciant, troubled and emboldened bodies of the young people in De Pian's study or the rogue 'resisters' and multiple 'acceptors' of Burrows's cohort, the palpable effects of policy work on the lives and bodies of young people is clear. What our collective work points to is the futility of thinking about or doing health policy work in schools in ways that presume a simplistic translation of health knowledge to health disposition and/or behaviour. Both within and across different cohorts of young people, markedly different orientations towards health imperatives arise. While there is substantive evidence to suggest children willingly and uncritically take up health policy messages, as we have briefly alluded to above, there are those who do not, and those who merely rehearse what they think researchers want to hear when asked about their views about health. Children's testimonies disrupt simplistic notions that telling children what to think and do will change what they think and do.

We also suggest that drawing on different theoretical resources, methodologies and orientations toward critical scholarship can yield nuanced understandings of what policy does, to whom, and with what effect. It can also sponsor different questions, different empirical foci and different 'solutions'. As we have signalled above, policy, as a way of solving problems (real or imagined), is the predominant disposition in both the UK and NZ. A post-structural perspective, however, urges a critical interrogation of the nature of the problem policy is hoping to solve (Bacchi, 2009). As we have tried to encapsulate through our snippets of empirical research, young people's experiences would suggest policy shapes problems rather than addresses them. It is not a stretch to conceive that some young people come to 'know' new problems via policy's posing of them. That is, health policy can give shape to and determine who emerges as the problem. As we have illustrated throughout, young people are differently positioned to deal with their categorization as 'problems' and the effects and affects of their positioning as such are differently experienced. This seems like common sense, yet health policy seems to assume a monolithic subject devoid of lived experience which will and does undoubtedly shape individual and collective capacity and desire to adhere to its missives.

The snippets of research shared throughout this chapter contribute to a PCS political and theoretical agenda in several ways. The testimonies of young people in both UK and NZ cohorts hone attention not simply to the bodies of young people, but their histories (and 'presents') in the specific contexts within which they live and learn. More specifically, the research, albeit briefly explored here, highlights the significance of school contexts as sites for exploring, understanding and critiquing taken-for-granted assumptions about HPE policy, curriculum and young people's embodiment. Schools are sites where empirical, theoretical and political matters come together. They afford opportunities for re-framing HPE policy, intervening in common-sense interpretations about what matters for young people, and are sites where it is possible (due to the containment of young people and their teachers in one place and national curriculum agendas) to impact what happens in the name of a health and/or physical education for youth. While PCS aims to retain a fluid, relational and pluralistic approach, PE, pedagogy, schools and educational endeavours have been less engaged with/by PCS scholars.

In so saying, there are clearly insights that socially critical HPE researchers can take from PCS. As with those ascribing to a PCS approach, socially critical HPE researchers are vitally interested in the contexts within which various expressions of physical culture exist. While historically focusing particularly on teaching and learning in school, pre-service or in-service environments, many scholars have broadened their sites of enquiry to places and spaces outside of formal institutions of learning. They recognize that boundaries between school, home and community are porous and that schools, their teachers and curricula, are not the only things shaping young people's engagement in physical culture. PCS orientations support this work and strengthen already emergent tendencies to engage with contexts other than schools.

Alongside PCS exponents, HPE researchers are also interested in using diverse theoretical resources to understand given corporeal phenomena, although a commitment to one particular theorist (e.g. Bourdieu, Bernstein, Foucault) or one kind of theoretical framework has tended to prevail. Drawing on PCS perspectives encourages those of us interested in HPE to embrace the kind of theoretical fluidity and interdisciplinary approaches characterizing PCS. The physical body, its movements, its meanings and representations and the power relations embedded in these cannot be apprehended by singular scientific approaches. Specifically, as we have endeavoured to illustrate in this chapter, understanding how young people think/do health and what/who shapes their cultural practices requires an openness to and willingness to engage theoretical resources and approaches from divergent locales. Policy studies, approaches to embodiment and the sociology of youth are just a few of these. Methodologically, ethnographic work can yield insights as to the meanings young people make of their own health and physicality, yet discourse analyses of policy, of youth health representations in media and professional resources, and embrace of the kind of methodological plurality PCS suggests may permit more holistic and nuanced understandings of health as cultural practice, lived and displayed. We hope that our work, briefly explored here, may offer a small opening for dialogue between PE scholarship and the work of PCS scholars.

References

Allwood, R. F. (2010). 'You asked what being healthy means to me and the answer is, it means everything': A feminist post-structural analysis of disordered eating, education and health. PhD thesis, Loughborough University, UK.

Bacchi, C. (2009). *Analysing Policy: What's the Problem Represented to Be?* Australia: Pearson.

Ball, S. J., Maguire, M. and Braun, A. (2012). *How Schools Do Policy: Policy Enactments in Secondary Schools.* New York: Routledge.

Bernstein, B. (1990). *Class, Codes and Control, Volume IV: The Structuring of Pedagogic Discourse.* London: Routledge.

Blackman, L. (2012). *Immaterial Bodies: Affect, Embodiment, Mediation.* London: Sage Publications Ltd.

Burrows, L. (2005). Proposed key competencies and health and physical education in the New Zealand curriculum. A commissioned Ministry of Education discussion paper. Available from http://centre4.interact.ac.nz/modules/group/group.php?space_key=468andmodule_key=15532andlink_key=16092andgroup_key=15532andjavascript=1#papers.

Burrows, L. (2009). Discursive dilemmas in New Zealand's health and physical education curriculum. In M. Dinan (ed.), *Health and Physical Education: Contemporary Issues for Curriculum in Australia and New Zealand.* Melbourne: Oxford University Press.

Burrows, L. (2010). Kiwi kids are Weet-Bix™ kids: Body matters in childhood. *Sport, Education and Society*, 15(2), 235–251.

Burrows, L. (2011). 'I'm proud to be me': Health, community and schooling. *Policy Futures in Education*, 9(3), 341–352.

Burrows, L. and McCormack, J. (2012). Teachers' talk about health, self and the student 'body'. *Discourse: Studies in the Cultural Politics of Education*, 33(5), 729–744.

Burrows, L. and McCormack, J. (2014). 'Doing it for themselves': A qualitative study of children's engagement with public health agendas in New Zealand. *Critical Public Health*, 24(2) 159–170.

Burrows, L. and Sinkinson, M. (2014). Mental health in corporeal times. In K. Fitzpatrick and R. Tinning (eds.), *Health Education: Critical Perspectives.* Abingdon: Routledge, 156–170.

Burrows, L. and Wright, J. (2004a). Being healthy: Young New Zealanders ideas about health. *Childrenz Issues*, 8(1), 7–12.

Burrows, L. and Wright, J. (2004b). The good life: New Zealand children's perspectives on health and self. *Sport, Education and Society*, 9(2), 193–205.

Burrows, L., Petrie, K. and Cosgriff, M. (2013). Health invaders in New Zealand primary schools. *Waikato Journal of Education*, 18(2), 12–24.

Burrows, L., Wright, J. and McCormack, J. (2009). Dosing up on food and physical activity: New Zealand children's ideas about health. *Health Education Journal*, 68, 157–169.

Cale, L. and Harris, J. (2013). Every child (of every size) matters in physical education! Physical education's role in childhood obesity. *Sport, Education and Society*, 18(4), 433–452.

Cosgriff, M., Burrows, L. and Petrie, K. with Keown, S., Devcich, J., Naera, J. and Duggan, D. (2013). 'You'll feel fat and no one will want to marry you': Responding to children's ideas about health, *Research Information for Teachers*, 1, 21–28.

De Pian, L. (2013). Embodying policy? Young people, health education and obesity discourse. Unpublished doctoral thesis, Loughborough University, UK.

Evans, J., Davies, B., Rich, E. and De Pian, L. (2013). Understanding policy: Why health education policy is important and why it does not appear to work. *British Education Research Journal*, 39(2), 320–337.

Evans, J., De Pian, L., Rich, E. and Davies, B. (2011). Health imperatives, policy and the corporeal device: Schools, subjectivity and children's health. *Policy Futures in Education*, 9(3), 328–340.

Evans, J., Rich E., Davies, B. and Allwood, R. (2008). *Education, Disordered Eating and Obesity Discourse.* Abingdon: Routledge.

Fitzpatrick, K. (2011). Obesity, health and physical education: A Bourdieuean perspective. *Policy Futures in Education*, 9(3), 353–366.

Fitzpatrick, K. and Tinning, R. (2014). Considering the politics and practice of health education. In K. Fitzpatrick and R. Tinning (eds), *Health Education: Critical Perspectives.* London: Routledge, 1–14.

Gard, M. (2004). An elephant in the room and a bridge too far, or physical education and the 'obesity epidemic'. In J. Evans, B. Davies and J. Wright (eds), *Body Knowledge and Control: Studies in the Sociology of Physical Education and Health.* London: Routledge, 68–82.

Gard, M. (2008). Producing little decision makers and goal setters in the age of the obesity crisis. *Quest*, 60(4), 488–502.

Gard, M. (2010). *The End of the Obesity Epidemic*. London: Routledge.

Gard, M. and Pluim, C. (2014). *Schools and Public Health: Past, Present, Future*. Baltimore, MD: Lexington Books.

Gard, M. and Wright, J. (2005). *The Obesity Epidemic: Science, Morality and Ideology*. London, UK: Routledge.

Gillespie, L. and Culpan, I. (2000). Critical thinking: Ensuring the 'education' aspect is evident in physical education. *Journal of Physical Education New Zealand*, 44(3), 84–96.

Halse, C. (2009). Bio-citizenship: Virtue discourses and the birth of the bio-citizen. In J. Wright and V. Harwood (eds), *Biopolitics and the 'Obesity Epidemic': Governing Bodies*. New York: Routledge, 45–59.

Halse, C., Honey, A. and Boughtwood, D. (2007). The paradox of virtue: (Re)thinking deviance, anorexia and schooling. *Gender and Education*, 19(2), 219–235.

Kirk, D. (2006). The 'obesity crisis' and school physical education. *Sport, Education and Society*, 11(2), 121–133.

Kunc, N. (1992). The need to belong: Rediscovering Maslow's hierarchy of needs. In R. A. Villa, J. S. Thousand, W. Stainback and S. Stainback (eds), *Restructuring for Caring and Effective Education: An Administrative Guide to Creating Heterogeneous Schools*. Baltimore, MD: Paul H. Brookes Publishing Co., 25–40.

McCormack, J. (2012). Obesity, parents and me. Unpublished doctoral thesis, University of Otago, Dunedin, New Zealand.

Ministry of Education. (2007). *The New Zealand Curriculum*. Wellington, New Zealand: Ministry of Education.

National Audit Office. (2012). An update on the government's approach to tackling obesity. Memorandum for the committee of public account, 17 July, National Audit Office.

Penney, D. and Chandler, T. (2000). Physical education: What futures? *Sport, Education and Society*, 5(1), 71–87.

Petrie, K., Penney, D. and Fellows, S. (2014). Health and physical education in Aotearoa New Zealand: An open market and open doors? *Asia-Pacific Journal of Health, Sport and Physical Education*, 5(1), 19–38.

Powell, D. (2011). Running in circles: Children's lessons in PE, fitness and fatness. Master of Education thesis, University of Auckland, New Zealand.

Powell, D. (2014). Childhood obesity, corporate philanthropy and the creeping privatisation of health education. *Critical Public Health*, 24(2), 226–238.

Powell, D. and Fitzpatrick, K. (2013). 'Getting fit basically means, like, non-fat': Children's lessons in fitness and fatness. *Sport, Education and Society*, 20(4), 463–484.

Rich, E. and Evans, J. (2009). Now I am nobody, see me for who I am: The paradox of performativity. *Gender and Education*, 21(1), 1–16.

Rich, E., De Pian, L. and Francombe-Webb, J. (2015). Physical cultures of stigmatisation: Health policy and social class. *Sociological Research Online*, 20(2), 10.

Tamboukou, M. (2003). Interrogating the 'emotional turn': Making connections with Foucault and Deleuze. *The European Journal of Psychotherapy, Counselling and Health*, 6(3), 209–223.

Tasker, G. (1996–1997). For whose benefit? The politics of developing a health education curriculum. *Delta*, 48(2), 187–202.

43
INTERNATIONAL DEVELOPMENT AND POLICY

Simon C. Darnell

Introduction

This chapter brings a critical cultural studies approach to understanding policy, and in particular the various policy approaches and politics that underpin the relationship between sport and international development. In this way, the chapter positions sport as an important element of the broader field of cultural policy. According to Cunningham (2003: 14): 'cultural policy embraces that broad field of public processes involved in formulating, implementing and contesting governmental intervention in, and support of, cultural activity'. Policies focused on sport fit under this general category and therefore constitute a site at which to deploy a cultural studies framework.

The question of whether cultural studies scholars should attend to policy, its development and impact constitutes a debate with some history. During (2007) suggests that cultural studies scholars have often been divided over whether to maintain a critical perspective in as 'pure' a form as possible, and therefore eschew engaging with policy, or instead embrace the study of cultural policy in order to increase the relevance and applicability of cultural studies and perhaps even contribute to policy formation or reform (also see McGuigan, 2003). Particularly in the face of criticism that a focus on signification and textual meaning resulted in insufficient attention paid to the political and institutional fields and forces that regulate cultural production (ibid.), some sought to include policy studies within the cultural studies approach. This shift acknowledged 'the need to locate a policy horizon within cultural studies as a necessary part of its theorization of, and effective practical engagement with, relations of culture and power' (Bennett, 2007: 108). This position also refuted a strict dichotomy between culture and policy – in theory and/or practice – and instead embraced permeability in the relations between cultural policy and cultural criticism (ibid.: 110). These cultural policy scholars did not seek to be policy makers, but did embrace the idea of engaging with the array of institutions, 'both public and private, that are involved in the cultural shaping and regulation of the population', and recognized the mutual inter-dependence between grassroots, community-led, and bottom-up cultural activities on the one hand, and top-down, state-led policy and dictums on the other (ibid.: 112). They embraced issues of economics, history, Politics (with a capital P) and geography, and grounded the study of policy in the specificities of these elements. This breadth of context, while still focused on specific policy fields, was seen as a way to bridge the divide between the 'critical and vocational' that had structured much of the study of culture previously (Cunningham, 2003: 21).

It is this approach to critical, cultural policy studies that serves as an organizing framework for this chapter. Indeed, this handbook of essays on physical cultural studies (PCS) presents an opportune moment to study sport, policy and international development from such a cultural studies perspective. Sport continues to be an important matter of public policy in many countries, as governments seek to develop elite athletes but also to reap social benefits such as health, inclusion and community development (see Coalter, 2007). In fact, the notion that sport can make a positive contribution to development and peace on an international scale has been significantly institutionalized in recent years, particularly through the emergence of the sport for development and peace (SDP) sector (see Giulianotti, 2011), a loose amalgam of national governments and civil society actors such as non-governmental organizations (NGOs), corporations, charities and international sport organizations. SDP activity is characterized by the organization and deployment of sport to meet international development goals like poverty reduction, conflict resolution, health promotion and gender empowerment. This chapter proposes that a PCS approach to international development and policy will need to consider (at least) the following factors: history and politics, social and political context, processes of subjectification(s), and futures. Each is attended to here in some detail and contemporary examples from policy, practice and research are used throughout. The chapter does not exhaust the ways to analyse sport, international development and policy from a cultural studies perspective but offers some direction and approaches through which to bring the PCS lens to the topic.

History and politics

The study of policy is contestable to the extent that the terms of analysis are not always obvious or agreed upon. For example, Thibault and Harvey's (2013: 3) recent assessment of public sport policy in Canada states that there is 'currently no consensus in the literature' on what precisely constitutes government policy or programming. In the face of such ambiguity, public policy is often understood as the 'intentions or actions' of government, government strategies or instruments, or a combination thereof (Page, 2006: 210).

From a PCS perspective, however, this understanding of policy offers only the most basic of starting points, for several reasons. First, it may underplay the historical and contextual factors that have led to the formation of specific policies, as well as the ways in which policies themselves are part of political processes. Second, it may overlook the increasing importance of civil society and non-governmental actors in the broader policy field, a fact that applies to the case of the SDP sector (Giulianotti, 2011). And third, it may privilege a focus on policy documents and outcomes more than the political logic and vision that such documents endorse or promote. Thus, analysing policies as strategies, instruments or policies is important but needs to be complemented by analysis of the ideologies, historically and politically constituted, to which policies subscribe.

From this perspective, deploying a PCS approach to sport, policy and international development calls for an appreciation of the ways in, and extent to which, both international development and sport, respectively, have always constituted political projects. With respect to the former, international development, as both a concept and a series of interventions, has never been a benign act of policy, but rather a deeply historicized and highly politicized regime of truth and action deployed along particular vectors of power. For example, while many recognize that the modern era of international development began with US President Harry Truman's inauguration speech of 1949, the ideological, political and practical roots of development can be traced to the late colonial period (Craggs, 2014). It was during this time that European imperial powers often justified their global expansion and domination on the grounds that they were bringing humanitarian assistance to native and underserved populations. Truman's invocation of a crusade against global poverty in the post-war era was thus less than novel, and more the peak of longstanding debates and policies regarding how best to access and utilize the resources of the colonized world (ibid.).

This is not to say that Truman suggested continuing the practices of colonialism apace, as his speech did signify important shifts in development policy and thinking. In point four of his four-point address, he called on nations to participate in a 'worldwide effort for the achievement of peace, plenty and freedom' in order that poverty and suffering in 'underdeveloped areas' of the world could be eradicated. Yet in so doing, he introduced the idea of 'underdeveloped' people and places, and proposed that the goals of development could form new links between the world's rich and poor (Rist, 2008). This laid the groundwork for emerging schools of thought about how to achieve development on a global scale. In the 1960s, modernization theory surfaced, largely championed by American scholars and policy makers advocating that the state could and should regulate societies in accordance with universal values of liberal democracy (Gilman, 2003). Technology, industrialization, and Keynesian economics based on state-led growth were to be the backbone of this modernist era. Eventually, dependency theorists and post development thinkers challenged the precepts of modernization theory as being variously Eurocentric, totalizing and ineffectual. Most recently, the Millennium Development Goals have sought to achieve development on a global scale, though many of the targets for 2015 have not been met.

These perspectives demonstrate that the practices and policies of international development have been produced at particular historical conjunctures and driven by specific political goals and desires. Notably, a similar historical approach can be brought to the study of sport. For example, in offering context for the current institutionalization of sport for development and peace, historians have shown that the instrumental notion of sport as a tool for social development existed, for example, within the Victorian era, as part of the production of Imperial subjects, and amidst the social reform edicts of the twentieth-century YMCA. In Kidd's words:

> To be sure, social development through sport has a long history. Its aspirations can be traced back to the 'rational recreation' interventions of the improving middle and working class in the late nineteenth century, the 'playground movement' of the early twentieth century, and the confessional and workers' sports movements of the inter-war period, among other antecedents ... International social development through sport dates back to nineteenth-century colonizing.
>
> *(Kidd, 2008: 371)*

Similarly, Coalter (2007: 8) suggests that the history of public policy for sport (in the UK and elsewhere) has been characterized by an essential duality: a goal to extend the social rights of citizens, while simultaneously emphasizing a range of wider social benefits presumed to be associated with participation in sport. From these perspectives, there is no essential or natural connection between sport and social development. Rather, political actors have built such relationships at ideological and policy levels and done so within particular contexts.

The recent institutionalization of SDP, then, is but the latest form of sport for the social good and is also a product of its time and place. At least three contextual factors help to explain the current popularity and novelty of SDP. First, shifts in the political and policy terrain of international development in the 1990s saw development thinkers and policy makers move

International development and policy

from a strict focus on economic development towards a more nuanced and softer approach that increasingly focused on developing social capital (Coalter, 2013b). In this context, champions of sport's social benefits, who Coalter (ibid.) refers to as 'conceptual entrepreneurs', were able to make the case that sport offered a new approach to tackling underdevelopment and marginalization, particularly in terms of economics and health. Second, and during the same general time frame, organizations like the United Nations began to change their approach to peacebuilding from one focused on international borders and state institutions to individual safety and security as well as social reform (Zanotti et al., 2015). It was in this context that sport-based programmes were able to secure some ideological footing (ibid.). Third, while sport and the SDP sector continues to be promoted as an original approach or response to the longstanding problems of development, Hartmann and Kwauk (2011) remind us that this novelty stems in part from the neo-liberal reforms of the last three to four decades that have seen the reduction of many of the public services that formed the social contract of the twentieth-century welfare state. Thus it can be argued that World Bank policies of structural adjustment in the 1980s, that made reduction in public spending a condition of lending to poor countries, effectively handicapped the ability of many nations to provide social development support for their citizens. It is this void of public services that many SDP projects now attempt to fill.

Thus, the organization, novelty and policy orientation of SDP has historical underpinnings and has been both produced and constrained by a variety of political forces. With that said, the policy documents designed to guide and govern sport for development and peace are also revelatory of relations of power on a global scale. Hayhurst's (2009) discourse analysis of six SDP policy documents published between 2003 and 2008, three by the United Nations and three by the Sport for Development and Peace International Working Group (SDP IWG), showed that citizens of the Global South or Two-Thirds World are often positioned as 'passive recipients' of SDP policies that are derived by the 'political agendas and interests of donors, UN agencies and NGOs' (Hayhurst, 2009: 215). In an era of neo-liberal globalization, these policies often advocate for entrepreneurial, competitive and largely unregulated responses to development inequalities of global poverty, lack of education and poor health. As Hayhurst (ibid.) argues, SDP policies often seek to facilitate partnerships between NGOs and the private sector in ways that will encourage people in the Two-Thirds World to become more efficient and self-sufficient within an increasingly global marketplace but tend *not* to support government oversight or regulation, nor call for welfare state assistance in the tradition of social democracy. From this perspective, SDP is a political activity.

Contemporary political contexts

Recognizing, then, that international development, sport and the nascent SDP sector are all historically constituted, socially and politically regulated, and connected to issues of public policy, it is reasonable to situate current SDP initiatives within national political contexts, particularly as SDP policies may reflect the national characteristics of donor countries (Hasselgård, 2015). A host of countries have included sport for international development in their public policy agendas in recent years, and while many of these initiatives share important characteristics, they also illustrate important political differences, as well as internal domestic tensions.

Norway, for example, has a strong tradition of international development assistance, and has been a leading international player in SDP since the 1980s (ibid.). However, Hasselgård (ibid.) argues that there are differences and tensions *within* Norwegian SDP policy and practice, specifically over whether to focus on delivering sport programmes in a service provision model or pursue broader, structural changes through a more politically engaged model of development through sport. According to Hasselgård, such ideological tensions are illustrative of Norwegian society generally, and show that SDP policy is never predetermined, but influenced by a host of factors including 'traditions, identity and mandate, values, available development tools, Norwegian development, foreign policy priorities and international trends' (ibid.: 21).

Kidd (2013) has brought a similar analysis to bear on SDP policy in Canada. In 1992, Canadian sport leaders designed what became the Commonwealth Sport Development Programme, housed by Commonwealth Games Canada (CGC) and supported by funding from Sport Canada and the Canadian International Development Agency (CIDA). The initial strategy of the programme was to support capacity within the sport systems of underserved Commonwealth countries. Eventually, though, the approach morphed to something more in line with the mainstream SDP model, with a greater focus on mobilizing sport in support of gender empowerment, disability rights and poverty reduction. More recently though, SDP – like international development more broadly – has seen its support reduced in Canada. CGC 'shifted its support back to sport development' which meant that CIDA did not renew its funding to the organization in 2011 (Kidd, 2013: 88).[1] And while domestic sport for development was included in the 2012 Canadian sport policy, international SDP is no longer a priority (ibid.). Such shifts are notable in relation to the Canadian government's steady move to the political Right in the last two decades, which has seen international development increasingly 'tied' to Canada's economic interests.[2]

These relatively rich western democracies like Norway and Canada – as well as the United Kingdom that saw sport for development gain support amidst Tony Blair's Third Way agenda of the late 1990s – can be productively compared to countries that differ in political and economic terms. Cuba, for example, has been using sport as part of its international outreach and cooperation for decades. Recent analyses suggest that while Cuban sport policy shares some of the main conceptual tenets of the SDP model (i.e. a belief that sport can support social development) its approaches and programmes value solidarity more than aid (Darnell and Huish, 2015). Further, that Cuba makes its sports training programmes available to international partners through fully subsidized scholarships illustrates foreign policy of South–South cooperation, a very different approach than the 'tied aid' that currently characterizes policy in countries like Canada.

It is also important to recognize the nations that are typically understood to be the 'recipient' countries within the global SDP landscape. Zambia, for example, has been the focus of much SDP activity, and has received funding and programme support from UK Sport, the Norwegian Olympic Committee, as well as CGC (Banda, 2010). A PCS approach encourages critical consideration of the context in which this donor activity is required and delivered. A largely socialist country upon gaining independence in 1964, Zambian sport provision – both participatory and elite – was provided by state-owned corporations, particularly from the mining sector. However, 'Zambia experienced its worst economic hardships during the Structural Adjustment Programme in the early 1980s' (ibid.: 249), which left the government unable to deliver basic public services and in turn exacerbated the HIV/AIDS pandemic that was experienced within many African countries. This absence of public services is still felt today and set the stage for SDP initiatives that emerged to fill the gap (ibid.). From this perspective, while SDP may be laudable in its intentions, it cannot be divorced from the political history that produced its necessity.

Given these different approaches to sport for development, scholars are left with a rather muddled picture of SDP on a global scale. While countries like Canada and Norway have shown that they have the luxury to debate the preferred policy model of SDP, or indeed whether to support SDP at all, countries like Zambia must grapple with the possibilities that SDP offers for filling gaps in the public sector. At the same time, while Cuba has demonstrated remarkable persistence and political will in investing in sport-based cooperation despite its limited resources, the new political realities under the leadership of Raul Castro mean that little is guaranteed in terms of Cuba's future investment in sport for international solidarity.

Further complicating this picture are emerging critiques that suggest sport may in fact be an insignificant part of the policy response to inequality. Coalter (2013a) has made a compelling case that if countries like the UK wish to emulate and achieve the sport participation rates of Scandinavian countries such as Finland, this would require making a commitment to social equality that characterizes these countries. It may be the case that meeting the goals of sport policy – either to increase participation or facilitate social inclusion – is epiphenomenal to the policies themselves and instead connected much more fundamentally to the broader structures and politics of (in)equality within and between nations themselves. Coalter's argument can be extended to a global scale; if tackling inequality is beyond the scope of sport policy, then global inequality may also be beyond the reasonable expectations of policies and organizations within the SDP sector. Such insights are compatible with a PCS approach to policy, as they call for placing sport policies in critical dialogue with their contexts and politics. Advocates of sport, as well as PCS scholars, who wish to support meaningful and sustainable social change, may need to investigate and attempt to challenge the structures of inequality more than expand or improve sport policies and programmes that strive for the improvement or inclusion of marginalized individuals. Such issues are discussed further in the next section.

Subjectification(s)

One of the reasons cited for the importance of cultural policy studies is that culture is inseparable from governmentality and governmental practices. In particular, Bennett (2007) argued that the key cultural studies questions of agency, production, interpretation and resistance are not compromised by studying the regulatory 'conduct of conduct' but rather are to be understood in relation to regulatory forces, of which the state remains paramount. Recognizing that practices and processes of governmentality reach far beyond the policies of government itself, this insight nevertheless has resonance, both theoretical and material, for the study of sport, policy and international development. Specifically, it leads to questions such as: What kinds of subjects do policies seek? Through what processes does this occur? Since the body is often an important aspect of the PCS approach, how is the body understood in the study of international development and policy as it relates to sport? And how do such policies affect particular bodies? While recognizing that much research still remains to be done around such questions, recent analyses offer some important insights and perspectives.

First and perhaps foremost, critical scholars have drawn attention to the ways in which the logic and practice of sport for development may reproduce social and material relations of inequality more than challenge or reduce them. One of the most cogent arguments in this regard has been provided by Hartmann and Kwauk (2011) who distinguish between the dominant vision of sport for development as reproduction and the interventionist approach that would seek more fundamental changes. In the dominant approach, rather than pursuing social change, participants or subjects are 'taught' the means to survive within social structures that are fundamentally inequitable. In their words, the dominant version

> is not really about structural transformation and change. Rather, it is primarily about sport's ability to resocialize and recalibrate individual youth and young people that, in

turn, serves to maintain power and hierarchy, cultural hegemony, and the institutionalization of poverty and privilege.

(Hartmann and Kwauk, 2011: 291)

SDP research published after Hartmann and Kwauk's critique has empirically corroborated their perspective. For example, Hayhurst's (2013) analysis of SDP initiatives in Uganda found that the dominant logic of neo-liberal development – particularly as framed by the concept of the 'girl effect', which argues for the importance of investment in girls and young women – tends to impel NGOs to seek change by preparing and training girls and young women to be successful entrepreneurs. While this may result in girls and young women attaining some important economic independence, it also demonstrates the regulatory effects of capitalism upon people as subjects. Similarly, Forde's analyses of SDP health curricula have demonstrated a tendency to reduce the history and politics of the HIV/AIDS pandemic to issues of individual deficiency and risk (Forde, 2014), and to describe and imagine a gendered subject that is static and heteronormative (Forde and Frisby, 2015). In such cases, self-governance is imagined as a core competency of the preferred SDP subject.

Such findings serve as a reminder that as an approach to or basis of international development, neo-liberal policy can include as much as exclude (Ong, 2006), but this does not necessarily result in a state of play in which people make 'free choices', nor does it lessen the burden they may face in meeting their basic needs within an increasingly competitive social and economic order.

Conclusion: futures of sport and international development

This chapter has put forth some suggestions for the constitutive elements of a PCS approach to sport, policy and international development. While the historical perspective advocated here, as well as the political logic and subjectifications that it produces, encourages PCS scholars to consider the ways in which sport, policy and international development have emerged within particular conjunctures, it is also necessary to attend to what is still to come.

Central to such concerns are the ongoing changes in the structure and distribution of national power on a global scale. The rise of the BRICS nations (Brazil, Russia, India, China and South Africa) has tilted the axis of global power away from a single superpower and opened new opportunities for development. Schulz (2015) argues that the IBSA triple alliance (between India, Brazil and South Africa) represents a series of possibilities for these three democracies to pursue their stated goal of 'fair, equitable and just development' (ibid.: 272), ranging from the continued entrenchment of the neo-liberal machine, to a neo-Keynesian investment in the public sphere, or even new solidarity-based relationships along the lines of the Latin American Bolivarian alliance (ALBA) currently led by Venezuela. The point here is that the future of international development is yet to be determined. Particularly given the significance of sport for each of the IBSA countries (e.g. each has hosted at least one sports mega-event in recent years) the question is raised as to how they may approach sport, international development and policy in the near future.

A PCS approach is thus tasked with conducting analyses of past and current policies, but also of what future policies can and should do. This requires situating these activities within their social, political and historical context and asking critical questions about their logic, interests and effects, both discursive and material. This approach may require radical re-evaluation at two levels. The first level is that of sport-based policies and interventions themselves, as Hartmann and Kwauk (2011), among others, have argued. A PCS approach will do more than contribute to the monitoring and evaluation of SDP projects; it will serve to politicize them as well.

The other level of analysis that may require revision is nothing less than the social sciences themselves, since the social sciences have often analysed social phenomena in relatively isolated, and even nationalistic and ethno-centric terms. In asking what kinds of frameworks should be deployed 'to create an international social science that may include in its analysis the recognition and debate of the conflictive and contradictory processes of domination-subordination that have organized its differential epistemes and silenced so many', Vessuri (2015: 308) calls for approaches that eschew reduction and binaries and embrace connection. In his words, we should 'go beyond the universal/particular and the global/national. Of vital importance is to assert the need of combining place (and not only that of the nation-state) with multiple voices in the process of becoming organically interconnected.'

Such invocations could serve as the guiding principles for a PCS approach to sport, policy and international development. This approach would embrace the intersections of culture, economics and politics stimulated by the post-colonial condition, the history of development and the continuing, albeit unstable, hegemony of neo-liberal globalization. In addition to local and/or national assessments of sport and international development, fundamental and far-reaching questions remain to be asked about how such sport policies, initiatives and interventions are shaped by, and in turn serve to shape, an array of social and political forces and subjectivities.

Notes

1   At the same time, in 2013 the Canadian government folded CIDA into the Department of Foreign Affairs, setting up a potentially significant tension between long-term development assistance on the one hand, and political and trade agendas on the other (CBC, 2013).
2   This practice – sometimes referred to as 'tied aid' – has seen Canada base its foreign aid decisions primarily on trade and investment opportunities (Mackrael, 2014).

References

Banda, D. 2010. Zambia: Government's role in colonial and modern times. *International Journal of Sport Policy*, 2(2), 237–252.
Bennett, T. 2007. Culture and policy. In S. During (ed.), *The cultural studies reader*, 3rd edn. Routledge, 106–118.
CBC. 2013. Federal budget folds CIDA into Foreign Affairs. *CBC News*, 21 March. Available from www.cbc.ca/news/politics/federal-budget-folds-cida-into-foreign-affairs-1.1412948.
Coalter, F. 2007. *A wider social role for sport: Who's keeping the score?* London: Taylor & Francis.
Coalter, F. 2013a. Game plan and the spirit level: The class ceiling and the limits of sports policy? *International Journal of Sport Policy and Politics*, 5(1), 3–19.
Coalter, F. 2013b. *Sport for development: What game are we playing?* London: Routledge.
Craggs, R. 2014. Development in a global-historical context. In V. Desai, and R. Potter (eds), *The companion to development studies*, 3rd edn. London: Routledge, 5–10.
Cunningham, S. 2003. Cultural studies from the viewpoint of cultural policy. In J. Lewis and T. Miller (eds), *Critical cultural policy studies: A reader*, 13–22.
Darnell, S. C., and Huish, R. 2015. Cuban sport policy and South–South development cooperation: An overview and analysis of the Escuela Internacional de Educación Física y Deporte. *International Journal of Sport Policy and Politics*, 7(1), 123–140.
During, S. 2007. Editor's introduction – culture and policy. In S. During (ed.), *The cultural studies reader*, 3rd edn. Routledge, 106.
Forde, S. D. 2014. Look after yourself, or look after one another? An analysis of life skills in sport for development and peace HIV prevention curriculum. *Sociology of Sport Journal*, 31(3), 287–303.
Forde, S. D., and Frisby, W. 2015. Just be empowered: How girls are represented in a sport for development and peace HIV/AIDS prevention manual. *Sport in Society*, 18(8), 882–894.

Gilman, N. 2003. *Mandarins of the future: Modernization theory in cold war America*. Baltimore, MD: Johns Hopkins University Press.

Giulianotti, R. 2011. Sport, transnational peacemaking, and global civil society: Exploring the reflective discourses of 'sport, development, and peace' project officials. *Journal of Sport and Social Issues*, 35(1), 50–71.

Hartmann, D., and Kwauk, C. 2011. Sport and development: An overview, critique, and reconstruction. *Journal of Sport and Social Issues*, 35(3), 284–305.

Hasselgård, A. 2015. Norwegian sports aid: Exploring the Norwegian 'Sport for Development and Peace' discourse. *Forum for Development Studies*, 42(1), 1–25.

Hayhurst, L. M. 2009. The power to shape policy: Charting sport for development and peace policy discourses. *International Journal of Sport Policy*, 1(2), 203–227.

Hayhurst, L. M. 2013. The 'girl effect' and martial arts: Social entrepreneurship and sport, gender and development in Uganda. *Gender, Place and Culture*, 21(3), 297–315.

Kidd, B. 2008. A new social movement: Sport for development and peace. *Sport in Society*, 11(4), 370–380.

Kidd, B. 2013. Canada and sport for development and peace. In L. Thibault, and J. Harvey (eds), *Sport policy in Canada*. Ottawa: University of Ottawa Press, 69–94.

McGuigan, J. 2003. Cultural policy studies. In J. Lewis and T. Miller (eds), *Critical cultural policy studies: A reader*. Chichester: Wiley-Blackwell, 23–42.

Mackrael, K. 2014. Commercial motives driving Canada's foreign aid, documents reveal. *The Globe and Mail*, 8 January. Available from www.theglobeandmail.com/news/politics/globe-politics-insider/commercial-interests-taking-focus-in-canadas-aid-to-developing-world/article16240406/#dashboard/follows.

Ong, A. 2006. *Neoliberalism as exception: Mutations in citizenship and sovereignty*. Durham, NC: Duke University Press.

Page, E. 2006. The origins of policy. In M. Moran, M. Rein and R. G. Goodin (eds), *The Oxford handbook of public policy*. Oxford: Oxford University Press, 207–227.

Rist, G. 2008. *The history of development: From western origins to global faith*, 3rd edn. London: Zed Books.

Schulz, M. S. 2015. Inequality, development, and the rising democracies of the global south. *Current Sociology Monograph*, 63(2), 261–279.

Thibault, L., and Harvey, J. 2013. *Sport policy in Canada*. Ottawa: University of Ottawa Press.

Vessuri, H. 2015. Global social science discourse: A southern perspective on the world. *Current Sociology Monograph*, 63(2), 297–313.

Zanotti, L., Stephenson Jr, M., and Schnitzer, M. 2015. Biopolitical and disciplinary peacebuilding: Sport, reforming bodies and rebuilding societies. *International Peacekeeping*, 22(2), 186–201.

44
GLOBAL MEGA-EVENTS, POLICY AND LEGACY

Barbara Schausteck de Almeida

Introduction

Some sport competitions go beyond physical contests of local interest and become global exhibitions that demand complex preparation and investments, generating significant impact for hosting cities and countries. In these cases, events reach stages on some criteria – most notably the international interest, number of visitors, media coverage and costs – to be classified as 'mega' events (Roche, 2000). More recently, the even greater magnitude of the Summer Olympic Games compared to other mega-events such as the FIFA World Cup, the Expos and the Winter Olympic Games motivated the creation of the term 'giga-event' to a more precise classification (Muller, 2015). Considering these variables, staging mega/giga-events does not rely on sporting purposes, but mostly on the possibility of perceived transformation of cities that last well beyond the event (Preuss, 2015).

Although policymakers and sport governing bodies tend to focus on the beneficial transformations of such events, mega-events also represent enormous challenges and risks. Grabher and Thiel (2014) argue that mega-events resemble natural disasters for their character of fixed deadline that triggers rigorous protocols of preparations and precautions. As a self-induced shock, mega-events are capable of changing routines and deliberately causing disruptions (ibid.), including a 'justification' for gentrification and displacement of low-income communities recently seen in Olympic Games host cities – Beijing 2008 (Wang, Bao and Lin, 2015), London 2012 (Watt, 2013) and Rio 2016 (Sánchez and Broudehoux, 2013).

The aim of this chapter is to point to some possibilities of a physical cultural studies (PCS) approach to the study of sport mega-events, particularly pointing to commonalities and differences that host cities and countries have been showing in the recent years. To do so, I use Silk (2011) and Silk and Manley (2012) as a starting point, as these are two examples of explicit adoption of a PCS approach to understand and reflect upon sports mega-events. Distinctly, the authors propose a radical contextualization of such events, and comparison across national contexts, through a framework of three axes. As a theoretical and a reflexive exercise, I use their propositions to 'test' and discuss to what extent they are applied to the case of Brazil and Rio de Janeiro, pointing to the factors that confirm, as well as may improve the potentialities of PCS for sports mega-events' studies. In other words, this chapter is driven by these two questions: is the PCS framework proposed by Silk (2011) and Silk and Manley (2012) useful to discuss and understand the cases of sports mega-events in Brazil (2014 FIFA World Cup and 2016 Rio de Janeiro Olympic and Paralympic Games)? To what extent these cases differ from the framework and can potentially suggest new approaches to the PCS studies of sports mega-events?

Then, engaging Silk's (2011) proposed agenda to analyze the London 2012 as a mediated mega-event (Roche, 2000), I describe some key points of the Brazilian experience on preparing and hosting the 2014 FIFA Men's World Cup and the 2016 Olympic and Paralympic Games in Rio de Janeiro. Then, I indicate convergences and particularities between these cases, as well as in comparison to those cases that were studied by PCS scholars, pointing to some of the possibilities to extend the study on sport mega-events through a PCS approach.

Contributions for the debate on sport mega-events

The complexity of mega-events can be related to their size and demand for investments, their international reach and the specificities of each host city and country. As a consequence, some questions appear to be local, according to the context and history of a city hosting the events, while others may be intrinsic to the events themselves. Frameworks are useful to allow comparison and the identification of commonalities and/or differences among cases of sports mega-events. In this sense, Silk (2011) proposed the academic reflection of London 2012 upon three 'productive avenues': the façade of 'glurbanization', the commodification of pastness and the quest for sameness. To some extent, Silk and Manley (2012) tested these avenues regarding four Pacific Asian cases of sporting events – the Commonwealth Games in Kuala Lumpur 1998 and in Delhi 2010, the 2008 Beijing Olympic Games and the Singapore Formula 1 Grand Prix. Following Silk's (2011) order, the authors discussed the 'avenues' as 3 Ps. The first 'P' is for places, discussing the 'glocal' (global plus local) and the 'grobal' (growth plus global). The second is pastness, pointing to 'heritage, histories and capital'. Lastly, peoples are discussed as 'the sanitized soul of the sporting spectacle'. I use both articles to address the three avenues and their examples.

First, Silk (2011) uses the concept of glurbanization – originally from Jessop (1997) – to describe the junction of globalization and urbanization, as the intent of a location to maintain a status of 'global city'. Then, the façade is built on creation or 'resuscitation' of an area, mostly on its aesthetic, to temporarily represent a few specific interests and images that are attractive to international branding and touristic influx. The main issue on this process is that voices and representations are ignored for not fitting to the narrative of interest, even if they are more concrete representations of local culture and landscape of the entire city (Silk, 2011). Silk and Manley (2012) argue that Pacific Asian cities in the context of sport mega-events are particularly interested in being part of the global economy and politics, balancing their images not only between showing global adaptation and local uniqueness (global plus local), but also as part of aspirations of global forces to be introduced in the region and in local markets to gain influence, profit and power (growth plus global). On both processes, glocal and grobal, there are mutual interferences; then, global and local should not be seen as opposed to each other. Within this context, sports mega-events become a 'short cut' to manifest an intended image at a global stage for an international audience and particularly to potential tourists and investments (Silk and Manley, 2012: 469).

Second, the commodification of pastness refers to how history and heritage are used to model a city within a range of interpretations that fit to the general representation of a global city attractive for tourists. Again, by selecting the images and what part of history matters, these representations reinforce existing power structures, ignore social struggles and incorporate some dominant political and ideological views. These selections are present in the Olympic Games ceremonies and, in some cases, facilities built as iconic buildings become a backdrop for competitions and television broadcasting (Silk, 2011). Even with the global and grobal forces intervening, local specificities are important to distinctiveness, as a point of positioning the city among its competitors in the global sphere. However, these specificities are frequently manipulated, using history and heritage as a tool to work in favor of political and ideological interests. In their analysis of the Asian Pacific sporting spectacles, Silk and Manley (2012: 472) described history as being 'neatly designed, decorative, commercial and manufactured forms palatable for consumption'.

Finally, the quest of sameness is the attempt to mask (mostly ethnic and class) differences, presenting a supposed common identity instead of embracing the plurality that composes the population. While some discourses may appear to be inclusive, forced evictions and displacement, as well as reducing differences to 'exotic' and distancing 'we' to 'them', are evidences of exclusion processes. Most of all, these attempts often present union, harmony and cohesion that are clearly utopic in any society, but are part of idealized identity and representations of the nation (Silk, 2011). While representing a 'world class city', rural and poor populations, for example, do not 'fit' into the discourse, leading to their isolation on the city's aesthetic. Then, representations tend to privilege middle and upper classes, private investors and businessmen, foreigners and tourists, as it was particularly in the case of Delhi 2010. In most of the cases, people in disadvantaged situations are likely to see their rights diminished with sport mega-events (Silk and Manley, 2012).

As useful as a framework potentially is, critical engagement is always necessary. This is particularly the case when the proposal is applied in different societies and periods of time. Then, local and national social, cultural, political and economic contexts have major importance, leading to adaptation or improvement for the framework when analyzing any given case. For this reason, the next section illustrates points of convergence and difference that one may identify regarding the framework proposal and the sport mega-events in Brazil. I build the arguments below based on the academic literature that are directly or indirectly linked to the preparations and analysis of these events, information from the media and from official documents of the bids.

Rio de Janeiro and Brazil on the sport mega-event circuit

The façade of glurbanization

Although the majority of interests to host sports mega-events have already been identified and analyzed in the past, some differentials are seen in candidatures and hosting in so-called peripheral or developing countries. For example, the media exposure is followed by image management on trying to change prejudices against a city or a country (Cornelissen, 2004). In the same way, the construction by the population of a collective view about themselves and about the future is accompanied by discourses using mega-events as an evidence of '"graduation" or "arrival" among the world's leading cities and countries—the achievement of "world class" or "world city"' (Black, 2007: 270). As observed in the 2010 FIFA Men's World Cup in South Africa and the bid of Cape Town for the Olympic Games, the discourses of a hosting country representing the integration or the whole continent is also an element that can be explored (Desai and Vahed, 2010; Pillay and Bass, 2008; Swart and Bob, 2004; Hiller, 2000).

These observations do not differ from what Brazil has mobilized during the bid and preparation for two sports mega-events: the 2014 FIFA Men's World Cup and the 2016 Olympic and Paralympic Games. When FIFA and the International Olympic Committee chose the country to host these events in 2007 and 2009, respectively, Brazil was living a golden era of economic growth and international visibility. The Brazilian gross domestic product (GDP) more than tripled from 2003 to 2010, ending the decade as the world's seventh biggest economy (World Bank, 2012). Politically, Brazil intended to use this position to establish partnership with developing countries and be their representative on global institutions such as the United Nations and the World Trade Organization, as well as proclaiming itself as a regional leader (Vigevani and Cepaluni, 2007; Soares de Lima and Hirst, 2006). These two key foreign policy strategies help to explain some of the discursive arguments during the Rio de Janeiro bid for the 2016 Olympic and Paralympic Games: in particular, the importance of being the first games in South America, to boost the structural improvements in the city that were already in progress and to be a platform to promote Brazil internationally (Comitê de Candidatura, 2009).

The Rio 2016 bid was part of the Brazilian foreign policy agenda to reinforce and establish multilateral relations, to show economic and political growth and its leadership in South America at an international platform of visibility such as the Olympic Games. Additionally, winning an international election against 'developed' countries (United States, Spain and Japan) temporarily positioned the country among the international leaders in both symbolic and discursive spheres (Almeida, 2015). For the 2014 FIFA Men's World Cup, a different process of selection disallowed the same strategic use, as the absent international concurrence and the initial perspective of a private endeavor did not appear at first as a national project. However, the preparations turned significantly to a public project of local and national spheres upon the building of football stadiums and the logistics on demand (Almeida et al., 2013). Disagreements with the demands of FIFA and particularly to the public spending on these facilities were some of the motivations for compelling protests in different cities during the month of June 2013, mobilizing one million people nationwide (see Watts, 2013).

To some extent, the public dissatisfaction evident through the protests represented the disagreements on using public resources to show the *façade of glurbanization*. Some of the 2013 protesters understood that investment in health and education services would be more important than having up-to-date sports facilities, according to the newest demands of FIFA. These protests disempowered part of the *glurbanization* discourse by bringing the hyper-visibility of mega-events to some of Brazil's most chronic problems, instead of ignoring or turning them invisible.

However, some of the *glurbanization* effects were strongly powerful over economically disadvantaged communities, where it worked together with gentrification (see Horne, 2015; Sánchez and Broudehoux, 2013; Silvestre and Oliveira, 2012). The 2014 FIFA World Cup and the 2016 Olympic and Paralympic Games opened a window of opportunity for massive urban interventions, particularly useful for a city like Rio de Janeiro, where the 'urban disorder' was mainly represented by slums (*favelas*), a point of great concern for politicians, middle-class inhabitants and real estate investors for some time. Then, the State implemented new policies and the term 'removal' became 'an important dimension of State management in some territories and population', justified by the idea that the events were bringing a 'legacy' for the city (Magalhães, 2013: 102). Appropriating the idea of La Barre (2016: 360) for this context, the mega-events represents 'two antagonistic temporalities' of the *façade of glurbanization*: first, the 'Rio Re-Marvelous', where 're' represents the opportunity for new possibilities for the city; and second, the 'Dystopian Rio', where the social human condition of removal and criminalization become part of the routine.

The commodification of pastness

History and heritage have relatively different patterns and characteristics in Brazil compared to other countries. For this reason, I describe one possible interpretation for the Brazilian identity building that may help to explain the discourses and images that were selected to represent Brazil within the context of sports mega-events. This possible interpretation begins on the so-called 'foundation myth', as the arrival of the Portuguese led by Pedro Álvares Cabral in 1500 and the exploitation of natural resources is understood as the country's 'discovery' (Chauí, 2010). The native indigenous inhabitants' history prior to the Portuguese arrival is mostly ignored by the 'official history'. After centuries of colonization in Brazil by Portugal and in other Latin American countries mostly by Spain, the Iberian/European heritage is alluded to in popular national histories, while the indigenous heritage is often omitted (Vargas, 2003). In Brazil, I would argue that the lack of visible material heritage about native indigenous lives, such as monuments and historical artifacts, is one of the aspects that differentiate Brazilian native indigenous people from others in Latin America (particularly Mayans, Incas and Aztecs), giving different meanings and importance to each people's history.

This background *per se* helps to explain why Brazilian history is relatively 'young'. From 1500 to 1822, Brazil was a colony of Portugal and in 1888 slavery was prohibited. The recent independence of a society formed by Portuguese, former African slaves and native indigenous required the building of a national identity to maintain the unity in the gigantic territory. The first positive element of reference used to the Brazilian identity was the natural environment, as a symbol of pride and singularity (Souza, 2011). The biodiversity, the size of the territory, the beauty and variety of forests and rivers that were not affected by environmental catastrophes would reinforce the idea of a 'divine gift' (Chauí, 2010: 9). At that point, the post-colonial elite thought that Brazil's mixed-ethnic character represented the worst of each group and were far from reaching European levels of 'development'. Then, nature would partially substitute the greatness and beauty that were non-existent in the population (Souza, 2006).

So far, this contextualization points to the fact that the *commodification of pastness* has specific contours that influence the national history discourses surrounding the sports mega-events in Brazil. As the 'official' history of Brazil starts with the arrival of the Portuguese in the year of 1500, the prior occupation of native indigenous populations and their struggles during the colonization period are ignored. Then, a selective view of heritage appears as the genuine or the sole explanation for the national history.

According to Vanolo (2008), cities use different metaphoric symbols as a strategy to urban branding, using material (roads, monuments, buildings) and immaterial (habits, routines, institutions) components. For Brazilian cities, the natural environment is one of the main metaphoric symbols, fitting the stereotype of what the whole country has to offer, particularly to tourists. For the 2014 FIFA World Cup, the visual identity was based on variations of a green and yellow stylized image that represent the sun, mountains, a river and leaves (see FIFA, 2010: 6). This image illustrated official documents and decorations inside and outside the stadiums. Some of the host cities' posters also had illustrations referring to nature, such as birds (Belo Horizonte, Cuiabá and Manaus), a typical tree (Curitiba), beaches (Fortaleza, Natal and Rio de Janeiro), mountains and sun (Rio de Janeiro). Fortaleza and Belo Horizonte also have illustrations on buildings and iconic touristic points. The cities of Porto Alegre and São Paulo represented buildings and industry; Recife focused on its local culture and Salvador and Brasília presented their iconic sightseeing (see Brasil, 2012a). These differences demonstrate that while FIFA's visual identity standardized an image for Brazil, the host cities chose other aspects to symbolize their particularities. While the majority of cities used nature as a subject of representation, the idea of glurbanization is also present, probably aiming to act against some of the country's stereotypes.

This appeal to the natural beauty of Brazil is also noticeable on the discourses surrounding the 2016 Olympic and Paralympic Games. The Rio 2016 bid committee defended in the introduction of its bid book that 'The Rio 2016 Games would use the most the city's natural landscape ... The athletes will compete among the most well-known sceneries of the planet. Extraordinary images will be broadcasted worldwide' (Comitê de Candidatura, 2009: 18). The former Brazilian president Luiz Inácio Lula da Silva used similar adjectives during his speech to praise the city of Rio de Janeiro on the election day for the voting members of the International Olympic Committee: 'the most beautiful and marvelous city' and 'one of the most beautiful and welcoming cities of the world' (Silva, 2009: 2–3). Nature was primarily seen as an asset, but it is proving to be a topic of controversies, as the governments failed to clean the pollution of bay's water as promised. Tests run by the Associated Press showed that the water offered high risk of infection to athletes at Guanabara Bay, where sailing competitions were to be held (Brooks, 2015). Despite promises and contestation from local authorities, it seemed that once again a potential point of virtue had, in fact, a hidden chronic problem.

In the next section of this chapter, I present the development that followed the use of the natural environment on the Brazilian identity building, when being a mixed-ethnic society became a virtue to be celebrated.

The quest for sameness

As briefly mentioned above, the mixture of ethnic influences was first seen as a problem for the Brazilian post-colonial elite. At that time, scientists used arguments supposedly based on biology to explain the superiority and inferiority of ethnic groups, reinforcing prejudice and serving as an explanation for the barriers to the country's modernization (Maio, 1999). From the 1920s to the 1940s, writings by Gilberto Freyre inverted these explanations and started to see the miscegenation as a cultural advantage. Freyre ([1933] 2003) saw and remarked on positive aspects of the three groups – Portuguese, native indigenous and African former slaves – and their descendants. By transforming the ethnic diversity into a merit, struggles were hidden or denied. At that historical moment, the idea of a 'racial democracy' was useful to direct the profile of Brazilians as a population ideally pacific and free of prejudices (Souza, 2011). Internationally, this idea inspired a study led by UNESCO during the 1940s to 1950s aiming to understand how Brazilian society was living with lower racial-ethnic tensions (Maio, 1999). Politically, this supposition was particularly useful for the nationalist government of Getúlio Vargas when it aimed to have a national unity around its project of State reform – then, the Brazilian football players served as a representation of the Brazilian people and the merits of a mixed-ethnic society (Drumond, 2009).

The belief of a 'racial democracy' is easily identifiable in Brazilian society. Through an individual manner of seeing the world, Brazilians notice daily the ethnic diversity and selectively recognize the 'democracy', instead of the prejudice and the struggles that happen every day. For this reason, the myths that support the national identity and its individual identification are still alive (Chauí, 2010). However, in 2015 the United Nations Special Rapporteur on minority issues, Ms Rita Izsák, visited Brazil and wrote that 'Poverty in Brazil has colour' (Izsák, 2015). She argued that Afro-Brazilians are marginalized, suffer discrimination and exclusion, and rarely occupy key positions, both in private and public organizations (ibid.). National data from 2010 showed that 43.1 percent of people auto-declared being *pardo* (more than one ethnic ascendance), 7.6 percent black and 47.7 percent white. Despite being the majority of the population, *pardos* and black are less represented as higher education students than white (31 percent are white, 12.8 percent are black and 13.4 percent are *pardos*); and salaries are still bigger for white people (Brasil, 2012b).

With this background of historical inequalities based on the blending of ethnicity and class, attempts of neutralizing the differences through discursive strategies are very much present on official political occasions. *The quest for sameness* is well observed when Brazil tried to show unity and a supposed particularity of its population during the bid for, and hosting of, sports mega-events.

During the speech for the IOC voting members, the former president Luiz Inácio Lula da Silva presented himself as a representative of all 190 million Brazilians, 'all united, supporting Rio de Janeiro' (Silva, 2009: 1). Then, he used the symbol of the Olympic five rings to refer to Brazil, arguing that the country is composed by people from all continents that are proud of being Brazilians without forgetting their origins. Then, in his words, 'We are not only a mixed people, but people that like to be mixed. This is what makes our identity' (ibid.). As these arguments compose the two first paragraphs of the discourse, he summarizes the whole country as a peaceful and harmonious unity that sees the miscegenation as a quality and as central to its identity. As the ethnic diversity is naturalized by society, official documents and discourses treat it as a positive reality. However, differences of class – that are intrinsically linked to ethnicity – are an unavoidable issue to mention.

The Rio 2016 Bid Committee pointed out that youth are part of the strategic vision, motivations and legacy to promote the Olympic Games. On the strategic vision, youth appeared on two occasions: first, to motivate young people to engage in the Games; second, to socially transform the city through sport, using the facilities to integrate young people and impoverished communities (Comitê de Candidatura, 2009). From these discourses, I argue that the youth of interest for Rio 2016 varies: on one hand, reference is to the poor youth Brazilians that would benefit from sports programs as an indirect effect from the Games. On the other hand, there is an interest on young consumers of sport not only from Brazil, but from South and Latin America, which are potentially interesting for sponsors and for sports governing bodies.

From the 2014 FIFA World Cup, the white majority of the public inside the stadiums were noticeable. A study of one match (Brazil v. Chile) showed that 67 percent of spectators declared to be white, 90 percent to upper economic classes and 86 percent had a higher degree of education (with a margin of error of 4 percent; Barbosa, 2014). This data supports the idea that *sameness* appears on discourses and public relation communication, whereas benefits go to privileged groups during preparation and hosting of sport mega-events.

Conclusion

This chapter aimed to present some of the debates on sports mega-events, pointing to the possibilities of a physical cultural studies approach to research on these phenomena. Engaging and extending Silk's (2011) proposed framework, I presented possibilities of interpretations on the recent Brazilian case of hosting the 2014 FIFA Men's World Cup and the 2016 Rio Olympic and Paralympic Games to analyze sports mega-events. More specifically, these two sports mega-events were discussed based on the façade of glurbanization, the commodification of pastness and the quest for sameness. As illustrated, to understand sports mega-events and particularly the society that bid to host them, these three topics of concern require careful contextualization. In fact, the effort was mostly to show what the evident face of glurbanization, pastness and sameness hide in the case of Brazil, similarly to what previous studies showed in other societies. Describing the history and the notion of heritage in a post-colonial country of mixed-ethnic populations has, in fact, reinforced the principles of the hidden social power struggles that mega-events tend to obfuscate. The junction of sport governing bodies aiming to sell their mega-events' products, and countries and cities aiming to show an attractive image to investors and tourists are likely to leave behind differences, diversity and human rights for unprivileged local communities. Although it seems that impoverished groups are visible in the invisibility of a society of enormous inequalities, sports mega-events tend to increase the gaps and, for this reason, need to be assessed and evaluated carefully.

Simultaneously, the framework is helpful to notice how these three factors reappear at different events and periods of time, even in very different societies where this visibility is not as evident. Then, PCS has the potential of pointing to the multitude of forces that influence and are influenced by mega-events, going beyond the limitations and the ephemerality of the event itself, as well as crossing geographical boarders at its assessments. However, the intensity in which the three axes appear is particular to each case. For instance, pastness receives a different significance in Brazil compared to other societies, such as those described by Silk and Manley (2012). Similarly, glurbanization and sameness related to the sports mega-events need to be appropriately addressed according to the specificities of the Brazilian history and society, as the preparations for the sports mega-events have made social, ethnic and geographical inequalities even more visible.

In sum, this chapter is a tentative collaboration to think how PCS can help to build upon and extend analysis on sports mega-events. Any intention of closing the debate or reaching every possible aspect on the subject would be unrealistic. Rather, I conclude by agreeing with Silk and Andrews (2011) that healthy contestations are welcomed to create an informed and growing body of knowledge in this area.

References

Almeida, BS (2015). Altius, citius, fortius … ditius? Lógicas e estratégias do Comitê Olímpico Internacional, Comitê de Candidatura e Governo brasileiro na candidatura e escolha dos Jogos Olímpicos e Paralímpicos Rio 2016. PhD dissertation, Physical Education Department, Universidade Federal do Paraná.

Almeida, BS, Bolsmann, C, Marchi Jr, W and Souza, J (2013). Rationales, rhetoric and realities: FIFA's World Cup in South Africa 2010 and Brazil 2014. *International Review for the Sociology of Sport*, 50(3): 265–282.

Barbosa, M (2014). Brancos e ricos são maioria na torcida do Brasil no Mineirão, diz Datafolha. *Folha de S. Paulo*, 29 June. Available from www1.folha.uol.com.br/poder/2014/06/1478120-brancos-e-ricos-sao-maioria-na-torcida-do-brasil-no-mineirao-diz-datafolha.shtml (accessed 15 March 2016).

Black, D (2007). The symbolic politics of sport mega-events: 2010 in comparative perspective. *Politikon*, 34(3): 261–276.

Brasil (2012a). Host cities unveil official World Cup posters. Available from www.copa2014.gov.br/en/noticia/host-cities-unveil-official-world-cup-posters (accessed 14 March 2016).

Brasil (2012b). Censo 2010 mostra as características da população brasileira. *Portal Brasil*, 2 July. Available from www.brasil.gov.br/educacao/2012/07/censo-2010-mostra-as-diferencas-entre-caracteristicas-gerais-da-populacao-brasileira (accessed 15 March 2016).

Brooks, B (2015). AP test: Rio Olympic water badly polluted, even far offshore. *The Associated Press*, 2 December. Available from http://bigstory.ap.org/article/cabd453515244bf2b1063e15f6b680c9/ap-test-rio-olympic-water-badly-polluted-even-far-offshore (accessed 14 March 2016).

Chauí, M (2010). *Brasil: mito fundador e sociedade autoritária*, 8th edn. São Paulo: Fundação Perseu Abramo.

Comitê de Candidatura (2009). *Sumário Executivo*, vol. 1. Rio de Janeiro. Available from www.rio2016.org.br/sites/default/files/parceiros/dossie_de_candidatura_v1.pdf (accessed 15 December 2015).

Cornelissen, S (2004). 'It's Africa's turn!' The narratives and legitimations surrounding the Moroccan and South African bids for the 2006 and 2010 FIFA finals. *Third World Quarterly*, 25(7): 1293–1309.

Desai, A and Vahed, G (2010). World Cup 2010: Africa's turn or the turn on Africa? *Soccer and Society*, 11(1–2): 154–167.

Drumond, M (2009). O esporte como política de estado: Vargas. In M Del Priore and VA Melo (eds), *História do Esporte no Brasil* (pp. 213–244). São Paulo: Editora Unesp.

FIFA (2010). FIFA public guidelines for use of FIFA's official marks. Available from http://resources.fifa.com/mm/document/affederation/marketing/01/37/85/97/2014_fifapublic guidelines_eng_13032014_neutral.pdf (accessed 14 March 2016).

Freyre, G ([1933] 2003). *Casa Grande e Senzala: formação da família brasileira sob o regime da economia patriarcal*, 48th edn. São Paulo: Global.

Grabher, G and Thiel, J (2014). Coping with a self-induced shock: the heterarchic organization of the London Olympic Games 2012. *Social Sciences*, 3: 527–548.

Hiller, HH (2000). Mega-events, urban boosterism and growth strategies: an analysis of the objectives and legitimations of the Cape Town 2004 Olympic bid. *International Journal of Urban and Regional Research*, 24(2): 439–458.

Horne, J (2015). Sports mega-events – three sites of contemporary political contestation. *Sport in Society* (online first). doi: 10.1080/17430437.2015.1088721.

Izsák, R (2015). End of mission statement of the United Nations Special Rapporteur on minority issues, Ms. Rita Izsák Brasilia, 24 September. Available from www.ohchr.org/EN/NewsEvents/Pages/DisplayNews.aspx?NewsID=16493andLangID=E (accessed 16 March 2016).

Jessop, B (1997). The entrepreneurial city: Re-imaging localities, redesigning economic governance, or, restructuring capital? In N. Jewson and S. Macgregor (eds). *Transforming cities: Contested governance and new spatial divisions* (pp. 28–41). London: Routledge.

La Barre, J (2016). Future shock: mega-events in Rio de Janeiro. *Leisure Studies*, 35(3): 352–368.

Magalhães, A (2013). O 'legado' dos megaeventos esportivos: a reatualização da remoção de favelas no Rio de Janeiro. *Horizontes Antropológicos*, 19(40): 89–118.

Maio, MC (1999). O projeto UNESCO e a agenda das Ciências Sociais no Brasil dos anos 40 e 50. *Revista Brasileira de Ciências Sociais*, 14(41): 141–158.

Muller, M (2015). What makes an event a mega-event? Definition and sizes. *Leisure Studies*, 34(6): 627–642.

Pillay, U and Bass, O (2008). Mega-events as a response to poverty reduction: the 2010 FIFA World Cup and its urban development implications. *Urban Forum*, 19: 329–346.

Preuss, H (2015). A framework for identifying the legacies of a mega sport event. *Leisure Studies*, 34(6): 643–664.

Roche, M (2000). *Mega-events and Modernity: Olympics and Expos in the Growth of Global Culture*. New York: Routledge.

Sánchez, F and Broudehoux, A-M (2013). Mega-events and urban regeneration in Rio de Janeiro: planning in a state of emergency. *International Journal of Urban Sustainable Development*, 5(2): 132–153.

Silk, M (2011). Towards a sociological analysis of London 2012. *Sociology*, 45(5): 733–748.

Silk, MK and Andrews, DL (2011). Toward a physical cultural studies. *Sociology of Sport Journal*, 28: 4–35.

Silk, M and Manley, A (2012). Globalization, urbanization and sporting spectacle in Pacific Asia: places, peoples and pastness. *Sociology of Sport Journal*, 29: 455–484.

Silva, LIL (2009). *Discurso do Presidente da República, Luiz Inácio Lula da Silva, na sessão de apresentação da Candidatura Rio 2016 ao Comitê Olímpico Internacional (COI)*. Copenhagen, Denmark. 2 October. Available from www.biblioteca.presidencia.gov.br/presidencia/ex-presidentes/luiz-inacio-lula-da-silva/discursos/2o-mandato/2009/copy_of_02-10-2009-discurso-do-presidente-da-republica-luiz-inacio-lula-da-silva-na-sessao-de-apresentacao-da-candidatura-rio-2016-ao-coi/view (accessed 14 March 2016).

Silvestre, G and Oliveira, N (2012). The revanchist logic of mega-events: community displacement in Rio de Janeiro's West End. *Visual Studies*, 27(2): 204–210.

Soares de Lima, MR and Hirst, M (2006). Brazil as an intermediate state and regional power: action, choice and responsibilities. *International Affairs*, 82(1): 21–40.

Souza, J (2006). *A invisibilidade da desigualdade brasileira*. Belo Horizonte: Editora UFMG.

Souza, J (2011). *A ralé brasileira: quem é e como vive*. Belo Horizonte: Editora UFMG.

Swart, K and Bob, U (2004). The seductive discourse of development: the Cape Town 2004 Olympic bid. *Third World Quarterly*, 25(7): 1311–1324.

Vanolo, A (2008). The image of the creative city: some reflections on urban branding in Turin. *Cities*, 25(6): 370–382.

Vargas, S (2003). Identidad, sujeto y resistencia en América Latina. *Confluencia*, 1(1): 1–12.

Vigevani, T and Cepaluni, G (2007). A política externa de Lula da Silva: a estratégia da autonomia pela diversificação. *Contexto internacional*, 29(2): 273–335.

Wang, M, Bao, HXH and Lin, P (2015). Behavioural insights into housing relocation decisions: the effects of the Beijing Olympics. *Habitat International*, 47: 20–28.

Watt, P (2013). 'It's not for us' – regeneration, the 2012 Olympics and the gentrification of East London. *Cities*, 17(1): 99–118.

Watts, J (2013). Brazil's protests raise fears for World Cup as a million take to the streets. *The Guardian*, 21 June 2013. Available from www.theguardian.com/world/2013/jun/21/brazil-protests-football-world-cup (accessed 22 December 2015).

World Bank (2012) GDP at market prices (current US$). Available from http://data.worldbank.org/indicator/NY.GDP.MKTP.CD (accessed 22 December 2015).

45
DIGITAL MEDIATION, CONNECTIVITY, AND NETWORKED TEENS

Jessica Ringrose and Laura Harvey

Introduction

While physical cultural studies takes active embodiment as its analytical starting point (Silk and Andrews, 2011), it has to date tended to focus on exercise, fitness, health, movement, leisure, recreation, dance and sport practices. Not surprisingly, there has been a plethora of technologies that articulate with our physical cultures – from m-health apps to 'smart' baby-grows, gaming to GPS fitness trackers such as RunKeeper, Runtastic; Nike+ Running, Endomono and so on – all of which demonstrate the crabgrass-like entanglements between everyday physical culture and new media technologies (Williamson, 2015). In this context, this chapter explores the embodiment of teen gender and sexual cultures and practices, examining their interconnectedness with media technologies. In doing so, we argue that the active embodiment of both technologies and sexualities are important questions for the emerging field of physical cultural studies.

danah boyd's (2008, 2014) work has consistently illustrated how much young people 'heart' social networking and find digital connections, including flirtation and sexual communication 'dramatic', exciting and fun (Marwick and boyd, 2011). Marwick and boyd (2011) and boyd (2014) have explored the notion of 'drama' as a concept youth use to identify, and to explain, often conflict-ridden relationships online, while rejecting the notion of bullying imposed on these events by adults. Drama references a more complex frame of 'testing out friendship and understanding the dynamics of popularity and status' (boyd, 2014: 138). Despite, however, noting that the escalation of conflict online is stereotypically viewed as 'girls' work', there is little attempt to understand how social networking practices may be reshaping gendered and sexualized discourses and power relations, both on and offline, in complex ways. As Van Doorn (2010: 584) notes, social networking research on young people has 'largely neglected the gendered and sexual dimensions of SNS participation'.

Our key interest in this chapter is in understanding how social networking affordances mediate gender and sexuality in the social lives of networked teens. As argued by boyd, mobile digital media platforms are characterized by common elements of 'Persistence: the durability of online expressions and content; Visibility: the potential audience who can bear witness; Spreadability: the ease with which content can be shared; and Searchability: the ability to find content' (boyd, 2014: 11). But how do these technological affordances shape youth intimacy, flirtation and sexual communication thereby transforming young people's networked gender and sexual cultures?

In this chapter we argue that what boyd calls social media 'drama' signals how social media affordances are *affective*. By affective we mean they mediate the bodily capacities to *affect or be affected* (Deleuze and Guattari, [1987] 2004; Massumi, 2002; Clough, 2008; Ringrose and Coleman, 2013). As new media theorists suggest, the digital reshapes the energetic flows and psychical qualities of social life including physical material 'reality' (Kuntsmen, 2012). Paasonen, Hillis and Petit (2015) argue theories of networked affect can help us to see 'how individual, collective, discursive and networked bodies both human and machine ... are modified by one another'. Social networking practices enable new flows of temporality and connectivity (Van Dijck, 2013) experienced as a range of modifications to bodies, or what Massumi (2002) would call variable 'intensities'.

Our contribution is to argue these flows, connectivities and intensities are not totally open – they filter through gendered and sexual discourses, as well as age and other axes of difference (race, ethnicity, locality etc.). As Van Doorn (2011: 536) maintains, we can't:

> separate bodies, gender and sexuality from the technological networks that give them form and meaning. Conversely, media technologies cannot be apprehended without accounting for the *embodied and gendered use cultures* that imbue them with significance by mobilizing them within larger everyday networks – both virtual and concrete.
> *(Van Doorn, 2011: 536; emphasis added)*

As such, to understand the concrete – that is physical culture, including everyday experiences of (in)active bodies in material space – we must also grasp the workings of online space given we are now dealing with what has been called a posthuman, *digitally mediated* cyborg body: the hybrid techno-corpus (Haraway, 1991; Braidotti, 2014). With this remit in mind, we approach digital mediation not as a 'transparent layer or intermediary between independently existing entities – such as young people *plus* their Blackberries and their Facebook profiles – but rather as a vital, temporal process, in which technologies, media and lives are intimately entangled and intra-meshed (Kember and Zylinska, 2012). We hold our understandings of mediation together with recent work on the affordances of digital technologies, examining these affordances not as separate entities but as part of what Kember and Zylinska (2012: 23–24) term the new 'lifeness of media ... which hold the potential to generate unprecedented connections and unexpected events'.

We develop the notion of digital *intra-actions* drawing on Barad (2007), to think about how digital life, particularly relationality around gender and sexuality unfolds online, suggesting digital flows are also, of course, experienced as variable intensities as 'subjective' affective states (Wetherell, 2012) with discursive, 'material' (that is physical) embodied effects offline. In relation to this volume, digital practices are thereby at the heart of young people's physical cultures, and we try to illuminate the temporality of these embodied practices in the merging of the online and offline in young people's peer cultures. We do this through a discussion of how young people negotiate *sexualized online* content, messaging and images in their networked content, and how it shapes on and offline relationships. In previous writing we have explored the negotiation of sexual content online in relation to research literature and debates on youth *sexting* (see for instance Ringrose et al., 2012, 2013; Ringrose and Harvey, 2015). Here we focus instead on how the relationships between *online digital space and offline material physical culture* intra-act (see also Ringrose and Renold, 2016) demonstrating some of the complexities associated with how young people perform and negotiate their mediated gender identity and sexual relationships online and in the shared physical space of the school.

To further understand this cyborgified, posthuman physical culture we draw on a research project that mapped experiences of digital sexual communication among economically and racially marginalized young people in London. We worked in-depth with a total of 35 young people aged 13–15, in two school communities located in two inner-city, multicultural London schools in 2011. Our methodology included first conducting focus groups where we asked young people to 'walk us through' their online and mobile phone practices. Young people were then invited to connect with us on Facebook for a three-month period during the research project. Next we conducted online ethnographic observation – 'netnography' (Kozinets, 2015) – of these young people's online interactions on their Facebook profile. Finally we returned for 22 in-depth individual case study interviews with research participants.

In this chapter we focus mostly on one of the schools, Langthorpe College,[1] located in a southeast London neighbourhood with high levels of economic deprivation and associated violence (Harvey et al., 2013). We focus on one school and only two interrelated case studies, one boy and one girl, Kamal and Cherelle, in order to understand how the 'affordances' (boyd, 2008, 2014) of social media technology work and 'mediate' everyday gendered and sexualized power relations and intimacies in youth peer groups. Moreover we have chosen to explore the experiences of two teens in our younger age range (aged 13–14) set, since we know less about the construction of teen sexual cultures among younger teens (Buckingham et al., 2009).

Through the two cases we consider how young people experience the new 'visibilities' of intimate relationships in a range of ways that shape the gender and sexual peer cultures. For instance, the searchability of contact information for 'flirting' and 'hooking up' can be seen as useful but also risky in gender-specific ways that extend into offline experience (Livingstone and Helsper, 2009). Visibility of personal information online can be both affirming and anxiety provoking (when unknown contacts suggest they know where you live). The sharing or 'spreadability' (Jenkins et al., 2013) of sexualized images of girls' bodies can also be something that is experienced as desirable and problematic at the same time. As an example, we explore the posting online of 'pornified' sexual content (Paasonen et al., 2007), which one can both enjoy but later come to 'regret' (Brown and Gregg, 2012), since posting a sexual shock or joke image has a 'persistence' or duration that can continue to shape the material possibilities of peer relationships long after the moment of posting. Overall, we show how our approach helps us to map out the 'doing' of teen femininity and masculinity online, through showing the affective dimensions of these technologically mediated gender and sexual power relations.

Hyper-connectivity: digitally mediated friendship and flirting

Mobile digital technologies cannot be treated like some add-on feature to young people's lives today. Technology has created posthuman cyborgs, where the mobile phone is an actant (Latour, 2005), and more like an additional limb or appendage, rather than separate object from the body (Haraway, 1991). These technologies are radically transforming the possibilities around connectivity with temporal and material affects (Van Dijck, 2013). Consider how year 10 girls discuss how their mobile phones shape their daily rhythms:

> Interviewer: So how much are you using your [mobile] phone do you think in an average day?
> Monique: Like all the time.

> Kylie: I use it to wake myself up, then I use it to phone Riley or you to see where you are to meet each other in the morning, and then when I get on the way to school I will be texting people from school.
> Tracy: Yeah and using it to get the time.
> Kylie: Yeah to get the time. I use my phone every second of the day. If I am not using it I feel a bit weird.
> Monique: I use it to go to sleep with my music on.
> Tracy: I talk on my phone all day long.

These technologies are loved and felt to be central to life, and to young people's sense of self. Indeed, life could be unthinkable without them. As Jodie (13) put it, 'I would die without my BlackBerry', and Claire (13) told us she found 'communicating on Facebook is easier than in real life'. Phone, Text, Facebook, BlackBerry Messenger (BBM), Twitter, Tumblr, Instagram, Snapchat and others are multiple overlapping, interfacing simultaneously (Kofoed and Ringrose, 2012) with one another, so texting, posts, image sharing or speaking on the phone can take place on multiple media at the same time, although some mobiles or apps can quickly overtake previous favourites. As Adam (15) explained, once the group at his school had BlackBerry (in 2011) 'everyone' had to get it to communicate and it mostly replaced texting and Facebook ('in-boxing') because it was cheaper and less easily monitored by adults. Similarly, Kaja (15) told us that 'BlackBerry Messenger is much better because it is kind of like portable. It is always in your pocket and it is like – and it is more secret as well. That is better. You don't need no internet connection.'

Currently, however, times have changed and BlackBerry is mostly obsolete. But what is critical for the purposes of this chapter, is how all of these rapidly changing technologies forge new bonds and intense degrees of connection:

> Kylie (15): My boyfriend, he got me to call him the other day, he stayed on the [mobile] phone for like three hours. That is like half my minutes gone and then he fell asleep ... But do you know what the weirdest thing is, once he fell asleep I couldn't hang up because I wanted to listen to him breathing.
> Interviewer: You wanted to listen to him breathing.
> Monique: When they are sleeping it is funny, it sort of has this cute, it is like, ahh, it is like listening to a little baby. It is cute. I have been on the phone like from six o'clock in the afternoon until maybe six o'clock the next morning.
> Interviewer: So you stay up all night?
> Monique: Because he won't come off the phone. But what we do is we drop in and out of sleep and then it is like, he will press the button and it will like make a noise so I will wake up, and be like, oh I'm awake now, so it is just weird, I don't know, it is just one of those things that you do.

Staying on your personal mobile phone with your boyfriend all night and reports of young people keeping Skype on all night long to be visibly and aurally 'in touch' with one another, or more recent disappearing media like snapchatting photos which erase after a few seconds, all show the radical or hyperconnectivity and its strange durations of mobile technologies. These degrees and forms of connection transform temporality and relationality initiating new forms of mediated intimacy. For instance, Year 10 boys explained how they only initiated flirting with people on BBM through the distance created by the BBM 'Broadcaster' of messages. The intra-action of mobile phone, messaging app, and flows of desire and emotion function to both create connection (such as the ability to communicate in private spaces and at any time) and dynamic temporal patterns of distance and closeness, in which both simultaneous and delayed communication are possible. As Kylie (15) stated:

> But like our phones play a massive part in relationships. Like phone calls until late hours. Texting, not as much because now we have got BBM. BBM is like Match.com basically, you have got everyone there and it is like – and people send broadcasts over BBM. Like there will be a smiley face and then next to the smiley face there will be something like 'Would you have sex with me?' 'Would you do this, would you do that?' and then by sending that broadcast, like the boy will answer it and then you will start talking to them … Like the question will be like, 'Would you have sex with me lights on/lights off. Socks on/socks off. What position? To what song? Condom or no condom?' Stuff like that.

Kylie refers to BBM as like match.com and also calls Facebook 'Baitbook'. These new hybrid terms point to how technological processes are reshaping and remediating teen sociality, connectivity and sexuality – friendship, dating and intimacy – in complex gendered ways, which we continue to explore through our two case studies of young people in year 8 (13–14 years old).

Cherelle

Facebook, BBM and the playground: on and offline sexual harassment

Cherelle is a British-born, black, 13-year-old girl. She lives in an economically deprived area surrounding Langthorpe College. She lives with her mum on a council estate. Cherelle described her attachment to the social media technology of BBM as a vehicle to stay in touch with existing friends and make new ones, saying she can't put the phone down. As we have been discussing, BBM was the dominant social media environment that the young people were using in 2011 in the research schools. In BlackBerry you have a profile image like Facebook, but contacts are added by circulating a pin number together with a description to the user's friend network, asking them to add the contact: this is called a pin 'broadcast', which is interesting because it requires a description of the user to be sent around the network. Cherelle explained that the body was central to these pin descriptions. She went on to describe the importance of the body parts, and the physical appearance of black girls, in particular, with 'big tits and a big bum' as desirable body parts (see also Weekes, 2002):

> If it is a boy and a girl told a boy to BC [broadcast] their pin then they will say, 'Oh she has big tits and a big bum and she's fit and if you get to know her, she's nice' … It's mad.

She went on to mention the idea of 'linking up' or meeting the people she's made contact with online, depending on their 'personality' and whether they are 'nice':

> Depending on the person, because if the person can't see your picture properly, they say 'Can you send me a picture of your face, so I can see you clearly?' and sometimes they can be very nasty, saying 'Can I have a picture of your tits?' or stuff like that, and yeah, sometimes they will get upset and overact and maybe delete you. But that's

alright, but when you are linking someone they want to know what you want to do when you link. But most boys will say 'We are gonna lips and hug and stuff' and yeah just go to the park and do stuff and yeah that's what most people do.

Cherelle talks about how sometimes boys will ask for a 'picture of your tits' and also ask if you want to 'link' or meet up in ways that seemed fun with banter around 'lips' (kissing) and hugging. She was also, however, very wary of too many 'facts' being posted about her which located her in real life, an aspect of 'searchability' that she felt threatening:

When I lost my BBM there is some girl in Year 10 and I told her to BC my pin, asked her, and … she BCd my pin she put lots of facts about me … so I had lots of adds and then for example, a boy, he said 'Oh you're peng' that means oh you're pretty and stuff and 'where do you live?' I said '[area] but I hang around [other area]'. They said, 'Oh I live in [area]'. 'Okay so what school do you go to?', they said [school] and then he was all like, 'Oh do you want to link?' I was like, 'Maybe' and he said, 'What would you do if we linked?' and I said, 'I dunno' and then he said, 'Oh would you give me blows?', that means suck my dick? and I was like, 'No not really' and then he said, 'Why?' and I said, 'Because I'm not like that', but he became furious when we got deep in a conversation and then I just ended up deleting him because of what he is saying.

Here Cherelle is wary of too many 'facts' being released about her, something that she felt exposed her in relation to a sexually aggressive boy who asked her 'would you give me blows'. Several of our year 8 girls described how being asked for blow jobs was a regular, everyday occurrence, and related to boys they did not know personally but also to boys in the school:

Cherelle: Well, I know lots of times I've been asked and sometimes I will say 'No' and they will say, 'Okay' and they will be like nice to you and then they will ask again and then they will put pressure on you and stuff like this and I will just be like, 'I'm sorry I don't want to' and they will say 'Why' and I will say 'I just don't want to', and they will say, like 'There's nothing wrong like all you need to do is just suck on it' and I will be like, 'But I don't want to do that' and just keep going and put the angry face on BBM and dedicate their status to you in a negative way.
Interviewer: Like say what kind of thing?
Cherelle: Like, 'Oh this girl is pissing me off'.
Interviewer: And do they say it to you or do you just kind of know?
Cherellle: You know, you can tell … I just delete them.
Interviewer: Okay, and do they ask you in person? …
Cherelle: Oh people in our school? … Some boys would say oh whatever and sometimes they would just get your head and go like that, but like you come up quick and just say, 'Get off me', but yeah that is as far as it goes.

The embodied and affective patterns of desire, pleasure, anger and aggression cannot be separated from the affordances of the media through which they are articulated and felt. Angry faces, deleting and negative statuses entangled with gendered and physical relations of power, which young people had to navigate online and offline. The relations between being online and being asked to perform a blow job, and having boys say something negative about a refusal online, is greatly complicated by knowing the contact as part of the wider peer group at school, to whom you cannot simply 'delete'. Cherelle describes being physically approached on the playground and head being pushed down towards the boys' groin. Despite saying 'this is as far as it goes' Cherelle recounted numerous other stories of boys 'rushing girls' pushing them over, touching them up on their 'tits' and 'bum', and daggering them (humping them from behind or front):

> Interviewer: So do you really feel concerned about them or do you just think, no they are not really going to do anything to me.
> Cherelle: I feel concerned most of the time because I'm okay with the boys now because before if I said something on BBM or Facebook and they got upset, I just like got into little arguments, like they would say, 'Watch tomorrow, gonna rush you' and this stuff. And tomorrow they will just floor you and kick and run, all this. But yeah.
> Interviewer: So they threaten to like basically beat you up?
> Cherelle: Mmm.
> Interviewer: But they don't do it?
> Cherelle: They do.
> Interviewer: They do. So you have been beaten up by a boy?
> Cherelle: Yeah, not like really hard and stuff, but like they will kick me, I have got punched quite a lot of times and yeah, but I haven't said anything about it, but since that assembly I know that I can trust – I can trust my mum. I had a talk to her.

What is critical here is the impotency of being able to 'delete' content or contacts online. The issue is not simply online persistence or duration, since the complex relations of the peer group bleed into the *material, physical offline* material space of school: 'watch out tomorrow I'm gonna rush you'. Cherelle also raises the important issue of not wanting to tell anyone, which girls and boys described could get you labelled a 'snitch' or a 'grass'.

Cherelle also described how BBM and Facebook has a really fun game of 'wifey and husband' that you play with a boy who is your 'best friend' on Facebook, who was Kamal, a black boy in her same year group, but how Kamal was 'changing' so she could not be 'close with him anymore':

> Cherelle: Like when Kamal first started school he used to hang around with Veronica and me so I became good friends with Kamal because he was quiet then, but then he met the boys in our year group who are popular and stuff and then he started hanging around with them and he became the same and worse.
> Interviewer: Like how, like what do they do?
> Cherelle: Like they rush people. Like they beat them up for no reason and just loud and yeah … you walk past and like a boy will pass and they will squeeze your bum or something and like just touch your tits … like every boy that I have on BBM, well not everyone but most have put nasty pictures … a girl naked or on top of a boy. The pictures what you will find on a dirty boy's display picture is either of him or his penis and a girl sucking it, or a girl naked or a dirty cartoon, things like that …
> Interviewer: Oh yeah, dirty cartoon. I wanted to ask you about this one. So this one is from Kamal
> Cherelle: Oh gosh …

Interviewer: because you commented on it [on Facebook] ... I was just wondering what you thought about that?
Cherelle: I was looking through his pictures and then I saw that and I was like, that is disgusting. I was talking to him about most of his pictures on the phone and yeah and he said, 'Oh why are you acting like it's all that and stuff' and I was like, 'It's disgusting and it's on your Facebook' and he was like, 'Yeah and' and I was like, 'Yeah'. But most boys just don't think that is – they don't take it seriously they take it like it is just normal and yeah.
Interviewer: It is interesting because you said, 'LOL ouch' and he says, 'Cherelle knows' and then you realize that and you said, 'Shut up' right?
Cherelle: Mmm.
Interviewer: And I am just wondering like, do you try to be jokey with him?
Cherelle: Mostly I am joking with him. I think that the way of joking that I can speak to him, because like when I speak to Kamal I have to speak to him in a way like for him to speak to me, for me to know stuff and understand stuff. And yeah –
Interviewer: So you feel like he listens to you then?
Cherelle: Yeah, that's how we became friends because like we was really close, but that was then when he started to change, that is when I saw this picture.

Cherelle is discussing an explicit cartoon image on Kamal's Facebook page of a black man entering a white blonde haired woman from behind who is crying. The man's penis is visible in the image, The comments on the photo were mostly 'Lool' and 'wooooow' but Cherelle said 'O:Lord', to which Kamal replied 'Cherelle knows' and Cherelle replies 'LOL shut up, Kamal'. There is a complex set of relations where it is supposed to be jokey and funny online, but Cherelle suggests the image is connected to how she felt Kamal 'started to change'. The image is consequently part of an affective entanglement of disgust, laughter and discomfort at a moment in which their friendship is shifting and both young people are negotiating their place within the peer group and their own friendship via online comments and physical interactions at school. These changes included offline 'touching up' in the playground as well as posting 'nasty' images. To continue discussing these affective intra-actions between Cherelle and Kamal, specifically, we turn to Kamal's interview next.

Kamal

Facebook, BBM and the playground: competitive, hierarchical heterosexual masculinity

As mentioned by Cherelle, Kamal is a British-born, black, 14-year-old boy, also living with his mum on a different estate, and he transferred only recently to Langthorpe College after being excluded from his previous school. As a newcomer to year 8, Kamal was negotiating his relationship with different peer groups at school and he worked hard in the focus groups and the individual interview to perform a kind of 'older', 'popular', hard masculinity. As part of this popular masculine bravado he proudly displayed his topless body on Facebook saying about one image of his back muscles:

Kamal: Wow this picture is good I think it should go on Facebook!
Interviewer: And like do you get ratings if lots of people like the picture?
Kamal: Yeah right now I've got 42 likes on the picture and lots of comments.

In this way, Kamal is negotiating the 'visibility' of displaying and showing your own and others bodies, but the relationalities around his image are dramatically different from those of girls. His image is publically available and rewarded, enabling him to describe pleasure and pride from its circulation, whereas the group described how girls' bodies in contrast are traded as part of a semi-private networked form of exchange. For instance, Kamal claimed he had around 30 images of girls on his phone, a number that also appeared to signal high status or 'ratings' in other focus groups with girls and boys. Kamal as with others suggested that getting images of pictures of girls in their bras was 'competition':

> Kamal: Because sometimes when you and your friend could have a competition of how many girls you can get and you can just do it and then just compare how much pictures you get.
> Interviewer: So you have got like 30 of them. So then do you go to your mates, 'Look at this I've got 30 pictures'?
> Kamal: No. I go, 'I've got bare pictures of girls here' and then when they say, 'How much?' I will tell them how much but I won't really show them.
> Interviewer: You won't really show them?
> Kamal: No, I will show them but like where they will like hold my phone and look at it and try to go through the next ones which might have a girl's face in it, for example, I won't let them. I won't let it out of my possession ... I wouldn't want them to know who the girl was because like I would only do it for someone I didn't like and I wouldn't have a picture of someone I didn't like, so yeah.

Having 30 images of girls was a number that had emerged in the data as a quantity signalling high popularity, and so we interpret this not as an accurate description of his 'collection', but more as part of macho bravado and the performance of heteronormative, desirable and conquering masculinity. Kamal also describes as a kind of heroic masculine code of honour of not revealing the faces of the images of the girls he's been sent, as if he has the power to 'expose' or reveal a girl's identity, To expose a girl's image meant to post it without consent publically on social media (commonly now understood as revenge porn). This was a form of digital 'visible', 'spreadable' and 'searchable' sexual 'stigma' (Trottier, 2014) attached to teen girls' bodies when they were publically posted, and it is worth noting that this practice was positioned as familiar although extreme across our sample of young people in both schools.

The power to expose the girls does not actually seem to be within Kamal's reach, however, since it is not clear if Kamal even knows the girls in the images he is posting. Indeed Kamal's BBM profile image was an image of a girl's breasts, which he claims is his girlfriend, but then says no one actually knows who it is because it is 'just her bra without her head' in the image. It is ambiguous as to whether the image is a girlfriend – the images are deployed to construct an older and knowing form of masculinity in conditions that are less certain than possibly claimed. Kamal also talked about tagging himself in girls' images he doesn't actually know:

> Kamal: I can tag it if I like the picture I could tag myself in it and then it will come to my profile. I could make it my profile picture ... it all leads to ratings because he's got that girl on Facebook and she's nice and how did he get her, they just want to find out, things like that.
> Interviewer: And what do the girls think if you tag yourself in their pictures?
> Kamal: Nothing, sometimes they will untag you, if they don't want you to tag them. But by the time they get to know that you are tagged in it, you could have made

it your profile picture already. They can untag you from it but then you have still got the picture.

Tagging technology allows for a form of connectivity and digital attachment to other girl's sites and images (Renold and Ringrose, 2016), although Kamal suggests it is not usually girls he is actually friends with offline whose images he tags himself in. So it is not clear if the 30 images he claims he has on his phone have been sent to him or he has tagged himself in them. Indeed, Kamal explains how the negotiation of asking for images of girls you *know* is actually quite complex:

> Kamal: Well you only get pictures from girls that like you or your girlfriend yeah. That is like mostly the only time you will get pictures …
> Interviewer: Do some people say 'No, I'm not sending you a picture'?
> Kamal: Yeah.
> Interviewer: And do you say, go on go on go on, or do you just go away?
> Kamal: No, I will ask why first. And if they don't give me a good reason then I can see that they don't really want to talk about it so I just change the subject.
> Interviewer: What counts as a good reason?
> Kamal: Like when they go, like for example they will go 'Because you are not my boyfriend' then that means that some people will do a wink face or an I can't watch face, and that is like okay, she wants you to move to her, like she wants you to be her boyfriend. Because she doesn't trust you as a friend but she trusts you as a boyfriend, if that makes sense?

Kamal suggests that girls want to have some sort of trust in you as a boyfriend before they will send an image to you, which is actually a much harder negotiation to sustain. These discussions all point to the discrepancy between having images on your phone and actually having a known girlfriend in the peer group. The digital mediation of masculinity then here involves a meshing of both girls' and boys' body parts via circulated images, but whose meaning is not always stable in the ever-changing affective interactions in the peer group (Ringrose and Harvey, 2015).

Indeed, recall that Cherelle has challenged Kamal's physical harassment and his posting of 'dirty' pictures on Facebook and BlackBerry, behaviour that seems to be potentially interfering with girls liking and trusting him, which Kamal is also struggling with. This became apparent when we discussed the sexually explicit cartoon on his Facebook page. It was a difficult part of the interview as Kamal became defensive, understandably saying at first that it was just funny and 'boys sense of humour is better than girls', but when the interviewer presses him about why it is funny because the woman is crying Kamal said 'I don't know' four times, and cracked his chewing gum loudly. This part of the interview is decidedly uncomfortable, and Kamal says he is tired, so the interviewer changes the topic to get back onto more neutral ground around Kamal having images of girls' breasts. A few minutes later when the tension has abated the interviewer returned to the issue of the cartoon:

> Interviewer: Do you think about that person and image them being a person or like what do you think? … What do you think she is thinking?
> Kamal: She is enjoying it. It is a way of expressing feelings yeah … Like people get hurt yeah but that like they enjoy getting hurt, because they know how it will feel next time or like see, erm, like they enjoying it. Not like they were enjoying

getting hurt the next time, but next time they will know what it feels like and they will like be prepared.

Interviewer: So like just generally like sex being painful then, like that prepares them for that?

Kamal: Yeah.

Interviewer: Do you feel that as a picture that is really realistic, as a picture of sex?

Kamal: No.

Interviewer: Why don't you think it is?

Kamal: Well for one it is a cartoon, two the people don't look real like, yeah. It just looks unreal but then it looks funny but real at the same time. Do you get what I'm saying?

Interviewer: Yeah, I get it. But I'm still not entirely sure what is funny about it. Maybe it is just because as you were saying not quite sure.

Kamal: Because people just find other people's pain funny. They find things like that funny.

Kamal insists that the cartoon is not 'real', but that what it depicts also makes it 'funny' at the same time. This is just one of many forms of images that circulate in the network that have the 'disgust', 'shock' and humour factor (Bale, 2011). Certainly not all boys liked these images or participated in this sexual shock/disgust dynamic. Kamal's comments that girls are preparing for pain in real-life sex is, however, an important site of discussion and intervention around young people's sexual cultures and versions of sexually aggressive masculinity (Haste, 2013). The cartoon is also racialized given it is a black man on top of a white woman, a complex sexual power dynamic which signals taboo boundary crossings in relation to racism and sexuality (Holland et al., 1998).

What is critical is that this image is tied in our findings to 'changing' the relationship with the girls in his school-based friendship group, namely Cherelle. These complex sexual power relations that Kamal is negotiating and his need to display access to collect, comment upon and possess girls and women's bodies also extended into the school space, where Kamal talked about touching up as a joke and part of the everyday experiences of being a 'teenage boy and girl':

Interviewer: Yeah, so does that happen quite a bit, like people just getting touched up in the corridor?

Kamal: Yeah.

Interviewer: What is going on there?

Kamal: Like boys just touch girls' breasts and their bums and that.

Interviewer: And what do the girls reckon about that?

Kamal: Nothing, most girls don't mind it.

Interviewer: How can you tell which girls mind it and which don't?

Kamal: Because say for example I touch a girl's breasts, if she doesn't say like stop or don't touch me then she doesn't mind it …

Interviewer: How does it work?

Kamal: It is like for example, my friend and my girlfriend yeah. My friend will do that to my girlfriend yeah. My other friends would rate him for that because it is my girlfriend and I am going out with her. So obviously like I won't get angry but I will go and do the same thing to his girlfriend.

Interviewer: Okay what do the girlfriends think about all of this?

Kamal: Nothing, they just think it is funny.

The interview illustrates a pattern across the year 8 interviews about consent and touching, as normative and expected by both girls and boys, as part of the dynamic of having access to girls' bodies both online and offline. There is a homosocial (Sedgwick, 1992) exchange where touching up of girlfriends is a funny competitive rivalry between the boys, as they navigate entry into competitive hierarchical masculinity with unclear boundaries around sexual consent and both in person and online sexual harassment (Powell, 2010). Many young people were critical of these practices and girls were angry but made excuses, such as the year 10 girls and boys who said it was year 8 boys 'crazy' hormones.

Conclusion

This chapter has begun to develop an analysis of how the 'affordances' of social media technology (boyd, 2014) are reshaping the possibilities of connectivity and relationality in young people's gender and sexual cultures. Cherelle's case study enabled us to explore how new norms of feminine desirability (visibility) were negotiated online, posing risks of searchability of information. Crucially, these online relations intra-acted with material and embodied experiences of being 'touched up' and sexually harassed at school from boys in her peer group.

Kamal's (14) case study showed how popular masculinity is performed (or attempted) via the ambiguous possibilities of tagging (connecting), and collecting images (visibility with material affective force as commodities that persist), afforded by new media technologies. We explored how the persistence of Kamal's pornographic cartoon image as well as his attitude to ownership and access to 'touching up' girls' bodies offline greatly impacted his friendship with girls, like Cherelle, in his peer group. Kamal's case study showed an attempt to perform 'older' popular masculinity and male bravado via the ambiguous possibilities of tagging (connecting) and collecting images (visibility with material affective force as commodities) afforded by new media technologies; we considered the persistence of his taboo image and how it shaped his relationship with Cherelle. We explored how issues of objectification and ownership over girls' bodies extended offline, with important implications for schools, which we mention briefly here but which deserve further attention. Significantly, our findings suggest that e-safety policies about stranger danger and 'deleting' online contacts are not especially helpful for coping with problems of relationships with *known contacts* from the school-based peer group online. Girls were dealing with sexual innuendo, tagging and comments online as well as being 'touched up' and sexually harassed in the physical spaces of the school playground. The flow of affect and material experiences online and offline was particularly evident in cases where girls were dealing with harassment from the *same boys* online and then offline in the corridors and outside spaces of the school. The mediation of physical culture here shows that the boundaries between what is considered 'online' and 'offline' are dissolving or indeed dissolved.

Overall our analysis shows the urgent need to continue unpacking how social networking affordances have a complex range of affective and material effects, which shape the possibilities of gender and sexual power relations in young people's school-based and wider peer relationships and physical cultures in profound ways. In line with Kember and Zylinska's (2012) arguments about the new forms of liveness and vitality emergent through new media practices, gender and sexuality take on new life-forms, but many of these are troubling and in need of further exploration. Indeed, many of the examples we discussed are reminiscent of older patterns of sexism and sexual double standards informing young teen femininities and masculinities.

What is perhaps 'new' about new media is how the digital affordances add more layers – extra temporal, spatial, affective and performative dimensions – to how we understand gendered and sexual (and racialized and classed) power relations, embodiment and identity work in teens' networked peer and everyday physical cultures. We have then, in this chapter, begun a discussion of how digital affordances shape the possibilities of connectivity and relationality in young people's gender and sexual cultures, and how this is played out in other physical cultural arenas and spaces. We have argued that sexual practices and cultures are an important site of analysis for physical cultural studies. We certainly need further work on how the new affordances of visibility, searchability, spreadability and persistance of social media may also present spaces for reworking and transforming age-old gender and sexual inequalities in ways as yet unforeseen. For instance we know little about how young people use social media to connect with gender and sexual activisms (e.g. feminism and LGBTQ rights) although there is now some emergent research on youth digital activisms like hashtag feminism, for instance (see Berridge and Portwood-Stacer, 2015; Keller et al., 2016; Retallack et al., 2016). We also need to continue to explore in far greater detail how social media technologies intra-act with embodied cultural practices. So doing will provide for enhanced possibilities of intervention into unequal power relations that coalesce around the hybrid physical techno-corpus.

Note

1   The school and participant names are all pseudonyms.

References

Bale, C. (2011) Raunch or romance? Framing and interpreting the relationship between sexualized culture and young people's sexual health. *Sex Education*, 11(3): 303–313.

Barad, K. (2007) *Meeting the Universe Halfway: Quantum Physics and the Entanglement of Matter and Meaning*. Durham, NC: Duke University Press.

Berridge, S. and Portwood-Stacer, L. (2015) Introduction: feminism, hashtags and violence against women and girls. *Feminist Media Studies*, 15(2): 341–344.

boyd, d. (2008) Why youth ♥ social network sites: the role of networked publics in teenage social life. In D. Buckingham (ed.), *Youth, Identity, and Digital Media*. Cambridge, MA: MIT Press, 119–142.

boyd, d. (2014) *It's Complicated: The Social Lives of Networked Teens*. New Haven, CT: Yale University Press.

Braidotti, R. (2014) *The Posthuman*. London: Routledge.

Brown, R. and Gregg, M. (2012) The pedagogy of regret: Facebook, binge drinking and young women. *Continuum* 26:3 (2012), 357–369.

Buckingham, D. et al. (2009) *The Impact of the Commercial World on Children's Wellbeing: Report of an Independent Assessment*. London: Department of Culture, Media & Sport.

Clough, P. (2008) The affective turn: Political economy, biomedia, and bodies. *Theory, Culture and Society*, 25(1), 1–22.

Deleuze, G. and Guattari, F. ([1987] 2004) *A Thousand Plateaus: Capitalism and Schizophrenia*. London: Continuum.

Haraway, D. (1991) A cyborg manifesto: science, technology, and socialist-feminism in the late twentieth century. In D. Haraway, *Simians, Cyborgs, and Women: The Reinvention of Nature*. New York: Routledge.

Harvey, L., Ringrose, J. and Gill, R. (2013) Swagger, ratings and masculinity: theorising the circulation of social and cultural value in teenage boys' digital peer networks. *Sociological Research Online*, 18(4).

Haste, P. (2013) Sex education and masculinity: the 'problem' of boys. *Gender And Education*, 25(4), 515–527.

Holland, J., Ramazanoglu, C., Sharpe, S. and Thomson, R. (1998) *The Male in the Head: Young People, Heterosexuality and Power*. London: Tufnell Press.

Jenkins, H., Ford, S. and Green, J. (2013) *Spreadable Media: Creating Value and Meaning in a Networked Culture*. New York: New York University Press.

Keller, J., Mendes, K. and Ringrose, J (2016) Speaking 'unspeakable things': documenting digital feminist responses to rape culture, *Journal of Gender Studies*, http://dx.doi.org/10.1080/09589236.2016.1211511

Kember, S. and Zylinska, J. (2012) *Life after New Media: Mediation as a Vital Process*. Cambridge, MA: MIT Press.

Kofoed, J. and Ringrose, J. (2012) Travelling and sticky affects: exploring teens and sexualized cyberbullying through a Butlerian-Deleuzian-Guattarian lens. *Discourse: Studies in the Cultural Politics of Education*, 33(1): 5–20.

Kozinets, R. V. (2015) *Netnography: Redefined*. London: Sage.

Kuntsmen, A. (2012) Introduction: affect fabrics of digital cultures. In E. Karatzogianni and A. Kuntsmen (eds), *Digital Cultures and the Politics of Emotion*. Basingstoke: Palgrave.

Latour, B. (2005) *Reassembling the Social: An Introduction to Actor–Network Theory*. New York: Oxford University Press.

Livingstone, S. and Helsper, E. (2009) Balancing opportunities and risks in teenagers' use of the internet: the role of online skills and internet self-efficacy. *New Media and Society*, 12(2): 309–329.

Marwick, A. and boyd, d. (2011) The drama! Teen conflict, gossip, and bullying in networked publics. Paper presented at A Decade in Internet Time: Symposium on the Dynamics of the Internet and Society, Oxford.

Massumi, B. (2002) *Parables for the Virtual: Movement, Affect, Sensation*. Durham, NC: Duke University Press.

Paasonen, S., Nikunen, K. and Saarenmaa, L. (2007) *Pornification: Sex and Sexuality in Media Culture*, Oxford: Berg Publishers.

Paasonen, S., Hillis, K. and Petit, M. (2015) Introduction: networks of transmission, intensity, sensation, value. In K. Hillis, S. Paasonen, and M. Petit (eds), *Networked Affect*, Cambridge, MIT Press, 1–26.

Powell, A. (2010) *Sex, Power and Consent: Youth Culture and the Unwritten Rules*. Melbourne: Cambridge University Press.

Renold, E. and Ringrose, J. (2016) Selfies, relfies and phallic tagging: Posthuman part-icipations in teen digital sexuality assemblages. *Educational Philosophy and Theory* doi:10.1080/00131857.2016.1185686

Retallack, H. Ringrose, J. and Lawrence, E. (2016) 'Fuck your body image': Teen girls' Twitter and Instagram feminism in and around school in J. Coffey, S. Budgeon and H. Cahill (eds), *Learning Bodies: The Body in Youth and Childhood Studies*. London: Springer.

Ringrose, J. and Coleman, B. (2013) Looking and desiring machines: a feminist Deleuzian mapping of affect and bodies. In B. Coleman and J. Ringrose (eds), *Deleuze and Research Methodologies*. Edinburgh: Edinburgh University Press.

Ringrose, J. and Harvey, L. (2015) Boobs, back-off, six packs and bits: mediated body parts, gendered reward, and sexual shame in teens' sexting images. *Continuum Journal of Media and Cultural Studies*, 29(2), 205–217.

Ringrose, J. and Renold, E. (2016) Cows, cabins and tweets: posthuman intra-acting affect and feminist fires in secondary school. In C. Taylor and C. Hughes (eds), *Posthuman Research Practices in Education*. London: Palgrave.

Ringrose, J., Gill, R., Livingstone, S. and Harvey, L. (2012) *A Qualitative Study of Children, Young People and 'Sexting'*. London: NSPCC.

Ringrose, J., Harvey, L., Gill, R. and Livingstone, S. (2013) Teen girls, sexual double standards and 'sexting': gendered value in digital image exchange. *Feminist Theory*, 14(3), 305–323.

Sedgwick, E. K. (1992) *Between Men: English Literature and Male Homosocial Desire*. New York: Columbia University Press.

Silk, M. L. and Andrews, D. L. (2011) Toward a physical cultural studies. *Sociology of Sport Journal*, 28(1), 4–35.

Trottier, D. (2014) *Identity Problems in the Facebook Era*. London: Routledge.

Van Dijck, J. (2013) *The Culture of Connectivity: A Critical History of Social Media*. Oxford: Oxford University Press.

Van Doorn, N. (2010) The ties that bind: the networked performance of gender, sexuality and friendship on MySpace. *New Media and Society*, 12(4): 583–602.

Van Doorn, N. (2011) Digital spaces, material traces: How matter comes to matter in online performances of gender, sexuality and embodiment. *Media, Culture & Society*, 33(4), 531–547.

Weekes, D. (2002) 'Get your freak on': how black girls sexualise identity. *Sex Education*, 2(3), 251–262.

Wetherell, M. (2012) *Affect and Emotion: A New Social Science Understanding*. London: Sage.

Williamson, B. (2015) Algorithmic skin: health-tracking technologies, personal analytics and the biopedagogies of digitized health and physical education. *Sport, Education and Society*, 20(1), 133–151.

PART VIII

Methodological contingencies

46
CRITICAL DISCOURSE ANALYSIS

Toni Bruce, Jenny Rankine and Raymond Nairn

In this chapter we discuss two critical discursive approaches that share important features with physical cultural studies, including the mutually constitutive relationships between language and culture, the concern with power and ideology, and an orientation towards social justice. *Critical discourse analysis* (CDA) and cultural studies *textual analysis* (TA) each emerged from a range of theoretical and methodological traditions and practices, making them difficult to summarize easily. Yet both offer much for what Silk, Andrews and Thorpe (Introduction, this volume) describe as a fluid sensibility for critical scholarship on physical culture, (in)active embodiment and power relations. We begin with one caveat. Our collaboration is an uncommon one because, despite the shared focus on discourses and texts, a foundation influenced by Marxist and post-structuralist theories, and potentially beneficial intersections, researchers employing CDA and TA have tended to work in separate disciplinary silos.

Some proponents describe CDA as 'a loosely connected set of different approaches' (Fairclough, 2012: 19) with 'fuzzy boundaries' (Blommaert, 2005: 24). Blommaert (ibid.: 22) identifies CDA's founding premise: that 'linguistic analysis could provide a valuable additional perspective for existing approaches to social critique'. CDA has recently been re-presented as critical discourse *studies* and described as a trans-disciplinary or interdisciplinary 'text-analytical approach to critical social research' (Hart and Cap, 2014: 1; Blommaert, 2005; Fairclough, 2012; Gee and Handford, 2012; Taylor, 2013). The socio-cultural traditions of CDA associated with Fairclough (e.g. Choudliaraki and Fairclough, 1999; Fairclough, 2001, 2012) and discursive psychology (Potter and Wetherell, 1987; Wetherell et al., 2001) may lend themselves best to the kinds of questions asked of sports media representations in physical cultural studies (Liao and Markula, 2009; Markula and Silk, 2011). CDA is integral to the work of Jenny Rankine and Raymond Nairn, who are Pākehā (white) members of Kupu Taea, a team of indigenous Māori and Pākehā researchers who analysed how New Zealand news media represent Māori, Māori issues and te Tiriti o Waitangi. This treaty was signed between the British Crown and numerous Māori hapu (sub-tribes) in 1840, and remains controversial. The group analysed three national, representative news samples that included Maori television news, supplemented with focus groups of Māori and non-Māori media consumers. Their use of CDA is underpinned by critical discursive psychology (e.g. McCreanor, 1989, 2012; Nairn and McCreanor, 1990, 1991; Potter and Wetherell, 1987; Wetherell et al., 2001).

Textual analysis (Jutel, 2004; McKee, 2003) or discursive analysis (Hall, 1997a) is conceptualized as a way of gathering information about people's 'sense-making practices' (McKee, 2003: 14). Researchers engage in 'a form of forensic analysis' seeking clues in texts that constitute the 'material traces ... the only empirical evidence' that remains of how people make sense of the world (ibid.: 15). In this approach, the researcher's sensitivity, immersion in the culture under investigation, and understanding of dominant discourses are what determine which texts might best reveal answers to the researcher's questions (ibid.). This approach drives Toni Bruce's cultural studies-informed (e.g. Grossberg, 1992; Hall, 1997a, 1997b; McKee, 2003; McRobbie, 1997) analyses of sports media, which share with CDA researchers a belief that sport is fundamentally constituted upon and through difference. She considers *how* and *why* elements of identity such as gender, ethnicity, dis/ability and national identity are highlighted if not hyper-emphasized in sport media narratives and images (e.g. Bruce, 2014; Bruce and Pringle, 2014; Bruce and Wensing, 2009). Her primary focus is representations of sportswomen (Bruce, 2009, 2014, 2016; Bruce and Hardin, 2014; Wensing and Bruce, 2003).

We share the belief that media representations matter because, like all discourses, they create reality and are neither transparent nor innocent (Hall, 1984; McRobbie, 1997; van Dijk, 1993; Potter and Wetherell, 1987). As the dominant story-tellers, mass media slowly transform 'the most plausible frameworks we have of telling ourselves a certain story about the world' (Hall, 1984: 8), structuring our consciousness in ways that have psychological, social and political consequences (Bennett, 1982; Fairclough, 2001; Moewaka Barnes et al., 2013). We believe it is vital for anyone analysing society critically to know how that society is being represented and affirmed through the range of media texts, including spoken, written, audio-visual and moving images.

Drawing on examples of our own critical analyses of media discourses, we identify the possibilities and limitations of CDA and TA in relation to three features they share with the physical cultural studies commitment to challenging power relations and contributing to social change.

The mutually constitutive relationship between language/texts and culture/social reality

The first focus is an understanding of the dialectical, and mutually constitutive, relationships between language, culture and social realities, which researchers explore by connecting specific texts to their wider socio-cultural contexts (e.g. Grossberg, 1992; Hall et al., 2013; McKee, 2003; Paltridge, 2012; Willig, 1999). In both analytical approaches, researchers aim to interpret texts, analyse their construction, and how they serve the speaker's interests, in relation to the specific cultural and historical contexts in which they were created. This shapes *how* researchers undertake their work, and one point of difference between CDA and TA may be the relative priority given to linguistic or discursive analysis within a broader focus on social issues. For example, Hall describes TA as focusing more on the '*effects and consequences*' of texts (a discursive concern) than on '*how meaning is produced through language*' (a linguistic concern) (Hall, 1997a: 6; see also Hall, Evans and Nixon, 2013). Thus, even working with similar texts, CDA is likely to require more attention to linguistic features than TA. Methodologically, the starting point for many forms of CDA involves formal analysis of linguistic features of a defined media corpus (KhosraviNik, 2013; for a sport example, see Liao and Markula, 2009). However, Kupu Taea, which integrates CDA with content and thematic analyses, focused on what speakers, writers and other communicators did in their talk, and the discursive resources they drew on to construct their version of events. Their first step is a thematic analysis of media texts that identifies common themes, including those identified in earlier work (Nairn and McCreanor,

1991; Rankine and McCreanor, 2004; Thompson, 1954), using repeated, careful, critical readings of news transcripts and software such as nVivo. Researchers then subject particular representations or clear examples of a theme to discourse analysis (Nairn and McCreanor, 1990, 1991). They identify and cluster statements and phrases that share linguistic and affective similarities (Rankine and McCreanor, 2004), with interactions between language and visuals. When re-readings of the data set no longer add to clusters, the researchers examine the family resemblances in each cluster (Rosch et al., 1976), until they can be expressed in a relatively simple sentence (Nairn, 2003). For example, a CDA analysis of a corpus of sports news (McCreanor et al., 2010) concluded that Pakeha definitions – 'Maori are marginal', 'Maori sport' is exclusive, and that Maori can't compete – were naturalized. These steps lead to identification of a set of what are variously called *discursive resources* (Nairn and Coverdale, 2005), *interpretative repertoires* (Potter and Wetherell, 1987) or *patterns* (Nairn and McCreanor, 1990) that can be tracked later through talk, television news, media materials, policy documents and other publications.

In contrast, TA seldom involves in-depth linguistic analysis of texts (Jutel, 2004) or clear methodological guidelines. Step 1, the question, is often contextual; triggered by what researchers see around them. For Bruce (2009), one study began with two questions related to the observed effect of unusually high levels of media visibility for sportswomen during Olympic or Commonwealth Games:

- Under what conditions are sportswomen able to gain space in mainstream media?
- What articulations need to be formed or disrupted for sportswomen to be seen as culturally important?

Step 2 involves gathering a wide range of texts and analysing 'bits' that appear 'relevant to the question', based on the researcher's cultural knowledge (McKee, 2003: 75). Thus, rarely are all elements of the text analysed in detail (Jutel, 2004). As a result, McKee (2003) describes textual analysis as having elements that 'are particularly unscientific' (ibid.: 118) and non-repeatable because they depend on the 'educated guesswork' (ibid.: 126) of a researcher immersed in the culture under investigation. Step 3, interpretation, depends on the researcher's contextual knowledge of other texts, or intertexts, on which the public are likely to draw for their sense-making, which may include Facebook sites, news coverage, letters to the editor, public comments, and texts in other cultural spaces where female athletes are visible, such as *Dancing with the Stars* or advertising campaigns (Bruce, 2009; Bruce and Hardin, 2014; Bruce and Wensing, 2009). Where the trigger is a single text, researchers must study enough texts in that genre or series 'to get a sense of its own rules, and how it works' (McKee, 2003: 94). In women's sport, this involves understanding the genre of sports media, including how athletes are usually represented. The final step of interpretation includes the wider public context in which the texts circulate, a step that McKee (ibid.: 99) calls 'the most vague and all-inclusive category'. Its main focus is discourses in specific contexts because it is only there that 'practices have specific effects, that identities and relations exist' (Grossberg, 1992: 55).

Power and ideology

The second shared focus is on issues of power and ideology. CDA has been defined as the study of social inequities 'focusing on *the role of discourse in the (re)production and challenge of dominance*' (van Dijk, 1993: 249–250). Similarly, McKee (2003: 51) argues that 'Cultural studies researchers are often the most overtly political of the researchers who use textual analysis, pushing for more equitable forms of social organization.'

For Kupu Taea, this involves establishing how patterned uses of discursive resources contribute to material impacts, as in the formation of policy or the repetitive naturalization of Pakeha dominance as natural (Rankine et al., 2011, 2014). This critical element of CDA demonstrates how telling the story in particular ways and drawing on certain repertoires creates preferred readings that favour powerful groups. An example is a front-page newspaper article that headlined an alleged Māori 'demand' for which the article provided no source (Nairn et al., 2009). Careful analysis drew on characteristics of news items, their discourse and production practices to identify how this non-event was constructed as newsworthy, and created an appearance of being factual while masking its unfounded nature.

Kupu Taea members identified eight anti-Māori discourses (McCreanor, 1989; Nairn and McCreanor, 1991) in Pākehā submissions in 1979 to the Human Rights Commission about race relations. Those discourses have been shown to be common in mass media from the early days of colonization (Colvin, 2010; Thompson, 1954; Ballara, 1986). They divorce Māori from exercises of power, while also enabling Pākehā to maintain a protective ignorance of the realities and impacts of colonial injustices (Nairn et al., 2011; Potter and Wetherell, 1987). More recent analyses of news media samples identified five further negative discourses (Moewaka Barnes et al., 2012). The most important was *Pākehā as the norm,* a pattern that underpinned all the previously identified discourses about Māori and minority ethnic groups and triggered a re-examination of the data to identify how this powerful position was simultaneously constructed and masked. Central to this discourse is the refusal to label Pākehā ethnicity, practices and institutions; instead Pākehā are identified only as Kiwis, or conflated with the public or the nation. Speakers are using this discourse when they use 'we', 'us' and 'our' to denote Pākehā, 'them', 'they' and 'their' about Māori, and routinely use 'Māori' to describe ethnicity and homogenize Māori peoples. Identifying this discourse enabled the team to begin exploring the power and privilege inherent in being naturalized as the ordinary, normative people against whom all others must be assessed, and usually found wanting in some respects (Kupu Taea, 2014). This powerful discourse, so naturalized that it seems obvious, translates to other axes of power – male, heterosexual, middle class and able-bodied norms, for example – that also position women and other groups as deviant or lacking. One of Kupu Taea's suggested alternatives is routinely to name the normalized group, making their vested interest clear; for example, for financial reporters to identify that three *Pākehā* directors of a collapsed company have been arrested; or for political reporters to write that a majority of *male* Members of Parliament voted against equal pay; or for sports reporters to identify the ethnicity of all players.

For Bruce, expressions of power and ideology reveal themselves in articulations, which represent ideas that are linked together so that they appear natural. As Hall describes it, 'ideas don't just float around in empty space. We know they are there because they are materialized in, they inform, social practices' (Hall, 1985: 103). We can think of articulations as the default settings or taken-for-granted frameworks for making sense of what we do, see and hear. However, any sense-making practice 'exists in multiple contexts across the space of a particular moment, articulated into different, sometimes competing and sometimes contradictory sets of relations' (Grossberg, 1992: 60). Despite articulations having no inherent connection, some constitute 'magnetic lines of tendency' that are very difficult, if not impossible, to break (ibid.: 141–142), such as the articulations of sport and masculinity or of athletes of colour and 'natural' athleticism. Even so, their constructed nature means it is important to investigate both their potencies and instabilities through revealing the 'variety of different ideological systems or logics … available in any social formation' (Hall, 1985: 104). For example, textual analysis of Olympic media coverage revealed that sportswomen competing on the global stage are frequently constructed within contradictory sets of discourses related to nationalism and femininity. In such contexts, the discursive hierarchy often privileges nationalism, so that female medallists are more likely to be represented as *national* citizens than as *female* athletes (Bruce, 2016). In another analysis, representations of Paralympic athletes oscillated between contradictory discourses of disability and nationalism: home-nation athletes were articulated to elite sport through the discourse of nationalism and represented as valued athletes, while Paralympians from other countries were primarily articulated to discourses of disability and represented as exotic, disabled others (Bruce, 2014).

Social justice orientation towards emancipation and political engagement

The third shared focus is a social justice orientation towards emancipation and political engagement (e.g. McKee, 2003; Saukko, 2003; Taylor, 2013; Willig, 1999). For example, CDA professes 'strong commitments to change, empowerment, and practice-orientedness' (Blommaert, 2005: 26). Thus critical analyses of texts not only direct us to pay attention to the play of power, but take seriously the idea of the public intellectual who actively intervenes in the public sphere. This resonates with the physical cultural studies commitment discussed earlier, especially consciousness raising and attempts to transform power relations. We see Kupu Taea as an excellent example of 'pragmatic political work' (McKee, 2003: 54) that embodies 'cultural workers and intellectuals engaging in intertextual negotiations across different sites of production to assume their roles as engaged critics and cultural theorists' (Andrews and Silk, 2015: 91).

In Kupu Taea's case, this commitment led to the production and wide dissemination, via 20,000 free booklets and a website, of alternatives to 14 dominant discourses that marginalize and disparage Māori and te Tiriti while naturalizing Pākehā dominance (Kupu Taea, 2014). These resources aim to contribute to the development of a speech community (Fitch, 2001) that uses and expects others to use discourses that are not intrinsically anti-Māori and unthinkingly pro-Pākehā. Each of the 14 anti-Māori discourses was summarized in a sentence, followed by wording that cues its use in news items, the assumptions underpinning it, its effects and, most importantly, alternative ways to talk about the issue. Māori media were interested and Kupu Taea received positive feedback from Māori organizations, which, with the persistent silence from mainstream newsrooms, suggests the team is on the right track in identifying the power relations affirmed through these discourses. However, the mass media silence also signals a weakness of CDA – or any media research – as the sole strategy for change. Results can be ignored by institutions that benefit from the status quo, or simply do not wish to change. CDA is not, by itself, a solution to that problem. Critical discourse analysts, like other critical qualitative researchers, often have to justify their approach because lay people see their work as subjective, making it easier to reject by political opponents (Burman and Parker, 1993). However, the nuanced understanding that CDA produces helps identify a greater variety of responses, potentially providing researchers and allied activists with the alternative discursive resources that might outflank dominant discourses.

Advocates for more and better quality media representation of sportswomen around the world have taken similar steps to Kupu Taea, producing media guides identifying problematic discourses and providing alternative ways of talking about and photographing sportswomen. However, the results are similar, in that the material is embraced by advocates for women's sport and ignored or actively trivialized by the media producers who have the power to create change. For example, rather than reflect on inequitable news coverage for sportswomen, an influential executive for a large New Zealand media company unapologetically explained to a packed crowd of women's sport fans that he ignored such research (Bruce, 2009). In New

Zealand, other attempts to change coverage by bringing analyses of gender imbalance to the attention of New Zealand sports journalists have also failed; being 'persistently rejected as irrelevant' and 'often ignored or trivialized' by media workers (Fountaine and McGregor, 1999: 113). So while researchers conducting CDA or TA are committed to action, what is less apparent is how best our research can inform interventions.

Conclusions

Exploring our own work has led us to the conclusion that CDA and TA both offer something different to physical cultural studies. At the same time, we see value in considering what might be achieved by investigating the unique strengths of both (e.g. Markula and Silk, 2011). We finish with a brief discussion of similarities in some of the opportunities and challenges we face, no matter which approach we take.

First, we conclude that critical analysis of media texts is vitally important; by doing this we can discover the range of people's discursive repertoires or sense-making practices, then propose alternatives to unjust dominant discourses. However, discursive analyses are only one element in creating change: a review of anti-racism campaigns found that they need to act on several levels (e.g. institutional *and* discursive *and* individual) as well as be well-funded and long-term (Rankine, 2014).

Second, we see the dangers of being limited by the theoretical lenses used to analyse media texts. In both our fields we have seen how early findings can blind researchers to emerging discourses or alternative interpretations. For example, in women's sport, the focus on inequality and difference may have blinded many researchers to discourses that emphasize similarities between men and women, and to ossifying interpretations of the meaning of specific discourses such as sexualization (Bruce, 2016).

Third, we both face challenges in convincing mainstream media workers to accept or act upon the results of our analyses. Although the results are embraced by communities with investments in change, those with the most power to shift representational practices appear unwilling to do so. We include ourselves among the many researchers that McKee (2003: 53) describes as wanting 'to change the kinds of texts that are published, particularly by journalists in newspapers and in television news, wishing for texts which are less racist, less sexist, less homophobic, less capitalist, for example'. However, one problem may lie in *how* we approach journalists. Even when researchers present their results as evidence of structural practices, the research often invites resistance because journalists feel insulted: they interpret results as suggesting they are racist or sexist because they produce racist or sexist stories (ibid.).

Fourth, we are investigating ways to use the strategy of conscientization or consciousness-raising more effectively. As McKee (ibid.) describes it, this approach means focusing less on brow-beating the producers of media texts and more on providing widely shared, accessible resources to enable people *to change how they interpret them*, while also remaining open to being educated ourselves about the sense-making practices of different groups (see also Fairclough, 2001). For Kupu Taea, this is what led to an earlier checklist for media consumers (Kupu Taea, 2008) and the *Alternatives to anti-Māori themes in news media* booklet and website. Advocates for change in media representations of sportswomen have written newspaper columns and blogs, given community talks, and produced extensive reports for relevant government agencies. Our results are also used in our teaching. Perhaps representing a nuance in approaches to conscientization, McKee (2003) argues that teaching is seen as an important domain of the strong cultural studies desire to intervene in sense-making practices: 'It's what we often do in our classes' (ibid.: 55). Fairclough (2001: 264), however, has suggested that research that stays within the academic sphere 'is unlikely to have much effect'. If we want to intervene strategically in public culture, we may need to take seriously Grossberg's (1992) argument that, 'We have to look at how both domination and subordination are lived, organized and resisted; we have to understand the possibilities of subordination that are open and allowed within the structures of domination, and perhaps point beyond them' (ibid.: 67). Thus, we conclude with Grossberg's suggestion that:

> by gaining a better sense of the state of play on the field of forces in popular culture and daily life, perhaps we can see more clearly where struggles are possible and, in some cases, even actual. Then we can try to find ways to oppose them, or help articulate them, to nurture and support them and perhaps, to bring them into visible relations with other struggles.
>
> (Grossberg, 1992: 66)

References

Andrews, D. and Silk, M. (2015). Physical cultural studies on sport. In R. Guilianotti (ed.), *The Routledge handbook of the sociology of sport* (pp. 83–93). London: Routledge.

Ballara, A. (1986). *Proud to be white: A survey of racial prejudice in New Zealand*. Auckland: Heinemann.

Bennett, T. (1982). Theories of media, theories of society. In M. Gurevitch, T. Bennett, J. Curran and J. Woollacott (eds), *Culture, society and the media*. London: Methuen.

Blommaert, J. (2005). *Discourse: A critical introduction*. Cambridge: Cambridge University Press.

Bruce, T. (2009). Winning space in sport: The Olympics in the New Zealand sports media. In P. Markula (ed.), *Olympic women and the media: International perspectives* (pp. 150–167). Basingstoke: Palgrave Macmillan.

Bruce, T. (2014). Us and them: The influence of discourses of nationalism on media coverage of the Paralympics. *Disability and Society*, 29(9), 1443–1459.

Bruce, T. (2016). New rules for new times: Sportswomen and media representation in the third wave. *Sex Roles*, 74(7), 361–376.

Bruce, T. and Hardin, M. (2014). Reclaiming our voices: Sportswomen and social media. In A. C. Billings and M. Hardin (eds), *Routledge handbook of sport and new media* (pp. 311–319). New York: Routledge.

Bruce, T. and Pringle R. (2014). Manliness and mountaineering: Sir Edmund Hillary as New Zealand adventurer and male icon. In J. Knijnik and D. Adair (eds), *Embodied masculinities in global perspective* (pp. 171–196). Morgantown, VA, USA: Fitness Information Technology Press.

Bruce, T. and Wensing, E. H. (2009). 'She's not one of us': Cathy Freeman and the place of Aboriginal people in Australian national culture. *Australian Aboriginal Studies*, 2, 90–100.

Burman, E. and Parker, I. (1993). Against discursive imperialism, empiricism and constructionism: Thirty-two problems with discourse analysis. In E. Burman and I. Parker (eds), *Discourse analytic research: Repertoires and readings of texts in action* (pp. 155–172). London: Routledge.

Choudliaraki, L. and Fairclough, N. (1999). *Discourse in late modernity: Rethinking critical discourse analysis*. Edinburgh: Edinburgh University Press.

Colvin, G. (2010). The soliloquy of whiteness: Colonial discourse and New Zealand's settler press 1839–1873. Unpublished PhD thesis, University of Canterbury, New Zealand.

Fairclough, N. (2001). The discourse of New Labour: Critical discourse analysis. In M. Wetherell, S. Taylor and S. J. Yates (eds), *Discourse as data: A guide for analysis* (pp. 229–266). Milton Keynes: The Open University.

Fairclough, N. (2012). Critical discourse analysis. In J. P. Gee and M. Handford (eds), *The Routledge handbook of discourse analysis* (pp. 9–20). New York: Routledge.

Fitch, K. (2001). The ethnography of speaking: Sapir/Whorf, Hymes and Moerman. In M. Wetherell, S. Taylor and S. J. Yates (eds), *Discourse theory and practice: A reader* (pp. 57–63). London: Sage.

Fountaine, S. and McGregor, J. (1999). The loneliness of the long distance gender researcher: Are journalists right about the coverage of women's sport? *Australian Journalism Review*, 21, 113–126.

Gee, J. P. and Handford, M. (2012). *The Routledge handbook of discourse analysis*. New York: Routledge.

Grossberg, L. (1992). *We gotta get out of this place: Popular conservatism and postmodern culture*. New York: Routledge.
Hall, S. (1984). The narrative construction of reality. *Southern Review*, 17, 3–17.
Hall, S. (1985). Signification, representation, ideology: Althusser and the post-structuralist debates. *Critical Studies in Mass Communication*, 2(2), 91–114.
Hall, S. (1997a). Introduction. In S. Hall (ed.), *Representation: Cultural representations and signifying practices* (pp. 1–12). London: Sage.
Hall, S. (1997b). The spectacle of the 'Other'. In S. Hall (ed.), *Representation: Cultural representations and signifying practices* (pp. 223–290). London: Sage.
Hall, S., Evans, J. and Nixon, S. (2013). *Representation*, 2nd edn. London: Sage.
Hart, C. and Cap, P. (eds). (2014). *Contemporary critical discourse studies*. New York: Bloomsbury Academic.
Jutel, T. (2004). Textual analysis and media studies. In L. Goode and N. Zuberi (eds), *Media studies in Aotearoa/New Zealand* (pp. 32–45). Auckland: Pearson Longman.
KhosraviNik, M. (2013). Actor descriptions, action attributions and argumentation: Towards a systematization of CDA analytical categories in the representation of social groups. In R. Wodak (ed.), *Critical discourse analysis, Volume II: Methodologies* (pp. 187–208). London: Sage.
Kupu Taea. (2008). *How news items represent Māori: A checklist for news media consumers to assess news stories*. Auckland: Kupu Taea. Available from www.trc.org.nz/research-about-media-and-te-tiriti.
Kupu Taea. (2014). *Alternatives to anti-Māori themes in news media*. Auckland: Kupu Taea. Available from www.trc.org.nz/alternatives-anti-maori-themes-news-media.
Liao, J. and Markula, P. (2009). Reading media texts in women's sport: Critical discourse analysis and Foucauldian discourse analysis. In P. Markula (ed.), *Olympic women and the media: International perspectives* (pp. 30–49). New York: Palgrave Macmillan.
McCreanor, T. (1989). Talking about race. In H. Yensen, K. Hague and T. McCreanor (eds), *Honouring the Treaty: An introduction for Pākehā to the Treaty of Waitangi*. Auckland: Penguin.
McCreanor, T. (2012). Challenging and countering anti-Maori discourse: Practices for decolonisation. In R. Nairn, P. Pehi, R. Black and W. Waitoki (eds), *Ka Tū, Ka Oho: Visions of a bicultural partnership in psychology* (pp. 289–310). Wellington, NZ: New Zealand Psychological Society.
McCreanor, T., Rankine, J., Moewaka Barnes, A., Borell, B., Nairn, R., Gregory, A. and Kaiwai, H. (2010). Maori sport and Maori in sport. *AlterNative*, 6(3), 235–247.
McKee, A. (2003). *Textual analysis: A beginner's guide*. Thousand Oaks, CA: Sage.
McRobbie, A. (1997). The Es and the Anti-Es: New questions for feminism and cultural studies. In M. Ferguson and P. Golding (eds), *Cultural studies in question* (pp. 170–186). London: Sage.
Markula, P. and Silk, M. (2011). *Qualitative research for physical culture*. Basingstoke: Palgrave Macmillan.
Moewaka Barnes, A., Borell, B., Taiapa, K., Rankine, J., Nairn, R. and McCreanor, T. (2012). Anti-Maori themes in New Zealand journalism; toward alternative practice. *Pacific Journalism Review*, 18(1), 195–216.
Moewaka Barnes, A., Taiapa, K., Borell, B. and McCreanor, T. (2013). Māori experiences and responses to racism in Aotearoa New Zealand, *MAI Journal*, 2(2), 63–77.
Nairn, R. G. R. (2003). Madness, media and mental illness: A social constructivist approach. Unpublished PhD thesis, University of Auckland, New Zealand.
Nairn, R. G. and Coverdale, J. H. (2005). People never see us living well: An appraisal of the personal stories about mental illness in a prospective print media sample. *Australian and New Zealand Journal of Psychiatry*, 39, 281–287.
Nairn, R. and McCreanor, T. (1990). Sensitivity and insensitivity: An imbalance in Pakeha accounts of Maori/Pakeha relations. *Journal of Language and Social Psychology*, 9(3), 293–308.
Nairn, R. and McCreanor, T. (1991). Race talk and common sense: Patterns in Pākehā discourse on Maori/Pakeha relations in New Zealand. *Journal of Language and Social Psychology*, 10(4), 245–262.
Nairn, R., McCreanor, T., Rankine, J., Barnes, A.M., Pega, F. and Gregory, A. (2009). Media surveillance of the natives: A New Zealand case study – Lake Taupo air space. *Pacific Journalism Review*, 15(1), 131–148.
Nairn, R., Moewaka Barnes, A., Rankine, J., Borell, B., Abel, S. and McCreanor, T. (2011). Mass media in Aotearoa: An obstacle to cultural competence. *NZ Journal of Psychology*, 40(3), 168–175.
Paltridge, B. (2012). *Discourse analysis: An introduction*, 2nd edn. New York: Bloomsbury.
Parker, I. (1992.) *Discourse dynamics: Critical analysis for social and individual psychology*. London: Routledge.
Potter, J. and Wetherell, M. (1987). *Discourse and social psychology: Beyond attitudes and behaviour*. Sage: London.

Rankine, J. (2014). *Creating effective anti-racism campaigns: Report to the Race Relations Commissioner.* Auckland: Kupu Taea. Available online at: www.researchgate.net/publication/284229016_Creating_effective_anti-racism_campaigns

Rankine, J. and McCreanor, T. (2004). Colonial coverage: Media reporting of a bicultural health research partnership. *Journalism, 5*(1), 5–29.

Rankine, J., Moewaka Barnes, A., Borell, B., McCreanor, T., Nairn, R. and Gregory A. (2011). Suburban newspapers' reporting of Maori news. *Pacific Journalism Review, 17*(2), 50–71.

Rankine J., Moewaka Barnes, A., McCreanor, T., Nairn, R., McManus, A.-L., Abel, S., Borell, B. and Gregory, A. (2014).Content and source analysis of newspaper items about Māori issues: Silencing the 'natives' in Aotearoa? *Pacific Journalism Review, 20*(1), 213–233.

Rosch, E., Mervis, C. B., Gray, W. D. et al. (1976). Basic objects in natural categories. *Cognitive Psychology, 8*, 382–439.

Saukko, P. (2003). *Doing research in cultural studies: An introduction to classical and new methodological approaches.* London: Sage.

Taylor, S. (2013). *What is discourse analysis?* London: Bloomsbury.

Thompson, R. (1954). Māori affairs and the New Zealand press, Part II. *Journal of the Polynesian Society, 63*(1), 1–16.

van Dijk, T. (1993). Principles of critical discourse analysis. *Discourse and Society, 4*, 249–283.

Wensing, E. H. and Bruce, T. (2003). Bending the rules: Media representations of gender during an international sporting event. *International Review for the Sociology of Sport, 38*(4), 387–396.

Wetherell, M., Taylor, S. and Yates, S. J. (2001). *Discourse as data: A guide for analysis.* Thousand Oaks, CA: Sage.

Willig, C. (ed.) (1999). *Applied discourse analysis: Social and psychological interventions.* Buckingham: Open University Press.

47
TEXT/REPRESENTATION

Cheryl Cooky

Introduction

As I write this chapter, I find myself in the curious position of having been invited to submit a chapter on 'text/representation' for a handbook on physical cultural studies (PCS). Having been part of conversations regarding this emergent, or perhaps not so emergent (see Ingham, 1997), area of scholarly inquiry and disciplinary perspective, I am somewhat aware of the central tenants, debates, and positions of those scholars who identify with PCS. I myself, however, do not overtly identify as a PCS scholar, although the theoretical, epistemological, and methodological frameworks of which I have been trained and utilize have certain shared affinities and sensibilities with those of PCS. My hesitance at self-identification is not due to any outright rejection of PCS, rather it resides in uncertainty regarding what is PCS, what is novel in the PCS project, and the intellectual, political, and professional risks and/or benefits in claiming an identity of 'PCS scholar'.

Moreover, my struggles with understanding PCS and its utility for my own scholarship is shaped by my academic biography, which is grounded in feminist theory, methodology, and epistemology. Indeed, from my vantage point, there seems to be much commonality between the theoretical, methodological, and epistemological orientation of feminist studies, and specifically feminist cultural studies of sport, and the 'key elements' of physical cultural studies articulated by Andrews and Silk (2015). In particular, the key elements of PCS (i.e. contextual, theoretical, political, qualitative, self-reflexive, pedagogical, and impact) as described by Andrews and Silk have historically been central concerns/projects of feminist studies, cultural studies, and even certain schools of thought within the discipline of sociology. This leads me to question what does PCS offer that these trans/inter disciplinary spaces do not provide? Is it simply the object of inquiry, the *physical context*? Is this a matter of nomenclature? As Andrews and Silk explain, 'PCS as a political project, is thereby driven by the need to *understand* and *expose* the complexities, experiences, and injustices of the physical cultural context it confronts (particularly with regard to relations, operations, and effects of power)' (ibid.; emphasis original).

Moreover, Andrews and Silk situate the 'promptings' for PCS in part due to the unrelenting (bio)scientization of kinesiology and the limitations of the term 'sociology of sport' to fully capture the contemporary diversity of thought, object of inquiry, and approach of scholarship. Noting a similar 'crisis-condition' in sport studies, Cole articulated the project of feminist cultural studies of sport, a project that reconsiders sport from a feminist standpoint and that recognizes 'sport' as a discursive construct that organizes multiple practices (science, medicine, technology, governing institutions, and the media) that intersect with and produce multiple bodies (raced, sexed, classed, heterosexualized, reproductive, prosthetic, cyborg, etc.) embedded in normalizing technologies (classification, hierarchization, identity production) and consumer culture.

(Cole, 1994: 6)

For the purpose of transparency, and to help situate this chapter, I identify as a 'feminist sports sociologist' in academic spaces (e.g. faculty websites, professional narratives, academic biographies) and on social media (twitter). My specific academic training (a bachelor's and a master's degree in kinesiology; an additional master's and a PhD in sociology, with women's/gender studies concentrations at both the master's and PhD levels) is intimately grounded in the 'traditions' of the parent discipline of sociology, yet is also engaged with the fields of media/communication studies, cultural studies, critical race studies, feminist studies, American studies, which coalesce and intersect in ways that parallel the orientations of other self-identified PCS scholars. And yet, despite these commonalities or shared affinities, I approach this chapter with a sense of ambiguity and uncertainty, as if I were a tour guide attempting to navigate a group of local citizens through a terrain of which only I myself am unfamiliar. My intersectional, interdisciplinary subject-position is the ground upon which I stand vis-à-vis PCS. Admittedly when considering the project of PCS, I wonder: *Indeed, haven't we* (sociology of sport) *been doing this all along*? As a result, I find myself occupying an intellectual space in this handbook as one of the 'outsiders within' (Collins, 1990); or perhaps the 'insider-other' (Cooky and McDonald, 2005) may be a more appropriate characterization of my positionality relative to the PCS project. Hence, I wish to approach this chapter with an explicit self-reflexivity and transparency in hopes that, based on this positionality, the reader can appropriately assess and evaluate the approach to the study of text/representation presented. As such, the goal of this chapter is not to provide an overview of text/representation as it is presumably understood in PCS, or to present grandiose knowledge claims as to definitional, theoretical, or methodological approaches of text/representation. Instead, the following discussion is grounded in the theoretical, epistemological, and methodological approach to studying gender and sport (as hegemonically defined) that I have found most useful in my own scholarly inquiry. This approach has also been shaped by my own intellectual struggles to produce knowledge with the potential, however small, to address issues regarding social justice and progressive social change (Cooky and Dworkin, 2013; Dworkin, Swarr and Cooky, 2013) while acknowledging the reality of the unevenness of social change (Cooky et al. 2015).

I first provide an overview of the three major levels of analysis of research on media text/representations. A brief discussion of the field of feminist cultural studies and theoretical frameworks is provided. I then discuss research my colleagues and I have conducted examining the representation of female athletes in media, primarily mainstream news media in the United States. As such, this chapter is admittedly narrow in its focus. I hope, however, it will offer insights into broader issues regarding feminist concerns of the ways in which the media texts/representations constitute and are constituted by bodies that are gendered, raced, classed, and sexualized.

Overview of research trajectories

Within media studies and specifically media studies of sport, there are three major levels of analysis and corresponding bodies of research. The first is *production*. This level of analysis examines the processes by which the producers of media content make decisions regarding what to represent and how, the demographic composition of those who are in positions to produce media content (for example: The Associated Press Sports Reporters Gender and Race Report Card; Schmidt, 2013), and the organizational practices of sports media outlets, to better discern why certain representations of sport circulate (Theberge and Cronk, 1986; Whiteside and Hardin, 2012). This particular area of research is the most challenging to conduct as there are barriers to accessing media producers, as well as difficulty in identifying the decision making processes of producers that do not simply reproduce common sense understandings of audiences (e.g. 'We give viewers what they want'). The second is *content*. This area of research is the most prevalent in sports studies and examines the distribution and type of coverage athletes/sports receive (e.g. Billings and Young, 2015; Cooky et al., 2015), the framing and representation of sports events or athletes (e.g. Boycoff and Yasuoka, 2015; Cooky et al., 2010, 2013), and the ways media representations reproduce or challenge wider societal ideologies. Changes in technology, the emergence of social media, the accessibility to the means of production of media content (in the form of blogs or YouTube videos, for example) have changed the ways in which media scholars envision the relationship between production and content, producer and consumer. Technology has enabled users/consumers to produce their own media content, and users may do so in ways that challenge the conventions of 'mainstream' (i.e. dominant) media. Researchers are turning their lens to examine these 'alternative' media texts/representations (e.g. Antunovic and Hardin, 2012, 2013). The third area is *reception*. Increasingly scholars are examining the ways in which audiences make meaning of the media representations/texts they see, and how athletes wish to be represented or portrayed, particularly female athletes who have historically been silenced, trivialized, or sexualized in texts/representations (e.g. Kane, LaVoi and Fink, 2013; Kane and Maxwell, 2011; Krane et al., 2011).

Feminist cultural studies

Feminist cultural studies is a theoretical and methodological orientation to understand how cultural images/texts/artifacts produce the category 'woman' or 'girl,' and thus articulate gender, gender difference, and gendered hierarchies of power. For feminist cultural studies scholars, an individual's identity in a postmodern, capitalist society is constructed primarily through consumption of popular culture products, images, and meanings (Sturken and Cartwright, 2009). In addition, feminist cultural studies consider questions regarding the role of pleasure, agency, and reception in the construction and maintenance of gender identities (Walters, 1999). Feminist cultural studies offer theoretical perspectives for understanding how individuals derive pleasure in consuming popular culture, despite the fact that their consumption may be reproductive of larger social structures and power dynamics. Feminist cultural studies also allow for an analysis of the ways in which social interactions, identities, institutions, and structures are shaped by discourses and media texts/representations and the ways media plays a significant role in the maintenance of the gender order (Driscoll, 2002).

My approach to the study of text/representation of sport as a contested terrain (Messner, 2002) is informed by feminist cultural studies, has focused primarily on media framing and content analyses, and includes the theoretical frameworks of a diverse array of scholars. In several studies, we have found the theoretical frameworks of hegemony, coding/encoding, and intersectionality/matrix of domination to be of particular utility in examining and analyzing mainstream news media texts/representations of women's sports/female athletes. In the following section, I discuss these frameworks as they have been articulated in our previous work (see Cooky et al., 2010, 2013).

Gramsci's concept of hegemony has proven useful for feminist sport studies scholars in contextualizing the gendered media texts/representations of athletes. According to Gramsci (1971), social order is maintained through a dynamic process of coercion and consent whereby dominant groups produce dominant cultural beliefs, or hegemonic ideologies, and given the power of hegemonic ideologies subordinated groups consent to structural conditions that may in fact maintain the status quo by which their subordinated status is maintained. Gramsci also acknowledged the agency of subordinated groups; opposition to hegemonic dominance can occur through the creation of counter-hegemonic ideologies/discourses. For Gramsci, coercion and consent is secured through the 'cultural leadership of the dominant grouping'. In contemporary cultures of the Global North, the mainstream media is a key institution by which cultural leadership is enacted, particularly when the lines between the corporate elite and the media elite are increasingly blurred.

Building upon Gramscian theories of hegemony, Stuart Hall (2000) developed theoretical and methodological frameworks for understanding how texts/representations are produced and consumed. As Hall notes, meanings are constructed through and within hierarchical structures of power wherein the preferred meanings, or the meanings intended by the producer, 'have institutional, political and ideological power imprinted in them, and themselves become institutionalized' (ibid.: 57). Media frames are both constructed within raced, classed, and gendered hierarchical relations of power and are read within those very same systems of domination. As such, preferred readings often limit the possible meanings encoded in texts by producers and thus limit the possible readings decoded by audiences (Hall, 2000; for examples in sports studies, see Cooky et al., 2010, 2013). Hall's theoretical framework is useful in that it situates texts/representations within social contexts and considers power dynamics in and through the ways texts/representations are produced and consumed. This theoretical orientation captures the complex processes of interpretation and negotiation that occur by both media producers and consumers.

Patricia Hill Collins's theories of intersectionality and the matrix of domination are also informed by Gramscian theories on the dynamics of domination and power in societies. Collins (1990) argued that dominant groups control social institutions in society, such as schools, the media, and popular culture, which produce controlling images that are rife with stereotypes about subordinated groups. These *controlling images* are not passively accepted by marginalized groups, as there are cultures of resistance within subordinated communities. Collins explained: 'Subjugated knowledges ... develop in cultural contexts controlled by oppressed groups. Dominant groups aim to replace subjugated knowledges with their own specialized thought because they realize that gaining control over this dimension of subordinate groups' lives amplifies control' (ibid.: 228). At the same time, Collins recognized there are segments of subordinated communities that internalize and perpetuate dominant ideologies. Thus, the processes of domination and oppression are complex.

Collins's concept of 'controlling images' has been particularly useful in explaining and contextualizing the ways in which women of Color are represented in the media, and particularly that of racialized media representations of female athletes (see Cooky and Rauscher, 2016; Cooky et al., 2010, 2013). Extensive research has documented the ways in which women's sport and female athletes are silenced, trivialized, and sexualized in mainstream media (Cooky et al., 2015; Daniels and LaVoi, 2013). The sexualization of female athletes in the mainstream media, particularly in the United States, has been well documented although the meanings of this particular representation are contested. Some scholars assert sexualized images are problematic not only because they detract from the accomplishments of female athletes but also because these images may have damaging impacts on the self-concept, self-confidence, and self-esteem of young girls (for a discussion, see Daniels and LaVoi, 2013). Other scholars argue sexualized images of contemporary sports media are more nuanced than the objectification thesis would allow, and are not simply oppressive, but can serve as sites for women's empowerment (see Dworkin and Wachs, 2009; Heywood and Dworkin, 2003).

In our recent work on racialized representations of female athletes, we were interested in exploring how girls, particularly girls of Color, envision themselves as athletes and how those imaginings may enable or constrain their sport participation in ways that contribute to racial disparities in girls' sport participation (Cooky and Rauscher, 2016). We were cautious to avoid engaging in moral debates

> regarding media imagery or the choices women make to co-produce or consume media images. Rather, we wish to contextualize the discussion within the larger structural context in which cultural imagery is produced, read, and negotiated. Given the ways in which sports that occupy the 'center' of our culture are masculine-identified, male-dominated, and male-controlled, along with the dearth of images of female athletes, and especially of female athletes as athletically competent, we must consider sexualized imagery within this broader context of sport
>
> *(Cooky and Rauscher, 2016: 74)*

Within these debates we suggest it is important to consider how arguments regarding the empowering potential of sexualized imagery of female athletic bodies in particular, and of women's bodies in general, often ignore considerations of sexism, racism, homophobia, and other axes of oppression (Gill, 2012). We argued, '*how* female athletes are sexualized in media and cultural representations is raced such that the sexualization of white female athletes upholds heteronormativity and white privilege while the sexualization of Black female athletes reproduces racist discourses of Black women more generally' (Cooky and Rauscher, 2016). As feminist scholars have noted, within the context of sport, the media discursively positions female athletes of Color, primarily Black female athletes in the United States, in a variety of ways that are simultaneously dynamic, contradictory, and contextually fluid. Drawing on contemporary scholars (Collins, 2004; Cooky, Dycus and Dworkin, 2013; Cooky et al., 2010; McDonald and Cooky, 2013; McKay and Johnson, 2008; Meân, 2013; Schultz, 2005), in our previous work we noted:

> Cultural images and discourses portray Black female athletes as 'respectable,' 'young ladies of class,' a 'racially neutralized American goddess,' aesthetically beautiful and feminine, and sexually attractive to men (Collins, 2004) exist alongside representations which situate them as 'bad girls,' 'nappy headed ho's,' 'sexually grotesque,' animalistic, and too muscular, thus transgressing the boundaries of traditional femininity and 'decency'.
>
> *(Cooky and Rauscher, 2016: 71–72)*

And while there has been an extensive body of literature on media representations of female athletes, very few studies engage critical whiteness studies and an intersectional analysis in the analysis of images of white female athletes. It is important not only to consider how representations of female athletes of Color are racialized, but how images of white athletes are also racialized (Cooky and Rauscher, 2016). Representations of white female athletes reproduce and are reproduced by whiteness and white privilege. Therefore, an absence of a critical examination of whiteness in the representation of female athletes, whiteness is able to retain its power by being unmarked and normative (Frankenberg, 1993).

Text/representation and the gendered body

Texts/representations often appear disconnected from embodied subjectivities and from the experiential. But texts/representation produce ways of knowing and thus constitute, and are constituted by, the possibilities of physicality. Feminist theorists have explicated the processes by which culture shapes and creates gendered bodies (Butler, 1993; Fausto-Sterling, 2000). Bodies are the products of historically specific practices and thus are not only determined exclusively by genetics but are also shaped by and through relations of power (Bordo, 1994; Fausto-Sterling, 2000) and are simultaneously produced by and constitutive of social meanings (Butler, 1993). These processes, as located within physical contexts such as sports, highlight the ways in which sport reaffirms the sex/gender binary as inherent, natural, and inevitable (Cole, 2000; Kane, 1995; Travers, 2008).

In our research on the mainstream media framings of sex testing/gender verification as manifested in the 'controversy' surrounding South African track and field athlete, Caster Semenya, we extended this scholarship to demonstrate how contemporary mainstream print news media framings of gender verification testing in sport reproduce, as natural and inevitable, the ideological foundation of the sex/gender binary (Cooky et al., 2013). Moreover, our framing analysis revealed 'conflicting accounts of how womanhood is defined in the United States and in South Africa, and which bodies are construed as "true" female athletes eligible to compete in international sport competitions' (ibid.: 37). In the paper, we argued Western scientific classifications of sex/gender are not 'objective' or 'value free' accounts of raced and gendered bodies but are themselves imbued with cultural meanings and informed by the socio-political contexts. This was evident in the differences we found in the framing of gender-verification tests. The United States print news media framed the tests as a 'scientific process necessary to "ensure" a level playing field', whereas the South African news media framed the tests as 'racist, a human rights violation, and a product of Westernized standards of femininity and beauty' (ibid.: 47). As we noted 'In the United States' media frames, gender-verification testing and Western definitions of sex/gender were 'global' processes by which capitalist, neoliberal notions of fairness, equality, and competition omitted the 'local' knowledge of Semenya's sex and gender (ibid.: 47). Our comparative media analysis illustrated 'how differing cultural contexts produce contradictory understandings of sex/gender, of gender-verification testing, and of notions of fairness in sport' (ibid.: 37).

Conclusion

Studies on media texts/representations of sports and physical cultures have dominated much of the current scholarship in the field of sociology of sport. This is due to a number of factors including but not limited to the prevalence, pervasiveness, and ubiquity of media coverage of sports along with the relative accessibility by which researchers can collect and analyze 'data' (i.e. texts/representations), an ease and accessibility not afforded by other areas of inquiry or methodologies (ethnographic research for example) which are often more time and resource intensive. Moreover, in a media-saturated culture, many of us have become primarily consumers of sports, thus, media texts/representations matter in that consuming mediated sports is the primary or sole entry point. And while sport studies scholars have increasingly turned to media texts/representations as a primary form of inquiry, feminist cultural studies, critical media studies, along with physical cultural studies, remind us of the importance of context in situating text/representation. Physical cultural studies compel researchers to consider how texts/representations are embodiments of the physicality of sporting spaces, as well as the processes by which bodies produce and are produced by texts/representations. Future research on text/representation should continue to extend the analysis of content to considerations of power and recognize media texts/representations are not simply reflections of gendered (or raced, classed, and sexed) subjects but instead constitute gendered subjectivities and athletic embodiment.

References

Andrews, D. and Silk, M. 2015. Physical cultural studies on sport. In R. Guilianotti (ed.), *The Routledge handbook of the sociology of sport*. London: Routledge, 83–93.
Antunoivc, D. and Hardin, M. 2012. Activism in women's sports blogs: Fandom and feminist potential. *International Journal of Sport Communication*, 5, 305–322.
Antunovic, D. and Hardin, M. 2013. Women in the blogosphere: Exploring feminist approaches to sport. *International Review for the Sociology of Sport*, 50(6), 661–677.
Billings, A. C. and Young, B. D. 2015. Comparing flagship news programs: Women's sports coverage in ESPN's *SportsCenter* and FOX Sports 1's *Sports Live*. *Electronic News*, 9(1), 3–16.
Bordo, S. 1994. *Unbearable weight: Feminism, Western culture and the body*. Berkeley, CA: University of California Press.
Boycoff, J. and Yasuoka, M. 2015. Gender and politics at the 2012 Olympics: Media coverage and its implications, *Sport and Society*, 18(2), 219–233.
Butler, J. 1993. *Bodies that matter: On the discursive limits of 'Sex'*. New York: Routledge.
Cole, C. L. 1994. Resisting the cannon: Feminist cultural studies, sport and technologies of the body. In S. Birrell and C. L. Cole (eds), *Women, sport and culture*, Champaign, IL: Human Kinetics, 5–30.
Cole, C. L. 2000. One chromosome too many? In K. Schaffer and S. Smith (eds), *The Olympics at the millennium: Power, politics and the games*. New Brunswick, NJ: Rutgers University Press, 128–146.
Collins, P. H. 1990. *Black feminist thought: Knowledge, consciousness, and the politics of empowerment*. London: Routledge.
Collins, P. H. 2004. *Black sexual politics: African Americans, gender and the new racism*. New York: Routledge.
Cooky, C. and Dworkin, S. L. 2013. Policing the boundaries of sex: A critical examination of gender verification and the Caster Semenya controversy. *Journal of Sex Research*, 50, 103–111.
Cooky, C. and McDonald, M. 2005. If you let me play: Young girls 'insider-other' narratives of sport. *Sociology of Sport Journal*, 22, 158–177.
Cooky, C. and Rauscher, L. 2016. Girls and the racialization of female bodies in sports contexts. In M. A. Messner and M. Musto (eds), *Child's play: Sport in kids' worlds*. New Brunswick, NJ: Rutgers University Press, 61–81.
Cooky, C., Wachs, F. L., Messner, M. A. and Dworkin, S. L. 2010. It's not about the game: Don Imus, race, class, gender and sexuality in contemporary media. *Sociology of Sport Journal*, 27, 139–159.
Cooky, C., Dycus, R. and Dworkin, S. L. 2013. 'What makes a woman a woman?' vs. 'Our First Lady of sport': A comparative analysis of Caster Semenya in US and South African news media. *Journal of Sport and Social Issues*, 37, 31–56.
Cooky, C., Messner, M. A. and Musto, M. 2015. 'It's dude time!': A quarter century of excluding women's sports in televised news and highlight shows. *Communication and Sport*, 1–27.
Daniels, E. A. and LaVoi, N. M. 2013. Athletics as solution and problem: Sports participation for girls and the sexualization of female athletes. In T. A. Roberts and E. L. Zubriggen (eds), *The sexualization of girls and girlhood*. New York: Oxford University Press, 63–83.
Driscoll, C. 2002. *Girls: Feminine adolescence in popular culture and cultural theory*. New York: Columbia University Press.
Dworkin, S. L. and Wachs, F. L. 2009. *Body panic: Gender, health and the selling of fitness*. New York: New York University Press.
Dworkin, S. L., Swarr, A. L. and Cooky, C. 2013. (In)justice in sport: The treatment of South African track star Caster Semenya. *Feminist Studies*, 39(1), 40–69.
Fausto-Sterling, A. 2000. *Sexing the body: Gender politics and the construction of sexuality*. New York: Basic Books.
Frankenberg, R. 1993. *White women, race matters: The social construction of whiteness*. Minneapolis, MN: University of Minnesota Press.
Gill, R. 2012. Media, empowerment and the 'sexualization of culture' debates. *Sex Roles*, 66, 736–745.

Gramsci, A. 1971. *Selections from the prison notebooks*. New York: International Publishers.
Hall, S. 2000. Encoding/decoding. In P. Marris and S. Thornham (eds), *Media studies reader*. New York: New York University Press, 51–61.
Heywood, L. and Dworkin, S. L. 2003. *Built to win: The female athlete as cultural icon*. Minneapolis, MN: University of Minnesota Press.
Ingham, A. G. 1997. Toward a department of physical cultural studies and an end to tribal warfare. In J. Fernandez-Balboa, ed. *Critical postmodernism in human movement, physical education, and sport*, Albany, NY: SUNY Press, 157–182.
Kane, M. J. 1995. Resistance/transformation of the oppositional binary: Exposing sport as a continuum. *Journal of Sport and Social Issues*, 19, 191–218.
Kane, M. J. and Maxwell, H. D. 2011. Expanding the boundaries of sport media research: Using critical theory to explore consumer responses to representations of women's sports, *Journal of Sport Management*, 25, 202–216.
Kane, M. J., LaVoi, N. M. and Fink, J. S. 2013. Exploring elite female athletes' interpretations of sport media images: A window into the construction of social identity and 'selling sex' in women's sports. *Communication and Sport*, 1, 1–31.
Krane, V., Ross, S. R., Miller, M., Ganoe, K., Lucas-Carr, C. and Sullivan Barak, K. 2011. 'It's cheesy when they smile': What girl athletes prefer in images of female athletes. *Research Quarterly for Exercise and Sport*, 82, 755–768.
McDonald, M. G. and Cooky, C. 2013. Interrogating discourses about the WNBA's 'bad girls': Intersectionality and the politics of representation. In L. Wenner (ed.), *Fallen heroes: Sport, media, and celebrity culture*. New York: Peter Lang, 193–207.
McKay, J. and Johnson, H. 2008. Pornographic eroticism and sexual grotesquerie in representations of African American sportswomen. *Social Identities: Journal for the Study of Race, Nation and Culture*, 14, 491–504.
Meân, L. J. 2013. On track, off track, on Oprah: The framing of Marion Jones as golden girl and American fraud. In L. Wenner (ed.), *Fallen heroes: Sport, media, and celebrity culture*. New York: Peter Lang, 77–91.
Messner, M. A. 2002. *Taking the field: Women, men, and sports*. Minneapolis, MN: University of Minnesota Press.
Schmidt, H. C. 2013. Women, sports, and journalism: Examining the limited role of women in student newspaper sports reporting. *Communication and Sport*, 1(3), 246–268.
Schultz, J. 2005. Reading the catsuit: Serena Williams and the production of blackness at the 2002 U.S. Open. *Journal of Sport and Social Issues*, 29, 338–357.
Sturken, M. and Cartwright, L. 2009. *Practices of looking: An introduction to visual culture*. New York: Oxford University Press.
Theberge, N. and Cronk, A. 1986. Work routines in newspaper sports departments and the coverage of women's sports. *Sociology of Sport Journal*, 3, 195–203.
Travers, A. 2008. The sport nexus and gender injustice. *Studies in Social Justice*, 2, 79–101.
Walters, S. 1999. Sex, text and context: (In)between feminism and cultural studies. In M. M. Ferree, J. Lorber, and B. B. Hess, eds. *Revisioning gender*. Thousand Oaks, CA: Sage Publications, 222–257
Whiteside, E. and Hardin, M. (2012). On being a 'good sport' in the workplace: Women, the glass ceiling, and negotiated resignation in sports information. *International Journal of Sport Communication*, 5, 51–68.

48
ETHNOGRAPHIC APPROACHES

Ryan King-White

From the earliest ethnographies practiced in Ancient Greece through today, research in this vein, in one way or the other, has always been about cultural description(s). Despite this binding feature, long-held traditions in ethnography regarding how it is practiced, whose voice holds sway, who or what is being studied, the authors' place in the research, and methods of representation (from the written to the performative) have radically changed in a relatively short period of time. Robin Patrick Clair (2003) has cogently outlined these developments in ethnography by tracing through four phases of (cultural) colonization, the linguistic turn, critical and radical feminism, post-modernism, and post-colonialism over the course of the past century. She concludes, 'after all, ethnography is not simply the methodological description of anthropological field trips; it is the expression of history, politics, and the essence of being' (ibid.: 20).

Tracing through the (short) history of ethnographic/ethnographically inspired research in physical cultural studies (PCS) reinforces Clair's basic timeline. Early studies in PCS primarily focused on a researcher entering a particular cultural setting, and telling the reader what happened from their (seemingly detached) perspective (cf. Silk, 2005). More contemporary research in PCS serves as an *exemplar* for how traditions in ethnographic inquiry have been unsettled (cf. King-White, 2013). These types of projects have focused on themes ranging from critical media literacy, feminism, autoethnography of the self, to participatory action research, and, in some cases, been at the forefront for new forms of representation via (performance) art, documentary film, and poetry.

Paying careful attention to the notion that 'it is as wrong to assume that all ethnography in past generations was conducted under the auspices of a positivistic and totalizing gaze as it is to imply that we are all postmodern now' (Coffey, 1999: 10), the following will be an attempt to describe what ethnography is, the key tensions shaping this form of research, and its relevance to PCS practice. Next, I critically explicate the major strands of ethnographic and ethnographically inspired research focused on various aspects/dimensions of physical culture. Along the way I point to specific research projects that have utilized (extensive) fieldwork components to provide deeply descriptive and critical accounts of cultural phenomena. Finally, I provide some considerations of the weakness/limitations of the extant research, and point to possible future research directions.

Central/contested ethnographic tenets

Access

Though there are many ongoing epistemological, ontological, and axiological debates regarding ethnography, most would agree that this type of research 'is perhaps best described as a practical activity that involves the ethnographer participating in people's lives, watching what happens, listening to what it said, and asking questions' (Silk, 2002: 780). This requires gaining *access* to a particular research site. Traditionally gaining access placed a mandate on the ethnographer to garner enough rapport with 'someone on the inside' of a (cultural) group in order to conduct research. More recently, the advent of cheap, durable, hand-held, high-quality smart phones, video cameras, digital cameras, audio recording equipment, and the internet has given rise to *virtual ethnography* where the physical presence of the researcher to gain access is not necessary, giving rise to a relatively new debate in ethnographic research.

According to Giampietro Godo (2008: 110) 'it is difficult to associate this research technique [virtual ethnography] with ethnography when it more closely resembles conversation analysis, discourse analysis, or more generally, text analysis'. Using his reasoning traditional ethnographic research required gaining access, conducting in-depth, first-hand analysis, and developing human relationships; the failure of virtual ethnography to meet this requirement leads to questions about its validity as a practice. Martyn Hammersley (2006: 8) counters that 'ordinary ethnography studies are also "virtual", in a certain sense: they are not objects that we can see or touch'. Thus, the very process of beginning an ethnographic research project is already controversial with respect to 'what counts' as ethnographic research practice.

Immersion

A second, no less contentious, act associated with ethnography is the *immersion* process. The primary objective during this process is to be in contact with a particular cultural phenomenon for an extended period of time so as to observe interactions as they 'naturally occur'. In so doing the ethnographer is better able to have observable data to rely on during the (re)presentation process, and reduce the number of interactions where they must infer what happened. Of course, the main issue here for contemporary ethnographic fieldworkers laboring in the neoliberal University, in this regard, is time.

Martyn Hammersley (2006: 4) speaks to this ongoing concern in ethnographic research stating that 'for most anthropologists, from the early twentieth century at least until fairly recently, ethnography involved actually living in the communities being studied ... [for] at least a year and often several years' to become *saturated* with information about a particular cultural phenomenon. Under extreme pressure to publish multiple peer-reviewed outputs, create 'impact', draw in external research income, enhance internationalization agendas and institutional metrics, engage in citizenship and administrative duties (and so on) just to earn tenure/pass probation periods (even at teaching institutions), many researchers simply cannot afford to follow this tradition and have moved to performing short-term *micro-ethnographies*.

No matter the approach, an ethnographer must choose how to spend their time in the field wisely. This normally requires finding *key informants* and *gatekeepers* who can provide access to important figures in the community, taking copious *field notes*, conducting and recording ethnographic and off-the-cuff *interviews*, obtaining *cultural artifacts*, taking pictures and video recordings, seeking out first-hand and mediated historical (re)presentations that provide more complexity and clarity to the researcher's understanding(s) of the researched (Van Maanen,

1988). Ethnographers must make tough choices about whom to follow, speak to, interview and when to do so. Thus, every split-second decision(s) the researcher and researched make during this process has a dramatic effect on the outcome of a study.

Interpretation

Ethnography certainly requires constant analysis and interpretation, about who and what to study and 'making sense' of it all. Eventually, however, there comes a point in the research process when the ethnographer must analyze the information they have collected. In so doing the ethnographer situates themselves on a continuum along a wide range of epistemological, ontological, and axiological approaches. These can range from, or between, utilizing a positivist, detached, 'god's eye' scientific perspective to 'going native' and actually being an integral part of the community (cf. Atkinson, Coffey and Delamont, 1999; Denzin and Lincoln, 2011).

No matter the methodological style utilized, interpretation (not a distinct phase and ongoing throughout immersion), generally involves making sense of copious mounds of documents, notes, boxes of video and audio recordings, pictures, and memories. Interpretation is almost certainly chaotic and (literally and figuratively) messy. Throughout this process the researcher's office/study space may have boxes of texts in folders strewn about, sometimes with notes scribbled on documents, others not, incompletely coded documents, and hours of recordings to sift through.

In order to organize all this information researchers can use a variety of interpretive methods that often speak to the methodological moorings outlined above. Ethnographers generally utilize a variety of *content analysis, discourse analysis, transcription, semiotics,* and sometimes computer software to (a)systematically organize their material in ways where key themes in the research can come to the fore (see Silk, 2005). Following this the researcher can, and often does, attempt to demonstrate that their interpretation(s) are credible and trustworthy. To do so an ethnographer can have disinterested peers critically evaluate their work (*peer debriefing*), send their interview transcripts and interpretations back to participants for further dialogue (*member checking*), all the while taking notes and thus creating an *audit trail* 'to add a dimension of reflexivity to [the research]' (Wheaton, 2013: 249).

Positivistic researchers refer to this process as *triangulation* to zero in on the *truth*, whereas those aligned with post-modern research paradigms tend to argue that this is better described as *crystallization*. To that end Laurel Richardson posits that the crystal serves as a better metaphor, because 'crystallization provides us with a deepened, complex, thoroughly partial, understanding of the topic. Paradoxically we know more and doubt what we know. Ingeniously we know that there is always more to know' (Richardson, 2000: 934). Thus, there exists no fixed point of 'truth' to be able to triangulate, rather multiple points of view/beliefs that only serve to complicate 'truth'. Either way, the primary goal in going through this arduous process is to put the researcher in the best position to (re)present the population they studied.

Representation

The next step, and attendant tensions, in ethnography is how to share what the researcher has learned about the researched. Traditionally, this was/is done by writing books and peer-reviewed journal articles from a perspective that lays out and interprets the data as what happened, attempts to provide anonymity to the researched population, and has no authorial presence in the text. However, more recently, researchers have argued that to best represent their research self-reflexively the authors' identities, and prejudice(s), must be written into the text so as to demonstrate how their background may have altered their interpretations (cf. King-White, 2012, 2013). Still others suggest that traditional journal articles and books are outdated forms of sharing ethnographic research. There is much to be said about the evocative nature that comes from ethnographic (re)presentations through poetry, such as Michael Silk's (2008) *Mow My Lawn*, performance pieces such as Jean Halley's (2012) *Death of a Cow*, artistic/creative outputs such as Jennifer Stirling's sport history turtle sculpture at the University of Maryland, and film, exemplified in Deb Roy's (2011) *The Birth of a Word*. Alternative forms of (re)presentation can be as, if not, more compelling and meaningful than traditional writing forms, have pedagogic potential, and can open scholarship to a wider academic audience.

Finally, 'exiting the field' can be wrought with tension; there exists no singular and systematic way to do this. Even the most detached observer in an ethnographic setting will form social bonds with the individuals they study, making (not so) fond memories, and having their lives forever altered by the research experience. The difficulties of physical and emotional detachment from a research site are amplified when the ethnographer engages in *reciprocity*, *participatory action research*, or even outright *activism*. Indeed, leaving the field may be least written about in ethnographic accounts and one of the most difficult elements of conducting ethnographic research. There is little doubt that entering and exiting the field as an ethnographer will forever change the researcher and researched in (un)anticipated ways, and may be another reason why scholars have turned to micro-ethnographies or opted for different research approaches.

Physical cultural ethnography

Silk's chapter in *Qualitative Methods in Sports Studies* (2005) sketches the landscape of ethnographic sport research through 2001. My work (King-White, 2013) focusing on moral, ethical, and political concerns that arise when conducting research in physical cultural studies serves as an updated companion piece – particularly through reference to studies that took place in the decade that followed Silk's chapter. The intent in this section is to further develop these arguments through discussion of recent advances and how they might (or not) come to bear on (physical cultural) ethnographic work.

Given an endless variety of research sites, methods, intentions, theoretical frames/locations that characterize ethnographic practice (and limited space), the section is organized through an admittedly overly simplistic structure. By my way of thinking, we generally research *marginalized sub-cultures*, *privileged sub-cultures* and *cultural intermediaries*, and this section will be organized under these sub-headings.

It goes without saying that all research sites have different power dynamics between the researcher and the researched, often depending on the identities, social backgrounds, and intentions of the project. Put very simply, we study along the continuum of power and privilege with the intention to advocate and/or intervene (King-White et al., forthcoming) in areas of injustice. Some forms of advocacy and intervention in research are made explicit by the ethnographer(s), whereas others achieve intervention by advancing critical theory, unsettling various taken-for-granted truths, and transforming knowledge (cf. ibid.). Throughout the following I hope to demonstrate the variety of ways that ethnographic PCS research has evolved empirically and methodologically.

Marginalized sub-cultures

The goals in researching marginalized sub-cultures are often the most clear. As I posit:

> Most individuals hailing from these various sub-cultures have been marginalized, suffer from various forms of abuse, and are relatively voiceless within contemporary society. As such, the primary moral and ethical concern for those working with these sub-cultures is to carefully help insert their voices into academic and public discussions and debates.
>
> *(King-White, 2013: 300)*

Thus ethnography along these lines is almost wholly situated around advocacy for disaffected populations.

Within PCS, and sport sociology broadly, a good example of this is the growing body of research focusing on Sport for Development and Peace (SDP) (e.g. Darnell, 2010; Darnell and Hayhurst, 2011; Donnelly et al., 2011; Giulianotti, 2011a, 2011b; Hayhurst et al., 2011; King-White, 2012; Tiessen, 2011). Simon Darnell is the foremost contemporary scholar practicing ethnography regarding SDP movements with research on right to play (Darnell, 2007), protesting the Brazilian Olympics (Darnell, 2014a) and ethical challenges in SDP (Darnell, 2014b) in addition to those mentioned above. Kyle Bunds (2014a, 2014b) has also conducted thoughtful research on water charities throughout the world, while Adam Beissel (2015) completed equally incisive work on Samoan football players.

Another developing body of (auto)ethnographic research focusing on marginalized bodies centers on the evolving place(s) women, femininity, and feminism has in sport and physical culture. Oftentimes research in this vein focuses on extreme, 'action, and lifestyle sport including surfing, windsurfing, snowboarding, skateboarding' (Olive, 2015: 100), and roller derby. Holly Thorpe, Rebecca Olive, Adele Pavlidis, Simone Fullagar, Becky Beal, Belinda Wheaton, Michelle Donnelly, and Janelle Joseph, among others, have worked individually and collaboratively to examine how women must navigate a number of problematic concerns within these sporting cultures in general and as individual researchers (e.g. Beal and Wilson, 2004; Donnelly, 2006; Joseph and Donnelly, 2012; Olive and Thorpe, 2011; Pavlidis and Fullagar, 2014; Thorpe, 2011; Wheaton and Beal, 2003).

Anita Harris's (2008) book *Next Wave Cultures* – as well as Takahiro Sato, Jennifer Fisette, and Theresa Walton (e.g. Sato et al., 2013; Walton and Fisette, 2013) – draws on themes from the aforementioned body of literature to address a variety of issues that young girls must contend with regarding physical activity, body image, and increased (yet still nowhere near equitable) acceptance of women in sport, and activism around the active female body. Their work dovetails nicely with a more explicitly activist-oriented form of ethnography – *participatory action research* (PAR). According to Greg Dimitriadis (2010: viii), 'PAR blurs the line between pedagogy, research, and politics', and requires the researcher to collaborate with the researched population in order to hear and, often, advocate for their needs. Julio Cammorota and Michelle Fine's (2008) book *Youth Participatory Action in Motion*, and Wendy Frisby's considerable contribution to the field (e.g. Frisby, 2005, 2011) serves as a beacon for how researchers can *intervene* in areas of injustice.

More generally, a recent special issue on bio-politics in *Cultural Studies ↔ Critical Methodologies* (vol. 14, no. 5, 2014) edited by Joshua Newman and Michael Giardina has provided a useful outline for contemporary developments in ethnographic research on marginalized sub-cultures. For instance Katie Flanagan (2014) utilizes feminist theories to underpin her historical and auto-ethnographical study about wearing a running skort. Jessica Francombe-Webb, Emma Rich and Laura De Pian (2014), Pirkko Markula (2014), and Brian Clift (2014) push at the edges of Giardina and Newman's (2011: 190) call to produce studies 'from the ground up' by considering new ways to include and represent a more radically 'embodied research' (Francombe-Webb et al., 2014: 471).

Privileged sub-cultures

Converse to the (radical) advocacy work conducted on disaffected populations, those that research privileged sub-cultures often attempt to expose the various ways people in these groups maintain, and perform, their relatively advantaged status in society. Often the researcher enters the field with a sense that something is amiss with the cultural phenomenon they are studying, but want to learn the historical and contemporary contexts forming taken-for-granted codes and norms of behavior in that particular setting. Since these bodily performances and activities are 'common sense' it can make matters more difficult for the researcher. For example, it can be a daunting task to ask someone why they fly the 'stars and bars' (the battle flag flown by US Confederacy in the American Civil War that has been utilized to promote racial supremacy in the United States), hurl racial epithets at people, or even join a country club when these are things that one is 'supposed to do' in that community (cf. Newman, 2013).

Gary Fine (1993) suggests that given the struggle for the researcher to garner access, meet key informants and gatekeepers, in addition to obtaining privileged information, research in this area requires a fair bit of 'lying' to the IRB and to research participants. Doing so runs the risk of being 'sued in court by participants that have been harmed by research participation' (LeCompte and Schensul, 2015: 104), but failing to be selectively truthful may shut down a research project before it ever begins. More to the point, in PCS research, both Joshua Newman's (2006) and my (White, 2005) dissertation and master's thesis projects could be conceived as 'infiltration' efforts to expose inequitable and often troublesome power relations (for example, privileged white, heteronormative, and nationalist behavior).

Exposing inequitable power relations are likely a common thread in PCS-oriented ethnographic works that focus on privileged populations. Given that the empirical emphasis for studies on privileged populations centers on the interwoven nature of whiteness, masculinity, and social class there have been two major developments in this type of study. The first continues in the tradition(s) of a typical ethnography whereby the researcher enters the field and writes about the cultural behaviors that they observe, and publish research on that population. The second, and for fairly obvious reasons, has been the marked uptick in autoethnographic research locating the PCS researcher as part and parcel of the very system being critiqued.

Traditional forms of ethnographic research in PCS can be seen in the work of scholars such as Lisa Swanson (2009) and Jaime DeLuca (2013) who conducted Bourdieusian studies on social class and what they termed upper middle-class (I would argue upper-class) soccer and swim cultures. Similarly, Maddox (2014) focused on upper-class tourists seeking 'authentic' yoga experiences in India, while expecting *essentialist* ideals about an India and its people that are juxtaposed to the hypercommodified West. These studies critiqued cultural entities that benefit from oft-unspoken levels of power and privilege, and describe the ways this power is inscribed and passed on to future generations.

Similar work on race, class, gender, and physical culture can be seen in a number of other studies. To wit: Caroline Fusco's (2005) research on the whitened social spaces in physical education and recreation locker rooms, Elizabeth Delia's (2014) deep understandings of the social identities of successful sport teams, Karl Spracklen's (2013) critique of racial divisions in northern England rugby culture, Thomas Fletcher's (2014) extensive fieldwork on racial constructions in northern England cricket clubs, and Stanley Thangaraj's (2012) analysis of how racial constructions pertaining to South Asian Americans were reinforced through recreational basketball in Atlanta. Other studies like Michael Atkinson's (2007) work on sport supplements, and Joanne Hill's (2015) research on boys and physical activity focus much more directly on constructions of masculinity.

As stated previously, parallel to developments in more traditional ethnographic research on physical culture, has been the rise of *autoethnographies*. What I believe is happening is that as those practicing qualitative inquiry have been encouraged to become even more self-reflexive in their work (cf. Giardina and Newman, 2011) researchers are finding that a number of us hail from identities that we seek to critique. In other words, many practicing research on physical culture are white, (fe)male, heterosexual, upwardly mobile (if not upper class), and able-bodied, and this certainly has an effect on the forms of physical culture that are studied, to what ends, the viewpoints used to interpret (objectivity or lack thereof) and ask questions, how access is granted, and so on.

Jennifer Metz's work on motherhood (2008) and teaching (2011), and Jennifer Giuliano's (2011) powerful (re)telling of her transformation from a consumer of Native American mascots to a passionate protester against them, are telling examples of the autoethnographic turn on privileged sub-cultures. More often, however, white male researchers produce these studies. For example, Silk (2008) offered self-reflexive accounts of his problematic relationship with Baltimore city and the place therein of recreational soccer, Jason Laurendeau (2011) compellingly writes about his entrance and exit from the BASE jumping community, Josh Newman (2011, 2013) critically considers his upward mobility with regard to social class, and Kyle Bunds (2014a) lays bare how he negotiates his privilege as a critical scholar. What each of these studies reveals is that despite working to undermine power relations in society through research, teaching, and activism those inequities still exist to the benefit of these scholars.

Cultural intermediaries

Similar to studies on privileged sub-cultures, ethnographic research on *cultural intermediaries* (Bourdieu, 1984) requires many similar 'infiltration' behaviors with the main difference being that the researched have even more power to shape public discourse through the dissemination of their mediated productions. Among others, Clarke and Clarke (1982), Gruneau (1989), MacNeill (1996), Silk (2001, 2002), and White, Silk and Andrews (2008) have engaged in ethnographic media production studies. As mentioned previously, morals and ethics driving any ethnographic study are tricky paths to traverse, but I assert that there are another set of challenging issues to confront when conducting studies on/in/with the media. More specifically, ethnographers in these types of studies are rarely production 'experts' (cf. Springwood and King, 2001). Therefore such work might not always make the desired impact, produce intended changes to production practices, or be well received by gatekeepers (cf. King-White, 2013; Silk, 2001, 2005).

Furthermore, the researcher's lack of expertise in production studies often results in (re)presentations that are closer to 'god's eye' accounts about what happened 'in the field'. Given the gradual shift away from this type of ethnographic (re)presentation in PCS it is possible that contemporary academics do not feel comfortable producing these types of projects. For, after situating the self as researcher and participant in these settings (e.g. King-White, 2013; Silk, 2005) it is difficult to provide much more than an outsider's or volunteer's account about what was taking place in these studies. Perhaps, the turn to complicate the self, uncertainty surrounding to whom the researcher is beholden, issues with access, and the amount of time that some of these studies require (cf. King-White, 2013; Silk, 2005) has led to a moment where these types of studies are almost non-existent in PCS over the past decade.

Future considerations

The aforementioned has demonstrated some of the major developments, ongoing arguments, and tensions within ethnography, a variety of ways it can be practiced, and how that has been taken up by a number of scholars in PCS. Within this final section I will make a call for where I would like to see further growth in ethnographic research. While eventually making an argument for the increased localization of ethnographic research, I must concede that work on (privileged) sub-cultures remains analytically useful, methodologically instructive, and can even drive progressive social change. I just find it *unmoving* – almost unemotional, detached reviews of *the author's* truth.

More to the point, it is one thing to possess the critical capacity and informational gathering abilities to present a cogent argument for why a particular sub-culture is behaving unjustly or is being oppressed. It is another thing to make the population being researched, reader, student, or audience at a conference presentation inspired to care. It is yet another to help (in whatever rudimentary ways) create a framework from which the critical ethnographer and others can intervene in productive and useful ways (cf. King-White, 2013; King-White et al., forthcoming). Thus I would like to see PCS research become more emotive, pedagogical, and *moving*.

By my way of thinking there have been a few recent studies that have fit that mold from a variety of perspectives. There exist sparse, yet emblematic, examples: Kyle Bunds's (2014b) autoethnographic explication of his own white, male, class privilege as a PCS practitioner proffered qualitatively different issues than Newman's (2011) account of a young man growing up poor in the rural American south; Renee Wikaire's (2013) inspired exploration of 'being' indigenous from New Zealand and recognizing Native American struggles in America as a graduate student at Florida State University; Jessica Francombe-Webb, Emma Rich and Laura De Pian's (2014) argument for considering the role of the body in ethnographic research; Jake Bustad and Oliver Rick's (2015) and Sean Edmonds's (2015) convincing calls for the (re)turn of *affect* in PCS; and Ryan King-White, Jaime DeLuca and Callie Batts's (forthcoming) reflections on the consequences of intervention based on our varied social identity backgrounds.

The term intervention is where I would like to offer my final consideration for future possibilities/requirements in PCS research. More to the point, Henry Giroux (2004: 74) writes that work in (P)CS needs to 'develop a pedagogy of commitment that puts into place modes of literacy in which competency and interpretation provide the basis for actually intervening in the world'. The issue that I have struggled with in respect to this compelling call is what exactly constitutes intervention? All too often, the term is included in PCS research projects, but the specifics for how, why, and to what ends the author is intervening are left out.

Being careful not to suggest that this is the *only* way for ethnographic research in PCS to progress, I would like to see more clarity and reasons for both utilizing the term and actually attempting to intervene in a particular setting. Further, I also encourage more localized ethnographic research on the institutions we work in, and where our expertise and (relative) power within the University can actually lead to progressive social change that can be *seen*. In this way the PCS scholar could be intervening by teaching in the classroom and in departmental meetings, speaking to, with, and against (athletic) administration about the inequities that our own student body, faculty, and staff must contend with, as well as developing a deeper understanding for the challenges that those in administration are confronted with in an increasingly devalued educational environment.

Work in this vein is not easy, particularly for untenured faculty members. However, I believe that this could prove to be a fruitful turn for PCS scholars to conduct what could be defined as a *natural ethnography*. Working on improving our everyday environments could help make our institutions positive examples from which other colleges and universities could draw. Certainly, educational institutions are not the only sites of inequity, but given the recent developments in (auto)ethnography regarding self-reflexivity and intervention I believe that more research in this area makes sense for the PCS scholar to engage in.

References

Atkinson, M. 2007. Playing with fire: Masculinity, health and sports supplements. *Sociology of Sport Journal*, 24 (2), 165–186.

Atkinson, P., Coffey, A. and Delamont, S. 1999. Ethnography: Post, past and present. *Journal of Contemporary Ethnography*, 28 (5), 460–471.

Beal, B. and Wilson, C. 2004. Chicks dig scars: Transformations in the subculture of skateboarding. In B. Wheaton (ed.), *Understanding lifestyle sports: Consumption, identity, and difference*. London: Routledge, 31–54.

Beissel, A. 2015. *Sons of Samoa*. Thesis (PhD) University of Otago.

Bourdieu, P. 1984. *Distinction: A Social critique on the judgment of taste*. Boston: Harvard University Press.

Bunds, K. 2014a. The Biopolitics of privilege: Negotiating class, masculinity, and relationships. *Cultural Studies ↔ Critical Methodologies*, 14 (5), 517–525.

Bunds, K. 2014b. Water for sport: The (re)production of global crisis. PhD thesis, Florida State University.

Bustad, J. and Rick, O. 2015. Physical cultures and affect: Leaning in to the affective turn. Paper presented at 8th Annual Physical Cultural Studies Graduate Student Conference, College Park, MD, April 17.

Cammorota, J. and Fine, M. 2008. *Revolutionizing education: Youth participatory research in motion*. New York: Routledge.

Clair, R. P. 2003. *Expressions of ethnography: Novel approaches to qualitative methods*. Albany, New York: State University of New York Press.

Clarke, A. and Clarke, J. 1982. Highlights and action replays. In J. Hargreaves (ed.), *Sport, Culture and Society*, London: Routledge, 62–87.

Clift, B. 2014. Suspect of smiles: Struggle, compassion, and running to reclaim the body in urban Baltimore. *Cultural Studies ↔ Critical Methodologies*, 14 (5), 496–505.

Coffey, A. 1999. *The Ethnographic self: Fieldwork and representations of identity*. London: Sage.

Darnell, S. 2007. Playing with 'race': Right to play and the production of whiteness in 'development' through sport. *Sport in Society*, 10 (4), 560–579.

Darnell, S. 2010. Power, politics, and 'sport for development and peace': Investigating the utility of sport for international development. *Sociology of Sport Journal*, 27 (1), 54–75.

Darnell, S. 2014a. Orientalism through sport: Toward a Said-ian analysis of imperialism and 'sport for development and peace'. *Sport in Society*, 17 (8), 1000–1014.

Darnell, S. 2014b. Constructing and contesting the Olympics online: The internet Rio 2016 and the politics of Brazilian development. *International Review for the Sociology of Sport*, 49 (2), 190–210.

Darnell, S. and Hayhurst, L. 2011. Sport for decolonization: Exploring a new praxis of sport for development. *Progress in Development Studies*, 11 (3), 183–196.

Delia, E. 2014. Subconscious (un)attachment to a sponsor: An irrational effect of stadium naming rights. *Journal of Sport Management*, 28 (5), 551–564.

DeLuca, J. 2013. Submersed in social segregation: The (re)production of social capital through swim club membership. *Journal of Sport and Social Issues*, 37 (4), 340–363.

Denzin, N. and Lincoln, Y. 2011. *The Sage handbook of qualitative inquiry*, 4th edn. London: Sage.

Dimitriadis, G. 2010. Introduction. In J. Cammorota and M. Fine (eds), *Revolutionizing education: Youth participatory action in motion*. New York: Routledge, vii–viii.

Donnelly, M. 2006. Studying extreme sports: Beyond the core participants. *Journal of Sport and Social Issues*, 30 (2), 219–224.

Donnelly, P., Atkinson, M., Boyle, S. and Szto, C. 2011. Sport for development and peace: A public sociology perspective. *Third World Quarterly*, 32 (3), 589–601.

Edmonds, S. 2015. This pain in my ass: An embodied narrative. *8th Annual PCS Graduate Student Conference*, College Park, MD, April 17th.

Fine, G. 1993. Ten lies of ethnography. *Journal of Contemporary Ethnography*, 22 (3), 267–294.

Flanagan, K. 2014. Sporting a skort: The biopolitics of materiality. *Cultural Studies ↔ Critical Methodologies*, 14 (5), 506–516.

Fletcher, T. 2014. 'Does he look like a Paki?': An exploration of 'whiteness' positionality and reflexivity in inter-racial sports research. *Qualitative Research in Exercise, Sport and Health*, 6 (20), 244–260.

Francombe-Webb, J., Rich, E. and De Pian, L. 2014. I move like you … but different: Biopolitics and embodied methodologies. *Cultural Studies ↔ Critical Methodologies*, 14 (5), 471–482.

Frisby, W. 2005. The Good, the bad, and the ugly: Critical sport management research. *Journal of Sport Management*, 19 (1), 1–13.

Frisby, W. 2011. Promising physical activity inclusion practices for Chinese immigrant women in Vancouver, Canada. *Quest*, 63 (1), 135–147.

Fusco, C. 2005. 'Healthification' and the promises of urban space: A textual analysis of place, activity, youth (PLAY-ing) in the city. *International Review for the Sociology of Sport*, 42 (1), 43–63.

Giardina, M. and Newman, J. 2011. Cultural studies: Performative imperatives and bodily articulations. In N. Denzin and Y. Lincoln (eds), *The Sage handbook of qualitative research*. Thousand Oaks, CA: Sage, 179–194.

Giroux, H. 2004. Cultural studies, public pedagogy and the responsibility of intellectuals. *Communication and Critical/Cultural Studies*, 1 (1), 59–79.

Giuliano, J. 2011. Chasing objectivity? Critical reflections on history, identity, and the public performance of Indian mascots. *Cultural Studies ↔ Critical Methodologies*, 11 (6), 535–543.

Giulianotti, R. 2011a. Sport, peacemaking and conflict resolution: A Contextual analysis and modeling of the sport, development and peace sector. *Ethnic and Racial Studies*, 34 (2), 207–228.

Giulianotti, R. 2011b. Sport, transnational peacemaking, and global civil society: Exploring the reflective discourses of 'sport, development, and peace' project officials. *Journal of Sport and Social Issues*, 35 (1), 50–71.

Godo, G. 2008. *Doing ethnography*. London: Sage.

Gruneau, R. 1989. Making spectacle: A case study in television sports production. In L. A. Wenner (ed.), *Media, sports, and society*. Newbury Park, CA: Sage, 134–156.

Halley, J. 2012. *The parallel lives of women and cows*. New York: Palgrave Macmillan.

Hammersley, M. 2006. Ethnography: Problems and prospects. *Ethnography and Education*, 1 (1), 3–14.

Harris, A. 2008. *Next wave cultures: Feminism, subcultures, activism*. London: Routledge.

Hayhurst, L. Wilson, B. and Frisby, W., 2011. Navigating neoliberal networks: Transnational internet platforms in sport for development and peace. *International Review for the Sociology of Sport*, 46 (3), 315–329.

Hill, J. 2015. 'If you miss the ball you look like a total muppet!': Boys investing in their bodies in physical education and sport. *Sport, Education and Society*, 20 (6), 762–779.

Joseph, J. and Donnelly, M. K. 2012. Reflections on ethnography, ethics, and inebriation. *Leisure*, 36 (3–4), 357–372.

King-White, R. 2012. Oh Henry!: Physical cultural studies critical pedagogical imperative. *Sociology of Sport Journal*, 29 (3), 385–408.

King-White, R. 2013. I am not a scientist: Being honest with oneself and the researched in critical interventionist research. *Sociology of Sport Journal*, 30 (3), 296–322.

King-White, R., DeLuca, J. and Batts, C., forthcoming. What 'counts' as critical intervention from three perspectives. *The Review of Education, Pedagogy, and Cultural Studies*.

Laurendeau, J. 2011. 'If you're reading this it's because I've died': Masculinity and relational risk in BASE jumping. *Sociology of Sport Journal*, 28 (4), 404–420.

LeCompte, M. and Schensul, J. 2015. *Ethics in ethnography: A mixed-methods approach*. London: Rowman & Littlefield.

MacNeill, M. 1996. Networks: Producing Olympic ice hockey for a national television audience. *Sociology of Sport Journal*, 13 (2), 103–124.

Maddox, C. 2014. Studying at the source: Ashtanga yoga tourism and the search for authenticity in Mysore, India. *Journal of Tourism and Cultural Change*, Published online, 1–21.

Markula, P. 2014. The moving body and social change. *Cultural Studies ↔ Critical Methodologies*, 14 (5), 483–495.

Metz, J. 2008. An Inter-view on motherhood: Racial politics and motherhood in late capitalist sport. *Cultural Studies ↔ Critical Methodologies*, 8 (2), 248–275.

Metz, J. 2011. Dancing in the shadows of war: Pedagogical reflections on the performance of gender normativity and racialized masculinity. *Cultural Studies ↔ Critical Methodologies*, 11 (6), 1–9.

Newman, J. 2006. Dixie's last stand: Ole Miss, the body, and the spectacle of Dixie south whiteness. PhD thesis, University of Maryland. College Park, MD.

Newman, J. 2011. [Un]comfortable in my own skin: Articulation, reflexicity and the duality of self. *Cultural Studies ↔ Critical Methodologies*, 11 (6), 545–557.
Newman, J. 2013. This pain in my neck: Living conscientization and/as paradox of praxis. *Qualitative Inquiry*, 19 (4), 247–260.
Olive, R. 2015. Reframing surfing: Physical culture in online spaces. *Media International Australia*, 155, 99–107.
Olive, R. and Thorpe, H. 2011. Negotiating the 'f-word' in the field: Doing feminist ethnography in feminist sport cultures. *Sociology of Sport Journal*, 28 (4), 421–440.
Pavlidis, A. and Fullagar, S. 2014. *Sport, gender, and power: The rise of roller derby*. Farnham: Ashgate.
Richardson, L. 2000. Writing: A method of inquiry. In N. Denzin and Y. Lincoln (eds), *Handbook of Qualitative Research*, 2nd edn. London: Sage.
Roy, D. 2011. The birth of a word. Available from www.ted.com/talks/deb_roy_the_birth_of_a_word?language=en (accessed February 25, 2016).
Sato, T., Fisette, J. and Walton, T. 2013. The experiences of African American physical education teacher candidates at secondary urban schools. *The Urban Review*, 45 (5), 611–631.
Silk, M. 2001. Together we're one? The 'place' of the nation in media representations of the 1998 Kuala Lumpur Commonwealth games. *Sociology of Sport Journal*, 18 (3), 277–301.
Silk, M. 2002. Bangsa Malaysia: Global sport, the city and the refurbishment of local identities. *Media, Culture and Society*, 24 (6), 775–794.
Silk, M. 2005. Sporting ethnography: Philosophy, methodology and reflection. In D. Andrews, D. Mason, and M. Silk (eds). *Qualitative Methods in Sports Studies*. New York: Berg, 65–103.
Silk, M. 2008. Mow my lawn. *Cultural Studies ↔ Critical Methodologies*, 8 (4), 477–478.
Spracklen, C. 2013. *Whiteness and leisure*. Basingstoke: Palgrave Macmillan.
Springwood, C. and King, R. 2001. Unsettling engagements: On the ends of rapport in critical ethnography. *Qualitative Inquiry*, 7 (4), 403–417.
Swanson, L. 2009. Soccer fields of cultural reproduction: Creating 'good' boys in suburban America. *Sociology of Sport Journal*, 26 (4), 404–424.
Thangaraj, S. 2012. Playing through differences: Black–white racial logic and interrogating South Asian American identity. *Ethnic and Racial Studies*, 35 (6), 988–1006.
Thorpe, H. 2011. *Snowboarding bodies in theory and practice*. New York: Palgrave Macmillan.
Tiessen, R. 2011. Global subjects or objects of globalization? The Promotion of global citizenship in organizations offering sport for development and/or peace programs. *Third World Quarterly*, 32 (3), 571–587.
Van Maanen, J. 1988. *Tales of the field: On writing ethnography*. Chicago, IL: University of Chicago Press.
Walton, T. and Fisette, J. 2013. 'Who are you': Exploring adolescent girls' process of identification. *Sociology of Sport Journal*, 30 (2), 197–222.
Wheaton, B. 2013. *The cultural politics of lifestyle sports*. New York: Routledge.
Wheaton, B. and Beal, B. 2003. 'Keeping it real': Subcultural media and the discourses of authenticity in alternative sport. *International Review for the Sociology of Sport*, 38 (2), 155–176.
White, R. 2005. Staging the American nation. Master's thesis, University of Maryland.
White, R., Silk, M. and Andrews, D. 2008. Revisiting the networked production of the 2003 Little League World Series: Narrative of American innocence. *International Journal of Media and Cultural Politics*, 4 (2), 183–202.
Wikaire, R. 2013. Neoliberalism as neocolonialism: Reflections on the waka ama in Aotearoa/New Zealand. Master's thesis, Florida State University.

49
PEOPLE IN CONTEXTS

Natalie Barker-Ruchti and Astrid Schubring

Introduction

Research does not merely report; it *instigates*.

(Frank, 2005: 968, emphasis in original)

What Arthur Frank refers to with the above claim is that research is a social activity that takes place between researchers and research participants in a shared space and at a shared time. As this occurs, they affect one another, in complicated and multiple ways, through their subjectivities and the research encounter these create, and will affect their lives after their meeting. Consequently, Frank (2005) regards trying to be impartial an empirical illusion and an ethical failure of responsibility. Instead, he proposes that researchers should acknowledge the situated, subjective and ongoing nature of science, and conduct dialogical research that allows researchers and research participants to share the scientific process.

In this chapter, our aim is to write about the complex social, embodied and relational process of researching people in physical cultural contexts. We specifically focus on the contexts researchers and research participants are situated in, how these backgrounds shape research situations, and finally, how they constitute a rich analytic potential. To reach this aim, we employ and outline two cultural studies terms that relate to researching people in contexts, namely 'research meeting' and 'research dialogue'. We further present an exemplary research encounter the first author experienced as part of her research into women's artistic gymnastics (WAG). In so doing, we illustrate how researchers and researched influence scientific work, how during such work, methodological contingencies occur, and lastly, how the capturing of and reflection on such incidents can generate valuable analytic potential. Finally, drawing on our own experiences of research encounters, we outline questions for three different research phases that we consider able to guide others' research practices.

Researching people in contexts

Andrews and Silk (2015) write that physical cultural studies are contextual in both form and objective. Indeed, the mapping of context, their complex relations, as well as the interactional effects they have on each other represent 'the contextual imperative and outcome of physical cultural studies'. To contextualize research encounters, (physical) cultural studies scholars argue for an alternative vocabulary to that traditionally accepted in interpretive science. *Research meeting* and *research dialogue* are two key terms, which we adopt from cultural studies scholars Richard Johnson, Deborah Chambers, Parvati Raghuram and Estella Tincknell's (2004) volume *The Practice of Cultural Studies*. In this book, and similar to Frank (2005), the authors acknowledge issues of politics and ethics, and provide strong arguments for the co-constructive and situated practice of cultural research. Within this assumption, the people-in-contexts approach applies to both researchers and research participants. In what follows, we take up the issue of subjectification as a form of social becoming and subjectivity as the embodied effect of this socialization process (Schubring, 2014: 38). We first look at subjectification and subjectivity with reference to researchers, then with reference to research participants. Finally, we discuss how such backgrounds and subjectivities shape the research process.

Researchers and research participants in contexts

Johnson and colleagues (2004) employ the concepts 'space', 'time' and 'place' to explain how researchers, research participants and research practice are shaped. What these scholars mean with the three concepts is that discursive forces and knowledge relating to social settings (read spaces), and dominant at one particular time, shape localities (read places), including research encounters. For the spatial factors that affect researchers, we see three contextual aspects to shape research practice: first, researchers' backgrounds influence what issues researchers are interested in, the questions they ask, the literature they read and the cultural knowledge they draw upon (Johnson et al., 2004). This may relate to particular childhood experiences, life-changing events and may be shaped by social structures, including gender, social class and sexuality. Second, socio-historical and cultural subjectification shapes scholars' understanding and practice of science. This may explain, for instance, why some scholars identify with statistical-type research and others prefer interpretive methodologies (Bloomer et al., 2004). Third, a variety of practical factors determine scientific work, including external instances such as ethical review boards, which may influence not only the timing, but also the research encounter and relational possibilities (Gibson et al., 2013). Other influential elements are available funding, time and facilities, and possibilities for collaboration.

Researchers as people-in-contexts reflect ideas of embodied research (Giardina and Newman, 2011; Schubring, 2014). In most research reports, however, this dimension is only acknowledged as part of a specific self-ethnographic or auto-ethnographic project design (Turner and Norwood, 2013). Researchers' embodied research practice seldom serves as data that is produced and analysed in its own right. Consequently, and as observed by Turner and Norwood (ibid.: 696) 'the ways our physicality matters as we move through the world in our own bodies of research are often veiled in the body of qualitative research literature' (exceptions are e.g. Allen-Collinson and Hockey, 2001; Punch, 2012). If we understand the research act as an embodied experience, however, researchers themselves can become 'pools of data' (Spry, 2010). Indeed, cultural studies scholars agree that researchers' 'entanglement in culture is one of our most powerful resources when studying culture' (Johnson et al., 2004: 55, see also Giardina and Newman, 2011).

As with researchers, research participants occupy and are shaped by contexts. Each participant brings an individual life history, personal backgrounds and embodied subjectivity to the research encounter. Thus, their motivation to participate in research and the knowledge that will be drawn from when providing insight into their lives are also shaped by particular subjectivities, as well as the spatial, temporal and local contexts they occupy at the time of the research encounter. Research participants may also bring experiences of earlier engagement in scientific research, as well as first-hand experiences of, or common sense preconceptions about, research aims and processes, including the research meeting. These circumstances influence the research encounters they participate in, if intended or not.

Research meeting and dialogue

A key moment within the practice of (physical) cultural studies is when researcher and research participant(s) come together in research *meetings*. Johnson and colleagues (2004: 201) stress that such appointments should not be reduced to events that allow scholars to extract specific information from a source, but rather as engagements that allow 'entry to a whole cultural world or scene'. This possibility to construct cultural information has indeed influenced scholars to conduct collaborative types of ethnographies (e.g. Gillespie, 2007; Campbell, 1999; Campbell and Lassiter, 2010; Kistler, 2010), also in physical cultural studies (e.g. Hoeber and Kerwin, 2013; Ortiz, 2005). This is not to say that research meetings do not involve traditional data production methods such as interviews and observations. Certainly, such means are employed; however, they are adapted to create research engagements that instigate *interactions* between researchers and research participants (Johnson et al., 2004). In this regard, a research meeting also conceptualizes and captures the interaction and relationality between context and phenomena, as well as the research encounter per se. That is, meeting acknowledges that research encounters are, for one, a means to tap into cultural contexts; but for two, are situations created by 'people-in-contexts', which offer cultural insights in their own right (see Figure 49.1 for a visualization of this co-construction).

A second important concept that Johnson and colleagues (2004) employ to describe the research process is *dialogue*. Dialogue refers to the analytic phase of research; however, in cultural studies terms, it is not separated from the meeting phase. In contrast, analysis is seen to begin during the meeting, as researchers gain understanding, have ideas and reflect upon what they have seen and have talked about with the research participants. Johnson and colleagues (ibid.) use the idea of 'double dialogue' to refer to, on the one hand, the face-to-face engagements with research participants and, on the other hand, the work with the record that documents what research participants have said/done. We would like to extend the double dialogue idea with a third dimension, namely that related to the preparation of the research engagement. Here too, contexts shape the decisions researchers make (see the specific contextual factors outlined above). For this preparation phase and the research encounter, consideration of space, time and place are particularly relevant and, if conducted in a self-reflexive way, have analytic potential (Hennink et al., 2011). For the analysis of data records produced from research meetings (i.e. interview transcript, field notes), various analytic procedures exist. Sticking with our cultural studies methodology, we consider Johnson and colleagues' (2004) four-step analytic procedure a generative option. The four steps these scholars suggest involve the following:

1. meanings of what participants voiced or did;
2. cultural forms participants employed to organize meanings;
3. contexts and power relations and their influence on participants' actions and meanings; and
4. participants' self-production and self-representation.

This procedure takes on a circulating and reflexive reading, moving from a focus on agency to its means and conditions and back again to agency, authorship and identity.

Physical cultural studies on people-in-contexts

Johnson and colleagues' ideas of research meeting and research dialogue urge researchers to acknowledge (their) partiality and their work's and research participants' socio-historical, political, spatial and temporal situatedness. Researching people in contexts thus involves researchers and research participants as people-in-contexts (see Figure 49.1). Such methodology is complex and perhaps even complicated, and may explain why scholars are reluctant to adopt such designs. Certainly, such an approach to research entails a degree of unpredictability, which makes the outlining of research outcomes tricky and, hence, may complicate the acquisition of research funds or consent from ethical organizations (Gibson, Benson and Brand, 2013). Further, Frank (2005) poses the question of whether research that flexibly works with research methodology and findings is negatively evaluated as inconclusive, rather than open-ended, which is what this scholar suggests is empirically and ethically appropriate.

Nonetheless, when scientific work is considered in terms of dialogic criteria, and if met with flexibility, open-(ended)ness and sensitivity, data production possibilities emerge that have the potential to produce useful alternative views (Fleming and Fullagar, 2007; Johnson et al., 2004; Frank, 2005). On one level, conducting research along such ideas has the potential to result in self-learning that can help understand research participants' experiences. Various physical cultural studies scholars have indeed achieved this through their research involving both self-/auto-ethnographic and ethnographic methods (e.g. Barker-Ruchti, 2011; McMahon, 2011; Carless and Douglas, 2012; Hoeber and Kerwin, 2013; Donnelly, 2012, 2014; Silk, 2008). On another level, researchers' self-learning can demonstrate the influence of socio-cultural forces and structural hierarchies. Useful examples of such research in physical culture have been conducted in a variety of contexts, including, for instance, roller derby (Donnelly, 2012, 2014), long-distance running (Allen-Collinson and Hockey, 2001), pain and injury experiences in competitive sport (Sparkes, 1996), writing collaboratively (Douglas and Carless, 2014; Barker-Ruchti and Schubring, 2015) and student-supervisor relationships (Fleming and Fullagar,

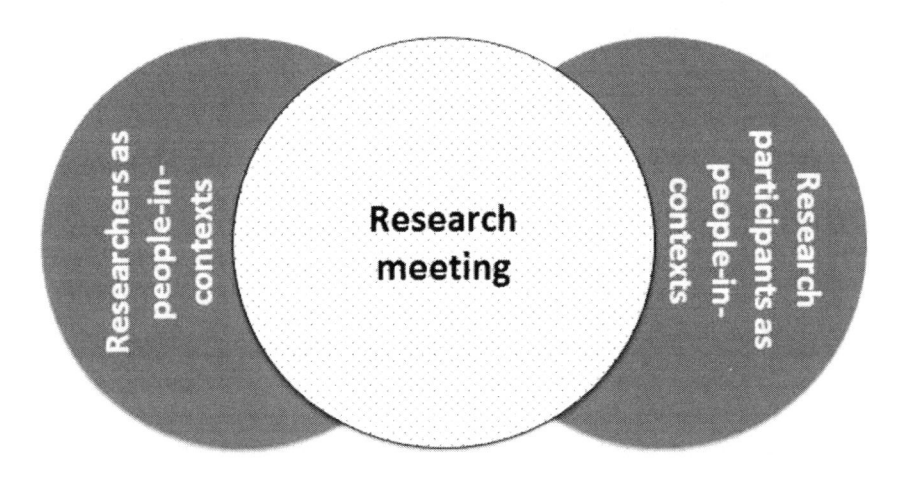

Figure 49.1 The research meeting that researchers and research participants (as people-in-contexts) create

2007). Indeed, Fleming and Fullagar reflect on their collaboration to argue that their considerations enabled them to 'mobilise other re-writings of self and forms of reflection that can be understood as transformations of knowledge in the present' (ibid.: 252). Had the relationship remained within typical patterns of apprentice and expert, these self-reflections may not have occurred and thus would not have stimulated (additional) epistemological constructions (Bartlett and Mercer, 2000).

So far, we have outlined methodological challenges relating to the subjectivities of researcher and research participants, the effects these backgrounds have on research meetings and research dialogues, and the analytic potential they may offer. To illustrate these factors, we will now present a research encounter Natalie experienced. This meeting was part of Natalie's doctoral research and, while not specifically anchored in physical cultural studies, entailed an (auto-)ethnographic design that aimed to study the realities of a sporting 'life-world' (Honer, 1985),[1] namely that of WAG. In this sense, we argue that the project reflects physical cultural studies research.

Methodological contingencies: a research case

Natalie's PhD project involved eight 10- to 15-year-old Australian high-performance women's artistic gymnasts and two coaches in their mid-fifties (for a full research account, see Barker-Ruchti, 2011). During the one-year ethnographic data production phase, Natalie produced field notes that she spoke into a voice recorder. The recordings covered all aspects relating to the gymnasts' training sessions, most prominently their spatial organization, use of equipment, the coach-athlete and athlete-athlete relationships, and training practices. The data demonstrated how disciplined the gymnasts were in each of the 10-weekly training instances amounting to 32 hours, how they trained in pain and with injuries, how the coach-athlete relationship was authoritarian and involved many instances of coach manipulation and verbal abuse, and lastly, how the gymnasts in only very limited ways were able to influence their sporting realities. During the research meeting, Natalie had developed an amiable relationship with the two coaches and a somewhat 'flat' relationship with the gymnasts. That is, the coaches welcomed Natalie into their gymnasium and home (which to outsiders, including parents, was closed) and were entirely open about their ambitions and approaches to coaching gymnasts. The gymnasts, in contrast, although seemingly unbothered by Natalie's regular visits and observations, appeared rather timid in their reactions to her informal questions.[2] Hence, approximately half way through the research engagement, Natalie decided that it was necessary to formally interview the gymnasts to hear more about their thoughts and motivations, future ambitions, and struggles. To do this, she approached each gymnast after one training session and handed out personalized interview invitations that outlined the intended interview content. This information was co-addressed to parents. However, only the three 10- and 11-year-old athletes agreed to participate; the older gymnasts never replied to Natalie's request for participation, even though they were reminded of the invite.

The lack of gymnast response was regrettable. With the benefit of hindsight, we now employ this example to consider the gymnasts' and Natalie's contexts that shaped the research meeting and provide interpretations that we see to help explain the gymnasts' reactions. For each entity, we cover a number of aspects, which are neither complete nor should be understood as independent from one another. Indeed, other factors influenced the research meeting, and all aspects relate in some way to form a network of influence.

Spatial and temporal factors that shaped Natalie's WAG research meeting

We have outlined earlier that spatial and temporal factors represent knowledge and discursive forces that are dominant at one particular time and that they refer to researchers' and research participants' previous life experiences, socio-historical and cultural subjectification and practical factors. For the gymnasts, the key spatial and temporal contexts that we see to have influenced the gymnasts' unwillingness to be interviewed relates to the culture of WAG, or 'WAG logic'. This logic emerged during the 1970s, within which gymnasts became viewed as immature and dependent individuals, whose child-like bodies can be trained and manipulated by coaches (Barker-Ruchti, 2009). The adult and often male coach-girl relationship is typical of this constellation and is supported by unequal age, perceived expertise and assumed leadership needs (Barker-Ruchti and Tinning, 2010). The gymnasts of Natalie's PhD study had become socialized by this WAG logic through their earlier training in this sport, which was on average a duration of seven years. This WAG logic, of course, also socialized the two coaches. Certainly, the coaches looked back on gymnastics careers, a multiple-year gymnastics education, and long-term coaching employment in the former Soviet Union.

At the time of the research encounter, the older gymnasts were aiming to establish their senior/junior national team status. As part of this phase, their training was intense and required multiple training camp participation at the country's national training centre. This occurred on top of their other commitments, of which schooling was most demanding (upper secondary education). This created an extremely demanding life schedule, which we would argue, prevented the gymnasts from agreeing to take on other responsibilities like Natalie's request for a research interview. Indeed, Natalie felt that after an initial reminder of her invite for an interview, she could not remind the gymnasts of her additional research intention. Further, the WAG logic had affected the gymnastics locality in that it did not provide gymnasts with private spheres or possibilities to voice thoughts and opinions. That is, the authoritarian gymnast-coach relationship involved little athlete input. In a similar way, apart from the bathroom, gymnasts could not access secluded spaces; even their locker room was located within the training area. This lack of input possibilities, as the lack of privacy or space to withdraw from others, especially the coaches, may have increased their uneasiness of talking to Natalie about private issues. Lastly, as the gymnasts were minors, the gymnasts' parents may have been involved in 'protecting' their daughters from additional commitments and possible scrutiny.

For Natalie, her long-term WAG involvement represents the key background that influenced the research encounter. She had competed in and coached this sport for many years and this drove her motivation to research WAG. Undoubtedly, her background as an 'insider' of the WAG culture influenced the head of the gymnasium agreeing for her to conduct research at his gymnastics institution. As this occurred, she became an 'approved intruder', an exclusive status that others, including gymnasts' parents, were not allowed. This gave Natalie and her work authority and through this, placed her closer to the two coaches and further away from the gymnasts. Indeed, as the relationship between the coaches and gymnasts was characterized by coach authority and athlete submission, the gymnasts may have perceived Natalie as a superior (as the coaches) and perhaps even feared that Natalie might pass on information they would have provided in their interviews. Natalie's positioning in relation to the coaches and gymnasts would thus have facilitated the amiable relationship she developed with the coaches and the 'flat' relationship with the gymnasts. Yet, Natalie's role was understood as to not directly contribute to the gymnasts' performance, and hence, she was asked to remain in the gymnasium's background. Again, this 'background status' may have limited Natalie's physical possibilities for encounters with the gymnasts and thus the development of a close(r) relationships with them.

Lastly, Natalie's academic socialization shaped the research encounter. In particular, her earlier work within interpretive science and employing qualitative data production methods affected her choice of PhD research methodology. Further, this form of science had influenced the type of literature she was reading and thus the research questions she wanted to answer through her study. At the time Natalie started this research, this type of scientific work had gained academic acceptance and, coupled with her desire to shape WAG, affected her choice of data representation – narrative writing style (Barker-Ruchti, 2008; Smith and Sparkes, 2009). Conveying high-performance gymnasts' realities in an as authentic and vivid way as possible was imperative to her because, as others have argued, evoking emotion has the potential to convince readers of significance (e.g. Tsang, 2000; Richardson, 2001). For Natalie, the hope was that such effects would communicate that the transformation of WAG is necessary.

Consequently, Natalie's and the research participants' contexts created methodological contingencies, which shaped the research meeting. In particular, it affected data production in that the observations needed to be conducted from the side of the gymnasium, Natalie's positioning close to the coaches created a friendly relationship that facilitated the informal talks and interviews, and the view the gymnasts gained of Natalie and her work created a distant and mistrusting relationship with athletes that (only) resulted in short and superficial informal talks. Yet, when considered within spatial and temporal dimensions, these contingencies offer additional valuable insight. Indeed, the gymnasts' refusal to be interviewed relates to the WAG logic and ultimately confirms Natalie's interpretations that gymnasts are positioned inferiorly within WAG and the coach-athlete relationship specifically. For Natalie, the contingencies also allowed processes of self-learning and stimulated reflections on the backgrounds she brought into the research encounter. Within this process, embodied reactions such as to the coach-athlete relationship, the disciplinary training practices and the gymnasts' suppression of emotionality were particularly strong stimuli that shaped her dialogue and the data representations Natalie produced.

Questions to prepare for people-in-contexts research

In this chapter, we have employed the concepts 'research meeting' and 'research dialogue' to illustrate the intricate, embodied and relational process of researchers-in-contexts researching people-in-contexts (see Figure 49.1). We presented a specific research case to demonstrate how the contexts researchers and research participants occupy shape research meetings. Within these meetings, methodological contingencies occur and we presented one such instance. The point here was to illustrate how, through considering spatial and temporal dimensions, research meetings and contingencies offer analytic potential. We would now like to close our chapter by referring to a number of research questions that we regard as important considerations for people-in-contexts research within physical cultural studies. We present these questions along the research phases we outlined earlier.

Preparing for a research engagement

In this phase of a research engagement, scholars will choose research topics, read literature and select a methodological procedure. Useful questions are:

- How have I been subjectified by my academic background, childhood and significant events in personal and work life?

- How does my subjectivity relate to the topic I plan to research? How does it affect the literature I read, the research objectives/questions I prepare and the research methods I choose?
- In which networks of collaboration and/or relations of dependency am I operating? How will these relationships influence my research?
- Which paradigms dominate my working context and what types of pressures might they create for my work?
- How do structural and practical aspects shape the research encounter I see possible?

Conducting a research meeting

In this phase, researcher and research participants come together in a research meeting. Useful questions are:

- In which contexts are the research participants I plan to engage with situated?
- How do other stakeholders relate to the research participants I aim to recruit?
- How may the subjectivities of my research participants and myself shape the research meeting and the relationships possible with them?
- What other relationships will I be a part of in the research setting, and how may these affect the research process?
- Which modes of documentation can I develop to capture empirical material relating to my embodied reactions throughout the research process?

Analysing the research encounter

In the research dialogue, although not limited to after the research meeting, researchers work with various research records, which may include reflections made during the preparation of research and research meetings. Useful questions are:

- What spatial (i.e. dominant ideologies, common practices, relationships and hierarchies) and temporal factors (i.e. life-stage, career phase, era, significant events) do methodological contingencies highlight?
- How may the specific spatial and temporal factors relate to the findings made in research records?
- How do my embodied reactions throughout the research process support/contradict what the research records offer?
- What roles can I give the research participants during the dialogue phase of my research?

Conclusion

Dominant assumptions about scientific work currently tell us that research projects must be rigorously planned. Physical cultural studies projects that are approached with a 'people-in-contexts' design situates research encounters so that through the research meeting, knowledge can be produced and learning occurs between and for both researchers and research participants. In such encounters, the relationships between the two entities and the knowledge that will emerge may be apprehended, but unexpected events will occur. While current research discourses devalue such contingencies, they can offer valuable analytic insight both regarding the research context and those situated within, as well as researchers' subjectivities. Although we could only briefly outline Natalie's attempt to recruit gymnasts, we hope to have been able to reveal relational patterns, the influence of power structures, participant subjectification and subjectivities, and researchers' dependencies on research participants. We thus hope that we have been able to point to the challenges scholars may experience when adopting a physical cultural studies approach and the paradigmatic openness, methodological flexibility and empirical sensitivity this requires. Further, physical cultural studies require time, and collegial support and a degree of 'freedom'. Despite these demands, not to mention the challenges bought by funding imperatives, the empirical insights that can be gained and the possibilities generated (including for learning) make 'people in contexts' research highly generative and worthwhile.

Notes

1. The German sociologist Anne Honer developed the concept of 'small social life world' in her research on people-in-contexts. Life-world can be understood as an 'intersubjectively constructed time-space of situated sense production and distribution, in which one engages in the course of a day or in the life course and which constitutes a more or less important element in the construction of individual identity' (Honer, 1985: 132, translation ours).
2. The questions were of superficial nature and covered issues such as general wellbeing, positive comments about having improved performance, and more specific questions relating to a particular occurrence during training (e.g. I saw that you hurt your ankle, what happened and what is wrong with the ankle?).

References

Allen-Collinson J and Hockey J (2001) Runners' tales: Autoethnography, injury and narrative. *Auto/Biography* 9: 95–106.

Andrews, D. and Silk, M. (2015) Physical cultural studies on sport. In R. Guilianotti (ed.). *The Routledge Handbook of the Sociology of Sport* (pp. 83–93). London: Routledge.

Barker-Ruchti N (2008) 'They *must* be working hard': An (auto-)ethnographic account of women's artistic gymnastics. *Cultural Studies ↔ Critical Methodologies* 8: 372–380.

Barker-Ruchti N (2009) Ballerinas and pixies: A genealogy of the changing female gymnastics body. *International Journal of the History of Sport* 26: 45–62.

Barker-Ruchti N (2011) *Women's artistic gymnastics: An (auto-)ethnographic Journey.* Basel: gesowip.

Barker-Ruchti N and Schubring A (2015) Moving into and out of high-performance sport: The cultural learning of an artistic gymnast. *Physical Education and Sport Pedagogy*. doi: 10.1080/17408989.2014.990371

Barker-Ruchti N and Tinning R (2010) Foucault in leotards: Corporal discipline and coaching practice in women's artistic gymnastics. *Sociology of Sport Journal* 27: 229–250.

Bartlett A and Mercer G (2000) Reconceptualising discourses of power in postgraduate pedagogies. *Teaching in Higher Education* 5: 195–204.

Bloomer M, Hodkinson P and Billett S (2004) The significance of ontogeny and habitus in constructing theories of learning. *Studies in Continuing Education* 26: 19–43.

Campbell E and Lassiter LE (2010) From collaborative ethnography to collaborative pedagogy: Reflections on the other side of Middletown project and community–university research partnerships. *Anthropology and Education Quarterly* 41: 370–385.

Campbell MR (1999) Learning to teach music: A collaborative ethnography. *Bulletin of the Council for Research in Music Education* 139: 12–36.

Carless D and Douglas K (2012) Stories of success: Cultural narratives and personal stories of elite and professional athletes. *Reflective Practice* 13: 387–398.

Donnelly MK (2012) The production of women onlyness: Women's flat track roller derby and women-only home improvement workshops. PhD thesis, McMaster University, USA.

Donnelly MK (2014) Drinking with the derby girls: Exploring the hidden ethnography in research of women's flat track roller derby. *International Review for the Sociology of Sport* 49: 346–366.

Douglas K and Carless D (2014) Sharing a different voice: attending to stories in collaborative writing.

Cultural Studies ↔ Critical Methodologies 14: 303–311.

Fleming C and Fullagar S (2007) Reflexive methodologies: An autoethnography of the gendered performance of sport/management. *Annals of Leisure Research* 10: 238–256.

Frank AW (2005) What is dialogical research, and why should we do it? *Qualitative Health Research* 15: 964–974.

Giardina MD and Newman JI (2011) What is this 'physical' in physical cultural studies? *Sociology of Sport Journal* 28: 36–63.

Gibson S, Benson O and Brand SL (2013) Talking about suicide: Confidentiality and anonymity in qualitative research. *Nursing Ethics* 20: 18–29.

Gillespie M (2007) Security, media and multicultural citizenship: A collaborative ethnography. *European Journal of Cultural Studies* 10: 275–293.

Hennink MM, Hutter I and Bailey A (2011) *Qualitative research methods*. London: Sage.

Hoeber L and Kerwin S (2013) Exploring the experiences of female sport fans: A collaborative self-ethnography. *Sport Management Review* 16: 326–336.

Honer A (1985) Beschreibung einer Lebens-Welt. Zur Empirie des Bodybuilding. *Zeitschrift für Soziologie* 14(2): 131–139.

Johnson R, Chambers D, Raghuram P and Tincknell E (2004) *The Practice of Cultural Studies*, London: Sage.

Kistler SA (2010) Discovering Aj Pop B'atz': Collaborative ethnography and the exploration of Q'eqchi' personhood. *Journal of Latin American and Caribbean Anthropology* 15: 411–433.

McMahon J (2011) Body practices: Exposure and effect? Stories from three Australian swimmers. *Sport, Education and Society* 17(2): 181–206.

Ortiz SM (2005) The ethnographic process of gender management: Doing the 'right' masculinity with wives of professional athletes. *Qualitative Inquiry* 11: 265–290.

Punch S (2012) Hidden struggles of fieldwork: Exploring the role and use of field diaries. *Emotion, Space and Society* 5: 86–93.

Richardson, L (2001) Getting personal: Writing-stories. *Qualitative Studies in Education* 14(1), 33–38.

Schubring A (2014) Growth as a challenge: A sociological analysis of the growth management of youth elite athletes, and their coaches. PhD thesis, University of Tübingen, Germany.

Silk, ML (2008) Mow my lawn. *Cultural Studies ↔ Critical Methodologies* 8: 477–478.

Smith B and Sparkes AC (2009) Narrative inquiry in sport and exercise psychology: What can it mean, and why might we do it? *Psychology of Sport and Exercise* 10: 1–11.

Sparkes AC (1996) The fatal flaw: A narrative of the fragile body/self. *Qualitative Inquiry* 2: 463–494.

Spry T (2010) Some ethical considerations in preparing students for performative autoethnography. In: Denzin NK and Giardina MD (eds), *Qualitative Inquiry and Human Rights*. Walnut Creek, CA: Left Coast Press, 158–170.

Tsang, T (2000) Let me tell you a story: A narrative exploration of identity in high-performance sport. *Sociology of Sport Journal* 17(1), 44–59.

Turner PK and Norwood KM (2013) Body of research: Impetus, instrument, and impediment. *Qualitative Inquiry* 19: 696–711.

50
NARRATIVE INQUIRY AND AUTOETHNOGRAPHY

Brett Smith

This chapter is concerned with narrative inquiry as a methodological contingency for physical cultural studies (PCS). After providing a definitional effort of narrative inquiry and some reasons as to why stories matter, one narrative approach, that is autoethnography, is focused on. Autoethnography in the plural is described and some reasons for using it offered. Several challenges that go with doing an autoethnography are also highlighted. The chapter closes with some future directions related to 'evidence' that physical cultural researchers might take up.

Narrative inquiry: a definitional effort

Just like defining PCS, no definitive definition of narrative inquiry can be given. This is because there are different theoretical positions to understanding narrative inquiry (see Schiff, 2013), differing definitions of narrative (see Frank, 2012), and diverse types of narrative analysis (see Holstein and Gubrium, 2012). This diversity and difference acknowledged, a definitional effort can be offered: narrative inquiry is a psychosocial approach that focuses on stories. But why stories? The seven claims and premises offered are neither exhaustive nor are they mutually exclusive, but they begin to map a vast terrain. Together they also add detail and depth to the definitional effort offered.

First, people are storytelling creatures (Frank, 2010). Stories are ubiquitous in culture and we have a tendency to tell and enact stories in our everyday lives. Given the ubiquity of stories and the human propensity for storytelling, it seems sensible then for researchers within PCS to consider attending to narrative rather than simply dismissing it as a very rare human activity undeserving of attention (Busanich, McGannon and Schinke, 2016; Fasting and Svela Sand, 2015).

Second, people need stories because of the work they *do* for us, which primarily, is to help make the world meaningful (Frank, 2010; Schiff, 2013). The world in itself is not naturally ordered or experientially meaningful but is rather what William James famously called a 'blooming, buzzing confusion'. What work narratives do for us is help turn the 'blooming, buzzing confusion' of the world into a meaningful place (Frank, 2010). Narratives do this by ordering events, providing a template to make sense of things, teaching us what to pay attention to, and showing us how to respond to what we attend to (ibid.). Third, stories connect and disconnect people and groups (ibid.; Caddick, Phoenix and Smith, 2015). Fourth, and extending the work of stories further, stories teach us who we are by constituting our identities and sense of self (Smith and Sparkes, 2008). Given these claims and premises of narrative inquiry, it would seem that stories matter in the lives of humans. To ignore stories would then be to disregard a key part of how humans make meaning and are able to live in society.

Fifth, stories are actors in that they shape what *becomes* experience (Frank, 2010). Stories neither emerge from the individual mind nor are simply representations of experience. Stories are developed from the menu of narratives culture supplies and, rather than being passive, these narratives do things. What these narratives crucially do, as actors in our world (ibid.), is shape what we come to know as experience. Sixth, stories also act on us by partly shaping human conduct. What we think, know, perceive, feel, and do is shaped by the stories that culture makes available to us (Caddick, Smith and Phoenix, 2015; Phoenix and Orr, 2014). If narrative is a key actor in our lives, then narratives cannot be simply dismissed. None of this is to claim that stories do everything or that our lives can be reduced to narrative. Rather it is to say that if stories partly shape human life, and affect what we do and don't do, then narrative needs to be attended to within PCS.

Seventh, humans are active storytellers. Stories might act on us by shaping experience and how we behave, but humans are also actors. One way to act – to perform agency – is through storytelling. For example, a person can act by selecting or editing a certain story in order to do something like motivate a group. Given that stories are a crucial means and medium of performing agency, focusing on stories provides insights into how people shape physical cultures.

Autoethnography: what is it and why do it?

As noted, there are different kinds of narrative inquiry. One way of sorting these is to make a distinction between work that takes the stance of the *story analyst* and work that takes the stance of the *storyteller* (Smith and Sparkes, 2009; Bochner and Riggs, 2013). A story analyst refers to a stance in which the researcher places narratives *under* analysis and produces an abstract account *of* narratives. To do this, stories are subjected to a narrative analysis (e.g. thematic narrative analysis) and results are communicated in the form of a realist tale. The upshot is research done *on* narratives. In contrast, when a researcher takes the stance of a storyteller the story *is* the analysis, meaning that the analysis itself *is* a form of storytelling. To do this, data is recast *as* a story by using a *creative analytical practice* (CAP). As described by Richardson (2000), CAP is an umbrella term for research that is cast into highly accessible storied forms, such as creative non-fiction or ethnodrama. Another type of CAP that a storyteller might use for certain purposes is autoethnography.

According to Allen-Collinson (2012: 192), autoethnography is 'a relatively novel research methodology within the range of qualitative forms utilized in research on sport and physical culture'. In general, it refers to a highly personalized form of qualitative research in which researchers tell stories that are based on their own lived experiences and interactions with others within social contexts, relating the personal to the cultural in the process and product. As Ellis and Bochner (2000) describe it, autoethnography is an autobiographical genre of research that displays multiple layers of consciousness, connecting personal lived experiences to the cultural.

> Back and forth autoethnographers gaze, first through an ethnographic wide-angle lens, focusing outward on social and cultural aspects of their personal experience; then, they look inward, exposing a vulnerable self that is moved by and may move

through, refract, and resist cultural interpretations ... Autoethnographers vary in their emphasis on the research process (graphy), on culture (ethnos), and on self (auto).

(Ellis and Bochner, 2000: 739–740)

Autoethnographic research can be represented in numerous ways. This includes short stories, poetry, vignettes, and layered accounts. Autoethnographies can be written, performed, visually communicated, produced digitally, and so on. Just as there are numerous ways to communicate autoethnographic research, there are now also different strands of autoethnography. As Allen-Collinson (2012: 196) noted, 'the autoethnographic genre is open to a vast range of styles and usages ... This openness to different forms, and refusal to be pigeonholed, is perhaps one of the great strengths of autoethnographic research.' The different strands and uses of autoethnography that have developed over the years include the following:

- *Evocative autoethnography*, or what is sometimes termed emotional autoethnography, takes a literary approach to research by seeking to show, rather than tell, theory through emotionally driven stories (Ellis and Bochner, 2006). The goal is evocation in terms of creating an emotional resonance with the reader and a heartfelt understanding of culture. Calling on the interpretive openness of stories (Frank, 2010), and the belief that stories are theoretical in their own right (Ellis and Bochner, 2006), another goal is to let the story do theoretical work, on its own, as a story. This is sought by showing theory through the story, rather than telling readers what the story is meant to theoretically convey. Or, put in the terms of Barone (2000), the autoethnographic researcher writes as an *artful writer-persuader* by relinquishing control over the interpretations placed on a story, inviting an aesthetic reading whereby readers interpret the text from their own unique vantage points, contributing their own questions-answers-experiences to the story as they read or watch it, as co-participants in the creation of meaning. Examples of an evocative autoethnography that connect with PCS can be found in the work of Smith (2013a) on how neo-liberalism that pervades the physical culture of universities can create artificial persons, and Ellis (2014) on chronic pain, arthritis, and exercise.
- Another autoethnographic option for physical cultural researchers, and perhaps the most popular to date in sport and PCS, is *analytic autoethnography* (Anderson, 2006). Like emotional autoethnographies, this type of autoethnography aims to deliver evocative stories. An analytic autoethnography differs, however, from an emotional autoethnography in that the author tells readers at some point what the story they crafted aims to theoretically do. Thus, analytic autoethnographers produce a theoretical autopsy of the story whereas in an emotional autoethnography this is resisted. Or put in the terms of Barone (2000), rather than operating as an artful writer-persuader, the autoethnographic researcher writes as a *declarative author-persuader* by seeking direct control over the interpretations placed on a story in the act of reading, listening, watching, and so on. Examples of analytic autoethnography that shed light on physical culture can be found in McGannon's (2012) story of her exercise identity and running experiences, Chawansky's (2015) vignettes of engaging in sport, development, and peace research, Fisette's (2015) tale of injury, illness, and a performing identity, Caudwell's (2015) narrative of the pleasures of moving, and Mills's (2015) deconstruction reconstruction of a coaching identity.
- *Autophenomenography*, as described by Allen-Collinson (2011, 2012), is an autobiographical genre that is framed by phenomenology (e.g. empirical phenomenology). The researcher in the process and product is positioned and acknowledged as both researcher and participant in her or his study of a particular phenomenon, instead of a particular social group that

shares a common culture. As Allen-Collinson (2012: 207) noted, although cultural location and lived experience are closely inter-twined, 'the primary focus is upon the researcher's lived experience of a phenomenon or phenomena rather than upon his or her cultural or subcultural location … In autophenomenography, the self is engaged with in a specific way: in relation to phenomena, or things as they appear to the conscious mind.' An example of how an autophenomenography might be done can be found in Allen-Collinson (2012).

- How autoethnographic work might be done within PCS has expanded further to include *meta-autoethnography* (Ellis, 2009). This is an autoethnography that builds on one previously produced by the researcher. It involves a researcher revisiting their previous autoethnography, considering the responses of others and the author to this former representation in the time that has elapsed since its production, and then generating an autoethnographic account about the original autoethnography to stimulate further reflection on key personal and cultural issues. Few meta-autoethnographies exist in sport and exercise (Smith and Sparkes, 2012). A rare physical culture example that mentions this kind of autoethnography can be found in Sparkes (2013).
- Most often evocative autoethnographies, analytical autoethnographies, autophenomenographies, and meta-autoethnographies are produced by one researcher. However, there is the option of two or more people working together to craft an autoethnography for certain purposes. When this occurs the researchers engage in producing what is known as a *collaborative autoethnography*, or what has also been termed a duoethnography or, when there are multiple people involved in the collaboration, a community autoethnography. An example of a collaborative autoethnography that connects with PCS can be found in the work of McMahon and Penny (2011) on the culture of body pedagogies within swimming in Australia, Smith and Sparkes's (2012) reflections of witnessing a chaos narrative, and Scarfe and Marlow's (2015) narrative of running with epilepsy.

Having highlighted what an autoethnography is along with its various strands, why might researchers studying physical culture consider using autoethnographies?

One response is that this kind of narrative inquiry has fidelity and connects with many of the key elements of the PCS project. For example, PCS and autoethnography are largely qualitative projects that are characterized by a commitment to social and cultural theory. Autoethnography is also faithful to the PCS project in that it promotes self-reflexivity. Both autoethnography and PCS foreground the body-self of the researcher as unavoidably situated within research practice. As such, there is a need for the researcher to critically turn their gaze on their own embodied selves, examining in the process how they themselves shape relationships in field, knowledge, and so forth. Indeed, according to Chang (2008: 13), part of the conceptual framework for autoethnography is based on the assumption that 'the reading and writing of self-narrative provides a window through which the self and others can be examined and understood'.

PCS and autoethnographic research additionally share a political commitment as well as promote a critical and public pedagogy. As Chang notes (ibid.: 13), conceptually autoethnography is based on the assumption that it 'is an excellent instructional tool to help not only social scientists but also practitioners gain profound understanding of self and other and function more effectively with others from diverse cultures'. For instance, like PCS, autoethnographies are often designed to impact learning communities within the academy, in the classroom, and throughout broader publics. In such contexts, the two often share a commitment to revealing socio-cultural inequities, injustices, and oppressive practices, how these are reproduced and resisted, and what might progressively be done to facilitate social change.

When crafted well, autoethnographies are particularly valuable for doing such political, critical, and public pedagogy for at least two reasons. First, autoethnographies carefully collect, analyse, and represent stories. Stories, unlike more traditional ways of 'writing up research', are highly accessible to the general public. As such, through stories physical culture researchers can reach audiences to facilitate a political, critical, and public pedagogy. Second, and as noted, stories are not passive but do things; they act on, for, and with people. Thus, this form of discourse can be harnessed to not only communicate and circulate knowledge to different audiences. It can be used as part of a critical and public pedagogy to do certain things in learning communities. This might include *conscientization*, that is, breaking through prevailing mythologies to reach new levels of awareness (Freire, 2000). As part of this process, oppressive bodily practices can be challenged, different ways of being opened up, and existing power relations as they are manifest within, and experienced through, the complex field of physical culture transformed. In such ways, autoethnographic stories become crucial equipment for the PCS project.

Another connection between PCS and autoethnography that, in turn, makes the latter a useful methodological option for physical culture researchers, is the focus on bodies. PCS often looks to explicate how active bodies become organized, disciplined, embodied, experienced, and represented in cultural sites and activities, like sport, fitness, leisure, wellness, and health-related movement practices. One way to help with this is through the collection, critical examination, and representation of stories through autoethnographic work. This is because in various ways narrative is central to being and having a body. For example, as Hydén (2014: 139) explains, 'telling and listening to stories is an activity that is accomplished through the use of bodies. Both telling and listening to stories involve bodily processes: the body and its parts are used as communicative instruments and as resources for structuring and interpreting stories.' As active storytellers, bodies also tell stories that can do things on, with, and for other bodies, thereby helping to organize, represent, and shape physical culture. At the same time, bodies are partly shaped by the narratives that circulate in culture. For instance, as actors in our world, narratives can shape our fleshy physicality, how we think about bodies, and how we make sense of our felt bodily emotions. They can perform the 'positive' and 'dangerous' work of teaching bodies who they ought to be, who they might like to be, who they can be, and which bodies to value and disregard (Frank, 2010). Moreover, the stories we are taught in the context of our social locations, and take on board, dwell and settle in our bodies, getting under our skin to develop and sustain embodied dispositions or habitual ways of acting. This is known as our narrative habitus (ibid.; Smith, 2013b). In such ways, then, narrative is not only entwined with physical culture. It is again crucial equipment for doing and advancing PCS.

Finally, though by no means least, according to Allen-Collinson (2012) when well-crafted autoethnographies are a means of gaining richly textured and nuanced insights into personal lived experience and emotions, and situating these within a wider socio-cultural context. We can thus learn a great deal from autoethnographies about the particular socio-cultural processes, experiences, emotions, and realities involved in the unfolding of physical culture.

> The 'insider' perspective gives autoethnographers the advantage of access to in-depth and often highly nuanced meanings, knowledge about, and lived experience of the field of study. This brings into play a wide range of resources, which would not normally be available to 'outsider' researchers. In inviting the reader to share the feeling and sensations, and to connect with the author's experience, autoethnographers often write highly readable, insightful and thought-provoking work, vividly bringing alive sub/cultural experiences for those unfamiliar with the social terrain under study.
> *(Allen-Collinson, 2012: 205–206)*

It would seem then that autoethnography holds great possibilities for developing PCS. This said, doing autoethnographic research is often difficult. It not only requires high levels of critical awareness, self-discipline, and reflexivity from the researcher. Strong literary writing skills are needed to craft a high-quality autoethnography. Further, irrespective of the quality, researchers may be accused of producing self-indulgent research. This accusation *can* have merit in that some autoethnographies can be self-indulgent. However, as Sparkes (2002) makes clear, any *universal* charge that *all* autoethnographic research is self-indulgent is problematic and needs challenging. For example, well-crafted autoethnographies move beyond the navel-gazing individual who looks just inside their own body to a deeper analysis in which lived experience is connected to the surrounding socio-cultural structures. Furthermore, argued Sparkes, autoethnographies can encourage acts of witnessing, empathy, and connection that extend beyond the self of the author and thereby contribute to understanding of physical culture in ways that, among others, are self-knowing, self-respectful, self-sacrificing, and self-luminous.

Ethics is another key issue facing researchers embarking on any autoethnography. For example, normally, in autoethnography the researcher is the central and identifiable character whose intimate thoughts and actions, often in sensitive contexts, are illuminated in great detail for the reader. This potentially places the author/researcher in a position of vulnerability as their life is laid bare to colleagues, family and friends, and actual and prospective employers. Publishing an autoethnography has the potential to harm the researcher in both the present and the future as s/he is unable to retract what has been written and also has no control over how readers might choose to interpret sensitive biographical information. In view of this, Muncey (2010) recommends that consideration be given to who can be harmed by the academic piece and what might be the consequences for them. She asks, 'In it the author is exposed for scrutiny; what risk can they do to themselves or the academy?' (ibid.: 106). In addition, the researcher needs to consider the implications on other people who are revealed, named, and implicated in the stories. Autoethnographers need to consider carefully how (and indeed if) certain others are included and represented within the write-up of the research. This raises tricky questions around anonymity, confidentiality, and informed consent.

Anonymity, confidentiality, and informed consent are ethical dilemmas in autoethnography in that, for example, people in the story may be deductively identified through their physical characteristics, attitudes, actions, and relationships with others. But, as Allen-Collinson (2012), Ellis (2004, 2007), Muncey (2010), and Tolich (2010) argue, none of this means that writing and publishing ethical autoethnographic is impossible. Here it is useful to go beyond traditional ethics, such as utilitarianism and principalism, and harness also various aspirational ethical positions (see Sparkes and Smith, 2014). For example, in discussing her own autoethnographic work Ellis (2007) aligns herself with an ethics in practice along with a relational ethics and an ethics of care.

Central to relational ethics is the question 'What should I do now?' rather than the statement 'This is what you should do now.' Relational ethics requires researchers to act from our hearts and our minds, to acknowledge our interpersonal bonds to others, and initiate and maintain conversations. As part of relational ethics we seek to deal with the reality and practice of changing relationships with our participants over time. If our participants become friends, what are our ethical responsibilities towards them? What are our ethical responsibilities toward intimate others who are implicated in the stories we write about ourselves? How can we act in a humane, non-exploitative way, while being mindful of our role as researchers (Ellis, 2007: 5)?

Reflecting on how she has grappled with relational ethical issues in her own work, Ellis (ibid.) offers the following advice to people who wish to engage in autoethnography (see also Ellis, 2004):

- You have to live the experience of doing research with intimate others, think it through, improvise, write and rewrite, anticipate and feel its consequences.
- There is no one set of rules to follow.
- Pay attention to research ethics committee (REC) or institutional review board (IRB) guidelines, but be warned that your ethical work is not done with the granting of REC or IRB approval.
- No matter how strictly you follow REC or IRB procedural guidelines, situations will come up in the field that will make your head spin and your heart ache.
- Make ethical decisions in research the way you would make them in your personal life.
- Question more and engage in more role taking than you normally do because of the authorial and privileged role that being a researcher gives you.
- Ask questions and talk about your research with others, constantly reflecting critically on ethical practices at every step.
- Relationships may change in the course of the research – you may become friends with those in your study – and so be aware that ethical considerations may change as well.
- Even when you get consent from those you study, you should be prepared for new complexities along the way.
- Practice 'process consent', checking at each stage to make sure participants still want to be part of your project.
- Include multiple voices and multiple interpretations in your studies when you can.
- Think about the greater good of your research – does it justify the potential risk to others? And, be careful that your definition of the greater good isn't one created for your own good.
- Deal with the ethics of what to tell. What strategies will you choose?
- When possible inform the people you write about. But, remember there are times when this might not be possible or might even irresponsible. Sometimes getting consent and informing characters would put them in harm's way.
- When appropriate, let the participants and those you write about read your work. But remember, sometimes giving your work back to participants could damage the very people and relationships you are intent on helping. If you decide not to take your work back to those you write about you should be able to defend your reasons for not doing so.
- Writing about people who have died will not solve your ethical dilemmas about what to tell and will actually make the dilemmas more poignant.
- You do not own your story. Your story is also other people's stories. You have no inalienable right to tell the stories of others. Intimate, identifiable others deserve as least as much consideration as strangers and probably more. You have to live in the world of those you write about and those you write for and to.
- Be careful how you present yourself in the writing.
- Be careful that your research does not negatively affect your life and relationships, hurt you, or others in your world.
- Hold relational concerns as high as research. When possible research from an ethic of care. That's the best you can do.
- You are not a therapist so you should seek assistance from professionals and mentors when you have problems.
- Not only are there ethical questions about doing ethnography but also autoethnography itself is an ethical practice with all that this entails.
- There is a care-giving function in autoethnography.

(adapted from Ellis, 2007: 22–26)

Supporting and adding to these suggestions, Tolich (2010) offers ten ethical guidelines for autoethnographers to consider as part of engaging with ethics as a process:

Consent
1   Respect participants' autonomy and the voluntary nature of participation, and document the informed consent processes that are foundational to qualitative inquiry.
2   Practice 'process consent', checking at each stage to make sure participants still want to be part of the project.
3   Recognize the conflict of interest or coercive influence when seeking informed consent after writing the manuscript.

Consultation
4   Consult with others, like an IRB.
5   Autoethnographers should not publish anything they would not show the persons mentioned in the text.

Vulnerability
6   Beware of internal confidentiality: the relationships at risk are not with the researcher exposing confidences to outsiders, but confidences exposed among the participants of family members themselves.
7   Treat any autoethnography as an inked tattoo by anticipating the author's future vulnerability.
8   No story should harm others, and if harm is unavoidable, take steps to minimize harm.
9   Those unable to minimize risk to self or others should use a nom de plume as the default.
10 Assume all people mentioned in the text will read it one day.

(Tolich, 2010: 1607–1608)

Clearly, there are numerous ethical issues involved in the process and production of autoethnographies. It is hoped the above advice is a useful starting point for carefully considering some of the ongoing ethical dilemmas.

A closing

Having offered a brief outline of narrative inquiry in general, and autoethnography in particular, this chapter closes with some modest thoughts about the future of doing this kind of work within PCS. There is much talk in narrative and autoethnographic research about what *potentially* each can offer. Like in PCS, this includes producing research that impacts on individuals, groups, and society. However, there is currently very little 'evidence' that autoethnographies, like much other work done within PCS, has a major impact.

Of course, what counts as 'evidence' and how 'it' can be captured is not simple. There are also important dangers concerning the uncritical promotion of 'evidence-based' work. For example, often it is suggested that only quantitative work and a positivist paradigm can produce 'evidence that counts'. In so doing, interpretive, qualitative research is discounted outright. Another danger is that when solely reliant on evidence-*based* work, the value of evidence-*informed* work (e.g. harnessing people's experiences in the field, tacit knowledge, practical wisdom, feel for the game, and witnessing stories) is dismissed. Such dangers recognized, the issue of 'evidence' within the current neo-liberal climate is here, and probably for some time. It should then be addressed.

As part of addressing impact and evidence, rather than shying away from these, the prevailing (and limited) ideas as to 'what counts as evidence' needs critically challenging much more (Silk, Bush and Andrews, 2010). Credible alternative understandings of what 'evidence' can mean needs developing. Likewise, how we might judge 'evidence' needs expanding (Amis and Silk, 2008). Further, autoethnographic and PCS research in the future needs to start providing 'evidence' (whatever that might mean) that our work can make a difference in and on physical culture. I am optimistic that it does (see Smith, Tomasone, Latimer-Cheung and Martin Gins, 2015). But this difference does not have to be at once 'big' in terms of producing 'solutions' and 'change'. As witnessed in numerous stories heard at conferences and in policy, medical, and sporting contexts, big solutions and change often do not arrive all in one piece. Solutions and change come about in imperceptibly small pieces, and they are recognized as solutions only after these small pieces have aggregated in ways that no one could often have predicted in advance (Frank, 2010). Perhaps this is how autoethnographic work and the PCS project might be best seen: as a boundless variety of infinitesimally small forces that, together, make a positive difference in the lives of those we work with.

References

Allen-Collinson, J. (2011). Intention and epochē in tension: Autophenomenography, bracketing and a novel approach to researching sporting embodiment. *Qualitative Research in Sport, Exercise and Health*, 3, 48–62.

Allen-Collinson, J. (2012). Autoethnography: Situating personal sporting narratives in socio-cultural contexts. In K. Young and M. Atkinson (eds), *Qualitative research on sport and physical culture* (pp. 191–212). Bingley: Emerald Group Publishing.

Amis, J. and Silk, M. (2008). The philosophy and politics of quality in qualitative organizational research. *Organizational Research Methods*, 11, 456–480.

Anderson, L. (2006). Analytic autoethnography. *Journal of Contemporary Ethnography*, 35, 373–395.

Barone, T. (2000). *Aesthetics, politics, and educational inquiry*. New York: Peter Lang.

Bochner, A. and Riggs, N. (2013). Practicing narrative inquiry. In P. Levy (ed.), *Oxford handbook of qualitative research* (pp. 195–222). Oxford: Oxford University Press.

Busanich, R., McGannon, K. R. and Schinke, R. J. (2016). Exploring disordered eating and embodiment in male distance runners through visual narrative methods. *Qualitative Research in Sport, Exercise and Health*, 8, 95–112.

Caddick, N., Phoenix, C. and Smith, B. (2015). Collective stories and well-being: Using a dialogical narrative approach to understand peer relationships among combat veterans experiencing post-traumatic stress disorder. *Journal of Health Psychology*, 20, 286–299.

Caddick, N., Smith, B. and Phoenix, C. (2015). The effects of surfing and the natural environment on the well-being of combat veterans. *Qualitative Health Research*, 25, 76–86.

Caudwell, J. (2015). 'Feeling blue': The ordinary pleasures of mundane motion. *Qualitative Research in Sport, Exercise and Health*, 7, 309–320.

Chang, H. (2008). *Autoethnography as method*. Walnut Creek, CA: Left Coast Press.

Chawansky, M. (2015). You're juicy: Autoethnography as evidence in sport for development and peace (SDP) research. *Qualitative Research in Sport, Exercise and Health*, 7, 1–12.

Ellis, C. (2004). *The ethnographic I*. Walnut Creek, CA: Altamira Press.

Ellis, C. (2007). Telling secrets, revealing lives: Relational ethics in research with intimate others. *Qualitative Inquiry*, 13, 3–29.

Ellis, C. (2009). *Revision: Autoethnographic reflections on life and work*. Walnut Creek, CA: Left Coast.

Ellis, C. (2014). No longer hip: Losing my balance and adapting to what ails me. *Qualitative Research in Sport, Exercise and Health*, 6, 1–19.

Ellis, C. and Bochner, A. (2000) Autoethnography, personal narrative, reflexivity: Researcher as subject. In N. Denzin and Y. Lincoln (eds), *Handbook of qualitative research*, 2nd edn (pp. 733–768). London: Sage.

Ellis, C. and Bochner, A. (2006). Analysing analytic autoethnography: An autopsy. *Journal of Contemporary Ethnography*, 35, 429–449.

Fasting, K. and Svela Sand, T. (2015). Narratives of sexual harassment experiences in sport. *Qualitative Research in Sport, Exercise and Health*, 7, 573–588.

Fisette, J. (2015). The marathon journey of my body-self and performing identity. *Sociology of Sport Journal*, 32, 68–88.
Frank, A. W. (2010). *Letting stories breathe*. Chicago, IL: University of Chicago Press.
Frank, A. W. (2012). Practicing dialogical narrative analysis. In J. Holstein and J. Gubrium (eds), *Varieties of narrative analysis* (pp. 33–52). London: Sage.
Freire, P. (2000). *Pedagogy of the oppressed*. New York: Continuum.
Holstein, J. and Gubrium, J. F. (2012). *Varieties of narrative analysis*. London: Sage.
Hydén, L.-C. (2014). Bodies, embodiment and stories. In M. Andrews, C. Squire and M. Tamboukou (eds), *Doing narrative research*, 2nd edn. London: Sage.
McGannon, K. R. (2012). Am 'I' a work of art(?): Understanding exercise and the self through critical self-awareness and aesthetic self-stylisation. *Athletic Insight*, 4, 79–95.
McMahon, J. and Penny, D. (2011). Empowering swimmers and their bodies in and through research. *Qualitative Research in Sport, Exercise and Health*, 3, 130–151.
Mills, J. (2015). An [auto]ethnographic account of constructing, deconstructing, and partially reconstructing a coaching identity. *Qualitative Research in Sport, Exercise and Health*, 7, 606–619.
Muncey, S. (2010). *Creating autoethnographies*. London: Sage.
Phoenix, C. and Orr, N. (2014). Pleasure: a forgotten dimension of ageing and physical activity. *Social Science and Medicine*, 115, 94–102.
Richardson, L. (2000). Writing: A method of inquiry. In N. Denzin and Y. Lincoln (eds), *Handbook of qualitative research*, 2nd edn (pp. 923–948). London: Sage.
Scarfe, S. and Marlow, C. (2015). Overcoming the fear: an autoethnographic narrative of running with epilepsy. *Qualitative Research in Sport, Exercise and Health*, 7, 688–697.
Schiff, B. (2013). Fractured narratives: Psychology's fragmented narrative psychology. In M. Hyvärinen, M. Hatavara and L. C. Hydén (eds), *The travelling concept of narrative* (pp. 245–264). Amsterdam: John Benjamins.
Silk, M., Bush, A. and Andrews, D. (2010). Contingent intellectual amateurism, or, the problem with evidence-based research. *Sport and Social Issues*, 34, 105–128.
Smith, B. (2013a). Artificial persons and the academy: A story. In N. Short. L. Turner and A. Grant (eds), *Contemporary British Autoethnography* (pp. 187–202). Rotterdam: Sense Publishers.
Smith, B. (2013b). Disability, sport, and men's narratives of health: A qualitative study. *Health Psychology*, 32, 110–119.
Smith, B. and Sparkes, A. C. (2008). Contrasting perspectives on narrating selves and identities: An invitation to dialogue. *Qualitative Research*, 8, 5–35.
Smith, B. and Sparkes, A. C. (2009). Narrative analysis and sport and exercise psychology: Understanding lives in diverse ways. *Psychology of Sport and Exercise*, 10, 279–288.
Smith, B. and Sparkes, A. C. (2012). Narrative analysis in sport and physical culture. In. K. Young and M. Atkinson (eds), *Qualitative research on sport and physical culture* (pp. 81–101). Bingley: Emerald Group Publishing.
Smith, B., Tomasone. J., Latimer-Cheung, A. and Martin Gins, K. (2015). Narrative as a knowledge translation tool for facilitating impact: Translating physical activity knowledge to disabled people and health professionals. *Health Psychology*, 34, 303–313.
Sparkes, A. C. (2002). *Telling tales in sport and physical activity: A qualitative journey*. Champaign, IL: Human Kinetics Press.
Sparkes, A. C. (2013). Autoethnography at the will of the body: Reflections on a failure to produce on time. In N. Short, L. Turner and A. Grant (eds), *Contemporary British Autoethnography* (pp. 203–212). Rotterdam: Sense Publishers.
Sparkes, A. C. and Smith, B. (2014). *Qualitative research methods in sport, exercise and health: From process to product*. London: Routledge.
Tolich, M. (2010). A critique of current practice: Ten foundational guidelines for autoethnographers. *Qualitative Health Research*, 20, 1599–1610.

51
POETRY, POIESIS AND PHYSICAL CULTURE

Katie Fitzpatrick

While 'realist' forms of research writing (Sparkes, 2002) dominate the field of physical cultural studies, a number of scholars use alternative forms of representation in their work. Alternative, that is, in the sense that their writing moves beyond the usual forms of communicating research that are consistent with academic prose or quantitative analyses.

>   Poetry
>   for example,
>   Might   move
>   the body
>   the hand to   craft, drift around the page
>   fall   over the margins
>   tackle   or reach toward
>   more nearly   embodied ways to write
>   to be
>   to make sense of
>   moving and being and moving and writing
>   writing and being   and moving and writing

The making of art forms such as poetry is only one example. Scholars also create theatre, visual art, performances, sculpture and dance (see other chapters in this volume). In this chapter, I draw on the notion of poiesis to understand how some scholars in the field of physical cultural studies have turned to the creative, the imaginative through poetry, not only as a means of expression, but also as a means of creating new knowledge. While these remain marginal in the field (Rinehart, 2010a), poetic research expressions are both methodological and representative; they, therefore, have implications for ontological and epistemological possibilities. For example, if, as an author, I create a poem, can this poem 'count' as a research text? Do the conditions of construction matter or can the poem itself be seen as an artefact, a knowledge remnant, as research evidence? Should this poem be used as a moment of 'data' or is it simply a way to represent research findings? What role does the creative process play? For the field of physical cultural studies, and the aligned fields of sport, movement and physical education (as well as dance), there is a further question: how might poetry engage with the body and movement in ways that other forms of writing, academic prose in particular, fail to do? In this chapter I address these questions, engaging them to think about the use of poetry and research in the field of physical cultural studies. I don't suggest that there are simple answers and, like other research questions, the answers very much depend on theoretical positioning.

Poetic representation is a form of arts-based research practice. Methodologically, arts-based approaches are gaining traction as a form of qualitative research, offering new forms of inquiry and expression. Atkins and Eberhart (2014: 44) note that 'art is not only a way of knowing but also a research method and an attitude toward inquiry that restores life and imagination to the research endeavor'. The notion of *poiesis* is useful here to think about production and creation in an artistic sense.

Poiesis

The term poiesis means to make, to create or to produce. In classical philosophy, Aristotle explained it according to three types of human thought: practical (praxis), productive (poiesis) and theoretical (theoria). Each of these have a 'mode of cognitive operation: *praxis* corresponds to *phronesis*, or practical wisdom; *poiesis* corresponds to *techne*, or craft; and, finally, *theoria* corresponds to *episteme*, or science' (Franchi, 2013: 359; emphasis original). According to this schema, these modes frame the possibilities of knowledge, but Atkins and Eberhart (2014) argue that theoria is the most valued of the three. Poiesis is, perhaps, the least popular mode in academic and scholarly work, perhaps because it is about creation, rather than product or outcome (jagodinski and Wallin, 2013). Atkinson (2009: 178) defines poiesis as 'an artistic, aesthetic, emotional, and public method of revealing "different" human truths'. He explains that:

> Poiesis arises from an act, a symbol, a thought, a feeling, or an expression that brings forth knowledge of the human condition falling outside of rationally technological ways of understanding human essences. Those interested in poiesis are less concerned then with measuring and accounting for something quantifiable in the world than the possibility of simultaneously experiencing the material and nonmaterial parameters of human existence.
>
> *(Atkinson, 2009: 178)*

Poiesis requires moving beyond what is, towards what might be or, what Martin (2004) calls, 'possible worlds'. jagodinski and Wallin (2013) argue that praxis, as informed action, is fundamentally different to poiesis. The latter, they maintain, has to be productive and novel, it must offer something hitherto unthinkable. Poiesis 'refers to the unveiling of *truth* connected to *neither* practical consideration or [*sic*] willing intent' (ibid.: 85; emphasis original). Rather than poiesis being (re)productive, it must be pro-ductive, an offering 'that dilates what *is* upon the virtual field of what might be' (ibid.; emphasis original). In this sense, poiesis expands the realm of what is or might be possible. In the first instance, poiesis may not be directly representative or even recognizable, because it comes from outside what is thought to be possible. Crucially, the expression of poiesis then requires praxis (action) (ibid.).

Poiesis has also been used to theorize the body and literature (Gallop, 1988). In this light, poiesis is employed as a process of analysing how the body is written and inscribed by discourse and, crucially, how it might be rewritten. Threadgold (1994) argues that the body and discourse can be remade and rethought through poiesis – indeed, that narrow subjectivities might be effectively challenged through poiesis.

Poiesis and poetry are not the same thing. But a poem may emerge as a product of poiesis and praxis. Gilbert (1994) distinguishes between poiesis, as the process, and poetics as the product. With reference to musical composition, she argues that there is a constant tension between musical creation and the end product, which is interpreted by an audience. She argues that 'music theorists' emphasis on the poetics of analytical procedure tends to erase subjective desires by neutralizing the subject'. Poiesis rather centralizes subjectivity through the creation. Franchi (2013: 359) argues that 'poiesis is always producing a *particular* work of "art" that comes into being at a specific moment in time, and in a specific time and place' (emphasis original).

While poiesis is a much broader philosophical concept relating to (unlimited) artistic creation, poetry is one possible result. Or, rather, a poem may be a form of poiesis in its intersection with praxis, if it is the result of novel production. The exposing of new thought via poiesis may be represented then in poetic form.

Why poetry?

Very much in line with the description of poiesis above, Zygmunt Bauman (2002) states that poets can uncover walls to expose newness. In this, he aligns pro-duction with the removal of boundaries, suggesting that concepts and modes of thinking are bounded by ideological 'walls' (what poststructuralists might call discourse). He argues that: 'the task of the poet … [is to] uncover … in ever new situations, human possibilities previously hidden' (ibid.: 359). In this, he suggests that sociologists should be more like poets:

> And for that reason we need to pierce the walls of the obvious and the self-evident, of that prevailing ideological fashion of the day whose commonality is taken for proof of its sense. Demolishing such walls is as much the sociologist's as the poet's calling, and for the same reason: The walling-up of possibilities belies human potential while obstructing the disclosure of its bluff.
>
> *(Bauman, 2002: 359–360)*

He insists here that if we do not look for newness, if we allow 'truths' to remain hidden behind the walls of 'ideological fashion' then, indeed, we are vulnerable to the bluff. In the field of physical cultural studies, poetry offers ways of viewing the body and physicality in ways that may undermine and speak back to oppressive, narrow and limited ways of understanding. Poetry is necessarily emotive, sensuous and empathetic; it can enable different kinds of knowledge and may directly subvert particular constructions of the body and movement. For example, the moving body is overtly medicalized in a great deal of scholarship addressing particular health problems, such as obesity (Gard and Wright, 2005). In this, the body is inscribed with moralistic judgements (body fat is viewed as a sign of personal failure to control eating and exercise). The body is prescribed 'treatments' (diet, physical activity) and monitored (heart rate, blood pressure, body fat, cholesterol …). The 'ideological fashion' involves capturing the moving body's data (sleep patterns, steps per day, breathing rate, weight …; Lupton, 2015). These trends for viewing the body and movement also reflect a neoliberalizing of the body and health that is increasingly digitized. Lupton (2014: 1352–1353) argues that digital body monitoring is reliant on discourses that 'conform to a general move in neoliberal political systems to encourage citizens to voluntarily engage in strategies to improve their lives and productivity'. The moving body then is captured by thinking that positions it according to particular digitized measures of health and economy; in Bauman's (2002) terms an 'ideological fashion' which obscures truths about movement for pleasure, emotional experience, the politics of the moving body and so forth. Poetry might be one way to reimagine (remember) other ways of thinking about physicality.

Poetry about the body and sport is, of course, not new. In ancient Greece, poetry was *the* way to comment on athleticism for writers like Pindar (Burnett, 2010) and sport remains a focus of creative writers, as is seen in the journal *Aethlon*.

Bob Rinehart says:

> Arguably, our 'areas' –
> that is, the
> subject matters of the body,   of how
> bodies
> adjust,   resist,   normalize,
> enjoy, grow, mortify,   d i s c i p l i n e ,   and   present themselves
> in the presence   and absence   of other bodies –
> are rife with possibilities for novel
> and nuanced,
> experimental and experiential
> ways of discovering and uncovering
> of meaning and   understanding.
>
> (Rinehart, 2010a: 185–186)

I am hearing his words poetically. I am reframing his words as poetry, taking liberties, invoking poetic licence. He is right, the body as subject lends itself to poetic expression. The body is a poem. Movement cultures are poetic.

In his exquisite poetic representation of racialization, social class and soccer, Silk (2008) engages (immerses) the reader in a two-page narrative dominated by colour, light, feeling and metaphor. Subverting standard academic prose, he instead gives a short and intense account of a sporting moment, which he refuses to contextualize, justify or explain. He lets the piece speak for itself. The account is deep, layered and rich. It invites one to read it several times, to experience along with the writer, the intensity of sensory experience. For Richardson (2004: 232), poetic representation is a 'method for seeing the conventions and discursive practices we take for granted'. She notes that poetry exposes the knowledge/truth relationship creating 'opportunities for rethinking how we think and who can think and what we can think' (ibid.). Richardson also argues that poetry creates 'the possibility of alternative criteria for evaluating social science production', including 'moral implications, practical applications, aesthetic pleasure, performativity, credibility' (ibid.). Poetry then allows for alternative ways to understand the body and movement that, in turn, expand the boundaries of thinking.

The use of poetry has (at least) several possibilities and advantages. In a beautiful piece published in the *International Review for the Sociology of Sport* in 1980, Zuchora argued for closer ties between sport and art. He reminds us art is a human need that has been with us since 'the dawn of history', permitting us 'to rise above surrounding reality, perceive in it the entire aspect of existence, grasp what is common to all, abstract, what has no genuine equivalent, to deepen the truth about life and the world'. Art, he says is 'a social necessity' (Zuchora, 1980: 50) but it is also political:

> the poet does not unfold his wings in ecstasy, he [sic] accuses. He challenges those who want to turn the stadiums into an oasis of peace in a world of 'crisis and bluff',

of social inequality, of the fight for markets and for colonial conquest.

(Zuchora, 1980: 61)

Poetry then can be disruptive, critical and challenge dominant conceptions. Salman Rushdie (1988: 97) maintains that a poet's task is to 'name the unnameable, to point at frauds, to take sides, start arguments, shape the world, and stop it going to sleep'. Poetry then has the potential to draw our attention to issues in the field, to push at the boundaries of our thinking and engage the audience. Such engagement is possible because poetry also has an emotional edge. In a moving poem about fishing with his daughter, Ritterbusch (2010: 70) reflects on how his daughter copes with the death of the pike they catch:

> My daughter watches
> intently as I gut the pike –
> she hates this, says this is
> the last one and she won't
> eat any more, not
> this one, not any other;
> we can catch them
> but we must let them go

He tells her a story about the one-legged seagull that feeds on the fish guts, imagining the pike taking the seagull's leg and implying a symmetry of nature. At the end of the poem, he admits:

> But she is nine, too old to buy such tales,
> and she grows quiet with a knowledge that strikes deep,
> that grabs hold and won't ever let go,
> burning through her life
> like evening sun
> red upon the water.

Poetry like this connects directly with the lived emotions of the body, it can make us feel and react in ways that are different to academic prose. It is an embodied form of writing. Reading and writing poetry can give a feeling of euphoria, a connection with our creative selves. Feminist poet Adrienne Rich (2003) insists that poems elicit an embodied response. She notes that 'you listen, if you do, not simply to the poem, but to a part of you reawakened by the poem, momentarily made aware, a need both emotional and physical, that can for a moment be affirmed there' (ibid.: 12). A (good) poem then can transport, awaken desire, move the reader in ways that may not be achieved by other forms of writing. Commenting on Wallace Steven's poem 'The house was quiet and the world was calm', Adrienne Rich reflects on why this poem is compelling despite its juxtaposition with her own world:

> if you go on listening, if the words can draw you in, it's surely for their music as much as for the meaning – music that calls up the state of which the words are speaking. You are drawn in not because this is a description of your world but because you begin to be reminded of your own desire and need, because the poem is not about integration and fulfilment, but about desire … for those conditions.
>
> *(Rich, 2003: 12)*

Sparkes and Smith (2014: 162) argue that 'people respond differently to poetry than they do to prose', and poetry, indeed, evokes embodied responses, which Faulkner (2007: 222) observes is 'about showing, not telling, our (in)humanity and all of its mysteries'. Miles Richardson (1998) agrees, stating that a poem should not (only) be about a thing but rather be the thing itself. As I argue elsewhere:

> I think there are some things
> that can only be said
> in poems
> or how   poems are the only ones to say
> some things
> this could be a physical site then,
> a kind of bounded unbound space to
> say the things we do not say in research
>   to cry in words when we can't bear the shame of the tears on
> our faces
> and why is that
>
> I think there are some things, some times that just call for the words
> we usually avoid, the ones that lurk at the edges and get put away.
>
> and how poetry goes right there to the edge, goes too far.
> reclaims our rage.
>
> *(Fitzpatrick and Fitzpatrick, 2015: 54)*

As a way to represent spoken words (such as interviews), poetry is also a mode of representation closer to actual speech, in that it includes natural emphases, pauses and silences (Richardson, 2000; Sparkes and Douglas, 2007). Poetry can also enable researchers to be more reflexive, to acknowledge their own subjectivities and to write themselves into the text. Brkich and Barko note that:

> poetry not only creates reality based on extant data ... but rather that it creates the data it represents while revealing reflexively the researchers' motives, interests, and concerns equally as data. We crave something less machine-like, formulaic, heuristic. We crave something more artistic, blurred between the two cultures – equally as science and as art.
>
> *(Brkich and Barko, 2013: 246)*

Poetry then reveals the authorial hand in the process of writing, allowing for more transparent and reflexive texts (Richardson, 2000, 2004).

A final point I want to make in this section is that, like narrative and other arts-based approaches, writing poetry requires some literary skill (Markula and Silk, 2011). Researchers using poetry debate whether the poetry itself should adhere to literary conventions in the sense that research poems should be judged on their artistic merits as well as their ability to communicate research contexts, or whether poetry can be seen in relation to process as well as product (Faulkner, 2007; Lahman et al., 2011; Lahman and Richard, 2014). Nevertheless, regardless of one's position, the effect of the poem lies with the reader and can be interpreted in unexpected ways (Rinehart, 1998).

Poetry and physical culture

There is not a singular way to use poetry in research; scholars have employed it as method as well as a form of representation. In the late 1980s and 1990s, there was increased interest in poetic representation in the fields of physical culture, physical education and sports studies (Sparkes and Silvennoinen, 1999; Sparkes, 2002), including a special issue of *Quest* (Hoffman, 1989). More recently, while several researchers argue for the use of poetry (e.g. Block and Weatherford, 2013; Hopper et al., 2008), examples remain rare. Poetry can be used to convey cultural nuance or an intense experience (e.g. Silk, 2008). It can communicate emotional experience (e.g. Popovic, 2012) or reflect the politics of sporting cultures (e.g. Rinehart, 2014). Others have used poetry at the intersection between moving and writing to capture the quality of movement as a text (see Longley, 2014, discussed below). Researchers also use poetry to interpret findings, as a way to rearrange the statements of participants and expose the hidden cadences and artistry of everyday speech (e.g. Fitzpatrick, 2013; Richardson, 1992, 2000; Sparkes and Douglas, 2007). Some use poetry as a method, asking participants to create poems or writing poems themselves as a part of fieldwork or note taking (e.g. Fitzpatrick, 2013; Sparkes and Douglas, 2007). Found poems involve choosing words or phrases that one might come across (spoken by people, written on signs or in graffiti, in text messages or websites) and structuring these words into a poem (Prendergast, 2006). A found poem is a kind of poetic discovery, one that requires the researcher/poet to attend to the poetry of the everyday. Sparkes and Smith (2014: 161) argue that 'constructing different poems about the same data can help a researcher to rethink the data and to work on additional ways to highlight these. Poetry is a form of knowing as well as representing, it invokes passion, which is 'a necessary condition for the possibility of thinking the politics and aesthetics of sport' (Farred, 2006: 460). In this section, I want to share and comment on a few poetic snapshots from work in the field to highlight how researchers are using poetry to explore physical culture.

The first example is from dance. Although this chapter has not explored the work in the field of dance studies specifically, I want to show here how one dance researcher, Alys Longley, uses poetry to reflect and intersect with movement in creative ways. Her methods perhaps push the boundaries of what might be considered physical cultural studies, into the realm of what she calls 'movement-initiated-writing'. Longley explores the intersections between moving and writing, explaining that

> sensorial information creates dance. Dancers listen kinaesthetically, read spaces with their muscles, make embodied decisions in the moments of falling. They experiment with how meaning is created by the timing of a gesture, or the quality of energy that creates dynamic feeling, or by the composition of bodies and objects in space, making some spaces alive and others invisible.
>
> *(Longley, 2014: 70)*

She notes that 'travelling between the highly physical complex world of kinaesthetic knowledge and the descriptive, documental, or conceptual register of written language is often uncomfortable' (ibid.). She uses a method of 'writing out of kinaesthetic sensation' to produce texts that interact with movement (Figure 51.1). Longley conceptualizes the page as performance (Figure 51.2).

The next example is from the work of Robert Rinehart who has experimented with several different forms of performative writing in sport sociology and qualitative research (e.g.

A procedure in touching the edges of a given concept

The foreign language of motion

Traversing uneven surfaces of sound

'This is a document made from the idea of glass"

Figure 51.1 'Intro 1' reproduced from Alys Longley

How to create space around the muscles of the eyes? Drawing eyelashes and eyebrows away from each other

Relationships with objects that underpin the day

Discontinuous levels of energy

And then when you hear it the second time you've already gotten it into your body

As we mix voices together

Travelling toward volume

Figure 51.2 'Intro 2' reproduced from Alys Longley

Rinehart, 1998, 2010b). This poem centres on the Olympic diver, US–Korean Sammy Lee (Rinehart, 2014: 655).

Diving practice: Fresno, 1937

For Sammy Lee

They stopped the plunge
up tight as three hundred
bronzed under the sun;
(while football doubles piled on,
even before Manzanar)
split vision, not even
mirages of drink,
hard shade almost
scuttled from itself.

The waters, reptilian, ran cool
as wet sand – or melting cubes
the iced drinks wasted.

Sign, wondrous and white,
delicately banal, a denial
to the Korean baby
who contaminated the sweetness
with his yellowed legs, stalks
of fat straws, ecrued waters,
now emptied, sucking, drained
because of his innocence.

The final example is an extract from the aforementioned prose-poem 'Mow my lawn' by Michael Silk (Silk, 2008: 477–478), which is an acerbic political and cultural sporting commentary on US soccer cultures; a self-reflexive discomfort (of place/body) combined with an awe for the colourful placelessness of Latino/a players and spectators.

We turned the corner from an eerie, evacuated, North Avenue; calm, a temporary hiatus, the only sign of life was the smoke, forced through the ramshackle chimney of Tyrone's Fried Chicken, preparation for the post-Church performances. A sharp left turn before the imposing grave yard, dark, thick skies, rain immanent, bump, potholes, gravel hits, windscreen survives. Shit hole. We were going to be playing here. Desolate. Barren. Destitute. Shit hole. Irritant. Irrational irritant. Despondency circles, creeping over and under my skin ('my "career" had come to this'?).

I looked up. A trick of another Sunday morning darkness?
      Beauty
     Celebration
    Grace
   Community
  Life, Lived

Color, dancing like sprites in the billowing smoke rising from the bbq's invaded the senses. Color, flags, slow motion, waved and feted. Music (so distorted to be unidentifiable to my adolescent auditors), internalized and celebrated by galacticos lined up like two rows of dominoes, hands on chests. Pride, performed. Smell, inhaled, home-cooking, reaching and touching the visceral clefts. Color, vibrancy, The male body, displayed and performed, clad in the luminous yellow of Arsenal's replica away kit, and the bright, bulls' blood red of the English replica away kit (my theoretical juices flowed, oh how I would be able to shape this amazing ethnographic turn, but, for now, 'hold back the interpretation'). Skin, radiant heat. Rays of sunshine fought their way between the accumulated nimbus. Glistening, gold. Awaiting the victor, posed toy soldiers perched atop oversized plastic trophies. The grass, unkempt, unmowed, somehow greener on the other[ed] side. In the shadow of deprivation, of Diaspora, of death, soccer supernova.

But.

Hearing.

Beauty
      Celebration
           Grace
               Community
                    Life, Living
My [ethnographic] reality.

Perform in the shadows.

Hope, dreams, desire. Dyeing in (my – our – their) perpetual whiteness.

Moving toward poetry?

It is an understatement to say that poetry is a marginal form of research representation in the field of physical cultural studies (and aligned fields). The reasons for this are diverse, not least the fact that 'most social scientists are trained to write analytically and less so evocatively' (Sparkes and Smith, 2012: 184). The 'ideological fashions' of the field of physical culture (and, indeed, physical activity, sport and physical education) seem on the whole to shun poetry as a form of knowing. In his presidential address to the North American sociology of sport conference, Rinehart (2010a: 184) observed that, despite embracing the social sciences, the field rarely allows 'for the existence of poets or even of poetic sensibilities'. However, as the work canvassed in this chapter shows, the field certainly lends itself to poetic expression, and writers are drawing on the concept of poiesis to push the boundaries of the field. There are, of course, many barriers to embracing poetic representation. Its marginal positioning in the social sciences prevents many from engaging with it (either as readers or writers) and, as Rinehart (2010a) also notes, there are a lack of research journals willing to publish this work. In addition, there may be consequences for scholars who choose to publish this form of work if it is not viewed (by colleagues, promotion committees and the like) as 'serious' research. Poetic writing is also personal; it exposes the writer's inner life in potentially vulnerable ways (Fitzpatrick, 2012).

Poetic representation does, however, also have several advantages for research. It introduces an overtly subjective and emotive edge to research writing and can connect with readers and policy makers in ways that other kinds of writing fail to do. As an art form it can "make us see" and connect and understand.' (Higgs, 2013: 158) or, as Sparkes et al. (2003: 169) attest, it can 'touch us where we live, in our bodies' and evoke passion. In this sense, poetic expression can be judged on different, more subjective, terms (Markula and Silk, 2011). Research poetry, along with other forms of poststructuralist qualitative research, then challenges the conventional measures of both research and the body (Denzin, 2008; Sparkes, 2002). As the work in this chapter also shows, research poetry can have an overtly political edge, challenging power relations in the field and drawing attention to inequities and injustice. Poetry has a lot to offer the field of physical cultural studies as we question how bodies express, reflect, articulate and challenge cultural and social norms. Indeed, researching at the intersection of bodies, movements and creative expression (poiesis, poetry) may be a productive point of expansion for the field. Barone (2010) argues that art has the power to 'challenge and disrupt prevailing regimes of truth by raising new questions without obvious answers'. He states that 'Poems … proffer a vision that is an alternative to the conventional, at odds with the commonplace, the usual lens through which we view the world' (ibid.: 331). Including poetry in physical cultural studies research is a move towards opening up texts to the political, the emotional and the subjective. Poetry (and the process of poiesis) may also challenge the boundaries (walls) at the edges of the field, which preclude particular ways of knowing and forms of knowledge coming to light.

References

Atkins, S. and Eberhart, H. (2014). *Presence and process in expressive arts work: At the edge of wonder*. London: Jessica Kingsley Publishers.

Atkinson, M. (2009). Parkour, anarcho-environmentalism and poiesis. *Journal of Sport and Social Issues*, 33(2), 169–194.

Barone, T. (2010). Educational poetry that shakes, rocks, and rattles. In T. Huber-Warring (ed.), *Storied inquiries in international landscapes: An anthology of educational research* (pp. 331–335). Charlotte, NC: Information Age Publishing.

Bauman, Z. (2002). Afterthought: On writing; on writing sociologically. *Cultural Studies ↔ Critical Methodologies*, 2(3), 359–370.

Block, B. A. and Weatherford, G. M. (2013). Narrative research methodologies: Learning lessons from disabilities research. *Quest*, 65(4), 498–514.

Brkich, C. A. and Barko, T. (2013). Fictive reality: Troubling our notions of truth and data in iambic pentameter. *Cultural Studies ↔ Critical Methodologies*, 13(4), 246–251.

Burnett, A. P. (ed.). (2010). *Pindar: Odes for victorious athletes*. Baltimore, MD: Johns Hopkins University Press.

Denzin, N. K. (2008). The practices and politics of interpretation. In N. K. Denzin, and Y. S. Lincoln (eds), *Collecting and interpreting qualitative materials* (pp. 458–498). Thousand Oaks, CA: Sage.

Farred, G. (2006). Careless whispers: The doubleness of Spanish love. *Cultural Studies ↔ Critical Methodologies*, 8(4), 453–476.

Faulkner, S. L. (2007). Using ars poetica as criteria for reading research poetry. *Qualitative Inquiry*, 13(2), 218–234.

Fitzpatrick, E. and Fitzpatrick, K. (2015). Disturbing the divide: Poetry as improvisation to disorder power relationships in research supervision. *Qualitative Inquiry*, 21(1), 50–58.

Fitzpatrick, K. (2012). 'That's how the light gets in': Poetry, self and representation in ethnographic research, *Cultural Studies ↔ Critical Methodologies*, 12(1), 8–14.

Fitzpatrick, K. (2013). *Critical pedagogy, physical education and urban schooling*. New York, NY: Peter Lang.

Franchi, S. (2013). The past, present, and future encounters between computation and the humanities. In V. Müller (ed.), *Philosophy and the theory of artificial intelligence* (pp. 249–364). Heidelberg Berlin: Springer.

Gallop, J. (1988). *Thinking through the body*. New York: Columbia University Press.

Gard, M. and Wright, J. (2005). *The obesity epidemic: Science, morality and ideology*. London: Routledge.

Gilbert, M. (1994). Of poetics and poiesis, pleasure and politics: Music theory and modes of the feminine. *Perspectives of New Music*, 32(1), 44–67.

Higgs, R. J. (2013). Stereotypes and archetypes in religion and American sport. In N. J. Watson, and A. J. Parker (eds), *Sports and Christianity: Historical and contemporary perspectives* (pp. 150–164). New York: Routledge.

Hoffman, S. J. (1989). Introduction. *Quest*, 41(2), 87.

Hopper, T., Madill, L. E., Bratseth, C. D., Cameron, K. A., Coble, J. D. and Nimmon, L. E. (2008). Multiple voices in health, sport, recreation, and physical education research: Revealing unfamiliar spaces in a polyvocal review of qualitative research genres. *Quest*, 60(2), 214–235.

jagodinski, j. and Wallin, J. (2013). *Arts-based research: A critique and a proposal*. Rotterdam, Netherlands: Sense.

Lahman, M. K. E. and Richard, V. M. (2014). Appropriated poetry: Archival poetry in research. *Qualitative Inquiry*, 20(3), 344–355.

Lahman, M. K. E., Rodriguez, K. L., Richard, V. M., Geist, M. R., Schendel, R. K. and Graglia, P. E. (2011). (Re)forming research poetry. *Qualitative Inquiry*, 17(9), 887–896.

Longley, A. (2014). Movement-initiated writing in dance ethnography. In N. K. Denzin (ed.), *Studies in Symbolic Interaction: 40th Anniversary of Studies in Symbolic Interaction* (pp. 69–93). Bingley: Emerald Group Publishing.

Lupton, D. (2014). Critical perspectives on digital health technologies. *Sociology Compass*, 8(12), 1344–1359.

Lupton, D. (2015). 'It's like having a physician in your pocket!' A critical analysis of self-diagnosis smart phone apps. *Social Science and Medicine*, 133, 128–135.

Markula, P. and Silk, M. (2011). *Qualitative research for physical culture*. Basingstoke: Palgrave Macmillan.

Martin, T. L. (2004). *Poiesis and possible worlds: A study in modality and literary theory*. Toronto: University of Toronto Press.

Popovic, M. L. (2012). Moksha rose from the heart: A prosaic and poetic embodiment of yoga autoethnography. *Cultural Studies ↔ Critical Methodologies*, 12(1), 30–42.

Prendergast, M. (2006). Found poetry as literature review: Research poems on audience and performance. *Qualitative Inquiry*, 12(2), 369–388.

Rich, A. (2003). *What is found there: Notes on poetry and politics*. New York: W. W. Norton and Co.

Richardson, L. (1992). The consequences of poetic representation: Writing the other, rewriting the self. In C. Ellis, and M. G. Flaherty (eds), *Investigating subjectivity: Research on lived experience* (pp. 125–137). Newbury Park, CA: Sage.

Richardson, L. (2000). Writing: A method of inquiry. In N. K. Denzin, and Y. S. Lincoln (eds), *Handbook of qualitative research*, 2nd edn (pp. 923–948). London: Sage.

Richardson, L. (2004). Poetic representation. In J. Flood, S. Brice-Heath and D. Lapp (eds), *Handbook of research on teaching literacy through the communicative and visual arts* (pp. 232–238). New York: Routledge.

Richardson, M. (1998). Poetics in the field and on the page. *Qualitative Inquiry*, 4, 451–462.

Rinehart, R. (1998). Fictional methods in ethnography. Believability, specks of glass, and Chekhov. *Qualitative Inquiry*, 4(2), 200–224.

Rinehart, R. (2010a). Poetic sensibilities, humanities, and wonder: Toward an e/affective sociology of sport. *Quest*, 62, 184–210.

Rinehart, R. (2010b). Sport performance in four acts: Players, workers, audience, and immortality. *Qualitative Inquiry*, 16(3), 197–199.

Rinehart, R. (2014). Reliquaries and a poetic sensibility. *Qualitative Inquiry*, 20(5), 653–658.

Ritterbusch, D. (2010). Pike. *Aethlon: The Journal of Sport Literature*, 28(1), 70.

Rushdie, S. (1988). *The satanic verses*. Wilmington, DE: The Consortium.

Silk, M. (2008). Mow my lawn. *Cultural Studies ↔ Critical Methodologies*, 8(4), 477–478.

Sparkes, A. C. (2002). *Telling tales in sport and physical activity*. Champaign, IL: Human Kinetics.

Sparkes, A. C. and Douglas, K. (2007). Making the case for poetic representations: An example in action. *The Sport Psychologist*, 21, 170–190.

Sparkes, A. C. and Silvennoinen, M. (eds). (1999). *Talking bodies*. Finland: SoPhi.

Sparkes, A. C. and Smith, B. (2012). Embodied research methodologies and seeking the senses in sport and physical culture: A fleshing out of problems and possibilities. In K. Young, and M. Atkinson (eds), *Qualitative research on sport and physical culture* (pp. 167–190). Bingley: Emerald Publishing Group.

Sparkes, A. C. and Smith, B. (2014). *Qualitative research methods in sport, exercise and health: From process to product*. Abingdon: Routledge.

Sparkes, A. C., Nilges, L., Swan, P. and Dowling, F. (2003). Poetic representations in sport and physical education: Insider perspectives 1, *Sport, Education and Society*, 8(2), 153–177.

Threadgold, T. (1994). *Feminist poetics: Poiesis, performance, histories*. New York: Routledge.

Zuchora, K. (1980). Closer ties between art and sport. *International Review for the Sociology of Sport*, 15(1), 49–64.

52
SENSORY, DIGITAL AND VISUAL METHODOLOGIES

Sarah Pink, Vaike Fors and Martin Berg

Introduction

Sensory, digital and visual research methods are increasingly established across the social sciences and humanities. In this chapter we focus on their potential for researching experiences of physical activity. We first outline the contexts where we understand contemporary physical activities are played out. These involve people moving through, in and around environments that are at simultaneously digital and material. This has two key implications. First, researching physical activity now often means researching activity in a world that traverses the online and offline, the digital and material. Second, we ask how technologies that are implicated in physical activity cross over into our research; how can we engage digital and visual technologies that are part of the world of physical activity to serve our research processes, and how can we use these technologies actively as researchers. We then discuss visual, digital and sensory methods with regard to this specific context, through three examples: digital autoethnography; digital video; data visualization.

These examples may vary from what would be expected in a discussion of physical activity. However, we argue that the very mundane and routine forms of physical activity that can be accounted for through the methods we propose are significant ways of moving through the world. They are modes of being physically active that underpin how we live and experience everyday life. The study of physical activity needs to focus beyond the intensity of sports, dance or performance, to engage with physical activity as embedded in, and as a way of knowing and being in, everyday life in its non-dramatic and mundane moments.

Defining physical activity and the places where it is played out

As Andrews and Silk have outlined, physical cultural studies has emerged partly to counter the sports activity emphasis in fields such as sociology of sport. We concur with this agenda, and where Andrews and Silk write of physical cultural studies that 'Its research object is the diverse realm of physical culture (including, but not restricted to sport, fitness, exercise, recreation, leisure, wellness, dance, and health related movement practices)' (Andrews and Silk, 2015), we argue for adding sleep to this list. Sleep is a way of being active that is rather different to exercise. We are thus interested in how we might go about researching physical activity in the form of our movement through everyday life, beyond sport, and in ways that are part of the doing of everyday activity.

While we do not engage extensively with the debates about what physical culture might be here, we stress that our approach goes beyond 'culture'. Although we are interested in physical activity and experience in ways that acknowledge how representations are layered into everyday life, we are also focused on how the experiential, unspoken or non-representational elements of physical activity can be researched. These ways of experiencing physical activity are normally invisible. Yet, we argue that we need to understand them in order to be able to comprehend what everyday movement through the world means, how it constitutes forms of wellbeing, and how it participates in the making of everyday environments. Therefore physical activity in our interpretation might involve something as mundane as a bedtime routine of switching off and on technologies, locking the doors and walking upstairs to bed (see Pink and Leder Mackley, 2016) or the everyday handling of touch screens on smartphones, computer keyboards and mice (Moores, 2012: 52). As we show below, the embodied and sensory knowledge that normally invisible activities, such as sleep, involve underpins how everyday life is organized. They are part of our physical ways of being in the world. Simultaneously, physical activity can be about how we get around in our everyday lives outside the home – walking or cycling to work and other activities are part of the ways in which we move around, know and experience the world.

Pink et al. (2016) have called for a re-focusing of digital ethnography practice towards how we inhabit a digital-material world where the online and offline are part of the same environment, which we need to account for in terms of the relationality between the digital-material, rather than seeing them as separate. The sensory experience of digital-material worlds (Pink et al., 2015) and the digital elements of sensory worlds (Pink, 2015) should be understood as fundamental to how physical activity becomes meaningful. Therefore, we argue that doing ethnographic research about physical activity should acknowledge this. There is now a growing market for, and use of, digitally mediated body monitoring and self-tracking devices – technologies that measure and report on everything from how fast you run, and what mood you are in, to devices that measure sleep patterns and pulse. Yet we know little about how these technologies are implicated in how we as humans perceive ourselves as bodies and selves from social and cultural perspectives. This knowledge gap has been acknowledged through research initiatives in medical anthropology and science studies through a science and technology studies perspective (Lupton, 2012, 2013). In this chapter, we push this field of research further by describing how body monitoring devices and apps can be used in studies of experiences of physical activity as they straddle the material and digital worlds, and in the process of doing so, bring to the fore experiential, tacit and unspoken aspects of physical activities in unanticipated ways.

We advance this nascent field of study in two ways. First, we situate the research methods we discuss specifically at the interface between these experiential sensory and embodied domains of everyday life activity and movement and how they are or can be visualized, heard or communicated through digital research practices. Second, we advance the discussion of such everyday physical movement and activity through a specific consideration of how we might engage digital media to research such activity, in the context of a digitally mediated world.

Sensory, digital and visual methodologies: an overview

Since around the turn of the century, visual and then sensory research approaches and methods have become increasingly popular across the social sciences and humanities (Rose, 2012; Fors and Bäckström, 2015; Pink, 2013, 2015). More recently there has been a surge in publications on virtual and digital methods (Berg, 2015; Kozinets, 2010; Boellstorff et al., 2012; Pink et al., 2016).

One of the core ideas that informs a sensory ethnography methodology is a theory of emplacement (Pink, 2015). This depends on a theory of place, as being what Doreen Massey has called an 'event' and a 'constellation of processes' and what Tim Ingold (2011) calls a 'meshwork'. Bringing together these ideas, we can see place as something that is not locality-bound, but that can include localities as elements of places, that is perpetually changing and is constituted through the trajectories of different things and processes of different qualities and affordances. As researchers we do not look at places from the outside and observe what is happening in them, but rather, according to a theory of emplacement we are ourselves part of, and constituents of place, along with other people, animals, plants, buildings, photographs, the weather and other diverse things. All of these, including us, are continually changing (although at different rates and in different ways) and continually moving (although again at different speeds and in different ways). The meanings of such emplaced things are always relational and situated. Emplaced as such, we as researchers and our roles as researchers are shaped by the environments we participate in, and they are also to some extent shaped by us. This approach enables us to consider the ways in which we connect with the things we research as being within a shared world with them, and also as being embodied, felt, sensory and experiential, as well as shared through verbal and written forms.

Another principle of sensory ethnography involves the need to be reflexive about our emplacement. That is to say we need to develop a strong understanding of how we are situated in the worlds in which we do research, and in our own research processes. This kind of reflexivity also involves considering the idea of the 'ethnographic place' (Pink, 2015). The ethnographic place refers to the place that is made through the ethnographic research – that meshwork or intensity of things and processes that cluster around the work of the ethnographer. This might include localities, participants, research materials, publications, readers, audiences of our films. All of these people and things participate somehow in what ethnographic research is, as it proceeds along a process.

Within the reflexive approach there always lies forms of autoethnography, often informal in that they involve reflecting on the research process rather than undertaking an in-depth interrogation of the researcher's experiences as they inform our understanding of the research problem. However, sensory ethnography also appreciates how forms of apprenticeship form an embodied element of ethnographic practice, which takes it closer to autoethnography, and we reflect further below on how autoethnographic approaches might be particularly useful for a sensory ethnography approach to physical cultural studies.

Researching the experience of body monitoring

There are debates in the literature about whether or not body monitoring technologies that measure and visualize our bodily activity are likely or not to improve our health. However, in this chapter we are less interested in the quantification of health improvement, but in the question of how quantification and visualization of bodily activity becomes a technology for experiencing the body as a sensory and living organism, and how this can become a way of imagining the body and its temporality. In this section we present three examples of how different visual methods can help us to understand physical experience in relation to body monitoring technologies, and how the body monitoring technologies actually becomes part of the methodology. In doing so we do not focus on what might be expected – that is on the question of how participants use the technologies – but on how physical activity is experienced when it is mediated through apps, and how digital–visual–sensory methods can be engaged to get access to these experiences. These three methods try to resolve the problem of how we might research experience which is very personal and individual, through: an autoethnography of using apps; digital–sensory video ethnography interviews with apps; and how data visualizations created by apps can become research tools.

Example 1: Digital autoethnography and body monitoring

Autoethnography is a well-established research method in physical cultural studies, used for example, by Allen-Collinson and Hockey (2008, 2013) to research and represent the experience of running, through powerful descriptive passages about the experience of running, interpreted theoretically through a phenomenological approach to experience. As a research method autoethnography involves reflexive self-observation and an exploration of the experiential interrelationship between researchers and the social world in which they are situated. When autoethnography is used to study how body monitoring technologies and practices affect the experience of physical activity it faces certain challenges and opportunities.

Body monitoring devices are increasingly turning into machines that not only track personal activity but also provide suggestions on how to lead a life that is assumed to be continuously improved. The Jawbone UP wristband and the 'Smart Coach' insight and coaching 'engine' are good examples of how these technologies work. The app 'UP' is connected to the wristband 'Jawbone', and this system crunches personal data to provide 'actionable insights and uniquely personalized guidance' (jawbone.com). By measuring, interpreting and correlating data sources, these devices provide an understanding that goes beyond everyday self-knowledge and add a digital voice to the practice of autoethnography.

The three of us have used the Jawbone UP on a daily basis during a period of time to record how far we had walked, run, cycled, travelled and how well (or badly) we have slept. The autoethnographic approach helped gain an understanding of how it feels to have our bodies monitored and how data could possibly impact on everyday life activities. Using this technology, we began to reflect on how our own physical activities were reconceptualized through the use of the app and the wristband. Physical activity was transformed into something we could talk about, compare and experience in ways not possible before. The data allowed us to reflect on our personal pasts by reading distances walked and nights slept. Through its very simplistic, yet problematic, way of presenting data, the app mediated our experiences of physical activity differently in ways that were both comforting and affirming. It did not necessarily compel us to exercise more, but instead provided a reassuring feeling that a number of km per day were covered, or the slightly stressful feeling of not having done so. Importantly we all gained a kind of personal companion that deciphered the complexities of our moving bodies, by reducing and translating their activities into steps, calories, kilometres and so forth.

Engaging body monitoring technologies as part of an autoethnographic research methodology implies that ethnographic self-observation thus involves yet another observer and a mechanism that partakes in writing the narrative of the self and body. When used to measure and record bodily activity, body monitoring devices are not merely devices that register bodily data. They also become interpretive filters between people and their bodies through a process where bodily movements and actions are quantified, and translated into a language or currency that can be communicated through the device's interface. This process involves transforming otherwise invisible or unknown processes into data that is tangible and possible to reflect upon. This means that the body is necessarily not so much monitored as it is created as an interpretable event. The autoethnographic practice thus becomes a practice through which one learns about oneself through the data that is generated by the devices. This is not so much a question of writing an ethnography of one's self as it is about learning the language of the devices and observing how they record and monitor one's bodily activities.

In contrast to traditional autoethnographic research that leaves researchers 'to their own devices', this digital autoethnography involves the wearable technologies by including an understanding of the relationship that forms between body and device. The technologies become involved in certain forms of mirroring and experiencing of the body that affect the practice of autoethnography. Body monitoring technologies necessarily become part of the autoethnographic practice and almost ethnographers themselves. This kind of autoethnography thus engages technology as means to understand oneself and observe the very process through which the learning of the technological language takes place.

Understanding how a body-monitoring device intervenes in autoethnographic practice is one way to involve digital technologies in ethnographic practice. However, in seeking to research physical cultures and experience through visual, digital and sensory methods such a methodological approach creates an important background to being able to understand how our sensory experiences and feelings are mediated by the digital and visual technologies that these activities involve. They also help us to understand more generally, how we and participants navigate a digital-material world where our physical experiences are quantified, visualized and then re-experienced by us.

Example 2: Video ethnography of use of apps

Researching how people use apps involves finding ways in which to approach and document how they use digital technologies (usually smart phones, tablets or laptops) to access data about their physical activity (e.g. walking, running, heart rate, sleep activity). This means effectively in our work, seeking to understand how they make connections between the sensory embodied experience of physical activity and the digital data that stands for it. Methods available for doing this vary, however, as for media use generally, because it tends to be something that people fit into moments in their daily routines, and that often is dispersed across the day temporally, this kind of activity is difficult to capture in real time. Body monitoring equipment is usually working in the background, via a smartphone or a wearable device on the wrist. People check the data that it collects at moments in their day that it is not necessarily easy to document. For instance one participant described how that day she had been sitting on the train and decided to check her sleep data to get a better understanding of how she had slept the night before. She also said that she checks her wrist wearable device two or three times a day. Participants might download spreadsheets of their data, but there was not necessarily a predictable moment that this would happen that would be observable. Therefore we needed to find ways in which to be able to get a sense of users' experiences that accounted for these issues of access. One way to achieve this was to turn to the traditional interview, but with some modifications. As Pink has argued (2015) the sensory ethnography interview is an important method in research, and once we take a sensory approach to understanding what is happening in an interview, the types of knowledge, or ways of knowing that it is able to produce about how people experience their worlds, become more clearly defined. There are two key points here. First, that the interview itself is a sensory encounter, in which the researcher needs to use her or his own experiences to empathetically engage with those of the participant. Second, interviews can involve sensory engagements with technologies (or other objects) through which participants can show their relationships to them, for example by showing, touching or using the technology in a particular way. Here we advance further the idea of the sensory interview to consider how it evolves when we understand the environment in which it is happening to be part of a sensory-digital-material world. In this section we discuss briefly how, by conducting interviews about and with body monitoring technologies it is possible to engage participants in the sharing of ways of knowing about their bodies, that involve what we would think of as a double translation. That is the embodied activity, which was experienced by participants is first collected as data, and visualized, it is then accessed through the corporeal and sensory engagements of participants with their devices – such as smart phones or wrist-bands. The double translation thus refers to the way in which the researcher's task is to engage first with understanding the physical experiences of exercise and *their* visualization, and second with the embodied experiences of using the technologies to access them. Both involve the researcher in empathetic ways in knowing and imagining. When combined with an autoethnographic awareness of what it can be like to use the technologies and apps, and to undertake certain forms of exercise then this technique becomes especially useful because the researcher has a specific resource of (reflexively moderated) personal experience to draw on to assist her/him in empathizing with the participant's experience.

For example, Christoph was a committed and longer-term user of body monitoring technologies who brought three devices with him to our interview. Christoph came to the RMIT Design Hub where we carried out a video interview, video was well suited to this particular discussion because in this case showing the technologies and apps was an important part of our conversation. This was the second of our interviews, and we turned back here to some aspects of the discussion we had had earlier as it seemed important to visually document these aspects of Christoph's use of apps and devices. From the beginning of our meeting his iPod, smartphone and tablet lay together on the table. As he had already explained, he used these with different apps and for different purposes. In this interview his demonstrations or re-enactments (Pink and Leder Mackley, 2014) were important. For example, as he showed how he used a stress monitoring app with the iPod, clipping a sensor on his ear, he showed how this was represented graphically on the device and discussed how he would be interested in the data produced through this for when he meditated. Likewise he demonstrated apps that mapped his movement through the city, not by showing how they would track his route through the city in practice, but by showing retrospectively the data that they had already collected. These different ways of showing the apps represented different ways of viewing the data, since it would seem less usual to consult a tracking app – like Moves, which tracks distance covered, and maps routes, among other things – while it was actually documenting and recording the route. Therefore in this interview the ways apps were shown also corresponded with how they might be consulted when used in real-life 'moments'. Because Sarah had been using the Moves app, and had started to do so between the two interviews, she could start to use her own experiences to understand those of the participant, and how physical activity was experienced not only as it was played out in practice but also later in relation to the representation of it when visualized on the app. This leads us to a third example on how video ethnography can teach researchers about physical cultures.

Example 3: Making physical culture visible through body monitoring devices

As we have shown above, the re-enactments of how the interviewees used their body monitoring apps and devices became important clues for understanding what these graphic illustrations of physical activity mean to people and how they use them to make meaning of both the app and other mundane aspects in their lives. We now discuss an interview with Pelle who had used digital devices and apps for body monitoring for the past 10–15 years. His interest in these technologies was personal and professional since he worked as both an interaction designer and a professional trainer. For him the success of the devices and apps depended on how they visualized physical activity in everyday life and the extent to which the monitoring was automated. During our interview, he often showed features of the UP app, connected to the Jawbone wristband (Figure 52.1).

However, is this a visualization of physical culture? It shows us when and how much we move, but tells us little about how the visualization is implicated as a constituent of place, along with other people and material/immaterial dimensions of the environment. Nevertheless data visualizations can be used as prompts when discussing experiences of physical activities. For Pelle, as for Christoph (above) during our interview, demonstrating these graphics was crucial for creating shared understandings of how to look at and use the different graphs, numbers and icons. For instance, Pelle showed how the ratio between the resting and active burn told him what he needed to make decisions about how to move during the day. He gave examples of how these considerations could have social effects since they may lead to people walking longer routes at work, giving them opportunities to meet people they may not have met otherwise. Thus the data visualizations opened up routes to knowing more than the number of steps

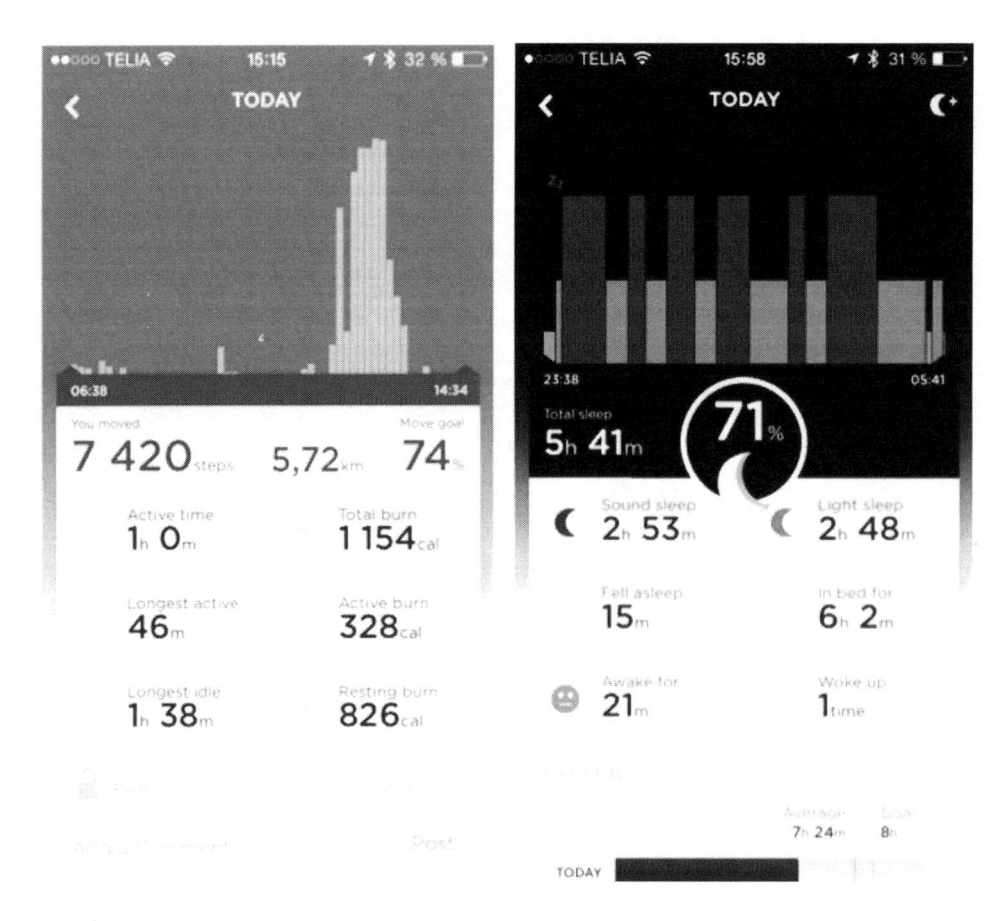

Figure 52.1 Screenshots from body monitoring app that automatically register body movement through a wristband, showing one day (left) and one night (right)

taken, because they gained meaning in relation to Pelle's wider social context. Pelle also explained how his views about what the apps could do for him had changed: 'I thought that I had bought a wristband that would measure my activities, but I have noticed that for me the most important data the wristband collects is my sleep patterns. Suddenly, I realized through the data collected by the wristband that I didn't need to sleep as much as I thought I needed to get a good nights' sleep.' Pelle was referring to how the wristband registered his sleep quality as well as how long he slept for, and how the sleep quality data visualization had taught him to understand his sleep differently and to adjust accordingly.

For Pelle the data visualizations were also conditioned by the contexts he viewed them in. For instance, by sharing data with his wife he could anticipate how she felt that day and what mood she was in. If her data showed that she hadn't had time to train, and/or had had a bad night sleep, then he would take that into consideration when coming home after work. However, when talking about the same data visualizations with his students as a physical trainer, he would use them as a site for inspiration. The shifting narratives within the trajectories of these visualizations can be understood as routes to knowing more about how they are part of creating what might be rendered as the tacit and unspoken dimensions of physical activity. As we have argued above, it is precisely these invisible ways of experiencing and understanding physical activity that we need to understand in order to be able to comprehend what everyday movement through the world means in relation to physical cultures. As our examples show, the visualizations of our moving bodies created by more or less automated body monitoring technologies in a growing market, can be used to make visible and articulate the experiential, social and cultural aspects of physical culture.

Critical discussion

This chapter proposes two advances for how we might research physical activity. The first is to support and push forward the argument that to understand physical culture the concept needs to be extended. This means going beyond the notion of physical culture as intentional and conscious activity developed in contexts such as sports. While sport and similar aspects of physical activity are relevant, they are just some among many ways that the body is active through everyday life. Instead if we include mundane everyday activity, such as sleeping, walking around at home, going to the shops and cycling to work – all of which can be monitored by people in their everyday lives – then we gain a much wider and richer conceptualization of how the moving body is part of the world we inhabit.

The second advance is focused on research methods and approach. We have demonstrated ways of researching physical experience, activity and the cultures around them in ways that go beyond conventional research methods in three ways. The first is the use of digital and shared autoethnographic methods. We have suggested using these both as a way to document and analyse the experience of using body monitoring technologies, but also as a means through which to be able to empathize with the experiences of participants. The second is an adaptation of the conventional interview, to use empathetic methods in the interview and to use enactments and tours of app use during these as ways of understanding how people use body monitoring technologies. Finally we have discussed the use of apps and data visualizations as ways in which to understand and engage with participants in the interview context. In this sense the body monitoring technology itself starts to play a key role in the process through which we seek to research and understand people's experience of it.

Conclusion

Through an alternative focus on everyday physical activity, including sleeping, we have shown how body monitoring and data visualization enable us to research and understand physical activity in new ways. In such a research process the digital-material-sensory configuration of the way in which the world and our activity in it is experienced comes to the fore as pivotal to how we now need to understand and investigate physical activity. Not only are such technologies becoming increasingly ubiquitous in everyday life, they are also becoming valuable technologies for doing research. This is precisely because they enable us to engage with the experiential and phenomenological elements of the way everyday life is lived, while at the same time examining how this is quantified, visualized and experienced as a representation. Indeed we are seeing how the experiential and representational aspects of our world are being brought together in personalized and individualized ways, which tend to go beyond the ways in which either experience or representation have been treated in cultural studies before. From the locus of a physical cultural studies – which is precisely situated at the nexus of the digital, material and sensory world – we have a key vantage point from which to study and theorize how new aspects of this relationship emerge.

Acknowledgements

The research discussed in this chapter is part of the 'Sensing, shaping, sharing: Imagining the body in a mediatized world' project funded by Riksbankens Jubileumsfond, the Swedish Foundation for Humanities and Social Sciences.

References

Allen-Collinson, J. and Hockey, J. (2008). Autoethnography as 'valid' methodology? A study of disrupted identity narratives. *The International Journal of Interdisciplinary Social Sciences*, 3(6), 209–217.
Allen-Collinson, J. and Hockey, J. (2013). From a certain point of view: Sensory phenomenological envisionings of running space and place. *Journal of Contemporary Ethnography*, 44(1), 63–83.
Andrews, D. and Silk, M. (2015). Physical cultural studies on sport. In R. Guilianotti (ed.), *The Routledge Handbook of the Sociology of Sport* (pp. 83–93). London: Routledge.
Berg, M. (2015). *Netnografi: Att forska om och med internet*. Lund, Sweden: Studentlitteratur.
Boellstorff, T., Nardi, B., Pearce, C. and Taylor, T. L. (2012). *Ethnography of Virtual Worlds: A Handbook of Method*. Princeton, NJ: Princeton University Press.
Fors, V. and Bäckström, Å. (2015). *Visuella metoder*. Lund, Sweden: Studentlitteratur.
Ingold, T. (2011). *Being Alive: Essays on Movement, Knowledge and Description*. New York: Routledge.
Kozinets, R. V. (2010). *Netnography: Doing Ethnographic Research Online*. London: Sage.
Lupton, D. (2012). M-health and health promotion: The digital cyborg and surveillance society. *Social Theory and Health*, 10, 229–244.
Lupton, D. (2013). Quantifying the body: Monitoring and measuring health in the age of mHealth technologies. *Critical Public Health*, 23(4), 393–403.
Moores, S. (2012). *Media, Place and Mobility*. New York: Palgrave Macmillan.
Pink, S. (2013). *Doing Visual Ethnography*. London: Sage.
Pink, S. (2015). *Doing Sensory Ethnography*. London: Sage.
Pink, S. and Leder Mackley, K. (2014) Reenactment methodologies for everyday life research: Art therapy insights for video ethnography. *Visual Studies*, 29(2), 146–154.
Pink, S. and Leder Mackley, K. (2016) Moving, making and atmosphere: Routines of home as sites for mundane improvisation. *Mobilities*, 11(2), 171–187.
Pink, S., Horst, H., Postill, J., Hjorth, L., Lewis, T. and Tacchi, J. (eds). (2016). *Digital Ethnography: Principles and Practices*. London: Sage.
Rose, G. (2012). *Visual Methodologies: An Introduction to Researching with Visual Materials*, 3rd edn. London: Sage.

53
DIGITAL MEDIA METHODOLOGIES

Steph MacKay

When John R. Mitrano (1999) investigated the meanings that fans involved in an online chat group read into the relocation of the Hartford Whalers hockey franchise, his study and others started a new era – a digital era – in physical cultural studies (PCS). Scholars[1] working in this digital era have used a variety of terms (e.g. new media, digital media) and definitions to describe the ubiquitous digital media phenomenon. This chapter defines digital media as LaVoi and Calhoun (2014: 321) proposed: 'forms of media content that combine and integrate data, text, sound and images of all kinds, are stored in digital formats; and are increasingly distributed through networks [the most obvious of which, and representing the focus of this chapter is the Internet]', with the added stipulation that they promote interactivity and group-forming. Examples include websites, blogs and social networking services such as Facebook, Twitter, Instagram and MySpace. From cradle to grave, digital technologies have become central to people's informational and social worlds (Lupton, 2012). Everyday life has become increasingly digitally technologically mediated and this increased mediation has had a remarkable impact on physical cultural communities (Leonard, 2009; Hutchins and Rowe, 2012). Given the revolutionary impact these technologies are having on people's lives, in order to understand contemporary physical culture, it is essential that PCS scholars understand digital culture.

Researchers have reached different conclusions about the roles that digital media play in physical culture. Some sport research projects have cautiously and critically lauded the revolutionary potential of the Internet's capacity to allow physical culture participants to reflexively create and sustain communities (e.g. MacKay and Dallaire, 2014; Pavlidis and Fullagar, 2013), participate in social movements (e.g. Wilson, 2007), garner support for sport to aid development and peace initiatives (e.g. Thorpe, 2015) and 'convert seemingly peripheral cultural activities into wider cultural [and economic] value' (Gilchrist and Wheaton, 2013: 181). On the flip side, some academics cast the digital media in a dystopian light by emphasizing their risks and dangers (e.g. Millington, 2014) and caution against extolling their democratizing potential (e.g. Baerg, 2007; Dart, 2009). Regardless of the perceived impact of digital media on physical culture communities, one point of consensus prevails: the Internet explosion has vastly changed how sport and physical culture are 'bought and sold, produced and consumed, accessed and experienced' (Hutchins and Rowe, 2013: 2). If Andrews and Silk (2015) are correct that we, as PCS scholars, hope to 'explicate how active bodies become organized, disciplined, represented, embodied, and experienced in mobilizing (or corroborating), or at times immobilizing (or resisting), the conjunctural inflections and operations of power within a society', further digital media research is needed.

Towards a PCS approach to digital media research

While all research entails executional challenges, digital media research requires particular ingenuity. Texts that address the 'how to' of PCS digital media research are emerging (e.g. Sparkes and Smith, 2013), but no canonical texts are available within PCS and few outside of it (see Hine, 2013). Guideposts for digital media inquiry, both in terms of method and ethics, are often lacking. Bayam and Markham (2009) note that although this situation creates challenges, it also affords opportunities. For example, at this point in time, research projects hold a great deal of potential for creativity. Some digital media scholars further suggest that a canonical 'how-to' text would be futile; they argue that 'the Internet's constant evolution necessitates continual reassessment of fieldwork methods' (Robinson and Schulz, 2009: 692).

Perhaps to the consternation of some readers, this chapter does not offer a ready-made recipe for scholarship that is 'rigorous, relevant and of high quality' (Andrews and Silk, 2015). Rather, it opens a dialogue about digital media methods by discussing the starting point for digital media research projects. It then outlines the ethical considerations applicable to projects exploring digital media representations of physical culture. Next, issues pertaining to data collection are discussed and, finally, data analysis methods are considered. My reflections are interwoven with experiences from my own case studies analysing the digital media texts, text production and user 'readings' of texts from (a) the blog by the Skirtboarders (an all-female skateboarding group from Montreal, Canada) and (b) the 2015 Facebook page of the Ladies of the Lakes (an annual surf social for women surfers/stand up paddle boarders of all ages on Lake Erie, Canada).

Where to start? Where to stop? Defining the edges of digital media projects

Explorations of physical culture participant experiences in producing and using digital or other media necessarily start with subject selection. While some scholars know the exact online content they plan to analyse (often a specific group or organization) in advance, others, like me, start with a concept or question and must then 'surf' for days or weeks before their search is complete. In reference to the latter situation, Hine (2009) notes that Internet project boundaries are often the outcome, rather than the precursor, of a project.

I chose the Skirtboarders' blog as the topic for my doctoral research because it seemed the most interesting of many produced by and for women active in sport. It also aligned with my research questions:

1 Do representations of sportswomen on digital media platforms such as the Internet differ from representations of sportswomen in 'traditional' media?
2 What gendered subject positions are adopted by individuals who interact with (produce and/or use) Internet-mediated sport texts?

Ultimately, I wanted to determine whether the producers of digital media texts challenge the dominant discursive construct[2] of sportswomen circulated in and through 'traditional' mainstream[3] and niche[4] sport media, believed by some authors to emphasize stereotypical, heterosexual femininity and hegemonic masculinity. Did the Internet provide producers with a platform they could use to 'talk back' (hooks, 1989) to these media? I also wanted to discover how users 'read' digital media texts.

Only after many hours of searching sites using the original search item (in multiple search engines) 'women and sport' did I happen upon the Skirtboarders' blog. Not being a female skateboarding insider,[5] or a woman currently interested in skateboarding, I had not intended to research female skateboarders. Despite my keen interest in skateboarding since my teenage years, when I hung out with and produced videos for a group of skateboarding boys, voraciously read skateboarding and surfing magazines (and occasionally watched videos), dressed daily in the 'skater style' with extremely baggy pants, t-shirts bearing anti-establishment messages and 'authentic' skate shoes sold at the 'authentic' local skateboarding shop, I never actually learned how to skate. As I transitioned from being a teenager to a young adult, I left behind my fascination with skateboard culture and did not revisit it until discovering the Skirtboarders' blog. My function in the community during high school and during my work with the Skirtboarders was primarily that of an observer who understood the inner workings of the culture with an insider's perspective of the communities' norms, and an outsider's insight into the particularities of those norms.

My position on the fringes of the women's skateboarding community allowed me to analyse in depth and ultimately determine that the Skirtboarders, through their blog and the collective female skateboarding community they built, were reflexively 'talking back' to mainstream and niche media through their digital media production (see MacKay and Dallaire, 2013). Furthermore, blog users were challenging male domination of skateboarding through their engagement with the virtual Skirtboarder community (see MacKay and Dallaire, 2014). For my postdoctoral project, I wanted to explore digital media projects produced by other (non-skateboarding) action sportswomen to see how their texts contributed to the construction of their individual and collective identities and whether these digital media projects ultimately increased participation. My painstaking efforts eventually led me to the Ladies of the Lakes' Facebook page and community.

While 'where to start' may not be a consideration for all researchers, 'where to stop' certainly is. Given that researchers could plausibly have access to unlimited data considering the usually limitless updating and intertextuality of digital media texts, Hine (2009) states that the research question must clearly specify the approach used in a hypermedia environment. Naturally, the 'where to stop' cannot necessarily be determined before the data collection and analysis has begun. However, this question should be kept in mind as scholars design their projects. In researching the Skirtboarders blog, I chose an end-date and collected and analysed all posts on the blog up until that date. This strategy provided me with comprehensive, but excessive data. To avoid this problem in my Ladies of the Lakes project, I followed boyd's (2009) recommendation to stop collecting data as soon as nothing more could be learned without expanding the scope of my questions. This strategy seems effective and worthwhile for PCS scholars.

Thoughts on Internet research ethics

After settling on where to start and where to stop the next step in digital media research is to design and conduct the project within acceptable ethical limits. Yet digital media research increasingly challenges the usual ethical frameworks and assumptions of researchers and research ethics boards (REBs). Part of the reason is the fact that individuals are sharing more personal information than ever before on platforms that morph in unpredictable ways, and that privacy policies and the terms of service of web-based services are constantly changing. Consequently, despite the many ethical commonalities involved in collecting, analysing and publishing research findings detailing online and offline materials,[6] differences exist.

As the Internet evolved, the academic community widely debated the possible ethical distinctions between projects using online or offline data. Some claimed that the ethical guidelines governing offline projects implicitly applied to online projects – or at least deserved serious attention. This debate, along with consideration of which issues require attention, has been the focus of attention since the mid-1990s by the Internet research ethics (IRE) subdiscipline. Scholarly associations (e.g. Association of Internet Researchers, AoIR), funding councils (e.g. Social Sciences and Humanities Research Council of Canada, SSHRC) and academics (e.g. Kitchin, 2007) have acknowledged the importance of IRE and have explored online inquiry issues such as: defining boundaries between the public and private domains of projects, obtaining free and informed consent (especially from minors), exploring notions of privacy and ensuring (or not) the anonymity, confidentiality and privacy of data. Some have also attempted to establish guidelines or sets of questions that researchers should consider throughout the research process.[7] However, no set of guidelines is static; ethical standards for Internet research continually and rapidly change as digital media evolves (Markham and Buchanan, 2012). Furthermore, as noted by the Markham and Buchanan (ibid.), a casuistic, or case-based approach accommodating the specific needs of each research project should be followed. PCS scholars using digital media in their projects must therefore be constantly reflexive and knowledgeable about the ethical standards, guidelines and notions that govern their work.

Additionally, while the above-mentioned questions are critical before and during the research process, scholars must first determine the nature of their digital media research, which invariably conditions the ethical questions they need to ask and the kind of REB, institutional review board (IRB) or human research ethics committee (HREC) clearance required (if any). Kitchin (2007) proposed a three-category typology that can be used by scholars and in government and agency documents (e.g. Blackstone et al., 2008). These categories are: non-intrusive web-based research, engaged web-based research and online research.

Non-intrusive web-based analyses include projects with content collected from spaces such as websites, blogs, public Facebook pages and Twitter accounts, without contributing in any way to these spaces; for examples of PCS scholarship, see Antonovic and Hardin's (2013) content analysis of profiles from the 'Sports Blog' directory or BlogHer, and Dart's (2009) analysis of how fans and journalists posing as fans blogged about their experiences at the 2006 FIFA World Cup). Engaged web-based research includes projects in which researchers identify themselves as users and somehow participate in the site (even if only by asking contextual questions about existing content). For online research, researchers identify themselves as users for the specific purpose of recruiting participants and subsequently using digital media to engage in participatory ethnographies (what Hine, 2000 called virtual ethnographies), conduct interviews or focus groups, or perform action research online (for examples of PCS research from this category, see Mitrano, 1999; Olive, 2013).

An important side note must be mentioned. Given that 'online' and 'offline' experiences and identities are now seamlessly interwoven in people's lives, some authors (Bailey and Steeves, 2015; Wilson, 2007; Ringrose and Harvey, Chapter 45, this volume) increasingly advocate the deconstruction of the online/offline binary and call for research that explores the convergence of the two. Relationships between participants' online and offline worlds are complex and scholars (e.g. Orgad, 2009) have expressed frustration over unsubstantiated claims about people's everyday lives made in research limited to online data. However, this does not necessarily mean that projects must combine online *and* offline data. Orgad (ibid.: 21) claims that 'online data such as, for example, online self-narratives, can be rich, detailed, and illuminating about information that could have not been gained using offline methodologies'.

While general consensus in the academic community holds that only engaged web-based research and online research require ethical approval, researchers performing non-intrusive, web-based research must ensure that the material collected falls in the public domain and is free and clear of intellectual rights or copyright issues. This brings us to one of the questions outlined above and widely discussed in IRE literature: where do we draw the line between the public and the private domains? Although Internet users run the risk of privacy violations when they decide to communicate on the Internet, what is the researcher's responsibility towards the people they study? Blackstone et al. (2008: 7) claim that 'social, academic, or regulatory delineations of public and private as a clearly recognizable binary no longer holds in everyday practice'. Furthermore, Whitty explains that:

> even if we conclude that these spaces are public spaces, the anonymity they afford can give the illusion that these are private spaces. Can we, as researchers, ethically take advantage of people's false sense of privacy and security? Is it ethically justifiable to lurk in these sites and download material without the knowledge or consent of the individuals who inhabit these sites?
>
> *(Whitty, 2004: 211)*

Thus, even researchers employing non-intrusive, web-based research confront this issue.

For my research on the Skirtboarders, I obtained ethical approval and began analysing the blog (considered a public, published text) with no intention of engaging with the Skirtboarders or their users until the interview recruitment process (i.e. non-intrusive web-based research). Like Wilson (2006), I planned to use the blog to 'case the joint' – that is, use blog data to decide how I would present myself to the Skirtboarders and blog users and to inform construction of the interview guide I intended to use for offline interviews. I quickly realized, however, that although the Skirtboarders and their users were operating in a public space (a blog), they still had sometimes strong perceptions or expectations of privacy, especially since the blog appeared to be part of their identity (as later confirmed through interviews). This realization led me to follow the suggestion of Blackstone et al. (2008), that researchers make themselves known and explain their research objectives. I clearly introduced myself by email (using addresses posted on the blog) to all members of the Skirtboarders crew, explaining my identity, purpose, role and intentions before continuing with my discourse analysis. This required me to demonstrate a different kind of sensitivity towards each Skirtboarder member post (now that they were all aware that I would be reading and analysing them). Regrettably, however, I never once considered asking the Skirtboarders to post an explanation about my research project or me on the blog to let all blog users know what I was up to (i.e. moving my research into the engaged web-based research category). Despite the approval of my institution's REB, I sensed that greater caution would have been preferable.

On beginning my project exploring the Ladies of the Lakes, Lisa Parkes, creator of the event and Facebook page, published a post identifying me to all users and explaining that I was in the process of writing about women great lake surfers and would be conducting interviews offline at the Ladies of the Lakes 2015 event. Based on what I had learned from my Skirtboarders' research, this step left me feeling more comfortable about my ethical conduct.

In both research experiences, while I had access to the content on the public digital media sites, the producers of the sites (i.e. Mathilde Pigeon, in the case of the Skirtboarders, and Lisa Parkes, in the case of the Ladies of the Lakes) acted as gatekeepers of sorts, providing me with the names and/or emails of women who they thought might sit down with me for interviews. That I still relied on the gatekeepers despite having full access to the public sites demonstrates how our relationships with digital media significantly impact our research in multiple ways, including our choice of research topic, the scope of study, the collection and analysis of data, maintenance of research rigour and, in this case, access to informants. In offline research projects, considerable debate has centred on the merits of being an 'insider', 'outsider' or 'somewhere in between'. In digital media research, however, researcher positioning becomes even more complex; we can be double 'insiders' (i.e. insiders in both the physical cultural communities *and* the digital media spaces we study, such as Olive, 2013 as both a participant in and a blogger about a small Australian town's women surfing community), double 'outsiders' (i.e. outsiders within the physical cultural communities and the digital media spaces), or a variation thereof. Critical digital media scholarship therefore requires scholars to be reflexive about their own digital media presence *and* their relationship to the physical cultural community they are exploring.

For my Ladies of the Lakes project, I was a 'middle-of-the-road' researcher, with daily access to the Internet and some social online networking services (e.g. Twitter) but consciously resisting others, such as Facebook, the very application I was studying. I am also a woman who surfs and participated in the Ladies of the Lakes event, but was not yet an 'insider' in the Great Lakes surfing scene. My 'middle' position in both the digital media world and the physical culture community also defined my work with the Skirtboarders: I was a blog 'user' despite never leaving comments and, as previously discussed, I dabbled in skate culture as a teenager.

Data collection and analysis

Once scholars know where to start (and roughly where to stop), and have reflected on ethical considerations and their researcher positioning, they can begin collecting and analysing their data. PCS scholars have explored the digital media phenomenon in nuanced ways. While researchers acknowledge that the rejigging of traditional methods of data collection and analysis to 'fit' the specificity of digital media content is both appropriate and perhaps inevitable (see Wilson, 2007), new methods are also emerging as more researchers engage with digital media projects. For example, in her ethnographic research on women's recreational surfing experiences, Olive (2013) created and maintained a blog for sharing experiences and knowledge with users, to learn from users about her local surfing culture and to reflect on her research. She noted that, although producing her blog 'Making friends with the neighbours' in no way replaced traditional/embodied methods including participation and interviewing, blogging provided multiple benefits, including aiding her to,

> write in ways that are culturally reflective, ... collect responses to the ideas I develop, showing me where and how the understandings and experiences of women who surf in my research field have resonance for other surfers, and helping me remain reflexive about my own subjective assumptions and experiences.
>
> *(Olive, 2013: 80–81)*

New collection and analysis methods, such as Olive's (2013) 'blogging as method' are emerging. However, 'rethought' (Wilson, 2007) approaches to collection and analysis continue to dominate the research landscape. For example, in terms of data collection, just like their counterparts exploring 'traditional media', scholars engaged in digital media research tend to pay vigilant attention to collecting and storing materials used in analysing online texts. In terms of data analysis methods, past PCS projects have turned to content analysis (Antunovic and Hardin, 2013), thematic analysis (Dart, 2009; Mitrano, 1999), Foucauldian discourse analysis (Hardin, 2011; MacKay and Dallaire, 2013), affect-based discourse analysis (Pavlidis and Fullagar, 2013) and virtual ethnography (Wilson, 2006). In all cases, scholars engaging with digital media projects have had to negotiate the unique data collection and analytical challenges that digital media present due to characteristics that differentiate them from 'traditional' media. Unlike most 'traditional' media texts, digital media texts are inherently intertextual; they lack linearity, are multimedia and polysemous, have the potential to reach a global audience, are impermanent and have an altered sense of authorship (e.g. the reader often is the writer) (Mitra and Cohen, 1999). Ultimately, as new applications and software enabling users to save online content appear, it is important for PCS scholars engaging in digital media research projects to 'keep up with the times' and familiarize themselves with these tools (and their costs), as well as the legal and ethical constraints involved in saving online content. Scrutiny of recent PCS and media studies literature for examples of analytical strategies and tools and constant and reflexive questioning of the concepts used to understand their digital media data are further approaches that might be beneficial for PCS digital media scholars to adopt.

PCS and the future of digital media research

The methodological challenges inherent in digital media research are constantly evolving as the research field deepens. Although there is no one 'correct' approach to studying a digital media phenomenon, the discussion in this chapter of where to start and stop, ethical considerations and researcher reflexivity and blended online and offline data collection and analysis are some of the issues that might affect researchers when completing their projects. Furthermore, while, research expounding productive and destructive accounts of digital media usage by physical culture communities should continue, more complex analyses of digital media that eschew utopian/dystopian descriptions of PCS participants, communities, fans, etc. are needed, that instead explore how digital platforms are:

> constructed within a capitalist marketplace, the social norms and practices of those who inhabit [them] and those who design [their] architecture, and any laws that regulate those spaces and those within them, as well as the interactions between all of these forces.
>
> *(Bailey and Steeves, 2015: 5)*

This is all the more relevant considering that, according to Andrews and Silk (2015), one of PCS's key elements is the 'contextual'.

Additionally, while physical cultural participants and communities have sometimes challenged relations of power, the prediction that the digital media shift would produce large-scale transformation in dominant notions of gender, sexuality, race, ethnicity, dis/ability and nation has not yet materialized. PCS scholars thus have a responsibility to shed light on the online/offline worlds of physical culture participants in a deeply contextual way but also to encourage them to use their platforms to enact social change, or even create their own sites to this end given that:

> PCS, as a political project, is ... driven by the need to understand *and expose* [emphasis added] the complexities, experiences, and injustices of the physical cultural context it confronts (particularly with regard to the relations, operations, and effects of power).
>
> *(Andrews and Silk, 2015: 90)*

Over a dozen PCS scholars (e.g. Rebecca Olive, Nicole LaVoi) are voluntarily 'stepping off the bench', to quote sports writer Dave Zirin, by producing and engaging with digital media.

While it is certainly unnecessary (nor methodologically prudent) for all PCS scholars researching physical culture participants' experiences with digital media to create their own media and/or to critically engage with the sites they explore, PCS academics are ultimately responsible for applying the skills and knowledge *they* consider essential in their effort to understand the digital media experiences of physical culture participants. In the process, they are responsible for sustaining a healthy level of critique and reflexivity on how their research (and, if applicable, engagement with digital media) may affect the social realities of physical culture participants since, like digital media itself, PCS research does not simply represent physical culture but actively constitutes it, as well. Given that we 'now live in a digital society' (Lupton, 2012: 2) and given that the infinite digital media content found online actively represents and constitutes global sport (see Leonard, 2009) and physical culture, developing a thorough understanding of physical culture necessitates engagement with digital media. In order to engage with digital media in empirical, contextual, transdisciplinary, theoretical, political, qualitative, self-reflexive and pedagogical ways (see Andrews and Silk, 2015) the dialogue about digital media methods in the PCS community should continue.

Acknowledgement

This work was produced during the period of my Social Sciences and Humanities Research Council of Canada (SSHRC) funded postdoctoral fellowship.

Notes

1. Some of whom would position themselves under the PCS umbrella and others who would not.
2. MacKay and Dallaire (2009) claim that the dominant discursive strategies that construct sportswomen focus on: gender marking, establishing heterosexuality, emphasizing female stereotypes, infantilizing women, non-sports related aspects, comparisons to men's performance and ambivalence.
3. Mainstream media are largely undemocratic, profit-centred, hierarchically organized (corporations and public companies that create and circulate media representations and their staff) and present voices that are largely exclusive due to the routinization and codification of the journalism profession.
4. Niche media are produced by non-commercial sources and aim to challenge existing power structures, represent marginalized groups and/or foster horizontal linkages among communities of interest.
5. While I do not identify as a female skateboarding insider, I also recognize that the insider/outsider binary is not only a highly unstable boundary but also ignores the dynamism of positionalities in time and through space.
6. According to Orgad (2009), online data is any text, image, sound, video or ethnographic material that researchers obtain from online exchanges with research participants. Offline data is data obtained through 'traditional methods' in 'traditional' offline settings.
7. For a particularly comprehensive list of questions, see the chart in Appendix I of Markham and Buchanan (2012).

References

Andrews, D. L and Silk, M. L. 2015. Physical cultural studies on sport. In R. Guilianotti (ed.), *The Routledge handbook of the sociology of sport*. London: Routledge, pp. 83–93.

Antunovic, D. and Hardin, M. 2013. Women and the blogosphere: Exploring feminist approaches to sport. *New Media and Society*, 15 (8), 1374–1392.

Baerg, A. 2007. Fight night round 2: Mediating the body and digital boxing. *Sociology of Sport Journal*, 24 (3), 325–345.

Bailey, J. and Steeves, V. 2015. Introduction: Cyber-utopia? Getting beyond the binary notion of technology as good or bad for girls. In J. Bailey and V. Steeves (eds), *eGirls, eCitizens*. Ottawa: University of Ottawa Press, pp. 1–20.

Bayam, N. K. and Markham, A. N. 2009. Introduction: Making smart choices on shifting ground. In A. N. Markham and N. K. Bayam (eds), *Internet inquiry: Conversations about method*. Thousand Oaks: Sage, vii–xix.

Blackstone, M., Given, L., Levy, J., McGinn, M., O'Neill, P. and Palys, T. et al. 2008. *Extending the spectrum: The TCPS and ethical issues in internet-based research*. Available from www.pre.ethics.gc.ca/policy-politique/initiatives/docs/Internet_Research_-_February_2008_-_EN.pdf.

boyd, d. 2009. Response to question one: How can qualitative Internet researchers define the boundaries of their projects? In A. N. Markham and N. K. Bayam (eds), *Internet inquiry: Conversations about method*. Thousand Oaks, CA: Sage, 26.

Dart, J. J. 2009. Blogging the FIFA 2006 World Cup finals. *Sociology of Sport Journal*, 26 (1), 107–126.

Gilchrist, P. and Wheaton, B. 2013. New media technologies in lifestyle sport. In B. Hutchins and D. Rowe (eds), *Digital media sport: Technology and power in the network society*. Abingdon: Routledge, pp. 169–185.

Hardin, M. 2011. The power of a fragmented collective: Radical pluralist feminism and technologies of the self in the sports blogosphere. In A. Billings (ed.), *Sports media: Transformation, integration, consumption*. New York: Routlege, 40–60.

Hine, C. 2000. *Virtual ethnography*. Thousand Oaks, CA: Sage.

Hine, C. 2009. Question one: How can qualitative Internet researchers define the boundaries of their projects? In A. N. Markham and N. K. Bayam (eds), *Internet inquiry: Conversations about method*. Thousand Oaks, CA: Sage, pp. 1–21.

Hine C. 2013. *Virtual research methods* (four-volume set). Thousand Oaks, CA: Sage.

hooks, b. 1989. *Talking back: Thinking feminist, thinking black*. Toronto: Between the Lines.

Hutchins, B. and Rowe, D. 2012. *Sport beyond television: The Internet, digital media and the rise of networked media sport*. London: Routledge.

Hutchins, B. and Rowe, D. (eds). 2013. *Digital media sport: Technology, power and culture in the network society*. New York: Routledge.

Kitchin, H. A. 2007. *Research ethics and the Internet: Negotiating Canada's Tri-Council Policy Statement*. Black Point, Nova Scotia: Fernwood Publishing.

LaVoi, N. M. and Calhoun, A. S. 2014. Digital media and female athletes. In A. C. Billings and M. Hardin (eds), *Routledge handbook of sport and new media*. New York: Routledge, 320–330.

Leonard, D. J. 2009. New media and global sporting cultures: Moving beyond the clichés and binaries. *Sociology of Sport Journal*, 26 (1), 1–16.

Lupton, D. 2012. *Digital sociology: An introduction*. Sydney: University of Sydney.

MacKay, S. and Dallaire, C. 2009. Campus newspaper coverage of varsity sports: Getting closer to equitable and sports-related (re)presentations of female athletes? *International Review for the Sociology of Sport*, 44 (1), 25–40.

MacKay, S. and Dallaire, C. 2013. Skirtboarder net-a-narratives: Young women creating their own skateboarding (re)presentations. *International Review for the Sociology of Sport*, 48 (2), 171–195.

MacKay, S. and Dallaire, C. 2014. Skateboarding women: Building collective identity in cyberspace. *Journal of Sport and Social Issues*, 38 (6), 548–566.

Markham, A. and Buchanan, E. 2012. *Ethical decision-making and internet research: Recommendations from the AoIR Ethics Working Committee (Version 2.0)*. Available from http://aoir.org/reports/ethics2.pdf (accessed 3 September 2015).

Millington, B. 2014. Smartphone apps and the mobile privatization of health and fitness. *Critical Studies in Media Communication*, 31 (5), 479–493.

Mitra, A. and Cohen, E. 1999. Analyzing the web: Directions and challenges. In S. Jones (ed.), *Doing Internet research*. Thousand Oaks, CA: Sage, 179–202.

Mitrano, J. R. 1999. The 'sudden death' of hockey in Hartford: Sports fans and franchise relocation. *Sociology of Sport Journal*, 16, 134–154.

Olive, R. 2013. 'Making friends with the neighbours': Blogging as a research method. *International Journal of Cultural Studies*, 16 (1), 71–84.

Orgad, S. 2009. Question two: How can researchers make sense of the issues involved in collecting and interpreting online and offline data. In A. N. Markham and N. K. Bayam (eds), *Internet inquiry: Conversations about method*. Thousand Oaks, CA: Sage, 33–53.

Pavlidis, A. and Fullagar, S. 2013. Becoming roller derby grrrls: Exploring the gendered play of affect in mediated sport cultures. *International Review for the Sociology of Sport*, 48 (6), 673–688.

Robinson, L. and Schulz, J. 2009. New avenues for sociological inquiry: Evolving forms of ethno-graphic practice. *Sociology,* 43 (4), 685–698.

Sparkes, A. C. and Smith, B. 2013. *Qualitative research methods in sport, exercise and health: From process to product.* New York: Routledge.

Thorpe, H. 2015. *Transnational mobilities in action sports cultures.* London: Palgrave Macmillan.

Whitty, M. 2004. Peering into online bedroom windows: Considering the ethical implications of investigating Internet relationships and sexuality. In E. A. Buchanan (ed.), *Readings in virtual research ethics: Issues and controversies.* London: Information Sciences, 203–218.

Wilson, B. 2006. Ethnography, the Internet and youth culture: Strategies for examining social resistance and 'online-offline' relationships. *Canadian Journal of Education*, 29 (1), 307–328.

Wilson, B. 2007. New media, social movements, and global sport studies. *Sociology of Sport Journal*, 24 (4), 457–477.

PART IX

Politics and praxis

54
PHYSICAL CULTURAL STUDIES AND PUBLIC PEDAGOGIES

Emma Rich and Jennifer A. Sandlin

Within the burgeoning physical cultural studies (PCS) scholarship, *pedagogy* has begun to emerge as a conceptual lens through which to understand the nexus between culture, the body, and learning. More recently, *public pedagogy* has become a driving force in the theorization and practice of PCS, and while the term is taken up in various ways, these usages are broadly situated within two key approaches. First, a number of studies explore how sites of physical culture operate pedagogically – that is, researchers analyze how various sites of physical culture in the public sphere act as pedagogical spaces and/or as pedagogues, as they teach us into certain ways of thinking about bodies, health, and physical activity. Second, the term *public pedagogy* is being deployed within PCS scholarship as a way to describe the 'public engagement' work that has become a fundamental aspect of the vision and enactment of PCS (Andrews and Silk, 2015). Andrews and Silk (ibid.) state, for example, that one key element of PCS is that it is 'pedagogical', and that 'PCS represents a form of public pedagogy designed to impact learning communities within the academy, in the classroom, and throughout broader publics'. Despite this ethos, how (public) pedagogy is conceptualized and/or enacted is often unclear. In offering some distinction, we begin this chapter by exploring how the construct of 'public pedagogy' (Sandlin, O'Malley and Burdick, 2011) challenges the idea that pedagogical phenomena reside only in formal educational spaces. Subsequently, we explore some of the ways in which scholars have problematized public pedagogy, its theoretical and practical conceptualizations and what this might mean for PCS.

We then discuss more fully how the concept of public pedagogy as 'public engagement' or 'public intellectualism' has been explicated and problematized within public pedagogy literature, focusing specifically on several interrelated issues we believe must be addressed by PCS scholars as they continue to theorize and enact public pedagogies of PCS in the broader public sphere: power dynamics embedded in individualized versus more collective enactments of public intellectualism; conflicting and complicated conceptualizations and enactments of 'public'; and tensions between more cognitive versus more embodied and affective approaches to social-justice-oriented action.

Seeing through the (cloudy) lens of public pedagogy

Public pedagogy refers to 'spaces, sites, and languages of education and learning' that occur outside of or beyond formal educational institutions (Sandlin, Schultz and Burdick, 2010: 1).

Such work registers processes of learning and education that take place in many sites and environments beyond formal education or schooling. As Giroux (2001c: 129) explains, public pedagogy implies that 'learning takes place across a spectrum of social practices and settings', including popular culture and everyday life, informal institutions and public spaces such as museums, zoos, and art installations, dominant cultural discourses such as neoliberalism, and public intellectualism and social activism (Sandlin, Schultz and Burdick, 2010). Similarly, Hickey-Moody, Savage and Windle (2010: 227) use the term 'pedagogy writ large' to capture a more general set of theoretical conceptualizations framing 'pedagogy in this broader sense'. There is now an emergent PCS literature that aligns with these public pedagogy approaches, exploring the pedagogical forces of a range of physical cultural sites (Markula, 2008; Rich, 2011a; Mansfield and Rich, 2013; Andreasson and Johansson, 2014). For example, Markula (2008: 382) describes the fitness industry 'as a promising educational field where it is possible to change the ways people view their bodies and their identities'. Similarly, Andreasson and Johansson (2014) analyze the fitness gym as a 'site of learning'.

Despite the enthusiasm with which many scholars have taken up the lenses of public pedagogy to explore extra-institutional sites of education, and despite the insights provided by such research, many scholars who have engaged with theorizing the field of public pedagogy have not only highlighted the promises such inquiry holds for understanding education, but have also outlined problems within current public pedagogy scholarship (Savage, 2010; Hickey-Moody et al., 2010; Sandlin, O'Malley and Burdick, 2011; Burdick and Sandlin, 2013; Rich, 2011a, 2011b; Savage, 2014). In this section, we briefly explore some more general issues, before turning, in the next section, to a more detailed discussion of issues surrounding the conceptualization of public pedagogy as public engagement. One issue raised by these scholars is that within public pedagogy literature, the concept of public pedagogy is often so broadly conceptualized that it runs the risk of losing explanatory power. Additionally, these scholars point out that despite some scholarship being clear about the theoretical lenses authors use to analyze sites of public pedagogy – drawing, for example, from Gramscian cultural studies, a/r/tography, or postcolonial theory, among many others – much work framed with public pedagogy lenses is unclear regarding its theoretical grounding (Sandlin, O'Malley and Burdick, 2011).

Also unclear are the processes or mechanisms through which such sites actually enact their pedagogies. Such processes are often obscured when authors over-rely on Williams's (1967) concept of 'permanent education' and his idea that 'our whole social and cultural experience' provides educational experiences (cited in Giroux, 2004: 63) without further explicating how these processes work or how they differ from cultural socialization. Giroux, for example, uses Williams's (1967) work as a starting point when arguing for the importance of taking seriously the education that happens within popular culture, as he stresses the role of 'cultural forms and processes' (Savage, 2010: 109) as educator. Some scholars have also gone further to provide important theoretical insights regarding how culture acts as pedagogy (see Burdick and Sandlin, 2013 for a review of this literature), and much of the work in PCS aligns with these critical analyses of popular texts. However, while Giroux (2001a, 2001d, 2002) and some other authors do explicate how such sites operate pedagogically, stressing, for example, pedagogical strategies such as the inversion of meaning (Bates, 2007) or exploring how 'power is mobilized' in mainstream films through the ways in which they use images, sounds, gestures, dialogue, and spectacle to 'structure everyday issues around particular assumptions, values, and social relations' (Giroux, 2001a: 591–592), the majority of public pedagogy literature seems to take these processes for granted without providing details about how they work. Instead, much of this literature, which is heavily reliant on and derived from Giroux's vast and influential body of work – which has, since the early 1990s, been central to the theorization of public pedagogy

– often takes up only Giroux's starting point, that culture educates, without engaging further in his or other scholars' attempts to outline *how* this educational process works.

Unsurprisingly therefore, a number of authors contributing to PCS (Andrews, 1998; Giardina, 2005; Silk and Andrews, 2011) deploy Giroux's approach to public pedagogy in their work focused on pedagogical forces of neoliberalism as expressed within particular physical cultures. In his critical reading of sport media, Andrews (1998: 186) made the case for a critical pedagogy of sporting representations and advocated for cultural studies scholars to 'counter the promotional colonization of everyday by creating insurgent narratives'. While some of Giroux's work does explicate specific processes of pedagogy, other areas of his work – especially his later work on the public pedagogy of discourses or narratives of neoliberalism – are much less explicit regarding pedagogical process, providing the sense that cultural processes and social and economic ideologies act as agents of 'repressive socialization (or more bluntly, forms of capitalist brainwashing), which placate individuals through containing and castrating their potential for critical thinking' (Savage, 2010: 109). As Savage (ibid.: 108) further points out, often specific or localized pedagogical mechanisms of culture are obscured, as pedagogy via culture comes to be seen as operating through the more 'hazy' concepts of socialization and interpellation, or as operating 'through the very broadest circuits of cultural life'. Giardina (2005: 7) in his book *Sporting Pedagogies*, for example, articulates a 'belief that global (cultural) sporting agents, intermediaries, and institutions actively work as pedagogical sites to hegemonically re-inscribe and re-present (hetero)-normative discourses on sport, culture, nation, and democracy throughout an ascendant global capitalist order'.

PCS work of this kind has produced important insights through critical explorations of the educative force of a range of physical cultural sites; focusing on pedagogy in the broadest sense, scholars have been able to identify the political, social and cultural norms that shape what and how people are learning about their bodies. However, we would argue that PCS is in danger of falling prey to 'totalizing' readings of physical culture and 'unidirectional' concepts of learning if it does not also explicate specific processes of pedagogy and engage with (Savage, 2014: 85) 'the complex interactions that occur in these spaces in between address and response'. Furthermore, PCS may provide some unique insights for advancement of knowledge within the field of public pedagogy because of its focus on the body and the 'emancipatory potential' of 'bodily praxis' (Giardina and Newman, 2011b: 37).

Problematizing 'public' 'interventions'

As Hickey-Moody et al. (2010: 229) argue, 'a sophisticated notion of pedagogy does not assume a simple movement of norms from society to individual. Instead, norms can be examined as they are developed and contested'. This space for contestation within sites of public pedagogy provides opportunities for PCS to intervene and disrupt and lead into discussions about the meanings of 'public' within conceptualizations and enactments of public pedagogy. As with 'pedagogy', however, how the 'public' is conceived of within public pedagogy scholarship is also a matter of contestation (Savage, 2010, 2014). Despite the growing interest in such explorations within PCS, there has been little engagement beyond the work of Giroux and with the more diverse and recent debates and scholars who 'enact' public pedagogy. Michael Giardina (2005) in his book *Sporting Pedagogies* embraces Giroux's (2001b: 14) call to 'accentuate the performative as a transitive act' and does so by 'enacting a performative cultural study of sport' (Giardina, 2005: 7), utilizing critical pedagogy to extend the scholarly practices of PCS. To this end, he describes his book as 'a reaction to and intervention into this context'. Elsewhere, Silk et al. (2015) in their paper on slowing the social sciences of sport, endorse a 'slow pedagogy' to counter 'neoliberal educational rationalities'. While inroads have been made into critical pedagogical engagements, criticisms have been levelled at PCS that while much of this work identifies oppressive political, social and cultural norms, it has been less successful at enacting social change (King-White, 2012; Markula, 2008).

It is hardly surprising therefore that in recent years some PCS scholars have been making the case for more political and public intervention (Giardina and Newman, 2011a; Atkinson, 2011). Markula (2008: 382) in her efforts to 'deterritorialize the current, molar feminine identity' taught a weekly exercise class where her 'instruction was informed by a deliberate agenda for social change'. Elsewhere King-White (2012) examines the possibilities of a critical pedagogical approach to PCS by detailing how it has shaped his formal teaching practices, drawing on Giroux's 'pedagogy of the privileged'. Mansfield and Rich (2013) cite examples where, as critical weight scholars, they have undertaken their own border crossings into politically engaged communities.

Despite this, Atkinson (2011: 142) argues that 'there is no possibility of hope offered in much of the extant PCS research'. Atkinson (ibid.) subsequently proposed a vision of radical PCS research whereby PCS must be 'flavoured by a political agenda' and researchers 'take point'. In response, we suggest that PCS would benefit from interrogating precisely terms such as 'resistance' and 'politics' as for many PCS scholars there may be no expressed particular political stance or end goal, other than 'the intention … to push against the given' (Gaztambide-Fernandez and Arraiz Matute, 2014: 59).

Nonetheless, even pushing against the given may be accompanied by risks; it may involve unsettling forms of communication, presentation and discourse which may provoke unexpected reactions or resistance in the contemporary moment. For example, Pavlidis (2013) explores some of the paradoxes and complexities of 'resistance' within the context of roller derby, suggesting that affects such as shame and hurt, while uncomfortable, might lead us to explore new questions.

There is also a tendency to employ the concept of 'pedagogy' as an inroad to 'public engagement' or 'politics' without adequately unpacking its meaning. Andrews and Silk (2015) claim that one PCS objective is thus to nurture dialogic 'reflection and action upon the world in order to transform it' (Freire, 2000: 51). But what might this look like? It has been over two decades since Giroux (1992) made a case for border crossing and the idea that research ought to bridge the gap between academe and various 'publics' is not particularly new; but is certainly invigorated by the recent public pedagogy scholarship examining issues of praxis, performance, activism and publicness, which we take up in the sections below.

Beyond individualized accounts of public intellectualism, towards collective enactments: who can be a PCS pedagogue?

The figure of the public intellectual is constructed most frequently in public pedagogy literature as an academic who educates the public 'in modes of critical praxis understood to foster agency, engaged citizenship, and sociopolitical imaginations' (Brass, 2014: 91). These imaginings are grounded in the neo-Marxist theoretical traditions of Antonio Gramsci and Edward Said and have been disseminated widely through the public pedagogy literature through the prolific work of Henry Giroux (ibid.). This conceptualization of the public intellectual as an individualized or 'solitary figure in a seat of epistemic power' (Sandlin, Schultz and Burdick, 2010: xxv) has prompted some scholars to question the locating of agency with(in) the 'institutionally or professionally identified pedagogue' (Sandlin, O'Malley and Burdick, 2011: 356), and to ask the question: 'On whose terms' (Mayo, 2002: 201) 'does this public intellectual work operate?'

Recent public pedagogy scholarship has also encouraged scholars to move beyond this more individualistic model of the 'public intellectual', towards more feminist and communal visions of public intellectualism (Dentith, O'Malley and Brady, 2014).

In these more communal and grassroots perspectives, 'the public' are positioned as multiple citizens and as potential educators or pedagogues through which more equitable forms of social justice within and through physical culture might be made readily apparent. As Brady (2006: 58) captures it, 'Education in this context is public in two ways. First, it opens a space for contesting conventional academic boundaries and, second, it raises questions about the capacity for citizens to engage as critical educators in their present, everyday lives.' In this regard, those who can practice public pedagogy are not just the 'public intellectuals' of PCS. This would align with understandings of PCS as a collective and democratic project. Brady (ibid.) argues that 'participating in scholarly communities that practice public pedagogy creates alternative discourses that focus on alliances rather than identities'. Rather than attempting to develop cohesive unity, she argues this is far more fluid and contextual and cannot be captured by fixed structures. It is a move perhaps towards collective narrative, and imagination to create physical cultural sites and practices that are yet 'unimagined'. This moves us to our next points about reimaging and moving across spaces, sites, and bodies.

Conflicting and complicated conceptualizations and enactments of 'public': from public instruction to publicness

Savage (2010, 2014) and Biesta (2012, 2014) have raised concerns about the lack of clarity around the concept of 'public' within public pedagogy scholarship, urging scholars to consider 'which public?' and 'whose public?' they are referring to when using the term (Savage, 2014: 79). Biesta (2012, 2014) argues that notions of the 'public' within public pedagogy have been paid little attention, and asks what it might mean to do pedagogy in a 'public way' (Biesta, 2014: 16), or in the 'interest of the public quality of human togetherness' (ibid.). For Biesta the question is less about *who* can be a public pedagogue, and more about *how* that pedagogy is enacted, and what issues of power arise in various enactments of public pedagogies. He conceptualizes three ways public pedagogy can be enacted. A pedagogy *for* the public is 'a pedagogy *aimed at* the public' (ibid.: 21), which uses instruction by 'educational agents' (ibid.: 22) as its main form and which places the logic of democratic politics under a logic of schooling. A pedagogy *of* the public is a pedagogy 'done *by* the public itself' through the mode of 'collective *learning*' (ibid.), which while more clearly linked to enactments of plurality still positions democracy under a 'regime of learning', which both demands something of the public, namely that they adopt a particular relationship of 'self to the self', and that they learn, and, in turning social problems into learning problems, turns the responsibility for those problems onto the individual rather than the collective (ibid.). Finally, a pedagogy in the interest of publicness operates at the '*intersection* of education and politics' (ibid.: 23) and as an 'enactment of a concern for 'publicness' – that is, a concern for the public quality of human togetherness and thus for the possibility of actors and events to become public' (ibid.), or to create a form of 'political existence … in which action is possible and freedom can appear' (ibid.). Here, Biesta reminds us of the importance of the public pedagogue who operates as 'neither an instructor nor a facilitator but rather someone who interrupts' (Biesta, 2006). Such interruptions are not *led*, and thus not *controlled*, by pedagogues, but emerge as enactments of human togetherness.

As an emergent field of study, PCS needs to be mindful of simply equating public pedagogy with the imperatives of public engagement, and to pay attention, following Biesta (2014), to demonstrate *how* that work is engaging the public. Space for engaging in more civic discourses or cultural and political movements is also constrained by the present neoliberal context of education that emphasizes excessive individualism (Brady, 2006). In the UK at least, there has been increased emphasis on the role of the University as a 'public institution' (Watermeyer, 2015) and of the academic as 'public intellectual'. Research by Watermeyer (ibid.: 334) with 'UK academics distinguished for their Public Engagement endeavours' revealed that 'for most respondents PE-HE remains an ancillary rather than integral component of the research process – especially or even, where it is mobilized for the purpose of evidencing the socio-economic impact of research – and that academic career progression' (ibid.: 344). The imperative to secure funds/demonstrate impact where scholars 'too often find that they must recast their work to highlight its 'relevance to public policy', a criterion imposed by national and international funding agencies' (Baviskar, 2008: 430) may shape the way we think about 'publicness' (Biesta, 2012).

In attending to the pedagogical addressivity of our public engagement work scholars are directed to imagine the publics they are seeking to inform. While there is pedagogical merit to this, we need to be cautious of definitions of public that are bound up in the imperatives of 'impact' solely as markers of productivity of the neoliberal academy. The risk is that scholars may draw on metaphors of 'knowledge already made' (Ellsworth, 2005: 5) to be transmitted to another, rather than constituted more relationally. Giardina (2005: 151) in his discussion of performing pedagogies of resistance suggests this 'involves communicating the skills that will empower students and citizens alike to become more open to and cognizant of the popular politics of representation of race, class, gender, sexuality, and other cultural form'. Similarly, Markula (2008: 382) described her public pedagogy where 'I assigned bodily performance in my exercise class as a "privileged site of experimentation" where I could teach participants new ways of thinking about larger social issues'.

While these approaches make important steps towards critical consciousness, they are reminiscent of Biesta's (2006, 2012, 2014) pedagogies *for* and *of* the public, where outcomes are driven by pedagogical imperatives and where pedagogy follows a 'curriculum that has to be taught or has to be learned' (Biesta, 2014: 23). That is, while we might provide learning opportunities for a range of publics (O'Malley and Nelson, 2013), if the goal is to foster spaces of publicness, which, for Biesta, cannot be decided in advance and are characterized by being 'spaces where freedom can appear' (Arendt, 1955, quoted in Biesta, 2014: 16) – these pedagogies are about 'new ways of being and doing' (ibid.: 23) – we cannot simply 'transmit' knowledge for purposes we have already decided in advance. Mansfield and Rich (2013: 367), for example, recognize how publicness means that enacted public pedagogy is a process of becoming: 'through border crossing there is the potential to challenge the bases of particular physical activity and health politics and policies. We do not know in advance what these new assemblages may bring forth.'

Cognition, embodiment, affect? Conflicting approaches to social-justice-oriented public engagement – reimagining spaces, sites and bodies

Moving from public instruction to publicness involves not only challenging tacit knowledge forms and public pedagogies as transfer, but also may require moving beyond conceptualizations of pedagogy as cognitive and rational to viewing public pedagogy as engaging with the public through relationality, affectivity, and embodiment (see Burdick et al., 2014). Within the public pedagogy literature, there is an enduring tension between a more critical-theory based public pedagogy that relies on rational, critical dialogue and a more arts-based public pedagogy that focuses on public engagement through embodied, holistic, performative, intersubjective, and aesthetic modes of pedagogy (Burdick and Sandlin, 2013). In Biesta's (2014: 23) model, described above, for example, he posits that it is *artistic* interruptions that are 'more activist, more experimental, and more demonstrative', and that can reignite the public sphere through civic action. Likewise, a number of feminist PCS scholars are beginning to recognize that a focus on critical dialogue obscures other more affective and embodied ways of knowing and being. In this move towards publicness, much may be gained by insights from the work on pedagogy and affect (Hickey-Moody, 2007, 2009; Probyn, 2004) and its focus on the relationalities between bodies. This turn to affect (Massumi, 2002) provides a different approach to public pedagogy than that taken up by Giroux. For example, in challenging the 'subjectivation' to femininity, Markula (2008) makes the case for a performative methodology to use the body's affect to create change. Focused on the context of fitness instruction, Markula utilizes a feminist reading of critical pedagogy and explores how a researcher can assume a role of public intellectual through performative pedagogy.

An arts-based public pedagogy approach also encourages us to develop forms of visual culture that provide new/alternative ways of imagining the physically active body. For example, such imagery may play a critical role in challenging prevailing discourses of ageing and engage more with the varied embodied and sensual experiences of the ageing body (Orr and Phoenix, 2015). Provocations through 'creative engagement' (Brady, 2006) with film, television, video, photography, art, new/digital/social media, performance arts provide opportunities to trouble and disrupt dominant discourses and narratives. As Brophy and Hladki (2012) suggest 'contemporary visual culture generates unsettled forms of communication, empathy politics, thereby inviting ongoing contestation'. As an example of such enactment, Emma's research (Rich, 2010) on schooling and eating disorders was the focus of an art exhibition Body Culture curated by artist Kerrie O'Connell. The intent of this public pedagogy enactment was to make visible the regulation and surveillance of young people's bodies in relation to contemporary discourses of fat and obesity. The translation of research into art was done with the expressed intent of seeking to trouble the normalcy of weightism dominant across a number of physical cultures.

Furthermore, while there is a literature dedicated to the presence of the researcher's body and methods, much less is written about the presence of the researcher's body in undertaking border crossing and performative pedagogies. Probyn (2004: 22) draws attention to 'what actual bodies do in classrooms'. We might ask similar questions about the politics of the researcher's body (Giardina and Newman, 2011a) as we cross borders into different disciplines, sites, institutions and spaces. Francombe-Webb, Rich and De Pian (2014) reflect on their presence as scholars undertaking research with the intention of disrupting biopolitical forces. Reflecting on their experience of crossing borders, they suggest that 'rather than simply considering border crossing as an exchange of ideas, knowledge, and practices; we explore the ways in which the presence of our sometimes 'normative' bodies can seemingly complicate and contradict our political agenda'. In this regard, while there is a pressing need to intervene, we need more reflections on the risks, experiences, and processes of enacting public pedagogy.

Concluding comments

In this chapter, we have attempted to illuminate how at this conjunctural moment, as PCS aspires towards pedagogical impact, it has much to gain from the ongoing literature, theory and practice of public pedagogy. In doing so, we have not and would not propose a single *method* of doing or researching public pedagogy with/in PCS. We would argue that any attempt would be rather futile given that, like other fields, PCS might be read as fluid and developing within relations of power and understood and experienced individually. As Beck's (2011: 715) autobiographical piece attests, PCS scholars' research experiences will shape their own 'understanding and practice of Public Pedagogy'. Rather, and to conclude, we would argue that such diversity and tension should be harnessed for more critical discussion of strategies for doing public pedagogy within PCS.

References

Andreasson, J. and Johansson, T. (2014). *The Global Gym: Gender, Health and Pedagogies*. Palgrave Macmillan.
Andrews, D. L. (1998). Excavating Michael Jordan: Notes on a Critical Pedagogy of Sporting Representations. In G. Rail (ed.), *Sport and Postmodern Times* (pp. 185–220). Albany, NY: State University of New York Press.
Andrews, D. and Silk, M. (2015). Physical Cultural Studies on Sport. In R. Guilianotti (ed.), *The Routledge Handbook of the Sociology of Sport* (pp. 83–93). London: Routledge.
Atkinson, M. (2011). Physical Cultural Studies [Redux]. *Sociology of Sport Journal*, 28: 135–144.
Bates, B. R. (2007). Race, Inversive Performance, and Public Pedagogy. In L. M. Cooks and J. S. Simpson (eds), *Whiteness, Pedagogy, Performance* (pp. 193–212). Lanham, MD: Lexington Books.
Baviskar, A. (2008). Pedagogy, Public Sociology and Politics in India: What is to Be Done? *Current Sociology*, 56(3), 425–433.
Beck, S. (2011). Public Anthropology as Public Pedagogy: An Autobiographical Account. *Policy Futures in Education*, 9(6), 715–734.
Biesta, G. (2006). What's the Point of Lifelong Learning if Lifelong Learning has No Point? On the Democratic Deficit of Policies for Lifelong Learning. *European Educational Research Journal*, 5(2–3), 169–180.
Biesta, G. (2012). Becoming Public: Public Pedagogy, Citizenship and the Public Sphere. *Social and Cultural Geography*, 13(7), 683–697.
Biesta, G. (2014) Making Pedagogy Public: For the Public, of the Public or in the Interest of Publicness. In J. Burdick, J. A. Sandlin, and M. P. O'Malley (eds), *Problematising Public Pedagogy* (pp. 15–26). New York: Routledge.
Brady, J. F. (2006). Public Pedagogy and Educational Leadership: Politically Engaged Scholarly Communities and Possibilities for Critical Engagement. *Journal of Curriculum and Pedagogy*, 3(1), 57–60.
Brass, J. (2014). Problematizing the Public Intellectual: Foucault, Activism, and Critical Public Pedagogy. In J. Burdick, J. A. Sandlin, and M. P. O'Malley (eds), *Problematizing Public Pedagogy* (pp. 91–104). New York: Routledge.
Brophy, S. and Hladki, J. (2012). Introduction: Pedagogy, Image Practices, and Contested Corporealities. *Review of Education, Pedagogy, and Cultural Studies*, 34, 3–4.
Burdick, J. and Sandlin, J. A. (2013). Learning, Becoming, and the Unknowable: Conceptualizations, Mechanisms, and Process in Public Pedagogy Literature. *Curriculum Inquiry*, 43(1), 142–177.
Burdick, J., Sandlin, J. and O'Malley, M. P. (2014). *Problematizing Public Pedagogy*. Routledge, New York.
Dentith, A. M., O'Malley, M. P. and Brady, J. F. (2014). Public Pedagogy as a Historically Feminist Project. In J. Burdick, J. A. Sandlin, and M. P. O'Malley (eds), *Problematizing Public Pedagogy* (pp. 26–39). New York: Routledge.
Ellsworth, E. (2005). *Places of Learning: Media, Architecture, and Pedagogy*. New York: Routledge.
Francombe-Webb, J., Rich, E. and De Pian, L. (2014). I Move Like You … But Different: Biopolitics and Embodied Methodologies. *Cultural Studies ↔ Critical Methodologies*, 14(5), 471–482.
Freire, P. (2000) *Pedagogy of the Oppressed*. New York: Continuum.
Gaztambide-Fernandez, R. A. and Azzaiz Matute, A. (2014). 'Pushing Against': Relationality, Intentionality and the Ethical Imperative of Pedagogy. In J. Burdick, J. A. Sandlin, and M. P. O'Malley (eds), *Problematising Public Pedagogy* (pp. 52–64). New York: Routledge.
Giardina, M. (2005). *Sporting Pedagogies: Performing Culture and Identity in the Global Arena*. New York: Peter Lang.
Giardina, M. and Newman, J. (2011a). Physical Cultural Studies and Embodied Research Acts. *Cultural Studies ↔ Critical Methodologies*, 11, 523–534.
Giardina, M. and Newman, J. (2011b). What is this 'Physical' in Physical Cultural Studies? *Sociology of Sport Journal*, 28(1), 36–63.
Giroux, H. (1992). *Border Crossings: Cultural Workers and the Politics of Education*. New York: Routledge.

Giroux, H. A. (2001a). Breaking into the Movies: Pedagogy and the Politics of Film. *JAC*, 21, 583–598.
Giroux, H. A. (2001b). Cultural Studies as Performative Politics. *Cultural Studies ↔ Critical Methodologies*, 1(1), 5–23.
Giroux, H. A. (2001c). *Public Spaces, Private Lives: Beyond the Culture of Cynicism*. Lanham, MD: Rowman & Littlefield.
Giroux, H. A. (2001d). *Stealing Innocence: Corporate Culture's War on Children*. New York: Palgrave Macmillan.
Giroux, H. A. (2002). *Breaking in to the Movies: Film and the Culture of Politics*. London: Blackwell.
Giroux, H. A. (2004). Cultural Studies, Public Pedagogy, and the Responsibility of Intellectuals. *Communication and Critical/Cultural Studies*, 1(1), 59–79.
Hickey-Moody, A. (2007). Re-imagining Intellectual Disability: Sensation and Outside of Thought. In A. C. Hickey-Moody and P. Malins (eds), *Deleuzian Encounters: Studies in Contemporary Social Issues* (pp. 79–98). London: Palgrave Macmillan.
Hickey-Moody, A. (2009). *Unimaginable Bodies: Intellectual Disability, Performance and Becomings*. Rotterdam, The Netherlands: Sense Publishers.
Hickey-Moody, A., Savage, G. C. and Windle, J. (2010). Pedagogy Writ Large: Public, Popular and Cultural Pedagogies in Motion. *Critical Studies in Education*, 51(3), 227–236.
King-White, R. (2012). Oh Henry! Physical Cultural Studies' Critical Pedagogical Imperative. *Sociology of Sport Journal*, 29, 385–408.
Mansfield, L. and Rich, E. (2013). Public Health Pedagogy, Border Crossings and Physical Activity at Every Size. *Critical Public Health*, 23(2), 356–370.
Markula, P. (2008). Affect[ing] Bodies: Performative Pedagogy of Pilates. *International Review of Qualitative Research*, 1(3), 381–408.
Massumi, B. (2002). *Parables for the Virtual: Movement, Affect, Sensation*. Durham, NC: Duke University Press.
Mayo, P. (2002). Public Pedagogy and the Quest for a Substantive Democracy. *Interchange*, 33, 193–207.
O'Malley, M. and Nelson, S. (2013). The Public Pedagogy of Student Activists in Chile: What Have We Learned from the Penguins Revolution. *Journal of Curriculum Theorizing*, 29(2), 41–56.
Orr, N. and Phoenix, C. (2015). Photographing Physical Activity: Using Visual Methods to 'Grasp at' the Sensual Experiences of the Ageing Body. *Qualitative Research*, 15(4), 454–472.
Pavlidis, A. (2013). Writing Resistance in Roller Derby. *Journal of Leisure Research*, 45(5), 661–676.
Probyn, E. (2004). Teaching Bodies: Affects in the Classroom. *Body and Society*, 10(4), 21–4.
Rich, E. (2010). Obesity Assemblages and Surveillance in Schools. *International Journal of Qualitative Studies in Education*, 23(7), 803–821.
Rich, E. (2011a). Exploring the Relationship Between Pedagogy and Physical Cultural Studies: The Case of New Health Imperatives in Schools. *Sociology of Sport Journal*, 28(1), 64–84.
Rich, E. (2011b). 'I See Her Being Obesed!': Public Pedagogy, Reality Media and the Obesity Crisis. *Health: An Interdisciplinary Journal for the Social Study of Health, Illness and Medicine*, 15(1), 3–2.
Sandlin, J. A., O'Malley, M. P. and Burdick, J. (2011). Mapping the Complexity of Public Pedagogy Scholarship: 1894–2010. *Review of Educational Research*, 81(3), 338–375.
Sandlin, J., Schultz, B. and Burdick, J. (2010). *Handbook of Public Pedagogy: Education and Learning beyond Schooling. New York: Routledge*. New York: Routledge.
Savage, G. (2010). Problematizing 'Public Pedagogy' in Educational Research. In J. A. Sandlin, B. D. Schultz and J. Burdick (eds), *Handbook of Public Pedagogy* (pp. 103–115). New York: Routledge
Savage, G. (2014). Chasing the Phantoms of Public Pedagogy: Political, Popular and Concrete Publics. In J. Burdick, J. A. Sandlin and M. P. O'Malley (eds), *Problematising Public Pedagogy* (pp. 79–90). New York: Routledge.
Silk, M. L. and Andrews, D. L. (2011). Towards a Physical Cultural Studies. *Sociology of Sport Journal*, 28(1), 4–35.
Silk, M., Francombe-Webb, J., Rich, E. and Merchant, S. (2015). On the Transgressive Possibilities of Physical Pedagogic Practices. *Qualitative Inquiry*, 21(9), 798–811.
Watermeyer, R. (2015). Lost in the 'Third Space': The Impact of Public Engagement in Higher Education on Academic Identity, Research Practice and Career Progression, *European Journal of Higher Education*, 5(3), 331–347.
Williams, R. (1967). Preface to Second Edition. In *Communications*, 2nd edn. New York: Barnes & Noble.

55
CRITICAL CORPOREAL CURRICULA, PRAXIS AND CHANGE

Jessica Francombe-Webb, Michael L. Silk and Anthony Bush

Albeit with differing degrees and intensities within various higher education systems, 'sport' as an academic discipline – in a similar fashion to other disciplinary enterprises – has become enmeshed within the dictates of neoliberalism; namely the 'logics' of the market, and the privileging of centrally controlled, efficiency oriented, rationally predictable, empirically calculable modes of knowledge generation and, ultimately, epistemologically restricted ways of knowing (cf. Ritzer, 2004; Giroux, 2010a, 2010b). Such processes have further wed the 'science of sport', the university and implicated subjects (students/professors) to the logics of the capital. Almost out of necessity there has been a tendency to downplay pedagogic practices and scholarly foci that empathize with, for example, human needs, civic and moral responsibilities, public values, fluid ways of knowing and becoming and critique (Giroux, 2010a). Perhaps more worryingly, such dictates question the very worth and perceived value of the 'social', and it follows, the social sciences of sport and physical activity. This is, of course, an alarming state given non-rational and incalculable pedagogical outcomes are crucial foundations for democracy, political freedom and equality (Brown, 2006), yet they appear devalued in the 'sciences of sport' as in other formations of (higher) education.

Our intent in this chapter is to build on a recent shift (at the very least in our own institutions) towards a democratisation of 'sport' that includes other(ed) practices, experiences and institutions and is not limited to exercise, physical activity, movement, dance and so on. We build on this in order to break down real or perceived hierarchies and boundaries (Giroux, 2001) within the critical, academic study of 'sport' and thereby open the field to a broader constitution of interests and possibilities. We are not alone in such practices, there are many social scientists and interdisciplinary, post-structural feminists (including those within 'sport') who value innovative and civic pedagogic practices and democratic curricula, values and practices; in spite, in part because, of a corporatized higher education system. Further, we suggest that any form of academic 'othering', any academic hierarchies or binaries, are unproductive in developing knowledge of sport, leisure and physical cultures. Ground within a feminist communitarian ethic/praxis (*sensu* hooks, 1994), we tentatively reflect on pedagogical approaches that, we believe, can aid in *opening up* the critical potentialities of *the* field, promote democratic knowledge, and ensure our curricula as spaces for praxis, vibrancy, innovation, critique, debate and equality. We locate our curricular development and pedagogical practices within the long histories of feminist work that bridge theory/practice, incorporate personal transformation, advocate for experiential, community, social-change oriented pedagogies and reflective teaching practices (see e.g. Naples, 2013; Naples and Bojar, 2013; E. C. Rose, 2013; St Peter, 1997; also Kirk, 2014 on physical education).

Moving beyond a bare physical pedagogy

With Giroux (2010a, 2010b), the dominant form of academic 'sport' programmes in higher education institutions embrace – to differing degrees – the economic and political rationalities of a neoliberal market. This 'bare pedagogy' 'strips education of its public values, critical contents and civic responsibilities as part of its broader goal of creating new subjects wedded to the logic of privatization, efficiency, flexibility, the accumulation of capital and the destruction of the social state' (Giroux, 2010a: 185). Moreover, compassion is deemed a weakness and moral responsibility is scorned given it places human needs over market considerations. Following Stephen Ball (2012), within the context of neoliberal 'reformation', 'sport' educators are increasingly being required to make themselves *more calculable than memorable*. Ball (ibid.: 18) argues that within a new paradigm of education built on competitive advantage, professionals themselves have to be re-invented as units whose productivity can be audited, in short this accountability and preoccupation with reporting on what we do rather than doing it has bought about 'a profound shift in our relationships to ourselves, our practice, and the possibilities of being an academic'. With Ball, this new academic performativity is built on the enterprising academic, who, drawing on Weber is a 'specialist without spirit' that makes it near on impossible for some universities to do what they do best – enabling people to think. The very performance then of pedagogic practice has become subjectified – the very structures of domination have been sedimented on the bodies of 'teachers' – with the realities of practice taking place within the 'constraining normativities of an increasingly corporatized academy' (Brenner, 2006: 3; cf. Sonu, 2012). For Ball (2012: 20) this results in an 'ontological insecurity' in which increasingly disconnected academics wander aimlessly – in a sort of third space distant from academic freedom, thinking space and the dictates of accountability and performativity – with a 'loss of a sense of meaning in what we do and of what is important in what we do'.

The epistemic corroboration of a bare and performative academic normativity is a positivist objectivism that underpins *scientific method*, as conventionally understood. Both are constituents, and simultaneously constitutors, of a particular understanding of modernity, centred around linear evolutionary assumptions pertaining to the (assumed) inexorable progress of human civilization through the advancement of empirically grounded – often a euphemism for quantitatively driven and objectively reasoned – science. Hence, the scientific hegemony presently in place within the corporatized university speaks not to the veracity of the scientific method *per se*, but to the political economy of the university (e.g. Nandy, 1988; Rutherford, 2005). By reinforcing the primacy of 'high-quality science' (Lather, 2006: 35), the meaning and purpose of higher education has become besieged by a phalanx of narrow economic and political interests (Giroux, 2010a: 188). Consequently, the corporate brand is more important than any mission to educate free moral agents (Giroux and Searls-Giroux, 2012; see also Barnett and Griffin, 1997; Evans, 2004; Readings, 1996). Science then reductively becomes a 'reason of state' (Nandy, 1988), far from an epistemological accident: it is quintessentially reductionist and related to the needs of a particular form of economic organization based on exploitation, profit maximization and capital accumulation (Shiva, 1988). 'Scientific knowledge' in this sense is political through and through; a knowledge ground within our contemporary social and political conditions that authorize particular regimes of truth (Murray et al., 2007). Of course, 'scientific knowledge' and 'scientists' in and of itself/themselves are far from homogeneous, and there exist an array of critical practitioners who understand the partisan and partial nature of knowledge and whom engage reflexively with new ideas. Furthermore, as Evans et al. (2013) pointed out, it is nothing but unhelpful and unproductive to 'other' science/scientists or to create binaries and academic polarizations. This is not our intent or indeed our point. Instead, to advance a holistic understanding of the body/of active embodiment we need multiple knowledges, truths and understandings (Pavlidis and Fullagar, 2014). With Dallas Rogers (2012), we are more concerned about the politics of (and technocratic right to) place boundaries around what can be counted as 'truth'. We thus are attuned to the problematics of a dangerously naïve commonsense view on truth (Murray et al., 2007) that fails to recognize the political workings of power which silently operate behind the mask of objectivity, inscribe rigid norms and standards that ensure political dominance, and set the agenda with regard to what questions about 'truth' can be asked and by whom. It is, quite simply, a mechanism of power that has co-opted and corporatized all aspects of learning (both the construction and understanding of learning) and re-interprets them as competition, privatization and profiteering (Cannella, 2011; see also Lincoln and Cannella, 2004; Lakoff, 2006; Stevenson, 2010).

The 'pornography' (Giroux and Searls-Giroux, 2012) of such a reductionist view of science (which perhaps impacts on the 'free-hand' of science as much as those positioned lower down the 'sport' pecking order, those in the 'social sciences') has materialized in the academic field of sport. Research, teaching and academic performativity and legitimacy have become infused with one of the most significant *irrationalities* of higher education *rationality*: namely, an epistemological empirical calculability that for the most part has embraced the doctrines and *standards* of logical positivism[1] and its correlative, constrictive curricular efficiency (see especially Andrews, 2008; Bairner, 2012; Gill, 2007). As Ingham and Donnelly famously opined (1990: 59), humanistic knowledge has definitely suffered at the hands of 'technocratic' scientific knowledge currently privileged within an epistemological prestige hierarchy that frames the field. While departments may pay 'lip service to the liberal education curriculum' within the 'contested terrain' of sport, the 'humanistic intellectual' is habitually forced to view the (scientific) 'technical intelligentsia' as an overbearing and resource-hogging adversary, as opposed to equal ally. The 'technological intelligentsia', however, oftentimes consider 'humanistic intellectualizing' to be superfluous, and thereby expendable, 'teachers' (used derogatively at best) that have been left behind within the neoliberal institution. As a consequence, and despite differential engagements/negotiations with a corporatized neoliberal agenda, 'sport' departments tend either to be exclusively bio-science focused, or unapologetically bio-science centric (the social sciences and humanities being grudgingly tolerated, but habitually under-funded and under-supported, and needing to 'prove' their worth and often 'conform' to prescribed, nee 'legitimate', standards). Any ontological or epistemological positions that may run counter to this, that might enable students to develop critical and analytical skills that hold power accountable, or that develop a sense of prophetic justice (Giroux, 2010a), are usually viewed with suspicion at best and outright hostility at worst. In short, the field is dominated (to its detriment) by self-destructive versions of reductionist science that (subconsciously) act as insidious components of the social and economic condition that privileges 'state' science (Murray et al., 2007) – science that is embedded within, and looks to expand, neoliberal, militarized, economic modes of governance and efficiency.

Such reductionist orthodoxies are not just damaging; they fail to do justice to the potentialities of 'the physical' and the work of academics from all disciplines interested in furthering inter-, trans- and multi-disciplinary understandings and overcoming social, political and health inequalities. Indeed, a *lean* and *mean* sport science (see Andrews et al., 2013) in which it is explicitly clear to see *whose knowledge counts* (Ingham and Donnelly, 1990) within the *prestige hierarchies* of the contemporary university, precludes the development of our disciplines and ultimately destabilizes the possibilities for higher education as a site of intellectual advancement, social justice and critical and autonomous thinking. Informed by Foucault (2005), privileging this type of knowledge that tells us *why* 'we, as humans, act this way or that' rather than '*how* it is that such ways of being are possible – what the conditions are that make certain subjectivities possible' (Pavlidis and Fullagar, 2014: 27 emphasis in original) puts higher education at risk of reinstating rather than rejecting 'truth claims' about absolute 'science' and a unified notion of 'human nature'. As such, forsaking such epistemological hierarchies in favour of more epistemologically balanced, empirically wholesome and intellectually stimulating fare can aid in providing the conditions for pedagogical practices that can do more than just reproduce the 'contemporary landscape of political intelligibility and possibility' (Brown, 2006: 693).

Towards the 'physical'

As with the tenor of this book generally, we use the term (the) 'physical' rather deliberately, for it marks our approach to displace and decentre dominant disciplinary approaches. Through democratizing 'sport', by moving beyond an over-determined focus on elite professional sport, we can begin to have conversations with students about all manner of iterations of being physical. Our starting point is that the physical can never be substantial (possessing some fixed, immutable essence), rather, it is unavoidably relational, and always in process, yet its contemporaneous iteration provides a persuasive – if illusionary – semblance of fixity within what is an ever-changing world. As such, our pedagogic practices/curricula cannot be limited to an understanding of sport or problems specific to physical cultural forms, practices, subjectivities and experiences (if there are any) – this would not do justice to the potentialities of the field. A critical 'sports studies' is not just about the physically active/sporting body; it is, as Denzin (2012) argues, and as we attempt to represent in our curricula and pedagogic practices, about the articulations between physically (in)active bodies and spaces of violence, global terror, neoliberal regimes, identity, self, gender, queer bodies of colour, bilingual belongings, and public education in globalizing times – it is about postcolonial intellectuals decolonizing the academy, freedom, social justice, border crossings, the voices of oppression, and democracy.

These articulations focus on debunking the compelling mythology within 'sport' that the body is an exclusively biological organism. Again, and with a great debt, Ingham's (1997: 176) theorizing shapes our approach to the curricula; the 'body is, at the same time, both physical and cultural … the genetically endowed is socially constituted or socially constructed, as well as socially constituting and constructing'. In this sense, the body is as much a social, cultural, philosophical and historical entity as it is a genetic, physiological and psychological vessel. There are important, interpretive engagements that are needed to render possible otherwise inaccessible interpretations and understandings of the active body/human movement. Such social and cultural dimensions of corporeality simply cannot be imagined, let alone understood, using a logical positivist predilection for identifying and testing the existence of objective rationalities and interventions. Nonetheless, within some circles, the myth of the natural body persists, and is effectively reinforced through the institutional (overt and covert) promotion of the *natural* bio-scientific dimensions of kinesiology.

In our previous work (see Andrews et al., 2013; Bush et al., 2012; Francombe-Webb, 2014; Silk et al., 2010, 2014, 2015) we have offered nothing but tentative thoughts and reflections on what a physical pedagogic approach might (not *ought* to) look like; a trans-/inter-disciplinary field as both constitutor and constituent of a *critical curriculum of the corporeal*. This draws on a range of sometimes innovative and mostly experimental pedagogic practices that we hope provide classrooms that encourage the development of politically progressive languages of, and possibilities for, social justice and democratic discussion/citizenship. Ground within a feminist communitarian and liberatory ethic and with the mores of the 'slow movement' (see Hartman and Darab, 2012; Silk et al., 2014) – albeit in tension with the use of fast technologies in practices such as 'flipped classrooms' (see Silk et al., 2015) – we have been finely attuned to the fact that having an 'impact', an agenda that sets out to 'make a difference', should not abandon the classroom. With Garbutt and Offord (2012), we advocate for a compelling and urgent need for curricula/pedagogy activated by ethical imperatives and concerns; forms of pedagogy that can consider relations of freedom, authority, democratic knowledge and responsibility, and which can do justice to the diverse narratives, issues, histories, embodied experiences, affective flows and contexts we are likely to encounter as part of the pedagogical process (Giroux, 2010a). We do so in the hope that our curricula and pedagogic practices are produced in the

> spirit of a critical democracy ... with the knowledge, passion, civic capacity, public value, and social responsibility necessary to address the problems facing the nation and the globe ... [an approach that challenges] the existence of rigid disciplinary boundaries, the cult of expertise or highly specialized scholarship unrelated to public life, and anti-democratic ideologies that scoff at the exercise of academic freedom.
> *(Giroux, 2010a: 187)*

Physical pedagogic possibilities

We do not 'have' a body; rather we 'are' bodily.
(Heidegger, 1997: 98–99)

Building on Heidegger (1997), if we 'are' bodily then claims to know the body through positivist scientific perspectives are remiss as, following Denzin (2012: 298), the 'active, agentic flesh-and-blood human body' is radically contextual and embodiment is complex. Such a starting point has implications for the ways in which we understand the process and experience of education and curriculum development and clearly raises questions about 'the constancy of immutable facts, scientific or otherwise, removed from the value inhered by active human observers' (Horn and Wilburn, 2005: 749). Instead of viewing our teaching and research as a positivist science, we understand it to be a practice, an 'art', and a site of pedagogic possibility that questions normalized cultural narrations of embodied existence (Denzin, 2012; Macintyre and Buck, 2008). This form of embodied learning entails that we 'seek to draw out complexities and create anew' (Pavlidis and Fullagar, 2014: 25) and it generates theories and knowledges in which the body is inseparable from our being in the world, our language, our histories and our politics. This challenges 'traditional views of learning that focus on either the gathering and cataloguing of pre-defined facts or the honing of prescribed methods of thinking' (Horn and Wilburn, 2005: 751–752) by instead acknowledging that our curricula are emergent. Thus, we need to read outwards from physically active/inactive bodies and situate these stories within the historical present, and open up a space for utopian imaginaries. As extant feminist theorizing has highlighted, this focus on embodied subject formations is wrought with complexity around the 'multiple affective layers, complex temporal variables, and internally contradictory time and memory lines that frame our embodied existence' (Braidotti, 2011: 25). As, Braidotti (ibid.) goes on to say, the feminist emphasis on embodiment, moving towards the affective and the process of becoming go 'hand in hand with a radical rejection of essentialism'.

In fact, our rejection of essentialism while embodied and concerned with affective repertoires is also framed by a 'commitment to radical democratic social transformation' (Kellner, 2001: 221). We advocate the development of a corporeal curriculum that is politically motivated and encourages students to take up positions as oppositional public intellectuals who intervene in and confront inequality. Building on Brophy and Hladki (2012), as well as Titchkosky (2012), this border work involves curricular development that is bound to a political and moral commitment to critically analyse the cultural and corporeal, locate the historical specificities of the conjuncture, and 'theorise out' in a way that not only names the problems in society but produces critical public spaces in which action can take place (Giroux, 2001). Such a corporeal curriculum can help in reshaping understandings of (ab)normalcy, wellness, inclusion/exclusion, the presence/absence of the body and its representations. With E. C. Rose (2013), this is a curriculum that recognizes the realities of our fleshly nature and examines the possibilities and constraints that flow from it.

Through our teaching practices we encourage our students to interrogate the power formations that flow and are expressed in forms of representation and social institutions. This is power that flows between the 'inner and the outer' (Braidotti, 2011: 17). We therefore, like many others within our various disciplines, are fostering curricula that take us beyond 'bare' physical pedagogy as an instrument of neoliberal legitimization; an approach that may require *slowing down* and reflection. With Giroux (2010a), we want to provide students with pedagogical practices that create a formative culture and safe space for development of humanistic bodily knowledges, technical knowledge, scientific skill and a mode of literacy that enables them to engage and transform (when necessary) the promise of a global democracy. A *slow* curricula centred on democratic values, identities and practices, can be a space for students to

> embrace pedagogical encounters as spaces of dialogue and unmitigated questioning, to imagine different futures, to become border crossers establishing a range of new connections and global relations, and to embrace a language of critique and possibility that responds to the urgent need to reclaim democratic values, identities and practices.
>
> *(Giroux, 2009: 691)*

We are thus strongly promoting the classroom as a space that connects the personal, the political and the cultural and that helps people experientially reflect, connect theory/practice, think critically, historically, sociologically, and think through affect. These approaches, and our future directions, are influenced by those whose work is constantly challenging the 'separations between nature and culture, the mind and the body, the corporeal and the textual, and the higher and the lower, which are naturalized' (Blackman, 2012: 45). In turning towards the affective we are attempting to further develop an embodied, corporeal curriculum predicated in relational ontologies and to advance our students' understandings of the concepts that already emerge across our research-led teaching – around governance, neoliberalism, Foucauldian analysis, technicity, consumer culture. To do this we initiate critical, dynamic, consciousness raising conversations that disrupt the discourses of the centre and the margins – moving in and between the inner and outer flows of power (Braidotti, 2011) – and we focus on the physical body. As such, we allow the body to move, gesture, exercise, dance, present, perform, work and so on, in ways that inevitable mean an entanglement of the embodied, emplaced (Pink, 2011), cognitive and epistemological in order to allow for a fuller exposition of the cultures of the body that are being experienced. Our role then, is to act as a catalyst for conscientization (Christians, 2005; Freire, 1973), to not only ask questions of *why* but also of *how*, and this 'involve[s] the use of human wisdom in the process of bringing about a better and more just world ... [we] are profoundly concerned with who we are, how we got this way, and where we might go from here' (Kincheloe and McLaren, 2005: 309).

Of course, theoretically, this all sounds logical, simplistic, easy! However, we appreciate, as Pavlidis and Fullagar (2014) do, that this is far from the case. They caution that the interruptions we initiate need to be considered carefully; 'we must be cautious about what our interruptions might do and how they may be received' (ibid.: 29). This is especially true given the orthodoxy of the scientific episteme within the corporatized university. In our own positions, we have had to have difficult conversations with colleagues in the hard sciences and with university administrators – sometimes with, and sometimes without, success – for the legitimacy and value of critical, interpretive and reflexive forms of intellectualizing in sport. We have aimed to centralize social justice and, as self-reflexive academics, attempted to hold on to the principles of democratic knowledge production. As such we have needed to *negotiate* principles *and* pragmatism, an institutionalized market ethos *and* our anti-/post-capitalist sensibilities, one of anomie *and* compromise, politics *and* Politics, tolerance *and* alienation, conformity *and* creativity, deference *and* the strategic decentring of academic prestige hierarchies.

We take 'teaching' *very* seriously and deem it to be crucial to the future shape, direction and relevance of both physical cultural studies and of the fields of employment our graduates enter. We have often found it very hard, within a highly competitive marketplace for students, to remain true to such values while at the same time serving a student body who, initially at least, want to know how we will aid them plug into an existing political and economic order. We also find it increasingly difficult to ensure diversity within the classroom when the possibilities of a higher education (at least in the UK) are increasingly foreclosed for anyone other than the middle/upper classes (see e.g. Reay et al., 2009) with 'good grades' (to ensure league table metrics are satisfied).

In our efforts to overcome – or *negotiate* – these tensions, we have engaged in, perhaps somewhat counter-intuitively, active relationships with employers as part of curriculum development and restructuring. We do not aim, however, to produce functional and productive clones; a production line of potential employees. Rather, we want our graduates to be relevantly skilled in the employment pathways chosen, but who are also engaged in transformative (as opposed to processual) knowledge and thinking, who have undertaken critical (self)reflexive learning (as opposed to followed an instrumental logic that celebrates the bottom line), who have at the heart of the subject matter broad values of democracy and who have engaged with critical physical pedagogies that draw attention to the production of knowledge and the way subject positions are 'brought into being' and affectively realized as part of day-to-day interactions between students, between employers and students and between staff and students. We aim for our curricula to provide the conditions that allow for behaviour to unfold and which offer skills for thinking critically and affectively about knowledge production and resources for creatively realizing and disseminating this knowledge. This, we hope, is far from just 'job training'.

Underpinning this approach has been the creation of thematic units which do not rely on a single discipline or theoretical assumption and in which views from history, sociology, cultural studies, psychology, gender studies, urban studies, media studies, women's studies, critical race theory, politics, geography and so on can come to bear relationally on understandings of physical culture. These units cover a gamut of issues, not exclusively limited to: globalization and (international) development; (un)healthy and physically (in)active bodies; mental health; abuses of power; the discursive constitution of the body; bio-pedagogies; physically active bodies and power relations; issues of surveillance, security, and governance within our city spaces and popular sporting texts; militarization and terrorism; the specificities of clinical populations;

cultural technologies (such as the internet, social media, popular and promotional cultures); social inequalities and social justice; ethics; the economic and political rationalities of neoliberalism and neoconservatism; and, the discursive constitution of bodies, health and well-being. We aim to link theory/practice/embodiment, and use theory as a resource to think and act, so that it allows us to situate physical culture within historical and institutional contexts, and to aid students to create the conditions for collective struggles over resources and power and where needed mobilize instances of collective outrage against discursive and material inequalities as they are manifest in our physical worlds (Giroux, 2001). This has of course been challenging, for students, for colleagues, for ourselves; not least in our efforts to influence units in sports coaching – an admittedly formative subject ensconced in an elite performance agenda. Our efforts here have been to question a staid, static and unquestioning ontological base, rethinking our curricula as a plurality of (often competing) approaches and perspectives and through which we can (re)imagine differing instances of 'coaching' as socially and culturally responsive, communitarian and justice oriented (see e.g. Bush and Silk, 2010; Bush et al., 2012). With differing degrees of success, our aim has been to provide multiple opportunities, spaces and possibilities where the body (ours and our students), again materially and discursively, is 'put to work' within what we hope are innovative, creative, and often individually designed *corporeal curricula*. These spaces include, for example, presentations, performance art, narrative writing, autoethnography, integration of innovative digital creativity, exhibitions, developing online personas and platforms that consider alternative realities and more equitable public/bodily pedagogies (see especially Silk et al., 2015 for a self-reflexive discussion of the types of pedagogic practice we have attempted).

We can, for sure, do far better than we have done (and we continue to learn from our colleagues around the world who do better than us) as we grapple with these tensions. At this juncture, there exist 'metrics' of success (such as in employability and student 'rankings' of satisfaction) but a corporeal curriculum of possibility warrants more malleable metrics reflective of 'learning the body' – how do we/should we 'measure' the citizens we hope we are producing? For now, our goal, following N. Rose (2013: 24), is to do our best within the orthodoxies of our current context to enable a pedagogic space that can 'accept that the social and human sciences are also sciences of the living, of living bodies, of living matter, of matter that has been made to live'; a recognition that we hope can aid our disciplines – through the curriculum as praxis – to help remake our human world for the better.

Note

1   We do not suggest discarding such advances, yet we do oppose parochialism and domination and the ways in which the conventions of this particular approach become accepted as the natural way of producing knowledge and viewing a particular aspect of the world.

References

Andrews, D. (2008). Kinesiology's Inconvenient Truth and the Physical Cultural Studies Imperative. *Quest*, 60 (1), 45–62.
Andrews, D. L., Silk, M. L., Bush, A. J. and Francombe, J. (2013). McKinesiology. *Review of Education, Pedagogy, and Cultural Studies*, 35 (5), 335–356.
Bairner, A. (2012). For a Sociology of Sport. *Sociology of Sport Journal*, 29 (1), 102–117.
Ball, S. J. (2012). Performativity, Commodification and Commitment: An I-Spy Guide to the Neoliberal University. *British Journal of Educational Studies*, 60, 17–28.
Barnett, R. and Griffin, A. (eds). (1997). *The End of Knowledge in Higher Education*. London: Cassell.
Blackman, L. (2012). *Immaterial Bodies: Affect, Embodiment, Mediation*. London: Sage.

Braidotti, R. (2011). *Nomadic Subjects*, 2nd edn. New York: Columbia University Press.
Brenner, D. (2006). Performative Pedagogy: Resignifying Teaching in the Corporatized University. *Review of Education, Pedagogy, and Cultural Studies*, 28 (1), 3–24.
Brophy, S. and Hladki, J. (2012). Introduction: Pedagogy, Image Practices, and Contested Corporealities. *The Review of Education*, 34, 75–81.
Brown, W. (2006). American Nightmare: Neoliberalism, Neoconservatism, and De-democratization. *Political Theory*, 34 (6), 690–714.
Bush, A. and Silk, M. (2010). Towards an Evolving Critical Consciousness in Coaching Research: The Physical Pedagogic Bricolage. *International Journal of Sport Science and Coaching*, 5 (4), 551–565.
Bush, A., Silk, M., Lauder, H. and Andrews, D. (2012). *Sports Coaching Research: Contexts, Consequences and Consciousness*. London: Routledge.
Cannella, G. S. (2011). Political Possibility, Hypercapitalism, and the 'Conservative Reeducation Machine'. *Cultural Studies ↔ Critical Methodologies*, 11 (4), 364–368.
Christians, C. (2005). Ethics and Politics in Qualitative Research. In N. K. Denzin and Y. S. Lincoln (eds), *Handbook of Qualitative Research*, 3rd edn (pp. 139–164). Thousand Oaks, CA: Sage.
Denzin, N. (2012). Afterword. In M. Silk, and D. Andrews (ed.), *Sport and Neoliberalism: Politics, Consumption and Culture* (pp. 294–302). Philadelphia, PA: Temple.
Evans, M. (2004). *Killing Thinking: The Death of the Universities*. London: Continuum.
Evans, J., Davies, B. and Rich, E. (2013). We/You Can Tell Talk from Matter: A Conversation with Hakan Larrson and Mikael Quennerstedt. *Sport, Education and Society*, 19 (5), 652–665.
Foucault, M. (2005). *Madness and Civilisation*. Abingdon: Routledge.
Francombe-Webb, J. (2014). Learning to Leisure: Femininity and Practices of the Body. *Leisure Studies*, 33 (6), 580–597.
Freire, P. (1973). *Education for Critical Consciousness*. New York: Continuum.
Garbutt, R. and Offord, B. (2012). A Scholarly Affair: Activating Cultural Studies. *Review of Education, Pedagogy, and Cultural Studies*, 34 (1–2), 3–7.
Gill, D. L. (2007). Integration: The Key to Sustaining Kinesiology in Higher Education. *Quest*, 59 (3), 270–286.
Giroux, H. (2001). 'Something's Missing': Cultural Studies, Neoliberalism and the Politics of Hope. *Strategies: Journal of Theory, Culture and the Politics*, 14 (2), 227–252.
Giroux, H. (2009). Democracy's Nemesis: The Rise of the Corporate University. *Cultural Studies ↔ Critical Methodologies*, 9 (5), 669–695.
Giroux, H. (2010a). Bare Pedagogy and the Scourge of Neoliberalism: Rethinking Higher Education as a Democratic Public Sphere. *The Educational Forum*, 74 (3), 184–196.
Giroux, H. (2010b). Dumbing Down Teachers: Rethinking the Crisis of Public Education and the Demise of the Social State. *Review of Education, Pedagogy and Cultural Studies*, 32 (4), 339–381.
Giroux, H. and Searls-Giroux, S. (2012). Universities Gone Wild: Big Money, Big Sports, and Scandalous Abuse at Penn State. *Cultural Studies ↔ Critical Methodologies*, 12 (4), 267–273.
Hartman, Y. and Darab, S. (2012). A Call for Slow Scholarship: A Case Study on the Intensification of Academic Life and its Implications for Pedagogy. *Review of Education, Pedagogy and Cultural Studies*, 34 (1–2), 49–60.
Heidegger, M. (1997). *Nietzsche*. San Francisco: Harper.
hooks, b. (1994). *Teaching to Transgress: Education as the Practice of Freedom*. Abingdon: Routledge.
Horn, J. and Wilburn, D. (2005). The Embodiment of Learning. *Educational Philosophy and Theory*, 37 (5), 745–760.
Ingham, A. G. (1997). Toward a Department of Physical Cultural Studies and an End to Tribal Warfare'. In J. Fernandez-Balboa (ed.), *Critical Postmoderism in Human Movement, Physical Education, and Sport* (pp. 157–182). Albany, NY: State University cf New York Press.
Ingham, A. G. and Donnelly, P. (1990). Whose Knowledge Counts? The Production of Knowledge and Issues of Application in the Sociology of Sport. *Sociology of Sport Journal*, 7 (1), 58–65.
Kellner, D. (2001). Critical Pedagogy, Cultural Studies, and Radical Democracy at the Turn of the Millennium: Reflections on the Work of Henry Giroux. *Cultural Studies ↔ Critical Methodologies*, 1 (2), 221–239.
Kincheloe, J. L. and McLaren, P. (2005). Rethinking Critical Theory and Qualitative Research. In Y. S. Lincoln and N. K. Denzin (eds), *The Sage Handbook of Qualitative Research*, 3rd edn (pp. 303–342). Thousand Oaks, CA: Sage.
Kirk, D. (2014). *Physical Education and Curriculum Study: A Critical Introduction*. London: Routledge.

Lakoff, G. (2006). *Whose Freedom? The Battle Over America's Most Important Idea*. New York: Farrar, Straus & Giroux.
Lather, P. (2006). This is Your Father's Paradigm: Government Intrusion and the Case of Qualitative Research in Education. In N. Denzin and M. Giardina (ed.), *Qualitative Research and the Conservative Challenge*. Walnut Creek, CA: Left Coast Press.
Lincoln, Y. and Cannella, G. (2004). Dangerous Discourses, Methodological Fundamentalism, and Governmental Regimes of Truth. *Qualitative Inquiry*, 10 (1), 5–14.
Macintyre, L. M. and Buck, G. (2008). Enfleshing Embodiment: 'Falling into Trust' with the Body's Role in Teaching and Learning. *Educational Philosophy and Theory*, 40 (2), 315–329.
Murray, S. J., Holmes, D., Perron, A. and Rail, G. (2007). No Exit? Intellectual Integrity Under the Regime of 'Evidence' and 'Best-Practices'. *Journal of Evaluation in Clinical Practice*, 13, 512–516.
Nandy, A. (1988). Science as a Reason of State. In A. Nandy (ed.), *Science, Hegemony and Violence: A Requiem for Modernity*. Oxford: Oxford University Press.
Naples, N. (2013). The Dynamics of Critical Pedagogy, Experiential Learning and Feminist Praxis in Women's Studies. In N. Naples and K. Bojar (eds), *Teaching Feminist Activism: Strategies from the Field*. London: Routledge.
Naples, N. and Bojar, K. (eds). (2013). *Teaching Feminist Activism: Strategies from the Field*. London: Routledge.
Pavlidis, A. and Fullagar, S. (2014). *Sport, Gender and Power: The Rise of Roller Derby*. Farnham: Ashgate.
Pink, S. (2011). From Embodiment to Emplacement: Re-thinking Competing Bodies, Senses and Spatialities. *Sport, Education and Society* 16 (3): 343–355.
Readings, B. (1996). *The University in Ruins*. Cambridge, MA: Harvard University Press.
Reay, D., Crozier, J. and Clayton, J. (2009). Strangers in Paradise: Working-class Students in Elite Universities. *Sociology*, 43 (6), 1103–1121.
Ritzer, G. (2004). *The McDonaldization of Society* (Revised New Century Edition ed.). London: Sage.
Rogers, D. (2012). Research, Practice and the Space Between: Care of the Self Within Neoliberalized Institutions. *Cultural Studies ↔ Critical Methodologies*, 12 (3), 242–254.
Rose, E. C. (2013). Activism and the Women's Studies Curriculum. In N. Naples and K. Bojar (eds), *Teaching Feminist Activism: Strategies from the Field*. London: Routledge.
Rose, N. (2013). The Human Sciences in a Biological Age. *Theory, Culture and Society*, 30 (3), 3–34.
Rutherford, J. (2005). Cultural Studies in the Corporate University, *Cultural Studies*, 19 (3), 297–317.
St Peter, C. (1997). Introduction to Women's Studies in Focus: Field-based Learning in the Practicum Course. *Atlantis*, 22 (1), 109.
Shiva, V. (1988). Reductionist Science as Epistemological Violence. In A. Nandy (ed.), *Science, Hegemony and Violence: A Requiem for Modernity*. Oxford: Oxford University Press.
Silk, M., Bush, A. and Andrews, D. (2010). Contingent Intellectual Amateurism; or, What is Wrong with Evidence Based Research. *Journal of Sport and Social Issues*, 34 (1), 105–128.
Silk, M., Francombe-Webb, J. and Andrews, D. (2014). Slowing the Social Sciences of Sport: On the Possibilities of Physical Culture. *Sport in Society*, 17 (9), 1–24.
Silk, M., Francombe-Webb, J., Rich, E. and Merchant, S. (2015). On the Transgressive Possibilities of Physical Pedagogic Practices. *Qualitative Inquiry*, 21 (9), 798–811.
Sonu, D. (2012). Illusions of Compliance: Performing the Public and Hidden Transcripts of Social Justice Education in Neoliberal Times. *Curriculum Inquiry*, 42 (2), 240–259.
Stevenson, N. (2010). Critical Pedagogy, Democracy and Capitalism: Education Without Enemies or Borders. *Review of Education, Pedagogy and Cultural Studies*, 32 (1), 66–92.
Titchkosky, T. (2012). The Ends of the Body as Pedagogic Possibility. *Review of Education, Pedagogy, and Cultural Studies*, 34 (3–4): 82–93.

56
SPORT, DEVELOPMENT AND SOCIAL CHANGE

Shawn Forde, Devra Waldman, Lyndsay M. C. Hayhurst and Wendy Frisby

Introduction: beginning the long walk towards social change

In beginning a chapter on social change and sport in a handbook on physical cultural studies (PCS), it is maybe fitting to draw inspiration from Paolo Freire. In outlining the process through which Myles Horton and Freire (Horton, Bell, Gaventa, and Peters, 1990: 6) would 'talk a book' about education and social change, Freire stated: 'I think that even though we need to have some outline, I am sure that we make the road by walking.' Freire's phrase is important for us for two reasons. First, it captures the spirit of our chapter. The four of us share an interest in discussing the relationships between sport and social change and we have conceived of this chapter as an open and ongoing dialogue, hopefully one that will interest, and be an invitation to, other scholars and practitioners passionate about sport, physical culture, and social change. Second, Freire's phrase parallels the thoughts of another prominent thinker. In his autobiography, Nelson Mandela stated:

> I have walked that long road to freedom. I have tried not to falter; I have made missteps along the way. But I have discovered the secret that after climbing a great hill, one only finds that there are many more hills to climb.
>
> (Mandela, 1994: 625)

Both Freire and Mandela draw on walking as a metaphor for struggle, learning, and social change. However, this quotation from Mandela is not what many interested in sport and social change draw from; instead, the common refrain is based on a speech in which Mandela (2000) stated 'sport has the power to change the world'. We believe that the latter quote is often mobilized in ways that privilege sport as a particular form of physical culture, and conflate conceptions of peace and social change with specific understandings of development. Drawing inspiration from the former quote, a metaphor relating to walking, we feel that engaging with a broader understanding of physical culture could promote discussion relating to how 'active bodies become organized, disciplined, represented, embodied, and experienced in mobilizing (or corroborating), or at times immobilizing (or resisting), the conjunctural inflections and operations of power within a society' (Andrews and Silk, 2015).

As we began to collaborate for this chapter, the second annual International Day of Sport for Development and Peace had recently concluded. In his speech on the inaugural day, United Nations Secretary-General Ban Ki-Moon stated that 'Sport empowers youth, promotes good health and deepens UN values such as equality, mutual respect and fair play. Sport helps us in spreading messages of peace, driving social change and meeting the Millennium Development Goals' (Moon, 2014). Within the blossoming sport for development and peace (SDP) sector, this line of rhetoric is quite common. Importantly, positioning sport as a tool to achieve development goals and conflating social change with this process can result in understandings of social change being limited to neoliberal conceptions of how individuals need to improve their own health, education, and income. In many contexts these are important goals, but imploring individuals to succeed within unequal societies, without questioning the roots of those inequalities, simply reproduces the status quo and we question how this can be understood as social change. The purpose of this chapter is not to critique dominant understandings of sport and development, or who has been able to construct them, as this has been done elsewhere (e.g. Darnell and Hayhurst, 2011; Hayhurst, 2009). Instead, we are interested in beginning a dialogue on how PCS and SDP might better inform one another, while more deeply interrogating the complexities of social change in different contexts.

Drawing on the work of Atkinson (2010; cf. Pronger, 2002), Wilson (2014) suggested that those in the field of SDP should not simply consider the rigid constructions of 'sport only' – but also activities such as yoga and fell running. The key argument to be made here is that these activities 'exist outside the capitalistic, hypercompetitive realm [that] might be understood as "post-sport" activities because they are sport-like (e.g. in their physicality), *but lack the dominant and institutionalized features*' of mainstream sports (Wilson, 2014: 24, italics added for emphasis). Indeed, it seems that those involved with SDP, or who identify with broader 'sport for social change' efforts, have been somewhat limited by an exclusive focus on 'sport', and perhaps even 'play', as they take place within dominant institutionalized forms and structures. In this way, we hope that bringing SDP and PCS into conversation with one another offers possibilities for more nuanced discussions relating to sport and social change. More specifically, and for the most part, we believe that those interested in SDP would benefit from considering the ways that physical culture bespeaks 'the broader political shifts and power relations the human body brings to life' (Giardina and Newman, 2011: 41); or, as David Harvey (2000: 119) stated, 'the body as a locus of political action'. To date, what has been relatively absent in conceptualizations of SDP and its positioning of sport for social change, has been an understanding of how we might illuminate and foreground the body as it moves through conjunctures of time and space, ideas and practice (cf. Giardina and Newman, 2011). In this light, we might ask: how does the body enact social change and challenge systems and practices of oppression – the very same systems and practices often (cl)aimed to be tackled through SDP programmes? Also, how can broader understandings of SDP, in conversation with PCS, work towards social change/praxis? Here, we are interested in Harvey's call for the study of the body to be conducted in ways so that 'real spatio-temporal relations between material practices, representations, imaginaries, institutions, social relations and the prevailing structures of political-economic power [are considered]' (Harvey, 2000: 130). Scholars involved in SDP have already begun this journey (see Darnell and Hayhurst, 2011; Spaaij and Jeanes, 2013), and in many ways we are following Hartmann and Kwauk (2011: 296), who posited that sport within SDP should be 'reconceptualized as a space of 'physical' education'. Although these authors do not refer to PCS specifically, they share a common interest in the ways that a critical pedagogy embedded in physical culture can 'generate and circulate the type of knowledge that would enable individuals and groups to discern, challenge, and potentially transform existing power structures and relations as they are manifest within, and experienced through, the complex field of physical culture' (Andrews and Silk, 2015).

The aim of our chapter is not to provide answers to the questions we posed earlier. Nor are we attempting to define social change, describe ways in which social change occurs, or prescribe ways to facilitate social change. Rather, our goals are to raise questions and provide examples from our own research programmes that grapple with just a few of the complexities involved in the long walk towards social change. Thus, we see our chapter as an unavoidably ongoing and incomplete journey. The Uruguayan poet Eduardo Galeano wrote:

> She's on the horizon ... I go two steps, she moves two steps away. I walk ten steps and the horizon runs ten steps ahead. No matter how much I walk, I'll never reach her. What good is utopia? That's what: it's good for walking.
>
> (as cited in Duncombe, 2007)

Although the above statement seems cynical, Galeano did not mean it as such. He believed that dreaming of and imagining a better world was imperative for social change and that utopia should not be visualized as a concrete and realizable paradise, but as an always unfinished project.

In the remainder of this chapter, and in the spirit of initiating a dialogue, each author presents a vignette that they feel challenges how sport and social change has been conceptualized. We use the term vignette, as our examples are meant to be brief, descriptive, and generative, as opposed to being complete analytical accounts. Devra begins by describing a partnership between a cricket club and an international corporation that are planning to develop cricket communities throughout India. Those involved in SDP may not connect these leisure-based, gated communities with their work. That being said, Devra's vignette offers an ideal place for us to begin our walk, as it demonstrates how a more open and active engagement with physical practices and the body across a multitude of spaces can challenge our assumptions relating to the boundaries of social change and development. In a very literal way, these cricket communities demonstrate an imaginary of development that arguably underpins a great deal of work in SDP. Our next two vignettes focus on the often unexamined lived physical cultural practices of SDP participants. In both these vignettes, practices that happen outside of institutional confines of sport are examined. Lyndsay's vignette describes how participants in an SDP programme in Eastern Uganda, which was designed to promote sexual and reproductive health, engaged in physical practices in their daily lives that they described as acts of resistance. Wendy's vignette explains how community development practices in non-sport spaces in the Global North broadened physical cultural practices in a low-income community. Both provide a way of reflecting on how researcher and practitioner conceptions of the impact of social change were challenged through the lived experiences of programme participants. Shawn's concluding vignette explores the common-place idiom that sport serves as a tool for social change by advocating that SDP scholars and practitioners consider the physical cultural practices involved in protest. In a similar vein to the vignettes presented by Lyndsay and Wendy, Shawn's examples aim to generate discussion relating to conceptions of social change within both SDP and PCS.

Devra's vignette

In 2011 the Marylebone Cricket Club (MCC) (an exclusive members club and custodian of international cricket laws that operates out of Lord's cricket ground in London, England) entered into a partnership with an international real estate investment company, Anglo Indian (a British-based corporation that looks to promote international sport/lifestyle brands in India). The goal of the partnership is to develop twelve MCC/Lord's branded communities throughout India that feature a Lord's cricket ground, an exclusive MCC members club, a Lord's tavern-themed restaurant, and residential housing geared towards the middle/upper classes. To date, such structures have not often been considered by scholars studying SDP, yet a more open depiction of these forms of development (as PCS is not over-determined by sport) allows for such projects to be included in our understandings of sport and international community development. Particularly, this example reflects a literal manifestation of the use of sport in development processes, and represents the incorporation of broad 'international development' philosophies into larger development assemblages by corporate actors rather than the state.

By creating communities targeting upper-class citizens, and creating spaces designed for consumption of British lifestyle brands, this project is reminiscent of broader international development practices focused on promoting neoliberal development characterized by privatization, free market capitalism, and economic growth (Rist, 2008). In promotional materials, Anglo Indian asserts that they will 'deploy all of its experience of entering the market and our local knowledge to open and clinch deals that fulfill overseas ambitions' (Anglo Indian, 2013). By positioning themselves as the appropriate entities to promote development because of their British status and historic cricket superiority, these organizations are reproducing a well-established (neocolonial) development discourse that continues to promote British groups as originators of development ideas and the legitimate institutions through which 'development' takes place (Waldman et al., 2015).

The role/place of the MCC/cricket is important because the roots of this 'development' through sport were laid by the role the MCC played in the imperial mission, and the construction of cricket as the imperial game. For example, historically, many MCC members played key roles in both the cricket and political empire, leading some to argue that these empires became synonymous (Stoddart and Sandiford, 1998). In this project, conceptions of 'development' are narrowed by these histories as the ability of the MCC to enact social change remains entwined within the logics of colonialism. In these communities, the MCC is incorporating common SDP rhetoric through promoting the 'spirit of cricket' (characteristics such as integrity, dedication, responsibility) by ensuring the cricket facilities are open to those who would be unable to afford access (Waldman and Wilson, in press). However, politics of exclusion remain present and the paradox of development is clear, as this project is promoted as inclusive, yet also creates (physical) boundaries between those who are (selectively) allowed access. Ultimately, the MCC continues to contribute to understandings that institutions in the Global North have a moral responsibility to promote development and define acceptable and desirable development practices that take place in the Global South (Darnell, 2007).

While perhaps not in the sense of 'critical consciousness' as alluded to by Hartmann and Kwauk (2011), these master-planned, leisure-based communities are sites where issues of power relations manifest and are experienced in the context of international development. Particularly, the geography of these communities are spaces of 'physical education'. In the imaginations of space, the mimicked Lord's cricket ground, MCC private club, Lord's tavern, and international retail are placed in the centre of the community – thus what is considered most valuable. These are features that encourage the consumption of imagined/faux Englishness, with these selective ideologies mobilized to produce specific meanings of space that will be experienced by those living within these environments (Silk, 2007; Waldman et al., 2015). Simultaneously, these spaces might have disciplining effects on the body. The MCC/Anglo Indian are in a position to control the aesthetics of the environment and the permeability of these spaces. By having control over how these communities will 'look' and 'feel', and who will be selectively invited in through outreach programmes, these sites will become locations where (postcolonial) hierarchies and class relations will be experienced, and boundaries between 'in' and 'out' groups will be carefully negotiated and maintained (Waldman et al., 2015).

In what ways can Devra's research relating to these cricket communities contribute to discussions about social change, sport, and development? We believe that her example prompts a couple of important questions. First, although a leisure-based urban development may not seem related to the work that SDP organizations are doing, would it be accurate to say that SDP organizations share a similar understanding of development and social change? Would an SDP programme in India be considered successful if the majority of the participants in the programme were able to achieve the personal success and wealth that enable them to live in the type of exclusive development that Devra describes? If so, can this be considered social change or development?

Lyndsay's vignette

The majority of SDP interventions seem to pivot on the use of a particular sport or 'sportscape' (cf. Bale, 1994), and the ways these aim to potentially control and regiment the body. Often, (bio)pedagogical messages (for example, Western conceptualizations of what counts as 'hygiene' and 'healthy living') are interwoven into SDP curricula through the very act of participation in a specific sport in a particular space (Hayhurst, Giles and Wright, in press; Forde and Frisby, 2015). Indeed, through a gender-based violence prevention programme in a rural community in Eastern Uganda, young women were taught sexual and reproductive health education through the practice of karate and taekwondo (Hayhurst et al., 2014). They pursued these activities through a precise curriculum and pedagogical strategies designed to train their bodies to act in specific ways that (arguably) enabled them to defend themselves against sexual predators, while also promoting these young women's awareness of their sexual and reproductive health rights, and their right to a life without violence. In many ways, this research demonstrated that the girls in this programme gained confidence, self-esteem, and the audacity to challenge gender and cultural norms in their communities – and thus, one may argue that this constitutes social change – though the onus is problematically on these young women to be the instigators of this change (see Hayhurst, 2014). This research also uncovered how, as an (indirect) result of their confidence gained through participating in martial arts vis-à-vis the SDP programme, many of these young women started to bicycle to the local markets – even though bicycling is deemed an 'inappropriate' activity for young women to pursue in this particular community, believed to be 'damaging' to girls' and women's bodies. That is, they pursued bicycling despite the perceived risks and consequences of doing so.

Encouraging young women in this community to bicycle to the local market was not the original intent of the SDP programme; instead, this intervention used focused, structured karate and taekwondo sessions to instil these young women with 'agency' and 'choice' to expand their embodied physical cultures. And yet, the decision made by these young women to bicycle to the market was arguably one that was largely influenced by their participation in the more structured karate and taekwondo activities. That is, these Ugandan young women did not bicycle to the market because they were directly trained to do so through an SDP programme; and yet, this very act is still arguably a political one that uses the body to facilitate social change in this particular community. Notably, and problematically, these young women may experience a number of risks to their safety through this very act of resistance, as they seek to shift these norms.

The above-mentioned example demonstrates the value in taking up a physical cultural approach to exploring sport for social change, expanding our perceptions as to what 'counts' under the banner of SDP and PCS. In this light, it seems the time is ripe to examine the body in SDP as it passes through spaces in capricious ways. Traditionally, SDP programmes, or studies, consider interventions that use what Bale (1994: 13) referred to as 'sports landscapes', which, as he noted, 'are often the result of the exercise of power by one group over another [where] power may be reflected in landscapes where a strong degree of control is needed over people ... or where exclusion is on the basis of social or economic criteria'. In line with Bale's notion of sports landscapes are the rigid monitoring and evaluation schemes used by SDP programmes – what I have referred to previously as 'technologies of aid evaluation' – often linear, rigid systems created by donors in the West/North to 'keep tabs' on the work of the NGOs and 'targeted beneficiaries' they fund (see Hayhurst, in press; Darnell and Hayhurst, 2014). Often, these structured, donor-driven evaluation schemes overlook, or sometimes discount, the nuanced and culturally specific lived experiences of SDP programme participants, the unintended outcomes of these interventions and/or how their outcomes are (un)problematically lived (M. Silk, personal communication, 24 August 2015). Furthermore, more often than not, the day-to-day lives and experiences of community or family members who are influenced by SDP activities, but who may not be directly participating or excluded from such programmes, are ignored through such strict monitoring and evaluation frameworks. Taken together, these concerns point to the question of how we might better understand the movement of the body *outside* of the unyielding sports landscapes – as it passes through time and space, and as it is entangled in the tensions and interfaces of political action and social change – both through and outside of SDP programmes, policies and physical practices?

In what ways can Lyndsay's research relating to a martial arts programme in Uganda contribute to discussions about social change, sport, and development? The example Lyndsay provided of the girls making the choice to ride bicycles to the market is instructive for a number of reasons. First, it raises questions about who dictates the intended, and in this case unintended, outcomes of SDP programmes. Often, the prescribed and intended outcomes of SDP programming relating to health focus on avoidance – avoiding sex, avoiding risky situations, avoiding certain 'unhealthy' attitudes and behaviours, and avoiding harmful peers. Lyndsay's example is strikingly different, as it provides an example of a SDP outcome that represents SDP participants as active, engaged, and political subjects. This example could have potential implications for how SDP organizations and scholars collect and analyse data relating to SDP programmes. For example, SDP is arguably following a similar path as the development sector in terms of prioritizing quantitative methods and randomized controlled trials. Lyndsay's example alludes to the importance of qualitative ethnographic work that goes beyond traditional outcome measures to engage with questions relating to how physical culture and social change intersect in people's daily lives.

Wendy's vignette

I will briefly reflect on the practices and spaces that may be neglected in SDP by considering several community-based action research projects that my colleagues and I have been involved in over the last several years. These projects have been conducted in a participatory manner with women living on low income and women who have recently immigrated to Canada.

In terms of *practices*, the professionals I have collaborated with, including community recreation staff, intercultural developers, and public health workers, typically operate from a community development approach that is arguably lacking in both SDP and PCS. As we have written about elsewhere (Carr and Frisby, 2016; Frisby and Millar, 2007; Frisby, Reid and Ponic, 2007), community development involves working collaboratively with people to find out what their interests, talents, and concerns are and finding ways to shift entrenched practices, power relations, and resources to move towards outcomes that they desire. Rarely, in our experience, has sport been identified as something that women living on low income and adult newcomers to Canada want to participate in. They have expressed much more interest in physical activities like walking, hiking, and dancing that include a social component so that meaningful friendships can be developed (Lee, Frisby and Ponic, 2014). Several recent immigrant women also expressed frustration that there were limited opportunities for them to teach physical cultural practices from their home countries to promote intercultural understanding (Forde, Lee, Mills and Frisby, 2014). Rather, as Donnelly and Nakamura (2006) have shown, the practice they encountered in Canada was one of assimilation where they were expected to fit into the existing sport and recreation system, rather than contributing their knowledge and experiences in ways that could broaden the country's physical culture. This is an example of how institutionally embedded power relations control the physical cultural practices of people within borders even though Canada's multiculturalism policy 'acknowledges the freedom of all members of Canadian society to preserve, enhance and share their cultural heritage' (Government of Canada, 2011: 3).

When considering *spaces,* we have conducted research in community centres and neighbourhood houses in a large urban Canadian city, which to date have not normally been considered to be spaces where SDP takes place. The physical cultural practices observed in community centres and neighbourhood houses (e.g. dancing, yoga, fitness, swimming, ping pong, martial arts) are much broader and are more communitarian focused than typically seen in competitive sport environments, and are sometimes connected to a gamut of other cultural practices such as music or art. For example, one neighbourhood house we worked with used a community development approach that involved artwork done by residents to beautify a park so that more people would feel safe to walk, cycle, and play in it (Carr and Frisby, 2016).

With a Freirean approach to social change (Freire, 2000), outcomes and actions are decided upon by those desiring them, rather than having social change forced upon them by others. As others have demonstrated (Forde and Frisby, 2015; Hayhurst, 2009), SDP programmes and desired outcomes are usually decided upon in a neocolonial fashion that does not adequately take lived experience, the broader context, and participant input into account. Examples of the types of social changes that women on low income and recent immigrants have expressed to us include reducing their social isolation, feeling more accepted in their communities, reducing their stress and depression, and increasing intercultural understanding about others in the community. Clearly, a narrow focus on sport would be very limiting in terms of accomplishing these desired changes. This poses implications for how social change is conceptualized because shifts in daily practices can be meaningful and could contribute to the longer-haul struggle of tackling larger structural issues like poverty, racism, sexism, and discrimination. Unfortunately, as others have argued (Doherty and Taylor, 2007; Tirone, Livingston, Miller, and Smith, 2010; Silk, Francombe-Webb, Rich and Merchant, 2015), sport professionals are often ill equipped and poorly positioned to be part of a movement that tackles the broader structural dimensions of inequality that are historically deeply entrenched and stifle social change. This is probably because those who receive training in kinesiology and physical education programmes are rarely exposed to the theory and practice of community development that has a long history in leisure studies and other disciplines (Carr and Frisby, 2016).

The ways in which Wendy's examples position social change should provoke discussion among those interested in practices and spaces related to sport and social change. As a field/discipline, PCS is inherently a political project with aims of progressive social change. For those in SDP, and arguably PCS, the idea of reducing social isolation or increasing intercultural understanding are seen as means to achieving social change, but for the women Wendy worked with, these things were seen as ends in themselves. The idea is that focusing on actively living in the world and engaging in daily collective practices that represent how people believe the world could and ought to be, is an integral part of collective action directed at challenging structures of power and domination (Reid, Tom and Frisby, 2006). Importantly, Wendy's examples demonstrate how practices like community development and an intercultural approach in spaces that are not dominated by assimilationist logics and the hypercompetitive sport ethos broadens possibilities for social change.

Shawn's vignette

In June and July of 2013, Brazil experienced protests on a scale that had not occurred in generations. The protests began with demonstrations against a proposed increase in bus fares, but as they grew to include hundreds of thousands of people, a number of different social movements, labour groups, and political parties took to the streets for various reasons (Saad-Filho, 2013). A narrative that dominated the global headlines during this time was the relationship between the protests and the Confederations Cup that Brazil was hosting. The FIFA (International Federation of Association Football) event is held every four years and is timed to occur one year prior to each men's football World Cup to serve as a 'warm-up' tournament for the host country. The protests, and the violent and militarized response to demonstrators, occupied a great deal of the international media coverage and a common narrative was that the protests began as a reaction to the bus fare increase, but galvanized around resistance to the pending World Cup and the amount of public money being spent (BBC News, 2013; Ramón, 2013).

Although the scale of protest was unique, the use of mega-events by various groups as platforms for political protest and social change is not new (Timms, 2012). Arguably, every World Cup and Olympics have been inextricably linked with various political groups and projects. In a chapter on sport and social change, these events and groups could easily be the focus, but my interest is slightly narrower. I will briefly present two examples from the World Cup in Rio de Janeiro where communities mobilized sport itself as a form of protest. On the eve of the Confederations Cup and then again during the World Cup in 2014, the Popular Committee for the World Cup and Olympics, a network of academics, activists, and community members, hosted the Copa Popular, or People's Cup in various favelas around Rio. The events had two main objectives: (1) raising awareness and protesting the forced removals that were the result of hosting the Olympics and World Cup; and (2) protesting the privatization of the Maracana football stadium and the commercialization of football in Brazil. Additionally, the event served to bring men and women from different communities that were facing similar issues together for dialogue. In reporting on the event, Borja and Steiker-Ginzberg stated that:

> The People's Cup was much more than a tournament to protest forced evictions in the city of Rio de Janeiro; it was also a form of creative resistance that challenges the culture of FIFA. While the staging of the World Cup is corporate, consumer-driven, and privatized, the Popular Cup exuded a spirit of openness and democracy, giving a voice to those disenfranchised by the events themselves.
>
> *(Borja and Steiker-Ginzberg, 2013)*

Protests organized by sex workers prior to and throughout the World Cup offer a second example. Even though sex work is legal in Brazil there were a number of incidents involving violent police raids, arrests, and closures of bars and apartments used by sex workers in the lead-up to the World Cup. In response, at the beginning of the World Cup, sex workers and allies participated in a protest march that concluded with a football match on the streets in front of the municipal building in Niteroi (Knoll, 2014). In this way, football was not simply a game, but also a form of protest and a way to occupy public space.

What was unique about these events was that people mobilized sport itself, as opposed to mobilizing around sport, as an act of resistance and as a political tool to achieve social change. Language relating to sport being used as a tool for social change is quite common among those involved in SDP, however, these sport-based protest events receive scant attention within SDP. Furthermore, this is somewhat surprising, because in many ways the use of sport for protest aligns with SDP in terms of sport being positioned as a social and physical practice that brings people together in collective, hopeful, and joyful experience. Ultimately, this raises questions about how social change is conceptualized within SDP and what would be the impact of discussions and dialogue relating to the use of sport, or other forms of physical culture, as protest or resistance.

Continuing our walk

Ultimately, our chapter has been about the need for broadening discussions relating to sport and social change by considering how a variety of physical cultural practices may be mobilized across a variety of spaces for a wide range of reasons. Our vignettes were meant to be 'conversation starters' based on the 'walking' we have done through our respective research programmes. With the hope that our chapter serves as an invitation for other people to join this journey we will conclude with the points of interest raised in our vignettes. We do not do this with the intention of defining a path for others, as arguably the four of us are on different paths, but instead these points of interest have offered us intersections to elucidate a praxis that would potentially offer different ways to think about and enact sport for social change. From our perspective, this praxis would be guided by the following tenets:

- Social change, development, and sport are concepts that need to be continually engaged with and challenged. Our chapter and our work relating to sport and social change have been and will continue to be (re)framed by questions relating to social change, such as what counts as social change, whose visions of social change are privileged, how do imaginaries of social change constructed by various groups manifest through physical cultural practices, what is the role of physical culture and SDP in social change over the short and long term, in what ways do traditional approaches to SDP and PCS thwart social change, and what are the risks of being involved in sport or physical culture programmes with a social change agenda?
- Discussions relating to sport and social change need to include reflexivity on the part of researchers and practitioners. That is, we need to ask: who is being targeted for development and for what purposes, are we complicit in unequal and unsustainable forms of development, and if so, should we be looking for ways that physical cultural practices may be able to intervene? For example, could the critical mass cycling events that periodically occur in cities as a way to reclaim public space and advocate for bike friendly cities be considered a form of SDP? Additionally, Devra's vignette offers potentially challenging questions relating to elite and exclusionary forms of sports-based development, while Shawn's vignette offers examples of how sport has been mobilized to protest these types of development.
- Understandings of social change, and knowledge relating to social change efforts need to be grounded in the actual struggles of people attempting to achieve social change. As illustrated by Lyndsay's, Wendy's, and Shawn's vignettes, social change is embedded in various physical cultural practices and manifests in multiple ways depending on particular historical, social, cultural, and political interests of those involved. We suggest that lived experiences and more nuanced physical cultural practices and spaces must be better

foregrounded and theorized in SDP programming, practice, and policy. As Wendy noted, this can come from embracing a community development approach and as Lyndsay discussed this has implications for how organizations decide to monitor and evaluate their work.

Overall, our aim is to encourage others involved in SDP and PCS to continue to mobilize this dialogue by further engaging in, and sharing, their own journeys relating to sport and social change. Let us continue walking.

References

Andrews, D. and Silk, M. 2015. Physical cultural studies. In R. Guilianotti (ed.), *Routledge handbook of sports studies*. Abingdon: Routledge, 83–93.

Anglo Indian. 2013. Gateway to India. Available from www.angloindian.net/gateway-to-india/your-gateway-to-india (accessed 3 September 2013).

Atkinson, M. 2010. Entering scapeland: Yoga, fell and post-sport physical cultures. *Sport in Society*, 13(7–8), 1249–1267.

Bale, J. 1994. *Sport, politics and culture: Landscapes of modern sport*. New York: Leicester University Press.

BBC News. 2013. Brazil unrest: 'Million' join protests in 100 cities. Available from www.bbc.com/news/world-latin-america-22992410 (accessed 2 July 2015).

Borja, E. and Steiker-Ginzberg, K. 2013. People's Cup brings together communities threatened with eviction. Available from www.rioonwatch.org/?p=9672 (accessed 2 July 2015).

Carr, P. and Frisby, W. 2016. An emergent case study of INTERactive: Promoting intercultural understanding using physical activity as the tool. In E. Sharpe, H. Mair and F. Yuen (eds), *Community development: Applications for leisure, sport and tourism*. State College, PA: Venture Publishing, pp. 201–210.

Darnell, S. C. 2007. Playing with race: Right to Play and the production of whiteness in 'development through sport'. *Sport in Society*, 10(4), 560–579.

Darnell, S. C. and Hayhurst, L. M. C. 2011. Sport for decolonization: Exploring a new praxis of sport for development. *Progress in Development Studies*, 11(3), 183–196.

Darnell, S. C. and Hayhurst, L. M. C. 2014. De-colonising sport-for-development: Critical insights from post-colonial feminist theory. In N. Schulenkorf and D. Adair (eds), *Global sport-for-development: Critical perspectives*. Basingstoke: Palgrave Macmillan, 33–61.

Doherty, A. and Taylor, T. 2007. Sport and physical recreation in the settlement of immigrant you. *Leisure/Loisir*, 31, 27–55.

Donnelly, P. and Nakamura, Y. 2006. *Sport and multiculturalism: A dialogue*. Toronto, ON: Centre for Sport and Policy Studies, University of Toronto.

Duncombe, S. 2007. Politics in an age of fantasy. Available from http://turbulence.org.uk/turbulence-1/politics-in-an-age-of-fantasy (accessed 2 July 2015).

Forde, S. D. and Frisby, W. 2015. Just be empowered: How girls are represented in a sport for development and peace HIV/AIDS prevention manual. *Sport in Society: Cultures, Commerce, Media, Politics*, 18(8), 882–894.

Forde, S., Lee, D., Mills, C. and Frisby, W. 2014. Moving towards social inclusion: Manager and staff perspectives on an award winning community sport and recreation program for immigrants. *Sport Management Review*, 18(1), 126–138.

Freire, P. 2000. *Pedagogy of the oppressed*. New York: Continuum.

Frisby, W. 2011. Learning from the local: Promising physical activity inclusion practices for Chinese immigrant women in Vancouver, Canada. *Quest*, 63, 135–147.

Frisby, W. and Millar, S. 2007. The actualities of doing community development to promote the inclusion of low-income populations in local sport and recreation. *European Sport Management Quarterly*, 2(3), 209–233.

Frisby, W., Reid, C. and Ponic, P. 2007. Levelling the playing field: Promoting the health of poor women through a community development approach to recreation. In K. Young and P. White (eds), *Sport and gender in Canada*. Don Mills, ON: Oxford University Press, 121–136.

Giardina, M. D. and Newman, J. I. 2011. What is this 'physical' in physical cultural studies? *Sociology of Sport*, 28, 36–63.

Government of Canada. 2011. Canadian Multiculturalism Act. Assented to 21 July 1988, current to 11 July 2011. Ottawa, ON: Minister of Justice. Available from http://laws-lois.justice.gc.ca/PDF/C-18.7.pdf (accessed 19 February 2011).

Hartmann, D. and Kwauk, C. 2011. Sport and development: An overview, critique, and reconstruction. *Journal of Sport and Social Issues*, 35(3), 284–305.

Harvey, D. 2000. *Spaces of hope*. Berkeley, CA: University of California Press.

Hayhurst, L. M. C. 2009. The power to shape policy: Charting sport for development and peace policy discourses. *International Journal of Sport Policy and Politics*, 1(2), 203–227.

Hayhurst, L. M. C. 2014. The Girl Effect and martial arts: Exploring social entrepreneurship and sport, gender and development in Uganda. *Gender, Place and Culture*, 21(3), 297–315.

Hayhurst, L. M. C. In press. Sport for development and peace: A call for transnational, multi-sited, post-colonial feminist research. *Qualitative Research in Sport, Exercise and Health*. doi: 1080/2159676X.2015.1056824.

Hayhurst, L. M., MacNeill, M., Kidd, B. and Knoppers, A. 2014. Gender relations, gender-based violence and sport for development and peace: Questions, concerns and cautions emerging from Uganda. *Women's Studies International Forum*, 47(1), 157–167.

Hayhurst, L. M. C., Giles, A. and Wright, J. In press. Biopedagogies and indigenous knowledge: Examining sport for development and peace (SDP) for indigenous young women in Canada and Australia. *Sport, Education and Society*.

Horton, M., Bell, B., Gaventa, J. and Peters, J. 1990. *We make the road by walking*. Philadelphia, PA: Temple University Press.

Knoll, A. 2014. Sex workers stage protests against police crackdowns at the World Cup. Available from https://bitchmedia.org/post/sex-workers-stage-protests-against-police-crackdowns-at-the-world-cup.

Lee, D., Frisby, W. and Ponic, P. 2014. Promoting the mental health of immigrant women by transforming community physical activity. In L. Greaves, A. Pederson, and N. Poole (eds), *Making it better: Gender-transformative health promotion*. Toronto, ON: Women's Press, 111–128.

Mandela, N. 1994. *Long walk to freedom: The autobiography of Nelson Mandela*. Boston, MA: Little, Brown.

Mandela, N. 2000. Sport has the power to change the world. Inaugural Ceremony Laureus Lifetime Achievement Award, Monte Carlo, Monaco, 25 May.

Moon, B. K. 2014. International day of sport for development and peace: Secretary-General's message for 2014. Available from www.un.org/en/events/sportday/2014/sgmessage.shtml (accessed 25 May 2015).

Pronger, B. 2002. *Body fascism: Salvation in the technology of physical fitness*. Toronto, ON: University of Toronto Press.

Ramón, P. 2013. Poor, middle class unite in Brazil protests. Available from www.cnn.com/2013/06/28/world/americas/brazil-protests-favelas (accessed 2 July 2015).

Reid, C., Tom, A. and Frisby, W. 2006. Finding the 'action' in feminist participatory action research. *Action Research*, 4(3), 313–330.

Rist, G. 2008. *The history of development: From western origins to global faith* (trans. P. Camiller). New York: Zed Books.

Saad-Filho, A. 2013. Mass protests under 'left neoliberalism': Brazil, June–July 2013. *Critical Sociology*, 39(5), 657–669.

Silk, M. L. 2007. Come downtown and play. *Leisure Studies*, 26(3), 253–277.

Silk, M, Francombe-Webb, J., Rich, E. and Merchant, S. 2015. On the transgressive possibilities of physical pedagogic practices. *Qualitative Inquiry*, 21(9), 798–811.

Spaaij, R. and Jeanes, R. 2013. Education for social change? A Freirean critique of sport for development and peace. *Physical Education and Sport Pedagogy*, 18(4), 442–457.

Stoddart, B. and Sandiford, K. 1998. *The imperial game: Cricket, culture and society*. New York: Manchester University Press.

Timms, J. 2012. The Olympics as a platform for protest: A case study of the London 2012 'ethical' Games and the Play Fair campaign for workers' rights. *Leisure Studies*, 31(3), 355–372.

Tirone, S., Livingston, L. A., Jordan Miller, A. and Smith, E. L. 2010. Including immigrants in elite and recreational sports: The experiences of athletes, sport providers and immigrants. *Leisure/Loisir*, 34(4), 403–420.

Waldman, D. and Wilson, B. In press. Behind the scenes of sport for development: Perspectives of executives of multinational sport organizations. *International Review for the Sociology of Sport*, Online First, doi:10.1177/1012690215620766.

Waldman, D., Silk, M. and Andrews, D. 2015. Transnational gentrification, the new Indian middle class and the socio/spatial creation of cloned cricket communities. Paper presented at Creating Leisure, the Annual Conference of the Leisure Studies Association, Bournemouth, United Kingdom, 7–9 July.

Wilson, B. 2014. Middle-walkers: Negotiating middle ground on the shifting terrain of sport, peace and development. In K. Young and C. Okada (eds), *Sport, social development and peace*. Bingley: Emerald Group Publishing, 19–43.

57
CORPORATE SOCIAL RESPONSIBILITY

Roger Levermore

Introduction

Being housed in a business school, you could be forgiven for thinking that some of the central tenets of business ontology (assuming that there is such a unified singularity) might appear at odds with the fluid trajectories of physical cultural studies (PCS) scholarship. However, given my interest in work that is multi-disciplinary (ranging from international relations and development studies to corporate governance and organizational studies) and the critical bent of much of my published work, there are clear convergences between PCS and work in corporate social responsibility (CSR) relational to power and emancipation. Moreover, it is my contention that there can, could and should be even more convergence in future examinations of CSR. This chapter therefore explores these convergences with respect to the ways in which CSR has engaged (and should engage further) with physical culture. Further, I explore how a PCS sensibility can be located in past, present and future research in this field; a debate I have previously addressed and in which I lamented the absence of what I see as key elements of a PCS sensibility in 'sport CSR' (see for example Levermore, 2013; Levermore and Moore, 2015). As such, the chapter offers an opportunity to deepen previous analyses and challenge previous assumptions that sport specifically (and physical culture in general) has engaged with CSR in a shallow/dominant perspective.

As a starting point, I take physical culture to encompass a range of activities that includes exercise, health (including rehabilitation), leisure, movement and different forms of sport (corporate/elite as well as grassroots). This definition is expanded below in an analysis of literature on PCS/sport and CSR to include the self-reflection and importance of qualitative, multi-disciplinary work (that is not dominated by adherence to a single theory) I see as being at the heart of guiding PCS.

The term corporate social responsibility is problematic partly because it means so many different things to many different people; it thus warrants deeper discussion at this juncture. Initially, the focus of CSR was on individual decision-making of leaders of companies (before the 1950s), which was subsequently expanded to that of the company itself (after the 1950s). In the current moment, CSR has been further extended to include a focus on the entire supply chain as well as industries (Carroll, 2008). Starting points for defining the application and purpose of contemporary CSR include Blowfield and Murray (2008: 10) who note the belief that business is a 'steward in society' and has duties to a wide range of stakeholders. The World Bank also refers to stakeholders, linking CSR directly to an empowerment-sounding resolution that 'CSR is the commitment of business to sustainable economic development ... to improve quality of life' (World Bank, 2003). Given the inter-contextual nature of CSR, it is not surprising that it has become the focus of many disciplines ranging from sociology to political economy, business and management to international relations and from accounting to health. However, I argue that CSR is more likely to be researched by those affiliated to business schools (which in themselves are both multi-disciplinary while being insular in their reluctance of interacting with other disciplines) rather than outside them.

A multitude of terms relate to, or are alternative names for, CSR. Dahlsrud (2008) has suggested 37 definitions. This includes corporate social performance, corporate social responsiveness, corporate sustainability (the environment features prominently in many CSR initiatives), corporate citizenship, corporate philanthropy, corporate social investment (CSI), creating shared value (CSV), economic/social governance (ESG), corporate accountability, corporate moral agency and social entrepreneurship. Employee volunteering, cause-related marketing and awareness campaigns supported by companies are also specific sub-categories of CSR. Some of these terms are skewed to regional or industry understandings (for example – CSI meaning CSR in South Africa; philanthropy forming much of CSR in the US; governance supposedly core to many European CSR ventures; ESG being a term used in some sectors of the finance industry and in Hong Kong).

CSR therefore runs the risk of being so all-encompassing, so ubiquitous, as to be rendered a meaningless term. Indeed, there are strong disagreements about whether some of these terms should constitute – or be included as – 'CSR'. For example, philanthropy and cause-related marketing are omitted from some definitions of CSR. The International Organization for Standardization, ISO 26000, for instance, explains CSR to be 'taking responsibility for your impact on society and environment, rather than as charity. It emphasizes sustainable aims, engaging with stakeholders and respecting international norms' (ISO, 2010). Some, including myself, are also critical of the inclusion of such all-encompassing terminology;[1] however, for the benefit of this chapter, these categories are included given the dominant understanding of CSR (academically and in business circles) tends toward such inclusive definitions.

Confounding the definitional complexity, CSR can also be understood as a discredited term. The 'shareholder' perspective tends to argue that CSR is a drain on financial and employee resources, with few indicators showing that CSR enhances corporate financial performance (Karnani, 2010). Furthermore, CSR can be unpopular within organizations, incurring the wrath of many staff as it takes them away from their core work as well as occasionally being used as a 'dumping ground' for employees that an organization either finds no other place for, or cannot dismiss.

It is critical theory, though, that provides the most damning critique of CSR (see especially in sport and physical activity, the work of Samantha King, 2008). It is variously seen as:

- An inadequate attempt to redress the gross exploitation and abuses (widespread bribery, breaking the law, exploiting employees, environmental destruction etcetera) with which business has traditionally treated many stakeholders and at its worst is a tool that further exploits and undermines them (Banerjee, 2008).
- A further weapon in distorting the political decision-making basis (Edward and Willmott, 2008). Shamir (2004) argued that CSR has been 'deradicalized' by corporate practices that have diffused the transformative impacts that might have initially been associated with CSR. Those practices include the creation of dubious corporate sponsored/created NGOs

created solely as a device to lobby for companies to show the extent to which CSR has meant companies are now responsible and therefore deserve to avoid being subjected to increasing regulation with respect to greater corporate accountability.
- Of having little substance. More specifically, being much more related to short-term and superficial marketing issues to help enhance public relations rather than a long-lasting, in-depth and well-thought series of programmes that address the governance of the company at the same time as respecting a wider range of stakeholders. This is exemplified by the ridiculously trivial, shallow and unsupported awards that are given out to sundry companies while core business interests that are detrimental to society remain unchecked (Waddock, 2008).

Despite these critiques, CSR can display loose attachments to notions of empowerment through review of the governance and structure of companies and how they interact with stakeholders inside and outside of those organizations or supply chains. Garriga and Melé (2004), in their review of the four overarching theories of CSR, include aspects of critical theory (universal rights, environmental protection, normative stakeholder relations etcetera) in the category 'ethical theories' of CSR. Even Banerjee (2008), in his widespread criticism of CSR, acknowledged that it often has 'emancipatory intent'. The empowering benefits of CSR are more likely if the layers of CSR have long-standing 'depth' to them. 'Depth' is defined by Ponte et al. (2010) to mean corporate 'actions' (core business + stakeholder engagement programmes) that take place more on a proximate and engaged – where CSR activity is located as close as possible both to where the business operates (such as in headquarters, branches, factories etcetera) and to business operations – level, rather than distant and disengaged. That is, CSR can potentially be more empowering at a localized level as opposed to taking place at distant junctures along the supply chain and/or in cause-related marketing, philanthropy or awareness campaigns that fail to relate to core business objectives.

Despite, if not because of, these critiques, some academic work on CSR (however broadly defined) identifies with some of the tenets that have to date been put forward as elements of a PCS sensibility (namely its orientation towards critical theory and opposition to dominant discourses and theories). This has tended to be CSR research that has a qualitative orientation and which is attuned to the relationships between CSR and broader social, economic, political and technological contexts (to include operations of power within society) and which aims to understand/expose complexities, experiences and injustices (e.g. CSR and gender-based violence, sexual health, neoliberal governance of the body, pathologized body, immigration, racisms, personal identity, citizenship, freedom, patriotism, political struggle, class relations etcetera).

The contemporary state of play: corporate social responsibility and physical cultural studies

The vast majority of research has tended to focus exclusively on sport over (for example) dance, exercise and health. This does not mean that there is an absence of CSR initiatives that connect with non-sporting aspects of PCS but research and reflection on them are scarce. Notable examples include the Norse company who have a cultural foundation that includes support for promising sports stars and includes dance in its awards. Likewise, the Serena group includes the support of dance in its philanthropy work. Furthermore, rehabilitation is a core theme associated with work that Transaero does in Russia. Commitment to health through initiatives such as wellness programmes are also well documented by company CSR initiatives;

so too, are contentious projects such as the pizza company – Domino's – with their 'healthy eating' initiative.

Similarly, there has been an overwhelming emphasis on professional/corporate sport over grassroots sport; with respect to the latter the admirable work of Hayhurst (2011) is groundbreaking, using postcolonial theory to examine and highlight the 'colonial residue' inherent in CSR-sponsored grassroots development initiatives that are financed by multinational corporations.

With respect to further convergence between CSR and PCS, and in line with the multi-disciplinarity of a PCS sensibility, research that emanates from outside the field of 'sport' adds to the contemporary state of play. Most articles in this intersection have been published in sport management, business and marketing journals. Further, cognate management and business journals have a sizeable segment of articles on CSR – which while not explicitly, add to the growing contribution towards understanding of CSR/physical culture. However, special editions (such as *Journal of Sport Management* and *Journal of Corporate Citizenship*) distort this somewhat. The most 'prestigious' journal (in terms of citation rating) to cover sport CSR is *Journal of Business Ethics*, while social science and health journals have also published academic research in this field. Therefore, it can be argued that there is a relatively healthy – if not overly robust – multi-disciplinary panoramic sheen to sport CSR research, with a small majority incorporating rich qualitative methodologies to aid understanding of lived experience of CSR. Furthermore, there is also something of a longer history than might be presumed; although articles relating to sport CSR have been published more regularly in the last decade, publications have made reference to sport CSR since at least the early 1980s. For instance, Latham and Stewart (1981) observed that a hierarchy of objectives exist in companies (including concern for employee, government and community stakeholders) and queried whether these objectives varied between successful, moderately successful and failing organizations in the National Football League (American Football). The results were somewhat unclear – as far as stakeholder relations were concerned, no significant difference existed between those organizations.

Albeit briefly, there also exists academic research in which 'sport CSR' is of peripheral concern, yet is nonetheless incorporated. Latham and Stewart (1981) – noted above – are one such example from the management-related journals. Mason (1999), for example, reflected on the unique character and orientation of the sports sector, where profit is not always the main driver and in which community relations assume greater importance (a theme that has permeated much of sports studies and sports management literature). Similarly, in social science, sociology, development and health studies, a number of peripheral articles have appeared (since 1985); their number escalating in the recent past (since 2010). For example, Hargreaves (1985) considered some forms of commercialized sport in power relations with passing reference to philanthropy.

Towards a critical sport corporate social responsibility

Perhaps most importantly, while there has been a limited application of core elements of PCS to sport CSR – I have stated previously (Levermore, 2013) that sport CSR has rather neglected critical theorizing – there have been a number of emblematic examples that offer a promising trajectory. Many of these engagements can be located in the expansion of 'sport CSR' into publications from outside of management disciplines. For example, Andersen and Skjoett-Larsen (2009) highlight the 'greenwashing' evident in much CSR activity, especially by multinational corporations, while Lund-Thomsen and Nadvi (2010) focus on the rigour of the monitoring process surrounding child labour practices in making footballs in Southeast Asia.

Hayhurst (2011) too, suggests through postcolonial feminist theory, that sport CSR is all too often infused with a 'colonial residue' to the detriment of those receiving sport CSR in poorer societies globally.

It is perhaps here – in the democratization of sport CSR research beyond the domain of management – that there lies exciting possibilities for CSR/PCS research agendas. To wit, Kidd (1995) for example explains the dominant hegemonic power relations within commercialized sport, while also recognizing that sport offers the chance for empowerment of the disadvantaged. Likewise, Shaw (2005) reminds those involved in corporate sport that they have a responsibility 'to strive consistently towards the development of a just society characterized by moral sensitivity'. Spaaj (2009) highlights how alternative approaches to development (often based around empowerment directed at the grassroots) rail against the way that 'linked up' partnerships (the epitome of many sport CSR initiatives) are used to support dominant development approaches (that largely support the status quo and fail to adequately address poverty). Meanwhile, Giulianotti (2011) reinforces the view that the corporate sector (and by extension, sport CSR) is one of the four core institutions supporting sport for development based on neo-liberal perspectives and that better objectives are required that stress social justice (grassroots empowerment) more prominently. Others, such as Kaufman and Wolff (2010), provide an overview of the extent to which athletes have tried to promote social change via radical direct, participant involvement (such as at sports events).

Some scholars have focused on the transformative and progressive role that corporate organizations can play in empowerments/societal transformation. Giardina (2009), for example, focused on how Puma has been credited with a rare philanthropy project, winning accolades for its 'transformative' initiative in Africa. Others, such as Drygas et al. (2011), note that the sport sector has missed golden opportunities to advance a range of empowering initiatives based around health as sports stadia sit largely in disadvantaged communities across Europe.

It might be at this intersection that critical CSR could help shift or radically reconceptualize CSR so that business more progressively helps transform society. Examples of where such reconceptualization has arguably occurred includes the pioneering work of King (2008) who highlighted that the NFL 'Pink October' breast cancer awareness programme was making little difference to survival rates of those who were diagnosed with breast cancer; the money raised through the campaign tended to be spent on awareness rather than breast cancer research (the figure was estimated at 8.01% in 2015; Gebreyes, 2015). A separate example of an attempt to critique existing sport CSR relates to the NGO, Corporate Accountability International, protesting against the way Olympic athletes receive considerable sums of sponsorship funding from fast food companies such as McDonald's – thereby sending out confusing message about the use of sport to address obesity and supporting companies that are accused of being partly responsible for the obesity epidemic (Weeks, 2014).

Conclusion: future directions

By way of summary, is all too clear that CSR research is dominated by analysis of professional sport, which can often miss the contributions from other(ed) physical cultural forms. Further, and despite a significant increase in highlighting and examining 'sport CSR' in the last five to ten years, much research has been from a dominant business-oriented approach that has tended to be, at best, acritical and acontextual, thereby the relationship between extant power relations and CSR has been relatively under-explored. There are of course notable exceptions, not limited to the progressive work of scholars such as Kidd, Shaw, Paaj, Hayhurst and King. There exist exciting and potentially transformative possibilities in holding together 'sport CSR' (as widely understood and not limited to work published in the sporting sub-disciplines) and PCS; work that could provide a more nuanced focus on emancipation and empowerment and that speaks against CSR and exploitation, corporate greed and corruption and the exacerbation of already deeply entrenched social inequalities. There exists scope for a more nuanced and critical approach to CSR – a more contextual CSR approach – that can not only critique hegemonic approaches, but can influence CSR so that it can become a potentially liberating and transformative practice that can make a difference in the lives of particular disadvantaged communities. To realize such potential will require a radical reconceptualization of CSR, the establishment of productive relationships between critical academics and corporate (sport) organizations, and a commitment (by organizations and academics) towards progressive social change (in the face, potentially, of the logics of the bottom line). A difficult realization for sure, but there are some promising signs in the literatures to date; future convergence between PCS and CSR might well be able to make further inroads into the complex relationships between social change, the 'logics' of capital and the supposed 'power' of sport.

Note

1 In the 'sport CSR' context, I have argued against the catchall phrase of CSR if possible (Levermore, 2013).

References

Andersen, M., and Skjoett-Larsen, T. (2009). Corporate social responsibility in global supply chains. *Supply Chain Management: An International Journal*, 14 (2), 75–86.

Banerjee, S. B. (2008). Corporate social responsibility: The good, the bad and the ugly. *Critical Sociology*, 34(1), 51–79.

Blowfield, M. and Murray, A. (2008). *Corporate responsibility*. Oxford: Oxford University Press.

Carroll, A. B. (2008). A history of corporate social responsibility: Concepts and practices. In A. Crane, D. Matten, A. McWilliams, J. Moon and D. S. Siegel (eds), *The Oxford handbook of corporate social responsibility*. Oxford: Oxford University Press, 19–46.

Dahlsrud, A. (2008). How corporate social responsibility is defined: An analysis of 37 definitions. *Corporate Social Responsibility and Environmental Management*, 15 (1), 1–13.

Drygas, W. et al. (2011). Good practices and health policy analysis in European sports stadia: Results from the 'Healthy Stadia' project. *Health Promotion International*, 28 (2), 157–165.

Edward, P. and Willmott, H. (2008). Dialogue. Corporate citizenship: Rise or demise of a myth?, *Academy of Management Review*, 33 (3), 771–775.

Garriga, E. and Melé, D. (2004). Corporate social responsibility theories: Mapping the territory. *Journal of Business Ethics*, 53 (1–2), 51–71.

Gebreyes, R. (2015). Does the NFL's Pink October campaign actually help breast cancer research? *Huffington Post*, 15 October. Available from www.huffingtonpost.com/entry/nfl-breast-cancer-pink-october_us_561ffc4ae4b0c5a1ce62988a (accessed 15 December 2015).

Giardina, M. D. (2009). One day, one goal? PUMA, corporate philanthropy and the cultural politics of brand 'Africa'. *Sport in Society*, 13 (1), 130–142.

Giulianotti, R. (2011). The sport, development and peace sector: A model of four social policy domains. *Journal of Social Policy*, 40, 757–776.

Hargreaves, J. (1985). The body, sport and power relations. *Sociological Review*, 33 (1), 139–159.

Hayhurst, L. (2011). Corporatising sport, gender and development: Postcolonial IR feminisms, transnational private governance and global corporate social engagement. *Third World Quarterly*, 32 (3), 531–549.

ISO. (2010). ISO 26000: Social responsibility. Available at www.iso.org/iso/home/standards/iso26000.htm (accessed 30 April 2015).

Karnani, A. (2010). The case against corporate social responsibility. *Wall Street Journal*, 23, 1–5.

Kaufman, P. and Wolff, E. A. (2010). Playing and protesting: Sport as a vehicle for social change. *Journal of Sport and Social Issues*, 34 (2), 154–175.

Kidd, B. (1995). Inequality in sport, the corporation, and the state: An agenda for social scientists. *Journal of Sport and Social Issues*, 19 (3), 232–248.

King, S. (2008). *Pink Ribbons, Inc.: Breast cancer and the politics of philanthropy.* Minnesota, MN: University of Minnesota Press.

Latham, D. R. and Stewart, D. W. (1981). Organizational objectives and winning: An examination of the NFL. *The Academy of Management Journal*, 24 (2), 403–408.

Levermore, R. (2013). CSR through sport from a critical perspective: Failing to address gross corporate misconduct? In J. L. Paramio Salcines, K. Babiak and G. Walters (eds), *The Routledge handbook of sport and corporate social responsibility*. London: Routledge, 52–61.

Levermore, R. and Moore, N. (2015). The need to apply new theories to 'sport CSR'. *Corporate Governance: The International Journal of Business in Society*, 15 (2), 249–253.

Lund-Thomsen, P. and Nadvi, K. (2010). Clusters, chains and compliance: Corporate social responsibility and governance in football manufacturing in South Asia. *Journal of Business Ethics*, 93, 201–222.

Mason, D. S. (1999). What is the sports product and who buys it? The marketing of professional sports leagues. *European Journal of Marketing*, 33 (3–4), 402–419.

Ponte, S., Richey, L. A. and Baab, M. (2010). Bono's product (RED) initiative: Corporate social responsibility that solves the problems of 'distant others'. *Third World Quarterly*, 30 (2), 301–317.

Shamir, R. (2004). The de-radicalization of corporate social responsibility. *Critical Sociology*, 30(3), 669–689.

Shaw, S. (2005). While the rich get richer … Challenging inequalities in conventional sport sponsorship. In J. Amis and T. B. Cornwall (eds), *Global sport sponsorship*. London: Berg, 265–280.

Spaaj, R. (2009). The social impact of sport: Diversities, complexities and contexts. *Sport in Society*, 12 (9), 1109–1117.

Waddock, S. (2008). Corporate citizenship: The dark-side paradoxes of success. In G. Flynn (ed.), *Leadership and Business Ethics*. Amsterdam: Springer Netherlands, 251–268.

Weeks, C. (2014). Olympic athletes urged to cut ties with sponsors like McDonald's and Coke. *Globe and Mail*, 21 February. Available from www.theglobeandmail.com/life/health-and-fitness/health/olympic-athletes-urged-to-cut-ties-with-sponsors-like-mcdonalds-and-coke/article17029611.

World Bank. (2003). Public policy for corporate social responsibility. Available from info.worldbank.org/etools/docs/library/…/publicpolicy_econference.pdf (accessed 30 April 2015).

58
EMBODIMENT AND REFLEXIVE BODY POLITICS

Joshua I. Newman, Michael D. Giardina and Christopher M. McLeod

We have been tasked within this chapter to write on and about 'embodiment and reflexive body politics' as (separately and conjointly) related to the broader physical cultural studies (PCS) project. Our work to date, individually and collectively, has focused on embodiment, reflecting upon how we as critical, interpretivist, anti-/non-foundationalist researchers might best make sense of the moving body in empirically nuanced, culturally attentive ways (see e.g. Bunds, Newman, and Giardina, 2014; Giardina and Newman, 2011b; Grainger, Falcous and Newman, 2012; Newman and Giardina, 2014). Further, we have recently written a series of articles seeking to unsettle the ontological and epistemological moorings seemingly inherent to such a deep culturally corporeal approach (see e.g. Giardina and Laurendeau, 2013; Giardina and Newman, 2011a, 2011c; Newman, 2011, 2013). Despite, if not because of, our recent forays into what we could define as the nascent PCS project, we have more questions than answers with regard to the interpretive body, and the disquiet thereof (and certainly as they relate to one another). In what follows, then, we offer a series of mediations about our struggles in coming to terms with the empirical and metaphysical bases of physical cultural studies. In particular, we deconstruct our chapter's title as a series of articulations which, in our estimation, need to be reconciled in order to move the physical cultural studies project forward – those being:

1 the body as and in *embodiment*;
2 the body politic and/as *body politics*; and
3 reflection and/as *reflexivity* (i.e. empirical *techne*).

We then offer a brief discussion of PCS's critical articulation(s) and how we might reorient the PCS project moving forward.

Cultural physicalities, or, the body and embodiment

'Culture', Raymond Williams ([1976] 1988: 87) famously wrote, is 'one of the two or three most complicated words in the English language.' Given this chapter resides within a collection dedicated to the study of *physical culture*, we will leave the task of un-complicating the 'culture' in physical cultural studies to its more etymologically inclined contributors (see e.g. Andrews,

2002). In our estimation, however, our first task is equally as unnerving: that being to explicate a working definition of *physicality* and its linguistic cousin, *embodiment*. But first, a brief review as to where the body has heretofore sat within the PCS project.

To begin, the (physical) cultural studies turn to the body resulted in research studies that reduced the body to textual patterns, media representations, semiotic systems, and/or grand corporeal narratives, or erased the researcher's own body, politics, and praxical dimensions from empirical field studies. This was, perhaps, the natural outcome, for the field of cultural studies writ large was going through similar permutations in the United States and elsewhere (i.e. a cultural studies of representational politics – if not convenience – rather than of political struggle that characterized its British forbearer). At the same time, it is undeniable that many such works provided critical interrogations of the body within popular/political culture, and offered insight into various topics of inquiry. Our critique of this *oeuvre* ultimately amounted to issues over 'the abstraction of politically-enfleshed bodies, the disappearance of authorial bodies, and the missing empirical dialectics of the self that have given way to a rhetorical bravado and, in some cases, what reads like educated guesswork' (Giardina and Newman, 2011c: 44), rather than a quarrel with its hopeful intent or even useful pedagogical illuminations, however unrealized they might have been.

Against such a trend, we argued for a PCS project (Giardina and Newman, 2011a, 2011b; but see also Carrington, 2008) that squarely located 'the body' (of the *researcher*) as part and parcel of the research act – a radically embodied, performative cultural studies project, if you will. Although this might not have seemed a very novel turn – feminist scholars have long considered the affective role of the body in the research act – our stressing of a physical co-presence, especially in terms of ethnographic musings, was aimed at the (physical) cultural studies of the past and its neglect in the flesh politics of moving with bodies. At the same time, and amongst similar calls, we witnessed an uptick in methodological reflexivity and 'embodied' (auto-)ethnographic engagement as overriding strategies of inquiry (see e.g. Clift, 2014; Francombe-Webb, 2014; Laurendeau, 2011). This is where we have stood for the last several years. And, we would argue, the field *has* moved forward in exciting if not provocative directions in the last few years (whether as a result of our particular calls for research in this area, or from research that has developed independently or in opposition to our calls).

Yet at the same time embodiment has been consistently deployed within such a PCS project as taken-for-granted, uncritical, or under-theorized. That is, *physicality* refers to the physical attributes of the human (and, in some cases, the object) – often with particular emphasis on the human body's capacity for physiological activity, force, or expression. Physicality is the state or quality of being physical, with an allusion to the corporeal body as an expression of, and articulation to, its mental, social, and spiritual capacities. By contrast, in its most common usage the term *embodiment* refers to a 'physical entity typifying an abstraction' or 'giving concrete form to an abstract concept'. The term is often used in anthropomorphic ways, to instill human or agentive qualities to a thing (e.g. 'the Confederate flag embodies racist ideologies'). In other instances, embodiment refers to a human who enfleshes an image or conception. And in still other cases, the term refers to the material thing's ability to evoke reference to other things (or, in some instances, ideas).

What, then, does it mean to embody? Or to be (an) embodiment? And, for our purposes, how does one go about studying embodiment? As a baseline, it would seem that embodiment as a construct deals in some ways with *surfacing*. That is, a shift in shape or a change in form: from immaterial to material, from static to fluid, from abstract to concrete, from backstage to frontstage. For *something* to be embodied it needs to become, or to surface as, *some thing*. Does that thing need to be expressed in and by a physical?; a physicality? This is a point of divergence for our decidedly Western author list above, just as it is for more contemporaneous scholars doing work on 'the body' and 'embodiment'.

A multiplicity of different engagements with embodiment currently abound, with scholars in fields as philosophically distinct and diverse as cognitive psychology, brain science, public health, sociology, anthropology, theology, and political economy charting new if conflicting territory (see e.g. Becker, 1962; Gibbs, 2005; Krieger, 2005; Niedenthal et al., 2005; Ziemke, 2003). The disparity and contradictions in the literature leave us wondering: how have *we* used embodiment? In short, we have been less clear than we should. And furthermore, in our work, we have sometimes used the very proximity of the body as the right to use this 'embodied' shorthand without due explanation. This is an unfortunate shortcoming, for as Holly Thorpe (2014: 667) has recently reminded us, our own bodies can 'rudely remind' us of 'the importance of the biological' that is 'beyond our sociological gaze'.

Our lack of clarity might be best captured in Thomas Csordas's (1990, 1994) distinction between 'embodiment as representation' and 'embodiment as being-in-the-world'. In reflecting on our previous work we admit that we have always implied both types of embodiment. Indeed, 'embodied' is a beautiful turn of phrase, a simple rhetorical device that nicely captures both these meanings and, as such, confers great importance on our topics of study. But, as we will argue shortly, the *only* type of embodiment *we have actually studied* has been the first – embodiment as representation. Csordas cautions social scientists venturing just past the cultural turn to take seriously the idea that 'culture is grounded in the human body' (Csordas, 1994: 6). He suggests that we avoid the 'representationalist trap' and – as Roland Barthes did – to make the distinction (and mindfully attend to the articulation) between the body as material, biological entity and embodiment as the field defined by 'perceptual experience and the mode of presence and engagement in the world' (ibid.: 12).

But what is so problematic about studying this type of embodiment exclusively? After all, as a surface, the body is surely discursive – in fact, those of the Derridian tradition might say that is *all* it ever can be (i.e. an assemblage of texts, the transcendental signifier). From this tradition – a tradition (physical) cultural studies seems so deeply rooted to (perhaps intentionally so, we would concede) – the body is in the first instance as in the last *cultural*. Embodiment is the surfacing of the corpus within systems of meaning (again with deference to Raymond Williams, as well as Richard Johnson and Stuart Hall). There is certainly a metaphysical coherence to the representationalist perspective: How can we ever know the body, and certainly embodiments of another, in any way other than through the communicative exchange? The cultural body is given to encoding and decoding, prisoner to the circuit(s) of culture. This perspective, a perspective that came to hold sway at the cultural turn, seems to privilege both a particular hermeneutics and ontology. With regard to hermeneutics, it is given that once we concede that to know the body (and its capacity for embodiment) is and can only be to know it as discourse (scientific, cultural, social text, etc.), then we can set out to demonstrate the body as ontologically subjected. The body and its capacity for movement, affect, expression, death, and living are made by and within systems of language. This is Foucault's allusive (illusive, elusive) body, bounded to a history of ideas and knowledge-power rationalities yet never capable of being, doing, feeling. But how, then, does the scholar of the cultural body account for human experience? As discursive formation? How do we concede to human action or choice? To pain and pleasure? Affect and impulse?

If we delve deeper into phenomenology, perhaps we might find an experiential body – a body of form and formation; a body with the capacity for being-in-the-world. In the early 1900s, Edmund Husserl brought the body in from the periphery of philosophical thought. But if the body becomes more central in Husserl's work it is there only as an afterthought to his main task of studying the essences of experience, to which the body has unique access. Martin Heidegger, a student and critic of Husserl, introduced the idea of *being-in-the-world* to explain the ontological rather than idealistic, or empirical, nature of bodies. However, it was arguably Maurice Merleau-Ponty who was the first to ground his ideas in the body, or body-subject, as he often called it. In *The Phenomenology of Perception*, Merleau-Ponty ([1945] 2002) takes issue at the traditional philosophical treatment of the body as an object separate from the conscious subject of the mind. Perception is a vital act that is not just of the body but is entangled with the body-subject and movements thereof. Hence, for Merleau-Ponty, our capacity for perception demonstrates that we are our bodies and that our bodies are always constituted by and constitutive of situations they inhabit. Of the broader phenomenological canon it is Merleau-Ponty's particular brand of existential phenomenology that provides a pathway forward to understanding the physically active body (Allen-Collinson, 2009).[1]

Thus, when compared to its rendering in cultural studies, the phenomenological body is often a more spatial, affective, and sensual corpus – a body that, following Chris Shilling (2005: 56), 'redirects our attention to the body's significance as a source of the self and society'. But such a body is not without its shortcomings. Shilling (ibid.), invoking Drew Leder's (1990) work, writes of the 'absent body' as being phenomenology's paradox, that state of being in which it is quite possible 'for the body to fade away within a phenomenological account of how the capacities and dispositions of the body are a source of society and shape people's practical experiences of the world', a body that 'ordinarily 'fades' and 'disappears' from our experience when we are engaged in that purposeful action that creates our environment and governs our daily routines, yet can abruptly reappear as a focus of attention when we are ill or in pain or when are bodies are at their least socially productive' (Shilling, 2005: 56–57).

Moreover, and in response to arguments that the phenomenological body 'has no developed conception of how the body can be shaped by social relations and contexts, or how its somatic experiences provide a means through which particular body-society relations can serve to attach people to or alienate them from their social milieu' (ibid.: 56), numerous scholars have sought to integrate such 'body work' with critical theory. Loïc Wacquant, for one, has been aggressive in pursuing a *carnal sociology*, one informed by phenomenology's view of the live body that 'is a sociology not *of* the body as sociocultural object but *from* the body as fount of social intelligence and sociological acumen', in which 'the human agent is a sentient and suffering being of flesh and blood' (Wacquant, 2015: 4, emphasis original). By this he means to suggest that we situate ourselves, '*not above or on the side of action but at its point of production*' (ibid., emphasis original). The trap here, though, and the one that (physical) cultural studies might avoid when put in conversation with carnal sociology, is to not privilege the corporeal at the expense of erasing context from one's research act.[2]

The forceful body and its members, or, body politics and the body politic

The following position has rightly been the ontological assumption guiding the fledgling PCS project: the body is cultural, and *culture embodied* is *political*. The body is ordered and made meaningful in culture, and orders and meaning are never neutral. Such a collective enterprise bent toward explication is thus necessary if we are to decouple meaning and being (and being as meaningful). We have sought to explain how, and the extent to which, the body is potentially given to cultural systems and political structures. Post-Derridian theories of (inter)subjectivity and biopolitics have been taken up in physical cultural studies to articulate embodied couplings (the body and self) to broader formations of capital, state sovereignty and geopolitical orders, patriarchy, colonialism, sexism, and ability (see e.g. Clift, 2014; Francombe-

Webb, Rich, and De Pian, 2014; Markula, 2014; Newman and Giardina, 2014; Shields, Newman, and McLeod, 2014; Weedon, 2014). Enter the theory and method of articulation: epistemological and hermeneutic bedrocks of the PCS project owing to New Left dialects and dialectics. In the realm of cultural politics, and following Hobbes, PCS scholars have taken up the portmanteau 'body politics' as more than a metaphor for the body politic and its many members. The term is a hermeneutic coupling of sorts, an allusion to the body conjoined to the state, the market, the community – the embodying one as part of, and bound to, the many.

More often than not, however, today we see this articulation of the one-as-enfleshed-to-the-many as a problem for our studies of physical culture. It provides a framework for understanding the *organized body* (structured in language, in social order, in economies of embodiment, in *communitas*, perhaps even in dimensions of time and space) but very little about the *body organic*. This is our Derridian burden, a structural and representational determinism that renders embodiment as discourse in/as/about context.[3] Owing a considerable debt to Derrida's significants and Foucault's hermeneutical genealogy, the PCS project has widely produced a body that is made real by language (as opposed to the opposition) and constituted by the history of ideas and ideology. This is an impossible, implicit body. A generation of scholars in anthropology, feminist studies, posthuman studies, and those working in contemporary continental philosophy camps haunted by Deleuze, Guattari, Braidotti, Agamben, Haraway, Barad, and Bordo, are now looking beyond the body as representation of ideas – the cultural body as articulated to the body politic – and toward the 'organ-ized and organ-izing body politic'.

One result of such a turn has seen scholars take up Deleuze to realize Derrida's implicit body. Whereas a Derridean deconstructive approach moves us beyond 'the self-grounding of a rational, meaningful sign system – the book of nature – to the inscription of marks in a world of (physiological/physical) force and signification – the "general text"', the Deleuzean injunction allows us to 'conduct a material analysis of forceful bodies politic' (Protevi, 2001: 2). It is our position that PCS scholars might benefit from following Deleuze's shift away from 'the transcendental from the conditions of possibility investigated by phenomenology' to the 'patterns and triggers of actual bodies, thus implicitly articulates a research programme for the investigation of forceful bodies politic' (ibid.: 2).[4]

Interpretive member-ship, or reflection and reflexivity

All this leads us to wonder, how does one *empiricize* embodiment in physical cultural studies? How do we situate the *forceful body*, its members and its becomings, among materially and historically constituted bodies and body politics. Interpretivist methods such as observation, ethnography, discourse and textual analysis have come to dominate the PCS project, our own work included (see e.g. Giardina, 2005, 2009; McLeod, 2013; Newman, 2010, 2011). Which is to say: in many of our past research endeavors, we practiced reflexivity through a combination of introspection, reflection, and projection. We used introspection in order to reveal both what we bring to the field, and in turn what brings us to a specific field. In this sense our introspections are often less explicit in our writing[5] but are nevertheless embedded within our choice of a given research field. Reflection differs from introspection in that we look for our presence, our actions, and our identities as they can be observed in the many 'reflective surfaces' of the field. Be they the jokes we are told at NASCAR races, the expectations of our teammates, or our literal reflections in airport windows, these reflective surfaces provide empirical material by which we can understand our culturally laden body as:

1 *Existent:* an embodied subject who enters the field and brings with him or herself a biographical and social history. A subject whose re-location, and tensions thereof illuminates to his/herself the locations he/she bears – our locatedness in both senses.
2 *Forceful:* an embodied subject who makes things happen either through action or inaction. A subject who tackles, who listens to racist jokes, or converses on politics.
3 *Malleable:* an embodied subject who recognizes him- or herself as corpus of habit and *hysteresis*. A subject who relishes how the field might change him or her, in terms of how he or she may be pained, pleasured, or gain great understanding of a social phenomenon.

Yet a key question still remains: how do we extend our observations of our own bodies as political and fleshy beings from the status of appearance to that of *occurrence*. That is, we focus here on what is required, ontologically and epistemologically, to say that our bodies matter. Put differently, the observations we make in these reflective surfaces are (perhaps) culturally and sociologically irrelevant unless we undertake the final step of the reflexive process – *projection*. To project – or to put the final and essential 'touch' on our reflexive praxis – *we interpret and explain how our existence, forcefulness and malleability are articulated to broader historical contexts and specific instances of political agency and oppression.* Projection, it seems to us, has always been the important step of making PCS 'matter' in the dual sense evoked by Judith Butler.

Projection is both an ontological *and* epistemological practice. That is, to project we both (a) assume that what we observe in reflection is something that occurs rather than something that appears (or perhaps even occurs in its appearance but does not only appear), and (b) describe and explain the specific mechanism by which this appearance is in fact an occurrence. For example, while it is interesting to note, in a *reflective* manner, that as white males we share a similar skin color to other spectators at a NASCAR race, and while it is even more interesting to note that as self-identified white males we may share some similar experiences as the other spectators at a NASCAR race, these observations ultimately have little *reflex*ive or sociological value until we demonstrate, for example, that we were read by our fellow spectators as white males with similar experiences (see Newman and Giardina, 2014). Put differently, our reflections on our white appearances have little value until we can demonstrate that they have also engendered a white *occurrence*. Often (perhaps too often) we resort to the quasi-ontological concept of 'articulation' alone to render these reflections as projections; to make our bodies matter. Here, in ruminating on this step of projection in our process of 'reflexive body politics' we would like to raise two questions:

1 How can we know that our bodies not only appear (to us) but also *occur* (to others)? Or in other words, how can we know our projections are ontologically meaningful?
2 How can we know that our bodies *occur* (to others) *in a manner that correlates with how they appear* (to us)? Or in other words, how can we know our projections are epistemologically meaningful?

For insight into these questions, we look to psychoanalyst Jacques Lacan ([1970] 2002) and his extended work on the mirror stage.

For Lacan, the mirror stage is the key phase in a child's development of an ego. This happens when the child first recognizes her own body as a total form in a reflective surface.[6] The child not only recognizes her own image but also distinguishes herself from other people and objects and, importantly, distinguishes herself from her own mirror reflection. This distinction is crucial because the child at once recognizes this image over which she has perfect, instantaneous control and yet recognizes, paradoxically, that she does not have perfect control over her own phenomenological body. Here the child identifies with an image, which at the same time is alienating in the sense that it is confused with the self. Out of this primary alienation the ego is born as an illusion of bodily and subjective coherence.

We are not so much concerned here with Lacan's insights into child development or the ego as much as how we can interpret the mirror stage as a repeating, constitutive, and confirmatory relationship of the subject to his or her own body and, *in turn,* the paradigm for reflexive body politics. We note two implications, one from Lacan's work, and one of our own design. First, in the imaginary relation to one's own body it is ultimately the other that becomes guarantor of our self. This is more so a pre-linguistic premise of psychoanalytic theory than a critique of using reflective methods in qualitative research. However, it does explain why reflexivity, a method grounded as it is in the reflected image, requires projection – the guarantee of which is ultimately and impossibly given over to the other.

Second, we wonder: what type of body do we see in Lacan's mirror and how does it compare with the bodies we discussed earlier? Just as the self in Lacan, and in reflexive body politics, is contingent on a body, we argue that the mirror can only present a body that is contingent on a self – *the reflected body can only be confirmatory*. The reflected body can only move as a better or worse illusion of the child. It may very well illuminate some previously unforeseen element of embodiment – our fullness and coordination, for example – but the body we view in reflection can only always ever be (a) the body of one who can perceive and (b) the parts of that body which are perceivable. The questions then are: how many and what types of forceful bodies are characterized by statements (a) and (b)? And, what degrees and variations of their forces are characterized by statements (a) and (b)? We can only see a Derridian body in the mirror. How many Deleuzean bodies are outside of our reflected gaze?

From this point of view, the type of reflexive PCS that we authors have privileged attains little more than, to use Karen Barad's (2007: 88) phrase, 'iterative mimesis' or 'mirrors on mirrors'. This is not because we reflect an artificially whole and coherent subject in our research – indeed we have always been profoundly suspicious of the illusion of a complete subject – but rather because the method (and theory) of reflexivity is premised upon an image, however shattered or warped we present it. And most importantly, we rely on the *other* to make this image into an occurrence. Even then, our body may occur in ways we cannot realistically describe, let alone connect to broader patterns of cultural politics. Reflexivity leaves us too often with a mirrored mirror – an articulation, yes; but a loose articulation of image to image.

By way of a conclusion

All of the above ruminations bring us back to the (our) crisis of embodiment with respect to the PCS project: a project we have heretofore held true to (and in many cases, explicitly argued for) may be at an impasse (an assertion one might find odd, given the title of this volume), at least when we view embodiment as a necessary component of such a project. But is it (a) methodology that is at an impasse, or the way we conceptualize that which informs the project? Do we in PCS, too often, privilege a methodology without theory (or a theory without method), but one that only exists because of (a) theory? We might propose, then, that our impasse with PCS is more a philosophical one than one of (a) method or (a) theory: what, again, is embodiment? As empirical material? As lived experience? As articulation of researcher to researcher? As disarticulative of the researcher's body? If only it was that easy.

Elizabeth Adams St Pierre (2015), we think, would contend that the answer to our question(s) lays in our re-orienting our strategic starting point: foregoing method or project and starting with theory. That is, getting outside of the idea that a PCS approach to the body or 'embodied research' should be 'formalized, precise, and methods-driven' (ibid.: 75), and turning instead to the ontological. Drawing especially from Deleuze and Guattari, St Pierre offers the following indictment:

> the very idea of method forces one into a prescribed order of thought and practices that prohibits the experimental nature of transcendental empiricism. Method proscribes and prohibits. It controls and disciplines. Further, method always comes too late, is immediately out-of-date and so inadequate to the task at hand. But method not only can't keep up with events, more seriously, it prevents them from coming into existence. One might say that 'method,' as we think of it in the methodological individualism of conventional humanist qualitative methodology with its methods of data collection and methods of data analysis, *cannot be thought or done in new empirical inquiry*. ... In fact, the new empiricist might well argue that attempting to follow a given research method will likely foreclose possibilities for the 'new.' The new empiricist researcher, then, is on her own, inventing inquiry in the doing. Hence, we have methods-driven research that mostly repeats what is recognizable, *what is already known*.
> (St Pierre, 2015: 79, 81; second emphasis ours)

This is what happens when inquiry is reduced to method and research design (which we are fearful of PCS becoming): we 'know' the outcome of our (research) acts, such that we are repeating the always already done. We need to, instead, after Foucault (1982), 'refuse what we are', to 'refuse the ontological assumptions, language, and practices' (St Pierre, 2015: 85) of a given methodology. Our disquiet, then, has come about by taking the ontological turn. For scholars of physical culture, we would do well to 'forget' the proscriptive nature of PCS, and in fact shift our focus 'from methodology' (which PCS most surely has become, however theoretically imbricated that methodology has been with [British] cultural studies. i.e. the theory and method of articulation) to one of 'onto-epistemology' (ibid.: 87).

So what, again, is embodiment? We would not be so presumptuous as to be so proscriptive. Ask that question for yourself, for your self will find a different answer than did we. And lead you down a different path than it lead us. The answer will probably be in the attempt.

Notes

1. A further specific focus on motility – or bodily movement – in phenomenology has recently been taken to the extreme by Erin Manning (2014) who displaces the body in favor of its movement. See *Body and Society* 20(3–4) (September–December 2014) for responses to Manning's article.
2. One possible way forward from this dilemma is found in the work of the new materialists and those arguing for (a) new empiricism (e.g. Sarah Ahmed, Karen Barad, Jane Bennett, Rosi Braidotti, Manuel De Landa, Elizabeth Grosz, etc.). Ahmed (2006), for example, writing in *Queer Phenomenology: Orientations, Objects, and Others*, expressly links the phenomenology of Husserl and Merleau-Ponty (among others) with feminist and critical theory to offer a queer model of orientations (rather than, we might say, articulations). This concept of orientation, she maintains, 'allows us then to rethink the phenomenality of space – that is, how space is dependent on bodily inhabitance' (ibid.: 6). What Ahmed is driving at is the need to disorient ourselves so that we may find our orientation. In so doing, we may find new planes (of affectivity) on which to act, new ways of seeing (if not experiencing) our reflected reflexion.
3. Of course, ours is certainly not an original critique of cultural studies or the cultural turn. See, for example, the arguments Protevi (2001) makes in his book *Political Physics*.
4. In *Nietzsche and Philosophy*, Deleuze (1983: 457) describes the production of forceful bodies in this fashion: 'Every relationship of forces constitutes a body – whether it is chemical, biological, social, or political'. Hence, Protevi argues, the study of forceful bodies requires both 'a politicized physics

(paying attention to the political ground of such basic physics terms as "law")' and a 'physicalized politics (paying attention to the physical ground of such basic political terms as "force")', as both are needed 'in order to understand politics as the forceful organ-ization of bodies' (Protevi, 2001: 3).
5 In fact we would contend that, in so far as this chapter is not a reflection on our work, it is one of introspection.
6 Homer (2005) notes that this surface may be the face of a parent or some other equally 'social' reflection.

References

Ahmed, S. (2006). *Queer phenomenology: Orientations, objects, others*. Durham, NC: Duke University Press.
Allen-Collinson, J. (2009). Sporting embodiment: Sports studies and the (continuing) promise of phenomenology. *Qualitative Research in Sport and Exercise*, 1(3), 279–296.
Andrews, D. L. (2002). Coming to terms with cultural studies. *Journal of Sport and Social Issues*, 26(1), 110–117.
Barad, K. (2007). *Meeting the universe halfway: Quantum physics and the entanglement of matter and meaning*. Durham, NC: Duke University Press.
Becker, G. S. (1962). Investment in human capital: A theoretical analysis. *The Journal of Political Economy*, 70(5), 9–49.
Bunds, K. S., Newman, J. I. and Giardina, M. D. (2014). The spectacle of disposability: Bumfights, commodity abjection, and bodies of the neoliberal street. *Critical Studies in Media Communication*, 32(4). doi:10.1080/15295036.2014.944928
Carrington, B. (2008). 'What's the footballer doing here?': Racialized performativity, reflexivity, and identity. *Cultural Studies ↔ Critical Methodologies*, 8(4), 423–452.
Clift, B. (2014). Suspect of smiles: Struggle, compassion, and running to reclaim the body in urban Baltimore. *Cultural Studies ↔ Critical Methodologies*, 14(5), 496–505.
Csordas, T. (1990). Embodiment as a paradigm for anthropology. *Ethos: Journal of the Society for Psychological Anthropology*, 18, 5–47.
Csordas, T. (1994). *Embodiment and experience: The existential ground of culture and self*. Cambridge: Cambridge University Press.
Deleuze, G. (1983). *Nietzsche and philosophy*. London: Continuum.
Foucault, M. (1982). The subject and power. *Critical Inquiry*, 8(4), 777–795.
Francombe-Webb, J. (2014). Learning to leisure: Femininity and practices of the body. *Leisure Studies*, 33(6), 580–597.
Francombe-Webb, J., Rich, E. and De Pian, L. (2014). I move like you … but different: Biopolitics and embodied methodologies. *Cultural Studies ↔ Critical Methodologies*, 14(5), 471–482.
Giardina, M. D. (2005). *Sporting pedagogies: Performing culture and identity in the global arena*. New York: Peter Lang.
Giardina, M. D. (2009). Flexibly global? Performing culture and identity in an age of uncertainty. *Policy Futures in Education*, 7(2), 172–184.
Giardina, M. D. and Laurendeau, J. (2013). Truth untold? Evidence, knowledge, and research practice(s). *Sociology of Sport Journal*, 30(3), 237–255.
Giardina, M. D. and Newman, J. I. (2011a). Physical cultural studies and embodied research acts. In N. K. Denzin and Y. S. Lincoln (eds), *The Sage handbook of qualitative research*, 4th edn (pp. 523–534). Thousand Oaks, CA: Sage.
Giardina, M. D. and Newman, J. I. (2011b). The physical and the possible. *Cultural Studies ↔ Critical Methodologies*, 11(4), 392–402.
Giardina, M. D. and Newman, J. I. (2011c). What is this 'physical' in physical cultural studies? *Sociology of Sport Journal*, 28(1), 36–63.
Gibbs, R. (2005). *Embodiment and cognitive science*. New York: Cambridge University Press.
Grainger, A. D., Falcous, M. and Newman, J. I. (2012). Postcolonial anxieties and the browning of New Zealand rugby. *The Contemporary Pacific*, 24(2), 267–295.
Homer, S. (2005). *Jacques Lacan*. London and New York: Routledge.
Krieger, N. (2005). Embodiment: A conceptual glossary for epidemiology. *Journal of Epidemiology and Community Health*, 59(5), 350–355.
Lacan, J. ([1970] 2002). *Écrits* (trans. B. Fink). New York: W. W. Norton & Company.
Laurendeau, J. (2011). 'If you're reading this, it's because I've died': Masculinity and relational risk in BASE jumping. *Sociology of Sport Journal*, 28(4), 404–420.

Leder, D. (1990). *The absent body*. Chicago, IL: University of Chicago Press.

Manning, E. (2014). Wondering the world directly – or, How movement outruns the subject. *Body and Society*, *20*(3–4), 162–188.

Markula, P. (2014). The moving body and social change. *Cultural Studies ↔ Critical Methodologies*, *14*(5), 483–495.

McLeod, C. (2013). Performing Kiwi citizenship in/through American rugby. Unpublished Master's thesis, Florida State University, Tallahassee, FL.

Merleau-Ponty, M. ([1945] 2002). *The phenomenology of perception* (trans. K. Paul). London: Routledge.

Newman, J. I. (2010). *Embodying Dixie: Studies in the body pedagogics of Southern whiteness*. Sydney: Common Ground.

Newman, J. I. (2011). [Un]comfortable in my own skin: Articulation, reflexivity, and the duality of self. *Cultural Studies ↔ Critical Methodologies*, *11*(6), 545–557.

Newman, J. I. (2013). This pain in my neck: Living conscientization and/as paradox of praxis. *Qualitative Inquiry*, *19*(4), 247–260.

Newman, J. I. and Giardina, M. D. (2014). Moving biopolitics. *Cultural Studies ↔ Critical Methodologies*, *14*(5), 419–424.

Niedenthal, P. M., Barsalou, L. W., Winkielman, P., Krauth-Gruber, S. and Ric, F. (2005). Embodiment in attitudes, social perception, and emotion. *Personality and Social Psychology Review*, *9*(3), 184–211.

Protevi, J. (2001). *Political physics*. New York: Athlone.

St Pierre, E. (2015). Practices for the 'new' in the new empiricisms, the new materialisms, and post qualitative inquiry. In N. K. Denzin and M. D. Giardina (eds), *Qualitative inquiry and the politics of research* (pp. 75–96). Walnut Creek, CA: Left Coast Press.

Shields, R., Newman, J. I. and McLeod, C. (2014). Life in three deaths: Thanatopolitical biopoiesis and militaristic nationalism. *Cultural Studies ↔ Critical Methodologies*, *14*(5), 425–437.

Shilling, C. (2005). *The body in culture, technology, and society*. Thousand Oaks, CA: Sage.

Thorpe, H. (2014). Moving bodies beyond the sociological/biological divide: Toward theoretical and transdisciplinary adventures. *Sport, Education, and Society*, *19*(5), 666–686.

Wacquant, L. (2015). For a sociology of flesh and blood. *Qualitative Sociology*, *38*(1), 1–11.

Weedon, G. (2014). Military resisters, war resistance, and the ethics of exposure and disclosure. *Cultural Studies ↔ Critical Methodologies*, *14*(5), 438–450.

Williams, R. ([1976] 1988). *Keywords*. London: Flamingo Fontana.

Ziemke, T. (2003). What's that thing called embodiment? In *Proceedings of the 25th annual meeting of the Cognitive Science Society* (pp. 1305–1310). Mahwah, NJ: Lawrence Erlbaum.

AFTERWORD
(Digital) physical cultural studies?

Tara Brabazon

Physical cultural studies (PCS) is an innovative, interdisciplinary, passionate and potent matrix for new knowledge. It re-orients an array of fields including sport and leisure studies, the sociology of sport and movement studies, creating what David Andrews and Michael Silk (2011: 1) have described as a 'relationship between physical culture, power, and power relations, and the body'. Too often, new intellectual labels are window dressing for grant applications, but the label in this case is prescient and agitating. It is 'intellectual migration' (ibid.). PCS's emergence as a new trajectory in an area formerly dominated by sport science recognizes and celebrates 'the physical cultural turn' and the extent of cultural studies scholars' interest in a range of new topics and tropes (Bandy, 2016: 726). Such a project requires not only an analysis of local, regional policies, sport and recreation and urban planning, but also an assessment of community developments. Certainly, PCS offers a solution to the disciplinary stalemate created by national research systems for evaluation, such as the Research Assessment Exercise (RAE), Research Excellence Framework (REF) and Excellence Research Australia (ERA). These systems codified knowledge and created artificial barriers blocking innovation in the quest for accountability and benchmarking. Certainly, PCS confronts and transforms the anti-theoretical and anti-humanities tendency of sports science, kinesiology and even sport and leisure studies. Most importantly, PCS offers a vision for movement and knowledge – and knowledge in movement – that hooks into debates as wide ranging as the obesity 'crisis', under-employment, over-employment, post-fordism, masculinity and femininity, the Precariat, health and technology.

It is the marinade of these topics that draws my attention in this Afterword. I write the phrase 'digital physical cultural studies' so that it will not have to be written again. Digital is a redundant adjective. Everything manages the challenge/threat/transformation of digitization. Such pervasiveness is beyond the internet of things (Couturier, Sola and Borioli, 2012). Instead, I summon the physical cultural studies of things. This Afterword operates through three intertwined concepts – digitization, deterritorialization and disintermediation – as a way to understand screens, sounds and movement in PCS.

Entering the digital

Digitization is the Kim Kardashian of sociological concepts. It is flashy, pushy and intrusive. It competitively builds Fitbit leader-boards, (over)shares RunKeeper distances and flaunts the completed 'Move', 'Exercise' and 'Stand' rings on the iWatch. Digitization has many characteristics. The most important is mobility: ideas move through space and time. The original uses of the internet were very basic, including electronic mail, file transfer, bulletin boards and news groups. These early functions involved connection and communication over geographical space, fulfilling the function of railways and cars in the nineteenth and twentieth century. This relationship between technology, space and time has been studied with power, passion and profile by outstanding scholars such as Harold Innis, Marshall McLuhan and James Carey. Digitization only increases and intensifies this contraction of time and space. The digitized movement of text, images and money is fast and convenient. As Virilio (1989) has shown, that which is fast dominates that which is slow. Such a mantra has profound consequences for theories of work, learning and leisure. The pleasures of the read-write web – to like a Facebook post, write a tweet or gather pins on Pinterest – create sedentary satiation. The movement is of text and images, not arms and legs.

Analogue aerobics videos in the 1980s ensured that a session could be played at the convenience of the user, delivered through home-based technology such as the video recorder or DVD player. With laptop computers, tablet-based platforms and smartphones, the mobility of these programmes has increased, delivered whenever and wherever a user presses play. From step aerobics to strength training, from walking programmes to yoga and meditation, movement and motivational plans are atomized and delivered to a person, regardless of their location. Walking and yoga sessions are located on a continuum of fitness (Wise and Hongu, 2014: 1), providing an entry point for most fitness levels. Podcasts and audiobooks on walking can accompany a walk through physical space. This just-in-time exercise and fitness slots into and through the work and family schedules of the user.

Such customized options can mitigate the assumptions about 'normal' mobility, movement and bodies. This is important as modes of ableism are profoundly damaging and inhibiting of motivation, not only for men, women and children with impairments, but for those with health conditions that limit the scale and scope of mobility. As Zoe Harcombe confirmed, 'we must be open to the idea that (quite logically) people are not, for example, overweight because they are sedentary, but they are sedentary because they are overweight' (Harcombe, 2010: 26). This is an important inversion. As we age, the capacities of our bodies transform. Therefore, customized, flexible, digital fitness applications can produce, encourage and enable a range of movement cultures.

A key and new pathway through digitization and movement is 'self-monitored fitness'. Considering the relative newness of the phrase 'self-monitored fitness', it is important to recognize its similarly young but, in digital terms, grandfather: the quantified self. It is no surprise that the phrase 'quantified self' was first summoned by *Wired* magazine editors, Gary Wolf and Kevin Kelly, in 2007 (Wolf, 2009). After this initial usage, a Quantified Self website was established, together with Quantified Self Labs. There is a Quantified Body podcast. As Wolf disclosed, the goal is to track 'every facet of life, from sleep to mood to pain' (ibid.). This tracking is also mapped, particularly through geosocial networking interfaces such as Foursquare, Facebook and RunKeeper. The statistics of life – at least with regard to the body and emotional state – are logged through weight, height, heart rate, diet, fitness and mood. Services such as Map My Walk connect analogue movements with digitized tracking and mapping. The Fitbit Surge reveals the walking or running journey through Google Maps. These hyper-individualized data collectors also collectivize and share this information with others, being known by the collective noun 'Quantified Selfers' (Choe, Lee, Lee, Pratt and Kientz, 2014).

The intricate intellectual rub emerges when this quantified self becomes a commodified self. This personal data has commercial value, targeting particular advertisements and featured links through Google and Facebook. The customized digital landscape transforms the World Wide Web into the narrow, personalized portal. This is self-tracking, life logging and constructing a database of personal analytics. The rise (and rise) of the quantified self in the last decade has a very precise context. Its initial usage in *Wired* magazine emerged just as the Global Financial Crisis erupted. Its popularity jutted from a period of austerity (Blyth, 2015), scarcity (Mullainathan and Shafir, 2014), zombie capitalism (Harman, 2010) and the Precariat (Standing, 2011). In this context, the quantified self rebounds between self-surveillance and narcissism, through to the 'excuse' (or mask) of eHealth in a time when public funding for preventative health and medical services is either threatened or in decline. In an environment of fear and threat – with an array of macro-cultural fears such as climate change, terrorism and the global financial crisis – Chris Till realized the costs and consequences of this hyper-measuring of the self. He argues that

> a thermodynamic model of the exploitation of potential energy underlies the interest that corporations have shown in self-tracking and that 'gamification' and the promotion of an entrepreneurial selfhood is the ideological frame that informs the strategy through which labour value is extracted without payment.
>
> *(Till, 2014: 446)*

The (ironic) gift of data generated by consumers who have purchased the hardware to enable post-fordist customization of fitness is fordist, disciplined standardization of steps, bodies and movements. This is digital labour where 'the forces at work ... coerce people into accepting the necessity of engaging in such productive activities for little or no pay' (Marx, 1990: 449). The key word in this interpretation is 'coerce'. This is not the coercion suffered through the moving assembly line or the brutality of textile mill masters. This is the coercion of deep and profound pressure – and surveillance – of bodies, gender, age and shape. In Althusserian terms, the ideological state apparatus is doing its job well (Althusser, 1970). Abuse, attacks and judgement are focused on the self rather than the state. The repressive state apparatus is not required. Online dashboards establish normative expectations that are carried on the body and updated to the phone's screen. What makes the power alignments so intricate in this case is that the citizen/user/consumer has chosen to purchase the wearable device that monitors, evaluates and ranks them. They have bought the instrument that surveys and commodifies them. They have consented to – and encouraged – their own surveillance and oppression.

With the radical transformations to the economy and workplace, it is no surprise that the economic value to be extracted from leisure is being realized by businesses. Physical exercise is linguistically tethered to work through such phrases as 'working out'. It is attached to institutionalized injustice via a 'fitness class'. This commodification of leisure is a form of reproletarianization (Gray, 2015; Brabazon and Redhead, 2014), to squeeze value out of non-working time. The gamification elements of the quantified self – through badges supplied for achieving goals – increases the objectification of the activity. Therefore, not only is work measured through key performance indicators (KPIs), performance management and time sheets, but productivity is also evaluated in leisure time. The quantified self – and self-monitored fitness that emerges from it – adds another layer to the measurement of health proxies. The quantified selfers share the numbers with a community of trackers. The encouragement and competition creates both support and gamification elements. This strategy can be deployed in specific workplaces with annual 'fitness challenges' as part of a wellness programme, geographically dispersed interest groups or healthy cities projects. This is a communitarian project at its best, and a ruthless commodification of a neo-liberal self at worst. As Lupton has described, 'self-tracking may be theorized as a practice of selfhood that conforms to cultural expectations concerning the importance of self-awareness, reflection and taking responsibility for managing, governing oneself and improving one's life chances' (Lupton, 2014: 12). Within this discourse, an individual becomes responsible for 'life choices'. A neo-liberal, libertarian and anti-statist framework is assumed. Within this discourse, an individual is free to make decisions and is therefore held responsible for the (poor) choices. Context and environment are displaced, to focus on 'the individual' making choices about food, exercise and – as a consequence – obesity. The wider cultural changes, such as unstable and sedentary work, digitized, home-based leisure, screen cultures in education and a fear about personal safety are all major points of consideration, beyond an individual's 'choice'.

Digital media are mobile media. For regional and remote communities lacking infrastructure for health, leisure, fitness and sport, digital platforms can deliver podcasts, YouTube videos, applications and digital connectivity to a range of locations with access to the internet (Brabazon, Redhead, and McRae, 2015). While some geographic locations may not feature the cycleways, pathways, lighting or safety for walking, running, cycling or skating on the streets, digitization can deliver fitness opportunities to the home, school, university or workplace, or while on the move. This movement matters. While much attention in sociology has focused on identity and/in place, how selfhood is managed on the move remains both a potent and under-theorized area. This is a key area of development for PCS.

Deterritorialization

In the early 1990s, Sherry Turkle (1995) wrote perhaps the most famous book in the early phase of the internet, titled *Life on the Screen*. This title captured the meaning of deterritorialization. We are no longer a body in space and time, but living a life on and through a screen that connects us to a network. This is a bespoke and customized digital self. Who we are in Pinterest is distinct from our Twitter handle or our Facebook or LinkedIn profile.

Deterritorialization, as a concept, captures how particular media platforms and communication systems de-emphasize our position in analogue space and time in favour of a virtual space and time. We may be in Singapore, Sheffield or Shanghai, but we can talk on the phone or via Skype, sharing time even if we do not share space. The satellite and telephone were twentieth-century manifestations of deterritorialization. But the digitized screens connected to the network are the most pervasive applications. This screen slices bodies from digitized identity, but also creates opportunities for scholars in PCS to consider new ways of thinking about bodies and movement. Fascinating and unstable compromises emerge between new and old ways of organizing space, time and identity. This is a malleable self, nesting and moving through a malleable place. Kevin Smiley, Wanda Rushing and Michele Scott realized that 'we can see that the malleability of place character can actually lead to it being reimagined and retained in a way that is constructive for places and inclusive of their residents' (Smiley et al., 2014: 4). They are describing how a place can be experienced, rather than bypassed and ignored on the way to a destination. The capacity to select 'mobility resources' (Aldred, 2014) and make choices is perhaps the most powerful act of all. The private car once signified control over the personal timetable. However, congestion and gridlock have reduced the freedom and self-efficacy possible through the automobile. Perhaps with greater affluence, many are choosing to reduce the space between work and home, so that an automobile is not required. Rachel Aldred's corrective is important: 'it is not just moving, but the power to choose to move that is important. While in some respects the rich are super-mobile, in some contexts, they benefit from being able to stay put' (ibid.).

The configuration of deterritorialization I configure in this Afterword is not synonymous with globalization. In its many definitions, globalization carries homogenization, standardization and domination with it. Deterritorialization can continue hyperlocal specificities but they can travel over digital networks. For example, Australian indigenous languages that exist in small geographical areas can be shared through deterritorialized media, in a way that globalizing ideologies – particularly inflected with neo-liberalism – would not enable. Therefore digitized deterritorialization can create new modes of researching place, space and identity.

The smartphone matters to this discussion. Over two-thirds of adults in the United States are in possession of smartphones (Klasnja and Pratt, 2014: 66). They can run complex applications, are connected to the internet and able to wirelessly deliver information on the behaviour of their owners. Predrag Klasnja and Wanda Pratt argued that 'smartphones and other mobile technologies might be the single most promising avenue we have to help individuals manage their health, and to do so at scale' (ibid.: 66). This transforms eHealth into mHealth, with the caveats that the individuals receiving information will not have the expertise to decode or understand it, in terms of diagnosis (Ghezzi, Chumber and Brabazon, 2014).

The meaning of an analogue place changes through deterritorialization. Digitally enabled reterritorialization emerges through geosocial networking. Locations can be 'checked in' on Facebook. But most significantly for the quantified self and self-monitored fitness 'movements', exercise routes can be tracked, uploaded and shared. Analogue places and movements are digitized, uploaded, tracked and shared. As argued in the introduction to this book, PCS is a way to reconfigure and reimagine exercise, fitness, health, movement, leisure, recreation and dance. Yet when 'digital' is not deployed as an adjective and – instead – marinates the field, much wider interdisciplinary disturbances are reviewed to theories of work, productivity, the political economy and social exclusion. This is the 'intellectual assemblage' of PCS so carefully configured by Michael Silk, Holly Thorpe and David Andrews in this book. By ensuring that digitization is woven with critical interrogation through PCS, there is no rip or division between the arts and sciences, HASS (humanities, arts and social sciences) and STEM (science, technology, engineering and mathematics). Technology does not belong to the sciences, just as meaning does not belong to the humanities.

Disintermediation

The final 'D' to be considered in this Afterword is disintermediation, which is a characteristic of peer-to-peer networks where links are removed from the traditional supply and distribution chain. In industrial, fordist business models, multiple layers and roles are involved in designing, creating, branding, marketing and the retail selling of a product. In other words, the person who sells lipstick did not develop the chemistry to make it. The person who designed a chair did not build or sell it. In the online environment, many of these layers between producers and consumers are either collapsed or removed. Content originators and businesses communicate with customers without mediation by wholesalers and retailers. Disintermediation has transformed the music and publishing industries, alongside banking, stock trading and the purchase of hardware and software. Some industries remain wedded to analogue supply chains. The selling of real estate, for example, still deploys real estate agents, although buyers do the early footwork online. Disintermediation is a flat model. Brokering is not required. Google is the midwife for online disintermediation, enabling the explosion of content from blogs, wikis, podcasts and vodcasts, to be found through an initiative search box. The challenge, particularly for university researchers, is how to manage the culture of equivalence between sources. I have described this as 'the Google effect' (Brabazon, 2006): the inability to discriminate between high and low quality information because of the scale of the data available and the ubiquity of a search engine that does not return results on the basis of intellectual quality. Power relationships are flattened. Expertise is decentred.

The key historical point from the users' perspective is that Google made the web – and indeed digitization – easier to use. However, there was confusion between quality, popularity and usefulness. New modes and forms of relationships were created. Is a Facebook friend a friend? What is the difference between a Facebook friend and a Twitter follower? Is Pinterest for ordinary people and Instagram for would-be celebrities? Intimacy and connectivity is transforming, as are our understandings of both digital objects and subjects. Digital PCS researchers can use unobtrusive research methods to view already existing data sets of exercise and motivation for a range of groups that (over)share their 'fitness journey' with participants in the online environment. Fitbit manages this community (over)sharing with much more public visibility than the iWatch. The key with the iWatch is its first letter. It is a monitoring of the self and the competition is with the self. Fitbit has a cascade of leaderboards, games and tokens for success. Every day, the individual's progress is assessed against others.

This Afterword has presented and probed a set of three interlinking variables: digitization, deterritorialization and disintermediation. Digital bodies are no longer tethered to Donna Haraway's cyborg or Howard Rheingold's virtual reality. They have a banal quality. Technology – when successful – disappears. When we make toast in the morning, we forget that the toaster is technology. Similarly, the ubiquity of consumerist objects to enable the quantified self are no longer special, quirky or worthy of comment. This information adds to the already expansive modes of interpreting the active body. They have been corporatized through annual corporate challenges. This is not emancipation through movement. This is not self-monitored fitness. This is self-regulated health for the purposes of the workplace. There is a desire for participants to – as Deborah Lupton (2016: 101) has described – 'optimize themselves'. Normative parameters of analogue bodies are patrolled. The fat and the thin are judged, labelled, medicalized and hospitalized. It is here that PCS scholars can struggle and agitate to create space for greater analogue, corporeal diversity. Physical cultural studies is not window dressing. It is not a desperate act from humanities scholars to strike back against kinesiology. Instead, through thinking about movement, PCS will rejuvenate and repurpose the entire field of cultural studies.

References

Aldred, R. (2014). A matter of utility? Rationalising cycling, cycling rationalities. *Mobilities*, 10(5), 686–705.
Althusser, L. (1970). Ideology and ideological state apparatuses. Available from www.marxists.org/reference/archive/althusser/1970/ideology.htm.
Andrews, D. and Silk, M. (2011). Physical cultural studies: engendering a productive dialogue. *Sociology of Sport Journal*, 28, 1–3.
Bandy, S. (2016). Gender and the 'cultural turn' in the study of sport and physical cultures. *Sport in Society*, 19(5), 726–735.
Blyth, M. (2015). *Austerity: The History of a Dangerous Idea*. Oxford: Oxford University Press.
Brabazon, T. (2006). The Google effect, *Libri*, 56(3), 157–167.
Brabazon, T. and Redhead, S. (2014). Theoretical times: reproletarianization. *Libsyn*, http://traffic.libsyn.com/tarabrabazon/Theoretical_times_-_reproletarianization.mp3.
Brabazon, T., Redhead, S. and McRae, L. (2015). Moving on up. *Libsyn*, March 19, http://traffic.libsyn.com/tarabrabazon/Moving_on_up_-_physical_cultural_studies_in_third_tier_cities.mp3.
Choe, E., Lee, N., Lee, B., Pratt, W. and Kientz, J. (2014). Understanding quantified-selfers' practices in collecting and exploring personal data. *Proceeding CHI*, 1143–1152.

Couturier, J., Sola, D. and Borioli, G. (2012). How can the internet of things help to overcome current healthcare challenges? *DigiWorld Economic Journal*, 87, 67–81.

Ghezzi, P., Chumber, S. and Brabazon, T. (2014). Educating medical students to evaluate the quality of health information on the web. In L. Floridi and P. Illari (eds), *The Philosophy of Information Quality*. Berlin: Springer.

Gray, J. (2015). *The Soul of a Marionette*. London: Allen Lane.

Harcombe, Z. (2010). *The Obesity Epidemic*. New York: Columbus.

Harman, C. (2010). *Zombie Capitalism: Global Crisis and the Relevance of Marx*. New York: Newmarket.

Klasnja, P. and Pratt, W. (2014). Managing health with mobile technology. *Interactions*, 21(1), 66–69.

Lupton, D. (2014). *Citizenships: Personhood and Identity Politics in the Information Age*. Canberra: ANU.

Lupton, D. (2016). The diverse domains of quantified selves: self-tracking modes and dataveillance. *Economy and Society*, 45(1), 101–122.

Marx, K. (1990). *Capital*, vol. 1. London: Penguin.

Mullainathan, S. and Shafir, E. (2014). *Scarcity: The True Cost of Not Having Enough*. London: Penguin.

Smiley, K., Rushing, W. and Scott, M. (2014). Behind a bicycling boom: governance, cultural change and place character in Memphis. *Urban Studies*, October 27.

Standing, G. (2011). *The Precariat*. London: Bloomsbury.

Till, C. (2014). Exercise as labour: quantified self and the transformation of exercise into labour. *Societies*, 4(3), 446–462.

Turkle, S. (1995). *Life on the Screen: Identity in the Age of the Internet*. New York: Simon & Schuster.

Virilio, P. (1989). *Speed and Politics: An Essay on Dromology*. New York: Semiotext(e).

Wise, J. and Hongu, N. (2014). Pedometer, accelerometer, and mobile technology for promoting physical activity. AZ1491. College of Agricultural Life Sciences, University of Arizona.

Wolf, G. (2009). Know thyself. *Wired*, 7 June, http://archive.wired.com/medtech/health/magazine/17-07/lbnp_knowthyself?

INDEX

2012 London Olympics and Paralympics 126, 336, 347, 349, 441, 442
2014 Brazil World Cup 443–447, 575
2014 Commonwealth Games Glasgow 126, 251
2016 Rio Olympics and Paralympics 287, 441, 443–447

able-bodied 243
able-bodied sport 213
ableism 212, 242, 598
action sports 107, 297, 305
activism 51, 52, 64, 137, 138, 151, 155, 159, 262, 335, 463, 487, 488, 490, 550, 552
advanced liberalism 402, 406
affect(s) 144, 298–300, 302, 325, 366, 371, 404, 452, 491
affective geographies 324, 325
affectivity 370
ageism 181
agencement 324
agency 20, 21, 27–29, 53, 74, 85–87, 111, 126, 136, 175, 180, 181, 196, 220, 269, 288, 290, 318, 324, 326, 340, 341, 385, 389, 405, 406, 437, 478, 479, 497, 50, 540, 552, 572, 581, 592
Ali, Muhammad 130, 136
Althusser, Louis 35
amateurism 64, 125, 238
American football 416
anatomo-politics 112, 114, 115
Andrews, David 18, 19, 21, 42, 49, 94, 295, 339, 467, 476, 601
Appadurai, Arjun 392, 393
Arendt, Hannah 26
Arnold, Thomas 210
assemblage(s) 2, 6, 8–10, 61, 64, 144, 170, 183, 201–206, 218, 220–225, 324–326, 341, 344, 345, 347, 350, 408, 571, 589, 601

at risk body 282
athletic bodies 194, 195
autoethnographic 271
autoethnography 36, 270–271, 274, 490, 505–513, 530–531
autophenomenography 270–271, 274, 507

Bale, John 335, 393–394, 572–573
Ball, Stephen 559
ballet 96–97
BASE jumping 36, 278, 490
baseball 159, 221–223, 249, 252, 257, 390
basketball 152, 241, 249, 257, 489
Berlin Marathon 373
Bernard, Michel 16
Biesta, Gert 554–555
biology 45, 47, 78, 142, 143, 145, 146, 180, 404, 446
biopedagogy 355–356, 572
biopolitics 21, 136, 405, 590
biopower 26, 169, 176, 260, 261
bird-watching 329
Birmingham Centre for Contemporary Cultural Studies 29, 62, 93, 103, 414
BlackBerry Messenger (BBM) 454–459
black cultural politics 131, 139
Black Lives Matter 138
black sporting politics 132, 134, 137
bodies 9–10, 16, 21, 24, 27, 38, 46, 52–54, 74, 84–87, 112, 121, 126, 133, 141, 150, 160, 167, 183, 191, 200, 214, 218, 237, 246, 258, 269, 286, 296, 305, 313, 323, 333, 355, 369, 378, 389, 425, 437, 452, 477, 496, 509, 521, 531, 549, 559, 572, 588, 592, 598, 602; active bodies 5, 15, 18–21, 45, 49, 139, 151, 192, 196, 210, 286, 420, 437, 477, 488, 496, 509, 521, 537, 549, 559, 564, 568; (im)mobile 291;

604

Index

(in)active 291, 452, 561, 564; able 160; aestheticized 218, 220; ageing 179–187, 268, 274; athletes', 112–115, 117, 196, 242; athletic 194–195, 197, 258; authorial 588; black 133, 136–137, 142; celebritized 239; children's 168, 200, 203, 205; classed 121; colonial 17; commodified 237–240; corporal 258, 259; cyborg 161, 201; damaged 196; dancing 95–99; Deleuzean 593; digital 200–206, 602; disabled 85, 159–166, 209, 212; disciplined 113, 167, 171–172, 175–176; disposable 137; disrupted 267, 274; docile 111–112, 117; emboldened 426, 428; exercising 9, 384; fat 228–229; forceful 593; gendered 46, 141–147, 481; girl's 453, 459, 462; government 333; healthy 167, 176, 402; heterosexualized 106, 477; insouciant 426; invisible 286–287; Japanese 261; living 565; male 136, 253; marginalized 488; masculine 155; medicalized and scientized 191; migrant 304, 347; moving 36, 49, 52–53, 78, 95, 160, 200, 289, 371, 531, 535; Muslim female 287–291; networked 452; normative 555; Other 401, 459, 509; Paralympic 159–160, 163; pleasurable 297, 298, 299, 302; political 258; pregnancy 317, 319; raced 130; racialized 346; regulatory 280; sexualized/sexed 9, 150–156, 237, 241–242, 477–480; spectacular and eroticized 246; spectacular 247; spiritualized/religious 209–215; sporting 9, 36, 62, 122, 131, 136–137, 152, 162, 227, 238–240, 246, 258, 299, 425; sports governing 441, 447; toned 296; transported 305; troubled 426; unhealthy 316; voluntourist 328; WAG, 251; white 150; women's 224, 287, 296, 346, 403, 461, 480, 572; working 122; young 167–178, 200, 203, 555
Body and Society 16, 20, 79
bodybuilding 159
body cultures 16, 17, 27
body image 75, 224, 225, 298–300, 488
body mass index (BMI) 229, 230, 232, 233
body techniques 16, 87, 88, 381, 382
body weight 229–233
body work 169, 218–223, 225, 405, 590
border crossing(s) 64, 317, 552, 554, 556, 561
Bourdieu, Pierre 16, 28, 32, 37, 104, 122, 123, 124, 144, 162
boxing 125, 130, 131, 162, 249, 257, 268, 381, 384, 385
Braidotti, Rosi 404, 409, 562
Brohm, Jean-Marie 16
bullfighting 305
Butler, Judith 39, 143, 592

capital space(s) 344–345, 350
Carby, Hazel 136

carnal sociology 590
citizen scientist 330
Clair, Robin Patrick 484
climbing 104, 305
coaching 111–117, 205, 499–500, 507, 531, 565
Cole, C.L., 54, 340, 476
Collins, Patricia Hill 417, 479
colonialism 132, 151, 152, 155, 288, 434, 571, 590
colonization 132, 156, 445, 470, 484, 551
commodification 27, 105, 131, 136, 202, 237–246, 292, 328, 442, 445, 447, 599; commodity aesthetics 249
Commonwealth Games 126, 251, 348, 436, 442, 469
communitas 414, 418–419, 591
community 159, 412–422, 537, 539, 543, 570–575, 583
community-based action research 573
community development 573–574, 597
complimentarity 141
Confederations Cup 575
conscientization 67, 472, 509, 563
consumer capitalism 378–382, 386
controlling images 479
Cooley, C.H., 86
corporal bodies 258
corporal punishment 257–276
corporate social responsibility 580–585
corporeal feminism 145
corporeal practices 19, 167
corporeal therapeutics 402, 405, 408
corporeality 13, 168, 179
creative analytical practice 506
cricket 121, 125–127, 489, 570–51
critical discourse analysis 467–473
critical golf studies 336, 338, 340
critical public health 314
crystallization 486
cultural capital 124, 128
cultural geography 323, 324, 326, 356
cultural intermediaries 490
cultural policy 432–440
cultural studies 19–20, 33–34, 42, 45, 47, 51, 58, 93, 102, 108, 122, 412, 416, 432
curriculum 10, 423, 425, 429, 554, 558, 560–565, 572
cyborg bodies 161, 201
cycling 126, 305, 307–310

Dace Trudell, Eryn 317–318
dance 93–101, 521, 582
Dance Dance Revolution (DDR) 372
dance/movement therapy (DMT) 74–76, 78
data visualization 528, 534–535, 536
Deleuze, Giles 16, 98, 220, 375, 591, 593, 594
Desmond, Jane 93

deterritorialization 600–601, 602
Developmental Origins of Health and Disease (DOHaD) 316
dieticians 317
digital: data 200, 202–206, 349, 532; ethnography 529; media 283, 451, 529, 537–544, 600; mediation 451–452, 460–462; technologies 200–208, 233–234, 452–453, 532, 537; video 528
digitization 597–598, 601, 602
disability 471
disabled sport 212
disablism 164
disintermediation 601–602
distance running 268, 270, 273, 498
Doctrine of Sexual Intermediaries 146
Douglass, Frederick 133–134
Durkheim, Émile 413

Edwards, Harry 137
embodiment 1–6, 9–10, 15, 42, 46, 49, 54, 63, 74, 99, 131, 138, 161, 164, 181, 201–203, 205–206, 211, 215, 218, 225, 241, 268, 271, 282, 292, 300, 307, 308, 310, 323, 330, 373, 403, 407, 424, 451, 462, 481, 554, 562, 587–594; (in)active 64, 179, 324, 467; active 16, 20, 94, 180, 184, 267, 286, 289, 291–292, 304, 402, 405, 451, 560; affective 371; ageing 184; as being-in-the-world 589; as representation 589; athletic 482; class 122; digitized 200; feminine 94; lived 46; personal 270; re-, 210, 213–215; reflexive embodiment 85–86; sporting 134; tough 301; young people's 426, 429
emotion(s) 297–299, 325, 371, 385
emplacement 38, 530
empowerment 36, 39, 46, 51, 62–63, 65, 107, 153, 167, 214, 289, 296, 306, 357, 387, 471, 582, 584; athlete 112–113; gender 433, 436; women's 58, 480
energy consumption 232
energy expenditure 232
entertainment industry 95, 97–98
environmental managerialism 338
essentialism 142, 562–563
ethics 36, 51, 53, 55, 58, 64–65, 112, 116, 117, 131, 197, 212–213, 244, 262, 407, 490, 496, 510, 512, 538–540, 565
ethnography 49, 88, 90, 94–96, 159 484–492, 511, 591; classic 164; digital 529; natural 492; public 67; sensory 530, 532; sensuous 159; video 531–533; virtual 485, 542
evidence-based research 18, 319, 512
exercise science 17, 315, 406–407
exercise 1, 4, 6, 10, 16, 18, 26, 27, 29, 39, 52, 63, 84–91, 99, 123, 124, 126, 151, 169, 173, 180, 182, 192, 200, 204, 22, 231, 260, 271, 279, 280, 286, 291, 308, 313–319, 369, 370–375, 378–388, 402–408, 424–427, 441, 451, 507, 508, 528, 531, 533, 546, 552, 554, 558, 562, 563, 572, 580, 582, 598–602
exergames 372
existentialism 28–29

Facebook 455, 457–458
Fanon, Frantz 132–133
faux sporting body 241
fell running 182, 569
femininity 96, 141–142, 223–224, 281–282, 301–302, 471, 481, 488, 555, 597; heterosexual 538; normative 154; pressures of 224; sexualized hyperfemininity 306; spectacular 219–220; teen 453; traditional 480
feminism 3, 26, 36, 51–53, 147, 463, 484, 488; corporeal 145; critical 415, 484; hashtag 463; radical 484; transnational 286–292; western 288
feminist cultural studies 54, 476, 481
feminist theory 15, 36, 63, 319, 476, 558, 562; postcolonial 584; transnational 287–290
FIFA 64, 243, 441–447, 540, 575
figure skating 249
fitness 1, 3, 5, 6, 9, 16, 56, 84–91, 113, 117, 183, 184, 191–197, 200, 211, 218, 219, 221, 238, 240, 246, 250, 259, 271, 286, 289, 290, 291, 296, 297, 315, 316, 345, 357, 370–375, 378–388, 451, 509, 528, 550, 555, 574, 598, 599–602
fitness boot camps 381
fitness gym 378–388, 550
football (soccer) 53, 113, 125–126, 153, 159, 194, 238, 241, 243, 249–253, 291–292, 369, 371, 390, 446, 489–490, 518, 523, 575, 583
Foucault, Michel 17, 25–26, 37, 47, 111–113, 115, 142–143, 169–171, 175, 203, 260, 314, 355, 424, 589, 591
Freire, Paolo 62, 67, 262, 568, 574,
Frisby, Wendy 419

Galeano, Eduardo 570
gamification 204
Gay Games 152, 155
gender identity disorder (GID) 154
gentrification 191, 346, 350, 441, 444
geographical information systems (GIS) 307
Giardina, Michael 551
Giles, Audrey 419
Gilroy, Paul 136
Giroux, Henry 491, 550–552, 555, 559
GLBTIQ athletes 152
global capitalism 391
global positioning technologies (GPS) 307, 310, 327, 372
globalization 27, 152, 258, 283, 288, 304, 335, 336, 393, 391, 395, 435, 439, 442, 564, 601

Index

glurbanization 443–448
Goffman, Erving 88
golf 128, 333, 335
Google 601–602
governmentality 170, 314, 316, 317, 437
Gramsci 479
grassroots sport 583
greenwashing 583
Guattari, Felix 16, 220, 591, 594

habitus 123–124, 127–128, 143–144
health 1–10, 16, 18, 30, 42, 43, 47, 62, 73, 77, 84–91, 95, 96, 99 125, 145, 146, 165, 168–176, 180–185, 192–197, 203–206, 218–222, 229–234, 246, 291, 296, 297, 313, 315, 316, 333, 336, 339, 341, 345, 355–360, 371, 378, 401, 404–408, 423–429, 435, 444, 451, 463, 517, 530, 549, 565, 569, 581–583, 597, 598, 600–602
health education (HE) 423–431
health inequality 345
health policy 424
healthification 355–356, 360, 362, 364, 366
healthified spaces 345
healthism 192, 193, 355, 378, 408, 425
health-optimizing physical education (HOPE) 423
Hebdige, Dick 415
hegemony 19, 26, 252, 479, 559
heteronormativity 53, 55, 153, 154, 362, 480
heteropatriarchy 150
heterosexism 154, 362
hexis 123, 144
higher education 446, 558–564
high-performance sport 9, 111–118, 124, 160, 164, 196
history 17, 209, 211, 231, 233, 249, 252, 258, 260, 313, 327, 378, 432, 433, 434, 436, 438, 439, 442–448, 484, 487, 496, 518, 564, 574, 583, 589, 591, 592
homophobia 155, 156, 164, 480
horse racing 238, 244
humane physical culture 197
Husserl, Edmund 589

ice hockey 416
identity work 267–269, 273
immersion 485
impaired body 164
Ingham, Alan 15, 17, 20–21
injury 76, 161, 181, 192, 195–197, 223, 238, 267–274, 278, 302, 317, 498, 507
intellectualism 7, 56, 62, 107, 108, 212, 549, 550, 553
interdisciplinary 34, 42–45, 48, 58, 94, 98, 108, 215, 253, 298, 304, 319, 323, 395, 429, 467, 477, 558, 597

international development 432–440, 571
International Olympic Committee (IOC) 152, 210, 443, 446, 447
internet of things 597
interpretation 6, 8, 19, 32, 33, 47, 49, 66, 93, 162, 181, 415, 417, 437, 444, 445, 469, 479, 486, 491, 524, 529, 599
intersectionality 288, 306, 479
intersex 142, 146
intervention 51, 61, 63, 64, 65, 159, 169, 182, 192, 202, 232, 233, 301, 313, 401, 405, 461, 463, 487, 491–493, 552, 572
invisible bodies 286–294
Ioannidis, John 228, 231, 234

Japanese physical cultures 258–259
Jawbone UP, 531
Johnson, Jack 135, 241
Jordan, Michael 136, 138

karate 572
keep-fit exercise 383, 385
kinaesthesia 371
kinesiology 17–18, 20–21, 49, 306, 476–477, 561, 597
kinesthesia 74, 78
kitesurfing 104
Kupu Taea 467, 470–472

Lacan, Jacques 592–593
landscape(s) 323–332, 358, 572–573
leisure 1, 3, 4, 6, 9, 76, 102, 107, 134, 142, 164, 218, 219, 239, 278, 286, 289, 290, 292, 296, 297, 301, 326, 350, 379, 383, 412, 451, 509, 528, 558, 598–601; activities 76, 123, 259, 292, 297, 339, 384; cultures 104; environments 344; institution 379; lifestyles 104; practices 73, 76, 79, 238, 329; studies 3, 58, 103, 329, 403, 574, 597; time 124, 382, 599; walking 326, 327
les autres 163
lesbian sporting celebrities 152–153
lifestyle sporting cultures 102–110
locker rooms 355, 489
Longley, Alys 521

MamaDances 317
marginalization 17, 53, 64, 161, 288, 297, 300, 435
martial arts 191, 258–260, 268, 381, 572–574
Marxism 19–20, 25–26, 33, 35, 121–125, 246, 249, 467, 552
Marylebone Cricket Club (MCC) 570
masculine 141, 152, 242, 250, 378, 381, 402, 458–459; aesthetic 221; appropriation 403; ideal 142, 222; identity 96, 297; normative 222, 407; physicality 160; sports 153

masculinity 36, 136, 141–142, 145, 154, 160, 184, 220–223, 241, 281, 458–462, 470, 489, 538, 597; female sporting 154; hegemonic 223, 252, 538; heteronormative 155; heterosexual 458–459; hyper-, 253; Japanese 154; popular 462; spectacular 219; stoic 210; teen 453; white 155
materiality 24, 44, 47, 145, 363, 370–371, 374
Mauss, Marcel 16, 87, 143–144
McRobbie, Angela 93
Mead, George Herbert 85
media representations 53, 259, 286, 292, 467–68, 472, 478–480, 588; of science 47; of surfing 57; of Mulsim female Olympians 287; of sportswomen 472; digital 538
mediation 237–245, 537, 587, 601
mediatization 237–244
medicalization 9, 154, 182, 191–198, 315, 318–319, 517, 602
mental health 76, 401–411
Merleau-Ponty, Maurice 16, 85–86, 201, 590
methodology 33, 43, 52, 63, 143, 453, 497–498, 501, 506, 530–531, 555, 593–594
mind-body dualism 74, 211, 241, 318, 402
mobilities 10, 304–312, 390–391
modernity 16, 48, 133, 169, 238, 288, 413–414, 559
modernization 260, 335–336, 413, 434, 446
Money, John 141
Motivation Scale for Sport Consumption 248
movement-spaces 371, 391
muscular Christianity 210

narrative inquiry 10, 34, 95, 505–513, 520
NASCAR, 591, 592
National Basketball Association (NBA) 138, 249
National Football League (NFL) 195, 249, 584
nationalism 152–153, 155, 413, 471
nature 10, 21, 46–48, 74–78, 143, 145–146, 323–332, 335, 340, 381–382, 404, 445–446, 519, 563, 591
neoconservatism 565
neoliberalism 28, 46, 155, 192–193, 224, 336, 344, 355, 507, 550–551, 558, 563, 565, 601
NEOsport 389, 392
neuroscience 42, 46, 402, 406–407
new materialism 146, 366
new media technologies 451–464
new prudentialism 359–360
new public health 345, 406
Nicolescu, Basarab 42, 44, 47
non-humans 10, 21, 145, 238, 310, 328, 330, 334, 336, 339–341, 404
non-representational theory (NRT) 305–306, 310, 324–326, 529
Nordic walking 372, 382

obesity 27, 175, 228–234, 313, 316–317, 362, 369, 406, 423–428, 517, 555, 584, 597, 600
objectification 64, 143, 169, 242, 246, 462, 480, 599
Olympic Games 56, 121, 125, 156, 161, 163, 209–210, 213, 242–243, 247–252, 287–288, 335–336, 341, 348, 370, 441–447, 469, 488, 575
organic golf 339
Otherness 287–288, 293

pain and injury 267–273, 498
Pan Am Games 56, 194–195
panopticism 112
Paralympic Games 159–165, 242, 288, 442–447
parkour 104–107, 305, 375, 382
participatory action research 418, 484, 487–488
pedagogy 67, 144, 167, 203, 317, 423, 429, 488, 491, 549, 562; critical 6, 569; public 7, 508–509, 549–555; body 168; embodied 423; bare 559, 563
personal, social, and health education (PSHE) 423
phenomenology 85, 147, 327, 507, 589–591
physical capital 218
physical education (PE) 15, 17, 103, 125–126, 151, 161, 168, 205, 232–233, 258, 361–362, 386, 423–431, 571
physicality 182, 184, 429, 481, 496, 509, 517–518, 569, 588
pilates 88, 191, 381, 384
pilgrimage walking 305
Pillow, Wanda 38
pleasure 9, 29–30, 75, 91, 133, 152, 175–176, 182–184, 212, 238, 253, 260, 286, 292, 295–301, 309, 317, 327, 330, 379, 382–383, 405, 456, 459, 478, 507, 517, 592, 598
poetry 515–525
poiesis 515–525
politics of touch 328
popular culture 3, 16, 97–98, 103–106, 136, 219, 381, 473
post-colonialism 25, 106, 131, 133, 155, 439, 445–447, 484, 550, 561, 571, 583–584
post-humanism 20, 43, 218, 225, 404, 453
post-modernism 234, 261, 373, 414, 484, 486,
post-sport 569
power relations 24–31, 39, 49, 53, 62–63, 95–96, 114–115, 131, 182, 260, 293, 305, 314, 358, 403, 418, 429, 435, 453, 481, 597
praxis 9–10, 24,–25, 51–58, 61–69, 94, 134, 159, 165, 257–258, 262–263, 284, 290, 299, 319, 420, 516, 551–552, 558
precautionary principle 277
pregnancy 313–320
privilege 55, 346, 356, 401, 404–406, 438, 447
projection 592

proprioconception 78
public intellectualism 549, 552–553
public spaces 10, 64, 180, 202, 374–375, 541, 550, 563, 575–576
publicness 374
Puma 584

qualitative research 7, 32–39, 44, 55, 94, 270, 404, 419, 471, 496, 506, 512, 516, 521, 525, 593
quantitative research 18, 44, 48, 146, 242, 306–307, 311, 329, 512, 515, 559, 573

racism 62, 130–131, 133, 137, 139, 150, 152, 193, 234, 362, 461, 472, 480, 574, 582
rad running 305
radical contextualism 34, 152, 155, 401, 441
reciprocity 54–55, 65, 213, 296, 328, 487
re-embodiment 213–215
reflexive body politics 592–593
reflexive body techniques 85, 87–89
reflexive sociology 34
reflexivity 32, 35–39, 55, 58, 108, 152, 258, 288, 335, 387, 407, 477, 486, 492, 508, 510, 513, 544, 587–588, 593
relational ethics 510
relational sociology 84, 91
representation 36–37, 93–94, 98–99, 108, 141, 145, 169, 237, 274, 287, 299–302, 348, 370–371, 413, 442–443, 468, 486–487, 515, 521, 524, 536, 538, 589
research dialogue 496–497, 501
research meeting 496–497, 501–502
Rich, Adrienne 519
Richardson, Miles 520
Rinehart, Robert 518, 521–522
risk sports 277–285
roller derby 295–303, 488, 498, 552
Rose, Nikolas 47, 402, 406,
rugby 238, 243, 268, 278, 489
running 73, 76, 89, 132, 160, 181, 182, 267–283, 305, 323, 345, 358, 369, 371–372, 375, 404, 427, 451, 488, 498, 507, 531–532, 598, 600

school health policies 423–431
Schooling Bodies 168–169
scientific method 8, 45, 48, 324, 559
scientism 7, 44
segregation 142, 350
self-reflexivity 5, 37, 288, 477, 492, 508
serious leisure 104, 379
sexism 154, 193, 234, 296, 362, 462, 480, 574, 590
sexual dysmorphia 142
sexualization 64, 150, 241, 472, 479–480
Silk, Michael 51, 94, 523, 597
skateboarding 53, 106, 299, 375, 488, 538–539

Skinner Releasing Technique (SRT) 317–318
Skinner, Joan 317
Skirtboarders 538–539, 541
snowboarding 53, 108, 159, 299, 306, 488
social class 65, 89, 121–129, 241, 274, 306, 415–416, 489–490, 496, 518
social identities 93, 269, 386–387, 415, 418, 489, 491
social interaction 84, 88, 164, 269, 478
social justice 7, 54, 58, 62–63, 131, 366, 425, 467, 471, 477, 549, 553–554, 561–565, 584
social media 56, 67, 107, 138–139, 201–202, 204–205, 218, 233, 237, 289, 291, 417, 452–455, 462–463, 477–478, 555, 565
social movements 104, 138–139, 408, 537, 575
social network 87–89, 91, 451–452, 462, 537, 598, 601
sociology of sport 17–19, 30, 34, 73, 94, 102–103, 108, 124, 279, 298, 301, 334, 339, 476–477, 481, 524, 528, 597
sociology of the body 15, 102, 168, 201
spectacular urban space 344
spinning 381, 384,
sport(s): fandom 286–287, 289, 291–292; history 96, 487; media 107, 138, 241, 291–292, 468, 478, 480, 538, 551; medicine 17–18, 191, 195–196, 258, 268; mega-events 152, 155, 288, 334–335, 346, 370, 394, 438, 441–448, 575; migration 389–397; science 182, 560, 597; spectatorship 124, 249–252, 292; studies 19, 42, 102–103, 107–108, 159, 215, 293, 476, 479, 481, 561
sport and environmental issues 333–343
sport and social change 568–576
sport for development and peace (SDP) 153, 433–439, 488, 569, 572–577
sporting 3, 19, 209, 214; achievement 125, 252; administration 53; agents 551; celebrity 152–153, 240, 248; environments 335; franchises 346; identity 291; institutions 391; life-cycle 244; life-world 499; mobility 306; organizations 53; paraphernalia 244; participation 215, 291; performance 205, 243; practices 123, 279, 287; Southern 38; spaces 55, 106, 335, 393, 481; spectacle 3, 247, 253, 346–348, 350, 442–443; structures 53; subjectivity 153; trauma 247
Sports Fans Motivation Scale 248
sportscapes 393–394
St Pierre, Elizabeth Adams 593–594
stadium 238–239, 242–243, 291, 345–346, 371, 393, 444–445, 447, 518, 575, 584
stakeholders 581–582, 583
Stoddart, Mark 341
structured variety 380
subaltern 132–133
subcultural capital 105

Index

subculture 102, 104–105, 415, 487–491
subjectification 152, 261, 404, 423, 433, 437–438, 496, 500, 503
surfing 54, 57, 104, 106–107, 488, 539, 542
surveillance 115, 117, 134, 167–168, 170, 173, 180, 203, 206, 239, 348–350, 555, 564, 599
sustainability 126, 334–335, 581
swimming 16, 38, 87–88, 132, 160, 183, 224, 241, 250, 323, 404, 489, 508, 574

taekwondo 572
T'ai Chi 183
Taiikukaikei 154
text/representation 476–482
textual analysis 467–473, 591
therapeutic landscapes 77–78
therapeutic leisure 379
therapeutic movement practices 73–74, 78–79
thirdspace 365
Thorpe, Holly 37, 42, 45, 55, 106–108, 159, 281, 488, 589
Thorpe, Ian 250–251
Tönnies, Ferdinand 413
Tonya Harding 124
transdisciplinary 1, 3, 6, 9, 42–49, 258, 267, 274, 333, 338, 402, 544
Truman, Harry 533

urban marathons 373–374
urbanization 369, 387, 442

Vigarello, Georges 16
voluntourism 328

Wacquant, Loïc 32, 144, 379, 384, 590
walking 16, 79, 87, 184, 271–272, 308, 315, 323, 326–327, 345, 361, 369, 371–372, 375, 404, 529, 532, 535, 568, 570, 573, 576, 598, 600
Wambach, Abby 153
Wheaton, Belinda 51, 107, 159, 488
white privilege 106, 480
whiteness 55, 106, 151, 154, 404, 480, 489, 524
Wii Fit 373
windsurfing 106, 488
wives and girlfriends (WAG) bodies 251–252
women's artistic gymnastics 495, 499–501
Women's National Basketball Association (WNBA) 138, 152
World OutGames 152, 155

yoga 17, 73, 76, 88, 90, 183, 299, 369, 404, 489, 191, 569, 574, 598

zumba 191, 381